Oahspe

Modern Language Edition, Volume 1 of 2

Seventh Era Faithists

Volume 1 of 2

From the Beginning through book 27, being the
Book of the Arc of Bon

(Volume 2 is a separate Book that contains books 28 through 39 and includes the glossary, index and afterword.)

Prepared by the Seventh Era Faithists
in 2010-2011 C.E.
also known as A.K. 162.

This Spiritual Guidebook called Oahspe Modern Language Edition is a print-on-demand version of the Oahspe Standard Edition
(http://oahspestandardedition.com/)

Dedicated to the Great Spirit

OAHSPE

Standard Edition
In Modern Language

A Practical Guidebook to the Spiritual Life

IN THE WORDS OF

JEHOVIH

AND HIS

ANGEL AMBASSADORS

BEING A

KOSMON BIBLE

CONTAINING

A History of the Dominions of the Higher and Lower Heavens on the Earth for the Past Twenty–Five Thousand Years;

Being from the Submersion of the Continent of Pan in the Pacific Ocean, Commonly Called the Flood or Deluge, to the Kosmon Era, the Present Time; Also a Brief History of the Preceding Years, from Man's Beginning on Earth to the Flood;

Together With:

A Synopsis of
the Cosmogony of the Universe;
the Creation of Planets;
the Creation of Man;
the Unseen Worlds;
the Labor and Glory of Gods and Goddesses in the Heavens of the Earth and in the Etherean Heavens above them;

With the
New Commandments of Jehovih
to Man of the Present Day,
and Other Revelations
from the Second Resurrection,
formed in Words in the Thirty–Third Year
of the Kosmon Era.

This present edition being placed into modern American Language; being an extraction, compilation and integration of materials from the First Published Edition

and from the
Second Published Edition
Published in 1891

and from
Extant pre-1882 Oahspe Source Materials
and from
the Heavens of Jehovih.

Oahspe Table Of Contents

Volume 1

Volume 2

Volume 2, in a separate book, completes the *Oahspe Modern Language Edition.*
Page numbers refer to those in Volume 2.

Oahspe Images List

Volume 1 images are in regular type. Volume 2 images are in *indented italic* type.

Forward

In this world of unknowns it sometimes happens that a person searches for definitive truths to life's mysteries. What is reality? Is there a Creator or are we simply coagulated dust whose consciousness arose from nothing? What is the system and order of the corporeal world? Is there a heaven? If yes, then what is the system and order of that spiritual world? What effect, if any, does heaven have upon earth and its people's lives? And does earth affect heaven? What is my place and destiny in all this?

As you first pick up this book you may be agnostic or skeptical† — if so, this may be just the book you need to weigh the many statements in favor of a Creator. Or, perhaps you are already convinced there is a Creator but you haven't found anyone who could explain what it all means without offending your sensibilities. In Oahspe, you are never asked to suspend judgment or reason in favor of blind belief.

Oahspe proclaims creation and the spirit world as a living reality and demonstrates how to prove this.‡ It also proclaims the Creator and reveals how to demonstrate the reality. In that regard Oahspe is unique in the world. Oahspe further explains Who the Creator is and also makes clear the difference between Lord, Lord God, God and the Creator. Through Oahspe, God makes known that he is not the Creator but a one-time mortal who was once even as we are. As an elder brother of tens of thousands of years experience, he now holds the office of God in the service of the Creator, and has been placed in charge of our planet and her heavens for a season.

Sometimes truths are shocking and sometimes they are a relief. Things may seem strange at first, but lack of familiarity does not reduce the intrinsic value of the information. The style of Oahspe is direct, yet it does not ask a person to accept without proof. Indeed, we learn through Oahspe that asking questions is an essential aspect of the human experience and that reaching spiritual maturity requires us to develop discernment. Yet much more than a book about self-enlightenment and self-development, Oahspe also teaches a timeless ethic.

---

† "Skeptical" here means that you want to be shown so you can make up your own mind. Also a skeptic allows for her or himself to be proved otherwise; a cynic won't allow for the possibility.

‡ If the reality is not clear, then caution is healthy—one wants to see proof so as to make up one's own mind. And in that regard, as Oahspe says, the light of truth can manifest to those who would know, yet those cannot become enlightened who shut themselves up in denial, saying: I defy you to prove the matter.||

For the closed mind or the mind full of itself has difficulty in being receptive. Such people have already made up their minds. They desire to hear no more, or, if they do listen it is only so they can find a weakness so as to attack the message. Perhaps it is vanity or fear that keeps closed-minded people unreceptive. But, as truly holy people show by their example, a humble mind need not be a gullible mind. And, as the skeptic can show, a fearless or receptive mind need not be a gullible mind either.

Yet humbleness and receptivity, while necessary, are insufficient to attain the desired proof in its fullness. To comprehensively perceive a confirmation requires a third attribute on the part of the seeker, that of 'action'. This not only means studying the issue and putting it to the test or putting it into practice, but working and behaving in ways that bring about a more perceptive mind, soul and spirit. For, to advance beyond the judgment level of a beast in the field, a person must develop the ability to more broadly perceive and to reason virtuously. To discipline oneself in that direction is to move toward greater knowledge and the blossoming of wisdom. Indeed, as any proficient teacher can testify to, the development of knowledge and wisdom requires practice. In that regard, generous suites of wholesome and desirable behaviors enrich many of the pages of Oahspe. From these the reader can develop the necessary discipline to advance in matters of perception. Also available to assist in that aim are many episodes in the lives of diverse persons worthy of emulation. ||

We read that it is okay or even healthy to be skeptical, but there also can be value in believing. How is this possible? Both the skeptic and the cynic cast doubt, but while the skeptic allows truth to prove otherwise, the cynic does not. Yet, instead of casting doubt the believer allows for the merit in the message to inform him of its meaning, knowing that the false falls aside of its own accord. According to Oahspe, there is a power in the soul to discern the truth, and it is called the ethe power, and it rests above the doubts that plague humankind.

May we all discern truth. Oahspe supplies invaluable keys such as how to find that essence within us that knows truth. Yet the book Oahspe not only provides basic answers, but reveals to us ways to find more. And while this book Oahspe doesn't claim to explain everything, it can start us on the way to finding all to our heart's content.

Many who have read Oahspe have called it the greatest of books. Should you find yourself without access to your copy of *Oahspe Modern Language Edition*, you can read it online or download a copy at: http://oahspestandardedition.com/

The Seventh Era Faithists

Preface

Since 1882, two published editions of Oahspe have been available to the public, the 1882 edition and the 1891 edition. All later editions have been essentially reprints of one or the other.

Now we welcome you to the new edition of Oahspe! Integrity, a hallmark of excellence, shines through the older editions. The *OAHSPE Modern Language Edition* strives to maintain that tradition. Comprised of past editions melded into an integrated coherency, all has been translated into modern language. Thus, while previous editions were written in antiquated English with "thee" and "thou", "wouldst" and "couldst", this new edition has been carefully translated into comprehensible modern English for today's reader. Moreover, this modern language edition includes assists for those who do not have English as their first or main language. This edition also eases the translation of Oahspe into other languages.

Previously unpublished in the 1882 or the 1891 editions but included in this edition are materials that originated from two prior unpublished editions of Oahspe. These were the original manuscript and the 1881 Oahspe. In general, the pre-1882 Oahspe material has been scattered and lost, and only copies of remnants remain. These have been carefully collected over the years and are now seamlessly woven into the fabric of this modern language edition. The gist and meaning of Oahspe, as a whole, remained through previous editions and into this one. And it is hoped that this new modern language edition makes for easier and broader comprehension.

Additionally, this new Oahspe edition is enhanced with:

- clean, clear images
- ample footnotes with definitions, clarifications and explanations
- an expanded index
- a Quickfind verse numbering system for easy identification and search of interior books, chapters and verses
- a glossary that combines two different glossaries, one from the 1882 and one from the 1891 Oahspe editions.

With all these enhancements, even longtime Oahspe readers should find this present Oahspe edition enlightening and informative.

The editors wish to thank all who have contributed. Oahspe carries no pretense as to being perfect. And yet, no matter which edition is read, the essential messages and wisdom come through clearly, and the stated purpose within Oahspe can be fulfilled.

Introduction

OAHSPE Modern Language Edition contains 39 interior books (books 01/ through 39/) that compose a wide-ranging but unified book that is greater than the sum of its parts. Accordingly, we look first at what Oahspe, as a whole, is about. Next, we look at a general key to reading Oahspe. Then we see thumbnail synopses of its interior books that indicate various issues focused on by Oahspe. We end with noting several literary conventions that assist the reader in understanding as well as navigating this edition of Oahspe.

What is Oahspe About?

Oahspe reports its main purpose this way:

> || 02/1.24. Not immaculate† is this book, Oahspe; but to teach mortals how to attain to hear the Creator's voice, and to see His heavens, in full consciousness, while still living on the earth; and to know, in truth, the place and condition waiting for them after death. ||
>
> † perfect, flawless, infallible

In fulfilling its purpose Oahspe introduces the reader to the magnificence and Person of the Creator, and the realm of the angels, and what heaven is like, and awareness of the spirit and the soul, and how to attain to hear the Creator's voice and to see His light and hand.

While Oahspe is a book of spiritual light and truths, it is also a historical record. Generally, books in Oahspe pertaining to heavenly history have a companion book containing concurrent earthly history. These various histories include the geological history of the planet, the history of the human race, and the history of major religions, past and present. The heavenly history books touch upon the genesis of the planet and the emergence of human life and continue to recent heavenly history.

In a book of such limited size, only the main flow that highlights pivotal events and principal concepts can be presented. Even so, Oahspe's authors made room for an examination of historical linguistics, anthropological and archeological subjects, science and especially cosmogony. Yet so concise and rich is Oahspe that it can become the springboard into vast numbers of previously unperceived realms and fields of study.

Also, encapsulating all or part of the foregoing, some of Oahspe's interior books include an analysis of today and a prospectus for tomorrow.

In summation, all throughout Oahspe a spiritual perspective is evident. The ways of heaven and earth are revealed, and from them we can draw wise conclusions as to the consequences of choices—and extract from them enlightened ways to conduct ourselves. A delightful journey of discovery and enlightenment lies ahead. May your journey be blessed.

Key to Reading Oahspe

Oahspe has many new and strange words. Its glossary should provide assistance for many of those words that are not names. In some instances a word can be understood in the context of the sentence or paragraph where found. Also, in this modern edition, as a general rule commonly re-used terms are defined in a footnote where the term is first mentioned in the text.

Numerous other footnotes help clarify or add information or testimony to the statements in Oahspe. For this reason, it is recommended that a new reader start Oahspe from the beginning and read straight through instead of skipping around.

Another, perhaps wiser, reason to start reading at the beginning and proceeding sequentially, is that in Oahspe, spiritual concepts develop along the course of the books. It is like laying a foundation before erecting the walls, and all this before setting the roof.

Even so, there are those who will skip around. Therefore, it is suggested that all readers read books 01/ 02/ 03/ and 04/ (being Tae's Prayer; Oahspe Prologue, Voice of Man, ant the Book of Jehovih). These relatively short books introduce the overview and gist of Oahspe as well as the reality of the spirit world and of all creation.

Here follows other key divisions for the reader:

Books 05/ through 30/, being the major portion of Oahspe, present a clear-headed and well-structured chronological history of heaven and earth. These books follow the development of man as mortal and angel, dramatically chronicling both the forces of good in their attempts to enlighten and resurrect humanity, and the forces of evil and self in their attempts to build for—and in—themselves and to thwart the good. These well-written narratives stretch the imagination to brighter fields of perception and provide a comprehensive framework useful in understanding today's realities.

If you are mainly interested in what Oahspe has to say about today, see books 31/ through 34/ (Book of Ouranothen, Book of Judgment, Book of Discipline, Book of Inspiration).

If your interest rests chiefly in the subtler part of life, see books 35/ through 37/, Book of Saphah (35/) contains ancient word origins, condensed histories, rites and ceremonies. God's Book of Ben and the Book of Knowledge (36/ and 37/) reveal underpinnings of the soul realm.

If you are interested in science and prediction, see books 37/ through 39/ (Book of Knowledge, Book of Cosmogony and Prophecy, Book of Jehovih's Kingdom on Earth); also see 04/ Book of Jehovih.

Synopses of Oahspe Books

The first four books of Oahspe (Tae's Prayer through the Book of Jehovih) lay the groundwork for understanding the nature of the Oahspe and include the inhabitation of earth. With that foundation it then sets course for a concise 25-book history of heaven and earth for the past 72,000 years.

The history of humanity is marked by a series of progressions. These lessons come in cycles: advancement followed by recession, being in turn succeeded by other cycles of improvement and regression. Cycles exist within cycles, but one important cycle, used in improving the grade of humanity, is an approximately 3000 year cycle of progression. It is this cycle around which most of the interior history books of Oahspe are organized so that the history in a typical book covers events for a 3000-year period.

At the tail end of the history books, being the Book of Es (book 29/), the text merges into a series of discourses intended to illumine for the reader the requirements of humanity for this day and age. That theme continues to the end of Oahspe.

Here follows a thumbnail sketch of the Oahspe books, based on the *OAHSPE Modern Language Edition*.

Tae's Prayer 01/ introduces the need for Oahspe.
Oahspe Prologue 02/ paints the scope of Oahspe in broad brush.
Voice of Man 03/ expresses the plight of humanity.
Book of Jehovih 04/ answers humanity.

The span of 25 history books from the Book of Sethantes 05/ through the Book of Es 29/, gives a history not only of people on earth but of the heavens of the earth.

Volume 1 ends with Books 26/ and 27/ (Book of Lika; Book of the Arc of Bon). These books respectively give the heavenly history and earthly history of the beginning of the last cycle (circa 1550 bce). [Due to size constraints the *OAHSPE Modern Language Edition* volumes had to split here.]

Volume 2 of the *OAHSPE Modern Language Edition* picks up with Books 28/ and 29/ (God's Book of Eskra; Book of Es). Book 28/ brings the history from the beginning of the last cycle (circa 1550 bce) to 400 years before the beginning of the new era (circa 1449 ce). Book 29/ highlights the final 400 years to (circa 1849 ce) and then briefly touches upon the early years of this present cycle.

The remaining part of Oahspe is organized thusly:

Bon's Book of Praise 30/ expresses the parting words of the last cycle, and some inspiration and guidelines for this new era.
Book of Ouranothen 31/ contains the opening words of our God for this new cycle.
Book of Judgment 32/ wherein God gives a state of the world address for the beginning of the new era.
Book of Discipline 33/ wherein God presents an aim for humanity, and each person, to move toward; and standards by which to gauge progress.
Book of Inspiration 34/ reveals the fundamentals of inspiration, including how to best tune into the highest inspirations in this present new era.
Book of Saphah 35/ gives a synopsis of past inspirations and what humanity did with them. That is, in language development, in selected condensed histories, and in rites and ceremonies.
God's Book of Ben 36/ — having looked at past explanatory and focusing structures (rites and ceremonies in Saphah), Ben now unveils a constant edifice present throughout the ages, namely the Nine Entities. The entities then proceed to dialog with a representative mortal concerning the nature of reality. The book closes with a symbolic battle with the beast (evil that is within humanity), which battle represents the triumph of light over darkness at the end of every ca. 3000-year cycle, this battle being fought near the beginning of the previous cycle.
Book of Knowledge 37/ continues and overlaps somewhat with the Book of Ben, again dialoging with the reader as to reality, and ending with a similar symbolic battle with the beast, but this time near the beginning of the present cycle; thus showing that at the end of every cycle the beast must be transcended. The Book of Knowledge also reveals to humanity profound "unseen" structures, orders and systems of the heavens and earth.
Book of Cosmogony and Prophecy 38/ elucidates the underlying structure, system and order of our "physical" universe, and then introduces some fundamentals of prophecy.
Book of Jehovih's Kingdom on Earth 39/ is an illustrative narrative of representative persons, from some of whom comes forth Jehovih's kingdom on earth. That is, a harmonious and peaceful social

order emerges in which the Ever Present is head and leader. This type of social order facilitates the growth of humanity, both individually and collectively, toward a balanced spiritual and physical life, which, according to Oahspe, is an outcome for this new era called Kosmon.

Notes on Literary Conventions

Gender References

Oahspe is one of the most pro-woman, pro-man, pro-humanity books available to mortals. It was written before attempts at neutral gender phrasing became socially aspired toward in America. Because new standards in such phrasing have yet to be formed and consensually accepted or acquiesced in, and to avoid confusion that would arise from introducing strange conventions, it has been decided to leave, in most instances, the gender phrasing as it is.

Firstly, then, Oahspe in its general statements employs the masculine gender "man, men, he, him, his, brother, brotherhood, etc." to refer to the generic person—this is the human personage, whether male or female. Thus, Oahspe usually employs the masculine to refer to both masculine and feminine. Secondly, the word "man" can also refer to humankind or humanity, and thus include both sexes. In these gender-inclusive or gender-neutral usages, the gender makes no difference to or is not important to the subject under discussion. In those places where Oahspe means only males or only females, it normally makes that clear by the context, and by using woman, women, girl, she, her, hers, sister, etc., as needed.

Dates

There are essentially two dating systems used in Oahspe. The American civil calendar is the one used by the editors in their footnotes and parenthetical statements and is marked by "bce" or "ce". The other calendar is based on what Oahspe calls cycles and these dates end in "BK" denoting "Before the Kosmon Era", which is the present cycle. In rounded number, this cycle started about 1850 ce. Dates after Kosmon end in AK meaning "year of Kosmon" (Anno Kosmon).

Footnotes

In the *OAHSPE Modern Language Edition*, where footnotes and parenthetical statements in the text are signed '–Ed.', they refer to an 1882 editor (whose footnotes in most cases also graced the 1891 edition). The modern edition editor in chief is referred to as '–ed.'; and where the statement is from a consulting editor for this modern edition, the signature is '–cns ed.' Unsigned footnotes are generally consensus footnotes from among the editors.

Verse Numbering System

Oahspe is a Book of books. Its general format consists of sequentially ordered interior books, each with chapter and verse numbers. The 1882 and 1891 Oahspe editions (and subsequent renditions) mostly numbered each verse, restarting the numbering sequence for each new chapter. Too, mostly each interior book started with a chapter, and thus began each with chapter one. The *Oahspe Modern Language Edition* builds and improves upon that design. For, example, it uniquely assigns a sequential number for each of Oahspe's interior books.

That simple act does more than enhance the unity and order that is Oahspe. By labeling each Oahspe verse with a book number, chapter number, and verse number, the *Oahspe Modern Language Edition* makes it easy to instantly and singularly identify a verse across the whole of Oahspe. This is part of its "Quickfind" verse numbering system.

The quickfind system itself is simple. Each verse starts with a verse identifier. That verse identifier consists of three parts: the book number followed by the chapter number followed by the verse number. It takes this form: Book/chapter.verse—*always* having the slash and the period. Thus, at the start of each verse in the modern language Oahspe is a verse identifier that has the "book number/chapter number.verse number" format, followed by the words of the verse. For example, the quickfind code that starts a verse with "20/2.16" denotes Book 20 (Book of Fragapatti), Chapter 2, Verse 16. And at that place in the Oahspe is found this: "20/2.16. And Oas was embellished..."

With the quickfind system comes many benefits. Because Oahspe with the quickfind system is both online and downloadable, so by using quickfind verse numbering the reader can easily find a given verse using the common find or search tools available with modern computer systems. For example, in a digital version of the modern language Oahspe, to easily go to that above mentioned 20/2.16 verse, simply place 20/2.16 into the 'find' or 'search' tool.

Moreover, since each verse has a simple quickfind number that distinguishes it from all other verses, this also means that a quickfind number by itself immediately reveals its corresponding location. This is helpful to know when coming upon quickfind referrals to the verse in other content areas of Oahspe such as the glossary or index. For instance, if an index entry referred to 20/2.16, it is clear that the reference is to chapter 2, verse 16 of the Book of Fragapatti. This gives rise to another benefit of using quickfind: it is easy to jot down the location of a desired passage and without the labor of writing out its corresponding interior book name. This is especially convenient when citing a diverse collection of Oahspe extracts.

Virtually all of Oahspe's quickfind verse identifiers are formatted as outlined above, namely: Book/*chapter*.verse. But one interior book, Oahspe's Book of Saphah, formats slightly differently. Saphah is divided by topics not by chapters. Accordingly, Saphah (book 35/) formats this way: Book/*Topic*.verse; or more specifically, 35/Topic.verse. Topics are identified by Letters instead of Chapter Numbers. For example, 35/D.1 refers to the Book of Saphah/the Tablet of Se'moin (labeled as topic D).verse 1, that is, 35/D.1 refers to Saphah/Se'moin.verse 1.

Saphah is a special case because it contains diverse topics. These topics have been categorized into sections, subordinate sections, and segments within them. These sections, subsections and segments do not necessarily follow each other in chronological order. To help indicate that, and to eliminate an implied chronology caused by sequencing of numbers, each segment or subsection has been allotted a letter of the alphabet instead of a chapter number; hence, e.g., Se'moin verse 1, is 35/D.1 but not 35/4.1.

A few of Saphah's segments have chapters within them. In those cases, the chapter number is inserted after the Topic. The quickfind formatting for that is: 35/Topic.chapter.verse. For example, 35/C.3.4 refers to the Book of Saphah/Topic C.chapter 3.verse 4. Topic C is the segment called Pan. Thus, 35/C.3.4 refers to chapter 3, verse 4 of Saphah's Pan. At that place in Oahspe this reads: 35/C.3.4. Many words were made sacred, so that they would be well learned and kept sacred. ||

In previous Oahspe editions the Saphah segments are not all clearly identified nor properly placed, and some have no verse numbers. But in this modern edition each segment not only has been clearly identified and given verse numbers, but now Saphah's various sections and sub-sections have been explicitly identified so that the context of any segment can be perceived more easily.

For easy reference, all quickfind book numbers and Saphah topics (letters) are shown in the Table of Contents of this *Oahspe Modern Language Edition*.

Numeration

Whenever the reader reads the word, billion, it is meant 10^9, which is the same thing as a thousand million; hence one billion = 1,000,000,000 or 1 x 10^9. Similarly, a trillion means 10^{12}, which is the same thing as a million million; so one trillion = 1,000,000,000,000 or 1 x 10^{12}.

Punctuation

Oahspe uses the double pipes symbol (||) generally to indicate a change. Thus, the symbol '||' is used to indicate the beginning or end of a quote or a statement by someone (Oahspe rarely uses quote marks). Also the double pipes symbol || is used to indicate an abrupt change of topic, such as at the end of an otherwise unmarked subsection within a chapter.

Tae's Prayer

Chapter 1 Tae's Prayer

01/1.1. JEHOVIH, the Creator, said: I blow My breath upon the planet, and man[1] comes forth, inquiring: Who am I, and what is my destiny? ||

01/1.2. So I send an elder brother of man, to teach him, and show him the light.

01/1.3. God said: Behold[2] me, O[3] man, I am an elder brother. I have passed through death and found the glory of the unseen worlds.

01/1.4. Jehovih gave to me, your God, dominion over the earth and her heavens.

01/1.5. Man said: I have found truth in corpor (physicality); I know I live; that trees grow and die. This is true knowledge. || Give me truth regarding the unseen; and a way that I can prove its truth?

01/1.6. And in the stirring up of man's soul, Jehovih spoke through His[4] sons and daughters. His voice came up out of the marsh and down from the heavens above, and the children of men heard and saw, and rose up because of the spirit in them. They responded to Him, Who is Almighty; and their voices were called Tae, because as it is the universal word of all children born, so it represents the universal prayer of man (humankind).

01/1.7. Tae said: Reveal, O Father, give me light! I see the wide earth, the sun, moon and stars. But the great vault of heaven appears to be just an empty sky. Where is the dwelling place[5] of the dead; the place of the souls of men?

01/1.8. In times past, You have quickened seers and prophets, and through them, lifted up Your children and proclaimed other worlds! Am I less worthy than those of past ages? All the while my forefathers, and now I, have abided by[6] Your mighty presence.

01/1.9. By Your own hand You have quickened my consciousness, to be dissatisfied with the old revelations, and made me peer deeper into the cause and place of things,[7] and to desire further light from Your holy place.

01/1.10. By Your power my manhood (womanhood) has been raised up. Only by Your power and wisdom will I be appeased.[8]

01/1.11. When I was a child I believed as a child, because it was told to me; but now that I am grown, I desire to know who Your prophets were, and how they attained their gifts, and wisdom of words.

01/1.12. The cosmogony You taught in ancient times was sufficient for that day; but now I am raised up by You to receive comprehensive knowledge of the sun, and the stars of other worlds, and of their travel in Your great firmament.[9]

01/1.13. And now I cry out to You, where is the promised heaven? Where is the proof of immortal life? By You I was quickened into life and made conscious that I am. To You I come in the majesty You made me, You my Father! By You I was made determined to sift all things to the bottom. In You I know there is capacity to encompass all my holy desires, and answer me.

01/1.14. Give me of Your Light, O Father. When I was a child I called to You as a child; now, I call out in the manhood (womanhood) You have bestowed upon me! I will know Your Lords, Gods, Saviors, and Your promised heaven.

01/1.15. I have scaled the mountain; the countless corporeal worlds traveling in the eternal sea of space speak of Your handiwork! I have perceived that all the stars in heaven would not fill the hollow of Your hand; that truly Your breath

---

[1] When Oahspe uses the word, man, as here, it refers to the human personage, whether male or female, and can also refer to the race of humankind. This generic meaning of 'man' is occasionally reinforced by the use of parentheses as in "Your son (Your daughter)." In those instances where Oahspe uses 'man, he, him, his' to mean 'male human only' the context makes it clear.

[2] perceive, look at, observe, discern

[3] The word "O" as in || O man, or O Jehovih || is a simplified construction of the word "Oh" and is used extensively throughout Oahspe.

[4] The Creator has had many names and is also feminine, as will be explained later in Oahspe.

[5] home, residence, domicile

[6] successfully lived with, endured, remained with, conformed to, undergone, borne up under, withstood

[7] the why and where of things

[8] satisfied, brought to peace and calm

[9] the world of space between the stars and planets. –1891 glossary. [sky, heaven, etc.]

moves the universe! The glory of Your works has inspired me with fervor[10] to come to Your Mighty Home!

01/1.16. Speak, O Jehovih! You alone can satisfy this soaring spirit that sprang from You, inspired. Give me light! O Father!

01/1.17. I have encompassed the earth and bridged its nations with assimilative words.[11] My geography is finished. O, give me a book of heaven! I have burrowed deep in corporeal knowledge, and have seen the drift of all on the earth. Where is the spirit world, and land of the dead? O give me light!

Chapter 2 Tae's Prayer

01/2.1. Jehovih heard Tae's prayer, and answered him. He said: Let the angels of heaven go down to the earth. My blessed son calls to Me in wisdom and truth. || And the angels of heaven descended to the earth, for it was in the early days of dan'ha (a time of great spiritual light) in the firmament of heaven, and the angels manifested and proved the immortal life of man.[12]

01/2.2. Jehovih said: Let this day be the beginning of the reign of Kosmon (the new era now upon us); for it is the beginning of the wisdom of earth joined with the wisdom of heaven,[13] in My name.

01/2.3. Tae said: Yet not even half is answered, O my Father in heaven. Since You have proved the immortal life, You have stirred me to my soul's foundation. Where do these inhabitants of the unseen world come from? Where lies this heavenly footstool of Your majesty?

01/2.4. If when I am dead I shall see the place, is the germ of that sight not already in me? How am I made that I see, but do not see this? Hear, but do not hear this? If I am now dead to[14] that which is to be, will I not then be dead to what is here now? Give me light, O Father!

01/2.5. Jehovih said: I gave a corporeal body to man so that he could learn corporeal things; but I made death so that he could rise in spirit, as an angel, and inhabit My etherean worlds.[15]

01/2.6. Tae said: You made both the seen and the unseen. Are they at war, or in harmony? My corporeal body is made of earth (flesh), and stone (minerals, bone) and water. Is the spiritual body, then, not made of air (oxygen, hydrogen) and imperceptible[16] dust?

01/2.7. The angels You have sent have feet and legs! Why? Do they walk on the air, or wade through it? They have no wings,[17] they cannot fly; they say they have not seen the illustrious angels who have long been dead. Must I also go into the es world (spirit world, heaven) simply to meet my neighbors, and never salute the wise of ancient days? Give me light, O Jehovih!

01/2.8. Something within me makes me anticipate the light and glory of what I have not seen; but I must have it tangible and demonstrable —the pure truth!

01/2.9. Have You not given me an inquiring spirit, so that I must prove all things to my own satisfaction? How and when, then, O Jehovih, shall I find growth for my own members,[18] so that I can know the es worlds and its inhabitants? I will not be appeased by merely seeing the spirits of the dead, or by their testimony. They may call themselves God, Christ, Buddha, Brahma, Allah, Confucius or Jesus, yet I will not rest on them or

[10] intense desire, enthusiasm, zeal, vitality

[11] words of amity and goodwill that help bring about harmony, fellowship, peace and unity, being welcoming and congenial

[12] This was the spiritualism movement, which flourished from about 1849 to 1882, being capped by the publication of Oahspe.

[13] physical awareness united with spiritual awareness

[14] unconscious of

[15] Etherean worlds are heavenly worlds existing in the highest heaven. To the corporeal eye peering up into the vastness of interstellar space, it looks mostly empty, but to the spiritual eye, it is filled with innumerable worlds—wondrous, awe-inspiring, full of beauty and joy.

[16] intangible, not perceived, subtle

[17] The depiction of angels having wings was an artistic device meant to symbolize the ability of an angel to rise to the higher heavenly realms, and, so, inspire mortals to understand that the soul was meant to rise beyond the earth.

[18] for example, spiritual senses such as spiritual ears and spiritual eyes; also soul, discernment and judgment

their word. I will put forward my plea to You only, O Jehovih. I am Your son (Your daughter).

01/2.10. You have quickened me to know things by my own knowledge; and though it is told me: Thus said the Lord of your God, yet I will raise my voice ever above them. And though a spirit says: I am your Jehovih, believe me, I will deny him.

01/2.11. For, You have quickened me to rise up above the tales of the ancients, and to demand knowledge from Your throne. By You, my soul is moved to this magnificence, and only Your magnificence can satisfy Your son (Your daughter).

01/2.12. As to the spirits of the dead, I desire to know their dwelling places, how they live, how they travel, their manner of growth, their food and clothes, and how they spend their time—whether they labor or live idly; and above all, to what extent, and in what way, their corporeal lives affected their spiritual happiness in heaven.

01/2.13. I desire to know, too, how it was with the ancients? Make clear, O Jehovih, the heavens and ways of my forefathers, for I would apply Your lessons wisely! The wisdom of today I would weigh against the crucible of the past, and set my star to the future, well prepared.

01/2.14. What then, O Father, is Your judgment upon the world today? For I desire to know how to live, so that tomorrow may prove an everlasting glory. Make plain the ways of heaven and earth, O my Creator! I would know Your creation, so that my just place in Your wide universe may become known to me.

01/2.15. Give me light, O Father! Not by word of mouth. I will have my members quickened so that I can comprehend within myself.

01/2.16. Then Jehovih, the Creator, spoke, saying: To all men and women I gave two senses, corpor and es. In the time of Seffas[19] (now finished) I allotted time for man to mature corpor (materiality). But now the time of Kosmon has come (the new era), and man shall mature es (spirituality).

01/2.17. It is well that you be believing toward men and angels; but it is better to develop yourself. You have desired to know the mysteries of My unseen worlds, and the past histories of the earth. Behold, I will give you a new sense, which will fulfill your soul's desire. And with it, you shall read the books in the libraries of heaven!

01/2.18. In the past, have I not said: All things shall be revealed! || Do not think that a loud-speaking messenger will come, for man would not believe; but I quickened the righteous with My own hand, and they will comprehend without belief.[20]

01/2.19. The time of preaching and believing is at an end.[21] Man shall know by his own knowledge, and practice that which he knows.[22] In this, My light is being manifested in this day. ||

01/2.20. And again Jehovih spoke in heaven, in answer to Tae's prayer; and OAHSPE came forth, being one of the first fruits, for this, the KOSMON era.

Oahspe

02/1.1. After the creation of man, the Creator, Jehovih, said to him: So that you shall know you are the work of My hand, I have given you capacity for knowledge, power and dominion. This was the first era.

02/1.2. But man was helpless; neither did he stand upright, nor understand the voice of the Almighty. And Jehovih called His angels, who were older than the earth, and He said to them: Go, raise man upright, and teach him to understand.

02/1.3. So the angels of heaven descended to the earth and raised man upright. And man wandered about on the earth. This was the second era.

02/1.4. Jehovih said to the angels who were with man: Behold, man has multiplied on the earth.

[19] Enforced culture

[20] That is, within themselves they shall perceive the truth or gist of the matter—and thus perceive beyond that which is accepted as true (believed to be true) merely because of tradition, guesswork, unsubstantiated testimony, manipulation of logic or emotion, etc.

[21] This may seem, by some, to contradict 01/2.17, which says, being believing is on the right road—but the verse also recommends developing beyond belief; and in 01/2.19 we learn it is because mere belief is insufficient to attain to Kosmon.

[22] That is, what knowledge man has, he will have acquired through his own understanding, and so put into practice that which he knows.

Bring them together; teach them to dwell in cities and nations.

02/1.5. So the angels of Jehovih taught the peoples of the earth to dwell together in cities and nations. This was the third era.

02/1.6. Now in that same time the Beast (self)[23] rose up before[24] man, and spoke to him, saying: Possess whatever you will, for all things are yours, and are good for you.

02/1.7. Man obeyed the Beast; and war came into the world. This was the fourth era.

02/1.8. And man became sick at heart, and he called out to the Beast, saying: You said: Possess all things for yourself, for they are good for you. Now, behold, war and death have encompassed me on all sides. I pray, therefore, teach me peace!

02/1.9. But the Beast said: Do not think I come to send peace on the earth; I come not to send peace, but a sword. I come to set man at variance against his father; and a daughter against her mother. Whatever you find to eat, whether fish or flesh, eat it, taking no thought of tomorrow.

02/1.10. So man ate fish and flesh, becoming carnivorous, and darkness came upon him, and he no longer heard the voice of Jehovih or believed in Him. This was the fifth era.

02/1.11. And the Beast divided itself into four great heads, and possessed the earth; and man fell down and worshipped them.

02/1.12. The names of the heads of the Beast were, Brahmin, Buddhist, Christian, and Mohammedan. And they divided the earth, and apportioned it between themselves, choosing soldiers and standing armies for the maintenance of their earthly aggrandizement.[25]

02/1.13. And the Brahmins had seven million soldiers; the Buddhists twenty million; the Christians seven million; and the Mohammedans two million; whose trade was killing man. And man, in service of the Beast, gave one-sixth of his life and his labor to war and standing armies; and one-third to dissipation and drunkenness. This was the sixth era.

02/1.14. Jehovih called out to man to desist from evil; but man did not hear Him. For, the cunning of the Beast had changed man's flesh, so that his soul was hidden as if in a cloud, and he loved sin.

02/1.15. Jehovih called to His angels in heaven, saying: Go down to the earth once more, to man, whom I created to inhabit the earth and enjoy it, and say to him: Thus says Jehovih:

02/1.16. Behold, the seventh era has begun. Your Creator commands your change from a carnivorous man of contention, to an herbivorous man of peace. The four heads of the Beast shall be put away; and there shall be no more war on the earth.

02/1.17. Your armies shall be disbanded. And, from this time forward, whoever desires to not war, you shall not impress (draft, conscript);[26] for it is the commandment of your Creator.

02/1.18. Neither shall you have any God, Lord or Savior, but only your Creator, Jehovih! And you shall worship none other, from this time forward forever. I am sufficient for My own creations.

02/1.19. And to all who separate themselves from the dominion of the Beast, making these covenants to Me, I have given the foundation of My kingdom on earth.

02/1.20. And all such people shall be My chosen; by their covenants and their works they shall be known on the earth from this time forward as Mine, and shall be called Faithists.

02/1.21. But to those who will not make these covenants, I have given the numbers of the Beast, and they shall be called Uzians, signifying destroyers. And from this time forward, these shall be the two kinds of people on earth, Faithists and Uzians.

02/1.22. So the angels of heaven descended to the earth, to man, and appeared before him, face to

---

[23] This is the animal part of man; the negative or shadow of the light; the identity or sense of being separate from others; egocentricity; possessiveness; self-concerns.

The beast or self, begins in the corporeal man and continues with him till he learns to transcend it. Whether that happens on earth or in the lower heavens, it must be done before rising to inherit the higher spirit worlds.

[24] into the perception of, in the presence of, in front of; that is, the beast rose to ascendancy in the thoughts and attention of man of that era

[25] expansion of: power, profit, status, reputation, honor (so-called), influence, hegemony, etc.

[26] i.e., shall not force into military service

face, hundreds of thousands of them, speaking as man speaks, writing as man writes, and teaching these things about Jehovih and His works.[27]

02/1.23. And in the thirty-third year of the angels' descent, the Ambassadors of the angel hosts of heaven, in the name of Jehovih revealed to man His heavenly kingdoms, through this OAHSPE, making known the plan of His delightful creations, for the resurrection of the peoples of the earth.

02/1.24. Not immaculate[28] is this book, OAHSPE; but to teach mortals HOW TO ATTAIN TO HEAR THE CREATOR'S VOICE, and to SEE HIS HEAVENS, in full consciousness, while still living on the earth; and to know, in truth, the place and condition waiting for them after death.[29]

02/1.25. Neither are, nor were, the revelations in this OAHSPE wholly new to mortals. The same things have been revealed at the same time to many, who live at remote distances from one another, but who were not in correspondence till afterward.

02/1.26. Because this light is comprehensive, embracing corporeal and spiritual things, it is called the beginning of the KOSMON ERA. And because it relates to earth, sky and spirit, it is called OAHSPE.[30]

The Voice of Man

03/1.1. O Jehovih, what am I that I should supplicate You? Do I know my own weakness, or do I understand the way of my thoughts? You have placed before me most wonderful creations. They impress me, and my senses rise up in remembrance of the Almighty. Where have I invented one thought other than by looking upon Your works? How can I do otherwise than remember my Creator, and out of Your creations, O Jehovih, find rich food for meditation all the days of my life?

03/1.2. And yet, though I have appropriated the earth to myself, I am neither happy nor perfect. Misery, crime and selfishness are upon my people.

03/1.3. What is my weakness that I cannot overcome it? Or, what is my strength that I give in to the desires of the earth? I build up my belief and courage in You; but before I know the way of my weakness, I stumble and fall. Am I made that I shall be forever a disappointment to myself, and a censure[31] to my own behavior?

03/1.4. How can I say to anyone: Be pure and holy, O man! || Are my flesh and blood not proof that man cannot be without sin? O this corruptible self, this tendency to fall from the right way! You, O my Creator, have proven to my senses, every day of my life, that You alone are mighty in purity and truth.

03/1.5. If only I had a starting point from which to estimate Your wonderful decrees, or could find a road in which I would never stumble! But yet, O Jehovih, I will not complain because of the way of Your works. You have invented a limit to my understanding, by which I am reminded of You, to call upon Your name. I perceive my own vanity; that were all knowledge mine, I would become less beholden[32] to You!

03/1.6. What am I, O Jehovih, without You; or how am I to find the glory of Your creations, other than by the light of Your countenance? You raised me up out of sin and darkness, and clothed me in light. I perceive the smallness of myself in Your great works. You have bound me to travel on the earth, to sojourn[33] with beasts and all types of creeping things; nor have You given me one attribute[34] in which I can boast over them, except in the power of destruction. The high firmament You have placed above me; the stars, moon and sun! I know You have been there, but I am bound down in a little corner of Your works! Neither do I have power to rise up to Your distant places, nor to know Your extended heavens.

03/1.7. No, I do not even have power to shape my own size and stature; but all things take form and dimension whether I will it or not. In Your own

[27] Again, this was the spiritualism movement.

[28] perfect, flawless, infallible

[29] That is, the purpose of writing Oahspe was not to produce the perfect book, but to show mortals how to attain to the Creator's Voice, see His Heavens, etc.

[30] From the Panic language (first language of the earth): O = sky, or heaven, Ah = earth, and Spe = spirit.

[31] reproof, critical eye

[32] appreciative, indebted, obliged, grateful, thankful, worshipful, prayerful

[33] to temporarily exist with

[34] characteristic, trait, quality

way the walls of the world are built; by their magnitude[35] I am confounded; by the majesty of Your hand, appalled.[36] Why have I vainly set myself up as the highest of Your works? My failures are worse than any other living creature under the sun. I cannot build my house in perfection as a bird does; my ingenuity cannot fashion a spider's net; I cannot sail up in the air like a bird, nor live in the water like the fish, nor dwell in harmony like the bee. Half of my offspring die in infancy; and the multitude of my household are quarrelers, fighters, drunkards and beggars; the best of my sons and daughters are less faithful than a dog! I go forth to war, to slay my brother, even while Your wide earth has room for all. Yes, I plague the earth with starvation, sin and untimely death. O, if only I could school myself to not boast of my greatness; instead I should be forever ashamed in Your sight, Jehovih!

03/1.8. But I will acknowledge my iniquities;[37] I can hide nothing from the eye of my Creator. Hear me then, O Father!

03/1.9. I took up arms[38] against my brother. With great armies I encompassed him, to despoil[39] him.

03/1.10. By the stroke of my sword I multiplied his widows and orphans; the cry of anguish that came out of their mouths I answered by the destruction of my brother's harvests.

03/1.11. To my captains and generals who showed great skill in killing, I built monuments in stone and iron. Yes, I inscribed them from top to bottom with their bloody victories.

03/1.12. And in my vanity I called out to the young, saying: Behold the glory of these great men! To honor them, I have built these great monuments!

03/1.13. And the youth of my household were whetted[40] with ambition for spoil. The example of my hand made them train themselves for warfare.

03/1.14. To my colonels and generals I gave badges of gold. I called to the young women, saying: Come, a great honor I give you; you shall dance with the officers of death!

03/1.15. And they fluttered up on tip-toe, elated by the honey of my words! O Jehovih, how gaping [41] my wickedness; how utterly I have failed, except in making the flow of my brother's blood the relish of satan![42]

03/1.16. To my destroying hosts I have given great honor and glory. In the pretense of enforcing peace I hewed[43] my way in flesh and blood.

03/1.17. I made an illusion, a kingdom. I called out to my people, saying: We must have a kingdom! I showed them no reason for it; but I pressed them to take up arms and follow me for patriotism's sake. And yet what was patriotism? Behold, I made it as something greater than You and Your commandment: YOU SHALL NOT KILL.

03/1.18. Yes, by the cunning of my words, I taught them my brother was my enemy; that to fall upon and destroy him and his people was great patriotism.

03/1.19. And they ran at the sound of my voice, for my glory in the greatness of my kingdom; and they committed great havoc.

03/1.20. Yes, I built colleges for training my young men in warfare. I drew boundaries, making borders here and there, saying: This is my kingdom! All others are my enemies!

03/1.21. I patted my young men on the head, saying: You dogs of war![44] Great shall be your glory!

03/1.22. And their judgment was turned away from peace; I made them think that righteousness was to stand up for me and my country, and to destroy my brother and his people.

03/1.23. Yes, they built me forts, castles and arsenals, without number.[45] I called to my people,

---

[35] great size and extent

[36] dumbstruck, overawed, sapped of audacity, paled, held in check, made fearful, overwhelmed, humbled

[37] sins, wickedness, immorality, evildoings

[38] weapons, instruments of war

[39] ruin, pillage, take by force, ravage, desecrate

[40] sharpened, stimulated, inspired

[41] open, obvious and extensive

[42] those who love evil and its practice; selfishness per se; self; the supposed opposite of Jehovih; the evil voice within man; the captain of the selfish passions; the captain of evil

[43] cut, hacked, slashed

[44] i.e., you warriors

[45] too many to be counted, endless numbers of them, innumerable

saying: Come, behold the glory of my defenses which I built for you!

03/1.24. And they gave me money, garrisons,[46] ships of war[47] and torpedoes,[48] shouting: Hurrah for our kingdom! We have faith in these things, but not in You, our Creator!

03/1.25. Thus I led them away from You. Their eyes I turned to look down, in the way of death. By the might of my armies, I put away righteousness.

03/1.26. Yes, I covered the earth over with drunkards, widows and orphans; to beggary I reduced them; but I whetted their pride by saying: Look what great standing armies we have!

03/1.27. To the man who said: There shall come a time of peace, when war shall be no more forever, I mocked and said: You fool! ||

03/1.28. I know the counts against me,[49] O Father. I cannot hide my iniquity from Your sight. I have said war was a necessary evil to prevent a too populous world! I turned my back on the wide, unsettled regions of the earth. With this falsehood in my mouth I stood up before You! Yes, I cried out as if for the righteous, saying: I war for righteousness, and for the protection of the weak! In the destruction of my brothers and sisters I stood as a murderer, pleading this excuse. Stubbornly I persisted in not seeing justice on the other side, while I cut down those whom You had created alive. Above the works of Your hand I raised myself up as a pruning knife in Your vineyard.

03/1.29. Even more than this, I persuaded my sons and daughters that to war for me was to war for our Father in heaven. By my blasphemy I led them into ruin. And when the battle was over for a day, I cried out: Behold the glory of those who were slain for the honor of their country! || Thus I have added crime to crime before You, Jehovih; and so, destroyed Your beautiful creation. Truly, I have not one word in justification of my deeds before You!

03/1.30. O, if only I had remained faithful with You, Jehovih! But I invented Gods to the glory of the evil one. In one place I called out to my sons and daughters, saying: Be Brahmins; Brahma saves whoever professes his name. In another place I said: Be Buddhists; Buddha saves whoever calls on his name. In another place I said: Be Christians; Christ saves whoever calls on his name. In another place I said: Be Mohammedans; whoever says: "There is only one God and Mohammed is his prophet!" shall have indulgence without sin. ||

03/1.31. Thus I have divided the earth, O Jehovih! Into four great idolatries I have established them, and into their hands put all manner of weapons of destruction; and they have become more terrible against one another than the beasts of the forest. O, if only I could put away these great iniquities which I raised up as everlasting torments to the earth. Truly, there is no salvation in any of these.

03/1.32. Their people are continually destroying one another. They quarrel and kill for their respective religions; setting aside Your commandment: You shall not kill. They love their own nation and hate all others. They set aside Your commandment: Love your neighbor as yourself.

03/1.33. They preach and pray in sufficient truth; but not one of these people practices peace, love and virtue, in any degree equal to their understanding. These religions have not saved from sin any nation or city on the whole earth.

03/1.34. In vain I have searched for a plan of redemption; a plan that would make the earth a paradise, and the life of man a glory to You our Creator, and a joy to himself. But alas, the two extremes, riches and poverty, have made the prospect of a millennium[50] a thing of mockery.

03/1.35. For one rich man there are a thousand poor, and their interests ceaselessly conflict with one another. Labor cries out in pain; but capital strikes him with a heartless blow.

03/1.36. Nation is against nation; king against king; merchant against merchant; consumer against producer; yes, man against man, in all things upon the earth.

03/1.37. Because the state is rotten, the politician feeds on it; because society is rotten, the lawyer and court have riches and sumptuous feasts; because the flesh of my people is rotten, the physician finds a harvest of comfort.

---

[46] fortifications, military posts and outposts

[47] war machinery

[48] weapons of destruction

[49] i.e., know the charges, indictments, accusations, particulars, specifics, etc.

[50] an enduring time of peace, virtue, happiness and prosperity

03/1.38. Now, O Jehovih, I come to You! You hold the secret of peace, harmony and goodwill among mortals. Give me of Your light, O Father! Show me the way to proceed so that war, crime and poverty, may come to an end. Open the way of peace, love, virtue and truth, so that Your children may rejoice in their lives, and glorify You and Your works forever.

03/1.39. Such is the voice of man, O Jehovih! In all the nations of the earth this voice rises up to You! As You spoke to Zarathustra, Abraham and Moses, leading them forth out of darkness, O speak, Jehovih!

03/1.40. Man has faith in You only; You alone were sufficient for the past: Today, You alone are sufficient for Your own creation. Speak, O Jehovih!

Book of Jehovih

In which is revealed the three great worlds (realms), corpor, atmospherea, and etherea. As in all other Bibles it is revealed that this world was created, so in this Bible, Oahspe, it is revealed how the Creator created it. As other Bibles have proclaimed heavens for the spirits of the dead, behold, this Bible reveals where these heavens are, and the manner, glory and work that the spirits of the dead enjoy; and through which the wisdom, power, love and glory of the Almighty is magnified for the understanding of man.

CHAPTER 1 Jehovih

04/1.1. ALL was. ALL is. ALL ever shall be. The ALL spoke, and Motion was, and is, and ever shall be; and, being positive, was called He and Him. The ALL MOTION was His speech.

04/1.2. He said, I AM! And He comprehended all things, the seen and the unseen. Nor is there anything in all the universe that is not part of Him.

04/1.3. He said, I am the soul of all; and all that is seen is part of My person and My body.

04/1.4. By virtue of My presence, all things are. By virtue of My presence, life is. By virtue of My presence, the living are brought forth into life. I am the QUICKENER, the MOVER, the CREATOR, the DESTROYER. I am FIRST and LAST.

04/1.5. I am two apparent entities, nevertheless I AM ONLY ONE. These entities are the UNSEEN, which is POTENT, and the SEEN, which is of itself IMPOTENT, and called CORPOR.

04/1.6. With these two entities, in likeness of Myself through them, I made all the living; for as the life is the potent part, so the corporeal part is the impotent part.

04/1.7. Chief over all that live on the earth I made Man; male and female I made them. And, so that man could distinguish Me, I commanded him to give Me a name; by virtue of My presence I commanded him. And man did not name Me after anything in heaven or on the earth. In obedience to My will he named Me after the sounds the wind utters, and he said, E–O–Ih! Which is now pronounced Jehovih, and is written thus:[51]

i001 **Symbol of the Creator's Name**.

CHAPTER 2 Jehovih

04/2.1. Jehovih said: By virtue of My presence I created the seen and unseen worlds. And I commanded man to name them; and man called the seen worlds Corpor, and the unseen worlds Es; and the inhabitants of Corpor, man called corporeans. But the inhabitants of Es he sometimes called

[51] Circle, cut twice, which is the true equal length cross, and with the leaf of life in the midst; see image i001.

es'eans and sometimes spirits and sometimes angels.

04/2.2. Jehovih said: I created the earth, and fashioned it, and placed it in the firmament; and by My presence, brought man forth a living being. I gave him a corporeal body so that he could learn corporeal things; and I made death so that he could rise in the firmament and inherit My etherean worlds.

04/2.3. To es I gave dominion over corpor; with es I filled all place in the firmament (even within corpor). But corpor I made into earths, moons, stars and suns; beyond number I made them, and I caused them to float in the places I allotted to them.

04/2.4. Es I divided into two parts, and I commanded man to name them, and he called one etherea and the other atmospherea. These are the three kinds of worlds I created (corporeal, atmospherean, and etherean); but I gave different densities to atmospherean worlds, and different densities to the etherean worlds.[52]

04/2.5. For the substance of My etherean worlds I created Ethe, the MOST RAREFIED.[53] Out of ethe I made them. And I made ethe the subtlest of all created things, and gave it power and place, not only by itself, but also power to penetrate and exist within all things, even within the corporeal worlds. And to ethe I gave dominion over both atmospherea and corpor.

04/2.6. In the ALL HIGHEST places I created the etherean worlds, and I made them of all shapes and sizes, similar to My corporeal worlds. But I made the etherean worlds inhabitable both within and without,[54] with entrances and exits, in arches and curves, thousands of miles high and wide; and in colors, movable chasms and mountains in endless change and brilliancy; and over them I ruled (rule) with ALL PERFECT mechanism. To them I gave motions, orbits and courses of their own; and I made them independent, and above all other worlds in potency and majesty.

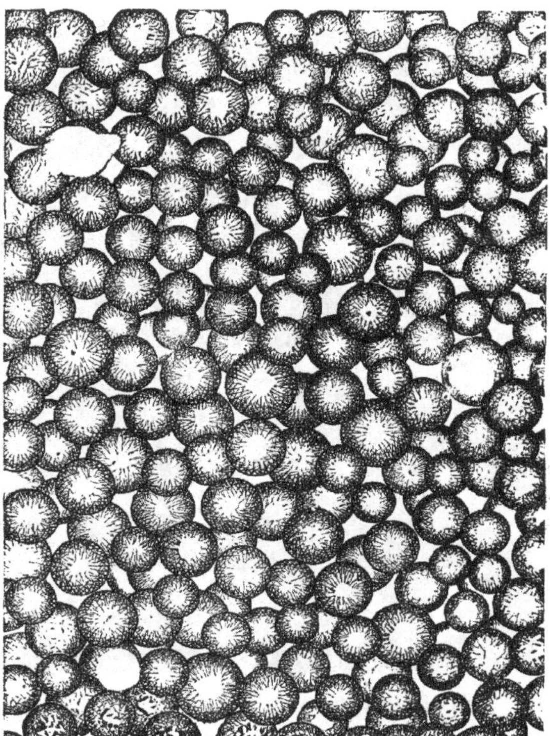

i002 **Etherea**. Jehovih said: For the substance of My etherean worlds I created Ethe, the MOST RAREFIED. Out of ethe I made them. And I made ethe the subtlest of all created things, and gave it power and place, not only by itself, but also power to penetrate and exist within all things, even within the corporeal worlds. And to ethe I gave dominion over both atmospherea and corpor.

04/2.7. Nor did I create one etherean world like another in size, density or in component parts, but every one differing from another, and with a glory matchless each in its own way.[55]

04/2.8. I also created atmospherean worlds in the firmament, and gave them places, orbits and courses for themselves. But atmospherean worlds I created shapeless and without fixed form, for they are in the process of condensation or dissolution, being intermediate in condition between My etherean and My corporeal worlds. Of three degrees of density I created them, and I commanded man to name them, and one he called Ji'ay, and one A'ji and one Nebulae.

---

[52] When a person dies, he lives first as a spirit (angel) in atmospherea. Afterward, in time he rises to etherea to live as an etherean. The dividing line between atmospherea and etherea is called Chinvat, which acts as a sort of bridge between atmospherea and etherea. Etherea is sometimes called Nirvania.

[53] see image i002

[54] i.e., on the surface; outside

[55] see image i003 next page

i003 **Snowflakes**. Jehovih said: I created the corporeal worlds round in shape, with land and water, and I made them impenetrable, for I bring forth the living on the surface of them. Man should not imagine that My etherean worlds are also round and impenetrable; for, of all I have created, I created no two alike. || Now, it came to pass in the lapse of time, that the atmosphereans so loved the lower heavens, that they did not strive to ascend to the emancipated heavens of Nirvania, never having reached the bridge of Chinvat. But they often returned to the earth and conversed with corporeans, and they lauded the glories of even the lower heavens, so that man looked up in wonder because of the magnificence of the Father's works. Yet these were bound spirits.* Then Jehovih made the snowflake and caused it to fall, so that man could behold the beauty and glory of its formation. And He sent ethereans down from the emancipated heavens, and these taught man that whatever glory he had yet heard of, was as darkness is to light, compared to the beauty and majesty of the etherean worlds. And the ethereans held up snowflakes, saying: In the name of Jehovih we declare to you, that the etherean worlds are larger than the earth, and penetrable—full of roadways of crystals, and arches, and curves, and angles, so that were man to travel a million years on one alone, he could not see half its beauty and glory. And the firmament of heaven has tens of billions of etherean worlds. Look at the snowflakes as though they were microscopic patterns of the worlds in high heaven; and you shall tint them like a rainbow, and people them with countless millions of angels, spotless, pure, holy, and rich in the knowledge of Jehovih and His works, and full of the majesty of His love.

* Atmosphereans reside in the lower heavens, and are called bound spirits because they are bound to atmospherea till they are emancipated.

04/2.9. But all of them are composed of the same substances, being like the earth, but rarefied. Nor is there on the earth or in it, one thing, whether iron, lead, gold, water, oil, or stones, that is not also in My atmospherean worlds. As I have given light to the earth so have I given light to many of them; and all these I have commanded man to call comets. And he named them so.

04/2.10. And I also created atmospherea around My corporeal worlds; together I made them.[56]

[56] see image i005

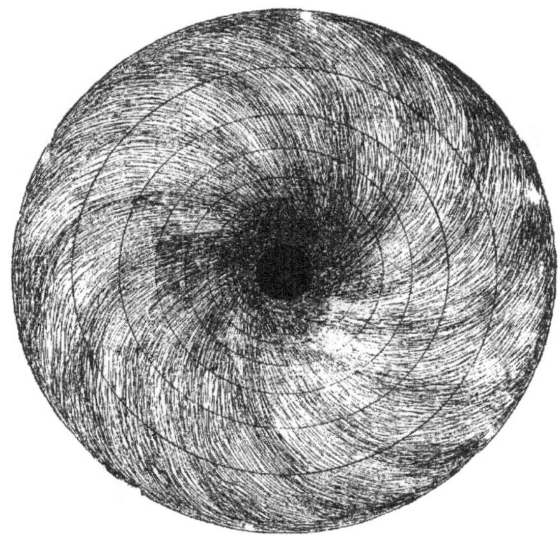

i005 **Earth and Atmospherea**, (as seen through spiritual eyes). Jehovih has said: Around My corporeal worlds I placed atmospherea; for, as the earth and other corporeal worlds provide a womb for the spirit of man, so have I made the substance of atmospherea to be a womb for the souls of men. And Jehovih made the atmosphere of the earth with a circumference of 1,504,000 miles, with the earth floating in the center of it. || The earth is the black center, and the surrounding swirled gradations of gray, her atmospherea. The rings symbolize plateaus; the outer rim, Chinvat.

CHAPTER 3 Jehovih

04/3.1. Thus spoke Jehovih; by the light of Kosmon He proclaimed these things among the nations of the earth.

04/3.2. Man looked upward in prayer, desiring to know the way of all created things, both on earth and in heaven. And Jehovih answered him, saying:

04/3.3. The whirlwind I made as a sign to man of the way of My created worlds. As you see the power of the whirlwind gathering up the dust of the earth, and driving it together, know that likewise I bring together the ji'ay, a'ji and nebulae in the firmament of heaven; by the power of the whirlwind I create the corporeal suns, moons and stars. And I commanded man to name the whirlwinds in the etherean firmament, and he named them according to their shape, calling them vortices and wark.

04/3.4. By the power of rotation, swift driving at the periphery, I condense the atmospherean worlds that float in the firmament; and these become My corporeal worlds. In the midst of the vortices I made them, and by the power of the vortices I turn them on their axes, and carry them in the orbits I allotted to them. Wider than to the moons of a planet I have created the vortices, and they carry the moons also.

04/3.5. Around some of My corporeal worlds I have given nebulous belts and rings, so that man could comprehend the rotation of My vortexan worlds.[57]

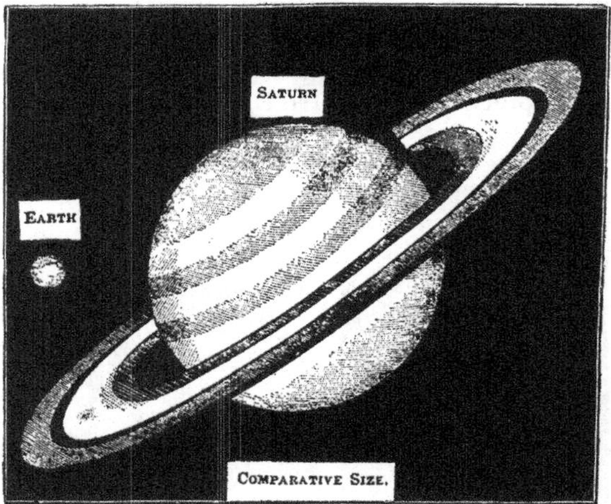

i060d2 **Earth and Saturn Compared**.

04/3.6. For each and every corporeal world I created a vortex first, and by its rotation and from the places in the firmament where it traveled, I caused the vortex to conceive the corporeal world.[58]

---

[57] The planet Saturn is one such example; see i060d2.

[58] In the general case, as a whirling vortex courses space, encountering atmospherean substance, it propels the substance toward the center of the vortex, where the atmospherea condenses to a thicker atmospherea and ultimately to a corporeal substance. This process is described in greater detail later in Oahspe, as are the four stages of vortex development shown in images i063, i064, i065, and i066, see next page.

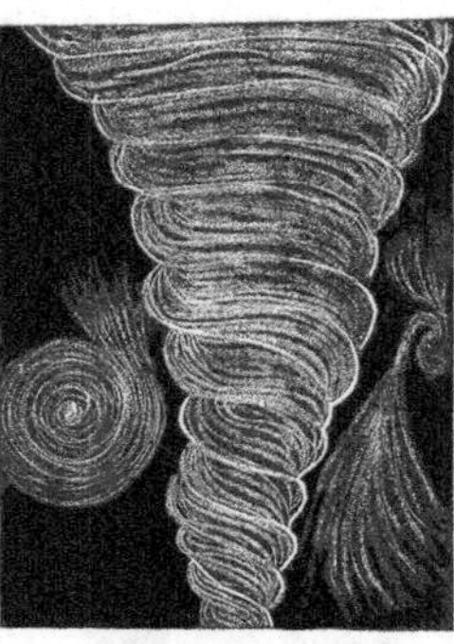

i063, i064, i065, i066 **The four stages of Vortex development** (above: L 1st, R 2nd; below: L 3rd, R 4th).

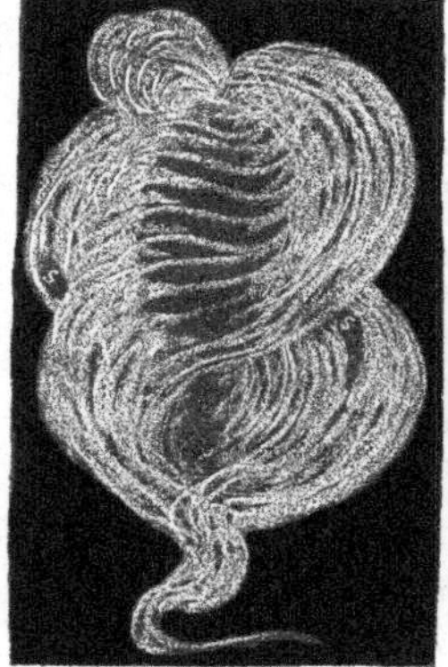

04/3.7. To make the sun I created a great vortex, and within this vortex and subject to it, I made the vortices of many of the corporeal worlds. The sun vortex I caused to rotate, and I gave it power to carry other vortices within it. According to their density and position, they are thus carried forth and around the sun.[59]

04/3.8. Do not think, O man, that I created the sky a barren waste, and void of use. Even as man in the corporeal form is adapted to the corporeal earth, so is he in the spiritual form adapted to My etherean worlds. Three great estates I have bestowed on man: the corporeal, the atmospherean and the etherean.[60]

[59] see image i073

[60] see image i004

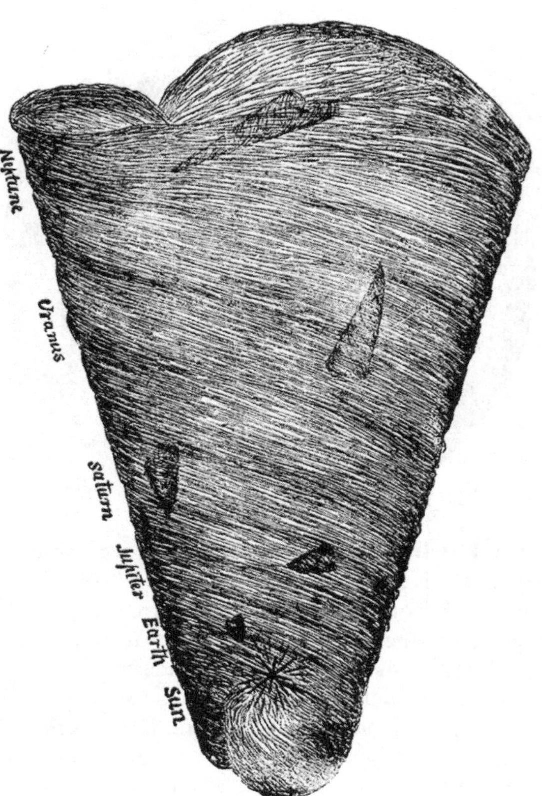

i073 **Tow'sang**. Solar Phalanx, that is, sun-family.

CHAPTER 4 Jehovih

04/4.1. Man perceived the general formation of the world, and he prayed that his eyes would be opened for a sign in heaven; and Jehovih answered him, saying:

04/4.2. The clouds in the air I bring into view suddenly; by different currents of wind I make the unseen visible and tangible to man's senses. In the same way, I cause etherean currents to bring forth ji'ay, a'ji and nebulae, prior to making corporeal worlds.

04/4.3. In all of the universe I have made the unseen to rule over the seen. Let the formation of clouds stand in view of man on earth, so that he may bear witness to the way the unseen becomes seen.

04/4.4. Man perceived, and he prayed for a sign of duration, and Jehovih answered him, saying:

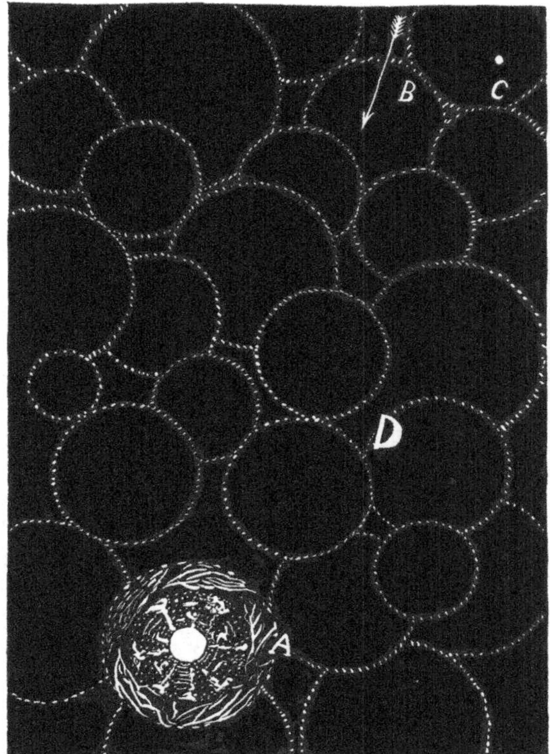

i004 **Photospheres**. Jehovih said: Let the sign of the corporeal worlds be as the signs of the etherean worlds;* nevertheless they shall be independent of one another. Neither shall the travel of corporea** disturb the motions and positions of etherea, but pass through, as if nothing were there. But the behavior (effect) of the etherean worlds on corporea shall be to bring them to maturity and old age, and final dissolution. || And it was so. And there floated within etherea certain types of densities, called ji'ay, a'ji, and nebula, which sometimes augmented the size of the traveling corporeal worlds, and sometimes illumed them on the borders of the vortices, and these corporeal worlds were called photospheres [suns –ed.], because they were the places of the generation of light. [D is etherea and the etherean worlds in dotted outline; A is a photosphere, i.e., a corporeal sun as it moves through etherea and the etherean worlds; B, the direction of the solar phalanx (photosphere plus planets) through etherea; and C, a corporeal planet (e.g., the earth) being carried in the master vortex of the solar system, that is, a planet being seemingly towed by the sun. –ed.]

* As there are countless billions of corporeal worlds, so are there countless billions of etherean worlds; and as stars, planets and moons have motions, orbits and courses, so do etherean worlds.
** any corpor body whatsoever; the corporeal realm.

04/4.5. Note the tree which has sprung up out of the ground and fulfilled its time; it falls and rots, and returns to the earth. But the wind, which you do not see, never ceases to blow. So also[61] is the comparative duration of all things. Do not think, O man, that corporeal things are annihilated because they disappear; for as a drop of water evaporates and rises in the air as unseen vapor, so do all corporeal things, even earth, stones, gold, silver and lead, become as nothing (loss of corporeality) in the firmament of heaven in course of time.[62]

04/4.6. Things that man sees, I created with a beginning and an end; but the unseen I made of endless duration.

04/4.7. I made the corporeal man belonging to the seen; but the spiritual man I made as one within the unseen, and everlasting.

04/4.8. As the corporeal man perceives corporeal things, so does the spiritual man follow upward the evaporated corporeal entities of things. As corporeal things are tangible to corporeans, so are es things[63] tangible to the spirits of the dead.

04/4.9. As I cause water to rise upward as vapor, and take a place in the air above, let it be a sign and testimony of other places (plateaus) in atmospherea where the spirits of the lower heaven dwell.[64]

04/4.10. As I made a limit to the ascent of clouds, so I made a limit to the places of the different kinds of substances in atmospherea; the more subtle and potent to the rim, and the more dense and impotent nearer to the earth.

---

[61] i.e., in the manner indicated

[62] That is, all things evaporate into subtler forms. The universe is constantly in the process of condensing and evaporating substances—from the most rarefied substances condensing downward toward corporeal form, and from corporeal substances evaporating upward toward ethereal form.

[63] heavenly things

[64] see image i007 next page

i007 **Earth, Needles in the Atmosphere, and Plateaus**. When Jehovih condensed the earth, and it became firm and crusted over, there rose up from the earth heat and moisture, which continue to this day. But Jehovih limited the ascent of the substances going upward, and the boundary of the limit of moisture was the same as the clouds that float in the air; and the heat was of similar ascent. And while the moisture and heat rise upward, they are met by the etheric substance of the vortex of the earth, and the moisture and the gases of the air assume the form of needles. On the side of the earth facing the sun the needles are polarized and acting, driving forth, which is called light; but on the face of the earth opposite from the sun the needles are in confusion, and this is called darkness. Jehovih said: So that man may comprehend the structure of the belt that holds the earth, I will give him a sign high up in the air. And Jehovih caused the vapor in the firmament to be frozen and fall to the earth, white, and it is called snow. For the snowflake shows the matrix in which it is molded. Jehovih said: Let this be a sign also, that even as heat and moisture rise up from the earth, so are there representatives of all things on the earth which have also evaporated upward, and all such things rise up to the level of density that is like themselves, every one to its own level, and they take their places in the strata of the vortex. These are called plateaus; or spheres, for they surround the whole earth. Some of them are ten miles high, some a thousand, some a hundred thousand or more miles. And all these spheres that rotate and travel with the earth are called atmospherea, or lower heavens.

04/4.11. According to the condition of these different plateaus in atmospherea, whether they are near the earth or high above,[65] so shall the spirit of man take its place in the first heaven;[66] according to his diet, desires and behavior, so shall he dwell in spirit on the plateau to which he has adapted himself during his earth life.

04/4.12. For I made the power of attraction manifest[67] in all things before man's eyes so that he might not err; so that like would attract like, I made them.

04/4.13. Man sought to know the progress of things. Jehovih answered him, saying:

[65] for an example of these see image i006

[66] Here atmospherea is the first heaven; etherea is the second heaven.

[67] be a reality, show itself, be apparent

04/4.14. Open your eyes, O man! There is a time of childhood, a time of propagation, a time of old age, and a time of death to all men. It is likewise with all the corporeal worlds I have created:

04/4.15. First as vapor the vortex carries it forth, and as it condenses, its friction engenders heat, and it is molten, becoming as a globe of fire in heaven. Then it takes its place as a newly born world, and I set it in the orbit prepared for it.

04/4.16. In the next age I bring it into se'mu,[68] for it is ripe for the bringing forth of living creatures; and I bestow the vegetable and animal kingdoms.

[68] commingled earth, air, water, heat and thick atmospherea; protoplasm-like; colloidal-like substance; also see image i008, p.32

04/4.17. Next it enters ho'tu,[69] for it is past the age of begetting,[70] even as the living who are advanced in years. Next it enters a'du,[71] and nothing can generate upon it. Then comes uz, and it is spirited away into unseen realms. Thus I create and dissipate planets, suns, moons and stars.

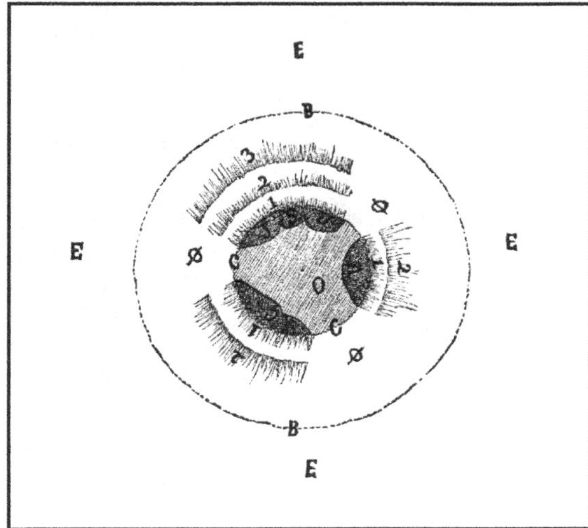

i006 **Earth and Plateaus of Lower Heaven**. E, Etherea; B, periphery of the earth's vortex. This line was called by the ancients the Bridge of Chinvat.* All within this area is called Atmospherea. The center circle is the earth; land mass is black; O, the ocean. 1, 2, 3, represent atmospherean plateaus on and near the earth. The O, O, O, with a line through it [∅], represent atmospherean oceans.

* Note that to make the earth, etc., apparent, this Chinvat line is not to scale. That is, were Chinvat drawn in actual proportion to the shown size of the earth, the B line would be drawn some 30 of earth's diameters distant from the center of the earth.

04/4.18. My examples are before all men. My witnesses are without number. I raise the tree up out of the ground; I give it a time to bring forth fruit, followed by a time of barrenness, then comes death and finally dissolution. I prepare the new field with rich soil, bringing forth; and the old field that is exhausted. And by My examples man shall weigh the progress and destiny of a whole world.

04/4.19. Let no man marvel because of the size of the mammoth and the ichthyosaurus,[72] for there was a time for them as there is a time for the infusoria[73] of this day.

04/4.20. I have given you a sign, O man, in the queen of the honeybee; because of the change of the cell, she comes forth a queen, even from the same kind of germ[74] as the other bees. Be wise, therefore, and remember that the earth is not in the place of the firmament of old. Let this be a testimony to you of the growth, change and travail[75] of the earth.

04/4.21. Nevertheless, O man, the seen and the unseen are only parts of My person; I am the Unity of the whole.

CHAPTER 5 Jehovih

04/5.1. Man perceived the magnitude and glory of the corporeal worlds. He said, How shall I speak of Your great works, O Jehovih, and of Your wisdom and power? Shall I open my mouth before You? I look upon Your countless stars, suns and moons, spread out over the heavens! The millions of years You have rolled them on in the never-ending firmament! Processions in and out, and round about,[76] of mighty worlds! By Your breath going forth!

04/5.2. O You All Highest! How can I hide my insignificance! I cannot create the smallest thing alive! Nor change the color of a hair on my head.[77] What am I, that You have seen me?

---

[69] barrenness. –1891 glossary

[70] generating new life forms

[71] death. –1891 glossary

[72] dinosaur

[73] microscopic life-forms

[74] seed, rudimentary form

[75] toil, struggles, labor pains

[76] in various directions; here to there; around about; on all sides; right and left, up and down

[77] Man can bring about the conditions conducive to the genesis of life, but he, himself, cannot command life to happen, cannot create life. Likewise, man may dye his hair, but it nevertheless grows out in its natural color. And even if someday man can determine and manipulate the color genes for hair, he can only alter what is already there and living. For, man can only assist in assembling or nurturing the conditions conducive to life coming forth, and in their combining.

04/5.3. Tell me, O my Creator, where did life come from—this unseen within me that is conscious of being? Tell me how all the living came into life?

04/5.4. Jehovih heard the words of man, and He answered him saying: Let a sign be given to man so that he may comprehend se'mu. || And so Jehovih caused the jellyfish and the green scum of water to be permanently coming forth in all ages, so that man could understand the age of se'mu, when the earth and the shores by the water, and the waters also, were covered over with commingled atmosphere and corporeal substance. This substance was called se'mu, because by His presence, Jehovih quickened it into life; and in that way, He made all the living, both the vegetable and animal worlds. Not that se'mu is jellyfish or the green scum of water; for in this day the earth does not produce se'mu abundantly; nevertheless the jellyfish and the green scum of water are signs of that which was in that day of the earth.

04/5.5. Jehovih said: Because of My presence I quickened into life all that live, or ever have lived.

04/5.6. Because I am male and female, even in My likeness, I made them thus.[78] Because I am the power to quicken into life, so, in likeness of Me, I made them with power to bring forth.[79]

04/5.7. According to their respective places, I created the living; not in pairs only, but in hundreds of pairs and in thousands and millions of pairs.

04/5.8. According to their respective places and the light upon se'mu, so I quickened them in their color, adapted to their dwelling places.

04/5.9. Each and every living thing I created new upon the earth, of a kind each to itself; and not one living thing did I create out of another.

04/5.10. Let a sign be upon the earth, so that man in his darkness may not believe that one animal changes and becomes another.

04/5.11. || And so, Jehovih gave permission for different animals to bring forth a new living animal, which would be unlike either its mother or father, but He caused the new product to be barren.[80] ||

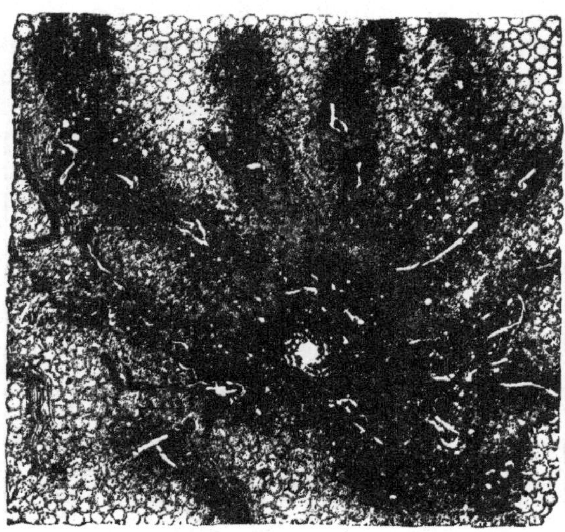

i008 **Se'muan Firmament**. Jehovih said: Behold, I caused all living creatures to gestate in darkness. And this shall be testimony to the end of the world, that, when I created life on the face of the earth, she traveled in My se'muan firmament. This is the triumphant entry of oxygen to the earth's surface. It is also the gestative age for the animal kingdom. Jehovih said: Let there be a sign for man that comes after, so that he shall understand the work of My hand. And Jehovih commanded that after that time, all the living should gestate in darkness. And it was so. || The white sphere in the middle of the dark se'mu is the earth.

04/5.12. Jehovih said: And this shall be testimony before all men that I created each and all the living, after their own kind only.[81]

---

[78] That is, made males and made females—but like Jehovih, each capable of imparting and receiving in the generic sense: of going forth or giving inspiration, thoughts, energy, etc., while also capable of receiving inspiration or accepting incoming energy, substance, thoughts, etc.

[79] to procreate, to beget, to bring forth life

[80] The mule has been instanced as proof that there is no such thing as one animal evolving into another. –Ed. [Capital 'E' in –Ed., indicates editor of the 1882 edition of Oahspe, which was Oahspe's first publication date; a small 'e' in ed., indicates editor of this present edition.]

[81] Accordingly, because all colors and cultures of man can have children together, it is obvious there is only one kind of Homo sapiens, namely humankind. But the varieties are sometimes called races, being nevertheless only varieties of one and the same kind (species).

04/5.13. Such is My person and My spirit, being from everlasting to everlasting; and when I bring a new world into the time of se'mu, My presence quickens the substance into life; and according to the locality and the surroundings, I bring forth the different species; for they are flesh of My flesh and spirit of My spirit. To themselves I give themselves; nevertheless, they are all members of My Person.

04/5.14. As a testimony to man, behold the earth was once a globe of liquid fire! Nor was there any seed on it. But in due season I rained down se'mu on the earth; and by virtue of My presence I quickened into life all the living. Without seed I created the life that is in them.

CHAPTER 6 Jehovih

04/6.1. When man comprehended the earth he looked upward; and Jehovih saw him and knew the desires of his soul. So Jehovih sent His son Uz, and Uz spoke, saying:

04/6.2. Hear me, O man; the mysteries of heaven and earth I will clear up before your judgment. You (the human race) are the highest of all creation, and come to the highest of all kingdoms;[82] from Great Jehovih you shall learn wisdom, and none shall stop you.

04/6.3. Contemplate, O man, on the magnitude of your Father's kingdoms and His places in the firmament on high. Unless I take you into the heavens above, you cannot comprehend its places.

04/6.4. Man then rose up in spirit, and ascended into the firmament, for his spirit had crystallized into separateness; and Uz and Es[83] ascended with him, speaking in the voice of the Father. And man saw that each and everything in the firmament was orderly, and still each to itself located. Then Es spoke, saying:

04/6.5. Observe, O man! As a farmer sows corn in one place, wheat in another, and flax in yet another—everything in a separate place; even so does Jehovih store the ingredients of which worlds are made—everything in its place: the substance of the iron in one place, the substance of the stones in another, the substance of the vegetable kingdom in another, and likewise for the substance of the animal kingdom, and the oils and sand; for He has places in the firmament of heaven for all of them. These that you saw are the ji'ay, the a'ji, and the nebulae;[84] and amid them, in places, there is se'mu also. Let no man say: Over there is hydrogen only, and over here, oxygen only. The divisions of the substances of His creations are not as man would make them. All the elements are to be found not only in places close by, but in distant places also.

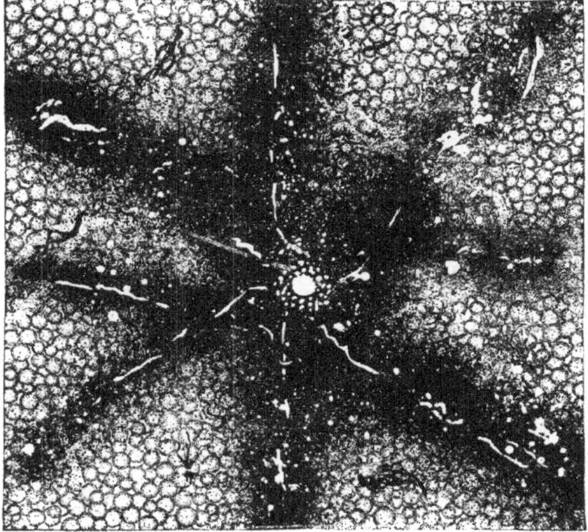

i010 **The Earth in Jy'ay**. The earth (white spot) in Jy'ay (ji'ay) during the glacial period, showing m'ha'k, the surrounding nebula, that caused the earth's crust to break and upheave, forming ranges of mountains. At the period referred to, the earth was turned from its axial course: the north becoming east, and the south becoming west.

04/6.6. When the Father drives forth His worlds in the heavens, they gather a sufficiency of all things. And when a corporeal world is yet new and young it is carried forth not by random, but purposely, in the regions suited to it.[85] Accordingly, as there is a time for se'mu; and a time for falling

---

[82] The kingdom over all other kingdoms is Jehovih's kingdom.

[83] Uz releases man's spirit from the flesh so that he can ascend into heaven; meanwhile, Es is the guide to heavenly things.

[84] That is, the "substance" of the things seen was atmospherean substance, and was either in the more rarefied ji'ayan form, or the comparatively thicker a'ji'an form, or in the thickly dense nebula form.

[85] see images i010 above, and i012 next page

nebulae to bury deep the forests and se'muan beds, to provide coal and manure for a time afterward; so is there a time when the earth passes a region in the firmament when sand and oil are rained upon it, then covered up, and gases bound and sealed for the coming generations of men.

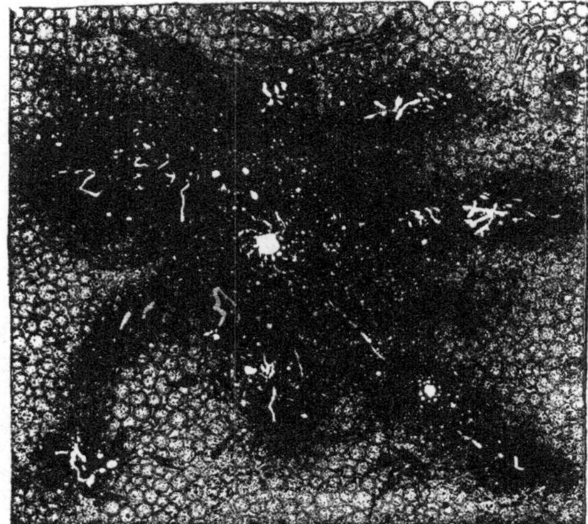

i012 **The Earth in Hyarti from Nebulae**. Showing the earth (white disk in center) eclipsed on all sides by nebulae. In the Hyartien period the earth was in darkness for one hundred and thirty years. This was the gestative age for the vegetable kingdom.

04/6.7. And man said: I am ashamed in Your sight, O Jehovih! I looked upward and said: The sky is vacant! Then I said: It is true, the corporeal worlds are made of condensed nebulae; but I did not see the wisdom and glory of Your works. I locked You up in coincidences and happenings. Your unseen world has become seen; the unreal has become the real.

04/6.8. O if only I had been mindful of You! If only I had not put You far off, nor imagined laws and decrees. Teach me, O Jehovih! How was the beginning of man? How was it with the first of the living that You brought forth?

04/6.9. Jehovih said: Have I not declared Myself in the past; in My works have I not provided thousands of years in advance? As I have shown system in the corporeal worlds, know then, O man, that system prevails in the firmament.

04/6.10. To the tree I gave life; to man I gave life and spirit also. And the spirit I made was separate from the corporeal life.

04/6.11. Out of se'mu I made man, and man was only like a tree, but dwelling in ha'k (darkness); and I called him Asu.[86]

04/6.12. I looked over the wide heavens that I had made, and I saw countless millions of spirits of the dead, who had lived and died on other corporeal worlds before the earth was made.

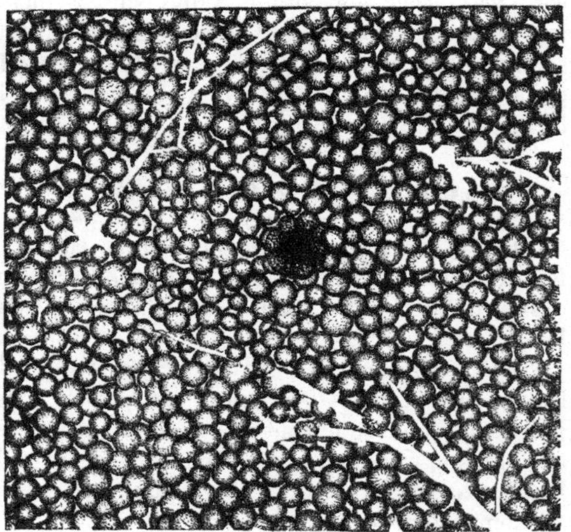

i009 **X'Sar'jis**, or end of the se'muan age; that is, the time of the termination of creating animal life. Jehovih said: Behold, I quickened the earth with living creatures; by My breath came forth all the living on the face of the earth, in its waters, and in the air above the earth. And I took the earth out of dark regions, and brought her into the light of My ethereal worlds. And I commanded the living to bring forth, by cohabitation, every species after its own kind. || And man was more dumb and helpless than any other living creature. Jehovih spoke to the angels that dwelt in His ethereal worlds, saying: Behold, I have created a new world, like the places where you were quickened into life; come and enjoy it, and raise man upright and give him words of speech. For these will also be angels in time to come.

04/6.13. I spoke in the firmament, and My voice reached to the uttermost places. And there

[86] See image i013 p.36. The Par'si'e'an (Persian) word for Asu was Adam.

came in answer to the sounds of My voice, myriads [87] of angels from the roadway in heaven, where the earth travels. I said to them, Behold! I have created a new world; come and enjoy it. Yes, you shall learn from it how it was with other worlds in ages past.

04/6.14. There alighted upon the new earth millions of angels from heaven; but many of them had never fulfilled a corporeal life, having died in infancy, and these angels did not comprehend procreation or corporeal life.

04/6.15. And I said, go and deliver Asu from darkness, for he shall also rise in spirit to inherit My etherean worlds.

04/6.16. And now the earth was in the latter days of se'mu,[88] and the angels could readily take on corporeal bodies for themselves; by force of their wills, clothing themselves with flesh and bones out of the elements of the earth. By the side of the Asuans they took on corporeal forms.

04/6.17. And I said: Go forth and partake of[89] all that is on the earth; but do not partake of the tree of life, lest in that labor you become procreators and as if dead to[90] the heavens from which you came.

04/6.18. || But those who had never learned corporeal things, being imperfect in wisdom, did not understand Jehovih's words, and they dwelt with the Asuans, and were tempted, and partook of the fruit of the tree of life; and lo and behold[91] they saw their own nakedness. And there was born of the first race (Asu) a new race called man;[92] and Jehovih took the earth out of the travail of se'mu and the angels gave up their corporeal bodies. ||

04/6.19. Jehovih said: Because you have raised up those who shall be joint heirs in heaven, you shall tread the earth with your feet, and walk by the sides of the new born, being guardian angels over them, for they are of your own flesh and kin.[93]

04/6.20. The fruit of your seed I have quickened with My spirit, and man shall come forth with a birthright to My etherean worlds.

04/6.21. As I have quickened the seed of the first born, so will I quicken all seed to the end of the earth. And each and every man-child and woman-child born into life I will quicken with a new spirit, which shall proceed out of Me at the time of conception. Neither will I give to any spirit of the higher or lower heaven power to enter a womb, or a fetus of a womb, and be born again.[94]

04/6.22. As the corporeal earth passes away, so shall the first race Asu pass away; but as I do not pass away, so shall the spirit of man not pass away. [95]

CHAPTER 7 Jehovih

04/7.1. Jehovih said: Let a sign be given to the inhabitants of the earth so that they may comprehend dan'ha[96] in the firmament of heaven. For even as I bequeathed[97] to the earth a time for creating the living, and a time for angels to come and partake of the first fruits of mortality and immortality, so shall man, at certain times and seasons, receive testimony from My hosts in heaven.

04/7.2. || And Jehovih caused the earth, and the family of the sun to travel in an orbit, the circuit of which requires of them four million seven hundred thousand years. And He placed in the line of the orbit, at distances of three thousand years, etherean lights, at which places, as the earth passes through, angels from the second heaven come into its corporeal presence. As ambassadors they come, in companies of hundreds, thousands, and tens of thousands, and these are called the etherean hosts of the Most High.

---

[87] great numbers

[88] see image i009

[89] experience, participate in, share, engage, acquaint yourself with, become involved with

[90] insensible of, deaf and blind toward

[91] lo and behold = look and see; used as an intensifier, an exclamation, meaning 'look! and see!' lo = look!; behold = see!

[92] This new race of man was also called I'hin.

[93] lineage, family, kinfolk, kindred; i.e., they are your relatives

[94] While here the doctrine of reincarnation is clearly repudiated, Oahspe later shows how the teaching of reincarnation came to be.

[95] Thus the second race, the I'hins and their descendants who obeyed the commandments, became capable of eternal life. (It has been said that everyone conceived or born on earth today, has capacity for eternal life.)

[96] a time of great light

[97] assigned, bestowed, granted, gave

i013 **Asu, the First Race**. Being the animal man (proto-man), wholly of the earth, and incapable of eternal life.

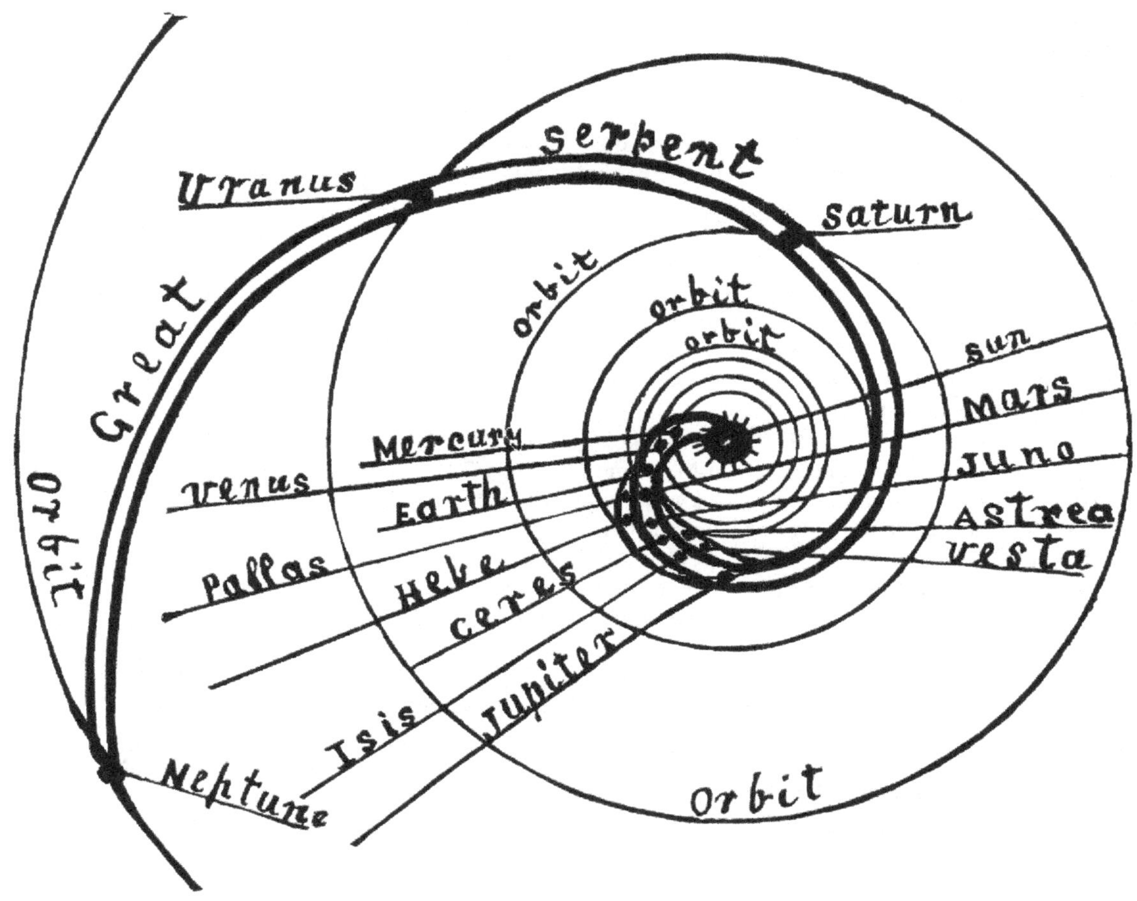

i072 **Dissection of the Great Serpent.**

04/7.3. They come not as single individuals; nor do they come for a single individual mortal.

04/7.4. And Jehovih gave this sign to man on earth; which is to say: In the beginning of the light of dan'ha, the spirits of the newly dead shall have power to take upon themselves the semblance[98] of corporeal bodies, and appear and talk face to face with mortals. Every three thousand years Jehovih gave this sign on earth, so that those, who learned the powers and capacities of such familiar spirits, could bear testimony regarding the origin of man on earth.[99] || Jehovih said: And when it shall come to pass in any of the times of dan'ha that these signs manifest, man shall know that the hosts of the Most High come soon after.[100] Let him who will become wise, enumerate[101] the great lights of My serpent,[102] for in such times I set aside things that are old, and establish My chosen anew. ||

04/7.5. In the time of the earth, when man was brought forth from mortal to immortal life, the earth passed beyond se'mu. The angels of heaven remained with corporeal man, but not in the semblance of mortals, but as spirits; and by virtue of their presence, strove to make man wise and upright before Jehovih. Upon the earth the number

[98] appearance, likeness, resemblance

[99] The Spiritualism movement fulfilled the sign mentioned in this verse.

[100] This bible *Oahspe* is one of their fruits.

[101] often more than merely getting a count, but gathering data, not unlike what a modern day census or scientist does

[102] solar system, solar phalanx, great serpent; see image i072 Dissection of the Great Serpent

of such angels was millions. To these angels Jehovih spoke:

04/7.6. Behold the work you have taken in hand! It was commanded to you all, to partake of all the fruits of the earth except of the fruit of the tree of life, which is of the knowledge of the earth and heaven, lest you lose your inheritance in etherea.

04/7.7. Behold, you now have sons and daughters on the earth; by your love to them you have become bound spirits of the lower heaven. Until you redeem them in wisdom and power even to the sixth generation, you shall not rise again and inherit My emancipated heavens.

04/7.8. To which end[103] you shall be co-workers with one another in system and order. In My name you shall become an organic body and known as the heaven of the earth, or lower heaven, which shall travel with the earth.

04/7.9. And I will allot to you a Chief, who is wise in experience in founding heavenly kingdoms; and he shall appoint from among you, officers, messengers, ashars, asaphs, and es'enaurs,[104] and you shall be numbered[105] and apportioned to your labor and places, like in My other lower heavens on other worlds.

04/7.10. He who is Chief shall be called God of this heaven and the earth, which are now bestowed[106] to his making.[107]

04/7.11. And God shall have a Council and throne within his heavenly city; and the place shall be called Hored, because it is the first kingdom of God in this firmament.

04/7.12. And God shall rule on his throne, for it is his; and his Council shall rule with him; in My name they shall have dominion over angels and mortals belonging to the earth.

04/7.13. And God shall appoint Chiefs under him who shall go down and dwell on the earth with mortals; and the labor of these Chiefs shall be with mortals for their resurrection. And these Chiefs shall be called Lords,[108] for they are Gods of land, which is the lowest rank of My commissioned Gods.

04/7.14. And God and his Lords shall have dominion from two hundred years to a thousand or more years; but never more than three thousand years. According to the regions of dan (light) into which I bring the earth, so shall the terms be for the office of My Gods and My Lords.

04/7.15. And God and his Lords shall raise up officers to be their successors; these officers shall be appointed and crowned in My name by God and his Lords.

04/7.16. At the termination of the dominion of My God and his Lords, they shall in these, My bound heavens, gather together all those angels who have been prepared in wisdom and strength for resurrection to My etherean kingdoms. And these angels shall be called Brides and Bridegrooms to Jehovih, for they are Mine and in My service.[109]

04/7.17. And in the time of dan I will send down ships from etherea to God, his Lords and the Brides and Bridegrooms; by My etherean Gods and Goddesses, these ships shall descend to these heavens to receive God, his Lords and the Brides and Bridegrooms, and carry them up to the exalted regions I have prepared for them.

04/7.18. All those who ascend shall be called a Harvest to Me, through My God and Lords. And the time of My Harvests shall be according to each dan, which is two hundred years, four hundred

---

103 outcome, result, purpose

104 Ashars are guardian angels over mortals, asaphs are guardian angels over the spirits of the newly dead, and es'enaurs are heavenly singers and musicians.

105 In Oahspe, to number or to be numbered is to count or be counted, but also other information is ascertained such as grade and rank of a person; and so a person is classified as well. This is not unlike a census, where not only a count is obtained, but other pertinent information collected.

106 presented, given, conferred, gifted

107 i.e., he (God) can make heaven in the way he sees fit

108 Collectively they are called Lords. A female Lord is called a Lordess. If undifferentiated in context, then Lord or Lords can refer to either male or female; same holds true for God; thus Goddess is the feminine.

109 Atmospherean spirits who, after sufficient spiritual maturation are prepared to be raised to etherean heavens, are called Brides and Bridegrooms, because they are then wedded to Jehovih. Greater description is found later in Oahspe.

years, six hundred years, and five hundred years; and these shall be called My lesser cycles, because they are the times of the tables of prophecy which I give to My servants.

04/7.19. But at no other times, nor in any other way, shall My Harvests ascend to My emancipated worlds in etherea. For each and every dan'ha I have created seven dans, and to each dan given six generations of mortals. ||

04/7.20. The angels understood the commandments of Jehovih according to their knowledge in the etherean heavens; being heirs of other planets, and having died in infancy, and having matured in the es worlds; but they did not understand the Creator regarding the practice of the lower heavenly kingdoms. And for that reason their knowledge was incomplete.

04/7.21. Jehovih said: I do not condemn you because you have become joint procreators with the asuans; for you have done two services to Me; which are first to teach yourselves corporeal things, so that you can understand and sympathize with corporeans, and second, you have caused the earth to become peopled with those who are capable of immortality.

04/7.22. Observe now what shall happen on the earth: Those who are of your flesh and kin who cohabit together shall rise in wisdom and virtue; but those who cohabit with the asuans will bring forth heirs in the descending grade of life. The first shall bring forth heirs to everlasting life; but the second shall bring forth heirs that shall go out in darkness.[110]

04/7.23. In the dominion of which matters your God and Lords will instruct you, so that you may, by inspiration and otherwise, learn to control the behavior of mortals to everlasting life. And so that these labors are not too severe upon you, I created the dans and dan'has in the firmament, at which times you can be relieved from the watch by other angels from other worlds coming to exchange with you.

04/7.24. This also I put upon you: That to rule over mortals to virtue, by your own wills governing them in all things, is contrary to My commandments. For what honor has any man if made to do a thing?

04/7.25. But you shall give My light to mortals, leaving them to choose. It is better for them to suffer some than to grow up in ignorance of the stings of disobedience.

04/7.26. Know that I make this a willing service on your part; because you have bound your affections on the earth, to your own kin, you willingly become guardian angels over mortals. Yet I did not make a separate law for you; as it is with you, so shall it be with the spirits of these mortals when they are born into the es world: They will also desire to become guardian angels over their mortal kin.

04/7.27. But these spirits, never having known My higher heavens, will be unsuitable for the office of ashars; they would only be the blind leading the blind.

04/7.28. To prevent which, God and the Lords shall provide these spirits in the first resurrection with places to dwell in; and with occupations and opportunities for education. For I do not desire them to remain bound to the earth, but to rise up and inherit My etherean kingdoms.

04/7.29. And in this also you shall be discreet in governing them, giving them the light of My heavens with some liberty to choose and to perfect themselves. Otherwise they would only be slaves in heaven. According to their weakness or strength, so shall you provide for these new spirits entering My es world.

04/7.30. Therefore those of you who are appointed by My God and My Lords as guardians over mortals shall be called Ashars, and you shall report to your respective Lords, according to the section of the earth where you may be. And ashars shall have many watches (work shifts).

04/7.31. And those of you who are appointed to receive the spirits of the dead into heaven shall be called Asaphs, and you shall report to your respective Lords and their kingdoms.

04/7.32. And the ashars shall make a record of every mortal as to the grade of his wisdom and good works; and when a mortal dies, and his spirit is delivered to the asaphs, the record shall be delivered with him; and the asaph, receiving, shall deliver this spirit, along with the record, into that place in these heavens which is adapted to his grade, where he shall be put to work and to school,

[110] cease to exist

according to the place of the resurrections which I created.[111]

04/7.33. As you shall thus become organic in heaven, with rulers, teachers and physicians; and with capitals, cities and provinces; and with hospitals, nurseries, schools and factories, so shall you also ultimately inspire man on the earth to the same things.[112]

04/7.34 And mortals who are raised up to dominion over mortals shall be called kings and emperors. As My Gods and My Lords are called My Sons, so shall kings and emperors be called sons of God; through him they shall be raised up to their places, and given dominion for My glory.

CHAPTER 8 Jehovih

04/8.1. Jehovih said: God shall cause a record to be kept in heaven, of his dominions and those of his Lords. And he and they shall enjoin[113] it upon their successors forever to keep a like record.

04/8.2. And in the times of My harvest a copy of these records shall be taken up to My etherean kingdoms and filed with My Orian Chiefs and Archangels[114] in the roadway of the travel of the great serpent,[115] for their deliberations regarding the progress and management of the inhabitants of the earth and her heavens.

04/8.3. Do not think, O angels, that the resurrection of your heirs and their descendants who come up out of the earth is an easy matter, and of steady progress devoid of mishaps and woeful darkness.

04/8.4. The angels under you shall become at times rebellious and defiant; disregarding your laws and decrees; and they shall desert your heavenly places and go down to the earth in millions and hundreds of millions. And they shall drive away the ashars, and then assume guardianship over mortals. But they shall develop no righteousness under the sun; and they will inspire mortals to war and destruction. And these angels will themselves take to war and evil throughout the place of your heavens.

04/8.5. With the foul gases of atmospherea they shall make weapons of war and places of torment. With these elements they shall make suffocating hells in order to cast one another into chaos.

04/8.6. And mortals slain in war shall be born in spirit into chaos on the battlefields; and entering the es world in chaos, they shall not know that they are dead (as to earth life), but shall still keep fighting right and left.

04/8.7. And enemy shall take enemy in these heavens, and cast them into the places of torment, which they shall have built, and they shall not know peace or wisdom.

04/8.8. And the work of your heavens shall become as nothing. You shall go about delivering hells and the spirits in chaos. And your labor shall become exhausting; truly you shall cry out because you came and peopled the earth.

04/8.9. For I have also created this possibility for My creations, so that both angels and mortals shall learn to know the elements of the heavens and the earth, and to know the trials of love and misfortune.

04/8.10. Nor have I made wisdom possible to any man or angel who does not know My elements, and the extremes of evil and good which I created.

04/8.11. But in the times of great darkness, which shall come upon earth and these heavens, I will bring the earth into dan'ha; and My ethereans shall come in My name and deliver them.

04/8.12. And again for another cycle they shall be left with the lessons given to them; but they shall fall again in course of time. But again I will deliver them; through My Gods and Goddesses I will cause them to comprehend the magnitude of My creations.

04/8.13. As you travel from heaven to heaven (via ships) in this atmospherea, so shall you also inspire mortals to build corporeal ships, and sail across the oceans, so that the inhabitants of different divisions of the earth may become known to one another.

---

[111] i.e., the type of work and schooling received depends upon one's place in the resurrections

[112] Thus, as we shall further see, civilization is not attained by any social evolution innate to man, but through the inspiration of angels reflecting the organization that is in heaven.

[113] impose, require, charge

[114] Both Orians and Archangels are ranks of ethereans. Orians are ranked above Archangels.

[115] The words *Great Serpent* means solar phalanx [solar system]. –Ed.

i017 **Pre-Flood Outline Map of the World**. Showing the Locality of Pan, the Submerged Continent.

04/8.14. And when the inhabitation of the earth shall have been completed and the nations shall have established civil communion around from east to west, in that same time I will bring the earth into the Kosmon era, and My angel ambassadors, Gods and Goddesses, shall render up the records of these heavenly kingdoms.[116]

04/8.15. Through them I will reveal to mortals the creation of My worlds, and the history and dominion of My Gods and Lords on the earth, even from this day down to the time of Kosmon. ||

04/8.16. And Jehovih caused the angels of atmospherea to assemble together and organize the first kingdom of the heaven of the earth. And the place was called Hored, because it was the place of the first organic abiding place for the first God of this world.

04/8.17. And Hored was situated over and above the mountains of Aotan in Ughoqui, east of Ul, of that country afterward called the continent of Pan.[117] ||

[116]And here they are, in part, in this Oahspe.

[117]The continent of Pan (see map i017) is covered in fuller detail later in Oahspe.

04/8.18. Thus ends the inorganic habitation of the earth and her atmospherea.

END OF BOOK OF JEHOVIH

i107 **Creator's name sign, with horizontal line only.**

Book of Sethantes, Son of Jehovih

First God of the first cycle of the earth after man's creation

CHAPTER 1 Sethantes

05/1.1. In the beginning of the inhabitation of the earth, the angels of heaven assembled in Hored, a heavenly plateau resting on the earth.

05/1.2. And the archangel Sethantes was the wisest of them all, and he said to them:

05/1.3. Behold, we have come from distant heavens; by the voice of Jehovih we came to partake of the glory of the red star, the earth. Jehovih said to us: Come and enjoy the new world I have created. Partake of all its fruits, except of the tree of knowledge, which is the fountain of life. Do not partake of this, lest you die.

05/1.4. But the voice of the earth spoke to us, saying: Partake, for indeed, mine is the tree of everlasting life.

05/1.5. And many did not obey the voice of the Father, and are now bound by the tie of life, which is in the blood.

05/1.6. And the voice of Jehovih came to me, saying: Sethantes, My son, behold, in My etherean heavens I gave into your charge millions of angels, whom you have brought to the earth, and they have fallen from their high estate. Go, deliver them.

05/1.7. And I said: What shall I do? And Jehovih said: Bring your angel hosts to Hored, for there I will crown you God of these heavens and earth for the redemption of angels and mortals. And it shall be a new heavenly kingdom from this time forward to the end of the world. For it is the time of the arc[118] of Wan, and I will bring from etherea My high-raised Goddess, Etisyai, chief factor[119] of Harmuts, and she shall crown you in My name: GOD OF HEAVEN AND EARTH.

05/1.8. God said: When I had thus spoken in Hored before the angels of heaven, a great light, like a sun, was seen descending from the firmament above. And I commanded my es'enaurs to chant in praise of the Father and His works.

05/1.9. Meanwhile I had the angels of Hored numbered, and there were twenty seven million six hundred thousand, being the same who were on an excursion in my charge when the voice of Jehovih commanded us to visit the earth.

05/1.10. The light above descended fast toward us; like a ship of fire it came nearer and nearer, till we saw it was far wider than the place of Hored and all my angel hosts.

05/1.11. And when the great light had descended to the plateau of Hored, there came forth out of the light one million archangels, from the arc of Wan in the Hosts of A'ji, in the orbit of Tow'sang in etherea, and they bore regalia[120] and crowns from the Orian chief of Harmuts. Foremost of the archangels was Etisyai, and her brother Ya'tiahaga, commissioners from the etherean heaven.

05/1.12. When they came near me, Etisyai gave the sign of Jehovih's name, greeting, halting, and saying: All hail! In Jehovih's name, and in the love of Harmuts, Orian Chief, we come to greet you, first God of the lower heaven, belonging to the corporeal earth!

05/1.13. I said: All hail, O emissaries of Harmuts, Chief of Orian worlds! Come, O Etisyai, and your brother and all this host! Come, honor my throne, in Great Jehovih's name!

05/1.14. The archangels then came forward, saluting, and Etisyai said: In Your name, O Jehovih, I found[121] here a throne!

05/1.15. And she caused the form and substance of it to rise, and she ascended onto it, and Ya'tiahaga with her. And the other archangels formed a crescent in front of the throne, all of them bearing crowns or diadems, but they stood upright. And now the angels of the host of God took their places, so that they could witness the testimony of Jehovih's commission, but the lights from the columns of fire, brilliant in all colors, shades and tints, baffled many of them from seeing plainly.

05/1.16. When all things were ready, Etisyai, standing erect and brilliant like a star, raised her

---

[118] great etherean light

[119] a title and position of responsibility in the etherean worlds

[120] official attire (clothing), insignia, ornamentation

[121] establish, create

right hand, saying: JEHOVIH! ALL-WISE AND POWERFUL! IN YOUR NAME, THIS YOUR SON, GOD, I CROWN! FROM THE ORIAN CHIEF, HARMUTS, RAISED TO THE RANK OF GOD, AND BY YOU, O JEHOVIH, ORDAINED! FROM THIS TIME FORWARD TO BE KNOWN FOREVER IN THE EMANCIPATED HEAVENS AS YOUR SON! PEACE! WISDOM! LOVE! POWER!

05/1.17. And now with her left hand she raised the crown high, so that all could see and bear witness, and upon giving the sign again of Jehovih's name above the crown, a flame of light shot forth brilliantly from it. And then she placed the crown on God's head, saying:

05/1.18. ARISE, O MY SON, SON OF JEHOVIH! Instantly there arose from the millions of souls one universal shout: All hail, O Son of Jehovih! And God rose up, having the crown on his head, and the people cheered him lustily, for he was well beloved.

05/1.19. Etisyai said: Bring forward your five chief Lords so I may crown them also. God then caused the five chief Lords, whom he had previously selected, to sit at the foot of the throne.

05/1.20. Again Etisyai raised her right hand, saying: O JEHOVIH! ALMIGHTY! FROM WHOM ALL GLORIES EMANATE! IN YOUR NAME, THESE YOUR SONS, I CROWN, LORDS OF THE EARTH, AND OF THE WATERS OF THE EARTH! FROM THE ORIAN CHIEF HARMUTS! BY MY COMMISSION I RAISE THEM TO THE RANK OF LORDS FOR KINGDOMS OF HEAVEN! PEACE! WISDOM! LOVE! POWER!

05/1.21. Then Etisyai took the crowns, which were handed to her by the other archangels, and placed them on the heads of the Lords, saying:

05/1.22. ARISE, O MY LORDS, AND BE LORDS OF JEHOVIH FOR HIS GLORY! AND BE THE LORDS OF GOD, HAVING DOMINION OVER THE EARTH AND THE WATERS OF THE EARTH, IN LOVE, WISDOM, AND POWER, AMEN!

05/1.23. The Lords rose up, having on their heads the crown of Lords, and again the multitude saluted with great cheering. When the applause ceased, Etisyai said:

05/1.24. My God and my Lords, give now the sign of Jehovih's name, so that His glory may be fulfilled. (For this was the oath of office.)[122]

[122] The sign is the circle twice cut. –Ed. [See image i001a.]

i001a **Circle Cut Twice.**

05/1.25. And God and the Lords saluted Jehovih before the hosts of heaven. And they stood apart a little distance, and Etisyai said:

05/1.26. Behold the All Light, Jehovih, encompasses me. My voice shall be His voice. By the glory of Faith in Him, I am One with the Father.

05/1.27. And a fleece of golden hue descended from above and encompassed Etisyai, and she was like a central star with rays of light emanating. She was entranced by Jehovih. Through her the Creator spoke, saying:

05/1.28. My Son, now God, I brought you forth out of corpor, quickened into life everlasting. By faith I inspired you to do whatever you have done. Faith I gave to you, as the tree on which ALL PERFECTION is the fruit. By that faith within man, which nurtures the I AM within himself to perfection, he becomes My Son,[123] doing by virtue of My presence. According to your wisdom and love I have given you strength; and by your strength, raised you up.

05/1.29. Behold, this day I have given you a kingdom in atmospherea, and made you God before all the kingdoms of heaven. This place shall be your place and Mine also. Here you shall dispense wisdom and laws, and appoint officers in My name and by virtue of My power.

05/1.30. And your kingdom shall be like two kingdoms: One here with the hosts of heaven, and one on the earth, over these your Lords. For you are the judgment seat and creator of order over the whole earth, and in the heaven belonging to the earth.

05/1.31. Stretch forth your hand, My Son, and clothe yourself in the golden fleece.

[123] or in the case of females: she becomes My Daughter

05/1.32. God made the sign, and then raised his hands upward, saying: Jehovih! Jehovih! By Your command I call upon You to array me in Your golden fleece! Behold I am Your Son.

05/1.33. And the archangels tossed up the raiment and regalia they had brought from their etherean arc in a'ji, and, by the faith that was in God, the substance flew to him and encompassed him in raiment of the upper heaven.

05/1.34. Then Jehovih spoke to the Lords, saying: As God has built a kingdom in Hored, and reigns over this heaven, and over you and your helpmates, so shall you build kingdoms on the earth, and you shall rule over mortals in My name, teaching them about Me and My everlasting kingdoms in the firmament above. In testimony of My voice, receive this raiment of silver and gold from My archangels.

05/1.35. The archangels then draped the Lords in shining raiment. And Etisyai came down from the throne, still entranced, saying:

05/1.36. Though My Daughter Etisyai will rise up in the flame of fire, yet I, Jehovih, will abide with you, O God, and with you, My Lords, now and forever! And then Etisyai took God's hand and led him to the center of the throne, saying: Sit on this throne for it is your Father's kingdom in the lower heaven of the earth![124]

05/1.37. When God sat down, the entrancement departed from Etisyai, and the Light of Jehovih went and settled upon God and the Lords. But Etisyai sat down at the foot of the throne, and immediately all the archangels sat down also.

05/1.38. God said: Behold, she who is greatest makes herself least of all. Arise, O Daughter of Jehovih, and enjoy my kingdom, for it is Jehovih's also. And God came down from the judgment seat and took Etisyai's hand and she rose up, at which point God proclaimed the freedom of the hour. Thus was established the first throne of God in these heavens. And now all of the hosts mingled together, angels and archangels, joyfully.

CHAPTER 2 Sethantes

05/2.1. When the hour ended, God again ascended the throne, and the marshals raised the signals of order, and the archangels went and stood in a crescent in front of the throne. Etisyai sat at the feet of God, and the splendor of her glory, unadorned, except with white and yellow drapery, shone through all the talents Jehovih had given her —the perfection of purity, wisdom, and love; the like of which only Gods had looked upon!

05/2.2. God said: In Your name, O Jehovih, I now found the session of Your kingdom in the lower heaven. As long as man and woman shall bring forth heirs to You, this kingdom shall not cease to glorify You. Let the Lords approach the throne.

05/2.3. The es'enaurs now sang, and the marshals and escorts conducted the Lords before the throne. When they were in order, the music ceased, and God said:

05/2.4. There are five great divisions of the earth, and I have ordained you the five Lords of them in Jehovih's name. I have placed you according to the number of inhabitants on the earth's divisions, and your relative rank before heaven. When you have seated yourselves in your respective kingdoms, you shall each have twelve messengers, whose duties shall be between you and me. Therefore choose your messengers this hour, so that, before the resurrection of the archangels, they may be confirmed and their registry[125] carried to heaven above.

05/2.5. The Lords chose their messengers, and they were confirmed in the name of Jehovih, and the swift messengers, who ply with the upper heavens,[126] made a record of their names and places. After which God said to them:

---

[124] Thrones in heaven consist of a raised platform with a judgment seat resting near the middle of it; the seat itself can be extended to accommodate many to sit on either side of the reigning God or Lord. At the front of the throne are steps leading up to the platform; the bottom step is called the foot of the throne. Facing the throne, at the foot of the throne, are one or more seats; and these are also considered to be part of the foot of the throne.

[125] book of official records with their name, office, place, etc., registered in it

[126] To ply is to regularly course or traverse. Messengers whose job it is to carry messages back and forth between atmospherea and etherea are called swift messengers. Those who ply only within atmospherea are called messengers.

05/2.6. You have been chosen according to your talents; according to your excellence you will be promoted to wider fields of labor. May the wisdom, love and power of Jehovih be with you all, amen!

05/2.7. And now Etisyai signaled that her time of departure had arrived.

05/2.8. God came down from the judgment seat, and standing one moment in sorrow, reached out and took Etisyai's hand, saying:

05/2.9. Arise, O Daughter of Jehovih, and go your way!

05/2.10. Etisyai rose up, pointing upward, saying: My house is in the arc of Wan. Jehovih dwells with you and me! My swift messengers shall come to you at times. My love will be with you and your Lords, and the harvest of your resurrection. In Jehovih's name, farewell!

05/2.11. Etisyai then walked to the ship of fire; but before she entered, she turned and took one more look at the hosts of Hored, and then, stripping from the frames, luminous drapery, cast it playfully over the es'enaurs, and quickly disappeared in the light.

05/2.12. The es'enaurs chanted, and the hosts of archangels joined in with them, and in that same moment of time the ship began to rise, and it was as thousands of columns of fire surrounding one majestic column, and the whole circle rising in spiral form, turning and rising, rising and turning. And when it was a little way up it seemed like an ascending sun; and then higher and higher, like a distant star, and then it passed beyond the vision of the angels of Hored.

05/2.13. When order was proclaimed, the All Light began to gather about the throne, covering over God and the Lords. Jehovih, through God, said:

05/2.14. Hear Me, for I reside also with these My Lords of the hosts of heaven.

05/2.15. The Lords said: What shall we do? And Jehovih answered: Summon all the angels to pass before the throne of God, one by one, so that I may judge them. For all those who dwelt on any of My corporeal worlds of the fifth of the second rate shall reside in the kingdom of Hored, and their labor shall be with es'yans only; but all of the full of the first rate shall reside in the kingdoms of My Lords, and their labor shall be with corporeans.

05/2.16. The marshals then arranged the angels and they passed in front of the throne, and so great was God's wisdom that, in looking on the angels as they passed, he perceived the rates of every man and woman. And those destined for labor in atmospherea only, he caused to turn one way, and those for the earth, as ministering spirits with mortals, to turn the other way; and when they had all passed, they were correctly divided according to Jehovih's commandment.

05/2.17. God said: Hear me, O Lords! Take your laborers and proceed to your respective places on the divisions of the earth and the waters of the earth. And you shall be Lords with me, your God, for the glory of Jehovih. Whatever you do on the earth I will ratify in heaven; whomever you deliver from the earth I will receive in heaven. As you shape and build up mortal man, delivering his spirit into my kingdom, so will I receive and award him.

05/2.18. So that your kingdoms may accord with me and mine, I give you sufficient messengers, and they shall pass daily between us: According to their proficiency and power to pass from place to place, so have I chosen them.

05/2.19. Let a record be kept within your own kingdoms, and these records shall be your own, to be carried upward with you in the next resurrection.

05/2.20. And separate from your own record, you shall also keep a record jointly with me, pertaining to your kingdom's relations with mine.

05/2.21. When mortals die and are born in spirit, you shall receive them and enter them in your records as es'yans, signifying newborn in heaven. And for these es'yans, you shall provide temporary dwellings where they shall reside, some for a few days, and some for the space of one year or more. Through the messengers you shall inform me of their numbers and conditions, and I will send ships to bring them to my kingdom.

05/2.22. You shall appoint asaphs, whose office it shall be to receive es'yans from the ashars.

05/2.23. While a mortal is alive on the earth, the ashars shall stay with him, guarding him in the name of the Lord, and in my name. But when he dies the ashar shall deliver the es'yan to the asaph,

---

[127] That is, 2 and 3/5 years old. "The full of the first rate" is infants under 2 and 3/5 years who, maturing in heaven, remember nothing of their corporeal lives. –Ed. [Es'yans are those whose birth into spirit life was recent.]

saying: In Jehovih's name, receive this newborn spirit. He was my protégé; for the good or evil in him, charge it to me. || And the ashar shall deliver up a record of the mortal life of the es'yan, and the record shall be kept within your own kingdoms.

05/2.24. And the asaph shall take the es'yan, saying: In Jehovih's name, I receive this newborn spirit. He shall be my protégé according to the commandments of the Lord my God. || He shall then take the es'yan to the place prepared for it, where it will have nurses and attendants according to its requirements.

05/2.25. When ships come to your kingdoms, the asaphs shall deliver all the es'yans they have received, and my officer shall receive them, and bring them to my place in heaven.

05/2.26. When God had ended the instructions to the Lords, the Lords answered, saying: We will be your Lords, O God, doing your commandments, for the glory of Jehovih, our Father.

05/2.27. God said: To each of you I have given a great division of the earth, and each division shall be named after you, each in its place.

05/2.28. This, then, was the rank assigned: Whaga (Pan); Jud (Asia); Thouri (America); Vohu (Africa); and Dis (Europe). And the lands were called after the names of the Lords and entered as such in the books of heaven in Hored, by command of God in the name of Jehovih.[128]

05/2.29. And the record of the Great Serpent showed the firmament of Tem'yi in the third circuit of c'v'wark'um and dan'ha twenty-four.[129]

05/2.30. When all was finished the Lords came and sat down at the foot of the throne, and the es'enaurs chanted a hymn of praise to Jehovih, and the entire multitude joined in the singing.

05/2.31. When the hymn ended, God rose up, standing amid a sea of light, and raising up both hands, said: O Jehovih! Almighty and everlasting! Help Your servants in founding this Your Kingdom for Your glory! Peace, Wisdom and Power!

05/2.32. Then making the sign of Jehovih's name with his right hand, he came down to the foot of the throne, and taking the hand of Whaga, Lord of Whaga, he said: Arise, my son, and go your way, and Jehovih will bless you.

[128] see image i017 p.41 (04/8.17)

[129] a dan'ha cycle is 3000 years average and a circuit is about 4,700,000 years

05/2.33. Whaga rose up and stood aside, and then in like manner God raised the other four Lords and they stood aside also.

05/2.34. The marshals filed past the throne, saluting, and after them the Lords, saluting also; and then came the asaphs, and lastly the ashars; and the procession was under way, passing between the pillars of fire, with which God's laborers had encircled and ornamented Hored.

05/2.35. This was the beginning of the first kingdom in the lower heaven, and the first of the reign of the Lords on earth.

CHAPTER 3 Sethantes

05/3.1. And in heaven God appointed angel surveyors, to survey the earth and atmospherea; and astronomers, to note the place of the stars; and enumerators, to number the inhabitants of the earth and atmospherea, to grade them and apportion[130] their places; and nurses and physicians, to receive the es'yans and administer to them; and builders of heavenly mansions; and weavers of fabrics for covering the newborn, the es'yans; and builders of heavenly ships for carrying the inhabitants from place to place. And God appointed officers and teachers, according to their grade, to all of these offices.

05/3.2. And when God had completed his appointments, the people were sent to their places, to begin the work allotted to them. And God called the asaphs, and he said to them:

05/3.3. Go down to the earth, and bring me the first fruit of the first resurrection.

05/3.4. And the asaphs said: Your will is our will, but what do you mean by the first fruit of the first resurrection?

05/3.5. God said: The spirits of the dead. The asaphs said: The spirits of the dead, who are they?

05/3.6. God said: When a corporean comes forth out of his corporeal body, this shall be called DEATH.

05/3.7. The asaphs said: Who then are the spirits of death? And God answered them, saying: O you who died in infancy, how can you learn corporeal things! Go then to my Lord, Whaga, and he will show you.

[130] determine and assign

05/3.8. The asaphs departed and went down to the earth, and the Lord, through the ashars, delivered five hundred es'yans to the asaphs, who brought them to Hored, before the throne of God. And God said to them: Who are these?

05/3.9. The asaphs said: These are the first fruit of the first resurrection. Behold, we know now the beginning and the end of corporeality; the earth body of these es'yans was only a womb from which they are now delivered.

05/3.10. God said: Well done. Take these es'yans and feed and clothe them, for this is your labor.

05/3.11. The asaphs answered: Alas, we have tried to feed them with all types of food on which we ourselves subsist, but they will not eat.

05/3.12. God said: Alas, O you innocents! You feed on ethereal food; these es'yans must have atmospherean food, even as corporeans subsist on corporeal food. Go, then, fulfill this first resurrection; for as much as you deliver them, so will you be delivered in time to come.

05/3.13. The asaphs then departed, taking the es'yans with them. But after a while they returned again to God, saying:

05/3.14. Behold, O God, we have gathered the atmosphere of trees of all kinds, and of seeds and plants that grow on the earth, all most beautiful to our senses, and savory to the smell, and we gave these to the es'yans, but lo, they will not eat. Being alarmed, we again hastened to you for information.

05/3.15. God said: O you of little wisdom, knowing so much of heaven and so little of earth. Go back to the place where you brought these es'yans from, and learn what kind of food they subsisted on.

05/3.16. The asaphs went back with all haste to learn in reference to the food. And in due time they came again before God, saluting, saying:

05/3.17. What shall we do, O God? Behold, these es'yans while in the corporeal form feasted on fish and worms. How can we bring them the atmospherean part of these things?

05/3.18. God said: The last time you were present you said you had gathered the atmospherean part of trees, seeds and plants growing out of the earth. Why, then, can you not gather the atmospherean part of fish and worms?

05/3.19. The asaphs said: Alas, we have observed this difference: The trees, plants and fruits emit delightful atmospheres, most nutritious to the spirit, but that which is emitted from the living fish and living worm is foul-smelling, being only the sweat and dead substance evaporating. What, then, shall we do?

05/3.20. God said: Go to the place where mortals kill fish and worms; and in the same time that mortals tear these things with their teeth, snatch from their hands and mouths the atmospherean parts of the food, and give it to these es'yans. Remember, also, that little by little you shall teach them to live on other kinds of food.

05/3.21. And as you do with these es'yans, do this also for others afterward, remembering that what men subsist on in corporeal life, is entailed[131] on them in spirit for a space of time after entering atmospherea; and they shall be fed spiritually with like substance. The asaphs then departed.

05/3.22. On the third day after that, the Voice of Jehovih came to God, saying:

05/3.23. My Son, behold what the asaphs have thoughtlessly done in your name! They came to the fishery and did as you directed, gathering food for the es'yans; and the es'yans stood at their side, saying: Why gather food for us? Behold, we are now strong in spirit; allow us to gather for ourselves. And the asaphs said: It seems well; do as you desire.

05/3.24. So the es'yans went to the fishermen and fisherwomen, who were eating raw flesh, and the es'yans laid hold of the atmospherean part, and ate a sufficiency of it. Then the asaphs said to them: You have feasted sufficiently; come away with us now.

05/3.25. But lo, the es'yans engrafted themselves on the fishermen and fisherwomen, and would not depart. The asaphs, not knowing what to do, called on My name. O God, quickly send to them those skilled in deliverance, so that My es'yans are preserved to everlasting life.

05/3.26. And God summoned those skilled in deliverance of engraftment, and dispatched them hastily with messengers to the fisheries.

05/3.27. Jehovih said: From the trees, fruits, flowers, grains, seeds, and roots that grow in the ground, I have created a ceaseless harvest going upward into the atmosphere, which shall be the sustenance of the spirits of men newborn in

[131] necessitated, bound

heaven. But whoever feasts on flesh on earth, shall not find spiritual food in heaven, but he shall return to the butcheries and eating-houses where flesh is eaten, and before it is rotten he shall feast on its atmospherean part. Place a guard, therefore, over the newborn, lest they engraft themselves on mortals, feasting on their feasts, and so go down to destruction.

05/3.28. After many days the asaphs came before God, saying: The physicians severed those who were bound, and we brought them away. Shall this be our labor, day and night, to lead these es'yans about, finding them clothes and food? For we have observed that the more we do for them, the less they do for themselves.

05/3.29. Jehovih spoke through God, saying: A nurse I provided for the newborn, but when he is grown I command him to provide for himself so that he may be a glory in My kingdoms. By charity alone you cannot raise man up; but be diligent in teaching him to continually try to raise himself, for in this lies the glory of manhood.

05/3.30. The asaphs said: If we leave the es'yans alone they will return again to the fisheries and fasten themselves upon mortals, doing nothing but eating.

05/3.31. God said: Near the fisheries, but in atmospherea, go and fashion a colony, and it shall be your colony in heaven. Take these es'yans there, not showing them the way to the fisheries. In the colony put them to work, weaving, making clothes and otherwise producing; but go yourselves for the food at the fisheries, and bring sufficient every day, giving only to those who labor, or to invalids and helpless ones. By this you shall inspire them to labor, which is the foundation of the growth of the spirit; and eventually they will not only care for themselves, but join you in helping others, which is the beginning of the second resurrection.

05/3.32. This then is the lesson you have learned, that according to the diet and the habit of mortals on earth, so must you provide the same for their spirits when first entered in heaven.

05/3.33. Choose therefore, from your own people, a sufficient number to make all things required for a delightful colony, whether it is food, clothing, nurseries, hospitals, place of worship, or place of dancing, and there receive all the es'yans who are delivered from the earth, raising them up in industry, virtue, wisdom, mirth, love, benevolence and adoration, and this shall be a new heaven to you all.

05/3.34. You are my chosen, and an example colony of all the kingdoms I shall build in my heaven. The time is coming when the whole atmosphere around the earth shall be filled with countless millions of angels born out of the earth.

05/3.35. Be swift in your labor; the people spring up from the earth rapidly into heaven, and every colony you now establish shall, in time to come, be a great kingdom, requiring experienced workmen. Whoever labors most efficiently for Jehovih, I will promote to wider fields.

05/3.36. You are one of the cornerstones of Seffas,[132] and his house shall embrace atmospherea and the whole earth. Words are already taking root in the mouths of mortals; and for tens of thousands of years, war will reign; might against might, darkness against darkness. Hundreds of millions will be slain in wars on the earth, and their souls be thrown into chaos. Even as you saw these spirits fastening onto mortals for food, so will spirits in chaos, millions of them, fasten themselves on the battlefields, still battling; or fasten themselves on mortals, obsessing them to madness and death.

CHAPTER 4 Sethantes

05/4.1. So God established colonies in heaven for the reception of the spirits of mortals; and the colonies embraced the arts of healing, education, industry, drapery, manufacturing, the building of ships, and all things required for the spirit, even as corporeal things are required by mortals.

05/4.2. And great labor came upon the hosts of God who established these things, toiling day and night, receiving the es'yans and providing food and clothing for them. And many of the hosts of God lamented that they had come to the corporeal earth, and they framed songs and anthems of lamentation, and these they chanted even while at labor.

05/4.3. God was troubled that they were lamenting in the presence of es'yans, and he called together the proper officers in order to rebuke them; but lo and behold, the light of Jehovih spoke from the throne, saying:

---

[132] established culture; also enforced culture, i.e., imposed and compelled culture

05/4.4. Do not rebuke them, O My Son. Did I not command them, saying: Behold I have created a new world, the earth; come and enjoy it. And when they had come, did I not say to them: Enjoy all the fruits of the earth, except the fruit of the tree of life, lest you die. But corpor spoke to them and they believed in corpor. Why then shall they not lament? Do they not remember their former homes in etherea, and thus aspire to regain them?

05/4.5. But seek, O My Son, to make their lamentations a glory in the souls of the es'yans, so that they may also aspire to a higher heaven.

05/4.6. The voice departed, and God, perceiving the wisdom of Jehovih, commanded certain officers to collect many of the anthems and deposit them in the library of Hored, in heaven; and it was done.

05/4.7. This, then, is representative of their lamentations:

05/4.8. Where is my home, O Jehovih? When I was happy and my feet wandered.

05/4.9. I dwelt with Your hosts, far above! Far above! Your glory shining.

05/4.10. O the songs in Your upraised kingdoms! When shall I rejoice in the music of my own house?

05/4.11. O those sparkling, running waters! O the pastimes and feasts of love!

05/4.12. Where is it, O Jehovih? It was my home in high heaven!

05/4.13. I fell, I fell in darkness! Wandering soul within me, that led me forth.

05/4.14. The gardens of Jehovih stood on every hand. O senseless feet to take me onward!

05/4.15. Into the darkness I was lured; sweet perfumes arose amid the darkness.

05/4.16. Intricate in Your glory, O Jehovih! I lost the way. I was lost!

05/4.17. The music of Your spheres was shut out. I was enveloped in darkness!

05/4.18. Where is my home, O Jehovih? Why have I forsaken[133] it?

05/4.19. Crystals, and high arches on every side. Full, standing out, shining.

05/4.20. And the songs of my sweet loves! Such was my home and place of revelry!

05/4.21. I bartered them all away, wandering forth. Buried myself in the opaque, in the dark!

[133] left it, abandoned it, turned my back on it

05/4.22. O for my home in high heaven! Mirth, song, rest, and love, clear shining.

05/4.23. You, O Jehovih, have given me sons and daughters. Out of this darkness my gems were born!

05/4.24. O I will polish them up. Kin of my kin, I will raise them up!

05/4.25. Your Goddesses in heaven above will come. In ships of fire descending!

05/4.26. My jewels shall enter and rise with me. We shall search for my home; the haven of rest!

05/4.27. I see You, O Jehovih, in the distance. Higher than the highest of heavens!

05/4.28. O hasten,[134] my home, and my rest! O ripen these, my precious diadems!

05/4.29. O take us to ethereal worlds.

05/4.30. But no one could repeat their numerous lamentations, for there were hundreds of thousands of them. And as the ethereans sang them, the es'yans, the newborn, the atmosphereans, listened, longing listened, and looked upward.

CHAPTER 5 Sethantes

05/5.1. In the first year of Hored, God's kingdom in heaven received one and a half million es'yans: men, women and children, born of the earth. And left within the different divisions of the earth, with the Lords, there were still three and a quarter million es'yans, being for the most part fetals.[135]

05/5.2. In the first one hundred years there were born from the earth, one hundred and seventy million es'yans. And this was the sum of three generations of I'hins; which is to say, that in those days the number of earth inhabitants (not including the asuans, who were not created to everlasting life) was fifty-four million. And already each of the Lords' heavenly places had become large kingdoms.

05/5.3. In those days the period of five years was allotted the es'yans as their time of infancy[136]

[134] expedite, quicken progress toward

[135] These are spirits wholly dependent upon another, feeding on another. Notice too that a fetus, when taken from the womb, continues to live on in spirit.

[136] As a mortal infant requires time and stages in which to learn and adapt to the corporeal life, so

in heaven, requiring nurses and helpers, but some of them required many more years.

05/5.4. After five years the es'yans were taken from the nurseries and, by symbols and objects, were taught the rudiments of education; and drilled in processions, music, dancing and gymnastics; but every day they were required to labor for a brief period, some at weaving, some spinning and some in transportation.[137]

05/5.5. The voice of Jehovih directed God, saying: The structure of My Kingdom in heaven requires you to make all labor an agreeable exercise for the growth of the spirits in your dominions.

05/5.6. And God commanded the officers of the realm of Hored to lengthen the hours of labor, according to the age and strength of the spirits received from the earth, and it was so.

05/5.7. Jehovih again spoke to God, saying: In all labor that you allot to those who have sprung up from the earth, freely allow them to do whatever they desire; but you shall not permit them to return to their earth kindred alone, unattended, lest because of their love they engraft themselves, becoming bound to mortals. But when they have lived fifty years in heaven, you shall not only permit them to return to mortals, but you shall direct them to do so, for, by this time, they shall have no further desire for engraftment.

05/5.8. Again Jehovih said: As fast as you can appropriate the labor of earth-born spirits to help in the resurrection of others, you shall do so in My name.

05/5.9. And God and the Lords under him labored so; and in one hundred years, there were twenty million souls, who had come forth out of the earth, and had been raised up to the second rate. And many of them fully comprehended the manufactories, nurseries, schools and hospitals in heaven, and they were in many things equal to the requirements of their teachers.

05/5.10. The voice of Jehovih came to God, saying: It is well, My Son, to take a rest. Behold, you have toiled a hundred years, day and night, without ceasing. You shall, therefore, appoint other officers, and spread out the kingdom of Hored to cover all the land of Whaga (the continent of Pan). And you shall appoint in My name your most efficient officer to sit on the throne for a short space of time, for you shall travel and visit the five Lords of the earth and their kingdoms.

05/5.11. And you shall take with you a thousand heralds, a thousand messengers, and five thousand musicians. And you shall have a ship sufficient to carry your host, and to be your house wherever you go. See to it, and set all things in order, and depart on a journey of one year.

05/5.12. So God called in the surveyors, who brought maps of earth and heaven showing the best places for extending the kingdom of Hored.

05/5.13. And God appointed fifty governors for the fifty places required, giving each of them five thousand men and women to accompany them. And when they were chosen God addressed them from the throne, saying:

05/5.14. You are chosen according to the commandment of the Father; and by His command I will come to your respective places before long, to bestow you with all that is required for building up colonies in Jehovih's name. As you witnessed the founding of Hored by the archangel Etisyai, so may you understand that I will come to you all and do likewise. Go forth, then, taking your hosts, and lay down the foundations for your cities. As you have learned from me, go forth also doing as I have done; and as you do with a small colony, and a small city, so will I give into your keeping that which is greater when you are prepared for it.

05/5.15. When God ceased, the marshals led the way, and with the hosts following their governors, filed in front of the throne, saluting with the sign of Jehovih's name, which was answered by God's hands upraised. Meanwhile the es'enaurs sang in glory to Jehovih. Presently the hosts passed beyond the pillars of fire.

05/5.16. When all had quieted, God said: Let the builders of ships begin now and build a ship for me and my hosts, for the time draws near. And from my laborers, who have toiled a hundred years, day and night, without ceasing, let the graders

---

does an es'yan (whether he died as an infant or adult) require time in which to learn and adapt himself to the spiritual life in atmospherea.

[137] Residents of the spirit worlds work with spiritual methods, spiritual equipment and spiritual materials, as in creating or transporting spiritual things.

choose those who, according to their grade, shall be my companions and hosts on this journey.

05/5.17. And they were chosen so, and notified.

05/5.18. God said: While I am absent, the one who stands highest in the grades shall sit on my throne, being God in my place; your God and my God shall be chosen according to the transcendence [138] of the one who has done the most for the resurrection of the es'yans.

05/5.19. So God commanded the graders to present the records before the throne, so that the Council of Hored could determine the matter.

05/5.20. And Ha'jah, an etherean, was chosen. So God commanded them to send word to Ha'jah, with an escort to conduct him to the capital.

05/5.21. In due time the escort brought Ha'jah into the palace of the kingdom of God, and God was sitting on the throne. With music, they came in and filed in front of the throne, forming a crescent, with Ha'jah between the horns.

05/5.22. God said: By command of Jehovih I have summoned you here, O Ha'jah. For a long time I have known you, even on other worlds. Of all virtues in man which stand highest, which is, never to mention one's self, you excel all others in my kingdom. Your labors for the general upraising of Hored excel all others. For this reason you are preferred; and chosen by Jehovih to be my assistant while I am here, and in my absence to be my very God in the Father's name.

05/5.23. Ha'jah said: This being the will of Jehovih, proceed.

05/5.24. God struck the gavel, and the Holy Council rose to their feet. God said: In Jehovih's name I salute you, Ha'jah, God of Tek,[139] to hold dominion in Hored. Come forward and receive my throne for the Father's sake. The marshals then conducted Ha'jah to the foot of the throne, and God came down and took his hand and led him up. And as they were going forth, a light, as golden fire, came down from the firmament above, sent by the kingdoms high exalted; and God and Ha'jah were covered over and illuminated.

05/5.25. God said: By Your Wisdom, Love and Power, O Jehovih, I receive Your Son on Your throne. Be with him in Wisdom and Strength for Your glory forever! Amen!

05/5.26. God raised up a rod, waving it, and rain came down from heaven. Ha'jah said: In Your name, O Jehovih! At which point God stretched up his hand to Jehovih, saying: Give me a crown for Your son, God of Tek, O Jehovih!

05/5.27. And there descended, like a small star streaming downward,[140] a light of gold and silver, and it settled on God's hand, and he fashioned it into a crown, and emblazoned it with the sign God of Tek, and placed it on Ha'jah's head, saying: In Jehovih's name, I crown you, to sit on the throne in Hored during my absence.

05/5.28. Ha'jah said: Your Son [Ha'jah], O Jehovih, shall fulfill Your commandments in wisdom and love. May the Father, Creator of worlds, give this, Your Son [Sethantes] rest and comfort for the glories he has wrought[141] in Your name! Amen!

05/5.29. The Council said: Amen! The es'enaurs chanted an anthem of praise to Jehovih. And God led Ha'jah forward and seated him on the throne, saying: You are God in my name and Jehovih's also. And since I now go down to the earth to sojourn (visit) for a season, you shall be known as God of both earth and heaven.

05/5.30. So God departed out of Hored and embarked on a ship, taking seven thousand men and women for his escort, plus a thousand es'enaurs and the crew of three thousand to work the ship.

CHAPTER 6 Sethantes

05/6.1. God went to the provinces of the governors of heaven, whom he had previously appointed and sent forth to dwell near the earth; and as he himself had been commissioned by Jehovih in Hored, so did he install the governors on their seats.

05/6.2. Now, the governors were situated at remote distances within Whaga (Pan), but God sent

[138] excellence; the one who stands above the rest

[139] Tek means two, so God of Tek probably means something like: Second God (of the earth and her heavens), or Second in Command, or, as we might say today, vice-God.

[140] i.e., like a falling star, a streamer or ribbon of light

[141] brought about, created, established

messengers to them, notifying them of the time he would appear.

05/6.3. And the Lord Whaga, being apprised[142] of God's journey, established a protectorate in the Lord's kingdom in the city of Ul'oo, on earth, and went and joined the ship of God, and traveled with him throughout Whaga, being present at the inauguration of the governors in these heavens.

05/6.4. To each and all the governors, God said: Remember that the responsibility given my governors pertains to things in heaven; for the Lord's matters[143] pertain to earthly things and to angels who labor with the corporeans. But you are to attend to the es'yans, receiving them in heaven, providing them with places to live in, and in their helplessness supply them with food, clothes and the rudiments of learning.

05/6.5. God said: Keep in mind also, the time will come when each of these governorships shall develop into an independent kingdom; and instead of being governors you shall be raised as sub-Gods.

05/6.6. After God established the governors, the Lord persuaded God to visit his place in Ul'oo, and from there, travel about over the earth and see the mortals with whom the Lord had to deal. And God consented, and the Lord sent messengers before him, so that the house of the Lord, which mortals had built, would be replenished and cleansed.

05/6.7. And the protectorate notified the ashars, and the ashars impressed mortals to go clean and purify the house of the Lord. And so mortals went to work cleaning the place, and they burned incense of sweet myrrh and hepatan, not knowing they were fulfilling the command of the Lord.

05/6.8. When the ship of the hosts of God came to the city of Ul'oo, mortals saw it high up in the air, and they feared and quickly ran to consult the prophet of the Lord. And the prophet said: Behold, God appears in a sea of fire in the firmament of heaven.

05/6.9. And God caused the ship to be made unseen, so that fear would subside on earth, and he descended with his hosts into the house of the Lord, and they went and touched the things mortals had built so that they could perceive corporeally.

05/6.10. Then the Lord gave a banquet, and the angels of God stayed four days, exchanging fellowship with the ashars, who ministered to mortals. And the ashars took the angels of God among mortals, both while mortals were asleep and awake, showing the angels all things.

05/6.11. And because of the presence of the hosts of God, mortals were roused up with new vigor to worship the Lord, rising early and going to the house of worship, and continuing all day; and not one of them knew the cause of it.

05/6.12. On the evening of the fourth day, God commanded his hosts to prepare to renew the journey, and the ship was again illumed and readied for its course.

05/6.13. God said: O Jehovih, Who creates all, look down and bless Your Lord! From his high estate in etherea he has descended to these poor mortals to lift them up. Already he has toiled with them a hundred years. Three generations have risen up out of the earth, and they begin to glorify You in Your kingdoms above the earth. Who but You, O Jehovih, can honor Your Lord or know his sore trials! Behold, man grows up out of the earth, saying: There is no Lord and no God. But his feet and his hands are guided every hour of the day. And when he enters the unseen worlds, these realms become seen; but he is helpless in a strange place. And Your Lord provides for him and teaches him Your kingdoms. Your Lord goes from place to place on the earth; he finds a corner and says: I will build a city here. He sends forth his angels and they inspire man on the earth to come and build a city. Yet when the city is built, man says: Behold, there is no God and no Lord.

05/6.14. Your Lord brings the corporeans together and guards them day and night; but man turns away in strife and destruction. Then Your Lord withdraws his angels from the city because of its wickedness; and lo, the city falls in ruins. But man does not know the cause. Yet Your Lord toils on, day and night, watching, guarding, and striving to lift man out of darkness. O Jehovih, Father, bless Your Lord and his hosts! Bring quickly, the time when man shall comprehend the foundations of Your kingdoms!

05/6.15. The Lord said: O Jehovih, Ever Present! Hear the words of Your God, he who comprehends the whole earth and the heaven of the earth, knowing no day or night. He deals with millions; his judgment is sufficient for all.

---

[142] notified, filled in on the details

[143] affairs, business, concerns, activities

05/6.16. Glorify him, Your Son, of heaven and earth. He fashions the homes of Your Lords and Your little ones in great wisdom. His love is the glory of all men; his strength fashioned after Your foundations. Give swiftness and rest, and joy in Your quickening of him, Your God! ||

05/6.17. The mortals of the city of Ul'oo had gathered together to worship, and they were singing and dancing to the Lord, and the angels joined in the singing also. And God went and sat on the altar and illuminated it, so the mortals could see him. Then the chief prophet came near the place of the Lord, and the Lord placed his hand on the forehead of the prophet, so he could speak in the name of God.

05/6.18. The prophet said: Behold me, I am the God of heaven and earth, and my words come out of the mouth of this my prophet. Keep holy the four days of the moon, for they are the Lord's days. Do no evil, but strive for wisdom and to do good. And when you are dead, behold, you shall live, for I have places prepared for you in my heaven. Rejoice and be merry, for the Lord lives and reigns.

05/6.19. When the prophet ceased, God rose up from the altar, and his traveling host also, and saluting the Lord in the name of Jehovih, disappeared in heaven above.

CHAPTER 7 Sethantes

05/7.1. As mortals sail corporeal ships across the corporeal ocean, so sailed the ship of God in the atmospherean ocean. As a man having five sons, sends four away to distant countries and keeps one at home, so did God do likewise with the five Lords bequeathed[144] him by Great Jehovih.

05/7.2. So God had departed from the foundation of Hored, in a ship, in heaven, to visit his four faraway sons, the Lords of the other four great divisions of the earth, whose labor was with both mortals and the spirits of the dead, for the glory of Jehovih.

05/7.3. First to Jud, Lord of Jud (Asia), he headed his ship, running close to the earth, bounding forth, and sapping up fuel from the tall forests to feed the phosphorescent flame, running easy till the wild coast on the west of Whaga was reached. Here he halted his ship, first God of the first Lords of earth, till his navigators determined the distance of the wide sea ahead; then gathering fuel and substance from the rich growing lands, he and his traveling host stowed the ship to the full.

05/7.4. And God went in, commanding: Go forth, go forth! Forth into the sea of heaven! And onward plunged the ship of God in the blue winds of the firmament, high soaring, above the black clouds sprung from the corporeal ocean. And the music of his thousand es'enaurs leaped forth in time and tune to the waves, plenteous and most defiant.

05/7.5. Jehovih looked down from the highest of all the heavens, His everlasting throne of thrones, saying: Onward! Onward! Tame the elements, O God! O man! The earth is yours; the air above is yours. Stretch forth your arm and tame the elements I have made.

05/7.6. Onward sped the ship of God, by the force of wills matured; and, by its hallowed light, displaying its purpose before other traveling Gods and men, those in other ships cruising on adventurous paths in Jehovih's wide oceans of splendor.

05/7.7. Merrily sang the crew, and danced, and viewed the wide expanse, premising about the scattered ships coursing here and there, in strange colors and marvelous swiftness.

05/7.8. On one side the rising moon, the setting sun on the other; beneath lay the black clouds and great corporeal ocean; and yet high above twinkled the stars and the planets of the Great Serpent on his long journey.

05/7.9. God came forth and surveyed the scene; and the power of Jehovih moved upon him. Then his seven thousand loves and traveling companions gathered around him. God said:

05/7.10. All Your places are new, Great Jehovih! For thousands of years I have gazed on Your matchless splendors, seen and unseen; but Your glory grows richer day by day. When Your voice came to me, more than a hundred years ago, saying: Go, My son, I have a new garden planted; take some workmen and till the soil; I foresaw the long labor of the generations that would spring up out of the earth. I feared and trembled. I said:

05/7.11. How shall it be, O Jehovih? Shall the new earth be peopled over, and mortals run their course like on other worlds before? First, in wholesome love, worship and due reverence to the

[144] given, granted, bestowed, assigned

Gods, and then for ages and ages bury themselves in bloody wars? O lead me forth, Father! Jehovih! I will take Your garden for a season, and fence it around with Lords, and wise kingdoms. And with Your potent spirit, hedge mortals on every side so that the earth shall bloom as a paradise for angels and men.

05/7.12. And Your sons and daughters came with me, and engrafted Your immortal kingdom.

05/7.13. How is it now? How does my labor compare with that of other Gods on other worlds?

05/7.14. O you archangels, Gods, and Goddesses! Look down on the great earth! Jehovih has filled my arms with a great load! I tremble on the immortal scales!

05/7.15. And God, transfixed, looked up into the swift-passing sky, for his voice reached to the thrones of etherean worlds on which the Orian regents reigned in all power. And down from amid the stars shot a single ray of light, embossed with the adorable words: JEHOVIH'S SON, ALL HAIL! HAIL, GOD OF EARTH, JEHOVIH'S SON! GLORY! GLORY TO GREAT JEHOVIH, FOR ALL THAT YOU HAVE DONE!

05/7.16. Then upward furled the shining light till it faded amid the distant stars. Anew the trumpeters and singers sent forth a strain of sweet music, spirited and sounding full of soul. And as the music glided forth across the waters, lo, other music, strange and welcome, came from the west lands to the borders of the ocean.

05/7.17. For the ship was across the sea, and the hosts of the Lord Jud had come to meet the God of earth and heaven. And now, saluting loud and long, the two ships drew to close anchorage. Presently the messengers interchanged, and in Jehovih's name greeted God and his hosts, who were old-time friends to the Lord and his hosts.

05/7.18. God said: By Your will, O Jehovih, let us take course for the Lord's kingdom and place of labor. And presently the two ships sped forth, close to the earth, unified in the music of anthems of olden times.

05/7.19. Far up into the heart of the country, where fertile lands, mountains and waters were close companioned[145] to the asuan race, the ships sped on till one pillar of fire, standing on a mountainside, proclaimed the place of the Lord, and here they halted and made fast[146] the vessels, unseen by mortals.

[145] i.e., the asuans populated these fertile regions where food was readily available

CHAPTER 8 Sethantes

05/8.1. These chieftains had long been friends on other worlds, and pledged to join in an adventure on some new corporeal world, to raise sons and daughters up to Jehovih. Now it was being fulfilled in the Lord and God, remotely situated, and this visit much looked forward to.

05/8.2. And so God and the Lord came forth, saying: In Jehovih's name! Met at last! And they embraced and reassured each other that it was really true, that which they had talked of a thousand years before.

05/8.3. And then all the hosts of God and the hosts of the Lord came forward, and knowing one another, saluted and embraced also. After that they proceeded to the house of the Lord, which mortals had been inspired to build of wood and clay. And when they were within, they joined in prayer and thanks to Jehovih, and they sang and danced, and rejoiced to their souls' content.

05/8.4. At sunrise the next morning the mortal priests and priestesses, led by a prophet, went into the house of the Lord, to pray, sing and dance as they had been taught by inspiration from the Lord, but many people lingered outside, saying to one another:

05/8.5. Ta hop! Ta hop! (I fear! I fear!) For last night I saw lights in the house of the Lord, and I heard sounds like singing and dancing before the altar of God!

05/8.6. Nevertheless their companions persuaded them, and they went in and sang and danced also.

05/8.7. After a time of rejoicing, followed by quiet, the Lord said: Behold, O God, the follies of judgment, and the vain calculations of even Lords and Gods! We look upon the mature man, saying: Alas, he is stubborn in his own way; we cannot convert him. Then we desire the immature, saying: Him I will raise up in my own way, and he shall not depart from my judgment. But we tire of his immaturity and slow growth.

05/8.8. God said: On that hangs the highest testimony of the Person of Great Jehovih. He

[146] secured, fastened, anchored

created man the nearest blank of all the living, purposely unlike all the rest and devoid of sense. Whereas, according to the order in the others of the animal world, a newborn babe should be already wise.

05/8.9. Jehovih says: I have provided all the living with certain paths to travel in; but man alone I created new out of all things dead and dissolved, and he shall grow forever. To the beast I gave an already created sense (so-called instinct); to man I allotted angels. And even these angels I have provided with others above them; and yet others above them, forever and ever. Thus the first of man, the newborn baby, I created a blank in sense and judgment, so that he may be a witness that even he himself was fashioned and created anew by My hand. Nor did I create him imperfectly, that he should re-enter a womb and be born over again. That which I do is well done. ||

05/8.10. The Lord said: You are wise, O God. The opposites prove Jehovih. Water runs downhill, but man walks up the hillside; the tree grows up out of the ground while it lives, but after death it falls. Man stands on the earth, but the earth rests on that which is lighter than the earth. Jehovih says: The life of the tree is of Me; the unseen that holds the corporeal earth in its place, is of Me. ||

05/8.11. And yet, O God, who can attain to know Jehovih? The mortal says: When I am dead and risen in heaven I shall see the Great Spirit; but he fails, still being helpless, yes, as helpless in his place as he was helpless on the earth. Then he says: When I am strong and wise, like Lords and Gods, and can traverse[147] the wide firmament, then I will see Jehovih. But when he rises and can course his vessel through the whirlwinds of the vortices of heaven, and he is called Lord or God, lo, he finds the arcs and the ethea[148] standing before him still. More and more he is appalled at the thought of the Great I Am Who lives still beyond.

05/8.12. He hurries down to the corporeal earth, to teach mortals and spirits of Jehovih and His endless worlds and exalted heavens. But lo, the darkness of men! They say: I do not see Him; I do not hear Him; I do not believe in Him. He is merely like the wind, going without sense; as water goes down the hill, so is He; He is dead. He is nothing.

05/8.13. And the Lord invents ways and means; yes, he teaches man to pray and sing to Jehovih, so that the sounds may lead his soul upward. The Lord tells him to wear clothes and hide his nakedness from the Lord; and the Lord sends angels to reward him for his good deeds. And the angels of the Lord lay plots and stratagems in man's pathway to stir him up. Yes, Jehovih gave man sleep, so that his corporeal-bound spirit could see and hear heavenly things. But man loads his stomach, and debauches on intoxicating smoke and drink till his soul is buried in darkness.

05/8.14. And the Lord cries out in despair: How weak I am, O Jehovih, before You! I took it upon myself to be Lord over men on the earth, to learn my lesson in the government of worlds. But O Jehovih, I know I fail in Your sight. What will Your God say when he sees my little good? What pity do the archangels have for Your struggling Lord of earth?

05/8.15. God perceived the sorrow of his friend, and he said: O Jehovih, You Who are Almighty, how keener You have made our sense of our own weakness, than those who look upon us! Your Lord is my God in the glories he has wrought out of such crude substance, and I sing to his praise and love. Lo I have looked upon the naked men and women of this great land, crawling on hands and feet, with no thought but to eat, and I have seen them raised up by Your Lord and his ashars, to walk upright and use words of speech, and to wear clothes and skins to hide their nakedness. Yes, O Father, I have cried out with great joy, and I called aloud to You, O Jehovih, saying: Who knows the labor of the Lord! Will man ever forget to sing praises to the Lord God?

05/8.16. But Jehovih says: I will keep some of the tribes of men in darkness till the last days; for man in his conceit shall be confounded; for he shall perceive that the tribes of darkness cannot put away their own darkness. Yes, man shall bow down in reverence to My Lords in the early days of the earth. ||

05/8.17. In this way God and his Lord conversed, as they went forth to see the work of the Lord, and to find the mortals who had given up the places of asu and came to live in villages and cities. Over the continent of Jud they traveled for many

147 trek about, travel throughout, course along

148 the whole of ethe everywhere, the etherean firmament

days and nights. And when God had seen all the work of the Lord, he said:

05/8.18. Behold it is good. Your toil and seclusion away from the Lords of the upper heavens are severe, but you are fashioning the love of millions, who shall bless you.

05/8.19. Now while God sojourned here, his hosts regaled[149] themselves with the company of the ashars and asaphs in the kingdom of the Lord, and great was the love and rejoicing among them.

CHAPTER 9 Sethantes

05/9.1. When God's visit was ended, and the hosts notified, the Lord gave a banquet lasting two days and nights, during which the angels sang, danced and trumpeted before God. After that, God and his hosts embarked on the ship, ready to proceed on the journey; and the Lord went up to the ship to say goodbye, and his host went with him.

05/9.2. God said: When dan approaches we shall meet again. May Jehovih prosper your harvests till then!

05/9.3. The Lord said: That is another hundred years! O God, I live almost in a wilderness. I have not ten million souls, mortals and spirits!

05/9.4. God said: Your kingdom shall be mighty when I come again. May it glorify Jehovih!

05/9.5. They embraced and separated! Each gave the sign of Jehovih's name. Upward rose the ship of God, with banners outstretched, and newly ornamented by the Lord's angels. And now, resuming its westward course, sped on above the mountaintops, like a meteor hurled from heaven. Meanwhile the trumpeters gave forth the gladly solemn sound of the march of God.

05/9.6. But before the ship had made half its journey, an approaching light emerged from the far west, radiant and laden with hosts from the Lord of Dis (Europe), and the Lord was also aboard.

05/9.7. When the ships drew near and halted, God called with a loud voice, saying: In Jehovih's name, all hail! I know my Lord comes.

05/9.8. And the Lord answered: Hail to you, O God, Son of Jehovih! || And they turned the Lord's ship and lashed the two together even as they sped on.

05/9.9. Now after they had all exchanged welcome and good wishes, the Lord said: Before we go to my central throne, let us survey the continent over which your servant is Lord of land and water.

05/9.10. And God answered: Your will be done, O Lord. And so they journeyed for many days, often descending to the earth in places where the Lord's angels had begun colonies with mortals, impressing man with words of speech, and to live in villages.

05/9.11. And God said that all he saw was good and well done. So they came to the throne of the Lord and halted and sojourned for sixty days.

05/9.12. And God and his hosts, and the Lord and his ashars and asaphs, were together in general reunion, praying, singing and dancing, and reasoning on the endless works of Jehovih. But one book could not contain all that was said and done, of the excursions made, and the visits over the plains and mountains where in thousands of years from then, man would live and build cities, and go to war and destroy them.

05/9.13. The mathematicians foretold the great cities and nations that would rise up; how this one and that one would move to battle; how their great cities would fall in ruins and be covered up by falling nebulae, and by denuding mountains[150] washing down upon them, so that even the memory of them would be lost. And yet, further on, the mathematicians foretold the coming of Kosmon when the ruined cities would be discovered and their histories deciphered by the su'is[151] of man in Great Jehovih's hand.

05/9.14. And now when all these things had been estimated, the prophets and mathematicians went before God, Son of Jehovih, according to the commandments of the Lord, and spoke, telling all these wonders.

05/9.15. When they had finished, God said: What is our service on the earth, O Lord? A few centuries at most and we will have risen up from the earth, taking our hosts with us to dwell in higher realms. But there shall be other Gods and Lords after us, to deal with mortals and newly born

[149] exchanged stories, nourished, feasted, delighted

[150] from mudslides, glacial activity, erosion, etc.

[151] spiritual comprehension

spirits. After awhile there shall be great warriors, and great cities and nations, and they shall have Gods and Lords of their times who will dwell many weary years, even centuries, in the darkness with man. After that, even the Gods and Lords will be forgotten. And man will turn against Great Jehovih, putting to death His adherents, preferring idols of stone and metal, and spirits born of woman.

05/9.16. The Lord said: And yet further on a brighter light adorns the way: Great Jehovih's hand sends the traveling worlds into the light of Kosmon, and new prophets arise, gathering up the histories lost and the glorious plan of the Great Spirit over all. Yes, even your labor and my ships will be seen by mortals of that day.

05/9.17. Thus they discoursed, reading the past and the future, and weighing the present; while angels less informed, gathered around to learn how worlds are peopled, and nations and cities destroyed; the far distant, and the near at hand, being as nothing[152] in Jehovih's vast universe.

05/9.18. But the time came for God's departure, and he and his traveling host embarked, and the Lord and his angels drew around to receive God's prayer before he left. And so after they had embraced and parted, God said:

05/9.19. Though I go away, my love abides with you all. And now, O Jehovih, bless these my fellow-laborers, and make them strong to endure their great trials. Yours is the power and glory, O Father! Amen!

05/9.20. The ship rose up and the trumpeters gave forth: Glory to You, O Jehovih, forever and ever!

CHAPTER 10 Sethantes

05/10.1. Jehovih spoke to God, saying: Steer your ship to the southland, My Son, and visit your Lord, who is God of Vohu (Africa). And God went as commanded, to the south, running close to the earth, over deserts and mountains.

05/10.2. But when they were a short way on the journey they were met by the Lord, who had been apprised of God's coming. And the ship of the Lord came alongside, and made fast to the vessel of God, and all the angels saluted and intermingled, having known one another hundreds of years, and some for more than a thousand years.

05/10.3. The Lord said: On our journey, let us run our ship through the valleys and along the banks of rivers, for it is here that both asu and men dwell. And so they journeyed, surveying the earth as they sailed above. The country was mostly barren, supporting neither man nor beast.

05/10.4. But man dwelt by the riversides, burrowing in the ground to avoid the heat by day and the cold by night. And they came to places where the angels of the Lord were dwelling with mortals, having inspired them to make villages and to hide their nakedness.

05/10.5. The Lord said: Behold, O God, only the unseen is potent over man. If the beasts or the stones or the forest could tell man to hide his nakedness, he would not; nor will he heed[153] his brother's voice. Without experience, man cannot be advised profitably regarding himself, for Jehovih has made him that way. Because man cannot discern angel presence, the angels alone can teach man and inspire him to new life. For they talk to him in his sleep, and show him what is for his own good. And when he wakes in the morning, he supposes it was himself talking, and he is ambitious to obey himself. Patient and of long endurance are the angels of the Lord.

05/10.6. God said: Will man ever know he has been raised up? Will he be believing? Or will he, too, need to go to some new world and raise up its first fruits and toil his hundreds of years with naked mortals? O Jehovih, how wisely You have shaped the labors of the believing and the unbelieving!

05/10.7. Lo, man comes forth out of the earth, boasting of his unbelief, saying: Unless I see with my own eyes, and feel with my own hands, I will not believe. But You, O Jehovih, have fitted a labor for his eyes and for his hands, to his heart's content.

05/10.8. And yet another man comes forth out of the earth, being believing, and quickly he mounts to the thrones of Your exalted heavens. Great is the work of Your Lord, O Father.

---

[152] 'Near at hand' here means that which is happening around the present time. || In viewing distant past and far future events, it is like one event happening—a short ribbon of time—the time between the endpoints seeming like nothing.

[153] listen to, pay attention to, consider, obey

05/10.9. The Lord said: Who knows Your wisdom, O Jehovih! Who cannot perceive You in the foundations of Your everlasting worlds? You have provided nurses for the new earth; and out of this, Your footstool, You will bring forth many, who will, in the far future, be laboring as Your Lord and his angels labor here. Of what expanse is Your wisdom, O Jehovih!

05/10.10. In this manner they conversed and journeyed onward, till they reached the throne and place of the Lord. And here they made fast their ships, and they descended, down to the city of Ong'oo, in upper middle of the continent of Vohu (Africa).

05/10.11. And the Lord now sent messengers to all the ashars in his dominions, appointing ten days of rest, and time for feasting, music, dancing, and worshipping Jehovih.

05/10.12. And so it came to pass that the angels of the Lord and those of God held a reunion, being the first one in over a hundred years.

05/10.13. And then God toured over all the continent of Vohu, inspecting the work the Lord had done, and he pronounced it good before Jehovih.

05/10.14. When God had rested the full time, he and his hosts entered the ship of God, and taking leave of the Lord and his hosts, departed on the journey, saluting the Lord with a thousand trumpeters in the name of Jehovih.

CHAPTER 11 Sethantes

05/11.1. And now the long journey across the ocean was about to begin. God said: Great is Your wisdom, O Jehovih, in the division of waters! Your barriers protect nations from nations. You have made a refuge beyond the waters, where the evil man cannot pursue. Yet greater still are Your spirit oceans, O Father. The spirits of darkness cannot cross over, and the spirits of newborn peoples are not contaminated. O You Far-seeing; You Bestower of thrift[154] into the hands of Your Gods and Lords.

05/11.2. The master of the ship provided well for the journey; and presently the vessel of fire sped over the water, high above the clouds that cover the ocean. Onward to the west, bleak and desolate, through the spirit sea, unseen by mortals. On the distant borders, where the lands come to the water's edge, the Lord of the land of Thouri (America) stood, stationed in a ship, to welcome God to the great west lands.

05/11.3. And this was the land that the angels later called North Guatama, signifying the meeting of nations and the dawn of Kosmon.

05/11.4. God came down out of the ship and stood on the land, and a light of etherean flame descended upon him, and Jehovih spoke out of the light, saying: Hear Me, O My Son! I have brought you here to this land, which is the last of the circle, even as Whaga is the first. Behold, when the earth is circumscribed[155] with those who choose Me, I will come here with a great awakening light to the souls of men.

05/11.5. On this land I will finish the dominion of the Gods and Lords on earth, even as begun on Whaga;[156] through you and your Lords I will now lay the foundation for My kingdoms. On this land I will raise up a people who shall be the fulfilling of that which the I'hins of Whaga profess; for My chosen shall come out boldly against all dominion except Mine, Jehovih's. Look over this land, My Son, and provide for the time of Kosmon.

05/11.6. My prophets will foretell[157] you what shall happen; and afterward you shall look upon the mountains and strong standing rocks, and the thought of your soul will pierce them, and its impression will be as a written book before the races of men in that day. Nor will they know the cause, but they shall come forth in tens of thousands, for My sake, putting away all Gods, Lords, and ancient tyranny. Your soul shall be My talisman, deeply engraved in the land, water and mountains.

05/11.7. On this land alone, no Lord or God shall be established by the sword, for it is My land, which I planned for the deliverance of the nations of the earth. ||

[154] wise provision

[155] encircled, surrounded, encompassed

[156] Thus the beginning of the end of mortals worshipping Gods and Lords is to start in North America, even as on the continent of Whaga (Pan) the worship of the Lord and the God was begun (see 05/6.11,17). This verse does not mean the end of Jehovih's God and Lords.

[157] prophesy, predict, reveal beforehand

05/11.8. The hosts of both the ships came and joined in gleesome reunion after a hundred years' absence; then they traveled over the land and waters of the great west continent.

05/11.9. And all the places that the Lord had searched out, to the east and west and north and south (i.e., in all directions), even to the farthest boundary, were revealed and recorded in the books of heaven.

05/11.10. God said: And you, my Lord, shall mark out the place of the dominion of Jehovih in the founding of His kingdom on earth. And a record of your labors shall descend through the Lords and Gods that come after you, even down to the time of the coming light of Kosmon.

05/11.11. And the people, who shall dwell here till that day, shall never be worshippers of any Lord or God, such as other people shall worship.[158]

05/11.12. Let my seal be put upon this land, in the name of Jehovih, and to Him I consecrate it forever!

05/11.13. When all that was accomplished, God and the Lord rested from their labors. And the Lord prepared a feast and reunion for all the angels in his dominions.

05/11.14. So they assembled; and they sang, prayed, danced, and conversed on things long past and things of the future, reassuring one another of their love and high esteem, even like mortals of this day do.

05/11.15. When the banquet had ended, God and his traveling host, in due ceremony and order, took their leave. And so God departed. And when the ship of God was raised up and under way, the voice of Jehovih came to God, saying:

05/11.16. Steer your ship, My Son, over all the other lands, islands and waters of the earth. Go low down to the earth so that your recording angels can witness the affairs of men, and all the places I created on the earth, and the waters of the earth.

05/11.17. So God visited all places on land and water, where man lived and where man did not live, and the angels made a record of them in the books of heaven.

05/11.18. And the time of God's journey since he left Hored was one year and seven days; and his rest was completed. So he sent messengers to Hored, his heavenly kingdom, announcing the time of his coming. And for there he set sail.[159]

CHAPTER 12 Sethantes

05/12.1. When it was known in Hored that God was about to return, Ha'jah prepared for God's reception.

05/12.2. And there volunteered ten thousand musicians, five thousand bearers of banners, one thousand marshals and officers of the throne, and one hundred thousand receivers, to go part way and meet God and his companions.

05/12.3. And Ha'jah granted their prayers and they started at once,[160] being the most majestic host that had as yet gone forth in the lower heaven.

05/12.4. And when they were a little way off, behold, God and his ship of fire approached in heavenly splendor. And the marshals met him and laid hold of the ship's han'iv,[161] at which, all the hosts did the same, except the musicians, who sang and played.

05/12.5. When they drew near and entered Hored, Ha'jah broke down from his high estate, and left the throne, running to meet God as a child would run to its father. And when the multitude saw this, they also broke loose from decorous behavior and gave full vent to their outbursting love for God and his hosts. And all the people became as a tumult[162] in rivalry of rejoicing.

05/12.6. In a little while God and Ha'jah turned and walked to the throne and ascended it; Ha'jah took his place, and God sat to his right, and order reigned.

---

[158] All the Algonquin tribes worshipped the Great Spirit, Jehovih, only. It was characteristic of them never to accept any God or Lord. And the American race, coming after them, are fast raising to the same exalted conception of the Great Spirit. –Ed.

[159] Messengers generally use smaller, fast moving ships. Therefore, they could arrive in Hored well before God in his excursion ship.

[160] immediately, right away, without delay

[161] the prow of a vessel. –1891 glossary. A prow is the front end of the body (hull) of the ship; bow.

[162] a jumble of commotion; here, they were passionately exhilarated, noisy, loud and exuberant in their uproar of love and joy

05/12.7. Ha'jah said: In Your name, O Jehovih, I welcome back Your First Son of earth, to the kingdom You have bestowed upon him and Your sons and daughters. Because he has glorified You, by his labor, wisdom and love, we honor him in Your name and for Your glory!

05/12.8. God said: In Your name, O Jehovih, I return to these, my loves! That I am returned I glorify You, O my Father. That You have made them rejoice, is the glory of my life.

05/12.9. And now a great light gathered up around the throne, so bright that many could not look upon it, and presently the power of Jehovih came upon Ha'jah, and the voice of Jehovih spoke through him, saying to God:

05/12.10. This is again your throne, O My Son! You shall finish that which I have put upon you. Your people shall learn the manner of My kingdoms, and know that even as I make all, so do I rule over all.

05/12.11. Hang up your traveling garb, My Son; dismiss your traveling hosts and resume your seat on the throne, for I gave it to you. The voice departed; Ha'jah rose up and stood aside, and the light fell upon God, and he resumed the throne and was hailed by the multitude in Jehovih's name.

05/12.12. God said to Ha'jah: Because you have prospered my kingdom during one whole year, you shall be my companion and assistant, with power and wisdom to superintend all matters not directly under my Lords.

05/12.13. Behold, I have set this day apart as a new day in heaven and earth; because on this day the sun takes its course from the north line; and from this time forward it shall be called the new year's day. So shall it be, from this time forward, the day of the relief watch in Hored.

05/12.14. Hear my voice, O Ha'jah, and members of the Council of the throne of heaven! That which I commanded, you shall proclaim throughout heaven and earth to all who serve me.

05/12.15. Because of the increase of the kingdom of Hored, I will have the place enlarged; and the Council shall no longer be called a Council, but Moeb, for it shall be an assembly over all councils below it.

05/12.16. And Moeb shall no longer deal with the affairs of individuals, even if they are Lords; but it shall have dominion with the cities and kingdoms of heaven, and with judgments and decrees.

05/12.17. But in all matters of less degree, this, my son Ha'jah, shall have dominion. And you, O Ha'jah, shall build a house in Hored, near this throne, and it shall be your residence and the place of your business.

CHAPTER 13 Sethantes

05/13.1. So God enlarged the place of Hored, and built one thousand more pillars of fire, enlarging the circle and otherwise making it a place of splendor. And God called together the recorders from the libraries of heaven, and caused them to select one hundred thousand new members for the house of Moeb (Parliament), choosing them from the highest on the lists. In this matter, God said:

05/13.2. Do not seek for the most learned, or the most prayerful, to be members; but choose those who rank highest in assimilating to Jehovih and to their fellows; for these are the first to become Gods and Goddesses. Jehovih says: A strong man may do more good works than a weak one; and yet the latter may stand fairer in My sight. I open the way to the weak and the strong; to the learned and the unlearned.

05/13.3. God said: In all these matters, whichever man or woman has put away self-desires for self's sake, serving the Father by laboring for others, is on the road to wisdom. And if the records show a sufficient time for growth in such a man or woman, through which these virtues become organic,[163] then choose that person, for Moeb shall be composed of such.

05/13.4. So the laborers gathered agni[164] from the heavens around them, and remodeled the interior of Moeb, so that its members would be

[163] That is, an integral part of a person; thus, for example, the automatic response (reflex) of such a person would be toward light. Compare this with those whose reflex (first reaction, knee-jerk reaction) is toward self, or darkness, or confusion.

[164] Agni is that kind of fire-light which Spiritualists have often seen produced by the spirits. It is often called phosphorus, but not correctly. [Although, it is phosphorescent (luminous), it is of spiritual origin.] Yet spirits can gather it and handle it. –Ed.

seated according to their rank. On the day it was finished, the recorders brought the new members, who went into the temple to their respective places.

05/13.5. When they were seated, God spoke from the throne, saying: To You, O Jehovih, I have built the house of Moeb in Hored; by Your wisdom I have chosen its members. To You, O Father, I dedicate this house, and it shall be Your house. Give us of Your light, O Jehovih, so that we may not err.

05/13.6. A light descended from the heavens above, and fell upon the members of Moeb, as a symbol of approval by the archangels; and presently the new members stood up of their own accord, but the old members remained seated.

05/13.7. God said: Above your heads I make the sign of Jehovih's name, in a circle of fire, and the cross, and the leaf of life; for by it, you are sworn to the Father's labor.

05/13.8. Hear me, then, O my beloved: From this day forward you are denied individual ministration with individuals, but you are now a unit with many, and your labor, love and wisdom must be in concerted action with these.

05/13.9. From now on you must no longer say: What can I do for this man or that man, or this woman or that woman, or this child or that child? || For this is individual labor; and on the earth such ministration belongs to the ashars; and in atmospherea, it belongs to the asaphs. But you shall minister to organic communities who are composed of individuals. For there are communities for factories, for education, for treatment of the sick, and so on; and such communities exist both on earth and in heaven.

05/13.10. You shall divide yourselves into groups for this purpose, and every group shall be in charge of its special business; and each group shall stand in Moeb as one member of Jehovih's judgment seat. You shall divide according to your talents, and group together, each of you choosing a department in which you have the greatest wisdom and strength. Withdraw now to complete your groups according to the rates my proper officers will assign, and then return again into Moeb, and in Jehovih's name, take the seats allotted to you all.

CHAPTER 14 Sethantes

05/14.1. On the second day after the house of Moeb was completed, and all the members were in their respective places, Jehovih spoke through God, saying:

05/14.2. Now is the beginning of the second resurrection. Even as the corporean puts off the corporeal body, and is born a spirit, becoming the first resurrection, so are you, in putting away individual self and becoming an organic community, the beginning of the second resurrection.

05/14.3. Because those of the first are for individual self, I have bound them close to the face of the earth; as they survived on the earth on corporeal food, so have I made them to survive in the lowest heaven on atmospherean food. Because Moeb has risen above these conditions, I will exalt the foundations of the house of Moeb higher up from the earth than Hored, and Moeb shall be the lower house of My kingdom.[165]

05/14.4. The voice of Jehovih departed and God saluted Ha'jah in the name of the Father. And a great light enveloped the house of Moeb, and the es'enaurs chanted a hymn of praise. Then God arose and stood in the throne of Jehovih, saying:

05/14.5. Hear me, O all you people of heaven above and heaven below, the house of Moeb in the beginning of the second resurrection is founded in Jehovih's name. Proclaim the words that have gone out of my mouth, to the east and west and north and south, and to the swift messengers of the arcs of the firmament above.

05/14.6. Glory, glory, to Jehovih! Boundless and Almighty Creator, Present, and full of love, wisdom and power, glory to You forever and ever, amen!

05/14.7. The house of Moeb chanted a proclamation. The swift messengers assumed their respective globes of light, and began to ascend in every direction, carrying the word to the exalted spheres.

05/14.8. And God crowned Ha'jah as sub-God of Hored,[166] and he was proclaimed to all the

[165] That is, Moeb, being in atmospherea, is the lower house, compared to the upper house of Jehovih's kingdom, being His kingdoms in etherea.

quarters of heaven and earth. And the history of his name exists to this day as Jah, among mortals.

CHAPTER 15 Sethantes

05/15.1. Ha'jah said: With the exaltation of Moeb, so too shall my places be exalted before Jehovih. Let the enumerators of the communities of heaven send representatives before me, and the communities of manufacturers who produce food and clothes for the es'yans, the communities for hospitals and nurseries, the communities for education, the communities for training messengers, and all other communities.

05/15.2. When the representatives came, according to the instructions of the marshals, and were before the throne, Ha'jah said:

05/15.3. The toilers shall not always be toilers; the physicians not always runners after the sick. Whoever is proficient, I will exalt. He who can walk shall no longer crawl.

05/15.4. Many are wise and strong, and some have passed beyond the boundary of self-desires for self's sake.

05/15.5. A child may not have self-desires, but then it lacks wisdom and strength. A full-grown man or woman may have wisdom and strength, but lack in the abnegation of self.

05/15.6. I will make every community a double from this time onward, and one shall be called Maga, and the other shall be called Minga. Maga shall be my promoted laborers, who are being prepared for the second resurrection.

05/15.7. And Maga's labor shall be in concert with Moeb, the house of Jehovih. But Minga's labor shall be as before, with individual affairs and the organizing of new places for the delivered es'yans, who are the fruit of the Lords and their kingdoms on the earth.

05/15.8. Let my marshals select judges to carry out these, my decrees, in the name of Jehovih.

CHAPTER 16 Sethantes

05/16.1. From the founding of Hored until the installment of Ha'jah, was one hundred and thirty years, and at that time the lower kingdom of heaven was fully organized according to the decree of Jehovih.

05/16.2. And the kingdoms of the Lords on earth were also fully established. And at that time the earth had passed into Hon'she, in the etherean space, where the Orian Shrevarhs[167] dwell, to whom the swift messengers from God had reported the condition of the earth's surface, with the tablets of Grade and Ingrade of mortals.[168]

05/16.3. The Shrevarhs said: The earth has not attained her fullness. The gases of her low regions must be purified to make more places for mortals.

05/16.4. So it came to pass that fire, brimstone, iron and phosphorus fell upon the earth, by command of the Shrevarhs, by the will of Jehovih, and this shower reached into the five divisions of the earth. But before its fall, God was notified, and he apprised the Lords, and they informed the ashars, and they impressed those mortals who were in rapport with heavenly things, and the chosen marched away from the places of destruction, so that not one perished.

05/16.5. But many of the asu'ans were consumed in the fire.

05/16.6. But God sent extra workmen, and surgeons and physicians, from heaven, down to those spirits who were falling into forgetfulness and dissolution, and commanded that they be engrafted on the surviving asu'ans for pity's sake; and this was accomplished through the Lords of the earth and their servants, the ashars.

05/16.7. At the end of two hundred years God enumerated the people in the lower heaven, and there were, besides the spirits of the fetals (many of whom were doubtful as to everlasting life), two hundred and ninety-six million souls. Of these more than thirty million, who were the first of the

[166] Sub-Gods are Gods who have heavenly kingdoms of their own, but who are, nonetheless, subsidiary to God.

[167] Hon'she is an Orian field, a place in etherea containing many etherean worlds, and through which corporeal worlds pass. According to the 1891 glossary a Shrevar [or Shrevarh or Shriever] is to a corporeal world as a guardian angel is to a mortal.

[168] In general a tablet of Grade and Ingrade contains the grades and rates of mortals, indicating their distribution (how many at each grade) in the population; and their ingrade indicates their future place in heaven. More later in Oahspe on this.

earth's production, had been raised up to the grade of Brides and Bridegrooms to Jehovih.

05/16.8. And now the sixth generation of the seed of the fallen angels was delivered, and this was the fullness of earth bondage for them.

05/16.9. God summoned the house of Moeb for the revelations of Jehovih on the first day of the first year of dan of Hon'she. And when they were assembled, and had chanted to Jehovih appropriate anthems for the times past, the All Light came upon God, and he said:

05/16.10. Behold, the time of dan of Hon'she is here. Before three days pass by, the hosts from the etherean heavens will descend to accomplish the resurrection of my hosts to the regions from which they came two hundred years ago.

05/16.11. Summon my Lords of the earth, and my people of heaven; proclaim my words to them.

05/16.12. You who peopled the earth with everlasting life, attend to my words; the harvest of the new year has ripened, it will be gathered into the heavens above. Let my people rejoice, for the glory of deliverance is at hand.[169]

05/16.13. In Orian fields, hosts of angels and archangels wait, full of hope and love, to receive these, the first fruits of the new earth.

05/16.14. Clothe them in quietness with the rays of light. Make ready; for etherean Gods and Goddesses set sail in the regions above to come and deliver us.

05/16.15. Proclaim my words in all places in the name of Jehovih. And add to them, saying: If you desire to ascend, come to Moeb, in the name of the Son of Jehovih!

05/16.16. Messengers went forth, both in heaven and on the earth, and proclaimed that which had been commanded.

05/16.17. And on the third day, ninety million angels assembled in Moeb and Hored, to witness the descending and ascending of Jehovih's chosen. And the archangels of Hon'she sent a hundred thousand Gods and Goddesses to guard Moeb and Hored, to dispel and keep away the clouds and sunshine, so as to add glory to the scene.

CHAPTER 17 Sethantes

05/17.1. The Loo'is came before God, and having organized themselves into one community so as to make it lawful to speak in Moeb, they appointed Ga'wasa to speak on behalf of the community. Ga'wasa said:

05/17.2. Hear me, O God, in the name of Jehovih! You have ordained me according to the custom of heaven, to be a master of generations with mortals, and yet one generation is incomplete, for which reason I have come before you. Today I have been summoned by Jehovih, through your messengers, saying: If you desire to enter the next resurrection, come, for the time of harvest has come. Thus says God, Son of Jehovih. || Yet, I also desire to dwell another generation on earth.

05/17.3. God said: The places of heaven are open to all. If you want to ascend now, do so. If you want to wait one generation, then you shall wait two hundred years, for that is the period of the next harvest.

05/17.4. Ga'wasa said: In Jehovih's name, let my brethren pass before you in judgment.

05/17.5. God said: Jehovih's will be done.

05/17.6. Ga'wasa withdrew and went and told his brethren what was said; and presently they came in and passed in judgment before God.

05/17.7. God said: You have said, let me pass in judgment before you! Hear me, then, for this is my judgment: If you ascend with your work incomplete, you will be the unhappiest of men. Remain, therefore, for a greater glory is within your reach.

05/17.8. The Loo'is passed to the left, signifying their determination to stay another two hundred years with mortals.

[169] 'At hand' means: is upon us, is now underway, is happening, is beginning, is very near the start, is ready to start, almost here, about to happen, thus it refers to the present. It can also mean: easily seen; in one's immediate presence; as in, the marshal of the throne was always at hand whenever the throne was approached. Or, as in: A'ji was at hand.

In contrast, 'near at hand' is not so immediate, but is approaching, and means: in the near future; is soon to happen; or, is close enough nearby in time, as to be in memory; as in, events near at hand. Near at hand can also mean: close by; or close enough nearby in location as to not be inconvenient to access or contact, as in, God's messengers were always near at hand.

05/17.9. After the Loo'is, others came desiring to be adjudged by God, and to all who had incomplete work, God said: Remain! And they remained.

05/17.10. Besides these, there were seventy thousand ethereans eligible to ascend, who volunteered to remain with mortals another two hundred years. Among these were the five Lords and Ha'jah, and four hundred messengers belonging to Hored, and seven hundred women in fetal,[170] in the western division of Hored under the Lord of Whaga.

CHAPTER 18 Sethantes

05/18.1. Jehovih spoke in the arc of O'wasti, in the Orian field of Hon'she, in the etherean heaven. Jehovih said: Earth's time is at hand; the deliverance of her first-born will fall at your doors. Come forth, O My sons and daughters, and receive them from My hand.

05/18.2. Onesyi, high aspiring Goddess of Hon'she, along with a thousand counselors,[171] gathered in a host of five million souls, emancipated, and to them the dignified Onesyi spoke, saying:

05/18.3. Unlike all harvests previously delivered to us from other corporeal worlds, Jehovih sends us the first-born of the earth. Let us rejoice and glorify Him, O my beloved. Send out to the boundaries of Hon'she and proclaim there the upraised hosts of earth. You, who volunteer to go to the earth to receive them, come quickly. And you, who remain at home, provide them with mansions and quarters.

05/18.4. Onesyi said: Swift messengers have just come to me from the arc of Wan; Etisyai will be there. She was the one who bestowed Jehovih's crown on the first God of the corporeal earth. Her hosts, a million strong, go by the way of Tiviyus, and ask that we meet them in O'wea. And you, Wistaw, shall sit on my throne. I will go to the earth, to receive the thirty million newborn, the glorious gift of Jehovih.

05/18.5. Onesyi said: The young virgin earth has given birth. O the joy of the firstborn! I will take with me a host of singers, a million strong. Their voices shall have power and sweetness to win the love and adoration of all thirty million. The glory of Jehovih's works shall shine so brilliantly upon them that all past trials shall be forgotten. Hasten, O Gods and Goddesses! Let down the curtains of fire! Here begins the play of Jehovih in the management of a new world!

05/18.6. Now men and women gathered together, being those long raised up in the emancipated heavens, whose wills were potent over a'ji and nebulae, and swift in appropriating what Jehovih had fashioned in the firmament. And they built a ship, the size of which was equal to the width of Hored, and filled it within with angels of the rank of Gods and Goddesses, many of whom had been brought forth into life before the earth was created, and whose native corporeal worlds had gone out of existence. And they let down curtains from the ship, and the curtains were like flames of fire, and they reached downward, equal to the breadth of the earth.

05/18.7. These Gods and Goddesses were like a unit in will; being potent and swift workmen, the ship was soon laden and on her course through the vault of heaven. Past the a'jian fields of Che'wang, she rode swiftly. Soon the hosts of the much-loved Etisyai were seen in a smaller craft, highly polished and swift, making way for O'wea.

05/18.8. Up goes a shout of joy from millions of throats, then a song of delight; heaven is joyful in Jehovih's boundless dominions. And now the two approach O'wea; and they slacken speed and draw near each other, nearer and nearer, till the ships touch and are joined by skilled workmen.

05/18.9. Forth leap the two Goddesses, Etisyai and Onesyi, and in no stateliness or ceremony, but like children in whom love is transcendent, they fly to each other's arms, amid the outburst of joy from the countless throng. Yet onward moves the etherean ship, majestic and meteor-like, steadily taking course to the new earth.

---

170 As a corporeal woman provides a corporeal womb for a fetus, and breasts for milk for the newborn, so are there angels capable of providing fetal to aborted fetuses, miscarriages, still births, etc.

171 advisors, consultants, confidants, luminaries; in other words, the governing body, being her cabinet for the work at hand

CHAPTER 19 Sethantes

05/19.1. And now the evening of the third day had come, and God and his hosts in Moeb were hastening all things, to be ready for the great light that was to descend from high heaven.

05/19.2. The ninety million angels looked upward, watching for the dawning of the light, waiting and watching. And many who remembered Etisyai, of two hundred years ago, wondered if she would return in glory, like when she came and crowned God by Jehovih's command. Some were robing themselves in white, and hastening nervously, like a bride about to wed; some were half inclined to sorrow for leaving the earth and lower heaven, where they had toiled so long; and some were stately and by their presence said: Your will be done, O Jehovih!

05/19.3. God ascended the throne, and Ha'jah came up and sat at his right hand; and the light of Jehovih shone upon them so that many newborn, especially of the es'yan spectators, could not look upon them.

05/19.4. God said: One dan has come and gone; this harvest is only thirty million.

05/19.5. Ha'jah said: Your son, O Jehovih, has shaped the destiny of a world. Great is his glory.

05/19.6. A light of golden hue gathered above the throne, and took the form of a triangle; and there was a graven image at every corner, which together read, I-O-D; and it was in the character of Whaga,[172] bestowed by the Lord on the altars in the houses of worship on earth, and its value was thirty-three million, which was the exact number prepared for the emancipated heaven in etherea; and the thirty-three was the years of a generation of mortals.

05/19.7. God said: Jehovih is one; the living is one; inanimate corpor is one; and these three are the entirety. To teach mortals this, O Ha'jah, is to give wisdom to the earth. Take this triangle, O Son of the Most High. And as long as Seffas endures on the earth it shall be the bequeathed[173] heirloom of heaven, descending from God to God who occupies the throne.

05/19.8. Then God stretched forth his hands, and the triangle became fixed and solid, and God hung it on Ha'jah's neck, adding: In the name of Jehovih, receive this jewel (the triangle), as my parting testimonial. Remember, that when mortals are raised up to understand this symbol of three in one, then Kosmon will begin to dawn on the earth.

05/19.9. Ha'jah said: O God, symbol of the three attributes, love, wisdom and power! You left your stately home, where you had Gods and Goddesses for companions, and came to the far-off earth, which was young and curtained around with poisonous gases, to guard the young and imperfect angels of other worlds in their wanderings forth, with your wisdom, love and power concealed. You gave them liberty and yet redeemed them. You stretched forth your hand over the earth and made it yield souls to glorify the Creator. And yet all the while you have never quoted yourself. O that this could be taught to angels and men! What person will not trip or mention himself, or make himself a manifested self?

05/19.10. This day I am to be crowned, to fill the place you have built up; but I falter and tremble like a child. Ha'jah burst into tears, and after a little while he added: O Jehovih, why have You laid Ha'jah's tears so close? You have created love in my soul, and it has grown to be a mountain. God, Your Son, who has been my tutor for a thousand years, and on many worlds, corpor and es, is now thrusting Your glory upon me.

05/19.11. God said: Heed[174] the earth and her heavens, for they are to be yours for one dan. And remember also, that though I ascend with my hosts to etherea, yet I have charge of this world until the completion of this cycle, two thousand eight hundred years; after I ascend, my archangels shall answer to your prayers to Jehovih.

05/19.12. Suddenly a light came down from the firmament, like a new star, twinkling, with a halo extending wide on every side. All eyes were turned up, full of expectancy. Hushed and still, the ninety million stood.

05/19.13. Presently the star assumed a brighter phase and spread its halo outward, with horns descending, like a crescent, like that formed in

[172] i.e., in the Panic language, the first language of the earth; Pan = earth; Panic language = earthly language. More on this later in Oahspe.

[173] given as an inheritance, bestowed, handed down, passed on

[174] Be mindful of, pay attention to

sacred worship when a God stands in the midst. Larger and brighter the light grew, tremulous[175] and waving like sheets of fire.

05/19.14. Then, three rays of light shot down toward Hored and Moeb, piercing, and in advance of the central orb. And the three rays were red, blue and yellow; but the crescent beyond was white, and it shone abroad over the heavens, so that the corporeal sun and stars in the firmament were invisible.[176]

05/19.15. Upon seeing the majesty and grandeur of Jehovih's host descending, millions of es'yans and clouded souls in the lower heaven broke and fled; some ran and hid to avoid the threatening light. For such is the magnifying power of the etherean flame, that all dark thoughts and hidden evil lurking in the soul are magnified, and made so plain that even the dumb can read them through.

05/19.16. Millions of the ethereans on God's staff had seen such scenes before, and now stood in glee, firmly riveted by the joy within them. To them, a hundred to one, clung the newly raised from earth, who had never known any other heaven, except the atmospherean heaven that travels with the earth around the sun every year. From these there arose millions of whispers, saying: It is like a new death; like a new birth. Behold a man dies on earth, and his spirit flies off to another world. And now yet again it flies off to still another world.

05/19.17. Quickly, now, projecting foremost came the three great rays; and these were the orders of marshals from the a'jian fields of O'wea and Hon'she; the red lights represented A'ji, the blue lights represented O'wea, and the yellow, Hon'she. Of these marshals, there were one million, and they cast curtains to cover around all of Hored, the great kingdom.

05/19.18. Chief of the marshals was Ah'jeng; and next to him were five sub-chiefs; and next to them one thousand tributary chiefs, who were masters of the ceremonies; and they came in the center of the descending three great rays of light, came swiftly and direct toward the throne of God. And the substance of the rays of light was like curtains of cloth,[177] one end of which reached up to the now near approaching crescent sea of fire.

i015 **The First Harvest**. Earth and lower heaven, with the fire-ship of Etisyai and Onesyi and their etherean hosts descending, for the deliverance of the first harvest of heavenly souls raised up from the earth.

05/19.19. When the light was nearly touching the pillars of fire surrounding Moeb, it slackened a little, and then gently slowed. The chieftains leaped

[175] quivering, fluttering, vibrating

[176] see image i015

[177] Spirit light can be formed into shapes, and into sheets by weaving. Other descriptions in Oahspe tell of how Crowns are woven into shape from the light.

from the etherean flames and stood at the foot of God's throne, saluting in Jehovih's name.

05/19.20. God and Ha'jah stood up and answered the sign, then descended and went to the left and right of Ah'jeng, and all three ascended; then Ah'jeng sat upon the throne, and the voice of Jehovih spoke through him, saying:

05/19.21. Hold up your heads and rejoice, O My sons and daughters! Behold, I come in a flame of fire! I am here, there, and throughout the place of heaven, boundless. I gather together and I put asunder[178] the loves of mortals and angels. For they shall go abroad in My firmament and behold My glorious works.

05/19.22. Down to the corporeal world I descend and carry away the loved, for they are Mine. I will make all people look up to My kingdoms. Down to the lower heaven I come in ships of light, curtained about with etherean mantles,[179] and gather in My harvest of new births to higher worlds, more radiant. My hosts below shall look up and glorify My everlasting splendors.

05/19.23. I give the tear of grief, sorrow and pity; but, in its flowing forth, I come with holier light and power to stir up the souls of My people. For they shall learn to speak to their Father, Who hears, and is attentive and full of love.

05/19.24. My joy is in the birth and growing up of souls, and in the joy of their joys, and in the proclaiming of their adoration for My boundless universe.

05/19.25. I call to them in darkness, and they come forth; but they halt in the darkness, and I call again, and I send My higher, upraised angels to them, and they call also. Yes, I fill the sky with the splendor of My worlds, es and corpor, so that I may stir man up to rise and enjoy the things I have made.

05/19.26. The voice departed, and Ah'jeng said: Behold the glory of the heavens, O my beloved, and the reward of the diligent in heart. Jehovih lives and reigns, the Highest and never to be reached, the Forever Beyond, and yet Ever Present.

05/19.27. O You Light of Light and Life of Life, how wonderful is the substance of Your creation! You have given me light to see Your splendors, which are forever new. O Jehovih, You Past, Present and Future of one time, which is and was and ever shall be. Jehovih, You Seen and Unseen, and Potent, Who have from Your very Self imparted a part to all the living! Who have raised up these of Hored! Glory be to You forever and ever!

05/19.28. And now, by certain signs and signals, Ah'jeng directed the officers of his hosts to take possession of Moeb and Hored. And the marshals extended out around the place, and by their presence added new light to the pillars of fire.

05/19.29. The marshals were decorated with colored raiment and signs and symbols, denoting the places from which they came, and their rank as Gods, and the experience they had passed through.

05/19.30. When Ah'jeng ceased speaking, the music of the chosen band of descending angels broke upon the place; first, faintly and far away. The work of the marshals was in keeping with the time of the music; and as the music drew nearer and stronger, so also more and more of the marshals descended and filed off to their respective places.

05/19.31. Presently the advance of the horns of the crescent, and the cold wave of the falling sea of fire, swept over the lower heaven fearfully and with unquestionable power. By a signal from God, the Brides and Bridegrooms joined in the music of the archangels, and great was its glory.

05/19.32. Between the horns of the crescent was a star of wonderful beauty; and it came toward God's throne, reflecting countless rays of light, brilliantly and awe-inspiring. And as the star drew near, it opened on the advance side, as a shell is opened, and there, with arms entwined, sat Etisyai and Onesyi, Goddesses.[180]

CHAPTER 20 Sethantes

05/20.1. Ah'jeng stepped down and stood at the foot of the throne. Masters of the inner temple gathered about the star, and unrolled a carpet reaching across the threshold, and the two Goddesses stepped forth from the crystalled cushion within the star, and glided, as if on a ray of light, up to the judgment seat of Jehovih.

---

[178] separate, set apart, disunite

[179] a mantle is a cloak, here of light

[180] Etisyai and Onesyi have been preserved in the tablet of the Zodiac under the name of Gemini. –Ed.

Meanwhile the musicians, a million voices, chanted: Glory, glory to Jehovih, Creator of worlds! Whose place is magnificence, and counterpart to endless time. The All, Whose Great Existence surpasses the grandest thoughts of men and Gods! Whose worlds in splendor are the scrolls, on which His hands write with the souls of mortals, His Almighty Will and Boundless Love!

05/20.2. And now the wheels of the great ship of fire, spread out and around; and all the millions of descended hosts formed a mighty amphitheater in which Moeb occupied the arena with its thirty-three million Brides and Bridegrooms of Jehovih arrayed in white, but differently from the Redeeming Hosts from the etherean worlds.

05/20.3. Moving in unison as one person, in time to the music, without a word of command, the hosts proceeded; each as a shining crystal in the place allotted, and void in nothing; and all so perfect, as if Jehovih had made each a special work of wonder to inspire men with reverence for the talents He had created.

05/20.4. The hosts, forming in place according to the music, were so perfectly timed that when the music ceased, all was still. The throne stood in the east, facing the west; the hosts of Moeb, who were the Brides and Bridegrooms of Jehovih, occupied the lower plane, and the ethereans surrounded them on all sides, rising higher and higher in the distance.[181]

05/20.5. God and Ha'jah met the Goddesses at the foot of the throne. God knew Onesyi hundreds of years before in other worlds, and he remembered Etisyai, who had crowned him two hundred years ago. Likewise Ha'jah also knew Etisyai and Onesyi. When they met they all saluted by touching the right hands; and immediately the Goddesses ascended to the center of the throne, and God went on the right and Ha'jah on the left.

05/20.6. Etisyai and Onesyi looked hopefully on the Brides and Bridegrooms, but were passive. Presently the voice of Jehovih spoke out of the light of the throne, saying:

05/20.7. Soul of My soul, substance of My substance, I created man. Out of My corporeal Self I clothed him with flesh, blood and bones. Man's spirit I gave from out of My own spirit, ever present; and I quickened him to move on the face of the earth.

05/20.8. God and the Brides and Bridegrooms responded, being quickened by the All Light: Out of corpor I came, quickened by Jehovih's Ever Presence. By virtue of His Wisdom, Power and Love I came into the world; to Jehovih all glory is due forever!

05/20.9. Again Jehovih spoke, saying: I allotted man a time to grow, to attain wisdom, power and love; a time to rejoice, and a time of sorrow; a time to beget offspring and know a father's love and care. In likeness of Me, I gave him attributes of My attributes, so that man could know Me and My Love.

05/20.10. Response: By the bondage of my love to my descendants, I know my Father lives and reigns, and will watch over me forever!

05/20.11. Again the voice of Jehovih said: I gave man a time in the corporeal form, so that he could learn corporeal things, and to learn where the tree of life springs from. I made man from no self-existence of his own, but from Myself; and in the place I quickened him into life, I bound him for a season. But when man has fulfilled his corporeal life I provide death to deliver him into a new world.

05/20.12. Response: Beautiful is Your Wisdom, O Jehovih, and far reaching. I was bound in the flesh even as a beast; like the attributes of a beast was my judgment, struggling for things of the corporeal world. With horror I looked upon death; as a sore calamity I judged Your cutting me off. But You delivered me into another world, preserving my judgment whole, bringing me to the heavens of my forefathers.

05/20.13. Then Jehovih said: At no time did I bring man, newborn into the world, without a mother and a nurse, and rich nourishment to feed him. Yes, I gave him angels to inspire him and lift him up; and I provided a Lord of the earth to manage his kingdoms and nations, and a God in heaven with a throne and judgment seat, so that man in the angel world would be provided and wisely instructed in soul, to comprehend the glory and harmony of My worlds.

---

[181] This arrangement of angels is reflected in corporeal theaters and sport stadiums where the seats rise as they recede farther from the central stage or arena. It not only allows for full view for everyone but also places the angels in orderly formations of grade and rank.

05/20.14. Response: Bountiful, O my Father Above! From nothing that I knew of, You brought me into conscious being, and in my helpless days fed me with rich nourishment. You gave me rulers and examples of government on the earth to discipline my soul to the order of men. And when I was born in heaven, I found God on his throne and a well-ordered haven of rest, with willing angels to clothe, feed and teach me the ways of Your kingdoms in the firmament.

05/20.15. Again Jehovih said: When man has fulfilled his time in the lower heaven, I prepare him by ample teachers for a higher resurrection. As Brides and Bridegrooms My hosts adorn them, and I come in a sea of fire. First man was wedded to the earth, by Me solemnized,[182] and without man's knowledge. Then to the lower heaven, he was wed, laboring with spirits and mortals.

05/20.16. The voice departed, and now Onesyi spoke, saying: Behold the Brides and Bridegrooms of Jehovih! When they were young they were wed first to the earth and then to the lower heaven, without their wills. Now they stand before the throne of God. In Your name, O Jehovih, I command them to speak their wills.

05/20.17. Response: I put away myself for You, O Jehovih! Make me one with You! I put away the earth for Your kingdom's sake, O Jehovih! Make me one with You! I put away Your Lord and Your God, O Jehovih, for sake of You! Your Lord and Your God raised me up and made me strong, but lo, the small spark of Yourself within my soul has grown to be a giant, bowing to none but You, O Jehovih! O make me Your Bride (Bridegroom), O Jehovih!

05/20.18. Onesyi said: The lame and the weak shall have a crutch, but the glory of the Father is to see His Brides and Bridegrooms walk alone. Whoever is wed to Jehovih shall never again, for self's sake, say to any man, woman, Lord, God, person or thing: Help!

05/20.19. Response: God and the Lord were my Saviors; without them I would never have known of Your exalted heavens, O Jehovih. Your Spirit calls me forever upward. Your Lord and Your God taught me to look upward; yes, they prayed for me. Now I am strong before You, O Jehovih! From now on, I will pray to You only; but never for my own benefit, nor for glory, ease, rest or exaltation; but that I may be quick, strong and wise to do Your will forever!

05/20.20. Onesyi said: Brides and Bridegrooms of Jehovih, All hail! All hail!

05/20.21. Response: Voice of Jehovih, All hail! All hail!

05/20.22. Onesyi said: To Jehovih and His everlasting kingdoms you are wed forever!

05/20.23. Response: To You, O Jehovih, I am wed forever!

05/20.24. Onesyi said: To be one with Him forever!

05/20.25. Response: To be one with Jehovih forever!

05/20.26. The voice of Jehovih said: They shall judge from My judgment seat; in them My Wisdom shall shine; for they are Mine forever!

05/20.27. Response: To consider You first, in all things, O Jehovih, this I shall do now and forever!

05/20.28. The Voice said: Behold, I have woven a crown for them; adorn them for My sake.

05/20.29. Response: I will have no crown, except that woven by You, O Jehovih! For Your sake, I will wear Your crown forever!

05/20.30. The Voice said: Behold, these who were My sons and daughters have become My Brides and Bridegrooms; they are Mine forever!

05/20.31. Response: I am Jehovih's forever!

05/20.32. Onesyi said: Pass before the throne, O my beloved. The testimony of Jehovih awaits His redeemed.[183] You shall dwell in the emancipated kingdoms forever!

05/20.33. And now the hosts of Brides and Bridegrooms passed singly before the throne of God; the whole thirty-three million passed. And during this time the es'enaurs chanted a hymn of glory, and mists of yellow, blue and red fell from the firmament above; and the mists descended into the archangels' hands as they stood about the

[182] made so, made binding, deep sealed, sanctified

[183] In other words, not just His words, but His actions (e.g., the crowns and crowning, resurrection into etherea) will confirm and be evidence of His declarations to the redeemed; the redeemed refers to the Brides and Bridegrooms because they had been saved or delivered from the animal mind, darkness and evil, and reclaimed and restored to goodness, purity, light, wholeness, etc.

throne, and by them were converted into crowns, which were placed on the heads of the Brides and Bridegrooms. And on the crowns were the words: IN WAN BROUGHT FORTH; DELIVERED IN HON'SHE.

05/20.34. As the hosts passed in front of the throne, Onesyi said: That which springs out of the earth feeds and clothes the atmospherean; but the etherean draws from the etherean worlds. Behold the crowns of the earth and of the lower heaven are only symbols of power, wisdom and love; but that which I bring from Jehovih's kingdom contains real virtue.

05/20.35. And lo and behold, the Brides and Bridegrooms became as archangels by virtue of the crowns from Jehovih's hand.

CHAPTER 21 Sethantes

05/21.1. When the ceremonies were ended, Onesyi said: Soon now in the name of the Father, we will rise and go on a long journey; and so that you may be apprised and consorted in love, I proclaim the freedom of the hour in Jehovih's name.

05/21.2. And the people went and mingled with each other, rejoicing and saluting. And Ha'jah, God and Etisyai greeted one another, and the Lords came forward and were greeted also; and then came the marshals, followed by the es'enaurs, and next came all long-serving laborers. And lastly, all who had redeemed any man or woman from darkness to light, came forward, and were saluted and duly honored.

05/21.3. And for the space of one hour all the angels indulged in revelry, reunion and fullness of heart; but no book could relate the thousandth part of the questions asked and love assurances expressed.

05/21.4. When the hour was ended, Onesyi signaled the proper officer, and he sounded the gavel thrice,[184] at which all was hushed and still. Onesyi said:

05/21.5. As Jehovih bestows a newborn child, and then takes the father and the mother away to the es world; so, likewise, Jehovih sent Etisyai, my sister, to establish the lower heaven, and now I come by His command to bear away this harvest to His everlasting kingdom. As a child bewails the loss of its father and mother, so will you who remain, bewail the loss of this rich harvest of archangels.

05/21.6. It is Jehovih's will that you drink deep of the sorrow of parting, for by this bondage you will be again reunited in the heavens still above. The progress of the soul of man is forever onward and in steps and plateaus; and the glory of the resurrection of the one who goes before is equally as great as is the sorrow of the one who remains behind. But the love that binds together is as a chain stretched out across the universe; neither time nor distance shall prevail against its inventions.

05/21.7. Swift messengers, well trained to course the vault of heaven, will pass between you, carrying the tidings of your soul's delight. And as Jehovih gives summer to follow winter, and the winter the summer, so also shall the time come again and again, forever, in which you shall mingle and part; again labor together, but in broader fields, and again part for a season.

05/21.8. Behold the wisdom of Jehovih in placing far apart the places of the souls of men; for all things abiding near each other equalize themselves. Even as there is glory in a new birth, so is there glory in death; as there is sorrow in death, so is there joy in resurrection. The time has now come when these whom you see, you shall not see for a long season; but you shall rejoice in this hour of parting, for they rise as Brides and Bridegrooms to Jehovih.

05/21.9. The es'enaurs sang an anthem of praise in which all the hosts united, and great was its glory. And now Onesyi arose, saying:

05/21.10. JEHOVIH, ALMIGHTY AND EVERLASTING! HOLY, HOLY CREATOR, RULER AND GIVER FORTH! LOOK UPON THIS YOUR SON, HA'JAH! O FATHER, IN YOUR NAME AND BY VIRTUE OF YOUR POWER VESTED IN ME, I PERPETUATE AND CROWN HIM GOD OF HEAVEN AND EARTH!

05/21.11. Ha'jah, now God, said: YOUR WILL BE DONE, O JEHOVIH! Then Onesyi turned to the five chief Lords of the five divisions of the earth, and bestowed them in like manner.

05/21.12. And Onesyi stretched forth her hand, saying: Give me a crown, O Jehovih, for Your Son, God of heaven and earth! And etherean substance descended into her hand, and she raised it up, and lo, it became a crown of great beauty, and she put it

[184] three raps with the gavel

on God's (Ha'jah's) head. Then, in like manner, she crowned the Lords of the earth.

05/21.13. And Etisyai and Onesyi came down and sat at the foot of the throne.

05/21.14. God (Ha'jah) came down from the throne with Whaga and Jud, and extending their hands, they said to Etisyai, Onesyi, and Sethantes, the retiring God:

Arise, O Goddess,
Arise, O Goddess,
Arise O God;
and go your way!

05/21.15. And they rose up and marched forth. The proper officers had already prepared the ship for its etherean journey; and soon as Etisyai and Onesyi had entered the central star, all the people who were to ascend went into the places assigned them.

05/21.16. God (Ha'jah) and the Lords returned, in tears, to the throne, and now the plateau of everlasting light began to ascend. Music sprang from every side, glorifying Jehovih and the magnificence of His bountiful worlds.

05/21.17. And those of the lower heaven echoed the music above; and the light of the ascending ship of fire made all else seem a shadow. But higher and higher it rose, in the form of a crescent, slowly turning on its upright axis, turning and rising, higher and higher, and the music faded away in the distance.

05/21.18. In a little while the meteor-like ascending ship of heaven looked like a star, till farther and farther off it disappeared in the distance.

05/21.19. And that was how the first harvest of angels born of the earth, ascended to the emancipated heavens in etherea.

CHAPTER 22 Sethantes

05/22.1. God said: Arise, O Lords of my realm, and go to the kingdoms of earth, which you received from Jehovih's hand; and may His wisdom, love and power be with you all!

05/22.2. And the Lords departed with their attendants, and went to their kingdoms over mortals.

05/22.3. And this was the beginning of the second dispensation of the first cycle of the Eoptian [185] age of the earth. And the lower heaven was well established in habitations,[186] angels, officers, and in all the requisites[187] for the upraised souls of mortals.

05/22.4. And God dispensed laws and government like his predecessor, enlarging all the places according to the increase in the number of spirits rising up from the earth.

05/22.5. And the voice of Jehovih was with God; and as the first kingdom had been called Hored, so the second was called Hored, signifying the place of God.

05/22.6. And as it had been with the Lords of the earth in their places, so it continued with the new Lords, and they enlarged their places also, even according to the increase in the number of inhabitants of the earth.

05/22.7. And as it had been in the past, that messengers plied constantly between Hored and the Lords' places, so it continued. By this means, through God and his Lords, all the affairs of the lower heaven were kept in harmony.

05/22.8. And God ruled in Hored four hundred years, and Hored spread over all the lands of the earth.

CHAPTER 23 Sethantes

05/23.1. When the time of God and his hosts was fulfilled, Jehovih brought the earth into dan of Eyon, in the arc Lais, whose angels descended in a ship of fire, and delivered God, his Lords, and all the hosts under them who were prepared for the etherean resurrection. At this time there were six hundred and twenty-five million inhabitants in atmospherea. And the number of the second harvest was two hundred and eighty million.

05/23.2. The ascent of the second harvest was like the ascent of the first harvest. And the place of the landing of the second harvest in the firmament of heaven was in Lais, and Bin, and the grade of

---

[185] From the time man comes into being on the earth with potential for eternal life, until his race becomes extinct, is the eoptian age of the earth.

[186] dwellings, residences, houses, buildings

[187] requirements, essentials, indispensables, necessities

the harvest was seventy-eight, being two less than the grade of the first harvest.

05/23.3. So the heavens of the earth passed into the care of the succeeding God and Lords, who had been raised up and prepared for those commissions. And for the present there were no more ethereans dwelling in these regions.

05/23.4. Jehovih had said: Those who come out of the earth shall be sufficient to themselves. As a mother provides for her child, so do I provide for the spirit generations of a corporeal world; but when they are mature in wisdom, strength and love, I command them to take the offices of Lords and God in the management of My kingdoms.

05/23.5. So it came to pass after the ascent of the ethereans, that the whole earth and its lower heavens were under the dominion of those who had sprung up out of the earth. And it became a saying: The first was etherean rule; the second was atmospherean rule. For the earth had Lords who had been on no other world, and a God who had never been on other worlds.

05/23.6. And it likewise came to pass that the atmospherean rulers were more lenient in their government, and less tyrannical[188] than the ethereans had been. For as the ethereans had forbidden the es'yans, the newly dead, to return to their mortal kindred, until their fiftieth year in spirit life, it was not so with the present Lords and God, for they indulged hundreds of thousands of es'yans for sympathy's sake to return to their mortal kindred. And these es'yans did not become workers in heaven, either for others, or for their own resurrection to higher regions; but they became idlers and vagabonds in the lower heaven, often living with their mortal kindred till their mortal kindred died, and then, in turn, persuading these es'yans to do even as they did.

05/23.7. And God perceived, when it was too late, that his leniency had laid the foundation for disorganizing the kingdom of heaven; for the strolling idlers, knowing no other heaven, sowed the spirit of disbelief throughout the places of learning and industry in the lower heaven, persuading others that they were toiling to no good purpose.

05/23.8. They said: Behold, it was told us on earth there was a Jehovih! But we are in heaven, and yet we do not find Him. Now we know, in truth, there is no All Person. Come, then, let us seek ease and the rich viands that rise up out of the earth. A man lives on the earth and dies, and his spirit floats about, and then there is no more of him. Why will you serve the Lord? Why will you serve God? Be free and live for yourselves instead of for others.

05/23.9. Thus it came to pass that little by little the lower heaven began to fall from its high estate.

05/23.10. The third dan was six hundred years, and God and his Lords, having provided successors, ascended with their harvest to etherea. And its number was four hundred and eight million Brides and Bridegrooms, and their grade was sixty-six.

05/23.11. The fourth dan was five hundred years, and the harvest was six hundred million Brides and Bridegrooms; and their grade was fifty-eight.

05/23.12. The fifth dan was three hundred years; and the harvest was two hundred million; and their grade was fifty, which was the lowest grade capable of emancipation, or capable of surviving in etherea.[189]

05/23.13. And now darkness set in and covered all the earth. And from this time until the end of the cycle, which was three thousand years from the birth of man on earth,[190] there were no more resurrections to the emancipated heavens.

05/23.14. The Kingdom of Hored was broken up and dissolved. The spirits did not love to labor or learn according to Jehovih's plan, but returned to

[188] In this case the meaning of the word tyrannical means directing and exacting rather than brutally despotic and unjust. For the Ethereans were strict, but for the sake of resurrection; not harsh for selfish reasons, as we today are accustomed to understand the context of the word tyranny.

[189] Below grade fifty the person is pulled more toward the earth then away; fifty and above and the person is drawn more toward light (etherea) than corpor.

[190] i.e., from the birth of the I'hins

the earth-attractions; and they were called DRUJAS,[191] because they did not desire resurrection.

05/23.15. And God, Lords, officers and teachers were without subjects and pupils. And mortals were overwhelmed by thousands and millions of drujas, so much so,[192] that the ashars were powerless to accomplish good inspiration.

05/23.16. At this time there were more than three billion[193] angels in atmospherea, and for the most part, they dwelt on earth.

05/23.17. Thus ended the first cycle of the first heaven of the earth.

END OF BOOK OF SETHANTES, SON OF JEHOVIH

[191] The ancients called the lost spirits by different names in all countries; in India, Druj; in China, Won-yeang; in the Algonquin tribes, O'spee; the Hebrews, Girapha (i.e., to be feared). Then we have the terms, ghosts, fairies, wraiths, etc., for modern terms. Under the name of familiar spirits the ancient Hebrews were well informed of these drujas. Druj is a Vedic name. The ancient Chinese called them M'spe. The Germans called them "The double" [doppelgänger] because when they take on forms they look like the mortal to whom they are engrafted. The term, familiar spirits, as now used, has a wider range. –Ed.

[192] so much so = to such an extent

[193] Billion means 1,000,000,000; thus three billion equals 3,000,000,000.

First Book of the First Lords

Being contemporary with the Book of Sethantes, Son of Jehovih. That is, when Sethantes was God of heaven, his Lords had dominion on the earth in the same period of time. And this is their book, even as the preceding one was God's book.

CHAPTER 1 First Book First Lords

06/1.1. In the beginning God created the heavens of the earth; and the Lord made man upright. Man was naked and not ashamed; neither did he know the sin of incest, but dwelt like the beasts of the field.

06/1.2. And the Lord brought the angels of heaven to man; by his side they took on forms like man, having all the organs and attributes of mortals, for it was the time of the earth for such things to be.

06/1.3. So it came to pass that a new race was born on the earth, and these were called I'hins, because they were begotten[194] of both heaven and earth. Consequently it became a saying: The earth conceived of the Lord.[195]

06/1.4. And the name of the first race was ASU, because they were of the earth only; and the name of the second race was I'HIN, because they were capable of being taught spiritual things.

06/1.5. The Lord said: Of all that live on the face of the earth, or in its waters, or in the air above, that breathes the breath of life, I have delivered only man to knowledge of his Creator.

06/1.6. And the Lord spoke to the I'hin through his angels, saying: Go hide your nakedness, for it is the commandment of God.

[194] impregnated, sired, generated, reproduced, born

[195] And this is the origin of the concept on earth that Father Spirit impregnated Mother Earth and brought forth life or man.

06/1.7. The I'hins were afraid, and they clothed themselves, and were no longer naked before the Lord.

06/1.8. Then the Lord commanded the angels to give up their forms, and to no longer be seen as mortals.[196] And it was done. And the Lord said to them: Because you brought forth life, which is in flesh and blood, you shall minister to man for six generations on the face of the earth. And it was so.

06/1.9. And so that man may continue to walk upright, you shall teach him the law of incest, for man on his own cannot attain to know this.

06/1.10. Nor shall you permit the I'hins to dwell with Asu, lest his seed go down in darkness.

06/1.11. And man was thus inspired of the Lord, and he walked upright, and prospered on the earth.

06/1.12. But after a season man became conceited in his own judgment, and he disobeyed the commandments of God.

06/1.13. And he strayed out of the garden of paradise and began to dwell with the asu'ans, and there was born into the world a new race called DRUK, and they did not have the light of the Father in them; neither could they be inspired with shame, nor with heavenly things.

06/1.14. But the I'hins were grateful to the Lord, and they gave sacrifice in burnt offerings. And they said to the Druks: Go sacrifice to the Lord, and he will prosper you. But the Druks did not understand; and they fell upon the Lord's chosen, and slew them, right and left, taking their possessions.

06/1.15. And the Lord said to the Druks: Because you have slain your brethren you shall depart out of the place of God; and so that you may be known to the ends of the earth I put my mark upon you.

06/1.16. And the mark of the Lord put upon the Druks was the shadow of blood, which, being interpreted, is WAR.[197]

06/1.17. And the Lord God said: By this sign, the tribes of Druk and their descendants shall be known to the end of the world.

06/1.18. And woman, being more helpless than man, cried out with fear, saying: O Lord, how shall I bring forth to you, and not to the sons of death?

06/1.19. And the Lord said: Because you have brought forth in pain, and yet called on my name, behold, I will be as a shield and protector to you. For I will also put a mark upon the I'hins, my chosen, so you shall know them when they come to you.

06/1.20. And the Lord commanded the male I'hins, old and young, to be circumcised, so that woman would not be deceived by the Druks. And the I'hins circumcised their males, old and young; for it was the testimony of the Lord to woman that seed of their seed was born to everlasting life.

06/1.21. And the Druks went away into the wilderness, and dwelt with the asu'ans and with one another.

06/1.22. God said: I will make a boundary line between the tribes of Druks and the I'hins; and this is the line that I the Lord God make between them:

06/1.23. The I'hins shall labor and clothe themselves, and I will remain with them; but the Druks shall wander in the wilderness, neither laboring nor clothing themselves.

06/1.24. And it was so.

CHAPTER 2 First Book First Lords

06/2.1. The time of the habitation of Asu was eight thousand years; and they survived two thousand years after the time of the birth of the I'hins, which is to say, Asu dwelt on the earth six thousand years, and then conceived of the chosen of God; and after that survived two thousand years more.

06/2.2. And Asu disappeared off the face of the earth.

---

[196] i.e., no longer seen in corporeal form

[197] Note that WAR is the distinguishing characteristic of the tribes of Druk and their descendants—but not their color, size, geographic location, etc. Every person alive today descends from both I'hins and Druks; and those who WAR are following their druk ancestry, rather than their I'hin ancestry. For, these races amalgamated, and also became extinct as to initial race; so that there is now no separate race of Druk or I'hin; but all peoples today are capable of eternal life. Yet, the Druk race and legacy was necessary to strengthen the races of man, imparting to them the necessary corporeal endurance and capacity, for that which was to come.

06/2.3. But the sacred people, the I'hins; and the carnivorous people, the Druks; remained on the earth.

06/2.4. The I'hins were white and yellow, but the Druks were brown and black; the I'hins were small and slender, but the Druks were tall and stout.[198]

06/2.5. Now, because the Druks had not previously obeyed the Lord, but went and dwelt with the asu'ans, there was a half-breed race born on the earth, called YAK, signifying ground people; and they burrowed in the ground like beasts of the forest. And the Yaks did not walk wholly upright, but also went on all fours.[199]

06/2.6. God said: Because the Yaks cannot be taught the crime of incest, behold, they shall not dwell forever on the earth. So shall it also be with the Druks, except where they cohabit with the I'hins, whose seed is born to everlasting life. But with the Druks, and their heirs that spring from the Yaks, there shall be an end, both in this world and the next.

06/2.7. And the arms of the Yaks were long, and their backs were stooped and curved. And the Lord said: Because they are the fruit of incest, and not capable of speech or eternal life in heaven, the I'hins shall make servants of them.

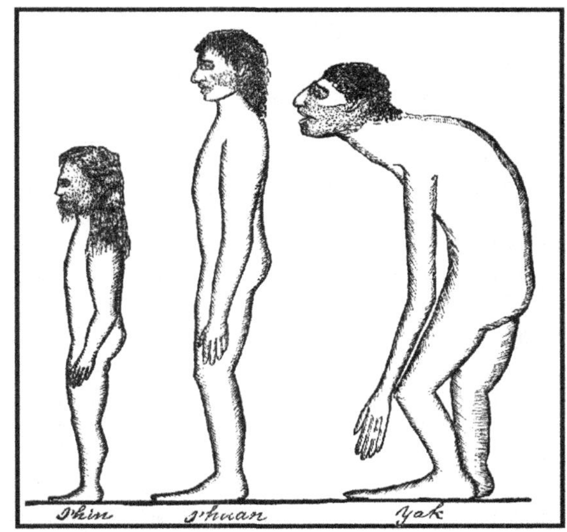

i014 **Some Races of Man**. I'hin, I'huan, Yak.

06/2.8. And so that they may not tempt my chosen to bring forth fruit to destruction, they shall be neutralized in my sight. So the angels of God taught the I'hins to make eunuchs of the Yaks. And after making eunuchs of both the male and female Yaks, the I'hins took them for servants.

06/2.9. And the Lord said: The Yaks shall serve the I'hins, and build and sow and reap for them. And it was so.

[198] The physical traits mentioned in this verse and in later verses, must be in the aggregate; that is, these are generalizations, being the statistical modes for a certain span of time. Used for reporting purposes, they are the simplified (generalized) extract of complex, continuous data.

For, logic, reason and experience in population studies and population description (statistical representation), would show that these supposed discrete units (e.g., white or yellow) are actually the modes of a continuum. For example, the offspring between a white I'hin and a yellow I'hin would be neither white nor yellow but lie between the two in color. And these offspring marrying with other in-betweens and with the white and yellow colors, for many generations, will ultimate in a continuous line (continuum, representation) of color from white to yellow.

And experience in population studies reveal the continuum line would be more or less curved in appearance; so that the Oahspe text indicates over-all bumps (modes, most frequent colors among Druks; most frequent colors among I'hins). And we read later in Oahspe of I'hins who were black, or brown, or red, or copper—in fact, they were of all colors.

This statistical representation applies as well to tallying the most frequent heights as well as the most frequent heft, for I'hins and Druks; with Oahspe giving their comparative general modes.

Thus, we may say regarding population physical traits, that there were gradations and pockets of differences. And more evidence supporting the application of statistical description will be given later. But as to skin color, today it is neither a sufficient nor necessary indicator of one's ancestry regarding these earliest of races; for everyone alive today has roots in both I'hin and Druk races as well as in Asu.

[199] as Asu did; see images i013 p.36, and i014 (the I'huan in image is explained in the next chapter)

06/2.10. The I'hins were disposed to live alone, but the Lord called them together, saying: Come and dwell together in cities. For it is fitting that you live in the manner of my kingdoms in heaven.

06/2.11. Build therefore, to the Lord your God; and my angels shall dwell with you, teaching you to sing and dance for the glory of your Creator.

06/2.12. And man built to the Lord, and established worship on earth in the manner of heaven.

06/2.13. Now it happened that the Druks came to witness the rites and ceremonies of the chosen, but they took no part in them, nor did they comprehend their meaning.

06/2.14. And God said to the I'hins: So that you can teach some of them about the Lord your God, build within the house of worship an image of me; build it in likeness of man. And I will manifest to those who are capable of everlasting life.

06/2.15. And the I'hins, men and women, with their servants, built images of stone and clay and wood to the Lord, and stood them by the altars of sacrifice.

06/2.16. And during the time of worship, the angels of the Lord came and possessed the idols, and spoke from them with audible voices in the presence of mortals.

06/2.17. And the Druks inquired of the I'hins as to the cause. And the I'hins said: Behold, there is a God in heaven, subtler than the air of heaven.[200] It was he who brought us forth out of darkness. He speaks in the idol so that you may know he abides with his people.

06/2.18. The Druks said: What does he say? The I'hins answered: That whoever has attained to remember God is on the way to everlasting life.

[200] That is, there is a God in the sky, who is more imperceptible or subtler than the air of the sky—which is why it is hard for you to see Him, hear Him, and even be aware of Him. You know the wind exists yet you do not see it; but you see its effects. In the same way, God exists; you do not see him, but you can see his effects. If you listen and watch closely enough to the subtle in the wind, closely enough to the subtle in the air, you may be able to catch a glimpse of Him, or feel His presence or hear His voice.

06/2.19. The Druks inquired, saying: How can a man live forever? Behold, you, who believe, also die!

06/2.20. The I'hins answered, saying: As the voice of the Lord is unseen but potent, so is there a spirit in man unseen and potent, which shall never die, but ascend in heaven to habitations prepared by the Lord.

06/2.21. And many of the Druks pondered on these things, and their thoughts quickened their souls within them, so that they brought forth heirs to eternal salvation.

06/2.22. And the Lord said to the I'hins: Because you have done a good thing, go abroad, by the roadsides and in other places, and build images to me and mine, and my angels shall bestow gifts, signs and miracles.

06/2.23. And the I'hins supplied the roadways of the earth with idols of stone, wood and clay, and the angels of heaven descended to the idols and established heavenly kingdoms close by.

06/2.24. And when man came there, and called on the name of the Lord, it was a password for the angels; and they wrought[201] miracles, and otherwise gave man evidence of the Unseen.

CHAPTER 3 First Book First Lords

06/3.1. And God gave commandments to man, so that the earth could be a place of rejoicing forever. And these are the commandments of the Lord God given in that day:

06/3.2. You shall strive to remember the Lord your God with all your heart and with all your soul.

06/3.3. You shall not kill man, beast, bird, or creeping thing, for they are the Lord's.

06/3.4. You shall build walls around your cities, so that beasts and serpents may not enter and do you harm. And if your habitation is in the wilderness, you shall build mounds of wood and earth to sleep on at night, so that serpents and beasts cannot molest you.

06/3.5. The I'hins inquired of the Lord, saying: If we build walls around our cities, how shall we get in and out? How shall we gather our harvests of fruit and nuts, and seeds of the field? How shall we ascend the mounds that we build in the wilderness?

[201] manifested, worked, brought forth

06/3.6. The Lord said: Behold, my angels shall teach you to build ladders and how to use them. And when you go into the city at night you shall take the ladders in after you; and when you come out in the morning you shall let the ladders down again.

06/3.7. And God's angels taught the chosen these things, and man provided the cities and mounds with ladders; according to the commandment of God these things were done.

06/3.8. And the I'hins prospered and spread over the face of the earth; hundreds of thousands of cities and mounds were built, and the I'hins rejoiced in the glory of all created things. Neither did they kill any man, beast, fish, bird, nor creeping thing that breathed the breath of life.

06/3.9. And God saw that man was good and grateful in all things; and God called to the angels of heaven, saying: Why are the I'hins good? For, as yet, they are ignorant!

06/3.10. And the angels answered, saying: They are good because you said to us: Go as guardian angels and inspire man to live without evil, || which we did; ministering to the I'hins, guarding and inspiring them night and day.

06/3.11. God said: Well then, the I'hins have no honor. Unless they learn by themselves to be good, they will be void of wisdom in heaven. For this reason you shall withdraw a little, so that man is tried as to his self-commandment.[202]

06/3.12. So the angels withdrew awhile from the I'hins. Now the I'hins had stored in their cities and on their mounds, ample provision of food and clothing for the winter; but the druks did not follow the example of the I'hins, for the druks stored up nothing.

06/3.13. And when the angels withdrew a little way, evil spirits came to the druks, and said to them: Behold, it is winter, and you are hungry. Go over the ladders and possess the stores of the I'hins.

06/3.14. So the druks plundered the I'hins; and evil spirits came upon the I'hins also, and many of them were inspired to defend their stores. And war ensued;[203] and it spread around the whole earth.

06/3.15. And the I'hins asked the Lord as to why God allowed evil to come upon his chosen.

06/3.16. And the Lord said: Because you depended upon me for all things, you did not develop yourselves. From now on, man shall learn to face evil on his own account; otherwise he cannot attain to the Godhead in heaven.

06/3.17. Your Creator has given you two entities, that which is flesh, and that which is spirit. And the flesh will desire earthly things; but the spirit will desire heavenly things.

06/3.18. Behold, when the druks came upon you for your stores, your flesh cried out WAR, and your people fell.

06/3.19. Now I have come again to raise you up; to make you understand the spirit within. It is that, and not the flesh, which shall learn to triumph.

06/3.20. The I'hins said: Our people are scattered and gone; will they not mingle with the druks, and thus go out in darkness?

06/3.21. The Lord said: Behold there were druks who had learned a little from the images; now because your people are scattered and gone, they shall go among the druks and teach the law of incest and the name of God; and the druks shall also begin to hide their nakedness.

06/3.22. So the Lord inspired other people besides the I'hins, to make and wear clothes, which they did.

06/3.23. And again the Lord brought the I'hins together in lodges and cities, and he said to them: From this time forward, you shall live upon the earth as an example of righteousness. And your brethren who have mingled with the tribes of darkness shall no longer molest you, but shall be your defenders and protectors.

06/3.24. And a new tribe began on the earth; and they were called I'HUANS, because they were half-breeds between the Druks and I'hins. The I'huans were red like copper; and they were taller and stronger than any other people in the world. And the Lord commanded the I'huans, saying:

---

[202] That is, man needs to learn why it is good to be good. Therefore he will be tested as to his ability to command himself to do right and to follow through in action. From this, he ultimately learns at least two lessons, why it is wise to be good, and why it is wise to be obedient to wisdom—especially that wisdom put forth by the Lord.

[203] followed, resulted, became a consequence

06/3.25. Protect the I'hins, the little people, white and yellow;[204] call them THE SACRED PEOPLE. For you are of them, and you are also of the Lord your God. And it was so.

CHAPTER 4 First Book First Lords

06/4.1. About this time man began to use his lips and tongue in enunciating words, prior to which he spoke in the thorax.[205]

06/4.2. And the Lord spoke to the I'hin, saying: So that the labor of the Lord your God may be remembered on the earth, go provide me a stone and I will engrave it with my own hand, and it shall be called Se'moin,[206] because it shall be a testimony to all nations and peoples, on the earth, of the first written language in all the world.

06/4.3. So the I'hins prepared a stone, hewed it flat, then polished it smooth; and the Lord came down in the night and engraved it. And the Lord explained it; through his angels he taught the I'hins the meaning of the characters engraved on it.

06/4.4. And the Lord said: Go into all cities in all the countries of the world, and provide copies of the tablet I have given. So it came to pass that the angels of heaven inspired the I'hins to make tablets and to read them, so that the first language of the earth (Panic) could be preserved to the races of men. And it was so.

06/4.5. Now the I'huans partly obeyed the Lord and partly obeyed the way of the flesh, and they became warriors and destroyers; nevertheless, they neither harmed the I'hins nor allowed harm to come upon them.

06/4.6. God had commanded the I'hins to make eunuchs of the Yaks, the monstrosities, and use them as servants; for the Lord saw that the Yaks were not capable of everlasting life in heaven.

06/4.7. Now the I'huans also made servants of the Yaks in the same way; but they disobeyed God by inflicting the neutral gender on their enemies whom they captured in war. And although they were themselves half-breeds with the druks, yet they hated the druks, and pursued them with vengeance.

06/4.8. In those days the relative proportion of the races of men were: I'hins, one hundred; I'huans, three hundred; druks, five thousand; yaks, five thousand; and of monstrosities between man and beast, three thousand; but the latter died each generation, for they did not have the power of procreation among themselves.

06/4.9. And God saw the work of destruction going on (of the I'huans slaughtering right and left), and he sent the I'hins to preach among them, saying to the I'hins:

06/4.10. Tell the I'huans: Do not kill whoever is created alive, for it is the commandment of the Lord.

06/4.11. For in the time of your most success in slaughtering your fellow-man, you are also peopling heaven with the spirits of vengeance. And they will return upon you, and even the I'huans shall turn upon one another; thus says God.

06/4.12. But the I'huans did not understand; did not believe. And it came to pass that great darkness covered the earth. And man, except the few I'hins, gave up his life to wickedness all his days.

06/4.13. And the Lord's people worshipped and preached in the temples, and the Lord and his heavenly hosts manifested to them; but all the other races of men did not hear; would not come to learn of God.

06/4.14. And the Lord became tired in his labor, and he called his angels to him, and he said to them: Behold, man on the earth has gone so far from my ways he will not heed my commandments; he cannot hear my voice.

06/4.15. And your labor is in vain also. For which reason we will persist no longer on the earth till man has exhausted the evil that is in him.

---

[204] Again, this is a generalization; see 06/2.4<fn-stout>. [Where reference is made, as above, to white people, it does not mean what we today call white people; but white in fact, with white hair also. The same remarks hold in reference to yellow people, etc. –Ed.]

Thus, white skin here is not the color of what in early kosmon was called the white race (being really a light or pale copper, or beige), but it would seem that the white of the I'hins was, in complexion, more a moon white. Moreover, being half angel, they may have had a more radiant or glowing skin tone, and a light in the eyes, compared to the druks.

[205] chest; guttural sounds

[206] see image i033 vol.2 p.227

06/4.16. So the Lord and his angel hosts departed away from the earth. And clouds came over the face of the earth; the moon did not shine, and the sun was only like a red coal of fire; and the stars shone in the firmament during the day as well as at night.

06/4.17. The harvests failed; the trees yielded no nuts, and the roots on which man feeds ceased to grow.

06/4.18. And the monstrosities, and the Yaks, and the druks, died off, tens of millions of them. And even then they were not extinct. Nevertheless, the I'huans suffered less; and the I'hins not at all. For the Lord had previously inspired them to provide against the coming famine.

06/4.19. And the Lord bewailed the earth and the generations of man: I made man upright and walked by his side, but he slipped aside and fell, said the Lord. I admonished[207] him, but he would not heed. I showed him that every living creature brought forth its own kind; but he did not understand, did not believe; and he dwelt with beasts; falling lower than all the rest.

END OF THE FIRST BOOK OF THE FIRST LORDS

Book of Ah'shong, Son of Jehovih

God of the second cycle after man's creation.

CHAPTER 1 Ah'shong

07/1.1. When God and his Lords of heaven and earth had lost their heavenly dominion, the swift messengers, who constantly ply through the atmospherean and etherean worlds, bore the report to Jehovih's kingdoms in etherea.

07/1.2. The earth had passed the ji'ayan eddies at Shrapah, in the etherean roadway Hi-abalk'yiv, and was heading for the eastern fields of Anakaron, having entered the dan'haian arches of Vehetaivi, where the great kingdoms of the Orian Chief, Hieu Wee, lay with his millions of Gods and Goddesses and high-raised ethereans.

07/1.3. Into Hieu Wee's presence, the swift messengers came, fresh from the heavens of the earth, with their pitiful tales of woe that had befallen its inhabitants.

07/1.4. Hieu Wee said: I see the red star, the earth, O Jehovih! I have heard the tale of horror. What shall be done, O Father?

07/1.5. Then Jehovih spoke, saying: Call your tributary Chief, Ah'shong. Let him hear the will of Jehovih!

07/1.6. Then Hieu Wee sent for Ah'shong, who had dominion over the fields of Anakaron in etherea, through which the roadway lay where the earth was to travel for three thousand years.

07/1.7. And when Ah'shong came before the Holy Council of Hieu Wee's million Gods and Goddesses, the All Light fell upon the throne like a sun; and the voice of the Creator spoke in the midst of the light, saying:

07/1.8. Hieu Wee, My Son! And Hieu Wee answered: Here I am, Your servant, O Jehovih!

07/1.9. Jehovih said: Behold the red star, the earth; she enters the fields of Anakaron. She is dripping wet and cold in the ji'ayan eddies. Her God and Lords are powerless in the spell of darkness. Send your son, Ah'shong, to deliver the earth and her heavens. For behold, I will bring them to his door.

07/1.10. Then Ah'shong spoke, saying: Your will be done, O Jehovih. Though I have long been honored in etherea, with many etherean worlds to command, I have not as yet redeemed one corporeal world and her heaven from a time of darkness.

07/1.11. Jehovih said: Go then, My Son, to the laboring earth and deliver her; but first appoint a successor for Anakaron.

07/1.12. Then spoke Hieu Wee, who was older than the red star, who had seen many corporeal worlds created; had seen them run their course, and then disappear as such. He said to Ah'shong:

07/1.13. Send to both Wan and Hivigat, in etherea, and get the history of the earth and her heaven; and also obtain an account of her harvests of Brides and Bridegrooms to Jehovih. And you shall call from my realms, as many million etherean angels as your labor may require, and with them proceed to the earth. There you shall establish

---

[207] gently corrected, instructed, counseled, reminded, warned, mildly reproved

a line of swift messengers between this place and yours, and, by the power of Jehovih, I will answer your prayers in whatever you may need.

07/1.14. Then Ah'shong went back to Anakaron, his etherean kingdom, and in the presence of his Holy Council, made known Jehovih's will and his. And Ah'shong called for sixty million volunteers, to go with him on his mission; and they came presently: some from Yohan; some from T'seing; some from Araith; some from Gon Loo and from various other places in Anakaron; came in millions; as many as Ah'shong called for.

07/1.15. So Ah'shong raised up a successor to Jehovih's throne in Anakaron, and he was installed and crowned according to the discipline of the etherean heavens.

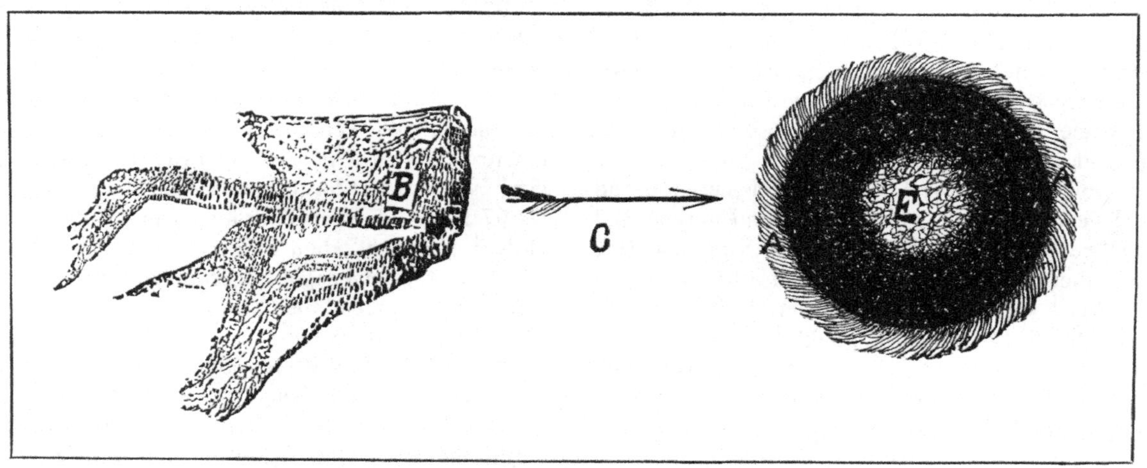

i016 **Ah'shong and Ethereans Come to the Red Star**. A, Atmospherea; B, Ethereans; C, Distance: 20,000 miles; E, Earth.

07/1.16. And Ah'shong sent swift messengers into the former roadway of the earth to obtain its history; its harvests of Brides and Bridegrooms.

07/1.17. Then Ah'shong and his sixty million volunteers gazed toward the red star, and watched her as she coursed along in the arches of Vehetaivi.

07/1.18. Thus Ah'shong, well skilled in the course and behavior of worlds, gathered together his millions of angels, trained in arduous enterprise and furtherance of Jehovih's will. Quickly they framed and equipped an Orian port-au-gon, and illuminated it with fire-lights and bolts. And these sons and daughters of Jehovih embarked and sped forth. A half a million miles, to the outskirts of Anakaron, where they stood close above the earth, so near that the sweeping moon would almost touch the down-hanging curtains of etherean fire. And here they halted, so that both mortals and angels belonging to the earth might see and fear; for Jehovih made man so that by unusual sights he would become weak and trembling, so as to change him to new purposes.

07/1.19. Jehovih's voice spoke to Ah'shong, saying: For three days and nights you shall stand in the firmament so that man on earth and in atmospherea may perceive the power and majesty of My chosen in heaven.[208]

07/1.20. Ah'shong said: On the fourth day, O Jehovih, I will cross Chinvat;[209] on the fifth, descend toward the earth. Bring me, O Father, Your messengers from the lower heaven. I will converse with them.

07/1.21. Jehovih sent the angels of the earth and lower heaven up to Ah'shong; disheartened they came, to know Jehovih's will:

07/1.22. Ah'shong said to them: The Father's hosts have come from their high estate and glorious ease, to redeem these fallen heavens and man on

[208] see image i016

[209] the border (bridge) between atmospherea and etherea; i.e., between the earth's vortex and etherea

the earth. It is our labor to come in love to the helpless, and teach them how to sing in Jehovih's praise. Then the swift messengers answered:

07/1.23. In the All Person's boundless love, may you find recompense for your holy words, most honored God. Down in darkness, long and earnestly, the Lords of earth have labored in unison with heaven's God, whose kingdom fell. Alas, our God, who ministered over the lower heaven, is crushed and humiliated. The enemies of high heaven, exulting in their spoil of Jehovih's kingdom and His name, mock us, saying: Where is Jehovih now? Where the Higher Light? O Faithists in an All Person boundless!

07/1.24. But now your high-shining sun, your ship of etherean fire, makes the sons and daughters of the earth and her heaven look up, fear and tremble. And when your Light appeared we made all haste in hope of succor.[210] Our souls are more than filled with thankfulness; and in Jehovih's name, we will go back and employ a million trumpeters to proclaim around the earth and heaven: JEHOVIH HAS COME!

07/1.25. After due salutation the swift messengers departed; and Ah'shong made all things ready for his descent at the proper time.

CHAPTER 2 Ah'shong

07/2.1. Jehovih spoke to Ah'shong, saying: On the evening of the third day you shall move your etherean ship toward the earth. And when you arrive within an arrafon[211] you shall halt for another three days, so that your magnificence may awe the mortals and angels of earth with the power and glory of My emancipated sons and daughters.

07/2.2. Ah'shong proceeded as commanded, and when he came within an arrafon, halted for three days, and the magnificence of the scene overcame the stubbornness of mortals on earth and angels in atmospherea. Again Jehovih said:

07/2.3. Proceed again, My Son, and when you are within half the breadth of the earth,[212] halt once more and make a plateau in that place, and it shall be your place of residence for the period of dawn, which shall be seven years and sixty days.

07/2.4. And from this time forward, My etherean hosts shall not remain in atmospherea more than eight years in any one cycle. This dawn that I give you shall be like every dawn of dan, some of one year, some of two, three, four or more years, as the time requires.

07/2.5. And you shall dwell in your kingdom seven years and sixty days, and the time shall be called the first dawn of dan, and the next succeeding shall be called the second dawn of dan, and so on, as long as the earth brings forth.

07/2.6. And the time from one dawn of dan to another shall be called one dan'ha; and four dan'ha shall be called one square, because this is the sum of one density, which is twelve thousand of the earth's years. And twelve squares shall be called one cube, which is the first dividend of the third space, in which there is no variation in the vortex of the earth. And four cubes shall be called one sum, because its magnitude embraces one equal of the Great Serpent.[213]

07/2.7. So Ah'shong proceeded again, and moved within four thousand miles of the earth, and the voice of Jehovih commanded Ah'shong to halt there, and found a new kingdom, using all things requisite[214] to that end. Jehovih said:

07/2.8. Your place shall be sufficiently distant from the earth, so that your dominion will not be disturbed by the confusion of fallen angels. Also, the distance of your kingdom will prevent those, whom you shall redeem away from earth and mortal contact, from returning to the earth.

07/2.9. Ah'shong perceived, and he proclaimed what Jehovih had spoken to him. And the hosts cast out fastenings to the plateau, so that the kingdom, together with the etherean sea of fire, could rotate with the earth and its atmosphere. Jehovih said:

07/2.10. Make the foundation of your place strong, and erect ten thousand pillars of fire around it; and in every direction provide roadways and mansions; but in the center you shall build the

[210] assistance, help, relief

[211] An arrafon is about 20,000 miles. –Ed. [circa 32,000 kilometers]

[212] about 4000 miles (ca. 6400 kilometers), or the distance from Atlanta to Los Angeles and back again

[213] Philosophers have long known that some certain measure of ethereal space must be equal to the density of the planets for a balance of power. –Ed.

[214] necessary, essential, indispensable

house of council, where your host of dominion shall sit during dawn.[215]

07/2.11. Ah'shong built the place as commanded by Jehovih, and when it was finished, Jehovih said: You shall call the place Yeshuah. And it was called that because it was a place of salvation. Again Jehovih said:

07/2.12. Now choose your council, My Son, and also your sub-officers, and when you have completed the list, leave the sub-officers in Yeshuah while you and your council of one million men and women proceed down to the earth and its heaven to cast your eyes upon its inhabitants, for they are in distress. And when you come to the place of My Lords and My God, deliver them and bring them to Yeshuah, for they need rest. And also bring away with you all I'hins in heaven who are capable, and place them into the care of your people.

07/2.13. Ah'shong did as commanded, first selecting his council and his officers, and then he and his hosts proceeded to the earth as commanded.

CHAPTER 3 Ah'shong

07/3.1. Up to this time the ancient names of the division of the lands of the earth had been maintained, and God and his Lords having been driven from the place of Hored, which had gone into dissolution, dwelt part of the time in Whaga and part in Jud and Vohu.

07/3.2. Accordingly God and the Lords had established three kingdoms, one in Whaga, one in Jud, and one in Vohu; and within these kingdoms of heaven there were two hundred million redeemed angels capable of the second resurrection, and one hundred million es'yans and unlearned apprentices. Whaga was chief of the three heavens, and there God, Lords and all chief officers had congregated as soon as the sign of the descending sea of Jehovih's kingdom appeared in the firmament above.

07/3.3. Jehovih spoke to God, saying: Make your places ready, O My Son, and your Lords with you. Behold, I come in a world of fire, and My faithful workers shall find rest and happiness.

07/3.4. Ah'shong will redeem your sons and daughters, for he will girdle the earth with new etherean light and great power.

07/3.5. Call your people together, O God, and have them rejoice and make merry, for the time of deliverance is at hand.

07/3.6. Then God communicated to the Lords, and they again to others, the words of Jehovih; and at seeing the sign in heaven, the faithful began to rejoice and gather together in their respective places. But of the unbelieving angels dwelling on earth, with mortals and in other abodes,[216] of whom there were hundreds of millions, this is what happened:

07/3.7. They were overcome by the sight of the ship of fire in heaven above, and fled, in fear, in all directions. And by their great numbers in the presence of mortals, caused mortals to also fear and flee in search of some secure place. And many of these spirits of darkness came beseechingly[217] to be admitted into the kingdoms of the Lords, where they had been invited for hundreds of years but would not come.

07/3.8. But God and the Lords surrounded their places with walls of light and would not receive the unbelieving. God said: Until Ah'shong arrives let order be maintained within my kingdoms. || But outside, the fear that prevailed for six days and nights on earth and in heaven was greater than anytime since the earth first was.

07/3.9. Meanwhile God and the Lords brought their es'enaurs out, and they sang and danced before Jehovih. And on the approach of Ah'shong with his hosts, God's musicians, heralds, and the great multitude arrayed in shining raiment, were all overcome by the splendor and magnificence, as were even God and his Lords.

07/3.10. These latter sat down on the improvised throne. The etherean marshals approached and divided their ranks, first into single columns, then double, then quadruple, and so on till the fifty thousand marshals had enclosed all sides, except the east, where there was an open space through which Ah'shong came, attended by his chief counselors, of whom there were five thousand. After them came the council of one million, interspersed here and there with groups of

[215] Dawn here means seven years and sixty days. –Ed.

[216] dwelling places, quarters, lodgings, locales

[217] urgently, imploringly, begging, pleading

thousands of es'enaurs, who were chanting hymns of praise to Jehovih and His kingdoms.

07/3.11. Above the continent of Whaga and parts of Jud and Vohu, the lower heaven was illuminated by the hosts of Ah'shong, the like of which had never been in atmospherea before. Nor was there any work being done on earth or in heaven, because of the fear and great stirring up.

07/3.12. But now Ah'shong approached before the throne of God and the Lords, saluting with the sign of the second degree of Jehovih, saying: In Jehovih's name, and by His Power, Wisdom and Love, I have come to give you joy.

07/3.13. God said: In Jehovih's name, all hail! Ah'shong, chief of Anakaron, all hail! And God went forward to the foot of the throne and received Ah'shong, at which, the Lords came forward saluting also. The es'enaurs ceased singing, and Ah'shong proceeded to the throne and sat on it, and God took off his own crown and gave it to Ah'shong, and also gave him the triangle, which was called the heirloom of the heavenly kingdoms of earth, bestowed by command of Jehovih.

07/3.14. The All Light was abundant around Ah'shong; and out of the light, the voice of Jehovih spoke, saying: Because these things are done in My name prayerfully, and in faith, so do I dwell with you all. My Son shall wear your crown, O God.

07/3.15. Behold, I come in might and swiftness, for it is the springtime of the earth. My Son, Seffas, is afoot on the earth; he has stirred up the earth-born. But I will establish My light anew in these heavens.

07/3.16. Have I not said: I brought the seed of everlasting life to the earth? || I gave responsibility to God and his Lords to teach mortals and spirits of My glories in the upper heavens. And I commanded that My God and My Lords in these realms would be from those who came up out of the earth.

07/3.17. You were installed by My hand, and have done a good work. Do not think that I curse because Hored and Moeb are fallen! Did I not know beforehand that these things would be? Behold, I have provided all My works so that man would be forever making new things. If Hored had remained standing, there would have been no heaven to rebuild on earth in this day. How, then, could My newborn Gods learn? Do not think that I come to teach with My own labor; I provide My people so that they shall teach one another.

07/3.18. What is so conceited as man? And yet I bring him into life the dumbest of animals. Man prides himself in his power and wisdom. I send the drought, the rains and winds, the weakest of My members, and they show man he is nothing. So also do My Gods and Lords of the lower heaven become conceited in their power and wisdom; but with the turn of a word, their heavens fall. Billions of souls turn from order and high estate, into confusion and anarchy. Thus I confound men and angels, and in their seeming misery lay the foundation for an everlasting good. The voice ceased.

07/3.19. Ah'shong said: In the name of Jehovih, I announce my presence over earth and the lower heaven.

07/3.20. The marshals said: ALL HAIL! AH'SHONG, GOD OF HEAVEN AND EARTH! Proclaim him in Jehovih's name.

07/3.21. Hardly had these words gone forth, when the voice of the entire hosts joined in proclaiming: ALL HAIL! O GOD! SON OF JEHOVIH!

07/3.22. Ah'shong, now God, said: Your crown shall be my crown, for under it, Jehovih's power shall triumph; otherwise people would say: Behold there is no virtue in Jehovih's crowns. So he placed it on his head, rose up, and saluted the retired God and Lords, saying to them:

07/3.23. I have a place for you; and it is called Yeshuah. Retire there with my proper officers, and partake of rest and the freedom of the place until I come also. But the retired God and Lords said: Put us to labor, we pray. To which, God (Ah'shong) said:

07/3.24. Jehovih's sons must not be humiliated; how, then, can you labor under me? Were you not Jehovih's God and Lords?

07/3.25. They perceived, and, after due salutations, were provided with an escort of five hundred thousand men and women; and they departed on their way to Yeshuah.

07/3.26. God (Ah'shong) said: Let M'ghi, Bing-fo and Nest come before me. They shall be my Lords of dawn in Jehovih's name.

07/3.27. The three came and stood before the throne. God said: I announce the presence of Jehovih's Lords of the earth. The marshals said:

All hail! O M'ghi, Bing-fo and Nest, Jehovih's Lords of Earth!

07/3.28. These were also proclaimed by the united voice of the assembled hosts. God said: In Jehovih's name, go your ways, O Lords of earth.

07/3.29. At that, the Lords crowned themselves and departed at once, saluting reverently.

07/3.30. God said: Bring the atmospherean marshals before me. They were brought and stationed in front of the throne. God said: Glory to You, O Jehovih! For I look upon Your sons and daughters who have withstood a great darkness, but retained faith in You. In Your name, and by virtue of Your power, I deliver them now. Let him who is chief, answer me: How many angels are prepared for the second resurrection?

07/3.31. Sawni, chief marshal, said: Two hundred million. God said: Retire, you and your companions, and assemble Jehovih's harvest of souls, and I will send them to Yeshuah.

07/3.32. The atmosphereans were then duly arranged as commanded, and God called a hundred swift messengers and one thousand etherean marshals, and they provided an abattos;[218] and the hosts who had been prepared for the second resurrection departed for Yeshuah, as commanded.

07/3.33. God said: I now have remaining, my etherean hosts and the atmosphereans in darkness. Of the latter, let them remain as they are for three days, for I will travel around the world with my etherean hosts, observing mortals and spirits in their places and habits, so that I may better judge them and provide accordingly.

07/3.34. So God and his etherean angels provided an abattos, and they embarked and started on their journey, traveling imperceptibly to mortals.

CHAPTER 4 Ah'shong

07/4.1. After God and his hosts visited the earth and the lower heaven, they returned to Yeshuah and sat in council on the affairs of mortals and atmosphereans.

07/4.2. The Council of Yeshuah, of which there were one million members, was formed in groups, and these again represented in groups, and these in still other groups. Consequently, a group of one thousand had one speaker, who became the voice of that thousand; of these speakers, one hundred had one voice in council; and of these, ten had one voice before God, and he was the voice of the whole, and Jehovih was his voice. Thus the whole council was represented in all its parts.[219] And this was the manner of proceeding:

07/4.3. God commanded the subject; the council deliberated in thousands, and each speaker became aware of the voice of his group. Then these speakers assembled in groups of one hundred and deliberated, and each of these groups again centered into one voice; and ten of these had one voice before God. Thus it came to pass that the decrees of God were both the wisdom of men and of Jehovih. From this sprang the saying: When God said this, or God commanded that, it was the word of Jehovih expressed by men and angels.

07/4.4. God said: Behold, the heavens and earth have become like gardens grown foul and rank, producing nothing. I have come with a pruning knife and a consuming fire.

07/4.5. God said: I withdraw from the druj and the druk the beneficence[220] of Jehovih's chosen; I leave them destitute. Who can approach the beggar with wisdom, or the king with inspiration to be good? A drowning man will try to swim; but the reveler in lust must perish before his soul can learn Jehovih.

---

[218] a type of spirit ship

[219] That is, the Council consisted of 10 groups, and each group consisted of 100 subgroups and each subgroup had 1000 members. Now, each subgroup selected one speaker. This made a total of 1000 speakers (1 speaker per subgroup x 100 subgroups per group x 10 groups = 1000 speakers).

Of those 1000 speakers, each 100 (i.e., each group) had one voice in council. That is, the one voice of each group had authority to speak before the whole council. As there were 10 groups, this meant there were 10 voices-in-council, who, together, had once voice before God.

Thus all of the one million received a voice: 1000 members per subgroup, 100 subgroups per group, and 10 groups to give one voice before God, i.e.,

1,000,000 = 1000 x 100 x 10 x 1 || or in reducing:

1,000,000 > 1000 > 100 > 10 > 1.

[220] presence and the good things arising from it

07/4.6. It is better to labor with a child from infancy, and then to maturity, to teach it rightly, than to strive with a score[221] of conceited adults and fail to redeem one. Who are the mockers of charity more than they who give to those who can help themselves but will not? Wisdom and uprightness of heart are like bread. Do not preach to unwelcome ears; are sermons of wisdom to be forced into men's souls?

07/4.7. Blessed Jehovih! He made hunger, and so men love bread. Without hunger they would not eat. A wise God drives home to man's understanding his helplessness in spirit when Jehovih is denied.

07/4.8. Pursue the earth, O my beloved; bring away all light. Pursue the lower heaven of the earth also; bring away all light. I will leave the earth and heaven in darkness one whole year. They shall cry out; their conceit in the dumb wind shall fail.[222]

07/4.9. Have the spirits of heaven not despoiled Hored and Moeb? Do evil spirits and evil men not say: Behold, there is enough! Let us divide the spoils. But they produce nothing. They are devourers; living on others' substance. The Great Spirit made man to exert; by exertion he grows in wisdom and strength.

07/4.10. They seek ease and comfort; helpless and more helpless they fall; they are on the road to everlasting destruction. Happy is the God who can arouse them.

CHAPTER 5 Ah'shong

07/5.1. God said: Blessed is the surgeon's knife; its burn is the capital of health regained; but yet a fool will cry out: Stop! Stop! Enough! You inflictor of pain!

07/5.2. Who has an eye like Jehovih? His whipping-posts are on all sides, but there is a clear road between them. Yet man does not follow it.

07/5.3. Withdraw all good men and good angels; and they who remain would not be half made up.[223] A man without an arm or a leg is only part of a man; a man without perception of the All Person is a deformity in soul. He seeks a home for his own ease and glory; but the Son of Jehovih seeks to find the severest[224] labor that will profit[225] his brethren.

07/5.4. Yeshuah shall be my homestead; here I will bring the fruit of heaven from below; here build my training schools. Seven years my service shall be; and they shall learn the ways of etherea. Build me a house of brotherhood and fill it with willing pupils sworn to labor. I will make them Gods and Lords with power and wisdom.

07/5.5. Behold a man makes a factory and turns out fabric for sale. I make a college and turn out sons and daughters of Jehovih, to give away. Bring me that material which will stand[226] in warp and filling;[227] Jehovih's fabric shall endure forever. Search out the seed of I'hin, and house them with care, for they shall redeem the earth-born after I ascend to the Father's kingdom. And there were brought from earth to Yeshuah one hundred million spirits. And these were divided into first and second best.

---

[221] A score is 20, and often used in the same way we use "dozen," indicating approximate amounts. Thus a score of adults would be about 20 adults.

[222] That is, their belief in: 'there is only the impersonal elements and nothing else,' shall fail. They shall come to acknowledge a higher power, a presence, even Jehovih.

[223] That is, those who remain would be less than half complete, meaning not able to grow and progress independently, but fall further from spiritual maturation by regressing toward the animal nature, fetalism and even unconsciousness (extinction).

[224] That is, in accordance with your bent (temperament and preferred field of labor) seek to find the most challenging and stimulating labor; or said another way, that which will stretch your mind, spirit, soul and talent to the limit of these abilities, and result in the highest best good in service to Jehovih. For such is key to reaching the highest grades; forever quickening; and a key to eternal joy, delight and happiness.

[225] benefit, be useful to, bless, help, do good to, be advantageous for, prosper, add to the well-being of

[226] be strong enough, persist, last, withstand

[227] In a woven fabric, warp consists of the vertical or lengthwise threads, and filling is the woof or horizontal threads.

CHAPTER 6 Ah'shong

07/6.1. All the first best angels of atmospherea, who were brought away from the earth and housed in Yeshuah, were placed at school and in factories newly made in heaven. These were I'hins.

07/6.2. And the second best spirits were placed in hospitals and nurseries.

07/6.3. Of those who had advanced to receive the second resurrection,[228] God said: Build an etherean ship and take them to Theistivi, in etherea.

07/6.4. So it came to pass there were two hundred million raised to the second resurrection, of grade thirty-five. Theistivi lies between etherea and Seven A'ji, which is the lowest of the etherean heavens next to an atmospherean abode.[229]

07/6.5. God said: Two qualities remain in Yeshuah, first and second. These shall be the new kingdom after I am ascended. From these I will raise up a God and Lords, and they shall rule over the lower heaven and the earth; and they shall bequeath others after them to rule in like manner.

07/6.6. And so the second light of Jehovih was founded on the fruit of the earth. God's etherean hosts became a training school to raise up a God, Lords, marshals, es'enaurs, and all other officers, men and women, for a lower heaven. God said: Yeshuah shall not approach nearer the earth; nor shall it be like Hored, where spirits of darkness could easily approach.

07/6.7. Now, the one hundred million spirits, whom God, his Lords and fellow-laborers had brought from the earth to Yeshuah, were placed in a brotherhood where they were assigned to the places suited to their talents. And God divided the time of study, recreation, music, discipline, marching, and so on, suited to all the people; and it was a place of order and glory.

07/6.8. For without discipline there is nothing; and discipline cannot be without ceremony; nor ceremony without rites, forms and established words. Is it not a foolish soldier who says: Behold, I am wise! I need no discipline, no manual of arms.[230] What more is he than one of an untutored mob?

07/6.9. God said: As I drill them in heaven to make them a unit, so shall you also give rites and ceremonies to mortals, so that, coming into heaven, they do not go back to their old haunts and fall in darkness. Whatever tends to harmonize the behavior of individuals is of the Father; the opposite tends to evil. It is better that men march to the sound of one monotonous word, than not march at all; the value lies not in the word, but in bringing into unison that which was void. A fool says: I do not need to pray, there is no virtue in words. But his soul grows up at variance with Jehovih. Nor is there more virtue in prayer or words, than in marching[231] before Jehovih; for whatever tends to unite men in one expression of soul in harmony, is Jehovih's.

07/6.10. Sacred dances as well as rites and ceremonies were established in Yeshuah in the name of Jehovih; and the new heaven became a place of delight.

07/6.11. God said: Teach my chosen to labor hard and wisely; and to dance with energy, and to sing with strength and fullness of soul. For what more is there in any man or woman than to learn to put forth? And what more pitiful thing is there in heaven than a man or woman who has but dragged along?

---

[228] These would be those two hundred million who were with God when Ah'shong first arrived in earth's heaven (07/3.30-31), and these were separate from those of the seed of I'hin brought up from the earth and divided into first and second best.

[229] Of these delivered, note two things. Being only grade 35, they were not emancipated because they were only ready to receive the second resurrection. Second, being only second resurrection and less than grade 50, which is the lowest grade required for survival in etherea only, they were not capable of surviving outside of atmospherea at their level; see 05/23.12. Accordingly Theistivi must have some characteristics similar to atmospherea and some characteristics similar to etherea.

[230] a drill in which soldiers practice in a specified way the use of their hand weapons; e.g., the sharp arm, hand and rifle movements done simultaneously by all members of the company

[231] This encompasses all movement in tune with Jehovih, such as sacred dance, marching in ceremony; and especially when in unison with others.

CHAPTER 7 Ah'shong

07/7.1. When all the best spirits of the lower heaven, and those who dwelt with mortals, were taken away and domiciled in Yeshuah, there were only druj (spirits of darkness)[232] left on the face of the earth. For one whole year, God left the earth void of Jehovih's light.

07/7.2. Mortals loved to commune more with the spirits of their kindred, who knew little of heaven, than they did with ethereans who were wise and holy.

07/7.3. God said: What man or woman have you found who says: Come angels of Jehovih, tell me where I can do more good works, for I thirst, and am hungry to serve Jehovih with all my wisdom and strength in doing good to my fellows?

07/7.4. Rather, they turn away from such angels, and drink in the tales of the strolling druj, and so wrap themselves up in darkness. For this reason they shall find darkness in heaven and earth; and they shall become like one who is sick and broken down in conceit.

07/7.5. When the year of darkness ended, God sent two million pruners around the earth and in the lower heaven of the earth, saying to them: Find all the evil spirits dwelling with mortals, whether they are fetals or familiars, and gather them into one place. Then find the spirits and fairies who have taken caves and waterfalls as their abode on earth, and bring them to the same place. Then find the idiotic and chaotic spirits who dwell on battlefields, and bring them to the same place. Then find the lusters, who dwell in old castles and ruined cities, and in houses of evil, and when they are going out for raids on mortals, seize them and bring them to the same place.

07/7.6. The ethereans went and collected all the evil spirits and the spirits of darkness belonging to the earth, and brought them to a place in atmospherea, and there were nine hundred million of them.

07/7.7. God said: Prepare a suitable ship to transport them to Hudaow, in Ji'ya,[233] and there provide them a kingdom to themselves, giving them a God, Lords and proper officers, to discipline and educate them for Jehovih's Kingdoms.

07/7.8. They were removed accordingly, and the earth and its lower heaven were purified from evil spirits by the decree of God in Yeshuah, in the second year of the first dawn of dan.

CHAPTER 8 Ah'shong

07/8.1. In the second year of Yeshuah, God (Ah'shong) caused to be established in his heaven, all required places of learning and industry, where es'yans could be educated to good works, and to a general knowledge of Jehovih's kingdoms. And sufficient ethereans volunteered as teachers and practitioners for all that was required.

07/8.2. God said: Now that the earth and heaven are purified from evil, my Lords shall deliver the es'yans to the asaphs, who shall deliver them to Yeshuah, which I have established a short distance from the earth as a barrier against their returning to mortals. Jehovih says: Do not permit the blind to lead the blind.

07/8.3. And it was so; at the time mortals died, their spirits were taken by the asaphs to Yeshuah; and to make this acceptable to the es'yans, God said: Tell my Lords of the earth to teach mortals by inspiration and otherwise about my kingdom of Yeshuah.

07/8.4. And so it came to pass, through the Lords and the ashars, that is, the guardian spirits with mortals, that the name, Yeshuah, was established on the earth. God said: In the time of kosmon, men shall say: Where did the name of heavenly things come from? But the origin of Yeshuah shall lie hidden away, and Jehovih will stretch forth His hand in that day and disclose all.

07/8.5. But mortals were thick in tongue, and could not say Yeshuah, and they said I. E. Su; from

[232] Elsewhere in Oahspe we learn that the plural of druj is drujas. However, the word druj is sometimes used in Oahspe to indicate the collective of drujas (drujas in general), or a group of drujas. It is similar to the way we use the word buffalo. We can say: Here is one *buffalo*. We saw five *buffalo* grazing. There go seven *buffaloes*. Likewise we can say: Here is one druj. We saw five druj repenting. There go seven drujas.

[233] Hudaow, in Ji'ya, is a place in the firmament like an atmosphere without a corporeal world. That is, an atmospherean vortex rotating and traveling in the firmament amid the etherean worlds. –Ed.

which came the name of many men, Iesu,[234] signifying, without evil, which is the ultimate salvation of the soul.

07/8.6. Jehovih spoke through God, saying: When the end of dawn comes, My emancipated sons and daughters shall return to their places, taking the resurrected with them. But, so that the earth and lower heaven may not be left in darkness, you shall provide a God, Lords, marshals, messengers and all other officers, to rule and teach in My name.

07/8.7. And you shall make them from those born of earth, and they shall hold office for two hundred years, four hundred years, and six hundred years, according to the atmospherean cycles.

07/8.8. Do not permit My etherean hosts to remain longer than dawn, either on the earth or within atmospherea, for I shall take the earth into dark regions in order to build it up to a higher state for the time that comes after.

07/8.9. The voice departed. God said: Let the voice of the council deliberate on this matter, and speak before the Father. For I will provide a heaven in the ancient place of Hored, and it shall be called Bispah, for it shall be a place of reception for the spirits of the dead preparatory to their being brought to Yeshuah.

07/8.10. In due course many of the earth-born were raised up, and God selected and appointed them to fill the places; and he founded Bispah, and officered it according to the command of Jehovih. After God established in Yeshuah, rites and ceremonies, processions and dances, with sacred words, he commanded his Lords to give the same things to mortals, and so they fulfilled all that was designed from the beginning.

07/8.11. In the seventh year of dawn, God commanded his council to select another God and Lords, and other officers. So the council proceeded according to the method of the ancients, selecting the most learned, purest and holiest, choosing them according to their rank in Godliness. And a record was made of these matters and deposited in the library of Yeshuah.

07/8.12. Then God called in his own Lords of the earth, and he set apart the first day of the new moon as the day on which he would consecrate the God and Lords, his successors; and he called the day Mas, which name endures to this day of kosmon. And further, God established the moon's day (mas) on the earth as a time of consecration. (And this is the origin of saying mass).

07/8.13. When the chosen were in place before the throne, God said: By command of Jehovih you are brought before me, His Son; in His name I will consecrate you to the places commanded by Him.

07/8.14. The marshals then conducted the one who ranked highest, up to the seat of the throne. God said:

07/8.15. In the name of Jehovih, and by His Power, Wisdom and Love, I ordain you God of heaven and earth. He who receives from my hand receives from my Father, Who raised me up.

07/8.16. The initiate said: All power comes from the Father. All wisdom comes from the Father. All love comes from the Father. In His name and by virtue of His commandments through His Son, I receive all that is put upon me, for His glory, forever!

07/8.17. God then said: Give me a crown, O Father, for Your Son! || A scarlet light descended from above, and God reached forth his hands and wove it into a crown and placed it on the initiate's head, saying: I crown you GOD OF HEAVEN AND EARTH. And now you shall also receive the Sacred Triangle, which is the heirloom of the Gods of earth. And he hung it around his neck, adding: And since there can be only one God on earth or in this heaven, I uncrown myself in Jehovih's name, and salute you, O God, GOD OF EARTH AND HEAVEN!

07/8.18. Ah'shong now stood to the right, and God, who was ordained, went and sat on the throne, and red and blue lights descended from above, enveloping him completely, and he was quickened.

07/8.19. He said: Let the initiates for Lords of earth approach the throne of the Most High Jehovih!

07/8.20. The five Lords came forward. God said: Join hands and receive from the Father. By virtue of the Power, Wisdom and Love of Jehovih, vested in me, I receive you as the highest chosen; and I proclaim you LORD OF EARTH,[235] in Jehovih's name! Accept this crown from heaven above, the like of which cannot be woven from earthly things;

---

[234] The original of iesus, or jesu, or jesus. –Ed.

[235] Where hands are joined the persons are addressed as one person. –Ed.

by its power, you shall remain in accord with Yeshuah and the kingdoms above.

07/8.21. God fashioned the crowns and then crowned them Lords of the five divisions of the earth. God said: Retire aside and choose your messengers and officers, and after ordaining them, depart to the kingdom prepared for you. The Lords said:

07/8.22. In Your name, O Jehovih, I accept that which You have put upon me. With all my wisdom, strength and love I will serve You, O my Father, Jehovih!

07/8.23. The Lords retired; and the es'enaurs sang, more than a million voices in concert!

CHAPTER 9 Ah'shong

07/9.1. Now the time had come for the end of the first dawn of dan after the creation of man. And this was known in the etherean heavens, where countless millions of Jehovih's emancipated sons and daughters lived. And, as might be expected, they decided to descend, which they did from all sides, to witness the labors of Ah'shong, and to receive his works as a profitable lesson for their own future on other new worlds.[236]

07/9.2. Consequently, distant stars began to appear in the firmament, approaching; and these were the etherean ships from remote places, where the name of Ah'shong had been known for thousands of years. From all sides they came, growing ever brighter and larger.

07/9.3. Ah'shong spoke to his companions, saying: Make ready, O my beloved. My friends and your friends are coming. Put our ship in order. Light the pillars of fire and spread out the sails, shining, so that they may be glorified in Jehovih's name.

07/9.4. The proper persons accomplished these things. Now, the etherean ship of Ah'shong was anchored east of Yeshuah; and so great was its size that there was room not only for the ethereans of Anakaron, but for more than three hundred million of the redeemed of earth to ascend with them.

07/9.5. Ah'shong said: When our friends arrive, we shall join them and make an excursion around the earth, discovering its rank and glorious promises; but as to the nine hundred million drujas which I sent off to Hudaow, in Ji'ya, we shall pass there on our way to Anakaron.

07/9.6. Brighter and brighter grew the descending stars, the etherean ships from faraway worlds; and larger and larger, till in majesty they neared Yeshuah. Ah'shong then came down and sat at the foot of the throne, according to the custom of Gods. God came down and took him by the hand, saying: Son of Jehovih, you who make yourself the least of men, arise, and take your hosts, and embark in Jehovih's ship, going wherever you will. Ah'shong rose up. The es'enaurs and trumpeters played and sang. Then Ah'shong said:

07/9.7. One more love I have in the world, O Jehovih. I go from Yeshuah, but my love remains. To you, O God, I will look back in hope and love, for you were raised by me. And to your Lords what less could I say? Yes, and to all the hosts I leave within these realms.

07/9.8. Ah'shong touched God's right hand, and then saluting, with the third sign of emeth[237] to Jehovih, departed, and the marshals conducted him off to the ship.

07/9.9. Ah'shong and his etherean hosts rose up in curtains of light; and presently the ship was loosened from its anchorage and floated upward, and all the angels entered it; and the sails were spread out, and the mantles suspended on every side, till the whole vessel, with its thousands of masts and arcs, looked like a world on fire. The inhabitants of Yeshuah feared and trembled at the mighty works of the Gods and Goddesses; and yet, as the es'enaurs on the departing ship chanted, more than a million voices, the Yeshuans sang with them, amid their tears, with souls overflowing, with awe, love and admiration.

07/9.10. In that same time the descending stars of other Gods and Goddesses, the etherean ships from faraway worlds, were drawing nearer and nearer; and, on every side, the firmament was alive with worlds on fire.

---

[236] Being the first dawn of dan upon the planet, it attracted many ethereans who were not directly involved in receiving the newly resurrected. This can be likened to a coming out party when a family brings out their first newborn baby for the first time into public (see 07/1.10), and friends and relatives come to view and remark about the child. And the family takes the visitors in to see the nursery.

[237] emeth means faith

07/9.11. Presently they came, first one and then another of the ethereans, and they made fast to Ah'shong's ship, until more than five hundred ships were united into one mighty vessel, and yet so near to Yeshuah that all could be seen.

07/9.12. And when they had united there were countless millions of angels in close proximity, many who had known one another for thousands of years; and some who were older than the earth, and knew its history. And these had companions as old as themselves; and they were ripe in experience with corporeal earths, stars and suns in other regions of Jehovih's kingdoms.

07/9.13. So great was the wisdom of these Gods and Goddesses, that to come within the earth's atmosphere was sufficient to enable them to read all the souls and prayers of mortals, and all the thoughts and desires of the spirits of the lower heaven belonging to the earth. To each and all of them, the voice of Jehovih was ever present, and their power was equal to their wisdom.

07/9.14. Jehovih has said: To the corporean I have given power to hear one or two things at the same time; but My Gods can intelligently hear tens of thousands of people speaking at the same time. Yes, they can find a way to answer them also.

07/9.15. When the ships were ready for departure, Ah'shong said: Let us pass low over Yeshuah, and you shall hear and see those I have founded in a new heaven. His companions said: Jehovih's will be done. So they proceeded; and after they had visited Yeshuah they descended to the earth, and throughout the places of the Lords; and when they had seen all, and heard the explanation from those with Ah'shong, regarding the state of the earth and its heavens, they rose higher and higher, and sailed toward Anakaron, where Ah'shong had invited them for repast[238] and social intercourse.

07/9.16. Thus the ethereans departed from the earth and atmospherea. This, then, was the beginning of the cycles of dan; and the first dawn was closed and past.

07/9.17. And the earth Gods, that is, the Lords, who were now called Adonya, were of those brought forth out of the earth. And God, who had dominion in the atmospherea of the earth, was also an earth-born; and so were all the angels in atmospherea the product of the earth.

07/9.18. And in Jehovih's name the Lords and God were appointed and crowned to rule in their respective places, and by this means they became the instruments of Jehovih for His glory.

07/9.19. Jehovih said: Whoever serves Me, in My name, is My son, or My daughter. The Light of My Judgment falls upon them sufficient for the time and place. To the extent that you honor them, you honor Me also. Through the flowers of the field I express Myself in color and perfume; through the lion and mastodon I express Myself with power and voraciousness; through the lamb and the dove I express Myself in meekness and docility. Through man I express Myself in words and actions; and all men, the wise and the ignorant, are channels of My expression. Some have thick tongues and poor speech, nevertheless they are My babes, My sons and daughters.

07/9.20. Jehovih said: After the Se'muan age, I gave to the earth from My etherean heavens sons and daughters, and they abode with mortals for three thousand years. And My ethereans established loo'is on the lands of the earth; and they commanded the loo'is, saying to them: Your office[239] is to lead mortals by inspiration to dwell together, man and woman, as husband and wife; and in such adaptation that their offspring shall rise higher in wisdom, love and power, than the father and mother.

07/9.21. Jehovih said: I will confound the wise man in the latter days; for he will not discover why man and woman did not live indiscriminately, like the beasts. Yes, I will show him that those who profess Me are led by Me; and those who deny Me go down to indiscriminate communion. Out of My works, the lessons of the early days of the earth shall show the presence of My hand from the beginning. By My loo'is, man and woman were inspired to raise up sons and daughters who would glorify Me and My works; by My loo'is, I have maintained My foothold among mortals.

07/9.22. Those who could comprehend Me, having faith that My presence in Person would ultimately triumph for the highest and best, I commanded to be called FAITHISTS. Since the

[238] food, refreshments and festivity; a banquet

[239] responsibility, duty, labor, charge

beginning, I have kept a thread of this line inhabiting the earth and her heavens. ||

07/9.23. The first harvest, then, was two hundred years, and the number of Brides and Bridegrooms was six hundred million, of grade ninety-two.

07/9.24. The second harvest was two hundred years, and was eight hundred million angels, of grade eighty-nine.

07/9.25. The third harvest was six hundred years, and was two billion angels, of grade eighty-three.

07/9.26. The fourth harvest was five hundred years, and was two billion three hundred million angels, of grade seventy-four.

07/9.27. The fifth harvest was three hundred years, and was six hundred million angels, of grade sixty-two.

07/9.28. The sixth harvest was four hundred years, and nine hundred million angels, of grade fifty-one.

07/9.29. And this was the last harvest; for none after that were of sufficient grade to live in the etherean heavens.

07/9.30. And now wars began in atmospherea, thousands of angels against thousands, and millions against millions.

07/9.31. For the possession of sections of the earth, and its mortal inhabitants, these millions of warring angels went forth. And it came to pass that mortals also fell to war; and, by the obsessing angels, were made to destroy their own cities and kingdoms.

07/9.32. And the attractions of this great wickedness caused other angels of heaven to desert their schools and factories, and descend down to mortals.

07/9.33. Thus again, the kingdoms of God and his Lords were reduced to impotence; the harvests of Brides and Bridegrooms had long since ceased to be.

07/9.34. At the end of the second cycle there were six billion angels in atmospherea, who, for the most part, were in darkness; not knowing who they were, or where they dwelt; neither knowing nor caring whether or not there were other heavens.

END OF BOOK OF AH'SHONG, SON OF JEHOVIH

Second Book of Lords

Of the second cycle, being contemporaneous with the Book of Ah'shong, Son of Jehovih.

CHAPTER 1 Second Lords

08/1.1. In the beginning man was naked and not ashamed; but the Lord raised him up and told him to hide his nakedness, and man obeyed, and was clothed.

08/1.2. And the Lord walked beside man for a long season, showing him the way of resurrection; and man was obedient, depending on the Lord for all things.

08/1.3. And the Lord said to man: Behold, I have walked with you, and taught you; but because of my indulgence, you have neglected to put forth your own energy.

08/1.4. Now I am going away from you for a season, so that you may learn to develop yourself.

08/1.5. But lest you stumble and fall, I leave certain commandments with you, and they shall be a guide to you and your heirs forever.

08/1.6. Hear, then, the commandments of the Lord your God.

08/1.7. You shall love your Creator with all your mind, heart and soul, all the days of your life.

08/1.8. And you shall love your neighbor as yourself.

08/1.9. Because you were born into the world without covering, you shall clothe yourself.

08/1.10. Then man inquired of the Lord: Behold, you have shown the ass[240] what is good for him to eat, and the fish, the serpent and the lion; you have shown every living creature except man. What then shall I eat?

08/1.11. The Lord said: I give you everything that grows up out of the ground that is good to eat, and they shall be food for you.

08/1.12. But you shall not eat anything of flesh and blood, in which life is.

08/1.13. For you shall not kill.

08/1.14. Man inquired of the Lord: You have shown the males and females of all the living, the

[240] donkey or burro—usually a beast of burden

times and periods to come together; but man and woman you have not shown.

08/1.15. The Lord said: You shall learn from the beasts, birds and fishes that the female during gestation is in the keeping of her Creator.

08/1.16. Therefore you shall also respect the times of woman.[241]

08/1.17. Man inquired of the Lord: You have shown the bird how to build her nest, the carnivore how to scent the subtle track of his prey, and the spider to weave his net; but as to the design of man's house, or the herbs that are good, or poisonous, you have not shown man.

08/1.18. The Lord said: All the instinct that is in the bird, beast, fish, insect, or creeping thing, was created with them, but man was created blank; and yet man shall attain to more subtle senses than any other living creature.

08/1.19. Man inquired: How shall man attain to these?

08/1.20. The Lord answered: Serve your Creator by doing good to others with all your wisdom and strength, and by being true to your own highest light, and all knowledge will come to you.

08/1.21. So the Lord left man to himself for a season; and man so loved the earth and whatever ministered to his ease and flesh desires, that he fell from his high estate. And great darkness came upon the earth. And man cast aside his clothes, went naked, and became carnal[242] in his desires.

CHAPTER 2 Second Lords

08/2.1. The Lord went abroad over the earth, calling: Come to me, O man! Behold your Lord has returned!

08/2.2. But man did not hear the voice of the Lord; for, by man's indulgence, the spirit of man was covered up in his own flesh.[243]

08/2.3. To the I'hins, the Lord sent his loo'is and they raised up heirs to the Lord; by controlling the parentage of the unborn, they brought into the world a new race of men, of the same seed and blood as of old, and these heard the voice of the Lord.

08/2.4. And the Lord said to man: Because you did not keep my commandments, you have brought affliction upon yourself and your people, to the farthest ends of the world.

08/2.5. Now I will raise you up once more, and deliver the tribes of men from darkness into light.

08/2.6. And the Lord delivered man into wisdom, peace and virtue; and the earth became like a garden of sweet-smelling flowers and luxurious fruit.

08/2.7. The Lord said: What do you say, O man? Shall you still require a keeper?

08/2.8. And man said: Behold, I am strong and wise. You can go away from the earth. I understand your commandments.

08/2.9. The Lord inquired: Do you know the meaning of: Love your Creator? And man said: Yes, Lord; and to love my neighbor as myself; and to do good to others with all my wisdom and strength. Yes, I have the All Highest Light. I am wiser than the ancients. Behold, I want no Lord, no God; I am the highest product of all the universe.

08/2.10. The Lord said: I will try you, O man; I will go away for a season.

08/2.11. So the Lord departed once more. And man had nothing to look up to, so he looked at himself and became vainglorious. And the tribes of men aspired to overcome one another; war and destruction followed.

08/2.12. Man forgot his Creator; he said: No Eye sees me, no Ear hears me. And he neglected to guard himself against the serpent (corporeality; self); and the serpent said to him: Partake of all things, for they are yours.

08/2.13. And man heeded, and, lo and behold, the race of man descended into utter darkness. And man did not distinguish his sister or mother; and woman did not distinguish her brother or father.[244]

---

[241] This injunction against sexual indulgence during pregnancy has been taught to Faithists in every cycle even to the Kosmon era, where it now stands as one of the standards that plays a crucial role in changing the generations born of the beast into those born of the spirit.

[242] flesh oriented; engrossed in fulfilling physical appetites, especially sexual; animalistic

[243] Once the spirit was obscured, lost to perception, buried amid darkness, then man became unaware of his spirit; being little attended to, it was overlooked then forgotten about.

[244] resulting in incest

08/2.14. And God saw the wickedness of man, and he called out, saying: Hear my voice, O man! Hear the voice of the Lord!

08/2.15. But because of man's darkness he could not hear the voice of God, his Lord.

08/2.16. And the Lord sent his angels down to man, so they could appeal to man's understanding.

08/2.17. But the angels also loved darkness, and did not strive to lift man out of darkness. And the Lord had no more influence among mortals, and he departed away from the earth. And on the earth, man became like a harvest that is blighted and rotten because of its rankness.

END OF THE SECOND BOOK OF LORDS

Synopsis of Sixteen Cycles

*Being forty-eight thousand years (i.e., two gadols);[245] covering a period from the creation of man down to the submersion of the continent of Pan, called by the ancients, **the flood, or deluge**, which was twenty-four thousand years B.K. (i.e., one gadol Before Kosmon[246]), selected from the records in the libraries of heaven.*

CHAPTER 1 Synopsis

09/1.1. First, the earth travels in a circuit around the sun, which is divided into four arcs called spring, summer, autumn and winter.

09/1.2. Second, the sun, with his family, travels in a large circuit, which is divided into one thousand five hundred arcs, the distance for each arc being about three thousand years, or one cycle. [247]

09/1.3. During a cycle, the earth and her heavens travel through the etherean regions of hundreds of etherean worlds, which are inhabited by Jehovih's high-raised angels, whose Chiefs are involved in the management of worlds.

09/1.4. During the time of a cycle, the earth is therefore under the control and management of such angels of Jehovih for the resurrection of man of the earth.

09/1.5. At the time of man's creation,[248] the earth was traveling in the arc of Wan, where thousands of Orian Chiefs live, with billions of high-raised angels.

09/1.6. The Holy Council of Orian Chiefs, through the Wisdom and Voice of Jehovih, appointed one of their number, Sethantes (an archangel), to take charge of the earth, and to people it with immortal beings, during its travel in Wan.

09/1.7. The rank and title of Sethantes, thus raised up by Jehovih, Creator of worlds, became, FIRST GOD OF THE EARTH AND HER HEAVENS.

09/1.8. And Sethantes had come with millions of angels, who had been previously raised up from other worlds, and he accomplished his work, and was known as God.

09/1.9. Sethantes was, then, the first God of the earth and her heavens, and his place was within the arc of Wan. And during his cycle of three thousand years, he raised up from the earth, one billion five hundred million Brides and Bridegrooms to Jehovih.

09/1.10. After Sethantes came Ah'shong, sub-Chief in the realms of Hieu Wee in the Haian arc of Vehetaivi. And during the cycle of Anakaron, also three thousand years, Ah'shong raised up from the earth, a harvest of seven billion two hundred million Brides and Bridegrooms.

---

[245] A gadol averages 24,000 years and is equivalent to one precession of the equinoxes; hence the 48,000 years is a rounded figure.

[246] which began about 1849 c.e. (common era, using the common civil calendar); also, again, the 24,000 years is a rounded figure; the actual duration of this third gadol was about 25,000 years

[247] That is, one dan'ha cycle. There are, of course, cycles of other lengths, but because the dan'ha cycle is the primary etherean administrative cycle for earth and her heavens, it is often simply referred to as a cycle in Oahspe. In fact, the format of Oahspe is structured around man's progress through the dan'ha cycles.

[248] i.e., at the time of the birth of the I'hin race

09/1.11. The third cycle was under the dominion of Hoo Le, surveyor of Kakayen'sta in the arc of Gimmel, and his harvest was three billion seven hundred million.

09/1.12. The fourth cycle was under C'pe Aban, Chieftainess of Sulgoweron in the arc of Yan, and her harvest was four billion eight hundred million.

09/1.13. The fifth cycle was under Pathodices, road-maker in Chitivya in the arc of Yahomitak, and his harvest was six billion four hundred million.

09/1.14. The sixth cycle was under Goemagak, God of Iseg, in the arc of Somgwothga, and his harvest was seven billion nine hundred million.

09/1.15. The seventh cycle was under Goepens, God of Kaim, in the arc of Srivat, and his harvest was nine billion three hundred million.

09/1.16. The eighth cycle was under Hycis, Goddess of Ruts, in the arc of Hohamagollak, and her harvest was nine billion four hundred million.

09/1.17. The ninth cycle was under See'itcicius, inspector of roads in Kammatra, in the arc of Jusyin, and his harvest was ten billion one hundred million.

09/1.18. The tenth cycle was under Miscelitivi, Chieftainess of the arches of Lawzgowbak, in the arc of Nu, and her harvest was ten billion eight hundred million.

09/1.19. And now the earth was full of people; all the continents and islands of the earth were inhabited by man; nor was there any wilderness left where man did not dwell.

09/1.20. But the generation of man had fallen from thirty-three years down to twelve years. And man and woman were at maturity at seven years old; and not many lived above thirty years; but they were prolific; many of the mothers bringing forth two score (40) sons and daughters, and from two to four babies at a birth.

09/1.21. And man dwelt in peace. The earth was tilled, and it brought forth abundantly everything that was good for man to eat and to clothe himself with. In those days, there were great cities of hundreds of thousands of inhabitants, and thousands and thousands of such cities in all the five great divisions of the earth. And man built ships and sailed over the ocean in all directions, around the whole world. By the angels of the Lord, he was taught and guided in all things. And man had books, both written and printed; and in schools, the young were taught knowledge regarding the sun, moon, stars, and all things that are upon the earth and in its waters. This was, therefore, called the first period of civilization on the earth.

09/1.22. Now, for the most part, all the people had become I'hins, small, white and yellow.[249] Nevertheless there were ground people, with long arms, who were large; but they dwelt by themselves, and their food was of all types of flesh, fish and creeping things. The ground people were brown and black, and they lived to be two hundred, and even four hundred years old.

09/1.23. Jehovih said: In the early days I raised up I'huans, and I gave them certain commandments, among which was, not to cohabit with the druks lest they go down in darkness. But they did not obey My words; and lo and behold, they are lost from the face of the earth.

09/1.24. Because the I'hins have become a spiritual people and have prospered in peace and spirit, behold, they have degenerated in the corporeal body. They yield abundant harvests for My etherean realms, but they are like untimely births.

09/1.25. Now I will bring the earth into a'jiyan fields and forests for a long season; for I shall again reproduce the I'huans; and the time of a generation shall be thirty-three years. For My harvests shall be of fruit that is mature and full of ripeness.

09/1.26. And Jehovih brought the earth into new regions in the etherean worlds, and covered it over with a'ji, east and west and north and south.[250]

09/1.27. And it came to pass that many of the I'hins lost the generative desire and, so, did not bring forth many heirs. But the brown people burnt with desires, and they laid hold of the I'hin women when they went into the fields, and forced them, and thus brought forth again the I'huan race, the copper-colored, strong, bright and quick.

---

[249] Again, while I'hins are described as white and yellow, we shall see later in Oahspe that they are also described as being of all colors (red, black, brown, etc.); see 06/2.4<fn-stout>. [Also, with regard to the population becoming mostly I'hins, the I'hins could have prevailed because the other races, aside from commingling with the druks (see next verse 09/1.23), may have died off through warfare, disease, famine, etc. –ed.]

[250] see, e.g., image i011

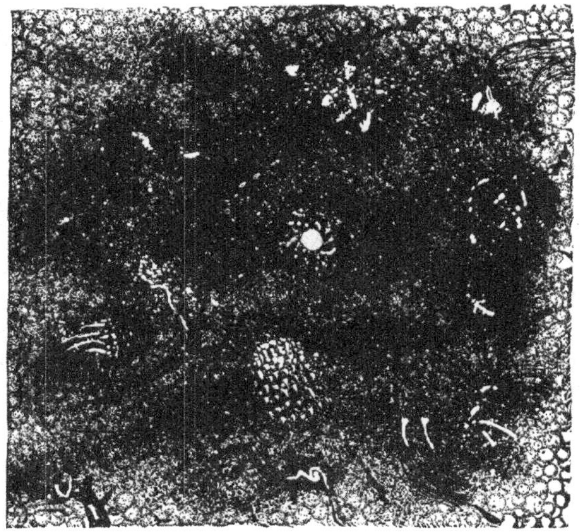

i011 **The Earth in A'ji**. Showing the earth (white spot in center) immersed in a'ji.

09/1.28. Accordingly the eleventh cycle, which was under Gobath, God of Tirongothaga, in the arc of Su'le, brought forth a harvest of six billion seven hundred million.

09/1.29. The twelfth cycle was under F'aiyis, Goddess of Looga, in the arc of Siyan, and her harvest was two billion six hundred million.

09/1.30. The thirteenth cycle was under Zineathaes, keeper of the Cross, in the arc of Oleganaya, and his harvest was one billion two hundred million.

09/1.31. The fourteenth cycle was under Tothsentaga, road-maker in Hapanogos, in the arc of Manechu, and his harvest was only six hundred million.

09/1.32. The fifteenth cycle was under Nimeas, God of Thosgothamachus, in the arc of Seigga, and his harvest was only forty million.

09/1.33. The sixteenth cycle was under Neph, God of Sogghonnes, in the arc of Arbroohk, but he failed to bring forth any harvest.

CHAPTER 2 Synopsis

09/2.1. God, who was Neph, said: Hear my prayer, O Jehovih! The earth and her heavens have gone down in darkness.

09/2.2. The I'hin has been destroyed in all the divisions of the earth except Whaga.

09/2.3. More than thirty billion angels are gathered on the surface of the earth, and they are too low in grade to be delivered.

09/2.4. What shall Your God do, O Father?

09/2.5. Mortals are descending in breed and blood; they inhabit the earth as diseased vermin.

09/2.6. Their cities are destroyed, and they live in the manner of four-footed beasts.

09/2.7. The inspiration of Your God and his angels can no longer reach them.

09/2.8. When they die and enter these heavens they are like festering sores on one another, billions of them.

09/2.9. For three thousand years I have labored with them, but the abundance of their darkness outmatches Your God.

09/2.10. What shall I do with them, O Father! How shall Your God deliver so great a carcass of death?

09/2.11. But Jehovih did not answer the prayer of God; left him to consult with other Gods in the higher heavens.

09/2.12. But in etherea, Jehovih spoke to His Orian Chiefs, saying: As I try mortals, so do I try angels; as I try them, so do I try My Gods. Forever and ever I keep before them the testimony of AN ALL HIGHER.

09/2.13. || Now on earth, it came about that the time of a generation of mortals had risen from twelve years to eighty years. Many mortals lived to be three hundred years old, and they had become very large, twice the size of men of this day.[251] But they were without judgment and of little sense,[252] and hardly knowing their own species. And they mingled together,[253] relatives as well as others; so that idiocy and disease were the general fate of the tribes of men; but they were large, strong and prolific. ||

09/2.14. The following is the grade of declension in the heavens of the earth; that is, including when Kishalon had changed the period of generation from twelve years into the upper grades, namely:

---

[251] making them about 10 feet tall (3 meters); but may have ranged up to 12 feet (3 2/3 meters)

[252] intelligence, astuteness, aptitude, acumen

[253] propagated

09/2.15. Abner, seventh cycle, enduring three thousand two hundred years in Hastaf, etherean a'ji seven, Hoe'tan, grade ninety-nine.

09/2.16. Enseeni, Goddess of Marsef, etherea, dan of Gem, enduring three thousand years, grade ninety-three.

09/2.17. Boaz, God of Hom, Orian field, dan of Josh, enduring two thousand seven hundred years, grade eighty-eight.

09/2.18. Da'ivi, Goddess of Wowitski in a'ji thirty-six, dan of Ruth, enduring two thousand nine hundred years, grade eighty-two.

09/2.19. Lia'mees, Goddess of War[254] in Broek, dan forty, Orian field, Semsi, enduring three thousand years, grade seventy-seven.

09/2.20. Divi'yas, God of Hut in Habak, ji'ya twenty-two, Neth, enduring three thousand one hundred years, grade sixty-nine.

09/2.21. Roa'yis'yis, Goddess of Tamak, Bent, one of Hud'du'owts, enduring three thousand seven hundred years, grade sixty-one.

09/2.22. Yij, Chief of Orian field, Lud in Goo, dan seventy-four, enduring two thousand six hundred years, grade fifty-eight.

09/2.23. Gul'yaniv, Chieftainess, Orian field, Ob'Low in ji'ya forty, enduring three thousand four hundred years, grade fifty-one.

09/2.24. From this time onward there was found no grade in the roadway of the solar phalanx (great serpent), sufficiently dense for the angels of the heavens of the earth.

CHAPTER 3 Synopsis

09/3.1. Jehovih moved upon the etherean worlds in the wide regions where the great serpent traveled. His voice went forth, and among the counselors, the high ruling chieftains of the exalted kingdoms in the firmament, He spoke, saying:

09/3.2. Hear me, O Chieftains! Be farseeing in My traveling worlds, and alert to My words. Behold the red star, the earth, has attained her maturity! As a daughter comes forth in the prime of life, so stands the young earth in her glory. For fifty thousand years she has played her part as an ornament of heaven and a harvester of bright souls for My exalted regions in the firmament.

09/3.3. Gather together, O you Orian Chiefs and you etherean Goddesses, and you who dwell in the roadway of the great serpent. Call a council of My everlasting rulers of worlds; and include those who plant My a'jian gardens and My ji'ay'an fields; and those who whirl My nebulous vortices in the firmament. ||

09/3.4. The voice of Jehovih extended across the wide universe, and those who were high raised in the management of worlds heard and comprehended.

09/3.5. And in the etherean gardens of Senaya, near the roadway of the solar phalanx, there assembled millions of Jehovih's highest; and the place was like a park, larger than a hundred times the size of the earth; and on every side lay the crystalline borders of etherean worlds. And when they were assembled, Jehovih spoke out of the light inherent, saying:

09/3.6. Sixteen times, My etherean hosts have redeemed the earth and her heavens from darkness into light, and yet before the end of a cycle she falls again, and her atmospherea with her. And now her heavens are again filled with billions of spirits who do not know Me and My emancipated worlds. Speak, O Gods and Goddesses.

09/3.7. Sut'Loo spoke first, saying: O Jehovih, I have heard; I have seen. Too prolific is the earth, the young daughter of heaven. Too prolific is the red star of the firmament.

09/3.8. Next spoke Ka'waha, saying: You have spoken, O Jehovih! The rich earth is too prolific, O Father. Her mortals are overpowered by her atmospherean hosts. Her people build up cities and nations for a season after dawn, but soon they are flooded over by fetals and drujas, and the mortals devour one another like beasts of prey.

09/3.9. Chi'jong said: Her people have tilled all the soil of the earth and covered it over with cities; but where are they? Her people have been learned in the matters of heaven and earth, but their knowledge is dissipated by the dread hand of war.

09/3.10. Dhu'itta said: Her people become wise in a day, but on the next, they are fools. One generation becomes skilled in books, and in knowledge of the sun, moon and stars, and in the

[254] Note that this has nothing to do with warfare as we on earth (English language) use that term. But in etherea, War is an etherean place, like an etherean world, but within the dominion of the etherean realm or province of Broek.

mathematics of corporeal things; but a generation follows, and lo, her people are cannibals again.

09/3.11. Gaw'zin said: I have heard, O Jehovih! I have witnessed, O Father! The red star is too prolific. She is like a garden too rich! Her products are overgrown, and they fall down and doubly enrich the soil again, to reproduce an imperfect giant stalk that is barren. So are her sons and daughters; they all run to earthly substances.

09/3.12. Loo'wan said: Great Spirit, I have heard, I have seen. We gather the earth's harvests for You, O Jehovih, but they are small. We gather the earth's harvests of dark spirits, O Jehovih, and they are ten times larger. Behold, there is no balance between them.

09/3.13. Thus spoke the Gods and Goddesses, till thousands of them had spoken. After that the voice of Jehovih spoke, saying:

09/3.14. You are blessed, My Sons and Daughters. How can you bequeath the administration of the earth and her heaven to the earth-born, till she is made suitable as a gift from My hand? Now hear Me, O My Sons and Daughters: I made five great divisions of the earth, and they have all been fully inhabited and tilled by mortals. Yes, on all the divisions of the earth there have been great cities and nations, and men and women of great learning.

09/3.15. And as often as they are raised up in light, so are they again cast down in darkness because of the great desire of the spirits of the dead to return back to the earth. These druj return to mortals and fasten upon them as fetals or as familiars, and inspire them to evil. Go now to the earth, O My beloved, and find the division of the earth where most of these druj congregate, for I will uproot their stronghold; I will break them from their haunts and they shall no longer carry My people down to destruction.

09/3.16. And now the council deliberated, and after a while, caused the records of the earth and her atmospherea to be examined, and they discovered that the heaven of the land of Whaga (Pan) was beyond redemption because of the great numbers of the spirits of the cannibals and the multitude of fetals. The condition of Whaga and her heaven was as if a disease in the flesh healed over externally, leaving the root of the disease within; accordingly, the redemption of the cycles did not remain with her, but evil broke out continually in a new way.

09/3.17. So Jehovih said: Now I will prune the earth and her heaven. Behold, the division of Whaga shall be hewn off and cast beneath the waters of the ocean. Her heaven shall no longer be tenable[255] by the spirits of destruction, for I will rend[256] its foundation and scatter them in the winds of heaven.

09/3.18. Go, therefore, down to the earth and provide nets and vanchas[257] for receiving the spirits of darkness, and for receiving the spirits of mortals who shall perish in the waters. Also provide a place in My exalted heavens suitable for them; and you shall put walls around them in heaven so they cannot escape, but can be weaned from evil.

09/3.19. And when you have come to the earth and its heavens, acquaint My God and his Lords with My decree. And say to them: Thus says Jehovih: Behold, behold, I will sink the land of Whaga beneath the waters of the ocean, and her heaven I will carry away to a place in My firmament, where she shall no longer engulf My people in darkness. And Jehovih says: Go, O God of heaven, and you, O Lord of Whaga, down to My chosen, the I'hins, and say to them: Thus says the Great Spirit: Behold, behold, I will sink the lands of the earth beneath the ocean, because of the evil of the spirits of darkness. Hear Me, O My chosen, and heed My commandments: Begin now, all hands, and build ships in all places, even in the valleys and on the mountains, and let My faithful gather together within the ships, for My hand is surely stretched over the earth. ||

09/3.20. And you shall also proclaim to the earth and her heaven that from the first, even in the ancient days, I proclaimed My three worlds to all people, which are: My corporeal world, the lower heavens belonging to it, and My etherean heavens, which are in the firmament above. And I said: The first glory is of the earth, on which is paradise when man obeys My commandments; and the second glory, which is greater than the first, I created for the spirits of the dead, but I bound the

---

[255] held, secured, maintained, defensible, livable

[256] tear, split, sever, pull apart, break up

[257] possibly a temporary holding cell prior to transport; or a combination medical-and-detention transport ship suitable for chaotic spirits

lower heaven to the earth so it would travel with it, so that the communion of the dead with the living could add a glory to both. But the upper heaven, I made the highest of all glories, and I filled the etherean firmament with countless etherean worlds for the dwelling places of those who rose in the third resurrection.

09/3.21. And I sent down from the exalted heavens to the lower heavens and earth, My holy angels, over whom I appointed Gods and Lords in the majesty of My dominions. And they came proclaiming these things in My name, teaching both mortals and spirits how to live so they could rise and inherit My illuminated worlds.

09/3.22. And because man was without knowledge, My Gods and Lords appointed certain masters of generations (loo'is), who were ethereans of great wisdom, to remain with mortals and inspire marriages that would best promote spiritual growth from the start. And there came forth among all people, certain ones capable of sar'gis and su'is,[258] and they obeyed the commandments of My Gods and Lords, forsaking[259] evil and striving to serve the spirit, choosing Me above all things. For which reason, I chose them also, and called them I'hins.

09/3.23. For as much as they commenced[260] putting away self and serving Me while they were yet in corpor, so were they not born in the spirit world before their full time. And yet there are others not of full birth[261] who have not, in the corporeal form, begun to triumph in spirit over their own flesh. ||

09/3.24. Jehovih said: Go forth, O My sons and daughters, and prune My vineyard.

09/3.25. Ask My God of the earth and his Lords with him, to gather together all the angels of the earth, from east to west and from north to south; and bring them to the land of Whaga.

09/3.26. My etherean ships of fire shall surround Whaga on every side. And I will cut loose the foundations of the earth, at the borders of the ocean and the mountains of Gan; neither shall any prop nor cornerstone stop My hand. And I will send rains, winds and thundering; and the waters of the great deep shall come upon the lands; and the great cities shall go down and be swallowed in the sea.

09/3.27. And the rich valleys of Mai, with her thousand cities, shall be pierced with the madness of men and women fleeing before the waters of the ocean. And women and children shall fall by the wayside and be drowned; and men shall go down in the water and not rise.

09/3.28. And the wide plains of Og, with her thousand cities and the great capital of Penj, and the temples of Khu, Bart, Gan and Saing, shall sink to rise no more. And in the deluge, the air of heaven shall be filled with the screaming and wailing of millions of mortals going down to destruction.

09/3.29. I will rescue them from darkness; I will carry them to a'jian regions, which I previously created for spirits of darkness; and I will appoint over them, Gods and Goddesses, to teach them of Me and My kingdoms.

09/3.30. And the earth and her heavens shall take a new start among My habitable worlds. ||

09/3.31. In all these ways, then, I have provided labor for My high-raised angels in the places I created, says Jehovih.

END OF THE SYNOPSIS OF HEAVENLY RECORDS FOR THE FIRST 16 CYCLES

---

[258] Sar'gis is the ability of a corporean to have the substance from either his body or his surroundings, be used by an angel to take on a corporeal appearance, or, in its unformed stages, to produce spirit raps from surroundings (sounding like a bang, thunderclap, popping sound, a snapping or a crack). Also a corporean or angel who can produce the semblance of a corporeal thing can be said to have the power of sar'gis.

Su'is, in general, is the ability to perceive spiritually, and sometimes used more narrowly, is the ability to perceive and/or see and/or hear angels (spirits) in their natural condition.

[259] giving up, stop doing, renouncing

[260] began, started, initiated

[261] i.e., those who are born into spirit life (corporeally die) before their full time in corpor is completed

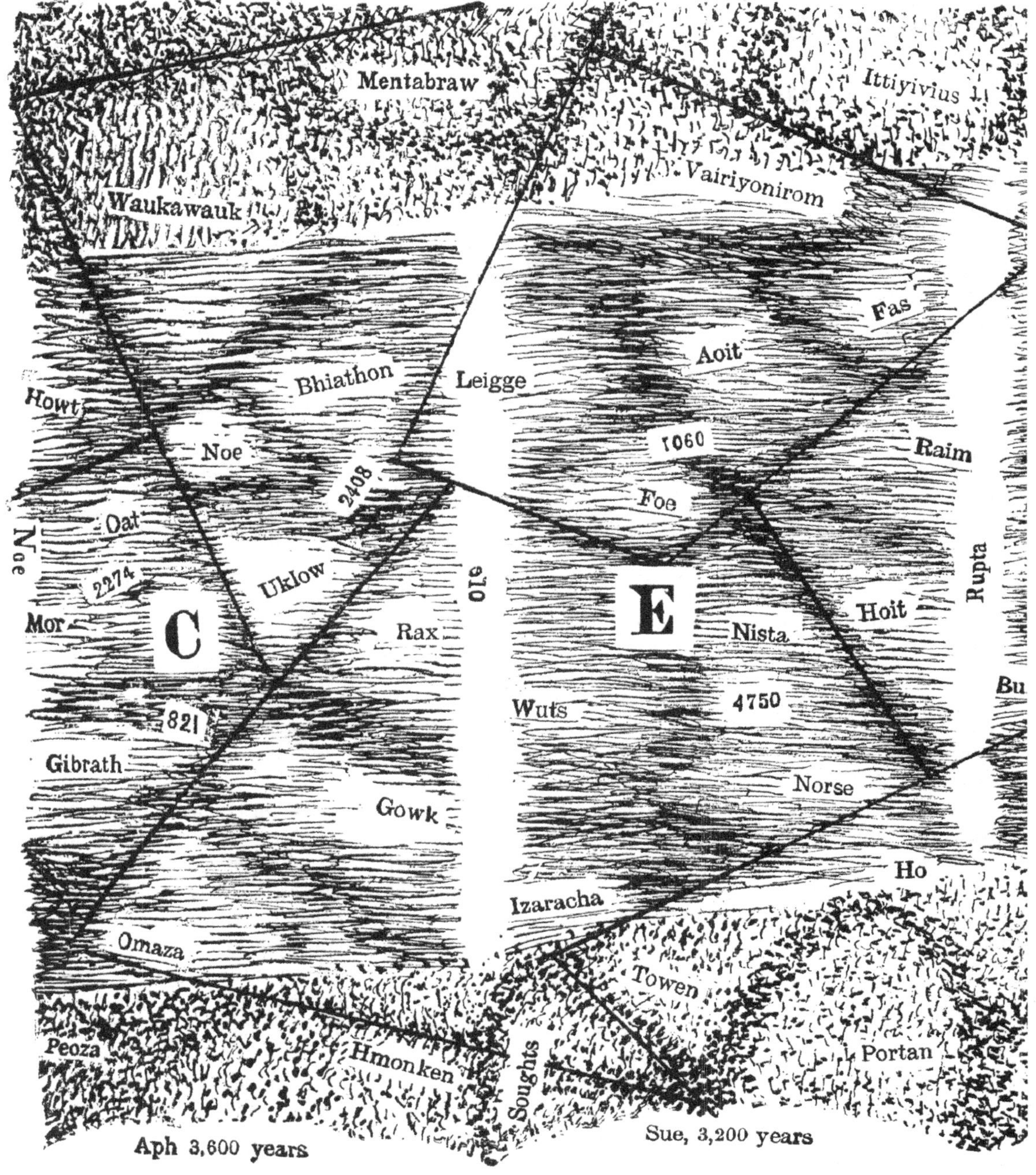

i084 **Map of the Etherean Roadway of the Solar Phalanx for the first two cycles of the past gadol, Plate 1 of 4**. The Roadway shown is that through which the sun and its family (including earth) traveled during the cycles of Aph and Sue. Numbers on the map represent grades. [Locations on the map represent relative positions of etherean realms in or near the pathway that the earth and its solar system traveled. A gadol averages 24,000 years; being closer to 25,000 years in this case. –ed.]

Book of Aph, Son of Jehovih

*Being the heavenly records of Aph, son of Nin'ya, Most Holy Daughter of Jehovih, and of his companion, Fiatisi, pertaining to the submersion of the continent of Whaga (afterward called Pan, signifying earth). And this period was commonly called the **deluge**, or **flood of waters**.*

CHAPTER 1 Aph

10/1.1. In the time of the world twenty-four thousand years[262] before the kosmon era, the great serpent being in the arc of Noe, in the etherean heavens, and of the Sum of Howt and ji'ya eighty-seven, the earth and her heavens were in great darkness. But the spirit of Jehovih moved upon His high-raised God, Aph, in etherea, to consecrate new dominions on the earth and her heavens. Aph said:

10/1.2. I, Aph, Son of Jehovih, God in the arc of Noe, in Sum of Howt, in etherea, came to hada, heaven of the red star, in Jehovih's name. In His wisdom, power and love, manifested in my own resurrection, to become companion to Gods, Goddesses and Orian Chiefs on the thrones of high heaven, proclaim:

10/1.3. To the atmospherean spirits of the earth, and to the spirits of the first, second and third resurrections,[263] abiding on the earth or near it, either with mortals or without; to their God and Lords, and to their Savior, and to all holy ones raised up by Jehovih for the redemption of men and angels:

10/1.4. The voice of Jehovih, Creator of worlds, came to me, in the arc of Noe, saying:

10/1.5. I am the All Highest! My service extends forever. I do not go, but I am far away. I do not come, and yet I am near. My voice is in all places. The light of the soul of man hears Me. I speak in the vine that creeps, and in the strong-standing oak.

10/1.6. Hear the voice of your Creator, O angels of heaven. Carry the wisdom of My utterance down to mortals. Call them to the glories of the heavens and the broad earth. Behold, My voice is in the rocks, and in the wind that blows, and in all things that do not have tongues.

10/1.7. Show them My suns and stars in the firmament above; for they are My written words. My voice proceeds in the space of heaven; the wise angels of My exalted places hear the sound going forth. Listen to My speech, O spirits of the dead; proclaim Me, O Gods and Goddesses.

10/1.8. They look for Me, like they look for things;[264] they listen for My voice, like they listen for a man's voice. And they do not find Me, or hear what I have spoken. Yet none can efface[265] My words; My wisdom endures forever. Behold, I do not come as a sound to the ear; My voice goes quickly into the soul from all sides.

10/1.9. Teach them, O angels; they do not look in the right way; their ears are turned after loud claps and noises. They cry out: Alas, I do not hear the voice of Jehovih; He has not spoken; no man has heard His voice; He is the All Silent, and dumber[266] than the things He created.

10/1.10. They have turned away from My God and My Lords; they have shut themselves up in conceit and darkness. They have peopled the air of the earth with spirits of darkness, the drujas of men of darkness, and cannibals. Their fetals float back upon them; like devouring vermin they burrow deep in pollution.

10/1.11. Remember them, O God, My Son, and you, My Lords of earth. Have no pity, but be like a

---

[262] That is, one gadol ago. The figure 24,000 years is a rounded number and used as a synonym for a gadol—24,000 years being the average duration of a gadol and used in the same way Oahspe uses the average of 3000 years as a synonym for a dan'ha cycle. The actual duration of this particular gadol was about 25,000 years.

[263] The first resurrection is for those who are chiefly concerned with their own selves. The second resurrection is for those who have united together in a brotherhood to accomplish good. The third resurrection here refers to the ethereans who were attempting to resurrect humanity.

[264] i.e., instead, Jehovih is found by perceiving inward, to the soul of things

[265] cancel, undo, delete, make impotent, erase

[266] unable to speak, non-expressive

surgeon's knife upon them. You have told them, O God, that Jehovih lives and reigns; His voice stands the All Highest. But they have mocked you and your Lords, and turned away, going after iniquity.

10/1.12. They are fearful lest they believe in My Person and My voice; but of their own gabble [267] they have no fear. They criticize Me and My God and Lords; but they own[268] that they do not know Me. They suppose My exalted heavens are without order and discipline; My captains they ignore, and the teachings of My holy ones are criticized by men of straw.[269]

10/1.13. Have they not said: Who is God, that I should adore? And the Lord, that I should listen? But I turn their eyes to the armies of earth; to the general and the captain. Then they say: Ah, our affairs on earth are officered and disciplined; we revere our highest, great captains.

10/1.14. Shall they turn God away, and the Lord? What shall the Creator do to please them? Is the name of My general (God), and My captain (Lord), not My own creation? Who founded the name of God and the name of the Lord? Why are they not pleased with My Gods and My Lords?

10/1.15. Hear Me, O you etherean Gods and Goddesses; they do not desire wisdom and resurrection. Their love lies in darkness. To eat, to sleep and to devour[270] are the delights of their souls. The first lesson of life they have not learned; the first heaven of the earth is to them the All of the created worlds.

10/1.16. Hear My judgment upon them, O My holy angels long risen. For I have raised them up again and again; I have founded lower heavens for them so they could learn; but they fall the moment My Gods leave them alone.

10/1.17. Now I will carry away their heaven and earth, and they shall be seen no more forever. But the drujas and fetals shall be carried to Hautuon and cast into walls of fire.[271] And they shall be divided up into groups; kin shall be torn away from kin, friend from friend, mother from daughter, and father from son; for they have become like absorbents, sucking one another continually.

10/1.18. And the walls of the fire shall go up around them without ceasing, and they shall not escape. And those who guard them shall keep them from one another, so that they do no evil. Neither shall they sleep nor rest, but they shall be stirred up and made to know that they are alive, and can exist independent of fetal (sucking).

10/1.19. Hear My voice, O God, and command your Lord to proclaim on the earth. Have I not made an example before mortals? See the carrion[272] that rots in the field. Is it not the feast of the hyena, wolf and buzzard? Do worms not come to life in it and in turn devour the carcass that brought them forth?

10/1.20. What more is the earth (Pan) to these spirits of evil and darkness? What more is their first heaven than a place of perpetual devouring? Have they not made it a place of everlasting destruction? They visit their evils upon mortals; the young child cannot escape them, nor can the middle-aged, nor the old man, nor the old woman.

10/1.21. The heavenly kingdoms founded by Gods and Lords have become pest houses for drujas and fetals; there is no place left for founding the upright and virtuous in heart.

10/1.22. Are My Gods and Lords servants to an evil world? And shall they find only rottenness to

---

[267] nonsense, expression, speech, chatter, babble

[268] acknowledge, make known; have as a trait

[269] those who have little to no substantiation to support their words

[270] That is, to destroy, to engage in fetalism, which is to live on (devour) the substance of others. Fetalism refers to breathing (sucking in) through the mouth, which thus sucks the essence from another, the fetal absorbing the essence and draining the other. For which reason, the Faithist in Jehovih is taught to nostril breathe only, if at all possible, even as the high-raised angels do. See verses 10/1.10; 10/1.17-20; 10/1.29; as well as elsewhere in Oahspe.

[271] These lights are seen in a small way in spirit circles; and they form in heaven, boundaries for certain dominions. This is most likely the original rendering of casting spirits of darkness into a place from which there was no escape. Not, however, that the place was one of punishment, but to the contrary. –Ed. [As prison walls are to mortals, so are walls of fire to low-grade and evil spirits, here keeping these isolated in small groups and in sections.]

[272] decaying dead body, corpse

deal with? Now I have answered in the firmament of My holy sons and daughters. I have called them from remote places in heaven to witness the work of My hand. For as I made the earth and its heaven, so do I rule over it to the same end for which I created it.

10/1.23. When they are short of My measure, I lengthen them out; when they run foul, I prune them to My own liking; for they are Mine. Behold, the fool has said: Jehovih has made a failure! He has created a world for a certain purpose, but it runs foul of His mark!

10/1.24. Hear Me, O God, and through your Lords answer him in his conceit. Did I not quicken man into life in My own way? At zero I created him, and I said: Two roads I have made, O man. One leads to everlasting light; and the other to everlasting darkness.

10/1.25. Now I have shown him the darkness; it is My witness, through which man knows My word is All Truth. Why, then, should I not create the world, and men, and angels, that they go down toward everlasting darkness? Is it not by darkness and pain that I push man forward?[273] Yes, the conceited man would fail himself were it not for the failures I set up before him. In what way, then, have I not created wisely?

10/1.26. Do I not have a right to do My own way? Are all things not Mine? If a man dies in the corporeal part, is he a failure? How else could man rise to My etherean worlds? Open his eyes, O My God and My Lords. He was not, and I created him. He presumes to look into My plans and judgments; by his little learning he exalts his conceit, and pretends to know all things.

10/1.27. I cause the grain to grow in the field, and the day before it is ripe I send wind and rains, and destroy it utterly. I bring forth man with shapely limbs and strong arms, but in the day of his prime I cut him down. I gave the passion of love to the mother, but I take away her first-born.

10/1.28. Do I not know that first, of all things, man shall be taught to know My power; and after that, My wisdom? Have they seen the places of the dead, and hell, and destruction? Teach them, O God; for their ultimate resurrection is My glory and My delight.

[273] Opposite this is the light and delight that call man forward (instead of pushing).

10/1.29. Shall man of earth say that the Creator was angry, and so sent the land beneath the ocean? He does not have wisdom to comprehend that in this day I cast out hell and destruction. The druj is his love, and, as vampires, they feed on each other to the ruin of both.

10/1.30. But I know what is for their own good; and My decree has gone forth.

CHAPTER 2 Aph

10/2.1. I, Aph, Son of Jehovih, high dwelling in the etherean worlds, and much trained in the change and tumult of corporeal worlds, answered Jehovih, saying:

10/2.2. Father of Worlds; Jehovih, Almighty! Your Son and servant has heard Your voice. Behold, my head is bowed, my knee bent to rush forth with the force of a billion, to the suffering earth and hada.

10/2.3. Hear me, O angels of the earth's heaven; from Jehovih's everlasting kingdoms I speak, and by His Power reveal! || Again His Voice coursed the high heavens along where angels dwell, older than the earth. Jehovih said:

10/2.4. Hear Me, O Chieftains, of Or, and of Oat,[274] and in the plains of Gibrathatova. Proclaim My word to your hosts of swift messengers from Wauk'awauk, Beliathon and Dor, and they shall speed it abroad in the a'ji'an mounds of Mentabraw and Rax of Gowh.

10/2.5. Hear My voice, O Goddesses of Ho'etaivi and of Vaivi'yoni'rom in the etherean arcs of Fas and Leigge, and Omaza. Proclaim My decrees of the red star and her heavens; in the crash of her rebellious sides, I will harvest in the forests of Seth and Raim.

10/2.6. Hear My voice, O H'monkensoughts, of millions of years' standing, and managers of corporeal worlds! I have proclaimed the uz and hiss of the red star in her pride and glory. Send word abroad in the highway of Plumf'goe to the great high Gods, Miantaf in the etherean vortices of Bain, and to Rome, Nesh'outoza and Du'ji.

10/2.7. Hear Me, O you Orian Kings and Queens of billions of Gods and Goddesses: I have

[274] see image i084 p.99; many of the names can be found there

spoken in the c'vork'um[275] of the great serpent of the sun! A wave of My breath speeds forth in the broad firmament. The red star flies toward the point of My sharpened sword.

10/2.8. Proclaim My voice in the Orian fields of Amal and Wawa; let the clear-tongued Shepherds of Zouias, Berk, Gaub, and Domfariana, fly with all speed in the road of Axyaya, where the red star's vortex first gathered up its nebulae, millions of years ago, and on the way, say: Jehovih has decreed a pruning-knife to a traveling world.

10/2.9. Shout it abroad in the crystal heavens of the summering Lords of Wok, Ghi, M'goe, and Ut'taw; call them to the red star speeding forth. Lo, she skips like a lamb to be shorn; her coming shock lies slumbering low. Let them carry the sound of My voice to the ji'ay'an swamps of exploded worlds, boiling in the roar of elements, where wise angels and Gods explore to find the mystery of My handiwork.

10/2.10. Tell them I have spoken, the earth and her heavens draw near the troughs, in the etherean seas of My rich-yielding worlds. I will scoop her up like a toy, and her vortex shall close about like a serpent hungry for its prey. Proclaim it in Thessa, Kau, and Tin'wak'wak, and send them to Gitchefom of Januk and Dun.

10/2.11. Hear Me, O Kriss'helmatsholdak, who have witnessed the creation of many worlds and their going out. Open your gardens and your mansions; the seine[276] of My fishing-pole is stretched; countless millions of druj and fetals will fall into My net. My voice has gone forth in Chem'gow, Loo and Abroth, Huitavi, and Kuts of Mas in the wide etherean fields of Rod'owkski.

10/2.12. Haleb has heard Me; Borg, Hom, Zi and Luth, of the Orian homestead, and Chor, where the central tones of music emanate, from Goddesses older than the corporeal worlds.[277] To them the crash of worlds is like a note created, and is rich in stirring the memory with things long past.

10/2.13. I have spoken, and My breath is a floating world; My speech is written in the lines where countless millions of suns and stars travel, and in the midst of the etherean firmament of the homes of Gods. Let them shout to the ends of the universe; invite them, in My name, to the hi'dan[278] of Mauk'beiang'jow.

10/2.14. Send swift messengers to the regions around the location of the great serpent, with the words of My decree; bring the Lords and Gods of Wan, Anah, Anakaron, and Sith.

10/2.15. Call up Ghad, Adonya, Etisyai, Onesyi, and the hosts of the upraised, for the pastime of Jehovih's sons and daughters in the high heavens, draws near.

CHAPTER 3 Aph

10/3.1. O angels of hada of the red star, and you, O God and Lords, upraised and mighty, with countless hosts, and quick answering the thoughts of mortals, hear the words of Aph, Son of Jehovih:

10/3.2. When I was in the Orian arc of Noe, and the red star passed the Utswowldayark, in the etherean group of Vorh, the voice of Jehovih came to me, saying: Go, My Son, deliver the earth. Take with you all whom I may send.

10/3.3. And I examined the records of the stars of heaven, and of the earth, and the accounts of Jehovih's harvests, and I perceived the bondage and labor of the red star were of the seventh magnitude in the advance of habitable worlds.

10/3.4. When His voice called the legions in high heaven, myriads[279] of shapely stars moved in from every side, even from below and above the earth; and these were ships of fire coursing the firmament, in which rode the Gods and Goddesses, called by Jehovih to the labor of earth and hada.

10/3.5. Closing in on every side they came, nearer and more compact, and brighter, with sparkling pillars of fire, and down-swaying curtains of light, till all the space surrounding the earth was hedged in with this army of Jehovih's etherean ships of fire.

---

[275] etherean roadway

[276] fishing net (long, like an extended volleyball net)

[277] That is, they were older than any of the corporeal worlds existing at that time.

[278] A dan'ha cycle begins with a hi'dan, which is the time of the greatest light in the firmament for that dan'ha cycle. Usually Oahspe just calls them dan'ha (when the reference is to the start of a dan'ha cycle); or calls them a dawn (of dan), which they technically are, but more precisely they can be called a dawn of hi'dan or simply hi'dan.

[279] a tremendously large number

10/3.6. Again I heard the Father's voice, saying: O Aph, My Son, My holy one, listen to the voice of Jehovih, Creator of Gods and Goddesses:

10/3.7. Behold, I sent My Son, Neph, to the red star, with wisdom and power. Long has he been gone, struggling with the black darkness of men and angels.

10/3.8. As a valiant soldier rushes into the heaviest part of battle, and forgets himself in desperate contest, but does not cease to struggle on, against all odds, even so, for three thousand years, My God Neph has hoped to save the whole limbs of the earth (the continents).

10/3.9. From My holy place I have watched the battle for everlasting life; but the too prolific earth contributes more to the corporeal than to the spiritual man. And now I bring My legions to the rescue of My valiant Son, Neph. Send word to him, O Aph, My Son. Proclaim to him and his Lords, and to his ethereans, My just decrees. || Aph said:

10/3.10. And I sent swift messengers down to hada, informing Neph, Son of Jehovih, of the march and presence of Gods, and of the decree of the Father; and I added to it, saying: O Neph, Son of Jehovih, come here, bringing your hosts with you.

10/3.11. Presently Neph answered me in Jehovih's name, saying: O Aph, Son of Jehovih, I come! My prayers are answered. All praise to the All Highest!

10/3.12. Then we saw in hada, the ship of Neph and his faithful hosts being prepared to ascend; and that which was seen from my ship was also seen by the myriads of Jehovih's vessels surrounding the earth. And my place became like a central throne, to which the hosts in their ships, now made speed, swift and orderly.

10/3.13. And as they arrived, the ship of Neph rose from hada. Meanwhile, my ship rested on the borders of Chinvat, in the Schood of Hein,[280] and seven agus[281] from the moon.

10/3.14. Again the voice of Jehovih came to me, saying: My Son, make fast[282] your ship, for your place shall be the head of the army of My hosts. And let your consorts[283] extend in a line from your place down to the earth, for this shall be the delivery of those whom I shall cut off.

10/3.15. So I made fast, and my messengers sped to the concentrating forces of heaven, informing the etherean groups on Jehovih's ships, of His commandments. And now Neph came, his ship filled with his long-laboring hosts. And I greeted him and said to him: By the power and wisdom of Jehovih, the continent of Whaga is to be cut loose and submerged, and her heavens carried away. Return to the earth; and from all the divisions of earth and heaven, bring all the spirits of darkness to Whaga, so that I may carry them away. || Then Neph and his hosts viewed the imposing scene and returned back to earth.

10/3.16. Quickly, now, the ships of fire formed in line, extending from my place down to hada, where Neph and his Lords of the earth rested, whose hosts extended to all the divisions of land and water, embracing the various heavenly kingdoms previously built by the Lords.

10/3.17. And in the line of the etherean ships the plateaus of rank were stationed; and the hosts of Gods and Goddesses took their places, according to the rank of wisdom, power and love manifested in the etherean departments from which they came; with the two Orian Chiefs at either extremity.[284]

10/3.18. And I divided the line into sections, each with two hundred and fifty ships, and there were one thousand sections. And every ship was contracted ten thousand fold,[285] which was the force required to break the crust of the earth and sink a continent.[286]

---

[280] a negative place, comparable with a calm on earth or a calm at sea. –1891 glossary

[281] An agus is about a thousand miles. –Ed.

[282] anchor, fasten, secure, tie

[283] the etherean ships that came to participate

[284] i.e., Aph (Orian Chief) at the top, and Fiatisi (Chief in Emuts) at the bottom

[285] ten thousandth times normal or 1 to 10,000

[286] I have seen a table held down by angels so that a strong man could not lift one end. –Ed. [This is just a small demonstration of the power available to knowledgeable and skilled angels. While that feat required only a little concerted power on the part of a few angels; by contrast the power of a large array of etherean angels in their ships, moving in concert with Jehovih, was required to do the work of breaking the crust of the earth, and sinking a continent.]

10/3.19. Along the line I stationed sentinels and talesmen,[287] and inexhaustible numbers of messengers so that Jehovih's voice and His sons' voices could traverse to every part in a moment of time. And after that I formed the tube of transit, which extended in front of the ships, and from the earth to beyond Chinvat; and I filled it with the earth's atmosphere even up to the high end, where it joined Io'sank, where I planned to deliver the drujas and fetals of those who were to perish in the ocean of the earth.

10/3.20. For every ten sections I appointed one hundred marshals and one God, and for every ten Gods one Chief in Emuts;[288] according to their rank in the heavens from which they came, so I appointed them. These, then, are the Chiefs in Emuts, namely:

10/3.21. Agar, of the order of Achav, Son of Jehovih, in Bowitch, from the corporeal star Godad, raised in Ben, of a'ji seventy, of seven hundred thousand years as inhabitant of Gon.

10/3.22. Hoe'ghi, Son of Jehovih, Marsh'wan of Hadom and Ag, nebulae four and Petrath; swift messenger of Jun, of the corporeal star Alanx, of one million two hundred thousand years as inhabitant of Roth'wok in Jois.

10/3.23. Fist'humitaivi, Daughter of Jehovih, ji'ya'an Oods'lon in Kaih; Goddess of Ine; Goddess of Ad; Governess of Wal'wal, of the corporeal star Ter'wig, and of the plains of Exwer and Gohen, in the etherean arc of Labis, of one million three hundred thousand years.

10/3.24. Hi'ata, Daughter of Jehovih, and nurse of Hue'enbak, in fifty-seven a'ji, of the corporeal star Heats, a milkmaid, Goddess of Luf, Goddess of the plateau of O'banf, in etherea, rank ninety, and of two million years as inhabitant of Nud and Ix.

10/3.25. Gon'leps, Son of Jehovih, God of Ney, God of Aper, God of Don, God of Mu, God of Reau; physician of Bo, and of Ir, and of Jan'er; marshal of Kute and Oblin of Sharar, in etherea, of the a'ji'an field of Do; of seven hundred thousand years as inhabitant of On'lof and Rick'tus.

10/3.26. Neo, God of Lun and Hintaya; God of Mors, and of Thespune; Master of Peh and Savior of Woh'haggai, a'ji plain seven, and risen from the corporeal star Se'etiyi, and inhabitant of Sirne one million seven hundred thousand years.

10/3.27. Sicci, Goddess of Nu, in Loots and Rab; Goddess of Bad; Goddess of Ture; Goddess of Red, a'ji twenty, from the corporeal star Ith'mule, inhabitant of Suga one million years; inhabitant of Ranna one million two hundred thousand years.

10/3.28. Listiac'ca, Goddess of Man; Goddess of Hirze; Goddess of Som and Nye; Weaver of Olt'bak and Agimus. Rank ninety, raised on the corporeal star Mem; inhabitant of Das'sawig and Gabriomety two million nine hundred thousand years.

10/3.29. Tussica, Goddess of Kol; Goddess of Lowst and Wittawhaggat; Goddess of Du'e'jhi and Loo of Maggatza; Goddess of Ep; Goddess of Gek of Hennasshalonkya; Goddess of Tur in the ji'ay'an swamp of Dobbokta, fifty-five, raised on the corporeal sun Nitz, of the serpent Tan, inhabitant of Tayay'hitsivi, two million years; inhabitant of Palla one million seven hundred thousand years.

10/3.30. Fiatisi, Goddess of Lubbuk; Goddess of Saran'ya, in Gowlolo; Goddess of Iz, Goddess of Serl; Goddess of Lok'low; Goddess of Um of a'ji, seventy-five; Goddess of Wartz and Do'e'huitta; Goddess of Crayya; Goddess of Bak'hoo; Goddess of Teel and Ros'itz; Goddess of Mutz'mutz; Goddess of La'errets of Wouk'humhowtz; Goddess of Bil and Dusk'wan'guessel; Goddess of Ork'sa; Goddess of Unksoot; Goddess of Sl'huitta; Goddess of Shein; Goddess of Isa; Goddess of Ham; Goddess of Reikowow and Shuitit; Goddess of Daing and Gou'wok; Goddess of Faitta'zammel; Goddess of Zittayya'howb of the gardens of Zittayya'bauf in a'ji seven; surgeon of Hualla; surgeon of Bos; surgeon of Rappaya; surgeon of Lum'zon; nurse of Paigga of Semathais; nurse of Zid; nurse of Loo'see; nurse of Home; nurse of Briathath; Queen of Ouppa; Queen of Rog'ga, disciplinarian of Tuh, of Kaibbi'summak, of Tootz'mutz, of Bir'bir, of Ctenski, of Rivvia, of Soon, of Hadab, of Fussuhowtz and Ceres; raised on the star Planzza, swift messenger in Bal and Wawa'lauk five

[287] Emergency-response teams, reinforcements, back-ups, troubleshooters

[288] Some of the high-raised officers in etherea devote their labors mostly to affairs in etherea, seldom dealing with the affairs of corporeal worlds. Others deal largely with the affairs of corporeal worlds; these latter are called Emuts. –1891 glossary

hundred thousand years; swift messenger in To'wakka and Runfwot five hundred thousand years; inhabitant of Terashash one million years; inhabitant of the fields of Ni'jayay one million years; inhabitant of Gun five hundred thousand years; maker of corporeal roadways five hundred thousand years.

10/3.31. So Fiatisi outranked all other Gods and Goddesses, and was special guest of honor to Aph, Chief over all the rest.

10/3.32. And the star that was Fiatisi's etherean ship was stationed near the earth, so that she could better oversee the deliverance of the spirits that were to be freed by the submersion of the land of Whaga; and of these spirits there were more than twenty-four billion four hundred million, of whom more than three billion were fetals, familiars, and spirits in chaos.

CHAPTER 4 Aph

10/4.1. Jehovih said: Aph, My Son, put a wall of pillars of fire around the land of Whaga; plant them close together, like a hedge. For the false Gods and false Goddesses of hada, when perceiving their habitation going down into the water, will endeavor to escape to Jud and Vohu, and other countries.

10/4.2. But you shall not let even one escape; for they have migrated to this division of the earth because of its sumptuous productions, the better to feast their evil desires.

10/4.3. And you shall spread a net around the borders of Whaga, against the line of the ocean and to the high north mountains; and the net shall encompass the continent of Whaga, and its height shall be a thousand miles, and in thickness, so deep that no spirit of darkness can escape and find the way abroad.

10/4.4. And when you have spread the net, you shall send a sufficient number of ethereans of great power to the large kingdoms in hada, and to the false kingdoms. And you shall also send a sufficient number of ethereans down to the earth, to Whaga, so that each and every mortal, whether man, woman or child, shall have five to attend them. And those who go to mortals shall take sufficient birth-blankets with them; for at the time of destruction, when the mortals go down in death, your servants shall receive the liberated spirits on the birth-blankets, and carry them to the atmospherean column of ascent. And here your hosts shall receive them, and provide them with food and clothes, as is required for es'yans.

10/4.5. But it shall happen that many who perish in the waters, will be mothers with children in the womb, which live by fetal, as is proper in My sight, for I created them so.

10/4.6. Therefore, give special care to all such fetals, for they are without sin. And when the mother is dead corporeally, and the fetal also, bring away their spirits, but together; and provide a volunteer angel of fetal power, and deliver the infant spirit to her to be nurtured until the proper time of weaning; and in the same place, provide a home for the mother of the child, so that she may inherit its love and mirth.

10/4.7. When the voice ceased, Aph, Son of Jehovih, looked over the hosts, as if in search of a sign that the time had come; but again Jehovih spoke, saying:

10/4.8. In the misfortunes of a fallen world, I created food for the warm love of My etherean Goddesses. See them here in millions; each one in hope of receiving a prize of that which was lost in darkness, and to thus raise up sons and daughters who shall rejoice in everlasting paradise. Do not think that I gave the talent of love only to a mother for her child, and there the talent ends; for as the talent in its incipient[289] age binds her soul to her child, so does the same talent, in My Goddesses, overspread a helpless world.

10/4.9. Are they not like midwives and mothers to thousands and millions of souls being delivered from corporeal bondage into everlasting light? And who can number them? Here stands a hundred million from Laygas; a hundred million from Inopta; two hundred million from Karduk; a hundred million from Buchk; two hundred million from Nin; two hundred and fifty million from Luth'wig; a hundred million from Pied; two hundred million from Raig; fifty million from Naivis; two hundred million from Dak'dak, and two hundred and fifty million from Od.

10/4.10. I spoke in the etherean firmament, and they have answered Me. But they do not come as curiosity seekers, nor with empty arms; but, see them, arrayed with their thousands and millions of

[289] beginning or initial

small equipments suited to the newborn! What thing is there under the sun that they have not remembered to bring with them in some part, whether regimen or drapery, to rejoice the souls of those who are to be cut off from corpor?

CHAPTER 5 Aph

10/5.1. Jehovih said: Now I will bewail you, O earth. The glories of your heavens that are past and gone, shall be a lesson to the Gods. Your heaven Hored, once the place of the wisdom of My Son, Sethantes, upraised, behold it is measured and gone down. And Moeb is no more. Yeshuah is fallen. Where the plateaus of many resurrections once floated, there are now miring[290] vampires and millions of souls that neither hear nor see, but are ceaselessly burrowing deep in everlasting darkness.

10/5.2. The plateaus are broken up, the substance scattered and unorganized; nor is there a vestige left to show the glorious work of the Gods from earth's past days.

10/5.3. Hear Me, O Gods and Goddesses, for in witnessing these deep miseries, the soul is quickened to retain great wisdom: Thus I created man; out of darkness I created him; and My holy angels taught him to walk upright, and gave him My commandments so that he could advance to eternal light. But because man did not obey the commandments of My God and Lords, he fell. Nevertheless, a few obeyed the commandments and did not fall, raising up heirs for the glory of My heavens above.

10/5.4. I have made an example of this kind of man, on all the corporeal worlds I have created; for those who did not fall, became exemplars[291] before the fallen; for having faith in Me and My works, they did not question My wisdom and justice.

10/5.5. But of those who fell, this is the history: They questioned first, My Person; next My Wisdom; then My Justice; finally My Power. And after that proclaimed the folly of God and his Lords; consequently they usurped[292] to themselves to say: There is nothing higher than man. And they said of themselves: I am the highest.

10/5.6. Hear My voice, O Gods and Goddesses; for, as out of a contrary wind I give a mortal sea-captain a wholesome lesson, or as out of a severe winter I give a corporeal farmer a lesson in providing for his household, even so, on the brink of a wicked world, I give you a lesson in the management of My kingdoms. For, from this time forward, the earth shall not fail, nor her heavens above her. How, then, shall My Gods not rule over her in wisdom and power?

10/5.7. Since many angels assumed they were the All Highest, they put aside the commandments, one of which was: to not permit the spirits of the newly dead to return and dwell with their mortal kindred; for they, not knowing about the higher heavens, will teach falsely concerning Jehovih and His everlasting kingdoms.

10/5.8. And it came to pass, that when one commandment was set aside, the others were also; and it followed that the spirits of the newly dead, who were without knowledge of heaven, led mortals in their own way.

10/5.9. For they dwelt together and slept together; and in dreams and visions, mortals judged themselves to be wise, not knowing they were obsessed in sleep; and for the desires of the flesh, they found acquiescence in spirit,[293] having no higher God or Lord.

10/5.10. And as one spirit returned and fastened itself on a mortal, so did another and another, till hundreds and thousands of spirits dwelt in one corporeal body, often driving away the natural spirit that I gave at the time of conception. And these mortals did not know it; and they became void of direct purpose because of the confusion of soul, and were worthless on the earth.

10/5.11. Jehovih further said: From this time forward, for a long season on earth, the spirits of the es'yans shall not be permitted to return and dwell with mortals. But the earth shall be encompassed on all sides with walls of emun,[294]

---

[290] plunging and sinking into the ooze, muck, slime and filth; and like in quicksand, they cannot pull away

[291] models representing a pattern and life of virtue

[292] arrogated, assumed control, claimed as a right

[293] no expressed objection, perhaps neutral silence, and certainly no inspiration to practice restraint

[294] choking atmosphere. –1891 glossary

and supplied with ashars to bear away the spirits of the dead in the hour of death.

10/5.12. But there shall come a time when mortals are capable of comprehending these matters, at which time, their kindred spirits shall return at intervals from their holy labors in heaven, to see them and talk with them face to face.

CHAPTER 6 Aph

10/6.1. And now Aph, Son of Jehovih, said: When the etherean hosts were arranged in due order, I called out to You, O Jehovih, saying: In Your Strength and Wisdom, O Father, join the heavens above with the earth below!

10/6.2. And the end of the etherean column that extended to Chinvat, on the border of the vortex of the earth, was made secure by the pressure of Your wide heavens.

10/6.3. Again I said: In Your Strength and Wisdom, O Jehovih, join the heavens above with the earth below!

10/6.4. And the end of the etherean column that extended down to the earth was made secure around the borders of Whaga, by the sea and the high mountains to the north.

10/6.5. Again I said: O Jehovih, deliver the earth from evil, for Your glory, forever!

10/6.6. And the vortex of the earth closed in from the rim, and lo, the earth was broken! A mighty continent was cut loose from its fastenings, and the fires of the earth came forth in flames and clouds, with loud roaring. And the land rocked to and fro like a ship at sea.

10/6.7. Again I said: O Jehovih, deliver Your heavens, which are bound like a chain, to a rotten carcass.

10/6.8. And again the vortex of the earth closed in on all sides, and by the pressure, the land sank beneath the water, to rise no more. And the corporeans went down to death; and the fetals and familiars gave up the battle; neither did they have anywhere to stand, nor did they know how to go to any place in all the heavens, but were lost and crying out for help.

10/6.9. And my hosts hastened in all directions with their birth-blankets, and received the druj, fetals and es'yans, in the millions and millions; gathered and delivered them to the fountain of light, where I had provided atmosphere for them; and they were placed within. So great were their numbers, that even Gods had scarcely seen anything like it before; and in order to attest before You, O Jehovih, I had them numbered, using the sections of the divisions of my Gods and Goddesses in order to do so.

10/6.10. Of druj and fetals, there were sixteen billion six hundred million. Many of these had lived on earth as fetals and druj for thousands of years, although many others of them were not capable of everlasting life. Next, of the first resurrection there were thirty-six billion; and of the second resurrection, three hundred and five million. But during the last hundred years, the earth brought forth no one capable of everlasting life except, indeed, the remnants of I'hins.

10/6.11. Now when the earth was delivered, and there was no escape for the spirits of the dead, or any returning to mortals, I called out to You, O Jehovih, saying: Give me of Your power, O Jehovih, and I will carry up all the plateaus of hell and the heavens of the buried continent! And Your hand came like the blade of a sword, flaming like fire, and swept over the ocean of the sunken land, cleaving all asunder. And, lo and behold, the anchorage of my feet was cut loose, and the spheres of heaven at my command.

10/6.12. Your voice, O Jehovih, came to me, saying: Descend, My Son, down to the floor of the resurrection; and go into the midst of the place of ascension, and take My Daughter, Fiatisi, with you, for I will add to your glory, the resurrection of all whom your eyes have seen.

10/6.13. So I descended; and there took Fiatisi, Daughter of Jehovih, with me; and when we had come into the place commanded, Your power came upon the place, and it started upward; and soon it turned on its vertical axis and rose higher and higher, turning and rising; and we saw we were loose from the earth, and we no longer rotated with the earth, but rose slowly upward, watching the earth rotating beneath us.

10/6.14. I said: Upward, O Jehovih! Upward, O Jehovih! Upward, O Jehovih! And all the hosts repeated the same words, for our wills and knowledge were as a unit, in which we had strength in You, our Creator!

CHAPTER 7 Aph

10/7.1. Jehovih spoke in the firmament, saying: Bring the newborn into the forests of Uk'loo and the ji'ay'an roads to the arc of Noe, in the etherean heaven of Hautuon; and when you have established them on a world of their own, leave Gods and Goddesses with them, to sort them, and provide according to their necessities; for all things shall be provided to them in such a way that they can attain to knowledge and individuality.

10/7.2. And when you have placed them, hasten with My Son, Neph, back to the earth, where I have labor awaiting regarding the ships of the I'hins. || And so, in that way, the newly born were delivered.

10/7.3. Then I (Aph) departed as soon as possible, taking leave of Fiatisi, thanking her for her assistance in this great deliverance. With me, I took Neph, Son of Jehovih, and another thirty thousand Gods and Goddesses, besides ten million ethereans, who each had thousands of years' experience in heaven and on various corporeal worlds; and we came back to the earth, to the ocean where the land had gone down.

10/7.4. And when I came to the ships in which the I'hins had escaped, finding the Gods who were in charge of them, even as I had previously commanded, Your voice, O Jehovih, came to me, saying: Bend the currents of the winds of heaven, O My Son; shape the course of the ships so that they fall into groups; and you shall divide the groups, making four groups in all. And by the winds of heaven you shall drive the groups (fleets) of ships, and bring them to the four different lands of the earth, according to its previous history and adaptation.

10/7.5. For in all countries, My chosen shall begin laying down the foundation of My everlasting kingdom, and they shall never again be destroyed by the people of darkness of earth or heaven.[295] ||

10/7.6. So according to the labor Your commandments put upon me, I divided my hosts, making four divisions of them. And I said to Neph: Direct them, O God, to those countries Jehovih has shown you, for you know all the earth; remember, you are still God of earth.

10/7.7. God (Neph) said: By Your light, Jehovih, I desire two ships to go to the north land, which was not sunk, for they shall be a testimony in time to come. Let Your Gods, therefore, shift the winds and drive two ships aside from the rest; and at the same time, my messengers will go and lead the way to the north land, in which direction Your Gods shall shape the winds of heaven.

10/7.8. Now those in charge of the wind currents divided the ships and drove two of them off to the northern land. And the Gods and angels turned the currents about and drove the four groups of ships in four different ways, according to the directions of God, Son of Jehovih. The messengers of God led the way, showing the Gods and angels of the wind, the countries designated by Jehovih.[296]

10/7.9. So it came to pass that in one hundred and fifty days, all the ships of the Faithists were in the ports; and the people went ashore, in the different countries where they had been taken. || Again Your voice, O Jehovih, came to me, saying: Behold, My people are few in the world, and lest they take the ships and sail about, and so get divided and lost, you shall send your hosts down to the sea at night to sink the ships.

10/7.10. When I told God (Neph) what You had said, God said to me: My angels shall inspire the I'hins to take all things out of the ships, and tonight your hosts shall fulfill the commandment of Jehovih. || And so it happened; the I'hins took all their goods out of the ships, not knowing they were inspired; and that night I sent angels down, and they sank the ships.

10/7.11. And in the morning the I'hins saw their ships had disappeared, and they said with one voice: Truly, I know I was inspired, for I would not rest till all the goods were taken out of the ships. Let us, therefore, build an altar to the Lord, and sing and dance, because he is with us. And when God (Neph) saw that their souls were propitious[297] for good works and miracles, he stationed his

---

[295] That is, never again would the earth be brought to such a low place of darkness as to be near unredeemable, nor would the Faithist ever be destroyed in entirety. The Faithist of today is living proof that the foundation was never destroyed.

[296] The countries directed to are Jaffeth (China), Shem (India), Ham (Egypt), and Guatama (America); the two ships to the north country going to Japan. More detail is given in the accompanying "The Lords' First Book" (11/).

ashars around the altars, and sent other ashars into the countryside where they gathered fruit which was growing wild, and brought it to the I'hins, casting it on the altars of the Lord, even while the people danced.

10/7.12. Thus I fulfilled the work You commanded of me, O Jehovih, and so I surrendered my commission to Your Son, Neph, God of heaven and earth.

CHAPTER 8 Aph

10/8.1. Neph, God of earth, said: Behold, O Aph, Son of Jehovih, by the power and magnificence of your work I am bewildered in your presence. Who can come so near the Almighty? Who but Jehovih has attained beyond the power of your soul? Who has wisdom like you, except the Great Creator? You have stretched a line beyond the moon, and by your spoken word crushed in the side of the great earth, as if it were nothing. You have said: Arise! And a world moved at your command! Yes, you have the love and esteem of millions of Gods and Goddesses.

10/8.2. And you came against the winds of the earth, saying: Turn here or turn there, and lo, the winds moved before your words as an obedient child to its father's voice. You call down the fire of heaven; it comes at your bidding; and you say: O Jehovih, put Your hand under the heavens of the earth, and immediately a light and floor, wide as the earth, fly into the place of your desire.

10/8.3. Now, behold, You have said: O Jehovih, I surrender my commission; I have finished that which You commanded me to do. For which reason, O Aph, my soul has great sorrow. But because you have labored a hundred days and cleaned up the whole earth and her heavens, as one might sweep the floor of a house, I am bowed down in gratitude.

10/8.4. Then Aph, Son of Jehovih, said: O Jehovih, what have I done that Your Son's love has come to me? The more I become one with You, O You Everlasting Creator, the more You show me plainer and plainer that I am nothing. And yet Your Son, seeing I am merely a figure moved by Your hand, heaps praise upon me. Shall a man lose sight of the Almighty!

10/8.5. Nevertheless, O Jehovih, who is so weak when it comes to love, as I, Your servant? Because You have quickened me in wisdom and power, so have You made my love as a place that can never be supplied to the full. How shall I find strength to leave this, Your Son, on the far-off earth? Will I not glory in his love and great esteem; and yet do I not know that I will repine[298] because I do not have him with me?

10/8.6. Hear me, O Jehovih, for I will swiftly measure Your Son. Scarcely forty thousand years raised up to etherea, and yet You made him God of heaven and earth. For three thousand years he struggled in the battle against evil and darkness; and the broad heavens in the etherean world looked on in sympathy, love and hope, because of his tenacity, wisdom and power.

10/8.7. It was like one man fighting against a house on fire, and the place filled with helpless babes. And yet Your God never ceased, not once rested and said: It is useless; but forever renewed the battle in new ways and stratagems. As a light shows better in the dark, so did Your Son Neph, O Jehovih, move the souls of even Gods and Goddesses in Your exalted heavens.

10/8.8. Then came Your voice, O Father, saying: Go, O Aph, My Son, and deliver the earth. || And, behold, the congregating of Gods and Goddesses! So eager to fly to the assistance of Your honored Son!

10/8.9. And God (Neph) said: One favor, O Aph, Son of Jehovih, I ask of you; which is that you shall stay three days and honor the throne of God. For I will have it founded and ready; and my Lords shall have the honor of speaking to you face to face?

10/8.10. Aph, Son of Jehovih, said: By Your permission, O Jehovih, I will stay three days and three nights with Your Son, God of heaven and earth, and I will honor his throne and speak face to face with his Lords, so that I may win their love.

10/8.11. In three days' time the kingdom of God was founded, and situated in atmospherea, near and over the land of Jaffeth (Chine'ya), but the plateaus extended with two wings, so as to embrace Shem

[297] favorably inclined, receptively disposed, auspicious, conducive

[298] desire someone's presence; feel their loss; miss them

and Ham (India and Egypt); and the Gods, with their Lords and attendants, went to the kingdom.

10/8.12. Now, there were with God (Neph), two million spirits (earth-born) in the second resurrection, who had volunteered to serve another two hundred years for the founding of the new kingdom of heaven, and they were well learned in official capacity, knowing how to found plateaus, with factories, mansions, hospitals, nurseries, and all places required in heaven for the newborn, so that God only had to say: Do this, or that; and it was done, and without error.

10/8.13. And now, five hundred thousand etherean volunteers from the hosts of Aph, Son of Jehovih, came before God; and they desired to remain two hundred years with God and his hosts.

10/8.14. God (Neph) said to them: Behold, the earth has passed Tryista, and it is no longer lawful for any but earth-born to hold the places of sub-Gods, sub-Lords and marshals; and since you are raised from different stars, and from different etherean circuits, what shall I do that you may be honored, and also profitable to yourselves in development?

10/8.15. Gaitivaya, chief spokesman for them, said: We desire only to be laborers. For what is two hundred years to us? Appoint us, we pray, not to the I'hins, for they are already advanced, but appoint us to the natives in the divisions of the earth, especially to those who speak only a little, and who burrow in the ground. Nor do we desire a place in your heaven, but we will abide with mortals, and in the first resurrection of those who are born in darkness.

10/8.16. God said: You shall remain, and your people with you. For, since you have volunteered to leave your high estate to come and dwell for one dan[299] on the lowest of all places, laboring for the blind and dumb,[300] you shall be recompensed with the love of millions in time to come.

10/8.17. Then God departed, and Aph, Son of Jehovih, went with him, and they came into the middle of the kingdom of God, where they halted, and God said: Here I will build my throne; and, as Sethantes, in the ancient time, called his place Hored, so will I also call my place Hored; and on the earth it shall be called the Mountain of God, for it shall be my home.

10/8.18. So God stretched forth his hand to Jehovih, saying: Throne of Your throne, O Father! And from the heavens above a great light came down and settled in the place of God and Aph, Jehovih's Son; and presently, the light gathered up from the atmospherea, substance, and made it shining and condensed, at which point, the attendants of such matters brought and laid the throne of God, and then fenced it around with pillars of fire, like Hored of the ancient days.

10/8.19. And God ascended and sat on the throne, and Aph also, sitting at the right hand of God, and the four Lords of the earth at the left hand; but the fifth Lord, Eolait, stood down at the foot of the throne. And he said: Behold, the division of the earth that was mine is sunk beneath the sea; how, then, shall I sit on the throne of God?

10/8.20. God said: Since your labor has been taken from you, you are a parable[301] on the newly dead, who have lost the earth, but have no place in heaven. Since the es'yan serves a time through the proxy[302] of others, so shall you, in that which I will bestow upon you. Know, then, that you shall sit at my right hand, for you shall be my assistant and Vice-God during the time of my sojourn;[303] and after that, whatever you will.

10/8.21. Eolait said: You have honored me, O God! Jehovih's will be done! So God rose up, raising his hand, and said: O You All Light, crown Your Son: Vice-God of Hored; for Your Own Glory, forever!

10/8.22. And as the light of etherea descended into God's right hand, he shaped it into a crown and placed it on Eolait's head, with the usual ceremony of such rank in heaven. And Eolait came and sat at the right hand of God. And in that same moment, Aph, Son of Jehovih, rose up; at which point, God, the Lords, and all others whatsoever, sat down, for the place was as if Jehovih had appeared in person.[304] Aph said:

---

[299] 200 years in this instance

[300] those unable to speak; the inarticulate

[301] counterpart, symbolic equivalent, a narrative

[302] agency, auspices, action, means

[303] referring here to the duration of God's administration

[304] This doesn't mean that the people mistook Aph for Jehovih, Who, after all, cannot be seen in form of man, but that the feeling in the place was

10/8.23. As a father is made to comprehend his own early life by looking upon his infant son, so have You, O Jehovih, forever raised up before my eyes the images of times and conditions long past. In these, Your Lords, You have called me back to the time and place when You and Your Son first crowned me a Lord and a Vice-God over one of the divisions of my native star.

10/8.24. And my soul rose up to You in fear and prayer; for I understood how unmindful mortals and angels are of the labor of Gods and Lords, and prone to rate themselves as Chiefs of all created things. But Your Voice, O Jehovih, came to me, saying: Do not complain, My Son, against the self-conceit of mortals and angels, nor of their criticisms of My Gods and Lords; for to such boasters I provide trials, which they do not perceive till they are encompassed by them. Suffer them,[305] therefore, to grow in their own glory within your dominions, for I have sufficient labor for them, either on earth or in heaven.

10/8.25. And I perceived Your wisdom, so I applied it through my angels; and when my people rose to the first resurrection, and the second resurrection, behold, I knew where to place them so that they could prove themselves all in all. And Your light came upon me in my place, saying: As you have profited in the first lesson, so shall you comprehend the second, and even up to the etherean heavens.

10/8.26. Nevertheless, O Father, You allowed all things to harass me and perplex my soul; and I was filled with fear and reverence because of the great responsibility You gave into my keeping. So great were my tribulations and trials that I called out to You in Your holy place to remember all other Gods and Lords in Your whole universe.

10/8.27. And You said: Hear the words of Your Creator, My God, My Son: For I created man to enter heaven as helpless as he entered earth life, and dependent on those above him, so that he might comprehend the unity between high and low, strong and weak, light and darkness; and I placed him in My mills, where he would learn that even as others grind for him, so should he grind for those beneath him.

10/8.28. For of what profit under the sun is it for My Lords to come down from their liberty and glory in My etherean firmament, and become Lords over the grovelers[306] in the flesh, or over the es'yans in darkness? Shall selfishness reign in heaven, and every one for himself? Have I not proved it on the earth that the love of doing good works to others is all that ensures a rich harvest of love in return?

10/8.29. Because they stoop from their high estate in order to promote My children whom I created alive, are they not becoming more one with Me? Even so is all exaltation in heaven; for as I stoop down to the dumb earth and water, and quicken them, making man, so have I stooped lower than anything can in all My universe. And those who follow My example, raising the low to make them have joy in life, are on the road to attain to all power, wisdom and love. ||

10/8.30. Aph, Son of Jehovih, said: I perceived Your wisdom, O Father; and Your power and wisdom came upon me tenfold. Then I sought forever after to go to the lowest and darkest places; but, lo, when I had grown in Your judgment, You spoke again to me, saying:

10/8.31. O Aph, My Son, because you have found the key to unlock the doors to the highest heavens, behold, you are too mighty for small labor. Come, therefore, with Your Creator, for I have a whole etherean world to be at your command, and your wisdom and power are required at My hand.

10/8.32. And I obeyed Your call, O Jehovih. And then, after a season, You called me again, and again, and made my labors extend into many etherean worlds. But I loved to look back and glorify You for my first Lord-dom, and to treasure the millions of loves I found in those days. And again, O Father, You have blessed me to meet many millions of them in this pruning of the red star, the earth.

10/8.33. Now You have called me to speak on the throne of Your God of earth. Alas, Your God has said: O Aph, Son of Jehovih, come and honor my throne! Whereas, O Jehovih, I am the most

---

such, that the presence of Jehovih was strongly felt when Aph stood up.

[305] bear the burden of them, allow them, permit them

[306] given to base pleasures; those who thus grovel

honored of men and Gods because I have again opened my mouth before You and in Your name. All glory to You, O Jehovih, now and forever!

10/8.34. Then Aph, Son of Jehovih, sat down, and God signaled the marshals, who proclaimed freedom for two whole days. At which point, the Gods and Goddesses of Aph's staff filed past the throne, and after them came the hosts of God, and then the hosts of the Lords, for they all desired to pass near and look upon Aph, and receive the signal of his blessing.

10/8.35. And afterward, all the people joined in with the es'enaurs in singing a song of glory to Jehovih, the All Highest. And when it was finished, the multitude turned to recreation and social intercourse.

CHAPTER 9 Aph

10/9.1. When the time came, God called his proper officers, and they proclaimed his presence, and the people came to order. Then God said:

10/9.2. Even as it was before the submersion, so shall it be now, and you shall fill the same places as before, every one to the place provided. Nevertheless, from this time forward, all work in heaven and on earth shall be new, and as if nothing had been. Let my Lords, their attendants and ashars, prepare for their departure; and they shall receive, as they desire, from other volunteers who have come into my kingdom, and these shall be assigned to labor suited to them, whether it be with mortals or with spirits in the first resurrection.

10/9.3. And to my marshals, messengers and asaphs: Hear the word of your God, which is that you proceed throughout atmospherea, selecting and appropriating all suitable places for the spirits of the dead; and that you apportion builders and workmen, and erect factories, schools, hospitals, nurseries, and all other suitable places, adapted to receiving those of the first resurrection, as is done in all atmospherean heavens. And all who are thus received shall be called es'yans for the first five years; but after that, they shall be called es'seans, signifying having separated from corporeal desire, being full residents of the es world. But those who will not become es'seans, being the spirits of druk-mortals and hard bound to the earth, shall be called druj, signifying wandering spirits of darkness and of evil; and those who engraft themselves on mortals shall be called fetals, signifying sucklings, and these names shall continue in heaven and on earth to the end of the world.

10/9.4. Where you may perceive the fault of leniency of the Gods and Lords of old, you shall be circumspect[307] in these times; for never again shall the rod of water chasten the living earth.

10/9.5. When God completed giving all his commandments, and the people were ready to depart, the es'enaurs and trumpeters sang and played a hymn adapted to the new heaven and new earth; and when this was finished, Aph, Son of Jehovih, spoke, saying:

10/9.6. Behold the light of the high heaven opens. Your Son, O Jehovih, longs for a great labor. I go on a journey farther than ten thousand suns. Fiatisi, Your Daughter, O Jehovih, and Goddess of a thousand worlds, has set apart (scheduled a time) to join two corporeal stars in a far-off heaven, on which a billion shall be delivered into spirit life in a single day. With her, by Your Will and Power, O Jehovih, I go! But yet do not let these, Your Gods and Lords and all their hosts, surmise[308] I will forget one single soul of all who are here. And when the next dan appears, behold, I will return to them to enjoy a portion of their sweet love. Aph is done.

10/9.7. And now the Chief descended and sat at the foot of the throne, and God, suffused with tears, came down and took his hand, saying: Behold, he who is greatest makes himself least of all. Arise, O Aph, Son of Jehovih, and crowned IMMORTAL GOD OF THE ARC OF NOE, SON OF THE ALMIGHTY, arise and go your way.

10/9.8. So Aph rose up, and shaking hands with God and his Lords, descended to the borders beyond the foot of the pillars of fire, and his hosts with him, being ten million in number, where the proper persons had in readiness an ascending otevan with wings, into which they all entered.

10/9.9. At a given signal the otevan started upward, but toward the east, and, swift as a

---

[307] mindful of all the circumstances of the matter, prudent, painstaking, careful, on guard, diligent

[308] be of the opinion that, conjecture, speculate, suppose, feel, think, believe, imagine

shooting star, it sped forth, and presently disappeared in the distance.

CHAPTER 10 Aph

10/10.1. Jehovih said: Neph, My Son, God of earth, hear the voice of Your Creator. For as you called on Me in your sore hour of trial, so did I come to you and deliver the earth and heaven, through My Son of the arc of Noe in etherea. Remember now the upraised of Hautuon, heaven of darkness, in Uk'loo, in the firmament, for they are yours until the next dan appears on the earth.

10/10.2. God said: I have heard Your voice, O Jehovih; but what shall Your servant do? Behold Aph, Your Arc-Son, has left the upraised children of darkness with Gods and Goddesses, who transcend Your servant so much in wisdom and power, that he can scarcely look upon them. How, then, shall it be with me, Your servant?

10/10.3. Jehovih said: Nevertheless, the upraised children of darkness are your own family, and the glory of your house in heaven shall be the light you shall make manifest in them. Do not fear, the Gods and Goddesses understand this matter.

10/10.4. Therefore, when you have put your kingdom in order, and established the heaven of the earth in all its parts, and stationed messengers between your throne and the thrones of your Lords on the earth, behold, you shall leave your Vice-God to rule in your place for a season, and you shall go to Hautuon, in the etherean forests, for you shall be expected by them.

10/10.5. God said: Your will be done, O Father. I perceive Your wisdom, glory and justice. Now I will sojourn on my throne one year, and then you, my Vice-God, shall relieve me while I go visit my rebellious children in Uk'loo, where Gods and Goddesses are overseeing them.

10/10.6. The Vice-God said: Your will be done, God of heaven and earth. So it came to pass that in one year, God had established heaven so well that he could control the affairs of angels and men into the way of everlasting life.

10/10.7. God informed his Council, which consisted of five hundred thousand etherean men and women, of the words of Jehovih, adding:

10/10.8. And I will stay one year in Hautuon, so that I may become known to them whom I have raised up. But at the end of that time I will return here, bringing back as many new volunteers from there as Jehovih may command.

10/10.9. It was known in heaven that God would leave at the proper time; and, to honor him in Jehovih's name, ten million of his hosts came from far and near to see him depart. And when God saw them, he proclaimed a day of recreation; and the people mingled together, and especially to re-converse on the matter of the deliverance of earth and heaven and the going down of Pan, as it had been.

10/10.10. On the following day, all hands being refreshed and assembled in order, according to the discipline of Gods, God spoke from the throne, saying:

10/10.11. Hear the words of your God, and rejoice in the founding of a new heaven. Be wise in heeding that which I shall utter, and make yourselves steadfast in all proven things.[309] Here are millions who stood by my side in the name of the Creator, in the days of darkness in heaven and earth. For three thousand years our battle lasted; and from out of the darkness, behold our prayers went up to Him Who is over and above all.

10/10.12. And your God said: Surely Jehovih will deliver when the vortex merges into Hi'dan; and you all repeated the same thing; and the unity of our souls' desire reached up to the Orian Chiefs, Jehovih's mighty Sons and Daughters.

10/10.13. For, as it is proven that a man in conflict with himself accomplishes nothing, while he who is in harmony with himself is mighty when he rules himself to a good purpose; so has it been proven that the unity of many angels can, by force of their own wills, control the place and proceedings of a world. And by your faith in this matter with your God, you became a star of faith in Jehovih, which is the mastering of all things to His glory.

10/10.14. And those who were without an All Highest in Person,[310] were without power, and of no effect, except to build up discord to our

---

[309] That is, be aware of, objective about, and supportive of that which has proven wise (so as to best sustain and advance the system and order of this kingdom and its resurrections).

[310] meaning the 'All Highest conceived of' is a Person and is always here In Person (being the Everpresence of Jehovih)

proceedings. While those who assumed to be Gods and Lords, but ignored Jehovih, were not sustained; for having nothing higher than themselves, they rose only to themselves.

10/10.15. Which is manifested on earth, even as it was in those days in heaven: boasting of good works or of good prayers, but housing themselves about with the earnings of others.[311] Did these false Gods and false Lords not set up self and worship it? And the fruits of their inspiration, and of their slaves under them, were the angels they sent to rule over mortals, for the glory of their philosophy. And so mortals of themselves also soon said the same things, which were: Behold, there is no God nor Lord of wisdom in heaven and earth.

10/10.16. And by that means, the doctrines of the false Gods and Lords overturned even their own kingdoms, changing heaven into hada.[312] But when the Light of Jehovih came, you and your God and Lords were one with His voice. For which reason, you have been preserved in victory. And now it has come to pass that your God and Lords have established a new heaven and new earth for the glory of the Father. And he[313] who labored so long in your love, now goes to the other wing of the battle, where your brothers and sisters, toiling with those in darkness, will rejoice to hear of your fruitful labors.

10/10.17. Then God turned to his right, and said to Eolait, Vice-God of Jehovih: Because you were robbed of your division of the earth, even while you were doing good work, Jehovih has bestowed [314] you well. You shall, therefore, hold the triangle of the Gods of heaven until your God returns.

10/10.18. With that, God hung the triangle on Eolait's neck, saying: In Jehovih's name, ALL HAIL, GOD OF HEAVEN AND EARTH? The hosts of millions responded: ALL HAIL, GOD OF HEAVEN AND EARTH!

10/10.19. And God (Neph) came down and sat on the foot of the throne, in the custom of Gods. And he who had been anointed came down and took his hand, saying: Arise, O God, and go your way! And God rose up, and the two, with their marshals and attendants, went down to the borders, at the line of the pillars of fire, where the proper persons had ready a ship with mantles and curtains; and God with his host of five hundred thousand, entered the ship.

10/10.20. Meanwhile the es'enaurs sang an appropriate anthem of GLORY TO JEHOVIH THE HIGHEST.

10/10.21. At a given signal the ship started upward, amid the applause of millions of angels assembled; and like a star it shot upward, higher and higher, till it was seen no more.

CHAPTER 11 Aph

10/11.1. The Council of Hored being still in session, God (Eolait), ascended the throne. And the light of Jehovih fell upon God, so that he was almost obscured from sight, and the voice of Jehovih spoke, saying:

10/11.2. Hear My voice; as by My Presence and of My Own Self I made each self, and gave to each, power of words, so am I in Light manifest by soul words to My etherean hosts. O Lords of earth, as you have provided ashars, and above them asaphs, and between all My kingdoms allotted messengers, so shall you also for barbarians provide familiar spirits, who shall be subject to the order of the ashars and their Lords.

10/11.3. I create alive all mortals, whether I'hins or barbarians; and your labor shall be not only with My chosen, whom it is easy to save, but also with those who do not know Me or My es worlds. For besides those destroyed by the flood, behold, the earth is still covered over with men, women and children.

10/11.4. In the time of Aph you received volunteers from Osi, in etherea; place this matter into their hands. ||

10/11.5. This was done, and they were divided up into groups. Then, since the angels of heaven had already numbered the corporeans, the ethereans were distributed accordingly. And these ethereans selected and apportioned familiar spirits to abide with the barbarians. And these familiar spirits were the fathers, mothers and friends who had recently died, but still sojourned in the first resurrection. So the officers provided places on earth for these spirits and persuaded them to

---

311 This is an abstract form of vampirism.

312 atmospherean regions of darkness, being comparatively darker than that to which it is being compared

313 God referring to himself

314 recompensed, rewarded, honored, blessed

reappear before mortals in order to prove continued life; but the officers never showed themselves.

10/11.6. Jehovih has said: Provide the way, but cause the familiars to do the labor. Neither shall you make a familiar of the spirit of a young man or a young woman, lest they become fetals.

10/11.7. So it came to pass that a new department of heaven and earth was opened and founded during the absence of Neph, and in one year it was prosperous.

10/11.8. At the end of one year God returned from the Hautuon Colony, bringing with him five million volunteers, who were of the third resurrection. And, it being known in Hored when he would return, a great concourse of angels gathered together to receive him in honor, and to welcome the volunteers.

10/11.9. So that, when God's etherean star descended, the Vice-God, Eolait, proclaimed a recreation of ten days, which was to follow immediately after God ascended the throne and regained his presence. And so, while the es'enaurs were singing, the star alighted, and the marshals and hosts of honor proceeded to their places, and received God, who, at once, ascended the throne and saluted Eolait, Son of Jehovih, saying:

10/11.10. By Your Will and Power, O Jehovih, Your Son[315] rejoices in the time of this proceeding. Eolait said: Welcome, God of heaven and earth. And he saluted with the sign of Jehovih's name, and was answered in like manner.

10/11.11. Without further ceremony, he took off the triangle of the Gods and placed it on God's neck, saying: In Jehovih's name, receive the gift of the ancient Gods.

10/11.12. Hardly had this been accomplished when the larger star-ship alighted on the floor of the Congress, before the Council, and near the altar of Jehovih; and the five million volunteers alighted, amid the applause of the many millions assembled.

10/11.13. God, being reinstated, said: Let the marshals proclaim ten days of recreation. For we shall account to our special loves how we found matters in Hautuon, and of the power of Jehovih manifested.

[315] this is God (Neph) referring to himself

CHAPTER 12 Aph

10/12.1. The voice of Jehovih spoke through God, saying: Because a new heaven is established, and because the old has been raised up, let signs be manifested, by which mortals and angels in later ages may know what has happened. Otherwise it shall come to pass, that mortals and angels will forget the flood and the purging of the earth. Consider now, O Gods and Goddesses, what shall be done?

10/12.2. Eolait spoke on behalf of the Council, saying: What shall we do, O Jehovih? And Jehovih answered, saying: Because I come near the earth in its early days, and farther off as it grows older, men will say: Alas, the folly of the ancients! || For I gave fear and faith as a heritage when men were weak in judgment; but with the growth of wisdom, I take away fear and the substance of things not proven to the judgment.

10/12.3. Jehovih said: In kosmon, men and angels shall ask for proofs. One will say: How is it possible to relate (report) the words spoken in the distant past? Another will say: How can it be proven that the old heaven was taken away?

10/12.4. Hear, therefore, the words of your Creator; and when one says: Behold, in those days few men had the gift of words and speech, answer him, saying: Yes, and heaven was the same way; because they did not have words, they could not be made to understand.

10/12.5. And another shall say: The Creator rules in large matters, but not in the small;[316] and another shall say: Because the angels come in kosmon, so could they have come in the distant past.[317] And you shall answer them, saying: Who

[316] For example, He creates the universe, but does not trifle Himself with causing a flood on some small planet; or, granting that, He may have made the world and made the flood to destroy the wicked, but He would not trifle Himself with words and languages of mortals.

[317] That is, the argument would seem to be: Since the familiar spirits in kosmon knew little more than mortals; and of heavenly matters, what they did impart was contradictory to one another; then would not the angels manifesting to mortals in that bygone era also have manifested similarly? And since the angels in kosmon came as familiars

knows the plan of an earthquake, whether it is small or large before Jehovih? Is He not ever present? And do certain conditions not bring certain results? And they will answer: Yes.

10/12.6. Say to them: Give, then, a name to the Highest Cause beyond all research; and they will say: By the ancients called Jehovih. And they shall perceive they have entangled themselves in a net. For if the condition of ignorance on earth begot ignorance in heaven, how could the light of heaven come afterward to the earth except from above (from a higher heaven of enlightenment, i.e., from etherea)? Since, then, the light of heaven came from above, who else could have invented the wisdom of a flood to come upon the speech of diverse nations?[318]

10/12.7. Give them, therefore, words in heaven and words on earth, pertaining to matters of this nature, and make these sounds sacred, so that it shall be proven in Jaffeth, Shem, Ham, Guatama, and in the heavens belonging to these lands. The voice of Jehovih ceased.

10/12.8. God said: You are All Wisdom, O Jehovih! Now I have a place for the new volunteers who came from etherea. For, this shall be their matter and business with the familiars who dwell with the barbarians. So, accordingly, they were allotted. And they were enjoined[319] to sing to mortals the song of the flood; and they thus established its history to endure forever on earth.

CHAPTER 13 Aph

10/13.1. All things prospered in heaven for many years; neither were there great wars on earth, nor famines, nor epidemics. And the Lords of the earth had sufficient loo'is for all the Faithists, so as to control I'hin marriages to bring forth sons and daughters who would rejoice in heaven.

10/13.2. And as fast as they died on the earth, these angels were carried to heavenly places suited to them, where they were handed into the care of asaphs and entered as es'yans. But the Lords appointed no loo'is over the barbarians; and only commanded the ashars to watch for their spirits in the hour of death, and, if possible, to bring them to the organic places of God in Hored; and mostly they were. This continued for many years; but eventually the familiar spirits aroused the barbarians, and they began to have dreams and see visions, for their familiars talked to them during sleep. And when this became common, Jehovih said:

10/13.3. Behold, the time has come to appoint loo'is to abide with the barbarians. For in this I will reveal a great secret, which is that My chosen on earth cannot subdue it; for they are a harmless and defenseless people. Therefore, I have wisely created the barbarian; for he shall drive away and destroy all evil beasts and serpents; and the forests shall fall down before him.

10/13.4. For this purpose, the loo'is shall select marriages with the intent of raising up great kings and queens. But, since in the old days, the kings depended on the prophets of God for counsel, and thus were advised against killing anything I had created alive, and they quarreled with God's prophets, so in this time of the new heaven, you shall permit the kings and queens to consult the

---

with only enough power to prove their existence after death, then the angels in the time of the flood were no more powerful nor advanced. Thus, angels labor in small matters, but not in the large. But even if they could plant words into mortals regarding a flood—on the large scale of things, why would it matter? Why bother with trivia?

[318] In summary, mortals did not make up the story of the flood because at the time of the flood they had neither the speech nor knowledge to make up the story of diverse nations undergoing a flood simultaneous to all.

Indeed, if earth was covered with animal-like humans who spoke in grunts punctuated with an occasional simple word, how could they spread tales of a worldwide flood, much less give a reason for it? How would they even know about the diverse nations of earth? How much less then, could they have perceived the wisdom of needing a flood?

Neither could the report have come from the lower heavens of the time, for they were also filled with the dumb. Therefore knowledge of the flood was passed down to mortals by angels from a higher heaven. Nor is it otherwise understandable that the nations under question all had the same explanation.

[319] instructed, commissioned, commanded

spirits of the dead with the talents I have given them.

10/13.5. This was done also; and the barbarians were attended by familiar spirits, many of whom took upon themselves any name pleasant to the ear, some of them calling themselves God or Lord, or after the name of some great king of the past. And these familiars, being stupid,[320] supposed themselves to be such persons.

10/13.6. The result of their stupid impressions was to inspire the barbarians to believe they were attended by Gods or Lords, or by the spirits of kings or queens; and so they held up their heads and began to think. For as it had been said by the Gods of ancient times: Some are led by flattery, some by self-conceit, some by duty, some by love of righteousness; but there are others who can be led to self-improvement by persuading them they are specially chosen by some God or Lord, or the spirit of a famous king or queen, to work wonders.

10/13.7. God said: There was a certain sick man who could not be cured by the physicians; and a foolish woman came along, seeing visions, and said to the sick man: Tomorrow you shall be healed. God has been trying you; but you have proven yourself in soul, and your God will withdraw the spell of your infirmity; behold, your God stands beside you.

10/13.8. Now on the following day, the sick man put forth his own spirit, rose up and was well; for which reason, it has been acknowledged that even deceit may accomplish what truth could not. Allow, then, the familiars to lead the barbarians on for a season, but be watchful, and at the proper time appoint new spirits to be with them.

10/13.9. God said: Instruct the Lords that the time has now come to reveal to mortals, especially to the I'hins, the seven tetracts; for, as the ashars are withdrawn a pace, so shall mortals advance a pace.

10/13.10. Which is to say: These are the inheritances of all men born on the earth: ANASH, which is persistent stubbornness, by word or thought; ZIMMAH, wicked device; RA, delight in being bad; BELYYAAL, worthlessness; AVEN, vanity and self-conceit; DIBBAH, slander and reporting of evils; and SA'TAN, to be a leader, and especially to the delight of the other six entities.

10/13.11. These are the members of the beast of all men and women under the sun; nor is any one without them in some manner or degree. Go, therefore, to the Lords and say to them: Jehovih has set the beginning of the resurrection through Aph, His Son, Chief of the arc of Noe, to lay the tetracts on the shoulders of mortals.[321]

10/13.12. The marshals of the Council provided messengers who were immediately sent down to the different divisions of the earth; for the tetracts were some of the words selected in heaven to be given as everlasting names, by which, in after ages, the tribes of Faithists could be discovered; and they were given alike to the Faithists of Guatama, Jaffeth, Shem and Ham, who were the sons of the arc of Noe preserved on the earth in that day. For these words, inherited by the Hebraic, Vedic and Algonquin languages, were provided to be synonymous till the coming of the Kosmon era.

CHAPTER 14 Aph

10/14.1. The voice of Jehovih came to God, saying: Behold, the time draws near when Aph, My Son, shall commit the care of Hored and her affairs to another God, for four hundred years. This, then, is the commandment of your Creator, O God: Hored shall advance to the second resurrection; but the first resurrection shall be established with My Lords.

10/14.2. And when the Lord has a sufficient number of souls who are advanced to take the second resurrection, then they shall be brought to this, My holy place, where they shall be further prepared, even for the next resurrection.

10/14.3. This was accomplished. And for the first resurrection, heavenly kingdoms with thrones for the Lords were established, both on the earth

[320] When Oahspe uses the word 'stupid' it is not in the pejorative (belittling, disparaging) nor derisive (abusive) sense, so common today, but refers to those in a mental and spiritual stupor, being dull and slow witted, generally devoid of wisdom and lacking much spiritual intelligence or mental acumen.

[321] And the mortals shall be made aware of the tetracts and learn to take responsibility for them. All, whether as mortals or angels, must transcend these expressions of the beast in order to inherit the higher heavens.

and also in the divisions of the Lords. Thirty-three years were allotted to these Lords' kingdoms for a resurrection, because thirty-three is the division of dan corresponding to one hundred dans to each cycle.[322]

10/14.4. Accordingly, every thirty-three years after that, there was one migration of a group from the Lord's first resurrection to that of Hored, which was God's second resurrection. In accordance with that, the light of dan fell on two hundred years, four hundred years, five hundred years, six hundred years and one thousand years, which became the base of prophecy for each cycle from that time forward, for a long period.

10/14.5. God said: Close the gates of Hored, and from this time forward, only those of the second resurrection may enter. And it was so. And God extended Hored over Jaffeth, Shem and Ham, to the second degree; but of Guatama, her heaven was as follows: The Lord made two kingdoms, the first and second resurrections, and allotted the first to a proxy in his own name, but over the second he presided in person, teaching his people by proxy of God in Hored. For the distance of the sea lay between these heavens, and the access could not be made in the diminutive light of thirty-three. Nevertheless, the Lord and his attendants maintained an etherean ship that enabled him to cross the sea at intervals of eleven years.

10/14.6. Accordingly now, in the second resurrection, new colleges were established in heaven, and the spirits began the study of elements and illustrations in es and uz,[323] and the process of travel and of carrying corporeal entities. And these spirits were at times, under ashars, taken down to mortals to assist in miracles and legerdemain.[324] For the lessons in the second resurrection embraced the mastery of corpor in analysis and synthesis.

10/14.7. After the first year of God in Hautuon, he went there every eleventh year and remained one year of the earth's time; so that in two hundred years he made eighteen visits. Now on his first visit he brought back with him a certain number of volunteers, who had been those raised by the arc of Noe; and the next visit he brought back twice as many as the first; and the next time, three times as many as the second, and increasing for each of the eighteen visits. And with the last visit, it was estimated that in total he had brought back one billion volunteers. And they were raised to the second resurrection, having been under the training of the Gods and Goddesses of Hautuon, under the direction of Aph, Son of Jehovih.

10/14.8. And now that the time of dan was drawing near, and Aph was expected to return to provide for the ascent of Jehovih's harvest, God looked up with a cheerful heart; for it was evident that by the expiration of the two hundred years from the submersion of Pan, many of the spirits delivered from the earth in that day would be prepared to take the second resurrection. And on that, God prophesied, saying: Through You, O Jehovih, in another hundred years I shall have delivered them into etherea as Your Brides and Bridegrooms.

CHAPTER 15 Aph

10/15.1. Jehovih spoke in the light of the throne of God in Hored, saying: Behold, a star comes!

10/15.2. The voice ceased, but God and his hosts knew the meaning, for it was the time for Aph to return and complete his deliverance of Neph and his hosts, and his Lords and their hosts.

10/15.3. So the Council members were moved to look into the firmament; and the messengers who had heard the voice, and who were departing on their various missions, also looked upward, even as they sped forth to their places; and they proclaimed it in all the heavens of the earth, and to the Lords and their divisions of the earth.

10/15.4. And the angels of heaven and those who resided with mortals, were stirred up, and because of their contiguity[325] to mortals, the latter comprehended that something unusual was about to happen.

---

[322] 33 x 100 = 3300; i.e., 3300 years would seem to be the ideal dan'ha length, while 3000 years is the average length.

[323] For example, illustrating the properties of an element in the spirit world (es), then condensing it to corpor and examining its properties, and then dissolving (uz) the element back to es (its atmospherean form).

[324] magic, sleight of hand, conjuring of things, etc.

[325] proximity; closeness; contact

10/15.5. The Council of Hored did not know how they should proceed, for the event was to surpass in magnificence anything they had ever witnessed.

10/15.6. God said: I have heard Your voice, O Jehovih. I know a star comes, and its glory shall be great. Give me light, O Father. How shall Your servant know the decorum[326] of Orian Chiefs? Behold, I am as one abashed with obscurity[327] in Your wide universe!

10/15.7. Jehovih's voice answered, saying: Do not fear, My Son. And let your Council be strong also. Proceed at once to decorate your people, in preparation for receiving the resurrection. And as to those who are to be My Brides and Bridegrooms, clothe them in white. ||

10/15.8. The whole Council heard Jehovih's voice, and they ordained officers to proceed throughout atmospherea and put in effect Jehovih's commandment. And the decorated angels, and those prepared as Brides and Bridegrooms for etherea, were ordered to form in companies near the throne of God in Hored; and the officers of companies were also provided with badges, on each of which was inscribed an account of their labor on earth and in heaven, the number and nature of their charities and self-sacrifices for others' good, and their grade in purity, power and wisdom. And the privates were decorated with stars to illustrate the same things, in degree and number; and the stations of their file[328] in Hored were provided in the order of music, rating them according to their chord and discord, and their social adaptability.

10/15.9. For these things were done before etherean judges, to whom Jehovih had said: Let the people pass before you so you may judge them, that being assorted and arranged, they shall make one harmonious whole; for it is only by this means that they will have power to ascend and endure in My regions of light. || There were one million of these judges, and they took up their stations in different parts of atmospherea, wherever the second resurrection had been established, every judge choosing a district for himself or herself, for they were both men and women.

10/15.10. And as the angels passed before them, the wisdom of the judges was so great that they could comprehend all each person had ever done, either on earth or in heaven. And by signals, the proper officers were advised how to decorate and adorn all of them.

10/15.11. And as fast as companies of one thousand passed, they were provided with conductors, who took them to their places, which had been previously determined by the command of God.

10/15.12. While this work was proceeding, lights began to appear in the firmament above; these were the marshals of the Orian fields in etherea, in their star-ships, taking course for Hored, and their number was legion.[329] But presently one brighter and more powerful than the rest made its way from the western arc of Onah'yi, and it steered directly to God's throne, growing brighter and larger as it came. And when it entered past Chinvat, and was well within the vortex of the earth, in the belt of the moon's orbit, its light spread across the whole atmosphere of heaven, and Hored was illuminated, and the angels of Hored were stirred up with enthusiasm.

10/15.13. The brilliant star did not prolong the suspense of the angel world, for he who sailed it was a God of millions of years; and by his wisdom, attained to such mastery that the elements of earth and atmospherea gave way, as if appalled by a heaven on fire. Down to the arena of the Council of Hored came the star-ship, whose majesty outweighed all ceremony, a very crown of magnificence. And he who came, attended by half a million, was Sue'ji, marshal for that which was soon to follow.

10/15.14. God rose up, saluting, and all the hosts rose up; at which, Sue'ji ascended the throne, greeted by God and his Council. Sue'ji said:

10/15.15. By Your will, O Jehovih! And God said: In Your name, O Father, Creator! Welcome to

---

[326] proper order and system, rites and ceremonies, standards of behavior, protocol, etiquette, proprieties; in other words, God wanted to know how to provide a reception suitable to Aph and his hosts

[327] abashed = humbled, humiliated, embarrassed; obscurity = a deficiency in light, a lack of light, relative darkness

[328] line, queue, array

[329] enormously large number; too large to estimate easily

Your Son! And presently all the place was aglow with a golden light, which, of all colors, ranks first in heaven, and the voice of Jehovih descended on Sue'ji, and He said:

10/15.16. Well beloved, come! Long enduring, come! Of patience and steadfastness, My sons and daughters! Behold, I came in the darkness and delivered Mi, for she was heavily laden with twins. And one dwelt with the mother, but the other I sent to nurse in Hautuon. And they are now grown to maturity, a son and daughter twin.

10/15.17. Turn to Hautuon: Lo, the twin comes! She was the puny child; but look upon her, O you Gods and Goddesses! Her billions come as an avalanche of ji'ay'an worlds. Open your arms, O My beloved sons and daughters.

10/15.18. The voice ceased, and Sue'ji said: When the harvest of Hautuon arrives, attended by the Gods and Goddesses who helped deliver the children of darkness, and who have changed them into beacons of light, behold, there shall be three days of recreation in atmospherea; for the hosts of Hautuon shall be shown their native world, and where they came from; and they shall read the lineage of kin and condition from which they were rescued by Jehovih's sons and daughters.

10/15.19. But on the first day, behold, Aph, the Orian Chief, will descend in all his glory. And on the fourth day all your upraised sons and daughters shall ascend into the etherean worlds, where there are waiting to receive you, trillions of souls, long since dwellers in Nirvania. Sue'ji ceased speaking, having given commands as to the stations of his marshals for the earth and her heaven.

10/15.20. God sent his messengers, saying: Go to Wak'hah and say: God says: My heavens have been numbered, and the account of my laborers rendered and recorded in the libraries of Hored. And of all the hosts who have labored with your God, behold, you, O Wak'hah, stand on the highest grade. Come, therefore, to the throne of your God and be anointed God of heaven and earth for the next four hundred years, and as long after that as Jehovih wills!

10/15.21. The messengers, attended by one thousand marshals, departed for Adjun, the place of labor where Wak'hah dwelt, being a physician's nurse for es'yans and still-born mortal children and those killed by abortion. And they delivered the message of God, to which Wak'hah replied: Thanks, O Jehovih! Tell God I will come. But first let me surmise: I have been all my life, now some thirty thousand earth years, trying to learn where I would be most serviceable to Jehovih and His sons and daughters. And when I judge that I have found it, lo, a summons comes from another direction, saying: Come here. And so it seems Jehovih forever hurries us onward, faster than our wisdom can discover the requirement. || So the marshals provided an otevan, and Wak'hah was conducted to Hored, even to the foot of the throne of God, where he was saluted and received under a rod with water, according to his rank.[330]

CHAPTER 16 Aph

10/16.1. Nearer and nearer came the visiting stars, the etherean ships from thousands of worlds, with countless millions of emancipated souls, dwellers in the Nirvanian regions of Jehovih. And when they reached the boundaries of the earth's vortex they halted a while, to form in ranks, so that their glory would add to one another. While they thus stood in the great vault of heaven, a gateway opened amid the stars on one side; and from far beyond came a strange and mottled sun, swaying to and fro; and this was the great fields and forests of Hautuon letting loose the billions of the delivered earth.

10/16.2. God and his hosts saw it. And every soul burst forth one universal shout of applause. It was coming straight to Hored. And as it came nearer, the curtains, sails and streamers, made of yellow, blue and red fire, began to wave and surge, like a ship in a rough sea, but steadily holding course in the undulating elements. Presently guardian ships could be seen, thousands and thousands, traveling beside the laboring sun, the hosts of Hautuon.

10/16.3. And the guardian ships were themselves like stars, and carried millions of etherean souls who had been Gods and Goddesses on many worlds; and they formed wings for the Hautuon avalanche, to hold steady the course to the

---

[330] Note here that rank is different from grade. For example, an angel may labor in a position of lower rank (a physician's nurse ranks lower than a physician, for example), and yet have a very high grade of service to others.

red star, the earth of mortals. And thus, in honored discipline, came the fleet of Jehovih's worshippers, who, only two hundred years before, were like vermin delving into darkness; deep buried in death, as their only knowledge; and to whom, Great Jehovih and His exalted worlds were unknown.

10/16.4. Brighter and brighter grew that great waving sun, sailed by the immortal Gods; growing larger and more imposing, till, when it entered the earth's vortex, it became like living fire, large as the earth, and of brilliant colors from black to adamant,[331] with blue, white, purple, yellow, scarlet, pink; of all shades; and living; and sparkling; with the broad curtains suspended, deep as the breadth of a world, and with sails and flags that reached upward, high as the moon.

10/16.5. Midway in the vortex of the earth it stopped; and the multitude of stars beyond, now gathered in, majestically, from every side, till nearly throughout the fabric of the earth's atmosphere, there was not a place that did not glow with Jehovih's fire of heaven. Music, which rose from the throne of God a little while before, now ceased; for here was the play of elements in harmony, which is the same as music to the ear of mortals.

10/16.6. The kaleidoscope of splendors hardly stood still, but kept moving, changing and forming by the decrees of the Gods and Goddesses; as a general on earth manipulates his armies, in the evolution of arms,[332] so in majesty and splendor, the marshaling stars constantly evolved new and glorious changes, stretching across the whole firmament of heaven.

10/16.7. And now another gateway opened amid the stars; and a cluster star was seen approaching from the southeast. It was like a star surrounded by stars, and brighter than all the others. This was the star-ship of Aph, the Orian Chief. At the sight of which, all souls in the firmament turned in pride and wonder. In the play and management of worlds, he had attained to be swift and mighty, above all the countless millions of Gods and Goddesses assembled. And at the sight of his etherean star, angels and Gods whispered: Aph! And the magic of his name, widely known in the Nirvanian fields of the emancipated heavens, spread abroad, till every soul uttered, APH! in all the regions of atmospherea and on the earth.

10/16.8. Nearer and nearer he came, nor did he stop at Chinvat, the boundary of the earth's vortex; but steadily, and with power, sailed on till his star stood in the doorway of heaven, and here halted as if to complete the immortal scene.

10/16.9. But a moment more, and all the avalanche of the glorious worlds around, moved onward toward the earth, surrounding it on every side, and with the star of Aph making headway for the throne of God in Hored.

10/16.10. This was the morning of the third day in the tide of dan, in which there were still four days left. But now the marshals took their parts. First, Sue'ji, Chief over all the rest, cried out from the throne of God: All hail, O Aph, Son of Jehovih! And the words were caught up on every side, and uttered in one breath around the world. All the while, the great star-ships and sun of Hautuon gathered in, nearer and nearer, till, like a net, they joined and filled the earth's atmosphere in the east and west and north and south, and below and above; on every side. And the words of the marshal: All hail, O Aph, Son of Jehovih! traveled like an echo over all the heavens.

10/16.11. Then Aph's fleet drew near; he and his hosts alighted, and he ascended the throne, saluting, saying: All hail, O Neph, God of heaven and earth! And this was also uttered by the millions of hosts. After which, the signs and ceremonies of the Gods were briefly concluded, and a recreation of three days proclaimed. So the angel hosts came forth out of their ships, or by the endless chain sped to any quarter of the earth they desired to visit. And for three days and nights the visitors dwelt on the earth and in the lower atmospherea; inspecting how the earth was made; its land and water; its mountains and valleys; its beasts of prey and beasts of burden; its birds and fishes, and, above all, its mortal people and spirits who lingered about the earth, the great story tellers, who knew no higher heaven. Then the visitors surveyed atmospherea and the works of God and his Lords, including their nurseries, hospitals, factories, schools and colleges.

10/16.12. On the fourth day the marshals called order; and so great was the discipline of the hosts and the arrangement of the starships, that in a

[331] sparkling, reflective, shiny clear like a diamond

[332] a set of disciplined and orderly movements in the field by military units

moment of time, order reigned among all these countless millions of people.

10/16.13. Now, during the recreation, the Chiefs from many worlds, as well as Gods and Goddesses, mingled together, and exchanged their varied experience in the wide regions of Jehovih's universe: of the management of both corporeal and es'ean worlds; of the cosmogony of etherean planets; the surveying of roadways; turning worlds from their orbital course, or changing their axial rotation; the deliverance of millions of souls into the ji'ay'an fields; the creation of new corporeal worlds and the dissolution of others, and the gathering together of the spirits disinherited, and of their final resurrection. Neither did there seem to be any end to Jehovih's universe, where such wonders go onward forever!

10/16.14. When order was restored, God commanded Wak'hah to rise to be anointed, and God said: In Your name, O Jehovih, I anoint this, Your Son, God of heaven and earth for the next four hundred years. Guide him in wisdom and love, O Father.

10/16.15. And God gathered from the abundance of eth'ic and made a crown and placed it on Wak'hah's head, saying: Hail God of heaven and earth, Jehovih's Son! This, in turn, was shouted by the hosts. Then God took off the triangle, the sam'gan, the heirloom of the Gods of the red star, the earth, and God hung it from Wak'hah's neck, saying: Take this heirloom, the symbol of three entities in one, and wear it for the glory of the Great Spirit, Jehovih.

10/16.16. To which Wak'hah, now God, answered: Your will be done, O Father, Creator and Ruler over all. And all on the throne stood aside, and God (Wak'hah) ascended the throne and sat in the center, at which time the es'enaurs chanted, and the hymn sounded around the whole earth. Then Aph, Son of Jehovih, spoke, saying:

10/16.17. In four hundred years, O God, I will come and deliver you and your harvest, and your Lords and their harvest, for the glory of Jehovih, the Unapproachable Almighty! Amen.

10/16.18. And now Aph went and sat down at the foot of the throne, at which, God came down according to custom, and took his hand, saying: Arise, O God, Son of Jehovih, and go your way! And Aph rose up, saluting, and he and his attendants departed and entered his star-ship. The es'enaurs chanted, the trumpeters played, and the solemn MARCH OF JEHOVIH'S SEA OF FIRE sounded from heaven and earth.

10/16.19. The marshals now put the great works in order: Neph and his attendants were stationed on the right of Aph in a ship newly built; next to him, the ships of his Lords and their attendants; after them, their marshals from the different divisions of the earth and atmospherea; next to them, the ships of the messengers; then the factors, then the nurses, then the physicians, and so on; and finally the divisions of earth-raised, who were now adjourned to the sun-avalanche, those raised from earth being of the same rank as those from Hautuon. These comprised the harvest of Neph for Jehovih's emancipated realms; and the number of souls exceeded all other harvests raised up from the earth.

10/16.20. And now came the time for the ascent, and Aph said: Give us of Your power, O Jehovih! And his words were echoed in all places in heaven and on earth. The plateaus trembled and oscillated. Again Aph said: Of Your power, O Jehovih! Arise, O Heaven! Arise, O Heaven!

10/16.21. And the plateaus of the sphere started from their foundations, and slowly moved back and outward away from the earth. The es'enaurs played the march; the ethereans tore off strips of fabric and threw them down to Hored, and then formed flowers and leaves and perfumed them, casting them out to fall in the lower heavens.

10/16.22. Outward, outward, moved the etherean world, then parted the breadth of the earth, and then rose slowly upward. Presently it turned on its own axis, up to now, one entire world; but with its rotation, the different stars began to individualize and separate, all except the harvest of Neph, which was the central figure, led onward and upward by Aph, Son of the Great Spirit.

10/16.23. Faster and faster rose the glorious scene, and more awe-inspiring, and sparkling with splendor! Nor could one from Hored scarcely look upon the dazzling light. But higher it rose, and onward, toward its far-off destiny, till it disappeared in the firmament above.

CHAPTER 17 Aph

10/17.1. Now atmospherea was like a new heaven, stripped of visitors and ready to resume labor after a glorious festival. So God at once dispatched all hands to their places, and the factories, schools, colleges, nurseries and hospitals, were once more alive with willing workers.

10/17.2. And Hored prospered in every department; and so did the departments of the Lords on earth; and mortals also prospered under the light of the Great Spirit.

10/17.3. For four hundred years God reigned in heaven, and his Lords under him, and the second dan of Aph fell upon earth and heaven. So God appointed AN'ON as his successor. And now Aph and his attendants came to deliver God, his Lords and those people prepared for their resurrection up into etherea.

10/17.4. And the number of Jehovih's harvest was one billion souls.

10/17.5. And God (An'on) reigned his time, and his Lords under him, and they were also delivered by Aph, but by proxy, and the harvest of Jehovih was eight hundred million souls.

10/17.6. And his successor, God of Hored and atmospherea, and his Lords fulfilled their dan, and they and their harvests were delivered by Aph's proxy also; and the number of souls delivered was six hundred million. And Jehovih commanded Aph to commit atmospherea and the earth to the successors of Ra'zan of Garowista, in Ems of the etherean phalanx of eighty Ar'doth.

10/17.7. The next harvest of God and his Lords was two hundred million souls. After that, the earth passed into the a'ji of Urk'stand for eight hundred years, and the light of the upper heaven was lost to earth and atmospherea; so there was no harvest for the etherean realms. And because of the darkness in atmospherea, it began to fall in hada; and the seven entities of tetracts took root in Hored, overspreading the dominions of God and his Lords. And many in heaven rose up, and, proclaiming themselves Gods or Lords, obtained followers, some to the extent of three million souls.

10/17.8. These false Gods made slaves of their followers, exacting service, and in return giving pitiful homes and regimen; and by the labor of their slaves, embellishing their mansions and cities in hada.

10/17.9. Jehovih had said of old: I keep death forever present before mortals so that they may not forget the change from corporeal to spirit life; otherwise they would dispute it possible for these things to be in My hands. But My resurrections in heaven are far apart, and its inhabitants lose faith in those above them. Through faith, all power and glory is attained; therefore I have exacted that angels cultivate faith in the next resurrection.[333] ||

10/17.10. But during the last thousand years in atmospherea, there being no resurrections to etherea, many fell into disbelief of the emancipated heavens, and so, began building up heavenly kingdoms on their own account, and for their own glory. And in order to have exalted kingdoms, they sent their slaves back to mortals to inspire them with the glory of their false God's kingdoms, so that others in turn might become slaves also.

10/17.11. So confusion began in heaven again, and it reacted on mortals, through the angels' presence, and war and misery spread over the nations and tribes of men on earth. Thus ended the cycle of Aph's arc of Noe, which was three thousand six hundred years.

END OF BOOK OF APH, SON OF JEHOVIH

The Lords' First Book

Being contemporaneous with the Book of Aph, Son of Jehovih. As the latter is of heaven, so is the Lords' Book of the earth.

CHAPTER 1 Lords' First

The History of the Flood

11/1.1. Hear me, O man, I am the Lord, the God of earth, Son of Jehovih! I am one of your elder brothers. I, your Lord, with my brother Lords and Gods, in the name of Jehovih, speak, saying:

11/1.2. Peace and patience to all men, so that you may comprehend my words, and bear witness that heaven and earth in every part is Jehovih's, and that all men and women are His sons and daughters, worlds without end.

11/1.3. As over mortal kingdoms, there are kings; as over empires, emperors; as over armies,

---

[333] That is, an angel is required to cultivate the faith that there will come a resurrection from those above.

generals; so has Jehovih in His heavens crowned certain chieftains for times and places, and given them certain names, by which they have been proclaimed to men and angels, so that the discipline of heavens could manifest the glory and dominion of Jehovih.

11/1.4. In all time, honored in high heaven, and known to the people on the earth as Jehovih's Lord, Commander of heavenly light on earth, and Pacificator between All Light and All Darkness, and titled LORD OF EARTH and LORD GOD, so have I and my predecessors, and my successors, been handed down for thousands of years among mortals.

11/1.5. So when it was said: The King said thus; and in after generations, if it is said: The King says thus; all men know it was not the same man, but was nevertheless The King, so I, the Lord, also proclaim the same thing of both my predecessors and successors; for all of them were, and have been The Lord.

11/1.6. For which reason, I, the Lord, by virtue of my own authority, and in Jehovih's name, proclaim the light and the darkness of the past. And as I have been exalted by the Father, so, too, are you all in waiting for your turn in the heavens above to become Lords and Gods and Goddesses.

11/1.7. To draw your souls up in heavenly aspirations, to become one with the Father in righteousness and good works, Jehovih sends His sons and daughters down to the earth, revealing the glory of His kingdoms in the etherean worlds.

11/1.8. But because of the darkness of man's soul, he sets himself up to mock the words of his Lord, saying: How can I become a Lord, or a God? Behold, his word has not been heard; none have written his speech.

11/1.9. Was it not so in all times on the earth? And because of this darkness among men, they have laid bare the iniquity of their own hearts. For out of the mouths of my chosen, who utter my words, come words of truth, love, wisdom, kindness, and the exaltation of virtue. But from those who deny me come corruption, war, avarice, [334] and the love of earthly things for self's sake.

11/1.10. Behold, they have quibbled about words and the meaning of words. One says: How much of this came from the Lord, and how much from the prophet? Making mathematicians of themselves on a matter separate from the subject of the righteousness of their own souls, which lies at the bottom[335] of God's desires.

11/1.11. Are not all words, at best, merely pictures and paintings for the spirit who finds them? And whether the Captain (Lord) or his private (angel) carry the light to the prophet, what does it matter to the man or woman who seeks to serve Jehovih by doing good works?

11/1.12. Some have said: Behold, I have given all I had to the poor, and I rise early and visit the sick; and in the night I sit up with them; and I gather up orphans and helpless ones, and make them so joyous of heart they thank Jehovih they are created into life. || Now, truly, all men know that such behavior comes from those who recognize my word, whether it comes from the mouth of a babe or the pen of a fool.

11/1.13. Who, then, shall not find delight in the word of the Lord? Do they not know that I am the same today, yesterday and forever? And in judgment, why will they not perceive that my word comes now as well as in the ancient times?

11/1.14. Behold, I am not for one man only, nor for one woman, nor for one book; but wherever the light of wisdom and the desire for virtue and holy deeds shine, there my speech will manifest. Is Jehovih not wide as the universe, and immutable? [336] And to be in harmony with Him, is this not the sum of all wisdom?

11/1.15. Therefore, if your Lord, or your God, has attained to be one with the Father, and he comes in dominion on the earth, with his millions of angels, who also know the higher light, and you are inspired by them to do Jehovih's will, what discussion shall man have against heaven or its representatives?

11/1.16. I declare freedom to all men in Jehovih's name, but with freedom I also give the experience of the Lords of earth. Permit, therefore, my prophets on all hands to embellish the pictures of the past in their own way; and to the extent that the pictures fortify faith in Jehovih and His Works, Power and Glory, be circumspect to desire nourishment from them. And rather than destroy that which is given in the name of Jehovih, go, and

---

334 greed, covetousness, insatiable preying

335 foundation, deepest part, core, base

336 permanent, persistent, stable, durable, certain

fall to work in like manner to build up His light in your own way.[337]

11/1.17. In this is wisdom; for those who strive for the light of my dominion shall receive my angels in my name; and by the words they find to express my commandments, they shall be known to be of me.

11/1.18. All words came from the Lord your God; by him, man was made upright on the earth. As the first race (Asu) went down into the earth, the second man rose up by my angels, becoming like Lords and Gods, and capable of knowing good and evil.

11/1.19. But as the light of a full grown man differs from that of a child's, so, in different degree, was the light of men; and those with the higher light were called Faithists, because they perceived that Wisdom shaped all things and ruled to the ultimate glory of the All One; but those of the lesser light were called Cain, the druk, because their trust was more in corporeal than in spiritual things.

11/1.20. And the Faithists were also called the chosen people, because they chose God, who is Lord over corpor; but the Cainites, the druks, were classed as enemies of the Lord, because they sacrificed by means of war and death, that which Jehovih made alive. And these two peoples have lived on the earth from the first, and even to this day.

11/1.21. And I, the Lord, Son of Jehovih, gave a certain commandment to man, saying: You shall love the Lord your God with all your soul, your wisdom and strength. But man had little strength in this matter; neither did I ask for more than he could give. And another commandment was: You shall not kill; which had man obeyed, there would have been no war in the world.

[337] That is, to the extent that they fortify faith in Jehovih, it is well to gain nourishment from the descriptions of the past; but take care to be judicious toward them. And if one discovers what seem to be errors, then instead of attacking or destroying, it is wiser to focus on that which one perceives to be the true nature of the past, and so build up Jehovih's light in one's own way, communicating (sharing) that light, as deemed wise.

11/1.22. In like manner I gave the light of heaven to all men, but my enemies perverted my words in order to justify themselves in sin. Yet the Father so dwells in man, that man can judge of truth and holiness. So if one man says: The Lord said, You shall not kill; and yet another man says: The Lord says, You shall kill; then let no man mistake which is of the Lord in fact. For the Lord does not make alive any man whom he desires to be killed.

11/1.23. And so, my word was perverted by man; and the little light which was not lost, man tried to obscure. Nevertheless, man multiplied and inhabited the earth over, building cities and nations, and prospering in certain seasons in all things earthly. But because my priority in coming to the earth was to develop the soul of man, and for his own ultimate happiness in the etherean worlds, I did not labor with those who did not heed me, but suffered them to go on in their own conceit. And they became divided against one another, and war, pestilence and diverse diseases came upon mortals, resulting in their further downfall.

11/1.24. And the spirits of those who denied me on earth, still denied me in heaven; and in their stubbornness and conceit, continued to dwell with man on the earth. So that in the course of time, the world was overrun by spirits of darkness who did not know heaven. And it came to pass that my enemies slew my chosen on all hands.

11/1.25. In four great divisions of the earth, Vohu, Jud, Thouri, and Dis (Africa, Asia, Americas, Europe) they did not leave one alive of the I'hin race. In Whaga (Pan) I had a remnant; and they were scattered far and near, in separate places hiding away from their evil pursuers.

11/1.26. I had said to them: Every living thing that grows up out of the ground shall be food for you; but everything within which is the breath of life, which is of blood and spirit, you shall not eat. Whoever sheds blood, in which is life, by that action invites his own blood and spirit to the spoil. In likeness of God, man was made heir[338] of the earth and all things on it.

11/1.27. Be fruitful and multiply; bring forth abundantly in remembrance of the Lord God of heaven and earth.

[338] inheritor; recipient of a heritage; beneficiary; given stewardship

11/1.28. And I gave the circumcision as a measure of the boundary of my chosen.

11/1.29. But there were giants (druks) in those days and in time after that; and my chosen came to them, and they bore children to them also. And their flesh became corrupt, so that vermin inhabited them from their birth to their death. And they became rotten in the head with catarrh; and in the throat with ulcers and running sores; and in the lungs and joints with the poison of death. And the offspring that was born to them came forth afflicted with the sins of their fathers and mothers, to linger in misery or to die in infancy.

11/1.30. And they thus peopled heaven with untimely births and with spirits of darkness, who, in return, came back and re-afflicted mortals.

11/1.31. And I said: I will destroy man from the face of the earth, for the flesh of man is corrupt; by the eating of flesh and unwise cohabitation he has corrupted his race upon the earth.

11/1.32. And I, the Lord, called to my chosen, who were persecuted and hidden away in the valleys and mountains, even on the tops of the mountains, in the land of Whaga.

11/1.33. And I said to them: Because you have kept my commandments, come forth and hear the word of the Lord your God. || And they came out from their hiding places, thousands and thousands of them. And I sent my angels to them, saying to my angels:

11/1.34. Say to my chosen: This is the word of the Lord your God: You have found favor in my sight, for of all that are on the earth, you alone have kept my commandments; and you have seen righteousness in the seed of your generations.

11/1.35. Go, therefore, and build enough ships for my chosen, and get within, where none can pursue or destroy.

11/1.36. For behold, I will bring a flood of waters upon the earth, even above the highest mountains; for I will destroy its corruption, and purge it of all uncleanness.

11/1.37. Take, therefore, food that is good to eat, and gather it into the ships; for the flood shall remain one hundred and fifty days, and you shall come forth and not find anything to eat.

11/1.38. And the angels of the Lord went to the Faithists in God and inspired them to build ships, both in the valleys and on the mountains; for two whole years they built them, and then they were completed.

11/1.39. And the angels of heaven numbered the ships, and there were one hundred and thirty-eight. And the ships stood on the mountains and in valleys; but of all the ships that had been built, not one stood near the waters.

11/1.40. And the earth stood in the arc of Noe in the firmament of heaven, in the place and grade of six hundred in the a'ji'an roads, twenty-four thousand years before kosmon.

11/1.41. And the Lord commanded the chosen to go into the ships; which they did; and in that same day the gates of heaven and earth were opened.

11/1.42. And the earth (that was Whaga) rocked to and fro, like a ship at sea; and the rains fell in torrents; and loud thunderings came up from beneath the floor of the world. And the sea came up on the land; first upon the valleys and then upon the mountains; so that the ships floated on the waters.

11/1.43. But the land was swallowed up, valleys and mountains; and all the living (on Whaga) perished, except the I'hins, who floated off in the ships.

11/1.44. And the Lord said: I numbered those who were saved, and there were twelve thousand four hundred and twenty; and these were all that remained of the first race of man that walked on two feet.

11/1.45. Behold, I will carry them to all the divisions of the earth, and people it anew with the seed of my chosen. ||

11/1.46. And Jehovih blew His breath upon the ships of His sons and daughters; blew them about upon the ocean; blew them to the east and west and north and south.

11/1.47. By the will of God, the ships were congregated into four fleets; thirty-four ships into each fleet, except two ships, which were carried together in a fleet by themselves.

11/1.48. The Lord said: I will name the fleets of my chosen, and their names shall be everlasting on the earth. And the Lord named them GUATAMA, SHEM, JAFFETH, HAM AND YISTA.

11/1.49. The Lord said: From these, my seed, I will people the earth over in all its divisions. And so that later generations, for thousands of years, may know the work of my hand, behold, I give them a sign, which is my covenant to them and their heirs forever:

11/1.50. Which is my crescent, in the form of a rainbow; and whatever people bear this, my sign, shall be a remembrance to me of my covenant. Nor shall they be destroyed from the inheritance that I have given to them.

11/1.51. And the chosen looked out of their ships; the sky was clearing, and a rainbow shone in the firmament; and by its light the land was found, where the Lord brought his people.

11/1.52. And in one hundred and fifty days from the beginning of the flood, the ships were brought into their respective places; for as the Lord destined them, so did they land in the different countries of the world.

11/1.53. The fleet named GUATAMA was carried eastward, and the country where it landed was also called Guatama.[339] The Lord said: From this place my chosen shall spread out north and south. But they shall not inhabit the lands to the east or west as far as the sea; for they shall be testimony in time to come, of this landing place from the continent of Pan.

11/1.54. God said: Permit my people to give names to the places where I lead them; for these names shall show in the Kosmon era, the work of my hand done in this day.

11/1.55. The fleet of two ships carried to the north was named YISTA, which in the Whaga tongue, was Zha'Pan, which is the same country that to this day is called Japan, signifying, RELIC OF THE CONTINENT OF PAN, for it lay to the north, where the land was cleaved in two.

11/1.56. And the Lord said to them: Behold, eight Hi'dan shall come and pass, and in that day, you shall be like a key to unlock the labors of heaven; for of all people you shall be reckoned the oldest in the world. And until I come and unlock the sea, you shall remain an exclusive people from all tribes and nations.[340]

11/1.57. Preserve, therefore, the names of my rites and ceremonies, and especially the names of land and water, and the firmament above, and ships that plow the water, and whatever sounds that man makes in the throat without the tongue and lips; for in the time of my glory on the earth you shall also be glorified. Preserve also peace, righteousness and industry, for you shall be a testimony in the later time, of the presence of my hand and of the Great Spirit also. Thus was Japan settled, and it continues to this day.

11/1.58. The fleet named JAFFETH was driven westward and north, and the country was called Jaffeth for thousands of years afterward, and is the same as that called Chine'ya (China) to this day.

11/1.59. The fleet named SHEM landed to the south, and the country was called Shem for thousands of years afterward, and is the same as that called Vind'yu (India) to this day.

11/1.60. The fleet named HAM landed southwest, and the country was called the land of Ham for thousands of years, and is the same as that called Egypt and Africa to this day.

11/1.61. God said: Behold, my chosen shall manifest many signs and words common to one another in these different divisions of the earth.

11/1.62. They shall remember the flood.

11/1.63. They shall repudiate idols, but worship the Great Spirit, Jehovih.

11/1.64. They shall have the crescent.

11/1.65. They shall have the triangle.

11/1.66. They shall preserve the four days of the change of the moon as sacred days, and they

---

[339] The meaning of this word [Guatama] is: Four Tribes United in One. The word Guatamala or Guatemala, would therefore mean: The Earth Place of Four Tribes of Men United in One. See maps of Central America. –Ed.

[340] It is true that the Japanese did remain an exclusive people until the dawn of kosmon, and that their belief is firm to this day that they are the oldest nation in all the world. The English word arc is Hak in both Japanese and Chinese, especially in the rural parts. Noe is Japanese for Lord, and No'eji is Chinese for spirit. Arc is Hebrew, and signifies a box, but more particularly a preserving box. Among the Phoenicians anything that was sacred was engraved with an arch on the front; for it was supposed to flatter the spirits who attended them, as much as to say, you are arc-angels. Is it not wonderful that the Japanese ports were opened by Americans and in the beginning of kosmon, and without war? Following in fact the manifestations of the spirits in America, as was prophesied in 1850. And the mark of the Faithist was still with them. –Ed.

shall be called mass (moon's) days [Sabbaths – Ed.].

11/1.67. They shall be circumcised.

11/1.68. They shall remember the seven tetracts: DIBBAH, the enticing evil; RA, the flesh evil; ZIMMAH, the joking evil; BELYYAAL, worthlessness; AVEN, vanity; ANASH, delight in destruction; and SA'TAN, desire for leadership, which is the captain of death.

11/1.69. They shall have three great lights: OR, the All Highest; GOD, son of Or; and LORD (Adonya), executor[341] of heaven and earth.

11/1.70. They shall have three lesser lights: God's angels and Lords; the prophets; and the rab'bahs.[342]

11/1.71. They shall have three representative symbols of light: The sun, the moon and the burning flame.

11/1.72. The Lord said: And my chosen shall use these lights and symbols, signs and seasons, in all the divisions of the earth where I have settled them.

11/1.73. And in the Kosmon era I will come and show them the framework of my building, which I raise up to the Almighty.

11/1.74. God said: Now the world was of one language and one speech; in all the places of my people, they spoke alike, person to person. ||

11/1.75. Nevertheless, in all parts of the earth there lived ground people, who were black and brown,[343] and burrowed in the ground; and they had long arms and curved backs, and were naked and not ashamed, for which reason they were called DRUKS.

11/1.76. The Lord spoke to the chosen (the I'hins), saying: Behold the earth! I give it to you, to be yours forever.

11/1.77. Do not mingle with the druks, for they are without understanding and are not heirs to everlasting life.

[341] person appointed to execute (carry out) the will of Or (Jehovih)

[342] Singular is Rab'bah: father, priest, one who is ordained as head of a family, tribe or nation. [The modern Chinese omit the first syllable, saying "bah," signifying "father." –Ed.]

[343] see footnotes 06/1.16<fn-WAR>, and 06/2.4<fn-stout>

11/1.78. Now many inquired of the Lord, saying: If these, having no understanding, are not heirs to everlasting life, how shall it be with our children who die in infancy?

11/1.79. The Lord said: This is a matter of the seed, and not of learning. Whoever is born from my chosen shall inherit my everlasting kingdom.

CHAPTER 2 Lords' First

11/2.1. The Lord said: A wise physician amputates a diseased limb and so preserves the trunk to become healed.

11/2.2. Did I not see the rankness of the tribes of darkness, the druks; and that the proceedings of man would render the earth void?

11/2.3. What worth has all the world, if it does not bring forth heirs to everlasting life?

11/2.4. Behold, I saw that my chosen had become exterminated on all the divisions of the earth except Pan. And I saw that those who had been their destroyers had, in turn, nearly exterminated one another.

11/2.5. And I saw that by bringing the remnants of my people here, they could re-establish themselves, and become the seed of a mighty people.

11/2.6. But, as for the land of Whaga (Pan), it was already in the throes of death. The druks had become a festering sore; and the spirits of the dead, tens of billions of them, would not quit their hold on mortals while life was on the earth.

11/2.7. And I sent my angels around the whole earth, and gathered in the spirits of darkness; gathered them to the land of Whaga.

11/2.8. And when my work was ready, I raised up my hand, as a surgeon that would lop off a diseased limb, and I cleft asunder the continent of Pan and sunk it beneath the waters.

11/2.9. And my angels conducted my chosen out of that land, and not one of them perished.

11/2.10. I said to the guardian angels whom I had given to man: In the lands where I will take my people, let them build mounds and walled cities, with ladders to enter, like the ancients. In all the divisions of the earth, they shall build alike.

11/2.11. For in the time of Kosmon, their relics shall be testimony that the I'hin foreran the I'huan, the copper-colored race, all over the world.

11/2.12. So also, I, the Lord, will provide in the Kosmon era to discover the sunken land of Whaga, so that mortals may comprehend the magnitude of the work of the Lord. ||

11/2.13. In those days the I'hins did not dwell alone, but in cities and villages; and they were clothed. They tilled the ground and brought forth grains and seeds good to eat; and flax and hemp, from which to make cloth for covering the body. And their food was of every herb, root, grain, seed, and fruit, that comes from the earth, and is good to eat; but they ate neither flesh nor fish, nor of anything that breathed the breath of life.

11/2.14. They toiled by day, bringing the fruit of their labor within their cities; and they slept at night within their cities, and on mounds, so they would not be molested by beasts of prey or by serpents.

11/2.15. And every city had one rab'bah (head father), who knew the way of the Lord; by the rab'bah, the altars of the Lord were built, and the times of the sacred days foretold.

11/2.16. And the rab'bah made written records on stone; which they taught to their successors, and to whoever desired to learn of the Lord.

11/2.17. And the Lord remained with them; and they kept the commandments and multiplied exceedingly, in all the divisions of the world.

11/2.18. Nor was there in those days, any war in any land under the sun.

11/2.19. In three thousand years time, behold, there were thousands of cities and hundreds of thousands of inhabitants who had spread abroad over the lands of the earth.

11/2.20. And they had built ships and sailed abroad on the seas, and inhabited its islands, north and south and east and west.

CHAPTER 3 Lords' First

The Scriptures of that day

11/3.1. God said: So that my people may remain upright, behold, I give to them and their successors forever, certain sacred words which shall be to them the bond of my covenant.

11/3.2. The Lord said: Seven degrees of sacred rites I bestow upon my people. And no man shall take the second till he has learned all the words of the first; nor shall he take the third till he has learned all the words of the second; and so on. Man shall learn all my sacred words; from mouth to ear they shall be learned, by every man and every woman of my people.[344]

11/3.3. Listen, then, to the words of the servants of the Lord:

11/3.4. I will serve the prophets of the Lord my God.

11/3.5. Heal my flesh, O God (Iod), and cure poison.

11/3.6. The Lord is my spirit (s'pe) unseen in the heavens.

11/3.7. He is all power, wisdom, love, and anger.

11/3.8. He can heal, and he can tear the flesh, and strike dead.

11/3.9. His prophets have his good grace; they can hear his voice and interpret him.

11/3.10. The Lord is my guardian; ten times a day I will remember him.

11/3.11. God who is Lord can stop blood; choke it up, O Lord.

11/3.12. He gave blood-stopping as a power of the prophet's hands.

11/3.13. Confound my enemies, O God.

11/3.14. The ashars (angels of the Lord) shield me.

11/3.15. I will honor the I'hins, the sacred people of God. They are my brethren.

11/3.16. This was the first lesson. Also the Lord said to his prophets: Go to the druks and sit them on the ground in a circle, and you stand in the center, saying: Behold, O druk, the Great Spirit has spoken; I have heard His voice. His words are holy words; whoever learns His words shall have power over sickness and poison, and the flowing of blood. And, if a woman, she shall become fruitful and have great rejoicing. Hold up your hands and repeat the words of the Lord.

11/3.17. And it was so, the prophets taught the words of the Lord. First, the first degree (as shown above); and when that was mastered, then the second:

11/3.18. Blessed is the name of the Lord. He can make me alive after I am dead, and this is all he requires of me, to say: Blessed is the name of the Lord. In the morning I will say it; at noon I will

---

[344] These seven degrees are also called lessons or commandments in the verses that follow.

say it; at night I will say it: Blessed is the name of the Lord.

11/3.19. I will wear clothes to hide my nakedness, because God requires it of me.

11/3.20. I will not steal, nor speak untruth.

11/3.21. If my brother takes what is mine, I will not be angry, nor judge him; but I will lay the matter before the prophets of God.

11/3.22. I will do no violence, for it is God's commandment.

11/3.23. This, then, that follows, was the third:

11/3.24. I will have only one wife; I will not go after other women while she lives. (I will have only one husband; I will receive no other man while my husband lives.)

11/3.25. I will permit no man or woman of poison (leprosy) to come near the oe'ugah [camp – Ed.]. In the Lord's name, I will drive them away.

11/3.26. I renounce[345] them; nor will I mingle with them, for it is God's commandment.

11/3.27. The fourth commandment was:

11/3.28. I forswear[346] the hunt; but whatever comes, and is fit food for man to eat, I will kill it.[347] I will take up fish in the name of the Lord, for they suffer no pain.

11/3.29. I will till the soil, gather roots to eat, and weave fibers of barks for clothing, and live like the I'hins, the chosen people of God.

11/3.30. I renounce murderers; nor will I marry with them, nor live as they live; they are the enemies of the Lord God.

11/3.31. I will curse no man, woman or child, for it is the Lord's commandment.

11/3.32. I renounce anger and all weapons of death; they are enemies of the Lord.

11/3.33. If a man injures me, I will lay the matter before the Lord's prophet, for his judgment is holy, says the Lord.

11/3.34. If a woman entices me, I will go secrete myself and repeat the sacred words.

11/3.35. I will respect the times of woman, for she is the gift of the Lord to be man's helpmate.

11/3.36. When my wife has a newborn child, I will do her labor for forty days, for it is God's commandment.

11/3.37. The fifth commandment, which is:

11/3.38. The four days of the moon are the Lord's; on those days I will not labor.

11/3.39. I will keep sacred the four days of every moon, and I will repeat the sacred words of the Lord three times.

11/3.40. And when the prophets say: Behold, the Lord says this is a sacred day; then I will keep that day holy, for the prophets hear the voice of God.

11/3.41. When the I'hins worship before the altar of the Lord, I will keep on the outer circle, for the I'hins are the chosen servants of God.

11/3.42. When the I'hins march forth, following the prophets, I will come after, for I will honor the Lord's chosen.

11/3.43. When the prophets say: Pitch the tents here, I will comply, for the prophets cannot err.

11/3.44. The sixth commandment, which is:

11/3.45. I will provide for the sick, and for the woman with a newborn child.

11/3.46. I will give, first to the I'hins, second to the druks, and lastly keep for my own self.

11/3.47. To warriors, I will give in time of sickness, but when they are healed, I will say: Go your way.

11/3.48. And if a man or woman is sick from poison, I will go to them. But before I go in I will say: O Lord, my God, in your name I go on a dangerous business; come through your ashars and protect me for your sake.

11/3.49. For the Lord can shield me around, and I shall not receive the poison.

11/3.50. The seventh commandment, which is:

11/3.51. I will keep these holy words secret in the name of the Lord my God.

11/3.52. When the Lord commands, saying: Go here, or go there, or build a city here, or a house or an altar; then I will do the Lord's bidding. ||

11/3.53. Thus the Lord established laws among men; and because of the sacredness of the Lord's words, man treasured them and kept holy the commandments of God. ||

11/3.54. Now I, the Lord, reveal in this, the Kosmon era:

11/3.55. My angels were with the chosen in the days of these sacred scriptures.

[345] reject, foreswear, refuse association with

[346] quit, give up, renounce

[347] It will be observed here that the druks had a different law given to them; for the I'hins killed nothing, and neither ate fish nor flesh. –Ed.

11/3.56. And when the words were repeated for the stopping of blood, behold, my angels compressed the veins. The words themselves did not stop the blood, but it was by the words that mortals came into concert with my hosts.

11/3.57. And when a man went into the presence of dangerous diseases, repeating the sacred words, behold, my angels enveloped that man with my unseen blankets, and the man was protected from the disease.

11/3.58. Without such words, there could be no concert of action between mortals and angels.

11/3.59. Do not think that your Lord taught a foolish thing; nor that the mumbling of words by my prophets was without wisdom and forethought by the Lord your God. ||

11/3.60. Now in those days the Lord caused the rab'bah to make a wheel, and hang it beside the altar. And its meaning was: As this wheel is without beginning or end, so is the Creator. Whoever turns the wheel once around has said: In you, my God, I trust.

11/3.61. And the Lord made an image to stand at the extreme of the altar,[348] where only holy men and women could pass, and the Lord called the emblem Fete,[349] signifying, BEYOND ME THERE IS NO APPEAL.

11/3.62. And the form of fete was a circle having an all-light center, with four dark corners cut off. And the Lord explained the meaning, which was:

11/3.63. There is a central light within man seeing clearly, but the four dark corners of the world (ignorance, lust, selfishness, and anger) beset [350] him on all sides.

11/3.64. And the Lord made an instrument and called it GAU, which was a triangle with a plumb line from the upper corner; and across the plumb line was a hollow reed for seeing through; and at the bottom end of the plumb line a weight was attached, which pointed to marks on the lower border of the triangle.[351] And the Lord explained to the prophets how to use the gau for proving all things, such as calculating the height of mountains, and the velocity of running waters, and how to lay the foundations of the temples, so that they would be square with the world. And the prophets taught the I'hins, but with them the mysteries were kept secret from all other people. So that, in after time, came the saying: Even the wicked were compelled to employ the I'hins, and were thus beholden to the Lord.

11/3.65. In all, there were two hundred and eighty signs, emblems, symbols, and implements given by the Lord to his people; and when they were all completed the Lord taught the prophets the meaning; and these became the sacred language of mortals in all the divisions of the earth.

END OF THE LORDS' FIRST BOOK

i033r07a **Fete**. i033r03f **Gau**.

Book of Sue, Son of Jehovih

Being the second cycle after the Flood.

CHAPTER 1 Sue

12/1.1. Jehovih spoke in the gardens of Atahavia, precinct of Sue, Orian Chief, in the etherean firmament, saying: Sue, My Son, what of the red star, the far-off earth? Behold, her harvests are blighted; she has become barren in imparting immortal souls to My unending realms.

[348] Apparently this means the Fete was situated a short distance in front of the altar, so that only the holiest of men and women could draw near the altar.

[349] See image i033r07a. More is given later in Oahspe regarding Fete.

[350] harass, beleaguer, plague, bedevil, besiege, attack, surround, hem in, assail

[351] see image i033r03f Gau

12/1.2. Sue heard the voice, and he said: In Your name, O Jehovih, I will summon my Gods of Hoit and Izaracha.

12/1.3. Swift messengers departed; and Sue, quick-perceiving God of two worlds in the etherean Seamar, foresaw the importance of the coming red star. He said: This, with my Gods of Hoit and Izaracha, who will come in swift speed, shall be the second deliverance.[352]

12/1.4. Then came Le Wing, God of Hoit; and presently, Sivian, Goddess of Izaracha, and they stood before Jehovih's throne. Sue said:

12/1.5. Jehovih has spoken. Behold, the red star no longer brings forth sons and daughters to Jehovih's realms. She is weak, unstrung, and out of tune, and comes this way. And I said:

12/1.6. In Your power and wisdom, O Jehovih, I will visit the red star! Six years I will stand on her soil, and course her heaven; and I will give such potency to her confused Gods and Lords as will make a billion sing for joy. || To accompany me, I have called you. Behold, I have charts and maps of her heaven and her corporeal parts; and a history of her, as yet, young adventures in the field of worlds.

12/1.7. Then spoke Le Wing and Sivian, saying: To do Jehovih's will and yours, behold, we have come to you. Give us to fulfill whatever you will.

12/1.8. Sue said to the swift messengers: You have heard; go proclaim my will throughout my etherean worlds; and summon up from Ithyivius a hundred million skilled volunteers. When the red star crosses the wing of Izaracha,[353] we will go forth in power, and land on her troubled parts in a sea of golden light.

CHAPTER 2 Sue

12/2.1. In the Ariniisca of Portan of the etherean worlds and division of Hoit and Izaracha, flew the call of the Gods for volunteers, of which a more welcome sound is not heard in high heaven than to do Jehovih's will. And with the voice and call there rose up hosts from every quarter, and from every subdivision, till the complement stood ready for the great work. And yet so vast were the fields and arcs of Izaracha that the hundred million chosen were only a small fraction compared to those left uncalled.

12/2.2. Coming near the throne of Sue in Aoit, the hundred million formed in squares and stars, and the chosen God[354] took his place at the head and front, looking to the low horizon, where rose the red star, the sick earth.

12/2.3. And now the builders, who had measured the elements lying in the route to the earth, formed their crescent ship of fire, and equipped it; and with mantles, curtains and banners, created of it a vessel of beauty and ornament as well as service.

12/2.4. Hardly was the ship completed when Jehovih's light encompassed it on all sides, so that what was beautiful before, was now illuminated, sparkling and bright as a sun, and rich in golden colors; for such was the quality of the ethe of the heavens created in this region.

12/2.5. When Sue entered the ship, the voice of Jehovih came, saying: Another cycle has come and gone on the earth and her heaven, but still they fall to barrenness before the succeeding dawn. Go now, O Sue, My Son, and give a wider range to the tetracts of both angels and mortals. Give a greater scope to tyrants, kings and queens on earth, and greater to the self-Gods and self-Lords in hada, and more responsibility.

12/2.6. Then all hands entered the etherean ship, singing and rejoicing, observed by countless millions come to wish them a haven of joy on their six years' visit to the corporeal earth.

12/2.7. Sue said: In Your name, O Jehovih, and by virtue of Your power vested in me, my hosts shall go forth at my command. Cut loose, you Gods, and you, O ship, born of heaven, to the red star, the earth, Go! And Sue stretched forth his hands and waved them, and lo, the mighty ship of heaven turned on its axis, cutting loose from the high firmament. And it turned, with its great curtains and banners sailing gracefully and swiftly through the blue ether.

12/2.8. The music of her es'enaurs swelled and rolled along on the spheres of many worlds unseen

[352] The arc of Noe was the first deliverance.

[353] see image i084, p.99

[354] That is, Sue, who was chosen by Jehovih to lead the mission. Note that the word God can be used to refer to anyone of that rank or higher; for, once having attained the Godhead, it is never lost or set aside.

to mortals, where live countless millions of spectators viewing the marvelous speed, power and brilliant colors of the great ship. Faster and faster she sped on, till nearing Chinvat, which now cut sharp into the fields and forests of Izaracha, over which was potent the name of Sue, the companion God and chiefest friend of Aph, Orian Chief, Son of Jehovih.

12/2.9. When the ship came to the bridge[355] and stopped, to take in the plan of the whirling earth, Sue said: A light! A light! You Gods! And at once, as high as the moon and bright as the sun, the illumined ship stood, to overawe the self-Gods, warrior kings, and murderers of the earth-born, whose plentiful souls in chaos polluted heaven.

12/2.10. For three days and nights Sue held his star-ship to the wonderful task of mastering by the marvelous scene.[356] Then slowly he entered the vortex of the earth, holding his course, but not with the rotation of the earth and her heaven; for he desired that both corporeans and atmosphereans would witness the coming power. So, slowly he came, only fifty thousand miles a day, so that when the ship neared the disorganized Hored, the self-Gods and self-Lords fled and left their well-supplied kingdoms desolate, and down to the earth they rushed in thousands, and with their hosts in millions, to hide or safely stow themselves from Agni's just hate.[357]

12/2.11. But the true God and Lords stood firm in their depleted kingdoms, fearing nothing, but in faith that this etherean ship was Jehovih's answer to their long cry for help from the heavenly spheres. And by their pillars of fire still standing, great Sue knew where to land in the lower heaven for safe anchorage. So to Hored he came, slowly, and toward the throne of God. When he neared the place, his es'enaurs chanted and the trumpeters played; and the sound of this music came to the ears of God and his hosts, and they were the hymns of more than a thousand years ago.

12/2.12. And God and his hosts sent up rockets (fireworks) that displayed the three primary colors,[358] the sign of Jehovih's name; and God's es'enaurs joined in chanting with the hosts above. Presently the ship of fire was at the landing place, and Sue, Jehovih's Son, cast out a ladder and descended, with his hosts, the hundred million angels, led by Gussitivi, marshaless of the throne of Sue, in Izaracha.

12/2.13. Sue said: Hail, O God of heaven and earth! In Jehovih's name, I have come in power and wisdom. And God answered: Glory to You, O Jehovih, that Your Son has come so far to bless Your bewildered kingdom! Then they saluted with the signs of the sixth resurrection, after which God said:

12/2.14. In the name of the Great Spirit, come and honor my throne. So Sue went forward, and they greeted by shaking hands; and Sue ascended and sat on the throne, saying: Keep your place, O God, for I have not come to displace you or your hosts of Jehovih, but to build up for His glory. Be seated, therefore, for I feel the light of the Father descending on my head.

12/2.15. Presently the All Light enveloped Sue, and the Father's voice spoke through him, saying: Hear the words of your Creator, My Son, and rejoice because I have not forgotten you and your people. Behold, this is the hour of your redemption from the trials of tetracts, which have run abroad in My dominions.

12/2.16. Was it not worse than this in the ancient days? And I came with My hosts and delivered them. I created man in darkness and gave him no judgment, so that the creation of his own thoughts might be for his own glory, forever. But instead of beautifying his thoughts, he listens to tetracts and clothes himself in clouds. The heaven I build for him, he digs to pieces, and then builds his own, but only to be displeased and turbulent. Nor

---

[355] i.e., Chinvat (07/1.20)

[356] That is, through the spectacle of his enormous illuminated ship, Sue gained the attention of low-grade spirits and mortals in such a way as to make them look up in awe and fill with fear, wonder and caution.

[357] Agni means fire, in this case, etherean fire. The etherean fire can illumine all so that if any darkness resides in the soul, it is seen plainly by those around. Thus, thoughts and sentiments of, say, hatred and vile cannot be hidden in the light of etherean agni, and, in turn, those of low grade can readily see their own deficiencies reflected in the light shining down upon them. To them, might the light not seem full of searing hatred, yet with the power of justice underscoring the light?

[358] yellow, blue and red

will he content himself with providing with his own hands, but searches out My most dutiful sons and daughters, making slaves of them for his own exaltation.

12/2.17. Behold, I have previously sent My sons and daughters to search out these traitors and self-Gods, declaring to them that only by forsaking evil and practicing righteousness could they attain to My exalted kingdoms. Their evil places I have cast down, and rebuilt in honor and glory, so that their own judgment could determine that virtue and good works are the sure foundation for happiness that will endure forever. But when I have raised them up in one cycle and made the lower heaven a paradise, alas, once My ethereans have gone away for just a little while, the tetracts take root, and grow, and turn all things upside down.

12/2.18. But now I will build them up in a new way. Yes, I will appropriate the evil of their inventions, applying this to their benefit in a way they do not dream of. The false Gods and false Lords shall be arrested and brought before this judgment seat, and I will judge them by their own behavior and desires; neither will I torment them nor abridge their happiness. Send, therefore, My Son, your marshals into the hidden places of these Gods and Lords, and say to them: Thus says the hosts of heaven: Come, my Son, and inherit a kingdom in hada, in your own way, for lo, there is room for all; but, so that you are not left behind, come quickly to Hored.

12/2.19. And they will come, hoping to embellish themselves in the old manner. But My Light shall come in due time in My own way.

12/2.20. The voice ceased, but Sue spoke on his own account, saying: What Jehovih has ordered, do so. Accordingly marshals and priests were sent in all directions in atmospherea, to gather in the false Gods and false Lords who had deserted their dominions in fear of the light of Sue's etherean ship. And after many days the false ones were brought to Hored, being seven thousand Lords and Gods.

12/2.21. Now when they were before Sue, Jehovih's Son, and arranged so that all could hear and see, including the whole Council, the Light gathered around the throne, and Sue addressed them, saying:

12/2.22. Hear me, O men and women! I have sent for you, and you are here. In this I am pleased. Know, then, that what I speak shall be in love and tenderness. You have deserted Jehovih's kingdoms, and it must be because it pleased you better than to remain. Is this not true? And you also deserted your own false kingdoms?

12/2.23. For a little while they consulted together, and then answered, saying: No, it did not please us to desert our own kingdoms; but we were afraid.

12/2.24. Sue said: Who do you think I am? They answered: A God from some far-off world, but where it lies, we do not know. We desire to know who you are?

12/2.25. Sue said: I am only a man; do not fear me. But since you feared, and so, deserted your kingdoms, does it not prove that you are not the All Highest? And do you not perceive that, because you had no All Highest, you were divided and inharmonious?

12/2.26. Hear, then, that which I say, and consider my words: I do not want your kingdoms or anything you have; but, so that harmony may reign in heaven, I will give every one of you more than you had, and increase your power also.

12/2.27. Since you see I have come to Hored, the throne of the ancients, do you not perceive that whoever accords with me is of my power also? Take, then, your kingdoms and be Gods and Goddesses, as you assumed before, and I will anoint you, and make you as part and parcel of one united whole. Again they counseled together, and then answered:

12/2.28. Why shall we take our kingdoms? Our slaves have deserted us; our kingdoms are pillaged of all their value. Indeed, our slaves have become wandering spirits, and have returned to the earth and are making their habitations with mortals, so that the people of earth are aroused because of miracles and wonders occurring on earth.

12/2.29. Sue said: What can you say to these wandering spirits that will induce[359] them to come up away from mortals? To which they answered: If we promise them provender,[360] clothes and plenty of rest, they will come; but when we put them to labor, having tasted of liberty, they will run away.

12/2.30. Sue said: How, then, did you make slaves of them in the first place? To which they

[359] persuade, influence

[360] provisions, food and drink, nourishment

answered: The day their mortal bodies died, we took them in, and they never saw or knew any other place in heaven; so we appropriated them to our service and they dutifully obeyed.

12/2.31. Sue said: Know, then, this is my conclusion: First, that you shall all be made as sub-Gods to one confederacy, and your kingdoms shall be fair to look upon, and well supplied with all things needed.

12/2.32. Behold, there are on earth, with the barbarians, hosts of familiars and fetals; whichever of you will go down to the earth and bring them away to Hored, shall have them for his slaves; and whoever brings the greatest number, I will award him the greatest kingdom. And if you can find emissaries to work for you in bringing fetals and familiars away from the barbarians, then such labor shall be accounted to your credit. And in the corporeal cities you shall station certain angels, whose labor shall be to receive newborn spirits on birth-blankets and bring them to your kingdoms also, for they shall be your slaves.

12/2.33. In that manner, Sue spoke, and the false Gods and Goddesses were highly pleased, and they divided themselves into certain districts over mortals and for the lower heaven, and were sent off at once to labor in their own way, and they were named sub-Gods.

12/2.34. Sue said: These sub-Gods have much weight with the barbarians, because they advise them in war. But, behold, it shall come to pass that when the sub-Gods have robbed the barbarians of their familiar spirits, the I'hin priests will have a greater weight with them.

12/2.35. And the sub-Gods will desire to find favor in my sight, and so, they will teach their slaves, and this will cause them to emancipate themselves in time to come.

CHAPTER 3 Sue

12/3.1. Jehovih spoke through Sue, saying: Mine is a strong government, and everlasting. Listen to the wisdom of your Creator, O My sons and daughters. Where have I not given liberty to all people? He who does right, where is he not free? He who does wrong, where does he have liberty? Whoever endeavors to surpass himself, have I not shown him his limit?

12/3.2. I created man at zero, but only for him to add to himself forever. I gave him liberty to add only that which perfects his own soul. For which reason, if he eats poison, it takes from him his body, which I gave. Here I made a boundary, both on earth and in heaven, which is to say, to the extent that man accumulates virtue, wisdom, patience, love, truth and pure words, he is free; because, in doing so, he follows Me in My works. But he who seeks to glorify himself in his possessions, binds himself, because he is unlike Me; for I gave All, and thus made the universe.

12/3.3. I have created two states, therefore, open to all men, both on earth and in atmospherea, which are, liberty and bondage. And I made man to choose that which he will; but, so that he might not err, behold, I send My emancipated angels to explain these things beforehand.[361]

12/3.4. Even so are governments ordained by My holy ones; accordingly, you may judge whether a government is of Me or against Me. For if it gives liberty to all righteous works, and for the promotion of knowledge, providing teachers to the extent of the demand, it is of Me. But if the government makes of itself a self, for which its aggrandizement[362] is at the expense of My children's liberty, then it is against Me.

12/3.5. For I have not created a people to be today as their forefathers were, but provided them with perpetual growth in wisdom and virtue; for which reason, the rising generations shall rebel against that which was well and good for their forefathers. All My governments understand this, whether on earth or in heaven. Whatever government does not accept this rule shall go down to destruction. For, as I have hedged man about with sentinels, such as pestilence, poverty and hunger, in order to awaken him to knowledge and industry, so have I hedged-in all governments under the sun with sentinels, such as rebellion, assassinations, war, and bankruptcy. As pestilence proves man's disobedience to My commandments, so do rebellion and anarchy prove the disobedience of governments to the progressive spirit which I created with man.

---

[361] Oahspe is such a vehicle.

[362] development; accumulation; greatness; increase in extent, power, might, prominence, stature, influence, significance, profit, etc.

12/3.6. The self-God says: I will make a strong government; by armies and cruel masters I will bind the subjects in my dominions. And he draws up a multitude of laws, and heaps up books to explain the laws, and finds judges to explain the books that explain the laws, and he says: Behold how wise I am! Behold the great wisdom of my judges! Behold the great learning of my books! Behold my most perfect laws! Behold my armies that stand in great power behind all!

12/3.7. But lo, a star appears in heaven, and all his fabric gives way like a spider's web. For instead of choosing his Creator, Who is strong, he erected things that were as nothing.

12/3.8. Hear your Creator, O My God, for through My Son I bequeath a new light to the lower heaven: For, as you have portioned to the self-Gods to take kingdoms, suffer them to hedge themselves around with a multitude of laws; but you yourself shall have no laws except the rites and ceremonies, which you shall adorn with music and processions.

12/3.9. And it shall come to pass that the dominions of the self-Gods will prosper for a season; and for the sake of self-glory, they will deplete the earth people of familiar spirits and fetals. But, afterward, their subjects will tire of the laws of the self-Gods, and hearing that you have no laws, except rites and ceremonies, they will, of their own accord, come to Hored.

12/3.10. Therefore, you shall convert the nurseries, hospitals, factories and places of education, into places of delight and recreation.

12/3.11. The voice ceased, but Sue said: Behold, a time comes in all the atmospherean heavens when the discipline of former days must give way to something new; and now is such a time in this kingdom. It may be compared to a young child who has been led by the hand for a long time, but now has become strong enough to walk alone.

12/3.12. For this purpose the earth has been brought through the fields of Izaracha, and my hosts have come with music and wisdom. Hear, then, my decree, O God of earth, and you shall be the most blessed of Gods: Send your messengers into all parts of atmospherea, proclaiming a recreation of ten days, of music, dancing and marching, with pageantry and feasting, to be in Hored on the first of the moon of Jaffeth.

12/3.13. The rest leave to the Father, for He will provide us in that time. And while the time is coming, I will go around the earth with my hosts in my etherean ship.

12/3.14. God said: I perceive Your wisdom, O Jehovih; in Your decrees I am raised up with new wisdom and power. O that I could have devised a way for them before they fell so low!

12/3.15. Sue called the Council and his own hosts from labor to recreation for one day, and the people mingled together rejoicing; for there were many ethereans with the hosts of Sue who had been earth-born, many thousands of years before, and their assurance of the emancipated heavens above had greater weight with the atmosphereans than anything that others could say. Then Sue and his hosts visited the earth and her heavens; and after that returned again to Hored.

CHAPTER 4 Sue

12/4.1. When the time of the festival came, more than a billion souls, besides the etherean hosts, had congregated in Hored, to witness and to participate in the ceremonies. Sue said: Here is wisdom and folly; false Gods and their dupes; laziness and industry; swiftness and sloth. Yes, here is a world worthless before Jehovih.

12/4.2. And why? Simply for lack of discipline and harmony. Everyone is for self, and none are producers for the general good. Alas, they are the same as mortals, but stripped of flesh. They are of no value to one another, and consequently of no value to themselves. Now I will show you, O God, that these hapless[363] beings, with no joy in life or hope of resurrection, shall become a great glory to the Father and His Kingdoms.

12/4.3. God said: Pity them, O Father! It is over a thousand years since they have been visited by the higher heaven. Many of them are learned, but doubting if there are other heavens, except the plateaus of the atmospherea of the earth. Millions and millions of them have never seen an etherean. Alas, I fear for them.

12/4.4. Sue said; Fear not, O God. They are like mortar in my hands. Neither shall there be preaching to them, nor praying for them. They are tired of these things. But I will found a new light among them, and it shall speak for us. Hear me, then; with the populace I shall be as one that is

[363] unfortunate, tragic, poor, pitiable

unknown. Call, then, your es'enaurs, and your trumpeters and harpists, and all the musicians belonging to your kingdom and to the kingdoms of your Lords, and let the procession begin.

12/4.5. For in all public matters those who are at the front, if wise, can lead on forever. Be politic,[364] therefore, and shape the populace while the self-Gods[365] are amazed at the immensity of the hosts assembled.

12/4.6. God did as commanded, and the people saw there was a head to the proceedings. Sue said: Send your marshals and decorators to follow close behind the musicians, distributing raiment to all who will follow in the procession. My etherean hosts are advised. They will stand by the way, and, with marvelous swiftness, provide the raiment. All possible extravagant colors and fabrics, hats and ornaments, shall be gratuitously[366] distributed.

12/4.7. My hosts shall be arrayed in plain white; and they shall not march, but be as servants and workmen. And when the atmosphereans have played and sung, over all the boundaries of Hored, then my etherean band shall sing and play, and start the dance.

12/4.8. All these things were done, and from the very start to the termination of the music there was harmony in every place and corner among the billions assembled. Nor was there ever a so extravagantly equipped multitude in the earth's heaven. And so completely captivated were the people, that their enthusiasm was boundless. Then came the etherean dance, which so surpassed the capacity of the atmosphereans that not one could join in. Nor could they take part in the etherean music.

12/4.9. So the atmosphereans looked on, confounded by the excellence of that which was before their eyes.

12/4.10. Thus ended the first day's proceedings, which to describe in full would require a large book. So the people were called to refreshment. And the ethereans, still dressed in white, and as servants and laborers, provided the viands.[367] For, they had previously prepared a supply of material. And so easily and swiftly did they do their work, that now, for the first time, the more learned of atmospherea began to observe them with surprise and wonder.

12/4.11. Presently inquiries were made as to who they were and where they came from. For so Jehovih created man, that when of his own accord, he admires the excellence of his neighbor, he goes to the extreme in praising him.

12/4.12. So God said: Tomorrow a new entertainment shall be given, and new raiment and new viands for the feast. And the hosts shouted with great vigor and praise. Then the people mingled together to converse on all they had witnessed; neither did they comprehend the object, except for pleasure only.

12/4.13. When the next day came, the ethereans had been divided into groups, and the rites of the ancients, and of the hosts of a'ji in Partha, were announced, requiring extravagant preparations[368] and millions of atmosphereans as assistants.

12/4.14. So great was their ambition to take part, that it was only by promises of something in the next rites, that the marshals were able to make selections.

12/4.15. Sue, Jehovih's Son, had previously stationed signal bells at remote distances from one another, but connected them so that the sounds would answer quickly. And in the intervening places, extemporized forests and waterfalls were arranged; and near the middle space, one thousand columns of fire were erected.

12/4.16. So, in the morning of the second day, when all these glorious scenes were completed, with the ethereans still plain and in white stationed here and there, the atmosphereans were more confounded than ever, and more loudly shouting in their praise.

12/4.17. First came the birth-rites; then marriage-rites; then death-rites and the first resurrection; then the rites of harmony. And the play represented a million ethereans who went to a corporeal world and followed it through its life, and to death and resurrection; its darkness, disharmony and terrible suffering in atmospherea; ending with a tableau[369] of a great sun of light

---

[364] be expedient, use to advantage

[365] Note that these left shortly after the procession got underway.

[366] without charge or obligation, freely

[367] delicious prepared foods

[368] including costuming and other accessories, grooming, set design, etc.

descending, to deliver them into everlasting paradise.

12/4.18. So grand was the spectacle and so sublime the music and spoken words, that the hosts of Hored wept, and laughed, and shouted, and prayed, as if their souls would break with joy.

12/4.19. Thus ended the second day, and so complete was the glorious work that every soul had sworn a solemn oath to forsake[370] the earth and lower heaven forever. Then God announced for the third day, the display of etherean power.

12/4.20. And the people were so bewildered already that a child could have led the most stubborn of all. For thus Jehovih created man, who, having become much conceited in himself, turns right around and makes himself a submissive fool.

12/4.21. So, on the third day, the ethereans displayed their power over the elements of the atmosphere; making corporeal substances and dissolving them at pleasure;[371] making light into darkness, and darkness into light; weaving fabrics; making diadems and precious stones; gathering viands from the essence of things evaporated up from the earth; founding plateaus and temples in heaven; making ships and chains and musical instruments. And, lastly, the etherean marshals, with half a million ethereans, turned the winds and sent a heavy shower of rain down to the corporeal earth.[372]

12/4.22. And all that time, the musicians of the hosts of Sue were playing music, the sweetness and grandeur of which so greatly surpassed that of atmosphereans, that any of theirs would be as nothing in comparison.

12/4.23. So, because of the exhibition of great power and wisdom, the third day had changed the fortunes and aspirations of every man and woman in the lower heaven. And they were running here and there, pleading to be taken as apprentices or servants, pledging themselves to do anything required of them. Neither would they be put off, demanding that half of the next day should be given to initiating them as real beginners in the second resurrection.

12/4.24. Then God spoke to them, saying: You do not know what you ask. Behold, I have commanded you for hundreds of years to put away your fine raiment and sparkling gems, and to begin adorning your souls, so as to become Brides and Bridegrooms of the Great Spirit.

12/4.25. But you would not, but strove continually to adorn yourselves, forgetting to labor for those beneath you. Behold, Jehovih's Brides and Bridegrooms now stand before you. What is their worth compared to yours? Are they not plain? And are you not decorated?

12/4.26. But millions of voices rose up, saying: We will do whatever you command, O God. There is no God like you. Then God spoke, saying: Hear me, then, further: To begin the second resurrection requires this; to put away your jewels, diadems, ornaments, and, above all things, to forsake self, and from this time forward to labor for others who are beneath you. If you do this in a brotherhood, you are already beginning the second resurrection. Neither is there any other road to wisdom and power.

12/4.27. Again the multitude cried out: We will do anything; we have faith. And God answered them, saying: Permit, then, a few to be initiated tomorrow; but be patient and of good judgment; slow to resolve, but firm forever.

12/4.28. So on the fourth day, in the morning, behold, more than a hundred million spirits had abandoned their showy raiment and stood arrayed in white, devoid of jewels and diadems, ready to be initiated and take the vows of the second resurrection. Accordingly new music was prepared, and the procession and ceremonies so arranged, that the greatest possible glory would be manifested.

12/4.29. Canopies were stretched overhead, and on the borders of the march, arches and columns were placed, decorated with flowers and vines; and amid these, half concealed, were nestled the response singers, who were to speak for and with the initiates. But concealed from view, and at a distance, were bells and explosives, which were the morning signals.

12/4.30. And the glad and solemn sound of the Immortal Voice came upon the souls of millions

---

[369] a portrayal, illustration, scene or representation that is dramatic and striking

[370] abandon, leave, desert

[371] i.e., effortlessly when and as they desired

[372] There are thousands and thousands of Spiritualists who have witnessed these things being done by the spirits, but of course not on so grand a scale. –Ed.

impatient to vow themselves to a new life; and God and his hosts welcomed them with great joy. So grand and imposing were the ceremonies, that, before midday, another hundred million came, robed in white, to be initiated also. Nor did the people desire any other entertainment.

12/4.31. And so the initiations were continued on the fifth day; and again, another hundred million applied, also robed in white. And this was continued on the sixth, seventh, eighth, ninth and tenth days. And, lo and behold, a billion angels had taken the vows of the second resurrection.

CHAPTER 5 Sue

12/5.1. The words of the initiation, led by the etherean hosts, were of this manner:

12/5.2. God on the throne said: O E-o-ih (Jehovih)! Almighty! Boundless!

12/5.3. Response: How shall I comprehend You, You Mighty One?

12/5.4. God: You, Higher than All Gods and Lords!

12/5.5. Response: Who moves the universe with power unlimited!

12/5.6. God: Creator and Controller of the corporeal worlds!

12/5.7. Response: In Whose hands the etherean firmament is like a fruitful garden, wider than the boundaries of time!

12/5.8. God: Whose members are All Space!

12/5.9. Response: Whose members are the All that is within place, beyond measure!

12/5.10. God: You, O E-o-ih! You Fountain and Terminus[373] of all things!

12/5.11. Response: E-o-ih! E-o-ih! Of Whom all things are simply parts, attuned to Your will!

12/5.12. God: You All Person, O E-o-ih! Incomprehensible!

12/5.13. Response: Who speaks in the Light! Whose voice is the progress of the universe!

12/5.14. God: E-o-ih! You All Giver! By giving, Creates!

12/5.15. Response: What are Your secrets, O Mighty One? O E-o-ih, Everlasting, and Greater than Magnitude!

12/5.16. God: I see nothing in all the universe but You! All selfs are merely fractions of Yourself, O E-o-ih!

12/5.17. Response: Who has not seen You, O E-o-ih? Your Person is in the east and west and north and south! Below and above; far and near.

12/5.18. God: Who has not heard Your voice? Who has not found Your hand, that pushes him along?

12/5.19. Response: Without You, O E-o-ih, I do not go; I do not move. I set out to do things of myself, and fail utterly.

12/5.20. God: What is man before You, O E-o-ih? He sets up a kingdom, and it falls like a house of straw.

12/5.21. Response: O E-o-ih, how I have wasted my time! My buildings were lighter than chaff![374] My virtues were merely bubbles, and they are burst and gone!

12/5.22. God: When will man learn to attune himself to You, O E-o-ih?

12/5.23. Response: How can I put away myself, O E-o-ih? Have I not said: I cannot put away my own judgment?

12/5.24. God: Man says, I will not put away my judgment! And lo, by that, he does it!

12/5.25. Response: Have I not said: To protect myself is the first law; and to preserve my own, the highest law?

12/5.26. God: Man assumes to protect himself, because he is without faith in You, O E-o-ih! And to preserve his own, which, in fact, is not his. ||

12/5.27. And here the Light fell upon the throne, and Jehovih spoke out of the Light, saying:

12/5.28. I have called you, O man, from your youth up! My voice has never ceased in your ear. Who can come into life without Me? Who can measure his own footsteps? Behold, he treads on My ground. Of all that he is made, the substance is Mine.

12/5.29. The kingdoms of the earth and the kingdoms of Gods and Lords in heaven, what more are they than imitations of My works? Where they imitate Me well, I am with them in wisdom, love and power. Shall a man butt his head against a wall to prove he is greater than his Creator? Behold, I came in the ancient days, saying: Strive to become

373 boundary, limit, end

374 the flakey, light covering of unprocessed grain

one with Me, and you shall rejoice that I created you. Strive to set up for yourself, and your vanity shall in time pierce you as a two-edged sword.

12/5.30. Hear the love of your Creator, O man! For, I made you with fondness for your sons and daughters. Of love like My Own, I gave you a part. And as you send communication to your wayward [375] son, beseeching him to return to you, so do I bring My messengers from higher worlds to call you. And, so that you may not mistake their higher place, I give them power and wisdom surpassing yours.

12/5.31. The Voice ceased, and the initiates said:

12/5.32. From this time forward I will serve only You, O E-o-ih! No more will I think what shall become of me. For I know You will appropriate me wisely, O E-o-ih!

12/5.33. Accordingly, as the stone is hewn and polished, so will You put it in the walls of Your house.

12/5.34. My labor is to hew, polish and perfect my own soul forever!

12/5.35. My soul shall become as a shining star.

12/5.36. My love like Your etherean angels.

12/5.37. And plain my raiment, and clean, forever![376]

12/5.38. Never more will I boast, nor speak untruth, forever!

12/5.39. Nor sloth attain me.

12/5.40. Nor vanity, nor self; nor will I talk of myself.

12/5.41. Nor criticize my brethren, nor my neighbors, for they are Yours, O E-o-ih!

12/5.42. To do righteous works and lift up my fellows shall be my labor from this time forward, forever!

12/5.43. Make me strong in You, O E-o-ih!

12/5.44. And wise to do Your will forever. Amen!

[375] disobedient, insubordinate, contempt for authority, delinquent, willful, headstrong, unruly, self-indulgent

[376] i.e., And plain shall be my raiment, and clean, forever.

CHAPTER 6 Sue

12/6.1. So great were the words and music of the ceremonies that the people were entranced beyond measure; the old and divided kingdoms, which were without unity and discipline, were now replaced by extreme sanctity and decorum.[377]

12/6.2. Sue said: Hear me, O God, I will counsel you further: Know, then, that the false Gods and false Lords have gone off to build up kingdoms of their own; nor do they know what has happened in Hored. Allow them to proceed until they have purified the corporeans from familiars and fetals; but when they have finished, call another festival of all these people, and also send word to the false Gods and false Lords who deny Jehovih, the All Person, and they will come adorned in extravagant raiment and jewelry, and bringing their slaves. For they will expect, by their pageantry, to triumph over all other Gods and men, hoping to carry back millions of subjects with them.

12/6.3. God said: I perceive, O Sue, Son of Jehovih. So God did as commanded, and sure enough, eventually the false Gods and false Lords stripped the mortal barbarians of their familiars and fetals, making slaves in heaven of these spirits. And it came to pass that God gave another festival, and it was greater than the first; and more than three billion angels were present, who had become enlisted in righteous works.

12/6.4. This was the beginning of the third year of Sue; and his wisdom and power were now manifested all around the world, on earth and in heaven.

12/6.5. And this is what happened in reference to the false Gods and false Lords. They came to the festival equipped in chariots and ships, with banners and flags, crowns and diadems, and with many other wonderful extravagances; and nothing like it had been in heaven since the flood. And each and every false God and false Lord endeavored to outdo the others in show and parade.

12/6.6. As might be expected, the first day of the festival neither won their applause nor censure. The second day they ceased to attract attention; for

[377] sanctity = holiness, saintliness, piety; decorum = polite behavior, deportment, manners, etiquette, conventions, propriety, formality

the thrift, purity and wisdom manifested in the countless millions of the second resurrection caused even children to receive more praise than the Gods and Lords with all their glitter and show.

12/6.7. On the third day one-half of the false Gods and false Lords cast aside their adornments and appeared in plain white, pleading to be initiated into the mysteries of the second resurrection. And on the day following, the rest of them came, seeking admission also.

12/6.8. At that, the Light of Jehovih spoke through God on the throne, saying:

12/6.9. Think, O Gods and Lords! What are you doing? It was barely yesterday that you asked for kingdoms, desiring to be leaders and great workers, over and above your fellows.

12/6.10. And you obtained your desires, becoming Gods and Lords over millions. And these became your dutiful subjects, and you adorned your thrones and your persons in great splendor.

12/6.11. Behold, I gave a festival, and you came as living witnesses of what self-made Gods and Lords could accomplish. And your dutiful subjects came with you to attest their loyalty and good faith in your wisdom and power.

12/6.12. Now you have cast aside your crowns and high estate, praying to become workers among the host of men and women! Are you not mad? And are you not making yourselves the destroyers of your own subjects? For, see, because of your abjuration[378] of self-pomp and self-glory, all your subjects are cast aside in ignorance and misery.

12/6.13. With one voice the self-Gods and self-Lords answered, saying: Alas, O God! What shall we do? Our crowns we can give away; our raiment and jewels, our thrones and kingdoms. But, O God, we cannot give away our subjects; they will not go. We have bound them to us; and we are bound to them because we accepted them. What shall we do, O God? The burden is more than we can bear!

12/6.14. God said: Do not be disconsolate,[379] O Gods and Lords! You have done a great work. You have rescued millions and millions of familiars and fetals. And even before you applied for the resurrection, behold, most of your subjects had already deserted you!

12/6.15. Hear the judgment of your Creator, which is that when all your subjects and fetals are risen in wisdom, virtue and good works, so as to take the second resurrection, then on that same day you shall be promoted. Only then can you have freedom of soul.

12/6.16. The voice ceased, and the self-Gods and self-Lords answered: You are just, O Jehovih. We will go to work among our poor and ignorant subjects, and make them comprehend Your wisdom, power and justice.

12/6.17. For ten days the festival lasted, and then it ended. And thus were rites and ceremonies first established in the lower heaven as a power to work wisdom and virtue. And from that time forward, music, marching and dancing were included in all ceremonies by the Gods and Lords of heaven.

CHAPTER 7 Sue

12/7.1. In the fifth year of Sue, he dispatched swift messengers to Opnetevoc, in etherea, saying: Thus says Sue, God of two etherean worlds: Behold, I am sojourning on the earth, and, with the God of heaven and his Lords, have prepared one billion Brides and Bridegrooms for Jehovih's etherean harvest. Greeting to Nista, of Ho and Tow'en, Goddess; in the name of Jehovih, send an airavagna and complete the resurrection of the Father's Brides and Bridegrooms!

12/7.2. So it came to pass in etherea that the Goddess Nista provided an airavagna, an etherean ship, resolving to come as commander in chief. Sue advised God, saying: Make of this matter a great testimony in your heaven. Send, therefore, your messengers into all parts, and to your Lords on the earth, inviting all people to be present to witness the ascent of Jehovih's Brides and Bridegrooms.

12/7.3. God did as commanded, and on the day of the appearance of Nista, daughter of Jehovih, in her sun-ship, in the firmament, there were assembled in Hored countless millions of souls inspired of Jehovih.

12/7.4. Great was the rejoicing and the manifestations of delight when the sun-ship came into full view, descending, like a world on fire. And when she passed Chinvat and was fully within the

---

378 rejection, repudiation, recanting, renouncing, cessation, discontinuance

379 dejected, despondent, disheartened

earth's vortex, the enthusiasm of the people knew no bounds.

12/7.5. They sang, prayed, danced and clapped their hands, as if mad with delight. Meanwhile, the Brides and Bridegrooms had been arrayed in etherean white, and were now saluting those whom they were soon to leave.

12/7.6. Quietly the etherean hosts fulfilled their part in the great play of the immortal resurrection; very Gods and Goddesses in demeanor.

12/7.7. Nearer and nearer came Nista in her sun-ship, slowly turning and descending, with ten thousand curtains suspended and waving; and ten times ten thousand banners and flags waving above and around.

12/7.8. And then slowly down, lower and lower, till the airavagna rested on the plateau of Hored, to the south of the Temple of Jehovih.

12/7.9. Gussitivi, marshaless to the throne of Sue, in Izaracha, with ten thousand deputies, went forward, and with open arms received Nista, Goddess descended, saluting with the sign of the star and square, having been warm friends two hundred thousand years in the plains of Oayad, in the etherean es'tu[380] of Hi'dan, the spiritual center of the orbit of the great serpent when in Zagagowthaka.

12/7.10. The es'enaurs of both hosts were chanting, and the angels of the airavagna were coming forth in hundreds of thousands, to be saluted by the previously trained Brides and Bridegrooms of Jehovih and by the hosts of Sue, the etherean laborers.

12/7.11. And when Nista came up to the throne, God and great Sue rose up amid the light, now gathering fast as a mantle of brilliant fire over the place of council.

12/7.12. Sue said: All hail, O Nista, Jehovih's Daughter! God said: In Jehovih's name, welcome, O Nista. To which Nista answered, saying: By the Wisdom and Power of Jehovih, O my beloved!

12/7.13. And Sue and God parted, and Nista ascended and sat in the middle of the throne. After the ceremonies of salutation, Nista said: Let the Brides and Bridegrooms of Jehovih approach the throne of God.

12/7.14. The marshals then ushered the billion of them to their places, and the swift messengers bound them on all sides, so that the responses would be uniform and spoken as if by one person. Then Nista spoke from the throne, and the Brides and Bridegrooms responded in the usual form of Gods and Goddesses, and after that, took the necessary vows and renunciations of the earth and lower heaven, according to Jehovih's commandments.

12/7.15. When the ceremonies were finished, God proclaimed one day of recreation, which was participated in joyously by more than four billion souls.

12/7.16. So, on the next day, Nista and her hosts, with the billion Brides and Bridegrooms, entered the airavagna amid the cheers and weeping of millions of atmosphereans, who had never witnessed so grand a spectacle.

12/7.17. And then Nista, by the power of the Great Spirit, set her ship in motion; raised it up from the lower heaven; moved it upward by her command, saying: Arise! Arise! Airavagna! By my will, arise! Embrace the realms of Great Jehovih! Arise!

12/7.18. The es'enaurs and trumpeters were singing and playing; and those ascending threw down flowers and perfumes, and all sorts of pleasant keepsakes, to the countless millions below.

12/7.19. In a little while the airavagna disappeared in high heaven.

12/7.20. This, then, is what followed of Sue's ministration: When six years expired, thus marking the end of dawn, he delivered God and his Lords and another billion Brides and Bridegrooms, taking them into the extreme borders of Izaracha, to which was assigned the a'ji'an field of Rus'tsoo with twelve etherean worlds.

12/7.21. And Sue left T-HI, as the anointed God of the lower heaven for the next four hundred years. And God (T-hi) anointed Lords for the divisions of the earth, the same divisions as before. And the earth and heaven prospered, so that in the dan following there were raised up two billion Brides and Bridegrooms.

12/7.22. After that there was a decrease in the etherean harvests for two thousand years, after which great darkness came on the earth and heaven belonging to it; and self-Gods filled all atmospherea. And, as for Lords, there rose up in every nation on the earth, thousands and thousands,

---

380 spiritual center. –1891 glossary

so that men and angels did not know if there were a true God or true Lord in all the universe.

12/7.23. Thus ended the cycle of Sue, being three thousand and two hundred years.

END OF BOOK OF SUE, SON OF JEHOVIH

The Lords' Second Book

Being contemporaneous with the Book of Sue, Son of Jehovih. As the latter is chiefly about the angels of heaven, so is the Lords' Book about man on the earth.

CHAPTER 1 Lords' Second

13/1.1. God said: I, the Lord, for my predecessors and successors and for myself, declare these things to mortals:

13/1.2. The chosen of God, called I'hins, because they were the fruit of both heaven and earth, were taken, under the protection of God, his Lords and angels, to all the divisions of the earth for the fulfillment of man on the earth for the glory of the Almighty.

13/1.3. And I, the Lord, a one-time mortal, with my holy angels, who had sprung from the earth in former times, walked with man to keep him upright in the way he should go.

13/1.4. By command of God, the angels watched over man, teaching him often unknowingly to himself, in all good works and industry. By constant changes of watch the angels relieved one another daily, weekly and monthly.

13/1.5. And at no time did the angels leave the I'hins alone, and without the light of heaven.

13/1.6. But wherever the I'hins went, the angels went also, often taking on sar'gis and being seen by man, even daily; and man talked with them face to face.

13/1.7. And the angels told man what was good for him; showing him the way of righteousness.

13/1.8. And man depended on the Lord and his angels for all things helpful to his understanding.

13/1.9. Now when the earth was inhabited in many places, and there were thousands of cities and villages, the Lord said to man:

13/1.10. Behold, you have made the earth the joy of the Lord; and now I give it into your keeping. What do you say?

13/1.11. And man answered: It is well; I can keep the earth, and I shall rejoice on it because it is the gift of God.

13/1.12. The Lord said: If I stay with you, day and night forever, you will not put forth your own power and judgment.

13/1.13. Man said: Go your way, O Lord.

13/1.14. Then the Lord withdrew awhile, taking his angels with him.

13/1.15. Now in those days, there were ground people dwelling in the wilderness who did not have the light of heaven in them, nor could they be made to understand.

13/1.16. As one may discourse to an ox, and it does not comprehend; so was speech to the people of darkness.

13/1.17. Nevertheless, in winter, when food was scarce, the ground people (druks) came to the cities of the I'hins, begging for food. And the I'hins, remembering the commandments of God, went out to them, treating them to everything good to eat.

13/1.18. Now, behold, the chosen were tempted by the people of darkness. And it came to pass that a new race was born on the earth, and they were called I'huans, after the ancient warriors that destroyed the chosen, before the flood.

13/1.19. These I'huans were copper colored and were capable of speech.

13/1.20. When God saw what had happened, he called to the I'hins, saying: O you that could dispense with the Lord! Did I not give to you the mark of the circumcision as a limit to the line of my chosen?

13/1.21. Hear me now in my prophecy: The I'huan shall be taught the name of Jehovih, the Great Spirit, and the plans of heaven and earth. And he shall one day inhabit the whole earth, holding dominion over everything on it and in its waters.

13/1.22. And ultimately the I'hin race shall disappear from the earth; their kind shall not be found on this my footstool.

13/1.23. The I'hins inquired of the Lord as to when these things would come to pass. The Lord said: In twenty thousand years.

13/1.24. The Lord said: From this time forward, the I'hins shall not mingle with any other people on the face of the earth. This is my commandment. And whoever violates my word shall be cast out of my cities, and go dwell with the barbarians.

13/1.25. Because the I'huans are your heirs, and are capable of everlasting life, you shall be the light of my kingdoms to them; teaching them peace, righteousness and mercy; but you shall in no case permit them to enter or reside in your cities.

13/1.26. Neither shall you raise a hand to do them harm. But if they come upon you in multitudes to take your stores, then you shall depart out of that city, leaving the I'huans to take the goods and food for themselves.

13/1.27. For you shall be an example of non-resistance for the sake of establishing the love of God in them.

CHAPTER 2 Lords' Second

13/2.1. God foresaw that the I'huans should be separated from the druks, otherwise Yaks would again be born into the world.

13/2.2. And he said to the I'hins: Behold, the I'huans cannot hear the voice of the Lord, therefore go to them, saying: Thus says the Lord: If you mingle with the druks, your seed shall not inherit everlasting life, but go down in darkness.

13/2.3. And the I'hins went and told the I'huans the words of God. Nevertheless many of the I'huans broke the commandment. And, indeed, Yaks were again born into the world.

13/2.4. The I'hins said to one another: Are these not like those of the legends of old, who were made eunuchs and servants?

13/2.5. The I'huans inquired the meaning; and when they were told, they made a law for themselves, making eunuchs and servants of both Yaks and the ground people wherever they came upon them.

13/2.6. The I'hins feared the judgments of God in this matter, and they called out to him for a remedy.

13/2.7. But God answered them, saying: Because of the enmity between these two races, behold, they will not marry. Suffer the I'huans to do in their own way. For of what profit is it to bring forth heirs that cannot inherit my exalted heavens? Because the tribes of darkness cannot be made to understand, behold, their souls go out of being as a lamp that is burned out.

13/2.8. So it came to pass that the I'huans made eunuchs of the tribes of darkness; from both sexes they made them, and made slaves of them also.

13/2.9. The Lord said: The I'huans shall have laws of their own. Let my chosen go to them and make laws for them, saying: Thus says the Lord:

13/2.10. The I'huans shall be guardians over the I'hins, the sacred people; and through the I'hins I will bless the I'huans, and make them mighty.

13/2.11. Since it is unlawful for the I'hins to kill any beast, bird or serpent, behold, their cities and mounds are invaded by all types of evil beasts and serpents.

13/2.12. The I'huans shall slay all such evil beasts and serpents.

13/2.13. And they shall guard the cities and mounds where my chosen reside.

13/2.14. The ground people and the Yaks shall be servants to the I'huans. And the latter shall cast [381] their servants, so they shall not multiply on the earth.

13/2.15. Hear, then, the law of God between the I'huans, one with another:

13/2.16. Whoever does an injury to his neighbor or to a stranger, the same shall be done to him.

13/2.17. Whoever takes from another, he shall restore a twofold equivalent.

13/2.18. Whoever kills a man, woman or child, shall be put to death.

13/2.19. Whoever marries his sister or mother, or his half-sister or half-mother, they shall all suffer death together.

13/2.20. Whoever oppresses another shall be cast out of the tribe of his people.

13/2.21. He who blasphemes the Great Spirit shall be put to death.

13/2.22. He who does not respect the time of woman shall be put to death.

13/2.23. The fields I have given to the I'hins, but the forests and wildernesses I, the Lord, have given to the I'huans.

13/2.24. And it was so; the I'huans began to be carnivorous. But both the I'hins and the tribes of darkness ate neither flesh nor fish.

---

[381] de-sex, neuter, spay or castrate, make eunuchs of them

CHAPTER 3 Lords' Second

13/3.1. In all the great divisions of the earth, these things were; nor did one division of the earth have much preference over another. But in the warm regions, where the earth brought forth abundantly, the I'huans and ground people dwelt most numerously.

13/3.2. In contrast, the I'hins dwelt in both the warm and the cold countries. For they clothed themselves; and built habitations. But the I'huans wore only a covering about the loins; neither did they build any habitations. And they roved about far and near.

13/3.3. But the ground people did not travel; and they mingled with their own kin, bringing forth heirs of darkness.

13/3.4. The I'huans learned the laws and obeyed them; and they looked upon the I'hins as a sacred people, doing them no harm.

13/3.5. And it came to pass that the I'huans became a very prolific people; four times more prolific than the I'hins, or the ground people.

13/3.6. And they spread rapidly over the earth, in all the regions where the earth brought forth fruit, roots, flesh and fish, that were good to eat.

13/3.7. For two thousand years the I'huans prospered; and they became mighty in many countries.

13/3.8. But in course of time they began to war upon one another.

13/3.9. And for hundreds of years they descended lower and lower in darkness.

13/3.10. And they no longer obeyed the commandments of God, but mingled with the ground people, bringing forth heirs of darkness.

END OF THE LORDS' SECOND BOOK

Book of Apollo, Son of Jehovih

Being the heavenly administration of Apollo, an etherean God.

CHAPTER 1 Apollo

14/1.1. Apollo, Son of Jehovih, resident of Pti'mus,[382] in etherea, and God of Suf'ad and Don'ga and Tah, in the South Province of Buru, Orian Chief, controller of vortices, said:

14/1.2. I, Apollo, once a mortal, proclaim: First, wisdom, peace and patience to all men, and comprehensive judgment concerning that which I speak. Second, to perceive the reason of things, as to what seems to have been, and of what comes after.

14/1.3. For the Great Spirit is all Harmony and Perfection, abounding[383] in time and in worlds to accomplish all possible imaginings; for which reason, be magnified in conception, not judging by the little understanding of mortals.

14/1.4. So that he who asserts harmony to be closer to the order of Jehovih, than that which is ill-formed or out of time, has little reason to prove his assertion before a wise man. As one may assert that ripe fruit is nearer perfection than that which is green, which assertion is self-evident without proof, so, in the understanding of Gods in the management of worlds, are things past and present, not things past and present in fact, but more like the immature and the mature.

14/1.5. Since, then, man perceives that words, at best, are just slow and coarse representations of the soul's conception of things, how much further lies a God's wisdom beyond the reach of mortal understanding! Remember, O man, that if you could recollect in a moment of time all you had ever learned, you would be wise indeed. If you were in tune with yourself, such would be your wisdom. To advance in such a way that man becomes attuned, first with himself, then with his immediate surroundings, then with the magnitude of worlds, and then with Jehovih, so that he moves,

[382] see image i085

[383] abundant, flourishing, richly supplied

acts and comprehends harmoniously, is to become one with the Father.

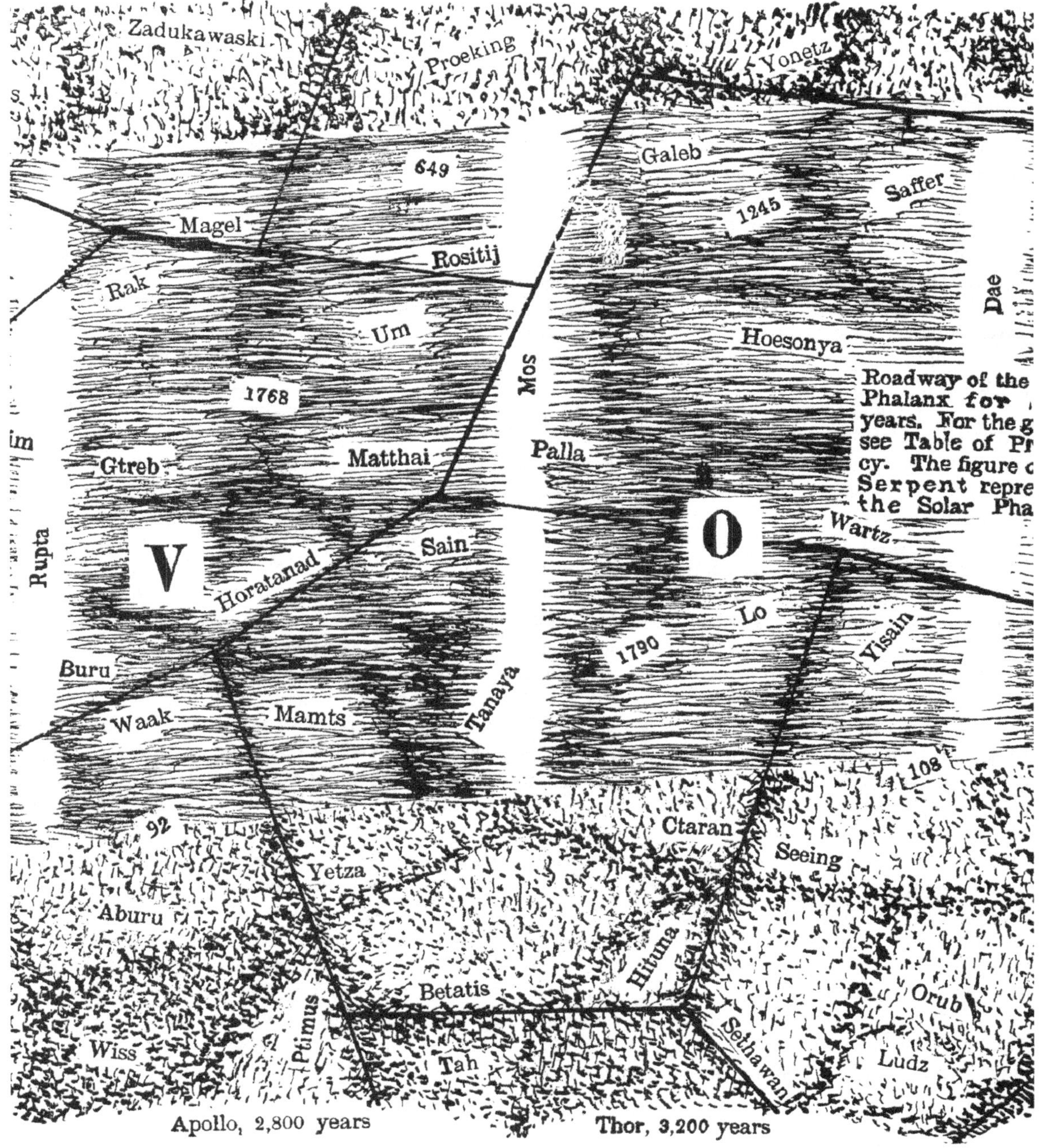

i085 **Map of the Etherean Roadway of the Solar Phalanx for the second set of two cycles of the past gadol, Plate 2 of 4**. The Roadway shown is that through which the sun and its family (including earth) traveled during the cycles of Apollo and Thor.

14/1.6. Which condition awaits all men, and is called in high heaven, Nirvania, because, to him who has attained it, things of the past and future are like an open book. He can look back to his own beginning in the world, and even beyond, and wherever he directs his eye, he can see and hear as if the matter was happening now.

14/1.7. Marvel not, O man, that the Gods reveal the words and signs of things long since perished corporeally; the proofs they could give, you could not understand, for the basis of spiritual entity does not lie within the measure of the corporeal senses. Nevertheless, Jehovih has given you comparisons; as a portrait of a man shows his looks even after his corporeal body has perished; and yet, the picture is only a representative.[384] To the spirit, a corporeal body is only a representative, being a manifested production of a spirit.

14/1.8. As out of corporeal things a new thing is produced and born into the world, so out of Jehovih is born the spirit of man; neither does the corporeal lead the spirit, nor the spirit the corporeal; but Jehovih does all. Do not think, then, that when the corporeal body is dead and molders back to original elements, that similarly the spirit of man will resolve itself back into Jehovih, for spirit is not bound by similar rules. As the corporeal body grows by aggregating to itself, not so grows the spirit of man, but by the opposite, which is giving away.

14/1.9. Remember, O man, the more you put forth your soul to give light and wisdom to others, the more you receive; and in this, you shall comprehend, in the reason of things, everlasting life to the spirit of man. So also, to him who desires to comprehend Jehovih, let him constantly describe the All Highest. To him who desires to comprehend the etherean worlds, the homes of spirits long risen in Nirvania, let him describe them. Fear not, O man, that you shall err; all the imagery you can devise is surpassed millions of times in the magnitude of the Father's kingdoms. Till you can shoot an arrow without striking the air, fear not for your weak thoughts shooting amiss in Jehovih's worlds.

[384] a likeness, an image, representation, emblem, indication

CHAPTER 2 Apollo

14/2.1. I Apollo, earth-born, of the continent Pan, submerged by Aph, the Orian Chief, by Jehovih's command, proclaim in the name of the Father, Creator of worlds, peace and wisdom to all nations and tribes of men: first, against all vanity and self-conceit in the souls of men; for in every cycle man asserts himself wise, great and learned, and the ancients, fools.

14/2.2. For the evidence of wisdom does not lie in learning one thing only, but in the adaptation of man to Jehovih and His works. In which measure, the modern and the ancient do not stand upon their own judgment in the matter, but by Jehovih's.

14/2.3. For if the ancient was not perfect in his place, neither are you, O man of this day. But, by the Gods, all the ages are adapted as Jehovih created them; do not judge Him, for your judgment is limited. That which was profitable to the soul of man, the Father revealed to the ancients; that which is profitable to the soul of man today, He reveals this day.

14/2.4. For which reason I, His Son, have come to fulfill my labor, even as all men, in time, must complete that which has been assigned them.

14/2.5. To rebuke vanity and self-conceit in those who do not perceive wisdom in things long past, but who applaud themselves without just measure before Jehovih. And the Gods perceive this vanity and pity them, hoping rather to exalt their minds, so that they may learn to perceive the Father's hand manifested in all things.

14/2.6. Turn your eyes inward, O man, and look at the spirit of things; imagine yourself a God looking down on a new earth, where man has been quickened into life, and attained to strength and learning. Take a look at his palaces and temples; his work in stone, iron, gold and silver; his knowledge of the sun, moon and stars; with written books to read; with clothes for the body and shoes for the feet; with great generals, and armies of soldiers; and with the land cultivated.

14/2.7. Are these civilized? And war abounding! By what right have you made yourself a judge, O man! Who has measured the inhabitants of the earth and found them pure and wise? Do more people now live on the land in peace and happiness than in many of the past cycles? Because you are different in many excellencies, you shall also remember that many great inventions are forgotten. The world has been peopled over many times, and many times laid desolate.

14/2.8. Who has been the chief enemy to man? Who is his chief enemy today? Is it not yourself? Do not think, O man, that because a few people perceive the Higher Light, the world is wise and good before the Gods. For in all ages there have been a few. Yes, today, there are a few more in number than in the ancient days. And this is the sum of the enlightenment of the world.

14/2.9. Hear me, O man of earth, and you angels of heaven: I proclaim harmony, symmetry and music. I am of the days of the fountain of these talents descending to mortals. I was like a shapely stone in Jehovih's edifice, and by hard toil, a fashioner of the flesh mold of man and woman.

14/2.10. As the ear of one man hears music, and he cries out with delight: A tune! A tune! And as the ear of another man hears music, which he cannot discern, and he cries out: A noise! A hideous noise! Why, then, shall you not judge them, and say: One of them has an ear for music, and the other has not? || One of them is at one with[385] the music; the other, being discordant himself, declares there is no tune, but only noise. To which will you give preference in judgment as to music?

14/2.11. Who has not seen Jehovih, the All Person? Who is it that cries out: I do not see Him? No harmony, no symmetry, no music, no complete whole? And to which will you give preference in judgment? Is not the judgment of the perceiver higher than he who does not perceive?

14/2.12. This I declare of Jehovih, that in all ages there are many who perceive the All Person, and many who deny Him. If, then, the lack of an ear for music makes a man dumb to a tune, is it not the lack of spiritual harmony which causes man to not perceive the everlasting presence of Jehovih the All Person?

14/2.13. Hear me, O angels and men: Can a man who does not hear the harmony of a tune, learn to sing? How much less, then, can man, or the spirits of the dead, harmonize with the Eternal Whole if they do not perceive Him?

[385] in unity with, unified with, in sync with

CHAPTER 3 Apollo

14/3.1. I Apollo, Jehovih's Son, proclaim an age when man on earth did not consider harmony, or symmetry, or music, as Gods!

14/3.2. And Jehovih's voice came to me in the etherean firmament, and place of Pti'mus, saying:

14/3.3. Apollo, My Son, God of Suf'ad, God of Don'ga, God of Tah, behold the red star, the earth, she comes through your dominions. Go to her with a sufficient number of your hosts, and give her a new God, and call his name Apollo.

14/3.4. Behold, neither men nor angels on the red star comprehend the harmony of My works; and because of their own disharmony, they deny Me, being blind to My Person. Go, My Son, and make them idolaters of harmony, symmetry and music, for a long season, so they may become organically attuned from the time of their birth upward.

14/3.5. I said: I perceive Your wisdom, O Jehovih. And I called together a hundred million of Your sons and daughters, and told them what You had said. With one accord, they said: We have examined the red star since the time of Wan,[386] and we perceive truly, the time has come for your labor, O Apollo.

14/3.6. I said: Send an oniy'yah to the heaven of the earth and deliver her God, Lords, and all persons capable of the second resurrection. And say to God and his Lords: Thus says Apollo, Son of Jehovih, and God of three etherean worlds: Greeting in the name of the Father, and love to you all. For your glorious work I have assigned seven Teres and Don'ga. There gather your hosts, where a place of rest and comfort is prepared for you. The earth and her heaven shall be left in darkness for thirty of her days, having neither God nor Lords.

14/3.7. So my legions departed for the earth in an etherean ship of fire, led by Tu'ain, Goddess of Proe'king, a place of great learning in the etherean mountains of Horatanad; and they delivered God and his hosts according to my decrees, and the earth was without a God and Lords for thirty days.

14/3.8. And the voice of Jehovih came to me again, saying: Hear your Creator, O My Son, you who sprang from the land long since submerged,

[386] when Sethantes was crowned as first God of the earth and heavens

who have spanned[387] many of My worlds, behold, the legions of Sue and his mighty resurrections are still preserved to mortals and earth-bound angels: Of the Gods and Goddesses who danced and sang before men; and of the uneven match between spirits and Gods.

14/3.9. Profiting in this, the people of the red star have become rich in rites and ceremonies, and in preferring the swift-footed to the slow, the nimble to the clumsy; indeed, the loo'is have well laid out the road to your success. ||

14/3.10. So, I perceived beforehand how I should proceed when I landed in the lower heaven and her earth.

14/3.11. When the time came, I departed, still remembering my native star with well-treasured pride. And so that all things would express the labor Jehovih put upon me, my oniy'yah excelled in beauty all other etherean vessels that had ever descended to the earth.

14/3.12. How shall I comprehend Your magnitude, O Jehovih? What is the journey of a God before You? We build a ship for a hundred million, and are vain of its size and beauty; but when we launch out into Your etherean realms, we feel like hiding our faces in shame of our vanity. We sail through a thousand of Your crystal worlds and talk of great distances, but the mirror of Your boundless creation lies before us still. We recall the red star, our native home, a single gem amid the countless millions You have cast into the universe, and we are speechless because of Your Awe-Inspiring Extent.

14/3.13. Where have You not excelled Yourself, O Jehovih? In one moment, we perceive Your Vastness; in another, Your Microscopic Hand in the smallest ethe'ic wave, and in the spear of grass down on the swift corporeal stars. We applaud You for Your handiwork, and yet before our thoughts have gone over even the smallest part, You turn our eyes inward to the soul of things, an endless wonder.

14/3.14. How shall I comprehend Your designs, O Jehovih? You take me back to the time Your angels came and stood man upright, saying: Be a man; and, be a woman! But they would not.

14/3.15. Again and again, Your pitying hand stood them up, and Your voice came, saying: Talk, O man! Come, you shall help perfect yourself. But man was slow in perceiving wisdom; he loved that which came to his flesh.

14/3.16. I remember the earth, O Father! Men and women with long hair hanging down; and hands with claw nails, fierce and war-like. And hair in tufts and short-curled. Whose eyes were drawn down like a lion's, and mouth wide and falling open, like a dog that is tired.

14/3.17. Therefore You have called me, O Jehovih; and I perceive Your double purpose: For man left alone would select and mate, and evolve to terrible war! And You store here an idol to unfit him for cruel deeds.

14/3.18. So, from Your etherean realms, where for fifty thousand years Your Gods and Goddesses had trained me to comprehend the discipline of Your created heavens, I came, descending, down to the red star, where You first quickened me into being, so that I could fulfill Your mandates.

14/3.19. Your hand took me up, Your hand sent me down; I had learned not to fear; the tree of faith had grown in me; I knew the secret of All Power. As a mortal goes into a dark cavern, where the air is damp and unacceptable to the nose, so came my hosts, O Jehovih, out of etherea into the vortex of the earth, into its dull atmosphere.

14/3.20. Your voice came to me, saying: Go around the earth with your oniy'yah, My Son. Stir up the atmosphereans, they who know no higher heaven. Behold, they have mutinied against My God and Lords; have rejected My proffered[388] wisdom. Their delight is in war and the deeds of mortals. As men on earth gather around to witness beasts in battle, so likewise these countless millions of spirits gather to witness kingdoms of mortals at war, or on fire, or plundering. And by their presence, urge men to cruelty and cunning horrors.

CHAPTER 4 Apollo

14/4.1. Hear me, O man and angels; from my words learn to be wise and deep perceiving. He who stands in darkness, does not see; no one can comprehend the time of Jehovih. The delight of all

[387] traversed, examined carefully, measured, labored in

[388] a beneficently offered or tendered or presented

men should be delight in the Light. But who practices to his highest knowledge? Before my days, time was no nearer the beginning of the universe than now. There were men who believed that for each and every man, with death came the end of that man's existence; and Jehovih sent angels to prove them in their folly;[389] yet though they saw them, and talked with them face to face, many would not believe that they were spirits of the dead.

14/4.2. And in the lower heaven, they were the same; they would not believe in a higher heaven. And though ethereans came to them to prove them in their folly, and talked with them face to face, yet many would not believe.

14/4.3. I searched the disbelievers, to understand their souls; and found they were begotten[390] in disharmony. They prided themselves in their wisdom; but that which they called wisdom was as a serpent in the soul.

14/4.4. Jehovih spoke to me, saying: Hear your Creator, O My Son. In atmospherea you shall appoint ten thousand Lords, with ten thousand kingdoms; and the earth and its inhabitants shall be divided among them.

14/4.5. And you shall build a new kingdom in heaven, and call it Gau,[391] and it shall be your judgment seat, with a Council of one hundred thousand men and women.

14/4.6. And all your Lords shall be called Apollo! And they shall inspire men to make images of stone and wood. And the images shall have short arms and long legs; and nails instead of claws on the fingers, and well-formed mouths, with shape to accomodate motion of the cheeks.

14/4.7. And your Lords shall find the loo'is who have been preparing these matters by birth; and the loo'is shall lead the angels in among mortals, finding the most comely-formed[392] men, women and young children. And when they have chosen them, they shall report the matter to the Lords, and they shall send ethereans to those mortals who are selected, and they shall be quickened by signs and miracles.

14/4.8. And it shall be proven before all the nations of the earth, including their kings, queens and governors, that the comeliness of the forms are pleasant in My sight, for which reason I come to them. And those who are thus selected shall sing and dance by entrancement; so that kings and queens shall be overcome by the achievements. And those that dance shall be made to float in the air, and sail about[393] in the dance.

14/4.9. For I will turn the judgment of man to beautify himself; and, in so doing, he shall learn to perceive beauty and harmony in My works.

CHAPTER 5 Apollo

14/5.1. Do not think, O man, that the Gods always deliver the nations of the earth in a day or by miracles. They go to the foundation of a matter; they make man a servant to help deliver himself. They stir up the nations in rites and ceremonies first; then come after, and appropriate the rites and ceremonies. And the women look on, receiving the spirit of the matter in their souls, the act of which entails[394] on their offspring that which is desired by the Gods.

14/5.2. With the hosts of high heaven, unseen by mortals, the Lords stir up the whole world. In one generation, behold, a new race is born. Man is unfitted for dangerous war, and no longer the delight of drujas hanging around.[395] So the drujas, and the familiars, turn from the peaceful earth (to them stale and unprofitable in bloody entertainments), to find their own petty kingdoms broken down and gone.

14/5.3. Be wise, O man, and angels of earth! Hear the voice of your brother, God of three worlds! I will tell you a great secret: These are the

[389] lack of understanding; absurdity; foolishness; i.e., to prove they were mistaken

[390] created, engendered, reproduced, gestated, born, came into existence, originated, conceived

[391] Gau here signifies plan of perfection. Gau is also mentioned in the Vedic Scriptures as the home of the God, Sughdha. –Ed.

[392] pleasingly-shaped, attractive to the eye that sees harmony and symmetry, pleasant to behold

[393] through the air for extended periods; and while on ground, glide about gracefully, nimble and light-footed

[394] necessitates, causes, inescapably brings about

[395] loitering, shady opportunists lurking about, searching for, sometimes only aimlessly alert for, self diversions

words of your Creator: Man and woman are pro-creators! Those whom they beget, are theirs, says Jehovih. Not for a day, but forever! Take notice of your offspring, O woman! Take notice, O man! Will you be entailed with druj, to pull you down? Will you choose offspring to glorify Jehovih?

14/5.4. Have your people not boasted, O earth? Have they not said: O the poor ancients! || What of them? Will they turn away from the idols of Apollo, and set up on their own account? Can the people hand down a name and models to live forever?

14/5.5. So I founded Gau in the place Hored had been, extending over Jaffeth, Shem and Ham; and the rest of the atmospherean heaven I divided among my ten thousand Lords and Lordesses, whom I selected and ordained in the manner of the ancients.

14/5.6. And the Lords established themselves in kingdoms, both on earth and in heaven. And they inspired kings and queens to erect images in the temples, and the images were given a name signifying Harmony, Symmetry and Music (Apollo). And the names varied in many countries, because of the languages of the people; but the signification was that these three entities comprised the All Light, the Creator, Jehovih!

14/5.7. And mortals were taught by the inspiration of angels how to make the images, for there were no corporeans sufficiently perfect for models.

14/5.8. According to the perfection of the images, so were they considered to be favored by Jehovih; and the sign of Jehovih's approval was manifested in the time of the sacred dance performed by the selected su'is; and the sign was, if the whirling dance caused many women to fall down by enchantment, then Jehovih was pleased.

14/5.9. Hear me, O man. The enchantment of the women was what the Lords desired, for the impression of the soul of woman shapes the unborn child.

14/5.10. In that regard, they worshipped blindly before the idols, not being sufficiently wise to understand how Jehovih was laying down the foundation for the coming race.

14/5.11. O you of little wisdom, compared with the Lords of heaven! How puffed up you are in judgment, not knowing the race from which you sprang! Jehovih's Gods and Lords mold the inhabitants of the earth as clay is molded in a potter's hand. They set them up, show them the way, and say to them: Go!

14/5.12. Mortals go on a little while, like a young child that totters and falls. And again the Lords set them up; and man, ungrateful, forgets and denies his God.

14/5.13. The unseen angels lead man and woman together, and say: Marry! And they wed, and bring forth of the Lord. Then man inquires: What do you mean: Bring forth of the Lord? But his judgment is under a cloud; he flatters himself that Jehovih created him, and then went away; and since then he has been his own master!

14/5.14. O man, what is your folly! How have you found such cunning ways to put off your Creator? What greater profit do you have in putting Him away, than in trying to perceive Him in all things? Why will you sing of man who is in darkness, and of the earth, which is just a fraction of the Great I Am? Do you not hope for wisdom, so that guardian angels may go away and rest?

14/5.15. Why should they stand over you day and night, to keep away familiars, fetals and drujas? Who shall close your mouth against falsehood, and your lips against cursing your Creator? Do you not hope, O man, that a wiser age will follow? When shall man learn harmony, symmetry and music? Who will hire a musician that constantly puts his instrument out of tune? Why should the Gods applaud men or angels who do not live attuned to the All Highest?

14/5.16. Show me one who is as good as his understanding; who lives as wisely as his goodness desires he should. He will understand my words; I can come to him and inspire him with great wisdom. He will comprehend the love a God has over mortals; and the patience of the toiling Lords and angels.

14/5.17. Hear me, O man! I will answer a great matter: The angels of heaven who are good, labor for those beneath them. This is their work, day and night. Do not think that they go away to idleness forever. To the etherean, industry becomes rest; to those who have attained to be Gods there is spontaneous growth forever. Remember this and be wise. To the atmospherean and to mortals, idleness of soul leads downward forever! Remember this also, and be wise.

14/5.18. Behold the rose and the lily; they are perfect in their order. Being one with Jehovih, they did not paint themselves. Let your soul practice with your Creator, and you shall become one with Him, even His Son. Find the symmetry of flesh; the symmetry of the spirit; the harmony of music,[396] and consider wisely your behavior.

14/5.19. The star of Jehovih is within your soul; feed it, O man, and you, O angel of heaven, and it will grow to be a God! Rob it, or starve it, and you shall remain nothing. It is weak and dim in the vain; it is bright and of great power in him who forgets himself in laboring for others.

CHAPTER 6 Apollo

14/6.1. Jehovih spoke in the light of the throne of Gau, saying: My Son, you have set the temples of earth wisely, and your ten thousand Lords have the voice of your Creator. But, behold, this dawn of dan has only five years and two hundred days. Five years are already gone. Call together your etherean hosts, and they shall report to you as to who the successors to you and your Lords shall be. I answered, saying: Your will be done, O Father!

14/6.2. So I sent messengers throughout the world repeating what Jehovih had commanded. And I added also: When the time of dan is completed, behold, my hosts shall assemble in Gau, where we shall ascend to our etherean worlds. Let my messengers invite all the people in all the kingdoms of atmospherea to be present. And these things were done.

14/6.3. Now, there were ten thousand kingdoms of the Lords of heaven and earth at that time. Many of them were located within the corporeal temples of worship, having spiritual thrones within them, where the hosts of angels assembled to counsel on the affairs of mortals, and to advise with them through the prophets and seers.

14/6.4. Neither was there in the entire world a temple, used for consulting the spirits and Gods, which escaped being usurped[397] by my etherean hosts. So that when kings or queens came to consult the oracle on matters of war or personal aggrandizement, my hosts answered, not to the consulter's own profit, but with the voice of Jehovih.

14/6.5. So it turned out,[398] that when the chief false Gods and false Lords were driven out of the corporeal temples, they lost interest in mortal affairs. And I classified them[399] and made new kingdoms in the lower heaven for them, forming them into confederacies. And they, too, became earnest workers to establish themselves in harmony, symmetry and music. And at the end of the time of hi'dan[400] there was not one false God or false Lord in atmospherea.

CHAPTER 7 Apollo

14/7.1. Apollo said: Hear the decrees of Jehovih, O Gods and Lords:[401] I, His Son, God of three worlds, speak! In my speech lies the wisdom of time; the evidence of fifty thousand years. Here is a great matter, O Gods; answer it, O Lords of heaven and earth: A child learns from that which is around about;[402] a man learns from that which is around about; a God and a Lord learn from that which is around about. Neither can they acquire anything more, forever. Jehovih says:

14/7.2. I have decreed the breaking up of old foundations; in new creations I provide food for the souls of Gods and men.

14/7.3. Apollo said: To condense and to expand; to expand and to condense, is this all? Who shall fashion a corporeal world by compressing ether? Or, by standing still, expand his own soul? How long will they be entailed with idle desires, self-ease, and self-glory?

14/7.4. Jehovih says: When the lower heaven turns into itself, it soon turns downward, also. And its cast molds the earth-born.[403] See to it, O My

---

[396] Music here refers to general expression or action; in other words, gracefulness in all things. The ancient Greeks gave a similar interpretation to the word music. –Ed.

[397] captured, taken over, possessed

[398] happened, eventuated, proved to be

[399] i.e., sorted them through noting their grades, ranks and rates, so as to most wisely provide for them

[400] i.e., at the end of Apollo's five years and 200 days

[401] referring to those who had been the false Gods and false Lords

[402] in one's milieu, surroundings, environment

sons and daughters, that you preserve the high estate of heaven. Apollo said:

14/7.5. To be a God is not all; to be a Lord is not all; you shall forever invent new stratagems[404] in Jehovih's kingdoms. Your people shall be endlessly infatuated with continual surprises, or your kingdoms in heaven will go down.

14/7.6. Jehovih says: Behold, I created man, and if he rests constantly, disease shall seize on his life parts. The kingdoms of men on earth that lack aspiration for the people shall bring destruction;[405] similarly in the kingdoms in the lower heaven, the lack of invented, new glories, shall breed up false Gods and false Lords.

14/7.7. Apollo said: To be a weak man, is nothing; to be a weak king, is nothing; to be a weak God, is nothing; but to be strong with Jehovih, furnishes food for the kingdoms of men and angels. Do not think, you Gods and Lords, that to be a good God is easy, or to be a good Lord is easy, or to be a good corporeal king is easy. He who rules in heavenly kingdoms, must constantly furnish food for the souls of angels and men.

14/7.8. I, Apollo, Son of Jehovih, will give you a parable suitable for Gods and kings: A multitude go into a forest; one man goes a little ahead of the rest, and he calls: Here! Here! Then he goes a little farther, and he calls: Here! Here! And the multitude follow. Concerning which, you reason well if you say: If the leader goes too fast for the multitude, they will not follow; and if he does not go fast enough, they cannot follow. Anarchy ensues in this latter condition, and new leaders are chosen.

[403] That is, as heaven is, so does earth become. Also, see to it = labor in such a way, make sure, make certain

[404] pursuits, goals, amusements, gambits, strategies and the like

[405] This seems to mean that a successful social order not only must provide ideas, vision, opportunities, means and impetus such as will give the people aims and ends to aspire toward, but also must provide for the fulfillment of people's individual, grassroots, or novel aspirations (assuming they are virtuous). Accordingly, too, for the social order, unifying themes must exist by which these aspirations can be seen to tie into a larger wholesome context.

14/7.9. And these conditions follow all peoples on earth, and in the lower heavens. But the glory of the emancipated heavens, in etherea, lies in the development of every soul into ripeness and bloom, with none too fast or too slow, but all as one, and one with Jehovih.

14/7.10. Is this not the testimony of the All Person: A ruler of a city; a ruler of a state; a ruler of a kingdom? Without a head to lead, and to govern, what people have been found? Without a God and Lords, and kingdoms in heaven, what angels are found: strollers, beggars, drujas and vampires. He who sets himself up against the king, what is he? He who sets himself up against the All Person, what is he? Where is the fruit he has brought to market?

14/7.11. His speech is cunning in denial; his arguments for liberty, the bait of hada. He cries out, in justification of his mutiny: Liberty! Liberty! But he leads to disharmony and darkness. After that, he rushes to the front, crying out: Follow me! Follow me! I will lead to truth and light. And he himself becomes a God, but in falsehood, even as by falsehood he denied the true God.

14/7.12. I declare to you a great fact, O Gods and Lords: A line lies between the man who has too much opinion of his own, and he who has no opinion at all. One is to be pitied, the other censured. So, which of these two do the Gods pity, and which do they censure?[406]

14/7.13. None could answer Apollo. So he spoke further, saying: Pity him who has too much opinion of his own; for of all men he stands the farthest from Jehovih. But the wise man and wise angel follow the median line between the two. In this lies the harmony of a man's soul.

CHAPTER 8 Apollo

14/8.1. Apollo, Son of Jehovih, said: In Jehovih's name I, Apollo, God of etherea, speak. Hear me, O Gods and Lords; the power of the Father rests in my soul; my words are of All Wisdom. Think of this great matter: The growth of love! As a man loves his city and his country—what, do you think Apollo has forgotten? Have I not told it in etherea? I sprang from the red star, the earth!

[406] rebuke, strongly disapprove, reprimand

14/8.2. For what reason shall I not take pride before Jehovih? And hold up my head in etherea, where I have neighbors that sprang from other stars. Shall a man forget his love because he is a God? No, truly. When I was mortal, I loved my neighbors; when I entered the second resurrection, in atmospherea, I loved all the people of the earth; and when I rose to etherea, my love expanded to a thousand worlds. But, of all places, how can I make the earth and her heaven second in the love of my soul?

14/8.3. As a mother invents diversions and employment for her children, shall I not gather fruit from Jehovih's repositories[407] to feed the atmospherean heavens? I came, and found you in a dark forest, with briars and thorns; but behold now, O Gods and Lords! The lower heaven has become a paradise.

14/8.4. Let me recall the philosophies I have overthrown: The false Gods and false Lords said: It is well that there is some war and destruction in heaven; otherwise, it would soon be too full! For they did not see the higher heavens; their arguments were framed in a dark corner. And, because of their evil inspiration, they gave mortals the same philosophy, saying: War is justifiable, lest the earth become too full. For these dark angels shut out from mortals, the higher light of FAITH IN JEHOVIH; justifying themselves in war, and the slaying of those whom Jehovih had created alive; by their behavior, thrusting condemnation in Jehovih's face for what Jehovih had done!

14/8.5. Neither did these mortal philosophers know that they were under the inspiration of spirits of darkness; nor would they wait till the earth was full of people, to prove whether their philosophy was true or false.

14/8.6. For, as you of heaven were addicted to deeds of darkness, your kingdoms reacted on earth, making druks out of men and women. Now all these heavens have turned from evil ways and become stars of glory in Jehovih's universe.

14/8.7. Do not think that only great thunders and terrible stratagems can govern heaven and earth righteously; for, as one man in an army may cause a panic, or one brave man's upraised hand lead a nation on to victory, so can you, O Gods and Lords, by wisdom, in the smallest of Jehovih's plans, rule over heaven and earth for the glory of His everlasting kingdoms.

14/8.8. That which I declare to you, go and declare throughout heaven; for the fruit of your teaching shall enrich the earth people, through their guardian spirits; and they shall, likewise, go about preaching among themselves.

CHAPTER 9 Apollo

14/9.1. When Apollo, Jehovih's Son, had finished his labor in the dawn of dan, God foresaw that his own resurrection, and his people with him, had come. So he sent his proper officers to the libraries of atmospherea, to learn who of all the etherean hosts should be selected to remain as God, and who as Lords, for the next four hundred years.

14/9.2. In twenty days the examiners returned and came before the throne of God and the Council of Gau. Za'dukawaski, chief speaker, said: By the grace of Jehovih, Creator, we stand before you, God of heaven and earth. We find by the ancient precepts,[408] which are adjudged wise in the foundation of atmospherea, one Gur, highest and most proficient of all the hosts of heaven, to be anointed God for the next four hundred years.

14/9.3. God said: I remember Gur, from Magel, in Sooftus, in etherea, God of Ra'yatuf and a'ji, seventy-two. Let the marshals go to him and acquaint him with Jehovih's decrees, in the name of God. And they shall provide suitable conveyance for Gur to come to Gau, according to his rate.

14/9.4. So the marshals, ten thousand in number, besides ten thousand musicians, went and brought Gur before the throne of God, coming in an otevan prepared for the purpose and adorned with one thousand pillars of light.

14/9.5. God said: I salute you, O Gur, in the name of Jehovih, Creator. Behold Apollo!

14/9.6. Apollo stretched forth his hand, and Gur came and shook hands with him, standing by the throne. Gur said: That I have lived to see this day, O Jehovih, I am blessed indeed! Your will, O God, and Jehovih's, be done!

14/9.7. God said: Behold, within thirty days the dawn of dan is to end, and all who choose, and are prepared for the third resurrection, shall be taken

[407] treasuries, stores, reservoirs, supplies

[408] teachings, commandments, laws, rules or principles regarding a course of action

up to etherea. Besides yourself, O Gur, there are two hundred thousand ethereans who have volunteered to remain another four hundred years in these atmospherean heavens, and on the earth. From them you shall select ten thousand Lords, and bestow them with kingdoms over mortals. I will raise two billion angels up with me to etherea.

14/9.8. To you, O Gur, I bequeath two billion atmosphereans who have been initiated into the second resurrection. And of the first resurrection, two hundred and fifty million; and of fetals three hundred million; and besides these, the inhabitants of the earth (men, women and children) seven hundred million.

14/9.9. God ceased speaking, and Gur said: Your will be done, O Jehovih! Then the es'enaurs sang, and the trumpeters played the March of Apollo, Jehovih's Son. Presently, the marshals and messengers filed before the throne; and a light of golden fire came down from etherea, cast out by the Gods of Helmatia, Orian arc of Tanaya, and it fell upon the throne of God, and many could not look upon it because of the brilliancy.

14/9.10. God raised up, as did Apollo by his side. God said: I stretch forth my hand to You, O Jehovih! Behold Your Son, Gur, God of Ra'yatuf, in etherea, an earth-born, forty thousand years inhabitant of Your emancipated realms. By Your power, and in Your name, O Jehovih, I proclaim him God of heaven and earth, to bestow You and Your kingdoms on angels and men! Be with him, O Father, Creator, that he may add to Your glory forever! Amen!

14/9.11. God took off the triangle, and hung it on Gur's (God's) neck, saying: I now bestow you with the heirloom of the Gods of the red star, the triangle of the ancients. And so that you may be still further honored, behold, one higher than I, even Apollo, shall weave a crown for your head.

14/9.12. Apollo walked to the left hand side, and raised his hand upward, and from unseen space a flame of yellow light came to rest on his hand, and he turned it just half around, and lo, a crown with sparkling gems stood upon his fingers' ends. Apollo had said:

14/9.13. Incomprehensible All Light! Weave me a crown for Your Son, God of heaven and earth! And even while he spoke, it was done, and he placed it on God's (Gur's) head. And God went and sat in the middle of the throne, saying: Throne of Your throne, O Jehovih! All things are Yours! For this shall be my resting-place, to do Your will.

14/9.14. During the ceremonies, the music was timed accordingly; and when the new God was crowned, the multitude of a billion applauded with great joy.

14/9.15. When all was quiet, God rose up from the throne, saying to Apollo and to him who had been God: In Jehovih's name, come and honor my throne! Accordingly, they both sat down at the right hand side of God.

14/9.16. God said: In thirty days, the dawn of dan will end. Let the marshals, through the messengers, proclaim the resurrection of two billion to the etherean heavens on that day. Proclaim it in all the heavens of the earth; inviting all to come who can; for it shall be a day of the feast of glory; but do not tell any of these that there has been a change of Gods, nor that great Apollo will rise also, lest sorrow come upon the people. The marshals then selected messengers, a great number, and sent them throughout the heavens of the earth, proclaiming the commandments of God.

14/9.17. God spoke further, saying: For thirty days the Council shall deliberate on my ten thousand Lords, selecting and allotting them; and I will crown them in the name of the Father.

14/9.18. Apollo then said: Now I will clothe myself in strange colors, so no one shall recognize me, and during the thirty days I yet remain, I will go about over the earth, so that I may again look upon the star of my birth.

14/9.19. And he who had given up the throne said: Your joy shall be my joy also. I, too, will again visit the star of my birth.

14/9.20. Accordingly, God said: Joy to you both, in Jehovih's name! Behold, I will throw a thick blanket over the throne, and you shall change your attire, and when I withdraw it, you shall walk forth unknown.

14/9.21. And this was done.

CHAPTER 10 Apollo

14/10.1. So Apollo visited all the divisions of the earth, and the islands in the ocean; and his traveling attendants, companions and officers, made a record of all the things they saw, especially those relating to the corporeans; their manners, sizes, color, habits, education and procreative capacities; and the records were taken with them, to be carried finally to etherea in the coming ascent.

14/10.2. And Apollo and his companions then visited atmospherea, making similar observations of the people in the first and second resurrections, recording the number and kind of nurseries, hospitals, factories, schools and colleges, together with the asaphs, teachers, physicians, nurses, and so on. And this record was also prepared so as to form a brief history of the earth's heaven.

14/10.3. On the twenty-eighth day Apollo and his hosts returned to Gau, the place of the throne of God in the lower heaven. In the meantime, the word of God, commanding the assembly for the ascent of two billion of Jehovih's Brides and Bridegrooms, had aroused the people of the lower heaven beyond measure—millions of them having never witnessed an ascent, nor, in fact, had seen an etherean adavaysit, a ship of fire.

14/10.4. In the evening of the twenty-ninth day, a light was seen high up in the firmament, to the northwest, brilliant, like a star of the first magnitude. Presently it grew larger and brighter, and shot across toward the southwest firmament, and then began to descend toward the earth, growing larger and brighter as it came.

14/10.5. The people of the lower heaven knew it was the adavaysit of the third resurrection, and they rejoiced before Jehovih, singing and praying. Now the marshals and proper persons for the purpose, commenced bringing into form the groups of Brides and Bridegrooms of Jehovih. And the groups were arrayed in stars, crescents, squares, circles and ovals, being classified according to their rates in these forms; and the groups had banners and signals of colored lights, according to their rank in love, or intelligence, or good works, or other characteristic virtues.

14/10.6. And these groups were arranged into combinations, every combination representing the work done by a sub-Lord or sub-God. And these combinations were further formed into four divisions, representing the four great divisions of the earth, and the four Lords, Jehovih's sons. So that when the whole two billion spirits were in due form, they characterized Harmony, Symmetry and Music, being the symbol of Apollo, Son of Jehovih, God of three etherean worlds, brevet[409] Orian Chief.

14/10.7. At midnight, the sea of fire, the adavaysit, which was twice the moon's diameter, reached Chinvat, the border of the earth's vortex, just beyond the orbit of the moon. Here the ship halted for four hours, and then began to descend, and rapidly, fearful to behold, becoming more scarlet within the vortex, but growing larger and definite in shape.

14/10.8. And, lo and behold, when the adavaysit drew near, it was in the form and configuration of the groups of Brides and Bridegrooms of Jehovih. It had fifty thousand curtains, and one hundred thousand banners, and of the hosts within the ship, seven million souls, each bore a streamer of phosphorescent light, which, together, were of all colors, shades and tints, and arrayed in symbols of the name, Apollo.

14/10.9. Unlike all other etherean ships of fire that had, as yet, visited the earth's heavens, it was provided with openings in the bottom, five hundred thousand of them, which were the places of entrance and exit. And the openings were studded with crystals of ceaseless fire of all conceivable colors, shades, tints, sizes, and shapes: curves, circles, angles, crescents, and so on. And up within the openings, were the crystal and opaque chambers, provided for the heirs of the third resurrection. And yet, within these chambers, were the reports of the guardian angels, of the lives and good work previously done by every man and woman of all the two billion who were to ascend to Jehovih's higher heavens. But in all the records there was not recorded one evil thing, or dark deed, or selfish thought; for of these things, the ascending hosts had long since purged themselves, till they were gems of the pure light of the Father of all. High up within the ship were the beams and network of timber, ropes and arches; and around the whole ship was the photosphere of its power, so that the whole adavaysit was like a crystal ship within a globe of phosphorescent light; and yet, in fact, the ship was the true light, and the angels the light of that light, while the photosphere was really the shell of darkness made reflective.

14/10.10. This, then, was the size of the adavaysit: of the photosphere, the diameters east

---

[409] honorary, nominal, vicarious, acting

and west, and north and south, were two thousand miles; and it was seven thousand miles high. And the ship within it was one hundred miles east and west and north and south, in diameters; and it was two hundred miles high.

14/10.11. As the earth is opaque, with a transparent vortex around it, so the opposite is the case regarding the structure of an etherean adavaysit, being light and habitable within as well as without, like the etherean worlds in the firmament. As Jehovih makes worlds, and sends them forth in the places of His firmament, so, in imitation of Him, His etherean Gods and Goddesses make adavaysits to traverse space from star to star, and from one etherean region to another. Great in wisdom and power are Jehovih's etherean Gods and Goddesses! Yet they, too, were once only men and women with corporeal bodies.

14/10.12. Jehovih said: I have given power to spirits of the newly dead to clothe themselves from the atmosphere with corporeal semblances of flesh and blood; and, to My exalted atmospherean angels, I have given power to clothe themselves from ethe in forms of light. But, to My exalted etherean angels, I have given power to clothe their hosts with ships of fire, and otevans, and adavaysits.

CHAPTER 11 Apollo

14/11.1. Cventi, marshalless for the hosts of Apollo, with ten thousand marshals and fifty thousand respondents of ceremonies, made preparations to receive the hosts of the adavaysit, commanded by Cim'iad, Goddess of Du'e'ghi, in etherea, Goddess of Noad and Rak, in Ji'ya, thirty-eight, well known to Apollo, and to Phaeja,[410] God of Norse, longtime residents of Um, in etherea.

14/11.2. Cim'iad was a small woman, dark, and of deep love, most jovial of Goddesses; and had long looked forward with joy to her pleasure of bringing so large a ship to deliver two billion of Jehovih's Brides and Bridegrooms into etherean worlds. And so, when the adavaysit was about to land in Gau, Cim'iad looked out from the clusters of central stars, the ornaments of the throne within the ship, to see the hosts who were assembled beneath, and joyously clapped her hands with delight, at which she was saluted by Apollo and Phaeja, and by God and his Lords.

14/11.3. Presently, the mighty vessel landed and anchored fast; and the ship of Apollo was moved up alongside and made fast to the adavaysit. Meanwhile, Cim'iad came forth out of the ship, and was received in the arms of Cventi, marshalless of Apollo, and then proceeded to the throne of God.

14/11.4. All the while, the musicians had been playing and singing; and the music of the lower heaven was thus united with the music of the upper heaven.

14/11.5. God said: Welcome, O Daughter of Jehovih! Come and honor my throne, in His name!

14/11.6. Cim'iad said: By the grace and love of Jehovih, I have come, O God! And to you, O Apollo, most wonderful of earth-born Gods, how can I express my boundless love! And to you, O Phaeja, long-enduring Son of Jehovih, my soul is as a twin, for the glory of our Everlasting Creator!

14/11.7. Behold, I have come in Jehovih's name to wed these two billion Brides and Bridegrooms to Jehovih!

14/11.8. Phaeja said: Your will and Jehovih's be done! And now they shook hands, as is the custom of Gods and Goddesses, and Cim'iad went and sat on the throne, saluting all the assemblage by making the sign of Jehovih's name with her right hand, which was answered by three billion spirits. And now the musicians played and sang the Stars of Jehovih! Meanwhile, the All Light began to descend thick and fast on Cim'iad's head, so brilliant that many could not look upon it.

14/11.9. And Jehovih spoke through Cim'iad, saying: I blow My breath upon a corporeal world, and man springs forth into life, the highest of My created lights. In the womb of Mi,[411] I fashion his spirit. When he is shapely and white,[412] I deliver him. I open the heaven of suns, and warm his soul.

---

[410] Apparently Phaeja was the predecessor to Gur as God of heaven and earth.

[411] Mi here refers to mother earth; it is another term along with Om that is used for the feminine attributes of Jehovih. –cns ed. [cns ed. refers to consulting editor for the present Oahspe edition.]

[412] This refers to the color of the purified soul, not body color. Note that Cim'iad herself had dark skin color (see 14/11.2).

Brighter than diamonds he comes forth; male and female they come; as stars for My everlasting worlds. Dressed as Brides and Bridegrooms for My chambers of Light and Love. In My arms they shall be blessed forever; in My mansions rejoice forever.

14/11.10. The respondents said (being led by the etherean hosts): I am Your bride (or bridegroom), O Jehovih! My soul finds love in You only, forever!

14/11.11. O Jehovih, my Father! I come to You to abide forever!

14/11.12. From Mi, my mother, the earth, who conceived me, I now rise up and go, forever.[413]

14/11.13. All praise to You, O Jehovih! And to you, O God of earth and heaven! And to you, O Lords of the earth, praise forever!

14/11.14. Your Lords, O Jehovih, raised me up. How can I render them joy for my stubbornness of heart! And Your God, for my second resurrection.

14/11.15. O how You have made us brothers and sisters, O Jehovih! And given me a higher world to abide in, forever!

14/11.16. O, Joy of my soul! To You I am beholden, O Father, everlasting Creator!

14/11.17. Jehovih said: Behold Me, O Brides and Bridegrooms! I am the ALL that is within all and over all. Members of My body are all things under the sun, seen and unseen, boundless, forever! I give them to you for your inheritance, forever!

14/11.18. Response: Who can give as You do, O Jehovih! Not only did You give myself to me, but You sent Your Gods and Lords to me to teach me how to live to enjoy Your Fullness, forever.

14/11.19. I will rise to Your immortal kingdoms, and learn the mysteries of Your glory and wisdom, O Jehovih! And when I am strong, I will go forth to those who are beneath me, and raise them up, to rejoice, forever!

14/11.20. Jehovih said: Laborers with Me; helpmates and companions, forever! With you I wed, from everlasting to everlasting.

14/11.21. Response: With You we wed, helpmates, forever! In the glory of Your worlds, without end!

14/11.22. Jehovih said: Mine are All Harmony; All Symmetry; All Love; and will endure forever!

14/11.23. Response: When I was in darkness, I fed on hate, anger, war, and lust. But You have taught me harmony, symmetry, and love, and I shall indulge in them forever!

14/11.24. Jehovih said: Receive My mantles[414] and My crowns, O My beloved! The darkness has come and gone; the rain has dried up, and My flowers are blooming for you, My beloved!

14/11.25. Response: Glory to You, My Creator and Preserver! All hail to Your Wondrous Works, O Jehovih! In all my giving I cannot attain to You, forever! Your Crown shall shine in my behavior, world without end! Amen! Amen! Amen!

14/11.26. Jehovih, You are mine, forever! Amen!

14/11.27. I am Yours, O Jehovih, forever! Amen! Amen!

CHAPTER 12 Apollo

14/12.1. The rites of the resurrection were completed, all of which would fill a book, were the words written down; and as for the music, for which there were five hundred thousand singers and players, a conception of it can scarcely be given to mortals. And when the light of the throne of God broke away a little, God announced six hours' recreation; and all the angels of Gau and of the etherean heavens, mingled together joyfully.

14/12.2. After this (for, behold, the end of the dawn of dan had come), Apollo, mightiest of all, rose up, and waved his hand in the sign, IN JEHOVIH'S NAME, and stood aside from the throne of God. After Apollo, Cim'iad rose up, and gave the same sign; followed by Phaeja. And when these three, high raised, stood aside on the floor of the throne, so that all the assembled millions could see them, so hushed were all things, it was as if time had come to an end.

14/12.3. Then the ten thousand Lords and Lordesses filed in front, they who had once been false Gods and false Lords, and in the past, arrayed in such gorgeous attire; now robed in plain white, and without ornaments.

---

[413] This doesn't necessarily mean they will never return as ethereans to raise other earthborn in the future. But they are resurrecting and leaving their earth mother, just as children grow up and leave home to live with their spouse.

[414] a loose, sleeveless covering like a cloak, here made of etherean light

14/12.4. The marshals opened the arches of the adavaysit, but yet not a soul moved from his or her place.

14/12.5. Then great Apollo, Cim'iad and Phaeja came down and sat at the foot of the throne, more loved than all the Gods who had as yet visited the earth and her heavens.

14/12.6. God came down from the throne and took Apollo's hand, saying: Arise, O Son of Jehovih, and go your way. Apollo rose up, in tears, and stood aside. Now God took the hand of Cim'iad, saying: Arise, O Daughter of Jehovih, and go your way. Next he raised up the long-tried Phaeja, when lo, both burst into tears, and fell in each other's arms! Phaeja, of few words at most, was last to slack the fond embrace; and then he and great Apollo, and Cim'iad, light of heaven, broke loose and marched forward to the etherean ship of fire. God resumed the throne, blinded by his tears.

14/12.7. Now fell the mantles of Jehovih, and His crowns, on the two billion Brides and Bridegrooms. The awakening LIGHT of the etherean firmament bespoke[415] Jehovih's Awe-Inspiring Presence! The hosts moved with one accord, and presently entered into the adavaysit, amid a shower of etherean flowers.

14/12.8. The marshals signaled, for the dawn was ended. The bright Cim'iad stretched forth her slender hand and arm to Jehovih, saying: By Your Power, O Father, I command! Arise! Arise! Ad-av-ay-sit! Arise!

14/12.9. And the mighty vessel, with the vessel of Apollo adjoined, rose from Gau, rocking, rising, and moving to the music of a million trumpeters and singers, who were joined by the es'enaurs of the lower heavens. Higher and higher rose the etherean fire-ships, turning and rising, passing beyond the vortex of the earth, beyond Chinvat, out into the firmament of etherea, higher and higher, till all was lost to sight in the distance.

CHAPTER 13 Apollo

14/13.1. Jehovih spoke in the light of the throne of God, saying: To the Council of Gau, heaven of My Heaven! Hear the words of your Creator, O My beloved: Sing songs to Apollo and his Lords; let my people rejoice; for the Glory of my Son is upon them.

14/13.2. From My kingdom comes the Light and the Life; out of My Wisdom Apollo has come. Sing to him, O you Lords of heaven; let My angels rejoice in his name, for he shall abide forever.

14/13.3. I created him for the glory of angels and men; in his idols and images My people shall perceive the harmony of My beloved. With My own hands, I molded the ankles and feet, and well-rounded thighs. Behold the arms of My Son, no longer than to the thighs, and with dimples, and small wrists.

14/13.4. His neck is straight and slender, and smooth and round, like the higin on an altar; and his shoulders like hewn stone, polished and tapering, like a woman's, who does not go to war.

14/13.5. His instep is high; he can spring like a deer, swift as the wind. He does not sit on his haunches all day, with his hands down, like a druk that is tired, waiting for food. He flees to the plain and the forest on his swift feet.

14/13.6. Proclaim Apollo in heaven and on earth. He is risen! Higher than the sun is the Holy Begotten of Jehovih! Out of the Virgin Mi he has come, Holy; in symmetry and music, there is none like Apollo.

14/13.7. She was My betrothed from the foundation of the world; Spouse of your Creator, O God! Her name was Mi, Mother of My Holy Begotten Son.

14/13.8. They were without shapeliness before Me; they lolled[416] about on earth; they lolled in heaven; on their haunches they waited hungrily.

14/13.9. The Virgin bowed down; for her first-born was the Redeemer of the world. In stone, wood, copper, gold, and silver, he is stronger than ten cities; and wiser than ten thousand men.

14/13.10. He comes to the young mother's dream, and shapes her unborn, with limbs like a racer, and with long hair on the head. He stands in the idol,[417] and knows the mother's prayer every

---

[415] gave evidence of, indicated, attested to, foretold of

[416] loitered, loafed, lazily lounged, idled

[417] In those times, idol worship was the way of raising the standard of human form. Mankind was raised from idol worship, to belief in a spirit in the sky, and now in Kosmon, to The Great Spirit that is in and over all. The sense of beauty of form remains an ideal and is applicable to these Kosmon

day. Whoever calls on the name, Apollo, calls on the Father, Creator of all things.

14/13.11. Blessed are the Lords of Apollo; blessed are the sons and daughters of Apollo; blessed are they who bring forth in shapeliness to look like My Son, Apollo.

14/13.12. This mark of shapeliness I have put up before all women under the sun; the young women prior to marriage; and also before the young men prior to marriage.

14/13.13. Choose a spouse from those who look like Apollo; and your heirs shall glorify your Creator.

14/13.14. Apollo is My judge; he sits at My right hand; swifter than an arrow is his judgment on a woman's first-born.

CHAPTER 14 Apollo

14/14.1. Jehovih spoke from the light of the throne of God, saying: Hear the words of your Creator, O you Counselors of heaven.

14/14.2. They spin, weave and make clothes; they learn in the places of learning; neither do I condemn them.

14/14.3. But My physicians are tired; My nurses are tired; My teachers are tired. Be wise, O My Sons and Daughters. Who has reformed a beggar by giving to him? What physician prevents sickness by healing?

14/14.4. They bring forth in deformity on the earth, and you must cure them in heaven. They squat on their haunches on earth, and they squat the same way in heaven, and you must cure them.

14/14.5. Go to the root of the matter, O My beloved. Send word down to the kingdoms of My Lords, and say to them: Thus says Jehovih: Follow them, O My Lords! Double the number of ashars, double the loo'is; leave no young man alone; leave no young woman alone. Keep watch over them day and night; give them visions and dreams of Apollo. For, I am concerted[418] in heaven and on earth to remold the forms of the earth-born.

14/14.6. Jehovih said: Hear your Creator, O Gau! Make seven more plateaus for the second resurrection. Out of the idolatry of My Son, Apollo, I will beautify the inhabitants of the earth. And the cast and mold of men and women shall become a great power.

14/14.7. Jealousies will overspread the earth; jealousies will rise in the first resurrection. Make seven more plateaus in the second resurrection, and sort the es'yans in the hour of birth.

14/14.8. God and the Council perceived; and so God appointed workmen, and fulfilled the commandments of Jehovih. And he established seven hundred tributary kingdoms of the second resurrection belonging to Gau.

14/14.9. These sub-kingdoms were provided with sub-Gods, second in rank below the Lords, of whom there were ten thousand who had direct supervision over mortals; and all the Lords had a sufficiency of guardian angels (ashars), and loo'is (masters of generations), so that they could direct any required number to particular mortals as they chose.

14/14.10. The Lords mostly established their heavenly kingdoms in the temples where mortals came to worship; and they inspired mortals to establish spirit chambers near the altars, where the prophets sat to learn the decrees of the Lord. The loo'is also came here (to the Lord's place) to receive their appointments over mortals, for the purpose of bringing about marriages acceptable before Jehovih.

14/14.11. On the other hand, the affairs of the sub-Gods were wholly with matters in heaven, except when commanded by the Lords for special work.

14/14.12. And it came to pass, that mortals and their affairs were directed and governed by the decrees of the lower heavens, and these again by the etherean heavens, which were of Jehovih direct.

14/14.13. So Jehovih changed the forms of the earth-born; but they became worshippers of Apollo, accrediting to one another Jehovih's perfection in them according to the form and figure [419] of the flesh. And because of the idolatry of the women for Apollo, their children were born of good flesh, and shapely; so that, in four hundred years, the hair on their heads grew long and straight, and men began to have beards. Neither did

---

times. –cns ed.

[418] united, organized and moving in coordinated manner; concerted like a symphony, thus organic in harmony, symmetry and music

[419] shapeliness; aesthetic appeal, symmetry, beauty of proportions, wholesomeness, etc.

any young man consider any virtue in a young woman so important as her form; nor did young women value any virtue in man so great as a well-molded form.

14/14.14. And when mortals died and their spirits entered the first resurrection, half the labor of the asaphs, the receiving angels, was accomplished.

14/14.15. So God changed the es'yan period to three years, except for the heirs of cousins, uncles and aunts, which was left at five years.

CHAPTER 15 Apollo

14/15.1. So perfect was the way of heaven, that, at the end of four hundred years, God, his Lords, and his sub-Gods, had eight and a half billion souls of grade eighty-eight ready for the third resurrection as Jehovih's harvest.

14/15.2. So Apollo sent Adova, division Goddess of Reth, in Coak, in etherea, down to the lower heaven, to deliver God and his hosts. And they were thus raised up to etherea in a sea of fire, and made one with Jehovih.

14/15.3. The next government in the lower heaven and on the earth was in like manner, and the next deliverance in dan was ten billion souls, of grade sixty-five.

14/15.4. Similarly was the next administration in the lower heaven and on the earth; and the deliverance was ten billion, of grade fifty.

14/15.5. Likewise was the next administration on the earth and in the lower heaven, and the deliverance was ten billion, of grade thirty-eight. So Apollo commanded these to be delivered in the a'ji'an fields of Oth, in Sanak and Orant, for they were unsuited for etherea.

14/15.6. The next administration in the lower heaven and on the earth continued in similar manner to those previous, and the deliverance was sixteen billion; but they were of grade twenty-four. So Apollo commanded them to be delivered in the nebulous straits of Koppawotchiakka, for further development.

14/15.7. The next administration in the lower heaven was as those previous, but not so on the earth. For the kings and queens carried the idolatry too far, and mortals began destroying ill-formed children and cripples, thus casting the ills of mortality into heaven. So there was no deliverance for the last dan of Apollo's cycle; and Jehovih received no harvest.

14/15.8. Thus ended the cycle of Apollo, being two thousand eight hundred years.

END OF BOOK OF APOLLO

The Lords' Third Book

Being contemporaneous with the Book of Apollo, Son of Jehovih. As the latter book is of heaven, so is the Lords' Book of earth, for the same period of time.

CHAPTER 1 Lords' Third

15/1.1. In the time of heaven known as the arc of Rupta to Mos, the Lord descended to the earth in a sea of fire, to the land of Guatama.

15/1.2. And the Lord spoke over the land and over the waters, calling and speaking: Where are the I'hins, the chosen of the Lord? Speak, O man; come forth at the call of your God.

15/1.3. Then spoke man, answering the call of God, saying:

15/1.4. More than a million; more than two, more than four million, are your people, O Lord!

15/1.5. The Lord inquired: Where are my people? Where is the place and boundary of the sacred people, the I'hins, whom I delivered in the time of the flood?

15/1.6. And man answered, saying: From the head of the Ca'ca'tsak, the mountain river of rivers (Amazon). In Thes'onka, wide as the ocean, and the mountain plains of Om (Mexico). To the great cities of O'wan'gache and Nathon; and Neshesh, and Tesumethgad, and Naphal; and Yeshuah, by the lake Owane (Nicaragua), here stands the tower of Rakowana, shining with copper, silver and gold. And by the river Raxaa and her lake, Jon'gan. And over the plains of Go'magat (crescent) and Takshan, where they build great boats with crossbeams and sails of cloth. And to the north land of Uphsic and E'chaung, where the still river (canal) Eph'su begins, running to the wide oceans. Vid and Sajins (Lakes Superior and Michigan), where the I'huans dig deep down and bring copper, silver and lead in boats to the King of Avaya, I'huan monarch and good protector.

15/1.7. The Lord said: The greatest place of all you have not named.[420] Your eyes have not seen, your ears have not heard. Search, therefore, and be wise. Man said:

15/1.8. I was ashamed before God, so I set out to get great learning to know of what the Lord spoke. And I traveled for one year to the north, and many moons to the south and east. And I found a rab'bah of great learning, both in books and spoken words; and many prophets of the Lord in the great cities. So I inquired, saying: Which is the greatest place of the Lord's chosen? And, lo and behold, they answered the same as I had answered the Lord. Then I came to the city of Ta'zuntqua, a place for the yearly dance in the valley of On-out-si, where the rab'bah's temple is covered with polished copper; and I asked the same question. For the che'ba[421] within me desired to make a record of all things valuable; but, alas, I got no other answer than the echo of my own words.

15/1.9. God said: Where are my chosen? Where is the greatest place of the I'hins? You have shown me the I'huans, their great cities and kingdoms; their places of great learning. But the greatest of all, you have not shown.

15/1.10. Man answered: I do not know, O Lord. Tell me?

15/1.11. The Lord said: In among the I'huans are the I'hins, the little sacred people. The little cities in the suburbs of the large cities of the I'huans, these are the greatest cities.

[420] In another place described, this country seems to have been inhabited first in Central or South America, and to have embraced South America, Mexico, Texas, and the Western Mississippi, from which a canal extended to the Lake Superior mines. Further research now shows that these wonderful people also extended over a large part of Tennessee and Ohio, and part of Kentucky, and a large portion of Kansas. The extent of the country inhabited by these sacred people shows that not less than four million could have occupied it. –Ed.

[421] the desire that comes of inspiration. –1891 glossary

15/1.12. Man inquired of God: How can that be? Behold, the I'huans are three to one, compared to the I'hins!

15/1.13. The Lord said: These that build temples of hewn stone, and cover them with polished copper, are not my people. These warrior kings, that fortify their cities with soldiers, are not my people. They are not great.

15/1.14. But my chosen are these who live in mounds, and in cities with wooden walls, and clay walls. They are the greatest of all people. They do not dress in gaudy colors, nor ornament themselves with copper, silver and gold.

15/1.15. They are the people of learning. They survey the way for the canals; they find the square and the arch; they lead the I'huan to the mines, where lead, copper and silver are buried. These are a great people.

15/1.16. Without them the I'huan could not build his own house; he could not find the level for a canal; nor provide the square of his temple. The I'hins are the greatest people.

15/1.17. My chosen have shapely legs, arms, feet and hands; and their hair grows long and straight, white and yellow.

15/1.18. The Lord said: Because the I'huan is of all shapes and sizes; and of all grades and judgment, even down to the ignorance of a beast, behold, he is bringing forth heirs of darkness.

15/1.19. Come to the Lord, O you who are chosen. You have built houses and temples for the I'huans, but of what avail[422] are these things?

15/1.20. Behold, they are at war, tribe against tribe, nation against nation. They no longer listen to my rab'bahs, the priests of my chosen.

15/1.21. Go, now, you shall build temples to God.

15/1.22. Then the I'hins inquired the meaning of God's words.

15/1.23. The Lord said: For a long time I have prophesied through my chosen, the I'hins. Now I will raise up prophets among the I'huans, the copper-colored race.

15/1.24. This is the temple you shall build to the Great Spirit and His kingdoms in haden.[423] ||

[422] benefit, help, advantage, purpose, value

[423] Haden is both the Chinese and Algonquin name for sky. Phoenicians said, Aden; the modern Hebrew, however, is sha-chag. Aven is the

15/1.25. There are two peoples before my judgment, says the Lord: The one that does not hear the voice of God, or know him; but the other people know me, and endeavor to obey my commandments.

15/1.26. And God was weary with laboring for the I'huans; for they went more after the way of darkness than light.

15/1.27. And the Lord called away his guardian angels, leaving the I'huans alone for a season. And spirits of darkness came upon them and obsessed them.

15/1.28. And in that same time, the Lord caused his chosen to display the mold of their thighs, and their short shapely arms. And the I'huans tempted them, contrary to law. So it came to pass that the I'huan women boasted of their conquests, bringing forth heirs of more shapeliness.

15/1.29. Now, when these heirs grew to be men and women, behold, they had the gift of prophecy, and of seeing visions and of hearing the voice of the angels of heaven. And they were called Ongwee-ghan, signifying, good-shaped men.

CHAPTER 2 Lords' Third

15/2.1. God said: Do not permit the Ongwee to dwell with the I'hins, lest the seed of my chosen become lost.

15/2.2. The Ongwees came suddenly into the world; by the thousands and thousands they came, in the north, south, east and west. And they had long hair, black and coarse; but their skin was brown, copper-colored; and their arms were short, like the I'hins. Very proud were the Ongwees; they would not mix with the I'huans; and they dared not mix with the sacred people, because of the commandment of the Lord.

15/2.3. So, the Ongwee-ghan became a new race in the world, having all the symmetry of the I'hin, and the savageness of the I'huans. And, being feeders on flesh and fish, fell under the dominion of angels of the lower heaven (inorganic heavens), and they rejected the Lord God.

15/2.4. The Lord said: Even this I will appropriate for their own salvation in time to come.

15/2.5. So the Lord commanded the I'hins to give the Ongwees laws, rites and ceremonies; and these things were done as commanded.

15/2.6. Then the angels of the lower heaven came, teaching the Ongwees the secret of making eunuchs of their enemies, the I'huans with the long arms; teaching them how to make spears, and bows with arrows, and darts, fishing-hooks and nets; teaching them how to make fire by striking flint stones; teaching them how to cook flesh and fish to make them more palatable. And this was the first cooked food for man since the days of the flood.

15/2.7. The I'hins feared the Lord would visit a judgment upon the land, because of the Ongwees' killing and eating flesh; but the Lord said to them: Suffer the Ongwees to fulfill their labor; for the land is too full of beasts and serpents. Nevertheless, it shall come to pass that great destruction shall come upon the I'huans and the ground people and the Ongwees. Their great cities shall be destroyed, and the lands laid desolate; but I will rebuild them again with greater glory than at present.

15/2.8. And so, that which the Lord had spoken through the I'hin prophets, came to pass. In three thousand years the large and handsome race, the Ongwees, transcended the long-armed I'huans, the short-legged race. ||

15/2.9. God said: Hear me, O man! Understand the labor of the Lord your God. Jehovih says to the Lord: Go to yonder earth,[424] and make man upright (on two feet). And the Lord accomplishes it. Then Jehovih says: Go yonder, and make man shapely on the earth. And the Lord finds a way to do this also.

15/2.10. Do not forget the Lord your God, for such labor will fall to your lot when you are long risen in heaven. Behold, there are millions of worlds, newly coming into existence every day. Expand your judgment; make yourself comprehensive so that you may fulfill in wisdom, the glory of the Almighty.

CHAPTER 3 Lords' Third

15/3.1. God said: Hear the word of the Lord, O man; in your little wisdom be considerate of[425] the magnitude of the labor of your Lord.

---

mythical Hebrew for an undefinable place or idol. Some scholars trace the English word Heaven to the same source. Galgal is a condition of the mind. –Ed.

---

[424] i.e., go to earth down there

15/3.2. Certain times and seasons are allotted by Jehovih for the development of new orders of men on the worlds He created. According to the times, seasons and condition of the earth, so has the Lord your God fittingly provided the race of man.

15/3.3. To raise man up so that he may comprehend the beautiful creation, and be adapted in harmony with it, this is the glory of your God.

15/3.4. Behold, I have spoken of the land of Guatama! Do not think that as one division of the earth is made answerable to my will by a certain rule, that another division of the earth is provided in the same way. The Lord your God finds one place filled with beasts of prey and great serpents, which must be destroyed; and he provides a race of men to accomplish this. And so, man is allowed by God to become carnivorous for a season. In another country the Lord finds drought and frequent famine; and so he provides man with knowledge adapted to those conditions.

15/3.5. Thus, as there are seasons to the earth when man shall be changed from one condition to another, according to the progress of the earth, even so does God accordingly lift up man for the glory of the Almighty.

15/3.6. Do not let your judgment mislead you as to a law of selection. There is no law of selection. Man has no inspiration of his own to select a mate and provide his progeny with shapeliness or judgment.

15/3.7. He marries because of the impulse of the flesh; nor does he care about the issue, whether they have long legs or short ones, or whether they become warriors or imbeciles.

15/3.8. And woman cares even less than man. Nevertheless a time comes upon the world, in a later age, when man and woman both consider these things, and somewhat govern themselves accordingly. But in such an era they are almost fruitless.

15/3.9. But in the early age of a world, man has inherent only two impulses, to eat and to indulge in cohabitation. Nor does he consider what may result from it. And the Lord and his angels lead man, without him knowing, to fulfill his times and seasons.

15/3.10. Now I have come to you in kosmon to reveal the government of heaven upon the earth, and the inspirations of your God and his angels upon the race of man. Behold, in the time of Apollo, man in his present form was brought into being on the earth. For the time and season of the earth was ready for such. Even as in this present day your Lord has come to change man from a race of warriors to a race of peace; for now the time and the season of the earth is propitious[426] to accomplish this.

15/3.11. In the time of Apollo, the first prophets of God were raised up from other than the I'hin race. In that day, the I'huan, the flesh-eating man, was first capable of hearing the voice of your Lord understandingly. And your God commanded man to remember the God of harmony, symmetry and music, and to build images of him in all the divisions of the earth.

15/3.12. Be most searching, O man; for you shall find in this present time and generation, the legends and history of Apollo in all the divisions of the earth.

15/3.13. And the word of his name, in all languages, has the same signification.

15/3.14. Behold, as in Guatama the Lord raised up seers, whom he instructed in the methods of slaying beasts of prey and serpents, so in the same period of time he raised up for the same purpose other seers in Shem, Ham and Jaffeth (India, Africa including the Fertile Crescent, and China). And the names of the great slayers are preserved to this day in the mortal histories of these countries. ||

15/3.15. Thus on the earth and in all its divisions, the Lord created a new race; it came of the I'hins and the I'huans. According to the different countries where they dwelt, so are they found to this day. In which, your God provided all these people who are of pure blood, to have no other God or Lord than the Great Spirit, Jehovih.

15/3.16. Nevertheless in the time of Apollo, this race (Ghan) was only a fraction compared to the hundreds of millions of I'huans and ground people and I'hins that dwelt on the earth. But the I'huans were at war for more than a thousand years.

---

[425] attentive to, thoughtful regarding, respectful of, contemplative toward

[426] favorably inclined, auspicious, conducive, amenable, responsive

15/3.17. They built great cities, and established mighty kingdoms; but as soon as they were built, lo, the wars laid them low or dissipated them. ||

15/3.18. God said: Now I will give man a new commandment, which is, to go forth and subdue the earth; to slay every beast of prey and every serpent that comes before him.

15/3.19. And of beasts of prey and of serpents, you shall not eat the flesh, or the blood, which contains the life.

15/3.20. Neither shall you eat the flesh of the beast with uncloven foot; nor shall you eat swine's flesh.

15/3.21. But all cloven-footed animals I give to you, for food to eat.[427] || For in the day you take the place of beasts of prey, you shall also take it upon yourself to eat the flesh they would have eaten. ||

15/3.22. Then the Lord sent I'hin priests to circumcise the new race, the Ghan. And he commanded the Ghans to marry among themselves, promising to give the whole world into their keeping.

15/3.23. And the Ghans began to wear clothes, like the I'hins; and the latter gave them rites and ceremonies, and taught them how to pray and dance before Jehovih.

END OF THE LORDS' THIRD BOOK

Book of Thor, Son of Jehovih

Being the records of Thor, Apollo's successor, on the earth and in her heavens, from the arc of Mos to the arc of Dae, in the etherean heavens, and of three thousand two hundred years.

CHAPTER 1 Thor

16/1.1. Thor, Orian Chief of Don'ga, in etherea, God of Palla, Surveyor of Yonetz and Thassa, God of Galeb, Receiver of Saffer and Hoesonya, God of Wartz, Lo, and Yisain, Counselor in the ethereal worlds Hituna, Ctaran, Seeing, Sethawan and Hababak, greeting:

16/1.2. In the Holy Council of Gods and Goddesses in Don'ga, the voice of Jehovih came to Thor, saying:

16/1.3. My Son, behold the red star, the earth; she courses from Mos to Dae,[428] and now drags in the swamps of Asath. Behold, you shall deliver her through your dominions, three thousand two hundred years. Even now the dawn of Ghan approaches.

16/1.4. Thor spoke before the Holy Council, on Jehovih's etherean throne, saying: Behold, the young world, the earth, comes our way. For three thousand two hundred years she will journey in the fields of Don'ga.

16/1.5. Then the Holy Council deliberated on the matters of the earth and her heavens, and all other corporeal worlds that were to pass through Don'ga for three thousand years. And it was found that the dawn of dan would fall upon the earth first of all.

16/1.6. Then Thor called for the swift messengers that course the firmament in the regions of Apperwaith, the roadway of the earth's past history. And the swift messengers came and laid their report before the throne of Jehovih, as to what world the earth was, and the harvests of angels she had yielded up to the emancipated heavens.

16/1.7. When their reports were finished, and deliberated on by the Holy Council, Thor, Son of Jehovih, said:

16/1.8. For further knowledge as to the present condition of this world, the earth, it is my command that Yathai, God of Gammotto, choose one million volunteers; and, in an airiata, proceed to the earth and her heavens to visit her God and Lords, and ascertain[429] the condition of their angels and mortals, and report back in Don'ga.

16/1.9. So, Yathai, God of Gammotto, in etherea, was appointed for this purpose, and he provided an airiata, and took with him one million othereans, and proceeded to the earth and her heavens, as commanded.

[427] i.e., all the cloven-footed except for pigs (swine, hogs). Cloven foot or cloven hoof is a cleft or divided hoof such as cows, deer, oxen, sheep, goats, etc., have.

[428] see image i085, p.147

[429] determine, discover, assess

16/1.10. And Yathai came to the throne of God in Gau, in atmospherea; and God sent his Lords an invitation to come also. And seventy-two of them came.

16/1.11. God said to Yathai: Behold, the earth and these atmospherean heavens are full of false Lords and false Gods. Yathai inquired how many there were. God said: More than thirty thousand Gods and one hundred and sixty thousand Lords. Behold, in every great city on earth there is a false God or a false Lord, and he has a small heavenly kingdom of his own, located on the earth. And the spirits of the dead of that place are his slaves, for his own exaltation.

16/1.12. And in many of these heavenly kingdoms there are wars, and anarchy (hells) where the angels torment one another endlessly. Nor will these false Gods and false Lords and their subjects admit that there are higher heavens than their own.

16/1.13. The spirits of the newly dead are captured and kept in ignorance of Jehovih and His vast creations; and made to bow in adoration and worship to the false Lord or false God. And these in turn, being in contiguity[430] to mortals, inspire them to the same worship. Which fits them at the time of their death to fall as slaves into the dominion of him whom they worshipped.

16/1.14. The wars in heaven have inspired mortals to wars on earth, so that all around the world, unending battles are going on.

16/1.15. And those who are slain on earthly battlefields are born into spirit in chaos, not knowing they are dead (as to the earth), and so they linger on the battlefields, still battling imaginary foes.

16/1.16. All over the earth these battlefields are covered with spirits in chaos, and with the spirits of druks, druj, yaks and ground people, who know nothing more than the beasts in the field.

16/1.17. Return therefore, O Yathai, to your Orian Chief, Thor, Son of Jehovih, and say to him: The God of earth is powerless to rescue her angels and mortals from the great darkness upon them. And beseech him in Jehovih's name to come and deliver me and my kingdoms.

16/1.18. Yathai inquired about the races of men on earth, and as to the times of their termination.

16/1.19. God said: In twelve thousand four hundred years the I'hin race, the mound builders, will come to an end. And at that time the Ghans will have triumphed over all the lands and waters of the earth.

16/1.20. When Yathai had obtained the required information, and also learned the localities of the divisions of the earth and her heavens, he departed in his airiata, with his companions, and visited all the chief places, and then returned to Don'ga, in etherea, before Thor, Son of Jehovih, to whom he reported all he had learned as to the condition of the earth and her heavens.

16/1.21. Then came the Light of Jehovih to Thor, saying: My Son, take a sufficient host of ethereans, and go to the red star and her heavens, and deliver them in My name.

CHAPTER 2 Thor

16/2.1. Thor called in thirty million volunteers; and he provided an avalanza, an ethereal ship of fire, in which they embarked for the red star, where they would remain four years two hundred and thirty-eight days, which was called the dawn of dan, for Thor, of Don'ga.

16/2.2. Then outward, onward, through etherea sped Thor and his thirty millions. Through the swamps of Asath, and the fields of Broddwuski; through the ethereal seas of Hoesonya toward the arc of Mos, and then to Chinvat; the boundary of the earth's vortex. Nor did he halt here, but sped onward in his ship of fire for Gau, the throne of God.

16/2.3. God and his Lords, being apprised of Thor's coming, had the capital prepared for his reception. And they also had gathered in all the angels of the second resurrection, and as many of the first as chose to come. In all, there were assembled in Gau, nine hundred million angels, Faithists in Jehovih. Of these, no more than one million had ever seen an etherean, nor had they visited farther outward from the earth than the seventh plateau in atmospherea.

16/2.4. Among these, even into the heavenly capital of Gau, alighted Thor and his thirty millions. And after due salutations in the manner of Gods and Goddesses, a day of recreation was proclaimed from the throne of God; and the

[430] close proximity including contact

atmosphereans and ethereans mingled together joyfully.

16/2.5. Then Thor ascended on the throne of God, and he ordained as follows:

16/2.6. One million constables to go to the false Lords and false Gods and arrest them, and bring them to Gau for judgment.

16/2.7. One million captors to possess the thrones and temples of the false Lords and false Gods, and hold them.

16/2.8. Eight million captors to gather in the angel slaves in all the hadan heavens.

16/2.9. Six million dispersers to overthrow and disperse the hells (heavenly battlefields of spirits in chaos).

16/2.10. Six million physicians to disrupt fetals from mortals.

16/2.11. Two million founders of es'yan nurseries, for the spirits of infants and helpless ones, born into heaven before their full time.

16/2.12. One million founders of hospitals, for chaotic angels and others stricken with disease.

16/2.13. Half a million marshals; half a million messengers; and three million builders.

16/2.14. And when these had been selected by the proper officers, they were dispatched to their places and duties.

16/2.15. Then Thor reorganized the Council of Gau for the period of dawn.

16/2.16. So God and his Lords rested for a season, while Thor and his hosts delivered earth and her heavens.

16/2.17. In one year all the false Lords and false Gods and Goddesses were captured and brought to Gau; nor did Thor pass judgment upon them until they were all brought in. And on this occasion, millions of angels were assembled in Gau to witness the proceedings.

16/2.18. Thor said to them: Do you not perceive that my power is greater than yours? How can that be? I have only thirty million; and of you there are more than thirty billion! What makes me more powerful? Behold, I have arrested all your heavens and heavenly rulers. How is this? Where did my power come from?

16/2.19. Not one could answer Thor.

16/2.20. Then Thor said: My army is a unit. Yours are divided, one against another. Yes, each one was in anarchy.

16/2.21. This I declare to you: Jehovih first of all; and His creations, which He has given to all His creatures.

16/2.22. To learn to master the elements of earth and heaven, this is the foundation for acquiring all power.

16/2.23. Because you bound yourselves in heavenly places on the earth, you did not rise up to the places prepared for you. Answer me now: How does the world stand as to what will come?[431]

16/2.24. Many of the false Lords and false Gods answered in the following manner: I fear to speak my mind, lest in anger you cast me in hell.

16/2.25. Thor said: He who has learned to know Jehovih and serve Him, fears nothing on earth or in heaven. Fear is nothing but the manifestation of weakness.

16/2.26. Speak, therefore, what you desire; no harm shall come to you.

16/2.27. Then many of them said: This I perceive, O God: Out there lie the earth and many heavens. The strongest mortals rule over the weaker mortals; the strongest Gods rule over the weaker Gods. Therefore, make me your slave. I am content.

16/2.28. Then Thor said: A greater hardship I give to you all; I give you your liberty and freedom. Go, therefore, wherever you desire. I ask not one to serve me; but instead I say: Go serve Jehovih by lifting up whoever is beneath you.

16/2.29. They answered: Where shall we go? We do not know the way from one heaven to another, nor the way down to the earth. You say: Go serve Jehovih by lifting up those who are beneath us. Now, truly, we cannot even lift up ourselves. If we had great riches, or power, or wisdom, then we would willingly assist those beneath us.

16/2.30. Thor said: Truly you are Gods of darkness. I say to you, do not wait for any of these things, but go at once and serve Jehovih.

16/2.31 They answered: When we have first provided a way for ourselves, then we will serve Him.

16/2.32. Thor said: You have spoken the darkness of the entire world. I say to you: Go serve

---

[431] That is, what is the condition, rank, grade, of the earth in reference to that which is coming?

Jehovih first; and after that come to me, so I may see if you lack anything.

16/2.33. They answered: How can one serve Jehovih by lifting others up, if he has no clothes, or food, or habitation?[432]

16/2.34. Thor said: It is well you ask that question; but I say: Direct that question to your own souls; and, behold, the Father will answer you. Let that be the question you ask yourselves every hour of the day; and be watchful for an opportunity to answer it by the labor of your own hands.

16/2.35. Then the false Gods and false Lords were dismissed from custody.

16/2.36. Thor commanded that the light of the throne and the pillars of heavenly fire be raised to a higher grade. The false Lords and false Gods desired to flee because of the brilliancy of the light, but did not know where to go.

16/2.37. Thor said to them: Why have you assumed to be Lords and Gods, since you cannot even master the elements in the lower heavens?

16/2.38. I say to you, the regions of Jehovih's universe are boundless. Let no one assume to do that which he cannot do; but, little by little, learn to master the elements surrounding him, and he will, in time, learn to traverse Jehovih's beautiful firmament, and indeed be a fit companion for Gods and Goddesses.

16/2.39. Then the false Lords and false Gods spoke, saying: O if only we had someone to teach us; someone to show us the way to learn!

16/2.40. Then Thor, perceiving they were in proper disposition for resurrection, allotted certain teachers and disciplinarians to them, and they were taken into educational colonies and put to work.

CHAPTER 3 Thor

16/3.1. Thor said: To induce men and angels to find the way of resurrection, this is the greatest of all teaching. Man says: O God, raise your servant up!

16/3.2. And the Lord says: Hold up your hands and I will lift you up. But man will not. Man says: Send wise and holy angels to me, O Lord, to guide me in righteousness and good works!

16/3.3. And the Lord says: That which you ask of God, even so do to your fellows. But man will not.[433]

16/3.4. As it is with man on earth, even so do we find it in hada.

16/3.5. To induce angels to develop themselves, by taking hold with their own hands,[434] and by the exercise of their own talents, this is the work of Lords and Gods. To rule over them without their knowing it, so as to lead them in the right way, this is wisdom.

16/3.6. The first passion of man is to eat; the second, the sexual desire; the third, to make others serve him. And if he accomplishes the latter, then he is indeed the prince of evil. For he then holds dominion to the hurt[435] of others.

16/3.7. As man builds these habitations in his soul on earth, how vain becomes his effort for happiness in heaven! To teach him to undo all his past, and to make full restitution to others, this is the work of Gods and Lords over spirits of darkness. ||

16/3.8. Thor established two thousand educational colonies in atmospherea, besides innumerable places of manufacturing and building; teaching the angels of heaven how to provide habitations for those born of earth into spirit life.

16/3.9. In three years of dawn, Thor had prepared four billion Brides and Bridegrooms for etherean ascension.

16/3.10. Now all this time, the angels of atmospherea had been taught much in regard to the emancipated kingdoms in etherea; and of the splendor, majesty and power of Gods and Goddesses living there.

---

[432] Thus, for example, how can one proceed without resources, the wherewithal, to induce others upward?

[433] So, for example, if you ask for love, then give love to your fellow humans; if you ask for wisdom, then impart wisdom for the wholesome benefit of others; if you ask for power, be willing to harmoniously work with others toward a good and worthy goal. But all too often man will not follow through on the second part of the arrangement for he desires the fruit without labor.

[434] i.e., hands on; by their own efforts, becoming actively involved, assuming ownership over their own behavior and thus taking responsibility

[435] injury, damage, detriment, impairment

16/3.11. Thor spoke from the throne of God, before the Holy Council, saying: Send swift messengers with greetings to Betatis, Goddess of Terow, in etherea, and say to her: Thus says Thor, Jehovih's Son, Orian Chief of Don'ga: Come to the heavens of the earth; I have four billion Brides and Bridegrooms as Jehovih's harvest. Provide an airiata of great size and splendor, for its presence shall enchant my people.

16/3.12. The swift messengers departed. And the appropriate officers at once began preparing to receive Betatis. Others were sent into other parts of atmospherea with fire-boats to bring atmosphereans to Gau, so they could perceive the glory of the higher heavens as manifested in the descent and ascent of the airiata.

16/3.13. All these things were accomplished. Betatis came in great splendor; and all the kingdoms and sub-kingdoms of Gau were filled with the billions who came to witness the ceremonies.

16/3.14. This, then, was the size of Betatis' airiata: The diameter, east and west and north and south, was two thousand miles to the borders of the photosphere, and nine thousand miles high. The ship within the photosphere was one hundred miles east and west and north and south, and was two hundred miles high. Of beams the entire length, there were twelve million four hundred thousand; and of uprights, two million; but of the short beams and short uprights, they were numerous accordingly. And there were a sufficient number of chambers within the airiata for every soul to have one; and, besides these, there were halls and temples within, also suitable for music and other entertainments.

16/3.15. The colors, shades and tints of the mirrors and opaque ornaments, both movable and fixed, were provided in all possible ways, for ornament and for service, the beauty of which had never been surpassed in Don'ga. And when the whole airiata was completed, it looked like an oval globe of light, with a framework. The transparent and opaque parts within, alternated, so as to add beauty to every part. And it was fitted and equipped for the third resurrection, having no storage places for atmosphere, or anything in common with the lower heavens.

16/3.16. To add still further to its splendor, Betatis had her airiata ornamented with illuminated banners and streamers, so that at a distance, when seen descending, the whole vessel looked like a sun surrounded on every side with movable stars and waving streams of light.

16/3.17. Among her hosts were one million trumpeters and players on harps; and two million singers.

16/3.18. In the center at the front of the ship was the Holy Council chamber, with four million members. Above the Council chamber was the chamber of worship; and at either side were the halls for dancing and social reunion.

16/3.19. When Betatis' ship neared the atmospherean kingdom of God, millions of her hosts stationed themselves on the galley-beams and stay-lines, adding a scene of life to the ethereal ship of surpassing beauty.

16/3.20. Betatis had provided her ship with ballast, so that, when she came within the earth's vortex, she could stand her ship where she desired, while the earth and her heavens turned their axial course, so that both mortals and angels could witness the brilliancy and glory of the works of Don'ga's chief Goddess.

16/3.21. And thus Betatis stood in her ship of fire, just beyond the plateau of Gau, while the earth and her heavens made one revolution.

16/3.22. The next day she descended into Gau, where God and his Lords, under the direction of Thor, Jehovih's Son, had prepared their mighty audience.

16/3.23. When the ship was made fast, the chief marshal of Gau and the chief marshal of Betatis' hosts met and conducted Betatis up in front of the throne of God.

16/3.24. Thor said: In Jehovih's name, welcome, Daughter of Light!

16/3.25. Betatis said: Praise the Almighty! In love, I have come to answer your prayer.

16/3.26. Then God spoke, saying: Welcome, O Goddess! Come and honor my throne!

16/3.27. Then Betatis went forward in a flame of light, and was greeted in the manner of Gods and Goddesses. After which she sat in the center of the throne. And at once the ceremonies of initiation for the Brides and Bridegrooms were accomplished.

16/3.28. Then came a day of recreation; and after that, Betatis and her hosts, together with the four billion Brides and Bridegrooms, entered her airiata and departed upward for the etherean heavens.

CHAPTER 4 Thor

16/4.1. In the fourth year of dawn under Thor, Son of Jehovih, he received from the Holy Council in Buru, of Don'ga, in etherea, a dispensation from the Orian Chiefs, decreeing to the earth one hundred years' travail[436] in vocent.[437]

16/4.2. Thor called up Waak, God of Rhines, and said to him: Jehovih has put a sore[438] travail upon these heavens. Go to Hey'loo and command him to provide an avalanza sufficient to deliver twenty billion atmosphereans to the a'ji'an forests of Gonaya.

16/4.3. For the inhabitants of these heavens are too dark to endure the vocent of a hundred years, and would be precipitated to the earth and engage in fetalism.

16/4.4. Waak, God of Rhines, knowing the condition of the atmosphereans, proceeded at once to Hey'loo, informing him of the decrees of the higher heavens, and of the command of Thor, Son of Jehovih.

16/4.5. Thor then sent word to his Lords and marshals, informing them also of his command, and, further, commanding them to bring all the lowest grades of angels from all parts of earth and heaven, to be concentrated in Gau, where the avalanza was to come for them.

16/4.6. Thor appointed Ti'See'inij, Goddess of Ares, to superintend the reception of the angels, and arrange them for entrance into the avalanza; and he gave into her command, to assist her, five hundred thousand marshals and captains, and one million es'enaurs. And she apportioned these to their respective duties and places.

16/4.7. To accomplish all this, Thor allotted seventy-seven days. And the proceedings were so wisely carried out that on the seventy-seventh day, the avalanza was present and all the angels ready to enter it.

16/4.8. Accordingly these things were accomplished: The twenty billion angels were carried away on the avalanza, which was walled around on every side with pillars of fire so that not one spirit could escape, even if he was chaotic or imbecile. Waak and Hey'loo had entire charge of the migration; and they proceeded upward and outward from the earth till they reached seven diameters of the earth's vortex, which brought them into the forests of Gonaya, where they landed them.

16/4.9. To provide for the reception, Ti'See'inij, Goddess of Ares, who had charge of the twenty billion, had previously sent there a sufficient force of angels, wise and strong.

16/4.10. So that when the avalanza landed, all things were ready. And according to their development, the angels were apportioned to different sections of the Gonaya forests, with suitable officers and teachers provided for them.

16/4.11. By Ti'See'inij, these things were done. And she established a throne of a'ji, provided a temple of Council, and provided all things that are required in the government of a new colony. And she provided a God in Gonaya to reign after the expiration of dawn; promoting to this one Hazedeka, a surveyor in Thalasia, the third heaven of Gau; and she gave him the title, GOD OF GONAYA, FOR FOUR HUNDRED YEARS.

16/4.12. Now, in reference to founding an a'ji'an habitation in etherea, this account is rendered to mortals and angels of the lower heaven: [439] The ethereans gather up the atomic elements floating amid the ethe'ic waves, and, giving them axial motion, they propel them forth. On their way, the atomic elements aggregate, till, from the size of a mite, the aggregation grows as large as the whole earth; but this world is habitable within and on its surface by the spirits of the dead, the angels.

16/4.13. || Jehovih said: In the same way that the solid earth, the stars and moon all float in the unseen firmament, so do atomic parts to all things float in ethe. As the earth is to the air and the ether above, so is an atom of corpor to the ethe'ic solution.

16/4.14. Jehovih said: Do not think, O man, that there is only one member in My Person, and that different conditions and states of that one comprise My universe. The foolish man has said, the blood is

[436] tribulation, trial, arduous times, adversity

[437] perpetual roaring of the atmospherean elements. –1891 glossary

[438] grievous, dire, bleak

[439] Notice that Oahspe was initially written for atmosphereans as well as for corporeans. This is stated more explicitly later in Oahspe.

the flesh and bones, and the flesh and bones are simply a state of blood; but he does not see that I do not make flesh out of blood, but out of that which the blood carries. And in the same way, I carry the corpor of My Person in the ethe of My Being.[440] ||

16/4.15. Now, as to Thor, Son of Jehovih, after the departure of the avalanza he provided a new God for the earth and her heavens, crowned him, and bestowed upon him the triangle which had been handed down since the inhabitation of the earth by man.

16/4.16. As for the remaining time of dawn, Thor traveled to all regions of the earth and her heavens, making records of these, to be carried with him to Buru in the time of his ascent.

16/4.17. In consequence of the depletion caused by the resurrection of the twenty billion to Gonaya, God and his Lords were greatly relieved of their burdens in Gau and on the earth.

CHAPTER 5 Thor

16/5.1. Peace and prosperity were established on earth and in heaven by the time the expiration of the dawn of Thor arrived. And now the time came for his own ascent, with his hosts, leaving the earth and her heavens in the care of God and his Lords.

16/5.2. So Thor, Son of Jehovih, sent swift messengers to etherea, asking to be delivered; and asking for the deliverance of six billion Brides and Bridegrooms to Jehovih.

16/5.3. See We'ing, Goddess of Hotosk, in etherea, was appointed by the Council in Buru to descend for Thor and his hosts, and his six billions.

16/5.4. Accordingly, See We'ing built her ship and gathered in ten million as her hosts for the journey. This, then, was the make of her ship, which she named Harp:

16/5.5. The photosphere was flat to the north and south, but oval east and west; the openings were on the flat sides, with passages through. The crescent described a circle of three thousand four hundred miles, and the depth of the harp north and south was three hundred miles. The pillars of fire that ascended from the midst were one thousand seven hundred miles high.

16/5.6. The stars within the photosphere were provided with five points; each star had one million chambers, and each chamber was allotted the habitation of one Bride or Bridegroom; and there were seven thousand of these stars.

16/5.7. The framework was crystalline, both opaque and transparent, and of all possible colors, shades and tints. Now, besides the stars and their chambers, the base of the crescent was provided with a large social hall, which, aside from accommodating others, was sufficient for and occupied by one million musicians.

16/5.8. God had knowledge of See We'ing's coming, and had commanded information to be sent throughout atmospherea, and to the Lords located on earth, inviting all who chose, to come and witness the ascent. And besides the Brides and Bridegrooms, two billion angels came; many not yet delivered from the first resurrection.

16/5.9. So it came to pass that See We'ing, Goddess of Hotosk, came down in her ship of fire to the foundation of Gau; came in great magnificence, and was received by Thor and by God and his Lords.

16/5.10. And she ascended the throne, and performed the marriage rite for the six billions. After that, a recreation time of one day was proclaimed in Gau, during which the atmosphereans and ethereans mingled freely together.

16/5.11. On the day following, Thor accompanied See We'ing into her ship; and their hosts went in also, being nearly seven billion. And then, amid a rain of etherean flowers, See We'ing started her fire-ship upward.

16/5.12. God and his hosts remaining in Gau saluted in the sign, JEHOVIH FOREVER! Which was properly answered by the ascending billions.

16/5.13. Then the great ship turned on its axis, rising and turning, higher and higher. And in a little while only an ascending star was seen, and then it disappeared in the distance.

16/5.14. Thus Thor fulfilled in dawn his great mission to the earth and her heavens.

---

[440] In other words, atmospherean worlds and corporeal worlds are not built from ethe, but from that which is carried by the ethe. Thus, the unseen is not just simply a rarefied form of corpor; that is, there is more than one member (i.e., there is more than corpor) in Jehovih's Person.

CHAPTER 6 Thor

16/6.1. Again the earth and heaven prospered for another season of two hundred years, and in the next dan there were five billion souls delivered. And new Gods and Lords succeeded, who also prospered, but not as well. The next harvest was four billion souls.

16/6.2. But once again, false Lords and false Gods began to set up kingdoms of their own, in heaven and in the cities of mortals. And, lo and behold, every one called himself either Thor or Apollo. And the spirits who manifested in the temples and for the oracles, all gave one of these names. And mortals who were obsessed, believed themselves to be the reincarnation of Apollo or Thor; the obsessing spirits calling themselves by these names. Others, more intelligent, said: Did the prophets not foretell that there was to be a second coming of Apollo? And are these spirits, who appear through the sar'gis, not the very person?

16/6.3. So great became the superstition of the nations of the earth, that in the fall of a leaf they found proof of the second coming of Apollo or Thor. Many of the spirits deserted the second resurrection in heaven and returned to the earth, to wait for information concerning the coming event, as they supposed, though there was no event coming.

16/6.4. Jehovih said: All corporeal worlds pass through the age of too much belief. As I gave man judgment so that he could examine and weigh a matter, so does he run into unbelief. Then My angels go to him, and show him where he believed too little; but, lo, he goes to the other extreme, believing all things, and not using his judgment.

16/6.5. God said: Why will men and angels not be patient, and wait till a matter is proven meritorious[441] before they pursue it to extremes? The same sun shines, the same stars stand in the heavens, and the earth travels steadily on her way; yes, her winds blow, her summers and winters come as in ancient time, yet man sets up a notion that a great wonder is near at hand. But no wonder comes, and nothing new is near.

16/6.6. How shall I restrain them, O Jehovih? Their desires for Apollo call down millions of spirits from my places of resurrection. And they fall in trials and hardships, and become suitable prey for designing false Gods and false Lords.

16/6.7. But no other salutation came other than the echo of God's own words. So God and his Lords bewailed the darkness of earth and her heavens.

16/6.8. But high up in the etherean heavens, came the Light of Jehovih; came the Voice of Jehovih, saying:

16/6.9. Hear your Creator, O you Gods and Goddesses! Behold the magnitude of My works! I do not labor for the profit of this man or that man; no, neither for this people nor that people; nor for the inhabitants of one star and one heaven; but for the glory of millions of stars and millions of heavens.

16/6.10. Does one corporeal man not bewail a shower of rain, and yet, his neighbor rejoices because of it? One man prays for sunshine, and another for shade. Do not think that I labor for each one separately, but for the perfection of the whole. For what reason, then, shall the God of earth and his Lords bewail the darkness that falls on the earth at this time?

16/6.11. I have prepared places of darkness in the etherean firmament, and places of light; and My corporeal worlds must travel through them, for so I created them. And these places of darkness and places of light are like changes of seasons for My harvests.

16/6.12. Now the earth passes into deep darkness, for I fructify the races of men in new corporeal growth, for things that shall come afterward. As they absorb from the a'ji of My places, in this age, so, also, do their souls become full of superstition and darkness. ||

16/6.13. Thus the earth went into great darkness during the last six hundred years of the cycle of Thor, and there was no harvest from her for the etherean heavens. But the spirits deserted atmospherea in millions upon millions, and went down to the earth, to dwell with mortals, and to find places to live on the corporeal earth.

16/6.14. And, except to the I'hins, the Light of Jehovih was shut out from men; thus ambition for improvement was at an end; they became like

[441] having merit, worthy, deserving, worthwhile, true, creditable

drones[442] and vagabonds;[443] and, when they died, their spirits continued to lie about in the places of their mortal life. And many of these spirits persuaded mortals to suicide, and they killed themselves by thousands and tens of thousands. Nor was there any courage among men to endure anything under the sun. They wanted to be with the spirits of the dead, to talk with them, to see them, and to be rid of earthly trials.

16/6.15. Neither did the spirits who congregated on earth have any knowledge of the higher heavens; nor could they impart knowledge as to where they dwelt, nor how they employed their time, for, in fact, they did nothing useful for heaven or earth, nor even for themselves.

16/6.16. Thus ended the cycle of Thor; and it was three thousand two hundred years.

END OF BOOK OF THOR

The Lords' Fourth Book

Being contemporaneous with the Book of Thor, cycle of Thor, Son of Jehovih. As the latter book is of the higher and lower heavens, so is the Lords' Book of the lower heavens and the earth, both books being for the same period of time.

CHAPTER 1 Lords' Fourth

17/1.1. God foresaw that the knowledge of one generation could be handed down to the next by altars and temples, by idols and images, and by painted signs and engraved words. And though all these things are in fact false, as a written word is not a word, but an image of an idea that has been spoken, so by symbols, God conveyed the living truth.

17/1.2. God said: Behold, with my sacred people I have established myself in written words. Now it has come to pass that all the races of man on earth shall be made to know me.

17/1.3. God commanded man to make stone and wooden images, and engravings also, of everything upon the earth. And so man made them; according to his own knowledge he made them.

17/1.4. God said: As every living creature has a name, so shall its image and its engraving have the same name. And so shall it be with all things on the earth, in its waters, and in the air above the earth; the image and the engravings shall have the same names as the real things themselves.

17/1.5. And God sent his angels down to man, to inspire him in the workmanship of images and engravings, and man thus accomplished the commandments of God.

17/1.6. And these were the first writings since the flood, other than those that were kept secret among the I'hins. And the writings were in the following manner, namely:

17/1.7. A picture of a man was a man; a picture of a tree was a tree; a picture of a bird was a bird; and so on, everything represented by its own name and image.

17/1.8. Then God said: When you have made the picture of a spear, behold it is a spear. And when you desire to show which way a man goes, you shall add to the graven image the likeness of a spear; and the way it points, shall show the way man goes. And you shall express the going of everything on earth and in heaven in the same way (with a spear showing its direction).

17/1.9. Thus man made a written language, and in every region of the earth. By many men these things were done; according to the light of God upon them, so they accomplished the written languages of thousands of tribes of men.

17/1.10. God said: This shall be called the Panic language Ah-ce-o-ga [earth language –Ed.], because it is made of earthly images. And, in later times, whoever desires to find the first written words of man, shall have recourse to the pictures of all things on earth, in the waters, and in the air above the earth.

17/1.11. God said: As in the ancient times man named all things according to their own spoken words and sounds uttered, so in the days of Thor the written words of everything on earth and in heaven came to the Ghans.

17/1.12. When man had written the name of all things, ONE only, he had not written, even the name of his Creator.

442 idlers, loafers, parasites, automatons

443 wanderers, rovers, drifters, ramblers, aimless, shiftless, of no fixed purpose

17/1.13. God said: Even that you shall also write. Then man inquired: O Lord, how can I find a word to express the Creator?

17/1.14. God said: I have raised many tribes upon the earth, and, behold, they have all written the names of all things, except only the Creator. Go, therefore, and write His name also.

17/1.15. Man said: Alas, O my God! I know no name, except the names I have already made. If I could hear the Creator, or see Him, then I could write His name.

17/1.16. God said: You have named the wind (wh-sh!), which you have not seen. Name, therefore, your Creator. And His name shall comprehend all things, far and near, seen and unseen.

17/1.17. Then man drew a circle and called it O, for it represented that which was without beginning or end, and which contained all within it. Then man drew a line cutting through the circle from east to west, to represent the light of the east traveling to the west. Then man drew a line from below upward, cutting the circle at right angles with the horizontal, to represent the one road of all things, from the bottom upward forever. The first line man called E, for it was the same as the wind speaks in the leaves. But the second line he called IH, for it represented that unseen shaft that cuts all things in two.

17/1.18. And when man had completed the engraving, he called it E-O-IH!

17/1.19. God said: In this symbol, you have found the way of a true square (true cross) and the four quarters of the world.

17/1.20. Keep His name and the image a secret between the rab'bahs and your God. Nor shall you utter it aloud, for it is sacred upon the earth.

17/1.21. Between you and your Creator stands your God, who is Lord of heaven and earth. Behold, I am the key of life and death; through me, your Lord, you shall unlock all the mysteries of heaven and earth.

17/1.22. Neither shall my rab'bah, nor my prophets, call on the name of any spirit, except the Lord, who is God. The words I give corporeally I also have recorded in heaven, neither can man alter my corporeal records and make them accord with that which is written above. But in the lapse of time I provide seers and prophets, through whom I can reveal to mortals the things of heaven.

17/1.23. On your behalf I have spoken the following to Jehovih: Man shall measure Your hand upon him; remember Your eye upon him; shall seek for Your wisdom within him; and he shall be thankful for Your good things before him. And he shall consider the little good of those who deny You, the conceit of those who claim to be self-made, and the folly of uttering other glories than Yours; and yet not mention any of these imperfections. For all these are the attaining of wisdom.

CHAPTER 2 Lords' Fourth

17/2.1. The Lord came down to man on the earth, and spoke to man in two ways: By the voice, as man speaks; and by the spirit, as soul answers to soul.

17/2.2. The Lord said: The voice of man is air in motion; by the mouth of man comes the word of knowledge.

17/2.3. But behind the voice, behind the air in motion, behind the mouth that gives voice, there lies the soul, which causes man to think of speaking. And the soul lies in the ocean of the Creator, Who is God of all.

17/2.4. The Lord said: That which speaks to your soul, O man, teaching you wisdom and good works; reproving[444] you for your faults, and enchanting you with the glories of all created things, is the voice of your Creator. And that is the road by which the Lord your God comes to you.

17/2.5. The Lord said: Behold, man has attained to written knowledge; now he shall have books, and learn to keep records, like the angels in heaven. Then God sent angels down to man, speaking both by the soul and by the voice; in different places and to different rab'bahs, teaching them how to make books of skins, of bark, and of cloth, for the graven words and images which he had taught man.

17/2.6. In these days the lands of Jaffeth, Shem and Ham were inhabited by millions of I'huans and Ghans; but the countries lying between them were inhabited by I'huans only.

17/2.7. And God spoke to the people of Ham, saying: Behold, there are two other countries inhabited by kin of your kin, flesh of your flesh,

---

[444] admonishing, revealing your relationship to the good, gentle correcting

and they are Ghans also. And they speak and write with Panic words, even as you do.

17/2.8. And the Hamites inquired: How far are the two other countries? Where are they?

17/2.9. The Lord said: Gather together two thousand men and women, and I will lead you to your brethren, whose forefathers were also saved from the flood; saved by the sacred little people, the I'hins. Provide oxen, asses, and all things requisite for a journey of four years, and I will lead you.

17/2.10. The Hamites obeyed God, and gathered provisions as commanded; they formed into two companies of a thousand each, equipped themselves, and started on their journey for Jaffeth and Shem.

17/2.11. Then God spoke to the people of Jaffeth, saying: Behold, there are two other countries inhabited by kin of your kin, flesh of your flesh, and they are Ghans also. And they speak and write with Panic words, even as you do.

17/2.12. The Jaffeth'yans said: How far are the two other countries? Where are they?

17/2.13. The Lord said: Gather together two thousand men and women, and I will lead you to your brethren, whose forefathers were also saved from the flood; saved by the sacred little people, the I'hins. Provide yourselves in all things requisite for a journey of four years, and I will lead you.

17/2.14. The Jaffeth'yans obeyed God, and gathered provisions as commanded; formed into two companies of a thousand each; equipped themselves and started for Ham and Shem.

17/2.15. Then the Lord spoke to the people of Shem in the same way, telling them of Jaffeth and Ham; and they also equipped themselves in two companies and started for Ham and Jaffeth.

17/2.16. Thus God provided for these three separate peoples to go and visit one another, and all in the same period of time. And God said to them before they started: The I'huans who inhabit the wildernesses on the way are very fierce and savage. Behold, they eat the flesh of both man and beast. But they will not harm the I'hins; therefore, O my beloved, take two score of I'hins (40) with you on your long journey. Through the I'hins, the Lord your God can speak all languages including the language of the barbarians, the I'huans.

17/2.17. Leave all things in the hands of the Lord God.

17/2.18. So it came to pass, after a journey of four years, the migrants from each country arrived at their destination. And they knew one another by their written and spoken words; and they called themselves the three children of the arc of Noe.[445]

17/2.19. And the Lord said to them in each of the countries where they had arrived: Provide records of the work of God; for these journeys shall be remembered to the end of the world.

17/2.20. And in all these countries, images of stone and copper, with engravings on them, were made pertaining to the children of Noe, and the flood, and the sacred tribes, Shem, Ham and Jaffeth.

17/2.21. God said: These shall be preserved as the first written names of these lands.[446] And it was so.

CHAPTER 3 Lords' Fourth

17/3.1. For two years the migrants remained in the countries they visited; traveling extensively, showing themselves, and relating a history of the country from which they came.

17/3.2. Then the Lord spoke to the migrants in their respective places, saying: Behold, the time has come for your departure. Gather together, O my beloved, and return to your own country, and relate there all the glories that your God has shown you.

17/3.3. So they departed, and returned to their own respective places. And, behold, it took four years to accomplish the journey.

17/3.4. Now during the migrants' travel, the Lord spoke to them every day through the I'hin priests.

17/3.5. The Lord said: Keep together, O my beloved. I will lead you; you shall not be lost.

17/3.6. Nevertheless, the journey was so long that many lost faith, and were not mindful of the

---

445 This is the origin of the story of the three sons of Noah, see Genesis 6.10, Ezra Bible.

446 Ja'fung is Chinese for Jaffeth, and is the oldest [corporeally known] original name of the country. Shem is the Vedic word for land, or country (India). Ham, as the student is aware, is A'ham, the original name of Egypt (Egupt). Legends of the flood, and of the journeys related above, are still existing in all those countries. –Ed.

words of God. And some of them strayed off among the I'huans, the barbarians, and were lost.

17/3.7. Of the six thousand migrants, ten tribes were lost; in all, three hundred and eighty-six people, men and women. Some were lost in one place and some in another.

17/3.8. God said: Sing songs of lamentations to my chosen who are lost, the Faithists in Jehovih. For this also shall become a matter of record to the end of the world.

17/3.9. Nevertheless, a time shall come when the Lord your God shall reveal the mystery of this day.

17/3.10. So, when the people had returned to their respective places, behold, they all sang songs of lamentation for the tribes that were lost.[447]

17/3.11. God said: I have shown you the far distant people; I have marked out the road. Keep the road open; keep the travel open between the great countries I have shown you.

17/3.12. Every eleven years one expedition shall start to the far-off countries. And if by chance you find my chosen, bring them home.

17/3.13 And on all the camping places of your journey, you shall build an altar to the Lord your God. You shall build it in the shape of a circle; and the congregation shall sit in this circle, but the priest shall sit in its center. And, behold, I will speak through the mouth of my priest, words of wisdom and comfort.

17/3.14. But in all your journeys, keep aloof[448] from the I'huans, the barbarians, the man-eaters. For they did not keep my commandments; nor did they preserve their seed through the circumcision.

17/3.15. But they mixed with the druks (ground people) and went down in darkness (barbarism).

17/3.16. Keep away from them, O my beloved; on all your expeditions, carry with you I'hin priests, the sacred people, the mound-builders.

17/3.17. In all your journeys you shall encounter your brethren coming and going, who dwell in the far-off countries. So that you may distinguish them, keep secret the sacred password [449] and the rites of my chavah (order).

CHAPTER 4 Lords' Fourth

17/4.1. Hear the word of your God, O man, and be considerate in your little learning, and so, interpret the records of the ancients rather by the spirit than by the word.

17/4.2. Where it was constantly commanded, in the ancient sacred writings, to avoid GOING DOWN TO DESTRUCTION, and they did not obey the commandments of the Lord, behold now the light of your God in this present day:

17/4.3. For the I'huan race, even before the flood, was in the first place, born capable of everlasting life. But they mixed with the druks until the seed of the spirit of eternal life became exhausted, and they brought forth heirs incapable of self-sustenance in heaven. Hence[450] it was said of them: They went down in darkness.

17/4.4. Now, after the flood a new race of I'huans was brought forth, and they were at first capable of All Light and of everlasting life. But they also did not keep the commandments of the Lord; but also mixed with the druks (the ground people), and they descended rapidly on the road of everlasting death (as a race).

17/4.5. But the Lord your God created the new race, the Ghans, capable of an upward inspiration.

17/4.6. And he gave to them the same commandments, to preserve their seed from the races beneath them, lest they go down in darkness also.

17/4.7. To which end, your Lord gave them certain rites and ceremonies, and passwords, in

---

[447] In all these countries, namely, China, India, Egypt and Persia, there is still in existence a legend that, long ago, the chosen of God went on a long journey in search of their ancient brethren, and that ten tribes were lost in the wilderness. –Ed.

[448] apart, separate, removed; distant in interaction, interest, emotional involvement, etc.

[449] E-O-IH, or Je-ho-vih, was the master's word among the ancient Jews. The Chinese said Che-hih-no, in their ceremonies, being the same phonetic word. The Algonquins (North American Indians) said U-he-no-win, accented on the second and fourth syllables. The Chinese word is accented on the first syllable. The Algonquin "U" is, most likely, without any signification. The word Git-che-ma-ne-to, of the Algonquins, means servant to the Great Spirit, that is, as the English word Lord means Land God, or an underling of Jehovih. –Ed.

[450] therefore, for that reason

addition to the circumcision, which would enable them to distinguish those with whom they should mingle according to the commandments of God.

17/4.8. Behold, then, the testimony that I lay before you, so that you may perceive the wisdom of my ways. For, it will be said by some that there is a law of evolution by which man rises from a lower to a higher state, as the earth grows older.

17/4.9. But I say to you, there is no such law. Without the labor of your Lord and your God, through their angels, man does not rise upward, but goes the other way.

17/4.10. In which matter, behold, before you to this day, I have left many nations and peoples who are on the downward road. And you have corporeal records before you, showing you, that in times past, these same countries were inhabited by a higher race.

17/4.11. For thus Jehovih created man, to go as readily down the mountain as up it.

17/4.12. Behold, all resurrection comes from above; all aspiration comes from the Lord and his angels. For man, being in the flesh, goes rather to the desires of the flesh than to the spirit.

17/4.13. As the light of the sun causes sleep to pass away, so does the light of Jehovih, through His Gods, Lords and angels, cause the soul of men to awaken to the possibilities of everlasting life in the exalted heavens.

17/4.14. This also, I, your Lord, have proven in the world: That those who fall from the light of the Father, lose their symmetry and beauty of proportions.

17/4.15. Behold, in the time of Thor, man did not consider the shapeliness of his spouse, nor the mold of her face, the clearness of her voice, her wit, nor her conversational powers.

17/4.16. The Gods and Lords have, by all stratagems, devices, rites and ceremonies, labored to make man mindful of the way of resurrection through the tree of life.

17/4.17. But even in the present time, behold, the mother barters off her daughter to a rich man; and the man seeks a spouse of wasted flesh for the sake of gold. And they bring forth heirs of crime.

17/4.18. And man cries out: He cannot be a good God who creates these!

17/4.19. But I say to you, they do not keep my commandments; they have gone astray in the wilderness.

17/4.20. Be wise, O man; learn from that which is before you, remember the times of the ancients, and the labor of the Lord your God.

17/4.21. In the beginning of the cycle of Thor, the Lord opened up many ways for the deliverance of the tribes of men on the earth; and man prospered in the way of God for a long season.

17/4.22. Then darkness came upon the races of men; millions of them returned to a state of savagery. And angels of darkness came upon the earth, taking upon themselves the semblance of corporeal forms, and dwelling with mortals, and engaging in practices about which it is unlawful to write or speak.

17/4.23. So that, at the termination of three thousand years, the lands of the earth were covered with darkness.

17/4.24. And Jehovih cast a veil over the face of the sun, and it did not shine brightly for many years.

END OF THE LORDS' FOURTH BOOK

Book of Osiris, Son of Jehovih

God of Lowtsin, an etherean world in the arc of Se'ing, known in the high heavens as Osire, Son of Jehovih.

CHAPTER 1 Osiris

18/1.1. To Osire, Son of Jehovih, on his throne in Lowtsin,[451] an ethereal world, where his reign a hundred thousand years had illumined many a corporeal star, came the Voice, Great Jehovih, Spirit over all, saying:

18/1.2. Osire! Osire! My Son: Go forth from these immortal worlds, and grasp the perishable earth in its debauched flight; and with uplifted rod proclaim yourself The One, the commanding God. As an indulgent father treads softly by his infant son, guiding him tenderly, and with wholesome advice, so, through My Gods and Chiefs, I have coaxed along the red star for many, many thousands of years. But as a wise father turns to his

[451] see image i086

truant son of later years, commanding you shall or shall not, so now in the same way, through you, My Godly Son, I stretch My hand over the earth and her heavens.

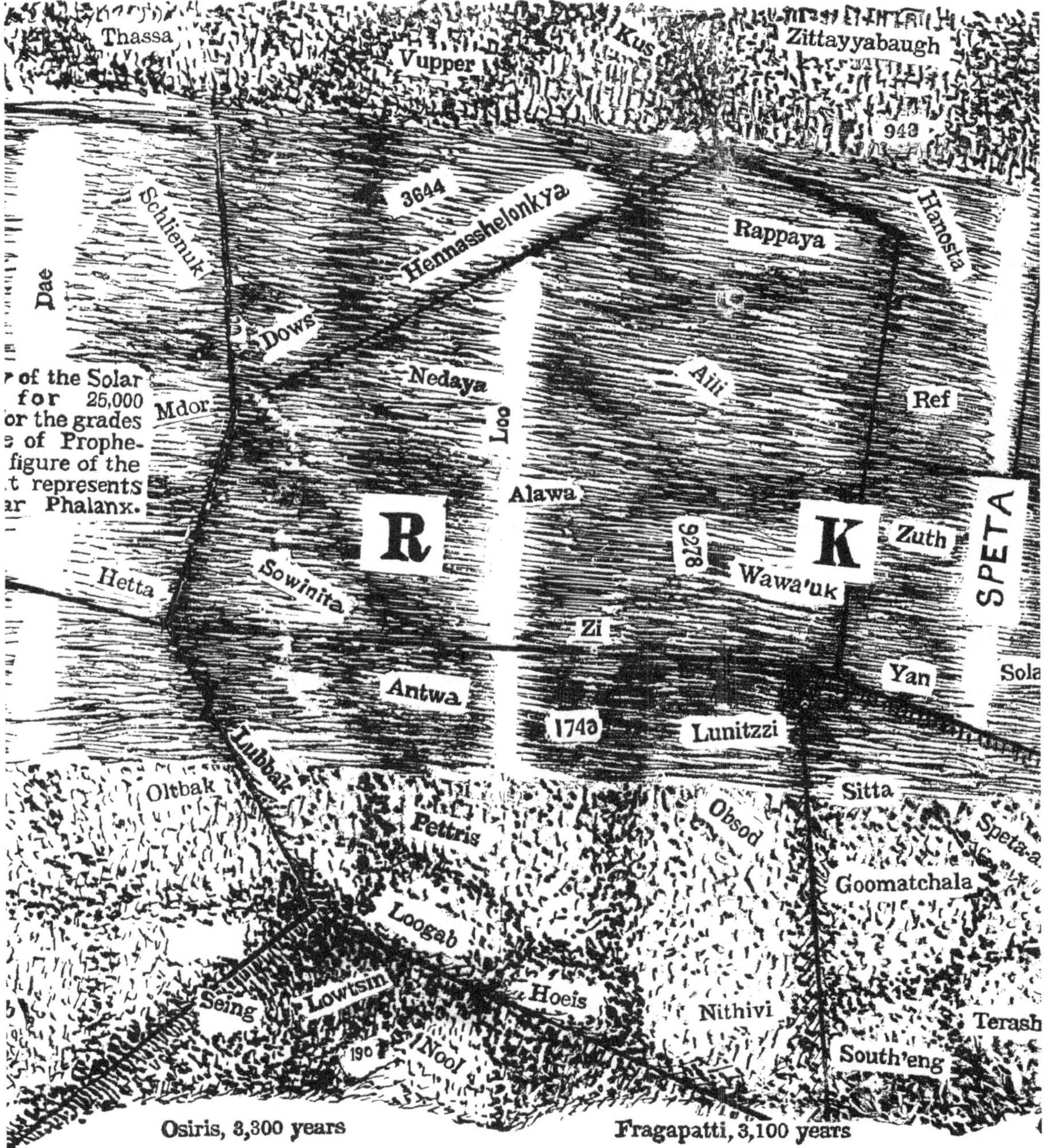

i086 **Map of the Etherean Roadway of the Solar Phalanx for the third set of two cycles of the past gadol, Plate 3 of 4**. The Roadway shown is that through which the sun and its family (including earth) traveled during the cycles of Osiris and Fragapatti.

18/1.3. Deep-buried she lies in anarchy; the false Gods and false Lords despoil her heavens in war, and cast down on the troubled earth, her millions of spirits of darkness, who glut themselves in crime. As driftwood on a surging sea now rises high on towering waves and quickly plunges down into the roaring waters, to rise and fall, and repeat endlessly the ceaseless struggle, so do the spirits of the dead, of earth, rise in heaven only to be plunged back again in unending toil and darkness on the low earth.

18/1.4. Where My most holy God and his Lords toil and struggle, powerless to divert the terrible heedlessness of men and angels. || Osire heard Jehovih's voice, and summoned a million swift messengers, well trained in the rise and fall of worlds, and bade[452] them go to the red star, the earth, at masterly speed, and survey the affairs of mortals and spirits, and promise succor[453] to God and his Lords of earth, then to quickly report back to Jehovih's throne, in Lowtsin.

18/1.5. In an arrow-ship, which Gods use for speed and light work in accomplishing Jehovih's will, the swift messengers shot forth through the ji'ay'an fields of darkness midway between the Serpent's coils, and were soon hidden deep in the whirling atmosphere of the warring earth. Meanwhile, Osire called long-risen Gods and Goddesses to council around Jehovih's throne, telling them the Voice's words, that had stirred his soul with compassion for those only recently quickened to life by the Creator's breath, but who persist in burrowing their souls down in hada, heedless of the call and persuasion of a loving God and Lords.

18/1.6. Jehovih's light spread over the Lowtsin throne of Osire and curtained around the stars, the Gods and Goddesses, revealing to them the full history of the earth and her heavens, so that all were clear to comprehend His Almighty Wisdom. Yet not one was moved with haste to answer; for scenes like these, concerning the countless millions of corporeal stars dotting the firmament, were their daily deliberation. And then, slowly, one at a time, the speakers, each a representative of a thousand Gods and Goddesses, gave words to Jehovih's light from their respective seats.

18/1.7. And when the multitude had spoken, and Osire, charged with the wisdom of all, perceived from human souls how the light matched his own, as to him Jehovih spoke, his first sphere of commandant God stood plain before him. And he rose up, mantled in white, standing in the throne of Jehovih like one newly illumined with a great change in his long life's administration.

18/1.8. To the council of Gods and Goddesses, he spoke: Attend to my words, for now the gift of the arc of Se'ing rises up before our hallowed shrine. As step by step, all things advance by Jehovih's will, and new roadways in etherea open up fields unexplored by traveling stars; so onward, step by step, our own endless realm takes the course of manhood in its giant strides. You have blessed the worlds of corpor and es for hundreds of thousands of years! Your busy scenes in an old routine change now to higher advent,[454] and an Orian arc comes upon us.

18/1.9. As an oscillating star feeds itself with a change of seasons, so has Jehovih coursed the wave of His traveling Serpents to give our etherean realms an endless life, diversified by change of scenes and constant surprises, which are the glory of the soul.

18/1.10. As thus Osire, the Mighty, with a soul full of words, engraved by Jehovih's hand, discoursed on the glories awaiting the high worlds, where he and his brother Gods and archangels dwelt in the All Perfect, there came back, hastening, as with Omnipotence impelled,[455] the swift messengers from the slow earth, with their etherean arrow-ship shooting like a meteor on fire. Then came Hagan, spokesman of the messengers, before Jehovih's throne, his mantle turned back,[456] and his eyes radiant with sure knowledge, saluting in Jehovih's sign and name. He said:

18/1.11. O Osire, Jehovih's Son, and you Gods and Goddesses, as the All Light gave Voice to our far-seeing God of Lowtsin, so do I stand here to corroborate, in Jehovih's name. The day of sweet persuasion to the earth-born, and their countless

---

[452] an oral command

[453] relief, aid, help, especially to one in difficulty

[454] dawn, beginning, start, level, arrival, event

[455] i.e., as if infused with and propelled by All Power

[456] apparently his mantle (cloak) had a hood

angels down in darkness, is done. Lo, the race of Ghans, planned by Jehovih from the foundation of the world, now stands triumphant on the earth. As Jehovih led the I'hins in paths fortuitous, by gentle words and love, but left them not strong before the warring elements, so has He created upon the earth the masters who shall subdue it, to the triumph of Gods.

18/1.12. Not like lambs are the Ghans, but lions untamed, born conquerors, with seed[457] to learn and reason about all things, faith in mastery, but not faith in Jehovih. As a man having two sons, one low-strung and passionless, the other in ceaseless mischief and desire for havoc, because of the fullness within, so on the earth stand the two races, the I'hins and the Ghans. And when they die, and enter heaven, the first, the I'hins, go like lambs, as they are directed; but the second, the Ghans, still full of inherent stubbornness and self-will, do not heed the God and Lords, but mock them. Back to the earth these well-formed and stately souls come, and set up heavenly kingdoms of their own, in darkness, and eagerly pursue with most relentless zeal their former enemies.

18/1.13. By their loud clamor and inspiring acts, they break up the weak Lords' kingdoms and deprive them of subjects, proclaiming heaven and earth free to all. So that even hapless[458] souls in the lower heaven, have been persuaded to fly from the hospitals and nurseries back to mortals, and there fasten themselves as fetals, shutting their eyes against all further light.

18/1.14. So, mortals have given themselves up to doing the wills of the spirits of darkness, turning looting and devastation into a holiday.[459]

18/1.15. We then came to God, Jehovih's Son, whose throne lies in Gau, and he said: Take this message to Osire, Jehovih's Son, God of Lowtsin: Greeting, in the Father's name. Behold, the arc of Se'ing is at hand. Send a ship, O God, and deliver my hosts, four billion. || With that, and in due salutation, we hastened here.

[457] potential, capability, susceptibility

[458] unfortunate, unlucky, poor

[459] amusement, sport, merriment, party, celebration

CHAPTER 2 Osiris

18/2.1. Osire said: In the name of the All Light, I will have fifty million conquerors to do my will, on earth and in heaven. But first, send an es'elene, with suitable attendants, to deliver God, his Lords, and their hosts, the Brides and Bridegrooms of Jehovih. And leave the earth in darkness thirty days. Meanwhile, let my builders provide a ship for me and my hosts; and let the heralds go abroad in Se'ing, announcing this, my decree.

18/2.2. Jehovih said: Do not think, O man, that I gave talents to men differently on earth, and there to end, making my exalted places to be even shorn and alike. I did not create man so; but as one on earth is mild, and leads on by smooth words and persuasive behavior; and as another, by quick perceiving and strong will, plunges in headlong; even so I carry them onward in My high heavens, perfecting them in their bent, but with wisdom and love, till each becomes as a sun in his sphere.

18/2.3. Do not fear, O man, whether I have labor for them in high heaven: I have worlds to be nurtured and coaxed at times; worlds to be pruned at times; and worlds to be commanded at times by most severe authority, and made to know that All Power lies in Me, through My Gods and Lords.

18/2.4. For these exalted extreme Gods I have places in the firmament, and numberless worlds on which they dwell as stars in My heavens. There I make roadways for My traveling corporeal worlds, where My etherean fields of pasture lie, to glorify Me, and lead on the mortal born. So, now, to My commanding God, Osire, who ruled in Lowtsin most amiably, with equals, but was high-strung with impatience toward self-willed ignorance, I brought the undisciplined earth to feel his giant power.

18/2.5. Say'ah, scribe of Ctaran, thus described the scene: Osire had spoken; his word had gone forth. Heaven was stirred up; Gods and Goddesses knew that work was on hand, new of its order in this place in the firmament. The earth had sons, at last, worthy of the will and service of Gods. Osire, impetuous and much-loved God of Lowtsin, was going to visit these earth-sons, wash them clean, and put jackets on them.

18/2.6. Osire said: In written words I will set down explicit laws for these unruly false Gods, the Ghans, and give them bondage, like the people of other worlds. O, if only they had received discipline before, instead of sweet persuasion!

18/2.7. Say'ah said: When some Gods give command, the people move along; but when Osire decreed, the whole heaven of Lowtsin ran. And quickly now the mandates[460] were filled; the ships were built: first, the es'elene, commanded by Yok, and equipped with five million souls, and started off in hot haste to the earth to deliver God, his Lords, and the Brides and Bridegrooms prepared for the resurrection; next, the ship, Buer, an adavaysit, built for Osire and his hosts, fifty million strong.

18/2.8. Osire said: So that no adventure runs foul, let swift messengers be stationed along the roadways; and they shall announce the proceedings of my Gods and Lords, and their whereabouts. || And the order of heaven was executed; the earth was stripped of her God and Lords, and darkness reigned on earth and in her heavens.

18/2.9. Then Osire left his high place, and with his hosts, aboard the etherean ship of fire, set out at break-neck speed toward the earth; for such was the disposition of this most determined God. Nor did he stop at Chinvat, the boundary of the earth's vortex, but sped on with banners and curtains flying, and with most martial music to stir up the souls of his hosts to sudden tittle.[461]

18/2.10. Down he came to the earth with his fire-ship, and sped around it, to learn its weak and salient points; and next rose up a little to view the atmospherean spirits who had presumed defiance toward high heaven. In the place where Gau had been (whose God, a most holy one, had learned to rule by love for eight hundred years, and was unappreciated by the crude boasters, the unlearned druj), there now stood castles and mansions of the false God, Utaya, around whom a million sentinels armed for battle were stationed to protect him, the false, and do his will.

18/2.11. To here came Osire, and over the battlements raised his ship, and brought it directly into the arena of the Council of hada. Then, halting, bade his marshals proclaim his voice:

18/2.12. Come forth, O Utaya; behold my power! Your sentinels stand appalled. I raised my hosts by higher law, and stand on my feet in your citadel.

18/2.13. Utaya said: Strange and audacious God! From what unmannerly region have you sprung? Know that Gods should kneel outside my walls, and beg to know my will, for an audience. Then Osire decided to hear his arguments, and thus spoke:

18/2.14. From Great Jehovih, I have come! I kneel to none except Him. To do His will in reverence I come in power and majesty. But before I demolish your pitiful walls, and cast you down, suppliant, to do my will, tell me, how do you excuse yourself in turning from the exalted heavens, and building here a kingdom of slaves, for your own glory?

18/2.15. Utaya said: O you jester! Before I demolish you and your ship, and enslave your hosts as mine, I will pacify your worthless curiosity, so that, from now on, you may know your lesson well. But first, you have mocked me for my slaves. What more are your hosts? Have you not tampered with their too willing love by stories of your unseen Jehovih, and persuaded them to let you lead them on to glory? Now I declare to you, there is no Jehovih, no All Person! Hence, your philosophy is founded on falsehood. The space is before us; the worlds are before us; there is nothing more. Let him who will, assume a kingdom; let him who will be a slave, be a slave. I am Apollo!

18/2.16. Osire said: After I have cast you down, you might say it was merely because it so happened that one was stronger than another. So, then, that you may remember my words are more in wisdom than in blind force, hear me while you can, for I cannot talk long with one like you: He who admits the universe moves in harmony and discipline (system and order), already admits the All Person, Jehovih. He who denies the All Person, Jehovih, denies unity in all things (for is your person not the unity of your members, and the All Person the unity of all things?). If all things are not in unity, then all things are divided, one against another. Whoever holds this conviction, is a disintegrator; and whoever holds that all things are a unit, is a unitor (unifier). Therefore, if there is greater strength in unison than in isolation (proving which of the two is the more potent), then unison has won the battle and so becomes the All Person (the Unifier of all).

---

[460] authoritative commands, orders, instructions

[461] excitement, exhilaration, fervor, vigor, zeal

18/2.17. Touching the matter of slaves: There is only One Master, and He rules over all; but it lies in the power of each and every soul to attune himself with the All Person, which is freedom. My hosts are of this kind. In contrast, your slaves attune themselves to you; they cannot rise higher than you; but my hosts have the universe for their model. Because you cannot find the Cause of your coming into life, why not say: I will call Him (that Cause) a name, and it shall be Jehovih!

18/2.18. And now Utaya began a long discourse, which Osire did not wait to hear, but turned to his marshals, saying: Break down the walls of Gau, and raise up ten thousand pillars of fire. Here I will rebuild Jehovih's kingdom. Let the es'enaurs chant, ALL HAIL TO OSIRE, GOD OF HEAVEN AND EARTH!

18/2.19. To which the astonished Utaya stood silently, as if wondering whether this was real, or a frenzied dream, that anyone should so disregard his power, now well established for three hundred years.

18/2.20. Out of the ship came the hosts, and without command, or waiting to know their parts, but everyone in time to the music, took their place in the citadel. Osire strode forward, and by the majesty of his power, overturned the throne of Utaya, the false God, and heaped the rubbish aside. Then, stretching forth his hand, he said:

18/2.21. In Your name, O Jehovih, and by virtue of Your power vested in me, I now command the elements to do my will, and raise a throne for me worthy of Your Immortal Son! And with his voice, his hosts, in concert, quickly piled the adamantine seat,[462] and hung it around with transparent tapestry, woven with the elements of silver and gold.

18/2.22. Meanwhile the laborers of Osire overturned the walls of Utaya's city, and set his millions of slaves free, even while Utaya's officers, panic-stricken, dropped onto their knees, pleading for pity, or fled precipitously off to the earth. And Utaya, conjecturing[463] the worthlessness of his stuff, compared to that which descended from the higher heavens, shouted and called in vain to those who were his most steadfast zealots in time of peace and easy rule, beholding them now, in thousands, vanquished without even a cruel deed or word.

18/2.23. Not long did the fray last, for Osire's work was like a man overturning the toys of a child; and Utaya, to prove his faith in himself, stood sole spectator, unmoved from his tracks, but helpless, wondering what would come next. But now Osire, with no words of explanation or excuse, ascended the new throne and gave the sign, IN JEHOVIH'S NAME, which was answered by his mighty hosts; at which, behold, from the vault of heaven above there descended mantles of light, matchless in brilliancy!

18/2.24. Utaya was illumined, and all his former evil deeds and cruelty stood out in huge black spots, quailing before the sea of light; for around on every side stood millions of souls, all pure, and transparent, washed by the ordeal of time and holy works. But Utaya was not all evil, or short in owning an honorable adversary; and so, quickly comprehending his awful plight in the midst of Purity, first let fall a tear, the which, in pity, blinded him from witnessing further his dire humiliation; and next, with the blubbering of a beaten schoolboy, he cried out:

18/2.25. Enough! Enough! You God Almighty! Take me away from your dissolving fire! I was only needing to witness some great God's deeds, to find proof of my own worthlessness!

18/2.26. But Osire was not new to such a situation, and proceeded with the affairs of heaven, appointing officers and laborers, and apportioning his High Council to do Jehovih's will, and so, left Utaya to sweat a while in his own torments.

18/2.27. O give me relief, cried Utaya, you God of heaven and earth! I consume, I burn in Purity's flame! For pity's sake, turn down the consuming light!

18/2.28. Osire halted from his labors long enough to answer thus: All Light cannot cease for the convenience of one man; clothe yourself, O false one, with robes of darkness, and hide your cruel butcheries. You, who would have made slaves

---

[462] The judgment seat was built using diamond-like stone (adamantine). To pile is to secure an underpinning or foundation; in construction, driving pile beams into the ground does this; perhaps similar to that, the adamantine throne was secured into the site.

[463] inferring, considering, anticipating, fearing

of my hosts, should be of holier metal[464] than to plead for help. Behold, I have not taken one of your slaves, or asked any to bow in obedience. To the righteous, the worlds are free; only evil men and evil Gods quail before Jehovih's ceaseless fire!

18/2.29. Meanwhile, Utaya hustled his glittering robes closely around himself, and pulled his flashing crown down over his scalded eyes, but its worthless fabric only fed the fury of the All Light, which came from the throne of God, Osire's resting-place. The slaves of Utaya had fled, or lay piteously prostrate, speechless with fear and wonder. Over these the hosts of Osire watched, and hastily took them beyond the now rapidly rising pillars of fire, where they were housed temporarily.

18/2.30. Still the voice of Utaya rang aloud for help and pity; but none came to him. Then he saw that the prostrate victims fared better, and were less conspicuous; so Utaya cast himself prostrate, along with the rubbish of his former throne. At this, Osire sent Yesta, sister of Atonas, Goddess of Opsa, in etherea, to rescue him, and mantle him around with balm from the upper heavens.

18/2.31. So Yesta and her band took Utaya away, far beyond the boundaries of the new-laid Gau.

CHAPTER 3 Osiris

18/3.1. Osire spoke from the throne, saying: Proclaim it in the east and west, and north and south, there is a God in heaven! That which has transpired in Gau, go tell the false Gods and false Lords in hada, adding: Osire has come!

18/3.2. Messengers started out for every quarter of the world, inspired by the impetuous utterances of the commanding God. And so, half breathless, and in hastening speed, these young Gods and young Goddesses, the messengers, dropped in upon the Lordly defamers of holiness, and told the tale of the overturned Gau, where proud Utaya fell. And they, in manner and custom, inspired the false rulers to imagine an even worse calamity had occurred; and that much[465] had been concealed out of deference to Utaya and other usurpers.

18/3.3. Osire called his Council and appointed new positions, with new officers, having nothing in common with all past administrations of the Gods of earth and heaven. So far, these appointments came from his etherean hosts, and, moved by the fire of his own energy, they quickly assumed their most honorable duties: some to build, some to survey and lay the course of streets, and places of habitations; and yet others to remove the old hospitals and nurseries, and make way for new ones, and for factories, and all requirements for the millions of souls now scattered, lost, or in dire confusion, currently struggling in the outside darkness.

18/3.4. From which arose a constant wail of fear and torment, strangely wild, compared to the glorious light spreading quickly from the rising pillars of fire around the throne of God. Osire's hosts of fifty million, attuned to harmony and precision, were proceeding briskly with their labor, each one knowing his part and playing close to the text in every motion; and yet in number these were as nothing compared to the millions scattered in the gloomy darkness, wailing beyond the walls.

18/3.5. Here, a road! Osire would say; or, with his hand, command: An otevan to those hapless slaves! And, as if his thoughts had spoken to his hosts, his etherean workmen rushed to make his will omnipotent. There was no loss of time or space to inquire how the matter should be done; for heaven's trained workmen have learned the power of concentrated effort, and the power of knowledge braced to a single point, by which the elements stoop to do their wills. To learn this simple harmony, FOR ALL TO BE AS ONE, how many countless millions must rise up from the earth, to be hurled back, discordant and powerless, before Jehovih's Sons and Daughters!

18/3.6. Yes, and kings, queens and potentates (rulers), high strung in unwarranted conceit, are cast down to beg, beseechingly like a child. Like a furious lion is tamed, his giant power worthless before the hands of man, whose strength by knowledge triumphs; so do the ethereans from high heaven descend to humiliate first, and then to teach the false Gods and false Lords of hada.

18/3.7. Jehovih says: What more, O man, have I put upon you than to learn? And strewn your path with lessons rich in happiness! To learn the elements, and master them; this it is to be a God or

---

[464] mettle, character, temperament, spirit, courage, fortitude, etc.

[465] information about this calamity

Goddess. And where one man is weak, let two or more unite; a simple thing, by which even the stars of heaven can be turned from their course.

18/3.8. Jehovih says: Have I not said: The weakest king is he who has the most soldiers; and the strongest nation, where no soldiers are required. How, then, do the false Gods expect by evil deeds to fortify their thrones? Lo, My etherean hosts come unarmed, and by a breath blow away their mighty kingdoms. ||

18/3.9. And so it was in Gau; only one earth-day had come and gone since Utaya reigned over a hundred million slaves, who daily brought up tribute[466] from the earth, to ornament this crown-like city; and now the dawn of another world stood supreme in the demolished kingdom.

18/3.10. What greater pity is there than to see the former slaves still loyal to their deposed master, here Utaya, coming to him in his banishment, fifty million swearing terrible oaths of fidelity to him forever; a most pitiful sight. For the Great Spirit created man capable of such, even to wed himself to misery, for zeal, in ignorance, to prove a most foolish love. And were it not for Utaya's guardians, his very slaves would have smothered him, in desperate effort to manifest fidelity.

18/3.11. Then Yesta spoke to him, saying: Raise your voice against this unseemly crowd, and be commander still, at least to save yourself. Remember how Jehovih gives this lesson to mortals, to say to evil: Away! For lo, to allow first one and then another to fasten upon one's self, is as great a crime as a debauched passion unchecked. Order them to go! For love of self, which is your gift from Great Jehovih, be yourself! It will better them also!

18/3.12. Utaya, struggling, said: Alas, fair angel! These were my slaves! The hardest blow of all is their acknowledged love. The fire of the throne of Osire was tame compared to this. For hundreds of years, I gave these creatures pangs and wretchedness, and now they give me love. Poor idiots! I cannot drive them away!

18/3.13. And so, sobbing, Utaya bowed his head, for such sudden great truths turned all his judgment into the darkness of his past deeds and wickedness, even while, crowding close on every side, the fifty million kept up their ceaseless assurances of endless love. Nor was there any way open to escape from their ignorant jargon and foul breath. So, when Yesta saw how helplessly Utaya had given up, she raised her hand, saying: What shall I do, O Jehovih?

18/3.14. Upon which, the Light descended, and Jehovih spoke through Yesta, saying: Flesh of My flesh I created man; from My Own Spirit I gave man a spirit also; and to all men alike I gave all things in My worlds. But some men are not content with what I gave, but ask for more, even that they may have their fellows for subjects. To these I have given in answer to their prayers. Behold, then, O man, why do you seek to put away today even that, which a day before, you did pray for? They are as good today as yesterday.

18/3.15. You have said: Man can make himself whatever he will! So, your Creator is worthless to you. If you do not desire to carry their love, which is the lightest of all burdens, how did you carry their hate for so long? Nevertheless, if you desire, you can put them away: They are yours; do as you will.

18/3.16. Utaya said: How can I put them away? I cannot reason with fifty million! No, before I persuaded twenty, the first ones, so ignorant, would forget what I said. Tell me, then, O Goddess, what shall I do to free myself from this great multitude?

18/3.17. Yesta said: Do not call on me, but on your Creator; and not to be freed for your own good, but for wisdom to do some good to them over whom you have long been a remorseless tyrant. These are a small curse to you, compared to your own judgment, for from yourself you can never flee. You shall undo your selfish deeds, which you have practiced for so long. So, turn at once, and make oath to Him Who made you, that from this time forward you will do good to others with all your wisdom and strength.

18/3.18. Utaya said: Alas, your words are wise and holy, but I have no faith! I have no faith!

18/3.19. Yesta said: Do not say this! Your words are another bondage on your soul. To say, I have no faith, is to imprison yourself away from All Light. Come, quickly, or lo, I leave you; for if you do not profess faith, why should I labor any more with you? Say: I have faith in You, O Jehovih! I can, I will, raise up these I have cast down. || Utaya wept,

---

[466] contribution, payment; usually exacted, forced; and demanded as evidence of loyalty or submission

and answered: O if only I had faith like yours! But for long years I taught myself that prayer to Jehovih was not required of one as great and strong as I. Alas, I smothered out the fire. And, amid his sobs, Utaya fell prostrate at Yesta's feet.

18/3.20. Quickly, now, she raised her slender hand toward high heaven, saying: O Jehovih, by Your power vested in me, I here encircle this, Your prostrate child, with adamantine light! Down from above came phosphorescent flames of light, with which Yesta drew a circle around her small group, at which the multitude stood back and looked on in wonder and fear. But the surging mass beyond pressed forward, shouting: Utaya! Utaya!

18/3.21. Little by little, Yesta extended the light, and her assistants put up a structure to guard the place, so that in a little while it was like a miniature throne in heaven. Yesta then assumed the power, and so, took command, placing helpless Utaya by her side. Meanwhile, her assistants sped through the multitude, making roadways, and selecting out the most intelligent of the former slaves, and making guards of them.

18/3.22. Yesta said to Utaya: Now I will give you a lesson in righteousness; for you shall educate and develop all this host, your former slaves, to your own level, before you raise yourself the tiniest fraction. Do not think it is easy to assume to be a God or a Lord, or even a mortal king. Those who make servants of others must also raise them up to be angels of light. Heaven is just, as well as bountiful. To whom Jehovih has given bountifully, it is commanded he shall give bountifully. For hundreds of years you have had the service of these hapless creatures; so now you shall serve them by making them intelligent men and women. Yes, till the lowest of them are your equals, of whom you can be proud, and say before the Father: Behold, my sister! Behold, my brother! || you, Utaya, shall not be free!

18/3.23. Utaya said: I perceive your words are from the All Highest. This is justice! I perceive now that while I rated myself supreme judge of right and wrong, I judged with partiality[467] to myself. Yes, without an All Highest, I perceive there can be no justice in heaven or earth. O You All Light, how can I approach You! I have been feeding myself with an endless poison; my darkness was my fortress. || Teach me the way, O angel of Light! Whatever Jehovih wills, that I will do, from this time onward, with all my wisdom and strength.

18/3.24. So Yesta restored order, and divided the multitude into many parts, and sent officers among them to select and assort them, so that, as soon as Osire would decree asylums and schools for them, they could be taken to them.

CHAPTER 4 Osiris

18/4.1. Osire lost no time, but officered Gau and established his Council in hot haste, making Ote as temporary God on the throne, while he himself went forth to other regions, to conquer and overturn false Gods and Lords. Leaving, therefore, a sufficient guard and council, Osire, with a host of twenty million, went westward in atmospherea, over and above the great central north lands, where a false God, Wotchak, was established with another hundred million slaves, to do his will.

18/4.2. Wotchak, having been advised by his messengers of Osire's approach to the earth's heavens, and supposing Osire to be from some remote star, and not knowing there were etherean worlds in the firmament, had laid his kingdom around with new walls, and doubly fortified his throne, and gaudily attired himself and officers, in hopes of overawing the coming God.

18/4.3. To Wotchak came Osire, not waiting to be announced, nor halting for Wotchak's sentinels, but driving his ship straight up to the throne.

18/4.4. Stop! Stop! cried the astonished Wotchak. Who dares to profane my throne, and set at defiance all the rules of virtuous Gods? Down from your ship, and crawl on your belly to your sovereign God! Know that I am great Apollo! || But Osire deigned only to say: By what authority have you made slaves of Jehovih's sons and daughters, to augment your own self-glory?

18/4.5. And, not waiting for a reply, alighted down before the throne, even while a thousand or more, well drilled, stood with him, in the form of a star, at which, the Upper Light descended in great brilliancy. Wotchak was frightened, and fled from his throne, and all his Council with him. Then spoke Osire, saying to his hosts:

18/4.6. Do not allow this false God and his Council to escape. Encircle them, and hold them, to

[467] bias, favor

know my will and the decree of Jehovih. Presently, the ethereans returned with Wotchak, who cried out: O, let me go! Take all, but let me go! What am I to you?

18/4.7. Osire answered him, saying: Such has been the history of these heavens. In past ages, the usurping false Gods were allowed to go their way, leaving their helpless former subjects in the hands of the etherean hosts. That day is past. I come to make such Gods know that their fate and responsibilities rest on the decrees of a Higher One, even the Creator, Jehovih. Behold, you have cast down and blighted a hundred million of Jehovih's children, making slaves of them, to do your will. As you were the cause of their fallen state, from liberty to bondage, so, now, you shall redeem them to freedom, wisdom and truth.

18/4.8. While Osire spoke, his proper officers let fall the light from the upper regions, the like of which Wotchak had never seen. Presently, all things became transparent, and the enraged Wotchak, foreseeing trouble ahead, answered in this way:

18/4.9. Do not accuse me, you audacious God! These, my Council, urged me hundreds of years ago to my course, their only condition being that they remain my close advisers. I was their tool, and if you desire justice, make them feel the sting of repentant labor. Let them have my slaves. I do not want them. I have been a most honest, upright God!

18/4.10. And now his counselors accused one another, and all of them heaping the blame on Wotchak. Meanwhile the etherean flames grew lighter and lighter, from which there was no concealment; and all their former falsehoods and cruel words, and evil deeds, were unveiled, disclosing souls dark and hideous, with long covered-up crimes, now laid bare for the gaze of every eye.

18/4.11. This scene brought the curious slaves, in millions, to witness it, and to reassure the suffering false God of their love and loyalty. And when Wotchak looked and saw the abject wretches who claimed him as their worshipful God, he cried out: Enough! Enough! Unfeeling God! You come in pretended right and peace; but, because of your power, execute on me and my Council torments more terrible than I ever gave to any slave of mine. Know that I am Apollo!

18/4.12. To which Osire answered: What are names to me! With that, Osire, by waving his hand, caused his hosts to cast aside the false God's throne, scattering all its glittering gems abroad, relics for the multitude. And now three pillars of light shot up and stood beside Osire and his attendants, at which all the strength and courage sapped out of Wotchak and his confederates, and they crouched down at Osire's feet.

18/4.13. Osire called Itu, saying: Take them outside the lights, and hand them over to their slaves for a while. So Itu and his guard gathered them from the light and bore them away. Quickly now, Osire officered this newly-conquered place in heaven, and called it Autat, signifying, foundation of perishable laws. And, on a new throne, appointed Luce as temporary God, giving him a Council of one thousand ethereans. After that, Osire drew the plans for roads, temples, schools, hospitals, nurseries, and all other habitations required by spirits newborn in heaven, leaving orders to have them completed by a given time.

18/4.14. Next, Osire ordered the divisions and selections to be made in the now scattered hosts of atmosphereans, and to have them all arrested and put into their proper places This labor he left in the charge of God, Luce.

18/4.15. Far out on the plateau, Itu and his attendants carried Wotchak and his confederates, followed by forty million of his former slaves. There Itu left Wotchak and his people, and Itu and his attendants stepped aside to witness whatever would transpire.

18/4.16. At this stage, Osire departed with his ship and steered southward over the land of Shem (India), coming to a place in the lower heaven called Vibhraj, signifying resplendent, where the false God, Daveas ruled,[468] having eight hundred million slaves, a thousand Lords and ten thousand Governors.

18/4.17. And, even as Osire had rushed in headlong upon the other false Gods, so in like manner he came with his fire-ship into the great city of Vibhraj, at this time the largest city of the lower heaven. Daveas had been warned by his

---

[468] In the English translations from the Vedic Scriptures, this God is spelled the same, Daveas. Evil men are also characterized as Daveas [devious]. –Ed.

sentinels, and so, came to the front of his capital, just in time to see the fearless Osire alight on the piazza in front of the Council House.

CHAPTER 5 Osiris

18/5.1. Osire said: In the name of Jehovih, peace to you! To which Daveas replied: No, in the name of Apollo, who I am! How dare you approach, except to crawl on your belly? For four hundred years the honor of my kingdom has been revered by all visiting Gods; but you come as a barbarian. Down, wretch! Before I have you bound and cast in prison!

18/5.2. Osire said: Why should I not come before you? Behold, the Great Spirit created the whole universe for His Sons and Daughters. By what right have you usurped a portion? And from what Source comes your authority to bid me kneel to you? But if you can show me where you have one just claim to enslave these people, rather let your argument run there, for I have come in the name of the Father to liberate them, so that they may be prepared for the second and third resurrections.

18/5.3. Daveas said: Do not think that I have neglected to prepare for rebellious Gods like you. Behold my millions of subjects! What is your handful? I tell you truly, I have prisons large enough to hold you and your hosts. Neither flatter yourself that I am ignorant. For two hundred years I labored in the so-called resurrections; I made myself a slave to the multitude, giving all my labor and time. Then I saw my folly, and so built a third resurrection myself. This is, therefore, my lawful kingdom. Moreover, I tell you to your face, you wretch, there is no higher heaven than mine. Neither do you come from a heaven as great as mine. But having great self-conceit, you have come for mischief. I have heard of you from other heavens! But now you have put your head into the halter. Seize him, marshals! Seize him and his hosts! Cast them into prison!

18/5.4. Osire did not speak, but raised his hand upward in the seventh sign, and suddenly his hosts cast forth sheets of light brighter than the sun. Daveas stood back frightened, and his marshals fled. Presently, Osire, with a thousand attendants, stepped forth in flames of light, and went up into the capital and surrounded Daveas, the usurper, but did not touch him. And now the ship was illumined, and lo, the sentinels of Daveas' Council broke and fled. Immediately after which, Osire spoke, saying:

18/5.5. Hand of Your hand, O Jehovih; voice of Your voice, overturn this house and throne! And, behold, the light of the upper heavens rested in Osire's palms, and he struck the house and the throne, and they tumbled over like straw before a hurricane. Alone stood Daveas, the evil God, half speechless and half blinded by the great Light of Jehovih. Down! Down! said Osire, to the walls and temples of the city. And his hosts concentrated at any point Osire's hand directed; and lo, everything fell and was scattered far.

18/5.6. Meanwhile, the officers of Daveas fled in all directions, except those who were overcome by the light, and these fell and buried themselves amid the rubbish.

18/5.7. Stop! Stop! cried Daveas. Give me air! I perish! I am a consuming fire! And he tossed his hands aloft; then cringed his face within his glittering robes. And now Osire called forth thunder and lightning, and sent shafts through, and over, and about the whole plateau of Vibhraj, and the din and roar confounded all the eight hundred million souls, so that they ran no farther, but stood and waited, watching for what would happen next.

18/5.8. Osire did not stop (in his proceedings), but went forward to a more suitable place, to build his throne. Jehovih! Almighty! he cried, Elements of Your elements, O Father! Found here a throne for Your Son! And even so it was accomplished, for while his words went forth, the elements rose to do his will, and there arose a most excellent throne, strong and adamantine, on which Osire ascended. Meanwhile, Daveas had fallen down flat, weeping and wailing; but Osire, by a motion of the hand, called Wang-te, a most enlightened archangel, with her attendants, to bear him away, which was quickly done.

18/5.9. Quickly now the place was cleared, and with pillars of light as brilliant as an arc in the etherean firmament, the hosts of Osire fenced around a sufficient space for a city of a billion souls. Now Osire appointed Klesta, to be Dawn Goddess, and he gave her a Council of fifty thousand ethereans. Outside of the walls of the pillars of agni were Daveas and his eight hundred million subjects, in dire confusion.

18/5.10. Wang-te, the archangel, said to Daveas: In your own falsehood you are favored to free yourself awhile, to organize a new kingdom, but in holiness, and then return and command obedience from this smothering host. Behold, you have taught them to believe you are Apollo; say to them now: I am not Apollo! I have been false!

18/5.11. Daveas madly replied: Never! Jehovih and His kingdoms be accursed forever! You strange spirits come from far-off kingdoms to despoil and overturn the most righteous place in heaven! Are Jehovih and His servants destroyers? To which Wang-te replied: This is no time for argument; see here these countless millions! If I and my attendants withdraw from you, you will be as one drowned amid this sea of ignorance and horrid smells. Assume at once, for pity's sake, to purge yourself of your life-long falsehoods and treacherous tyranny. Announce yourself as Daveas, as you are, and I can save you!

18/5.12. Daveas rudely thrust her aside, saying: Never! I acknowledge to no one! If there is a higher heaven, I will ascend there as I am, Apollo! Apollo! Wang-te said: Do not put me off; in Jehovih's name! Remember what you are, and from the little you have seen, how powerless you are before Omnipotence! Your fate is like that of all dictators on the verge of a chasm of horrors. Daveas did not wait to hear her further, but proclaimed aloud, Apollo! Apollo! and stood aside. Presently his former officers rushed to him, and with that came the sea of millions of spirits, unorganized, unwashed, unfed, frightened and mad, for love of the name Apollo, the meaning of which they did not know; and they became as a knot of serpents, entwined around the central figure, Daveas and his officers. And in the terrible brawl not one voice could be distinguished from another. And the outer extreme pressed inward, on every side, and presently the eight hundred million resembled a ball, a knot of darkness, with a dull and rumbling moan within, and fearful clamor on the surface, from which horrid smells issued in all directions.

18/5.13. Wang-te and her attendants hastened back to the throne of Osire, Son of Jehovih, to tell what had happened. Osire said: What shall I do, O Father? Then the Light of Jehovih came, and Jehovih spoke, saying: Consider My creation, My Son. I made the young child to fall with few bruises; but the full-grown man falls heavily. Shall I make a separate rule to favor kings and queens on earth, and false Gods in heaven? No, truly. Behold, I will make of Daveas an example in heaven, and on earth also. Because he has spurned his own name, so will I make both angels and mortals to curse and shun the name, Daveas.[469]

18/5.14. Osire said: Proceed with my kingdom, in the name of the Father. Let Daveas rest awhile as he is.

18/5.15. After that, Osire departed, taking the remainder of his hosts with him in his fire-ship; and he went to a heavenly place to the westward, where Seru was, being a false God, with ten million slaves; and Osire destroyed Seru's kingdom also. Next, he went to a heavenly place in the north, where Raka, a false God, had seventy million slaves; and Osire destroyed his kingdom also, liberating his slaves, and putting a guard over Raka. ||

18/5.16. So in that way, Osire traveled throughout atmospherea, demolishing all the heavenly kingdoms of the false Gods, of whom there were, in all, seven hundred and eighty; but many of them had less than a million subjects. For a total of thirty days, Osire was engaged in destroying all the evil kingdoms in the lower heavens, and then the work was finished.

18/5.17. Osire said to his hosts: For thirty days we labored in destroying that which was; now we will rebuild to Jehovih for another thirty days. Take the ship, therefore, to Vibhraj, for there I will found my central kingdom. And, after we have completed the work of starting the second resurrection on a sure foundation, then we will go down to the earth and overturn the kingdoms of the false Lords and men.

CHAPTER 6 Osiris

18/6.1. Jehovih said: Vibhraj shall be My place; your throne, Osire, shall be My throne. Send sheriffs out into all the divisions of heaven where you have destroyed the evil kingdoms. And your

[469] Most interpreters of the Hindu Scriptures spell this name, Daevas. As the natives pronounce it, it sounds more like Dah-we-oz, but it is identical with Daveas of the ancient Vedes. –Ed. [In Persia (Par'si'e) this became Darius.]

sheriffs shall arrest all the false Gods whom you have dispossessed, and bring them here, so I may speak with them face to face.

18/6.2. Then Osire spoke to the sheriffs, saying: Go out into all the divisions of atmospherea, and arrest and bring here all the false Gods whom I have dethroned, saying to each of them: Osire, God of the lower heavens, commands your presence. Come, and hear the voice of your Creator. || But it shall happen that many will fear to come, because of the light, lest their evil deeds be seen; say to all these: The light will be lowered for a short space of time; come, therefore, quickly.

18/6.3. To all the knots, where the false Gods are enveloped, you shall take a sufficiency of umbrae,[470] so that you may release them. But leave a sufficient guard with the knot to keep them in their places.

18/6.4. The sheriffs went abroad, as commanded, being sufficiently provided with attendants and all things required for such adventures; and after many days, the false Gods were arrested and brought before the throne of God, Osire, Jehovih's Son. And on that occasion there were assembled one hundred thousand archangels, of whom two thousand had risen to the rank of Gods and Goddesses, and thirty thousand to the rank of Lords and Lordesses.

18/6.5. Osire said to the false ones: Brothers, greeting, in the name of Jehovih! Neither shall you fear, nor be expectant of torture or punishment. Though I come in All Power, my words shall be tempered with wisdom. But I can be no respecter of persons,[471] nor swerve one fraction from Jehovih's commandments.

18/6.6. The bondage of all men was in the Father; for, before you were conscious individuals, Jehovih stretched forth His hand, and you came forth from Void, which was your prison in which your selfs had been as nothing.

18/6.7. In likeness of the Father, I came to deliver those you had bound; and through Him I have attained power to that end. So, in likeness of Him, also, I cannot bind you, or cast you in prison. No, indeed, my sheriffs have just delivered you from bondage, and I am now holding you free from the knots.

18/6.8. Most of you are learned men of the second resurrection; but you have used your wisdom for self-glorification, being proud to call yourselves Gods; not teaching the unlearned of Jehovih and His kingdoms, but falsely teaching that your own kingdoms were the All Highest, and so, shutting out the true light from the unlearned.

18/6.9. Jehovih has blessed you all with strong minds and handsome forms, as a result of which, you have each falsely proclaimed you were Apollo. Do not think that this matter was unknown in high heaven. I have here the reports of swift messengers, which were brought to me in the firmament above. I did not come in ignorance of what you were doing; neither did I come in weakness. More than a hundred billion, who have been raised up to etherea from the earth and its heavens, stand at my side. Beside these, a million times as many ethereans, from other worlds; and above all of these, the Great Orian Chiefs; and yet beyond, and over all, Great Jehovih!

18/6.10. Have I not proved my power before you all? Did I go away in a corner and say: Come, I will show you my power? No, I came close to you all. As the Father first proves power, so have I. After that, wisdom. So that I may talk to you in wisdom, I had you arrested and brought here. Hear me then, and remember my words.

18/6.11. In former cycles, the high Gods who descended to these heavens, finding false Gods, simply liberated their slaves, but put no labor of restitution on the false Gods. This was because the false Gods of those periods were too imbecile and unlearned. But the earth and her heavens have progressed to a higher state. And with progression comes, also, responsibility. With learning comes responsibility; and with wisdom, also.

---

[470] great darkness occasioned by the falling of nebulae. –1891 glossary. [In this verse umbrae would seem to refer to a type of thick nebula, perhaps thick enough to immobilize the members of the knot. Obviously as these ethereans can manifest sheets of light, likewise they can manifest vast cohesive conglomerations of dense nebulae (umbrae).]

[471] Such as pretenders who claim to be more than what they are, as in professing to be Apollo; and, anyone placed above Jehovih and His will, cannot be given respect as to person (i.e., because of name, title, position, etc.); and so, the false ones should not expect favor on that basis.

18/6.12. You bound your subjects to your kingdoms; and you now perceive you cannot put them aside. You taught them your kingdoms were the All Highest; of this they must now be unlearned. You taught them that you were the All Highest Gods! They must be unlearned in this, also. You put aside the ancient rites and ceremonies in which the name of Jehovih was used, teaching them to sing to you only. They must be taught new songs, substituting the Great Spirit, to Whom none can attain, forever. You taught them to be unthinking, and contented as slaves; they must now be taught to think for themselves, and to labor for everlasting liberty.

18/6.13. And now, touching the law of the resurrection, remember, this is the same in all the created worlds, which is, that the spirit of man grows by giving away whatever the spirit has to give. If you have great learning, and you give of it, then more learning shall be added to you; if you have goodness of heart, and gentle words, then, by giving this away, more shall be added to you. If you have craft in inventions or mechanics, and you bestow of these talents to others, then more will be added to you. As the corporeal man accumulates corporeal things by not giving them away, not so accumulates the spirit of any man.

18/6.14. For he who locks up the light of the Father that is in him, cannot obtain more light; he who locks up goodness of heart, cannot obtain strength of spirit. And without strength of spirit, no man can attain to the third resurrection. But, so that men may learn to obtain strength of spirit, the second resurrection has been established in atmospherea belonging to all the habitable corporeal worlds.

18/6.15. The chief delight of man shall be, therefore, to find some way to impart his spiritual talents and strength, and to the greatest possible number of people. Do not think that preaching to the ignorant is sufficient; but you shall take hold with your own hands and show them how to accomplish. Yet labor alone is not sufficient; for some are so created that you cannot inspire them without rites and ceremonies and music.

18/6.16. Nor shall a man, after having taught and raised up a few, say: Behold, what a good work I have done! But as long as he finds a man or woman or child, who lacks in anything, he shall feel to say: Alas, what I have done is as nothing in the resurrection of my fellows.

18/6.17. For the rule holds for all men alike, to desire exaltation, everlasting liberty, and unlimited power; and unless you are prepared to give these to others, then you cannot attain them yourselves. Neither is it possible for man to turn away from responsibility; to whom the Father has given, from him the Father requires. You have had your kingdoms. Yes, and boasted of them. Your boasts have ascended to etherea. Will you go there and be asked: Where is your kingdom? Shall it be said you shirked from the care of those the Father gave into your keeping?

18/6.18. Consider now, O brothers! When the conscience of man burns inward, there is still darkness slumbering in his soul. The etherean lights will burn him. He whose conscience no longer burns inward, becomes himself a brilliant flame of light. Through him Jehovih speaks.

18/6.19. Osire ceased; and now a brilliant light descended about the throne, and presently Jehovih spoke through Osire, saying:

18/6.20. Times and half-times I have given to My corporeal worlds and their heavens. In a time I have made a full resurrection to those who aspire to My heavens above. Nor do I go away from any place I created, saying: Go alone for a season. But in a time I manifest a new light, for such, also, are My creations. Do not think that I have given seasons to corporeal worlds only; I gave seasons to atmospherea, also.

18/6.21. Is a summer on the earth not half a time? And the winter half a time? And the two, one full time? So also I created for atmospherea a time of four hundred years, and a half-time of two hundred years. And in seven times and one half-time I created one dan'ha.

18/6.22. For thousands of years I sent My Gods to teach these things, so that My angels could know the times of My resurrections. Does a farmer not have knowledge of the resurrection of spring, when I cover the earth over with new-growing things, which I raise up out of the earth? How much more knowledge should My angels have of My spring-times, in atmospherea, when My archangels come to gather in My harvests of emancipated souls?

18/6.23. I commanded My etherean hosts, saying: Go to the lower heaven and teach them there is no such thing as individual resurrection. And they came proclaiming My word, showing all people that any number of individuals were as nothing unless united, which is the salvation I provided to all My worlds.

18/6.24. For I created progress to be in compact; nor did I give to any person individual salvation or resurrection. So that men could learn the advantage of compact, I caused mortals to have corporeal languages, and to live in cities. So that you in atmospherea could learn the All Perfection of being one with one another, I gave you the second resurrection; teaching you, through My Gods and Lords, to abnegate self-aspiration, for self-aspiration is at the expense of others; but commanding you to learn to assimilate with one another.

18/6.25. And I gave rites and ceremonies, among which was the oath of service to Me and My kingdoms, and to none other, in which many bound themselves, which was, and is, the beginning of liberty. Touching this matter, I created types (of rites and ceremonies) on earth and in the lower heavens, so that even the unlearned might understand Me and My works.

18/6.26. For to him who begets children I gave bondage, to them and to him conjointly. But this is a bondage that does not circumvent liberty in time to come, for they can ascend to heaven, and progress conjointly, better than alone. But some gave themselves up to love earthly things, such as houses, money and kingdoms, which things have no resurrection. Therefore, such bondage holds the person after death to the thing he loved.

18/6.27. Similarly, many have set up kingdoms in the lower heavens, binding themselves to things that have no higher resurrection, which things belong on the plateau of atmospherea where I created them. But to them who have bound themselves to their fellow, saying: I am the salvation! || It is like a young man saying to a maiden: Come, I will be your husband. And she goes to him in confidence. Here, then, is bondage; and she holds him as the way of her salvation. Neither can he alone annul that which has been united, nor yet can they together annul this; for, by their bondage, I am also a party to the contract.

18/6.28. In like manner, they who assume kingdoms, professing to be Gods of salvation, and thus enticing My innocent ones to themselves, become bound, not only to their subjects, but to the contract of deliverance to salvation; for so I created them.

18/6.29. The Voice ceased, and Osire said: If a man weds a woman with an evil temper, his glory lies in not going away from her, but in teaching her to overcome her temper; or, if her husband is evil, her glory lies not in going away from him, but in reforming him. It is wise to accomplish whatever work Jehovih has put in your way, rather than to desert it for sake of personal comfort.

18/6.30. Nevertheless, there is a limit to all things, except Jehovih; and with the wise there is power to accomplish much that seems impossible at first. Hear, then, my judgment upon you, which is that:

18/6.31. You shall again assume kingdoms, and everyone shall have all the subjects he had before. And you shall be provided with places and thrones by my archangels, and with councils of my archangels, also. And I will give each and every one of you an assistant God, who shall sit at your right hand for four years, the time of this dawn, teaching how and what to teach.

18/6.32. My hosts will now conduct you to the places prepared for you, around which are erected walls of agni. And when you are safely seated on your thrones, your former subjects shall be brought before you in groups, and adjudged to the labor, and to the schools, and to other places that are suited to them, according to their strength and talents.

18/6.33. And I pronounce it upon you that you shall deliver your respective subjects sufficiently for the third resurrection. And according to your zeal and faithfulness, my hosts will labor with you, to the end that Jehovih may be glorified in your harvests for the emancipated worlds. Attend, therefore, to give the sign, In Jehovih's Name, and prepare to receive ordination from my hands, by the power and wisdom of the Great Spirit.

18/6.34. The sheriffs showed them how to make the sign, and how to stand before the throne; and then Osire said: By Your Wisdom, and Love, and Power, O Jehovih, which rest in me, I anoint these, Your Gods, for Your service, and for the exaltation of Your kingdoms, forever! Amen.

18/6.35. The light was now becoming so brilliant that many of the newly-made Gods quailed before it. But the marshals conducted them, and they passed before the throne of Osire, where they were crowned and arrayed as Gods of the second resurrection; after which they were again conducted before the Council, and saluted on the sign; and then, to martial music, they were taken to the kingdoms prepared for them.

CHAPTER 7 Osiris

18/7.1. Who shall tell the story of the Gods of heaven! Their mighty kingdoms, overspreading the whole earth! Hundreds and hundreds of them, and thousands! Their libraries of records of valorous and holy deeds! A council chamber of half a million souls! Hundreds of departments; thousands! Here a board to select young students to the colleges of messengers. Another board to select students to the colleges of arts. Another to select students to mathematics. Another for prophecy. Another for great learning. Another for factories. Another for compounding and dissolving elements. Then come the departments of the cosmogony of the stars; then, of the ethereal worlds; then, the roadways of the firmament; then, ji'ya, a'ji, and nebulae; then, se'mu; then, hi'dan and dan; then, the dawn of dan; then, histories of corporeal affairs, and of the affairs of the heavens far and near; then, genealogy of thousands of Orian Chiefs; the creation of mineral, vegetable and animal kingdoms. Yes, just to enumerate[472] even half of what comes before a God and his council would itself fill a book.

18/7.2. Who, then, O Jehovih, shall venture to unveil the labor and wisdom of Your etherean Gods! How shall the second resurrection give up its mysteries? Shall Your recorder follow the young student for messenger, and disclose the training put upon him? How, like a carrier dove, he is taught to go from place to place, but holding the message in his head? Then follow the student in another department, and make a record of how he is taught? And of the multitude of questions that come before the Council from far-off places. Then the rites and ceremonies, and the unending variety and magnificence of the music. Can a man describe a million men, women and children? A hundred million! A billion! Five billion! Who has seen so great a man, to do this! And yet this is only Your lower heaven, O Jehovih!

18/7.3. A strange voice rises up from the earth, saying: Have they anything to do in heaven? O you Gods! And one half of the earth-born coming here in infancy! And the countless millions who know little more than the beasts of the field! Yet mortals are falsely taught that these unfortunates would skip off to paradise and possess great learning in the hour of death!

18/7.4. O that[473] their understanding could be opened up to Your kingdoms, You All-Extending Creator! That their eyes could look upon the greatness of even Your lower heaven! To behold a thousand departments reaching as wide as the earth! And then the hundreds of thousands of branch departments, of hundreds of grades, adapted to every soul that rises up from the earth.

18/7.5. O that they could look into the dark places in atmospherea! That they could see a million souls, plunged into chaos by terrible war! Crazed spirits, wild and battling! Not knowing they are dead! The ceaseless toil of a million nurses and physicians, laboring day and night with them! O the darkness upon them! O the glory of Your exalted ones! Who is there, having seen the magnificence of Your glories, who will not stir himself up every moment to lift up his brother and point the way to Your throne?

18/7.6. O that they could see Your swift Gods of dawn! How they hear a hundred tongues at one time, and frame answers for all of them, and, by a motion of the hand, dispatch messengers to fulfill the same (answer them) in words! How they select officers, to know a hundred at a glance, and know where to place them, so that every one shall fit his place! Who is there, O Father, that can frame into words the proceedings of heaven, so that mortals can comprehend even a fraction of Your great glories!

18/7.7. Shall a man light a candle and say it represents the sun? How, then, can they find the affairs of mortals comparable to Your kingdoms? O that they knew the meaning of the difference

---

[472] list, perhaps epitomizing or summarizing the subjects

[473] that = 'if only' or 'were it the case that' or 'if it could be the case that;' in other words, expressing a desire or wish that something were true

between All Light and the darkness of man's judgment!

18/7.8. O that they knew You, You Central Sun of All Light! They have put away Your Person, and they go in any direction. Your Great Gods are only myths to them, because of the darkness of their souls. Behold, they look for a small man with a large sword! The power of great wisdom they do not know.

18/7.9. O that they could observe the coming and going of thousands of messengers, from far-off kingdoms, before the throne of Your God! How he has answered their matters instantly! And all the while heeded the voices of a thousand marshals! O that man knew the glory of Order! The power of Harmony!

18/7.10. They have seen a clock with a hundred wheels, and the eye of its maker overseeing its every part in motion, and they call it wonderful! But how can they know Your Councils, O Jehovih? Your millions? And Your God on his throne, mantled in Your Light, overseeing a whole heaven! What majesty of words can make mortals comprehend his wisdom, and power, and great labors!

CHAPTER 8 Osiris

18/8.1. Thus Osire established Vibhraj, the resplendent heaven, with one thousand eight hundred sub-kingdoms, in atmospherea, all under the commandments of the central kingdom. Then he established the roadways between them, and appointed seven hundred thousand messengers. After that he ordained proper officers for inter-communion; and the several sub-kingdoms established their places of learning and places of labor, their hospitals and nurseries, and their innumerable asaphs, the receivers of es'yans, the newborn spirits of the dead of earth.

18/8.2. Osire said: Behold, there is order in heaven. Now I will appoint a God to hold dominion two hundred years. For while the dawn of dan yet remains, I will assist him. Let the examiners search, then, among my hosts, and find from those who sprang from the earth, one who stands clear on the record, and chief in rank.

18/8.3. So the examiners searched; and after thirty days, they selected Konas; and when Osire was informed, he sent a thousand of his own attendants in an otevan, and they brought Konas to Vibhraj, to Jehovih's throne. Osire said:

18/8.4. Greeting, in the name of the Father! You are chosen above all others; and, after the dawn of dan is ended, you shall be God of heaven and earth for two hundred years. Prior to the ascent of my hosts and myself, behold, I will crown you. Till then, you shall sit on my throne and fill my place while I am absent.

18/8.5. I have now restored order in heaven, having given all the inhabitants a single purpose in concert, by which, their resurrection is surely founded. Now I will go down to the false Lords' kingdoms, on the earth, and to the mortal kings and queens, and restore order there also.

18/8.6. Konas said: Your will and Jehovih's be done! I am exalted and rejoiced in what is bestowed upon me. Make me strong and wise, O Jehovih, so I may glorify Your kingdoms!

18/8.7. So, after due preparation, Osire departed privately, taking with him one hundred thousand attendants, going down to the earth and to the false Lords' kingdoms, in the cities and temples of mortals.

18/8.8. Seven days Osire spent traveling around the earth, visiting angels and mortals, but telling no one who he was, or what his object was; and then he halted his otevan, which had been built for the purpose, in the regions of the mountains of We-ont-ka-woh, in Western Jaffeth (China). He said:

18/8.9. We-ont-ka-woh shall be my headquarters for a season. Here, then, I will found the first Lord's kingdom for mortals; and because mortals have made an idol of Apollo, I will cast down Apollo and make them know that I, Osire, am Lord of the earth. Then spoke We'taing, saying:

18/8.10. Behold the glory of Jehovih from the start! In our journey around the earth, we have found the I'hins not as idolaters, but still worshippers of the Great Spirit, Jehovih. But as to the half-breeds, who can understand them? They believe nothing; they believe everything. They ask the idol for rain, and for dry weather! For strength to slay the druks; for flesh to eat, and for famine to be visited on their enemies.

18/8.11. They are as living prey for druj to feast on; they invite the darkest of all evil. And to do their wills in return, the druj, the evil spirits, busy themselves inoculating the air with poison to kill the mortal's enemies.

18/8.12. Osire said: With the I'hins we have little to accomplish; but as to the Ghans and the I'huans, they shall be converted into disbelievers of the presence of all spirits, except two, Jehovih and satan.

18/8.13. To accomplish this, I will give them three figures: The signs of seasons,[474] which shall represent the Creator in all the parts of the living; the sign of the sun, with motion and all life coming forth; and the hand of man.[475]

CHAPTER 9 Osiris

18/9.1. Through Osire, Jehovih said:

18/9.2. I created man with a corporeal life so that he could learn corporeal things. But behold, the I'huans have lost all energy to acquire earthly knowledge, depending on their familiar spirits for information on everything, thus wasting their mortal lives in non-improvement. So that when they die, and enter heaven, they are easily made slaves of by evil spirits.

18/9.3. It would be better for them if they had no knowledge of spirit life, so that they would put into service, the talents I created within them. See to this matter, O My Sons and Daughters; for their desire for the presence of the spirits of the dead will draw fetals upon themselves, and they will go down in darkness, like the ancients.

18/9.4. The Voice departed, and then Osire said: Hear me, O brothers, O sisters; this is my commandment upon you, and for you to render to your successors after I call you for the resurrection:

18/9.5. Possess the temples and oracles, where the familiar spirits speak; do not allow familiars to come any more to kings, queens, governors, leaders or rulers of men; but take possession of all these places, and answer the corporeans with corporean knowledge only.

18/9.6. And so that you may be as a unit to mortals, you shall all give the same name, even Jehovih, through His Son, Osire. For when you answer at the oracle, or in the altar or temple, they will ask who the spirit is; and you shall say: "Osire, Son of Jehovih;" doing this in my name and the Father's.

18/9.7. And when you speak by entrancement, through the seers and prophets, also assert the same thing. And they will ask: Why has the Son of Jehovih come to us? And you shall say:

18/9.8. Because you are an idolatrous people, worshipping before stone and wood; by which, evil spirits take advantage of you, and rule you to your own detriment.

18/9.9. And they will reason among themselves, saying: How do we know, then, that you are not an evil spirit? And you shall say: It is well that you ask this, for I declare to you, you shall not worship Osire, but only Jehovih, the Creator. This doctrine, only, is safe.

18/9.10. Again they will say: Who is satan and his attendants? You shall answer: Whoever professes any name except the Great Spirit, is of satan, which pertains to self.

18/9.11. Now, while you are thus reasoning with them, certain ones in the temples will be worked by the familiar spirits, writhing and

---

[474] Zodiac is called, sometimes, the signs of the seasons. The Osirian religion was really the directing of man's attention to the power and grandeur of corporeal worlds. In other words, the God Osiris' labor was to call mortals away from idol worship and make them scientists. –Ed. [It was also the time when man greatly developed his cognitive, intellectual, reasoning, etc., abilities.]

[475] Osiris established and fortified inspiration for man to build in the corporeal field. The fruits of that inspiration continue to this day; and for convenience' sake, adherents can be called Osirians.

The hand of man still represents the ability to accomplish. And in early kosmon, while man considers the sun essential to life, it is no longer viewed as a creator, as earlier Osirians came to believe; but instead, today's Osirians believe in nothingness, or rather random chance occurring in favorable circumstances.

Accordingly, building upon the Osirian past, a teaching to this day is that man has built himself by his own hands, and therefore, by extension, the highest standard used to measure man is man himself—not some mythical God or hallucination of the mind called angels—for the teaching in its strictest sense considers all Gods and angels to be fabrications from the mind of man. Even the sun and universe can be understood by man, and someday mastered, or so the hope of the Osirian is.

twisting, and you shall say to the next of kin: Behold, I will tell you how to cast out the evil spirit. You shall say: I charge you, in the name of Jehovih, to depart!

18/9.12. It shall come to pass that they will do this, and at the time they use the words: In the name of Jehovih, Depart! || you shall drive away the familiars, thus proving the power of Jehovih greater than all spirits.

18/9.13. But so that this matter may spread rapidly, and be valued highly, impart the name of the Great Spirit, in secret, not permitting them to speak it aloud. Choose, therefore, certain mortals, and ordain them through the king, and their labor shall be to cast out evil spirits.

18/9.14. It will come to pass in many places where you dispossess the false Lords and their confederates, that these evil spirits will inoculate the cattle and beasts of burden with poison, and they will die; and the evil spirits will show themselves to the dogs, and cause them to howl; and the evil spirits will obsess the swine, which are easily influenced, and the swine will appear drunk and foolish. And all these things you shall prophesy to mortals beforehand, thus supplying evidence of the Great Spirit's wisdom.

18/9.15. After these things are accomplished, mortals will further say: Behold, O Son of Jehovih, before you came, Apollo told us when to plant, and when to reap; when to bring the male and female cattle together; but now that we have put him aside, what shall we do? And you shall answer them:

18/9.16. Come into the starlight, and I will give you the signs, so that you may know these things yourselves. || And where you speak in the oracle, or by entrancement, you shall point out to them certain stars, and give them the names of these stars; and certain groups of stars (constellations) with their names also; and you shall show them the travel of the sun, north and south, and give them a tablet of onk (zodiac), divided into twelve groups, with twelve lines coming from the sun.[476]

18/9.17. And you shall raise up priests by inspiration, and by entrancement, and through them illustrate the position of the um[477] in the signs of the zodiac (onk). And the priests shall explain these things to the unlearned, so they may comprehend through their own knowledge.

i033r10g **Um**. Direction or place.

i033r10i **Git'um**. Direction or place of moon.

i033r10j **Git'ow'um**. Direction or place of sun.

i033r10k **V'work'um**. Direction or place of vortex.

18/9.18. When these things are accomplished, you shall inspire the I'huans and Ghans to go to the I'hins and ask to be circumcised to Jehovih; and the I'hins, also being under inspiration, will confess them[478] and bestow them with the sign.[479]

---

[476] see Onk or Zodiac, image i020

[477] Um means direction, and in this case the place and direction of movement was illustrated by the priest. Note that there was um not only for the signs, but for individual stars, sun, moon and planets as well. For some symbols of um, see images i033r10g, i033r10i, i033r10j, i033r10k from the Tablet of Se'moin (vol.2 p.227).

[478] That is, will acknowledge them to be worshippers of the Great Spirit, and so bestow them with the circumcision—most likely this came with a rite and ceremony; perhaps also a sacred name of the Creator was imparted, to be kept in secret.

[479] being the circumcision, which signified the person had seed capable of eternal life

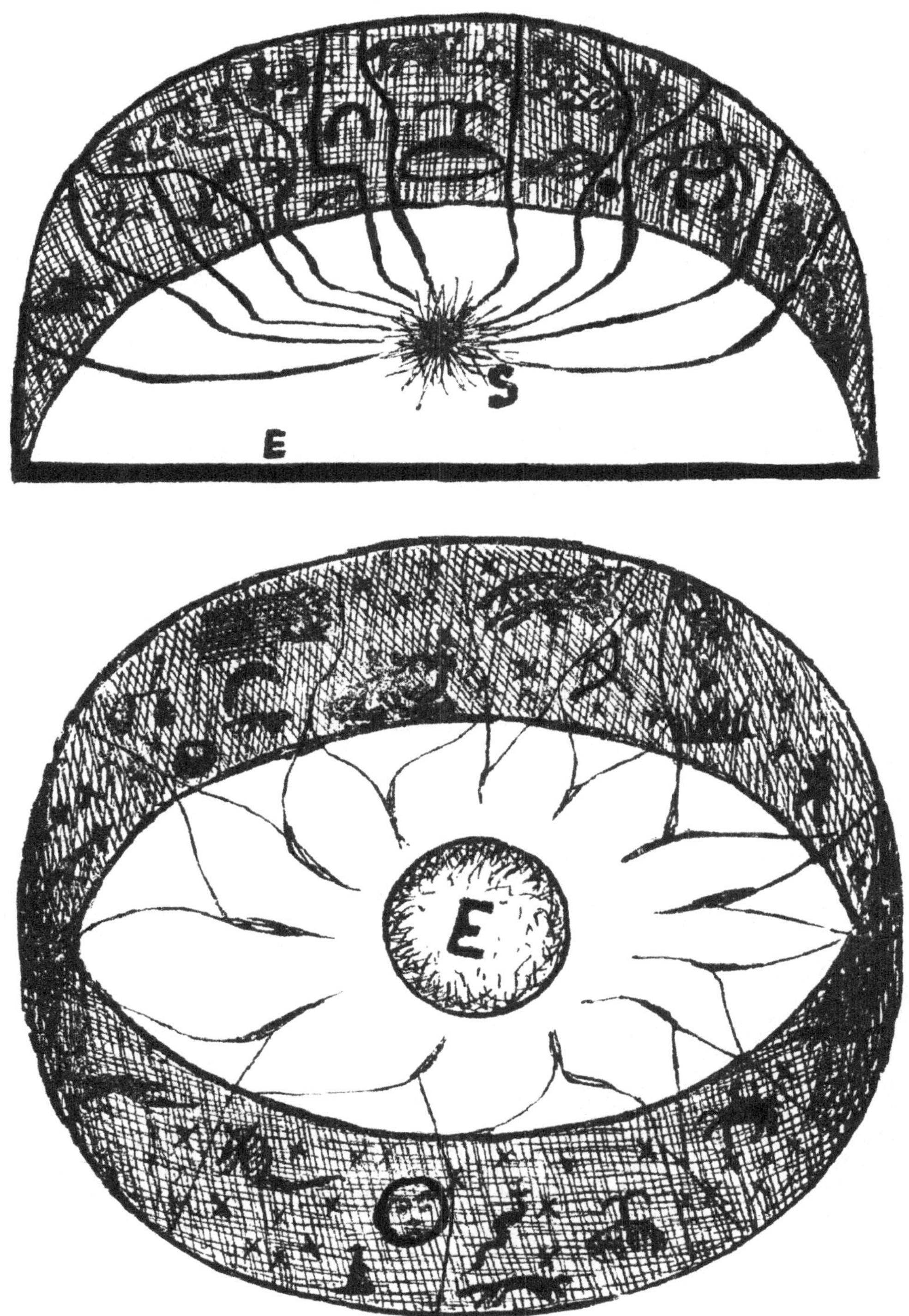

i020 **Onk or Zodiac**. First revealed to man (other than I'hin) 12,200 years before kosmon. E, Earth; S, Sun.

CHAPTER 10 Osiris

18/10.1. When Osire had completed his instructions to his hosts, he sent messengers to Vibhraj, saluting, in the name of Jehovih, calling for one million more ethereans, who came presently; and Osire divided them into ten thousand groups, giving each group one or more of his attendants, to whom he had previously given instructions. When all of them were ready for the work, Osire said:

18/10.2. Experience has proven that to dispossess familiar spirits in one place, is only to drive them to another. It is wise, therefore, that in the same day that you make the attack in one city or temple, you do so in the principal places all over the earth, giving the familiars no place to fasten upon. Therefore, let the beginning of sunrise tomorrow in each and every place be the sign of attack; and you shall possess all the temples, places of the oracles, cities, kings, queens, rulers, and leaders of men, driving away, by stratagem or by force, all the false Lords, and all spirits professing the name of Apollo, or any representative[480] spirit in the name of Apollo or Thor.

18/10.3. And immediately mortals will recognize that some change is going on in the unseen world; and they will go to the places of spirit communion, asking for Apollo to explain; and you shall answer: Apollo is cast out! Hear the wisdom of the Great Spirit, Jehovih!

18/10.4. And then you shall instruct them as I have commanded.

18/10.5. So it came to pass as Osire had decreed; the ethereans drove out the false Lords of the earth and they banished the familiars of all the kings, queens and leaders of men. And the ethereans taught in the temples and oracles, and by entrancement, and by inspiration, as commanded by Jehovih, through His Son, Osire.

18/10.6. But in all places the Great Spirit's name was made a secret; and it was commanded of mortals that His name only be spoken in whisper, or low breath, because Jehovih speaks to the soul of man silently. And these things were established; and this was the first universal teaching of the Great Spirit given to mortals other than the sacred people, the I'hins.

[480] agent, deputy, delegate, functionary

18/10.7. And Osire decreed: You shall give one Lord to every city and oracle; but every Lord shall profess Jehovih, and to being His Son.

18/10.8. And this was also accomplished; and when the people consulted the oracles as to who the spirit was, the answer was: Jehovih, through His Son, Lord of earth (or God of earth). But it was made lawful to use the names, Lord and God, with audible voice; and they were thus used, and spoken of by mortals as the substitutive words, permissible in public, in place of the name, JEHOVIH. After this, the names LORD and GOD were worshipful.

18/10.9. Osire said: It is an easy matter to rule over the kings, queens, prophets, and all learned people; but not so easy to rule over the ignorant. They, having been accustomed to worship Apollo through the idols, will continue to do so for a long time; therefore, you shall cause the kings to issue edicts prohibiting familiar spirits, and forbidding soothsayers[481] and workers of magic; for you shall teach mortals that these things come from satan (the evil disposition of men).

18/10.10. This was also done, according to the commandments; and now there was no place left for familiar spirits to obsess mortals. And these spirits distributed themselves like the spirits of ancient times; some going into swine, and living with them; concerning which, Osire commanded his hosts to inspire the kings and queens to pass laws prohibiting the eating of swine's flesh, lest mortals become bound with fetals. Accordingly, this law was established on the earth. Some of the dispossessed spirits went into the forests to dwell, and some to the fountains and mists in waterfalls; others, who were depraved, dwelt in the fisheries and slaughter-houses; and still others, in the kennels, with dogs and cats. Nevertheless, there were many mortals who were dealers in magic and witchery, and these had an abundance of familiars. And when such mortals would die, the familiars would go to their sons or daughters; consequently it was said of them, they inherited the gift of magic.

18/10.11. Osire, having overcome the evil spirits, now called a council at We-ont-ka-woh; and five hundred thousand angels came.

[481] those who profess to foretell events concerning self; fortune tellers

18/10.12. Osire said: In Jehovih's name, I will now deliver those[482] I have cast out; and you shall labor in conjunction with the Gods of atmospherea to accomplish this end. Behold, I have had the familiars enumerated, and there are more than six billion of them on earth. You shall go, therefore, to all the divisions of the earth that they inhabit, and proclaim a great festival, to be held in We-ont-ka-woh, inviting them here. And you shall provide them with conveyance, bringing them across the seas in suitable vessels. For, when I have congregated them here, I will destroy the ships so they cannot return.

18/10.13. This was accomplished, and more than five billion spirits came to the festival, where food was provided for them, and also clothes of fantastic colors, to please the eye of the ignorant; and after they were provided in decency, they were entertained with music and dancing, and taught to take part also. For seventy days the festival lasted, and every day varied from another; and the multitude became so intoxicated with delight, and also, so broken off from their old habits and associations, that they forgot all about the ships and conveyances.

18/10.14. Osire spoke to his Council privately, saying: Provide an airiata large enough for all these people. I will show you what shall happen! So, while the festival was going on, the proper workmen built the vessel, and its capacity was sufficient to carry all the multitude of spirits, besides a sufficiency of regimen for them on a long journey.

18/10.15. Now after the festival had lasted seventy days, Osire proclaimed order so that he could speak to them. He said:

18/10.16. Brothers and sisters, in the name of the Great Spirit, greeting to you all. I am about to depart to a higher world. So that you could hear my voice, I proclaimed order. So that you may rejoice in my words, I speak in love and tenderness. My home is in a world far away. Where there is no suffering; no sorrow. And the spirit of my people is radiant with light. I would tell you of the beauty and glory of my home, but it would not be fair to you. You would no longer be content to remain here. So I seal up my mouth.

[482] the false Lords and familiars

18/10.17. Because you suffered, and my soul was full of pity, I made this festival. The Great Spirit taught me how to make food and clothes, and to travel far, and not be afraid. All the people where I live can hear the voice of the Great Spirit. They learn all things by first learning to hear Him. His Wisdom supplies every want.

18/10.18. It will be a long time before I come again; my heart of love will come back to you. The time of the festival is ended; your time has come to return to your old places. These Lords of yours, whom you have had so long, should provide for you.

18/10.19. Almost at once, when Osire began to speak, the people desired to go where he would decree; and when he suggested for them to return to their former Lords, who were also present, they answered with a universal shout: No, never more with them!

18/10.20. Osire said: I perceive you desire to go with me and my hosts. I have learned to understand the souls of people. But do you understand me? I mentioned the great glories in my heavens; but I did not tell you we worked to make them. Yes, we work every day. The Great Spirit made the tree to get its food and clothes without labor; but, behold, it has no power to travel. Some things in the world do not labor; but man, who has neither feathers nor hair to cover his body, is provided with talents. Talents are the greatest of all gifts. The air and the ground provide the substance of fruit and foliage to the tree; but the spirit who has talent can find the substance of fruit and foliage in the air, and gather it. ||

18/10.21. Lights of various colors were now being set up by the ethereans, and the place enriched with the most enticing perfumes.

18/10.22. Osire proceeded: By the cultivation of talent, all things are possible to all men and women. With a sufficiency of talent, you need no Lords or oppressive rulers. I mentioned the great beauties in my etherean home. You go to the spray of fountains, and amuse yourselves in rainbows; but you are in a small corner, at best, and the substances of your joys are in perpetual failure. Behold the sprays and bows made by my hosts! Hear the music played in the elements of their handiwork!

18/10.23. At that, the hosts overcast the entire multitude with the vapor of the air, converted into millions of kaleidoscopic pictures, and filled the place with the music of wind currents trained to tunes.

18/10.24. The hosts were overjoyed beyond measure. Again Osire said: Hear me yet further; the festival must cease. You forget, I told you I must go. My marshals will now conduct me and my hosts to my fire-ship. As for you, my heart is broken. I know the toil and hardships put upon you. But if you desire these things, they are yours.

18/10.25. The universal shout was: We will go with you! Take us in your fire-ship. Teach us how to improve our talents!

18/10.26. Osire said: What will the Lords do? Shall they remain without subjects? But the false Lords answered quickly: We will also go with you, and be servants to do your bidding!

18/10.27. Osire said: When I am on the ship I will answer. So he departed, and went into the airiata, to the side of which his own fire-ship was made fast; and presently he commanded all who chose, to come aboard; and lo and behold, all of them, more than five billion, went in. At which point, Osire commanded immediate ascent; and he thus delivered them high up in atmospherea, where his proper officers had already provided a plateau of habitation for them; and the name of the plateau was Assan, signifying, no escape, for here Osire decreed to have them educated, and purged from evil; nor was it possible for them to return to the earth by their own power and learning.

CHAPTER 11 Osiris

18/11.1. In Assan, Osire appointed Sha'bon as God over the delivered hosts; and Sha'bon selected officers and teachers, and then divided the people into groups and sections, according to their development, and then erected schools, nurseries and factories, and put the inhabitants to work, feasting them aplenty with rites and ceremonies.

18/11.2. After Assan was duly organized, Osire departed, and went and sojourned in various kingdoms that had been established by his Lords.

18/11.3. And all the heavens of the earth were thus organized anew under Osire, being accomplished in three years; and Osire spent the remainder of dawn in Vibhraj, perfecting it as the central kingdom of atmospherea. And lastly, he decreed the appointment of ten thousand Lords, to dwell on earth. Some at the temples of worship, or at oracles; and some within the cities of the Ghans; and he decreed for his Lords as follows:

18/11.4. You shall not teach mortals of heavenly things, neither by inspiration, nor through the oracles.

18/11.5. You shall not let them commune with the spirits of the dead, not even their own kin.

18/11.6. You shall not permit spirits to come to their mortal kin. And the spirits of those who die in infancy, you shall deliver to the asaphs in Vibhraj.

18/11.7. You shall not permit spirits to inhabit deserted houses; nor permit them to form habitations on the graveyards, on the earth.

18/11.8. You shall not permit spirits to inhabit caves or waterfalls on the earth.

18/11.9. You shall not permit spirits to obsess mortals, nor to speak through them by entrancement, unless they are spirits you appoint, in order to carry out these, my decrees; or unless they are masters of generation (loo'is), whom you shall appoint over mortals for other purposes.

18/11.10. You shall control the selecting and appointing of guardian spirits over newborn mortals.

18/11.11. And all such guardian spirits shall teach their wards nothing of heaven near the earth, but inspire them to believe that it lies far away, and very high, from which none return.

18/11.12. And the guardians shall also inspire their wards to consult God only, or his Lord, and to do this by secret prayer.

18/11.13. And that the Lord and God are all goodness, and all wisdom, and all love, and all power.

18/11.14. And that all evil comes from tetracts, [483] born with man's mortal condition.

18/11.15. And you shall inspire mortals to acquire a knowledge of the sun, moon and stars, giving names to them, together with their places in the firmament.

18/11.16. And give them temples for observation, and tablets for instruction.

18/11.17. For in all things you shall direct man's soul to the acquisition of corporeal knowledge, causing him to look into corporeal

[483] that is, evil disposition –Ed. [see 10/13.9-10; 11/1.68.]

things to find a reason for the behavior of all created substance.

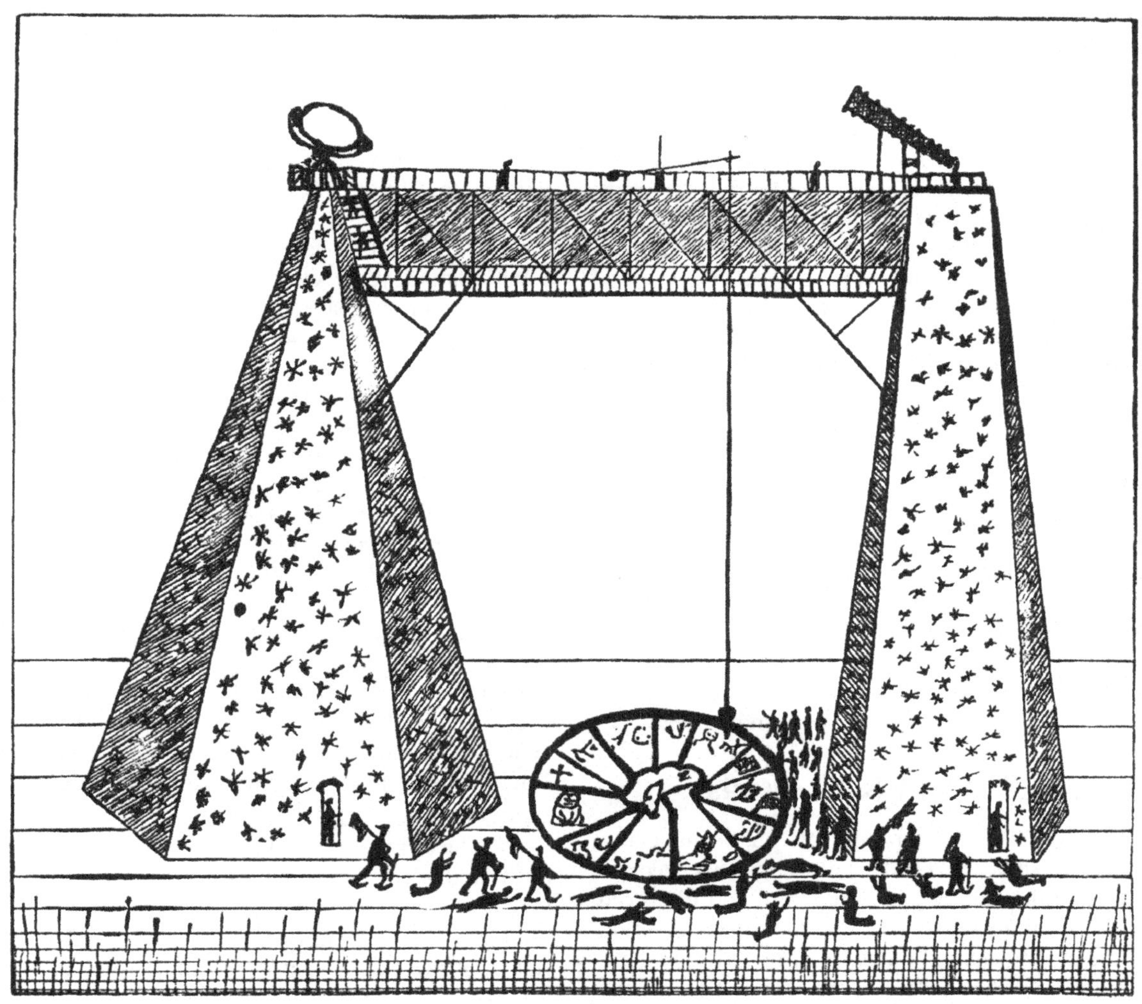

i019 **Star-Worshippers**. Arose during the cycle of Osiris, some 12,000 years before kosmon.

18/11.22. All these things must come to pass on the corporeal world; nor can there be any resurrection in the latter days, unless those of this day go through the fall that I am preparing for them.

18/11.18. And they shall no longer depend, in any sense, on the spirits for knowledge, or truth.

18/11.19. For I am not laying the foundation for spiritual knowledge on earth; that must come after. For as Jehovih first gave man a corporeal life, and then a spiritual life, so am I now laying a foundation for a new race (Ghans with corporeal intelligence and corporeal judgment) on the earth. For from their kin shall spring the heirs of Kosmon, who shall embrace both corporeal and spiritual knowledge.

18/11.20. But these shall rise in corporeal knowledge, and go down in it, suffering death in that which I now rain on the earth.

18/11.21. You shall teach them in truth; but future generations will contort your teachings into corporeal worship, prostrating themselves before the sun, moon and stars, going down in disbelief in not only the spiritual life, but in the Great Spirit, and His Gods and Lords.[484]

18/11.23. For which reason, you shall found[485] corporeal knowledge in the stars, and name them; for these things will be testimony in kosmon, of the fate of the worshippers of corporeal knowledge, in the time of the Osirian cycle.

18/11.24. In this you shall leave nothing undone that can be done, in order to make mortals put aside all spirituality, except to believe in the Great Spirit and a distant heaven; instead make them pursue knowledge wholly corporeal.

18/11.25. For the labor of God and his Lords shall not always be to fetch spirits back to earth, to learn of corpor, for this is not Jehovih's plan.

18/11.26. A heaven of corporeal knowledge shall be built up, which shall have a base in the firmament of heaven, where spirits can be taught in time to come.

18/11.27. Do not fear that man, during this period before us, can become too unbelieving in spiritual things; for Jehovih requires even perfection in unbelief, in certain periods of time. And this is the founding of that era on the earth.

18/11.28. Therefore, attend to these matters with all your wisdom and strength; and may the Light of Jehovih be with you, now and forever.

CHAPTER 12 Osiris

18/12.1. Osire, through his mathematicians, now furnished the Lords with maps of corporeal stars and the sun-belt (zodiac, onk), and bestowed names of animals upon them. Showed the position of the moon, sun and the earth in it; showed where the region of Cows[486] was; the place of Bulls; the place of Bears; the place of Horses; the place of Fishes; the place of Scorpions; the place of Sheep; the place of Lions; the place of Crabs; the place of Death [Sagittarius –Ed.]; the place of Life [Gemini –Ed.]; the place of Capricornus; and marked the seasons, and made twelve sections to the year, which was the width of the sun-belt.

18/12.2. And he placed the sun in the center of the belt and made lines from there to the stars, with explanations of the powers of the seasons on all the living.[487]

18/12.3. And he gave the times of Jehovih: the four hundred years of the ancients, and the half times of dan, the base of prophecy; the variations of thirty-three years; the times of eleven; and the seven and a half times of the vortices of the stars; so that the seasons could be foretold, and famines averted on the earth.

18/12.4. When the tablets were completed and ready to deliver to the Lords, Osire said: Take these and bestow them on mortals, both through the oracles and by inspiration, making them sacred with the prophets, seers, priests, and their kings and queens.

18/12.5. And you shall inspire them to build temples of observation, to study the stars; teaching by the gau, and by the travel of the sun north and south, and by Cnest [north star –Ed.], and by dark chambers, so that they can prove the Fichtus of Haal;[488] for all that can be done or taught, shall be,

---

[484] see image i019 Star-Worshippers, p.201

[485] initiate, establish, lay the base of; thus man would base his corporeal knowledge on the stars; said another way, all corporeal knowledge originates from (can be reduced to, linked to, traced to) the stars; the origin of astrology and astronomy. Note that originally the constellations and stars (including planets) were identified so that man (through correlation) could learn the timing of corporeal events. It was only later that man attributed the CAUSE of these events to the stars or constellations themselves.

[486] The terms cows and horses, or mares and bulls, in the Vedic Scriptures, do not refer to the animals themselves, but to groups of stars, with reference to their power on the male and female; or rather, positive and negative forces. In some of the astrological maps, in Upper Thibet [Tibet], the star groups are still set with animal outlines.

Osiris was sent to the earth to develop corporeal brains in man [mind, corporeal knowledge, corporeal judgment]; and he will stand to the end of time as the God of natural philosophy [science], as that term is understood. The names of many of the stars, and of most of the signs of the zodiac, are today as they were given by this God, Osiris, more than ten thousand years ago. –Ed.

[487] see image i020 Onk or Zodiac, p.197

[488] Fichtus of Haal refers to 24,000 years' periods, as will be seen in another place, when great changes take place on the earth. It also refers to an average position of the north star. And yet

to prove man's corporeal senses adequate for a perfect corporeal life.

18/12.6. For this rule follows on all corporeal worlds; that with the culture of the corporeal senses, man becomes vigorous, strong, and independent; and with the culture of the spiritual senses in corporeans, they become weak, sensitive and dependent.

18/12.7. In the first case, they ultimately become selfish and wicked; in the second case, they become impotent, and unadapted to corporeal life, and thus become extinct.

18/12.8. On all corporeal worlds, for every race He created, Jehovih has provided these two seasons: a season for the development of the corporeal senses, and a season for the development of the spiritual senses. To find the mean between these is to find Kosmon, which lies far in the future.

18/12.9. Now, therefore, I place the matter into your charge, in the name of Jehovih, that you shall not consider the spiritual nature of the corporeans in any respect, leaving that matter to God and his sub-Gods, who will receive them at the time of their mortal death.

18/12.10. But you shall teach them to fear no spirit, Lord or God; teaching them that by their own wills they can cast out the tetracts, which assume to be spirits. Indeed, you shall inspire them to be Gods and Goddesses themselves; and by their aspirations they will become large and powerful, and of fearless disposition.

---

again, the same term applies to certain distances from the sun, where planets have orbits. It is by this rule that astronomers, to this day, judge of the place where a planet is likely to be discovered. The ruined temples of India and Eastern Persia suggest that, in the time of their building, the astronomers of those days knew nearly as much of the heavens as we do today. Some five thousand years afterward these things were taught in Egypt, when the first pyramids were built. According to the rules in prophecy, these astronomical desires came to man every eleven thousand, and six and five thousand years. –Ed.

CHAPTER 13 Osiris

18/13.1. When great Osire had thus spoken, and commissioned his God and Lords to the harvesting of earth and heaven for another cycle, then the dawn of dan was finished. Order reigned in heaven and on earth, because a man, a God, had spoken. Men and angels had their eyes turned inward, to know of what capacity Jehovih had made them. And the earth, moon, sun and stars were shown in a new light to the sense of men; not to be shunned and despised, but glories given by the Great Spirit for useful purposes.

18/13.2. Jehovih had said: Some men I created to reason upon events near at hand, others to speculate upon events in remote regions; with thoughts diverse and unalike in procedure. Do not think, O man, that in high heaven such men become all alike; for I did not create them so, but to run in their various extremes forever!

18/13.3. Of the first, Osire, My Son, enthroned to give reason practice, did not come at a random period, but just when I had designed to sow the seed of unbelief and broadcast it over earth and heaven. ||

18/13.4. For such seasons appear in all peoples under the sun; a season of belief; a season of unbelief. And with the believing is the practice of truth and love; and with the unbelieving is the practice of great research and learning, with cruelty and disputation.

18/13.5. Osire said: Send for my resurrection, O Jehovih; I have uprooted the evil of idol worship, the extreme that follows too much belief. I have opened man's eyes to Your corporeal worlds, and set a mark on man's souls, so that no more shall man come from earth to heaven, saying: Alas, I have no corporeal knowledge!

18/13.6. Jehovih said: To further man's ultimate glory, I have decreed the earth to ji'ay'an fields for three thousand years, in which your fruit shall have its full growth.

18/13.7. Osire foresaw the times and places in the future road of earth and heaven, and that from his decrees would spring corporeal philosophy, the first of earth, to which man would look back in future ages, saying: From there sprang the Osirian system; from there, the Asyrian[489] races. Yet he looked further on, when men would become idolaters in disbelief of spiritual things, doing worship to the sun, moon and stars; and in very corpor profess to find the cause and foundation of all.

18/13.8. Jehovih said: Man shall search all things in order to find Me; but I gave this labor not to one generation of men, nor to those of a hundred or a thousand years, but to cycles.[490] For when I come in kosmon to found My kingdom on earth, man shall have the testimony of all speculations and philosophies before him, together with their fruits. And he shall judge that which is good by the evidence of past practices. ||

18/13.9. High in the arc of Se'ing rose Osire's call, where millions waited, knowing the dawn of dan on the red star was near its end. Swift messengers told the story of Jehovih's work, through His Son, Osire; and, measuring the width of his harvest, laid the scheme at the feet of the reigning Goddess, Antwa. And she gave the word, Go, to her legions in waiting, who had moored an obegia, a float, a fire-ship, ready to proceed for the hosts redeemed by Great Osire.

18/13.10. And amid music and dancing, they cut her loose, the obegia, with five million souls aboard, commanded by Eticene, Goddess of Antwa's Garden—an etherean plain, where ten billion souls dwelt; a place of rest, for Gods and Goddesses to regale[491] themselves with stories of redemptions of mortals on the countless stars floating in Jehovih's etherean veins.[492]

18/13.11. The obegia, the pride of Eticene, steered off to the red star, the earth, for the marriage festival of seven billion Brides and Bridegrooms, the yield of Osire's harvest for the upper kingdoms.

18/13.12. Meanwhile, Osire and his hosts, prepared in the usual way, waited for the signal, the coming of Jehovih's light within the earth's vortex. For strange as it may seem to Gods and men, everything in the firmament is upward; those who leave a star (a planet), rise upward; those who leave an etherean world for the stars, also rise upward, but call it downward, to suit the understanding of mortals. In that way, then, the obegia, with the hosts of Eticene, pierced the vortex of atmospherea.[493] The Brides and Bridegrooms shouted with joy.

18/13.13. And the millions of guests, assembled to witness the awe-inspiring ceremonies, joined in applause.

18/13.14. Then down came the ship of fire, broad as a sea, with all her appurtenances[494] in trim; and, adorned in majesty, descended to the floors of Vibhraj. And from the mantles of light came Eticene, to salute great Osire, in the name of the Great Spirit, and receive his contribution to the unchangeable worlds!

18/13.15. Osire, with his attendants, the archangels of Lowtsin, received Eticene under the Sign of Ormadz, Master Creator of Power, and then presented his delivered sons and daughters, seven billion.

18/13.16. Due ceremonies were proclaimed, and upon completion, the Brides and Bridegrooms of Jehovih entered the obegia. Osire saluted God, who was ordained to be ruler of heaven and earth for the next two hundred years, and, with sorrow in his soul, Osire departed, going into the obegia, the fire-ship, for a higher heaven, where waited millions of loves, calling to him to come home.

18/13.17. Then upward rose the mighty ship, commanded by the slender Eticene, the young Goddess of Antwa's Garden; her little hands stretched upward to Jehovih, by her mighty faith, Commander of the elements.

END OF THE BOOK OF OSIRIS

---

[489] The sound, "Ah," substituted for "Oh," makes a word earthly that was heavenly. Asyrian, and Aysyrian, and Aysirian, and Assyrian, are synonymous terms. –Ed.

[490] i.e., dan'ha cycles

[491] delight each other, tell stories, entertain

[492] i.e., through the roadways; see image i098

[493] Thus, Eticene and her hosts were still traveling upward when it pierced the atmospherea of earth. But then, perhaps as they reorient the ship, they must seem to themselves to be traveling downward, for their orientation must change at some point.

[494] equipment and accessories

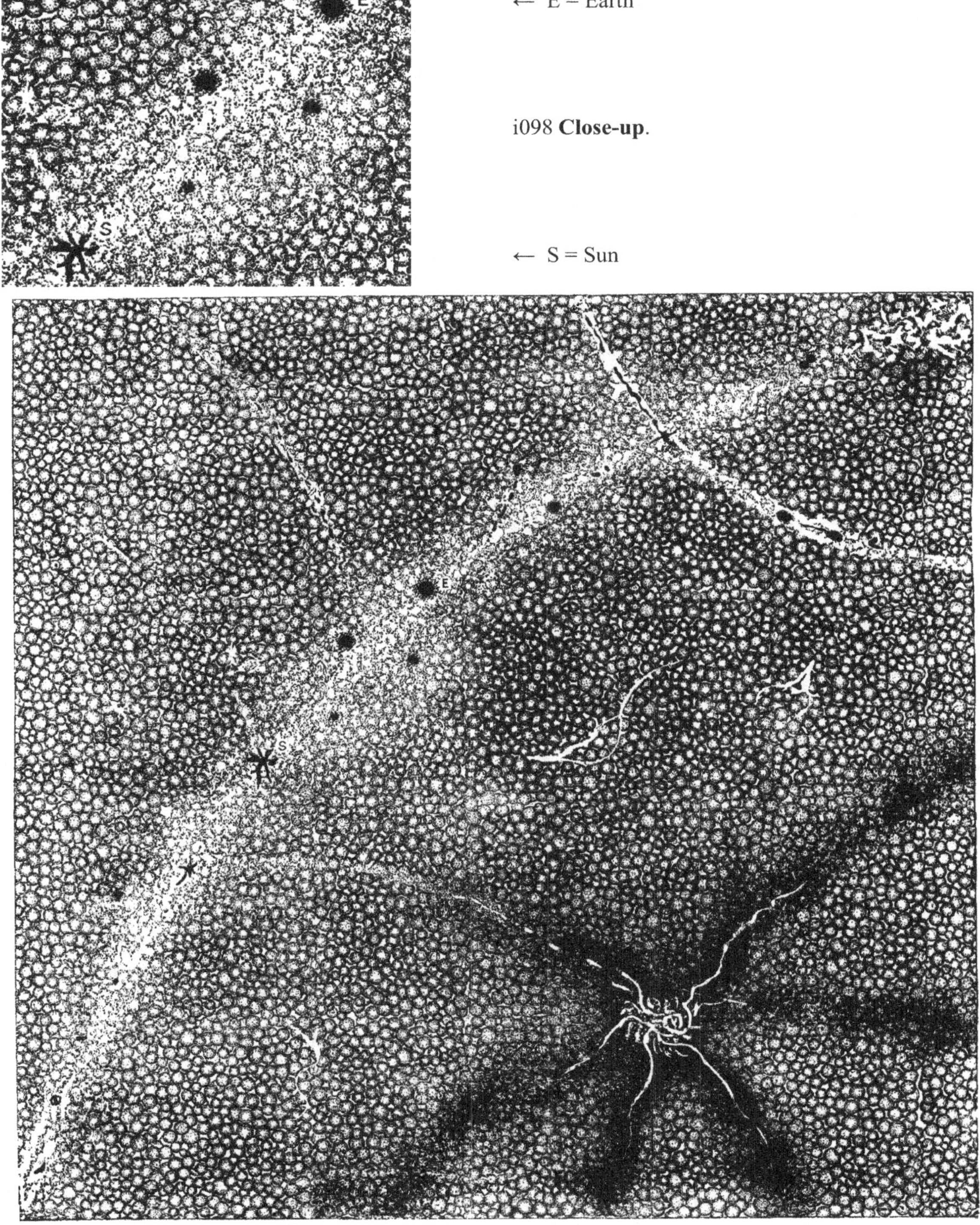

← E = Earth

i098 **Close-up**.

← S = Sun

i098 **Etherean Worlds and Roadways for Sun-phalanxes**. S = Sun; E = Earth.

The Lords' Fifth Book

Being contemporaneous with the Book of Osiris, Son of Jehovih. As Osiris is of the higher heavens and the lower heavens, so is the Lords' Book of the lower heavens and of the earth, for the same period of time.

CHAPTER 1 Lords' Fifth

Of Vind'yu (Hindu) Scriptures

19/1.1. God apportioned certain parts of the earth for the tribes of Shem of the arc of Noe'chi, a heavenly place, seat of mountains, and Lords, All Wise; and from his Wisdom directed Hirto into his pastures.

19/1.2. Hirto, Son of Neph, born of an egg, descended out of the highest heaven. He was a most gracious Lord, and in deference to Om, struck himself (in his egg) against the rocks of heaven. So, when the egg was broken, one-half of the shell ascended (becoming the dome of heaven), the other half became the foundation of the world.

19/1.3. The evil voice spoke to the children of men, and polluted them. About which, the Great Spirit spoke in the firmament of heaven, saying: To Hirto, son of Neph, I bequeath[495] the tribes of Shem forever. For they have withstood Anra'mainyus,[496] My everlasting enemy. So Hirto became Lord of Shem, and he banished Anra'mainyus down under the earth, where he busies himself building fires for the furnaces of hell, the smoke and flames of which come up through the earth and are called Agni (volcanoes), so that his existence would be known to men.

19/1.4. Thus came Evil from Good; but so that Everlasting Wisdom would prevail with mortals and the spirits of heaven, All Light created Visvasrij (universal system and order)[497] as a creator to abide forever. Before this time there were two things in the world: Voidness was one, and Vachis was the other. Vachis vach [that is, Speech spoke –Ed.], and the world was. So it came to pass that Voidness was divided into two parts, the seen and the unseen worlds.

19/1.5. The unseen spoke in the wind three sounds, E-O-IH, and was called by mortals Eolin, God of the wind; so Eolin showed Himself in three colors: yellow, which is the highest color; blue, which is the coldest color; and red, which is the warmest color.

19/1.6. Eolin said: Out of My three sounds, all sounds are made; out of My three colors, all colors are made. He was the All Master.

19/1.7. He said: Three worlds I have made: the earth world, which is for mortals; the all high heavens, which are for pure and wise angels; and the intermediate world, which rests on the earth.

19/1.8. Eolin said: Three lights I have created: the sun, to rule the day; the moon, to rule the night; and the burning fire, for the use of man.

19/1.9. Three spirit lights I created: Ruch, which issues out of My soul; Shem, which comes from My Lords in heaven to the souls of men; and Vas, which comes from the spirits of the intermediate world.

19/1.10. Eolin said: I am in three states: Ghost, which is ever-present and unchangeable; Corpor, which is in places, like the earth, stars, sun and moon; and Motion, which is everlasting unrest. Such am I, Eolin, Mightiest in three, in All Place and All Time.

19/1.11. When the egg was broken and the shell distributed, lo and behold, the se'mu of the egg had nowhere to rest, and being void of compact[498] distributed itself in the void world and was not seen. Then Hirto, High Lord of the upper heavens, sent whirlwinds abroad, and they gathered of the substance of the egg and rained it down on the earth.

19/1.12. Uz, son of Eolin, ran quickly and turned Anra'mainyus' fires to the north, and Eolin touched the earth with His quickening hand, and instantly all the living were created.

19/1.13. So Eolin said: To you, My first-begotten Son, I bequeath the earth, it shall be yours to keep forever. Neither shall there be any other God.

---

[495] give as an inheritance, grant, assign, bestow

[496] the evil voice; satan

[497] origin of the concept of what is today called natural law, laws of physics, Nature or Mother Nature

[498] cohesion, ability to amass

19/1.14. But in course of time the evil voice (satan) encompassed the earth with serpents that spoke like men and angels, and the serpents made friends with All Evil, Father of Anra'mainyus; and the women of the tribes of A'su went and tempted the first men, the I'hins, and so, evil offspring were born into the world.

19/1.15. Hirto, Lord of the earth, drove the first men out of the region of light, and set high-born angels on the boundaries of Chinvat, at the gates of the upper heaven, to guard the tribes of Faithists for ever after. Nevertheless, evil, being set on foot, soon overspread the earth. So Hirto rested his hands on his thighs, and swore an oath to All Light that he would drown the world and all the living. And in answer to the Lord a seraphim, a mighty fire-ship, came down out of the sun region, opening the floodgate of heaven with a sea of water, and all the people perished, except the I'hins, the sacred people, friends of the Lord of earth.

19/1.16. So the Lord took the hollow of his hand and lifted up his people, and gave them doves' wings, and they flew far and came to the land where the Lord dwells; so it was called Shem as a proof to all the world.

19/1.17. In those days God was so near to mortals, that when an honest man spoke, the Lord answered him. And Anra'mainyus was near also, and when an evil man spoke an evil voice answered him. For that reason, the Lord singled out the purest and most virtuous of women; the wisest, strongest and most faithful, best of men, and married them, giving two women to one man, according to law. And the heirs of the wisest and most virtuous of men and women were wiser than their parents. And the Lord gave this secret to his people (prophets, priests) in the house of God, and they gave the knowledge to the chosen people.

19/1.18. Hirto said: For this reason, O my beloved, you shall not wed with the druks, the dark people, that burrow in the ground, lest your seed become polluted, and your heirs go down to hell with Anra'mainyus.

19/1.19. But Anra'mainyus, evil creator of evil, went to the druk women; speaking to them in a dark corner, he said: You have the root of Babao to make delirious; fetch it to the white people that came with doves' wings; fetch, and they will eat and get drunk. And when the young men are drunk, go to them, for they are my gift.

19/1.20. So, of those who came out of the arc of Noe'chi, sin was newborn; for the druks went in where they were drunk, saying: Lest the white people and the yellow people fall upon us, and our seed perish on the earth, make us of flesh and kin, bone and bone, blood and blood.

19/1.21. Hirto, the Lord God, saw into the darkness, and being compassionate, said: I will visit great punishment on Anra'mainyus for this; his head shall droop in sorrow. But as for the I'hins, being drunk, I will forgive them. And as to the newborn people, they shall become the mightiest of all people in the whole world, because they came out of both darkness and light. The darkness in them shall battle all darkness; the light that is in them shall then master over their own darkness. But as for the druks, they shall go down in darkness forever. ||

CHAPTER 2 Lords' Fifth

19/2.1. Shem had many tribes, who settled on the borders of the sea at Haventi and Gats; and the Lord (Hirto) dwelt with them, speaking through the chief prophet, Tah (Tae), who made a record on stone, and wood, and cloth, of the Lord's word, and these were preserved in the Valens (house) of God (Hirto).

19/2.2. And when Tah was old, and died, the mantle of the Lord's gifts fell on Tah's son; who also had power to hear the Voice; and he also kept a record of the Lord's words.

19/2.3. And when he died, his son succeeded in the same way; and, because of this truth, the Lord called all of them by the sacred name, Tah, the order of which continued for a hundred generations. And it came to pass that the I'hins filled the country far and near with cities; and yet, in all that time, they killed nothing that had been created alive to breathe, on the earth, or in the water, or in the air above.

19/2.4. In the early days of the I'hins, the Lord spoke through the chief prophet, saying: When the inhabitants of one city or tribe marry with those of another city or tribe, behold, it is only just that the names of father and mother be given to the offspring.

19/2.5. But men were in darkness in those days, and did not understand God. So, accordingly, the inhabitants combined the names belonging to the neighboring tribes. That is to say, one tribe said, ut (wheat); another tribe for the same thing, said, yat; and another tribe said, wat; and another, hoot; and so on. So, the later generations said, utyatwathoot (wheat), and this was called the Yi-ha language; and so great were the number and the size of words used, that the writings of the ancient prophets were lost, because none could understand them.

19/2.6. The Lord spoke, saying: Because I desired to preserve the genealogy of my chosen, you have applied the law to things that are worthless in my sight. You have built a babble [babel; i.e., bah'bah'i –Ed.], a tower of words, so that your tongues are confounded one with another. You strove to reach to heaven with a multitude of words, but made food for hada (hades).

19/2.7. The Lord said: Come, now, into murdhan (sacred spirit communion), and I will deliver you. So the people sat in crescent, and the Lord came between the horns, saying: Behold, you are Tau,[499] but I am the S'ri (Spirit). My word shall stand against the entire world.[500]

19/2.8. Hear, then, the commandments of God (Hautot). Because you have built a tower of words, you are confounded. However I do not come in anger, but to deliver you. Neither will I write anymore, nor teach written words, for they are only folly, except to the learned.

19/2.9. By spoken words I will teach, and you shall repeat after me. And these shall be sacred words to the end of the world.

19/2.10. So the Lord taught orally in the temple, face to face with the people, and they learned the words and their meaning.

19/2.11. And those who learned the best, the Lord named Ritvij,[501] because he made them teachers over others. The Lord said: Because you have confounded the language of the ancients, I will give you a new language, and it shall be vede [perfect –Ed.], against all my enemies; nor shall any man anymore meddle with the words I give.[502]

19/2.12. Hirto (Lord) said: Love your Lord God only, and with all your soul. Turn your face away from the angels who come to you; they are the emissaries of Anra'mainyus.

19/2.13. Hirto said: Love the sun and moon, and all things on the earth, for they are the Lord's gift. What is spirit? It flies away; it is nothing.

19/2.14. Banish the druj (spirits) that prophesy. They are nothing but lies; they are Anra'mainyus' emissaries.

19/2.15. Learn to prophesy by the sun, and by the moon and by the stars. They tell no lies.

19/2.16. || The Lord then gave the signs of zodiac (the horses, cows, lions, sheep and birds) that rule upon the earth, and upon the winds of heaven, and on the heat and cold, and the sun, moon and stars, and spring, summer, fall and winter. But these things are omitted here in this book, because they are known in mortal histories to this day. ||

19/2.17. The Lord says in this day, the Kosmon era: Behold, O man, in the time of Osiris, I, the Lord, raised up many philosophers on the earth, and inspired them not only to fulfill the legends of the ancients, but also to write books of disputation, in order to turn man's mind away from the consultation of familiar spirits. I inspired men to write in this manner, namely:

19/2.18. Touching the matter of the egg, and also of Anra'mainyus, they appear never to have been proven; neither are they given on the authority of Hirto, the Lord of earth. It is reasonable to suppose that the Great Spirit divided up the worlds

---

[499] A crescent is often compared to a bull's horns. Most likely, the word Taurus had its origin as here described. Taw and Tawri are bull in the Yi-ha language. The word, of later date, signified force, or bull-like. The laws issued in a spirit circle are called "bulls," or Tau. Taurus, force, manifested especially in the procreative element, at a certain season of the year, as manifested in animals. Known by signs in the zodiac. Hence, as the Pope issues bulls. –Ed.

[500] That is, there is no power in all the world that can prevail against the word of the Lord.

[501] The word ritual, in English, can be traced back to ritvij, the present Sanscrit [Sanskrit] word for priest, or teacher of sacred things. Nearly all the Hebrew words pertaining to the mythical Tower of Babel, and the confusion of languages, correspond with Yi-ha, and its descendant language, the Sanscrit. In English we have babble, and gad, and gab, which are real Sanscrit words, as spoken. –Ed.

[502] The new language given was called Vede. Although it later became (with other languages) part of Sanskrit, this latter word still means "perfect."

among His Gods and Lords, and that the earth (Bhu) fell to Hirto as his portion; while the stars, which are also worlds like this, fell to other Lords and Gods. But as for evil Gods, like Anra'mainyus, who has ever seen one?

19/2.19. As for Hirto, the Lord, I have seen him myself, and so have thousands of other honest prophets. But when the Lord spoke it was not about foolish stories, but to teach man how to live, so that he could be happy and a glory to the Great Spirit. Neither did I ever hear the Lord assert that he was more than the spirit of a man risen from the earth. In my opinion, therefore, the Lord is the captain over the earth, and over all other spirits. But to know even this, is not so great a good truth as to know how to do righteously.

19/2.20. Therefore, of all things man should learn, it should especially be what he can see and hear and prove, rather than about spirits whom he cannot prove, nor find when he wants them.

CHAPTER 3 Lords' Fifth

19/3.1. The Lord said: As a farmer plants wheat in one field, rice in another and flax in a third, so do I, the Lord, inhabit the earth with the seed of man. Neither shall any wise man say: These things came by chance; that one people just happened to settle in Jaffeth (China), another in Vind'yu (India), and another in Arabin'ya [Ham, or Africa plus part of Near East; see i018 (p.228 –ed.]. Such is the argument of my enemies, says the Lord. Not perceiving the wisdom of my work as it happens [as it is unfolding –ed.], they fail to extend judgment into my plans of thousands of years, and so, stubbornly, shut themselves up in ignorance, saying: There is no God.

19/3.2. For I foresaw the breadth of the earth, and that it should be subdued for the glory of man; and in the early days, I divided my armies with wisdom.

19/3.3. To Ham I allotted the foundation of the migratory tribes of the earth. And of the tribes of Ham, behold, I selected many colors of men; through which I foreordained the name Ham to stand as a living testimony to the end of the world. For I foresaw that the time would come when the nations would look back searching for histories of my peoples, and I erected certain words and signs which would be testimony in the later times of earth.

19/3.4. The tribes of Ham were of all colors (black, white, yellow, copper, red and brown); nevertheless, they were I'hins (Faithists), having flat nails and short arms, and desiring to acquire knowledge.[503] And I brought them to a country of sand fields and with fields of rich pastures interspersed, where lived only a few natives, the dark people, with short hair. Neither did I omit even the hair of the head of man without providing testimony of my word.

19/3.5. I provided testimony of the I'hins in all the divisions of the earth, with long hair belonging to the tribes that worshipped Jehovih, so that man of the Kosmon era might perceive that the land from which they (I'hin ancestors) sprang is not above the water.[504]

---

[503] This is the key phrase for understanding the homogeneity of races of today. If you have flat nails instead of claws, arms that don't extend to the knees, and the desire to acquire knowledge, then you are indeed so because of the I'hins. (See 19/4.24-25 for more I'hin ancestry signs.)

Also, here we see explicitly that not all I'hins were yellow or white, but Africa, for one, had I'hins of all colors; and enough so, that there was no mode or general color. Because the I'hins came to Ham from Pan, this means the I'hins of Pan were also of all colors, although the modes (greatest numbers) there were in the white category and the yellow category. (See 06/2.4<fn-stout> with regard to color.)

[504] I'hins had long hair; see comparison at image i014, p.75. For man, hair length was an outward sign of spiritual capacity, although not necessarily of spiritual attainment (practice, competence, proficiency, facility). The capacity for eternal life comes because of one's I'hin ancestry; and, while in the past, hair length was an outward sign of I'hin ancestry, today virtually all humans, regardless of hair length, have capacity for eternal life (thus showing their I'hin ancestry). For it is in the Line of Light, which is of the Tree of Light through the Tree of Life, that one's identity is procured; remembering, that, while the caterpillar (flesh body) crawls along the ground, it is the butterfly (spirit within) that rises into the air (enters heaven).

19/3.6. Behold the multiple (Yi-ha) language of the tribes of Shem! Side by side with the tribes of Jaffeth I raised them. And, behold, the latter use the derivation of the Panic language to this day.[505]

19/3.7. For I gave to the tribes of these two different lands my ten commandments and ten invocations, not to be written, but to be spoken and taught from mouth to ear, to be sacred in the language given.

19/3.8. In which man shall perceive that the same stories of the egg, and of the origin of evil in the world, could not have been communicated by mortals.[506]

19/3.9. For I locked up enough of the Panic language in Jaffeth as a testimony to be discovered in future years; showing that, unlike Ham and Shem, a mighty nation could retain one language for thousands of years.

19/3.10. For I foresaw that philosophers would try to prove that languages were of mortal origin, and that they would change according to the growth of knowledge among men.

19/3.11. Behold, I gave scriptures to all my people, enjoining[507] some to adhere to the text; and, so, I preserved the work of my hand.

19/3.12. The tribes of Ham were previously ordained with characteristics to make them love to emigrate westward; and the tribes of Jaffeth and Shem with characteristics to make them love to stay within their own countries. And the tribes of Guatama were ordained with characteristics to make them love to go eastward. For I set a boundary to the tribes of Guatama, that they would not reach the ocean on the east.[508]

19/3.13. The Lord said: Having designed Ham for teaching the barbarian world of me and my dominion, I also prepared them so that, through their seed, men and women would have hair neither straight nor short, but long and curled, and red, and white, and brown, by which the genealogy of nations might be traced in future times. ||

19/3.14. Now, nestled in between the three great countries, Jaffeth, Shem and Ham, was located the chief place of the I'huans, and here they founded a new nation; and the Lord called them Par'si'e,[509] signifying, warrior Faithists, because he created them as a shield, to guard his chosen, the I'hins.

19/3.15. The difference between the I'huans and the Par'si'e was that the I'huans lived scattered about near the I'hins, but the Par'si'e'ans lived in a nation by themselves.

19/3.16. Nevertheless, they were all of the same blood and kin, being half-breeds between the I'hins and the native druks; and they were large, and mostly of the color of new copper.

19/3.17. And because the Par'si'e were favored by the Lord, the Lord gave them separate laws, and commanded them not to mix with the druks; which commandment they kept for more than a thousand years.

19/3.18. But in course of time, the Par'si'e'ans were tempted by the druks, and fell from their high estate, and they became cannibals.

---

505 The two languages are exactly opposite in construction; one monosyllabic [* the language of Jaffeth], and the other composed of a wonderful combination of syllables, sometimes as many as thirty to forty to one word. Think of the following: Vahhomvokwijomyissitiviyubuyhhomavashstbahh yodahuittayaivi, for the word FIRMAMENT. –Ed. [* Note that this is a generalization, for while the language of Jaffeth (China) was chiefly monosyllabic, it did have some polysyllabic words, although generally of not more than two or three syllables.]

506 The same legend exists in China, in regard to the egg and the origin of evil; the only difference being the name signifying satan or serpent. "Hiss" or "h'ce" is Chinese for serpent. This is Panic, that is, what the serpent says; but when "AH" speaks, we know "ah" means earth. In the Ezra Bible, the serpent spoke to Eve, i.e., the earth spoke; or, in plain English, the flesh tempted the spirit. In the Hindu scriptures, the first race, A'su, tempted the white people with wings. Had one of these countries obtained the legend from the other, the languages would have corresponded. In the Chinese version, the Tower of Babel (babbling languages) is not referred to. Why? Certainly, because in that country there was no confusion of languages. –Ed.

507 instructing, requiring, compelling, impelling

508 The mound builders came from the west, but never reached as far as to the Atlantic Ocean. –Ed.

509 Par'si'e is the origin of the nation and term Persia.

19/3.19. And the Lord sent the Ghans to travel in search of his people; and lo and behold, ten tribes of the Lord's people were lost in the wilderness; and this was the country of the Par'si'e'ans, and that land was filled with wild goats. From which came the name, LAND OF GOATS.

19/3.20. And the lost tribes, not being flesh eaters, were at a loss for food; and they said: Come, let us live on goat's milk.

19/3.21. And they lived like this for a long season, taming the goats, and keeping herds of them. And they roved about, driving their herds with them, for which reason they took the name of SHEPHERD KINGS.

19/3.22. And the Lord looked on them with favor, saying: These that call themselves shepherd kings shall have this country. Behold, out of the seed of these people, I will do mighty wonders.[510]

19/3.23. The Lord said: What man could discover, I, the Lord, left for him to discover; what man could not discover, I, the Lord, taught him.

19/3.24. To the shepherd kings I revealed how to make leather out of skins; nor had man any means of his own to make this discovery. || The shepherd kings made bags of leather in which they carried milk, which was thus churned; and they made butter, which was the first butter made in this world.

CHAPTER 4 Lords' Fifth

19/4.1. God said: I preserved the I'hin race to be without evil, as the foundation of my light, from whom I could reach forth to the tribes of darkness.

19/4.2. For I foreordained[511] not to go within darkness to battle it, but to stand outside it, and give an example of righteousness (the I'hin) for man to look upon.

19/4.3. And I planned from the beginning that my chosen would labor through examples of cities and kingdoms of righteousness.

19/4.4. The evil man and evil priest, who are subjects to satan and his hosts, remain in evil,[512] preaching righteousness without a city or kingdom of example. But my chosen go away by themselves and build their cities, as a testimony of their faith in the Father.

19/4.5. And they practice the fullness of my commandments in their lives toward one another.

19/4.6. To him who says: THIS IS MINE, I have not spoken. To him who says: MY HOUSE, MY LANDS, I have not spoken.

19/4.7. For inasmuch as these things belong to them, such men belong to such things, and not to me.

19/4.8. To illustrate this truth, I raised up separate from the world's people, the I'hins, who were my living examples of righteousness.

19/4.9. Do not think, however, that the I'hins were the perfection of manhood and womanhood. They were not a developed race, nor righteous because of their own knowledge.

19/4.10. By the constant presence of my exalted angels, they were obsessed to righteousness, being restrained away from evil. They were my sermon before the tribes of druks and cannibals that covered the earth over; and, by virtue of signs and miracles, and by nonresistance, I preserved them.

19/4.11. For man of himself evolves only to power in evil; and for this reason, O man, you shall discern[513] my dominion over the races of men, to work righteousness and goodwill.

19/4.12. And my examples reached into the souls of the barbarians, so that, in future ages, I could prepare them to hear my voice, and to comprehend my commandments.

19/4.13. For it is the fullness of light among men, when, without my presence or the presence of my hosts, they shall understand virtue and knowledge, practicing them of their own accord. In which time, men shall perceive that righteousness, peace, and love toward one another, are the foundation of the happiness of the spirit, and the only light of its resurrection.

19/4.14. The Lord said: Do not think that I came to one nation alone, leaving the others in darkness; I did not come to one alone, but to all the divisions of the earth. I held my hand over them according to what was required for them according to the times, and they accomplished that which was designed from the beginning.

---

[510] See 17/2.6 through 17/3.17, especially 17/2.16 and 17/3.4-9 for the story of how the ten tribes of Ghans got lost; and now we see these became the start of the shepherd kings.

[511] set beforehand as strategy, predetermined

[512] That is, with the world's people. –Ed.

[513] recognize, make out clearly, behold, detect

19/4.15. The will of Jehovih is not for man to be forever led, because, lo, his Lord says; but for man to ultimately have the light of practicing good works organically, from infancy up.

19/4.16. The Lord said: A teacher who does all things for his pupil, also sacrifices his pupil; he who teaches his pupil wrongly, sins against the Father; he who teaches his pupil not at all, is accessory to evil. In this light the Lord, your God, stands over the children of men.

19/4.17. Behold, I have demonstrated that my chosen can maintain themselves unharmed among barbarians; also that by unrestrained marriages a sacred people is quickly lost among barbarians.

19/4.18. For man, witnessing terrible conflicts, would rather have sons of strong limbs and arms, and crafty minds, to do abundant murderous work; from which condition he has no incentive to rise in gentleness and love, for the glory of the spirit.

19/4.19. So that I, your Lord, could show future generations, first, that without my hand in the work, no good nor peace could come among men; and, second, that only by a race of I'hins, as examples of my power, through signs and miracles, could the barbarians be reached for their own good.

19/4.20. Not only did I leave the ruins of my cities, which had no gates of entrance, and houses without doors of entrance, so that you would have testimony of the race of I'hins, but I have shown you that only by such a procedure could the barbarians be induced to a higher evolution.

19/4.21. Do not think, O man, that I did not foresee the time when men would question whether the Great Spirit ever placed a Lord over the earth; and that man would say: Behold, there is no Lord and no God. For I foresaw these times, and provided angels to go in advance, to show, first, the evolution of the races of men from out of the lowest darkness; and, second, that the cause of the evolution came from the Great Spirit, and was directed to righteousness; but would not have been so, except for the Lord, your God.

19/4.22. For I left sufficient tribes to this day, who dwell in darkness, even cannibals, as a testimony, that of themselves they possess nothing to cause a desire for evolution into knowledge, peace, industry, love, and good works to one another.

19/4.23. Will man not say: One people is raised up in consequence of the presence of their neighbor, and without a Lord or God, and the angels of heaven?

19/4.24. Now, behold, I have left savages at your door, and you do not raise them up, but destroy them. Showing you, that even your wisest and most learned have no power in resurrection. Neither have I left any way open for the resurrection of barbarians, except by examples of Faithists, who shall practice righteousness and miracles.[514]

19/4.25. And there shall rise up those who will do these things; and because of their success, they shall also be testimony of the I'hin race, in whom I laid the foundation for the redemption of the whole earth.

CHAPTER 5 Lords' Fifth

19/5.1. Thus the Lord established the five peoples who were saved from Pan; and he commanded them to preserve Panic words in their respective countries, which they did, and many of which exist to this day.[515]

19/5.2. Here follows what became of these I'hins, namely:

19/5.3. Those that came to Guatama survived twenty-one thousand years, and then became extinct.

19/5.4. Those that came to Jaffeth survived twenty-one thousand years, and then became extinct.

19/5.5. Those that came to Shem survived twelve thousand years, and then became extinct by amalgamation.[516]

---

[514] Miracle here likely means proof of the spirit world, and especially of the dominion of Jehovih and His heavens. But more generally, a miracle may refer to the fortuitous circumstances or results, which often attend the course of good works.

[515] Many Japanese words, Chinese words, East Indian [India], Central American, Algonquin and Phoenician words, are nearly identical in sound and meaning, especially as spoken by the uneducated. The sound, "An," sharp, plays a conspicuous part. –Ed.

[516] 1891 Editor: Nevertheless in hundreds of years after, there came into Shem I'hins from Jaffeth who survived thousands of years. [Also there were I'hin migrants from Ham coming into

19/5.6. Those that came to Ham survived twenty-one thousand years, and then became extinct by amalgamation.

19/5.7. Those of Guatama attained to one thousand large cities, and three thousand small cities, being more than four million souls. And they never had any king or queen, or other ruler, except the Lord, who ministered to them through the city fathers. And they retained their sacred name of Guatama to the last of them; but the I'huans called them Oech'lo'pan, signifying, people of another world [continent –Ed.].[517]

19/5.8. And in the course of time they became diminutive, and lost their desire to marry. And there came great darkness (ocgokok) on the earth, with falling ashes, heat, and fevers; and so the Lord took them up to heaven.

19/5.9. Those of Jaffeth attained to two thousand large cities, and seven thousand small ones, being more than eight million souls. And they had no king, serving the Lord only. And they retained to the end of their line, the name Jaf-fa; but the I'huans called them Tua Git, signifying, people of spirit light.

19/5.10. And there came a'ji on the earth, and it touched them with impotency, and they brought forth no more heirs; so the Lord took them home.

19/5.11. Those of Shem attained to six hundred large cities, and two thousand small cities, being more than two million souls. Nor did they have any king, but they served the Lord through the city fathers. And they retained their name, Shem, to the last of them; but the I'huans called them Sri-vede-iyi, signifying, people of the true light, woman-like. And impotence came upon them, and they disappeared, even as a drop of water in the sunlight, and no man knew when they ceased to be.

19/5.12. But hoping to preserve their seed to the Lord, many of them married with the I'huans; but their children became I'huans also, having neither the silken hair nor the musical voices of the I'hins, nor the light of the upper heavens.

Shem. –ed.]

[517] The North American Indians still have a legend of the mound-builders, that they were people who came from another world and dwelt on earth for a long season, to teach them of the Great Spirit, and of the Summer Land in the sky. –Ed.

19/5.13. Those of Ham attained to one thousand two hundred large cities, and three thousand small cities, being four million souls. But, being of mixed colors, they did not become impotent. But they broke the law of God more than all other Faithists, being of warm blood; and they mixed greatly with the I'huans. And they had no kings or queens, serving the Lord only, through the city fathers. And they retained the name of Ham to the end of their line, when they ceased to exist as a separate people because of their amalgamation with the I'huans.

19/5.14. Regarding the tribes that went in the two ships to the north land (Japan), after a thousand years, no man could draw the line between them and the I'huans, for they mingled with them, and were lost, as I'hins. Nevertheless, they redeemed the barbarians into wisdom and peace.

CHAPTER 6 Lords' Fifth

19/6.1. God said: In the time of Osiris, your Lord provided for the light and knowledge that had been with the I'hins, to be merged into the new races, the Ghans and I'huans. This foundation was laid by the Lord and his angels.

19/6.2. Before this time, the I'hins could not inspire the barbarians to make leather and cloth; nor could they inspire them to industries of any kind in the ways of virtue and peace.

19/6.3. The Lord provided the inhabitants of the earth with oracle houses; in which, the Lord could speak face to face with mortals, through his angels, chosen for this purpose. In this manner the Lord taught mortals.

19/6.4. Persuading them to industries, peace and righteousness, imitating the ways of the I'hins.

19/6.5. Teaching them about the stars, sun and moon; showing them how to find the times and seasons of the earth.

19/6.6. Inspiring them to observe the stars, and to name them, which names are preserved to this day. ||

19/6.7. I have established landmarks, says the Lord. What I do, man cannot do. I lift the barbarian up; he gives up his cruel practices by my command.

19/6.8. I call him to the observation of the stars, and he heeds my voice.

19/6.9. Behold, O all you who say there is no Lord, I have left a remnant of barbarians. Go try your hand. Let them, who find the cause of the progress of man to come of the earth [i.e., physical causes –ed.], go raise up the barbarian.

19/6.10. I say to man: Go commune with the spirits of the dead, and man does it. I say: Come away from such worship, and fall down before the stars, and man does it.

19/6.11. Jehovih said: My Lord, My God, go; call man to one thing today, and let him worship it. And tomorrow call him to another, and let him worship it. For man shall fall down and worship everything in heaven and earth. By trying them man shall know them. For in the day of My glory, kosmon, man shall put away all worshipful things except Me, his Creator. ||

19/6.12. The Lord God said: Through his worshipful talents man can be raised up. Even as to great learning, man will not pursue it till he first worships it. ||

19/6.13. In the time of Osiris, the Lord named the stars in heaven after the legendary names of Gods and Lords. And the Lord did not teach that man should worship them, but that he should learn their glory and majesty in the firmament.

19/6.14. But man forgot the Creator because of the wonder of His works. Even to this day, man inclines to view as substantial and real, things that are seen, and to reject the All Potent, which is unseen.

19/6.15. This was the command of God: for man to learn corporeal things as well as spiritual. And I, the Lord, carried away the spirits of the dead, not permitting man and angels to commune together. For they had done this previously, and, so, both had rejected the higher heavens.

19/6.16. Jehovih says: It is not the plan of My heavens for the spirits of the dead to remain on the earth forever, engaging in mortal servitude and practices.

19/6.17. Behold, the way of My kingdom is upward; man on the earth shall seek to rise upward, rather than call the angels of heaven downward.

19/6.18. And so the Lord carried away the spirits of the dead, and he turned man's judgment to learning the glories of the lower kingdoms (corpor).

19/6.19. And man advanced in great learning; both of the sun, moon and stars, and of all things on the face of the earth.

19/6.20. The Lord said: These signs I have given man, so that he may comprehend the cycles of his Creator: When spiritual research is chief among men, they do not advance in science, art, or inventions, that belong to the earth. But when man is bereft[518] of spiritual aspiration, he advances in corporeal knowledge, inventions, and investigations.

19/6.21. These signs foretell the changes being wrought on mortals by the hand of the Almighty, through His Gods and Lords.

19/6.22. God said: Behold, I raised up great kings and queens on the earth; and I gave them pageantry, rites and ceremonies, like that in heaven. And these (the rulers and grandeur of court life) I made to be an object of aspiration by the multitude, so that they would learn to provide themselves with the luxuries of all created things.

19/6.23. For I did not desire man to become spiritual until the earth and all manner of savage beasts and serpents were subdued. Otherwise man would have descended into impotence, and failed on the earth.

19/6.24. I have left these testimonies before you to this day: that the spiritual man inclines to shut himself up in seclusion and prayer; but the Osirians [519] go forth to work manfully.[520] ||

---

[518] lacking, deprived of, cut off from, left unprovided for, stripped of, dispossessed of

[519] whoever is a materialist; or searcher exclusively after corporeal knowledge; or who has man or the sun, or corporea, as the central figure or All Highest

[520] To work manfully is to cast one's spirit forth with power to congregate and make.

Though these two qualities (corporeal and spiritual) may seem incompatible, yet, now, in kosmon, as people reach spiritual maturity, both qualities (spiritual and corporeal) will become as a unit in balance. Moreover, since the unseen (spiritual) has dominion over the seen (corporeal), then the corporeal qualities will become subject to the spirit—resulting in the physical talents and corporeal knowledge serving the good of all.

And, even though the spiritual and the corporeal come into balance as a unit, the distinction still stands regarding the two, that the corpor in man will tend to go forth manfully and the spiritual in man will tend to inward.

19/6.25. In those days the Lord established reciprocities between kings and queens. And they proceeded in this manner:

19/6.26. The central kingdom was called the sun-kingdom, and the others were called satellites. And the chief ruler was called THE SUN-KING, or KING OF THE SUN.

19/6.27. And the king maintained an observatory, for determining the times and seasons of the sun, moon, earth and stars. The name of the observatory was TEMPLE OF THE STARS (OKE'I'GIT'HI).

19/6.28. The Lord said to man: Build a chamber for God within the temple of the stars.

19/6.29. And so man built it. And the Lord chose seers, one for every STAR CHAMBER; and the seer sat within, with a table before him, on which sand was sprinkled. And the Lord wrote in the sand, with his finger, the laws of heaven and earth.

19/6.30. Thus God gave to man the names of the stars and their seasons, and the seasons of the sun, moon and earth.

19/6.31. And the seer gave the table to the king; and the king proclaimed its words. And God gave man sacred days, for feasts, and rites and ceremonies; and they were set according to the times of the moon and stars.

19/6.32. And the king, by command of God, caused the people to watch the stars, moon and sun, so they would know the sacred days.

19/6.33. The Lord said: I have days for planting, and days for reaping, days for sailing of ships, and days for males and females.[521] By the stars in the firmament, and by the moon's changes, man shall learn to know my times and seasons.

19/6.34. So man took to learning from the stars, moon and sun, to ascertain the will of God.

19/6.35. And nowhere in all the world did man prosper so greatly in the Osirian philosophy as he did in Par'si'e, and in Jaffeth (China), and most of all among the shepherd kings.

[521] Most likely this refers to the time of rut or estrus of the various types of animals, perhaps also duration of gestation and general time of birth. As to ships sailing, this perhaps refers to tides, prevailing winds and seasonal variation of ocean currents.

CHAPTER 7 Lords' Fifth

19/7.1. Great became the wisdom of man in that day, and his power and glory were greater than had ever been since the world began. He established mighty kingdoms and sub-kingdoms, over the lands of Jaffeth, Shem, Par'si'e, and Arabin'ya (Ham).

19/7.2. He excelled in building temples and palaces; and in all manner of inventions; in fabrics of linen and silk, and wool and fine leather; in writing books and tablets; in mathematics; in laws and reciprocities; in navigation, and in inland travel; in making thermometers, barometers, magnetic needles, telescopes and microscopes; and in chemistry and botany.

19/7.3. Truly the philosophers of those days knew the mysteries of heaven[522] and earth.

19/7.4. And man grew no longer thankful to God and his Lords; but man became conceited, saying:

19/7.5. The Gods are fools! All things are Nature, and of growth. Man had become wise in spite of God and his Lords. All things evolve into higher states; it is the natural order. Neither is there any All Person, Jehovih! He is void, like the wind. ||

19/7.6. And God saw the conceit of man, and he said: Behold, he whom I have raised up, turns against me. Now I will go away from man for a season, so that he may learn wisdom. Behold, man shall also find that many of his fellows whom he raises up, turn against him also.

19/7.7. So the Lord departed out of the star chambers; and, lo and behold, the places became filled with spirits of the newly dead, who did not know the heavens above or the way of the Almighty.

19/7.8. And man inquired of them: Behold, you are now a spirit! Tell me, is there any God, or Lord, or Jehovih?

19/7.9. And the spirits, desiring to flatter man, and also not knowing the heavenly kingdoms, answered, saying: No, there is no God, no Lord, no All Person, Jehovih!

19/7.10. So the kings issued edicts, commanding the people to no longer worship God, or Lord, or Jehovih!

[522] Heaven here must mean the corporeal sky.

19/7.11. But woe, for the judgment of kings and queens. Man, having inherent worship in his soul, ceased indeed to worship God and his Lords, and even Jehovih; but, instead, he took to worshipping the stars.

19/7.12. Now, the spirits manifesting in the temples advised one thing through one seer, and something else through another; for they were of little knowledge, and wholly unorganized.

19/7.13. So, presently, the kings took to war against one another. Anarchy ensued, and man fell to destroying all the glories he had made.

19/7.14. Thus again, after three thousand years, man went down in darkness; again fell under the obsession of drujas, and again became a barbarian.

END OF THE LORDS' FIFTH BOOK

Book of Fragapatti, Son of Jehovih

CHAPTER 1 Fragapatti

20/1.1. In Horub, an etherean world on the borders of the arc of Aza, in the procession of Sayutivi, Cnod and Gorce, a region of light, of ten thousand earth years, and one hundred vesperes,[523] where reigned Fragapatti, Orian Chief of Obsod and Goomatchala[524] one thousand years; God of Varit, God of Lunitzi and Witchka, and Schleinaka, and Dows, thirty thousand years; Surveyor of Gies, roadway and trail of Fetisi, and Mark, seventy thousand years; Prim of Vaga, Tsein, Loo-Gaab, and Zaan, forty thousand years.

20/1.2. Fragapatti said: Jehovih spoke to me in the Council of Obsod, capital of Horub, where my million Gods sat, our throne itself an arc of light, and from the Almighty's throne there came a greater light, all brilliant, and, with it, the Matchless Voice. Jehovih said:

20/1.3. My Son! My Son! Go to the red star, the earth. She comes your way; her coat is red with mortal blood!

20/1.4. Fragapatti said: The Father says: The red star comes this way; her coat is red with mortal blood!

20/1.5. || The Gods and Goddesses turned to their tables, to mark the time; and now, quickly, the whisper ran to the million ears: The red star! The earth! Remember, it was the little star where Sethantes stood man upright, now some sixty thousand years ago. And Aph crushed in her walls, and pruned her to the quick. ||

20/1.6. And then they examined thoroughly the earth's history, these Gods and Goddesses; measured her course to learn just when she would pass; and they found five years and fifty days would be her dawn of dan, her time to cross the arc of Aza. And as yet she roamed two hundred years away.

20/1.7. Fragapatti said: Because this sudden light has given such long warning, so, great work comes our way. Let my swift messengers come; I will speak to them.

20/1.8. Then the marshals ushered in the swift messengers, saluting, before Jehovih's throne.

20/1.9. Fragapatti said: Autevat, my son, the All Light fell upon me, saying: My Son, go to the red star, the earth; her coat is red with mortal blood! Now, by her time, she stands more than two hundred years beyond the boundaries of Horub. For that reason I called you and your attendants. How long will it take you to go there, survey the earth and her heavens, and return here?

20/1.10. Autevat, well trained in such matters, said: Of the earth's time, forty days. Fragapatti said: What number of attendants will you require for so great a distance? And Autevat said: Twenty thousand.

20/1.11. Fragapatti said: Provide yourself, then, with all you require, and go at once. And if you shall find the inhabitants of the earth suitable for sacred records, then commission the God or Lords to send loo'is to raise up an heir for Jehovih's kingdom.

20/1.12. Autevat said: Your will and Jehovih's be done. And duly saluting, he and his attendants withdrew, and, coming to Gat-wawa, ordered an arrow-ship of twenty thousand gauge. In two days it was completed; and during that time, Autevat had chosen his attendants. And so Autevat and his attendants departed, swiftly, like a ray of light, for the red star, the earth, to see what the matter was,

---

[523] administration[s]. –1891 glossary

[524] see image i086, p.179

that a God as far away as Fragapatti, could feel and know the flow of human blood!

20/1.13. For such is the all perfection of Jehovih's Sons and Daughters. Even mortals can sense things a little way off; but Jehovih's upraised Gods feel the breath of the stars, and know when they are disordered.

CHAPTER 2 Fragapatti

20/2.1. Fragapatti and the Council were deeply engaged in the Sortiv of an Orian arc, through which the phalanx of Inihab and her constellation pass every thousand years. This was an etherean region where the star, Unhowitchata, was dissolved some twenty days before by the chief, Avaia, and his band of etherean Gods, who had drawn largely on the inhabitants of Ful, a garden of Horub, in Fragapatti's dominions. Thirty billion bound spirits, wrapped in corporeality, were cut loose from Unhowitchata.

20/2.2. And Avaia had quartered the dismembered hosts near Sortiv, where the light of the arc fell sharply on them; and to deplete this concourse[525] taxed the Gods for more help than was at hand. To remedy this, Fragapatti's hosts were extending the ji'ay'an fields of Uth, thus lowering the grade, suitable to the spirits of darkness rescued from Unhowitchata, a prolific world, bringing forth imperfect human souls too abundantly for the quality.

20/2.3. And near at hand to pass the arc of Sortiv was Inihab with her hundred stars, many of them larger than the earth, to seventy of which the inhabitants of Horub would need go as redeeming Gods and Goddesses for the dawns of dan upon them. To apportion all of which, Fragapatti and his million Council had work on hand, so that the condition of the earth and her heavens did not weigh seriously upon them.

20/2.4. But in forty days' time, or in that period which would be forty days on the earth, Autevat and his twenty thousand attendants, with the arrow-ship of fire, returned from the earth and her heavens, speeding close to Obsod, where the marshals received them, and announced them to the Council. Fragapatti said: Let Autevat and his attendants approach the throne.

20/2.5. And Autevat went in, saluting, and stood before the Chief, Fragapatti. Autevat said: In Jehovih's name, and by His power and wisdom, I am here to proclaim regarding the red star and her heaven: First, then:

20/2.6. It has been three thousand one hundred years since great Osire sowed the seed of mental culture among mortals, which has grown to be a giant, and a most merciless tyrant. To learn about that which I speak, even God and his Lords, to honor you, O Fragapatti, gave me voice and word, and opened the libraries of their heavens, and accompanied me all around the earth, to all nations, tribes and wanderers. To me, the God of earth said:

20/2.7. Greeting to Fragapatti, in the name of the Father! And to you, His Son! Take this record to him, and his Council, in Horub. For against such odds I am powerless through my Lords and hosts.

20/2.8. God said: From the time great Osire ascended to his etherean realm, our heaven yielded ample harvests for one thousand five hundred years. And God and Lords succeeded in regular order for every dan put upon the earth.

20/2.9. But then came a change, for the a'ji'an fields pressed close on every side of heaven, and the souls of angels and mortals turned down to the gross earth. After which time, only those who were already within the second resurrection came and strove for the upper worlds.

20/2.10. These depleted the constant rise, and left our colleges, schools and factories vacant; for the hosts of es'yans, newborn from the earth, were stubborn in their much earthly learning, spurning wise counsel and association.

20/2.11. And there were born from the earth into atmospherea, millions and millions of spirits who could not believe they were dead, but maintained they were confined in dark dungeons,[526] howling and cursing day and night.

20/2.12. For the seed of corporeal knowledge had taken root in the I'huan race.[527] They had learned the motions, names and places of the stars,

---

[525] throng, crowd, gathering, of angels

[526] One of the first surprises a novice in Su'is receives, is to see and hear so many spirits in the spirit world who do not know they are dead; or rather, that they have left their mortal bodies. And they very generally believe they are confined in a dark chamber, from which they cannot escape. – Ed.

the moon and sun; and from these, prophesied the affairs of nations and men. And they duly marked out, with maps and charts, the destiny of things, according to the dates of corporeal births and movements, attributing the highest central cause to the sun and stars in conjunction.

20/2.13. And thus they cast aside all spirit, even Jehovih; reasoning, that if the sun made winter and summer, and grass to grow and die, so it also ruled over animals and men. And so, the temples built to observe the stars, before which men once fell down and worshipped Jehovih, became the places where decrees of horrid deaths were pronounced against all who taught of or believed in spirit.

20/2.14. And now a mighty nation of I'huans rose on earth, called Par'si'e,[528] and they ignored the decrees of Gods and Lords to build no city larger than two thousand souls; indeed, declaring the Lords and Gods to be only inspirations from the quickening power of the sun and stars, made dark and personal by the credibility of past ages.

20/2.15. And so, in representation of the solar phalanx, they built Oas, a sun city, which stands to this day a million souls, sworn to make it the central governor over all the earth, with all other places tributary and paying for its glory. And over Oas they made a king, and called him, King of the Sun, this title to be his and his successor heirs, forever.

20/2.16. And Oas was embellished and adorned above all other places that had ever been on the earth; the fame of which spread abroad over Jaffeth, Shem and Ham, between which it lies centrally. Its colleges became famous, and its observatories were of such magnificence that their roofs were covered with silver and gold. The mirrors, lenses, and dark chambers within the towers were so constructed that the stars could be read in the day as well as at night; and the records of observation, by men of great learning, covered more than a thousand years.

20/2.17. But now, alas, Oas aspires not only to be the central sun in knowledge, but in power and dominion, over the whole earth. And so, relying on her ample treasures, she sends forth armies to conquer and destroy, to gather and plunder, to build still greater her magnificence.

20/2.18. So Jaffeth, Shem and Ham run red with human blood, at which, I raised my voice to high heaven, that Jehovih would send deliverance for the souls of men.

20/2.19. For of the millions slain, whose spirits still lie on the battlefields in chaos, or madly fighting some unseen horror of hallucination, none can be persuaded to come to holier places in heaven; while hosts of them rush madly into Oas, to find even their souls accursed by mortals.

20/2.20. God said: So the heaven of the earth has fallen to the earth, except the I'hins and the far-off I'huans, whose spirits my Lords gather in and prepare for the coming resurrection. But among the Par'si'e nation, none believe anymore that the dead shall rise, nor that spirit exists; but that with the mortal death, there is the end. To which, the king has made a decree that man shall never again teach or preach of a heaven for spirits of the dead, nor proclaim a Great Spirit, a Creator.

20/2.21. Autevat said: In this manner God disclosed the affairs of earth and heaven, now deadlocked in everlasting destruction; which things, I, with my attendants, saw in fuller detail in every land and kingdom. And as we sat in Vibhraj, in the sacred circle, a light, a single star, appeared before us, at the throne of God; and from its center the book of heaven fell, as if to broadcast before mortals the plan and will of Jehovih, near at hand.

20/2.22. At this, God said: Tell me, Autevat, you who travel across the mighty heavens, and are stored with the knowledge of Gods ruling over other worlds, what is the signal of this light, and sacred book? To which I replied: This, O God: The time has come to earth to prove to mortals the things that the Gods and Lords have taught. History shall no longer be locked up privately with the chosen race, the I'hins; but it shall stand before both saints and sinners.

20/2.23. You shall prove the resurrection before these stubborn kings, the slaughterers of men, so that they may say, not as the I'hins, we believe the soul immortal, because (the teaching is) handed

---

[527] From here to the end of Oahspe, the word, I'huan, generally becomes an umbrella term encompassing a continuum consisting of pure I'huans on one end to pure Ghans on the other end, and all types in between these two. The Ghan end represents the advancing edge of humanity.

[528] descendents of the Shepherd Kings mixed with the I'huans and Ghans –cns ed.

down from the ancients, but because it has been demonstrated before our eyes.

20/2.24. God said: How shall this be? To which I replied: I cannot tell, great God, for that department is not in my keeping. But this much I know: You shall send loo'is into the city of Oas, and they shall raise up a su'is'sar'gis of the fourth grade. All else leave till Fragapatti comes.

20/2.25. God said: To reach the fourth grade will require five generations, which shall spring from the I'hin race commingling with the I'huans. Go, then, O Autevat, to your etherean home, before the Council of Obsod, to Jehovih's throne, and say to great Fragapatti: An heir to the light of resurrection shall be born before the dawn of dan of Horub.

20/2.26. Autevat said: On learning these truths, I took my leave, and rose and came swiftly back to your realm.

20/2.27. Fragapatti said: It is well. During the next dawn of dan on the earth, I will take a resting spell in which to fulfill Jehovih's plan on earth and in her heavens.

20/2.28. So, saluting Autevat, who retired, Fragapatti proceeded with his Council in the affairs of other worlds, making a memorandum[529] of the time and place the earth would draw near the plains of Horub, in the etherean worlds, some two hundred years yet to come.

CHAPTER 3 Fragapatti

20/3.1. But the dawn came; and in the wing of Goomatchala, home of Fragapatti, Orian Chief in the etherean worlds high standing, came the Voice, Jehovih's word, saying: My Son! Behold, the dawn of dan nears the border of Horub. The wailing earth, the red star, comes swiftly. And God and Lords call out the name of My infant Son, Zarathustra.

20/3.2. Fragapatti rose up, hearing the Voice, and saw that a little over two hundred years had passed, that the time had ripened for the coming world, that the time had come for the revealed word to mortals. He said: To You, O Jehovih! Boundless! I come with my hosts, ten million strong.

20/3.3. Fragapatti went into the etherean Council of Gods and Goddesses. He said: The time has come; the red star borders on the plains of Horub. Jehovih calls!

20/3.4. Then the Council rejoiced, for the weighty matters of hundreds of etherean worlds were settled for a space of time, with promised rest and recreation in corporeal fields. First spoke Ad'ar, God of many worlds, a decreer of time in a'ji'an vortices, in the regions of Hispiain suns, saying: O Jehovih, give Your Son, Fragapatti, five years' rest, the dawn of earth in dan. Only the earth and her heavens to deal with!

20/3.5. Next spoke Fivaka, Goddess of three etherean worlds, the white-haired Wielder of the Scimetar of Bars, period of Os, Carbon fashioner for the arcs of Job and Sawl. She said: O Jehovih, Almighty! What shall be the prayer of Your Daughter, Fivaka? What can her love devise for the rest and glory of our high God, Fragapatti, Orian Chief! Then spoke Che'sin, marshal in chief for seven etherean worlds, small man, with flowing beard, brought forth from the star, Indr. He said: O Jehovih, make me contributor of my much love to the rest and glory of our Holy Chief, Fragapatti!

20/3.6. Thus spoke ten thousand Gods and Goddesses of their love and high esteem for the worker, Fragapatti, rich in power, wisdom and love, above all etherean Gods in Horub.

20/3.7. Fragapatti said: Ten million strong my hosts shall be. On the earth and her heavens, during her dawn of dan, five years and fifty days, we shall have no other labor, thus making it like a holiday for Gods and Goddesses to redeem the fallen world!

20/3.8. Fragapatti had spoken. So the proper officers and workmen proceeded to their parts; and in seven days the Yattal announced the fire-ship, the beyan float, ready for the journey. Meanwhile, the selection of the ten million Redeemers had been made, and they came, every one like a brilliant star, to take their rooms in the monarch[530] vessel.

20/3.9. Fragapatti made Huod Commander in Chief, and gave him ten thousand aides. For the curtains and tallij, he made Metrav, Goddess of Rook, Mistress to the Flowing East. And for the spires, he made Iata Mistress of Restless Morn. She was Weaver to Ga'ing, in Reth, four thousand

[529] made a memo, scheduled it into the calendar

[530] preeminent, surpassing other vessels

years, and much loved, with black eyes, piercing. Of music, Fragapatti made Theritiviv conductor. She was Goddess of Helm, an etherean world in the roadway of Zi and Olus, four thousand years Mistress of Ne'alt and Exan; one time companion to Etisyai, the Vruiji, loved in Wan and Sangawitch, for her mirth in adversity. Of the trumpeters, Fragapatti made Boan conductor; he was God of Ixalata, now on leave of absence. For Chartist, he made Yan the Chief; he was Surveyor of Oatha, an etherean sea in the Orian arc of Wede and Hollenpoitchava, also on leave of absence during the red star dawn. Of the libraries, he made Hetta Chief Mistress; she was Goddess of Vitia in the Wails of South Eng; thirty thousand years Teacher of Imes, and ten thousand years Counselor of the Orian Chief, Erris, of the arc Wiamesse.

20/3.10. Besides these, Fragapatti distributed the minor offices of the float to such Gods and Goddesses whose most exalted states were the extreme opposite, so that the great journey through etherea would be the inverse of all serious purpose. And thus they started on their course, amid the applause of billions of ethereans, wishing them love and joy on their mirthful cruise in furtherance of Jehovih's will.

20/3.11. Ahead lay the swamps of Ull, where seven corporeal stars were dismembered a billion years ago, now set with a'ji'an fields, and forming nebulae; where they bring, at times, the drujas, the dark spirits of other worlds, so that they may take on the semblance of corporeal forms to complete their neglected good works in times past. Speeding swiftly across, the ship rose freely; and then shot into the pastures of Ze, where Lepsa, God of the corporeal star, Tessa, four hundred years, feeds seventy million es'yans, colonizing them to truth and good works. Lepsa knew the float was coming, and so had called a billion spectators, to look on, knowing they desired to see great Fragapatti; and they sang and blew their trumpets, rejoicing; to which the Gods and Goddesses of the float cast out myriads of arc'ian flowers, and sweet perfumes, mementos of love.

20/3.12. To Evul, now, the ship made its way; where seven etherean worlds lie bordered in the arc of Nu, being pastures of Elim, God of Ooh'sin, where another host of two billion congregated, to see them pass, cheering with singing, trumpets and stringed instruments; and to this God, Elim, being friends for ninety thousand years, Fragapatti caused the banners of the float to salute on the sign, JEHOVIH'S NAME, and Elim answered him with a million posts of light, amid the waving of innumerable banners.

20/3.13. Onward moved the float, the fire-ship, with its ten million joyous souls, now nearing the borders of Horub, the boundary of Fragapatti's honored regions, where he was known for hundreds of thousands of years, and for his work on many worlds. Here, reaching C'vork'um, the roadway of the solar phalanx, near the post of dan, where a half billion ethereans were quartered,[531] on a voyage of exploration of more than four million years, rich stored with the glories of Great Jehovih's universe. Their koa'loo, their ship, was almost like a world, so vast, and stored with all appurtenances. They talked of going home! Their pilots had been coursing the firmament since long before the earth was made,[532] and knew more than a million roadways in the etherean worlds, and where best to travel to witness the grandest contrasting scenes.

20/3.14. By their invitation, Fragapatti halted here awhile, and the hosts interchanged their love, and discoursed on their purposes, rejoicing in the glories of Jehovih's everlasting kingdoms; and though they had lived so long, and seen so much, every one had new and wondrous works to tell of; for so great is the inventive power of the Great Spirit, that never twice alike will one find the scenes in the etherean worlds—but radiant, each different; all moving into everlasting changes, as if each one were to outdo the former in beauty and magnificence.

20/3.15. And then again they sped onward, now richly stored with the awe-stirring wonders they had just heard from strange travelers. Presently, now, the float neared the borders of Chinvat, the earth's vortex, just beyond the orbit of the moon. Here Fragapatti halted for a day, sending swift messengers down to the lower heavens, and to the

---

[531] accommodated on a vessel, i.e., they all lived on the ship

[532] This would not necessarily mean that the earth was less than four million years old, because these pilots would likely have been coursing the firmament long before their current voyage of four million years. –cns ed.

earth, to resolve where he should anchor during dawn.

20/3.16. And, the next day, he ordered the lights lowered, and now slowly moved toward the rolling earth; down, down, till he reached the third grade of plateaus from the earth's surface, called Haraiti.

CHAPTER 4 Fragapatti

20/4.1. Jehovih said: Here, O My Son, Fragapatti! Here in Haraiti I have laid the foundation of your kingdom. Make fast here the fire-ship, five years and fifty days.

20/4.2. Call forth your hosts; build a throne of My throne; the voice of your Creator is with you. Fragapatti said: Throne of Your throne, O Jehovih, I will build here. Haraiti shall be my headquarters for the dawn of dan. Come forth, O you Gods of dawn! Come forth, O you Goddesses of dawn! Hear the voice of the Son of Jehovih. Bow down, O you heavens!

20/4.3. The ship was anchored, and the ten million came forth and assembled in a living altar. Fragapatti raised his hand, saying: Throne of Your throne, O Jehovih! And the hosts raised their hands, and the elements took shape and majesty, rising into a throne brilliant as fire. Then Fragapatti ascended and sat on the throne, saying: Glory to You, O Father, the Highest!

20/4.4. A light came down from the etherean firmament, and covered the throne over with a canopy, wide enough for five million men to sit under; and at the borders of the canopy, the ethereans, whose work it fell to, set up columns of crystals, opaque and transparent, illuminated in all possible colors, shades and tints.

20/4.5. Fragapatti said: From Your Council Chamber, O Jehovih, I will build to You forever! And now the hosts, Gods and Goddesses, held up their arms, lifting and casting in; and, lo and behold, there rose and stood the habitable Mouru, council chamber and capital of Haraiti.

20/4.6. Then all hands turned to prayers, glorifying the Father; then in singing with praise.

20/4.7. After which, Fragapatti said: In Your name, and by Your Power and Wisdom, O Jehovih, I will now establish heaven anew over the earth. My marshals shall now proceed down to the earth and command the presence of God and his Lords, and all others who can endure this light. They shall hear my voice, and learn my decrees.

20/4.8. Ten thousand marshals, saluting, departed for the regions below and to earth.

20/4.9. Fragapatti said: Meanwhile, I will appoint my High Council of the first house of Mouru, Gods and Goddesses of dawn. Hear me, then, in the name of Jehovih, the All Light:

20/4.10. Caoka, God of Airram; Ata-kasha, God of Beraitis; Airyama, God of Kruse; Pathema, Goddess of Rhon; Maidhyarrya, Mistress of Karyem; Gatha-Ahunavaiti, Goddess of Halonij; Rama-quactra, God of Veres; Vahista, God of Vohu [speech –Ed.]; Airam-ishya, God of Icisi, the Myazdas; Haptanhaiti, God of Samatras; Yima, God of Aom; Sudhga, God of Laka; I'ragha, God of Buhk-dhi; Elicic, Goddess of N'Syrus; Harrwaiti, Goddess of Haut-mat, in a'ji; Dews, Goddess of Vaerethagna; Wettemaiti, Goddess of Dyhama; Quactra, Goddess of Ægima (AEgima); Ustavaiti, Goddess of Maha-Meru; Cura, Goddess of Coronea; Yenne, Goddess of Aka; Caoshyanto, God of Aberet; Rathweiska, God of Huri; Cpentas, God of Butts; Vairyo, God of Nuga-gala; D'Zoata and her brother, Zaota, God and Goddess of Atarevasksha; Ratheweiskare, God of Nece; Yatha, God of Ameshas, and Canha, God of Srawak.

20/4.11. Fragapatti said: O Jehovih, behold the glory of my house! I have chosen only those who have ruled over whole worlds. Was ever a God so favored, with such a Council! Was ever so great a light sent to so small a world as the red star?

20/4.12. Jehovih said: As I have created man to need relaxation at times, so have I made the same conditions to be desired by My highest of Gods. Neither have I exalted any God so high, that he cannot labor in the most menial office without it also being his glory. Neither shall the autocrat learn sympathy till he lives with a beggar; nor the highest best man learn love and tenderness without taking a season in the depths of misery.

20/4.13. Fragapatti said: Shall the strong man forget he was once a child; can an Orian Chief forget he was once a slave; can he who is in the light forget those who are in the dark?

20/4.14. Mighty You are, O Jehovih! I came to the earth and her heavens to rest myself in Your service; but You were here before me; Your voice rises up to rebuke me; yes, I am still only a child to You! ||

CHAPTER 5 Fragapatti

20/5.1. When Fragapatti had selected both departments of his Council, which comprised one hundred thousand souls, he said:

20/5.2. When a God espouses[533] a new kingdom, it is customary for him to create his own capital, and affix the boundaries of his lights and hall of audience; but when he has Gods and Goddesses for his assistants, it is meet[534] and proper for them to help in the building. In this case, I give into your hands to provide[535] this realm.

20/5.3. Hardly had his words gone forth when the Gods and Goddesses stretched forth their hands to Jehovih, and, lo and behold, the elements of the plateau took shape, and there stood the canopy of the new kingdom; then again they stretched forth their hands to Jehovih, and there came the walls of the house of heaven; and yet again they stretched forth their hands to Jehovih, and there came the floor and foundation.

20/5.4. And the house was called the House of Mouru, the place of the throne of Fragapatti, in the lower heavens. On the plains beyond the house, Fragapatti created a thousand fields and pastures; and in each and every one he created ten thousand mansions, and every mansion was capable of accommodating one thousand souls. Fragapatti created these with roadways from one to another, his hosts being the workmen, in the wisdom and power of Jehovih.

20/5.5. While this work was going on, the marshals who went down to the earth returned, bringing God and his Lords with them, and also bringing with them one million two hundred thousand spirits of the second resurrection. Fragapatti commanded them to bring God and his Lords into the House of Mouru, and they were brought in.

20/5.6. Fragapatti said: In the name of Jehovih, I salute you, O God, and your Lords, and your hosts.

20/5.7. God said: In Your name, O Jehovih, I am, as are my Lords and my hosts, blessed with great joy. That you, O Fragapatti, have come to redeem the earth-born and the spirits of these heavens, is a joyful period in the time of worlds.

20/5.8. The Lords said: For ourselves and our hosts, O Jehovih, we thank Your Son, Fragapatti.

20/5.9. Fragapatti said: So you, O God, could know my decrees, I commanded you and your Lords, and your exalted hosts, to come here. Hear me, then, and to those whom I shall send to you to do my commandments, in the name of Jehovih: The time has come when mortals on the earth shall begin their lessons in spiritual things proven, with themselves taking part in the building of Jehovih's kingdoms.

20/5.10. Through you, the present reigning God of the earth and her heavens, must be carried out the death and resurrection of your chosen heir, Zarathustra; to prove, first, that man on the corporeal earth can live All Pure and without sin; second, that corporeal death belongs to the earth-body of man, and not to the spirit; and, third, that after death, the same person can rise in spirit and appear to mortals, to be seen and known; after which, he shall show his final ascent toward the upper heavens, in the arms of his God.

20/5.11. While this comes upon you in person to carry out, you shall also, through your ministering angels, prove to mortals the advantage of virtue and truth over sin and darkness. For you shall cause also to be stricken in death two evil men who are all impure; and they shall suffer death at the same time with your heir, Zarathustra; but these shall not have power of their own to appear before mortals after death. For from now on, mortals shall be a testimony to one another of the reward of virtue, and the power of being one with the Gods, Sons of Jehovih.

20/5.12. But since all attestation[536] by spirits can be set at defiance by the craft of philosophers, you shall not wait till after the death of your heir, to teach the truths of the Father's kingdoms; but beforehand. Causing Zarathustra, while yet mortal, to write down rules of mortal life, and doctrines, faith, repentance, and praise of the Great Spirit; and of prophecy, and all manner of righteous gifts, and the power of miracles, and the triumph of the spirit of man over corporeal elements.

---

[533] takes up; marries oneself to; begins a life with; commits to

[534] fitting; suitable; good

[535] create and furnish

[536] testimony, confirmation, evidence, disclosure

20/5.13. And when you have completed these things, you shall bring the spirit of Zarathustra to this House; but the druks, who suffer death with him, you shall deliver in the usual way to the places prepared for their resurrection.

20/5.14. Tell me now about your heir; and ask of me whatever you want, to assist you in carrying out my decrees, and it shall be granted to you.

20/5.15. God said: Zarathustra has attained his twentieth year, and comprehends the destiny put upon him. He is pure and wise, with faith and gentleness; but he is larger and more powerful than any other man in the world. He is instructed, both in the spiritual and corporeal senses, having a knowledge of the books of the ancients, and of writing and making tablets.

20/5.16. Fragapatti said: Five years you shall have in which to complete your labor. Depart, therefore, to your place, taking with you those of your Lords and hosts as you may require. I will appoint a thousand messengers to travel between your place and this place, so that every time you ask for this or that, it shall be granted to you. To which God replied:

20/5.17. I will go now and cause Zarathustra to write a book of wisdom,[537] and give him prophecy over the kings, nations and tribes of men. What I do shall be proven to you in Mouru. Then God withdrew a little, and selected his Lords and such other assistants as he desired; and, after this, Fragapatti granted a day of recreation, during which time the ethereans were made well acquainted with the conditions of mortals and of the billions of spirits still lingering in the first resurrection, and in darkness and chaos.

20/5.18. On the next day God and his hosts departed for the earth, well attended by thousands of volunteers from the etherean sojourners of Haraiti.

CHAPTER 6 Fragapatti

20/6.1. Fragapatti said: The voice of Jehovih comes to me, saying: My Son, appoint an assistant chief to sit on your throne, and go throughout atmospherea, taking surveyors and inspectors with you; for you shall see with your own eyes the condition of billions of spirits in hada.

[537] see image i075

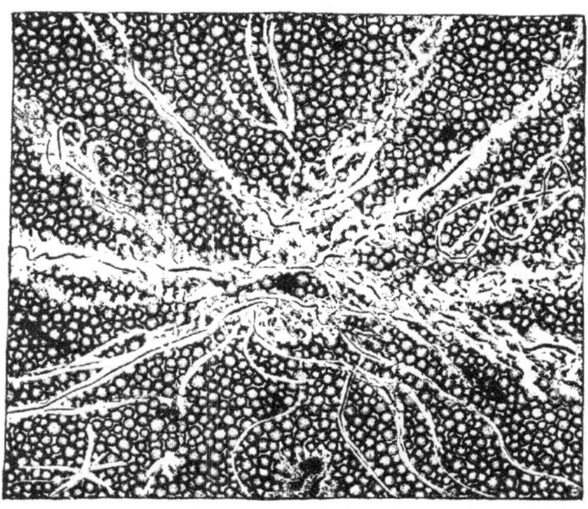

i075 **The Earth in the Crossroads of Horub**. Showing the position of the earth in the time of Zarathustra, 8,900 years B.K. Jehovih said: In Horub I delivered My first Holy Book to mortals, through My Son, Zarathustra. After that, I carried the earth into darkness, so that it would be perfected for the generations of men to come afterward. In this way, I provided the nations that I delivered through Capilya, Moses and Chine.

20/6.2. Fragapatti said: In Jehovih's name, I announce Athrava my assistant, God of Mouru. || There was great rejoicing in the Council at this. Then Athrava came forward, and ascended Jehovih's throne and sat at the right hand of Fragapatti. Etherean lights fell upon the place from every side, and Fragapatti gathered from the elements and made a crown for Athrava, and crowned him.

20/6.3. Officers and workmen were sent to build a conveyance for Fragapatti, and for the attendants he would take with him. So, the next day, Fragapatti chose thirty thousand companions, making Verethragna speaker, and they departed for their inspection of hada and the earth.

20/6.4. His ship was built without lights or curtains, so they could travel unobserved. First he inspected the plateau of Haraiti, which, prior to this, had never been inhabited; and he found its distance from the earth was equal to ten diameters of the earth; and its east and west and north and south diameters corresponded in size to what the earth would be were it that volume; that is to say, the surface of the plateau was five hundred and twenty-eight thousand miles in every direction. And in the ratio of the number of mortals on the earth, this plateau would inhabit five hundred and twenty-eight billion souls. And yet this was not the thousandth part of the number it could sustain, in fact, within and on its surface.

20/6.5. Fragapatti said: Such is Haraiti, O Jehovih. And yet there have been, till now, no spirits to come and inhabit it! Who can survey Your works, O Father! Who will fear that he shall reach the limit of Your handiwork!

20/6.6. Verethragna said: And yet we shall find in the lowest hadas (atmospherean heavens) spirits huddled together like bees in a hive. And yet why, O Chief, for is it not so with mortals also? They cluster together in cities and tribes, warring for inches of ground, while vast divisions of the earth lie waste and vacant!

20/6.7. Fragapatti said: Is this not the sum of the darkness of mortals and of spirits in the lowest realms—they do not know how to live? A spider or an ant is more one with the Creator than these!

20/6.8. Next they visited Zeredho, six diameters of the earth distant. Here they found a colony, of two billion spirits, that had been founded by Osire three thousand three hundred years before; but not the same people, but those who came up from the earth afterward. They had a God named Hoab, an atmospherean from the earth, two thousand one hundred years. And he was upright and wise, and of good works most excellent; but knowing nothing of etherea, he had no ambition to rise there. And his contentment had visited itself on the colony, and they were contented also.

20/6.9. Fragapatti said: To remain here forever, is this the extent of your desires, O Hoab? And Hoab answered him, saying: Yes, Master. What more is life than to reach the highest place and remain there? To which Fragapatti said: Is this the all highest? And Hoab said: Yes, Master. Any place and condition is the all highest, if man makes it so. None can attain higher than I; no people higher than my people. We are freed from the earth and hada, and we have no desire to return there, nor to go to any other place.

20/6.10. Fragapatti said: Let us walk a little, so I may see your kingdom? Hoab consented, and they walked along, seeing the inhabitants lying at ease, some amusing themselves weaving threads of light, then unraveling them and weaving them over again; others playing with crystals, lenses, and opaque and transparent elements, but not one doing anything for another; nor, in fact, did they need to, for all were capable of doing for themselves. Now, after they had traveled a while, Fragapatti said: Do you not have, O Hoab, a desire to return to the plateaus below you, where the inhabitants are in misery and darkness, and bring them into your own realm? To which Hoab said:

20/6.11. No, Master. Let them shift for themselves. Even if we helped them up they would be thankless. No, my doctrine is: Man is the all highest of all things. The elements are dumb; the worlds are many and wide. Let man choose a corner for himself, and settle there forever. Fragapatti asked: Because a man chooses a corner, is it necessarily his own? Hoab said: Our place was bequeathed to us by our forefathers; of course it is ours, and to remain so forever. Nor do we allow any other spirits to settle in our dominions. Being far away from the rest of the world, we are not much molested.

20/6.12. Fragapatti said: How did you come here? Hoab said: Long ago a God named Osire came here, bringing six billion drujas up from the earth. With them he founded a colony here, with factories, colleges, hospitals, and all things necessary to enlighten the people, giving them ample teachers. In time, many of the inhabitants migrated away from this place, and it was almost depleted of its people. But the Gods below this sent new supplies of inhabitants, of which we are the second and third installments; so we inherited the place, with all its factories, educational facilities, and other places.

20/6.13. Fragapatti said. As you were raised up by the Gods of other places, would it not give you joy to raise up others, who are still in darkness? Hoab said: No, Master. We are pure and refined; the atmosphere of drujas is unpleasant to us. They would vitiate[538] our own happiness, besides entailing toil and responsibilities upon us. We cannot mix with any people but the refined and holy. We take care of ourselves; let others do the same, and all will be well.

20/6.14. Fragapatti said: Who do you think I am, and my people with me? Hoab said: Visitors

---

[538] diminish, reduce the quality of, debase, corrupt, impair, annul

from some far-off realm, who are either discordant with yourselves, or bent to meddle in the affairs of other peoples. We have had visitors before, and we never grieved when they left us. To which Fragapatti replied:

20/6.15. You are strong in your philosophy. If no nation or people had such ambition as this, there would be no contentment in the world. To be satisfied with one's own self and behavior is to be a God in fact. If only you had nothing to fear from immigration coming to your shore, or from some new philosophy undermining your long-established convictions, you might indeed be the happiest of Gods, and your people the happiest of people.

20/6.16. Hoab said: True! You perceive wisely. Oh, if only there was nothing to fear; nothing to dread, forever!

20/6.17. Then Fragapatti said: And I declare to you, Hoab, that such a condition can be attained. For I have seen kingdoms in heaven fortified so. And if you and your people were prepared to receive the sacred secrets pertaining to this, I would most willingly unfold them before you. Hoab said: You are a wise God; please stay and teach us.

20/6.18. Fragapatti said: I am now on a journey, and cannot remain longer; but, on one condition, I will return here and disclose these matters, so that never more shall you be afraid of immigration into your country, nor for any philosophy which any man or God may teach: Exact a promise of secrecy from all your people. Hoab said: It shall be done.

20/6.19. And Fragapatti and his hosts withdrew, departing out of that plateau, and promising to return when notification had been served on his people. But Fragapatti inspected the whole surface, and found it capable of educating and providing for a thousand billion[539] spirits; and there were only two billion in Hoab's kingdom, inhabiting only a small corner of the plateau; nevertheless, Hoab laid claim to the whole.

20/6.20. After this, Fragapatti descended to the next plateau, the first grade of plateau above the earth, called Aoasu, signifying, land and sky world, meant for the first spirit life after mortal death. Aoasu has its foundation on the earth, and it undulates with mountains and valleys, like the earth, having seas over the corporeal seas. And the outer surface of Aoasu is from twenty to a hundred miles above the earth's surface; and in the manner of all spirit worlds, it is habitable within and without. But the first resurrections were within it and on the earth's surface; and the second resurrections, mostly on the plateau's upper surface; although all atmospherean plateaus are also made for the second and third resurrections. On the roadway next descending between Zeredho and Aoasu, was where Osire established Vibhraj, which was now so depleted of its people that Fragapatti did not stop to examine it, but proceeded directly to Aoasu.[540]

20/6.21. Here the mountains of Morn and Eve lie, and the mountains of the Moon, Sun and Stars; chief of which groups are:

20/6.22. Ushidaho; Ushidarena; Erezifya; Fraorepa; Ezora; Arezura; Tudae; Bumya; Doitya; Raiodhita; Mazassavao; Autare, a place of light, inhabited by Hura, Lord of Vouta; Ereasho; Vata-gaiko, a place of Uz, signifying torments, because of its darkness.

20/6.23. This group of mountains is ninety miles higher than the earth mountains of Jaffeth. South of these are Adarana, Aayana, Isakata, Somya, Kanaka-tafegrhao, Vahra, and the double mountain, Hamanakanna; eight ranges of the round mountains, Fravanku; the four peaks, the Vidwaana.[541]

20/6.24. These extend over the earth mountains of Shem (India), and have an altitude above the earth of one hundred miles. These are the oldest inhabited spirit worlds since the submersion of Pan, whose spirit worlds were carried up to a higher heaven, which has since been called Haraiti.

20/6.25. Extending east and west lie the group called the Red Men's group: Aezaka, Maenaka, Vakhedrakae, Akaia, Tudhakkae, Ishvakhaya, Draoshisvao, Cairivao, Nanhusmao, Kahayuyu, Autarekanhae, and Karayaia, which were the first places in heaven for colonizing the spirits of the I'huan race.

20/6.26. The next group lies to the west and south, which are: Gichindava, I'huna-Varya,

---

[539] i.e., a trillion (1,000,000,000,000)

[540] see image i021 p.227 Atmospherean heavens founded by Fragapatti, showing plateaus

[541] Many of the names of these spiritual mountains are still retained in the Vedic Scriptures. –Ed.

Raegamna, Akaya, Asha-cteambana, Urinyovadidhkae, Asnahovao, Ushaoma, Utsagaerenao, Cyamakhama, Cyamaka, Vafrayaotso, Vafrayao Vourrusha, and Uasoakhao.

20/6.27. To the south of this group are the Towering Eagles, which are: Ijatarra, Adhutuvavata, Ceptimavarenao, Cpentodata, Asnavoaya, Kairogakhaivacao, Tauraiosa, Baroyo, Barocrayama, Fraayapoa, Udrya, Usayaokhava, and Raevao. || All of which groups were named by the Gods and Lords of the intermediate worlds during the time of the Yi-ha language among mortals, being named after the amalgamation of the tribes of I'hins, every syllable, in former ages, being one tribe, of which the Gods have made this a testimony to endure from before the time of Fragapatti and Zarathustra, in which it may be proven to mortals and spirits that this division of the spirit world was revealed to man at the time language was carried to its highest compounding.[542]

20/6.28. Besides these mountains in the lowest heavens, there were four thousand others, the names of which were duly registered in the libraries of heaven, by Thor and his sub-Gods; but more than two thousand of them were uninhabited, owing to the fact that Jehovih had not, as yet, created a sufficient number of people for them. But the mountains mentioned here and previously (all in Aoasu), were mostly those where the false Gods and false Lords set up kingdoms of their own after Apollo's time; and the names of the mountains are also the names they espoused to themselves.

20/6.29. Fragapatti said: Alas, these heavens! Who can measure the vanity of men and angels, who cut loose from the Great Spirit, endeavoring to set up kingdoms on their own account! Their places perish; sorrowful histories! Behold these vagrant spirits, strolling about, or hiding amid the ruins! Ashamed of their rags, and nakedness! Prowling around; millions of them; hundreds of millions!

20/6.30. Verethragna said: I thank You, O Jehovih, that I am once again among the lowest! Keep me, O Father, amid this darkness, till I shall never again forget the lowest of my brothers and sisters. I behold Your Wisdom, O Jehovih! Were it not for these cycles of time, in the dawns of which Your ethereans can come down to witness the bound in hell, they themselves would forget the horrors. O, do not allow me to rest till I have helped to raise them up to know You, and to be a glory within Your works!

[542] All these divisions in the spirit heavens are still found in the Vedic Scriptures. Some corporeal mountains have been named after them. –Ed.

CHAPTER 7 Fragapatti

20/7.1. Fragapatti surveyed Aoasu in all the Morn of East Birth, and his officers enumerated the spirits, and recorded their condition, and then he called his conductors, saying:

20/7.2. I have measured the Morn of the East Birth; take me now to the Setting Eve of Death.[543]

20/7.3. So the ship, with its passengers, was raised a little, and started for the west, running low over the regions lying west of Ham, Shem and Jaffeth. Fragapatti said:

20/7.4. I perceive that the plan of the Gods on this star was to complete its inhabitation by going westward. For this reason, I will see where they designed to have the Eve of Death and the birth of the Father's kingdom on the corporeal part.

20/7.5. When they came to the Atlantic Ocean (Uzocea), they raised their ship still higher, and sped across for the regions inhabited by the I'hins and I'huans.

20/7.6. Arriving there, they came to Ipseogee, a region in the lower heaven where Hapacha, Lord of the I'hins, had a kingdom of seventy million souls, many of whom were I'huan spirits. Here Fragapatti stopped, and fastened his ship, remaining seven days. And Hapacha received him and his hosts, and entertained them. And during their sojourn, Hapacha sent his otevan over all the heavens belonging to Guatama, north and south, taking the surveyors and inspectors of the hosts of Fragapatti into all inhabited places, so they could complete their records.

20/7.7. Meanwhile, Hapacha conducted Fragapatti throughout his kingdom, exhibiting the factories, schools, colleges, hospitals, and all places that belong to the second resurrection.

[543] In these verses Fragapatti is referring to the birth of Seffas upon the earth when he refers to the Morn of the East Birth (note he could go no farther east because Pan lay sunken). The Setting Eve of Death refers to the death of Seffas and the subsequent birth of Kosmon (the Kosmon era).

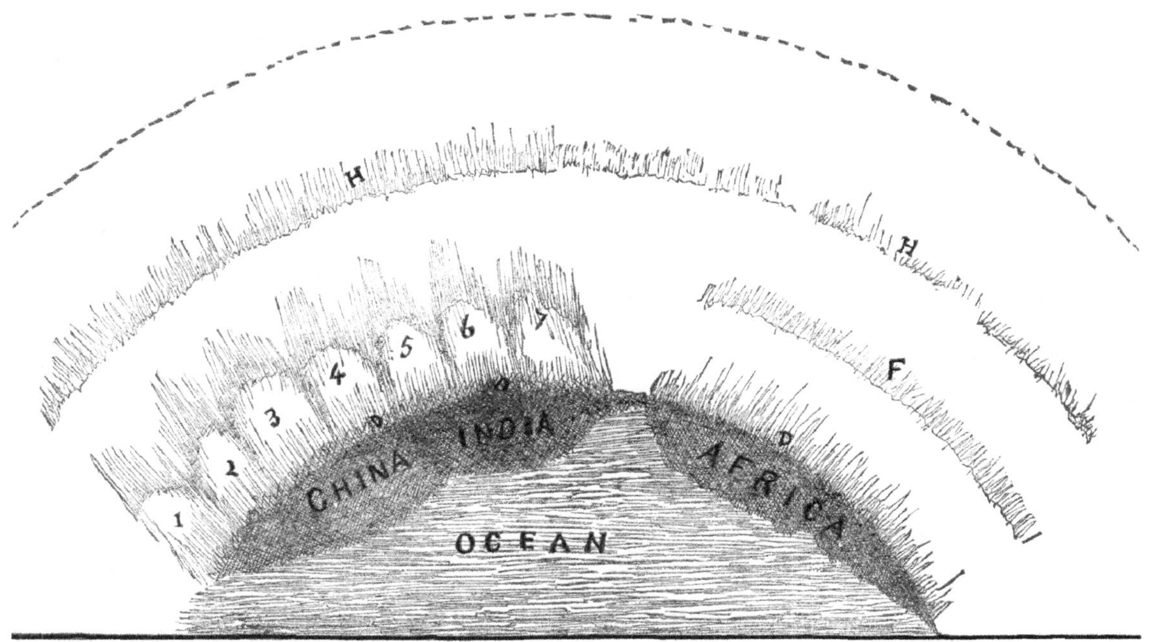

i021 **Atmospherean heavens founded by Fragapatti showing their relative position to earth**. All that lies between the dotted line (Chinvat) and the earth is atmospherea;* etherea lies beyond. H, Haraiti, highest lower (atmospherean) heaven, founded by Fragapatti. F, Zeredho, second highest lower heaven, founded by Fragapatti. 1, 2, 3, 4, 5, 6, 7, third lowest heavens, founded by Fragapatti. These seven were called the Seven Heavenly Mountains, and known by the name Aoasu.**

* The line Chinvat is not to scale; it is actually some 30 of earth's diameters distant from the center of the earth; other heavenly plateaus shown are not to scale, but are shown relative to earth.
** See Vedas.

20/7.8. Fragapatti said to Hapacha: I am well pleased with you and your kingdom. You shall hear from me before many days. At present I must depart. So Fragapatti did not reveal who he was, or what his mission was; but gathering together his hosts, he departed, still going westward, until he completed the circumference of the earth.

20/7.9. Now I will go around the earth again, said Fragapatti, and inspect mortals and their kingdoms. So, his conductors ran the ship just above the lands, being guided by messengers familiar with the earth and with all the habitable places. And they zigzagged their course, going into all kingdoms and into all large cities, and into forests and plains, determining the condition of the earth, and its capabilities, as well as the conditions of mortals and their capabilities.

20/7.10. And when Fragapatti had completed this latter inspection, he returned to Mouru in Haraiti; and the duration of his absence was seventy-seven days.

20/7.11. And all the records obtained on the expedition were immediately filed in Mouru, where the High Council and all others who chose could read them. And on the third day after his return, Fragapatti resumed the throne of Jehovih, and was prepared to found anew the kingdoms of atmospherea, and also those of earth; to overthrow or set aside what was not good, and to raise up both mortals and spirits who had proved themselves worthy.

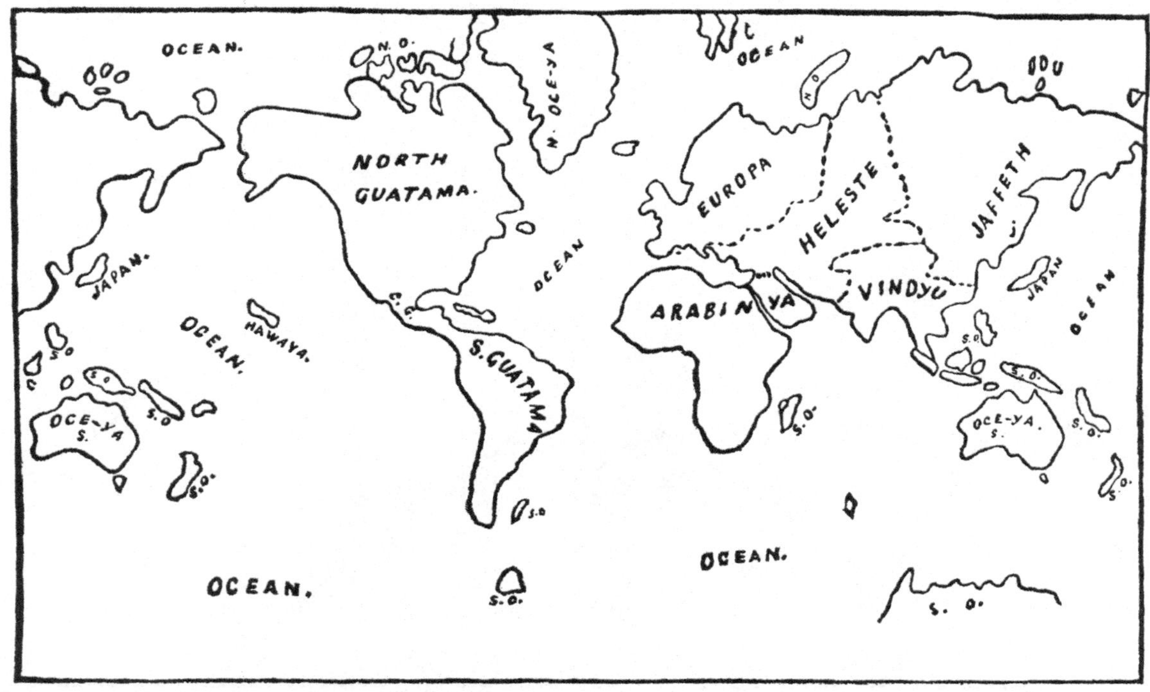

i018 **Post-Flood Outline Map of the World**. Showing the chief political divisions used by heaven from the time of Fragapatti (and subsequently used by mortals). [The map shows the names of places as described in this volume. The spelling is not always the same, owing to the different periods of time mentioned, but phonetic in a general sense. The submersion of the continent of Pan is a good explanation of the four peoples, Chinese, East Indian [India], Hebrews and American Indians. In phonetecy it accounts for the sounds of words used in Central America, Sandwich Islands and Japan. –Ed.] [The mid-Pacific land is Hawaya (Hawaii). –ed.]

CHAPTER 8 Fragapatti

20/8.1. This, then, is the manner of the House of Mouru: Fragapatti would announce the subject; then, rank and rank, according to exaltation, the representatives of hundreds and of thousands would speak on the subject. When all had spoken who either desired to, or were those whom Fragapatti asked to speak, then Fragapatti would pronounce in the name of Jehovih. And these were the decrees. For example:

20/8.2. Fragapatti asked: What shall be the divisions of the earth, and who shall be the Lords of these? || And when the House had expressed, then Fragapatti said: In the name of Jehovih, these shall be the divisions of the earth, namely: Jaffeth bounded on the east and north, by the sea and to the ice regions, and on the west to the mountains of Oh'e'loo, which shall be called the first division.[544]

20/8.3. To the east and south, water and water; and to the west, the highlands of E'zar; and its name shall be Shem.

20/8.4. From this day forward, the south land shall be called Arabin'ya, encompassed by the sea. And north of this, the first country of the brown red race shall be called Heleste,[545] bordering on Shem and Jaffeth on the east, and extending half way to the sea on the west.

20/8.5. Uropa shall be Goddess of the west part, and it shall be called after her. And the two great west lands shall be called North Guatama and South Guatama. And all the islands of the earth shall be called Oce'ya; and the waters of the earth

---

[544] see image i018

[545] note that Par'si'e is part of Heleste

shall be called Oce'a, signifying, in likeness of the earth and sky.

20/8.6. For the seven divisions of the earth there shall be seven rulers of the rank Lord God; and for South Oce'ya, one ruler of the rank Lord; and for North Oce'ya, one ruler of the rank Lord; and for Japan (Zha'pahn), one ruler of the rank sub-God.

20/8.7. Hear me, O Gods and Goddesses: He whom I shall proclaim from among you shall reign only during dawn of dan, and you shall raise up a successor in your own name, and in Jehovih's name, to the same rank, to hold dominion for two hundred years, being the next succeeding resurrection.

20/8.8. Fragapatti said: I proclaim, in the name of Jehovih, Ah'oan, Lord God of Jaffeth; Yima, Lord God of Shem; E'chad, Lord God of Arabin'ya; Gir-ak-shi, Lord God of Heleste; Uropa, Lord Goddess of Uropa; Yaton'te, Lord God of North Guatama; Kow'anea, Lord God of South Guatama; M'wing'mi, Lord of South Oce'ya; Ots'ha'ta, Lord of North Oce'ya; and Soo'fwa, sub-God of Japan.

20/8.9. Approach the throne, you Lord Gods, Lords and sub-God, so you may be anointed in the name of the Father, and duly crowned with the emblem of All Light.

20/8.10. The Lord Gods came first; and they stood before the throne of Jehovih, now illumed brilliantly, in gold and white. Fragapatti said: By Your Power and Wisdom, O Jehovih, which rest in me, I anoint and bestow to Your kingdoms, these, Your Lord Gods, for Your glory. Amen! (And now speaking to the Lord Gods:) Receive this fire (ethe fire), for it is His anointing with power and wisdom, so that all men, women and children, mortals and spirits, coming under your dominion, may rejoice in their Creator, rising forever. Amen!

20/8.11. The Lord Gods responded: May I glorify You, O Jehovih, in the kingdom You have bestowed upon me! In Your name I receive this fire, for it is Your baptism with power and wisdom. Whomever You have entrusted to my dominion I will cause to rejoice at all times, and to rise up forever in Your numberless kingdoms!

20/8.12. Fragapatti said: And to you I bequeath, in the Father's name, power to exalt successors, so that you may also bequeath to your successors power for them to exalt successors also; and so on, till the next dawn of dan from the etherean kingdoms, for this shall be the manner of the dominion of the Gods and Lords of earth, and her heavens, for a long season after now.

20/8.13. The Lord Gods responded: I accept Your power, O Jehovih, to exalt a successor to me in my dominions, with power to bequeath the exalting power to his successors after him, till the next etherean dawn of dan.

20/8.14. Fragapatti said: Crown of Your Crown, O Jehovih, I weave from Your golden light, for these, Your exalted Sons and Daughter; and with my hand, in Your name, crown them. Jehovih, be with them, now and forever. Amen!

20/8.15. Then Fragapatti gathered of the light present, and fashioned crowns for them, and they came forward to the foot of the throne, and he crowned them. And as they said: I receive Your fire! There came down from above a stream of light, bright as the sun, and settled upon them.

20/8.16. And now they sat down at the foot of the throne, in ancient custom, and Fragapatti came down from the throne, bringing attendant Gods with him; and they took the hands of the newly-anointed Gods, and raised them up; and Fragapatti said: Arise, O Lord God, and go your way. Jehovih is with you. Then they stood aside, a little way off.

20/8.17. Then the two Lords came forward. Fragapatti said: O Jehovih, by Your power and wisdom vested in me, I appoint and announce these, Your Lords, to their divisions of the earth; and with my hands, and in Your name, I weave a crown for each of them, and crown them Lords of Your light, for Your glory. Amen!

20/8.18. Hear me, O Lords; that which I bestow in the name of the Father, and you receive, you shall also bestow in the name of the Father upon your successors at the end of this dawn of dan. Though a Lord God has dominion, first, with mortals, and, second, with the first heaven in his division which rests on the earth; and though a Lord has dominion with mortals only, and with those ashars who minister to them, you are both made Lords of far-distant islands, where you shall determine many things in your own way, often being Gods also, which I also bequeath to you, and your successors forever.

20/8.19. The Lords said: What You have put upon me, O Jehovih, I will do, with Your power and wisdom, for Your glory, forever. Amen! I receive Your crown with praise and thanksgiving, and will bestow it in Your name upon my successor, as bright as I now receive it.

20/8.20. Fragapatti then laid the crowns upon them, and they also sat at the foot of the throne. Then Fragapatti took them by the hand, and raised them up, saying: Arise, O Lords of Jehovih, and go your ways.

20/8.21. And when they stood aside, Soo'fwa came forward. Fragapatti said: In Your name, O Jehovih, and by Your power in me vested, I crown this, Your Son, to be sub-God of his division of the earth and its heavens. I crown him with Your LIGHT, and bestow him with a rod of water and a rod of fire, so that he may have dominion in Your name, and for Your glory. Amen!

20/8.22. Hear me, O God: Your duties make you both Lord and God; but your second resurrections shall be removed at short intervals, as you shall presently be informed. But you shall have power to appoint assistant Lords to be with you, in my name, and the Father's. And you shall also exalt a successor after you, with power to his successor also.

20/8.23. In Jehovih's name, receive this crown of yellow light, for it is the emblem of the oldest habitable country above the waters of the earth! And may the Father be with you, now and forever. Amen!

20/8.24. He also sat at the foot of the throne; and as he had raised the others, Fragapatti raised him up, saying: Arise, O God, and go your way. So he stood aside. And now the es'enaurs sang and chanted, and the marshals led the way; and the newly empowered Gods departed out of the House of Mouru. Once outside they proceeded to a vessel that previously had been provided them, for it was to re-conduct them back to the earth. And so, amid the flying of banners and the music of the trumpeters, they entered the vessel, and sped forward, soon out of sight.

CHAPTER 9 Fragapatti

20/9.1. The hosts of the second resurrection were now conducted to the mansions previously created in Haraiti by Fragapatti; and they were provided with teachers and occupations, according to their development.

20/9.2. Fragapatti said: The marshals-in-chief will now send the builders of fire-ships before me; I want to speak to them. Now when the builders came, and duly saluted before the throne, Fragapatti said:

20/9.3. Go build me an avalanza capable of carrying three billion angels, with as many rooms, and make it capable of descent and ascent, and with east and west and north and south motion, and prepare it with a magnet, so that it may face to the north, while traveling.

20/9.4. The builders saluted, withdrew, then went and built the vessel. And it was two hundred thousand paces east and west, and the same north and south; its height was one thousand lengths, and the vesture[546] around it was a thousand paces thick; and it was provided with etherean curtains, two hundred thousand; and with four hundred thousand banners, of all possible colors, shades and tints. Besides these, were fifty thousand small flags and streamers. The floor was woven in the form of a spider's net, extending from the center outward, and with circular bars at crosses; and the framework within was constructed with one million uprights, the entire height of the vessel; and yet across these were twenty million bars; and within the whole, were the rooms and halls, and places for musicians.

20/9.5. When it was completed, the builders notified Fragapatti. He said: Athrava, come and sit on the throne. I promised to go and see Hoab and his colony, in Zeredho, when he sent word[547] to me regarding certain matters. Behold, messengers have notified me, and Hoab desires to know how he can establish his colony, so that he may never again fear being bothered by other Gods and angels.

20/9.6. Let fifty thousand musicians enter the ship with me, besides a sufficient number of captains and officers to manage the ship. The marshals at once made the proper selections, and took them to the ship, where they all entered, Fragapatti with them, and they departed.

20/9.7. So Fragapatti returned to Zeredho, the second highest lower heaven, of which the ambitious Hoab, with his colony, desired to be sole occupant forever.

[546] This would appear to be a mantle of light covering the ship, but not a photosphere, however.

[547] notice, a message

20/9.8. Hoab was waiting to receive him, having aroused up a sufficient number of his indolent[548] subjects to maintain the semblance of a heavenly Council. But what a surprise! He had expected only a small vessel, with a few attendants. And now, when he saw the magnificence of the avalanza, and the majesty of the band of musicians, so far transcending anything he had ever seen, he feared, and was awe-stricken.

20/9.9. Fragapatti approached slowly, but with Avom lights, and when the ship was close, the hosts aboard cast out hundreds of thousands of perfumed ovaries, which exploded with beautiful colors, filling the surrounding atmosphere with the most delightful perfume. Finally the avalanza came to anchor and Fragapatti, without any ceremony, alighted, taking a thousand attendants with him, and came directly up to Hoab, who was abashed somewhat on account of his shabby appearance.

20/9.10. Fragapatti said: Friend and brother, peace and joy to you and your house! To which Hoab replied: All hail, great Chief! Happiness attend you and your hosts! And if I had not previously discovered you were a philosopher like myself, I would apologize for the vast difference between the respective appearances of our hosts. But you are welcome all the same!

20/9.11. Fragapatti said: A mere incident of conditions, most noble God. You are aware that when children go on a holiday excursion, they attire themselves in their best; so it is better that I find an apology than that you should.

20/9.12. Hoab said: No, Chief, there is a philosophy in this matter which has worried me lately: A thousand years ago my colony was ambitious to attire itself in grandeur, and to build fine ships and go on excursions also. Five hundred years later, they ceased building ships and going on excursions, saying: What is the use? Lately, they are all utilitarians, doing just as little as possible. In fact, many of my subjects deny themselves comforts, on the plea that they can do without them.

20/9.13. Fragapatti said: You remember when I was here before, I said to you that without contentment no people had attained to peace; and you did acquiesce. Why, then, should you not rejoice that your people have thus subdued ambition and curiosity? Has your mind lost its contentment in so short a time? You know I came here to impart to you and your people the great secret, that you may fortify yourselves in such a way that you shall never fear for Gods or angels molesting you.

20/9.14. Hoab said: Hear me, O Chief: If my people lose all ambition for rites and ceremonies, and dancings, and excursions; and keep constantly striving to deny themselves of everything except what necessity calls for; and if that necessity becomes smaller and smaller, where will the end be? Will not all inspiration die out? For, to tell the truth, since my people have given up rites and ceremonies, and prayers and singing, they have also given up rejoicings of soul, and are becoming like a dead people.

20/9.15. Fragapatti said: Then you would seem to prove that to hold on only to the useful in life would ultimately end in suicide to the state, to the family, to the individual, and even to the soul?

20/9.16. Hoab said: Many of my people are too lazy to clothe themselves; and because of shame, they seek secluded places, as they say, to live as they please. Do such people not commit suicide against the state? Has a man a right to withdraw himself from his fellows, saying: It suits me better? We have been told that in the first age of mortals, they had no ambition to live together, being void of all talents, and that the Gods inspired them to language and to society, giving them rites and ceremonies as an inducement to make them harmonious and attractive to one another.

20/9.17. Fragapatti said: How shall I account for the difference between your arguments now and the other time I was with you? You desired me to believe that you and your people were the highest, best, happiest of all people in all the heavens. Why this change?

20/9.18. Hoab said: You promised me you would teach us some way of protection against being molested by other Gods and spirits from other kingdoms. Since then I have reasoned on the subject, and I perceive that if such a state of security could be given to my people, they would wander off into isolation, and even forget language and judgment. But, you told me you had been in heavens where such a state of seeming impossibility exists?

[548] lazy, idle, sluggish

20/9.19. Fragapatti said: Do not let arguments sway you, O Hoab. But rather, examine proofs for yourself. I thought that my statement to you was too extravagant to be believed without evidence. Behold, then, what I have done: I brought a vessel large enough for all your people, desiring that you go with me to my kingdom, newly founded in Haraiti; and if at the end of a few years, and you desire it, I will take you and your people to still another kingdom, in a far-off world. After that, if you desire it, I will provide the same conveyance back to Zeredho, with power to rule over it to your heart's content.

20/9.20. Hoab said: Fairest of Gods! I feared, indeed, that you had come with the old story; to worship the All Light, the Unknowable Nothingness; with foolish ceremonies and rites, and prayers and songs of praise; which, however good for the ignorant and superstitious, are worthless to a God as enlightened as I am. This you perceive with your own judgment. I will gladly go with you, and I will persuade as many of my people as possible to go also. You are the first God who ever came to our heaven, who did not want to circumscribe[549] our liberties, which neither I nor my people can tolerate. ||

20/9.21. These things were then communicated to the people of Zeredho; and after a few days they gathered together, and went into the avalanza, every one of them. Fragapatti signaled the commander not to go direct to Haraiti, but by way of Utza, one of the hells in the Aoasu mountains, inhabited by billions of spirits in darkness, many of whom did not know who they were, nor even have names, being infants and idiots, chaotic and foul smelling.

CHAPTER 10 Fragapatti

20/10.1. When they came to Utza, Hoab cried out: What do my eyes behold! As I live, here are people who once belonged to Zeredho, my own heaven! By what strange law did they leave my kingdom to come and dwell in these torments?

20/10.2. Fragapatti caused the avalanza to stop so that information could be obtained. Then he called the druj to the ship, and thousands of them came, ragged and debauched. Hoab knew many of them, and he said: Do you know who I am? And they answered: Yes, Hoab, God of Zeredho. Again Hoab spoke, saying: Why did you leave my glorious kingdom to come and dwell in this hell of iniquity?

20/10.3. They answered, saying: A pity that we left, indeed! But since it is so, it is so. Hear us, then, O Hoab, this is the reason: Even as mortals often leave Purity in order to revel in sin. Other than that, we do not know.

20/10.4. Then Fragapatti spoke, saying: Jehovih says: I have given man many talents. Because the roadways are not open for their growth, he plunges into darkness. Do not think that you can draw a line, and say: O man, you shall not do this, or, you shall do that. || For you are powerless to hold him, whom I created to go forward. And if he does not find a way to go forward, he will turn and go backward.

20/10.5. The drujas said: Yes, master, Zeredho did not fill our souls; we were thirsty for amusement and lightheartedness. We heard no voice but Utility. We sheared off all ornament and diversion, and art, and, finally, even music. We would gladly hear from Zeredho, to find out if they have ceased to talk, and perhaps to live, because, in fact, Utility has spoken!

20/10.6. And they laughed, and frolicked about like idiots and fools, mingling with harlots, thieves, liars and drunkards.

20/10.7. Fragapatti caused the ship to move on a while, and then stopped, and called other drujas, and questioned them in the same manner, and received answers of the same character.

20/10.8. Again they moved onward, and the same was repeated; finally, they came to a place where all was darkness and noise and confusion, where the denizens did not even heed the ship, nor the calls made to them. Then Fragapatti spoke to Hoab, saying: Has it been proven to you that man cannot stand still? Hoab said: It is true. This matter comes home close to me. I perceive now that had I not come out of Zeredho, I would not have witnessed these things, nor would I have seen Zeredho as I now see it.

20/10.9. Fragapatti said: Do not be hasty against your own philosophy, for I will show you your own wisdom by and by. So they traveled seven days in hell, the lowest division of hada,

[549] limit, restrict, circumvent, thwart, deny, prohibit, restrain, hinder, impede

where there was neither government, nor order, nor truth, nor virtue, but torments, wailings, and cursings.

20/10.10. Fragapatti said: You have seen that all these many people do not know their own darkness.

20/10.11. Hoab said: Is it not true, O Chief, that no man knows his own darkness? Who, then, is safe? Who knows he is not on the downward road?

20/10.12. Fragapatti said: You have said man is the All Highest. But does it not come home to us all, as it did to the ancients, that to do good with all our wisdom and strength, and have faith in this, that we are on the road to the All Highest?

20/10.13. Certainly you have proven, said Hoab, that Zeredho is not the All Highest, for it cannot retain its people. Even hell has prevailed over her. And does not hell prevail over all self-righteousness, and over riches, kingdoms and empires? If, therefore, hell prevails, is not hell the most powerful? And if the most powerful is not hell, then the All Highest possible must be most powerful. The ancients were happy in ignorance, for in believing in an All Person, a Creator, and that they would ultimately see Him, they had an object in view. But with the growth of wisdom, we find we cannot realize such a Person, and so have no object in view ahead of us. And with that, we recoil upon ourselves, and all is dead.

20/10.14. Fragapatti said: Has man no lesson from the past? In the ancient times the Gods persuaded mortals to make stone idols and worship them. And they were sufficient until man attained more knowledge. Again the Gods came to mortals, inventing a large man-God in the sky, persuading them to worship him. He was a sufficient God till man learned to commune with angels; and the angels contradicted that philosophy. But hear me, O Hoab, do we not have a lesson in this, which is, that we must ever have an All Highest Person so far ahead that we cannot attain Him? If this is true, then when we have surpassed a Person whose figure[550] and condition we can comprehend, is it not incumbent upon us to create within our own souls the thought of an All Person beyond our comprehensibility?

20/10.15. Hoab said: It seems so. But how can you teach your soul to think of an All Person beyond man's comprehensibility?

20/10.16. Fragapatti said: For a basis to reason from, let us consider the etherean, the atmospherean and the corporeal worlds to constitute His body; and the motion within and between these as the manifestations of His Power and His Wisdom. Since, then, we ourselves have these things in part, we find, also, we have another attribute embracing all the others, which is combination concentrated into one person. Shall we not, then, give to Him, Who embraces all things within Himself, combination concentrated into one Person? Otherwise, He is our inferior, which cannot be. Therefore, being ourselves persons, are we not mere offshoots from the All Person? Otherwise, we could not have attained personality. Does a child not take its personality because its mother was a person? Can man have an entity unless he receives it from an entity? Could man be a person, unless he sprang from a Person?

20/10.17. Hoab said: You are a great light, O Chief! Truly, you have unfolded a universe before me! Yes, there must be an All Person! O if only I had seen this philosophy before!

20/10.18. Fragapatti said: Do not be infatuated, O Hoab, with sudden appearances. For were I to show you, first, what it is to believe in an All Person, Whose magnificence surpasses the universe itself, and then that man can attain to be one with Him, even as a note in music is one within a tune, I would so far enrapture your soul that you would do nothing but listen. Let us, therefore, suspend our research awhile, so that we may devise some resurrection for this hell of suffering millions.

CHAPTER 11 Fragapatti

20/11.1. The avalanza was constructed in such a way that the words spoken by Fragapatti and Hoab could be heard by all who chose, of whom there were two billion on board. And when Hoab expressed conviction, the same sentiment seized upon the whole assembly; at which point, Fragapatti raised his hand, saying: By virtue of Your power, O Jehovih, I will illume this hell!

20/11.2. And by Fragapatti's will a sudden light was created, so brilliant, none present, except the ethereans, could look upon him. Hoab bowed

550 attributes, stature

down, and hid his face, and Hoab's hosts were overcome with fear, prostrating themselves on the floors of the avalanza.

20/11.3. Fragapatti said to the swift messengers: Go at once to Mouru, greeting, and say that Fragapatti demands, at once, a million etherean volunteers, for signal centers in Aoasu's lowest hells, bringing rods of fire and water.

20/11.4. The swift messengers departed hastily. Fragapatti then commanded that the avalanza be anchored for a day; and he and many of his hosts went out into hell, where the spirits were weeping, wailing and cursing, or lying in drunkenness and lethargy. Many of them were naked and foul smelling; and hundreds of thousands of them, having had diseased corporeal bodies while on earth, now carried with them into hell the substance of their corruptions, even the rottenness of plagues and consumptions, and of other diseases it is not even lawful to mention.

20/11.5. Fragapatti said: By Your Power, O Jehovih, a wall of fire shall encompass these people around. They shall not escape. For, were they to return to a nation of mortals, they would inoculate them to death. Fire, O Jehovih, Fire! You All Purifier!

20/11.6. And he cast his hands outward and upward, in majesty, and there rose up walls of fire on the face of the mountains; and its light fell into the valleys of Ugh'sa, the pit of hell. To the east and west and north and south, Fragapatti turned, saying: A wall of fire! A wall of fire! And he, himself, shone as a sun, united with the Eternal All Creator, Whose voice was power to wield the elements to His will.

20/11.7. Presently, there were hemmed into one field more than five hundred million drujas, who, by the sudden transformation, were roused up to desperate wildness, with bated breath,[551] running here and there, first one way and then another.

20/11.8. And yet there were other millions of them, so low, stupid, and crazed, that the others ran over them as if they were only a heap of rubbish, death!

20/11.9. Then Fragapatti went to Hoab, saying: For pity's sake, come and help me, and persuade your hosts also.

[551] breath held in due to terror; not doing any breathing due to fearful anticipation

20/11.10. Hoab said: O friend, and brother, do not mock me! You have undone me entirely. I am nothing. My hosts are nothing. For pity's sake, temper your own light. It pierces me through!

20/11.11. Fragapatti said: Shall I not send you back quickly to Zeredho, with your hosts? Hoab said: My wish is nothing; my will is nothing! Yours and the Great All Power's will be done. Fragapatti said: If ever you had faith in your life, I charge you now to quickly summon it to your soul, for Great Jehovih is with me now, and just ask and speak in faith by the Creator, and it shall be granted to you. Speak quickly, while yet the power holds upon me: Shall I put on a thousand-fold more light? Say: In Faith I will endure all, for the glory of Jehovih! Give me fire or torments, or whatever You will, O Jehovih!

20/11.12. Hoab trembled, and then strained in every part, and at last, suddenly sprang up facing the light, melting in the flame of fire; and he said: I will endure all, in faith of You, O Jehovih! Give me fire or torments, or whatever You will. From this time forward, I will do for You, forever!

20/11.13. Presently, his spirit took the crystal form, and the victory dawned upon his soul. A smile, denoting knowledge of All Holiness and Majesty gleamed in his countenance! The light began to retract and to reflect from his face, brilliant and sun-like. He had conquered and won! He said: Thanks, O Jehovih!

20/11.14. Fragapatti said: Quick, now, seize the goal; go forth practicing your light for others, and it will grow, giant-like. And Hoab was strong in faith, almost mad with the delight of such wondrous change; and he rushed forth, commanding, in the name of Jehovih, raising up hundreds and thousands, even as he had been raised, crystallizing.

20/11.15. They labored one full day and night, and all the ethereans with them; and they rescued, and divided, and subdivided the spirits of darkness into grades and sections. And many of the spirits belonging to the hosts of Hoab were thus raised to the second resurrection, with light and power.

20/11.16. But of the hundreds of millions of spirits in the torments of hell none were as yet raised even to the first resurrection. But, they were stirred up and routed out of lethargy; and the supplies for their drunkenness were cut off by the walls of fire, created by Fragapatti, which flamed upward ceaselessly day and night.

20/11.17. And Fragapatti stationed sentinels with power, near the walls of fire, commanding them to cast in the elements of ughs and brimstone, [552] so that the suffocating smell would prevent the drujas from escaping.

20/11.18. On the second day, a million ethereans, with rods of water and rods of fire, came from Mouru, in answer to Fragapatti's commandment. And when they arrived before him, and had saluted in the sign of Jehovih's name, he said to them: Behold, I have established one signal center in hell. It will require a thousand more centers before we have broken them up and delivered them. The marshals shall select from among you ten thousand of the rank of DAS, to remain in this center and complete the work I have laid out.

20/11.19. So the marshals selected ten thousand from the ethereans of the rank of DAS. Now the das are those who have attained to power with the rod [wand –Ed.] with water, and the rod with fire, but not with the hand, like the ranks above them. They go among the denizens of a signal center (in hell) with the two rods, casting water with one and fire with the other. And the hosts of spirits in darkness run for them, like cattle for salt; and the das thus discover and sort them; for the lowest spirits go for the rods with water, and the highest for the rods of fire. Because the lowest spirits dread the light; and because the highest desire to be rescued from the lowest.

20/11.20. On the second day, therefore, the das began work; and many millions were baptized with water; but with fire only one million. The latter were then taken beyond the walls of fire, and colonized, clothed and fed, and guardians placed over them, in preparation for the nurseries, hospitals, schools, factories, and such other educationals as belong in the lowest heaven.

20/11.21. On the third day the das went through the same labor again, and again many millions were baptized with water, and only two million with fire. The latter were also taken beyond the walls of fire, and colonized in the same manner as those of the previous day.

20/11.22. Such, then, is the labor of the das in hell, baptizing and selecting; and it continues until all the people are taken beyond the walls. The last taken are, therefore, the lowest grade, and the first taken are the highest grade. But the last are usually so low in knowledge and ambition that they cannot move by themselves, and are placed in nurseries and hospitals, to be cleansed from their foulness, and to be healed of their infirmities.

CHAPTER 12 Fragapatti

20/12.1. Fragapatti caused the ship, the avalanza, to be moved to other black mountains, buried deep in revolting crimes and misery; into which no one with Godlike power had ventured for hundreds of years. Again he called down Jehovih's fire, and raised walls, impenetrable, high on every side, frightening and stirring up the self-condemned with frenzied fear. And with oaths, curses and imprecations against all righteousness, they ran, all polluted with foul thoughts, which had clothed them about with foulness terrible.

20/12.2. And Hoab, too, now a very sun, desperate to do overwhelming good things, even a thousand times more than in his self-ease of other days when he refrained from dark company lest he be polluted, now rushed in headlong to the very worst and foulest. Proclaiming Jehovih and active work to stir them up; and by his quick and unmistakable zeal, proving his soul's connection with the Almighty's Power.

20/12.3. After Fragapatti and Hoab rushed in, so did hundreds of thousands of ethereans; laboring for the Father's kingdom, with flames of fire they cut loose the demons' grips of torture on the helpless, and hurled them separate. None could escape because of the surrounding walls, now seething with the choking smell of brimstone; and so, weeping and wailing before the crystallizing lights thrust at them, they had no recourse but to fall prostrate.

[552] Ughs: foul air from dead people. –1891 glossary. || Brimstone is sulfurous gas. By ughs we may presume the smell of rotting corpses. In other words, to keep the drujas contained, they were surrounded by ughs and brimstone; and the ethereans (knowing the chemical composition of such things even as today we know how to make suffocating sulfur odor) could easily cast a thick wall of them.

20/12.4. All day long, and all night, Fragapatti and Hoab (now a powerful worker, which Fragapatti had previously seen would be the case) and the etherean hosts, did not rest; but waded into the hell of death, turning to the right or to the left the miserable, devouring wretches, brothers and sisters of mortals and spirits, now engulfed in their own depravity, and by their desperate desire for sin, holding millions of the moderately good as officers of torture, in order to gratify their horrid love of witnessing horrors. Into groups and series they roughly selected them, as a starting point for the das that were to come afterward and more carefully divide them.

20/12.5. Then Fragapatti called the das and put them to work with their rods of water and rods of fire, making stations beyond the walls of fire, where the naked, trembling, rescued sufferers and drujas were housed and fed, restrained by guardians of ample strength and foresight. For such is the nature of the low man and low woman, that the love of evil, in time, delights to feed itself in evil more than in good, and will even turn against benefactors, and spurn good offerings.

20/12.6. Of whom Jehovih says: As by fire the dross (impurity) of metal is burned and cast out, leaving that which is pure; so I created the righteous with light from My countenance, to burn out the dross (darkness, evil) which the wicked nestle into their bosoms. In this, man shall perceive that it is Me and My chosen, casting out the dross, that heals. Go, then, deliver the wicked in hell, and make them clean with water and with fire, and you shall find a star in every soul. And as many of these as you deliver, so is your glory in My etherean kingdoms.

20/12.7. For each deliverer is like a sun around which these stars congregate, and they magnify one another forever. And when these stars have grown, they also go and do the same. Such are My exalted ones in the highest heavens, whom you call Gods and Lords, and justly so, because of their supremacy. ||

20/12.8. Thus went Fragapatti through the lowest regions of Aoasu; for forty days and nights he and his hosts labored, and he broke up the regions of hell, and cast out the souls of the tortured, billions of them. Nor was any place left standing in all the lower heavens where evil held dominion.

20/12.9. Now established in those regions were two hundred thousand colonies for the rescued evil ones. Aside from those were the very lowest, being nine hundred million who did not know anything: Some were infants who died at the time of birth; some, infants of drunkards, who came to the lower heavens with the intoxicating liquors or smoke of their mother's debauchery; some were very young abortions, slain by their mothers and fathers; and some were chaotic, killed in wars, mad and crazed, howling, screaming and fighting. And Fragapatti had all these unfortunates brought away from the others, putting guardians over them for the present.

20/12.10. Then he called together the crew of the avalanza and Hoab with all his hosts; and when they were duly in order, Fragapatti extemporized[553] a throne, sat on it, and spoke, saying:

20/12.11. Without You, O Jehovih, man is nothing. Neither can he stand upright, nor hold up his head, nor his soul after he is up, except by You. When he cuts himself off from You, he falls like a limb of a tree that is severed.

20/12.12. He goes about boasting: There is no All Person. But his words are like a severing knife, and he does not know it. He sets up his judgment, saying: You were good for fools, O Jehovih; but as for me, You are a foolish encumbrance!

20/12.13. Yes, he says: Who has seen Jehovih! And he laughs because of his cleverness. He says: What did Jehovih stand upon when He created the worlds? How long did He sleep before He created? He says: What a foolish Creator! He created sin and death! He says: Who knows the size of His head; the length of His arm; the place He lives; or who has heard His voice!

20/12.14. He says: Truly, there is no All Person; no All Highest; no Light. This is the second downward stage, and in the third, he says: A curse upon Faith! A curse upon all things! A curse upon myself! And then comes hell and her horrors to swallow him up.

20/12.15. But You are near, O Jehovih! Your hosts traverse the universe. They come in Your name, and Your power and glory are with them. In their majesty they encounter all evil; they cast out hell and its prisoners.

---

[553] improvised, created only with the elements at hand; made impromptu

20/12.16. Then Fragapatti turned to Hoab, saying: Speak, O Hoab. Nine hundred million dead, who are still sleeping in death, lie at our feet. These regions are unsuited for their treatment; where shall we take them? Or shall we, because they are so dead, leave them to shift for themselves?

20/12.17. Then Hoab rose, saluting, and tears were in his eyes. He said: Mighty You are, O Jehovih! Lo, I was on the verge of an everlasting fall! I was on a steep precipice, but did not see it. With blinded eyes I walked about. I lost Your countenance. My family became strangers to You, and we were becoming strangers to one another!

20/12.18. Yes, I was ungrateful before You. I forgot that You created me. I forgot that all the joys I had ever had were bestowed by You; and that by You I had been made capable of appreciating my own enjoyment. And then I raised up my voice against You, and turned You out of the world.

20/12.19. Yes, I chose a corner and appropriated it for my own ease and glory. I said: To keep other Gods and angels away from my lands, this is all I desire. But You were mindful of me, O Jehovih! Your voice sounded in the heavens above, and Your Son came down in Your glory. He saw my vanity and my weakness, but he did not rebuke me. Yes, I told him I did not love to go to those beneath me and raise them up. I said: Let them shift for themselves!

20/12.20. Now I am rebuked in my own words! I have now cast myself out of hell. Behold, I said: Zeredho shall be a place for me and my people forever! None shall come here to make us afraid or to bother us. And Your Son said to me: I can teach you and your people so that you shall never again fear to be bothered by the low or by the evil-minded; nor shall you fear that Gods or angels shall come and inhabit Zeredho!

20/12.21. Thus spoke Your Son, O Jehovih! And he has given us the secret. We no longer fear that others will encroach upon Zeredho. Behold, Zeredho is Your place, O Jehovih. These unfortunates, these drujas, are Your children. They shall go to Zeredho. I do not fear pollution now, nor do my hosts. We will wade into this filth, like scavengers into a filthy street, and we will make these children be like shining stars in Your firmament!

20/12.22. Yes, O Jehovih, nothing can make us afraid again! We have nothing; we have nothing to lose. We are Your servants, now and forever!

20/12.23. Then Fragapatti spoke, saying: Behold the size of my avalanza, O Hoab! If you will take its measurement, you shall find it is just the size and build to take you and your hosts and these drujas. Do not think this matter is mere coincidence, for I sent scouts beforehand, and had all these unfortunates enumerated, and your people enumerated also.

20/12.24. When Hoab perceived this great wisdom in Fragapatti, and comprehended the care that had been used to accomplish so much, he made no reply at first, but, looking at him, burst into tears. Presently, he said: By Your Power and Wisdom, O Jehovih, I will also lift my fellows up out of darkness and misery!

CHAPTER 13 Fragapatti

20/13.1. Then Fragapatti sent swift messengers to Mouru, relating all that had been accomplished, also giving the names of the generals and captains over the newly established colonies redeemed from Utza, in the Aoasuan mountains, so they could be registered in the libraries of Haraiti. And Fragapatti established a line of messengers between the colonies, and also from the colonies to Mouru, selecting and appointing the messengers, to hold office during dawn.

20/13.2. And when the affairs of this region of the lower heavens were completed and in working order, Fragapatti was ready to ascend with the mad and dumb drujas rescued from hell. Accordingly, the proper persons fell to[554] work and carried them into the avalanza; being obliged to blindfold them because of the light. Nor did the drujas cease wailing and crying with fear, pain and craziness. But because of the multitude of infants, Fragapatti had previously provided five hundred thousand women of fetal, so that the infants might be redeemed to everlasting life.

20/13.3. Fragapatti had aboard sixty thousand physicians, and they went to work, resuscitating and restoring to consciousness the unfortunates. And of the hosts of Hoab, every single one wanted

[554] energetically began

to help, and so, willingly worked as nurse and helper.

20/13.4. Now thirty thousand es'enaurs began the music, soft and gentle as a breath of wind, carrying the tones throughout the ship, sounding like an endless echo, calling and answering from all possible directions, a continuous and enrapturing change, as if near, and as if far away. So that the uninformed did not know where the music came from, nor how it was produced.

20/13.5. All these things were set to working order just as the great avalanza was ready to start. Then Fragapatti went into the ship, being almost the last one to enter. Already the light was gathering bright and dense about him, his head almost hid in the brilliancy of the halo. And then he called out:

20/13.6. Arise! Arise! In Jehovih's name, upward rise! And as he spoke, behold, the avalanza moved with his will, for all the hosts joined in the same expression, and presently the great fire-ship started upward; leaving the burning walls and signal centers flickering below, so that even hell overthrown shone with great grandeur.

20/13.7. Fragapatti spoke to Hoab, saying: When I took you and your hosts from Zeredho, I promised to take you to Mouru, the capital city of my kingdom, Haraiti. Now you desire me to go to Zeredho with these drujas. I ask you now, do you think that you can plan their salvation, and restore them to light?

20/13.8. To which Hoab replied, saying: I perceive that of myself I can do nothing but go downhill; or, at best, keep on a level road. As I now comprehend All Light, there is not one thing in the whole universe that can rise of itself; but, by the external pressure of other things, all tend downward, even man. To attain to be one with Jehovih is the beginning of the resurrection of the individual; but he who has attained power to resurrect others is strong indeed. There are many who spasmodically resurrect others, but, alas, how few can keep them resurrected! Not only must he have the Light of Jehovih within himself, but power to make others obtain the Light for themselves. Alas, I am weak!

20/13.9. Fragapatti said: Understand yourself, O Hoab. Do not be deceived, nor short in faith to accomplish; for in this lies the key to all Wisdom and Power. Yet do not allow yourself to go to the other extreme, saying, man of himself can accomplish nothing. To teach a child this, is to cut off its legs and arms. To teach it that it can accomplish, is to make it giant-like and effective.

20/13.10. Hoab said: I perceive your wisdom, O Chief. How, then, shall we find a line by which we can train this economy?[555] If we do not inspire them with faith to accomplish, they will accomplish nothing; if we teach them they are dependent on Jehovih for all things, that Jehovih does all things, that no man can change his own destiny, that he is moved as a machine, then we will make nonentities of our people. On the other hand, if we inspire them that they can accomplish, it will grow upon them, and, finally, they will believe that they do all, and Jehovih nothing. This was the mire my other kingdom ran into.

20/13.11. Then Fragapatti spoke, saying: You perceive that reason cannot solve the matter. Let us, then, suspend the subject, and I will take you to Mouru and her kingdoms, and there we may obtain facts more pertinent than opinion or reason.

CHAPTER 14 Fragapatti

20/14.1. The avalanza rose upward with its contrasting assemblage of the souls of Light, and the souls of darkness, the drujas. The holy es'enaurs were chanting anthems of praise and thanksgiving, while the drujas were engaged in ——— or cursing everything in heaven or earth, or in weeping and moaning, or in stupor, dull as if dead.

20/14.2. Fragapatti had previously sent swift messengers to Athrava and the Holy Council of Mouru, where the Light of Jehovih had descended, Whose voice came upon them, saying:

20/14.3. Lo, My hosts come in the avalanza; prepare to house them, using thirty million volunteers. Choose from among My ethereans and My atmosphereans, those who shall receive the hosts of the avalanza, the nine hundred million in darkness. Go, therefore, to the borders of the sea, Che-wan, near the crossroads, Tse-loo, where I have created the plains of Hoo'e'tse-gam, ample for their resurrection. And you shall provide houses, hospitals and nurseries, suitable for them to

[555] i.e., the wise balance between too much and too little; a fruitful policy

dwell in, so that you shall be ready, when the avalanza comes, to deliver them.

20/14.4. Athrava and the Holy Council had responded to this, and the swift messengers in turn had informed Fragapatti of the prepared place. Accordingly, the avalanza landed in Hoo'e'tse-gam, where the thirty million were waiting to receive them, having been disciplined by Ardi'atta, Goddess of Zhei, in etherea, first of the seven Ie'tas in Gom. And they had ten thousand trumpeters, besides four thousand two hundred other players.

20/14.5. Ardi'atta had provided the pastures in green and in red and brown, but the green she had laid near Che-wan, where the avalanza would land; so it was called, Hoo'e'tse-gam, signifying, green for the newborn. Consequently, the drujas were delivered from the avalanza on an open green plain, neither dark nor light, suited to the diseased in mind.

20/14.6. Fragapatti knew Ardi'atta, for her former kingdom in etherea lay in one of his own provinces, and it was easy for him to commune with her at a distance, and without messengers. So, even before the avalanza landed, he said to her:

20/14.7. I will cast the drujas on the green fields, and as fast as you and your hosts can resuscitate them to consciousness, they shall be selected and carried into the houses and nurseries you have provided for them.

20/14.8. The avalanza was thus discharged of the drujas, in Haraiti for the present, to receive treatment prior to being carried to Zeredho. And Ardi'atta and her hosts took charge of them, although more than four million of Hoab's hosts also remained, as volunteers with them to assist in the redemption.

20/14.9. Then Fragapatti directed the ship to be steered for Mouru, where it arrived in due season; and waiting to receive him were more than one billion souls, and they had provided musicians, one million players and singers, so that far and near it was like a sea of music.

20/14.10. When Hoab looked upon the beauty and magnificence of the scene, and especially the discipline, his soul was so filled with thanks to the Great Spirit that he scarcely could speak. And when he mastered himself a little, he said: O Chief, Fragapatti! How could one so exalted as you are, come to me in Zeredho! Every hour I am rebuked by myself because of my former vanity.

20/14.11. Fragapatti said: To learn not to speak of one's self, nor to think of one's self, whether praised or rebuked, is this not the right road to Jehovih? Hoab said: It is true. Therefore, the opposite, is going on the wrong road.

CHAPTER 15 Fragapatti

20/15.1. When the avalanza was made fast, and the hosts came forth, many of the Zeredho'ans, fearing the brilliancy of the lights of Mouru, were permitted to go and dwell a little way off; but the others, led by Fragapatti and Hoab, entered the capital city, and came before the throne of Jehovih, greeted by Athrava and the Holy Council.

20/15.2. Athrava said: In the name of Jehovih, O Chief, greeting: And to you, O Hoab. Come, and honor the throne of Mouru.

20/15.3. Fragapatti said: Greeting to you, Athrava; and to you, most Holy Council, in the name of our Father! Hoab said: Greeting, in Jehovih's name!

20/15.4. And then Fragapatti and Hoab went forward and ascended the throne, and sat at the left hand of Athrava. At once the Light from the etherean worlds began to fall upon the throne, and even upon the whole Council, and the light was brilliant and golden yellow, the most sacred color. Hoab had never seen such light before, and was overwhelmed with fear and delight; but many of his hosts were obliged to hide their faces.

20/15.5. Presently, while three billion looked on, the light condensed over the throne, till like a very sun it stood above Fragapatti's head. And then the Voice of the Almighty, Jehovih, came out of the midst of the light. Jehovih said:

20/15.6. Hear the words of your Creator, O man! I, Who created the corporeal and the es'ean worlds! Behold the works of My hands! Who can find a place where I have not created!

20/15.7. Do not think that I cannot also create a voice and words. For is this not easier than to create a man who shall create words? Behold My corporeal suns amid My corporeal star-worlds! Behold My etherean suns amid My es'ean worlds.

20/15.8. I made corporeal darkness, and I made corporeal light. I made spiritual darkness, and I made spiritual light. But I am the Light of light. I am the Word of words.

20/15.9. As the wisdom of man invents words, so does the light of My Light come in words to those who can bear My Light.

20/15.10. Behold My wisdom, O man, in creating souls out of the substance of corporeal darkness! Their souls can thus hear Me and not be afraid. But to those who become pure souls, I come openly. Their throne becomes My throne! Their voice becomes My voice. Their hosts look upon My throne, and My Light shines before My people.

20/15.11. Hear, then, your Creator, O Zeredho. Your people called to Me in their darkness, but I did not come. Your hand was upon them. You had said to them: Behold my wide countries; my mountains and valleys; my bright rivers and refreshing winds. Come, they are yours to keep forever!

20/15.12. And because your hand was upon them, they were beset with darkness; they could not find their way out; nor did they perceive anymore the glory of My kingdoms. Yes, you were like a wanton[556] going after My chosen, and your voice lured them away from Me!

20/15.13. But I spoke in Nirvania, high above, in My thrones of light. And My Sons and Daughters heard My voice. I said to them: Lo, the red star and her heavens are fallen in darkness! Go to them and deliver them into a new resurrection. ||

20/15.14. Had I not spoken in the ancient days, saying: If you raise up those who are beneath you, so will I send those who are above down to you, to raise you up also.

20/15.15. But they forgot My words; nor did they strive any more to raise up those who were in the hells below. And I said to My Nirvanians: Go to Zeredho, for she has enticed My holy ones away from Me. And you shall give them a parable of compensation openly, and they shall come before My Light and hear My Voice. For you shall take them to hell and cause them to deliver the drujas, through the light of My countenance; and afterward you shall bring them to Mouru, so that I may speak with them face to face.

20/15.16. Hear the commandments of your Creator, O you Sons and Daughters of Zeredho, for that which I give you shall be inviolate. Which is, that you shall have dominion over the earth and her heavens for two hundred years, commencing at the close of this dawn of dan.

20/15.17. And you, O Hoab, shall be God over all the rest, and you shall be anointed with power to raise up successors with power and wisdom. Be wise, O My children, and profit in the wisdom of My etherean hosts while yet the dawn of dan remains.

20/15.18. The Voice ceased. Then Athrava spoke, saying: In Your name, O Jehovih, I now suspend myself from Your throne, till it is the will of Fragapatti and Your will also, that I resume it. And he rose up and stood aside. Then Fragapatti went and sat in the middle of the throne.

20/15.19. Fragapatti said: I proclaim three days' recreation to the Holy Council, and to the city of Mouru. Behold, my people shall mingle together as brothers and sisters, rejoicing in the Light of the Father. Be joyful, singing and dancing. The ascent to Jehovih's kingdoms may be compared to a ladder with steps, and not a level plain, and you shall call this the first step in the resurrection of the earth's heavens in this dawn.

20/15.20. The hosts then mingled together, greeting and rejoicing, for the Zeredho'ans had long desired to see the ethereans now dwelling in Mouru; and the ethereans were equally desirous of seeing the atmosphereans. Consequently, there was great rejoicing and merriment.

CHAPTER 16 Fragapatti

20/16.1. When the time of recreation ended, Fragapatti ascended the throne of Jehovih, and signaled to the marshals to proclaim order and labor; and the vast multitude took their places at once; and in the same instant, the es'enaurs played music, with anthems, which, when finished, was the signal for heavenly business. Fragapatti said:

20/16.2. Again I am about to depart, and again I shall leave the God of Mouru, Athrava, with you. But Hoab, and those of his hosts as I may choose, shall go with me. For, according to the rank and glory of Gods, I must now deliver Hapacha and his kingdom of Ipseogee, raised up from Guatama.

20/16.3. So Fragapatti descended to the foot of the throne and sat down; and Athrava, God of dawn of Mouru, came down and took him by the hand, in ancient manner, and said: Behold, you have

556 one who seduces

honored my throne, and the time of your departure is upon you. Arise, then, O God, and go your way.

20/16.4. And Fragapatti rose up and stood aside, and signaled for Hoab to go and be raised in the same manner; which he did, becoming wise in the behavior of Gods toward one another.

20/16.5. The marshals had lined up fifty thousand attendants, as well as ten thousand es'enaurs, and, at a signal from Fragapatti, marched forth out of the capital, followed by the hosts of Hoab and one hundred thousand ethereans.

20/16.6. And once they were beyond the lights of Mouru, behold, some of the hosts of Hoab rejoiced, because they were more pleased to be where there was less light. Yet there were seven hundred million of them who did not rejoice, but rather loved the light more.

20/16.7. Then Fragapatti said: It is well that not all are of one mind. The seven hundred million, who love the light more, shall be my traveling companions to Ipseogee. Because they are strong in light, I have work for them. But the others shall be taken back to Zeredho, where I will also come in due time.

20/16.8. And after they are settled in Zeredho, behold, I will send a God to them, and they shall found a new kingdom, in Jehovih's name. Let all hands, therefore, enter the avalanza, following me.

20/16.9. At once the hosts entered the ship, and Fragapatti gave the word to be off, and they sped forth directly for Zeredho, led by swift messengers who well knew the nearest route and the lightest places. And the route taken was through the sea of Foo'witchah and the Oram of Haiti.

20/16.10. Hardly had they gotten under way, when the light of the upper heavens began to descend on Hoab, whose excitement, from the wondrous scenes, made him propitious to the change; and feeling the buoyancy of the light, he thus spoke, saying:

20/16.11. How could I forget You, O Jehovih? Or in observing your purposes, deny Your designs? How did I not see that at my quickening in my mother's womb, I was the farthest from You? And yet, even then, Your breath was upon me!

20/16.12. And when You had fashioned me and bade me walk upright, You sent Your angels to me, saying: Behold, Your Creator lives. You are life of His Life; flesh of His Flesh He created you. And He gave you yourself in proof of Himself.

20/16.13. I was conceived in the earth; housed up in darkness; of Yourself built up; nor of myself was I anything under the sun.

20/16.14. And You created the honeybee, and bade him speak to me for my own benefit. He said: Behold me, O man! I am a worker. In a community I live with my brothers and sisters. I shut my eyes to things sour and bitter, and I store my house with sweet provender only. Soul of man, hear me! I am the voice of your Creator. Behold the harmony of my house, and the provision I make for my newborn!

20/16.15. And You created the ant, and bade him speak to me for my own benefit. He said: Behold me, O man! I am a worker. In a community I live with my brothers and sisters. Soul of man, hear me. I am the voice of your Creator. Behold the industry of my house, and the burdens we bear jointly into our stores.

20/16.16. And You created the spider, and bade him speak to me. He said: Behold me, O man! I am one with your Creator. I move by the spirit of things; I build my house by the geometrical figures of the unseen worlds. Do not think that I reason or take lessons from other spiders; I take no lessons; I move by the spirit within me, and it moves in concert with the spirit of things outside. Hear me, spirit of man! There are two ways to knowledge before you; one is by the soul of things, and one by reason. ||

20/16.17. And You continually held up before my eyes that the unseen ruled over the seen. Then I became vain before You, O Jehovih! I said: When I am dead, and born a spirit, then I will see the unseen, and cannot err anymore.

20/16.18. But lo, my folly in Your sight! When I was risen in spirit, I saw the spirit of things; but, alas, the soul lay still beyond. And to me the soul was now the unseen cause, and ruler over the spirit.

20/16.19. Again Your holy ones came from the etherean worlds, speaking to me, saying: And yet beyond the soul comes Nirvania.

20/16.20. Now I have seen Your crystal spheres, and Your matchless glories. Yes, I look into this sea of Foo'witchah, where I had often gazed before, seeing nothing then; but now, seeing ships laden with Gods and Goddesses from Your Nirvanian fields, moving in higher works and worlds.

20/16.21. And Your Fire stirs me to the soul, to expand to the mastery of these atmospherean heavens. O if I could express the hallowed glory You have bestowed upon me! O if only I could thank You for the happiness I have because You created me!

20/16.22. O that I could open up the souls of men to behold Your wondrous works, and the majesty of becoming one with You, You Almighty, Jehovih! O if they would hear me and believe! O if only they would not turn away from Light! O that they could learn to glorify You every day, for the little Light and little joy they receive! How like Gods and Goddesses they would become in Your kingdoms.

20/16.23. But they harbor discontent; they discourse on the little they have received from You. Like the cankerworm, that grows to devour, they feed their sorrows by recounting them over and over. For pain they cry out; and for disappointment they weep. Yes, they feed their own darkness with darkness, and in the end forget You, You All Light!

20/16.24. Hoab ceased, but gazed at the coursing ships in the atmospherean heavens; in a little while Fragapatti said:

20/16.25. Behold Your wisdom, O Jehovih! Those whom You would make strong, You have made to feel adversity's sting. For the emergencies that lie ahead, You plan Your Gods to run near the cliff's edge where millions perish.

20/16.26. Who can attain to know Your wisdom, O Jehovih! Who can comprehend the trillions of Your Sons and Daughters! And yet You know every one, and carry them by a breath, so gently they do not feel You, or know You. To a very hair's breadth You take them; and in the time of desperation, Your hand comes to the rescue of the righteous.

20/16.27. Man says: Now I will fortify myself with riches and houses, and all manner of possessions; adversity shall not come upon me; I have more faith in my possessions than in Jehovih. Mine is a kingdom I can see; but Jehovih is far off. ||

20/16.28. But You are suffering him, in his vanity, to go away from You for a season. Sooner or later You bring him in with a short turn; either on earth or in heaven. And he goes down as an example to hundreds and thousands that envied him.

20/16.29. You have set up the poor man in faith; he toils day and night; he is weary and sore; he cries out with hunger; his rags are a shame to him; but he remembers You, O Jehovih! In Your praise he sings a song in his soul every day. To do good to others is his great delight.

20/16.30. And afterward Your hand reaches down to him; his soul is like a giant. You have planned him for a very God in heaven!

20/16.31. The spark of faith that was in him, he nurtured, and it became like a mighty tree that did not fall before the blast. The good he received he exalted, and it fructified and grew as a harvest in rich soil; and he stood mighty in all places.

20/16.32. His songs are in Your praise, and they endure forever; his psalms are the voice of Your loves; and the multitude of Your people remember him, while all else are cut down and destroyed. Your work has a sure foundation; Your Wisdom stands before man's wisdom; not one has found a failure in Your word, as it speaks to his own soul.

20/16.33. Your labor is from the subtle and unseen; Your footstool the cause of causes. But the vain man looks to Your object; he turns Your ways upside down; he makes the cart push the horse. And You suffer him to drink to the full of his own vanity; and when he runs himself into torments, You find a way to reach him and bring him home to You.

20/16.34. Great is his glory when he finds You; his voice becomes the love of Your loves forever! For You had shaped him as an example, and given him scope to run to his extreme, for his own glory. Yes, You had planned him to be one of Your great workers, who would not go down afterward.

CHAPTER 17 Fragapatti

20/17.1. On the way to Zeredho, Fragapatti and his hosts in the avalanza were joined by a ship of a billion explorers from the north regions, a thousand times farther than the north star, of the seventh magnitude of light, even three higher than Fragapatti. Ctu, the Chief in command of the expedition, greeted in the sign, Jehovih's Name, which Fragapatti answered; and by certain signals the ships approached and made fast, with the es'enaurs of both singing and playing the same anthem, being five million voices, and half as many trumpeters.

20/17.2. Then Ctu came near Fragapatti, saluting, and the hosts stood in line, so they could hear what was said. So, after due ceremonies, and acquainting each other as to who they were, where they came from, and so forth, then Ctu spoke, saying: I see you have your ship ballasted with a north magnet?

20/17.3. Fragapatti said: This is only a five years' dawn, and I teach my hosts how to ballast so they may better read the maps, roadways, stars and suns. Of these, my hosts, five hundred million have become capable of being delivered into etherea, except in cosmogony. I am providing for them, so that when they ascend, they may not be lost in the etherean worlds, nor be dependent on others.

20/17.4. Ctu said: What is the length of this serpent? Fragapatti said: Seven and one-eighth Hoitumu. And he asked Ctu what distance he had come from his home; and Ctu said: One million four hundred and twelve thousand eight hundred and thirty and two Hoitumu!

20/17.5. How long is your journey yet before you? Ctu said: Five hundred thousand years! Then Fragapatti inquired as to how many star-worlds (planets) Ctu had so far passed on his journey, and Ctu said: We have passed twenty thousand star-worlds, some smaller than this red star, and some ten thousand times larger; some of them yet liquid balls of fire, some newly crusted over, some with atmosphere, water, earth, and minerals not yet separated, but boiling, seething, whirling; some firm and just entering the age of se'mu; and some old and worn out. And we passed one that had become barren as to living creatures; and the God, through whose pastures it passed, dissolved and dissipated it before us, having invited billions of guests to witness the scene.

20/17.6. Of atmospherean worlds, we have passed more than ninety thousand; some of them larger than the vortex of this red star, and capable of providing homes to trillions of inhabitants; and yet, on many of them, there were no people.

20/17.7. Thus they discoursed on the size and wonder of Jehovih's kingdoms; but their numbers and descriptions only the Gods themselves could comprehend, they were so vast; and, when they had nearly concluded, Ctu, himself an Eon,[557] remarked:

20/17.8. The mortal desires to become a spirit; then his ambition is to become an etherean; next, an Orian; next, a Nirvanian; next, an Oe'tan,[558] and then to travel (as Eons) in the surveys of magnitudes. But those ahead still call to us to hasten, because the glories ahead are still more surpassing in magnificence! Who, then, can approach the Unapproachable, All Highest! He Who fashioned the plan of all creations! Who is there that is not swallowed up with devotion and awe of Him Who is Ever Present, that extends beyond all limit, our Father, Jehovih!

CHAPTER 18 Fragapatti

20/18.1. When they drew near Zeredho, Ctu, with his ship and hosts, withdrew, duly saluting, and they sped on their journey. But Fragapatti halted on the borders of Zeredho and landed seven hundred million of his hosts, the others remaining aboard.

20/18.2. Again the avalanza put forth. Fragapatti said: Now I will visit Yaton'te, Lord God of North Guatama, and see what he has accomplished, and perhaps he will accompany us to Ipseogee, to see Hapacha, my well-loved God of the West Wind.

20/18.3. Now, when they came to the sea of Ctevahwitich,[559] they raised the avalanza fifty thousand miles for the benefit of Hoab and his hosts, for the roadway of Tems lies here, where pass countless numbers of fleets filled with students learning about the dismembered warks belonging to the earth.

20/18.4. Here the students learn the processes of condensation and dissolution of meteoric stones and small planets, of such diameter that a mortal

---

[557] travelers (in the surveys of magnitudes) who notify the Oe'tans of the available places for new worlds, and the time for dissipating old ones. – 1891 glossary

[558] an angel who had attained to wisdom and power to make worlds. –1891 glossary

[559] This sea in the spirit world is over and above the Atlantic and Pacific oceans; or, in other words, outward from the earth's center, in atmospherea. – Ed.

could walk around one of them in a day. On the outer extreme of this sea, the nebulae is in constant waves, where the vortices play, condensing and bursting, like whirlwinds on the earth or corporeal ocean.

20/18.5. Here Fragapatti explained, saying: In this you shall behold the wisdom of Jehovih, and the uniformity of His works. Here lies the first belt away from the earth capable of having nebulae condensed into meteoric stones. All nebulae lying nearer than this to the earth's surface is either attracted to the earth or repulsed from it. Therefore, calculate the distance of this belt from the earth, together with its density, and you shall find that it is the same distance as wark belts belonging to the stars in the firmament of similar size, density and velocity as the earth. The first wark belt of the sun is, therefore, the place of its nearest planet; the second wark belt is the place of its next nearest planet, and so on; and these wark belts are all graded in distances according to what I previously stated.

20/18.6. Jehovih has said: I have created two ways for My mathematicians to prove My works; one is to measure that which is near at hand, in order to determine that which is far off; the other is to observe that which is far off, in order to determine that which is near. For, since man could not measure the wark belts of this world, I provided him with the means to determine the wark belts of the sun, so that he might better comprehend his own world.

20/18.7. So that man might find still further evidence of the earth's wark belts, I created the nearest one with different densities, so that not every year on earth would be alike as to heat and cold. And in certain cycles of dan I condense the first wark belts so that to mortals the sun seems as if in eclipse. For it is through this belt that My cycles of dan'ha give either light or darkness to mortals spiritually.

20/18.8. Let man compute My times for his own benefit; I created the first wark to gain in rotation faster than the earth, one year for every eleven. So that when the wark has made twelve of its own years, the earth shall have completed eleven years. ||

20/18.9. Fragapatti caused the avalanza to be driven into a forest of whirlwinds, so that the hosts could observe, as he illustrated and explained, saying: You shall perceive now, that those stones that are condensed beneath the apex fall to the earth, while those ascending frequently rise toward the lighter plateau and explode, to be attracted back within the wark belt. This belt compares to the cloud belt near the earth. There the wind currents make raindrops and snowflakes; here the currents make the first nebulous formations that come under the name corpor.

20/18.10. While Fragapatti was thus discoursing, the avalanza rocked to and fro, and many of the people perceived now, more than ever, the knowledge and power required by angels and Gods, to contend successfully with the elements. But the beauty and grandeur of these fountains, these fire-spouts, and whirlwinds on fire, together with the roar and whistling of the flying stones, so enraptured Hoab and his hosts, they could do nothing but look and wonder at the glory of it.

20/18.11. For seven days and seven nights Fragapatti and his hosts traveled in this wark belt, observing and studying these miniature worlds, creating (condensing) and dissipating; and on the eighth day the avalanza was lowered beneath the currents, and they sailed directly for the kingdom of Yaton'te, Lord God of North Guatama, piloted by messengers well acquainted with the course. But not being in a much frequented roadway, they encountered few ships or processions of other Gods.

20/18.12. Yaton'te had been apprised of Fragapatti's coming, and had accordingly notified his kingdom, and summoned seventy of his Lords to his capital, which was named after himself. So Yaton'te commanded his otevan to be put in order and illumed, and having provided five hundred es'enaurs in addition to his crew, together with his Lords and ten thousand attendants, he went forth a thousand miles to the borders of Hagak, to meet Fragapatti.

20/18.13. But, lo and behold, when compared to the avalanza, the otevan was only as a small boat is to a large ship. Accordingly, when they approached each other, Fragapatti caused the front of the avalanza to be opened, and the otevan entered within the walls and was made fast. And the hosts of the otevan came out and were received with great joy by Fragapatti and his people.

CHAPTER 19 Fragapatti

20/19.1. A thousand miles north of the northern line of the sun on the earth, in the middle between the east and west front of North Guatama,[560] and from the earth upward, and without intervening space, five hundred miles, Yaton'te had founded his kingdom, and it was here that Fragapatti came to see him. Five hundred miles westward lay Ipseogee, extending north and south two thousand miles, where reigned the good Faithist, Hapacha, styled[561] God of the West Wind.

20/19.2. After the avalanza reached Yaton'te's capital, and the hosts duly landed in the lower heaven, Yaton'te ascended his throne, and after due ceremonies of welcome and thanksgiving, and with music rendering praise to the All High, Yaton'te proclaimed recreation for three days and three nights.

20/19.3. Then Fragapatti spoke to him, saying: I am glad to have this recreation time, for I desire to hear the story of your adventures, and of your success in this kingdom, for your record must also be my record, to be taken with us, at the end of this dawn, to heaven above. Hoab and his hosts shall also hear your words.

20/19.4. Yaton'te replied: What I have done, I have done. Nevertheless, he who has built great kingdoms may find little to admire in a small one.

20/19.5. Fragapatti said: I have seen old men who doted more on a grandchild than on a large family they had bred themselves. And is it not a wise provision of our Creator that He bestowed us with such means as enables us at all times to live over again our past history in the young? Every hour we find a new way open to remind us of our follies in youth; and also a new channel in which to witness Jehovih's wisdom.

20/19.6. Yaton'te said: If a man converts his neighbor from evil into good, two great things are accomplished, the triumph of the man and the reformation of the neighbor. If, on the other hand, a man fails to convert his neighbor from evil to good, two misfortunes have transpired, which are, the disappointment of one and the loss of glory to Jehovih. It is a strong man who can recount his own failures and say he glorifies the Father because of them.

20/19.7. Fragapatti said: How shall we measure magnitudes,[562] O Yaton'te? Does a mortal, who has delivered one druk into light, not have as great a glory as a God who delivers hundreds of thousands? Is the one not as great in magnitude as the other? According to our worthiness in righteous persistence, no matter what our limit is, is this not the greatest glory? Jehovih granted to man to first learn to deliver himself, to master himself, to rule himself in the All Highest. He who can do this is a great ruler. And in the next time, Jehovih entrusts him with a small kingdom, perhaps a drunkard, or a wanton,[563] or even over his own family, to rule over to righteousness. He who does this is a great ruler. Is not, then, man's persistence in righteousness the whole glory of his kingdom?

20/19.8. Yaton'te said: The Father knows! To try, and to try, and to try; this is the sum of the good a man does. And yet what man is there in heaven or on earth who cannot find an apology for falling short in the good work he accomplishes? Does the poor man not say: O, if I had this, what great good I would accomplish? And the rich man makes the same speech, and the king also. And yet Jehovih has given a kingdom to each and every one of them. But he who can say: I have done all I could, according to my strength and wisdom, rates among the highest of men and Gods.

20/19.9. Hear me, then, O Fragapatti, so you may best understand; imagine yourself to be absent from all light of high heaven, and to be in a place of darkness, where three billion spirits are vagrants, scattered far and wide on the corporeal earth. Such was Aoasu in this kingdom; but the spirits did not congregate together in hells, as they did in the east, for they had no association; no Gods, no Lords. They were perpetual migrants, except those who dwelt with the druks as familiars.

20/19.10. And as to the spirits of those who died in infancy, they were taken by the spirits of their fathers and mothers, or others, and cared for until they also gained sufficient knowledge to serve

[560] i.e., one thousand miles north of the Tropic of Cancer, and halfway between the East and West Coasts of North America

[561] called, named

[562] scale, importance, greatness

[563] one who is more or less undisciplined, unrestrained, unchaste or libidinous; a seducer

them as vagrants; and this was the end of their aspiration.

20/19.11. And strange to say, all these spirits were without clothes or drapery of any kind, and devoid[564] of shame; neither were they good or evil, nor did they have any desire for, or knowledge of, a higher heaven, being content to rove about, to sleep, and to eat. And they had a thousand languages; or, at least, a thousand different kinds of signs and utterances, which they had acquired on earth, but lost and mixed up so that neither Lords nor Gods could converse with them.

20/19.12. Thus I surveyed them and found them before I built this capital, for which reason I located it centrally among them. Know also, O Chief, that I traveled among them with music and with fire, and gaudy apparel, in the hope of gaining their aspiration; but, alas, they neither smiled nor frowned at my fine shows, but vacantly gazed at us, or even fell asleep while our otevan was paraded before them!

20/19.13. Then I came here and built this capital, and founded Jehovih's throne, on which you now honor me. And then I sent to them, here and there, presents of gaudy attire, in the hope of inspiring the multitude through the few; but, alas, those I attired soon removed their clothes, preferring nakedness. Thus ended my second failure.

20/19.14. After this, I sent a hundred thousand preachers to them, to portray the greater glory of a higher heaven. But, alas, they did not listen, or, if paying attention, in a day would forget all that had been told to them. And thus ended the third failure.

20/19.15. Then we held a holy council, imploring Jehovih for light and power; and His voice came upon me, saying: Go to their loves, My Son; go to mortals. Begin with es'yans.

20/19.16. Then I commanded my hosts to go and live for a season among mortals; and they brought the es'yans to Yaton'te, under guard of the asaphs. And the next of kin followed, desiring to remain. And I said to them: Behold, my place is fair, and my people are clothed. Unless you are clothed also, you cannot dwell with us, nor shall you look any more upon your next of kin, whom I have taken for myself.

20/19.17. And for love there came many mothers and fathers, and brothers and sisters, belonging to the recent dead; and they suffered themselves to be clothed; and these were the first in my kingdom.

20/19.18. Again I called my hosts together, and I said to them: A thousand Lords I must have. I will divide North Guatama among my Lords, and they shall dwell with mortals, having enough ashars to give one to each and every mortal, man, woman and child. And whether by natural death or by war, it does not matter, the es'yans shall be brought to my kingdom.

20/19.19. This I accomplished, providing nurseries and places of entertainment for those who were brought here. But, alas, the tens of thousands of spirits, who, because of their kin, came, and accepted clothing for sake of remaining, had little talent to talk, or even desire for anything.

20/19.20. At the next holy council the Light came to me, saying: Hear the voice of your Creator, O My Son; because you have been diligent in striving for the resurrection of My children, I have come to you. Behold, I created man naked, and with shame, as the foundation of industry. But because this people followed, in the Osirian age, the abandonment of spirit communion, while they were yet mortal, they lost the light of My countenance.

20/19.21. Neither can you inspire them to industry, except through clothing the body; but, first of all, you shall make them ashamed of nakedness; otherwise, there is no higher resurrection for them.

20/19.22. Then I inquired of the Creator as to how I should teach them shame. He said: Of themselves, to themselves, for themselves, you can do little. But you shall inspire them through mortals.

20/19.23. Every plateau shall be a thousand miles in breadth every way,[565] except the lowest, which shall be two thousand miles; with a rise of one degree to the next, so that the plateaus shall

[564] completely lacking; destitute, void

[565] What is the geometric shape of this plateau? Does it follow the land border contours? Most likely, the 2000 miles breadth would stretch from the Rocky Mountains eastward, to the coast of North America.

extend from the earth up to your kingdom, like a stairway, one plateau higher than another.

20/19.24. And for both the lowest and second lowest plateaus, your Lords shall provide subjective entertainments, subjective teaching and subjective things in general. Nor shall there be anything real on these two plateaus, except the inhabitants and their food, and the mirrors, lenses, and machinery for producing subjectives.[566]

20/19.25. And the lowest plateau, being on the earth, shall be provided as a mirage, having everything spiritual in appearance, as they are corporeally on the earth. And it shall be provided with forests, lakes and rivers, and with all types of animals, birds and fish, and with whatever is suitable food for mortals.[567] And the lowest plateau shall be called Hochedowa, signifying, happy hunting ground.[568]

20/19.26. And you shall send word to your Lords, saying: Thus says your Creator: Behold, I have created a good place, and called it Hochedowa. Teach this to mortals, by inspiration and otherwise, saying also to them: Go tell one another, for, after death, the soul shall go there in great delight. And you shall say to them: Unless you wear garments to hide your nakedness, you shall not enter Hochedowa.

20/19.27. Yaton'te said: When the lowest plateau was made habitable, covering a large portion of North Guatama, the Voice came again, saying: Through your Lords, My Son, you shall possess all mortals, every man, woman and child, allowing not one of the drujas to come near them.

20/19.28. And because of the construction of your plateau, behold, I will send in many places upon the land, great droughts, and these wandering spirits shall not find sustenance, except through you and your Lords. And as fast as they come, you shall oblige them to be clothed, or draped about the loins; but you shall show preference to all those who wear ornaments.

20/19.29. Yaton'te said: This much we have accomplished, O Fragapatti: The foundation of my heavenly kingdom is broad and sure, but as yet I have few subjects to show you.

20/19.30. Fragapatti said: Behold, I will take two days of rest, and then I will inspect your places. Proclaim, therefore, recreation for two days.

CHAPTER 20 Fragapatti

20/20.1. When the recreation was ended, Yaton'te called his council together and he sat on the throne, and Fragapatti and Hoab sat at his left hand, on the throne also.

20/20.2. The Voice of Jehovih came to Yaton'te, saying: Behold, O My Sons and Daughters, this heaven and this land shall not be like any other place; for here shall rise in time after, those who shall begin the founding of My kingdom among mortals. For in the lands of the East, and the heavens of the East, I have given them Lords and Gods before whom they fall down and worship. But in this heaven, and this land beneath it, there shall not be given any Lord, or God, or any person born of woman for their resurrection.

20/20.3. To this end I have created this subjective heaven and her plateaus, and they shall endure till the dawn of kosmon, and the overthrow of war and mortal kingdoms. From this throne I will come in that day, through My Chiefs, and reveal the histories of My kingdoms. And I will radiate outward, around about from this heaven, until My kingdoms encircle the whole earth, and until the earth's heavens are Mine also.

20/20.4. And whether the I'huans are mortals or spirits, you shall not teach them to worship anyone, except the Great Spirit.

20/20.5. For a question will rise among mortals in the beginning of kosmon, as to whether mortals are ruled by the angels of heaven. And I will prove it before them that in this land, all Gods, Lords and Saviors shall be cast out, and mortals shall become worshippers of the Great Spirit, being ruled to that end by the inspiration that shall descend from this heaven, through the spirits of the I'huan race. And

---

[566] These days, circa 150 ak, we may think of this type of production as similar to creating virtual realities, using such things as projected realities (environments, images, holograms, tangible and otherwise, etc), production equipment, and the like. Mortals experiencing films, television, internet, holograms, music recordings, etc., are all corporeal examples of subjective encounters.

[567] Meaning the sort of food that these spirits had been used to eating when they were mortals; plus plenty of spiritually healthy foods.

[568] The happy hunting ground has been known in Guatama even to the coming of kosmon.

they shall know that I, Jehovih, alone rule over all, and within all My works.

20/20.6. Be wise, My Sons and Daughters, for as you now find little aspiration among the hosts of wandering spirits, so the same lack of aspiration will be manifested among mortals in the beginning of kosmon. The Voice ceased.

20/20.7. Yaton'te called Et'seing, his assistant God, saying: Come and sit on the throne. I will now go for forty days with Fragapatti and show him all my works. Then I will go with him to Hapacha, God of Ipseogee, after which I will return here.

20/20.8. Et'seing, having been anointed and crowned previously, came and sat on the throne, duly saluting. Then Fragapatti rose up to speak, perceiving that the great multitude desired to hear him. He said:

20/20.9. In what they have done I am well pleased, O Jehovih. Through Your voice I selected them, and being Your servants, they deserve neither praise nor censure. You have wisely chosen them, for in this dawn I perceive the foundation of that which will reach mortals in the third dan'ha[569] that comes after. And because You have chosen this place, O Father, great is the responsibility of these, Your Lords, and Your Lord God.

20/20.10. Because they have supplicated You, You have guided them, and they cannot err. Because their work has been slow, they have great honor in patience and persistence. May Your Wisdom, Power and Love continue with them, for Your glory, now and forever. Amen! Fragapatti ceased, but the light became brilliant above his head; and the Voice came out of the Light, saying:

20/20.11. They shall concern themselves more in a righteous foundation of My kingdom, than in a multitude of conversions and resurrections. For the standard of their Lords and Gods, and their successors, is of more value than tens of thousands of redeemed who are of little wisdom and strength. For these latter will be raised up afterward.

20/20.12. The Voice ceased, and Fragapatti came down from the throne, followed by Yaton'te and Hoab. The es'enaurs chanted: ALL HAIL, GREAT JEHOVIH'S POWER! HIS LIGHT THE IMMORTAL VOICE! And when the Gods advanced to Ctius,[570] they halted, standing abreast, and then filed in front of the throne, saluting in the SIGN OF OM, and were answered by Et'seing. Lastly came the marshals of the traveling hosts; and when they had passed, the Gods followed them, thus passing out of the capital to the place of the ships of fire, followed by the inhabitants of Yaton'te.

20/20.13. There they entered the avalanza, amid music and cheering, and then departed, first to survey the kingdom of Yaton'te, and then to go to Ipseogee.

[569] This would be the present dan'ha cycle and which launched the Kosmon era.

[570] The etherean Ctius was probably chief marshal of the throne. He was stationed in front of the throne.

CHAPTER 21 Fragapatti

20/21.1. After Fragapatti had examined the places of the asaphs and of the physicians, and other such places that belong in the lower heavens, he descended to Hochedowa, the land of delusion (illusion) for teaching by subjective illustrations; the happy hunting ground. He was to witness the games and tournaments, which were, so far, maintained by a great expenditure of labor on the part of the ethereans. Jehovih said:

20/21.2. As mortal children can be taught by objective illustration, so have I created My es worlds capable of a similar process subjectively. My rules are not man's rules; nor are My worlds illustrated as man illustrates. Witness My rainbow, which is a subjective illustration to mortals of a bow without the substance of a bow. But man bends a stick, and says: Behold, a bow! And he holds it in his hand; but Mine he cannot touch.

20/21.3. I gave to mortals to teach their sons and daughters many combinations by the use of objects; thus they would know a circle, a square, a triangle, or learn to compute numbers by the use of objects. In the same way, but inversely, I created subjective means for the spirits of the dead, so that they could be taught and amused with My works.

20/21.4. To corporeans I give corporeal eyes and corporeal ears, so that they may attain to wisdom on the earth; but to a few I give su'is, so they may see and hear things spiritually.

20/21.5. To the spirits of mortals who die in infancy, I give spiritual eyes and spiritual ears; but without cultivation they do not hear corporeal things, nor see corporeal things. But to those spirits who have fulfilled an earth-life, I created them to see and hear after death, the matters of both worlds.

20/21.6. Nevertheless, there are many spirits in heaven who have not fulfilled either a spiritual or a corporeal life, and they can only see and hear a little; for which reason I commanded that they should be called drujas, signifying, spirits of darkness.

20/21.7. And I sent My Gods and My Lords, saying to them: Go to the spirits of darkness, for they neither see nor hear heaven or earth, and are wandering about indifferent even to their own nakedness.

20/21.8. And you shall create mirrors and lenses, and optical illusions and delusions, and provide games and entertainments for them, so that their understanding may be opened up for the glory of My kingdoms.

20/21.9. When the avalanza arrived at Hochedowa, it was lowered and made as a floating observatory, in order to witness what was going on; and yet it was so provided, that it could be moved about from place to place.

20/21.10. And they witnessed the heavenly tournaments and games; the boating, fishing, hunting, and all other entertainments representative of what these angels had been engaged at in mortal life; and yet these things were only subjective, and not real.

20/21.11. But it came to pass that many drujas were restored to their memory of earth-life; restored to seeing and hearing, and, in fact, came to know they had entered another world; all of which illustrated to their dull senses that it was possible for them to learn to see things, and to hear things, understandingly.

20/21.12. Nevertheless, within these regions there were hundreds of millions of angels so stupid as to be void of form and expression.

20/21.13. Jehovih had said: When a man has fainted, you shall arouse him by calling his memory to things past. And when the druj in heaven has seen who he is, and his place also, you shall show him symbols of things past, and thus awaken him.

20/21.14. Jehovih had said: Behold, O man, you are the chief glory of My creations. Neither did I create any animal that walks on land, or flies in the air, or swims in the water, or crawls on its belly, with desire for spiritual life, nor with capacity to accumulate spiritually. But I have given only to you, O man, power to aggregate the spiritual entity.

20/21.15. For I bestowed My animals to be like a vessel that is full of water; no more can be put into them; and also when the vessel is destroyed, the water runs back to the ocean. I quickened them into life by My Own hand; but when I take away My hand, lo, they go back into dissolution. As a drop of water that has no power before the sun, but evaporates and is seen no more, so is the spirit of all the animals I created before the light of My countenance. But to you, O man, I gave power for everlasting life.

20/21.16. Nevertheless, as a man may take a drop of water and put it in a vial, and keep it for a long time, so have I given to My exalted angels, power to take the spirit of a fish or animal,[571] suddenly dead, and re-clothe it for a season with the semblance of a body;[572] but yet it is only a subjective existence. And, even as a man lets a stone fall out of his hand, and it drops to the ground, so, when My angels release their hold on My spiritual animals, their spirits fall into the sea of My body, and are seen no more. Even so, but in less degree, I also created the trees, the grass, the moss, and all vegetable things that grow on the face of the earth. And I gave to My exalted angels power to take the spirit out of a tree, or a bush, or a plant, and to carry it away and re-clothe it with corporeal substance. But to My exalted Gods I gave power to do the same things, not with one plant only, but with whole forests, and with animals, fishes and serpents. And when they do these things in atmospherea, they are called subjective heavens.

20/21.17. So it began, in the ancient days, when spirits of darkness returned to mortals, that they told them heaven was like the earth, with everlasting life for all animals as well as for man. || Do not turn away from such spirits, O man, but learn from them, so when you also become a spirit, you do not linger in My bound heavens.[573]

---

[571] this includes birds

[572] atmospherean body

[573] There are spiritualist books describing the spirit world as having animals, and spirits who have animals as pets, including exotic animals such

20/21.18. For if you set your soul to feed on animals, and to dwell with them, the Gods cannot deliver you to My emancipated heavens, till you have served your time in the lower heavens. One great light I have bestowed upon all men, which is that they can progress forever. Though the waters of the ocean rise up and make clouds; and the clouds fall down as rain and run to the rivers, and from there back into the ocean, and this repeats a thousand times, ten thousands of times, yet that water has not progressed. Neither have I given progress to a stone, nor to a tree, nor to an animal; but I have given progress to man only.

20/21.19. Be wise, O man, and do not tie yourself to things that do not progress, nor set your soul upon them, lest they become a bondage to you in the next world. But for the druks (those who have tied themselves to things that do not progress), I have created heavens midway between light and darkness, subjective and objective, so that they may be redeemed. ||

20/21.20. Fragapatti also visited the Washa'wow'wow, the great hunting fields; and the place of tournaments, the Se'ka'to'si, where tens of thousands of drujas were being amused, instructed, and awakened to their condition and to their possibilities. And when Fragapatti and his hosts had seen the beauty and grandeur of this lowest of heavens, and made a record of the affairs, Yaton'te said:

20/21.21. Now I have shown you, O Fragapatti, the foundation of a great house, even my kingdom, which is Jehovih's. I am at your service, to go wherever you may desire. So Fragapatti spoke, saying:

20/21.22. I desire to descend to the earth's surface, and survey the plains, rivers and lakes, in the regions where the Father's kingdom will be founded. Let my mathematicians calculate the time when these things shall be, and also record this in the etherean libraries, for the benefit of the angels of that day.

20/21.23. The mathematicians calculated the time, and then Yo'tse'putu, the chief, said: In eight thousand nine hundred years, the foundation! So Fragapatti caused the avalanza to be lowered down to the earth's surface, and he coursed over the land to the east, west, north and south, and when he saw it was a fair country as to land and water, he said:

20/21.24. Behold the Wisdom of Jehovih in the foundation and plans for inhabiting and subduing the earth. And yet, eight thousand nine hundred years! O what innumerable millions on the earth will go down in darkness before that day! Here the light will fall! Here the beginning of the death of Seffas! Yet Your Hand, O Jehovih, is over all.

CHAPTER 22 Fragapatti

20/22.1. Fragapatti sent messengers to Hapacha, God of Ipseogee, apprising him of the visit. So Hapacha hastily called in his Lords, captains, and fathers, and began preparing a time of recreation, including suitable reception and entertainment.

20/22.2. And Hapacha provided in this manner: first, one hundred thousand musicians, formed in eight parts of a circle, with eight intervening spaces. With each group he provided one thousand marshals, and they stood in front of the musicians, with eight intervening spaces also. Next within, he provided places for the messengers, of whom there were three hundred thousand. Outside the musicians were the asaphs, of whom there were one million; then came the ashars, of whom there were two million. Next came the nurses and physicians; next, the teachers in factories, schools and colleges; and of all these there were fourteen million six hundred thousand.

20/22.3. Of the grade first above the es'yans there were twenty million; of the second grade, which was the highest, there were thirty million; but no es'yans were present.

20/22.4. In the middle of the circle was the throne of Hapacha, now extended to accommodate his Lords. To the south of his throne were the seats of the captains of the hosts. In a crescent were Hapacha's counselors, of whom there were one million.

20/22.5. Hapacha, having them thus called together, and having previously explained to only a few the purpose, now addressed them all, saying:

20/22.6. By the Wisdom and Power of Jehovih I speak before you. That which I say is not of myself, but of the faith I have in Jehovih, of which faith you are likewise blessed.

---

as a leopard. Through reading these accounts, one can learn subjectively about the spirit realm at that level.

20/22.7. Since our youth up we have been advised by the guardian angels, their Lords and God, to be firm in faith in Jehovih above all things. For it was declared to us, in the earlier times, that there was a higher heaven and a lower heaven, and that through faith in the Father we would all ultimately ascend and dwell in His Holiest Kingdoms.

20/22.8. For which reason, ever since your mortal lives have been put away, you have been steady workers, even for this kingdom, raising up many, and causing them to rejoice in everlasting life. But as it has been promised you beforehand, that the Gods above us would surely come and deliver all who are prepared for the next resurrection, even so, to this day, you cherish the hope for wider fields of labor, where you may overtake[574] your kindred and others who have become wise in Jehovih's light.

20/22.9. The time of that resurrection is at hand for many of you. Our Father has brought this heaven into a lighter region, so that you may be prepared for that still greater light beyond. And, as you have seen, because of the new light that is with us, many of the I'huan es'yans have deserted our nurseries and gone back to the earth, for they love the darkness of earth more than they love the light of heaven.

20/22.10. My Lords have sent messengers to me from various parts of the earth (Guatama), saying to me: To the extent that the es'yans have deserted your places in heaven, even so have they returned to mortals in those great numbers. || And it has come to pass that great manifestations of spirit presence are now common to men, women and children, on earth.

20/22.11. Many of these es'yans, falling in with drujas, have adopted their roving habits, denying that there is any higher heaven, honestly believing they will have an opportunity to reincarnate themselves and dwell again in mortal form. Knowing no higher heaven than the earth, and knowing no happiness except in the indulgence of lust, they appear to mortals and marry in manifestation, falsely pretending to be the kin of the living.

[574] catch up with, rank with; i.e., enter etherea, even as others who became wise in Jehovih's light

20/22.12. And this sign foreruns the approach of a new dawn of dan near at hand. Being thus doubly armed in prophecy, your God called you to witness the words and proceedings of Fragapatti, who is on his way here, accompanied by Yaton'te, God of Yaton'te, Creator (founder) of Hochedowa.

20/22.13. For more than six hundred years many of us have labored in this field, and our harvests for Gau have been the most esteemed of all the resurrections contributed by the Lords of earth. To comport with our dignity, and to represent these harvests, I have commanded the builders of otevans to have a vessel ready for my Lords and their attendants, and my chief marshal, to go part way and meet our visitors, bearing the sign of the triangle, and of fruit, and the altar. ||

20/22.14. Hapacha then gave full instructions; and, presently, the receiving hosts departed in the otevan, with music, rejoicing, being cheered by the remaining hosts. In the interim, Hapacha caused the house to be put in order.

CHAPTER 23 Fragapatti

20/23.1. Fragapatti had previously visited Hapacha, but did not say who he was, except that he was God of Lunitzi, in etherea; consequently, Hapacha, now knowing that Fragapatti was coming, did not know it was the same person, and expected to see one coming in great pomp and glory. For he had heard of the wonders Fragapatti had already accomplished in the eastern heavens, particularly the breaking up of the hells of Aoasu and the deliverance of the tortured inmates.

20/23.2. That was the situation when Fragapatti came to Ipseogee in his avalanza, but displaying neither lights nor curtains; coming with the receiving hosts within his vessel, anchoring near the throne of Hapacha.

20/23.3. Presently Fragapatti came down out of the ship, Yaton'te and Hoab with him, also the marshals, who were on the left, the receiving hosts being on the right. Hapacha's es'enaurs struck up, PROCLAIM JEHOVIH'S NAME, O YOU LORDS AND GODS! And the hosts of the avalanza joined in with singing, and with trumpets, harps and triangles, knowing they were the symbols of Hapacha's kingdom, and great was the glory of their music.

20/23.4. When Fragapatti approached the throne, the music ceased. Hapacha said: Who comes here? And he made the ancient sign of Jehovih's name. Fragapatti said: A Faithist in Jehovih; and he gave the countersign. Upon which, Hapacha said: In His name, welcome brother, and welcome to your hosts also. May His love and wisdom be manifested in me and my people during your sojourn with us.

20/23.5. Fragapatti said: Jehovih is All Wise. He fashions some men like suns, and out of their souls the light extends into the far-off spheres. And Jehovih sends swift messengers from His most exalted heavens to course these vast fields at certain times and seasons. And these messengers, passing through both light and darkness, with their great wisdom, scan the distant kingdoms where mortals and angels dwell, and quickly catch (perceive) from the guardian hosts, and from the scenes around, the brightest, best stars, and carry the record to the reigning Gods above. And when these Gods descend to the regions and places of these immortal gems, they go visit them.

20/23.6. Even so, O Hapacha, stands your record in the higher heavens. And when the Father called me to visit the red star and her heavens, I looked over Jehovih's messengers' reports, where your name was set, radiant with love and fire. So I made haste to you, and came unknown because I was as yet unproved in these heavens; and your much worth, and the amity[575] of your hosts, won my love. I told you that you would hear from me soon, and so you have. Behold, Fragapatti is before you!

20/23.7. Hapacha said: Blessed, O Jehovih! Come, O Fragapatti, and honor my throne, in the name of the Father! And come also, O Yaton'te, and you, O Hoab! And they went up and sat on the throne, and Fragapatti sat in the middle.

20/23.8. Again the es'enaurs sang and played, and during the singing the light of the upper kingdoms began to envelop the throne. Then Fragapatti spoke, explaining:

20/23.9. Hear me, O all you people, and be attentive to my words:

20/23.10. Because you have been faithful from the start, you have become the light of the earth and of this heaven; and because you have maintained your altar and times of sacrifice (worship), there have been maintained in the upper heavens altars and sacrifices in conjunction with you.

20/23.11. By which, you have been blessed in hearing the Voice during all the darkness through which the earth and her heavens have passed.

20/23.12. As the Father has given voice between mother and child, though they are distant from each other, so, in like manner, are Jehovih's kingdoms, which are in sympathy in righteousness and love.

20/23.13. As you see the light gathering about this throne, do not think that I bring the light, nor that it is sent to me in person. There is a cord between me and my etherean kingdoms, and I am one end of it; the other end is the throne in etherea. When I sit in the midst of this throne, behold, it is also illuminated by the higher heavens.

20/23.14. Yet, do not think that my heavens are the highest of all, for the All Highest, as such, can never be attained. Nevertheless, my heavens are connected as with a cord to them above me, and they to others still above, and so on forever, upward, upward! The All Highest conceived of, is called Jehovih; and no matter how long it descends, still the Voice is His Voice.

20/23.15. So that you may hear Jehovih's Voice, I will now set my sun above the throne.

20/23.16. Fragapatti ceased, and a light most brilliant, in the figure of the sun, settled above his head and centered behind the throne. Many could not look upon it because of its brightness. Presently Jehovih spoke out of the Light, saying:

20/23.17. Rejoice, O Hapacha, in the name of your Creator! Sing your songs of delight, and let your people hold up their heads. Behold, I have watched over you and your hosts; with faith in My promises, you have fulfilled the dawn of My Light!

20/23.18. Three thousand years are like one day in My sight. Yesterday I said: Sit here, stand there, for tomorrow I come again. And this was My commandment for thousands, and tens of thousands of years.

20/23.19. But others did not remember Me; in the night they went down, like a child who falls asleep. And when I came in the morning, behold, they had not awakened. But I roused them up, and showed them My great Light.

20/23.20. Again I said to them: Three thousand years are like one day in My sight. Sit here, stand there, and remember Me. Tomorrow I come again.

[575] friendliness, goodwill

But lo, they went down in sleep; again they failed to remember Me, their Creator.

20/23.21. But you, O Hapacha, have maintained the watch all night long. You are the first of Gods who has kept this kingdom whole from dawn to dawn. You are the first of Gods who has kept My kingdom safe in the lower heavens till the morning came.

20/23.22. Now I have come to you to deliver you and your kingdom to Haraiti, where you shall reside till the close of dawn, when My Sons and Daughters shall bear you upward to My emancipated worlds; and your hosts shall go with you.

20/23.23. The Voice ceased. Then Fragapatti spoke, saying: For three days I will tarry[576] here; you shall have two days of recreation, but on the third day you shall appoint your successor, and then I will speak again before you and your people.

20/23.24. So Hapacha proclaimed two days of recreation, and the hosts mingled freely together, those of the avalanza coming out and rejoicing with the Ipseogee'ans, and great was the glory of those two days.

CHAPTER 24 Fragapatti

20/24.1. Hoab did not rejoice; for he alone, of all the people assembled, was burdened in soul. He said: Jehovih! You have rebuked me, and I am cast down. You have shown me Your Son Hapacha, one of Your Gods in the lowest of heavens. And Hapacha, Your Son, has maintained his kingdom to You till this dawn of light has come.

20/24.2. Yet You gave into my keeping a kingdom far higher than this, even Zeredho; and I went down, like a child who falls asleep. My kingdom forgot You; my people ceased to sing songs to Your name. We buried ourselves in darkness.

20/24.3. And You have chosen me to be the next succeeding God of earth and her heavens! How shall I fulfill Your commandments? How shall I know the way to choose Gods and Lords under me who will be steadfast and zealous?

20/24.4. As he thus communed with Jehovih, Fragapatti said to him: Through faith all things are accomplished; without faith, all things are uncertain. He who says: I know Jehovih lives and reigns, has said wisely. But he who says: I go forth in You, O Jehovih, for I know You will accomplish, has said much more. For his words maintain the power of the Father in him. ||

20/24.5. When the morning of the third day came, Hapacha called the hosts from recreation to labor; and the es'enaurs chanted a hymn of rejoicing; and after that, Hapacha said:

20/24.6. To You, O Jehovih, all things are committed, even as from You they came forth. Your Voice is ever upon all men, but they do not hear You. Your eye is observant of all men, but they do not believe it. To teach men these simple things, is to make Gods of them. To open up their understanding, to find You, to know You, and to realize Your Ever Presence, to become one with You, this is the labor with Your Gods, Your Lords, and Your holy angels.

20/24.7. In Your name I have raised up one who is to succeed me in this, Your kingdom. From Your Light Your Orian Chief shall weave a crown for him. With my own hands I will crown him to You and Your kingdom.

20/24.8. The marshals now brought forward, Penoto, of Caracas, highly learned in discipline, and he stood before the throne of God. Then Fragapatti rose up, saying:

20/24.9. Without a keynote a number of instruments cannot be attuned to harmony. Without a faith in an All Highest Person, neither angels nor mortals can live in harmony.

20/24.10. Individuals may be strong, but many in concerted action comprise the Father's kingdoms.

20/24.11. Neither angels nor mortals can assimilate of themselves;[577] but all can assimilate with the Father, every one perfecting himself differently. Such persons are then assimilated to one another.

20/24.12. Whoever serves his own conception of the All Highest, making himself a servant to it, is on the right road; and, in the plan of the universe, will drift into an association adapted to himself.

20/24.13. Many such persons, becoming a unit, are powerful over the elements surrounding them. Disbelief in an All Highest Person is caused by

576 stay temporarily, sojourn, remain

577 on their own account; by their own means; by themselves

weakness of spirit, resulting from disease or from pre-natal sin,[578] or by laudation of one's own self. Such persons cannot harmonize, because each one is his own self-esteemed all highest. They are without power, without unison and without sacrifice, accomplishing little good in heaven or on earth.

20/24.14. Do not think that darkness belongs only to the earth and the lowest heavens;[579] there are those who rise to the second resurrection, and then fall into unbelief, and then fall to the first resurrection, and afterward become wandering spirits. And some of them even fall into hell, which is belief in evil and destruction being good; and yet others become drujas, engrossed in the affairs of mortals, and in lust, teaching reincarnation; and they finally become fetals and vampires on mortals.

20/24.15. Whoever has attained to the height of his own ideal, is on the precipice of hell; but he who, finding the God of his forefathers too small for himself, and so, invents one much higher, is a great benefactor. A fool can ridicule the ancient Person; his delight is to pull down; but a wise man furnishes a greater Great Person. To pull down the All Person, is to pull down His people.

20/24.16. To try to make a non-appreciable Person out of Jehovih is to make one's self the opposite of a creator.[580] To learn to create, to invent, to cast one's spirit forth with power to congregate and make,[581] is to go on the right road.

20/24.17. To learn to pull down, to scatter, to annul, to disintegrate, to set things apart from one another, to find evil instead of good, to find folly instead of wisdom, to expose the ignorance of others instead of finding wisdom in them; all these follow after the first inception of disbelief in the All Person.

20/24.18. And since, from disintegration of the compact between the Creator and His children, the cord of communication is cut off with the exalted kingdoms in etherea, they have indeed double grounds for disbelief; nor can they comprehend how others can be believers in an All Person, much less have Faith in Him.

20/24.19. And the same rule that applies to individuals also applies to communities and to kingdoms, in regard to the fall which is consequent to unbelief in an All Person. For a community becomes One Person; a kingdom in etherea becomes One Person; a kingdom in the lower heavens becomes One Person; a kingdom (state, nation) on earth becomes One Person; with each and every kingdom being a single figurehead; and for as many of these kingdoms as become united with each other, they also become One Person, being a single figurehead of many parts, which is the perfection of each and every individual.[582]

---

[578] sins that were committed by the parents or previous ancestors

[579] That is, to the heavens resting on or very close to the surface of the earth. Note that those who ascend to etherea as Brides and Bridegrooms, being wedded to the All-Light, cannot fall into unbelief.

[580] To give the Creator properties that cannot be related to, aspired toward, or comprehended in the sense of measuring one's closeness or distance to those traits of His, is to make Him non-appreciable, i.e., not capable of being understood and appreciated; not seen as a Person.

In that case, to use a metaphor, one has no safe Port toward which to aim the ship of one's being; nor anywhere against which one may take safe bearing; and being without direction, one becomes adrift at sea and the possibility of capsizing under the waves increases dramatically. In regards to being a creator, it is elsewhere in this Oahspe said that man is to become a co-creator with his/her Creator. –ed.

In those who, having fallen from the second resurrection, refer to the Creator as unknowable, we have an example of how this idea makes the All Person un-appreciable. For, although we will never know Jehovih in His full form and extent, everlasting resurrection (spiritual growth) means we will be forever growing in our knowledge of Him, and forever attaining in His attributes. –cns ed.

In sum, Jehovih is not unknowable (impossible to know; beyond the capacity of human understanding), but to those in darkness, it may seem so for a season. –ed.

[581] This attribute is that which is stated elsewhere in Oahspe as going forth manfully (19/6.24<fn-manfully>), and is part of that which Oahspe calls manliness; note this refers to both males and females.

20/24.20. Hence, as a single individual can cut himself off from the Father, so can a community, or a kingdom, and so go down to destruction.[583]

20/24.21. The strongest, best man in the community is he who labors most to perfect the unit, that is, the Person of the community; the strongest man in the kingdom is he who labors most to perfect the Person of the kingdom; the strongest man in heaven is he who labors most to perfect the All Person of heaven.

20/24.22. The weakest of men is the opposite of these; he labors to show there is no All Person in anything; truly, he is already falling away from the Father. Yes, he accuses himself, for he says: I neither see nor hear an All Person, nor do I believe in one.

20/24.23. It is a wise man who, finding he is going into disbelief too much, corrects himself. And he is not less wise who, finding he believes too much, and hence, investigates not at all, corrects himself.

20/24.24. It was said of old, first, testimony; second, belief; third, faith; and fourth, works; but I declare to you that, with the expansion of knowledge, testimony must be strengthened. For in the ancient times, angels and men could be commanded to believe, and they believed.

20/24.25. And here many of the Lords and the Gods of the lower heavens have erred; for they did not furnish to those beneath them the necessary testimony comporting with the advanced knowledge in heaven or on earth. A God shall be swift in devising food for meditation; for angels, as well as mortals, without an advanced teacher, are as well off with none at all.

20/24.26. It was said of old that a God taught the people on one of the stars to believe Jehovih lived in a straw, and they rose in wisdom, harmony, and unity. Then afterward, another God came and taught them there was no Jehovih, because, in truth, He could not live in a straw; and the people fell into disbelief, disharmony and disunion. Which, then, of these, was the better God?

20/24.27. Yet I declare to you, they were both necessary. For without a habitation and a figure, the Great Spirit cannot be taught in the first place to either angels or mortals. The labor of the Gods is to lead the people upward, step by step, until they learn to be Gods and Goddesses themselves.

20/24.28. On this earth, mortals were taught through stone and wooden idols; and afterward by engraved images. In some of the mixed tribes it will be necessary to teach them incarnated Jehovih in mortal form, and by sympathy for his sufferings, teach them how to follow his spirit up to heaven. But all these subterfuges shall be set aside in the Kosmon era.

20/24.29. This heaven, more than any other heaven of the earth, will be regarded[584] by the etherean kingdoms. Beneath you, even on this part of the earth,[585] mortals will first espouse the Father's kingdom.

20/24.30. Of all things, let your labor be first of all to sow the seed of belief in an All Person, the Great Spirit. As you now sow, and build Jehovih's kingdom in your heaven, so, in the coming of the Kosmon era, the same teaching will take root in the souls of mortals.

20/24.31. Nor shall you, under any circumstances, permit Gods, Lords, or Saviors to

---

[582] This can be likened to a body with many organs, each of which must function perfectly for the whole to function perfectly; and for each organ to function perfectly, each component cell (individual) must function perfectly.

[583] Starting from a single cancerous cell, an entire body can ultimately die. Accordingly, health or unity of the whole requires the perfecting of each and every member within that entity.

From this we can see the bondage of those who lead. For as an individual's pending union with Jehovih requires perfecting himself, so does the leader's compact with Jehovih (acknowledged by the leader or not) require that the person of the whole (the group) also perfect itself in the ways of Jehovih. And the compact also requires the component parts of the group be allowed to perfect themselves. Where the leader disallows for that, then he (or she or they) become bound. Where the leader does provide wholesome ways that lead to perfection of members, then so do the members and the whole, benefit spiritually.

Also note that in these Kosmon times, the United Nations of the world are also rated as One Person; and so the same applies.

[584] special attention paid to it; given priority

[585] that is, over that portion of North Guatama that became the United States of America

be established as worshipful beings, either in these heavens or on this part of the earth. For this land is dedicated by Jehovih for the overthrow of all idols, of God, and Lord, and Savior, and of everything that is worshipped, except Jehovih, the Great Spirit. Neither shall any of these idols be established with effect in these heavens or on this land. But be most circumspect to establish Jehovih, the Light of light, the All Person, in the souls of angels and mortals.

20/24.32. Fragapatti ceased, but signaled for Hapacha to ordain Penoto, to be God of Ipseogee. Hapacha rose up, saying: Penoto, Son of Jehovih! You have been chosen to be God of Ipseogee for six hundred years, and even after, if Jehovih so wills. You have passed the examination, and stand above all others.

20/24.33. You have been favored with much traveling in heaven; and for your benefit many swift messengers, from the emancipated worlds, have explained to you the dominions of the Great Chiefs.

20/24.34. He, through whose fields this world is now traveling, has stood up before you. He has spoken to you and your people. Heed his words, and you shall be one with his kingdoms in wisdom and power.

20/24.35. By proxy I have visited the etherean worlds; you have not. By being one with this Chief, you will inure[586] to All Light, and soon you shall visit his places by proxy also.

20/24.36. And at the end of six hundred years, you and your harvest will be called for by the etherean hosts. Be ready for them! And before you depart, you shall raise up one sufficient to take your place, and you shall bestow him.

20/24.37. Penoto said: Your will and Jehovih's be done! That which is given me to do, I will do with all my wisdom and strength, so help me, O Jehovih!

20/24.38. Hapacha said: By virtue of Your Wisdom, Power and Love, O Jehovih, vested in me, I ordain this, Your Son, God of Ipseogee for the period of six hundred years. Be with him, O Jehovih, and may he and his works glorify You forever! Amen!

[586] become as one, habituate, become increasingly accustomed

20/24.39. Penoto said: Which I accept and covenant with You, O Jehovih, for Your glory forever. Amen!

20/24.40. The es'enaurs now sang: YOU LIGHT AND PERSON, APPROVED AND SUNG ON HIGH JEHOVIH! OUR GOD HAPACHA; JEHOVIH YOU HAVE CALLED HIM! WELCOME, PENOTO! YOU, ALONE, JEHOVIH, REMAIN FOREVER! GLORY, GLORY TO YOU, O CREATOR!

20/24.41. The light gathered brilliantly over Fragapatti's head, and when the music ceased, the Voice of Jehovih spoke out of the Light, saying:

20/24.42. In the first days I blew My breath upon the lands of the earth, and man became a living soul. Then, in the second time, I moved My hand upon the earth, and man went forth in power.

20/24.43. Thus My Voice has approached near the earth. Be steadfast in My commandments. The time shall surely come, in the third season, when My Voice shall be heard by mortals.

20/24.44. The Voice ceased, and then Fragapatti took the light in his hands, as one would take fine flax, and he turned it about three times, and lo, a crown was woven, most brilliant, but of a reddish hue. He said:

20/24.45. Crown of Your Crown, O Jehovih, I have woven for Your Son, God of Ipseogee. And he handed it to Hapacha, who said: And in Your name, O Father, I crown him, second God of Ipseogee, six hundred years. Be with him, O Father! Amen!

CHAPTER 25 Fragapatti

20/25.1. It being now the end of the fourth day, Fragapatti commanded the hosts to embark in the avalanza; and the marshals conducted them in, taking first the sons and daughters of Ipseogee, being sixty million; next the Zeredho'ans, ten million; and then Fragapatti's attendants, being mostly ethereans, five million.

20/25.2. When the hosts were aboard, Fragapatti, Hoab, Yaton'te and Hapacha rose up, and after making the sign of the Setting Sun, went down and sat at the foot of the throne.

20/25.3. God (Penoto) went down and took Fragapatti's hand, saying: Arise, O Chief! The Father calls. Fragapatti rose up and stood aside. Next, God raised Yaton'te, and he stood aside; and then he raised Hoab, and he stood aside. And now came the greatest trial of all—he took Hapacha's hand, saying: Arise, O God, Great Jehovih calls you! Go your way and His.

20/25.4. But they both burst into tears, and fell into each other's arms. Hapacha said: O Father! Penoto said: His will be done! || And now the light gathered brilliantly over the scene; Fragapatti moved forward, then Yaton'te, then Hoab, and next Hapacha!

20/25.5. Penoto resumed the throne. The es'enaurs chanted, and the fire-light of the higher heavens descended over the entire place. Like a sweet dream, the scene closed. Fragapatti and his hosts were gone.

20/25.6. Like a bee that is laden with nectar, flying from a field of flowers to its home, Fragapatti returned to Haraiti with his avalanza laden, flying swiftly through the vault of heaven, a shooting star in Jehovih's hand.

20/25.7. Athrava, God of Haraiti, and assistant to Fragapatti, knew that the avalanza was coming, and that Hapacha and his hosts were aboard; so he resolved to provide a glorious reception.

20/25.8. Accordingly, for the length of a thousand miles, he caused pillars of fire to be erected, in two rows, so that the avalanza would pass between them; and near the pillars he stationed one million trumpeters and harpers, divided into one hundred groups. And they were arranged so that when the avalanza passed them, they could come aboard.

20/25.9. Now during Fragapatti's absence, many of the spirits who had been rescued from torture and madness in the hells of Aoasu had been restored to consciousness, more than one hundred and fifty million of them.

20/25.10. Of these, Athrava said: Clothe them in most gaudy apparel, and let them be the bearers of perfumes, flowers and torches, as presents for the I'hin hosts of Hapacha. And the lights shall be lowered at the landing place, to make it acceptable to those newly raised, who are aboard.

20/25.11. Athrava said: As for Mouru, within the walls of light it shall be rated seven; but when Fragapatti has ascended the throne, it shall be raised to nine. || And in those days, nine, in Haraiti, was fifty percent of the capacity of endurance in the plateau.

20/25.12. Jehovih had said: If they raise the light, it will be more acceptable to My etherean hosts, for they have dwelt a long time near the earth, and are thirsting for etherean light. But yet consider, here are billions of atmosphereans who cannot endure the etherean light, but delight in a lower percent. See to it, then, that the walls of light protect My hosts in the dark on one side, but raise the grade to nine within.

20/25.13. Athrava said: There shall be flights of stairs leading over the walls of Mouru, and they shall be white and illumed on that day, which will be sufficient for dividing the people according to the light suited to them. The I'hins with Hapacha will go over the walls, for they entered their corporeal cities in the same way; besides, they are capable of enduring the light; but the I'huans with Hapacha will desire to remain outside. For them you shall prepare a place of delight and rest.

20/25.14. But Athrava gave no orders regarding the ethereans, for they were capable of perceiving all necessary things, and without instruction.

CHAPTER 26 Fragapatti

20/26.1. When Fragapatti entered the Road of Fire with his avalanza, where Athrava had stationed the musicians and groups of furlers,[587] the hosts aboard broke loose from all bounds of propriety,[588] so great was their delight; and they shouted and sang with the trumpeters with most exalted enthusiasm. Many of them entered the Orian state, and not a few, even the Nirvanian. And they became even as Gods and Goddesses by their own entrancement, seeing, hearing and realizing, even to the third rate above the Brides and Bridegrooms of Jehovih!

20/26.2. These were just spasmodic conditions of light, from which they presently returned, being able to give descriptions of their visions. For so Jehovih created man, with spells of clearness far in advance of his growth; and having realized such, he returns to his normal condition, to prepare himself constitutionally.

20/26.3. Along the road, on either side, were mottoes and sayings peculiar to the hosts of Hapacha, and to mortals of Guatama. When Hapacha saw these, he said: How is it possible?

---

[587] evidently holders of banners that they unfurled, with wording on them, for reasons shortly made clear

[588] decorum, composure, formality, stateliness

How did these Gods derive this information? But the light came to his own soul, saying: The wise and good sayings of men below, are borne[589] by Jehovih's swift messengers to realms above. || Hoab, standing nearby, heard Hapacha's words, and Hoab said: How can men and spirits be inspired to wise and good sayings? Who thought to erect such signboards on the road to All Light! And yet what darker deeds are done, when the soul of man finds curses and evil words to vent his awful sins, and walls himself around with horrid imprecations![590] And which he must face in after time only to be appalled at the havoc of his own deadly weapons. How few, indeed, comprehend the direful thrust of hateful words, imagining them to be only wind, to pass away and be seen no more, but which are placarded on the signboard of heaven, as his fruit sent to market! The poison dealt out of his mouth to his brother man! A man throws a spear, deadly, but it falls on the earth and lies there; but words and sayings are more potent, scoring deep in the soul of things. Fair, indeed, it is with you, O Hapacha, and with your hosts also, to enter Haraiti with these pure scroll!

20/26.4. As fast as the ship passed the lights, the etherean musicians came aboard, being anxious to meet Hapacha and his hosts, especially the I'hins, and to congratulate them on being the first harvest from the lowest heaven at the end of a cycle. And strange to say, there were just twice as many as Sethantes had prepared in the first dawn on earth. Fragapatti called the swift messengers belonging to the Roads of Gon, in etherea, and he said to them: Go to Sethantes, whose fields lie in the Roads of Gon, and say to him: Greeting, in the name of Jehovih! The earth has reached Obsod and Goomatchala, home of Fragapatti, who sends love and joy on behalf of sixty million, first harvest of ha'k, grade sixty-five.

20/26.5. Of these messengers, four hundred departed, leaving a reserve of eight hundred, who continued on the avalanza.

20/26.6. The drujas, who were arrayed in gaudy attire, withdrew a little from the landing, fearing the light. When the ship drew near the walls, and was made fast, two million of the marshals of Mouru came to the front, as an escort to conduct all who chose over the ascending stairs.

20/26.7. And so great was the faith of Hapacha's hosts, that over fifty million of them passed within the sea of fire, singing: GLORY TO YOU, O JEHOVIH! CREATOR OF WORLDS!

20/26.8. Seeing this great faith in them, Athrava commanded red and blue lights, to favor them; and not one of them quailed, or turned from the light. And now, many of them had their first view of the glories and powers of Gods and Goddesses. Every part of Mouru was illuminated. The structure of the temple, its extent and magnificence in conception, with its hundreds of thousands of mirrors and lenses, its transparent and opaque crystals, translucent and opaque circles and arches, hundreds of millions, all of which, when viewed from any one place, was unalike when viewed from another place, as if each position were striving to outdo the others in beauty and perfection. So that, were a person to walk for a thousand years in the temple, every moment he would see, as it were, a new palace of surpassing grandeur.

20/26.9. And so wonderfully was it arranged, that the faces of one billion people could be seen from any place a person might be; and yet all these people constituted a part and principle in the building, being as jewel stones, created by Jehovih for the ornamentation of His celestial abodes.

20/26.10. Hoab, always quick to speak, said: O if only angels and mortals would strive to make of themselves such jewels as these! Hapacha, being overwhelmed with the beauty and magnificence, did not speak. Yaton'te said: When you are on the throne, Fragapatti, I will leave for the kingdom of Yaton'te. Here, then, I will take my leave. Fragapatti shook hands with him, saying: Jehovih be with you!

20/26.11. So Yaton'te remained where he was, but Hoab and Hapacha continued on with Fragapatti. All eyes were turned to them, and especially to Hapacha, whose persistence in faith in Jehovih had won the lower heavens to Wisdom and Love. And as they moved toward the throne, great Athrava rose up, smiling, holding out his hands to receive them. Next, and behind Athrava, were the five Goddesses, Ethro, of Uche and Rok; Guissaya, of Hemitza, of the Valley of M'boid, in etherea; Si'tissaya, of Woh'tabak, the one-time home of Fuevitiv; Ctevi, of Nu of Porte'Auga; and Rinava,

---

[589] carried, conveyed

[590] fierce denunciations, maledictions, invoking of evil, cursing

of the Swamps of Tholiji, in South Suyarc of Roads, near Zuh'ta and Hitch'ow, in the South etherean vault of Obsod.

20/26.12. And the Goddesses also rose up with extended hands; and now, because of the brilliancy of their presence, the throne became a scene of hallowed light, and threads of light extended to all the Council members, and by these, were radiated outward so that every person in the Temple of Jehovih was connected with the throne, which made every spoken word plain to all.

20/26.13. Athrava said: In Jehovih's name, welcome, O Fragapatti! And your hosts with you! The Goddesses repeated the same words, and they were echoed by the entire audience. Fragapatti said: In Your name, O Jehovih, I am delivered to my loves. Be with us, O Father, so we may glorify You! O my people, receive Hapacha, Son of Jehovih, who rose up and stood in the dark all night long, in faith in Jehovih. Behold, I have delivered him in dawn, and his hosts with him.

20/26.14. And now Jehovih's light appeared beyond the throne, rising like a new sun, reddish tinged, emblem of the Western Light, in honor of Hapacha. And it rose and stood above Fragapatti's head in great brilliancy. Then Jehovih spoke out of the Light, saying:

20/26.15. With My breath I create alive the earth-born child; with My hand I quicken the newborn spirit; and with My Light I illume the soul of My Faithist. Behold, I dwell in the All Highest place, and in the lowest of created things; whoever finds Me, I find also; whoever proclaims Me, I proclaim in return. Hapacha, My Son, Savior of men! Of My Light you shall be crowned!

20/26.16. The Voice ceased, and now Fragapatti advanced to the middle of the throne, and took of the light and fashioned a crown, and placed it on Hapacha's head, saying: Crown of Your Crown, O Jehovih, I crown Your Son! In Your Light he shall be wise and powerful, with Love to all Your created beings, from now and forever.

20/26.17. The Goddesses then received them, and after due ceremonies they all took their seats, Fragapatti in the middle of the throne. Athrava resigned at once, during the stay of Fragapatti. The es'enaurs now chanted: GLORY BE TO YOU, O ALL LIGHT; THE PERSON OF EVERY KINGDOM HIGH AND LOW; WHO HAS BROUGHT OUR BROTHERS AND SISTERS HOME!

20/26.18. By natural impulse of thanks, Hapacha's hosts, fifty million, rose up and responded, singing: TO YOU, O JEHOVIH, HOW SHALL OUR SOULS FIND WORDS! YOUR SONS' AND DAUGHTERS' LOVE, HOW CAN WE RECOMPENSE? MAKE US LIGHT AND CLEAR, O FATHER! SPOTLESS BEFORE THEM AND YOU!

20/26.19. But the anthems were long, and sung with brilliancy, rejoicing and responding, millions to millions, as an opera of high heaven.

20/26.20. When the music ceased, Fragapatti said: With the close of dawn of dan, these hosts shall be received as Brides and Bridegrooms of Jehovih, and ascend with us to the regions of Goomatchala, in etherea. The apportioners will therefore divide them into groups in Haraiti; with etherean teachers to prepare them. So that this may be accomplished, I proclaim one day's recreation, to assemble on the next day in order of business.

20/26.21. The marshals then proclaimed as had been commanded, and the hosts went into recreation, the ethereans rushing to Hapacha's atmosphereans with great glee, every one desiring some of them.

CHAPTER 27 Fragapatti

20/27.1. When they were called to labor, Fragapatti said: For the convenience of my own hosts, the light shall now be raised two degrees. In which case it will be well to permit the hosts of Hapacha to retire to the fields of Hukaira (in Haraiti), where Athrava already has a place and teachers for them.

20/27.2. Accordingly, the conductors now removed Hapacha's hosts, except about one million who resolved to endure the light. The es'enaurs chanted while these arrangements were being carried out, and when they were accomplished the music ceased.

20/27.3. The chief marshal said: Swift messengers, who are waiting outside, salute Jehovih's throne, and His God, and ask an audience. Fragapatti said: Where do they come from? And what is the nature of their business?

20/27.4. The marshal said: From the Aoasu'an fields of Howts. Their business concerns the Osivi knots. Fragapatti said: Admit them on the sign of Emuts, greeting from God, in the Father's name.

20/27.5. The marshal withdrew for a short while, and then returned, bringing in one thousand swift messengers, of whom Arieune was Goddess. She advanced near the throne to the left. Fragapatti said: Goddess Arieune, Greeting to you, in Jehovih's name! Please proceed.

20/27.6. Arieune said: Greeting, in love to you, Fragapatti, and to all your hosts. I hastened here from the fields of Howts, section twelve, on the one-time plateau and place of Hored, where there are a billion in knot, and have been for many days. I reported this to the Lord God of Jaffeth, Ah'oan, but his forces are all employed, so he sent me here.

20/27.7. Fragapatti said: It is well. You are at liberty! Hoab, can you untie the knot? Hoab said: I have faith to try. To which Fragapatti replied: Athrava will go with you, but you do the labor. Choose, therefore, your hosts from my ethereans, and have a vessel made of sufficient size, so that if you find it advisable to bring them away, you can do so. Retire, then, with the captain of the files, and make your selections, and, meanwhile, give commands for the vessel to be made, and put in readiness for you.

20/27.8. Hoab said: With Jehovih's help I will deliver them. And he saluted, and, with the captain of the files, he withdrew and made his selections, choosing five million in all, of whom half were physicians and nurses. Meanwhile he had the proper workmen build a vessel of sufficient capacity and strength, as commanded by Fragapatti. And in seven days everything was completed, and Hoab commanded his hosts to enter the ship, and he and Athrava went in also; and presently they were off, being conducted by the Goddess Arieune, in her arrow-ship, to the place of the knot.

CHAPTER 28 Fragapatti

20/28.1. The Goddess Arieune slackened the speed of her arrow-ship to suit that of Hoab's vessel; so onward together they sped in a direct line, propelled as a rocket is propelled, by constant emissions from the hulk (body of the ship); this expenditure being manufactured by the crew and commanders, skilled in wielding Jehovih's elements. For as mortals find means to traverse the ocean and to raise a balloon, so do the Gods and spirits build and propel mightier vessels through the firmament, between the stars and over and under and beyond the sun.

20/28.2. And when the ethereans, highest raised in the most subtle spheres, send their ships coursing downward in the denser strata of a corporeal world, their ready workmen take in ballast, and turn the fans, and reverse the whirling screws to match the space and course of travel; for which purpose men learn the trade, having rank and grade according to proficiency. Many of them serve a thousand years' apprenticeship, becoming so skilled in wielding the elements, and in the knowledge of the degrees of density, that billions of miles of roadways in heaven are as a well-learned book to them.

20/28.3. And, thus conversant with Jehovih's wide domains, they are eagerly sought after, especially in emergent cases, or on journeys of millions of years; for they know the requirements so well, the places of delight, the dangers of vortices, eddies and whirlpools, that when a God says: Take me here, or over there, they know the nearest way and the power required.

20/28.4. For, as Jehovih has made icebergs on the corporeal ocean, dangerous to ships; and made strong currents of trade winds, and currents in the oceans, so are there in the etherean firmament currents and densities which the well-skilled God can take advantage of, whether for a slow trip of pleasure, or a swift one on urgent business to suffering angels or mortals.

20/28.5. And if a God or Goddess is suddenly dispatched by a higher Council, to a distant place, he or she must already be acquainted with navigators sufficiently to know whom to choose; and, likewise, understand the matter well enough to lend a helping hand if required. For often, the navigators have no swift messengers to pilot them; and yet a short journey of fifty thousand miles may require as much skill as a million, especially when descending to a corporeal world.

20/28.6. Hoab knew, and he managed well, following close on the arrow's trail till they neared the ruined plateau. And then, amid the broken currents, Arieune, perceiving that Hoab's vessel was less wieldy, dropped alongside and made fast. She said to Hoab:

20/28.7. Behold, we are near the place. Then Hoab asked: How did you discover a knot in such a wasted country? Arieune answered him:

20/28.8. When Jehovih created woman, He gave to her two chief attributes, curiosity and solicitude for others. So, passing here, surveying the place where the first heavenly kingdom was, I remembered it had been said that Aph left some island places where once a colony in heaven had been built, and I stopped to examine it. A moan and terrible sound greeted me! I heard the Osivi knots, as I had often heard others before.

20/28.9. We landed and made fast, and presently went about searching, led by the sad, sad noise. Then we came to the great mound, the knot, a billion drujas bound in a heap! Wailing, muffled, moaning as if the whole heap of them were in the throes of death, but could not die!

20/28.10. Being powerless myself to overcome such fearful odds, I took the bearing of the regions where I would find the nearest God; and so, having measured the knot, I set sail as you have heard.

20/28.11. Hoab said: Every day I behold Your wisdom, O Jehovih! In a new light Your wondrous judgment rises up before me. Who but You, O Father, had seen the fruitage of Curiosity made perfect in Your daughters? From the little bud seen in mortal form, to the over-scanning of Your heavens by such Goddesses! ||

20/28.12. As Hoab thus discoursed, they arrived at a suitable landing-place, where they anchored their vessels, and then hurried to the knot. Without much ado, Hoab walled the knot around with low fire, leaving a gateway to the east, where he placed a thousand sentinels. One million of his army (his hosts) he stationed outside of and beyond the walls, and these were divided into groups of selectors, guardsmen, physicians, nurses, bearers, and manufacturers of fire and water. The selectors were provided with rods of fire and water, and the guardsmen with shields and blinds.

20/28.13. Then Hoab stationed another million between the knot and the gateway, and these were stationed in four rows, each two rows facing one another and only two paces apart, so that, in all, there were two passages, each like a walled alleyway. And the other three million Hoab caused to surround the knot on every side. Each and every one of these was provided with a fire lamp, which they held in the right hand. And when all things were thus ready, Hoab commanded the attack to begin. And at once the attackers thrust their fire lamps in the face of the nearest druj, and, seizing them with the other hand, pulled them away. The drujas do not all relinquish their grip in the knot at sight of the lamp, but often require to be nearly burned and stifled with the light before they release their hold. Nor is this a grip of evil, but of fear.

20/28.14. || The knot is nothing more nor less than a mass of millions and millions of spirits becoming panic-stricken and falling upon their chief, or leader, who becomes powerless in their grip, and is quickly rolled up in the midst of the knot. ||

20/28.15. And when the deliverers thus begin at the exterior of the knot, peeling off the crazed and moaning spirits, they hurl them backward, where they are caught by the seconds, who, in turn, hurl them into the alleyways, where they are again thrust forward till past the gate in the wall of fire. From the time, therefore, that the druj receives the thrust of the fire lamp in his face, he is not allowed to linger, but is whirled suddenly from one to another so quickly, he cannot fasten to any person or thing. For if they were to fasten, even on the deliverers, first one and then another would fasten, and soon a second knot would result. Because of which, to untie a knot of a billion crazed angels is not only a dangerous proceeding, but a feat of unusual grandeur to be undertaken by five million ethereans.

20/28.16. To provide against accident, Hoab appointed Athrava to take charge of the delivered after they were beyond the walls; for in such matters Athrava had experience spanning thousands of years. So Athrava divided and arranged the drujas into groups, placing guardians with fire rods over them; and in some cases taking the groups away and walling them around with fire also.

20/28.17. Now by the time five hundred million of the knot were released, some of the external, delivered groups, began to tie themselves in knots. And when Athrava saw this, he said to Hoab: Behold, they are becoming too numerous for my hosts. I lack sufficient guardsmen. Hoab said:

20/28.18. Then my army and I will cease awhile, and, instead of delivering, come and assist you. Accordingly, Hoab suspended the battle for a time, and together they labored with those outside, untying the small knots and arranging them in safer ways, placing a greater number of guards over them.

20/28.19. This done, the es'enaurs struck up lively music, starting dancings and marchings; for such is the routine of the restoring process practiced by the Gods. Then come the nurses with cheerful words, with mirth and gaiety, following one diversion with another in rapid succession. But to the raving maniacs, and to the stupid, and to the helpless blind, the physicians now turn their attention.

20/28.20. Again Hoab and his army fell upon the knot, pulling the external ones away and hurling them out, but not so rapidly, having fewer deliverers, for he had bequeathed an extra million to Athrava, outside the walls. And after another three hundred million were delivered, Hoab again ceased, and joined with Athrava to assist, divide and group them in the same way. And he bequeathed another million of his army to Athrava, and then again resumed the attack on the knot, and thus continued till he reached the core of the knot, having untied the whole billion drujas, gradually lessening his own army and enlarging that of Athrava.

20/28.21. And when Hoab came to the core of the knot, behold, he found Oibe, the false God, who falsely styled himself Thor, the etherean. And in the midst of the knot they had jewels of rare value and stolen crowns and stolen symbols, and rods, holy water, urns, incense, a broken Wheel of Jehovih, a broken triangle of the Gods, and, in fact, so many things that one could write a book to describe it all. Suffice it to say, a false God and his kingdom had collapsed, and he fell, crushed in the glory of his throne. And there were with him seven false Lords, who were also crushed in the terrible fall.

20/28.22. Oibe and his Lords, from their confinement in the knot, were also crazed and wild with fear, screaming and crying with all their strength, even as all the others were, like drunkards long debauched, delirious and fearful of imaginary horrors, which have no existence. Or as one's hand, when long compressed, becomes numb, so that when the pressure is taken away it still seems not free, so Oibe and his Lords would not believe they were free, but still cried, calling for help.

20/28.23. At this time, a messenger with forty companions and with five hundred apprentices, came from Ah'oan, God of Jaffeth; and the messenger's name was Turbe, an atmospherean, three hundred years, grade two. Turbe said: Greeting from Ah'oan, in Jehovih's name! To whom shall I speak; to whose honor, aside from Jehovih's, shall I credit this deliverance? Athrava said:

20/28.24. To Hoab, a Zeredho'an disciple of Fragapatti, who is sojourning in Mouru, capital of Haraiti. And Athrava asked Turbe his name, where he came from, and especially if he knew about this knot before, and the history of its cause? To which Turbe replied:

20/28.25. This I have learned from Ah'oan: Some four hundred years ago, one of the sub-Gods, named Oibe, because of his modesty and birdlike fleetness, was promoted by Samati, who is now commissioned by Fragapatti to be master of the I'huans. This, whom Hoab has delivered, is Oibe, the one-time faithful sub-God of honorable purposes. His kingdom prospered for two hundred years, and his name and fame spread throughout all these heavens, and even down to mortals, who were inspired by his admiring spirits to make images of birds (oibe or ibis), and dedicate them to Oibe.[591]

20/28.26. He became vain because of the flattery, and, losing faith in Jehovih, finally came out in unbelief, saying there was no All Highest, except as each and every God chose to exalt himself. Within his dominions, which numbered nearly a billion angels, were twenty or more of Lords under him; to the wisest of whom he began to preach his views, looking to personal laudation and glory.

20/28.27. In some twenty years, the matter culminated with Oibe and a few of his favored Lords proclaiming a new kingdom, styled, THE ALL HIGHEST KINGDOM IN THE ALL HIGHEST HEAVEN! And the title he assumed was, THOR, THE ONLY BEGOTTEN SON OF ALL LIGHT! THOR THE ALL LIGHT PERSONATED! [592] THOR, THE PERSONAL SON OF MI, THE VIRGIN UNIVERSE!

20/28.28. Thus Oibe cut loose from the true God and his kingdoms; and he immediately walled his kingdom around with a standing army; promoting seven of his most efficient admirers as Lords; and others as generals and captains. And at once he set about enlarging and enriching his throne and capital, which he called Osivi, but known as Howts on the true charts.

---

[591] This is the origin of Ibis worship. –Ed.

[592] in person, embodied, personified, incarnated

20/28.29. In one hundred years his kingdom became a place of two billion souls. His chief city, Osivi, was the richest and gaudiest city that had ever been in these heavens. The streets were paved with precious stones; the palaces for himself, his Lords, marshals and generals, were built of the costliest jewels with pillars, arches and chambers of the most elaborate workmanship, and of the costliest material.

20/28.30. Oibe became a tyrant; and, except for his Lords and a few favored friends, none were permitted to approach his throne except by crawling on their bellies while under guard. Nor were they permitted to raise their eyes upon him, except at a very great distance. And all his subjects, although under progressive discipline, were in fact his slaves. These slaves were sent far away into atmospherea, or else down to the earth, to gather tribute for the glory of Thor (Oibe) and his favorites; nor did these slaves distrust, but believed they were working for Jehovih, believing that he lived in the capital, Osivi!

20/28.31. At first, Thor educated and otherwise improved his slaves; but, finding them less obedient as a consequence of gaining knowledge, he finally destroyed all the heavenly schools and colleges, and resolved to keep his subjects forever ignorant. Consequently, the wiser ones deserted him, except his officers, and his angels were without knowledge, knowing nothing, except that they had to work for Thor forever!

20/28.32. In addition to ignorance, Thor kept his subjects forever in fear of himself, continually threatening them with terrible punishments if they ceased to pray to him as the only personified All Light, Jehovih. And in time, his people forgot all aspiration for any other heaven or any other God. Many of these were deputized to dwell with mortals as guardian spirits, persuading mortals to worship Thor and Ibis, threatening them with being turned into serpents and toads after death if they did not obey these injunctions.

20/28.33. In that way, then, Thor, the false, ruled for four hundred years in Osivi; nor was it possible for Samati to send an army of sufficient strength to overcome such a kingdom. But a change finally came. A light descended from the higher heavens six generations ago; and, according to the legends of old, it was ominous that the Gods of higher worlds would intercede.

20/28.34. So Samati, taking advantage of this, sent emissaries to Thor, otherwise Oibe, and solicited him to give up his evil ways, and reestablish Jehovih. Thor, the false, sent word back, saying: When I was a child, I was taught to fear Jehovih, and I feared Him. After long experience I have discovered there is nothing to fear in all the worlds. If there is any Jehovih, He is without form or person or sense! I do not fear Him! I do not revere Him! My heaven is good enough for me and my Lords. As for my subjects, let no man, no God, no Lord, meddle with them.

20/28.35. Samati, who was the lawful God of all these heavens and of the earth, thus perceived no way to reach Thor's slaves, for the slaves were too ignorant to desire anybody or anything except Thor. Nevertheless, Samati sent word the second time to Thor, this time saying: Your kingdom is even now destitute of enough intelligent people to protect you in case of panic. If a comet, or any sudden light, or the passage of an avalanza through your dominions should take place, you would surely find yourself overthrown in a knot. Your subjects look upon you as the All Highest; they will surely rush upon you.

20/28.36. Thor sent the messengers back with an insulting answer. Thus the matter stood till after Ah'oan's appointment as God of Jaffeth and her heavens, which at once cut off Thor's emissaries to mortals, and confined him within his own kingdom. At this time, Samati was commissioned to establish the word of God among mortals, but he communicated Thor's position to Ah'oan.

20/28.37. Ah'oan sent ambassadors to Thor, the false, beseeching him in the same manner to give up his (false) personality, and return with his kingdom to Jehovih, promising him the best of assistance. To this, Thor, the false, replied, by the messengers, saying:

20/28.38. Ah'oan, you usurper! If you desire favors of me, you shall approach me as all Gods and angels do, by crawling on your belly before me. Do not encroach the tiniest fraction on my Most High Kingdom, or I will banish you back to your miscreant[593] regions with stripes and curses!

20/28.39. Ah'oan was surprised, but perceived that till trouble came upon Oibe nothing could be done for him. So, the time came; Jehovih allowed

---

[593] wretched, infidel, good-for-nothing, abject

him to go the full period of self-glory. Thus Oibe fell!

20/28.40. Turbe ceased, and Athrava said: O Jehovih, when will man cease to fall? You have proclaimed Yourself in all places, high and low; Your Gods and Lords and countless angels have proclaimed You! You alone are the password to all the universe! Your name has a thousand exalted devices to win the souls of mortals and angels from darkness to light, and yet they turn away from You, You Creator of suns and stars and countless etherean worlds! And they set up themselves as an object of worship! O the smallness of Gods and men! O the vanity of Your little children!

20/28.41. You have said to mortals: Do not go into the marshes, for there is fever; do not build large cities, for there is sin; do not go after lust, for there is death! But they go in headlong, and they are bruised and dead!

20/28.42. To those who are risen in heaven, You have said: Remember the lessons of earth, lest you fall! Remember the fate of self-conceit, lest you be scourged.[594] Remember the king and the queen of earth, how they become bound in heaven, lest you also become bound.

20/28.43. But they will not heed; vain self rises up in the soul; they behold no other God but themselves in whom they acknowledge wisdom.

CHAPTER 29 Fragapatti

20/29.1. Hoab heard the story of Turbe, and he said to him: Since I have heard these things, I am resolved to bind Thor, the false, and his Lords, and send them with you to Ah'oan! Turbe said: This would be my delight. Because Thor insulted Ah'oan, it would be well for Ah'oan to restore him to his senses.

20/29.2. Hoab said: Wait, then, a little while, and my physicians will bind them so they can do no harm in their madness, and I will have them delivered into the boat. So the proper persons bound Thor and his Lords with bands of cord, for they were wild and delirious; and after that, they were put into Turbe's boat, ready to be carried away. Hoab said to Turbe:

20/29.3. Greeting to Ah'oan, in the name of Jehovih. And say to him that, according to the laws of these heavens, a false God, or false Lord, who has led the people away from the Father, shall, after his deliverance, be made to re-teach the truth to his deceived subjects; nor shall he be promoted higher or faster than the lowest of his former subjects. For which reason, after Ah'oan's companions have restored Oibe and his Lords to soundness of mind, he and his Lords shall again be bequeathed with their own kingdoms. Meanwhile, in this same plateau (Howts), I will begin the establishment of a new kingdom to the Father out of these crazed drujas.

20/29.4. Turbe and his companions then re-entered their boat and set sail at once for Ah'oan's kingdom; with Thor, the false, and his Lords, wailing and crying with fear, not knowing any man, woman or child.

20/29.5. Hoab now turned his attention to the hosts of panic-stricken drujas, who were constantly forming themselves in knots, and yet being as rapidly severed by the ethereans. To Athrava he said: How more helpless a deranged spirit is than a mortal! They float on their own wild thoughts. At one time they fly from us before the wind; at another they run together, or upon us, like molten gum, and we cannot keep them off.

20/29.6. Athrava said: Behold the wisdom of the Father in creating man in a corporeal body! What a glorious anchorage for a young, weak, or deranged spirit! What a home a corporeal body is! How much easier we could manage these crazed ones were they provided thus!

20/29.7. Hoab said: Which shows us the way we must proceed to restore them. Since we cannot create corporeal bodies for them, the Father has given us power to provide them subjectively for the time being.

20/29.8. So Hoab and Athrava proceeded as follows: First by walling the place around with fire, so that none of the druj could escape, and then dividing them into thousands of groups, by means of fire also; then creating subjective bodies for them, to which they bound themselves willingly, and which prevented them from fastening to one another. (This is what drujas call reincarnation in another world.)

20/29.9. And while they were thus provided temporarily by their teachers, governors and nurses, many of them imagined themselves to be

---

[594] afflicted, ravaged, the object of vengeance

kings and queens, and high priests, and even Lords and Gods!

20/29.10. For more than a hundred days, Hoab and Athrava labored in the above manner; and the physicians, nurses and es'enaurs labored to restore the minds of the people; and they mastered the adversity, having nearly all restored and disciplined when messengers came from Fragapatti, greeting, saying:

20/29.11. Behold, the dawn of dan is passing swiftly, and I must yet visit the Lord Gods in the different heavens of the earth. It is therefore my decree that Athrava return to Mouru and resume the throne; and that Hoab return also, and join me as my student and companion on my journeys. Send these, my commandments, to Ah'oan, greeting, in my name, and he will provide a Lord to rule over the delivered knot of Osivi.

20/29.12. So, Hoab and Athrava were relieved by a Lord appointed by Ah'oan, and his name was Su'kah'witchow, an atmospherean pupil of Samati, of four hundred years, and of great resolution and proficiency. So Hoab provided Su'kah'witchow with a throne, and left four million teachers, nurses and physicians with him. And with the other million, Hoab and Athrava departed for Mouru, in Haraiti.

20/29.13. Now as for the cruisers, the swift messengers with Arieune, as soon as the knot was safely untied and Oibe and his Lords bound and delivered into Turbe's keeping, to be sent to Ah'oan, they departed, having recorded the proceeding in Arieune's diary.

20/29.14. Fragapatti, having heard of Hoab's success in delivering the knot, decided to honor him on his reception at Mouru. Accordingly, Fragapatti sent heralds out into Haraiti, proclaiming a day of recreation, and inviting as many as chose to come to Mouru to receive Hoab. The proper officers provided musicians, flags, banners and fireworks, suitable for the enjoyment of hundreds of millions of the inhabitants of Haraiti. Others provided one thousand reception boats, to go part way and meet Hoab's ship.

20/29.15. So when Hoab returned to Mouru, he was received in great honor and majesty, and in lights of unusual splendor.

20/29.16. Regarding this matter, Fragapatti said afterward: I had policy[595] in this; Hoab was to be the next God of earth and her heavens. And whatever would win the love, admiration and awe of his unlearned subjects would contribute to their resurrection.

CHAPTER 30 Fragapatti

20/30.1. So for one day there was great rejoicing in Mouru; and when it ended and the people retired to their respective places, the lights were raised for business.

20/30.2. Fragapatti said to Athrava: Come and resume Jehovih's throne. As for me, I will go now and establish another habitation in Zeredho; and after that I will visit the Lord Gods of the divisions of the earth.

20/30.3. And when I have completed these labors, it will be near the end of the dawn of dan. See to it, therefore, that all who wish to prepare for the third resurrection are duly notified.

20/30.4. And now, when Fragapatti had risen from the throne, swift messengers were announced from Sethantes, the inhabitor[596] of earth. The marshals were commanded to admit them; and presently the swift messengers came in, greeting in Jehovih's name. They said: Sethantes sends love to Fragapatti. When the resurrection of this dawn comes, Sethantes will visit Mouru. And he will also bring with him Onesyi, first deliverer of Brides and Bridegrooms of the first harvest of the earth.

20/30.5. When the message had been delivered, there was great rejoicing in the capital. Fragapatti thanked the messengers in the Father's name, and then the swift messengers withdrew.

20/30.6. Presently Fragapatti also withdrew, taking Hoab and Hapacha with him; and when they departed out of the capital, and came to the avalanza, the marshals already had assembled the ten million accompanying hosts, and so they entered the ship, and, amid music and rejoicings, they departed for Zeredho, and afterward went directly to the kingdom of Yima, Lord God of Shem and her heavens.

---

595 strategy, concealed purpose

596 that is, he who was responsible for having filled the earth with those capable of eternal life

20/30.7. Yima had been notified of their coming, and so had a piedmazr (an oar-boat) made, in order to go and meet them. The piedmazr was sufficient to carry the ten thousand musicians, thirty thousand rowers and two hundred thousand travelers who embarked on her to meet Fragapatti.

20/30.8. Three years had now elapsed since Yima set out to establish the Father's kingdom in the heavens of Shem; and, except through messengers, little was known in Mouru of Yima's labors. Fragapatti had said of him: Yima lives with the Voice; he cannot err.

20/30.9. In the seventh diaphragm of the east Apie, the vessels met, and Fragapatti opened the lower division of the avalanza, and, amid music and rejoicings, took in Yima's boat with crew and passengers. After due ceremonies, Fragapatti caused the avalanza to proceed, conducted[597] by Leaps, one of Yima's messengers, and they proceeded rapidly until they arrived at Astoreth, the capital of Yima's kingdom in atmospherea, first grade, and resting upon the earth.

CHAPTER 31 Fragapatti

20/31.1. After Yima's appointment by Fragapatti, he had come to these regions; and, finding great darkness upon both spirits and mortals, he appealed to Jehovih, to know the cause and cure.

20/31.2. The Voice of Jehovih came to Yima, saying: Whether spirits or mortals, they seek rather to obey their own self-desires than My commandments. Behold, I sent them Apollo and he gave them intercourse between the two worlds, angels and mortals. And for a season they held up their heads and remembered Me and My kingdoms.

20/31.3. But presently, they turned everything upside down, and built on their own account. I had shown them that by industry and perseverance they could attain to knowledge and power. But because mortals discovered that prophecy could come from the spirits of the dead, they ceased to perfect themselves, and so, grew up in idleness.

20/31.4. The angels loved not to labor, loved not to achieve My exalted heavens, being contented with the lowest. And they likewise fell in darkness, forgetting Me and My higher places above.

[597] directed, navigated or piloted

20/31.5. I called out to My Son, Osiris, saying: Go down to the earth and her heavens, and build them up, in My name. Yes, you shall wall them apart, so there shall be no communion between the two worlds, except to My chosen.

20/31.6. And Osiris came and fulfilled My commandments, providing for mortals in such ways that no spirit could come to them; and, as for the spirits that infested the earth, he drove them away and colonized them, thus cutting them off from the earth. And for a season, mortals prospered under My judgments; and they sought to improve the talents I created with them.

20/31.7. But again they confounded My judgments and perverted My laws. Every man on the earth has a philosophy of his own; every spirit in these heavens has a philosophy of his own. And there is no uniformity between any of them. Hear Me then, My Son; you shall not teach as Osiris did, nor yet as Apollo, but pursue a mean between the two.

20/31.8. You shall select them, permitting certain spirits to return to mortals, and permitting certain mortals to attain su'is and sar'gis, and to see and commune with spirits. But you shall provide them in judgment;[598] making the process of inter-communion a secret among mortals. For by this you shall shut off the drujas of heaven and the druks on earth.

20/31.9. Behold, My Son Samati will come this way; therefore labor with him and Zarathustra. I have given My decrees into God's (Samati's) hands; he shall build on the earth. But you shall build in heaven. As he builds for mortals, you shall build for the spirits of the intermediate world. But keep open the doorway to My holy places in the heavens above.

CHAPTER 32 Fragapatti

20/32.1. Yima inquired of Jehovih as to proceeding, and the Voice answered him, saying:

20/32.2. Go from place to place in these heavens, and prove your power. To the ignorant,

[598] Apparently this means discretion, and to provide for the participants' development in discernment, circumspection, reasoning and prudence regarding the spirits who manifest to them.

power is antecedent[599] in gaining the judgment; after power comes wisdom. The fool says: What can you do that I cannot? But when he sees the power that comes from My hand, he opens his ears and eyes. To teach men and angels to unite—how have they done anything but fail on all hands!

20/32.3. Mortals have said: It is good to be good, but it is not practical. They have said: It is wise to be wise, but wisdom runs in a thousand roadways; every man for himself.

20/32.4. The angels of these regions have said: It is good for us to unite into kingdoms; to have Gods and Lords; but who can unite us? Shall we sell our liberty to one person? But they will not unite; they dwell in disharmony. Every one takes the earnings of another; the profit of one is the injury of others; they are barren of united good.

20/32.5. Jehovih said: One kingdom may have many good men and many good women, but be of no good as a kingdom. I do not measure the individuals, but the entire household. I judge the virtue of a kingdom by its combined harvest delivered to My keeping.

20/32.6. When a kingdom is aggregating to itself more wisdom and virtue, the amount of its increase is My harvest. When a kingdom cannot retain its own members, it is falling away from Me. The uprightness of its few is as nothing in My sight. The secret of the power of a kingdom lies in its capacity to aggregate in My name and obey My commandments. ||

20/32.7. For a hundred days Yima went through the lower heavens, displaying the miracles of the upper heavens; and his hosts, many of whom traveled with him, enlisted pupils, particularly collecting the spirits of young children. And in a hundred days he had many millions of spirits, abracadabras,[600] mostly helpless wanderers.

20/32.8. With these he returned to Astoreth, and prepared to found his kingdom. Jehovih spoke to him, saying: Do not fear, My Son, because of the helplessness of your subjects. He who would start a new kingdom is wise in choosing none who have hobbies of their own. Whoever goes forth in My name, I will be with him.

20/32.9. Yima inquired of Jehovih as to who should be appointed assistant God, and the Voice answered: Thulae. So Yima anointed Thulae; and he made Habal chief marshal of the capital.

20/32.10. Again the Voice of Jehovih came to Yima, saying: You shall appoint one hundred Lords to Shem, and they shall have dominion over mortals. Hear the Voice of your Creator: Through My Son, Zarathustra, I will establish temples to My Lords and Gods; and you shall provide your heavenly kingdom in such a way that your Lords shall inhabit the temples, communing with the rab'bahs [priests –Ed.], who shall be called God-irs; but the communion between spirits and mortals shall be known only to the God-irs, and to the sub-priests under them. But mortals shall be left to believe that these fathers have attained to spirit communion by great purity and wisdom.

20/32.11. Likewise, when drujas manifest to mortals, it shall not be countenanced[601] in any way other than as a mark of evil, raised up against truth.

20/32.12. And when you have established your kingdom, you shall cut off the supplies of the drujas so that they will become borrowers from your people. In this manner, they will, in time, consent to labor.

20/32.13. Yima then appointed one hundred Lords, who became as the roots to the tree of heaven. The Aoshoan Lords were:

20/32.14. Ithwa, Yaztas, Micros, Jube, Zarust, Hom, Paoiris, Vadeve, Niasha, Cope, Drhon, Yus'ak, Cood'ayay and Thracton.

20/32.15. The Thestasias Lords were: Kashvre, Tusht, Yain, Amesh and Amesha; Armait, Wai'iv, Vahois, Vstavia and Comek.

20/32.16. The general Lords were called Ashem, with voice; that is to say, Ashem-vohu; and these were the Lords in chief, given for the kingdoms of the Sun in the land of Shem. They were: Shnaota, Zathias, Mutu, Aoirio, Kaeshas, Cter'ay, Shahkya, Thraetem, Gahnaetobirischae, Habarshya, Paitis'gomya, Huiyus, Hakdodt, Anerana, Tibalath, Kevar, Darunasya, Hors, Maidoyeshemo, Runnas, Gayomoratischi, Ba'ahraya, Zartushta, Kai'boryawich'wich'toe'benyas and Cpitama. And

[599] something that must come first, a prerequisite, a prior circumstance

[600] in this case being those in the first resurrection, which is aspiration toward a higher condition for self's sake, that is, the desire to improve one's condition

[601] looked upon or acknowledged

Yima made these twenty-five Lords controllers of the Voice, with mortals, to take Samati's place after the death and ascension of Zarathustra, for which reason they were called the Ashem-vohu.[602]

20/32.17. The Lords of farmers and herdsmen were: Gaomah, Hoshag, Tamur, Jamshed, Freden, Minochihr-bani and Hus.

20/32.18. The Lords of sea-faring men were: Thaetas, Mirh-jan, Nyas, Khaftras, Thivia, Agreft, Ardus'lor, Tanafar, Avoitas, Marganesiachta, Hoakastanya and Vartuan.

20/32.19. The Lordesses of births and mothers, the Hotche'che, were: Kaviti, Way'huts, Howd, Anechorhaite, Juveas, Wisseta, Hopaeny, Ctnevirchow, Aivipohu, Cadhan, Hucrova, Dion, Balkwoh and Gamosyi.

20/32.20. The Lords of buildings were: Irathama, Haira'thracna, Heidas, Hutu, Coy'gaga, Haira'Wahti, Vivi'seeon, Muta'hagga, Kaoyas, Macyo, Aims, Hodo, Trusivi, Verecopagga and Suyi.

20/32.21. The Lords of time-keeping [Ah'ches –Ed.], who had dominion of the change of watch, were: Copurasastras, Vaitimohu and Howitchwak.

20/32.22. Jehovih spoke to Yima, saying: In this day I will bless your labor. Because mortals have ceased to believe in immortality, they have shut off the intercourse with drujas. For which reason you shall establish pure communion with your pure Lords, and none other.

20/32.23. Yima sent his Lords to their separate places, and every Lord took a thousand attendant angels with him. Yima said to them before they departed: See to it, O Lords, that in your respective places you stir the people up. And wherever you find kings or queens or generals surrounded by spirits that urge them on in their affairs, cut off those spirits, leaving the mortals destitute of inspiration, and their kingdoms and armies will become disorganized and helpless.

20/32.24. And whenever Samati (God) and Zarathustra come to a city, you shall go also, laboring with them. And when Zarathustra holds up his hands and says: O Father, Light of Your Light! || Then gather of the substance around, and shield him with a wall of fire. And if Zarathustra should say: O Father, Ormazd, give Your children food || then you shall cast down, from the air above, fish and fruit.

20/32.25. And if a king or a captain raises a hand against Zarathustra, you shall gather about him and shield him. And if a man draws a sword against Zarathustra, catch the blade and break it to pieces.[603]

20/32.26. Jehovih spoke to Yima, saying: The time will come when the present mortal kingdoms will fall. But the followers of Zarathustra, who will succeed them under the Zarathustrian law, shall be protected, even as you, during dawn, protect Zarathustra.

20/32.27. For which reason, your Lords shall raise up other Lords to take their places after the ascent of this dawn. And it shall come to pass that All Light and All Truth and All Success shall come to mortals through the priests (rab'bahs), who shall succeed Zarathustra. But as for the kings of great cities, who will not accept My Light, they shall go down in darkness, and their kingdoms shall fall to pieces.

20/32.28. Yima having established his Lords, now turned his attention to the heavenly kingdoms of hada.

CHAPTER 33 Fragapatti

20/33.1. Jehovih said to Yima: You shall separate the spirits, the partly light from the wholly dark. Therefore, build a throne and a plateau sufficient for three billion souls; and because there are more females than males, you shall call the place of your throne Astoreth. And when you have provided a house for your Council, you shall send forth selectors, who shall bring you as many as

[602] See the Vedic Scripture. –Ed. [i.e., mortal records referring to that time]

[603] Many Spiritualists have witnessed the power of spirits to break things. Some have supposed that they break steel by electric or magnetic currents. I have witnessed the breaking of things when the sound was strong as the report of a musket [sound of a gun firing]. Where there is sufficient number of spirits, it is possible for them to erect walls of fire, or pillars of fire. The value [power] of manifestations is greatly increased by a su'is or sar'gis leading such a life that he may have an extensive army of spirits with him. –Eng. Ed. [1882]

choose to come; and these shall be the foundation of your kingdom.

20/33.2. Yima proceeded as commanded by the Father, and presently he had congregated, around about[604] Astoreth, a sufficient number so as to establish places of amusement, places of worship, and places of learning. Again the Voice came to Yima, saying:

20/33.3. Because your kingdom is attractive, you are flooded with idlers, who are of no profit to any person in heaven or earth. To keep them away, you shall wall your kingdom around with pillars of fire. For thus I have created man, that he will return with zeal to those who turned him away. Because you shall make your labors seclusive,[605] they will run for you.

20/33.4. And when they come to you, you shall bargain with them for righteous behavior before you feed them. And when you have thus gathered in all who come in this way, you will not yet have the half of them.

20/33.5. But those who are left will be without judgment, so you shall take possession of them, and bestow them in colonies. And you shall rank them. The lowest of all shall be the first rank; those who come after the pillars of fire are built shall be the second rank; and those who come with the selectors shall be called the third rank.

20/33.6. And you shall divide your own hosts; those who go with your Lords down to mortals as guardian spirits shall be called ashars, and they shall bring the spirits of the newly dead and deliver them to your hosts in heaven, which hosts shall be called asaphs.

20/33.7. And the ashars shall drive all spirits away from mortals, except those who are appointed by you or your Lords. For above all things you shall seek to become controller over mortals, so that they become Faithists in Me and My dominion.

20/33.8. Yima then divided the spirits of heaven according to the commandments of the Creator. After that he took possession of the wandering spirits of darkness, whether they were on earth or in heaven, and he had them taken into places prepared for them. And he provided them with physicians, nurses and teachers, and they were made to understand they were dead as to their earth bodies, and that they must give up the earth.

20/33.9. After this, Yima established places of learning in heaven, and places of labor, teaching the angels to clothe and feed themselves by their own industry.

20/33.10. Again the Voice of Jehovih came to Yima, saying: Behold, My Son, the lower heaven has reached S'pe'oke.[606] It is, therefore, the time in which angels of the first grade shall be taught to build heavenly mansions.

20/33.11. Yima commanded the teachers and the superintendents of factories to prohibit the spirits from returning to mortals, except by permission. Yima said:

20/33.12. It is wiser to inspire mortals to aspire to rise in heaven after death than to have mortals ever drawing the angels down to the earth. And my Lords on the earth shall labor for this outcome also. So Yima taught new inspirations, both in heaven and on earth, which were that the spirits of the dead should build homes in heaven for their kindred, and that mortals should be taught that there were mansions in heaven ready for their souls after death.

20/33.13. Yima said: Mortals becoming founded in this belief, will not so readily become wandering spirits after death.

20/33.14. While Yima was thus building in heaven, his Lords, with their attendant spirits, were manifesting on earth, as had never been before since the foundation of this world.

20/33.15. The temples of the stars[607] were broken and thrown down by the spirits; the iron gates of the cities were taken off and carried into the forests; the palaces of kings and queens were unroofed, and the stones of the walls of the palaces were hurled from their places; even to the

---

[604] centered around; surrounding; within the vicinity of

[605] exclusive, restricted, private, secretive

[606] Spirit house; that is, prior to this time the angels from the earth had not grown sufficiently to desire homesteads; neither had the heavens of the earth been prepared with plateaus sufficient for such spirits. Prior to this period angels of low grade were kept with mortals, and taught subjectively. – 1891 glossary

[607] In the early days, in India, the observatories were called oka'se'iang; that is, temples of the stars. –Ed.

foundation, one stone was not left upon another; and these things were done by the spirits of heaven.

20/33.16. And men and women and children were carried in the air by the angels, and unharmed. The household goods were carried out, and the food of the tables stripped off, even as mortals sat down to feast, and they were made to see the food going away; with their own eyes they saw these things.

20/33.17. And mortals were made to see visions and to dream dreams of prophecy, and to have unusual powers. And in many places the spirits took on sar'gis, and walked about among mortals, being seen and felt; and they talked audibly, explaining to mortals the dominion of Yima and his Lords.

20/33.18. In all things that Yima and his hosts did in heaven, his Lords worked in harmony with him in their labor on the earth. Nevertheless, there were also vagrant spirits on earth who did not belong to the kingdoms of heaven, but who made manifestations on their own account; and they were given to lying, and to flattery, and to evil generally. Little by little, Yima cut off these evil spirits, and took them away to his colonies, and disciplined them.

20/33.19. Such, then, were Yima's labors when Fragapatti came to see him. To honor this occasion, Yima had proclaimed recreation in Astoreth, and invited his Lords and captains and others to be present, and take part in a season of enjoyment.

CHAPTER 34 Fragapatti

20/34.1. Upon arrival of the avalanza, the es'enaurs of Astoreth and the trumpeters of the colonies sang and played, being joined by the hosts aboard the vessels. And when they ceased, Thulae, assistant God of Astoreth, commanded the marshals to receive the hosts, foremost of whom were Yima and his attendants, preceded by his traveling marshals and five thousand female harpers led by We'aytris, Goddess of Foes'ana, in etherea. After these came ten thousand marshals of Fragapatti; then ten thousand swift messengers; then Fragapatti with Hapacha to his left and Hoab to his right. And these were followed by the musicians, and finally came the hosts in general.

20/34.2. Yima ascended the throne at once, but Fragapatti and his hosts stopped in the arena, within the circuit of the altar. Beyond these were the guards of the lights; and still outside of these were the Crescent Members of the Council.

20/34.3. Yima said: In the name of Jehovih, I welcome you, O Fragapatti, Chief of Obsod and Goomatchala, to the throne of God! In His Wisdom and Power I would have you honor Astoreth by taking possession, in the Father's name!

20/34.4. Without replying, Fragapatti walked alone to the throne, saluting on the sign of HIGH NOON, which Yima answered IN THE SETTING SUN! Yima stood aside, and Fragapatti ascended and stood in front of the middle of the throne. He said:

20/34.5. Into Your possession, O Jehovih, receive this, Your Throne! Hardly had Fragapatti spoken, when a light, bright as the sun, settled above his head, and a Voice came out of the midst of the light, saying:

20/34.6. To you, My son (Fragapatti), and to your son (Yima), and to your Gods and Lords, and to all who follow them in My name, I bequeath this, My Throne, forever! Whoever becomes one with Me, shall not only hear My Voice and receive My Power, but also inherit that which he creates out of My creation.

20/34.7. Jehovih's Voice continued, saying: Whoever looks upon My works and says: Behold, I cannot cope with these elements! is short in faith and wisdom. For I have not created in vain, that mortals or spirits cannot control My elements in their respective places. They shall improve the talents I have given them.

20/34.8. I made the earth wide and filled it with many things; but I gave man a foundation so that he could attain to the mastery of land and water, and minerals, and of all the living. Yes, I gave him a corporeal body to practice with, and as an abiding place for the assistance of his own soul.

20/34.9. And I created atmospherea wider than the earth, and filled it with all manner of spiritual things, and with the substance of plateaus; but I also gave to the spirits of the dead, talents, by which they can attain to the mastery of all things in atmospherea.

20/34.10. Whoever has attained to these things is like a traveling sun: My light is upon him; he prepares the place, and My Voice comes out of the Light of it. Let My Sons and Daughters stir themselves up; where they are gathered together in My name, I am there also. My hand is upon them;

My Power becomes one with them, and My Voice is possible in their midst. || The Voice ceased.

20/34.11. There were many present who had not previously heard the Voice of All Light, and because of the brilliancy they were blinded for a while, but presently restored. Fragapatti then said: Hoab and Hapacha, come and sit on the throne. And they went up and sat on the throne; and in the same time the es'enaurs chanted: Hail to Great Jehovih's Voice! His Sons and Daughters, of thousands of years, have returned once more to their native red star, to proclaim His boundless glory!

20/34.12. Fragapatti said: In the Father's name, I proclaim a day of recreation; to resume labor at the sound of the trumpet in the east. And now the hosts mingled together freely, buoyant with cheerfulness. And during the recreation, millions of ethereans went out into the plateau, visiting the places of learning, the factories and hospitals, and such places as belong to the lower heavens.

20/34.13. On the next day, at the call of the trumpet, the people resumed their places, and after the music, Fragapatti said: To you, O Thulae, I will speak in the name of Jehovih. You are chosen by the Father to be assistant to Yima, Jehovih's Son, during this dawn, which is near its end, and after that you shall be Lord and God of these heavens and of the earth beneath, for two hundred years.

20/34.14. Because you are wise and good, the Father has raised you up, and great is your glory. So you may have strength and power, you shall also be called Yima during your reign; for the time has now come to the earth when mortals must learn to know the Lords and Gods who rule over them.

20/34.15. During the coming two hundred years, the earth will be traveling in my Orian field, Goomatchala, and you shall be one with me in your dominions. Whatever you shall require from my hand, I will send to you. You shall, therefore, keep your place in order; and if you need a'ji, I will send it; if you need dan, I will send it.

20/34.16. Most importantly, be less concerned about the spirits in your heavens than about mortals on the earth. Mortals must have sufficient a'ji, so that the race does not become extinct; they must have sufficient dan, so that they do not become like beasts. For which reason, every eleventh year you shall number abracadabra[608] and supply my swift messengers with these lists. And I will bring the elements of Goomatchala to bear upon your labor profitably to the Father!

20/34.17. Secondly, be careful of too much leniency toward the spirits in the first resurrection. Do not allow them to abide with mortals as teachers. Remember that mortals love their dead kindred to the extent that they would deprive them of heavenly education, for the sake of having them around. Remember, also, that the spirits of the recently dead, who are entered as es'yans in all good heavens, love their mortal kindred to the extent that they would seek no higher heaven, than to linger around them on earth. Which habit grows upon them, so that in two or three generations they become drujas, worthless to themselves, knowing little of earth and less of heaven.

20/34.18. Be firm, therefore, in holding dominion over the es'yans, permitting them only to return to mortals under guard; and especially preventing them from teaching mortals anything other than the Ormazdian religion.

20/34.19. After this, you shall be circumspect in Astoreth; remembering that it is the role of a God to provide his kingdom for the development of all the talents Jehovih has created with them. For you shall so intersperse labor and recreation, and rest and learning, so that each and every one is of equal attraction.

20/34.20. And whether your commandments are for angels or for mortals, you shall first of all and last of all, inspire them to faith in the Creator, and to follow the little star of light He has given to every soul. Fragapatti ceased.

20/34.21. Jehovih said: I have drawn My crescent and My altar. Whoever would hear My Voice and heed My commandments, let them hearken to[609] the forms and ceremonies that shape the soul of things. I am Order; I am Stateliness

---

[608] A census of mortals and angels would be made; and part of the enumeration was a listing of the grade and rate of each individual. Those individuals in the resurrection were tallied into a tablet called the abracadabra. There is more on this later in Oahspe.

[609] be alert to, pay attention to, heed, observe, attend to, help fulfill, abide by, be mindful of, be guided by

without severity; I am Love without passion; I am Wisdom by suggestion, and without dictation; I am the most Silent, but most Powerful; I am the Least Seen, but Always Present when asked for.

20/34.22. And now, since the people knew Fragapatti was about to depart, the proper officers arranged matters so that all could pass in front of the throne to receive his blessing. Accordingly, the es'enaurs commenced singing, and the procession began. The master of the lights of the Council lowered them, and Fragapatti lowered his own lights, and came down and stood at the foot of the throne, covered with light drapery, which fell down to his feet.

20/34.23. His hands he held upward, waving gently; and he created drapery and perfume, and wreaths of flowers, and bestowed something upon every soul that passed, of whom there were more than a billion!

20/34.24. And when the procession had all passed, Fragapatti sat down at the foot of the throne. Then Yima came down and took his hand, saying: Son of Jehovih, arise and go your way, and the Father be with you! So Fragapatti rose up and departed, and Hoab, Hapacha, Yima and Thulae with him; and Yima left Hi'etra, Goddess of Me'Loo, on the throne of Astoreth.

20/34.25. So they entered the avalanza, and, with music and rejoicing, departed on their journey. And Yima conducted them throughout his dominions, both in heaven and on earth. For many days Fragapatti thus dwelt with Yima and Thulae; and after he had inspected their labors, and his recorders completed their record, which was to be taken afterward to etherea and deposited in the libraries of Fragapatti's dominions, Yima took leave, and his piedmazr was discharged, and he departed for Astoreth, where he arrived in due season. But Fragapatti proceeded to the dominions of Ah'oan, Lord God of Jaffeth and her heavens.

CHAPTER 35 Fragapatti

20/35.1. The Voice of the Creator was with Ah'oan from the time of his landing in these lower heavens. And Ah'oan chose from his hosts a Council of ten thousand, and they sat in a living altar; and the Voice directed him to build a capital and a throne, and to call the plateau Sang'hi; which he did.

20/35.2. And when it was completed, Jehovih said to Ah'oan: You are My Lord and My God; the labor of your hand shall endure on the earth and in heaven. Whatever you build, I will build, for you are of My holy place. Make yourself an otevan, and go about in your dominions, and inspect all things, making a record of the same, which shall be deposited in the libraries of these heavens, so that angels and mortals, in after ages, may read them.

20/35.3. Ah'oan made an otevan, and traveled as commanded, making a record, and preparing also a place of records, in Sang'hi, where these things were deposited; of which these words are a brief transcript. That is:

20/35.4. These heavens are without order or organization, except one kingdom, ruled over by Oibe, who falsely styles himself Thor, the only begotten Son of Jehovih.

20/35.5. The spirits of these heavens are mostly of the first resurrection; nevertheless, there are millions of them who believe they are not dead; and the majority of these are in chaos, still lingering on battlefields or in the places where they were cut off from the earth.

20/35.6. In many places there are spirits who set up colonies, trying to provide themselves with homes and clothing, and to found heavenly abodes; but they are forever overrun and pillaged by drujas.

20/35.7. With and among the people of Jaffeth there are more than two billion angels who do not know how to get away from the earth. Of these, millions of them are fetals, making themselves twin spirits to mortals. These spirits often show themselves to mortals, but are believed to be doubles; yet these bound spirits do not know who they themselves are, or where they came from; nor can they go away from the mortals to whom they are bound, and on whom they live.

20/35.8. As for the mortals of Jaffeth, they have cities of warriors, and are large and fierce. The earth of this region has been in a'ji thirteen hundred years.

20/35.9. After Ah'oan had thus discovered the condition of things, he returned to Sang'hi, and they sat in Council, and Jehovih said to Ah'oan: You shall appoint forty Lords to dwell on the earth; and to each Lord you shall give ten thousand assistants. And these Lords shall go down to the earth, and drive away the drujas, and take possession of the kings' and queens' palaces and the temples of the stars; and they shall obtain control over the captains and generals of armies, and blind their judgment, and lead them astray, so that they will be powerless in war and destruction.

20/35.10. And when Samati, God of Zarathustra, travels in Jaffeth, your Lords shall go with him, with a sufficient number of angels to accomplish successfully all that Zarathustra professes in My name. And your Lords shall shield Zarathustra around, so that no harm comes to him; and when enemies pursue him, your Lords shall lead them astray or detain them long enough to enable Zarathustra to escape. For in this dawn My word shall be established on the earth, never to perish.

20/35.11. And when you have established your Lords, you shall colonize your heavens, giving them seventy colonies; but Sang'hi shall be the central kingdom. You shall choose from among the atmosphereans one who shall be your assistant God, who shall sit on your throne during your absence.

20/35.12. And you and your Holy Council shall instruct your assistant God, so that when this dawn is ended, he shall become God of Sang'hi in My name for the next two hundred years.

20/35.13. Ah'oan informed the Council of the words of Jehovih. And Ah'oan appointed the forty Lords, as commanded, and appointed an assistant.

20/35.14. These, then, were the Lords appointed: First, to have control over the Word of God on earth: The, Seung-bin, Go-magit, Ben-hong, She-ang, Bog-wi, Ah-tdong, Mwing-wi, Ah-tchook, Gonk-boy, Yuk-hoh and Ahwotch.[610]

20/35.15. Second, to have control over the palaces of kings and queens, and temples: Mina, Ahchaung, Ahyot, Yowgong, Ohonto, Yon-gwe and Ahma.

20/35.16. Third, to have control over armies and kingdoms: Kear-ak-a, Geeouh-young, Bi, Gwan-gouk, Gee-ooh-young, Sam-sin and Deth.

20/35.17. Fourth, to have control over sea-farers: Shopgee, Agan-ha, Rax and Lo.

20/35.18. Fifth, to have control over mothers and births: Songheng, Someconc, Yahiti, Ogne-ka-was and Hoah'ava.

[610] These names still exist in the ancient Chinese and Indian [India] mythologies and sacred books. –Ed.

20/35.19. Sixth, to have control over marriages: First, the loo'is in general, and then: Ahsam, Oanis, Yotsam, Ivitgom and Sap-sang.

20/35.20. So Ah'oan sent his Lords to their various places, with their assistants. After that he began colonizing the angels in his heavens. And in one year he raised up from Jaffeth more than a billion angels, having supplied them with houses, hospitals, nurseries, factories, and all such things and places as are required in hada for resurrection.

20/35.21. In the second year he delivered another billion, and of these, more than half had to be taken away from the earth by force. And this billion he also housed and provided with teachers and overseers in similar manner as before.

20/35.22. So by the time Samati, God of Zarathustra, was prepared to travel in Jaffeth, visiting the kings and queens, the Lords of Ah'oan had banished the drujas to such an extent that they were powerless to prevent the decrees of the Father's word. And when Zarathustra went into Jaffeth, behold, the Lords of heaven were with him as was God of the Word (Samati), and the kings and queens of earth were powerless before him.

20/35.23. And when Zarathustra went to a city, and being inspired by God, said: Fall down, you walls! Behold, the angels of heaven broke the walls, and they fell. And when Zarathustra said: Come forth, you spirits of the dead! || Behold, the Lords seized the drujas and held them up so that mortals could see them. And when Zarathustra said: O Ormazd, give Your children food! Behold, the angels had fish and fruit ready, which they let fall to the people, the time and place being previously arranged between them and God of the Word!

20/35.24. Thus Ah'oan's dominions extended down to mortals; thus the word of Zarathustra became Jehovih's Word to mortals.

20/35.25. And now Fragapatti, Chief over all, was coming to inspect the labors of his Lord God, Ah'oan, and of Samati. Ah'oan had sent commands to his Lords, and to their assistants, to return to Sang'hi and remain three days in recreation. And Ah'oan commanded the captains of the colonies of heaven to come, and to bring with them as many of their pupils and subjects as possible.

20/35.26. And it came to pass that when Fragapatti's avalanza came to Sang'hi, there were more than two billion souls assembled to witness the pageantry and proceedings. For, Ah'oan had provided the means and facilities, so that these things could manifest in magnificence.

CHAPTER 36 Fragapatti

20/36.1. Never in these heavens had there been such pageantry and display as when Fragapatti's avalanza entered Sang'hi; never had so many musicians, two million, been distributed to lend so great an effect to a procession.

20/36.2. Of this matter, Ah'oan said: By the pageantry and the music, my hosts of delivered drujas were made to realize the glory of the upper heavens; by the glory of those three days' recreation I shut out the attractions of the lower world. My people were entranced with delight; they were born for the first time into the kingdom of heaven!

20/36.3. Ah'oan said: But the greatest glory of all was when Fragapatti honored the throne of Sang'hi. Jehovih cast a sun upon the place; and the Voice spoke from the Light, so that the whole multitude saw the Light and heard the words of the Father! And when Fragapatti rose up and stood in the middle of the throne, the Light was so great that millions of the people fell down because of its glory.

20/36.4. The lights were lowered to suit the newly born in heaven,[611] and the people of etherea mingled with the atmosphereans, diverting, explaining, and inspiring them with the magnitude and glory of the higher heavens.

20/36.5. After the recreation, and when the multitude were in order, Fragapatti spoke from Jehovih's throne, first, to Es'pacia, assistant Goddess to Ah'oan, who was to succeed him after dawn. To her he said: Es'pacia, Daughter of Jehovih, hear my words; I am one with the Father, and in His name salute you. Behold, from this time forward the Father's Word shall dwell with mortals.

20/36.6. It shall become anchored to the earth, never to depart; though it may be mutilated and perverted, yet His hand is over it, and it shall not fail. As a mother delights in the first spoken words of her child, so shall we all take delight that the Father's Word has become engrafted on the earth. Before this time, the Word was with the I'hin tribe, but locked up in secret. It could not be maintained on the earth except by locking it up in secret, and with a people prepared as seed for delivering all the races of men. But now the Word is delivered openly to mortals.

20/36.7. After this, if the spirits of the lower heavens do not know the Father's Word, they can be taken down to the earth and there taught His commandments. Prior to this time, the angels of these lower heavens had no anchored Word; they constantly fell in darkness, and pulled mortals down with them. Behold, the Word is now engraved, through our Sons, Samati and Zarathustra; it cannot be lost.

20/36.8. You have been exalted first Goddess of these heavens, and Lordess of this division of the earth, to maintain the light of this dawn, to angels and mortals. You shall first of all labor to protect the Word to mortals; the wisest of your angel hosts you shall appoint to all the priests and cities of Zarathustra, to protect them and to maintain the Word.

20/36.9. You shall maintain your hosts in the temples of worship, where they worship the Great Spirit. But to those mortals who deny the Word, and to those who seek to destroy the Word, you shall lend no assistance, but leave them either without angels, or with only those who will lead them into failure.

20/36.10. Throughout Jaffeth you shall inspire mortals to hang the wheel of the altar in country places, by the roadsides. And when mortals pass the places, they shall turn the wheel, in remembrance of the Creator. Therefore, you shall station angel sentinels at each and every one of these altars, and these shall have messengers to your throne. And when a mortal passes the wheel and turns it, and is afflicted with sickness, you shall send angels to him to heal him. But if he is afflicted with sickness and does not turn the wheel in remembrance of the Father, your sentinel shall not send notice to you, and you shall not send angels to heal him. Nevertheless, the wheel and the altar

---

[611] Newly born in heaven does not seem to mean only those who recently died on earth, but those who are for the first time awakened to the Light of the Father's kingdoms. In another place we read of spirits having been in the lower conditions for hundreds of years, not knowing the heavens above them. –Ed.

shall cause men to think; for, after a disbeliever afflicted with sickness has passed the wheel without turning it, and if he repents and goes back and turns the wheel, then you shall send angels to him quickly and heal him, so that he may proclaim abroad what the Creator has done for him.

20/36.11. For as long as you carry out these decrees of All Light, so shall you remain united with my heavens above, which are united with those above, which are united with the Creator. And should you lack in power or wisdom, ask the Father, and I will answer you in His name.

20/36.12. Fragapatti then spoke to the Council in words similar to those spoken in Astoreth. After that, he walked down to the foot of the throne, where the marshals had provided a place for the people to pass before him, even as they had done in Astoreth. Accordingly, when the musicians began singing and playing, the people marched before him, and by the waving of his hands he created drapery, and flowers, and wreaths, and gave something to all the people, even though two billion angels passed before him!

CHAPTER 37 Fragapatti

20/37.1. So, Fragapatti departed, and sailed for Hi-rom, the heavenly kingdom of E'chad, Lord God of Arabin'ya and its heavens.

20/37.2. E'chad also had the Voice of Jehovih with him, and could not err. After his appointment to this division of earth and heaven, Jehovih commanded him, even as He had Ah'oan, to make an otevan and visit all the places, and make a record, before he established his kingdom. And E'chad did these things, taking thirty thousand companions with him, being surveyors, inspectors, recorders, numerators, and others of such order as are required in preliminary examinations of the earth and lower heavens. Besides these, he had also his hosts of musicians, his heralds and messengers.

20/37.3. Forty days he spent in this labor, and then the record was completed, of which E'chad had two copies made, one for his own kingdom in etherea, and one for the heaven he was about to found. According to these records, which are everlasting in heaven, the numerators estimated there were one billion eight hundred thousand spirits wandering about, mostly on the earth, many of them falling into forgetfulness and dissolution. And many of them had forgotten who they were, and had no memory of once having lived mortal lives. Millions and millions of them had forgotten their speech, and were dumb. Millions of them lived with mortals as fetals and familiars, depending for their own existence upon the spiritual part of the food mortals drank and ate. And yet other millions of them pursued evil for evil's sake; inspiring mortals to war, for the delight of seeing them destroy one another; delighting in persuading mortals to suicide or to all manner of wickedness.

20/37.4. In the region of Gavies there were four hells, containing sixty million souls in torments, tormenting one another in perpetual horrors, especially males and females doing what is even unlawful to mention. And these tormentors would bring es'yans, fresh from the earth life, and cast them into their hells for these wicked purposes. For even as mortals delight in vengeance, so can the talent grow until its feast lies in the fruit of hell; nor do such spirits desire to have even their own torments lessened; nor could they of themselves escape were they to try.

20/37.5. E'chad's inclination was to rush in and deliver these hells, but Jehovih said to him: Go first and establish Hi-rom, with suitable habitations, and then return and deliver these hells, and you shall have places for them. So E'chad established Hi-rom, and appointed the Holy Council of one hundred thousand men and women. Sa-ac he made chief marshal; and he appointed Geth'ya to be assistant God. Jehovih said to E'chad: You shall appoint sixty Lords to your division of the earth; and they shall dwell in the principal cities of Arabin'ya, and have dominion over mortals. And each and every Lord shall have ten thousand ashars to do their commands.

20/37.6. These, then, are the Lords appointed by the Lord God, for Arabin'ya: First, to have dominion over the revealed Word: Tsdasag, Bachar, Raab, Nathan, Neshu, Dath, Shephat, Gaon-ay, Cha'ya and Zeker.

20/37.7. Second, the loo'is in general; but for special masters of generations: Achuzeh, Chata, Galah, Dayyan, Aphsi, Ishsah, Basar and Goi. Third, for destroying evil cities, and for protecting good ones, and for building new ones: Atsil, Sherngoth, Matshebah, Achime, Amos, Ahio, Yat-gaab, Zer, Howdawitch, Beodi, Machal,

Yay-baoth, Ammah, Fakir, Cephets, Bachre and Hiv-iv.

20/37.8. Fourth, to abide on earth with rab'bahs (priests) and shield them in danger: Machaveh, Emul, Ashshaph, Alcmosum, Lai-awotch, Trivi-yab, Herivir, Beli-gib, Barat'ay, Shav'ya, Tir and Bowd-wahtal. Fifth, to inspire to inventions: Kartum-mim, Moses, Beged, Chakasat, Mih-gad, Jagri, Hen-di, Sru, Amothes and Benguda. Sixth, to have control over altars and temples: Atman, Krit and Anach.

20/37.9. In addition to these, the Lord God appointed censors[612] of Hi-rom and her colonies in heaven; and the ashars, appointed over mortals as guardians, were directed by the censors as to which colony to take their es'yans, where the asaphs, the receivers, were stationed.

20/37.10. As soon as E'chad had these matters completed, he descended into the four hells with his otevan, taking three million angels to help him deliver them. And when he arrived at the place, behold, the power and light of Jehovih was upon him! And he surrounded the four hells with his hosts of angels.

20/37.11. Fire of Your Fire, O Jehovih! he cried; Give me here walls of fire, to enclose these suffering hells! And along the line of his hosts there fell, from the firmament above, sheets of fire, and he walled the places around in such brilliant flames and suffocating flames that not one of the inhabitants of hell could escape.

20/37.12. And E'chad and his hosts poured into them from all sides, building fires in pillars and walls, blinding to the drujas, so they fell flat down and hid their faces. And they marched thoroughly through the four hells, until all the inhabitants were fallen prostrate before them, crying out. And they were all naked, men and women; and only the recent victims were ashamed.

20/37.13. E'chad said: Turn now, and deliver those who are ashamed, making a place beyond the walls of fire; but wall that place around also, and then clothe and feed them. So E'chad's hosts delivered those who were ashamed. Again E'chad called out: Begin now in sections and deliver the others into prisons surrounded by suffocating fire so they cannot escape. And do not let the light cease to fall upon those who will not be clothed. It is better that they lie prostrate than to display themselves nakedly. But as fast as they will accept and wear clothes, and cease cursing, so deliver them into genial[613] lights.

20/37.14. For six days and six nights E'chad labored in delivering the four hells, and on the seventh day they were all delivered. And among these drujas there were three and a half million in chaos, spirits who had lost their minds by the torments that other spirits had inflicted upon them. E'chad had these placed in his otevan and sent to Hi-rom, to be treated by the physicians.

20/37.15. But E'chad and many of his hosts remained with the groups of the delivered, preparing them further for resurrection. And now E'chad had them inspected, and he further searched the es'pe[614] of the earth to establish the origin of these hells, and as to who they were. This, then, is the substance of the history of that matter, namely:

20/37.16. In the lower country of Arabin'ya, on the earth, there had been an I'huan tribe of hundreds of years, who had attained to thirty cities, chief of which was Os'nu, which was the capital over all the rest. Os'nu was ruled over by Che-muts, a king of great wisdom and power in his youth; but, after subjugating all the large cities of Arabin'ya, he became a tyrant and a man of wickedness.

20/37.17. Being learned in the earth, moon and stars, he drew to his palace other men, and not a few women, of great learning, and together they resolved upon obtaining from the I'hins, the sacred people, the secrets of their miracles and religion. Up until this time all the people in the world respected the I'hins, neither did they deny them in anything, for they were the forefathers and foremothers of the I'huans.

20/37.18. Che-muts, the tyrant, said: Because from our youth we have been taught to revere the I'hins, we have become superstitious regarding them. Now it is evident that they have some other means (than consulting the stars) of prophecy. It is my command, therefore, that the different cities of I'hins be seized, and the people put to death,

[612] magistrates in charge of suitability, aptness and other information required for destination placement of es'yans

[613] lights that were gracious, hospitable, pleasant, calm, comforting, soothing

[614] spiritual history. –1891 glossary

offering relief only to those who reveal their secrets. With their gifts of miracles and power of prophecy, I can march successfully against Par'si'e, Jaffeth and Ashem, and I shall become king of all the world. And you who help me in this matter, instead of having merely cities to rule over, as you now have, shall have kingdoms with many cities.

20/37.19. The learned men acceded to this, and shortly after, the king's people fell upon the I'hins, pulled down their flimsy walls, putting them to flight or slaying them outright, offering no salvation unless they would reveal their secrets, and give themselves up to marriage with the I'huans.

20/37.20. Hab-bak, a chief rab'bah of the I'hins, went to see the king and expostulate.[615] He said to Che-muts: Behold, my people are older than this country. Our wisdom does not come like other men's, but through marriage. How can we reveal? We are born gifted. No other people are thus born. How can you obtain the secrets of the womb? Besides this, we are sworn before our birth by our fathers and mothers to secrecy in our religion.

20/37.21. You desire us to intermarry with your people. I foresee your aims. You hope for the gift of prophecy, which, if given to evil men, would give them all power. But know, O king, he who desires prophecy for such purpose can never obtain it. Prophecy comes by the other road.

20/37.22. If my people intermarry with yours, it is simply the loss of mine. If you had our passwords and our signs, they would benefit you nothing, being born as you are. According to our number, we pay you your just tribute. I pray, then, change your decree and permit my people to remain as they have, for thousands of years!

20/37.23. Che-muts, the king, said: Why do you call yourselves I'hins? Hab-bak said: Because we are Faithists in One Great Spirit. The king asked: What is the secret name of the Great Spirit? Hab-bak said: I can only repeat that name under certain rules; otherwise I will lose my power of prophecy. Besides, if you knew the name, it would be worthless to utter it. To whoever utters His name not in faith, it is void. Whoever utters His name for earthly gain or earthly glory, utters in vain also. Of what value, then, would the name be to you, even if I violated my own oath and revealed it to you?

20/37.24. The king mocked him, and had him seized and taken to the lions' den, of which all kings and rich people, in those days, had one or more, as a place for casting in their disobedient servants. And when Hab-bak was at the lions' den, the king again offered to save him if he would reveal even the name of the Great Spirit, hoping that by its utterance he could also heal the sick, restore the blind and deaf, and especially prophesy. Hab-bak said: Though you may cast me in, and I be devoured, allow me beforehand to prophesy concerning you and your kingdom. Yes, I will even prophesy concerning myself. Hear, then, my words:

20/37.25. You have sought to destroy my people, who are, compared to yours, only as one little finger to a man's whole arm. In Os'nu you have hundreds of thousands of people, and in other cities tens of thousands and tens of thousands; so many that one man in his whole life could not count them. Yet, as to my people, what are they? Not more than ten thousand altogether. Hear, then, my words: You cannot destroy even one thousand of my people. Nor will my people raise a hand in self-defense.

20/37.26. But you will cast me into the lions' den, and I will be devoured. And this little hat, without a brim, will come out of the lions' den, and it will be a mighty power for thousands of years. It will be red with my blood, shed because I am faithful to the Great Spirit in my oath. And it will be restored to my people, and it shall be called THE SCARLET HAT! And in the day that it is carried in the streets of Os'nu, you will be slain by your own people.

20/37.27. The king laughed, saying: A prophecy often causes fools to carry it out. With that, he gave the executioners the sign, and they pushed Hab-bak onto the trapdoor, and cast him into the den, where there were thirty lions. And they fell upon him and devoured him. And his hat was colored red with blood; and some of the people, who were superstitious regarding the I'hins, procured the hat and went about repeating the prophecy of Hab-bak, and the multitude were anxious for some pretext to justify themselves in destroying the tyrant. So presently the city was in riot, and the people fell upon the king and slew him, and also slew the

[615] earnestly reason with, so as to change the other's view; to remonstrate; protest and plea

learned men and women who were his counselors and subsidiaries.

20/37.28. In the libraries of heaven it is recorded as follows: Because of the cruelty of Che-muts, king of Os'nu, on earth, thousands and tens of thousands of people had been put to death; and because they died in anger, and because of the injustice, their souls went into torment in hada, and they came and incited the king to greater wickedness, in order to have him slain. And so it came to pass that Che-muts, chief king of Arabin'ya, was slain by his own people, and the king's counselors were slain with him.

20/37.29. And when their spirits were delivered from their mortal bodies, the drujas fell upon the spirits of the king and his counselors, and bore them off to a foul-smelling place in hada, and cast them in, and the drujas went in after them, beating them. At which point it became known in hada that there was a newly-started hell, and other spirits brought other victims there and cast them in. And the drujas went about on the earth, in Arabin'ya, finding whomever they hated, bringing their spirits into hell, beating them and otherwise punishing them, until these four hells became the habitation of sixty million souls.

CHAPTER 38 Fragapatti

20/38.1. When E'chad had discovered the history of these hells, he searched and found the spirits of the king and counselors, but alas, they knew nothing, being in chaos, or more like one in a troublesome nightmare from which there is no awakening.

20/38.2. But E'chad appointed physicians and nurses for them, and it was three years before they began to awaken; but at the time of Fragapatti's visit they were not sufficiently restored to know who they were, or, if knowing one moment, would forget in the next. Yet it was not many days after the deliverance of the hells that E'chad had the inhabitants removed to Hi-rom and its colonies.

20/38.3. E'chad, having been informed by heralds that Fragapatti was coming, sent word to his Lords, generals and captains, and to superintendents of schools, factories and hospitals, to come to Hi-rom and enjoy three days' recreation, bringing as many atmosphereans as they could with them.

20/38.4. So Fragapatti came, as did the hosts of E'chad, and there was great rejoicing for the space of three days; during which time Fragapatti visited all the places and labors of E'chad, having records made of these, to take with him to etherea at the end of dawn. Now at the end of the three days' recreation, the trumpet in the east called the Council to labor and the hosts to order. Fragapatti sat in the middle of the throne, with E'chad next to him, and then Hoab and Hapacha, and then Thulae, Es'pacia and Geth'ya, and others of lesser rank.

20/38.5. A light immediately gathered above the throne, but this time, deep scarlet, with white border. Fragapatti said: Your Voice, O Jehovih, be upon these people! At which, the es'enaurs chanted a hymn, and after that the Voice of Jehovih spoke out of the light, saying:

20/38.6. Whoever raises up My children, I raise up with My own hand. To whoever utters My words in wisdom and truth, I speak from My judgment seat. Because you have come down from your exalted kingdoms in the upper heavens and raised up the drujas of these heavens, so do I come from My All Highest Holy Place to raise you up. As you have prepared to found My Word with mortals, so I prepare here in Hi-rom a heavenly place of delight.

20/38.7. Was I not with the I'hins since the creation of man on the earth? And where they have been faithful to Me I have come in great security. Now, behold, the earth rose up against My chosen and sought to destroy them, but they failed utterly. And when they cast My faithful servant into the lions' den, yet he would not violate his oath, even though he suffered death. And I stretched forth My hand and took his hat, red with blood, out of the lions' den; and I gave power to the hat. And into the far-off country of Jaffeth I will take the title of KING OF THE SUN, and bestow it upon Ya'seang, and neither Arabin'ya nor Par'si'e shall endure in holiness.

20/38.8. Behold, I give you a new sign, in addition to the triangle, and it (scarlet hat) shall be the sign of Hi-rom from this time forth, signifying, FAITH EVEN TO DEATH.[616]

---

[616] The Cardinals of the Christian religion have no right to wear the red hat. Their faith is in Christ, the idol, and not in Jehovih. In the Masonic order, however, the master is entitled to wear it, because

20/38.9. The Voice ceased, and Fragapatti turned to the red light and stretched forth his hand and took of it, saying: OF YOUR SCARLET, O JEHOVIH! GIVE TO YOUR SERVANT A HI-ROM, AS AN EMBLEM OF THIS HEAVEN! And he fashioned it into a hat without a brim, and laid it on the throne. Presently a swift messenger, from without, desired admittance before Fragapatti, and he was permitted to come. He said:

20/38.10. Greeting to you, O Fragapatti, Son of Jehovih! And by the love of E'och, God of Tshi, in Ude, grade six, I am sent before you in Jehovih's name. Behold, one Hab-bak is outside, who was the wearer of Hi-rom!

20/38.11. Fragapatti said: Admit him, and bid him approach the throne of God. The swift messenger retired and presently returned, bringing in Hab-bak, faithful to death. And he went up to the throne, and Fragapatti took the scarlet hat, saying: In the name of the Creator, I cover your head with Hi-rom, second only to Jehovih's crown! And he placed it on Hab-bak's head, and the light of it was so great that hardly any but ethereans could look upon it.

20/38.12. Then Hab-bak said: By this, Your Power, O Jehovih, I will go now and deliver to everlasting light the soul of the king who slew me. And I will restore the Council also. For they will remember the scarlet hat, and it will be like an anchorage for their crazed minds to rest upon! So Hab-bak saluted on the sign of the triangle and departed.

20/38.13. And now came the time of departure for Fragapatti and his hosts. So he instructed Geth'ya, and bade him travel with him. Then Fragapatti instructed the Council, which was like his instruction to the preceding Councils. And then he descended to the foot of the throne, and the marshals had the people march before him. And Fragapatti created flowers, drapery and ornaments, and gave every one something as they passed, though there were more than a billion souls!

20/38.14. And when they had all passed, and resumed the places assigned them, Fragapatti sat down at the foot of the throne in ancient custom, and E'chad descended to him, taking his hand; and he said to him: Arise, O Chief, Son of the Most High, and go your way! Fragapatti rose up and departed, followed by the officiating Gods and Goddesses, and they all went into the avalanza and departed, going to the kingdom of Gir-ak-shi, Lord God over Heleste and her heaven.

---

they profess only the Great Spirit, Jehovih, the ARCHITECT. The hat should be blood red, and have no rim, and its name, evidently, should be Hi-rom. –Ed.

CHAPTER 39 Fragapatti

20/39.1. When Gir-ak-shi arrived at his division of the earth and heaven, the Voice of Jehovih came to him, saying: My Lord and God, hear the Voice of your Father. In your division I have no I'hins left upon the earth, and the place is like a field without seed. The I'huans have degenerated also, by marrying with the druks. And you have come to this, My farm, when it is grown up full of weeds and thistles.

20/39.2. Look about your division, and you shall find no loo'is or ashars of any benefit to righteousness. Consider, then, what shall be done, so that both mortals and spirits may be made to know Me and My kingdoms. ||

20/39.3. Gir-ak-shi found the mortals of Heleste to be barbarians, many of them naked, or at best clothed with the skins of animals to keep them warm in winter. Some of them burrowed in the ground, and some lived in houses made of bark, leaves and grass. And their food was mostly fish and flesh. Their cities were numerous, but small, and every city spoke a different language.

20/39.4. Their weapons of war were clubs, spears, and bows and arrows, but they had neither iron nor copper, and used stone for cutting.

20/39.5. Gir-ak-shi said: What incentive can I give such a people that will raise them up?

20/39.6. Gir-ak-shi then surveyed his heavens, but alas, there were no kingdoms, no organizations, no societies. As mortals lived and died, so did their spirits continue in the same places, procuring subsistence in the same way, but spiritually; and often taking part in mortal wars and hunting, seeing and hearing through their mortal kin's eyes and ears.

20/39.7. Gir-ak-shi said: What incentive can I give such angels that will raise them up?

20/39.8. If I tell the mortals to till the soil and make clothes of flax and wool, my words will be interpreted as folly, or as implying hardships. If I tell the angels there are higher heavens, more beautiful, my words will be disbelieved. If I tell them that all growth depends upon exercise and labor, they will decline to grow. Have I not seen rich men and rich women in other countries whom I told that, in order to rise, they must learn to labor? But they ignored me.

20/39.9. Jehovih said to Gir-ak-shi: You have more than a billion drujas in your department. The mountains, valleys and forests are filled with them, roving about. As you would entrap birds by rich bait, so shall you gather together all you can of these drujas. But as to your mortals, you shall call famines into certain places, and thus drive them to observe the Unseen Cause of things.

20/39.10. Gir-ak-shi called together his hosts, millions and millions. He said to them: Form in sacred circles, hundreds of thousands of them, and go to the places I will point out, and invoke the higher heavens in Jehovih's name. Cast a famine here, and a blight in the animals of the forest. Cast imbrele[617] into the water so that the fish will die. Make mortals stop and consider.

20/39.11. Let the ashars go, then, and find the most prophetic among mortals, and make them prophesy concerning the famines and the blight. Make their prophets objects of worship; then I can rule the inhabitants of the earth through the prophets.

20/39.12. Concerning the angels, Gir-ak-shi said: Five heavenly places I will build for the drujas. One shall be called Monk, one Acha, one Troy, one Be-yome and one Hellen. I shall have five Lords to rule in my heavenly divisions: Ki-liope, Lord of Monk; I'tius, Lord of Acha; Foebe, Lordess of Troy; Liriyi, Lordess of Be-yome, and Co'ye, Lord of Hellen. These shall be heavenly places in the mountains, pure and delightful.

20/39.13. And you shall make them places of feasting and sporting for one whole year; anything that can be done to make them attractive for drujas shall not be left undone.

20/39.14. My hosts shall be selected and apportioned into five divisions of half a million each; and their mission shall be to go throughout Heleste, bringing in drujas to my five heavenly places.

[617] poison worms materialized. –1891 glossary

20/39.15. As for myself, I will build a plateau in these mountains, the Aguaadica, with a Council of half a million. Let my Lords stand aside, and I will apportion to each of them their attendants; by the star-lights that fall upon them they shall be known and come forth.

20/39.16. The Lords stood aside, in different places. Gir-ak-shi then cast stars until the three million were selected. After that Gir-ak-shi proceeded according to the Voice of Jehovih; and he conducted his hosts to the places the Father commanded.

20/39.17. After they were all placed, Gir-ak-shi chose his own Council, and built a plateau and a throne to Jehovih on Mount Aguaadica; and when he considered the wisdom of the manner Jehovih had directed him, to thus lay a foundation for so great a work, he soliloquized,[618] saying: O Jehovih, will these drujas ever understand the manner of Your armies? Will these mortals ever understand the proceedings of Your Lords and Gods?

20/39.18. For one year the hosts entertained, fed and clothed the drujas sumptuously, and they won them away from the earth; won them to the kingdoms prepared for them. And then Gir-ak-shi commanded the founding of schools, factories and hospitals in heaven; and he appointed ashars and asaphs, and began the resurrection through his Lords. And by the fourth year he had colonized nearly all the drujas in his heaven, giving them sufficient recreation to restrain them from returning to the earth.

20/39.19. As to Fragapatti's coming, for a long time prior to this Gir-ak-shi had it proclaimed to his newly delivered, giving invitations to them to be present. This he communicated to Fragapatti, through messengers. So, Fragapatti, knowing the grade of the place, decided to come in gaudy colors, and with very loud but suitable music, and for the manifestation of power.

20/39.20. To match which, Gir-ak-shi had his people attire themselves in the gaudiest colors. For it is by these things that the unlearned judge, as to the glory and possibilities of high heaven.

20/39.21. So it came to pass that Fragapatti's avalanza descended from above like a sea of fire, but decorated in thousands of ways with banners,

[618] apostrophized; the asking of rhetorical questions; so-called 'thinking out loud'

flags, curtains and such other ornaments as would convey the idea of greatness to the minds of the es'yans. On the other hand, Gir-ak-shi had decorated Aguaadica, his place and kingdom and throne, in the most extravagant splendor. And he and his Lords, and his captains and generals, and his Holy Council, were arrayed majestically.

20/39.22. In addition to these things, Gir-ak-shi had provided a feast, which was to succeed the ceremonies; and after the feast there were to be diverse entertainments. But of these matters, who knows the thought of Jehovih! How He has provided ingenuities to bring the dark soul to understanding!

20/39.23. Gir-ak-shi said: To teach mortal teachers how to teach the barbarian, O Jehovih! To teach Cold-Awe in order to impart Warm-Mirth, O Jehovih! Shall they build a prison and decorate the convict in fine clothes, and bid him take his ease, watching the virtuous working for him, O Jehovih! Will they ever learn Your power in resurrection, O Jehovih!

CHAPTER 40 Fragapatti

20/40.1. Fragapatti and his hosts remained thirty days with Gir-ak-shi, and great was the enjoyment of the people; and then Fragapatti departed, going to the kingdoms of Uropa, first Goddess of a barbarian division of the earth. The Voice of Jehovih had been with her from the beginning, but there were few corporeans in her division, and only six hundred million angels, mostly drujas.

20/40.2. Nevertheless, Jehovih said to Uropa: You shall found here a kingdom in My name, and it shall become mighty in heaven and earth. Uropa said: What is the best way, O Jehovih? Jehovih answered, saying: As for the drujas, you know. But as for the corporeans, behold, they have neither copper nor iron, but use stone. Therefore send five hundred of your ashars, who are well skilled in the art of inspiring mortals, to Arabin'ya; and you shall cause fifty men to migrate into your lands. And the fifty men shall be skilled in mining and working copper and iron.

20/40.3. And your ashars shall inspire them to go to the mountains and find the ore, and then to work it, making tools, and implements for hunting and fishing.

20/40.4. So Uropa sent angels to Arabin'ya, and they inspired fifty men to go to Uropa, and find copper and iron, and work it. And in four years, behold, not less than twenty thousand men had migrated from Arabin'ya. And the ashars inspired them to marry with the druks and half-breed I'huans. And in this way a new people of higher light was born into Uropa's division.

20/40.5. In Zeigl, Uropa built her heavenly kingdom and founded the city of Oitch. Five hundred thousand angels were her Holy Council; and there were fifty thousand captains; and two million ashars, partly ethereans and partly atmosphereans.

20/40.6. Her heavenly kingdom was of the kind and manner of Gir-ak-shi's, and her administration in the same way. And in four years she had rescued nearly all the drujas in these regions of atmospherea. So when Fragapatti came to see her, having all her hosts present, she provided entertainments in the same manner as Gir-ak-shi did.

20/40.7. After this, Fragapatti visited Kow'anea and his heavenly kingdoms, and also his earth divisions. Next Fragapatti visited M'wing'mi and his heavenly kingdoms and earth divisions. Next he visited Ots'ha'ta and his places, and then Soo'fwa.

20/40.8. With all these Lords and Gods Fragapatti spent many days, examining and recording all the labor done; and he spoke before them all, so that his voice was heard by nearly all the people in the lower heavens. And so great was the work accomplished by Fragapatti with any one of these Lords or Gods, that should a history of it be written it would require the whole lifetime of a man to read it. Nor is it possible with earth words to describe adequately the beauty and glory of a single one of these recreations in his travels.

CHAPTER 41 Fragapatti

20/41.1. The close of dawn was near at hand. Fragapatti, richly stored with knowledge of the earth and her heavens, returned to Mouru, the heavenly kingdom of Haraiti, in atmospherea. The capital was illuminated, and the decorum of the higher heavens prevailed.

20/41.2. Already assembled were more than four billion angels prepared for the third resurrection. Fragapatti sent word to his Lord

Gods, and to his Lords and Gods, and to Samati, God in inherent right, up to the end of dawn. And he notified them all of the day and hour when he would accomplish the resurrection.

20/41.3. And then Fragapatti called his swift messengers, whose labor is with the thrones of Jehovih in etherea. He said: Behold, the dawn of dan is near the close. The Brides and Bridegrooms of Jehovih will number ten billion souls. Two divisions I will make, of grades fifty-five and seventy, for the forests and plains of Goomatchala. This you shall communicate to Hoseis, Goddess of Alawatcha, on the road of Affolkistan, saluting in Jehovih's name, from His Son, Fragapatti, Chief.

20/41.4. The swift messengers saluted, and then departed. Next he called the messengers for the kingdoms below, and of these there were twenty thousand, divided into twelve groups, and they had been previously apportioned to certain divisions of heaven and earth.

20/41.5. To them Fragapatti said: To the Lord God of each division, and to the Lords and Gods, and through them to the officers under them, greeting, in the name of Jehovih! Appoint and anoint the successors in Jehovih's name; and when your kingdom is in order, you shall appear at the throne of Mouru, for the resurrection of my hosts is near at hand. You shall also provide ships and suitable vessels, and bring, as visitors, from your kingdoms and most-holy places, as many atmosphereans as desire to come, so that they may witness the ceremonies and the ascent of Jehovih's Sons and Daughters.

20/41.6. And these commandments were carried to all the divisions of the corporeal earth and her heavens. Fragapatti then said to Athrava: You shall receive the Brides and Bridegrooms. As for myself, I will go down to the earth and receive God and Zarathustra, and they shall be borne in my own ship, to this place, and then to etherea. ||

20/41.7. In all places on earth and in heaven the spirit inhabitants were stirred to the utmost. In Haraiti there were already more than four thousand colonies, and every one had thousands and thousands eligible to the third resurrection, who would depart in the coming ascension. Of these there were persons of every occupation, and they were perfect in their order, belonging to groups and series of groups. And now the captains and generals were reorganizing them into phalanxes; and the Gods again organizing the phalanxes into kingdoms.

20/41.8. Zeredho sent her contribution of four hundred million souls to Haraiti. The Lord Gods were making their groups in their own several divisions, to be further organized after arriving at Mouru, the place where the final ascension would take place. Some of these had over a billion of their own ready for resurrection, including those whom they had previously sent to Haraiti.

20/41.9. Fragapatti sent special messengers to God, Samati, to learn the day appointed for Zarathustra's death; and he further allotted to Zarathustra three days in hada, in which to preach to mortals by the inspiration of God, and appointed the fourth day after his death as the time of his ascension from the earth.

20/41.10. And now, when all these matters had been organized, Fragapatti ordered the assembling of the sacred circle of the Holy Council, Sons and Daughters of the Most High. The lights were raised, and only Gods and Goddesses could remain in sight of, or near the throne of Jehovih. Fragapatti commanded Hoab to stand in the center of the circle, facing the judgment seat.

20/41.11. Fragapatti said: Hear the words of your Creator, O Hoab. I called you up out of the ground, and with My own spirit I quickened you into life. From your youth up I have followed you day by day. I have called out to you from My holy hill; with a woman's tenderness I came after you. When you tried to run away from Me, I followed after. Yes, I called My Son, high raised in My everlasting kingdoms, and I said to him: O My Son, run quickly, for Hoab, My well-beloved, runs away from Me. Go and bring him; for he is My Chosen.

20/41.12. He shall be My God of the red star; her heavens shall bow down before him. I will raise him up and anoint him with My holy fire; his countenance shall shine like a sun in My firmament.

20/41.13. And Fragapatti, My Son, overtook you in your flight; with great cunning he captured you to My labors. And you have raised up your voice and glorified Me; your arms have been bared to the harvest; your fruit is a song of glory.

20/41.14. Have I not given you experience in all things? Even to the precipice of hell I made you to walk and not fall. I made the darkness of everlasting death encompass you; and in the hour of your despair I came to you and raised you up.

20/41.15. Have I not great profit in you, My Son? My countless millions cry out in all places; they do not perceive Me; they do not know of Me and My heavenly places. Like a troubled sea that knows no rest, the voices of mortals and angels forever cry out: There is no light!

20/41.16. In what way, then, was I not wise in you, O Hoab? I made you of strong limb, and with arms that reach far; your judgment I fashioned for the great multitudes.

20/41.17. I say to the young bird with feathers: Fly! And it flies away. I say to man: Go forth in My name! But he looks around. Again I say to him: Go forth! But he turns to his neighbor for his opinion. Again I speak, calling: Come to Me! But he stands wondering. Again I say: Come! But he says: By and by. Again I say: Come! He replies: I do not have all light! Again I call, and he says: Alas, there is nothing!

20/41.18. And he goes down in darkness; he curses Me and accuses Me of errors! He preaches My shortness, but in his words, cuts himself off from Me. In the foul-smelling place of his darkness, My holy angels cannot come; he burrows himself in stubbornness that is blind and deaf.

20/41.19. But I blow My breath upon the earth and the stars; I drive them into new roads in the firmament of heaven. Into the dwelling-places of My high Gods I drive them as chaff before the wind. And when the light of My heavens has cleared away the darkness, I send My Gods with great power.

20/41.20. To this end I have raised you up, O Hoab. My shield is upon you; you shall wear the triangle of the red star; for two hundred years you shall hold dominion over the earth and her heavens. In My name speak, O Hoab!

20/41.21. Then spoke Hoab, saying: Your Voice is upon me, O Father! My limbs are weak; my hands tremble like an old man that is palsied. Behold, I have sought in vain to find anything perfect in me; I am like a trumpet that is bruised and split; there is no harmony or power within me.

20/41.22. You first gave me a wife, and sons and daughters, to rule over and to raise up for Your glory, but I failed utterly. My wife did not see with my eyes, nor hear with my ears, nor judge with my judgment; we were like two instruments, broken and out of tune. As for my sons, they went astray, like sheep without a herdsman; my advice was as weak to them as the shadow is to the tree. And my daughters went away from my love, and chose young men, even before my eyes.

20/41.23. Then I cried out to You, saying: O Jehovih, why did You give me a kingdom? Behold, it is scattered and gone! Then I went down into the grave in sorrow. But Your hand raised up my soul in heaven; and You gave me another kingdom. But my people would not see through my eyes nor hear through my ears. Then I sought to know if my eyes were wrong, and my ears wrong, and my judgment wrong.

20/41.24. And I turned about, like one who is lost in a forest, and shuts his eyes to the direction of the sun, going instead by the sound of a multitude of tongues. And my kingdom drew a boundary around itself, and shut out all light. But Your Son came and delivered me and my people.

20/41.25. Behold, I was as weak as a child; in my weakness Your light came upon me. Never again shall I desire others to see through my eyes, or hear through my ears, or judge by my judgment. You have healed me of infirmity, O Jehovih. Only by one Eye can things be seen through; by one Ear can things be heard through; by one Judgment can things be judged.

20/41.26. You have said: Go forth in My name! I will go, O Father! You have said: You shall have dominion over the earth and her heavens! This I will accomplish also, by Your Light and Power, O Jehovih!

20/41.27. Then spoke Jehovih through Fragapatti, saying: Accept the earth, O Hoab, My Son, My God! It is yours to keep and to rule over! Accept atmospherea, O Hoab, My Son, My God! It is yours to keep and to rule over!

20/41.28. Hoab said: I will be Your Son, O Jehovih! I will be Your God, O Jehovih! From You I accept the earth to keep and to rule over! From You I accept the earth's heavens, to keep and to rule over! || Again Jehovih spoke through Fragapatti, saying:

20/41.29. What you do now and forever, do in My name, for it is of Me and is Me in you!

20/41.30. Hoab said: What I do now and forever, I do in Your name, O Jehovih! For I know it is You in me that does all glorious things!

20/41.31. Jehovih spoke through Fragapatti, saying: With My Own hands I weave a crown for you My Son, My God of the red star! I place it on your head for the glory of My kingdoms, which are endless in number and full of holiness! Wear My Crown, for it is with Wisdom and Power!

20/41.32. Then Fragapatti's hands were waved about by the Great Spirit, and a crown was woven and placed on Hoab's head, and it was brilliant and white, studded with countless millions of gems. Hoab said: This crown from Your hand, O Father! I accept it and wear it, emblem of Your kingdoms, endless in number and full of holiness. I know that You will always be with me in Wisdom and Power! I will glorify You forever! My kingdoms shall glorify You forever!

20/41.33. The chief marshal now conducted Hoab to the throne of Jehovih, which had been previously vacated, and Hoab sat in the middle of the throne. Meanwhile, the es'enaurs chanted a hymn of glory. Hoab then said: Fragapatti, Son of Jehovih, Orian Chief, come and honor my throne in the name of the Father. Then Fragapatti went to the throne and sat on it. Next Hoab called up Athrava, then Hapacha, and then other Gods and Goddesses.

20/41.34. And now, while the Council remained assembled, Fragapatti said: Behold, the time of the death of Zarathustra has come. Remain here, and I will go quickly down to the earth and receive God and Zarathustra, and the hosts of God and his Lords.

20/41.35. So Fragapatti departed, and sailed swiftly down to Par'si'e, on the earth, and came to the meeting place of the corporeans who had charge of the Holy Word. And it was on the morning of the fourth day after Zarathustra's death. For three days and nights his spirit had been preaching to the Faithists, explaining the kingdoms of Jehovih.

20/41.36. So Fragapatti called to God, saying: Behold, my Son, your labor is done. In you I have great delight. Behold, my ship lies by the river; my lights are raised for the everlasting thrones! God (Samati) said: It is finished! That which you put upon me I have done! Behold, here stands Zarathustra, my Son. ||

20/41.37. Zarathustra was at that time taking leave of his corporeal friends, for his soul was fast becoming illuminated. Yes, he had looked up and saw the ship of All Light, and he knew now the Voice of the Father.

20/41.38. So Fragapatti went and took Zarathustra in his arms saying: Come, my beloved. Your home is up there! So they went into the ship of fire, and ascended to Mouru.

CHAPTER 42 Fragapatti

20/42.1. And now the Lord Gods, and Lords and Gods, began to arrive in Mouru. The marshals, and their officers and workmen, had extended the landing-places for the hosts of ships; receivers had been appointed and allotted their various places. Heralds and messengers had been provided with places of announcement; and lines of intercommunion had been laid, so that the words of heralds and messengers could be heard by all the millions in waiting.

20/42.2. Know, O angels and mortals, that such is the glory of Jehovih's works, for stand where you will, His kingdoms are always seeming above. As you of the earth look upward and see the stars, so they that live on the stars look upward to see the earth. If, therefore, you were receiving messengers from the stars, it would seem to you that they came downward; but to them, as if they rose upward, even until near the landing-place, when it would be downward to them also. This is because the feet of a mortal or the feet of an angel are on the foundation of his place, and because his head stands in the opposite way from his feet. ||

20/42.3. First came Ardi'atta, Goddess over the spirits who had been delivered out of the hells of Aoasu by Fragapatti and Hoab, and then housed in Zeredho and Haraiti. And with her was her successor, Gaipon, manager of the hosts. Ardi'atta brought one billion three hundred million souls in her ship, mostly visitors who had been delivered out of hell. Besides these, were twenty million raised to light [the degree of the third resurrection – Ed.], clothed as Brides and Bridegrooms of Jehovih. These latter were the harvest of Ardi'atta, and in her charge. The receivers of her ship stationed it in its place, and then the receivers of her hosts conducted them to their places.

20/42.4. And now E'chad, Lord God of Arabin'ya, came in his ship with more than four billion souls, half of whom were Brides and Bridegrooms. His ship was received by the proper officers, and stationed in its place; and his hosts received by the proper persons, and conducted to their respective places. With the Brides and Bridegrooms E'chad entered the south wing of the capital; and E'chad's successor remained with the visiting hosts. When E'chad entered before the throne, Fragapatti saluted him on the sign JEHOVIH'S REST, and E'chad answered in THE GLORY OF EVENING!

20/42.5. Before the hosts of E'chad were landed and placed, there came Ots-ha-ta, Lord of North Oceya, with his successor, in a ship of thirty million, of whom Ots-ha-ta had two million Brides and Bridegrooms. His ship was received and stationed in its place; and his hosts received and assigned to their places.

20/42.6. Meanwhile, Kow'anea, God of South Guatama, came in his ship, with his successor, bringing seven hundred million souls, of whom Kow'anea had sixty million Brides and Bridegrooms. And they were received by the proper officers and assigned to their places.

20/42.7. Hardly had Kow'anea landed, when Yaton'te came, with his successor and his hosts. Yaton'te's ship was the most beautiful of all that had yet arrived. His hosts were four billion souls; but of Brides and Bridegrooms he had only thirty million. Fragapatti saluted him on the sign of STAR OF THE WEST, and Yaton'te answered in the sign of the GOLDEN CIRCLE! He and his hosts were then assigned their places.

20/42.8. Now came M'wing'mi, God of South Oceya, and his little ship was laden with four hundred million souls, and he had three million Brides and Bridegrooms. His ship was received and stationed in its place, and his hosts received and stationed in their places.

20/42.9. Next came Soo'fwa, God of Japan and her heavens. His was the most brilliant of all the ships, and he had three billion five hundred million souls aboard, of whom two hundred million were Brides and Bridegrooms. His ship was received and stationed, and his hosts also; and when he entered before the throne, Fragapatti saluted him on the sign of BEFORE THE ANCIENTS! And Soo'fwa answered him in the sign of LITTLE STAR!

20/42.10. And now the most loved of all came, Uropa, Goddess of the barbarians! Her ship was the swiftest and best trimmed, and she brought one billion souls, of whom she had eighty million Brides and Bridegrooms as her harvest. When she entered before the throne of Jehovih, leading in her Brides and Bridegrooms, Fragapatti saluted on the sign, PERSISTENT FIRE! And Uropa answered him the sign, JEHOVIH'S TRUST!

20/42.11. Now came great Ah'oan, Lord God of Jaffeth and her heavens. His ship was the largest of all, and he brought five billion souls, of whom nearly two billion were Brides and Bridegrooms. When he came before Jehovih's throne, Fragapatti saluted him on the sign, THE POWER OF LOVE! Ah'oan answered him in the sign, EVERLASTING LIFE!

20/42.12. And now the ship of Gir-ak-shi came in, bringing a billion souls, of whom eighty million were Brides and Bridegrooms.

20/42.13. Besides these, there were seventy-six other Gods, from departments of the grand divisions of the heavens, some bringing five million souls and some even twenty million. And there were Lords of islands and Lords of small places on the earth, who had also come in small ships, some bringing five and some ten million souls. And all these Gods and Lords had Brides and Bridegrooms according to the place and number and condition from where they came. And they were all received and stationed in their proper places.

20/42.14. Thus there came to Mouru more than thirty billion atmosphereans that had sprung up from the earth by Jehovih's will; and of these there were ten billion eight hundred million spirits prepared as Brides and Bridegrooms to the Great Spirit. Besides these, there were the hosts of Fragapatti, the ethereans, ten million, mostly Gods and Goddesses, and these formed the inner sacred circle of the Holy Council. Next to these were their ten million successors, who were to be the Holy Council of Mouru after the ascension. And next outside of these were stationed the Lord Gods and their attendants, behind whom stood their Brides and Bridegrooms. Next stood the Gods, their attendants and their Brides and Bridegrooms; and then the Lords, their attendants and their Brides and Bridegrooms.

20/42.15. And next outside of these stood the successors, the Gods and Lords, with their attendants; and yet behind them, their visiting hosts. And within and among them all, the musicians, marshals, messengers, swift messengers and heralds, were assigned their respective places.

But so vast was the multitude of angels, and so great the glory, that one could look upon the scene all day and not even see the millionth part; nor is it possible for corporeal words to convey anything but a crude picture of the magnificent scene.

CHAPTER 43 Fragapatti

20/43.1. God (Samati) said: You gave the red star and her heavens, into my hands, O Jehovih! Your Sons bestowed upon me the triangle as an emblem of Your first three worlds, and of the first, second and third resurrections. Behold, the time of my reign has come to an end. With Your holy harvest You call me to a higher world.

20/43.2. But You have raised up Your Son, Hoab, who is of great Wisdom and Power in You. He shall be Your God and Your Son in the places I have been. To him, in Your name, O Father, I bestow the triangle, symbol of You and of Your created worlds, and of the individuals within them. By my parting with it, the end of this dawn is recorded; by Hoab's reception of it, his dominion is begun.

20/43.3. God then took off the triangle and hung it on Hoab's neck, saying: I salute you, God of earth and heaven! Immediately the es'enaurs chanted, Hail to you, O God, Son of Jehovih!

20/43.4. Now during the arrival of the hosts of Gods and Lords and their resurrections, there were to be seen, high in the firmament above, two stars, like twins, descending. These were the avalanzas of Hoseis, Goddess of Alawatcha, coming to receive the Brides and Bridegrooms of Jehovih, to take them to the etherean realms prepared for them by the Orians of the higher heavens.

20/43.5. Her avalanzas were descending by the road of Affolkistan, and coming swiftly. Now, between the glory of these lights, and the ceremonies in Mouru, one did not know where best to look, for the awe and grandeur on every side was overwhelming. And not less to move so vast a host were the es'enaurs, the singers, and the far-off trumpeters. There stood also the great multitude of Brides and Bridegrooms, arrayed in white, like a vast sea of white, more than ten billion!

20/43.6. But the waiting was not long, for the Gods so time their labors that every adventure fits to another. The twin stars grew and grew in size, till, like two suns descending, they seemed as wide as the borders of Haraiti! And while the multitude thus gazed and watched, Fragapatti rose in his place on the throne and called out, saying:

20/43.7. Behold, the time has now arrived for the brotherhood of Gods and Lords to be bestowed upon the earth and her heavens. As the earth is divided into many sections, so have I bequeathed on the earth many Lords, to hold dominion over mortals; and yet over all of these, I have chosen and appointed one God.

20/43.8. For, in this manner the first heavenly kingdoms of the red star were founded by Sethantes, Son of Jehovih. In the history that followed since his day, it has turned out that first one Lord, and then another, lost power in his kingdom, and finally, even the Gods were powerless to rule angels and mortals to righteousness.

20/43.9. So that you may be strong from now on, like the heavenly kingdoms on other worlds, I now decree Diva, in the name of Jehovih! And God and his Lord Gods, and his Gods and Lords of divisions, shall comprise the Diva; nor shall any other person be eligible to the order here, whether they be of this world or of any other world; and the Diva shall be male and female members.

20/43.10. And he who is God, who was Hoab, high raised from Zeredho, shall be Div over all the rest. Nevertheless, the name Div shall be used by all the members of Diva, when abiding in their respective dominions. But no other person, either on earth or in heaven, shall be entitled to the rank of Div.

20/43.11. And in this capital, Mouru, the Diva shall meet three times every earth year, to render to one another the matters of their respective dominions; and when the meetings take place, each and every Lord and God, and Lordess and Goddess, shall be present and fulfill these, my commandments.

20/43.12. And when the members are thus assembled, Div only shall have the title of Div; and the members shall salute him as Div, Son of All Light; but no other person shall have the title of Div, Son of All Light. And the meetings of the Diva shall be private; nor shall any person be eligible to be present in Diva, except the novices who may be in preparation to become Lords and Gods by succession. But none of the novices shall be entitled to speak in Diva.

20/43.13. And each and every member of Diva shall report his department, as to whether in need of assistance, or his capacity to provide emigrants to other plateaus, and these reports shall be made in person before Div; and when all the reports are given, then Div shall render judgment on them, giving to or exacting from any one or more of the dominions, according to the Voice of Jehovih.

20/43.14. And the judgments of Div, Son of All Light, shall be called Divan law,[619] from which there shall be no appeal. And the Lords and Gods shall carry these decrees down to mortals, in their respective dominions, rendering them to the God-irs on earth, by which mortals through the Rab'bah, shall receive communion from the All Light.

20/43.15. During the assembly of Diva, swift messengers shall be present and witness all the laws that shall be passed; and immediately afterward these swift messengers shall depart from Mouru and come to the etherean kingdoms in the roadway of the earth and her heavens, and render the same to the nearest Orian Chief, or other etherean God, Son of Jehovih.

20/43.16. Therefore, so that my commandments shall be in the name of Jehovih, let God and Lord Gods, and Gods and Lords, and Goddesses and Lordesses, approach the Father's throne, so I may bestow them according to the rites and ceremonies of the Gods of other corporeal and atmospherean worlds.

20/43.17. The marshals now conducted all of them, except God, before the throne: First, Thulae, then Es'pacia, then Geth'ya, and so on, until the hosts of the dominions were before Fragapatti. And then God (Hoab) rose up and faced toward the west. Fragapatti said:

20/43.18. In Your name, O All Light, I create a Diva for the earth and her heavens; and this, Your God, I anoint as Div, with power to him to anoint his successor in like manner. May Your Voice and Judgment be with him forever! And these, Your Lord Gods, and these, Your Gods and Your Lords, and these, Your Goddesses and Your Lordesses, I now anoint as members of Diva; and to each and all of them I give power in Your name to appoint successors after them for Your allotted seasons. May Your Wisdom and Power be with them forever. Amen!

20/43.19. God said: In Your name, O All Light, I accept the Diva. And, on behalf of my Gods and Lords, proclaim Your Divan Power to heaven and earth.

20/43.20. The others responded: We will fulfill Your decrees, O All Light, now and forever. Be with us in wisdom and strength for Your glory!

20/43.21. Fragapatti then extended his hand upward, saying: Inqua git's'ang, of Your Inqua git's'ang, O All Light! (Dominion within dominion, give me Your symbol, O Jehovih!) And there came out of the light before the throne a substance, and Fragapatti seized it and formed from it, first, a hollow ball, and within it another ball; and second, two interlocked triangles; and he gave to each of the Diva a pair, that is, an inqua and a git's'ang [a ball within a ball, and interlocked triangles –ed.];[620] and he said to them:

i033r03k **Inqua.**

i033r04g **Git's'ang.**

20/43.22. Behold, O Jehovih, You called me from my high place in heaven, saying: Go to the red star, the earth; her soil is wet with human blood! Her heavens are dead; My harvest is nothing! || And I came and delivered Your Word to mortals; in blood I gave it, and then washed clean the whole earth. And I gathered together Your lost children in the lower heavens, and raised them up with power. Regarding which, in token of Your Light that was within me, I have become one within Your labors, and I have raised up Gods and Lords in You also; and so that one perfect thing may be within another, in the manner of Your

[619] In English we call this Divine Law. In the Vedic, and in modern religious ceremonies in India and China, the terms, Div and Divan law, are still in use. Here we behold the origin of the terms, Divine and Divinity. –Ed.

[620] see images i033r03k and i033r04g, from the Se'moin tablet (vol.2 p.227)

created worlds, this, Your holy sign, I bequeath to them, to be theirs and their successors' forever!

20/43.23. So Fragapatti bestowed the Lords and Gods, and his labors were finished.

20/43.24. Meanwhile, the sun-ships of Hoseis drew near and landed, both to south and west of Mouru, and so mighty and full of grandeur were they, that the billions looking on were breathless in awe and wonder. Then out of the fire-ships the marshals of Hoseis' hosts descended, of whom there were thirty million aboard. And they spread a frowas[621] from the ship to Jehovih's throne, and Hoseis alighted from the ship and walked briskly forward on the frowas, and Fragapatti and his hosts went and received her, and conducted her to the throne.

20/43.25. And now, after due ceremonies between the Gods and Goddesses, Athrava rose up and said: To you, O Hoseis, Goddess of Alawatcha, in the name of Jehovih, I bestow the Brides and Bridegrooms of heaven and earth. They are the harvest of Samati, God of the division of Haniostu, and his Lords and Gods, through the Orian Chief, Fragapatti, for the Father's emancipated heavens!

20/43.26. Hoseis said: Brides and Bridegrooms of Jehovih, in His name I receive you, to deliver to the All High Worlds.

20/43.27. And then Hoseis and Athrava proceeded in the ceremonies in the usual way, and were responded to by the ten billion Brides and Bridegrooms.

20/43.28. When the ceremonies were finished, the time of the ascension was at hand. So Fragapatti and Hoseis, accompanied by their Gods and Lords, went down to the foot of the throne and sat down, and God (Hoab) sat alone in the middle of the throne. The es'enaurs then sang a hymn on THE MARCH OF JEHOVIH'S WORLDS! When it concluded, God went down and took Fragapatti's hand and Hoseis' hand, saying: Arise, O Son, and you, O Daughter of Jehovih! The Father calls! Go your way! Fragapatti and Hoseis rose up, and then all the Gods and Lords rose up.

20/43.29. Hoab, that is God, fell into Fragapatti's arms! And when they had embraced, God withdrew and returned to the throne. Fragapatti saluted him on the sign, FAITHIST, and God answered him in the sign, FOREVER! After which the hosts followed Fragapatti and Hoseis, and entered the great avalanzas.

20/43.30. Fragapatti gave his own avalanza to Athrava and his attendants, and they took the magnet from it and made it rotary also. And when they were all aboard, Hoseis commanded the ascension, and the mighty fire-ships rose up, turning and rising.

20/43.31. Fragapatti and the ethereans created flowers and drapery, and cast overboard sufficient, so that every one of the twenty billion remaining had some memento. In a little while the resurrection was complete; the sun-ships rose higher and higher; passing the earth's vortex and entering etherea, going to the kingdoms prepared for them by the high-raised Sons and Daughters of Jehovih!

END OF BOOK OF FRAGAPATTI

---

[621] likely similar to a walkway or bridge-way with red carpet (formal, stately) treatment

Book of God's Word

Being contemporaneous with the cycle of Fragapatti, Son of Jehovih. As the upper book [Book of Fragapatti] is of heavenly things, so is this lower book of the earthly administration of God for the same period of time. And it is called the Book of God's Word, because it is about the first descent of God to the earth to establish his word with man. Through Zarathustra, a man of Par'si'e, God came for that purpose, eight thousand nine hundred years before the Kosmon era.[622]

CHAPTER 1 God's Word

21/1.1. Hear my word, O man, said I'hua'Mazda.[623] Perceive my utterances in things that have been and that will be. Remember the lapse of time; open your understanding to the substance of the affairs of the ancients.

21/1.2. Do not quibble over names, said I'hua'Mazda. Nor over places, nor words. All places are my places; all words, my words; all names, my names. All truth is my speech. All fact is my voice. By my commandments all the nations of the earth shall be made to know me and my works.

21/1.3. The Master of the I'huans, Samati, High God of heaven, whose home was in Mount Vibhraj, a heaven created in heaven, a thousand miles high.

21/1.4. I'hua'Mazda said: How shall they know me, I, Holy Mazda? They are sealed up; their souls blind as death. Behold, the king, high ruler of Oas, king So-qi; valorous with a strong sword. So-qi! So-qi! I call, but he does not hear. I go to the temple; it is closed against God, I'hua'Mazda!

21/1.5. Where are the altars of your God? The place of the holy dance. So-qi does not hear. None can hear the Voice of I'hua'Mazda. Angels and Gods are rejected with disdain.[624]

21/1.6. O man, can you measure swords with your Creator? If only you could open the curtains of heaven, and see! What does your little learning amount to? Shall a chick that is not hatched discourse on the philosophy of life?

21/1.7. Behold, O man, I have told you that the natural senses (corporeal senses) cannot understand spiritual things. But I will reach you, you vain city, Oas. You, king So-qi! Your sword shall fall from the hilt; your mandates shall be like a breath blown away.

21/1.8. Hear me, O man, said I'hua'Mazda: I opened the door a little, so that you might learn a little about the stars. And now that you are puffed up; vain boaster of your knowledge, you slam the door in the face of your Master!

21/1.9. You had gone in darkness; a driveler[625] to familiar spirits; lazy and longing to die. Then I said to you: Behold, it is a good world; go, then, and be wise. Quickly you were changed; bewailing the stupidity of the ancients. How much better are you than them? Because I delivered you from darkness, you kill my prophets.

21/1.10. I'hua'Mazda said: I make you free, O man, but you deny my person. When I suffer you to fall in bondage, you cry: O God, my God! When I deliver you into freedom, you go with a sword and spear to lay your fellows in death.

[622] God's Word is an important book, because it is the father and mother of all other religions in the world. The best historical accounts place Zoroaster [Zoraaster, Zarathustra] about six thousand years before Moses' time. That the Persians and Indians [Hindus] were far advanced in learning in those days, we have the proof that the stars and planets were then named and mapped. As much of the astronomy of that period is blended with our astronomy of today, so is the Zoroasterian [Zarathustrian] religion the framework and foundation of modern Buddhism and Christianity. The student will find that a thorough knowledge of the sacred books of the Chinese, Hindoos [Hindus], Persians, etc., will facilitate the classification of names here used. I'hua'Mazda, is synonymous with God; Mazda, [Ormazd] synonymous with Jehovih. –Ed.

[623] I'hua'Mazda, The Master Voice, or, as we would say, thus says God, or, God said, etc. –Ed.

[624] contempt, beneath oneself to consider

[625] one who follows another like a drooling dog follows its master; one who eagerly embraces drivel (nonsense, foolishness); a minion, a flunky

21/1.11. Hear me, O man, in what I have done for you, said I'hua'Mazda. Of A'su I cleft a rib[626] and stood it up, saying: Be a man, upright in likeness of your God. And my voice made you—what you are, but were not, proves I am. I said: Save your seed, O man. I'hins stood aloof from the Asu'ans, and were holy; but your brother dwelt with A'su and brought forth to destruction.

21/1.12. Be admonished, said I'hua'Mazda. I struck the earth and broke it like an egg is broken; for I would cut loose the bound in heaven. Then all the tribes of men cried out: There is a Mazda! An All Power Unseen!

CHAPTER 2 God's Word

21/2.1. In those days when an army captured a large city, slaying the people, they carried back the spoil to So-qi, king of Oas, capital of Par'si'e, and received rewards according to the amount of plunder. The wars were between the different nations of I'huans. The sacred people, the I'hins, had nothing to be plundered; and they were unmolested.

21/2.2. I said: Whoever lays up treasures in this world, shall find no peace! But you have built so great a city, you hope nothing can break it down. Now I will show you, O king: Your city shall prove to be the weakest of cities. I will raise up one man out of the seed of the I'hins; and Oas, the mighty city, shall fall before his hand.

21/2.3. I'hua'Mazda, God of heaven, sent certain loo'is, highly knowledgeable angels, to look around, and afterward he called them and asked what they saw. They said: Work! Work! I'hua'Mazda said: Work it shall be! Go, you holy masters of generations, down to mortals close about the city of Oas. And search out seed of the I'hin race, and by inspiration lead them to the fairest daughters of I'hua, in the city of Oas; and they shall be tempted, and soon a quickened fruit shall ripen in the city, sons and daughters. Again go to the I'hins, and by inspiration bring others and have them tempted by the improved fruit. And yet again repeat this method, and in the sixth generation you shall raise up a son having the gifts of su'is and sar'gis, and you shall call him Zarathustra.

21/2.4. The loo'is, the angels who were guardians over mortals for such purpose, went and accomplished what had been commanded by God. And the child's mother's name was Too'che, and the father's name Lo'ab. Too'che herself was su'is born, and before she conceived, was obsessed by Sa'moan, an angel; and during the time of maternity she was not suffered[627] to wake from her unconscious trance. And by the loo'is, her soul was often taken to high heaven (etherea) to see its glories, and then returned to inhabit her own body. Thus, the child was born of All Light, and at that same time the obsession fled, and Too'che proclaimed within the city that no man was father to the child, but that she conceived from All Light, believing so, because she was unconscious during gestation.

21/2.5. The learned men cast the horoscope, but found nothing in the stars to alarm the kings, found nothing to support the maiden's story. The loo'is went before God, saying: Behold, a child is born, capable of All Light. Then God spoke, saying: I will come; go and lead the way.

21/2.6. When the child was still a nursling, I'hua'Mazda spoke through the child, while its own spirit slept. Then again came the learned men, chief of whom was Asha, son of Zista, learned in a thousand stars and all living creatures and in the bones of animals no longer living. So Asha spoke to Too'che, saying: Can your suckling talk? And God answered him, saying:

21/2.7. Not the child, but I, I'hua'Mazda. Do not think, O man, these small lips utter words prompted by this child's soul. I come to stop the cruel hand of war; to make man know there is an Unseen Master. Behold, this child has no sex! He is an Yeshuah (Iesu), a passionless birth.

21/2.8. To which Asha said: Can it be this woman has a man hidden under her cloak, and hopes to evade the just punishment of the king! O harlot! You who told a shameful tale of conception without a man! Your lies are now added to others to make good the first. Out of the city, wretch! or you shall be stoned to death, and your child with you!

[626] that is, much as one would cleft a scion (insert a shoot into a stock plant), so into the stock of Asu a scion (a bud or shoot, i.e., soul of light from angels) was grafted

[627] not given scope or latitude, not allowed

21/2.9. Too'che made no answer, except with a flood of tears. Then I'hua'Mazda spoke, saying: Hold your hand on these lips; and perceive how I gesticulate[628] with these little hands. Yes, take the little form in your own arms.

21/2.10. Then Asha feared, but wanted to hide his fear and so took the child, while I'hua'Mazda spoke, saying: O man, if only you could behold the spirit, and would temper your judgment with patience and wisdom!

21/2.11. Asha said: If in truth you are the Mazda of the I'huan race, why have you come in such questionable weakness? What can a child do? Can you wield a sword with these little hands? I would have hoped to see a God come in stronger shape, and in majesty of a thousand angels, winged, and in flames of fire!

21/2.12. I'hua'Mazda said: My wisdom is not man's wisdom; my weapons, not arrows and sharp swords. What is great in man's judgment is as nothing to me; what is as nothing to man, I will make great, for I shall overturn this mighty city. Because I come in peace and love, the city shall be divided, man against man, and bloody war run riot in this walled kingdom.

21/2.13. Asha said: To what end have you come? For if it is true you are a God born in this questionable shape, you have some greater motive than to overthrow the town. I charge you, then, most precocious youth, tell me what your purpose is, so justice may be done?

21/2.14. I'hua'Mazda said: The cities of man are as nothing in my sight; I come to teach man of other worlds, and that the souls of the righteous shall live forever; I come to deliver man from darkness into everlasting light.

21/2.15. Asha said: Your words are wisdom, or else my sudden surprise has affected my judgment. I will go now, so that I may reflect on this wonder. Tomorrow I will come again. Keep this matter private. For if it is known that I, of such high estate, have talked with tolerance regarding spiritual things, I will be doomed to death.

[628] make gestures with the hands and arms; speak with the hands

CHAPTER 3 God's Word

21/3.1. When Asha had gone, I'hua'Mazda spoke to Too'che, the virgin mother, saying: Take your child away and hide yourself, lest the king has you and your child put to death. So Too'che departed with her child, and hid in another part of the city.

21/3.2. Now Asha went directly to So-qi, the king, and related what had transpired. When he had finished, the king said: According to the histories of the ancients, when a God appeared among mortals, there were signs and miracles. You have told me only words. Go, therefore again to the child and say: The king desires a miracle.

21/3.3. Asha returned the next day, but lo and behold, woman and child were gone, and not one of the neighbors knew where. Asha said: If I go before the king with this story, he will have me slain as an inventor of lies. So he did not return to the king.

21/3.4. But where Too'che and her child dwelt, there came a maker of songs, by name Choe'jon, and he spoke to the virgin, saying: Where is the child? She answered: He sleeps in the rack of hay; I will fetch him. So she brought the child from his bed of new hay; and straws stuck to the baby's mantle, and these straws had no roots.

21/3.5. I'hua'Mazda spoke through the child while its own spirit slept, saying: I came to you, O Choe'jon; I brought you here, for you shall frame songs about the virgin's baby. Choe'jon was frightened, but nevertheless he said: Can it be true, in this enlightened age! A miracle! Shall I talk to you, O child? Then I'hua'Mazda said:

21/3.6. Behold, you do not speak to the child, but to I'hua'Mazda. Take these straws to your writing-box and plant them in new earth, and in one day they shall grow and bear ripe wheat. So Choe'jon departed and planted the straws, and in one day, they grew and bore ripe wheat.

21/3.7. Choe'jon had previously sung his songs before the king, and so had permission to approach the court; and he went and told the king of the miracle. The king said: The philosopher, Asha, told me about this child, and I sent him for a miracle, but he does not return. Now you have come and said: Behold, a miracle! || What value is a miracle, except to those who witness it? Shall your king accept a thing because of belief? Is not belief the fruit of darkness? Go, therefore, again to the child and bring it before me, so I may see with my own eyes.

21/3.8. Choe'jon returned to the place, but lo and behold, virgin and child were gone; nor did the neighbors know where. But she was concealed in another part of the city. And now there came before her one Os'shan, who was weeping because of the apparent death of his son. To him I'hua'Mazda spoke, saying: Do not weep, for I have healed your son and also given sight to your daughter.

21/3.9. Os'shan trembled at such words coming from the lips of a child, and he ran away; and he found his son healed, and his daughter restored to sight. In his joy he returned to the place, but the virgin and child were gone. Os'shan was hostler[629] to the king, and capable of audience, and so he went and told the king of his good fortune.

21/3.10. The king said: Asha, the philosopher, told me a fine story of this child, but when I sent him for information he did not return. Then came Choe'jon, the maker of songs, telling me what he had witnessed. I sent him to have mother and child brought before me, but he did not return. Now you come with tale of a miracle, like those told in the dark ages. Go, therefore, and search the city over till you find this wonder, and bring him before me.

21/3.11. On the next day another man, the king's brother's son, came before the king, saying: Today I have seen such a wonder that it would have been marvelous in the days of angels and Gods. Behold, a little child spoke to me such words of philosophy that they made me tremble. And yet, O king, you know I am no coward. My house is hung with a hundred scalps. Yes, and this child already proclaims itself Zarathustra in communion with the God I'hua'Mazda! To me it said: Why do you kill the sons and daughters of your God? Do not think that your many scalps are a glory before heaven. Behold, I am stronger with my little finger than So-qi, your king.

21/3.12. So-qi, the king, said: Enough! Unless this mother and child are brought at once before me, so I may see the truth of these wonders, every male child in Oas shall be cast into fire! || The king's brother's wife had a child, and the son's wife had a child, and they foresaw that the decree of the king would affect them dearly; so many went forth searching for Too'che and Zarathustra.

21/3.13. But the spirit, I'hua'Mazda, had previously directed the mother to go beyond the gates, and led her far off into the Forest of Goats, where the tribes of Listians lived by fishing and hunting, and on goats' milk. I'hua'Mazda talked to the virgin, saying: Twenty years you shall dwell in the forest, fearing nothing, for your God will provide for you. And when your son has grown to be larger and stronger than other men, behold, your God will manifest for the redemption of the races of men who are hunted and slain for the glory of the kings.

21/3.14. So the virgin and her son dwelt in the Forest of Goats until Zarathustra was a large man and grown to maturity, and his stature was equal to three ordinary men; nor could any number of men lay him on his back. But because of his gentleness like a young goat, the tribes of the forest called him the Lamb of God, signifying, strength and goodwill.[630]

CHAPTER 4 God's Word

21/4.1. When So-qi, the king, issued the decree to have Zarathustra found and brought before him or else all the male infants of Oas were to be slain, the Lords sent travail on the king's wife and on the king's daughter, wife of Asha, the philosopher, and the two women gave birth that same day to two sons, a month before their time, but nevertheless to life and strength and beauty. Now, according to the laws of Oas, a king could not rescind or change his own decrees, for he had assumed the position of infallibility, in consequence of which, he had doomed to death kin of his kin, flesh of his flesh.

21/4.2. Accordingly, after search had been made in vain to find Zarathustra, the king repented of his decree, but knew no way to justify a change of commandment. Asha, hearing of this, came out of concealment, saying to himself: Now I will go to the king and hold him to his decree, even demanding that he slay me also. So Asha came before So-qi, and after saluting, said: O king, I have heard of your strait,[631] and have come to you so that I may counsel you.

---

[629] one who tends horses and stables; Os'shan was most likely supervisor over this department

[630] see image i108 Zarathustra

[631] predicament, difficulty, plight, distress

i108 **Zarathustra.**

21/4.3. The king was angry, and he said: Asha, my friend, hear your king: You came before me, relating a marvelous story regarding an infant son of the virgin who says she never knew a man. Now, according to the laws of the City of the Sun, any man stating as truth that which he cannot prove, is already adjudged to death. Shall the law be unfulfilled, because, in fact, you are near me in blood?

21/4.4. Asha said: Most assuredly, O king, the laws must be carried out. Are they not the all highest? For it follows that if man is the all highest, then his laws, above all else, must never be set aside. Therefore, you shall have me slain. Do not think I come before you to plead an excuse, in order to save myself; rather let all men perish than allow the king's decrees to go amiss.

21/4.5. The king said: You are wise, O Asha. The laws cannot err, for they are the standard by which to judge all else. And he who has risen to be king stands, by nature, the infallible highest of all things. History has proven this. But hear me yet, for you have wisdom from the movements of the sun and moon and stars: The king, being the all highest, how can he be bound? Can he not decree new decrees forever?

21/4.6. Asha said: I will not deceive you, O king! I know you are not arguing for me, but for your own infant son, and for your daughter's infant son. Nor have I come before you in prowess[632] (to save you from your decrees), although I love life. But here is the dilemma: By changing one law, you admit that all laws made by man may also need changing; which is to say, wisdom is folly.[633] How, then, shall the judge try any man by the laws? Is it not setting up error in order to find truth?[634]

21/4.7. The king said: You reason well. This morning, in my walk in the market gardens, when the soldiers were spreading the scalps of their enemies in the sun to dry, I wondered whether or not, in ages to come, the weaker nations and tribes of men might attempt to justify their right to life. So, if the kings admit to fallibility in their decrees and laws, then no man can foresee the end; for even slaves, servants and women will rise up against the laws, and claim their right to life. How, then, would the earth be large enough for all the people? Yet, for what reason, O Asha, comes this heartache of mine against killing my own son?

21/4.8. Asha said: What are your sympathies, O king? If you were to justify the escape of your child's death for sympathy's sake, would my wife and my children not justify their sympathy in desiring me to live? No, sympathy is the enemy of law and justice; it is the evil in our natures that cries out for evil. The laws must be maintained; the decrees must be maintained; the king's word must be maintained. No man must permit his judgment to go higher than the law, or the decree, or the king.

21/4.9. Asha said: This is the City of the Sun. If this city goes back on its own laws, what will the tributary cities do? Will they not also begin to disrespect the laws, or say: Perhaps the laws are in error? This will result in anarchy. To one purpose only can a great city be maintained. To divide the purposes and judgment of men is to scatter to the four winds the glory of our civil liberty. Was it not disrespect of the laws, combined with superstition, that caused the nations of ancients to perish?

21/4.10. The king said: What shall I do, O Asha? My son has smiled in my face!

21/4.11. Asha said: You shall send me and your son and your daughter's son, and all male infants to the slaughter pen, and have us all beheaded and cast into the fire. Otherwise, it will come true what the infant Zarathustra has said: Behold, my hand shall strike the city of Oas, and it shall fall like a heap of straw.

21/4.12. Do not think, O king, I am superstitious and fear such threats; but this I perceive: Permit the laws to be impeached, and every man in Oas will set himself up to interpret the laws to be wrong and himself right. And your

[632] a display of expertise (being here: superior reasoning)

[633] i.e., wisdom is imperfect (and therefore cannot be trusted)

[634] Asha's argument eventuates to: Man must have an all highest perfection against which to judge; all lesser wisdom flows down from the all highest wisdom; if the all highest wisdom is imperfect, then all lesser wisdom must be imperfect, and man is left without a standard by which to judge. This sets the stage for the disintegration of man's society, and eventually anarchy ensues—for without a perfect all highest, there is no unity and the whole system comes crashing down.

officers will rebel against you on all sides, and the glory of your kingdom will perish. ||

21/4.13. After the city had been searched for thirty days, and the virgin and child still not found, the king appointed a day for the slaughter, according to his former decree; and there were ninety thousand male infants adjudged to death, the king's son among the rest.

21/4.14. While these matters were maturing, the Lord went to Choe'jon, and inspired him to make songs about Zarathustra, the infant who was stronger than a king; and also songs about the decree of death to the ninety thousand infant sons of Oas. And the beauty of the songs, together with the nature of these proceedings, caused the songs to be sung in the streets day and night; and the songs, in satire, approved of the horrors, so that even the king could not interdict the singing.

CHAPTER 5 God's Word

21/5.1. When the day arrived for the slaughter of the male infants, no more than a thousand mothers appeared at the place of execution with their infants, the others having risen in the previous night and departed out of the gates, more than eighty-nine thousand mothers!

21/5.2. When the king went to the place of execution, having set aside the day as a holiday, and finding only a thousand infants present, he inquired the reason, and, having been told, he said: Can it be that mothers love their offspring more than they respect the decrees of the king? Asha was standing near, having stripped himself ready for execution, and he answered the king, saying:

21/5.3. Because they love their offspring, is it not the love of the flesh? And does the law not stand above all flesh? In this matter, then, because they have evaded the law, they have also adjudged themselves to death.

21/5.4. Then came Betraj, the king's wife, bringing the infant. Betraj said: Here is your son, O king, ready for the sacrifice. Asha reasons well; there must be an All Highest, which never errs; which is the law of the king. Take your flesh and blood and prove your decrees. What! Why hesitate? If you swerve the tiniest bit, then you shall open the door for all men to find an excuse against the law. Does the sun not blight a harvest when he will? Yes, and strike dead our most beloved? Are you not descended from the Sun Gods? Who will obey the laws if you, yourself, do not?

21/5.5. The king said: Behold, it is yet early morning; let the officers go fetch all who have escaped beyond the walls, and both mothers and children shall be put to death. Till then, let the proceedings be suspended. || Now, a vast multitude had congregated, anxious to witness the slaughter; and when the king suspended matters, there went up cries of disappointment. And many said: When a thing touches the king, he is a coward.

21/5.6. The king departed for his palace, leaving Asha standing stripped for the execution. And the multitude cried out: Asha is more like a king than So-qi. Let us make him king. (As to) King So-qi! We will not have a sheep for a king! || And none could restrain them, or be heard above their noise; and they ran after the king and slew him with stones, and they made Asha King of the Sun. And not one infant was slain according to the decrees.

21/5.7. God said: Do not think, O man, that things happen without a cause, or that all things are left to chance. In my works I plan the way ahead of time, even more carefully than a captain lays siege to a city. Before Zarathustra was born I sent out ashars to choose my personages. Do not think that Asha made his own arguments; but by virtue of the presence of my ashars, whom he did not see, he spoke and behaved in my commandments, all the while not knowing it. And it was the same with the king's wife; my angels also inspired her to speak before the king. And those who fled out of the city, were inspired by my hosts of angels.

21/5.8. God said: Yet with the king's decree I had no part, for I foresaw he would do this of his own will; and with the multitude in slaying the king I had no part, for I saw they would do this on their own account. Nor would the multitude hear my voice, even though I had spoken to every man's soul; for in them tetracts were the ascendant power.

21/5.9. God said: The multitude slew the king because he had gone so far from me he no longer heeded me. And I made Asha king because he came so near me, that my power was with him through my ashars.

CHAPTER 6 God's Word

21/6.1. During the infant age of Zarathustra, God did not manifest through him again; but he sent Ejah, one of his Lords, to be with Zarathustra, day and night. And Ejah taught the infant wisdom in all things, but showed himself to none other.

21/6.2. When Zarathustra was half grown, the Lord began to manifest through him, giving signs, miracles and prophecy before the Listians who lived in the Forest of Goats. This forest was of the width in every direction, except the east, of forty days' walking journey for a man; and in all that region, there were no houses, the inhabitants living in tents made of bark and skins.

21/6.3. The Lord inspired Zarathustra to teach them to build houses, and tame the goats, and to live in cities, and otherwise subdue the earth through righteousness; the chief center of their habitations being on the river Apherteon and its tributaries. And it was from these inhabitants that sprang in after years the migrants called Fonece'ans, signifying, out of the mountains. Nevertheless, these people were I'huans, but because of the cruelties of the Par'si'ean kings, they fled and lived in the forests.

21/6.4. The Lord said to Zarathustra: Behold the people who fly from the kings! I have made them kings over goats and over the beasts of the fields.

21/6.5. And from this time forward the Listians styled themselves shepherd kings. And Zarathustra taught them about the Lord, and that man should have dominion over the beasts of the forests, but that no man should hold dominion over his neighbor. Consequently, every man of the Listians styled himself a king, and every woman styled herself a queen.

21/6.6. Again the Lord said to Zarathustra: Go, my son, where I will lead you, and you shall find a people sacred to the Great Spirit. So Zarathustra wandered beyond the Forest of Goats, and came to Hara'woetchij, to the south of the mountains of Oe-tahka, where there were three large cities and twelve small ones, inhabited by I'hins.

21/6.7. And the Lord had been with the I'hins, and foretold them Zarathustra was coming, so that it was confirmed to both sides. The Lord said to the high priest: You shall permit Zarathustra to come within the walls of the cities, for he is pure.

21/6.8. So Zarathustra went in; and in the time of worship before the altar of God, the Lord appeared in a great light and commanded the high priest, saying: Behold, I have brought my son to you. Him you shall anoint as a priest according to the I'hin laws; and you shall teach him the rites and ceremonies of the ancients.

21/6.9. Accordingly, Zarathustra was made a priest and was otherwise accepted as an I'hin and bestowed under the rod with water and with fire. And he was also taught the sacred words and the art of writing and making tablets; and of weaving cloth and making clothes from flax.

21/6.10. Seven years Zarathustra remained with the I'hins, fasting and praying, and singing and dancing before the Lord. And then the Lord commanded him to return through the Forest of Goats, which he did, teaching the Listians wherever he stopped for a rest, and the Lord was with him, working miracles.

21/6.11. The Lord said to Zarathustra: Behold, the dawn of light has come! You shall, therefore, leave your mother with your people, and I will lead you to the city of your birth. Zarathustra said: Tell me, O Lord, about the city of my birth?

21/6.12. The Lord said: It is a great city, but it shall fall before your hand; for I'hua'Mazda has turned his favor away from its kings.

21/6.13. In two days' time, Zarathustra came to Oas, and entered into the city, but he brought no provender[635] with him. Now, it was a law of Oas that all strangers coming into the city should bring provender, as a testimony of fidelity to the laws and to the king. So, when he came to the inner gate, the keeper asked him for provender; but Zarathustra answered him, saying:

21/6.14. Naked I came into the world, and Ormazd[636] did not ask me for provender.[637] Is your king greater than the Creator?

21/6.15. The keeper said: I do not understand your words; shall a servant explain laws? To which

---

[635] In essence, this food and/or drink was an admission fee for strangers to enter the city.

[636] Ormazd, signifies Jehovih, the Creator; more definitely, Master of Light. OR is both Hebraic and Vedic for LIGHT. Mazda, or Mazd, is the origin of our word Master. –Ed.

[637] That is, I was born with nothing, and Jehovih didn't require anything from me to enter the world.

Zarathustra said: You are wise; neither shall you suffer for disobedience in letting me pass. The Lord will give you food.

21/6.16. When he had spoken thus, an abundance of fruit fell at the feet of the keeper, and the keeper feared and stood aside, permitting Zarathustra to pass into the city. The keeper not only told the people of the miracle, but ran and likewise told the king. This was Asha, who had reigned since the death of So-qi; and Asha no sooner heard of the miracle than he imagined the person to be the same whom he had seen in infancy.

21/6.17. Asha, the king, sent officers at once to find Zarathustra, and bring him before the court. But the Lord, knowing these things, inspired Zarathustra to go on his own account; and he went accordingly before the king, even before the officers returned.

21/6.18. The king said: Who are you? And for what purpose have you come before the king?

21/6.19. Then spoke I'hua'Mazda through Zarathustra, saying: I am I'hua'Mazda, God of the I'huans. The one through whom I speak, is Zarathustra, whom you saw in his mother's arms. We two are one. I have come before you, O king, because of two reasons: You have sent for me; and I desire to use you.

21/6.20. The king said: Speak further, stranger, so that I may approve of your words.

21/6.21. In the time of So-qi, said I'hua'Mazda, I made you king of Oas, and from that day to this my ashars have been with you and heard you often praying privately for information about the infant you saw; for it rests heavily on your judgment whether or not man is immortal. Sit with me privately tonight, and I will show you So-qi's soul.

21/6.22. Asha said: You were to strike the city and it would fall. Behold, it stands! Yet I desire not to stand in my own light.[638] || Then Zarathustra spoke on his own account, saying: Do not fear, O king, regarding this prophecy. As you would bend a straw, so do the Gods wield the nations of the earth. The city will fall before six years pass, and you shall be reduced to beggary, and yet you shall be happier than now.

CHAPTER 7 God's Word

21/7.1. When night came, the king sat privately with Zarathustra; and I'hua'Mazda cast a light on the wall, and the soul of So-qi came and appeared before Asha. So-qi said: Do you know who I am? And Asha said: Yes, So-qi.

21/7.2. So-qi said: True, O king, the soul is immortal! || And then it disappeared. Asha said: It seems to be So-qi. And yet if it were he, would he not have called me, Asha, instead of, O king? Then spoke Zarathustra, saying: Call for some other spirit? Asha said: Permit, then, the soul of my wife to appear.

21/7.3. Again the light appeared, and the soul of Asha's wife inhabited it, and he saw her. Asha said: It is, indeed. And then she disappeared. Asha said: Had it been my wife, she would have spoken. Zarathustra said: Call for another spirit. Asha called for Choe'jon, the songster, who looked like no other man under the sun. And Choe'jon also appeared; and even sang one of the songs about the slaughter of the infants.

21/7.4. Asha said: It was like Choe'jon; but had it been he, he surely would have mentioned the miracle. Then Zarathustra said: Call yet for another spirit. And Asha called, and another appeared; and thus it continued until twenty souls of the dead had shown themselves, and talked with him, face to face, and every one had related things pertinent to themselves.[639]

21/7.5. Then Zarathustra spoke, saying: Tomorrow night you shall sit with me again. Now on the next night, twenty other spirits of the dead appeared and spoke face to face with the king. But yet he did not believe. So I'hua'Mazda spoke through Zarathustra, saying: What will satisfy you,

[638] i.e., I don't want to judge before hearing your side of the story; in other words, it is not my light (thoughts, reasoning, meaning) that I wish to examine, it is yours; I wish to hear you speak further.

[639] Even today, the spirits who communicate to their mortal kin and friends either directly or through psychics, usually relate details about themselves or about the mortals to whom they are communicating, as a verification that they are who they appear or claim to be. This is to assure the persons still on earth that their loved one lives on in spirit, and that is why the messages are usually insignificant. –cns ed.

O man? For I declare to you, that spirit is not provable by corpor, nor corpor by spirit. There are two things: one grows by aggregating; and the other grows by dissemination, of which All Light is the highest. As by darkness light is known, and by light darkness known, similarly diverse are corpor and spirit known.

21/7.6. I'hua'Mazda said: Your generations, O king, have long been bred in unbelief in spirit, and unbelief is so entailed upon you that evidence is worthless before you. Who do you think I am?

21/7.7. Asha said: Zarathustra. Then Zarathustra asked him, saying: Who do you think I am?

21/7.8. Again Asha said: Zarathustra. To which I'hua'Mazda said: Because you see this corporeal body with your eyes, and hear this corporeal voice with your ears, even so does your corporeal judgment find an answer.

21/7.9. But I declare to you, O king, there is a spiritual judgment as well as a corporeal judgment. There is a spiritual man within all men, and it never dies. The spiritual man, which is within, is the only one that can discern spiritual things. It is the only one that can recognize the spirits of the dead.

21/7.10. Then Asha said: How can I be sure that there is not some element belonging to you personally, that is like a mirror, reproducing a semblance (likeness, copy, image), of whatever is within your thoughts?

21/7.11. I'hua'Mazda said: What would that benefit you, if proven? And what benefit if not proven?[640] Hear me, then, for this is wisdom: There are millions of souls in heaven who are in the same doubt you are now in, not knowing that they themselves are dead; especially those slain in war and in unbelief of spirit life.

21/7.12. The king said: Who, then, do you say you are? I'hua'Mazda said: First, there is Ormazd, Creator, Who is over all and within all, Whose Person is the Whole All. Then there are the unseen worlds in the sky; then this world, and the stars, sun and moon. After them, mortals, and the spirits of the dead.

21/7.13. Hear me, O king; because the dead do not know the All High heavens, the Ormazd, Whose name signifies Master of All Light, sends His exalted angels down to the earth as masters and teachers, having captains and high captains, so that their labor is orderly. The highest captain is therefore called I'hua'Mazda, that is, master voice over mortals and spirits for their exaltation.

21/7.14. Know, then, O king, I, who speak, have you and your city and your country within my keeping. I come to stop man's bloody hand. And through Zarathustra I will reveal the laws of Ormazd; and they shall stand above all other laws. Because you are the most skilled of men, I made you king; because you have seen that man must have an All Highest Law, I have come to you. Yes, from your youth up, during your long life, I have spoken to your soul, saying: Asha, find the All Highest; Asha, you shall have a strange labor before you die! Asha, you, who have attained to the measurement of the stars, shall find a Power behind the stars!

21/7.15. The king said. Enough! Enough! O stranger! You turned my head with wonders. I hardly know if I am living or dead, because of the mastery of your wisdom. Alas, my kindred are dead; my friends are fools! I have no one to tell these wonders to. You shall live all your days in my palace, and whoever you demand for wife, shall be granted to you.

21/7.16. I'hua'Mazda said: Till I come again to you, O king, keep your own counsel. For the present, I must return to the forest. Give me, therefore, some of your choicest ink, brushes and writing cloth, and send two servants with me. Asha said: Allow me to be one of your servants, and I will abdicate my throne!

21/7.17. I'hua'Mazda said: I shall need you where you are. Thus ended the interview with the king. The next day Zarathustra returned to the forest, to write the Zarathustrian laws.

CHAPTER 8 God's Word

21/8.1. These, then, are the Zarathustrian laws; the I'hua'Mazdian laws; which, being interpreted

[640] For are you not still left in darkness concerning the unseen? –ed. || Asha's need to have his corporeal understanding satisfied, is not the issue here, for whether an explanation is found in the physical or not, the cause is still in the spiritual. For the issue, as God indicates, is not proof but belief, for Asha is rationalizing to support his belief that spirit is nothing and all cause lies in the physical. –cns ed.

into the English language, should be described as God's Word, transcribed from the libraries of heaven by the will of Jehovih!

21/8.2. That is to say:

21/8.3. Zarathustra said: Interpret to me, O Holy One.

21/8.4. I'hua'Mazda said: O Pure One, All Pure! Hear and I will interpret; therefore, write.

21/8.5. Zarathustra wrote. Then spoke I'hua'Mazda to Zarathustra, the All Pure!

21/8.6. First, Ormazd was, and He created all created things. He was All; He is All. He was All Round, and put forth hands and wings. Then began the beginning of things seen, and of things unseen.

21/8.7. The first best highest place He created was the All Possibility. And the second best highest place He created was the All Good. With Him all things are Possible. With Him all things are Good.

21/8.8. Ormazd then created the highest of good creation, the Airyana-vaja (etherea), the longest enduring.

21/8.9. The third best of created places created by Ormazd, was Haraiti, a high heavenly good place, a Home of Fragapatti, a Creator Son of the heavenly Airyana-vaja, a rescuer of men and spirits from Anra'mainyus, the evil of blood and bone.

21/8.10. The fourth best of created places created by Ormazd, the Creator, was Gau, the dwelling-place of Sooghda,[641] of heavenly shape, with straight limbs and arms, and ample chest, full of music.

21/8.11. Out of Mouru, of the regions of Haraiti, came the Voice, created by the Creator Ormazd; came to I'hua'Mazda; and now comes to you, Zarathustra, you All Pure.

21/8.12. The fifth best place created by the Creator was the Bakhdhi,[642] with lofty standards.

21/8.13. Then came Anra'mainyus, the Black Doubt, the Sa-gwan, sowing seeds.

21/8.14. After that, the Creator created Tee-Sughi, the reason of man, and turned his eyes inward, so that he could see his own soul.

[641] Sooghda, or, improperly, Sughda, is known as Apollo to English and Latin students. –Ed.

[642] The plan of salvation; the word that leads to everlasting life. In the Chinese language this "dhi" is a separate word, and pronounced "jhi." –Ed.

CHAPTER 9 God's Word

21/9.1. By the hosts of Haraiti, the voice of I'hua'Mazda came to Zarathustra, the All Pure: Hear me, O Zarathustra; I am I'hua'Mazda. Hear about your Creator, Who created all created things.

21/9.2. These are the chief best places created: First, the earth, the air and the water, and all the living that are on them and in them.

21/9.3. Out of darkness came Void! Waste! And nothing was; as seeming nothing. And He, the Creator, Ormazd, shaped the shape of things.

21/9.4. The living that live; the living that are dead; the first of all that breathed; these the Creator, Ormazd, created.

21/9.5. With legs or wings; and with hair, feathers or naked; meant to crawl, walk or fly—so created the Creator, Ormazd, all the living.

21/9.6. To all to live a life; a right to live and die: Out of the life of Ormazd, He gave them life and death.

21/9.7. Then asked Zarathustra, the All Pure, inquiring of I'hua'Mazda, saying: To whom else have you spoken these things?

21/9.8. I'hua'Mazda said: Since I told you, a million! Before I told you, a million! More than a thousand millions! Then asked Zarathustra: Tell me one, one to whom you have revealed? Then answered I'hua'Mazda: To Vivanho, the first of men who had words; the first of women who had words. In the first days when pure men and pure women were created, I came, I revealed. Then Zarathustra, the All Pure, said:

21/9.9. To be all pure; to be all good; to be all wise; to be all holy; to do all good works; what are these?

21/9.10. I'hua'Mazda said: These are to hear my voice, O Zarathustra. Then Zarathustra said: To be all bad; to be all foolish; to be all evil thinking; to do evil works, what are these?

21/9.11. I'hua'Mazda said: These are not to hear my voice; these are Anra'mainyus, O Zarathustra! Then Zarathustra inquired, saying: Is the 'not to hear your voice' a person? Is the 'to hear your voice' a person? (i.e., Is Anra'mainyus a person? Is Vivanho a person?)

21/9.12. I'hua'Mazda said to Zarathustra, the All Pure: Anra'mainyus was a person, but he is dead; Vivanho is a person, and he lives to all the holy, to all the good, to all the wise. But to all the evil, to all the bad, to all the foolish, Anra'mainyus is not dead.

21/9.13. Then inquired Zarathustra, the All Pure: Where did all good come from; where did all evil come from? Who is the All Good; who is the All Evil? Then answered I'hua'Mazda to Zarathustra, saying: You perceive now, All Evil must have a name; All Good must have a name. Without names, no man could talk. Behold, I will write for you, O Zarathustra, you All Pure. The mark I make first, you shall call the All Good, the Creator, the Master, the Light! Here, then, I have made a circle and a cross and a leaf.[643]

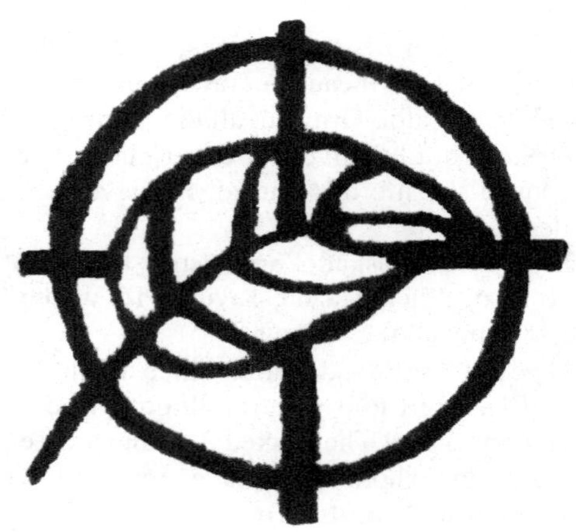

i033r01i **Jehovih** or **Ormazd.**

21/9.14. I'hua'Mazda said to Zarathustra, the All Pure: Whoever looks upon this mark, whoever sees it, sees the Name of All Names, the Creator. Whoever makes this mark, writes the name of the All Good; whoever pronounces this mark, pronounces the name of Ormazd, the All Master.

21/9.15. Then I'hua'Mazda made a circle, and painted four dark corners in it, and called it Anra'mainyus, the Uh-druk, the opposition to All Truth, and All Light, and All Good. And I'hua'Mazda explained to Zarathustra.

21/9.16. And, behold, there stood within the circle of evil, the name of All Good, the cross, and it was light, and the corners were black. I'hua'Mazda called this mark Fate, explaining to Zarathustra, the All Pure, saying: These three marks embrace all the created creation; hence, the name of the third one is Fate, from which there is no escape, nor separation, forever.

i122 **Fate.**

21/9.17. Zarathustra inquired of I'hua'Mazda, saying: Is evil, evil; is good, good? I'hua'Mazda said: Evil is evil to man, but evil is not evil to Ormazd. Good is good to man; but good is not good to Ormazd. Only two conditions are before Ormazd; neither evil, nor good; but ripe and unripe. To Ormazd, that which man calls evil is unripe; to Ormazd, that which man calls good is ripe.

21/9.18. I'hua'Mazda went on explaining, saying: For the sake of understanding, O Zarathustra; for the sake of not confounding, you shall call evil, evil; and good, good. Hear me, then, my son:

21/9.19. Without green fruit, none could be ripe; without evil none could be good. So Ormazd created all creation, and called it good; but lo and behold, there was nothing to do. All things never moved, as if dead; all things were as nothing.

21/9.20. Then Ormazd blew His breath outward, and every created thing went into motion. And those at the front were called All Good, and those at the rear were called All Evil. Thus the Creator created the Good Creation and the Evil Creation; the I'hua'Mazda and the Anra'mainyus.

CHAPTER 10 God's Word

21/10.1. Then I'hua'Mazda spoke to Zarathustra, the All Pure, saying: Thus your Creator created all things; and the time of the creation was as a time, and a time, and a time, and without measure.

21/10.2. I'hua'Mazda said to Zarathustra: Thus are the created creations; thus were the created creations; thus shall ever be the created creations. The Light of all light is Ormazd; He, the Soul of all

[643] see image i033r01i; or i001, p.24

souls. These are the things seen and things unseen, created by Ormazd, your Creator: Mi, the Mother Almighty: Then is Voice, the Expression of things, the All Speech, the All Communion, created by Ormazd, your Creator, and by Mi, the Almighty Mother, a virgin never before conceived; and this was Vivanho, the Son.

21/10.3. I'hua'Mazda said to Zarathustra, the All Pure: Watch me, O Zarathustra! Here I make one straight line; and now I make another straight line, and now another, all joined.

21/10.4. Then Zarathustra answered, saying: You have made a triangle: What is the meaning, O I'hua'Mazda? Then I'hua'Mazda answered, saying: Three in one, O Zarathustra: Father, Mother and Son; Ormazd, the ghost of things;[644] Mi, the seen and unseen;[645] and Vivanho, the expression of things.[646]

21/10.5. I'hua'Mazda said to Zarathustra: These three comprise all things; and all things are just one; nor were there more, nor ever shall be. Nevertheless, O my son, each of these has a million parts, a billion parts, a trillion parts. And every part is like the whole; you, O Zarathustra, also. For you have within yourself those three attributes, and no more. And each and all created things have these three attributes in them. Thus Ormazd created all the living creation; brothers and sisters He created them, in likeness of Himself, with three entities embraced in one, which are: first, the ghost, the soul, which is incomprehensible; second, the beast, the figure, the person, which is called individual; and third, the expression, to receive and to impart.

21/10.6. I'hua'Mazda said to Zarathustra, the All Pure: To receive and to impart; what else has man; what more does he desire? Then I'hua'Mazda drew a picture of a cow, and a picture of a horse, a strong male horse dashing forth. And he asked Zarathustra, saying: Which of these signifies receiving; which of these signifies to impart? And Zarathustra perceived.

21/10.7. I'hua'Mazda said to Zarathustra: To be negative is to be a cow (receiving); to be positive is to be a horse (imparting).

21/10.8. Zarathustra inquired of I'hua'Mazda, saying: How many words are there, that can be written words! You have now written many wise words, full of meaning. How many more words are there? Then answered I'hua'Mazda, saying: A thousand words and ten thousand words would not be all; but ten times ten thousand hundred thousand, and those are all the words created.

21/10.9. Then Zarathustra, the All Pure, said: Write down all the words for me, and explain the meaning of them to me, so that I may go before the world teaching All Truth, so that men will no longer be in darkness.

21/10.10. Then I'hua'Mazda wrote down tens of hundreds, and thousands of words, and explained the meaning. After that, Zarathustra sat in the bushes for thirty days and thirty nights, neither eating nor drinking nor sleeping. And then I'hua'Mazda revealed the secrets of heaven and earth to him, and commanded him to write them in a book; which he did; and this was the first book, the Zarathustrian law, the I'hua'Mazdian law.

CHAPTER 11 God's Word

21/11.1. By this authority then, I, Zarathustra, by the power of I'hua'Mazda, reveal the created creations.

21/11.2. Ormazd created a good creation. First, the land and water and firm things; out of the unseen and void He created them. Second, the heavenly lights; and the heat and the cold everywhere. Third, all living animals, fish, and birds. Fourth, man and woman.

21/11.3. Then Ormazd spoke through His Son, Vivanho, saying: Speech! Voice! Words! And man and woman were the only talking animals created in all the created world.

21/11.4. Ormazd then created death, Anra'mainyus; creating him with seven heads. First vanity (uk), then tattling (owow), then worthlessness (hoe'zee), then lying (ugs'ga), then incurable wickedness (hiss'ce), then evil inventions

[644] i.e., the intangible essence of things, which, for convenience or ease of understanding, is here called soul

[645] i.e., all form (shape and structure) whether in corpor, atmospherea or etherea

[646] Thus we have an unseen essence, the form around it, and its expression.

for evil (bowh-hiss), then king and leader (daevas).[647]

21/11.5. Ormazd then created association (clans) by words bringing men together, Haroyu.

21/11.6. Ormazd then created habitations (oke'a); and then He created dwelling-places for the Gods, Varena; with four good corners and four evil corners He created them.

21/11.7. And Ormazd created sustenance for the living and the dead, haoma. Then He created the boon[648] of rest, for the weary, haraquaiti. After that He created sweet-smelling and rich-growing pastures (meadows), Urva.[649]

21/11.8. And Ormazd created combination (unity), which is strength, chakhra. Then power to receive knowledge, haden'amazd.

21/11.9. Ormazd then created the holy day (rak). Then He made the four signs of the moon, Uk'git, E'git, Ki'git and M'git, for all holiness.

21/11.10. And He said: Six days you shall labor, O man; and worship on the seventh, because they are the moon's times.

21/11.11. Then Ormazd, the Creator, created the power to live without kings, like the I'hins in the east, and the name of this power He created was Ranha. ||

21/11.12. Then spoke I'hua'Mazda to Zarathustra, the All Pure, saying: To attain to Ranha; how to attain to Ranha; this, then, is the holy Mazdian law:

21/11.13. Ormazd shall be King, and you shall acknowledge no other. He shall be your All Highest love forever, and above all other loves.

21/11.14. You shall disown all other rulers, kings, queens, Lords, and Gods.

21/11.15. You shall not bow down in reverence except to Ormazd your Creator.

21/11.16. You shall covenant yourself to your Creator every day, and teach your children to do so also.

21/11.17. You shall keep holy the four moon days, for they are the change of watch of the Gods and angels over man.

21/11.18. You shall not kill what your Creator created alive.

21/11.19. You shall love your father next to your Creator, and obey his voice, and honor your mother, because she brought you forth by the will of your Creator.

21/11.20. You shall not allow your desires to lead you after woman.[650]

21/11.21. You shall not take that which is another's.

21/11.22. You shall not be vain, for nothing is yours.

21/11.23. You shall not speak untruth.

21/11.24. You shall not talk about your neighbor behind his back, for Ormazd hears you, and the angels will go tell your neighbor's soul what you have said.

21/11.25. You shall not be idle or lazy, or your flesh will become weak and bear down your soul.

21/11.26. You shall not envy, nor harbor hatred against any man, woman or child.

21/11.27. You shall not reprove[651] any man or woman for their evil, for they are the Creator's.

21/11.28. You shall reprove your own child, and teach him the right way.

21/11.29. You shall not lie with your wife during pregnancy.[652]

21/11.30. You shall not marry any of your kin, except beyond the fifth generation.

21/11.31. You shall not take to wife a woman of unclean habits.[653]

21/11.32. You shall not commit the self-habit.

21/11.33. You shall not desire of your neighbor more than you would give.

21/11.34. You shall fast one day of the fourth moon all your life, neither eating fish nor flesh, nor bread nor fruit; nor shall anything but water enter your mouth.

21/11.35. One whole year of your life you shall dwell with the poor, live with the poor, sleep with the poor, begging for alms for the poor.

---

[647] These are the same as the seven tetracts of the Hebrew Scriptures. –Ed. [For more on the seven tetracts see 10/13.9-12; 11/1.68.]

[648] blessing, benefit

[649] Much of this subject matter is still to be found in the Vedas. –Ed.

[650] Was there a parallel rule for woman regarding her desires?

[651] express disapproval of, rebuke, criticize

[652] Was there a parallel rule regarding a pregnant wife not lying with her husband?

[653] And was there a parallel rule here?

CHAPTER 12 God's Word

21/12.1. I'hua'Mazda said to Zarathustra, the All Pure: Three castes I have made; the first are the I'hins, sacred above all other people, because they keep my commandments; second, the I'huans, whom I created more powerful than other people, because by them I will subdue the earth; and third, the druks, the evil people, who will not learn.

21/12.2. I'hua'Mazda said to Zarathustra, the All Pure: Remember the caste of men; keep your blood in the place I created you; nor shall you marry except in the caste I created you.

21/12.3. I'hua'Mazda said: A thousand castes I created among the I'huans: The king; the doctor; the magician; the priest; the farmer; the bearer of burdens; the messenger, swift footed; and for all other occupations under the sun. I created them each and all within their own castes; nor shall they marry except in the caste I created them.

21/12.4. Zarathustra responded to I'hua'Mazda, saying: I will keep your commandments. Your seventy commandments, and seven hundred and seven thousand.

21/12.5. I will preserve as sacred the castes you have created, O I'hua'Mazda. And I will teach these holy truths to my children; to my servants, and to all men.

21/12.6. Then I'hua'Mazda wrote all the commandments, those previously mentioned, and he stooped down and kissed the books, which were made of stone and cloth, saying: This is my holy book. Take it, O Zarathustra, you All Pure, and go forth into all the world, teaching it, and explaining it.

21/12.7. Then Zarathustra, the All Pure, stooped down and kissed the book, saying: This is your holy book, O I'hua'Mazda. I take it; and I will go into all the world, teaching it, and explaining it.

21/12.8. Thus was completed the first sacred, most holy book created for mortals. And Zarathustra rose up from his writing, tall and handsome, inquiring of I'hua'Mazda, saying: Where shall I go first, O master?

21/12.9. Then answered I'hua'Mazda, creator of the Ormazdian law, the Zarathustrian law, saying:

21/12.10. Take my holy book, the Ormazdian law, the Zarathustrian law, first, to Asha, king of the I'huans, king of Oas, the City of the Sun. Him I have prepared for you and your work since the day of his birth, since the day of your birth, since the day I spoke to him in your infancy.

21/12.11. Then Zarathustra went forth, strong in faith; and he came to Asha, the king. And the king said to him: You have been gone so long! Behold, I have cast the horoscope a hundred times, a thousand times. I have proved all the stars in heaven and named them, and made maps of them. And I have measured the power of one star over another star; and the powers of the stars on this world, and the powers of the sun and moon.

21/12.12. Yes, I have sent into the great cities of the east, to men of great learning; and to the south and north and west, to men of great learning. And then I sent to the kings of Jaffeth and Shem; to Bow-ghan-ghad; to Bing-thah; and to the great city of Huug-sin, where the great philosopher, Ah-tdong, lives. And from all of these I have obtained great wisdom.

21/12.13. Hear me, then, O Zarathustra; although I do not believe your philosophy, I will speak to you as if it were true: First, then, in all the stars there is nothing but lies; nor does it matter if a man is born under this star or that star! I am old now and have observed thousands of men, yes, even kings and queens, as to whether the stars rule over them, and I declare to you that the philosophy of the stars is nothing but lies. Moreover, I have searched my own behavior, and I find I am often doing things contrary to my first intentions; but as to the cause, I do not know.

21/12.14. This also I have discovered; there is one kind of cause that lies with individuals; and there is another kind of cause that lies with kings and kingdoms; but, yet, I perceive that each and every man is bound in his own channel[654] by something stronger than himself. To find the cause of this, I have searched even to the extent of all the stars in the firmament, but did not find the truth.

21/12.15. Now I ask you, in the name of your Gods, if you can prove this matter to your king?

21/12.16. Then Zarathustra answered, saying: Through my hand I'hua'Mazda has written a most holy book, explaining many philosophies. This book I have brought to you, according to the commandments of my God, so that you may read it.

---

[654] station, path, habit, destiny, fate

21/12.17. Then the king took the book and read it; and the next day Zarathustra came again before the king. The king said: Your book says thus and so, but it proves little. Your God asserts he has done thus and so, and that he created thus and so. First of all, then, I do not know if there is a God; second, if there is a God, I do not know that he comes to you; and, third, if he comes to you, and he is a just God, why does he not come to me? And yet, after all this, for I do not doubt your wisdom will give sufficient answers to these questions, if it is true there are Gods unseen that rule over us, and spirits of the dead that come to us, persuading our souls unconsciously to ourselves, what does it matter whether we try or not, to obtain truth and wisdom? Shall all things not be left to the spirits and Gods and Lords? Do you not know that the ancients believed these things?

21/12.18. And yet what of the ancients? Were they not in darkness, and addicted to horrid rites and ceremonies, and murders, and savagery? With our wisdom of disbelief in their religions, have we not attained to great cities and empires? Behold our thousands and tens of thousands of large cities! And do they not all have just reason to be proud? For there is not one city without walls and gates being adorned with thousands of skeletons and skulls of serpents and lions, and the scalps of druks.

21/12.19. Then I'hua'Mazda spoke to the king, speaking through the voice of Zarathustra, saying: Hear your God, O king, and consider my words. There are two births to all men; the first is from the mother's womb, and the second is from the corporeal body. Prior to the first birth, the will and power of the child has nothing to do with shaping its own destiny. But prior to the spiritual birth, which is the mortal death, the man has much to do with shaping his future destiny in the next world.

21/12.20. I declare to you, O king, that the corporeal man is, therefore, only half accomplished as to his real life. He is only half his own master; only half the controller of his place and behavior in the mortal world; nevertheless, he is the first half, the first chooser. Do not think that spirits and Gods rule men as if they were slaves or toys; for another power also lies over man, which is neither spirits nor Gods nor stars, nor moon nor sun; but the corporeal surroundings that feed his earthly desires.

21/12.21. This is the Ormazdian law; neither the corporeal stars, nor corporeal earth, nor corporeal moon, nor corporeal man, rules over the spirit; but the subtle, the unseen to mortals, is the cause and ruler of all things.

21/12.22. Asha said: O if only I could believe this! If only I knew this were true! O, if only the unseen worlds could be opened up to my understanding! For I perceive there is more power and virtue in your philosophy than in my decrees. || But touching on your book, O Zarathustra, answer me this: Who do the people in the world belong to, if not to me, the Sun King? Are the people not mine?

21/12.23. I'hua'Mazda said: All belong to Ormazd. Is it not here taught (in the book) that man shall acknowledge obedience and worship to Ormazd only?

21/12.24. Asha said: I so perceive. Answer me this, O Zarathustra: To disown the king and the king's kings; will this not bring anarchy? For will the rulers not declare your doctrine robs them of subjects? To which I'hua'Mazda permitted Zarathustra to reply. He said:

21/12.25. Is it not hard for a man to be denied the privilege of choosing his own master? Behold, they are now impressed into war; yes, you keep standing armies, trained in the labor of death; and this for the glory of the Sun Kingdom. Now hear me, O king, for I am now speaking on my own accord, and no God is speaking through me. And I declare to you, I have attained power to go in soul into the unseen worlds and see with my own eyes how it is with the souls of the dead. And I declare to you there are great torments for the wicked. I have seen them in hell, with walls of fire going up around them day and night; suffocating fires of brimstone, from which they cannot escape. And those slain in war, both those who are for the king, and those against the king, are equally cast into ceaseless torments, and even kings and queens with them, where all are wailing and gnashing their teeth, and cursing; and in their madness, doing wickedly toward others with all their might.

21/12.26. The king said: If it is true that you can go into heaven and hell, it must be true you can go to places on the corporeal earth in the same way. Prove this to me, and I will believe all you have said. Then Zarathustra said: Tell me where I shall go, so I may convince you, O king?

21/12.27. Asha said: Go to the tower of the horoscope and find the words on the calendar.

21/12.28. While Zarathustra was gone in spirit, I'hua'Mazda spoke, saying: Have I not said, spirit cannot be proved except to spirit! Have I not said I am I'hua'Mazda; and Zarathustra has said he is Zarathustra. But this you cannot see. Behold, you shall witness now your own craft (unbelief). Here returns Zarathustra.

21/12.29. Then Zarathustra spoke, saying: You said to me: Go to the tower of the horoscope and find the words of the calendar. Lo, I have been there, and am already returned before you. These, then, are the words of the calendar: To-ka, Seis, ctvai tnong, biang loo-sin-gooh wotchich; an porh, an oot, an dhi, an git.

21/12.30. Asha said: This is true. But how shall I determine whether or not you gathered the calendar information from my heart? For I had the knowledge in my heart since sunrise. Then Zarathustra answered, saying: Try me once again; yes, you shall ask me for some toy of yours, and I will go fetch it.

21/12.31. Asha said: When I was a boy I let fall into the river, between the cliffs, at the outer wall, a golden case; go, bring it.

21/12.32. Again while Zarathustra was gone in spirit, I'hua'Mazda spoke: Two conditions belong to all men, belief and unbelief. They are like seeds, planted in the soul of man while he is yet in his mother's womb; and when he is born into the world, they begin to grow within him. If man favors one only, it will grow at the expense of the other. Because of unbelief in man, he searches after truth and knowledge; but because of belief in man, he finds happiness; but the latter may lead to stupidity, and the former to cruelty. It is a wise man, therefore, who keeps these two talents evenly balanced.

21/12.33. Now, even while I'hua'Mazda spoke, the long-lost golden case fell at the king's feet, and it was still dripping with water. The king examined it, and then exclaimed: This is true! And yet, if there are spirits and Gods, how shall I determine which one brought this? May it not have been an evil spirit as well as a good one?

21/12.34. Then I'hua'Mazda spoke, saying: Have I not said, I will show you your own craft in finding some other reason than the right one?

21/12.35. Asha said: O you Gods, can you not heal me of my unbelief? My judgment shows me I am diseased in my heart. O, if only my mother had been a believing woman before I was born! Tell me, O Zarathustra, or I'hua'Mazda, whoever you are, for I perceive you are not like any man under the sun, tell me what I shall do, so that I may become your servant?

21/12.36. I'hua'Mazda said: Tomorrow at sunrise I will come to you, with Zarathustra, and I will tell you many things.

CHAPTER 13 God's Word

21/13.1. The following morning, the king said: I have not slept. All night I was like one burning with fever; for your wondrous words and your miracles have very nearly turned my judgment upside down.

21/13.2. I'hua'Mazda said: Because a man cannot understand a thing, shall he cry out, MIRACLE! Now I declare I have done no miracle; nor has Zarathustra. Yet to mortals these things are miracles! If so, is a man not a miracle to himself? Is procreation (having children) not a miracle?

21/13.3. This, then, I have found, O Asha, what man is not accustomed to, he calls a miracle; after he has seen a matter frequently, he calls it a natural law. What man have you found who comprehends the first cause of anything under the sun?

21/13.4. Why, then, should man waste his time in unprofitable research? Is it not wiser that man labor to raise his fellow-men out of misery and darkness, than to gratify his own personal desire for great learning?

21/13.5. The king said: You reason well. And yet, what learned good man have you found who will not say: Yes, to do good is a pretty philosophy! And there ends his aspiration. What, then, can I say, or what can you say, that will render the words fruitful?

21/13.6. I'hua'Mazda said: You are this day king of all the world; nor is there any other kingdom that does not pay you tribute. Whatever you desire is as a law to all other kingdoms. For that reason I come to you. Indeed, you were born to this end. Hear, then, the voice of your God, and you shall do what is good for your soul and good for all other people.

21/13.7. Asha said: I am almost tempted to accede to your wishes before you have revealed; but yet hear the voice of your king; what does it matter to me about the good of other people? Even if it is proven that great men have souls that live after death, it is not yet proven that the druks have souls also. If they have souls, then heaven must be a stupid place indeed. For you have not shown me that man obtains wisdom by dying, nor is it reasonable that he should do so. Rather tell me, O Zarathustra, how I may get rid of the world; for of what use is life at most?

21/13.8. I'hua'Mazda said: Because you do not rejoice in your life, you perceive that it is your philosophy that is deficient, and not that the world is. Yet I will prove to you that you are overflowing with happiness. To believe what I reveal and have faith in it, is to become happy. The king then answered him, saying: To believe, there is the matter. I declare to you, there is not a grain of belief in my heart. How, then, can it grow?

21/13.9. I'hua'Mazda said: He who can say, I can think of an All Highest, has the seed of everlasting life in him. He who lives the all highest he can; he who thinks of the All Highest; he who talks to the All Highest; he who tries to perceive from the standpoint of the All Highest, quickly transcends belief and becomes a very God in faith. He becomes master of himself, and feeds himself with happiness, even as men feed themselves with bread.

21/13.10. Asha said: What would you have me do? To which I'hua'Mazda said: With the people, you have greater authority than a God, greater than miracles. Your decrees are all powerful. You shall have a copy of this book written on stone and cloth, one copy for every sub-kingdom in your dominions. And you shall send it to them with a sword and a serpent, saying to them: Receive this book, for it is a Holy Book, the ALL HIGHEST LAW, the I'hua'Mazdian law, the Zarathustrian law, the Ormazdian law. And it shall be a rule and guide to you and your kingdom forever. And every king in the KINGDOM OF THE SUN shall serve one year in living with the poor, carrying the alms-bowl for sacrifices to Ormazd.

21/13.11. And when you have sent forth this decree into all the world, you shall yourself give up your kingdom; and you shall give to the poor all your gold, silver and cases, and all your treasures whatsoever, having nothing left to yourself but the clothes that cover you. And you shall go and live with the poor, carrying the alms-bowl yourself in the streets of Oas. And of the food you gather in the bowl, you shall give the choicest parts to the poor, saying: THIS IS THE SACRIFICE OF THE MANY GIVEN TO YOU; EAT OF IT, FOR IT IS THE VERY BODY AND BLOOD OF ORMAZD, OUR FATHER IN HEAVEN! But the poorest of all that is in the bowl shall be your portion.

21/13.12. At the end of one year you shall go about preaching the Ormazdian law, commanding the cessation of war and the abandonment of evil, and the acceptance of righteousness.

21/13.13. The king said: What can you promise me if I do all these things? Then I'hua'Mazda suffered Zarathustra to answer him: He said, NOTHING! Did the Creator ask this, before He made the world? If you desire to approach (draw closer to) your Creator, do as He does. Nor is it my place, nor the angels' place, nor the place of God, to promise you anything. You are not my servant; and you shall serve only the Master, All Light (Jehovih).

21/13.14. And as I have taught you, so shall you go and teach others, explaining the Ormazdian law.

21/13.15. Asha said: Do the Gods in heaven give rewards for good works and sacrifices[655] done on earth? Zarathustra said: He who does good works and makes sacrifices to Ormazd has his reward. For it is by this means, that the soul of man becomes strong, and especially strong for the first and second resurrections in the next world.

21/13.16. Asha said: To be with you, O Zarathustra, and feast on the wisdom of your words, I would make any sacrifice. Will you go with me among the poor?

21/13.17. I'hua'Mazda said: No, you shall go alone. And for company you shall pray to your Creator, and make songs of praise to Him, nor think any more of yourself than as if you were dead.[656]

---

[655] The word sacrifice here [as used by Asha] is evidently used in the same sense as in the Vedic Scriptures, and signifies, "Contributions to the poor and afflicted." –Ed.

[656] That is, as if he no longer existed; which is to say, as the people in the Kingdom of the Sun no more think of a person after he is dead (because they think he no longer exists), so likewise Asha

21/13.18. The king said: It is said of madmen that they think they are not mad. How, then, am I to know if I am mad? Will the world not adjudge me so, if I obey your commandments? And can the world not judge me better than I can judge myself? It was said of the ancients that Sughdha (Apollo) obsessed old men and weak-hearted women; and it was for that reason Osiris came and slew him. If there are Gods in heaven, as you say, maybe you have come to slay Osiris?

21/13.19. I'hua'Mazda said: You are a great multiplier of arguments; but in all your speech I have seen nothing that planned the resurrection of men from darkness into light. And is this not the All Highest that man should aim at?

21/13.20. Asha said: I am done. Your judgment is greater than mine. All you have commanded of me I will do. From this time forth I will serve only Ormazd, the Creator. Your God, O Zarathustra, shall be my God. Your ways shall be my ways. Starting now, I will argue forever on the side of the Creator. And in all matters, I will first ask myself what I shall say that would be like your God would say it; and what I shall do that will fulfill the Ormazdian law.

CHAPTER 14 God's Word

21/14.1. ASHA, KING OF OAS, the City of the Sun, KING OF THE SUN, ruler over the whole corporeal world, owner and possessor of all mortals, men, women and children, COMMANDER OF ALL FLESH, descended from the SUN GODS thousands of years, and whose forefathers were the fathers of all living creatures, HIGHEST OF MEN, and by whose good grace the inhabitants of the earth are permitted to live, and whose decrees are the standard of all things, MAKER OF JUSTICE and MAKER OF TRUTH, and whom none dare question, and on whose word the sun and moon and stars bow down, greeting:

21/14.2. To the kings and queens of the east and west and north and south, over all the cities in the world; rulers in the temples of the stars (observatories); slayers of dragons, slayers of lions, slayers of tigers, men, women, children and serpents, honored in the golgothas,[657] and by millions of cowering slaves; owners of thousands of wives, and whose boats sail in lakes of mortal blood, and whose crowns are honored by ten thousand men slain every year, sworn on the flesh of the thigh, whose words are life and death; and most obedient to the SUN KING, I command:

21/14.3. First, that there is an Ormazd, Creator, Person! Whose Soul is in all the world, and in all things in the firmament above; Who is Father; Who is the Light of light, Creator of darkness and men, Who is forever The Going Forth; Who is Cause of causes; larger than all things seen and unseen; the Power of all power.

21/14.4. Second, I'hua'Mazda, His Only Begotten Son, born of the Virgin Mi (the Substance Seen). Pure and All Holy; Master of Men; Person of Word; Essence of Ormazd revealed in WORD; SAVIOR OF MEN; Holder of the keys of heaven; through WHOSE GOOD GRACE ONLY the souls of men can rise to Nirvania, the HIGH HEAVEN:

21/14.5. Third, Zarathustra, A man, All Pure, conceived by a Virgin, and born wise, being one with I'hua'Mazda, who is one with Ormazd. Of whom The Word says: He does without miracle THE RAISING OF THE DEAD; THE HEALING THE SICK BY THE LAYING ON OF HANDS; WHOSE WORD OF COMMAND BRINGS FORTH RIPE WHEAT, FULL GROWN, IN A DAY; and doing all things that the ancients accredited to the Gods as miracles, but which the Ormazdian law shows to be NATURAL LAW TO ANYONE WHO IS ALL PURE, and who draws power from Ormazd the Creator, and His holy angels.

21/14.6. Fourth, A Book, holy and sacred, revealed by I'hua'Mazda to Zarathustra, the All Pure; and written on stone and cloth, revealing All Wisdom, which is styled, the Ormazdian law, the I'hua'Mazdian law, the Zarathustrian law, which is the All Highest Law in All the world, approved by ASHA, I, THE KING OF KINGS!

21/14.7. Fifth, by ten thousand learned scribes in my command, written copies of The Holy Book, with one now sent along with commands by the KING OF THE SUN! That this book shall be the All Highest law in all my sub-kingdoms, and that all my kings shall believe it and command the same of their slaves [subjects –Ed.]. Nor shall any man stand up against this, my decree, and live; nor shall

---

was to void himself of any thoughts or concerns of himself.

[657] Temples made of skulls and teeth. –Ed.

any man alter one word or sign in this Holy Book; nor disbelieve one word it contains.

21/14.8. And my kings and sub-kings; and my queens and sub-queens, shall obey all the commandments, even as I obey them; nor shall any man, woman, or child, question these things, as to whether they are the All Highest, or whether there is error in whatever comes from my hand; for by my decree they are made All Truth!

21/14.9. For I was raised up to the High Estate by Ormazd, for this purpose; and not one in the whole world has power like me.

21/14.10. And you, to whom these holy words come, shall make oath on a serpent and a sword to obey these, my commandments, now and forever. ||

21/14.11. Thus Asha sent officers to carry the books he had made to the kings and queens in the east and west and north and south; and those he sent were men of great learning, and of the highest caste; and they took with them serpents and swords, and gave the books as commanded, exacting an oath from all who received them.

CHAPTER 15 God's Word

21/15.1. When Asha, the king, had thus completed the labor of making the books, and sending them as commanded by I'hua'Mazda, he sent for Zarathustra, for further counsel as to how he should abdicate the throne according to the Highest Light. And when I'hua'Mazda was in his presence, even before Zarathustra had yet come, Asha said: Here comes that quickened thought again! Behold, I sent for Zarathustra in order to ask certain questions, and lo, my heart answers me!

21/15.2. Yes, of course, I have nothing to do with what is not my own! Now, while he thus framed his own answer, Zarathustra came and said to him: You desire to counsel in regard to abdicating your throne? Behold, I'hua'Mazda has been to you even now, saying: What have you to do with that which is not your own!

21/15.3. Asha said: I have asked before: That which speaks to my heart, what is it? Now according to your wisdom, that which speaks to my heart is I'hua'Mazda! How shall one know it to be so? Zarathustra said: If a man asks the All Light in reference to his own affairs, and for his own concerns, then he receives an answer from the tetracts; but if he asks the All Light in reference to what he shall do for others, to render the highest good to them, then the answer is from I'hua'Mazda. I declare to you, O Asha, he is a dark man indeed to whom the Creator does not speak every day.

21/15.4. Asha said: What, then, shall I do in a matter like this? As yet, all the world belongs to me. Presently I shall deliver it to itself; should I not provide a ruler for them?

21/15.5. Zarathustra said: Why, then, you will be bound to give them one as good and as wise as yourself, otherwise you will cheat them! Furthermore, does the Ormazdian law not say: You shall not have any king but your Creator?

21/15.6. Asha said: I so perceive. What then, shall I go away saying nothing? Then I'hua'Mazda answered, saying: You shall do more than this; for you shall give liberty to all men, and proclaim to them, commanding that they shall obey the doctrines of the Holy Book, serving no master but the Creator. And when the old order over the people is completely broken up by your decree, you shall go away, leaving your throne and your capital to whatever may come to them.

21/15.7. Asha said: I perceive. That which has been given me to do, I will do. Behold, I will bestow freedom on all the world; and with my alms-bowl go about begging. Heaven must be just, and it is right that I should have the experience of the poor as well as of the rich. How else would I ever become sufficiently wise to be a God in heaven?

21/15.8. Yet one more thing, O Zarathustra, and I will ask you no more questions; you have said I must pray to Ormazd: Now, behold, I never prayed in my life! Who will teach me to pray?

21/15.9. I'hua'Mazda said: Let your lips utter your holiest desires, and let your soul seek constantly for new expressions magnifying the wisdom, love and power of Ormazd, the Creator.

21/15.10. Nor shall you be concerned about rules of prayer; the rules are for the unlearned. He who invents a new prayer to Ormazd every day of his life has done wisely indeed. For the glory of prayer is the strengthening of one's own soul to perceive the Higher Light.

21/15.11. The purpose of prayer is not to change the decrees of Ormazd, but to change one's own self for the better. Yet he who repeats words of prayer like a parrot repeats, improves himself but little.

21/15.12. Asha said: If a man thinks a prayer, and uses no words, is it well with him?

21/15.13. I'hua'Mazda said: It is well with him; but it is better to add words also. It is well for Ormazd to think a universe, but better to create it. To begin to learn creating, you shall use spoken words; the perfection of creating is to have the words bear fruit. He who omits words of prayer will in time omit prayer also, and his soul thus tends to barrenness.

21/15.14. A vain man says: I have no need to pray; Ormazd knows my soul! In that case, then, shall the field not say: I shall produce no harvest, because Ormazd knows my capacity! I declare to you, O Asha, the secret of all spiritual growth lies in giving out the spirit: He who would grow in wisdom, must give wisdom; he who would grow in love, must give love; he who would grow in power of spirit, must give out power of spirit.

21/15.15. Think, then; if you pray silently, your power goes weakly to your audience; but if you pray with words, openly, you give to your audience of your fruit; and, for this glory, Ormazd provides you abundantly.

21/15.16. When you go with your bowl to feed the feeble, the old, the helpless, and the blind, you shall teach them prayer and confessions; and you shall absolve those who are depressed because of their sins, so that they may rejoice in their own lives.

CHAPTER 16 God's Word

21/16.1. So Asha, being converted, gave up all he had on earth, and went and lived with the poor, carrying the alms-bowl for one year, preaching and praying for the poor. And it came to pass that at the end of the year he had thousands of followers.

21/16.2. And he built altars for them, teaching them to worship the Creator; to restore the mark of circumcision; to be upright before men; to labor for the helpless and distressed, and to not do to any man that which they desire not to be done to themselves.

21/16.3. And these people took the name of Zarathustrians, in contradistinction to the Par'si'e'ans. Nevertheless, they were the I'huan race, and the Ghans.

21/16.4. And because of their religion, they could not own property, neither houses, nor lands, nor cattle, nor beasts of burden. Many of them gave themselves into servitude to the Par'si'e'ans, but many of them lived on the contributions brought by converts who had owned great possessions.

21/16.5. Now it so turned out, that when Asha abdicated the throne, there were many aspirants to take his place, and the Council of the Sun was puzzled over whom to select, so peace would remain in Oas; but they finally made Hi'ya'tseing king, because he was a great warrior, having bestowed the city's walls and gates with more than ten thousand skulls, from the refractory[658] tribes adjacent.

21/16.6. Hi'ya'tseing assumed the titles of his predecessors, chief of which were King of the Sun, King of Kings, and King of Oas, the central city of all the world; and sent his proclamations to the chief cities of Jaffeth, Shem and Ham, commanding that earth, water and fruit be sent to him from every place under the sun. And he stipulated certain presents that must be sent to him every year, among which were thousands of subjects (slaves).

21/16.7. Hi'ya'tseing was a man of great learning, and had traveled far and near. He knew the people and lands of the earth, and the different products of the different lands, and the number of peoples in the great cities of the world, and the number of warriors belonging to the different sub-kings under him. Besides these things he knew the stars and their places, and the constellations of cows, horses, bulls, bears, lions, fishes, and serpents, even as they had been taught in the Hyartien[659] period among the ancients.

21/16.8. Hi'ya'tseing said: The Fete has made me king of the world; hence, it is right that I am king. He said: It is evident, because Asha abdicated the throne, that man must have a religion. Because I know all the rites and ceremonies of the ancients, I will give man a religion on my own account. Because Asha commanded the Zarathustrian religion to the far-off kingdoms, then Asha and Zarathustra are my enemies. Let my officers arrest

---

[658] stubbornly resisting submission to authority or control; unruly; ungovernable

[659] Hyarti is a period of darkness, especially a time of spiritual darkness.

Asha and Zarathustra and bring them before me. I will make an example of them.

21/16.9. And on the day that Asha was arrested, behold, the year of his carrying the alms-bowl was ended. Asha and Hi'ya'tseing had known each other for many years. When Asha was before the king, he said: I have nothing in this world; why, then, have you arrested me? The king said: Because you gave away your possessions, you are the most dangerous of men. I have decreed you to be put to death. Are you prepared?

21/16.10. Asha said: Yes, O king. And yet, because of our long acquaintance, I ask of you one favor, which is, that I be put to death according to the Panic rites, which were before the flood. And if, by chance, it is proved to you there is a God with power to release me, and he does it, then your hand shall not be raised against me? The king said: Your request is granted.

21/16.11. Accordingly, a wheel of uh'ga[660] was built and Asha was bound upon it, the king having appointed a guard to watch him till he would die. But because of the king's fear that the test might be tampered with, he caused the yogernot[661] to be set up in his private piazza, with the uh'ga facing the Gate of Lions, so that his private attendants could also watch.

21/16.12. Great was the wailing and crying of the people when it was known that Asha had been decreed to death. The city of Oas became like a house of mourning and madness, and it was divided against itself, some for Asha and some for the king.

21/16.13. Because Asha was old, and being in view of the king all day, the king repented, but he had no power under the laws to set aside his own decree. And when the sun went down, the king went before Asha, saying: Behold, you have been on the wheel for six hours, and yet your God has not come to release you. This is a great torture, and I weep for you. If you will, therefore, slay yourself with a sword, I will have you taken down.

21/16.14. Asha said: I declare to you, O king, I have no pain. Whether it is my madness, or whether it is because the Gods favor me, what does it matter, since I do not suffer? Nor do I have a right to slay myself, since I did not create myself alive. Moreover, if it is the will of my Creator, Ormazd, that I die on the wheel, then it is just. If it is not His will, then He will release me. Therefore, O king, I am content.

i022 **Ug-sa or Uh-ga**. The test on the wheel. In ancient times, true prophets were distinguished from false prophets by being bound upon the wheel. Angels of Jehovih would release the true prophets, while the false ones would perish on the wheel.

21/16.15. The king said: This indifference comes from madness. And your madness has affected the City of the Sun. Have your way, then, and die!

21/16.16. The king returned into his palace, but the next morning he came again, making the same proposal, and receiving similar answers. And at night he came again, repeating his offer, and again being refused, he resolved to come no more.

21/16.17. Now on the night of the third day, Asha felt the power of I'hua'Mazda coming upon him, and he said to the guard: Behold, this night I

---

[660] the ancient wheel, the jaugernot (juggernaut); see image i022 Ug-sa or Uh-ga; also image i033 in volume 2 p.227, second row, second image from left

[661] jaugernot, the wheel; i.e., the uh'ga

shall be released! Make certain, therefore, that the thongs are well fastened. For, if it turns out that the Father releases me, then you will stand before the king accused of conniving at my release. Accordingly, the guard re-examined the fastenings, and sent word to the king of what Asha had said. And the king replied: No, if he is released, then I will know of a truth there is a God; nor shall one man of my guardsmen stand accused.

21/16.18. This they told to Asha, and Asha said: I say to you, not only one shall stand accused, but all of you. And there were one hundred of them, being two watches of fifty each; but it being the change of watch, they all heard, and they laughed in derision.

21/16.19. And behold, in that same moment, the thongs fell off, and I'hua'Mazda delivered Asha down from the uh'ga.[662] And the spirit of I'hua'Mazda was in Asha, nor was Asha himself, though conscious of the things done through him.

21/16.20. I'hua'Mazda said: Go and say to the king: Behold, Asha is delivered by the power of his God. Then the guardsmen said: It is not morning; the king sleeps.

21/16.21. I'hua'Mazda said: I say to you, the king is not sleeping, but is joyful from drinking wine with his courtiers. They went then and told the king, finding that, in truth, he was not asleep. And the king commanded them to bring Asha before him, which they did.

21/16.22. Hi'ya'tseing said: What profit do my guardsmen have in releasing this old man? Behold, it has been said that you, Asha, had gold and silver hidden away. I know now it is true, for you bribed these guardsmen to set you free. For that reason, every man of these guardsmen shall be put to death, and their skulls mounted on the walls of Oas, and their skins tanned for leather. Away with them, you marshals; bind them till the rising sun, and at that hour hew off their heads, as I have decreed.

21/16.23. And now as for you, you old hypocrite and destroyer of liberty! What do you say?

21/16.24. Asha said: According to your promise I should now be free. There was no stipulation in your decree that I could not bribe your guardsmen. Behold, then, my wisdom! Have I not revealed to you that you cannot trust any man?

21/16.25. The king said: You are the wisest of men. I had hoped to hear you say your God released you, in which case I had here twelve swordsmen ready to hew off your head. But because you have shown me great craft, you shall live for a season, but only on the condition that you shall leave Oas and never return.

21/16.26. Then I'hua'Mazda spoke through Asha, saying: You have decreed the guardsmen to death at sunrise! Now I declare to you, O king, not one of them shall die as you have decreed. But I, I'hua'Mazda, will deliver them. Do not think that I am Asha; I am not Asha, but a spirit, the God of the I'huans. Nor will I spirit away your guardsmen by a miracle, but I will deliver them by natural means, and thus show you that I am mightier than all kings.

21/16.27. The king said: It cannot be that there are Gods or spirits. Is man's judgment nothing? These things were suited to the dark ages. They frightened men to justice, and as such served a purpose. But in this enlightened age man shall know justice and wisdom by himself.

21/16.28. While the king was speaking, I'hua'Mazda caused the attending spirits to assume mortal form by the curtains of Arizzi, behind the king, and they made a noise, so that the king turned to look, and lo and behold, he saw them. He feared, thinking they were evil persons concealed, and he said: Robbers! Murderers! And he drew his sword and thrust at them; but they vanished! He said:

21/16.29. Truly you are a devil, O Asha! And he thrust his sword at Asha, but it fell from the handle. He said: You Fetes! Kill him! Kill him! And while he was thus confused, Asha walked forth out of the palace, nor would the king's guards lay hands on him.

---

[662] The mediums of today [circa 1849-1882] are tested in many cruel ways, in order to prove es'sean power. Professor Crooks of England, the inventor of the radiometer, relates some wonderful experience in his investigations, to test the unseen power. I have seen mediums bound and tied in many ways, even till the blood exuded from the wrists and ankles, and yet the angels released them, in a moment of time; and frequently without untying a knot. –Ed.

CHAPTER 17 God's Word

21/17.1. When Asha went away from the king's palace, Zarathustra met him, and they went together to the prison where the guardsmen were confined, awaiting execution scheduled for sunrise; and four hundred of the converts of Asha also came. And when they were near the prison, Zarathustra said to them:

21/17.2. Stand in the altar (crescent) of the living God, for his power is upon me, and I will deliver this prison! || And the keeper of the prison and also his attendants, woke up, and came with spears, saying: Disperse! Disperse! Or, by the King of the Sun, you shall die!

21/17.3. Zarathustra said: Are you greater than I'hua'Mazda? Thrust, then, your spear against my breast. The keeper did so, saying: Your size is nothing to me, you boaster! But, lo, the shaft was broken in a thousand pieces, nor did the blade touch his garments. Seeing which, the other spearmen feared, and Zarathustra walked up to them and took their spears from them.

21/17.4. And the Zarathustrians stood in the form of a living altar, and Zarathustra laid his hands against the front wall of the prison, saying: In your wisdom and power, O I'hua'Mazda, deliver this prison! And, behold, the front wall opened as a door opens (swung open), and the prisoners came out unharmed.

21/17.5. Zarathustra said: Tomorrow the king will decree to death every Faithist within the city. Go, therefore, while it is yet night, and command all my people to rise and depart out of the city at once, and I will lead them to a place of safety. So that same night the Faithists fled beyond the walls.

21/17.6. And it came to pass that on the next day, when the king heard what had transpired regarding the prison, he decreed to death every Zarathustrian found within the city, even as prophesied by Zarathustra. But they were already gone and into the Forest of Goats, being four thousand six hundred and thirty men, women and children.

CHAPTER 18 God's Word

21/18.1. I'hua'Mazda spoke to Zarathustra, the All Pure, saying: Explain these things to my people, for they shall not dwell in darkness or fear. Zarathustra said: What shall I tell them, O I'hua'Mazda?

21/18.2. I'hua'Mazda said: My people are united; My people are delivered out of the evil city. To themselves, of themselves, and by themselves, I have delivered them, as a separate people.

21/18.3. I found an easy way to unite them; I went not by a dark road. This is no miracle, but the manifestation of Faith in the All Light.

21/18.4. Take them farther away from Oas; far away into the forest. And since Asha is an old man, and learned above all other men, he shall be the ara'ba[663] over them.

21/18.5. I'hua'Mazda said: But as for you, O Zarathustra, you are young and strong. You shall choose fifty men from among my people, well learned and strong, full of vigor. And they shall be your companions; and you shall visit the large cities of Jaffeth, Shem and Ham. For four years you shall travel, delivering the Zarathustrian law; but at the end of that time you shall return to Oas, and to this people, my first chosen.

21/18.6. And behold, after that, Asha shall go with you to Oas, and you shall raise your hand against the city, and it shall fall. ||

21/18.7. Zarathustra then explained these things to the people, and afterward took them to the valley of Yan'she, by the river Witch'owitch; and he divided them into three large cities and four small ones, after the manner of[664] the I'hins, the sacred people, white and yellow.

21/18.8. And he gave them fathers (rab'bahs), and made Asha chief father over all the others. Thus was founded the Zarathustrian religion; the I'hua'Mazdian law, the Ormazdian law, the Zarathustrian law.

21/18.9. And Zarathustra chose fifty men, who were well learned, and vigorous, not old; and they departed, to establish the Zarathustrian law in the cities of the east and south. I'hua'Mazda led them forth, speaking to Zarathustra, the All Pure, telling him where to go, and directing him along in the

---

[663] Rab'bah is spelled in many ways in different places, because the pronunciation of different people makes it so. Ara'ba signifies, ground of fathers, or, foundation of the order of fathers. –Ed.

[664] following the example of, doing things similarly to, using as a template or cynosure, in the manner of, like

nearest roads, over the mountains and plains, and across the rivers. And wherever they went, I'hua'Mazda provided them with beasts of burden, and beasts to ride on, converting their owners to the Ormazdian law, who gave them all things required.

21/18.10. The first large city Zarathustra came to was Tse'gow, on the plains of Jo'ab, high walled with wood and stone; and when he came to its gate the keeper demanded his name and business, speaking in another language, and Zarathustra did not understood him. Then came I'hua'Mazda, answering the keeper in his own tongue, saying:

21/18.11. I am a servant of the Creator, Ormazd; I come to prove immortal life before the king. Send word, therefore, to your king, and he will admit me and my people. So the keeper sent word to the king, who commanded that Zarathustra come before him.

21/18.12. And when he and his attendants were before the king, the king said: Are you the one of whom the King of the Sun has spoken? And what is your business with me? Your king, the king of kings, is mad. Then I'hua'Mazda answered, saying:

21/18.13. Zarathustra, of whom the Sun King spoke, is before you. I am here to prove to you many things pertaining to what is written in the Book of Holies. But before I utter many words, I ask that your son, Ha'sing, and your wife, Hi'ti'us, and your daughters, Peutu, Zoo, He'in and Zabee, be present also.

21/18.14. The king said: How do you know the names of my people? And I'hua'Mazda said: Here stand guardian spirits, ashars, and they speak to me. Chief among them is Ay'ay, your grandfather, who slew himself; and next to him are your kinspeople[665] in spirit, Noa, Wess, Lut, Gan'ce, Mith'ce, Nim'och, Wo'huin, Ruks and Pa'stcue.

21/18.15. The king was concerned, for many of these had been slain in wars, nor did he know how Zarathustra discovered their names. So he sent for his wife and children, and they all went into an inner chamber with Zarathustra. Then I'hua'Mazda spoke to the king, saying:

21/18.16. Do not think that Asha is mad[666] because he has given up all he had and gone to live with the poor. The Gods call all men mad who do otherwise, especially rich men, kings, and rulers. For such men set value on things that they cannot retain except during earth life at most. Asha sets value on that which will last forever. I wish that all men would do as Asha has done.

21/18.17. Because of unbelief in the Great Spirit, man has set himself up as the All Highest, and his trade has become war and destruction. I did not come to persuade you to give away your kingdom nor your riches, nor yet for any glory or profit to myself. I speak for the hosts being slain, tribe against tribe, city against city; I speak for the millions of spirits in darkness, who dwell on the battlefields.

21/18.18. I'hua'Mazda thus gained the attention of the king, and, meanwhile, the angels who accompanied him took on forms, looking like mortals; and presently the king and his family looked about and saw them, and were frightened; and the king drew his sword, saying: Who have entered, uncalled! But as he advanced, behold, the spirits disappeared. The king was amazed, I'hua'Mazda continued, saying:

21/18.19. Do not be concerned that the spirits show themselves; neither call these appearances miracles. Spirits are always present; but because they clothed themselves with corporeal parts, you have seen them for the first time. While you were quiet, they came; with your sudden passion they disappeared.

21/18.20. The king said: Will they come again? Then I'hua'Mazda answered, saying: Since your wife and your daughters are frightened, why should they appear again? Yet hear me, O king! Since your youth up you have been prepared for this. Your wife is half-breed with the I'hins, the sacred people. The I'hins were preserved by the Gods for this purpose, for they are like leaven,[667] prepared for the resurrection of all the races of men. Because of this great virtue in your wife, the spirits of the dead can show themselves before you.

21/18.21. While I'hua'Mazda thus spoke, the angels again assumed sar'gis, and present were several spirits whose mortal lives had been cut short by the king's own sword. Chief of these was Awetakeytha, one time king of the city of Tse'gow.

21/18.22. The sar'gis spoke to the king, saying: Do not think that I am dead, O king! I am not dead,

[665] relatives, kinfolk, extended family

[666] crazy, foolish

[667] that which causes bread to rise; agents for uplifting

except in the corporeal part. As by your sword you cut me off, so by the sword you shall be pierced through. Next spoke Too'Sain, another sar'gis, saying: Till you are dead, O king, and your soul cast into hell, I will not cease to torment you! Next spoke Ghon, another sar'gis, saying: Before yesterday I brought venom from rotten flesh, and inoculated you in the breath of your mouth! You shall cough blood and foul-smelling corruption! Next spoke Owd, saying: I come from the land of the dead, O king, with the torments of hell for you! Then spoke We'Seay, a sar'gis, saying: I am your first wife; why did you slay me? Was the world not wide enough?

21/18.23. In that manner the spirits continued to speak, suffered by I'hua'Mazda to express their evil desires and passions in their own way; nor did one spirit appear who had a single good word of cheer for the king. Then the king spoke, saying:

21/18.24. Go away, spirits, or devils! I will see no more! And, with that, he swung his sword about fiercely; but when he quieted a little, I'hua'Mazda spoke to him, saying:

21/18.25. I declare to you, O king, the air is filled with the spirits of the dead; and because they were slain by you, they lie in wait for your soul, when you die. Do not think that by slaying a man you are rid of him; only the corporeal part is within your power to destroy. The soul never dies. Ormazd is just. Those you have injured, you shall restore.

21/18.26. The king said: If a man is a bad man, and I kill him, is it not a great good? I'hua'Mazda said: To kill him is a great evil. You should convert him to good. The king said: But if he belongs to me? Then I'hua'Mazda said: No man belongs to you. The same Creator created all men; from Him all men are created; and they belong to Him.

21/18.27. The king said: But I have possession of them. They are mine. If your Creator is stronger than I, let Him take them. I'hua'Mazda said: To take them from you would be no honor; but for you to deliver them is your own honor.

21/18.28. Now while the king's mind was thus engaged, the angels fell to work to demonstrate their presence and power, in some unusual way; and, accordingly, they cut loose the tapestry hanging on the walls, and let it fall to the floor, with a great explosion of sound. The queen and her daughters rose up and fled.

21/18.29. The king was angered, and thrust his sword at Zarathustra; but, lo, it broke into a hundred pieces, and yet no part touched Zarathustra. I'hua'Mazda said: Unless you repent of your evil ways, I will withdraw my holy angels from this house, and you shall bear witness that before the morning sun appears, this palace shall not be left standing.

21/18.30. But the king was hardened. So, when I'hua'Mazda perceived there was no repentance in the king, he withdrew the Lord and his ashars, abandoning the palace to evil spirits, but he sent guardian spirits to inspire the queen and her daughters to flee from the house that night, which they did. And the spirits of darkness went to the king's enemies and inspired them to go against the palace; which they did, and destroyed it.

21/18.31. The next day, Zarathustra went about in the city, which was in great tumult, and I'hua'Mazda spoke through him to the people. And in one day he gained more than a thousand followers; and when the king saw this, he decreed Zarathustra to death, offering a reward to whoever would slay him.

21/18.32. The next day he preached again before the people, and gained a great addition to his followers; and then the king ordered his soldiers, of whom there were ten thousand, to attack Zarathustra and his people, and destroy them. But I'hua'Mazda had prophesied this to his adherents beforehand, and had advised them to flee. And many escaped before morning; but there were also many who were still within the walls when the soldiers came upon them.

21/18.33. I'hua'Mazda stretched his hand upward, saying: Fire of Your fire, O Father! Give me here a wall of fire! And a wall of fire rose up between them and the soldiers; and the latter, seeing this, turned and fled, crying out: Shri! Shri! (signifying spirit.)

21/18.34. Thus Zarathustra led them out of the city, and not one man, woman or child was injured. But it came to pass that the deeds done through Zarathustra were greatly exaggerated by those reporting them, so that people who had not yet seen him believed the world was about to come to an end.

21/18.35. Thus the king lost all discipline over the city; and the people lived without law or order;

robbing one another, or destroying whatever stood before them.

CHAPTER 19 God's Word

21/19.1. Zarathustra called his fifty companions before him, saying: Because these people are delivered from the tyrant, they will become his enemies. A people long oppressed, love vengeance. This would thwart the Ormazdian law. Take them, therefore, away from the city, dividing them into groups among yourselves, and I will send angels, capable of interpreting languages.

21/19.2. I'hua'Mazda said: Behold, a God does not come to accomplish at random. Nor does he come to one man only, in order to overthrow the evil of a whole world. You have been prepared for this work since the day of your birth. My angels have been with you, and you are a part of my army. Now this shall happen to you: After you have divided these people, and conducted them into the forests, you shall begin to speak with new tongues, and these people will understand you. And you shall build altars of worship to Ormazd, teaching these people songs, prayers and dancing, explaining to them the Ormazdian law.

21/19.3. Zarathustra said: Do not wait for me to come, nor for the voice of I'hua'Mazda, but do in faith as I have commanded, and the Voice will be with you.

21/19.4. So those who fled from the anarchy of the city, were led away, half a day's journey, and there encamped. And the companions of Zarathustra, who were called Inquas, were entranced, and comprehended the language of the people, and could talk with them understandingly.

21/19.5. So they built altars to Ormazd and taught the people worship, and caused them to take an oath to not kill any man, woman or child, nor any beast or bird, nor any animal created alive. And they bound them on the oath taken under the thigh, to eat only fruit, nuts, roots and bread, according to the Ormazdian law. And they divided them into families of tens and families of hundreds, and of a thousand, giving them one rab'bah for each, according to the Zarathustrian law.

21/19.6. But Zarathustra returned into the city, and I'hua'Mazda clothed him around with fire, at night, and with clouds in the daylight, so that the people could behold his power, and no man dared raise a hand against him.

21/19.7. Then he commanded the people to gather together all the skulls on the walls, and the scalps that were hung about the houses and on the poles; and they were taken away and burned. And as for the soldiers, he disbanded them; and thus, the king was rendered helpless, left to stroll about, cursing.

21/19.8. And Zarathustra advised the people to go out of the city to live; and so they went forth by thousands, beginning new lives. After that, Zarathustra left the place; and at once it was filled with drujas, and they went to the druks and inspired them to fire and plunder. And it came to pass, in not many days, the great city of Tse'gow, with all its temples, towers, and palaces, was reduced to a heap of ashes.

21/19.9. Zarathustra went before the hundreds of thousands of people, speaking by the voice of I'hua'Mazda, saying: I hear certain ones saying: Whoever sets value on earthly things, above heavenly things, it is good for him to have fire and destruction. But I say to you, all things come from the Father, Ormazd, or by His permission. When He withdraws His hand from a wicked city, evil spirits rush in.

21/19.10. You have said: Who are evil spirits? Why does Ormazd not destroy them? I say to you, evil spirits are both yourselves and the dead. Those whom you have slain in passion, still live to torment you in spirit. You had their skulls hung on the gates and walls; the doorways to your temples of science were hung with the scalps of your enemies. The spirits of these people still live, though their bodies are dead, and for vengeance' sake they obsess you to deeds of wickedness.

21/19.11. This is the Ormazdian law; when a man is dead, you shall either burn the body, or bury it in the ground, so that the spirit is not troubled. But you have bound them in spirit; Tse'gow was an eyesore in the sight of those who were slain for its glory. They delighted to see it destroyed.

21/19.12. Compared to what you lost by the fire, these spirits have gained tenfold; for now the Gods can deliver them in heaven. For which reasons, I declare to you that it is a great good that Tse'gow is destroyed. The world is large; the lands are very wide. Kill no man, woman or child. They are Ormazd's.

21/19.13. Neither shall you build large cities; they are a curse on the face of the earth. Nor shall you live alone, for such people become bound to self; but you shall dwell in families of tens, hundreds and thousands. Has the Father not given you an example in the I'hins? They do not kill, nor take that which is another's; nor are they given to lust, war, or quarrelsomeness.

21/19.14. The Voice said: Where is the king's wife, Hi'ti'us? Where is Ha'sing, the prince? And the princesses, Peutu, Zoo, He'in, and Zabee? The multitude answered: They are gone!

21/19.15. After that the Voice said: I say to you, they were gone, but they are returning. Presently they will be here. They shall speak before you. || And sure enough, presently the king's wife, son, and daughters came. Hi'ti'us said: Behold, Tse'gow of Oas is burned. Who has seen the king? || He'in and Zabee, the princesses, were very young girls, and they cried for their father. He had slain himself, cutting his bowels across with his sword.

21/19.16. I'hua'Mazda spoke through Zarathustra, saying: Come, Hi'ti'us, and stand on the rocks so that all can see, and bring your children. She came and stood beside Zarathustra. And now the Voice said: Let these bear witness whether or not the dead live in spirit.

21/19.17. Hi'ti'us said: With my own eyes I have seen the spirits of the dead; with my own ears, heard them talk. My children shall hold up their hands if these things are true. The children held up their hands. Again Hi'ti'us said: Where is my husband, the king?

21/19.18. While they were still standing on the rocks, lo and behold, the ghost of the king rose up before all the people, and He'in and Zabee cried out: Here is my father! Then I'hua'Mazda spoke, saying to the soul of the king: Do you know you are dead? The soul of the king spoke loud, so that all could hear him; he said: No, I am not dead, but I have done a foolish thing, I cut my bowels across.

21/19.19. Then Hi'ti'us said: I fear, indeed, the king is dead, and this is his spirit. He looks strange! I'hua'Mazda said: There is no cut. Your belly is unharmed. But the spirit persisted, saying: I thrust my hands in the hole, and yet you say, there is no wound! You are mad! I remember you; it was you who brought back these phantom enemies to torment me!

21/19.20. I'hua'Mazda said: What enemies do you see? The spirit answered: All I ever slew; a thousand or more! Away, you torments! You mockers! I will thrust you through.

21/19.21. The soul of the king then stamped and raved, for he saw the spirits of the dead; but the audience did not see them, though they saw him, for he was in sar'gis form.

21/19.22. I'hua'Mazda said: I say to you, O king, you are dead, and risen from the dead. If you could only awaken to this fact, you would be risen in spirit. Nor can you be delivered till these, your enemies, are also delivered. Then the spirit of the king answered, saying: I banish you from the city of Tse'gow! Nor shall you ever return, under penalty of death!

21/19.23. I'hua'Mazda said: I tell you, O king, the city of Tse'gow is destroyed. Truly there is not one house standing in the entire place! The soul of the king answered, saying: You torment me! You madman! You assert lies in the face of facts! Be gone, wretch! O if only my belly were not cut across, I would go at you with vengeance!

21/19.24. I'hua'Mazda withdrew the sar'gis, and the king could not be seen; nevertheless, his spirit continued cursing and raging all the same. The queen, Hi'ti'us, comprehended the matter fully, and her heart was heavy with sorrow.

21/19.25. I'hua'Mazda said to her: Remember the faith of your forefathers, the I'hins. Be strong in the Ormazdian law, and these sorrows will pass away. Nor is there anything in heaven or earth that can satisfy the soul that is short before the law. To her who can say, I live the all highest, happiness has a sure foundation.

21/19.26. And whoever perceives the dead in torments, let such pray for them, singing anthems to the Father. Let such intercede with the All Light, to bestow them with peace. Do not think that because of your prayers the All Light runs with haoma, to feed the spirits of the dead. But this I declare to you, that by the peace and joy in your devotions to the Father, the spirits are reclaimed to virtue and exaltation.

21/19.27. These things I will show to you this night; be steadfast and hopeful in Faith, and when the evening has come, I will again call up the spirits of the dead before you.

CHAPTER 20 God's Word

21/20.1. Because of the destruction of Tse'gow, there were hundreds of thousands of people rendered homeless and destitute, and groups were surging about, crying out for food, or for some needful thing. I'hua'Mazda said to Zarathustra, the All Pure: The ill-fortune of mortals is the good fortune of the righteous Gods; but the good fortune of mortals is the glory of the evil Gods. Do not think because Tse'gow is burned, and the people hungry, that the Voice of the Father is out of place. Now is the time they will listen. By the loss of earthly treasures, the soul seeks for that which will endure forever.

21/20.2. Go, therefore, O Zarathustra, and I will go with you; and criers shall be sent out, calling the people to the valley of Tsoak'ya tonight.

21/20.3. So it came about, when night set in, that Zarathustra came before the people, and there were tens of thousands of them. I'hua'Mazda spoke to them, explaining the Ormazdian law.

21/20.4. When he was done speaking, Zarathustra took Hi'ti'us, the king's widow; her children, and forty others, and made a crescent of them; and he stood between its horns. And to his left and right were many of his companions. Thus prepared, Zarathustra sang a song, which the I'hins had taught him in his youth.

21/20.5. And the drujas were ushered into the crescent, taking on sar'gis, the king among them. And the spirit of the king was softened, for they sang peace to his soul and joy forever; and presently, he awoke from his craziness, and remembered he was dead; and he rejoiced in Zarathustra, and applauded him before all the people. And likewise the spirits of darkness who were with him did the same.

21/20.6. Zarathustra said: Behold, I have not come in a dark age. You shall not worship any man born of woman, nor call him sacred. One only shall you worship, Who is Ormazd, the Creator, and Master over all the world. Hear now my voice to Him!

21/20.7. Zarathustra stretched his arms upward, full of energy, and I'hua'Mazda spoke through him, saying: Light of Light, O Father, hear Your Son! With Your Almighty Hand bless these faithful sufferers! || Hardly had these words been spoken, when there fell from the air above, fish, fruit, grains, roots, and all things good to eat, more than enough to feed the famished people for three days; and there were more than thirty thousand of them.

21/20.8. And all the while the sar'gis of the king looked on, and saw what had been done; and he cried out with a loud voice: Blessed are You, O Ormazd! O if only I had known You! If only I had sought to find You! || Hi'ti'us, my wife! And my blessed babes! Swear to the king, you will proclaim the I'hua'Mazdian law, forever! Swear it! Give me joy! Swear! Swear! Swear!

21/20.9. Then Hi'ti'us and the children held up their hands as directed by I'hua'Mazda, swearing a solemn oath to maintain the love of Ormazd and the Zarathustrian law, forever. After these, there came thousands and thousands of others, who also swore in the same way. I'hua'Mazda then took away the sar'gis, and the spirits could no longer be seen by mortals.

CHAPTER 21 God's Word

21/21.1. The next day Zarathustra appeared before the multitude, and I'hua'Mazda spoke through him, saying:

21/21.2. I did not come in an age of darkness, but of light and knowledge. I am not here to proclaim miracles; I serve the Father, Whose Son I am.

21/21.3. In heaven above there are two kinds of spirits; those who serve the earth and those who serve the Father. If you serve the earth you shall be ministered to by the spirits of the lower heavens, who are bound to the earth. If you serve the Father, you are ministered to by the spirits of the higher heavens.

21/21.4. Because last night you were united in prayer to the Father, His holy angels brought you food. His harvests are over all the earth; His fields are broad. It is not just[668] that He also gather it and bring it to you. To be just to Him, you shall go and bring forth out of the fat earth all you need, rejoicing in Him. Cease warring; do not kill anything He created alive that runs on the ground or flies in the air. And no flesh except fish, which is without blood, and is cold in life, shall enter your mouths.

[668] right, proper, fit, fair, wise

21/21.5. In the morning, when you first awake, pray to the Creator, Ormazd, praying in this manner: Glory to You, You All Light! Because You have created me alive, I will strive with all my might to be upright before You. I have faith You created me wisely; and I know You will show me the right way.

21/21.6. Make my eyes see sharper into my own soul than into anything else in the world; I will discover its dark spots and wash them clean. Seal up my eyes from the sins of others, but magnify their goodness to me, so I may be ashamed of my unworthiness before You.

21/21.7. Today I will run quickly to the distressed and helpless, and give them joy by some deed or word. Seal up my tongue against slandering any man, woman or child, for they are of Your creation, and of Your Own handiwork.

21/21.8. What You feed me with, is sufficient for the day; complaint shall not escape from my mouth. Quicken me all day, O Ormazd, with this, my prayer, so that I may become a glory in Your works. Amen! ||

21/21.9. I'hua'Mazda said: Touching on prayer, remember, that to utter words, but to not practice, is of little value. He who is true to his own light is strong in soul; to be false to one's own light is to put out the eyes and stop up the ears. He who would rise in heaven, let him begin to rise on earth. The resurrection lies in following the All Highest Light one already has. He who does not do this, is a fool to ask the Father to raise him up. Hell fire is his boundary in the next world.

21/21.10. Because Ormazd sacrificed Himself, He created all things. By sacrifice[669] for the elevation of others, a man starts the beginning of approaching Ormazd. This is resurrection, in fact.

CHAPTER 22 God's Word

21/22.1. I'hua'Mazda called together those who swore allegiance to the Zarathustrian law; and he separated them from the others, and in ten days there were thirty thousand professed followers.

21/22.2. Nevertheless, I'hua'Mazda spoke to Zarathustra, saying: Of all these, only one in ten will remain long[670] in faith. And to establish the tenth firmly is more valuable than to have ten times as many who do not understand what they profess. Zarathustra asked: How can a tenth be made firm?

21/22.3. I'hua'Mazda said: Long ago I told you to go and live with the I'hins. Zarathustra said: I understand. I learned the Wheel of Ormazd from the I'hins. Then I'hua'Mazda said: Make a Wheel of Ormazd.

21/22.4. Zarathustra made a wheel, and hung it slanting, to face the sun at high noon. Then I'hua'Mazda explained to the people, saying: This is a symbol of the name of the Creator, Ormazd, the All Light Master! Put it in the place between the horns of the crescent, for it is sacred; it is the Sign of the Altar; it is called the Altar. Let the Faithists go with me, and I will explain.

21/22.5. They carried it to the meeting-place and faced it in the same direction. And when the people stood in a circle around it, I'hua'Mazda said: The name of this place shall be Harel,[671] and the name of the wheel shall be Altar. Behold, you have already sworn an oath under the thigh, in the custom of your forefathers, but you shall now renew your oath on the Altar of Ormazd, and His Holy Book.

21/22.6. I'hua'Mazda then administered the oath to many, in which they covenanted to turn from evil and strive to do good; and each and every one turned the wheel once around, as a witness before the Father. When they had all covenanted, I'hua'Mazda said: You shall make many wheels, and carry them along the roadways, and wherever one road crosses another you shall fix an Altar; and you shall dedicate the wheel to the Creator.

21/22.7. And whoever passes that way afterward shall halt and remember his Creator; and he shall renew his covenant, to turn from evil and strive to do good; and in testimony before the Father, he shall turn the wheel once around.

21/22.8. Thus was established the sacred wheel of Zarathustra among the I'huan race.

21/22.9. I'hua'Mazda spoke to Zarathustra, saying: What is the most potent thing? Zarathustra said: The eye is the most potent. The eye is most to

[669] Sacrifice here evidently means contributing. –Ed.

[670] persistent, lasting, ingrained, deep-rooted, firm, unfading, reliable, enduring

[671] In Hebrew, the word Harel, i.e., Hill of God, is sometimes synonymous with altar. –Ed.

be feared; yet the most desirable. The eye of man can go away from man; his hand cannot go away from him, nor his foot. Man's eye can go to the mountains; to the clouds, the moon, sun and stars.

21/22.10. I'hua'Mazda said: If the eye of man is his most potent instrument, what then? Zarathustra said: The eye of Ormazd is His most potent power over man. So Zarathustra made a picture of an eye, and placed it over the altar. Then I'hua'Mazda made the people covenant anew, but this time to the I'hua'Mazdian law, the Ormazdian law. And they said: I know Your Eye is upon me night and day; nothing is hidden from Your sight, O Ormazd!

21/22.11. And I'hua'Mazda commanded them to place a picture of an eye over the altars in all places of worship.

21/22.12. Then came the first night of the new moon, and Zarathustra went into the place of worship, followed by a great multitude. So I'hua'Mazda said: This is mas[672] night for the spirits of the dead. So that the widow, Hi'ti'us, may have joy this night, I will sing and pray for the spirit of the king. And, afterward, for all spirits who are in darkness.

21/22.13. When they sang and prayed, the spirit of the king came in sar'gis, and talked to Hi'ti'us, and to others. And after that, the spirit of the king prayed and sang with I'hua'Mazda. Thus was established the first night of the new moon as moon's night (mass) for the spirits of the dead, and it was demonstrated before the living.

21/22.14. I'hua'Mazda taught through Zarathustra for forty days and nights; teaching the Zarathustrian law, the Ormazdian law. And thousands and thousands of people were converted to righteousness; and these were called disciples (ga'spe Zarathustra) of Zarathustra.

21/22.15. Zarathustra inquired of I'hua'Mazda as to what was the best, most potent thing for the generations of men. Then I'hua'Mazda answered, saying: The best, most potent thing for the generations of men is to teach the very young child the ever presence of the All Potent Eye, which sees into the body of mortals, and into the soul.

21/22.16. Zarathustra inquired concerning very young children. Then I'hua'Mazda answered, saying: In three days and five days and seven days the rite of circumcision for the males, and piercing the ears for the females. And, when they are old enough, they shall be consecrated on the wheel.

21/22.17. Zarathustra said: To consecrate, what is that? Then I'hua'Mazda answered: To profess the All Highest, the Creator, Ormazd. And from that time forward the young child shall pray to Ormazd every night before going to sleep, and pray every morning as soon as awake, to Ormazd, renewing its covenant and acknowledging the presence of the All Potent Eye.

21/22.18. Zarathustra inquired concerning children who were not thus provided. I'hua'Mazda answered, saying: Such children may live, or they may die. If they die, they fall into the care of drujas and become drujas themselves; but if they live, they will grow up liars and druks, killing and stealing.

21/22.19. Zarathustra inquired concerning the death of a consecrated child? Then I'hua'Mazda answered: If a consecrated child dies, its soul is received in heaven by the consecrated spirits of Ormazd. It is then taken to a place of all good, a place of delight.

21/22.20. When these things were explained to the disciples, the mothers brought their children before Zarathustra; and I'hua'Mazda consecrated them on the altar, and they were baptized with water and fire, and given names by the rab'bah.

CHAPTER 23 God's Word

21/23.1. Zarathustra, the All Pure, inquired concerning protection against impostors. To which I'hua'Mazda answered, saying: Prove all things on the altar. If a man comes before the people saying: Behold, I am a prophet! and he teaches strange doctrines, he shall be tied on the wheel with his face toward the sun at high noon. And if he is a true prophet, the spirits who dwell by the altar will set him free. But, if he is not released on the third night, the wheel shall be carried out into the forest and stood up by the bushes. And if he is an impostor, the wild beasts will come and devour his flesh.

21/23.2. Zarathustra inquired concerning the wheel after an imposter had perished on it. I'hua'Mazda said: When an impostor has perished on the wheel, behold, the wheel shall no longer be used as before. But the disciples shall cut away the

[672] Mas is also Sanscrit for moon. –Ed.

rim of the wheel, and cast it away, for it is useless. But the cross-bars of the center of the wheel shall be retained, for it was on the bars that he was bound, and the cross of the bars is sacred; and it shall be hung in the place of worship, for it is a true cross.

CHAPTER 24 God's Word

21/24.1. Zarathustra inquired concerning the government. To which I'hua'Mazda replied, saying:

21/24.2. To the All Pure disciples there is no need of government, except to do the Will of Ormazd. But no people are all pure; no people are all wise. Two kinds of governments the Creator created; the first is His Own, the Government of Ormazd; the second is the government mortals have among themselves.

21/24.3. Zarathustra inquired if government did not abridge[673] liberty. I'hua'Mazda said: The Ormazdian government gives liberty; so far as man's government takes after the Ormazdian government, it gives liberty also.

21/24.4. Zarathustra inquired: What is the best, most potent, man's government? To which I'hua'Mazda replied: This is the best, most potent, man's government: First, there shall be no more than two thousand people, so that they can know one another; and no city shall be larger than that.

21/24.5. The oldest, wisest, best man shall be the high rab'bah; but the families of tens and families of hundreds within the city shall each have one rab'bah, being the oldest, wisest, best man among them.

21/24.6. These rab'bahs shall be the government of the city. They shall have a government house, and it shall be the place of decrees.

21/24.7. Zarathustra said: How shall they make decrees, so that the decrees do not pervert liberty? I'hua'Mazda said: Do not ask this, O man! He who cries out constantly for his liberty is a selfish man, he is a druk. Unless a man is willing to sacrifice his liberty somewhat, for the public good, he is unworthy before Ormazd. To find the amount of sacrifice, this is the business of the decrees.

[673] constrict, lessen, curtail

21/24.8. Zarathustra said: How, then, shall the rab'bah proceed? I'hua'Mazda said: When they are seated, the chief rab'bah shall announce the subject; neither shall any other rab'bah announce the subject. But if a rab'bah has a subject, he shall state it beforehand to the chief rab'bah.

21/24.9. After the subject is announced, then all the rab'bahs shall speak on the subject; but they shall not speak against one another; but each one declaring his highest light.

21/24.10. When they have all spoken, then the chief rab'bah shall speak his highest light, which he gathers from the others in the first place, but which is afterward illuminated by the Light of Ormazd, and this shall be the decree.

21/24.11. Zarathustra inquired concerning the laws between cities. I'hua'Mazda spoke to Zarathustra, the All Pure, explaining the Ormazdian law. He said: A city is a family of one.[674] A small village is a family of one; for which reason a city is called Ir.[675] And every city shall have one God-ir, who shall be the oldest, best, wise man. The God-irs shall meet in council to consider what is good for all the cities jointly. For cities are situated in varying places with diverse resources; some are suitable for flax and wool, some for iron, some for copper, and some for ships.

21/24.12. Zarathustra inquired concerning the Council of God-irs. I'hua'Mazda answered him, saying: The God-irs shall choose the oldest, best, wise man among them, and he shall be called God-ir Chief. And he shall sit in the east in the Council chamber, and he shall present the subjects,

[674] That is, the entire city is considered to be as one person; the collective whole is considered to be as one person. This verse does not mean a single individual human being is considered to be a city or a family.

[675] Ir is the same in Hebraic, Hebrew, Phoenician and Vedic literature, and signifies city. God-ir signifies, or is equivalent to, City-God. The God-irs were without written laws, being themselves supreme. The representation of districts by Congressmen is a crude example of the Zarathustrian law. Were Congressmen the oldest, best, wise men, they would be more like the God-irs than at present. The God-irs were entitled to carry the Fete (true cross). Hence the term, *The Fates decree* thus and so. –Ed.

after they have been told to him by the other God-irs. And when he has presented a subject, all the members shall speak upon it. And after they have all spoken, then the God-ir Chief shall speak, and his words shall be the decree, which shall be called the Zarathustrian law, because the All Light dwells with the Chief, and he cannot err. This is the Ormazdian law, the I'hua'Mazdian law, the Zarathustrian law.

21/24.13. Zarathustra asked: What is the Ormazdian law regarding a walled city (giryah)? I'hua'Mazda answered, saying: To the I'hins, walled cities; to the I'huans, cities without walls. To the cities of the druks, walls. This is the kingdom of I'hua'Mazda: Why should those who have faith, build walls? For, as they shall not hoard up gold and silver, none will rob them. After Zarathustra, there will be two kinds of people living. One shall be the people of this world; the other shall be the people of Ormazd. The former shall strive for earthly things; the latter for spiritual things. And there shall be no affinity between these two people. From this time forward, the Zarathustrian people, who have faith in the Father, shall not have walled cities.[676] But this world's people, having no faith in the Father, shall have faith in stone walls; by which sign, you can know which people are righteous in my sight.[677]

21/24.14. Zarathustra inquired concerning the smallest of cities. I'hua'Mazda answered him, saying: The smallest city is a man, his wife and their children. And even as the people in a large city are one with one another, so shall a man, his wife and their children be one with one another.

21/24.15. And as a large city must have a head father, so shall a small one. Whatever has no head is nothing.

21/24.16. Zarathustra said: In the government of a large city, the fathers speak on a subject, and after them, the head father decrees.

21/24.17. I'hua'Mazda said: It shall be the same in a family of husband and wife. The wife shall speak first, and the children next, if old enough; and after that the father shall decree. That which is a good law for a large city, is good for a small one. As the kingdoms in heaven are governed, so shall the kingdoms of earth be governed.

21/24.18. Zarathustra inquired concerning a bad husband and a good wife, and a bad wife and a good husband? I'hua'Mazda spoke to Zarathustra, the All Pure, saying:

21/24.19. Who knows what is good and what is bad? Are all men not to give themselves as sacrifice to the Father, and all women also? If a good woman is not willing to sacrifice herself to a bad husband, after having sworn to Ormazd, then she is not good, but a lover of herself. A good woman has no self to serve. Because her husband turns out bad, shall she also? Is it not good for her in the place Ormazd provided? Shall she set up her judgment against the Father's?[678]

21/24.20. There are men of evil, and of passion, who abuse their wives. Does every damsel[679] not know this? For this reason, if she commits herself to her husband in the name of the Father, He hears her. And He establishes His Kingdom in her house. And that man and that woman have no longer themselves to consult as to their desires; for if the Father desires her to leave her husband, or the husband to leave the wife, He takes one of them to heaven. Do not think that He changes as the wind, or bends Himself to please the caprice of man or woman. Rather let the good wife, with a bad husband, say to Ormazd:

21/24.21. Because I was vain, You have rebuked me, O Father. Because I sought to change my condition, You have shown me I knew not what

---

[676] Note that the I'hins, although Faithists in the Great Spirit, are not considered Zarathustrians (followers of Zarathustra); but I'hua'Mazda (God) is here addressing the situation regarding I'huans.

[677] The distinction here drawn between them is true to the history of the Zarathustrians, to the Israelites, Brahmans [followers of the original Brahma, not the ones known in today's religion], and the Algonquins. Only those who fell from faith deviated from this condition. In later times, since the doctrine of Saviors was introduced, the world's people have used standing armies instead of walls. The same rule applies to them; having no faith in the Father, they have faith in standing armies. Their treasures being earthly, they build earthly; having an idol in heaven, they make an idol of their army's pageantry and power, boastingly. –Ed.

[678] It may be expected that the same applies to the good man who marries a bad woman. –cns ed.

[679] young woman or girl, maiden, virgin

was good for me. Yes, you have shown me the folly of my judgment before You, and I will profit in turning to Your Will. I will not open my mouth in complaint anymore. Though I be scourged[680] with stripes, and made ashamed of my household, yet I will glorify You. The city You have founded in me, I will begin at the foundation, and build up as a holy city, in Your name.

21/24.22. And she shall say to her husband, who beats her: Because the Father gave you to me, I will rejoice and sing in your praise. Before I sleep at night, I will ask His blessing upon you, and in the early morning, and at high noon. Though you may hate me, yet I will do so great good works for you, that you shall love me. Though you may kill me, yet I will go into heaven and build a house for you.[681]

CHAPTER 25 God's Word

21/25.1. Zarathustra, the All Pure, divided the people, leading his followers away from the others, taking them into good places of delight. After that, he looked back with compassion, and he said to I'hua'Mazda:

21/25.2. What about those who will not accept the Ormazdian law? I'hua'Mazda answered him, saying: Behold, your arms are full! Let the dead have dominion with the dead. Not only this generation, but many that come after you, will not be alive to the Ormazdian law.

21/25.3. Zarathustra apportioned his people into cities, villages and families, but over all of them he appointed Yus'avak as Chief, one of his companions who came with him from Oas.

[680] whipped

[681] This condition of and commitment to staying in the marriage till death parts them, and all the while attempting to uplift the other spouse (even if abusive), apparently needed to be rooted in humanity at that time. Without such a grave initial commitment to monogamic marriage being grounded in the soul of I'huans, perhaps in later times the institution of marriage would have fallen apart or at least suffered greatly, maybe irreparably. Compare this to the heavenly teaching in Kosmon times regarding marriage, mentioned in later books of Oahspe.

21/25.4. And when Yus'avak was established, Zarathustra and his companions traveled farther, and came to the city of Ne'ki'ro, kingdom of Aboatha, king of twelve generations through his forefathers, whose title was, ABOATHA, SON OF UZZA, SON OF NIMROD, SON OF THE HOUSE OF TUS'IANG, WHO WAS DESCENDED FROM BEFORE THE WORLD WAS!

21/25.5. Ne'ki'ro was a walled city, but the Zarathustrians gained entrance without paying tribute, because the law thus favored strangers. Aboatha, in his youth, had traveled among the Par'si'e'ans, and knew the language; and when Zarathustra was before him, speaking in the Oas'an tongue, the king inquired his business, and how long he intended to stay, adding that he, Aboatha, had received the tablets of the Ormazdian law, with the interpretations, from the King of the Sun, Asha; and that he had desired to see Zarathustra.

21/25.6. Zarathustra said: I came to establish the Ormazdian law. In the name of the All Light I will blunt the edge of the sword and the spear. Until I have fulfilled the commandments upon me, I shall remain within your city. I come in the Person of I'hua'Mazda to address things you have read in the holy book.

21/25.7. The king said: My city is not large; yet I have more scalps and skulls, for the size of my city, than any other king in the world. But know, O man, I am a philosopher. Many of my people are also learned people. Hear me, then, and if you have a greater philosophy than I have, I will not only bequeath to you the public skulls and scalps, to be your treasures forever, but I will also give my skull and scalp into your hand, as the most valuable treasure in the Jaffeth'an empire.

21/25.8. Zarathustra said: Though you set great value on skulls and scalps, because they are the product of labor, yet they are of no value to me, or to the Father in heaven. Neither have I any philosophy for you, nor for the Father's begotten. To accept His will; to be servant to Him, by doing good to others, comprise the whole of the law, by which all men may be made to rejoice in their creation.

21/25.9. The king said: Do not think I am like other men. I am not like other men. At the start of all things, there were SEVEN and NINE things. I was one of them. By division, we created all there is in heaven and earth. I have divided myself seven thousand and seven millions, and nine thousand

and nine millions of times. One-seventh and one-ninth of all there are of created things is my very self. Tell me, then, have you as great a philosophy as this?

21/25.10. Zarathustra said: O the folly of men before You, O Ormazd! They run after that which flatters self, seeing their fellows going down in death, and they do not raise their hands to lift them up! I tell you, O king, your poorest slave that brings out of the earth food for two men, has a greater philosophy than yours! He who can rule over his own self-conceit, who does not speak of himself, gives a better philosophy of himself than you have. He who has not yet risen from his mother's breast, has more treasures to give than you have obtained with all your philosophy. Before three days have passed by, the city's skulls and scalps will be burned to dust. Nor will your philosophy help you to stop the hand of I'hua'Mazda.

21/25.11. The king said: Do you propose to battle my army with this handful of men? Zarathustra said: I have spoken. There is no value in discoursing with any man who has an opinion to establish, nor is man's opinion of value to raise up the souls of men. Bring, therefore, your army, and command them to fall upon me and mine!

21/25.12. The king said: You have no weapons; do not think that I battle with men who use their tongues, like women!

21/25.13. Zarathustra said: Why boast? Your soldiers will turn and flee when you bring them against me!

21/25.14. The king turned away then, and ordered his officers to bring soldiers to dispatch Zarathustra and his companions, and to hang their skulls and scalps on the walls. Zarathustra and his companions went into the king's garden, and formed in an altar. When the sun had set, and evening came, the king's soldiers, more than ten thousand, came upon them.

21/25.15. I'hua'Mazda had great power, because of Zarathustra's faith, and he spoke with a loud voice, saying: Light of Your Light, O Ormazd! Build me here a wall of fire! And behold, there fell from heaven curtains of fire, till a great wall stood between the two peoples; nor would any soldier throw a spear or sling a stone; and many of them broke and fled.

21/25.16. When the king saw Zarathustra's power, he feared for his kingdom; and being undecided about what course to pursue, he went into his palace. Then Zarathustra and his companions came out of the garden, but the light extended up above Zarathustra's head like a pillar of fire. I'hua'Mazda spoke to some who were nearest, saying:

21/25.17. Run quickly and call the soldiers back, saying to them they shall be my soldiers, and I will give them the weapons of the Creator. So the messengers ran and brought many of them back. I'hua'Mazda commanded them to gather the skulls and scalps from the city walls, and from the gates, and go and burn them; and the soldiers did these things.

21/25.18. The next day after they were consumed, I'hua'Mazda began to preach, explaining the Ormazdian law; and he gained many followers. The king had tried by all means to gather his soldiers together, but no one obeyed him. After that, Zarathustra went to him, saying: If you are one-seventh and one-ninth of all things, who do you think I am?

21/25.19. The king said: They say you are a very Creator! But, in my opinion, you are only a magician. You cannot do anything real; which is why I was hoping you would come before me. Know, then, your end has come! With that, the king struck at Zarathustra; but the king's sword was broken into pieces, and had no effect.

21/25.20. The king had two trained cheetahs, large as the largest lions, and he ordered them to be set loose upon Zarathustra. And it was done; but, lo and behold, the cheetahs came and licked his hands. But the king was hardened, and would not believe. I'hua'Mazda called the king to come near.

21/25.21. When the king approached, I'hua'Mazda said to him: I am not your enemy, but the enemy of evil; I have not come to take your kingdom. In a few days I shall leave this place. So, your kingdom would be worthless to me. And yet I come to establish another kingdom, which is the Father's. I come to overthrow sin and wickedness, and to build up that which is good. And in doing that, it shall be known among men that the soul is immortal.

21/25.22. I would rather see you and your people alive and full of joy, than to see them dead.

You have said you understand the Ormazdian law; perceiving there is also a king's law.

21/25.23. The king's laws are for the earth-world; to punish the wicked and reward the valorous; the Ormazdian law is for the Zarathustrians, who need no kings. Your subjects are for war and plunder; but the subjects of the Great Spirit are for doing good, and in love and mercy. And have I not shown you that the Ormazdian laws are the stronger of the two? Yes, a hundred times stronger. It would be wiser for you to espouse the stronger law. You have gathered certain treasures, boasting of your treasures' value. Because you have made a law of exchange for skulls and scalps; what have you achieved? Have you in fact made them valuable? Because a man brings a skull to you, you give him bread; does that make the skulls valuable? Now I declare to you, values consist not in the rate of exchange between men. Shall a man gather a heap of stones, and say: Behold, they are valuable! Or iron, gold, or copper, and say: Behold, they are valuable! Or say: A piece of bread is valuable, or flax, or wool?

21/25.24. Because man has set value on things not valuable, he builds in falsehood and death. Ormazd alone is valuable; the man who has the most All Light, has the greatest valuables. For by the Light of the Father all righteous things can be obtained easily. || While I'hua'Mazda was yet speaking, the spirit of Zarathustra went abroad, and, with ten thousand other spirits, brought fish and fruit, and let them fall to the ground. The people ran and gathered them up for food. || The king made no reply at first, for he was encompassed with evil spirits, who were angered with I'hua'Mazda and his proceedings. Presently the king said:

21/25.25. Because I am transcended by you, it is no longer useful for me to live. With that, he cut his belly across, and fell dead. And Zarathustra commanded that the king's body be laid straight for three days; and it was done; and thousands of people came to look upon the king, to witness that he was dead. And they saw that, in fact, the bowels were gushed out of the wound, and that there was no breath in him.

21/25.26. So I'hua'Mazda suffered the spirit of the king to live three days in torments, and then he called his disciples around him, saying: Now I will raise the king to life, and it shall be testimony in Jaffeth.

21/25.27. And Zarathustra pushed the bowels back into the belly, and drew it shut, saying: In Your name, O Father, I heal this man's body, as a testimony of Your Wisdom and Power! And when Zarathustra had drawn his hand over the belly twice, it was healed. And then Zarathustra said: O Father, as by Your spirit You quickened into life this, Your child, in his mother's womb, restore him now to life!

21/25.28. And the king was healed, and restored to life before the people; he awoke, looked around, and then rose up. He said: Even now I was dead and in hell, and I saw millions of the dead, and they were in hell also. And there went up around them fires of burning brimstone, and none could escape.

CHAPTER 26 God's Word

21/26.1. When the king was restored, he was another man, having su'is, and believing with full conviction; and he asked Zarathustra what he should do now so that he could escape the fires of hell after death.

21/26.2. I'hua'Mazda spoke through Zarathustra, saying: Do not think what you can do to escape hell fire, for that would be laboring for self. Think what you can do to save others. For which reason you shall practice the Ormazdian law. You shall dwell one year with the poor, carrying the alms-bowl, according to the Zarathustrian law. After that you shall preach the I'hua'Mazdian law, of the denial of self for the good of the city, teaching the turning away from earthly things, and striving for spiritual things, having faith in Ormazd.

21/26.3. The king said: I can do all these things, but one thing I cannot do, which is, having faith in Ormazd. If He is a Person, and created all the creation, is He not the foundation of evil as well as good? If He created evil in the past, or by incompetence permitted it to enter into creation, might He not do so in the future, even after death?

21/26.4. I'hua'Mazda said: When a potter has a pot half made, do you say it is an evil pot? No, surely not, but you say that it is not yet completed. Even so are all men, created by Ormazd. Those who are good are completed, but those who are evil are unfinished work. But the Creator also gave man knowledge, so that he could see himself in the unfinished state; and the Creator gave man power and judgment, so that he could work in helping to complete himself, and by this, share the glory of his creation. The man who does this is already clear of hell fire; he who does not do it shall not escape.

21/26.5. The king inquired concerning animals, to which I'hua'Mazda answered, saying: Animals are of the earth creation, and are completed in the place of their dwelling. Nor does any animal have aspiration to make itself better or wiser, so that it may contribute to the creation. And some men have no more aspiration than an animal, serving the beast (the flesh) only. Only the torments of hell can stir them up.

21/26.6. When I'hua'Mazda explained the Ormazdian law, of which not even one-fourth is described here, the king comprehended, and so took the vows on the altar, under the eye, according to Zarathustrian law. || So when the people of Ne'ki'ro were restored, Zarathustra left one of his traveling companions with them, as God-ir in Chief, and Zarathustra departed, taking his other companions with him.

21/26.7. Regarding which, it is recorded in the libraries of heaven, showing that the next city kingdom was likewise delivered, and the people became Zarathustrians.

21/26.8. And again Zarathustra departed, and came to another city, which was overthrown and delivered also. Until it came to pass that Zarathustra overthrew and delivered twenty-four cities and kingdoms in Jaffeth.

21/26.9. After that he departed to the upper lands of Shem, where he also overthrew and delivered many cities and kingdoms, establishing the Zarathustrian law. For two whole years he labored in Shem; and so great was the power of Ormazd upon Zarathustra that all the cities and kingdoms of Shem threw off the bondage of the Sun Kingdom of Par'si'e.

21/26.10. After that, Zarathustra traveled toward Ham, which was called Arabin'ya. But in those countries Zarathustra did not have such great success because the people were not learned in books, or in the stars, or tablets. Nevertheless, Zarathustra delivered many cities.

21/26.11. So I'hua'Mazda said to Zarathustra: Go back now to your own country; and you shall overthrow yet another seven cities and seven great kingdoms; and after that you shall return to Oas, and it shall fall before your hand, so that the prophecies of your childhood are fulfilled.

21/26.12. So Zarathustra returned to Par'si'e and went to the seven great cities and kingdoms, and overthrew them; and many of them were destroyed utterly by fire and by war; but Zarathustra delivered the faithful and established the Zarathustrian law with all of them.

21/26.13. And now he returned to his native city, Oas, according to the commandment of I'hua'Mazda.

CHAPTER 27 God's Word

21/27.1. In those days, Pon'yah was king of Oas, and, by title, KING OF THE SUN; KING OF THE MIDDLE OF THE WORLD; KING OF KINGS; MIGHTIEST OF MORTALS; OWNER OF ALL HUMAN FLESH; RULER OF THE EARTH, AND MASTER OF LIFE AND DEATH!

21/27.2. For nearly four years Zarathustra had been absent, and the effect of his preaching in foreign lands had been to cut off the paying of tribute to the City of the Sun. Which was why Pon'yah, king of Oas, had sworn an oath under his own thigh, to pursue Zarathustra and have him slain.

21/27.3. Accordingly, the king had equipped many different armies and sent them in search of Zarathustra; but while I'hua'Mazda led Zarathustra one way, he sent spirits to inspire the soldiers to go another way. Consequently, none of the armies sent to capture Zarathustra ever found him. When he was heard of in one city, and the soldiers came to that city, he was already gone. And so it continued, until now Zarathustra had returned to the very gates of Oas.

21/27.4. Because Zarathustra was the largest man in the world, he was easily known; and from a description of him, even those who had never seen him, would know him the first time they laid their eyes on him.

21/27.5. Asha had continued with the Zarathustrians; but in consequence of the persecutions of the kings of Oas, they had been obliged to retire farther into the forests, plains and unsettled regions, where the Listians, the wild people roved. To these the Zarathustrians were friends, and the Listians came in great numbers, and dwelt near the Zarathustrians.

21/27.6. After Zarathustra had completed his travels, he returned first to the Forest of Goats, to meet his followers, and to rejoice with them for the great light I'hua'Mazda had bestowed upon them. So when Zarathustra returned to them, there was great rejoicing; and there were present Zarathustra's mother, and many of the Listians who knew him in his childhood.

21/27.7. After many days of rest and rejoicing, I'hua'Mazda came to Zarathustra, saying: Behold, the time has now come to go against the city of your birth. Take Asha with you, and I will cause Oas to fall before your hand.

21/27.8. Accordingly, Zarathustra took Asha and returned to the gates of Oas; but he was known at once; and when he demanded admittance, he was refused, because the king had previously decreed his banishment and death, there being an offer of reward to whoever would destroy him and bring his skull to the king.

21/27.9. The keeper of the gate, whose name was Zhoo'das,[682] wanted to obtain the reward, and hit upon the following plan, saying to Zarathustra: I know you; you are Zarathustra, who is banished under penalty of death. I have no right to admit you within the city, nor do I have a desire to witness your sure death. But if you will hide yourself, till the change of watch, when I am absent on the king's reports, you may take your own risk. But if I admit you, I will also be put to death.

21/27.10. Zarathustra said: I do not fear for myself, but I would not have you put to death on my account. Where, then, can I hide myself, till the change of watch?

21/27.11. Zhoo'das, the keeper of the gate, said: Within the chamber of the wall. Go, and your friend with you.

21/27.12. So Zarathustra went into the chamber of the wall, and Asha went with him. And now, when they were concealed, Zhoo'das called his wife and said to her: Stay here, walking back and forth, so that they who are concealed will think it is I. And I will run quickly to the guards, and they shall come and seize Zarathustra, for whom the reward is offered.

21/27.13. And the keeper's wife came and walked back and forth; and the keeper ran quickly and brought the guards, one thousand men, with spears, swords, war clubs, slings, and bows and arrows, and they surrounded the chamber on all sides. And then Zhoo'das spoke ironically, saying: Come forth, Zarathustra, now is the change of watch!

21/27.14. And Zarathustra and Asha came forth and saw what was done. Zarathustra said to Asha: The Light is upon me. Go with me. No harm shall come to you. But the time has come when I shall fulfill what has been prophesied of me in my youth.

CHAPTER 28 God's Word

21/28.1. So Zarathustra allowed himself to fall into the power of the Sun King; and the soldiers caused him and Asha to march in their midst to the place of the skulls. And thousands and tens of thousands of people came forth to witness the proceedings; for there were many who were in sympathy with Zarathustra, as well as many against him.

21/28.2. And in order to restrain the multitude, the captain of the army called out many soldiers in addition to those who made the arrest. Others ran to the king's palace, carrying the news of his arrest, and the place he had been taken to.

21/28.3. The king said to the heralds: Though this man shall die, it is fit that proper judgment be rendered against him, as an example before all men. Go, therefore, to the executioners, and command them to bring Zarathustra into my presence, so that I may adjudge him to death according to law.

21/28.4. Thus Zarathustra was brought before the king, who accosted him, saying:

21/28.5. By your behavior you are accused before your king, and I adjudge you to death. But so that you may be an example before the world, I will render my judgments before the heralds, who shall proclaim my words to all who desire to witness your death.

21/28.6. First, then, my predecessor ordered your arrest, and you did not deliver yourself to my soldiers; nor could they find you. For which you are adjudged to death.

21/28.7. Second. Without permission from the KING OF THE SUN, you have traveled in foreign lands, sowing seeds of dis-allegiance against the CENTRAL KINGDOM. For which you are adjudged to death.

---

[682] Judas is not a Hebrew name, but Parsee. – Ed.

21/28.8. Third. The King of Kings offered a reward for your head, and the king's soldiers were unable to find you. For which you are adjudged to death.

21/28.9. Fourth. In your youth you threatened to overthrow the city of Oas, the City of the Sun, and failed to make your word good, thus being a teacher of lies. For which you are adjudged to death.

21/28.10. Fifth. You have cut off the foreign tribute to the rightful Owner of the whole world! For which you are adjudged to death.

21/28.11. Sixth. You have revived the doctrines of the dark ages, teaching of spirits and Gods, which things cannot exist, because they are contrary to nature, and contrary to the laws of the King of the world! For which you are adjudged to death.

21/28.12. Seventh. You have taught that there is an unseen Creator greater than your king; which is contrary to reason. For which you are adjudged to death.

21/28.13. Eighth. You did not return to Oas openly, but as a thief, and hid yourself in a chamber of the wall. For which reason you are adjudged to die in the manner of thieves, which is the most ignoble of all deaths.

21/28.14. Therefore, I command the executioners to take you to the den of thieves and cast you in; and tomorrow, at high noon, you shall be hung up by your feet along with the thieves, where you shall be left hanging till you are dead.

21/28.15. So that my judgment may appease your best friends, do you have anything to say against my decrees?

21/28.16. Zarathustra said: All the charges you have made against me are true today; but before tomorrow's setting sun I will have disproved some of them. Today your kingdom is large; in two days I will be dead, and you will be dead also; and this great city will be destroyed. Even the Temple of the Sun will be split in two, and fall like a heap of rubbish.

21/28.17. The king laughed in derision, and then spoke to Asha, saying: You are an old fool. Go your way. So, Asha was liberated, and Zarathustra was taken to the den of thieves and cast in. Now the den of thieves was surrounded by the dens of lions that belonged to the king's gardens; and a bridge was passed over, so that when the prisoners were within, the bridge was withdrawn. And no prisoner could escape, but would fall prey to the lions, which were fed on the flesh of the persons executed according to law.

CHAPTER 29 God's Word

21/29.1. During the night, Pon'yah, King of the Sun, thought that perhaps he could obtain the secrets of Zarathustra, regarding his powers with uz, and he sent him the following message: If you will reveal the secrets of your power to your king, your life shall be spared; and if you will prostrate yourself before the King of Kings, saying: There is none higher! You shall have five cities to rule over all your days.

21/29.2. To which Zarathustra sent back the following reply: Zarathustra has no secrets to reveal; neither does he desire five cities, nor one city, to rule over. Tomorrow I shall die, and on the following night you shall die also. And yet, before you die, you shall see the temple of the stars split in two and fall down; and the city of Oas shall fall and rise no more; and Ya'seang, in Jaffeth, shall become King of the Sun, and his dynasty shall stand thousands of years.[683]

21/29.3. The king was surprised at such an answer, and so angered that he struck the messenger with his sling, and he fell dead, and the king ordered his body to be cast into the den of lions.

21/29.4. It was nearly midnight when the body was brought, and Zarathustra, being tall, saw above the wall, and he called out, saying: Do not cast the body into the lions' den; for I will call him to life in the name of Ormazd. And the men laid the body down by the outer wall, and Zarathustra said: He who is standing by the body shall lay his hand upon it, for the power of life is through life.

21/29.5. And the man laid his hand on the flesh of the man's body between the neck and the back, and Zarathustra said: Repeat after me: Life of Your Life, O Ormazd! Restore this, Your son, to life!

21/29.6. And, lo and behold, the man awoke to life, opened his eyes, and presently rose up; and Zarathustra told him to depart out of the city. Now,

---

[683] The title, King of the Sun, has existed from the time of Zarathustra to the present, in one part or another of the Chinese Empire. –Ed.

the arrest and condemnation of Zarathustra had caused thousands of people to assemble around the prison; and they saw the man restored to life; and some of them went with him out of the city. And all night, after that, Zarathustra healed the sick, and restored the blind and deaf, by calling over the walls in the name of the Father.

21/29.7. When it was nearly sunrise the next morning, the place of the executions was crowded with spectators. Many of the Zarathustrians believed that Zarathustra would liberate himself by the power upon him; and on the other hand, the king's people, especially the learned, desired to realize his execution, for they denounced him as an impostor.

21/29.8. The latter said: If he is the Master of the I'huans, let him prove his powers while he is hanging by the feet.

21/29.9. It was the law of Oas to keep twelve executioners, representing twelve moons, and at sunrise every morning they put to death whoever had been adjudged to death the previous day. Now, there were two thieves in prison with Zarathustra, condemned to the same ignoble death. And they were weeping and moaning! Zarathustra said to them: Do not weep, nor moan, but rather rejoice. He who gave you life is still with you. He will provide another and better home for your souls.

21/29.10. Behold, I do not weep, nor moan. They who put us to death do not know what they do. The multitude should rather pity them than us. Today you shall escape from the tyranny of Oas.

21/29.11. Zarathustra preached till high noon, and when the light fell on the top of the temple of the stars, the twelve executioners entered the prison and bound the prisoners' hands together behind their backs; then with another rope they tied the feet, bringing the rope up the back of the legs and passing it between the arms; and they carried the end of the rope up over a beam and down again; and the executioners seized the rope and pulled upon it. And they swung the bodies of the victims high above the walls and secured the rope, leaving them hanging there.

21/29.12. Zarathustra was thus hung between two thieves; and while he was still alive a bolt of light fell upon the temple of the stars, splitting it in two, and it fell to the ground. From that, a cloud of dust arose that grew till the air of the whole city was choking; and then down came another bolt of light, and, lo and behold, the walls of the city fell down, and Zhoo'das perished in the chamber of the wall.

21/29.13. The multitude ran for the king; and when they brought him out of the palace, another bolt of light fell on the palace, and it crumbled into dust. The king called to his guards, but they did not obey him, but fled; and, so, the multitude slew the king.

21/29.14. The learned men then went down to the place of executions, and Zarathustra was not dead yet; but the two thieves were dead. And Zarathustra said to the learned men: Now I will give up my body, and behold, you shall say I am dead. Let the executioners then take down my body and cast it into the lions' den, and you shall witness that they will not eat my flesh. And some shall say: Behold, the lions are not hungry. At that time you shall cast in the bodies of the two thieves, and lo, the lions will fall upon them and eat their flesh.

21/29.15. Then the learned men shall say: Behold, that happened because Zarathustra's virtue lay in his flesh, which was different. Now I declare to you, these things are not of the flesh, but of the spirit. For angels shall gather around my body and prevent the lions from tearing my flesh. Of which matter you shall testify before the multitude; for when the lions are devouring the flesh of the thieves, the angels will go away from my body, and, behold, the lions will return and eat my flesh also. By which it shall be proved to you that even lions, the most savage of beasts, have spiritual sight, and are governed by the unseen world, even more than man.

21/29.16. After Zarathustra had thus spoken to the learned men, he spoke to the Father, saying: Receive my soul, O Ormazd! And his spirit departed out of the body, and in that same moment the whole earth shook and trembled, and many houses fell down. So they cast the body into one of the dens, in which were seventeen lions, but they fled from the body. Then the executioners cast in the bodies of the thieves, and, lo and behold, the lions fell upon them instantly.

21/29.17. And when the angels went away from Zarathustra's body, the lions returned to it and ate also. And the keepers turned in other lions, and all the flesh was eaten. And the multitude ran and brought the body of Zhoo'das and cast it in, and the lions ate it also. And next they cast in the king's body, and the lions ate it, and were appeased of hunger.

21/29.18. Now when it was night, some of the Zarathustrians gathered together at a neighbor's house; and Asha was present, and they formed a living altar in order to pray for the soul of Zarathustra, and for the two thieves, and for Zhoo'das, and lastly, for the king. And now the learned men came, saying: Why have you not, during all these years, notified us of these things? Behold, Zarathustra is dead! Asha said:

21/29.19. Have I not carried the alms-bowl publicly, proclaiming them from day to day? And the learned people said: Pity, old Asha! A knave[684] has dethroned his reason! || Now I declare to you, it is the same now as in the olden time; the learned men are farther away from the Father than are those devouring lions. You look into the corporeal world for light, truth, and power, but are blind to the spirit, which underlies all things. I declare to you, whether it is heat, light, or disease that floats in the air, or growth that comes out of the air, in all things it is the unseen that rules over the seen. And more powerful than heat and light, and life and death, is Ormazd, the Person of all things.

21/29.20. Till you have learned this, I can explain nothing that you can comprehend. And yet, to know this, is the beginning of the foundation of everlasting happiness.

21/29.21. While Asha was thus speaking, behold, the soul of Zarathustra came and stood before them, and he was arrayed in the semblance of his own flesh and color, and in his own clothes. And he spoke, saying: Do not fear; I am the same who was with you and was hanged and died, whose flesh was devoured by the lions; I am Zarathustra! Do not marvel that I have the semblance of a corporeal body, for its substance is held together by the power of my spirit. Nor is this a miracle, for the spirits of all the living each hold in the same way, its own corporeal body. As iron attracts iron, the spirit learns to attract from the air a corporeal body of its like and measure.

21/29.22. Then someone present inquired: Where are the two thieves? To which Zarathustra said: As steam rises from boiling water, without shape or form, so are their souls this hour. For this reason I was sent into the world by the Father. Let him who would become controller of his own spirit toward everlasting life, learn the Ormazdian law, seeking to grow in spirit, instead of living for the things of this world.

21/29.23. Behold, in attendance here are Lords of the Hosts of Heaven, who are Sons and Daughters of the Most High Ormazd, the Creator. They will now gather together and re-clothe the thieves, and show you what they are like. || Presently the two drujas, the thieves who were hanged with Zarathustra, stood before the people in sar'gis, and they raved, cursed, and moaned; but they were blind and dumb as to where they were. Then Asha asked them who they were and what they wanted, but they only cursed him, and added that they were to be hanged.

21/29.24. Asha said: Behold, you are already dead, and your spirits risen from the earth! To which they replied by curses against the king. And now the Lords of heaven re-clothed the spirit of the king, but he also did not know that he was dead, and he also cursed, at which, the spirits of the thieves attacked him with evil intent, and all the people saw these things. But the Lords of heaven took away the sar'gis, and mortals could no longer see the drujas.

21/29.25. Zarathustra said: As they were angered and spiritually dumb while in their earthly lives, so do they even now cling to the earth. For which reason you shall sing anthems and pray for them three mornings at sunrise; three high-noons, and three evenings at sunset. Do this also for all your kindred who die, or who are slain, from this time forward, forever.

21/29.26. And you shall utter only words of love for the dead; for whoever utters curses for the dead, brings drujas upon himself. In your love and forgiveness, you raise them out of the torments of hell. And because you raise up others, so does Ormazd raise up your own souls.

21/29.27. Then someone asked how long a spirit lingered about? To which Zarathustra said: Some for three days, some for a year, some for a hundred years, and some for a thousand years! Until they have wisdom and strength to get away. But after three days you shall no longer desire the spirit of the dead to remain with you; rather you shall say to Ormazd: Deal with him and with us in Your Own way, O Father; we are content. || It is better for the spirits that you do not call them back

[684] a boy or young man; or a deceiver

from the higher heavens down to the earth; it is better for you that you remember them high up in paradise; for these thoughts will enable you to rise after you are dead.

21/29.28. Remember that All Light answers everything in heaven and earth after its own manner: If you kill, you are answered in torments sooner or later: If you utter falsehood, you are answered in falsehood: If you curse, you will be cursed in return: If you hate, you will be hated: If you seclude yourselves, you will be excluded: If you keep evil company in this world, you will be bound in evil company in heaven: If you seek to become a leader of men, remember that they whom you rule over will be your burden in heaven: If you do not teach, you shall not be taught: If you do not lift others up, none will lift you up: For in all things the same rule applies in heaven as on earth, for it is a continuation in spirit of that which is practiced in the flesh.

CHAPTER 30 God's Word

21/30.1. The following evening, when the Zarathustrians were assembled for prayer and singing, the soul of Zarathustra again appeared before them in sar'gis, teaching the Word of Ormazd. He said:

21/30.2. There are two types of people on the earth; one is engrossed in the affairs of earth; the other in the affairs of heaven. It is better for you to be of the latter. The fool will say: If all people are engrossed with the affairs of heaven, then who will provide on the earth? Such is the argument of all druks. Do not fear, therefore, for the earth people becoming short of votaries.[685]

21/30.3. Similarly it will be said of celibacy also; the druks will say: If all people become celibates, then the race of man will terminate. For which reason, I say again to you, do not fear, for there will be plenty left who are full of passion, and are unmindful of the kingdoms of heaven.

21/30.4. Let all who can, live for the Higher Light; the lower will always be supplied sufficiently.

21/30.5. Even as you find the two types of people on earth, so also in heaven these two types exist. One follows the Highest Light, and ever rises toward the highest heavens. The other follows the affairs of earth, and does not rise, and hence is called druj. The latter engages in sensualism,[686] and in quarrels among mortals, inspiring them to evil and low desires.

21/30.6. One person present asked: How shall we know one another, whether we are of heaven or of earth? Then Zarathustra answered, saying: Seek to know yourself; you are not your neighbor's keeper. Search your own soul a hundred times every day, to know if you practice the All Highest according to your own light. Neither shall you find excuses for your shortness; nor reflect overmuch on past errors, but use them as inspiration to perfect yourself from now onward.

21/30.7. Another one present asked: What about thieves, falsifiers, and murderers? Zarathustra said: The man who serves himself only, is worse than any of these; there is no resurrection for him. But if a man ceases his evil way to practice virtue, he is on the right road.

21/30.8. A falsifier is like one wearing a clean gown, going about casting filth upon it; he soils his own spirit.

21/30.9. A thief is in a worse condition than an overburdened beast; he carries his stolen goods not only in this world, but also in heaven, to the end of his memory.

21/30.10. A murderer is like a naked man, who is ashamed, and cannot hide from the multitude. When he is in heaven, his memory of the deed writes, in human blood, a stain on his soul, which all others see.

21/30.11. Another one asked: According to the I'hua'Mazdian law, the highest, best men forsake the world, laboring to raise up the poor and ignorant, reciting prayers and anthems; taking no part in the affairs of people who are engrossed in the matters of earth; who, then, shall govern the wicked? To which Zarathustra answered, saying:

21/30.12. When there are no men and women sufficient for such purpose, there will be no wicked to govern. Despite all your preaching that the highest life is celibacy, there will be plenty left who will marry; with all your preaching that the highest, best man will not be a leader of men, or a king or governor, yet there will be plenty left who will fill

[685] one dedicated to, in this instance, pursuing earthly matters

[686] sensuality, pleasures of the senses

these places, even though they see the walls of hell opened up to receive them.

21/30.13. Another one asked: If the Zarathustrians separate from the disbelievers, and live by themselves, what will be their power to do good among the evil? To which Zarathustra said:

21/30.14. As the highest heavens send Lords and masters down to mortals, so shall the Zarathustrians send emissaries among the wicked, preaching the truth, and citing the example of the Zarathustrian cities (communities).

21/30.15. For above all philosophy that man may preach, practice holds the highest place, and is most potent. See to it, therefore, that you practice the Ormazdian law toward one another in all things. Avoid men of opinion; men of learning who pride themselves in it; men of argument; men who quibble for proofs in unprovable things; men who wish to be known as wise men; men who deny; men who can see defects in everything, and have no good alternative to offer.

21/30.16. Shun the disbelieving man, for he is diseased and may infect you; the flatterer, for he is purchasing you; a woman for woman's sake; or a man for man's sake; or company for company's sake; for all these imply that the Creator is less in your sight, and not so well loved.

21/30.17. One asked concerning spirits; to which Zarathustra said: For the affairs of earth, consult the spirits of the earth, the drujas; for the affairs of everlasting resurrection, consult your Creator, and His holy spirits will answer you in His name. And to whichever you have made yourself companion, there will be your abiding place after death.

21/30.18. See to it that you do not become inveigled[687] by drujas, for spirits can assume any name and form; but weigh their words, whether they are wise, and according to the Ormazdian law. If they do not teach the higher heavens, but profess a long life in the lower heavens, consider them by their words. To flatter you, they will profess to remember you in another life; and to please you, say you were a king, and have had many successions of lives on the earth.

21/30.19. But of what value under the sun is such philosophy? Instead, to rise up, away from the earth, and from the lower heavens also; it was for bestowing this word upon men that I was sent into the world. It is to teach you to know the Father's upper heavens, and the way to reach them, that His words were given to men.

21/30.20. As it was in ancient times, so will it be again before another generation passes away. Drujas will teach that the spirits of the dead go into trees and flowers, and inhabit them; and into swine, cattle, and birds, and into woman, and are born over again in mortal form. Do not argue with them; do not let their philosophy trouble you. You can judge whether they are in darkness or in light, by the glory and beauty of the heavens where they live. If their words are of the earth, they belong to the earth; if they are servants to false Gods or false Lords, they will preach him whom they serve. But these matters are nothing to you, for you shall serve the All Highest, the Creator. In this, no man can err.

21/30.21. And in regard to the heaven you wish to ascend to after death, magnify it with all your ingenuity to the All Highest Perfection. People it with your highest ideals for your companions. Then see to it that you make yourself a fit companion for them also. If you do this with all your wisdom and strength all the days of your life, the Father will be with you, and you shall be a glory in His works. ||

21/30.22. In that manner, Zarathustra preached after his resurrection from death; for three days and three nights he preached before his disciples; and Asha wrote down the substance of his words, and they were preserved to the generations of Faithists from that time onward. And the words were called the Zarathustrian law, the I'hua'Mazdian law, and the Ormazdian law. And they, along with the previous holy book, were the first heavenly words given on tablets, skins, cloth, and in books, to mortals, except for those words given in secret to the tribes of I'hins, of which the different nations of the earth knew nothing of their own knowledge as to what they were.

21/30.23. On the morning of the fourth day, when the disciples sat in crescent, which was called the living altar of God, Zarathustra again came in sar'gis. He said: Behold, the time has come for me to rise out of hada, where I have dwelt for three days.

21/30.24. The Gods who were with me all my earth life are gathered together here, and there are millions of them. Just near the river over there,

[687] influenced, persuaded, deceived, enticed, urged on, tricked, lured

stands the boundary line of a heavenly ship of light! It is wider than the eye can see, and higher than the eye can see! A million angels are singing in that ship! And there are great Gods and great Lords in it. So bright, my eyes dare not look upon them. They are all Sons and Daughters of the Great Spirit.

21/30.25. The drujas have all run away now. Their foolish gabble is hushed, gone! It is as if another world came alongside, so majestic that this one was lost. Above, high, very high, up there, something like a sun illumes the ship of fire! I know it is he who has come for me. I go now! Where I go I will build for you all.

21/30.26. And you, O Asha! The Gods have thrown a mantle of light over you! A chain reaches from you to Ormazd! || Asha was overcome, and gladly would have gone to the spirit Zarathustra. But the latter said: Stand, so I may kiss you! So, Zarathustra kissed Asha, and departed.

END OF BOOK OF GOD'S WORD

Book of Divinity

Which descended to the earth and became known by the names, Div, and Diva, and Divan laws [Divinity and Divine Laws –ed.]. Being God's labors in atmospherea, for a period of three thousand and one hundred years, during the passage of the earth from the arc of Loo to the arc of Spe-ta, in etherea; and on the earth, from the time of Zarathustra to the time of Abraham, Brahma, Po and Ea-wah-tah.

CHAPTER 1 Divinity

22/1.1. God, Son of Jehovih, said: By virtue of my own authority, and in the name of Jehovih, Creator of all things: Peace and comprehensive judgment to angels and mortals.

22/1.2. That from the little that has been demonstrated in the world, of governments and principalities being manifested on earth, you may be taught that similar organic bodies exist in the heavens belonging to the earth.

22/1.3. Which heavenly places and governments were the cause and forerunners of good governments manifested among mortals.

22/1.4. Jehovih said: He who is chief of a government on earth shall be called king, but he who is chief of My heavenly government shall be called God. And it was so.

22/1.5. I, who am God in my own behalf, for the enlightenment of the world, declare the Glory and Wisdom of Jehovih above all things on the earth or in the heavens above.

22/1.6. As Jehovih provided that no man could be a king forever, but must give way to a successor, even so, in His heavens, He also provided for His Gods and Lords to have successors at certain periods of time.

22/1.7. So that the way would be open for the everlasting resurrection of all men,[688] by which, all who choose may, in time, become also Lords and Gods for the countless worlds that now are, and shall yet be created.

22/1.8. Jehovih said: I blow My breath outward, and, behold, all things are created. They go away in disorder, but they come back to Me orderly and in organic companies. And every individual member is like a tree, bloomed to perfection in every branch.

22/1.9. Jehovih said: These companies, returning to Me in all their glory, are marshaled in decorum and discipline by My Gods, for such is their labor.

22/1.10. Jehovih said: The labors of My Gods shall be chiefly in atmospherea. Nevertheless, My Gods and Lords shall not only labor with the spirits of the dead to teach them organic discipline and harmony, but they shall provide for mortals so that they also may learn the system and glory of My creations. ||

22/1.11. During Fragapatti's time in the dawn of the cycle of Loo in heaven, Jehovih commanded the founding of an organic Congress for His God, Lords, and Lord Gods.

22/1.12 And Fragapatti created the organic body, and named it the Diva, making God its chief, with the title, Div, even as it is known to this day in the sacred books of mortals.

22/1.13. Jehovih said: In the early days of a world I give the races of man (on the earth) a

[688] males and females

despot to rule over them. But in time after I give them representative governments with many voices, having a right to help make the laws. Similarly I provide for the hadan heavens: In the early days I provide a God who shall be dictator and governor in his own way. But in later times I provide a parliament in heaven, in which My God and My Lords shall jointly consult together in framing laws for angels and mortals. And these shall be called Divan laws.

22/1.14. Jehovih said: Behold, My God, Lords and sub-Gods, shall teach the same things in the different parts of the earth and in these heavens. I will not have one Lord teaching one thing in one place, and another teaching the same thing differently in another place.

22/1.15. Jehovih said: My God and Lords shall provide comprehensively,[689] so that all peoples, on earth and in heaven, may be drawn toward Me in harmony and discipline.

22/1.16. God said: I, God of earth, being made Div, by Jehovih's will, through His Son, Fragapatti, heard the Creator's voice, saying:

22/1.17. Div, My Son, proclaim the Ormazdian law, and the I'hua'Mazdian law, and the Zarathustrian law.

22/1.18. God said: This, then, is the Ormazdian law: Ormazd, the Creator, displays His creations, which He created. He set the stars in the firmament; these are the words of the book of the Almighty. He made the substances of the earth, and all the things on and in it. These are the words of the Creator, Ormazd, the Jehovih.

22/1.19. The substances of things going and coming forever; creating and dissolving from one shape into another, these are the Ormazdian law, the Jehovih'yan law. By virtue of His presence these things speak (impress) upon one another forever. What these things speak upon the soul of man, write upon the soul of man, these are man's knowledge, acquired by the Ormazdian law, the Jehovih'yan law. What these things speak upon the souls of angels, write upon the souls of angels, these are the angels' knowledge, acquired by the Ormazdian law, the Jehovih'yan law.

22/1.20. God said: This also is the Ormazdian law: Perpetual growth. As a man, being brought forth out of what was not an entity, thereby becoming an entity;[690] this then is brought about by the Ormazdian law.

22/1.21. With capacity in man for life everlasting; with capacity to acquire knowledge and power forever, and never attain to the Almighty. Like a road on which a man may run in full liberty forever, and never come to its end, rejoicing on his journey; this is the Ormazdian law.[691]

22/1.22. As the actions of corporeal substances produce light; as light is the expression and speech of certain corporeal changes, so is Ormazd, the Master Light, the Creator, that which illuminates the soul of man, making man conscious that he is; making man express his impressions. This is the Ormazdian law, this is the Ever Presence that never terminates.

22/1.23. Though worlds come into being and go out of being (as such), yet Ormazd remains; He is the Forever; and within Him all creations are created. These are the Ormazdian law, the Jehovih'yan law.

22/1.24. God said: This, then, that follows is the I'hua'Mazdian law: The school of knowledge, kept by God and his Lords, for teaching mortals and angels.

22/1.25. In which certain discipline and words are necessary to cause the congregating of men and angels, to dwell together and to travel onward forever, in harmony and rejoicing.

22/1.26. Behold, a great multitude was in disorder and in confusion, and unhappiness resulted. Then came order and discipline, and the multitude was harmonized and filled with rejoicing. What accomplished this was the I'hua'Mazdian law.

22/1.27. Jehovih had said: Behold, I create man with the possibility of becoming a creator under Me. The first lesson of creation that I give into man's hands, is that he shall create harmony and affiliation within himself and with his neighbors, so that the many may become in concert, even as one man.

---

[689] through one unified plan

[690] That is, you came forth out of the elements; in other words, before conception you were not an entity, and with conception you became an entity.

[691] And of course the further along the road of light one gets, the closer one gets to Jehovih (in attributes) compared to those starting out.

22/1.28. God said: Such was the Ormazdian law; to create man with the possibility of becoming a creator under Jehovih (Ormazd). But where man and angels, through their God and Lords, began to make, and to create, harmony and discipline; this was the I'hua'Mazdian law.

22/1.29. As the manual of arms is to soldiers, making them a unit in motion, so is the I'hua'Mazdian law in making and teaching peace, order and unity among mortals on earth and angels in heaven.

22/1.30. By the I'hua'Mazdian law the heavenly kingdoms in hada are maintained; and by the same law great kingdoms and nations on earth are built up. The discipline of God and the Lords, through their ashars, in ruling over mortals, for the comprehensive benefit of the whole; this is the I'hua'Mazdian law. It is called the I'hua'Mazdian law because God and his Lords, through their ashars, keep guard and rule over all good mortals and angels for their own exaltation in the heavens above.

22/1.31. God said: The following is the Zarathustrian law: The bestowal of words to mortals, illuminating the dominion of God and his Lords: The making of all good mortals joint heirs and members of the same heavenly kingdoms, in which, God and his Lords and Holy Council in heaven devise and administer laws for the ultimate resurrection of all men.

22/1.32. The revealed word of heaven, to mortals; this is the Zarathustrian law.

22/1.33. The word was with God, and God became the word; this is the Zarathustrian law.

22/1.34. For the word being established through Zarathustra became the life of God in flesh, being perpetual to the end of the world.

22/1.35. For though Zarathustra may be forgotten, and the words of his mouth not remembered on the whole earth, yet the Zarathustrian law (the Word of Light expressed through corpor) became everlasting in the souls of mortals from that time forward, forever and ever.[692]

22/1.36. For man to know of, and to desire to become one with the All Highest, this is the Zarathustrian law. Nor does it matter through what name he strives, as long as he strives to know the will of God.

22/1.37. When a king desires soldiers for his army, he sends recruiting emissaries, calling: Come, join the armies of the king. Even so, but for peace and righteousness, God sends his Lords and holy angels down to mortals, saying: Come, join the kingdom of God. And when they come, behold, they use certain rites and ceremonies, with words and sacred days: The names of these rites and ceremonies and the words revealed by God, these are the Zarathustrian laws. For they are the initiative (the first steps), by which mortals become joint workers with God and his Lords.

CHAPTER 2 Divinity

22/2.1. God said: Be attentive, O man, to the voice of your Lord and his angels; be patient, so that you may understand the dominion of your God, and add glory to the Almighty. ||

22/2.2. The Div was the chief, and the Lords and their officers comprised the Divan Congress, during the period of time covered by this book (Divinity).

22/2.3. And the mortals of that day, who joined in the armies of God, were represented by the voice of guardian angels (ashars) through their Lord, according to the nation or place represented.

22/2.4. And the ashars reported to their Lord, regarding the conditions and places of mortals, and the conditions and places of angels also, and the Lords spoke about this in the Diva.

22/2.5. And the Div decreed laws and governments, to mortals and angels, according to what was best for them. ||

22/2.6. Jehovih said: I am the Light and the Life; behold Me, I am Ormazd. When I shape My thoughts into words, behold, I am I'hua'Mazda; I am the Word. When the words of My kingdom are registered with mortals, behold Me; I am the Zarathustrian law. I am three in one.

22/2.7. In that way I have given to you, O Div, and to My angels and My mortals; for you three shall be a unit in the furtherance of My kingdoms.

22/2.8. Behold, from this time onward your labors shall be called Divinity (Divan). And whoever falls under your inspiration shall be called Divine (Divas).

---

[692] This means we each and all have access to the Word of Light within our souls, if we would take advantage of it; and it calls us along the path of light, ever drawing closer toward the All Light.

22/2.9. God said: Consider, O man, the wisdom of your God, and perceive what is feasible[693] according to your own judgment, and be far-reaching with your own members.[694]

22/2.10. || The Div decreed: To carry birth rites down to mortals; to teach them to consecrate to Diva their newborn children, under a rod with water, in the same manner es'yans are baptized in heaven. And with rites and ceremonies, and words, according to the Zarathustrian law, the I'hua'Mazdian law, and the Ormazdian law. ||

22/2.11. God said: At the time of the baptism of mortal children, behold, my Lords appointed ashars to those children, to keep them in the way of the Almighty.

22/2.12. And that was the first Divan law.

22/2.13. || The Div decreed: To establish wedding rites and ceremonies with words and processions, in order to firmly bind monogamic[695] marriages, according to the Zarathustrian law, the I'hua'Mazdian law, and the Ormazdian law. ||

22/2.14. God said: At the time of marriage, behold my Lords appointed new ashars to man and wife, whose duties were to minister to them as to a small kingdom, for the glory of Jehovih.[696]

22/2.15. This was the second Divan law.

22/2.16. || The Div decreed: To establish funeral rites and ceremonies, with words, according to the Diva, that is, the Zarathustrian, the I'hua'Mazdian, and the Ormazdian law. ||

22/2.17. This was the third Divan law.

22/2.18. God said: In the birth rites; in the marriage rites, and in the funeral rites, recording angels of the Lord were present; and afterward, they reported these things to my kingdom in heaven.

22/2.19. And all those mortals who carried out these rites and ceremonies, with words, were named Zarathustrians. Nevertheless there were many others, who, not being capable of the inspiration, stood aloof from me and my kingdoms.

22/2.20. Jehovih said: I do not blame My God and My Lords for their love favoring more those mortals who became Zarathustrians, than those who rejected God and his Lords. Nor do I censure God and his Lords for favoring their chosen in building cities, nations and empires, and leaving other mortals that were enemies to perish in their cities, kingdoms and nations.

22/2.21. God said: You who are one with the Divine law, are free from the law; but they who reject me and my kingdom are bound by the law.

22/2.22. Regarding the first three Divan laws, God said: These are the sacred words decreed to mortals: By father or mother: I bestow this, my child, to be a good Zarathustrian, according to the Diva. || And in marriage, by the Bride and Bridegroom: I bestow myself to this my mate, a good Zarathustrian, according to the Diva. || And in sacrament previous to death: I, a good Zarathustrian, confess, with repentance, to You, O Ormazd; and to Your Lords of the heavenly hosts of Diva.

CHAPTER 3 Divinity

22/3.1. God said: Behold, I come to reveal what was done in heaven, so that you, O man, may understand the cause of things being done on earth. ||

22/3.2. These Divan laws were made in heaven; and by the Lords of that day, through their angels, given to mortals, by which mortals became a manifestation of heavenly things.

22/3.3. Here follows a continuation of these laws, namely:

22/3.4. Of the third Divan law: If a man is not too weak, he shall confess to all the Lords with repentance. On the other hand, if he is too weak to utter words, then the priest shall confess him by holding the right hand while saying the holy words. And while this is being done, the ashars shall provide a sufficient number of spirits to receive the newborn, and bring him to the place in heaven that has been previously selected for him.

22/3.5. The third Divan law also decreed as follows: If the es'yan is a Zarathustrian, and his kin (family) in heaven are drujas, he shall not be taken to the heaven where they are; nor shall his kin be

[693] able to be accomplished, possible, suitable, achievable, attainable, sustainable

[694] Thus we can stretch our thoughts upward to consider God's wisdom, and determine what is attainable and accomplishes the greatest good.

[695] literally "one seed," meaning monogamous marriage; in its pure sense, marrying only once during one's lifetime

[696] In other words, a marriage was considered to be the beginning of a small kingdom.

permitted to see him for thirty days. But after thirty days, his kin, if drujas, may be permitted to see him in his own place in heaven, but only if they are under guard.

22/3.6. The fourth Divan law: If the es'yan is a Zarathustrian, and his kin in heaven belong to the organic heavens, then he shall be taken to them, and his abiding place shall be with them for a season.

22/3.7. The fifth Divan law: If the es'yan is a Zarathustrian, his spirit shall not be allowed to remain longer than three days and three nights with his mortal kindred. And then he shall be taken to his place in heaven, and given into the keeping of the asaphs, who shall explain all things to him.

22/3.8. God said: While the mortal priest is reciting prayers after death, in the morning, at noon, and at sunset, the ashars shall assemble in the same house, along with the newborn spirit, and join in the singing and praying, for it will pacify the spirit, and restore him to know what has taken place. And this shall be called the sixth Divan law.

22/3.9. God said: And the same laws shall apply in the case of a Zarathustrian woman. In the case of a Zarathustrian child, who died in infancy, the Div decreed:

22/3.10. The seventh Divan law: The child of a Zarathustrian being too young to speak, shall not make confession, even through the priest. The mortal priest shall say: O You Master Light! Behold, my child is dead! Receive its little, tender spirit! Take it to Your heavenly place of delight! || And the ashars shall take the young es'yan to a place suited to it, and deliver it to the asaphs; and the asaphs shall examine it, and, if it requires fetal, they shall provide it in heaven, if possible. But if it is too young, then the asaphs, with a sufficient guard, shall take it back to its mortal mother, or to its mortal father, or to its brother, or its sister, or other near kin, or to whomever the asaphs find most advisable. And the spirit child shall be put to bed every night with its fetal mother, fetal father, or fetal host, so that its spirit may draw sufficient sustenance to grow into everlasting life. But the asaphs who have it in charge shall bring it away in the morning to its place in heaven. But in no case shall a Zarathustrian spirit child be left to fetal with a contentious mortal woman, or with a drunken mortal man.

22/3.11. God propounded:[697] If a Zarathustrian is dead, and his spirit has resided many years in a place of heavenly delight, and then his mortal wife dies, and she is not a Zarathustrian?

22/3.12. The members of the Diva all spoke. Then God decreed the eighth Divan law, which was: The spirit of such a woman shall not be allowed to go to the place of her husband. For thirty days she shall be kept in a place suitable for her. After that she may, under guard, visit her husband; but until she accepts the Ormazdian law, she shall not dwell with the husband in heaven, nor with her children in heaven. And if she has mortal children, she shall not be permitted to see them, except under guard.

22/3.13. The ninth Divan law was the same, but for a Zarathustrian woman whose husband was not a Zarathustrian; for he was bound by the same law, and thus kept separate in heaven until he accepted the Ormazdian law.

22/3.14. God propounded: If a Zarathustrian has a wife who is not a Zarathustrian, and she gives premature birth, whether by accident (miscarriage) or abortion, what happens to the spirit of that child? On this all the members of Diva spoke, and after that, God decreed:

22/3.15. Such spirit shall not be brought to heaven for a season, but shall be fetaled day and night on its natural mother or father, until the full nine months are completed, and then it shall be delivered with due ceremonies by the ashars. After that it shall be fetaled the same as in the seventh Divan law. And this was the tenth Divan law.

22/3.16. The eleventh Divan law: If a Zarathustrian attains to maturity before he dies, his spirit shall be es'yan for two years. And during this time he shall be attended by not less than two asaphs when he goes away from his heavenly home; and the asaphs shall teach him the mode of travel, the manner of knowing localities, both on the earth and in the first resurrection. And they shall teach him the varieties and kinds of food suited to the highest, best education of a spirit. But when he travels with his companions of his own heavenly group, then the asaphs of the group shall go along with them. And, during the two years, he shall be provided with food and clothes from the

[697] put forward for consideration

stores in heaven, and he shall not labor to provide himself with anything.

22/3.17. The twelfth Divan law was in reference to the same spirit, which was: At the end of two years the asaphs shall deliver him, and those of his group who are prepared, into the department of first instruction, and his name shall be entered in the library of that department of heaven as ENTERED APPRENTICE, IN THE FIRST RESURRECTION. Here his first lessons shall be making clothes and providing food for himself and others. And he shall be entitled to participate, if he so desires, in the recreations of the entered apprentices, such as music, dancing, marching, painting, or other arts.

22/3.18. The thirteenth Divan law was in reference to the same spirit, which was: He shall serve not less than two years as entered apprentice, and longer if his proficiency is not sufficient for advancement. But when he is advanced, he shall no longer be called entered apprentice, but a CRAFTSMAN. And he shall be taken to a suitable place, where his labor will contribute to the heavenly kingdoms. And his recreations shall entitle him to instruction in both corporeal and es'ean knowledge, and their correspondence.[698] As a craftsman he shall serve seven years.

22/3.19. The fourteenth Divan law was in reference to the same spirit, which was: The craftsman's examination being completed, he shall then return to labor in the nurseries in heaven, becoming assistant to the asaphs. And during this period he shall report at the roll call. And his teachers shall take him with them down to mortals and teach him how to see and hear corporeal things. And they shall also explain to him fetalism and the obsession of mortals by drujas, so that he may understand the cause of lying, stealing, tattling, conspiracies, and murders, among mortals.

22/3.20. The fifteenth Divan law pertained to the same spirit, which was: After he has served three years as nurse-assistant to the asaphs, he shall be promoted to the hospitals in heaven, as assistant to the physicians. And they shall teach him the restoration of spirits in chaos, and crazy spirits, and deformed spirits, and of sick spirits, and of spirits afflicted with foul smells, who cannot clean themselves, especially of the spirits of women who produced abortion on themselves, or suffered it to be done to them, and of monomaniacs, and all manner of diseased spirits. And the physicians shall take him with them when they go down to mortals to remove fetals, and he shall learn how they are severed, safely to both. And they shall take him to the battlefields, where mortals have slain one another, whose spirits are in chaos, or are still fighting, and he shall assist in bringing them away from the corporeal place, and also learn how to restore them, and where to deliver them when restored. And if there are knots in any region near at hand, the physician shall take him to the knot, and show him how they are untied, and how they are mastered and delivered. And if there is any hell near at hand, the physicians shall take him there and teach him how hell is delivered and its people restored. For ten years he shall serve as assistant to the physicians.

22/3.21. The sixteenth Divan law applied to the same spirit, which was: Having fulfilled the part of assistant physician, he shall be promoted to the full rank of NURSE. And in that department he shall serve ten years, which completes his emancipation in that order, and after that, any and all the nurseries of the lower heavens shall be free and open to him, and he shall go to whichever one he desires, except when specially commanded for a certain work by his Lord, or by the God of his division.

22/3.22. The seventeenth Divan law referred to the same spirit, which was: Having passed a satisfactory examination by his Lord, or his Lord's attendants, he shall be promoted to the full rank of PHYSICIAN. And in that department in heaven he shall serve fifty years. And then his emancipation in that order shall be complete. And all the hospitals in the lower heavens shall be open to him, and he shall choose whichever of them he desires as his place of labor, unless specially required by his Lord, or by the God of his division.

22/3.23. The eighteenth Divan law affected the same spirit, which was: He shall now pass an examination by his Lord or his Lord's deputy, and if he proves himself in a knowledge of the structure of both the corporeal and spiritual man, he shall be registered as ENTERED FACTOR, and he shall serve twelve years in forming and making fabrics for

[698] Meaning how Es things match up with corporeal things, and how corporeal things match up with Es things.

raiment, and for other useful and ornamental purposes.

22/3.24. The nineteenth Divan law was like the eighteenth, except that his labor shall be gathering and transporting food for another twelve years. And the twentieth Divan law was like the nineteenth, except that his labor shall be the wielding of large bodies, and of carrying them long distances.

22/3.25. The twenty-first Divan law dealt with the same spirit: He shall now enter the CREATIF as an apprentice. Thirty years he shall serve in the CREATIF, learning how to create. And the twenty-second Divan law was like the twenty-first, except that he shall dwell in Uz and serve twelve years in learning Uz.[699]

22/3.26. The twenty-third Divan law, meant for the same spirit, was: He shall now enter college, and serve according to his talents, from five to forty years, learning corporeal and es'sean measuring, and distances, rotations, velocities, magnets; currents of vortices; roadways in vortices, and how to measure vortices by their spiral force; how to find the center and the periphery of vortices. And if he serves the full term of forty years, he shall have the freedom of the eighteenth, nineteenth, twentieth, twenty-first, twenty-second and twenty-third commandments; and all those places shall be forever open for him. And if he chooses to go into any of them he shall do so, unless specially ordered to some other emergent place by his Lord, or the God of his division.

22/3.27. The twenty-fourth Divan law, for the same spirit, was: He shall now enter architecture as an apprentice, and learn the building of heavenly mansions and cities; and he shall serve eight years, and be promoted to build judgment seats and thrones, and serve another sixteen years.

22/3.28. The twenty-fifth Divan law, for the same spirit, was: He shall now be eligible to enter the SCHOOL OF LIGHT AND DARKNESS, and learn the relative power of attraction and propulsion belonging to them; and his education here shall embrace practice and experiment; and he shall serve seventy years for the full course. After which, if he is proficient in creating light and darkness, he shall be emancipated from the twenty-fourth and twenty-fifth Divan laws, and all those places shall be open and free to him forever.

22/3.29. The twenty-sixth Divan law, for the same spirit, was: He shall now serve twenty-four years in building and propelling heavenly boats, and small ships. And the twenty-seventh Divan law was similar, which was: That he shall now travel fifty years in atmospherea, and on the earth, and on the oceans of the earth.

22/3.30. This completed the primary education in the first resurrection.

CHAPTER 4 Divinity

22/4.1. God said: For the spirit of a Zarathustrian who has completed his primary education, what then? On which, all the members spoke. After that Div decreed:

22/4.2. He shall serve two hundred years as an apprenticed loo'is. He shall become proficient in the knowledge of procreation of mortals. Learning to prophesy what the offspring will be, according to the parentage; to become wise in discerning how the es of a living mortal governs the flesh, to good or evil; how the es of a mortal controls the sex and ultimate size, health and strength of the offspring.

22/4.3. To learn which, the loo'is shall take him to thousands of mortals, and he shall make a record of what he has under observation; and when those mortals have offspring born to them, he shall make a record of it; and he shall observe the character of the birth, and the foundation of the child, together with what conditions surrounded the mother of the child. And he shall follow that child till it has grown up, and also married, and begotten a child, or children, and so on to the sixth generation. This is the twenty-eighth Divan law.

22/4.4. Div decreed: After he has served two hundred years he shall be examined by his Lord, or his Lord's deputy, and if proficient in prophesying to the sixth generation, he shall be entered as an ashar on a list of four twelves for every moon's change. But the forty-eight ashars shall not be ashars to more than one hundred and ninety-two mortals, unless otherwise specially allotted by the Lord or God in dominion.

22/4.5. For four generations, of one hundred and thirty-three years, he shall serve as an ashar. And he shall learn to have dominion over his

---

[699] Many Spiritualists have seen spirits perform Uz. I have seen flowers passed through a board without injury or abrasion to either board or flowers. –Ed.

mortal protégés night and day, not letting them, however, know his presence. To accomplish which, he shall begin with his protégés in their first infancy; remaining with them while they sleep, talking to the spirit of the mortal, teaching and persuading. This was the twenty-ninth Divan law.

22/4.6. Div decreed: Having served the full term of ashar, he shall be entitled to examination by his Lord or deputy. But now a new type of examination begins; which is, that the examination pertains to his protégés, as to what kind of fruit he has sent to heaven, the grade of his es'yans being the standard.[700] This was the thirtieth Divan law.

22/4.7. Div decreed: Having passed the examination as ashar, he shall now be promoted as asaph, where he shall serve sixty-six years. Here again his examination shall be not of himself but of the harvest of his department. This was the thirty-first Divan law.

22/4.8. Div decreed: His examination being complete, he shall now receive emancipation from all preceding departments and decrees; and he shall have his choice in all places he has passed, unless otherwise specially detailed by his Lord or God of his division. This was the thirty-second Divan law.

22/4.9. Div decreed: He shall now be entitled to enter the CHAPTER OF THE PRIMARY SOUL. His first lessons shall be in colors and sounds, both of corpor and es. First, beginning with gray of not more than three combinations; and when he has mastered these, he shall have four, then five, then ten, then a hundred, and so on, until, when any combination of colors is placed before him, he can instantly perceive every color, shade, and tint, and the apparent velocity of light, and its force (actinic) emanating. And he shall pursue this study until he can create in es the counterpart of anything in corpor, or create in corpor the counterpart of anything in es. And of sounds he shall proceed in the same way; first, learning a combination of three, so that when his teacher produces any three sounds (notes) together, he can hear them and determine the exact velocity of each wave. Then he shall begin with four sounds, then five, then ten, then a hundred, and even a thousand, which, even though made in the same instant, he shall detect every one, and the velocity and force of each. This was the thirty-third Divan law.

22/4.10. Div decreed: He shall now begin the practice of combining and creating color by sounds, and sounds by colors, both in corpor and es. His teachers shall make explosions with light, and explosions without light, and by using only his eye and ear he shall be able to determine the elements by which the explosions were made. This was the thirty-fourth Divan law.

22/4.11. Div decreed: He shall go far away from the explosions, and when the waves come to him, even though he does not hear the explosion, he shall be able to determine, by the waves, of what substance the explosion was made, and whether in light or darkness. And, if in light, what colors were manifested. This was the thirty-fifth Divan law.

22/4.12. Div decreed: He shall now receive instruction in the sounds of conversation. First, his teacher shall cause him to hear two people conversing at the same time, missing nothing that is said; then three, then four, then five, then ten, then a hundred, and then a thousand, but no greater number in this department. This was the thirty-sixth Divan law.

22/4.13. Div decreed: He shall now analyze the waves of voice, in which he cannot hear the sounds. His teacher shall station him in a certain place and cause him to read the waves of light and sound that come to him, so that he knows not only the words spoken, but the kind of person speaking or singing. This was the thirty-seventh Divan law.

22/4.14. Div decreed: His teacher shall now cause him to read the waves of light and sound emanating from two persons talking at the same time, whom he cannot hear, and he shall understand not only the words spoken, but the kind of persons speaking. Then he shall read the waves in the same way for three persons, then four, then eight, then a hundred, and even a thousand. This was the thirty-eighth Divan law.

22/4.15. Div decreed: Then he shall be taken near a battlefield, where mortals are in deadly conflict, and he shall be stationed far enough away so he does not hear the sounds; but when the waves come to him, he shall read them and know the number of the men in battle, the kind of weapons in use, and the cause of contention. This was the thirty-ninth Divan law.

22/4.16. Div decreed: He shall now be promoted to be a messenger between Lords, and

[700] criterion, measure, summation, précis

between Lords and Gods. This was the fortieth Divan law.

22/4.17. Div decreed: For one hundred years he shall serve as messenger, and at the end of that time his Lords and Gods shall render his record and promote him to marshal. And at this, his emancipation from all the preceding decrees and departments shall open these latter to him, to choose whatever department he desires, except on such time and occasion as specially required by his Lord or God. This was the forty-first Divan law.

22/4.18. Div decreed: For two hundred years he shall serve as marshal, and under as many as forty Lords and Gods, and in as many as twenty heavenly kingdoms. This was the forty-second Divan law.

22/4.19. Div decreed: He shall now be promoted Lord, and have dominion over a city or nation of mortals, and over the spirits belonging to that city or nation. This was the forty-third Divan law.

CHAPTER 5 Divinity

22/5.1. God propounded: If a man dies, and is not a Zarathustrian, what then? All the members spoke, and then:

22/5.2. Div decreed: Because he did not accept the Zarathustrian law while mortal, he is unsuitable for the highest exalted places of delight. For all official preference shall be to the Zarathustrian. This was the forty-fourth Divan law.

22/5.3. Div decreed regarding the same spirit, one who had not been a Zarathustrian: His education shall not run to the Lord-head, nor to the God-head. He shall not be a column in the Father's building, nor one of the arch-stones of great strength, but he shall stand as a plain brick in the wall. This was the forty-fifth Divan law.

22/5.4. Div said: I am not created God to merely serve my time and nothing more. I am to look far ahead as to who shall be Lords and Gods over the earth and atmospherea.

22/5.5. Div propounded: What, then, shall be the course of a spirit who was not a Zarathustrian? And this was made the forty-sixth Divan law: He shall be delivered to the asaphs, who shall enter him in the nurseries as an es'yan, where he shall remain six years, learning the elementary powers and expressions.

22/5.6. Div decreed the forty-seventh Divan law: The same spirit shall then be apprenticed in manufacturing and general labor, where he shall serve twelve years, unless previously instructed in these things while mortal.

22/5.7. Div decreed the forty-eighth Divan law: He shall now enter school and learn surveying and measuring without instruments, and determining the kind of emanations that rise up from earth, their altitude and density; and he shall learn exploration and enumeration in both corpor and es; the building of piedmazrs and otevans; the constructing of arrow-ships, and all other vessels used in the heavens to carry things from place to place. And he shall serve thirty years in these things.

22/5.8. Div decreed the forty-ninth Divan law: He shall now be promoted to restoring, nursing and caring for the drujas who are being rescued by the captains, generals and Lords; in which service he shall work thirty years. But in both the forty-eighth and forty-ninth Divan laws it was afterward decreed: Whatever service he did in these areas in mortal life, shall stand twofold to his credit in Spirit.

22/5.9. Div decreed: If he now acknowledges and practices faith in the Great Spirit, he shall be promoted to the COLLEGE OF CREATION, and taught to create light and darkness. After this, he shall be taught to sar'gis flowers, trees and clothes, and take elementary lessons in music and expression, in which branches he shall serve fifty years. And then he shall be entitled to examination, and if he can withstand the third grade of light, he shall be ranked BRIDEGROOM OF OM.[701] This was the fiftieth Divan law. The fifty-first thus provides:

22/5.10. If he does not yet comprehend faith in the All Person, he shall be granted freedom to all the places where he has served, and he shall be emancipated from all Lords and Gods, and from all labor and education, and honorably discharged, to pursue whatever he desires in any place in heaven or earth. Nor shall the Lords or Gods take any more notice of him other than due respect and honor.

22/5.11. Regarding this, DIV, SON OF ALL LIGHT, spoke, saying: This also shall be part and parcel of

---

[701] Om is female for Jehovih. Bridegrooms marry Om. Brides marry Jehovih. –Ed. [Hence a female reaching this level would be ranked BRIDE OF JEHOVIH.]

the Divan law, which is to say: From the latter class rise the false Gods and false Lords, who often set up kingdoms of their own in atmospherea. They shall not rise above the second resurrection.

22/5.12. The Voice of Jehovih came to God, saying: Without the disbeliever in spirits, mortals could not find courage to kill serpents; without false Gods and false Lords the lowest drujas would never be put to work. Those who cannot be raised by persuasion, may be aroused by less scrupulous masters, who make slaves of them.

CHAPTER 6 Divinity

22/6.1. In the twelfth moon of the Diva the Voice of Jehovih came to Div, saying: So that My Lords and My Gods may not err, you shall promulgate[702] the foundation of the Divan law. God perceived, and in the name of Div he decreed:

22/6.2. Hear me, O Gods and Lords! This is the foundation of Divan law: The decrees of God and his Lords, his Lord Gods, his Gods, and his Lords; not singly, but by all members, and ratified by the Council of Diva under Div, Son of All Light. That is to say:

22/6.3. A kingdom in heaven rises or falls by Divan law; a kingdom or nation on earth rises or falls by Divan law. The virtuous are rewarded and exalted by Divan law; the wicked are cast into trials by Divan law.

22/6.4. But this is not Divan law: Man to be created and live; to live a time on earth, then die and enter heaven. These are done by the Ever Presence, the All Light, the Creator, and not by the Diva.

22/6.5. This is Divan law, namely: To assist man out of darkness into light; to give security to the helpless; to raise the souls of men to everlasting light; to minister to the needy; to deliver those who are in pain; to teach man to desist laboring for himself; to teach him to labor for others.

22/6.6. But this is not Divan law: For seed to grow; for a tree to grow; for a spider to weave its web; these are done by the Ever Living Presence, the All Master, Creator!

22/6.7. This is Divan law, namely: To regulate the affairs of angels and mortals, for their ultimate resurrection; to lay the foundation for harmony in community; to gather together the inharmonious, and put them in tune.

22/6.8. But this is not Divan law: To provide the earth with life, or to hold it in its place; to build the place of the higher or lower heavens; to provide corpor or to provide es; these things are by the Ever Personal Presence, the Creator, and shaped and molded by His hand through the Chiefs of the higher heavens.

22/6.9. This is Divan law: To bring man and woman together in marriage, wisely, for the (potential) child's sake, and for the joy of all.

22/6.10. But this is not Divan law: To give desire for marriage, or desire from marriage; these are from the All Person, the Master Light.

22/6.11. This is Divan law: When a man walks along, to take him by the hand and bend him to the right or left.

22/6.12. But this is not Divan law: For the man to go forth; this he does by the Ever Presence, Jehovih, the Ormazd.

22/6.13. A carpenter builds a house, but he did not build the logs or the stone. The Diva builds kingdoms in heaven and kingdoms on earth, and shapes them for usefulness and beauty; and when they are old and out of sorts, the Diva abandons them, and they fall to pieces. Nevertheless, Ormazd provided and provides the wherewithal[703] for the whole.

22/6.14. Div decreed: This also you shall promulgate in heaven and earth, lest angels and mortals worship Div and Diva. For though the Diva appoints mortal kings,[704] yet mortals shall not worship Div (Divinity).

CHAPTER 7 Divinity

22/7.1. In the sixth Diva, Div decreed: The Divan law shall be the higher law; and you shall give mortals a law copied from it, and the mortal law shall be called the lower law.

22/7.2. One of the members of Diva said: If a mortal judge is judging between certain men, by which law shall he judge? On this matter the members spoke at great length.

---

[702] make known

[703] the substances, resources and necessary means

[704] This is the origin of the now defunct notion of the divine right of kings.

22/7.3. And Div decreed: He can discern the higher law only dimly; but the lower law he can read plainly in a book. He shall therefore judge by the lower, but by the highest interpretation. And then Div on his own account said:

22/7.4. For the priests of the Zarathustrians, who have carried the alms-bowl and lived pure in all things, being celibates, serving the Creator, Ormazd, only, going about doing good, they have the higher law, the Divan law, within their hearts; they shall judge by it. Nevertheless, trouble does not come into any of the worlds by those who strive to do right, but by those who evade. The time shall come when the judge shall not interpret according to the higher law; he will strive to hide justice in a corner, using words to conceal his own perversity. It is by such men and angels that heaven and earth will be blighted in coming time.

22/7.5. For, as through Zarathustra, God's Word has been established on the earth, and since words themselves perish and are supplemented by new words, the time shall come when the higher law will fall, like a house on sand. For there are no words that are everlasting, or that are understood by all men alike; words themselves are only like husks that surround the corn. Men in darkness quibble on the husks, but do not discern the fruit within. ||

22/7.6. Jehovih spoke to Div, saying: Man builds a house, and it perishes. Succeeding generations must also build, otherwise the art of building would perish. It is better for the building to perish, than the art of building. I created all men to labor and to learn. Should My Gods and angels require less? Because language melts away, the language-makers, being My Lords and ashars, have constant employment of delight. ||

22/7.7. Div said: Foolish men chase a language that is dead and moldered away; but the wise seek language to express the spirit of things. The latter is under the Divan law; the former is bound as a druk. And so, you shall be circumspect regarding words and language, because mortal judges who judge by the lower law, are bound in words. ||

22/7.8. Copies of these Divan laws were given to mortals through the Lords and ashars, either by inspiration or by words spoken in sar'gissa. And in Jaffeth, Shem and Arabin'ya, mortal kings decreed mortal laws and revelations, based on the Divan laws, and on the Zarathustrian laws. ||

22/7.9. Div propounded: A man and woman in mortal life were as druks, being filthy, idle, and begging from day to day, and yet they had many children born to them. And the children were like the parents, lazy and worthless, being beggars also. Now in the course of time, the man and woman die, and later the children die also, and none of them are yet entered into the first resurrection in heaven, still being beggars and dwelling around their old haunts: What of them?

22/7.10. The Lords all spoke on this subject, and after that Div decreed: Such spirits shall be reported by the ashars to the Lord, and the Lord shall send a captain with a sufficient army to arrest them, and bring them away from the earth, and place them into a colony for such spirits. This was called Divan act, the first.

22/7.11. Act, the second: Such drujas shall be clothed and fed for thirty days. If, by this time, they manifest no inclination to labor, but are still lazy, they shall be removed into another region, where food can be obtained only by exertion.

22/7.12. Act, the third: This law shall apply also to mortals; they shall be inspired, through the ashars, to migrate to cold and unproductive regions. Div said: You have planned wisely in this, O Jehovih! For all Your places in heaven and earth shall be subdued, and made to glorify You!

CHAPTER 8 Divinity

22/8.1. The Diva met three times every year in Mouru, and enacted many acts like those previously related; and there were so many, that all the spirits in heaven and mortals on the earth were fore-planned, from before birth until they became Brides and Bridegrooms in heaven.

22/8.2. And heaven and earth became as one country, with one king, who was God; and his word ruled over all. The Lords' kingdoms prospered, as did the kingdoms of the sub-Gods and the sub-Goddesses. Never before on earth and in her heavens had such glory manifested. And there were rites and ceremonies, recreations, games and pageantry, on earth and in heaven, so great, that one could write a thousand books describing them, and yet not have told a tenth of it.

22/8.3. So, after God had reigned one hundred and ninety years, he descended from his heavenly place, and traveled about through all of the Lords' dominions, and the sub-Gods' dominions in the lower heavens, so that he might rejoice before Jehovih in the great good works he had done.

22/8.4. And in all the heavenly places great rejoicing arose because God came there; and the singers made and sang hymns of rejoicing; and trumpeters and harpists proclaimed the glory of Jehovih's Presence.

22/8.5. So God had the people counted for the Gods of the etherean worlds, who were to send receivers in the time of dan for the great resurrection. And the number of Brides and Bridegrooms to Jehovih would be sixteen billion!

22/8.6. After that, God directed his fire-ship to run close to the earth, so that he could survey mortals and their kingdoms. And he visited all the great nations of earth, to the south, north, east, and west. And now his soul cried out with great sorrow! The great peoples of the earth were turning into celibates!

22/8.7. And the voice of Jehovih came to him, saying: God, My Son, Hoab, why do you sorrow? And God answered, saying: Behold, the earth is not populated everywhere; the plains and mountains are not subdued; the wilderness is filled with beasts of prey; the Zarathustrians are running into the same line as the I'hins; they kill nothing; they live for the soul only. And since they have learned the bondage of the lower heavens, they will not marry and beget offspring.

22/8.8. Again Jehovih spoke to God, saying: Do not call down a'ji or ji'ay, My Son! Do not fear. In ten years, behold, I will bring the earth into dan, and you shall bring your harvest into My emancipated worlds.

22/8.9. So God sorrowed no more; and on his return to Mouru, and in the next meeting of the Diva, he propounded: If a husband and wife have a child born to them, they both being Zarathustrians: What then? When the members had spoken:

22/8.10. Div decreed: They shall have rites and ceremonies, so that the ashars of the order of Zarathustra may be appointed to it. What the ashars do in spirit, the corporeans shall do in corpor. And this was the first supplemental Divan law.

22/8.11. Through the commandment of the presiding Lord, the ashars assembled in the house of a Zarathustrian at the time of the birth of a child; and these spirits baptized the child with a rod, sprinkling water on its head in the same way as when selecting victims who have been delivered out of hell. And by inspiration, the angels induced the mortals to go through the same ceremony, having a priest perform with the rod, which had been dipped in water.

22/8.12. Div decreed: A baptized child shows it has sprung from Zarathustrians, and has high possibilities inherent in it. And if it dies in infancy, it shall not be placed with the children of druks in heaven, but in a place that will enable the parents, after death, to visit it with delight. This was the second supplemental Divan law.

22/8.13. So it became common on the earth for mortals to have their children baptized in infancy, so that in case of death, they could be taken to a place of delight, and not fall into the power of drujas, the evil spirits.

22/8.14. Div propounded: If a young man, who is a Zarathustrian, and a young woman who is also a Zarathustrian, seek to marry, and both every way obedient to the Ormazdian law, and to the I'hua'Mazdian law, what shall be the rites and ceremonies of marriage for them? On this all the members spoke, and after that:

22/8.15. Div decreed: They shall be married by a rab'bah, with kin and friends present. The rab'bah shall say: Ormazd has united you forever; live in peace and love on earth, and you shall dwell together in a heavenly place of delight after death. What Ormazd has joined, no man can separate forever. || And while the mortal ceremony is being performed, the ashars and the kindred spirits shall have rites and ceremonies in the same house, and this shall be called the beginning of a new heavenly kingdom. This was the third supplemental Divan law.

22/8.16. Besides these, a hundred and eight supplemental Divan laws were passed; and they comprehended all things in the life and death of mortals, and all things pertaining to the resurrection after death. And so great was the power of the Zarathustrian religion on earth that war ceased, and the tribes and nations dwelt together in peace. The people ceased to build large cities, and ceased striving for the things of earth.

22/8.17. But they learned little, except rites and ceremonies, prayers, and singing hymns of praise to Ormazd, and to His Gods and Lords, and to Zarathustra, the All Pure. Thus ended the dominion of Hoab's reign in heaven and earth, whose greatness had never been surpassed.

22/8.18. So Jehovih brought the regions of dan, and sent seven ships, and delivered God and his harvest of sixteen billion angels into places of delight, the Nirvanian fields of Niscrossawotcha, in etherea.

CHAPTER 9 Divinity

22/9.1. Then God bewailed the state of the earth, because man ceased to love anything on it. His whole mind and heart were set upon heavenly things, and the earth was becoming like a neglected farm grown over with weeds and briars. So Jehovih answered God's prayers, saying: Behold, I will bring darkness to cover the earth on all sides. Prepare for it, My Son, for not only will man desire of the earth, but the angels in your high heavenly places will forsake them, and go down to the earth.

22/9.2. So it came to pass, Jehovih brought ji'ya upon the earth, and it was in a state of darkness for four hundred years, and the sun did not shine, but was like a red ball of fire, and mortal things were without lights and shadows.

22/9.3. And men's minds and hearts took after the nature of the corporeal world, losing sight of Ormazd and His heavenly promises, and they focused on the desires of earth, and of the pleasures of the flesh-life. Now during ji'ay, there fell perpetual atmospherean substance on the earth, and it was of the nature and kind of substance of which the earth is made, but atmospheric, and this is that which is called ji'ya.[705]

22/9.4. And the plateau of Haraiti and Zeredho were driven down to the earth and near the earth; and the belt of meteoris was moved nearer by thousands of miles, and in many places upon the earth, meteoric stones fell like a rain shower, but burning hot, and with suffocating smell. And the affairs of mortals were changed; they built new cities, and became great hunters, applying the wisdom of their forefathers to the matters of the earth.

22/9.5. And the heavenly places of delight were broken up and descended to the earth; and the angels were cast upon the earth, turning away from faith in Ormazd, seeking joy in the affairs of earth. And God and his Lords were powerless to inspire righteous works, either with mortals or angels. But man and woman became prolific, and they grew large, and full of resolution and power.

22/9.6. The Voice of Jehovih spoke to God, saying: Maintain your kingdom; and your Gods and Lords under you shall also maintain their kingdoms. Nor shall you let My people become discouraged with My works.

22/9.7. Because I have sent darkness upon the earth to benefit mortals in mortality, so also in that same time I have given My heavenly hosts lessons in My es worlds. Neither shall they call this a judgment upon them, nor say that I do these things in anger, or as punishment, or for benefit of one to the injury of others.

22/9.8. Because you were guided by My voice and My commandments in bestowing the Divan law, behold the strength and wisdom of your pupils! For, to the extent that they learn to master the elements I created in atmospherea, so will they become triumphant in My etherean worlds.

22/9.9. God perceived, and he and his Lords and sub-Gods fortified their kingdoms on all hands, and provided assistance to their colleges, factories, hospitals and places of education, in order to maintain the angels who had sought resurrection.

22/9.10. Nevertheless, it came to pass that many angels believed a new order of light was coming on the earth, in which the earth would become the all-highest abode for angels and Gods. Others having lived two or three hundred years in atmospherea, and never having been in etherea, began to disbelieve in the higher heavens, and finally to disbelieve in Jehovih, also.

22/9.11. And in two hundred years time, God and his Lords lost influence and power with both angels and mortals. And the latter took to war, and the angels who had ministered to them became wanderers and adventurers, without organization, and cared neither for truth nor wisdom, but flattered mortals for their own glory.

22/9.12. And the kings and queens of the earth built temples for their familiar spirits, who assumed the ancient names of Gods and Lords. Now when the next arc of dan was near at hand, God enumerated his upraised hosts, and there were twelve billion prepared as Brides and Bridegrooms for Jehovih's higher heavens.

---

[705] Ji'ay is the Panic word and ji'ya is the Gau word for the same thing.

22/9.13. And because it was less than the number of his predecessor, he cried out to Jehovih, bewailing his weakness. And Jehovih answered him, saying: Do not bewail, My Son! You have done a great work. Nor ask that you may remain another dan, for the next will not be so fair a harvest. So God grieved no more, but bestowed his kingdom on his successor; and his Lords did likewise, and so did his sub-Gods and all other persons having protégés. And God called together the Brides and Bridegrooms of Jehovih; and Jehovih sent five great ships of fire down from etherea, and delivered God and his hosts into the emancipated worlds.

CHAPTER 10 Divinity

22/10.1. In the twelve hundredth year after Fragapatti, in the east colony of Haraiti, one Ctusk, a former Lord of Jehovih's host, renounced Jehovih, the Creator, and falsely proclaimed himself Ahura, the All Master; and he took with him three Lords of grade eighty-eight, as well as twelve sub-Gods of grade sixty-four, and one thousand six hundred students of eight hundred years' resurrection, none of whom were less than grade sixty, and were sufficient to pass as Brides and Bridegrooms. And these students took with them thirty-six thousand teachers, factors, physicians and nurses, all of whom were higher than grade forty.

22/10.2. And Ahura appropriated to himself one colony of one hundred and ten million angels, together with the colleges, schools, factories, and all the things belonging in them. And the three Lords took their kingdoms, and by annexation made them part and parcel with Ahura's kingdom. Now these three Lords' kingdoms comprised the largest habitable places of mortals in Vind'yu and Jaffeth, and the greatest heavenly places of angels in the first resurrection.

22/10.3. And Ahura divided up the regions he thus obtained, making confederate heavenly kingdoms, sufficient in number to give place of dominion to his Lords and Gods, and to make sub-Gods out of all the one thousand six hundred students. And after that, Ahura counted his people, and there were more than three billion souls in his heavens!

22/10.4. God sent messengers to Ctusk, who had assumed the name, Ahura'Mazda, admonishing and inquiring: My Lord, whom I have loved, whom by my own hand was crowned in the name of Jehovih, why have you deserted the Father's kingdoms? In what way have you had cause to complain against Jehovih? Or against me, your God? O my son, my Lord, do not say you have gone so far you cannot return! What can you ask of me that I will not grant you? No, even judge me, and if you desire all the heavens and the earth in my place, I will abdicate to you, and become your lowest servant, or whatever you will put upon me.

22/10.5. Ahura returned this answer: Because I have nothing against you, I have alienated myself and my kingdom from you. I do not desire your kingdom, nor even my own. Behold, I looked upon you, and you were pure and holy. I looked upon the kingdoms of heaven and the kingdoms of earth, and they were impure and unholy. Then came certain brother Lords to me, most wise Lords, and they said: A less pure God, a less holy God, would be more efficient. So, I was persuaded to my course.

22/10.6. God replied to this, saying: Behold, we have a Diva! Why did you not speak thus before me, face to face? And your three great Lords were also Divans; and they likewise were silent on the matter. The Div would have decreed whatever was all wise. Because I was in darkness, I did not see your thoughts, nor those of your Lords, and you have heaped shame upon me. How shall I send my record to etherea? Shall I say: Behold, certain Lords consulted clandestinely,[706] and then concluded to overthrow the Creator; and in fact they have gone and set up a kingdom of their own, calling it the All Highest?

22/10.7. Hear me yet, and I will endeavor to speak wisely to you. Some days ago your messengers notified me that you had repudiated Jehovih, saying: There is no All Highest Person; I can make myself high as the highest! Then your messenger gave me a map, saying: Behold, here are the boundaries of the kingdom of Ahura'Mazda, the All Sufficient High God!

22/10.8. I looked over the map, and saw its great extent; and I surmised to myself: He is a great God who can rule over all that! For I knew you and

---

[706] secretly, on the sly, covertly

your education, which is as great as any Lord's in atmospherea. But you know you cannot control even a plateau! Can you raise your hand and stop the a'ji, or the ji'ya, or the nebulae! You can barely change a single current of wind; nor can you cast a drought on any land. And yet you know there are Gods who can do these things by a motion of one finger! How, then, do you dare proclaim yourself an All Sufficient High God?

22/10.9. But I will not rebuke you, for I desire your love and your help. I would win you by any sacrifice I can make. Behold, there is great darkness in heaven and on earth. Whatever I may be short in, I will rebuke myself in after ages. I pray, then, return to me, and make exactions upon me and my kingdoms. With your loss, behold, Diva is broken up. With your dismemberment of heavens, others will follow. Alas, I will not look upon even that which my soul sees. I plead for your love and assistance. Nevertheless, if the All Highest Light, for the All Best Good, shows you that you are right, do not come to me! I know the Great Spirit will sustain me, even though my soul is well nigh crushed to pieces by the loss of so fair a love.

22/10.10. To this Ahura replied: If it were not the wisest, best course to do as I did, how did the thought come to me?

22/10.11. God replied: Because of the long reign of ji'ya, you were inoculated with darkness; even as a mortal, on a rainy day, loses his patience to be wise.

22/10.12. Then Ahura sent the following: I have been patient in my answers; but now I will speak plainly. First of all, you are All Pure, and Most Wise, above all other Gods. For more than two hundred years I have been a faithful Lord to you and your kingdoms. At first the Great Light came to you, and a voice came out of the light! Then I was afraid, and awe-struck. Because I believed you were so near the Creator, your every word and act were worshipful to me.

22/10.13. At last I rebuked myself, saying to myself: Fool! Giving worship to man born of woman! Remember your Creator only!

22/10.14. But the times changed; ji'ya fell upon heaven and earth. Our glorious kingdoms were cast down by the great darkness. Then I reasoned with myself, saying: Behold, when we were in light, Jehovih's Voice spoke to us. When the darkness came, the Voice no longer came. || We sat in the Diva, in the altar circle, praying for light from the Father, but it did not come. And I said: We need the Voice in darkness even more than in light. || For a hundred years we did not see the light of the Voice, nor hear the Voice speak. You have said you heard in your soul! Who is there in heaven or earth that cannot say as much?

22/10.15. In my soul I no longer believe there is an All Person. There are great Gods, a thousand times greater than I; but that is all! Yes, some of those great Gods may have cast the ji'ya upon us. But that is not my concern. There is room for you and your people. Here is room for me and my people.

22/10.16. Jehovih spoke to God, saying: Do not answer Ahura anymore. Behold, I will interpret him to you: He will eventually persuade angels and mortals that it was he who inspired Zarathustra. But he himself does not foresee this. Permit him, therefore, to go his own way; nor should you take sorrow to your soul because of it. Have I not given to all men, from the lowest to the highest, even that which they desired? Behold, I can use even bad men in the far future!

22/10.17. Jehovih said: For a long season Ahura will strive to walk upright, but because he has cut Me off, he will also cut himself off in time to come. Behold, a mortal man strives for riches honorably, and when he is rich, his riches cut him off from Me by the ruin he casts upon his competitors. Nor can he extricate himself. Even so will it be with Ahura: His kingdom and his sub-kingdoms, and his multitude of officers will cause him to enslave hundreds of millions of drujas, and they will draw him into a vortex from which he cannot escape. ||

22/10.18. So God answered Ahura no more; but nevertheless, his heart was full of sorrow. Now when the time of the meeting of Diva came, God foresaw that not more than one-half of them would be present, and he feared the questions that might come up.

22/10.19. But Jehovih said to him: Do not fear, My Son; for even though many more leave you, yet you shall preserve the Diva to the end of this cycle. So it came to pass that Jehovih stilled the tongues of all the Gods and Lords of the Diva in reference to Ahura, even as if they had never known him. And Ahura sent quizzers to different Gods and Lords afterward, to learn what action the Diva had taken in his case. But when he was told that he had not been mentioned, he became angered and swore an oath that he would build the largest of all heavenly kingdoms.

22/10.20. Because of the great darkness on heaven and earth, God sent hope and promise into all the kingdoms, urging his Lords and his sub-Gods to maintain faith, not only within themselves, but also within the hearts of their respective inhabitants. Now, from the time of the secession of Ahura to the next dan would be three hundred years, and God knew this, though the multitudes in heaven and earth did not. And God commanded great recreations and extensive labors in order to prevent further dismemberment. But in the course of a hundred years many were carried away by the extravagant stories told about Ahura's kingdoms being places of great delight, and of ease and idleness.

22/10.21. Ahura's Lords said to him: You shall adorn your kingdom, your throne and your capital; Ctusk shall be the largest and most ornamental of all places in the universe; and our subkingdoms shall be places of great delight. And Ahura was persuaded, and so, began his self-glorification, and his Lords with him.

22/10.22. And in another hundred years Ahura had withdrawn and annexed to him the following provinces in heaven, along with their sub-Gods: Etyisiv, with seventy million souls; Howwak, with one hundred million souls; Hyn, with twenty million souls; D'nayotto, with eighty million souls; Erefrovish, with one hundred and ninety million souls; the whole of the kingdom of Gir-ak-shi, six hundred million souls; the whole of the kingdom of Soo'fwa, with eight hundred million souls. And all of these confederated in the lower heavens, making the kingdom of Ctusk the central kingdom, with Ahura as MAZDA IN CHIEF.

22/10.23. This reduced the Diva to seven members, but these remained faithful. And God kept up the standard of resurrection for one hundred years more. And then Jehovih sent a region of dan to heaven and earth, and the Most High heavenly hosts descended in fire-ships and took God and his harvest up to Jehovih. And with all the misfortune that befell God and his Lords, there were, nevertheless, six billion Brides and Bridegrooms to Jehovih raised up to the higher heavens.

22/10.24. Now when the etherean hosts came for the resurrection, knowing the darkness that was upon the lower heaven and the earth, they sent otevans, with heralds and trumpeters around the earth, proclaiming the resurrection at hand, and asking all who chose, to go to Mouru, in Haraiti. And the word was whispered throughout Ahura's kingdom: What! Then, in truth, there must be higher heavens than this! Alas, had we been faithful till now, we would have been Brides and Bridegrooms! || So strong was this disaffection for Ahura, that five of his Lords broke membership, and re-affiliated with God and his kingdoms.

22/10.25. And thus matters stood when God's successor came to the throne.

CHAPTER 11 Divinity

22/11.1. The next dan was five hundred years, and God and his heavenly kingdoms prospered under Jehovih. But as to the Lords' kingdoms on earth, and mortal kingdoms and empires, not much light was manifested in them.

22/11.2. For Ahura, who had falsely taken and was known by the name Ahura'Mazda, established Lords to rule over mortals. And these Lords were in direct opposition to God's Lords; for the latter taught the higher heavens and the All Person, Jehovih, or Ormazd, according to the language of mortals. But Ahura's Lords taught only one heavenly kingdom, which was Ahura's, called Ctusk, the All Holy Highest Heaven.

22/11.3. God's Lords inspired mortals to everlasting resurrection; Ahura's Lords inspired mortals to Ahura's kingdom, and there the end. And since mortals had built temples for their priests (rab'bahs), who were gifted with su'is, the spirits congregated in the temples, and often appeared in sar'gis, teaching openly their differing doctrines. And the ashars that labored for Ahura extolled the glory and the delight of Ctusk, and the wonderful majesty and power of Ahura. But the ashars of God's hosts inspired and taught of the Great Spirit, Unapproachable.

22/11.4. For five hundred years God's hosts were confronted with this opposition; and it came to pass that mortals, especially in Vind'yu, were divided into two great classes of worshippers. And just before God's successor came into dominion, he propounded the matter in Diva; upon which all the members spoke at great length. Afterward, Div decreed:

22/11.5. Whatever is worshipped, having comprehensible form or figure, is an idol. He, who worships an idol, whether of stone or wood, or whether it is a man or an angel, sins against the Creator. || This was given to all of God's Lords, and by them to the ashars, and commanded to be taught to mortals by inspiration and otherwise.

22/11.6. When the time of dan came there were seven billion Brides and Bridegrooms raised up to Jehovih's emancipated worlds, and the succeeding God and Lords came into dominion under more favorable auspices,[707] but which were not to continue long.

22/11.7. The Diva had extended to fourteen members; and God's Lords had succeeded in securing kingdoms in the principal parts of Jaffeth, Vind'yu and Arabin'ya. On the other hand, the emissaries of Ahura, the false, had been most active in extending the kingdom of their idol. Ahura was most cunning with the last Divan act: Instead of interdicting it, he altered it, so it read as follows: Whatever is worshipped, having comprehensible form or figure, is an idol. He who worships an idol, whether it is made of stone or wood, or whether it is a man or an angel, sins against the All Highest, who is personated in Ahura'Mazda, the Holy Begotten Son of all created creations!

22/11.8. And next, Ahura decided to found a second heaven, decreeing to his emissaries as follows: Behold Gir-ak-shi, the heavenly region above the lands of Heleste! There I will build a new heaven, greater than all other heavens, except Ctusk. And when Gir-ak-shi is well founded, I will people it with many millions of mighty angels, Gods and Lords. And my hosts shall descend to the corporeal earth; to the lands of Par'si'e and Arabin'ya, and they shall obsess mortals day and night, and inspire them to go to Heleste,[708] where they shall build great cities and kingdoms devoted to me and my hosts.

22/11.9. And when these things are fulfilled, behold, I will send my hosts to Uropa, and there also build heavenly kingdoms and mortal kingdoms; and when these are established, behold, I will send my hosts into other countries, one after another, until my heavenly kingdoms embrace all places, and until all the earth is mine.

22/11.10. For I will be God over all, and you who labor with me shall be my Lords and sub-Gods forever. And my kingdoms and your kingdoms shall be bestowed with glories and ornaments, like never before. And the Gods of other worlds shall not be permitted to come against me or mine to carry away my people. They shall no longer flatter them, calling them Brides and Bridegrooms to Jehovih, a thing, none can see or comprehend. ||

22/11.11. And Ahura and his emissaries went to work to carry out these decrees, and in two hundred years they had inspired the Par'si'e'ans and the Arabin'yans to emigrate by tens of thousands to the land of Heleste,[709] which was inhabited by druks and wanderers, full of wickedness. Ahura inspired his immigrants to fall upon the native druks, and destroy them. By which came to pass, that which Jehovih spoke in Mouru, saying: Those who cannot be raised by persuasion may be aroused by less scrupulous masters.

22/11.12 And while Ahura's hosts were slaying the druks of Heleste by tens of thousands, God's heavenly hosts were receiving their spirits and conducting them away to other atmospherean regions.

22/11.13. These, then, were the divisions of mortals on earth at this time: First, the I'hins, who were the original Faithists. And they were capable of prophecies and miracles to such an extent that all other people called them the sacred people. Nor did the great warriors of other nations and peoples molest them. The I'hins lived secluded and separate from all other people. Nevertheless, they were the seed of everlasting life on the earth, and the foundation for raising up prophets and seers for other peoples. Even as Zarathustra's mother was of the I'hins, so was it with all men and women born into the world having su'is and sar'gis. For being near Jehovih, they had faith in Him, and Him only. The second race, equally ancient, was the druks,

[707] good conditions, favorable signs

[708] Par'si'e is located in the southern part of Heleste of the i018 Post-Flood World Map (p.228); so "Heleste" here probably refers to the rest of Heleste.

[709] In another place it is shown that the languages [of Heleste] were Parsee, Indian [India], Chinese and Arabic. –Ed.

the barbarian hordes, incapable of inspiration, except for their stomachs' sake. And though they were told a thousand times: Behold, you have a spiritual body! || They neither understood, nor cared, and forgot it a moment later. And though it was said to them: Behold, there is a Great Spirit! || They did not hear, nor understand, nor heeded the words. The third race was the I'huans,[710] born between the I'hins and the druks. To this race, in its early days, a commandment was given by God not to marry with the druks, and they had maintained that law among themselves by the sign of the circumcision. || The following, then, was the first beginning of persecution against Faithists in Jehovih:

22/11.14. When Ahura usurped his heavenly kingdom, and appointed guardian angels over mortals, he was determined to leave nothing undone in order to overthrow the doctrine of Jehovih, the All Person. So he decreed as follows:

22/11.15. Since by the mark of the circumcision, they have pride in being Faithists, I will not have circumcision. After the third generation (one hundred years) whoever has this mark upon him is my enemy. He shall be pursued, and no profit shall fall to his lot. Do not permit little children to be maimed for my sake; rather let them be circumcised in heart.[711]

22/11.16. And Ahura put no restriction upon his mortal followers marrying, and so it came to pass that those druks not slain in Heleste married with the worshippers of Ahura.

22/11.17. And about this same period of time Jehovih brought the earth into a light region for two hundred years. And when the Diva was in session, Jehovih's Voice spoke to Div, saying: Do not let My Sons be cast down because of the sins of Ahura; rather be wise and appropriate from his wickedness that which will be good in the end. For, as it was not lawful for My people to marry with the druks, behold, Ahura has made a law on his own account against circumcision, and it shall come to pass that by their (Ahura and his cohorts) sins, even druks shall be raised up to learn of Me and My kingdoms.

22/11.18. And it came to pass that a fourth race rose up in the world, and it was mongrel, being dark and short and less noble. The I'huans were red, and brown, and tall and majestic; the I'hins small, and white, and yellow. And Jehovih put these marks upon His peoples so that the races could be read in thousands of years.[712]

22/11.19. Ahura perceived this. One of his Lords said to him: Behold, the marks of su'is are written! Then Ahura sought to disprove Jehovih in this. He said:

22/11.20. Behold, there are two senses to all men, the es and the corpor. When one is in abeyance the other acts. This is su'is. Call together your companions, and find a remedy; for I will prove all things in heaven and earth.

---

[710] Here we can understand that the Ghans were considered to be a division of the I'huan, that is, Ghans were the advanced part of the I'huans, being the leading edge toward the perfect human. And now in kosmon, the Ghans are no longer the cutting edge, as man is still progressing, ever drawing closer to becoming perfected in his order. More is said later in Oahspe regarding this.

[711] This Vedic expression, it seems to me, signifies: Rather let them [be willing to] have their hearts cut out than to [worship falsehood (meaning the Creator)], etc. –Ed.

[Or: Rather than cutting away part of their body, let them cut out falsehood from their hearts (meaning stopping worship of Jehovih).

Ahura also seems to be saying: Let my chosen be known by their goodness of heart (an inner mark) rather than be known by an outer mark (circumcision). Here we can see Ahura's craft in using this edict so as to appear compassionate in order to ingratiate himself upon mortals; for, rather than to protect children, his real motives were to make a law against Faithists and to prove his wisdom greater than Jehovih's.]

[712] Again, the reader should keep in mind that these traits indicate the common case, being the statistical mode of each race, or overall impression, some seven to eight thousand years ago. Accordingly, while painting with the broad brush of generalities is undoubtedly useful and has a tenor of accuracy, still, one should avoid oversimplifying, lest one fails to remember the non-average cases, or, with unwarranted presumption of infallibility, one rigidly applies the stereotype to individual cases. See elsewhere in this Oahspe regarding the races of man including color.

22/11.21. For fifty years Ahura and his hosts tried by other means[713] to have a great prophet and seer born into the world, but failed. Ahura said: I know the way of the loo'is: They decoy[714] the I'hin men to go with the I'huan damsels. But I have sworn there is no Jehovih; how, then, can I go to the sacred people? And, after all, such a prophet might prove treacherous to my kingdom. So Ahura commanded his emissaries to weigh the matter for another fifty years, and then to solve the problem.

22/11.22. So Ahura's emissaries inspired thousands of experiments to be made, by which a prophet or seer could be made among the mongrels. And Jehovih allowed them to discover that by pressing down the front brain of infants they could be made capable of su'is. And infants were strapped on boards, and another board strapped on the forehead to press the head flat; and every day the headboard was re-strapped tighter than the day before, until the forehead, which holds the corporeal judgment, was pressed flat, and the judgment of the brain driven up into light-perceiving regions at the top of the head.[715]

22/11.23. Ahura thus raised up prophets and seers, and they were willing instruments in his hands. And he sent tens of thousands of angels into all the divisions of the earth, teaching this to mortals, thus laying down the foundation for his grand scheme of reducing heaven and earth into his own kingdoms.

22/11.24. Jehovih spoke in the Diva, saying: Permit even this. The druks will heed what one of their own people says as a seer, more than if the same thing were said a hundred times over by an I'hin.

CHAPTER 12 Divinity

22/12.1. The next resurrection was six billion souls, and God and his Lords and his sub-Gods had maintained the Diva, and maintained all the orders of heaven, and the divisions and kingdoms, except those that had confederated with Ahura and his kingdoms. And God and his Lords had preserved their own colleges, schools, factories, hospitals and nurseries, as well as their standard in the temples with mortals. And as to mortals who remained Faithist, that is, the I'huan race preserved in purity, God and his Lords and ashars held command over them for the glory of Jehovih.

22/12.2. But over the mongrels, who were multiplying fast on the earth, Ahura and his Lords and ashars held command. But alas for the grade of Ahura's host in heaven! In less than one thousand years he had abolished his colleges and schools, except what pertained to acquiring knowledge of the earth and atmospherea. He did not teach his people to look higher for other worlds, and in this he began the work that was later to be his own downfall.

22/12.3. Jehovih had said: Whoever fails to provide a philosophy for the endless acquisition of knowledge, dams up the running waters I have made. Let Ahura teach what he will; the time will come when he will be obliged to find an outlet for My created beings. And rather than acknowledge Me in My Person, he will profess to send souls back into earth to be reincarnated.

22/12.4. Ahura's heavenly kingdoms numbered more than six billion souls, and half of them were little better than drujas, being slaves to certain masters, doing whatever they were told without knowing, or desiring to know, the reason for it.

22/12.5. As yet there were six hundred years to pass before another dawn of dan,[716] in which God, his Lords and their people had faith that Jehovih's hosts would come from on high to help deliver heaven and earth out of darkness.

22/12.6. On the other hand, Ahura, although having been taught the cycles in his early education, spread the word abroad in heaven and earth that there were no cycles; that, as things are, they had always been, and would continue to be.

22/12.7. So, as much as God's hosts prophesied a coming light, Ahura and his hosts prophesied that nothing of the kind would come. Ahura, moreover, sent the following order to his Lords, to be taught in heaven and earth, as follows: Am I not He Who inspired Zarathustra, the All Pure? Did I not speak to him, face to face? Are all created things not My own? Who, then, knows except Me if I will light up the world again? Behold, I am the Personation[717] of Ormazd, Who was VOIDANCE, but now is Me,

---

[713] i.e., without resorting to use of an I'hin

[714] lure, entice, trap, ensnare

[715] for examples, see images i023 and i024 p.435

[716] i.e., a new dan'ha cycle

Ahura'Mazda. In Me only is life and death and resurrection. Whoever calls: Ahura'Mazda, Ahura'Mazda! is Mine, and within My keeping. Do not allow your judgment to be warped by prophets who hope for impossible things. ||

22/12.8. Now, in the eightieth year of the final dan, Ahura's many heavenly kingdoms began to be disturbed by his sub-Gods' lack of advancement, and so, sixty of them congregated together, and, by messenger, appealed to Ahura, saying:

22/12.9. In reverence to you, O you All Highest God! Many hundreds of years we have served you. And we have paid you tribute whenever you required it of us. We have helped to adorn your capital, Ctusk; we have laid your streets with diamonds and pearls, we have built your mansions with precious gems. And as to your throne, what one of us is here who has not contributed to glorify it before you? Yes, in all ways we have been most loyal and tributary to you.

22/12.10. Nor are we unmindful of our own wisdom. We remember your arguments of old. Before seceding from your God you said to him: Behold, you have long promised we would be raised to more exalted kingdoms, but, behold, two hundred years have elapsed, and there is no advancement. || This is the argument you used for seceding from your God's kingdoms. Behold, we have now served you and your kingdoms more than a thousand years. We come to you to know how we can now serve you so that you may exalt us into kingdoms commensurate with[718] our wisdom and power?

22/12.11. To this Ahura replied, saying: Most humble and well-meaning Lords and sub-Gods, why did you not come to me, face to face? Why have you consorted in private? Was not my capital, and before my throne, the proper place for your argument? Had you suggested any way by which advancement for you was possible, I would have answered your demands.

22/12.12. But his Lords and sub-Gods did not come before him, but sent this answer: As you promised us advancement provided we served you, so we likewise promised our ashars, and our marshals and captains. Now they come to us, saying: We have served for hundreds of years; give us preferment. But we have nothing to give. Do not think, O God, that we are unwise, or that we hunger and come begging; or that diadems, gems or costly thrones would satisfy us. We know what you have to give—promises! We know every corner of your vast kingdom, and that all places are full, and that you cannot exalt us. Why, then, should we have spoken before the throne in Ctusk? Would not our voices merely breed mischief among your other Gods and Lords? Rather let us err in our proceeding, bringing just punishment upon ourselves, than injure you and your kingdoms. Hear us then, O Ahura'Mazda:

22/12.13. Where does the desire for endless advancement come from, if this heaven is all? If a little knowledge gives power, why then is great knowledge not desirable? We have destroyed our great colleges, saying: You must not go higher than us. Remember, O Ahura, we were students under the Faithists' God and Lords when you seceded; and you said to us: Behold the long training of your course; a curriculum of a thousand years! Come with me; I will give you kingdoms at once!

22/12.14. So we came to you, and we were suddenly puffed up with great pride. Behold now, we look abroad and the same stars shine upon us. We have not visited them. We do not know how to go so far. The countless etherean worlds lay beyond ours. We are told that they are habitable. We do not know. We have no knowledge enabling us to get away from these heavens; except, indeed, back to the filthy earth.

22/12.15. To this Ahura replied, saying: It is plain to me you are beside yourselves.[719] This heaven is good enough. If there are higher heavens, let them come or stay. I do not go to them. But, in truth, with your present convictions, I would be an unwise God not to grant you dismissal from my kingdoms.

22/12.16. This ended the matter, and the sixty sub-Gods then deliberated on their course, and finally sent the following address to God, in Mouru:

22/12.17. In reverence to you, God of the Faithists in Jehovih: We have had sub-kingdoms, and know our rank is beneath yours. But we are reaching outward and onward; we submit our cause

[717] voidance coming forth as a person, being the embodiment

[718] corresponding to, sufficient for, equal to

[719] distraught, agitated, unable to think clearly

to you. First, then, there are sixty of us, of the rank of sub-Gods, and we hold seven hundred million subjects. Disaffection has risen between ourselves and Ahura'Mazda, from whom we are alienated. But whether we shall unite our hosts into a new kingdom of our own, or affiliate with some mighty God—that is our question.

22/12.18. What preferment can you give to us if we turn our subjects over to you?

22/12.19. God answered them, saying: Brothers, hear me patiently, and consider my words. First, then, I am not God of the Faithists, or of any other people, but God of the locality that was assigned to me by the Father, through His Son. Nor can you give your subjects to me; for by my service to Jehovih I can have nothing, and, least of all, my brothers and sisters.

22/12.20. Moreover, I can give you no preferment; I have nothing, neither to give nor to sell. When the Father gives me wisdom and power, I impart them to others. Besides, until you have also learned to know that you have nothing, neither subjects nor jewels, also desiring nothing, except wisdom and strength to impart to others, how can you hope to gain admittance into my places of learning?

22/12.21. And lastly, since you have kingdoms of your own already, raise them up, and thus prove to me your just merit.

22/12.22. To this the confederated Gods replied: What do you mean? That Gods and angels must labor for others, rather than themselves, forever, and receive nothing for it?

22/12.23. God answered them: Even so; except you shall receive an abundance of happiness, and it will endure forever! || Here the matter ended for two whole years; and the sub-Gods did not understand the plan of Jehovih's kingdoms. But their kingdoms were out of sorts, having no head; and hundreds of thousands of their subjects were deserting them and returning down to the corporeal earth, becoming wanderers and drujas.

22/12.24. Finally the sub-Gods again appealed to God in Mouru, inquiring as follows: Is a God not a God, whether he is for another or for himself? Behold, we have helped to build up Ahura; he is a mighty God! If we affiliate with you, we will labor to build you up also. Yes, we will adorn your throne and your great heavenly city. But since we have been sub-Gods we do not desire to enter your service as menials and servants. What, then, shall we do, so that both you and ourselves may have honor and glory?

22/12.25. God answered them, saying: You cannot serve me; I have no servants. Serve Jehovih only. Behold, we are all brothers, being sons of the same Great Spirit. As for building me up, it is sufficient for me that He Who created me will build me up according to my just deserts. As for adorning my throne, you can only bring substance to it from the lower kingdoms, which I do not desire. Why would you adorn the heavenly city of Mouru? Behold, it is merely a resting place on the great journey to the kingdoms of endless light. In a few hundred years, at most, not only I but my hosts will rise from this place, never to return.

22/12.26. And lastly, to be a self-God, like Ahura, is to own all things possible, and hold on to them; to be a God as I am, is to own nothing, and to retain nothing; but to be forever giving away all one receives. Did I not say to you before: Begin with your own hosts and exalt them. Because you asked for subjects, behold, the Father gave to you. Do not think that He will permit you now to cast them aside or barter them off. Neither shall you allow them to become wanderers, nor return back to the earth as drujas. To the extent that you raise up the kingdoms that have been entrusted to you, so will you also be raised up.

22/12.27. Nevertheless, if you desire to affiliate with Jehovih's kingdoms, the way is open to you; and your first labor would be to gather together all your own hosts, and to labor among them, teaching them wisdom, strength and individuality, equal with yourselves; and when the lowest of them all is risen so, then you can enter the kingdoms of the Father. As you have had the profit of your subjects for hundreds of years, return now to them service for service. Jehovih is Justice!

22/12.28. The sub-Gods made no answer to this for awhile, but Jehovih moved upon their hearts, and they perceived wisdom and justice, and they repented, bitterly bewailing the loss of the thousand years in which they had espoused kingdoms. But they did not have sufficient power or learning to extricate themselves; so they petitioned God for more light. And so, God affiliated them, and appointed Vishnu as Lord to them and their hosts.

22/12.29. And Vishnu took three hundred thousand teachers, captains, physicians, nurses and laborers, and went to them in Maitraias, a heavenly place to the west of Vind'yu, and there established a Lordly division, with messengers connecting them to Mouru, in Haraiti. And Vishnu sent his captains with sufficient forces, under command of the sub-Gods, to arrest those who had become wandering spirits, or had returned to the earth as drujas. And while they were on this duty, Vishnu organized his Lord-dom, and this was the first Lord-dom established in heaven, which is to say, as mortals on earth have military stations, so was the Lord-dom of Vishnu.

22/12.30. Jehovih's Voice had spoken to God in Diva, saying: Behold, the time is coming when the sub-kingdoms of Ahura, the false, will begin to revolt. And they have billions of slaves who will strive to go back to the earth to dwell with mortals. They dwell in darkness, and you shall not allow them to regain the earth, lest the races of men go down in darkness, even as before the submersion of Pan. For which reason, you shall establish a Lord-dom, and raise a sufficient army to shield the inhabitants of the earth. And you shall make Vishnu your Lord in My behalf.

22/12.31. When it was known in Ctusk, the heavenly place of Ahura, that sixty sub-Gods, with their hosts, had affiliated with Jehovih's kingdoms, general disobedience to Ahura was manifested by the remaining sub-Gods, of whom there were yet more than eight hundred. And these had within their dominions more than two billion angels, all slaves, who had light from no other heavenly place than the small precinct where they had been kept in drudgery for hundreds of years.

22/12.32. The Voice of Jehovih came to God, saying: My Son, take advantage of the seed of disaffection in Ahura's kingdom. Send an otevan of great power throughout the heavenly kingdoms. And you shall put trumpeters in the otevan, and they shall prophesy the dawn of dan within two hundred years.

22/12.33. God perceived, and he had his workmen build an otevan of great power; and he provided trumpeters, and sent them forth, saying to them: You shall travel ten years in the heavenly places around the whole earth, prophesying: In less than two hundred years Jehovih's etherean hosts are coming. Prepare for the resurrection; His kingdoms are open for the weary; His Lords and Gods will give you rest!

22/12.34. Ahura summoned his Council of false Gods, hoping they might invent a remedy to counteract so great a prophecy. And he and his Council sat forty days and forty nights in their heavenly capital; but there was no high light among them, merely each one giving his opinion. But at the end of forty days Ahura resolved upon the following method: to send a prophecy of his own.

22/12.35. Accordingly he had an otevan built, and sent trumpeters forth with these words: I, Ahura'Mazda, Only Son of the All Nothing Presence, personated in My Very Self, proclaim from My All Highest Heavenly Judgment Seat! Hear My words, O Gods, and tremble! Hear Me, O angels, and fall down! Hear Me, O mortals, and bow down to My decrees. Behold, I sent My fire-ship, prophesying that in less than two hundred years I would come in a dawn of dan! But you did not obey; you were defiant before Me! Then I swore an oath against the whole world! You shall know My power! Then I came down out of My holy, high heaven; and I have already come. Now is the dawn of dan! I send My trumpeters first; after them come My lashers and enchainers,[720] whose captain is Daevas, whose God is Anra'mainyus. I will have Mine, and I will cast into everlasting torments, druks and drujas by the thousands and tens of thousands.

22/12.36. Ahura's Gods had become acquainted with him during the hundreds and hundreds of years, and they no longer trembled at his commandments. In their hearts they knew he could not do what he professed; they knew his prophecies were vain boastings. Indeed, his very trumpeters did not believe what they proclaimed.

CHAPTER 13 Divinity

Jehovih prepares a way for the birth of Abram, Po, Brahma and Ea-wah-tah[721]

22/13.1. In the one hundred and eightieth year preceding the dawn of dan; that is to say, two thousand nine hundred and twenty years after

[720] Lashers are those who use the whip. Enchainers are those who bind others using chains and shackles; those who fetter or manacle.

[721] known in early kosmon, through legends, as Hiawatha, as well as other names

Fragapatti and Zarathustra, Jehovih sent swift messengers with six thousand etherean loo'is from the Nirvanian fields of Chen-gotha [Jen-go-ha – Ed.] in etherea.

22/13.2. And the swift messengers brought these words with them: Greeting to you, God of the red star and her heavens, in the name of Jehovih! By the love and wisdom of Cpenta-armij, Nirvanian Goddess of Haot-saiti, we speak in the Father's name. Peace and joy to you, O God, and to your sub-Gods and Lords, and Lord Gods and Goddesses. One hundred and eighty years of darkness will now come upon your kingdoms. And then the darkness will go away, and dawn will come. And during the darkness, behold, the nations of the earth will go down in great darkness.

22/13.3. But the light of the Father's Presence will not be destroyed. A little seed shall endure among mortals. In order for that seed to be ready for the labor of your Goddess, who will come in that day, she sends here with us two thousand etherean loo'is for Vind'yu; two thousand for Jaffeth, and two thousand for Arabin'ya.

22/13.4. And your Goddess decrees that you shall appoint to these loo'is one of your high raised Gods, and he shall go and labor with them.

22/13.5. And the business of this, your God, and of these, my loo'is, shall be to raise up heirs and followers, who shall be grown to maturity when I come. For through these that they raise up, I will deliver the Father's chosen out of the afflictions that will be upon them in that day.

22/13.6. To this, God replied: In the name of Jehovih, greeting and love to Cpenta-armij, Goddess of Haot-saiti. I receive your loo'is with joy, and I appoint to them my favored God, Yima, God of a thousand years' tuition, namesake of Yima, son of Vivanho, the Sweet Singer.

22/13.7. So the swift messengers, with due ceremonies, left the six thousand etherean loo'is and departed. And God sent messengers to Yima, commanding him to come to Mouru at once, deputing[722] his assistant God to take his place and to retain it until dawn. So Yima appeared presently before the throne of God, and the latter instructed him in all that had been commanded from on high. And Yima sent word to his former kingdom for a thousand of his attendants, and they also came. Meanwhile, Yima conferred with the loo'is, who explained to him all that they required. And after this they provided a piedmazr, and descended to the earth, to Jaffeth, Vind'yu and Arabin'ya.

22/13.8. And Yima stationed his piedmazr midway between the three countries, in the first plateau above the clouds, and called the place Hored, in honor of the first heavenly kingdom on the earth. And when he had founded his place and named it, he sent word to God, Jehovih's Son, who gave him five hundred messengers, mostly college students. And God gave them, to deliver, heine currents,[723] so the ethereans could be supplied with regimen of their own order.

22/13.9. Yima made the watches twenty-four hours duration, changing at dawn of sunrise every morning, half on and half off. And he called in all ashars from the regions of mortals where he planned to labor; and when they had assembled in Hored, he addressed them, saying:

22/13.10. Behold, it is still one hundred and eighty years till dawn of dan. In that time Cpenta-armij, Goddess of Haot-saiti, situated in the Nirvanian fields of Chen-gotha, will come in the Father's name, and with wisdom and power!

22/13.11. But until that time, alas, great darkness will be in heaven and earth, especially in these regions. And it shall come to pass that the mongrels, the worshippers of Ahura'Mazda, will triumph in these lands. They will build great cities and kingdoms, and they will rule over the I'huans to great injury. But the druks will be redeemed to everlasting life during this period; for the mongrels will wed with them, and their progeny will be capable of receiving light [es light –ed.], even in mortality.

22/13.12. Nevertheless these mongrels will be great savages, and there will be cannibals over all these three great lands. And those who are slain in battle will be cut up and put in vessels with salt, and thus their flesh will be preserved for food.

22/13.13. But because the I'huans, the Zarathustrians, will not war, the mongrels will enslave them, except for those who escape to the forests. And between celibacy and torments, the Zarathustrians will have great suffering and

[722] delegating, assigning, committing, deputizing

[723] etherean food. –1891 glossary

bondage, and many of them will be discouraged and lose faith in the Creator.

22/13.14. But in order for their seed to be preserved and delivered out of bondage, you shall raise up many who are capable of su'is; and in the time of dawn they shall be rescued from their enemies. Behold, present here are etherean loo'is who will go with you throughout these lands and survey the people, and also provide for the great lights who shall lead the people.

22/13.15. After Yima thus instructed the ashars in a general way, he handed them over to the loo'is, who divided them into companies of thousands, and each and every loo'is had one company of ashars. And when this was completed they departed out of Hored, going to their various places.

22/13.16. And eleven days after that, behold, a'ji began to fall on heaven and earth. The belt of meteoris gave up its stones, and showers of them rained down on the earth, and the sun became like a red ball of fire, and it remained so for one hundred and sixty-six years. And the peoples of Arabin'ya, Vind'yu and Jaffeth, fell from holiness; the Zarathustrians gave up celibacy by hundreds of thousands, and married, and begot children in great numbers; many women giving birth to twenty, and some even to twenty-five children. And some men were the fathers of seventy children, and not a few even of a hundred. And the Zarathustrians, even the Faithists with the mark of circumcision, went and married with the mongrels, and they with the druks, so that the foundations of caste were broken up.

22/13.17. So great was the power of a'ji that even the I'hins often broke their vows and lived clandestinely with the world's people, begetting offspring in great numbers, not eligible to enter their sacred cities. And yet mortals did not see the a'ji; but they saw their cities and temples sinking, as it were, into the ground; yet in truth they were not sinking, but were covered by the a'ji falling and condensing.

22/13.18. Jehovih had said: What I give that grows the corpor, inspires man to corpor; what I give that grows the es, inspires man to es. || And in the days of a'ji, neither angels nor men can enthuse mortals with spiritual things; only those who are organically grown in spirit can withstand the a'ji.

CHAPTER 14 Divinity

22/14.1. Jehovih said: When a'ji comes near a dawn of dan, let My loo'is be swift in duty; far-seeing in the races of men. I not only break up the old foundations of temples and cities in those days, but the foundations of the abuse of the caste of men. My Voice is upon the races of men. Today I say: Preserve the caste of men; marry thus and so, every one to their own line. For I perceive it is wisdom. Tomorrow I say: I will have no caste, for the races are becoming impoverished in blood; marry here, marry there! And I give them a'ji, and their desires break all bounds, and I raise them up giants and strong limbed.

22/14.2. But in those days My loo'is shall fly swiftly and with great power, so that a seed may be preserved for Me and My kingdoms. I do not come for one race alone; but to all men; as by My Spirit I created them all alive, so likewise My hand is over them to all eternity.

22/14.3. And when the shower of a'ji is over and gone, I send My high-raised Gods and Goddesses to gather together My flocks, and to proclaim to them anew, My Wisdom and Power. And those who have been selected and preserved by My loo'is are the foundations of My new order. ||

22/14.4. Ahura took advantage of the age of darkness to sow disbelief in Jehovih, which he broadcast over earth and heaven, and to gather in his harvest for the glory of his own kingdom. And when war, murder and lust were thus reigning on earth, Ahura decreed to his Lords, and they decreed to his ashars, and they decreed to mortals: That all that was required of any man or woman was not celibacy, nor carrying the alms-bowl, nor any sacrifice at all; but that saying prayers to Ahura'Mazda, and to his Lords, and to wish them here with praise, was sufficient for all situations; and that by doing so, on the third day after death they would ascend and dwell in Ahura's paradise. || However this was not true, for Ahura's emissaries caught the newborn spirits, and made slaves of them, commanding them to gather regimen and substance for the glory of Ahura's heavenly kingdoms.

22/14.5. In the fortieth year before dawn, the Voice of the Father came to God, saying: Mouru is becoming uninhabitable; Haraiti shall be moved into the earth; Zeredho shall be no more. Do not go to Ahura with this prophecy; he has denied My Voice; he will not hear. But I will take the foundations of Ctusk from under him, and it shall go down into the earth.

22/14.6. But you, O God, My Son, I forewarn; for your kingdoms and your upraised sons and daughters shall be preserved through the darkness. They shall become My Brides and Bridegrooms; I will prepare a place for them in great glory.

22/14.7. Call the Diva together, and I will speak before them, and My Voice shall be proclaimed throughout all these heavens, except in the heavens of Ahura, where My Voice shall not be proclaimed.

22/14.8. So God called the Diva, and they came and sat in the sacred circle, and the light, like a sun, gathered above God's head, saying: Come up above Haraiti; behold, I have broken up meteoris; I have fashioned a new plateau in the firmament above, upon which all things are plentiful for heavenly kingdoms. Come with your Lord Gods, and with your Lords and Gods, and I will show you. And when you have seen it, you shall possess the place and begin its inhabitation, taking there your hosts of billions.

22/14.9. When the Light ceased speaking, it took wing and rose upward, and Div and Diva rose also and followed after; and thus Jehovih led them to the plateau; hence it was called Craoshivi, signifying, THE LIGHT HAS CHOSEN.

22/14.10. And God and his sub-Gods possessed the place, and laid the foundation for inhabitation; and after that he and his Lords and Gods returned and counseled on the manner of removal.

22/14.11. At this time there were four billion Faithists belonging to God's kingdoms, most wise and upright, full of purity and good works. But God and his Lords, and Lord Gods, did not have sufficient power to remove so many angels, especially as many of them were still below grade fifty, and so were inclined downward more than upward. So, after due counsel, God decreed to build an avalanza capable of transporting two hundred thousand at a time, and to begin by removing the highest grades.

22/14.12. And God foresaw of his own wisdom that he should send to Vishnu and his Lord-dom an all-sufficient force to protect the mortals of Vind'yu, Jaffeth and Arabin'ya, which were soon to be flooded by the hosts of Ahura being cast down on the earth. Accordingly he sent for Vishnu, and when Vishnu was before the throne of God, the latter told him all the words Jehovih had said in regard to Ahura and his kingdoms and their ultimate precipitation to the earth; and told him about the new plateau, Craoshivi, where the Light had conducted them. And he further commanded Vishnu to return to his own place, Maitraias, and survey the dominions, and estimate what force he would require in order to protect the mortals of those three earth divisions.

22/14.13. Vishnu replied: As to the latter part of your commandment, O God, I have already accomplished it. For I feared these things might come to pass, and I provided accordingly. The number I will require of and above grade eighty will be six hundred million! For, I must have at least one angel for each and every mortal.

22/14.14. God answered him, saying: You shall have eight hundred million! Upon hearing this, Vishnu took leave and returned to his own place, Maitraias. God immediately sent forth selectors with power; and they went into all the colleges and factories, and other places of Jehovih's kingdoms, and selected out the eight hundred million angels required by Vishnu, and God sent them to Maitraias as soon as possible. ||

22/14.15. Now, of the six hundred million angels taken to Maitraias, who had been subjects to sub-Gods, besides a hundred million that had strayed off, becoming wanderers and drujas, Vishnu found thirty million above grade fifty, and these he appropriated at once, to work in concert with the sub-Gods in building schools, colleges, factories, and all of the required places for the elevation of man. When he had thus established order, he called together the sub-Gods and said to them:

22/14.16. Do not think I am about to leave you on your own; I am not. But you are not mine to keep; nor are your hosts mine. You asked for them in the first place, and Jehovih gave them to you. I have restored order; the time has now come when one of you must be chief captain over all the rest, and he shall apportion the rest of you according to his highest light. Choose, therefore, your captain, and I will give him a judgment seat and badge of office, and together you shall comprise a Council. For I will make this a kingdom when the majority has passed grade fifty.

22/14.17. The sub-Gods deliberated for eight days, but, perceiving the responsibility of leadership, not one of them would accept the place. So they came before Vishnu, saying: Release us, we pray, and raise up another person, and he shall be our captain.

22/14.18. Vishnu said: A certain man and woman married, and they prayed to Jehovih for offspring, and He answered their prayer, and they had many children. And now, when they perceived their responsibility to the children, they said to the Great Spirit: We pray that You give the responsibility to some other persons. || What do you think of them?

22/14.19. Now I say to you, Jehovih heard their first prayer, but not the second. If I serve Jehovih, how, then, shall I answer your prayers and appoint another person in your place? It is a wise man who does not rush not into leadership and responsibility; but he is a good man, indeed, who, having gotten in, says: Now I will go ahead in Jehovih's wisdom and power with all my might. || The Gods who are above us come to such a man and help him! Go, then, once more into Council, and appoint a chief captain.

22/14.20. Barely had Vishnu finished saying this, when the sub-Gods perceived what was meant by the higher light, and the whole sixty held up their hands, saying: I will serve You, O Jehovih! Give me whatever You will!

22/14.21. With that, Vishnu commanded them to appoint the one with the highest grade, which they did. And it fell upon Subdga; and accordingly, Subdga was made captain-in-chief of Maitraias, with rank sixty on the first list. So Vishnu created a judgment seat for Subdga and gave him a badge of office. And the other sub-Gods were made captains of divisions, and numbered according to their assignment, and none of them were humiliated before their former subjects, but became trainers and disciplinarians in new fields of labor. And their former subjects were no longer called subjects, but hosts, and they were liberated in all things, except with no liberty to return to mortals.

22/14.22. Vishnu no more than had these matters settled, when the new hosts, the eight hundred million, came as the guard and shields of mortals. Vishnu organized them, making Maitraias the central throne over them; and he divided them into companies of one million, and gave to each company one marshal and one thousand messengers. And the marshals again sub-divided their hosts into thousands, and numbered them, and to each thousand he gave one master, with his quota of messengers.

22/14.23. Next, Vishnu divided the three great countries, Vind'yu, Jaffeth and Arabin'ya, into as many parts as he had appointed marshals; and the lands were mapped out, showing cities, towns and country places, and each marshal was assigned his place. And a record of these things was made, including the maps, the divisions, and the names of the marshals and masters; and it was registered in the libraries of heaven.

22/14.24. So Vishnu's hosts were sent to their places and commanded to give daily reports of their labors, which were to be carried by the messengers to Vishnu.

CHAPTER 15 Divinity

22/15.1. In Mouru, God and his officers were using all their strength and wisdom to provide for the removal of his hosts to Craoshivi. The demand for builders, surveyors and carriers, with power, was so great that God decided to send trumpeters through the kingdoms of Ahura, the false, asking for volunteers.

22/15.2. For this purpose he sent twelve otevans in different directions, some even going through the city of Ctusk, Ahura's capital, and they proclaimed aloud what they wanted. And it came to pass that in less than one year the otevans gathered out of Ahura's kingdoms, seven million angels capable of grade seventy, who were able to fill the places required.

22/15.3. This was the most damaging blow of all to Ahura's kingdoms, for he thus lost the wisest and most powerful of his people. And this news spread like fire before the wind. His sub-Gods began to revolt against him, and laid claim to their own kingdoms. Many of them openly preached against him in their heavenly places, accusing him of falsehood and of being a mere pretender, with little power.

22/15.4. Nevertheless, he had great power in the name Ahura'Mazda, for he was believed in heaven, to be the same God, even I'hua'Mazda, who inspired Zarathustra. And mortals also, living and dying in this belief, could not be convinced otherwise. And when their spirits left their mortal bodies, Ahura's angels took them to the heavenly city of Ctusk, where they saw its glory, shining and magnificent. And they took them within sight of Ahura's throne, but not near it, and they were obliged to crawl on their bellies a long distance even for this purpose. And the throne was kept radiant with perpetual fire. Then they were made to re-crawl their way back again, until out of the city. After that it was said to them: Behold, we have shown you Ahura'Mazda's heavenly city and the glory of his throne. But him you cannot look upon, until you have performed the service required of all souls entering heaven. Nor can you come again to this most brilliant and majestic of cities, till you have served under your Lords and masters for your allotted time. After that you shall come here and dwell in peace, rest, and happiness forever!

22/15.5. And these spirits had no way of knowing otherwise, nor would they believe, if told; and they thus willingly made slaves of themselves for hundreds of years, carrying provender, or doing drudgery to certain masters who were again serving the Lords and the sub-Gods, going through the same rites and ceremonies in heaven as they were accustomed to on earth.

22/15.6. But Jehovih provides for all things, wiser than the wisest Gods. He created His creations with a door on every side, full of glory and freedom. Out of earth and atmosphere conjoined, He created animal and vegetable kingdoms. And He created the trees of the earth and the flesh of animals out of these two things, the dust of the earth and the air of heaven.

22/15.7. And Jehovih made it so that in death, their corporeal elements would go to their respective places, where they belong. But the Creator created this possibility, that in the death of a vegetable and in the death of an animal, when the atmospherean part flies upward, it would carry with it a small part of the dust of the earth, and it thus does His bidding.

22/15.8. He created His creations with this possibility also: that the earth gives away of its substance into atmospherea over hundreds of years; and the fields become barren and cease producing; and certain animals become barren and cease reproducing, and their species go out of existence. And He created man subject to the same forces; and when the earth is in the giving-off period, behold, man ceases to desire of the earth; and he cries out to his Father in heaven for the light of heaven.

22/15.9. The Creator also created this possibility for the earth and the heavens above the earth: a season, hundreds of years, for the earth to give off its substance, which flies upward (outward); and for hundreds of years, a season for the earth to receive an addition of substance from the atmosphere, surcharged from the regions far away. And when it is thus receiving, it is called the time of a'ji, because that which falls (condenses) is a'ji.

22/15.10. When a'ji comes upon the earth, the drujas come also. The days of the darkness of earth are their delight; their harvest is in the rich falling a'ji; it suits their laziness and their inclination to bask about. In those days they become like over-fed animals; and to their masters, the false Gods, they become worthless, for they derive their sustenance without labor. A'ji is their delight; but they are also like a foolish man drinking wine with delight, who continues till his delight turns to madness. So the drujas feast and disobey their masters; and then they become boisterous and unruly, full of disorder and evil intent, defiant, believing themselves to be Gods and Goddesses. Like a beggar with a pocket full of money, who lacks discipline and is determined to glut his passions to the full, so it is with the drujas in the time of a'ji.

22/15.11. Thus Ahura calculated without Jehovih; in his heart he had conceived great power in his kingdom; but the long a'ji seriously affected his heavenly places. His sub-Gods no longer paid him tribute, which had been used to support in ease and glory his five million heralds, his five million musicians, and his five million ceremonious paraders; who had been thus constantly provided with new costumes, new palaces and new decorations.

22/15.12. So, first one and then another of his sub-Gods revolted; and Ahura was powerless to enforce obedience, for so dense was a'ji that whoever Ahura sent forth only reveled in sumptuous feastings. And it came to pass in the years after a'ji set in, that over six hundred of Ahura's sub-Gods had dissolved all connection with him; and of the two hundred yet remaining, who were situated close to Ctusk, Ahura's heavenly place, not ten of them could be relied upon in an emergency.

22/15.13. At this time Ahura resolved upon regaining his lost dominions, and he was like a man who, having lost heavily at the games, resolved to win all or lose all. Accordingly, Ahura set his workmen to building fifty thousand parade ships. He said to his remaining sub-Gods: Behold, I will traverse the heavens in such magnificence and glory that all angels and mortals shall fall down and worship me. And surely, too, this time of a'ji must come to an end; and in that day I will remember those who have been faithful to me. And I will also remember, with a curse, those who have been unfaithful to me.

22/15.14. For fourteen years the workmen were building Ahura's fleet, and yet they had built only thirty thousand ships. For, so great was the desertion of his skilled men that failure met him on all sides. But with these thirty thousand ships Ahura determined to travel throughout all the atmospherean heavens.

22/15.15. Accordingly, he called together his five million heralds; five million musicians; five million masters of ceremonies; five million masters of rites; ten million marshals; twenty million captains; three million generals; one million Lords; and one hundred fifty of his sub-Gods, with their twenty million attendants; his ten million bearers of trophies; ten million light-makers; ten million waterers; five million torch-bearers; and his body-guard of thirty million. Besides these there were the bearers of banners, the proclaimers, the road-makers, the surveyors, the directors, and so on, more than fifty million of them. In addition there were one hundred million traveling hosts, and one hundred million waiters for them. In all, there were more than four hundred million spirits that went within the thirty thousand ships, and the ships were not full.

22/15.16. And the ships traveled in the form of a pyramid, but not touching one another, and yet fastened together. And the base of the pyramid was four hundred miles wide in each direction, and four hundred miles high. And the belt of light around the pyramid was a thousand miles in diameter every direction; and it was ballasted to run within fifty miles of the earth's surface.

22/15.17. Thus Ahura set out for a whole year's cruise in atmospherea; and wherever he went he proclaimed himself thus: Ahura'Mazda, the Creator! The Only Begotten Son of the Unknowable! Behold, I come; I, the Creator! I have come to judge heaven and earth! Whoever is for Me I will raise up to Nirvana; whoever is against Me I will cast into hell. ||

22/15.18. The pyramid reflected light in its travel; and Ahura's emissaries on earth used this as a testimony that all things were about to come to an end; the earth to be cast out, and heaven and hell to be filled up with spirits, each to its place, according to its obedience or disobedience to Ahura'Mazda.

22/15.19. On the other hand, Ahura's rebel sub-Gods laughed at him; and, as for the over-fed and debauched drujas, they mocked him. So it came to pass that when Ahura visited his rebel sub-Gods in their kingdoms, instead of regaining their allegiance, he was sent on his way with hisses and groans. And yet never, since the earth and her heavens were, had there been such great show and pageantry.

22/15.20. Before Ahura had visited half the kingdoms in atmospherea he foresaw the futility of his project; the probable downfall of his own mighty kingdoms began to break in on his heart. Enthusiasm for his name was on the wane, and all his magnificence had failed to restore him to what he had been.

22/15.21. Now, while he was absent from Ctusk, the capital of his kingdoms, he had deputed Fravaitiwagga to reign in his place, and to maintain the order and glory of his throne. Fravaitiwagga was a deserter from God's Haienne colony in Haraiti, where he had been educated for two hundred years, and was expert in primary surveys and buildings, but became impatient for advancement beyond his capacity. He had now been with Ahura for three hundred years, learning little, but feasting and frolicking, being a great flatterer of Ahura, and given to long speeches and flowery words.

22/15.22. While Fravaitiwagga was on the throne, and after the departure of Ahura on his excursion, there came to him one Ootgowski, a deserter from Hestinai in Zeredho, who had been in Ahura's service a hundred and fifty years, but banished from his heavenly place by Ahura on account of gluttony and drunkenness, after which he became a wandering spirit, dwelling sometimes in one kingdom and then in another, and often visiting the earth and gaining access to the oracles, and even to mortal priests, where he represented himself sometimes as Ahura'Mazda, sometimes as God, sometimes as a favorite Lord, sometimes as Fragapatti, or Thor, or Osire, and, in fact, using any name he chose, issuing decrees and commandments to mortals, then flying away to return no more.

22/15.23. Ootgowski came to Fravaitiwagga, and said to him: Greeting to you, O God, in the name of Ahura'Mazda! Behold, I have been sent to come to you in great haste by our Creator, Ahura; who commands your presence in the province of Veatsagh, where a mighty Council is being held with Ahura's re-affiliated sub-Gods. What preferment Ahura'Mazda has fashioned for you, I do not know. To this Fravaitiwagga answered as follows:

22/15.24. Who are you, and from what kingdom? And above all, why have you come without heralds and attendants? To this Ootgowski answered, saying: Behold me! Do you not know me? I am Haaron, God of Sutuyotha! Who else could come so quickly? Who else, but I, runs fearlessly unattended between the kingdoms of the Gods?

22/15.25. Fravaitiwagga had been drunk many days, and was so dazed with the pretentious Ootgowski that he took for granted that he was indeed Haaron, a great friend to Ahura. Fravaitiwagga called his Council together and appointed Semmes to be God in his place; and so Fravaitiwagga departed in an arrow-ship, with messengers, for Veatsagh, which lay in an entirely different direction to where Ahura was traveling.

22/15.26. Semmes, the deputized God of Ctusk, was faithful to his office for four days, and then proclaimed recreation until the trumpet call from the throne. And in this interval the debauchee, Ootgowski, obtained access to the floor of the inner chamber, and seduced Semmes to accompany him, carrying off all the costly gems and jewels of the throne! And when outside the capital, they embarked with their plunder in an arrow-ship to some unknown region.

22/15.27. For many days the members of the Council waited for the trumpet call, but not hearing it, resolved to learn the cause. And after a diligent search, not finding Semmes, but discovering that the throne had been plundered of its valuables, they were thrown into great confusion. By two days later, the throne was destroyed, the Council divided and gone, and the heavenly city of Ctusk had turned to riot and plunder.

22/15.28. And so in Ctusk and near about, there were more than four billion angels with no God, nor leader, nor any head at all. Thus it came to pass that Jehovih took the throne from Ahura, as had been prophesied.

22/15.29. And while this was going on, Ahura was away with his pyramid fleet, being discomfited wherever he went. But two hundred and twelve days after his journey began, messengers came to him and told him what had happened in Ctusk.

22/15.30. Ahura gave orders to sail at once for his capital; and his pyramid fleet hastened with all possible power. Suffice it to say, in a few days he was back in Ctusk, a witness to the rioting and plundering going on. But the majesty and splendor of his fleet calmed the people, and restored order for the time being; nevertheless he was without a throne and without a Council.

CHAPTER 16 Divinity

22/16.1. Near the beginning of the fall of a'ji, God decreed to his Lord Gods, to his Gods and Lords, and Goddesses, as follows: As in the past you have gathered of the rising atmospherean part of the living earth-substance, so shall you now turn above for your regimen. The condition now in heaven can be compared to the waters of the earth. When it does not rain, mortals go to the well and fetch up water out of the earth; but when it rains they do not go to the well for water, but set out vessels, and the rain fills them.

22/16.2. So, in the times of dan and half dan and quarter dan, our hosts bring their regimen up from the earth. In which work you have many employed as laborers. Behold now, a'ji will rain down upon us ample regimen for one hundred and eighty years. Therefore, do not allow your laborers to fall into idleness, for this will lead to mischief. But immediately put them to work in other occupations; and do not permit them to have spare time.

22/16.3. || The mathematicians discovered that no a'ji would fall in Yaton'te, or on the lands of Guatama. So for those regions, God sent laborers from several divisions in the heavens. ||

22/16.4. Two heavenly kingdoms, Gir-ak-shi of Heleste and Soo'fwa of Japan, grieved God more than all the rest. For these had become strongholds for Ahura, who had pursued warfare on earth till in those two great divisions all the Faithists, the Zarathustrians, had been put to death. And the mortal kings of those countries had issued laws commanding all people to be put to death who professed the Great Spirit, Ormazd (Jehovih). And the law had been carried out effectively.

22/16.5. So God bewailed Soo'fwa with lamentations. He said: O Japan, my beloved, down stricken! How can I restore mortal seed to you? You are far away; no man on your soil hears the Creator's voice! How can I carry her; she lies down with cold feet.

22/16.6. While God lamented, the voice of the Father came to him, saying: Hear Me in My wisdom, O My Son. I will not let Ahura go there (Japan). Withdraw your guards from the evilest of men. Allow him to go his own way. Ahura shall be brought home before he visits Soo'fwa and Gir-ak-shi.

22/16.7. God perceived; and he sent messengers to the guard over Ootgowski, saying to them: When you come to the guard, even to the captains, ask permission to speak to Ootgowski; and the captain will permit. And you shall say to Ootgowski: My son, you came here saying: Put a guard over me, for I am obsessed by Satan with the seven horns (tetracts). And God appointed a guard over you. Today, behold, God sends word to you, saying: I will no longer guard Ootgowski. For his glory he shall enter the kingdoms of Jehovih and become a worker for righteousness' sake.

22/16.8. When the messengers had said this much to Ootgowski, the latter said to them: God is wise; I volunteered to have myself put under guard, but I am tired of it. Say to God, his Lords and sub-Gods: I will come to Jehovih's kingdoms and work for righteousness' sake. But first I desire a little rest and travel? || So Ootgowski was purposely granted freedom, and of his own accord he went and destroyed the foundations of Ahura's throne, as has been told. And Ahura thus hastened home without completing the travel of the heavens.

22/16.9. Jehovih said: What does a name matter? Let them call the Creator Ahura'Mazda, and call Ahura'Mazda the Creator. Since He has not shown Himself in a ship, or in the figure of a man, behold, your inspirers shall teach His Ever Presence.

22/16.10. God perceived, and a record of the name was made and entered in the libraries of heaven. And God looked abroad and saw that the same thing also pertained to Gir-ak-shi and Heleste. So God entered this also in the libraries of heaven. And its reading, translated, is as follows: In the land of Heleste, the highest, most sacred name of the Great Spirit, the Creator, was decreed by God to be Mazda; and the same thing is decreed for Japan.

22/16.11. Thus it was known from that time forward, that the origin of the word Master, as applied to the Creator, sprang from those two countries only, and from no other division of the earth. Of this matter, God said: In thousands of years this word shall be testimony to mortals of the war in heaven of this day, which did not reach to the heavens of these two lands. And it was so, and will continue forever![724]

22/16.12. However, God had no footing in Japan or Heleste, nor did he have sufficient power to establish a God or Lord in either country, or in the heavens belonging to them.

22/16.13. And when Diva assembled, God propounded this matter, on which the fourteen members spoke at length. And then Div decreed: To the swift messengers in attendance, and through them to the etherean Goddess, Cpenta-armij, deploring[725] of Diva in Jehovih's name: Two heavenly kingdoms and two corporeal divisions have walled themselves around in idolatry. A'ji has yet six years, and dawn twenty-six.

22/16.14. Thirty days later the star-ship, Gee'onea, from Haot-saiti, in etherea, appeared in the heavens above, being first observed when it was on the borders of the bridge Chinvat. Immediately God sent a swift-rising Ometr to meet the star-ship and conduct it to Craoshivi, where he had gone with one of the transports, with two hundred million, well selected, to found a new city in heaven. Suffice it to say that in three days' time,

---

[724] The term Master, applied to Christ, came by way of the Grecians [Greeks], and not by the Hebrews. The Hebrews never rejoiced in a word that implied servitude in the sense of master. –Ed.

[725] sorrowing over, lamenting, expressing regrets

the star-ship landed in Craoshivi with one million laborers provided to endure till the coming dawn.

22/16.15. After due salutations, Os, chief captain of the ethereans, said to God: In Jehovih's name I come to possess the heavenly places, Soo'fwa and Gir-ak-shi, and their lands, Japan and Heleste. This work must be accomplished before dawn, before the coming of Cpenta-armij. Therefore, send for your messengers who know the places, so that I may conduct my hosts there to labor.

22/16.16. God then gave messengers to Os, and the latter departed and went to the kingdoms named; and it so happened, by the wisdom of Jehovih, that this took place at the same time that Ahura had returned and found his capital and throne demolished. Hence Ahura was powerless to interfere with the labor of Os and his hosts.

22/16.17. So Os divided his forces and possessed both Soo'fwa and Gir-ak-shi, together with the divisions of the earth belonging to them. And Os possessed the corporeal temples of worship, and the places of the oracles, and all places for consulting spirits. And he did not teach the name Jehovih, nor Great Spirit, nor Father, for none of these would be received. But he taught and extolled[726] this: That heaven (the voice of the oracle, etc.) was thus inspired OF THE MAZDA, THE CREATOR; OF THE VOICE THAT SPOKE TO ZARATHUSTRA, THE ALL PURE. That man should strive to goodness and good works; to self-denial and love; to justice and truth; and cultivate the state of mercy and obedience to the all highest light in the soul.

CHAPTER 17 Divinity

22/17.1. But even Gods fail at times. For all persons learn by failures that there are higher powers. Only Jehovih never fails.

22/17.2. In the last month of the last year of a'ji, even while God, Jehovih's Son, and his Lord Gods, and his Lords and sub-Gods, were proud of heart that they would carry the earth and her heavens through safely, they met sore trials. This, then, is what happened: A comet came within the earth's vortex, and was drawn in, just like floating debris is drawn within a whirlpool in a river. The substance of the comet was condensed, and fell on the earth in mist and dust and ashes. Consequently, the earth and its heavens were in darkness for twelve days, and the darkness was so great that a man could not see his hand before him.

22/17.3. And during those days of darkness there were more than four score hells founded within Ahura's heavenly regions, and he himself was cast into one of them, and he was walled about by more than three billion angels; pilfered and stripped of all he had. And his remaining sub-Gods were also bound in hell and robbed of all they had.

22/17.4. And presently the spirits ran for the kings' and queens' souls (of those who had been tyrants on earth), and they caught them, and brought them and cast them into hell also, taking vengeance on them with stripes[727] and foul smells. And hundreds of thousands of spirits went and gathered foul smells and cast them into hell, and surrounded the hells on every side with foul gases, so that none could escape.

22/17.5. The madness upon them became so desperate, that even the tormentors rushed in, making a frolic of madness. And those who ever had an enemy on earth now ran for him and caught him in hada and brought him with the help of others, and cast him into the torments of hell. And those who had been slaves for hundreds of years to Ahura and his Gods, now caught everyone they could lay hands on, and dragged them into hell.

22/17.6. As soon as God's messengers came and told him what happened, God sent all his available forces to overthrow the place, if possible. Vishnu, full of hope and courage, sent one-half of his forces to God's assistance, thus risking the guardianship of the three great mortal kingdoms, Vind'yu, Jaffeth and Arabin'ya. And God sent messengers to the heavenly kingdoms of North and South Guatama, saying to the Gods of those places: Behold, Ahura, the false, is involved in torments; upon him are his hosts, three billion! Send all above grade seventy at once. To Uropa he sent also, saying the same thing, and adding: Alas, my little wisdom in sending off a billion of my own hosts to Craoshivi at such a time!

---

[726] promoted, placed positive energy into; not only to make it acceptable and desirable, but irresistible so as to make man take to heart, practice, and venerate that which the message proclaimed

[727] whippings

22/17.7. Craoshivi was the new plateau, difficult to access, and it was hardly possible to recall his hosts in the time required. So God summoned the Diva, so that they could sit for the Father's Voice; and the members came and sat in the usual way, and Jehovih spoke to God, saying:

22/17.8. Peace to you, My Son! Do not regret having sent your most exalted hosts to Craoshivi. Did I not lead you there? And I said to you: Possess this place, and send your hosts here. Nor should you grieve because I sent the nebulae and the darkness of that time. Is it a greater tragedy for you to see these things, than for mortals to witness the spring floods that wash away the summer's coming harvest?

22/17.9. To learn to provide against contingencies, this is wisdom. Yet not all wisdom is in man's heart, nor yet with My Gods. How can you perceive how it is with Ahura's soul, whether this hell is good or evil for him in the end?

22/17.10. If you behold My sudden power, how much more must Ahura feel it? (For his whole kingdom is gone, and he is now in hell.) Yet you shall deliver him out of hell; by your hosts, he and his sub-Gods shall be delivered. But the torments of his own soul shall be far greater, than what his drujas can heap upon him.

22/17.11. Then God inquired of Jehovih, saying: What is the best, most perfect way, to deliver Ahura and his subjects out of hell?

22/17.12. Jehovih answered him, saying: Send those whom he has despised, or ill-treated, or humbled. And when your Lords and Gods have come to the place, let these, his abused enemies, take the hand of your Lord or your God, and they shall call out to Me in the name, Ormazd, which name Ahura has tried to destroy for the glory of his own. And at the sound of the name, Ormazd, your hosts shall cast burning light into the faces of the drujas, and thus scatter them away till Ahura is released; and he shall witness that he has been released through the name, Ormazd.

22/17.13. God sent E'chad and Ah'oan[728] to deliver Ahura out of hell; and they labored four years in accomplishing it, and then Ahura was free. And Ahura's hosts were divided into groups of tens of thousands, and hundreds of thousands; and God appointed generals and captains over them, except for eight hundred million drujas, who had escaped from hell and through the guards' fires, and descended back to the earth, to torment and deceive mortals.

22/17.14. So it turned out that Vishnu failed in some degree to save the nations of the earth from the approach of evil spirits. Jehovih spoke to Vishnu, comforting, saying: Because you have helped to deliver Ahura, you shall not take sorrow to your heart. What are eight hundred million to you? So Vishnu grieved no more.

22/17.15. Now during the deliverance of Ahura's hell, no less than six knots had been tied, and in one of these Ahura and his sub-Gods had become bound, so there was no escape for them. But the outer and extreme knots were untied first; and as fast as the delirious spirits were rescued, they were carried outside, beyond the fire-walls, and placed under guard.

22/17.16. Thus, in sections, Ahura's hell was cast out; and when the deliverers came to Ahura and his confederates, they were all, except Ahura, in a state of chaos, frenzied with fear. But Ahura was not beside himself,[729] though in serious fright. Ah'oan, Lord of Jaffeth, spoke to him, saying: In the name of God, and of Ormazd, I have delivered you. How is it with you?

22/17.17. Ahura said: I am done! I am nothing! One God alone can do nothing. Do with me whatever you will. I am your servant.

22/17.18. Ah'oan said: No, be servant to none except Ormazd, your Creator. His name is the watchword and the power in all the high heavens. By His name you shall become one among Godly companions.

22/17.19. Ahura said: But you must torment me first! Ah'oan said: For what reason? My work is not to cast down but to lift up. So it is with all of Ormazd's Gods. Behold here even your sub-Gods, and those whom you have evilly used in the past! See, they hold up their hands in prayer to Ormazd for you!

22/17.20. And is this not the way of knowing whether angels and mortals are of the Creator? If they pull down, they are not His. If they slander or torment, or speak evil of one another, or give pain,

[728] These are the namesakes of the first Lord Gods at the time of Fragapatti.

[729] not hysterical, not wholly unnerved or uncontrolled, mind not in chaos

they are not His. Why, then, shall I not do good to you and restore you to your kingdom?

22/17.21. Ahura said: Give me anything, but do not give me my kingdom again, for of all torments this is the worst. Ah'oan said: Would you treat evilly those who have been your subjects? If so, you are not of the everlasting resurrection. Ahura said: No, I never want to see them again! Never hear them again! Never know them again! If, therefore, you will do me good instead of evil, take me, I pray, far away, and alone, so that I may meditate forever on the horrors I have passed through.

22/17.22. Ah'oan said: Hear me now, once and for all, and I speak in the name of God and the Great Spirit, Ormazd: Because you have served yourself and compelled others to serve you for nearly two thousand years, you have become blind to the Ormazdian law, which is, that your own peace and happiness can only come by making restitution to your servants, and by lifting up those whom you have cast down. How can I deliver you away from them? I could take your person away from here, but I cannot deliver your memory. No man can be delivered from himself.

22/17.23. Only one way is open for you, and it is under the Ormazdian law, which is, that you shall take your kingdom again, and deliver it to righteousness, intelligence and good works. Serving Ormazd by doing good to them whom the Creator gave you. Many of them have served you more than a thousand years; would you now cast them off without recompense?

22/17.24. Ahura said: You are just, O Ormazd! I perceive the wisdom of Your Gods, and the bondage of men. Take me, O Ah'oan, put me in a way to carry out this great light.

22/17.25. Ah'oan said: Hear your sentence, in the name of Ormazd, the Creator; which is, that you shall be taken to a place of safety, which E'chad shall select; and there your best, most exalted people shall be taken, and put to work and to school, and in nurseries and hospitals; and you shall go among them, teaching and encouraging them in industry and righteousness, for Ormazd's sake. And when you have them disciplined in this way, you shall receive another installment of your people, and they shall be likewise disciplined. And then another installment, and so on, until you have all your kingdom.

22/17.26. And to ensure your success, these, my Lords and generals and captains, shall go and labor with you and your hosts. And you and your people shall have no ornaments; and all your raiment shall be white-gray, teachers and pupils alike, except when specially ordered otherwise by God and his deputies.

22/17.27. And when you and the majority of your hosts have risen above grade fifty, you shall be crowned in the name of Ormazd, and your kingdom shall have a throne, and you shall be one among the united hosts of the higher heavens. Till then, go to your labors diligently, and may Ormazd abide with you in wisdom and power.

22/17.28. Ahura said: You are just, O Ormazd. I will from this time forward, forever, serve You with all my wisdom and strength!

22/17.29. And then E'chad and his attendants led the way, and the marshals, generals and captains brought the first installment of Ahura's hosts, and they went to a place called Ailkin, a heavenly place capable of seven billion, and there they founded the new colony for Ahura.

22/17.30. But Ah'oan and his hosts continued their labors in delivering the hells, until they delivered them all, more than eighty, and placed all the spirits under guard and discipline.

CHAPTER 18 Divinity

22/18.1. Thus drew to a close the cycle of Fragapatti, being three thousand one hundred years. And at this time there were few people on earth or in heaven who were not capable of everlasting life, including the druks and drujas.

22/18.2. Jehovih spoke to God, saying: Now you shall enumerate earth and heaven, as to all that I have created capable of everlasting life; and of My harvests since the habitation of the earth, when man first walked upright. And your numbers shall be entered in the libraries of heaven, to remain forever.

22/18.3. So God called together a council of mathematicians, and they counted mortals and angels, and recorded this labor in the libraries of heaven, where the wise men of heaven and earth may read the records.

22/18.4. In Fragapatti's cycle ninety-two billion were born alive. Of these ninety percent were born to everlasting life. Ten percent went into dissolution, as a drop of water evaporates before the sun and is seen no more.

22/18.5. In Osiris' cycle, ninety-one billion were born. Of these eighty-seven percent were born to everlasting life. Thirteen percent went into dissolution and were seen no more.

22/18.6. In Thor's cycle, eighty-eight billion were born. Of these eighty-five percent were born to everlasting life, and fifteen percent to dissolution.

22/18.7. In Apollo's cycle, eighty billion were born. Of these seventy-two percent were born to everlasting life, and twenty-eight percent to dissolution.

22/18.8. In Sue's cycle, eighty-seven billion were born. Of these sixty-two percent were born to everlasting life, and thirty-eight percent went into dissolution.

22/18.9. In Aph's cycle, sixty-six billion were born. Of these fifty-four percent were born to everlasting life, and forty-six percent went into dissolution.

22/18.10. In Neph's cycle, before the submersion of Pan, one hundred and twenty-four billion were born. Of these twenty-one percent were born to everlasting life, and seventy-nine percent went into dissolution.

22/18.11. And these comprised one-sixth of the people that had been created alive on the earth since man walked upright; that is to say, three trillion seven hundred and sixty-eight billion.

22/18.12. But in the early days of man, only a small percentage were born to everlasting life; and, first of all, only one percent.

22/18.13. And God gave thanks to Jehovih, the Creator, because all the races of men on earth were now capable of everlasting life.

22/18.14. Of the hells and knots springing out of hada since the days of Wan,[730] this was the proportion:

22/18.15. In the cycle of Fragapatti, two hundred and seventy-six hells, of average duration, thirty years. Involved in these hells, two billion angels. Sixty-four knots, of average duration, two years. Involved in these knots, one billion angels.

22/18.16. In the cycle of Osiris, three hundred and eighty-nine hells, of average duration, four hundred years. Involved in these hells, seven billion. Two hundred and twelve knots, of average duration, three years. Involved in these knots, three billion.

22/18.17. In the cycle of Thor, five hundred and ninety-one hells, of average duration, six hundred years. Involved in these hells, nine billion angels. Four hundred and thirty-six knots, of average duration, six years. Involved in these knots, four billion angels.

22/18.18. In Apollo's cycle, seven hundred and forty-two hells, of average duration, eight hundred years. Involved in these hells, ten billion angels. Six hundred and four knots, of average duration, twelve years. Involved in these knots, five billion.

22/18.19. In Sue's cycle, twelve hundred and seventy-three hells, of average duration, one thousand years. Involved in these hells, thirteen billion angels. One thousand and five knots, of average duration, thirty years. Involved in these knots, eight billion.

22/18.20. In Aph's cycle, three thousand five hundred hells, of average duration, two thousand years. Involved in these hells, twenty-eight billion angels. Two thousand knots, of average duration, fifty years. Involved in these knots, twenty-five billion. And these were the numbers of spirits cast into hell and into knots, from the submersion of Pan to the end of the cycle of Zarathustra (Fragapatti); but at the dawn of each and every cycle, both the hells and the knots were delivered by the etherean Gods. Except in Fragapatti's cycle, when they were almost entirely delivered by the atmospherean God.

22/18.21. Prior to the submersion of Pan, commonly called the flood, more than half the people entering the first es world went into hell and knots. And in all ages of the world there have been thousands and millions of spirits who delight in hell for certain seasons, even as the same tendency is manifested in mortals who delight in debauchery, vengeance and war. Nor is a hell very different, as to spirit, from what war is among mortals. And as mortals of this day glorify themselves, their generals and their captains, for the magnitude of their havoc in war, so in ancient times in atmospherea, there were great boastings and laudations for those who inflicted the greatest torments and horrors in hell.

22/18.22. As mortals of the druk order often leave their evil ways for a season, and become

[730] i.e., the arc of Wan, time of Sethantes

upright and virtuous, loving decency and righteousness, and then break away and indulge in a season of debauchery, so has it been in the es world with millions and billions of angels. In one day the teachers and physicians were rejoicing before Jehovih because of the steadfastness of their wards to righteousness; and in the next day were left to deplore the loss of hundreds and thousands who had broken faith and gone off for indulgence's sake into some of the hells. And these had to be rescued, persuaded, threatened and coaxed back again and again to the nurseries and hospitals, or to the factories and colleges.

22/18.23. Nor does anyone know, except Jehovih, the labor, fretting, and anxiety that were undergone by the teachers and physicians, and Lords and Gods, who had such drujas in charge. For even as it is seen on earth that men of great learning and high estate often fall, becoming lower than the beasts of the fields, so were there in heaven, hundreds of thousands, even millions, often high raised in the grades, who would stumble and fall into the lowest of hells, and even into the knots.

22/18.24. So Jehovih brought the earth and her heavens into another dawn of dan, in the arc of Spe-ta, in the Nirvanian roads of Salkwatka, in etherea.

22/18.25. Now, through the entire cycle till dawn of dan'ha, God and his Lords maintained the Diva; and mortals understood the matter somewhat, that there were certain Divine laws in heaven that ruled over mortal kingdoms and empires. So that, the words Div, Diva, and Divine rights, began to be realized as a concerted power in heaven greater than man's power.

END OF BOOK OF DIVINITY

Book of Cpenta-armij, Daughter of Jehovih

Being of the first deliverance of God's chosen people.

CHAPTER 1 Cpenta-armij

23/1.1. Jehovih spoke to Cpenta-armij, Goddess of Haot-saiti,[731] in Nirvania, in the arc of Spe-ta, Commander of the South fields of Abarom, in the Orian Plains of Bilothowitchieun, of a reign of two hundred thousand years; Surveyor for Otaias, ten thousand years; Leader of the Oixan, seventy thousand years; Captain of Geliyas' roadways, in the forest of Lugga, twenty thousand years; Founder and Ruler of Isaas, thirty thousand years; Trencher of the Haigusets swamps, four thousand years; Goddess of Nor, Goddess of Eunigi, Goddess of Poutu, each ten thousand years, saying:

23/1.2. My Daughter, behold, the red star and her heavens come your way. She will cross the arc of Spe-ta, four years and thirty-two days' riding. Open your fields in Abarom, and give her forty years' indulgence, for this is the first of her deliverance.

23/1.3. Cpenta-armij answered, saying: I see the red star, the earth, O Jehovih! Like a wandering ship in a wide ocean, she comes through my fields, the young earth, traveling on, carefully, in the roads of Salkwatka. Has she so soon, in just little more than sixty thousand years, overcome her enduring knots and torturing hells?

23/1.4. In Your Wisdom and Power, O Jehovih! I will go in person to this corporeal world, and encourage her God and Lords for the excellent labor done.

23/1.5. Jehovih said: Call your Council, and proclaim from My throne the FEAST OF THE ARC OF SPE-TA. Then Cpenta-armij called her High Council of a hundred million, Sons and Daughters of

[731] see image i087

Jehovih, and she ascended to her place in the center of the throne of the Great Spirit.

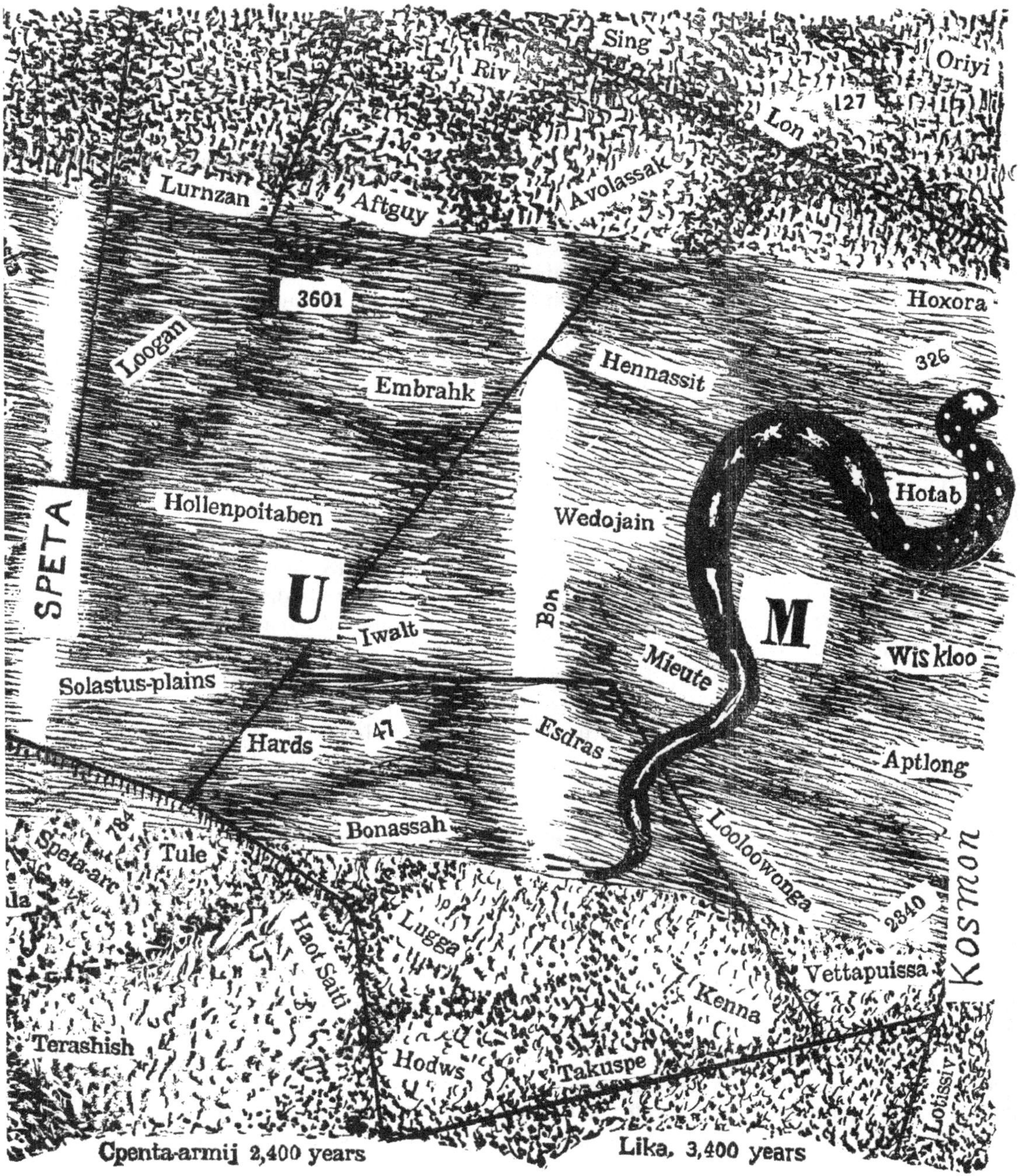

i087 **Map of the Etherean Roadway of the Solar Phalanx for the fourth set of two cycles of the past gadol, Plate 4 of 4**. The Roadway shown is that through which the sun and its family (including earth) traveled during the cycles of Cpenta-armij and Lika.

23/1.6. And present with her were: Obed, God of Oise, in Embrahk; Gavaini, Goddess of Ipthor, of the Solastis Plains; Ab, First Shriever of Riv-Sing; Holon-ho, God of Loo-Gam; Raisi, Goddess of Esdras; Wish-tse, God of Zuth, in Ronega; and all these Gods and Goddesses were more than a hundred thousand years raised in etherean realms, and knew the earth before she was inhabited by man.

23/1.7. On a visit to Cpenta-armij were: Owks, Orian Chief of Maiter-lan, fifty thousand years, Marshal of Wiski-loo, thirty thousand years, God of Tunsin, in the Tarps Roads, ninety thousand years; and See-wah-Gon, Chieftainess of the Orian arc of Su-los, two hundred thousand years, Mistress of Aftong, in the Plains of Bel, three hundred thousand years, Pilotess of Lu-wow-lu, one hundred thousand years, Goddess of Eune, in the Mountains of Gem-king; and Ha-o-ha, Founder of Ogee, of Siam, of Wick-a-wick, and the twelve Nirvanian Old-tse, in Lo-owtz, Eli-hagam; together with their traveling hosts, five million each.

23/1.8. Cpenta-armij said: For Your glory, O Jehovih, I proclaim the Feast of the Arc of Spe-ta. And these, my visiting hosts, shall enjoy the four years' deliverance of the red star and her heavens!

23/1.9. Then Owks responded, and then See-wah-Gon, then Ha-o-ha, speaking at great length, and rejoicing for the invitation. And they related many adventures on other stars in the time of the arc of deliverance, the arc of Spe-ta, and with what Gods and Goddesses they journeyed and what Chiefs and Chieftainesses.

23/1.10. So Cpenta-armij spoke to her chief marshal, saying: Send heralds to the builders, and order me an airavagna capable of five hundred million, and of speed, grade sixty. After this you shall select one hundred million from my attendants, and after that three hundred million of the Egisi.[732]

23/1.11. With these, and my visitors, I will start for the red star in twenty days. The proper officers attended to these things, and while they were going about their business, behold, the red star, the earth, rose up in the roadway far away, and the es'enaurs saw it, and they chanted:

23/1.12. What is over there? The red star, Jehovih! Your breath has spoken. Your voice, the silent motion. O Your endless power, Jehovih!

23/1.13. Around her, close about; what is that filled with angels, billions! Wondrous are Your works, O Jehovih, and measureless! She rides around the sun, in her orbit of two hundred and seventy million miles.

23/1.14. It is her atmosphere, traveling with her; its boundary, Chinvat. How fearfully[733] You have created, O Jehovih! And the magnitude of Your places! That little red star is a world, O Father! And the billions of angels, why do they stay in such heavens, O Jehovih!

23/1.15. Then from far away, the trumpeters answered: She that spins around the sun, the red star, the earth, a new world, a generator of the souls of men. The Gods have called her, but she will not hear. Her atmosphere is full of angels struggling for the earth. But Your hand is upon them, O Jehovih. Your trumpeters will line the roads of Salkwatka.

23/1.16. Then sang the es'enaurs: How lovely Your works are, O Jehovih! Too lovely Your Places are, O Jehovih! Too lovely is the red star, the earth, O Jehovih! Your children love it while in mortal form; and after death they love it too much, O Jehovih!

23/1.17. The pipers answer for Jehovih from the Wide East: I made the earth, the red star, with oh so little to love. I gave her poisoned weeds, vines and grasses, and millions of death-dealing serpents. Then I created poisoned marshes and terrible fevers. Yes, I created man on the earth, with sore travail and full of misery, so that he would turn and look upward for a holier place.

23/1.18. Then sang the es'enaurs: You created Your atmospherean heavens too lovely, O Jehovih! —Your bound heavens that travel with the red star, the earth. The spirits raised up from the mortal earth find too much to love in Your lower heavens, O Jehovih!

23/1.19. The pipers again answered for Jehovih: I created My lower heavens full of darkness and evil possibilities. As a place for madness, I created it; a place for lying and deceit; full of hell and

---

[732] volunteers who may have previously registered themselves for such an excursion. –1891 glossary

[733] awe-inspiringly majestic; in such grandeur as to induce reverence to the utmost degree; awesomely; magnificently; impressively; strikingly; to an appalling extent

torments. To drive man upward; to blow My breath upon him, to lift him up, as one lights the fire by blowing.

23/1.20. Cpenta-armij spoke from Jehovih's throne, saying: What is the deliverance of man? Is it from his mother's womb? Is it from his corporeal body? Is it from the corporeal world and her atmosphere? The Father has given three births to all men. In the first, man has nothing to do with his shaping or time in his mother's womb. In the second, he has a little more to do in directing his course during his mortal life; but for the third, for the higher heavens, he must work for his own deliverance.

23/1.21. Cpenta-armij said: The Creator created three kinds of earth deliverance for man: first, from his mother's womb, coming crying, blank and helpless; second, from the tetracts (earthly passions and desires), serious and full of fear; third, from the enemies of the Great Spirit. This last is the Feast of Spe-ta.

CHAPTER 2 Cpenta-armij

23/2.1. Cpenta-armij said: I looked far off in the distance, and saw the earth and her heavens traveling on. I listened to the voice of mortals! A merchant counted over his gains; he said: This is heaven! A drunkard quaffed a cup of poison;[734] he said: This is heaven! A wanton said: This is heaven! A general, red with blood, counted the badges on his breast; he said: This is heaven! A tyrant, rich in toiling slaves, said: This is heaven! Then a vast multitude, all smeared with the blood of war, pointed to a field of mortals slain, and said: This is heaven! A farmer stretched wide his arms, toward his great, uncultivated possessions; he said: This is heaven! A little child with a toy said: This is heaven!

23/2.2. || Then Jehovih spoke, saying: You cannot convince any of these to the contrary. They are not ready for deliverance. ||

23/2.3. Cpenta-armij continued: I listened to the voice of spirits, the angels traveling with the earth. A wanderer, going about, with nothing to do, said: This is heaven! An obsessor[735] of mortals and of other angels said: This is heaven! The fairies, the butterfly angels, the triflers, that forever look in crystal waters to behold their own forms, said: This is heaven! The rollicking, deceiving angels, who went and inspired mortals to falsehood, said: This is heaven! Vampire angels, that nestle in the atmosphere of mortals, largely living on their substance, said: This is heaven! Evil angels obsessing mortals for murder's sake, to make mortals burn houses and torture helpless creatures, said: This is heaven!

23/2.4. || Again Jehovih spoke, saying: You can convince none of these to the contrary. They are not ready for deliverance. ||

23/2.5. So once more I listened to the sounds coming from the far-off earth. And I heard the prayers of mortals. The king prayed for his kingdom and for himself. The general prayed for success in war. The merchant for great gains; the tyrant for great authority.

23/2.6. || Jehovih said: Only the earth can answer such prayers. ||

23/2.7. I listened again for the prayers of mortals; they had great afflictions, dire diseases, famines, and wars; the merchants were bankrupt, and there was great suffering, and they prayed for deliverance.

23/2.8. || Jehovih said: If you deliver them they would return to their old, evil habits. I say to you, the merchant shall be bankrupt; the king shall fail; the general be overthrown; the healthy shall be sick for a season. Until they know My power, they cannot learn; unless they feel affliction, they will not help one another. If a man says: O Jehovih, come and heal the sick. || Should he not first of all recognize My will and know My power?

23/2.9. To give money to the drunkard, what good is that? To give wealth and earthly prosperity to those who do not acknowledge Me, is to set them against Me. To give healing to the fevered, is to teach them that I have no power in the unseen air. Do not answer the prayers of these. ||

23/2.10. I listened once more to the prayers of mortals. And they were from those who lived according to their highest light; they purified the flesh by pure food, and by bathing every day; and they went about doing good constantly, hoarding up neither clothes, nor silver, nor gold, nor

---

[734] drank his alcohol

[735] one who obsesses (dominates, wills, brow beats, nags, hounds, haunts, etc.) another persistently with insistent inspiration

anything earthly. And they purified their thoughts by putting away the evil tongue, the evil eye, and the evil ear;[736] and many of them were bound by the kings, and the tyrants, and the laws of mortals; and some of them were sick. And they prayed, saying: Great is my affliction, O Jehovih. I know that in Your sight I am justly punished.

23/2.11. But hear my prayer, O Father! Make me strong, so I may carry heavy burdens for the weary; give me liberty, so I may go about helping the poor forever. Give me wisdom, so I may uncover Your glories before men.

23/2.12. || Jehovih said: Go, My Daughter, and deliver them. They are ready for deliverance! Answer the prayers of these. ||

23/2.13. Then I called together my hosts of five hundred million, in the Nirvanian heavens in Haot-saiti, in etherea, the highest heaven. And we entered the airavagna, while, swelling high on every side, the music of millions cheered us on. Upward, high up, shone the glimmering red star, toward which our steersman now pointed the fire-arrow, to shoot meteor-like across Jehovih's pathway; and in that direction our buoyant souls turned, saluting our starters with a happy goodbye!

23/2.14. || Arise! Arise! By my vested power in You, O Jehovih, the elements shall fall before my will! Arise; onward! To the red star, speed on! Airavagna, upward, on! ||

23/2.15. Thus spoke Cpenta-armij, her voice mellow and sweet, but so tuned to the spheres, it could be heard across the breadth of a world. And Jehovih—Whose power and will she had learned to be as one with, by long experience and studying submission to His will—lent a willing ear and strong hand. Out shot the flames, the buoyant force manufactured by less skilled workmen learning the trade of Gods, where the million screws of fire whirled, propelling, till the mighty ship reeled, and turned, and rose from its foundation, with all its joyous hosts aboard, shouting loud, and singing praise to Him Who rules over all. Then turning round and round, slowly, spiral-like (manifesting the great secret form and force of vortices, now first revealed to man to show the plan of worlds, and how they are held in their places and moved in universal harmony and endless creation), so began the great airavagna on her course in the roadway of Salkwatka, in etherea, shooting toward the red star, the young earth.

23/2.16. And the first place they came near was the Oixanian Spars of Ochesu, where ten million spectators were gathered near the road to see the Goddess pass in her ship; and their banners waved, and their music burst forth most exhilarating; which was answered by the airavagna's cheering hosts and sailing streamers. Here Cpenta-armij paused with her ship, to salute in honor, the Goddess Yuetisiv, and then shot suddenly upward a thousand miles.

23/2.17. Again onward, turning to the right across the breadth of the road, a million miles, to salute Vultanya, Goddess of the swamps of Ailassasak, where, by the portico[737] of her heavenly palace, seventy million pupils, in their thousandth year of tuition, stood to receive the passing blessing of the Orian Chieftainess, Cpenta-armij. And there, with just a brief pause, like a nod from the ship, then Cpenta-armij sent downward on their heads a shower of newly created flowers from the sphere above, and in turn heard their chorus rise joyfully, in as many million words of love and admiration.

23/2.18. Still onward, upward sped the airavagna, her hosts viewing the scenes on every side. Here were the richest and most glorious places of Salkwatka; where the etherean worlds, rich in the glitter of swamps shining on the countless rainbow arches and crystal pyramids, afford an extensive view of the new Orian boundaries of Oteson's broad kingdoms. Here, where the thousands of excursionist ships, from the measureless regions of the Huan lights, course along. Here, where a million varieties of fire-ships are to be seen, of sizes from ten miles across to the breadth of a world, in unceasing travel, in tens of thousands of directions, onward in their ways, every single one a history of millions of years; and with billions of souls, and every soul rich in the knowledge of thousands of worlds.

23/2.19. Some propelled their ships by music alone; the vibratory chords affording sufficient power in such highly skilled hands, and the tunes

[736] This means not only to speak no evil, to see no evil, and to hear no evil, but also to put away the desire to speak, see, or hear expressions of evil.

[737] a covered walkway or porch, with columns, found at the entry of a building

changing according to the regions traversed. Others went forward powered by colors made in the waves of sound, carrying millions of angels, every one attuned so perfectly that his very presence lent power and beauty to the monarch vessel. And their directions were downward and upward, and east and west, and north and south, and of every angle and course. Such were the traveling regions of Wellagowthiij, in the etherean fields of Oteson.

23/2.20. And of the million ships, with their tens of billions of spirits, who of them had so great a Goddess, as Cpenta-armij, who could turn her well-learned eyes on any one, and know its home regions, and from what Orian pastures or Nirvanian rivers it sailed! Or, who was like her visiting friends, great Owks, See-wah-Gon, and Ha-o-ha, now standing side by side with her, reading the coursing fleets, and relating to one another who these were, and of the great Chiefs aboard, and with whom thousands of years ago they had been together taming some rambling star and calming its disturbed vortex, or perhaps surveying a roadway many millions of miles through an a'ji'an forest.

23/2.21. And during all this, their own airavagna was shooting on in the hands of her proper officers, everyone to his part and all the hosts in varied amusement; for such is the labor of the high raised in heaven, labor itself becomes an amusement of great relish. Coming then to the Crossings, near Bilothowitchieun, there was a small colony of ninety million etherean weavers, superintended by Cpenta-armij's ward, Hoewuel, God of two thousand years, who knew she was coming his way, and had lit the roadway a hundred thousand miles in her honor, so she turned the airavagna and cast the streamers and banners, saluting. Here again Cpenta-armij sent down flowers and keepsakes to every one of her beloved sons and daughters; and the history and mission to the earth and her heavens was written on every flower. And once again the airavagna rose upward and sped on.

23/2.22. Thus the Goddess, the Chieftainess, Cpenta-armij, went forth in Jehovih's wide universe, toward the red star; passing through ten thousand varieties of etherean worlds and roadways in the ji'ay'an fields and forests of high heaven, seeing millions of etherean ships going here and there, every one knowing its own mission and field of labor, while the highest raised Gods and Goddesses could exchange courtesies with the fiery vehicles, and speak to them, to know where they were headed, and for what purpose.

23/2.23. Then rising high; here on a level lies the earth; here the boundary of her vortex, Chinvat, just beyond the sweep of the moon. Cpenta-armij halts here to view the rolling earth, her land and water; and her atmospherean heavens, the sojourning place of the newly dead, and those who have not aspired to rise to holier heavens.

23/2.24. Quickly now Cpenta-armij takes in the situation, and orders the airavagna onward; which now takes a downward course, steering straight toward the habitable earth; slowly now, turning slowly, and descending. Viewing all the regions on every side in the great vortex, she spies the plateau Craoshivi, the newly founded place of God.

23/2.25. And Cpenta-armij, of the Nirvanian Chen-gotha, quickly explains the place to her companions and to her hosts; and, stretching forth her slender hand, itself almost like a stream of fire, she cries out: Behold my anchorage! Bring my ship here and make fast, where the voices of my weary God and his Lords now rise, long expecting me. In Your wisdom and power, O Jehovih, I will raise them up!

CHAPTER 3 Cpenta-armij

23/3.1. Jehovih spoke to God, ruler of atmospherea and the earth, saying: Well done, O My Son! The beginning of the end of your trials is at hand. I have spoken in the highest heavens, in My etherean worlds; in the gardens of Haot-saiti, near the arc of Spe-ta, to My Daughter, who has attained to be One with Me, a Nirvanian in the regions of Chen-gotha, the holy Cpenta-armij.

23/3.2. Her ship, an airavagna, with five hundred million etherean deliverers on board, has started on the road of Salkwatka, bound swiftly for your regions, to your new plateau, Craoshivi.

23/3.3. Send word to Yima, Vishnu and Os to come to Craoshivi, each to come in rank, attended by ten million with grade above seventy, with es'enaurs, marshals, captains and generals.

23/3.4. And send invitations to your Diva to come; and to your sub-Gods, Lord Gods, and Lords, in all the divisions of heaven and earth, have them bring all their people above grade fifty. And give to your marshals a list of all who will be with you in Craoshivi on that day. And your marshals shall apportion, divide and arrange all your hosts thus assembled in Craoshivi, according to grade, approaching your throne in four lines, east and west and north and south, and your throne shall stand in the center but to the east.

23/3.5. Also in the center of the cross, your marshal shall provide sufficient space for the hosts of Cpenta-armij to land her airavagna, and to disembark. But at the outer boundary of the four lines of your hosts you shall draw a circle, and there your light makers shall erect pillars of light, making the circle as a wall of light; and, as the diameter of the circle is to the distance down to the earth's surface, so one-tenth of that distance shall be the height of the apex summit for the canopy over your capital chamber, which shall hold the Holy Council of your Goddess, Cpenta-armij.

23/3.6. God said: Your will be done, O Jehovih! And immediately he sent invitations by messengers, as commanded by the Great Spirit, inviting all the Gods and Lords of heaven and earth, commanding them to come to Craoshivi.

23/3.7. When the Lord Gods, Gods and Lords were thus notified, they appointed substitutes to rule in their places. And they made otevans, every one suitable to the number of angels he was to take with him, and they embarked and rose up from their various places in atmospherea and the earth. And being guided in their courses by experts who had learned the way, they came to Craoshivi, where they were received by the chief marshal of God and his officers, and allotted their various places, according to their respective grades. But as the plateau was above grade fifty in the earth's vortex, accordingly there were no angels of lesser grade than fifty among all the hosts assembled.

23/3.8. And Jehovih commanded God to count the angels thus assembled in Craoshivi, and there were seven billion nine hundred seventy-five million eight hundred thousand, officers and all.

23/3.9. And the day and the hour of their assembling, when they were counted, was exactly the same time that Cpenta-armij's fire-ship arrived at Chinvat, when her light burst in full view to the hosts of God in Craoshivi. And they all saw her coming; saw the manner in which a Chieftainess comes to the lower heavens. And because of the great glory before them, the seven billion burst forth in a song of praise to Jehovih.

23/3.10. Jehovih spoke to God, saying: Ascend your throne, My Son, and allot the Council and your officers to their place, for behold, My Daughter will descend quickly now. And when she comes, My Voice will be with her for the years and days of the dawn of dan.

23/3.11. So God caused his Council, marshal and Diva to take their places and be ready for the emancipated Sons and Daughters. And presently the descending star grew brighter and larger, larger and brighter, till like a sun she shone abroad over all the plateau of Craoshivi.

23/3.12. The Gods stood in awe at sight of the sublime spectacle, for the light of the airavagna was brilliant, and unlike all the lights of the lower heavens, and new to nearly all the people.

23/3.13. Nearer and nearer descended the ship of light, till soon the music of her hosts descended to those beneath, who, awe-stricken and buoyant with delight, burst forth, entranced with the glory of the scene, singing, by the force of Jehovih's light upon them, the same glorious anthem.

23/3.14. And now the marshals spread the way, for the airavagna came close at hand; and over the bows of the airavagna Cpenta-armij shone like a central sun, as did her visiting hosts, Owks, Ha-o-ha and See-wah-Gon; so that were it not for Cpenta-armij holding out her slender hand, the hosts below would hardly have known which of the four great lights Jehovih had sent. Presently the ship's curtains swept across the high pyramid of the capital, and then across the transparent blankets and crystal framework; and now three hundred thousand anchors shot down; slowly the mighty ship lowered itself, till her screen-work, from which the anchors hung, touched the very floors of the capital; and standing before God and his hosts, were the ethereans, all radiant with holiness, the glory of the most high heavens.

23/3.15. The attendants then quickly spread the homa;[738] the masters of arches opened the floor and sides of the airavagna, and there, with its members already seated or standing, was the central part of the etherean Council chamber even as if the throne of God had been built for it. Then the Chieftainess Cpenta-armij came forth, accompanied by Owks, Ha-o-ha and See-wah-Gon, and arriving before the

[738] refreshing fragrance, more delicate than haoma. –1891 glossary

throne, stood, waiting for the salutation and the sign.

23/3.16. God, still sitting on the throne, said: Daughter of Jehovih, Chieftainess of Haot-saiti, in the name of the Father! And he gave the sign Arc of Spe-ta! Cpenta-armij and her three companions saluted in the Sign of the Circuit![739] Which was the highest compliment any God of the earth had ever received.

23/3.17. Cpenta-armij said: By Jehovih's command I am before you, O God. I come in Love, Wisdom and Power. Behold, my Voice is His Voice, Creator of Worlds!

23/3.18. God said: My throne is founded in Jehovih's name. Come and honor it, and bring your most high Gods and Goddesses with you.

23/3.19. They went forward then, and all the Gods and Goddesses, and Lords and Lordesses, stood up, saluting by shaking hands; and then Cpenta-armij went and sat in the middle of the throne. Meanwhile, the es'enaurs chanted a hymn of thanksgiving.

23/3.20. Cpenta-armij, being under the Voice of Jehovih, said: For joy I created man and woman; for seasons of labor and seasons of recreation. Be mirthful before Me, and jubilant toward one another, in remembrance[740] of My creations. And when I call you to labor, behold, My hand will move upon you for the furtherance of My kingdoms in their resurrections.

23/3.21. At this, the multitude broke off from their places and stateliness, and commingled together joyfully. And all those who were on the throne came down and went into the multitude, saluting and rejoicing.

CHAPTER 4 Cpenta-armij

Of the birth of Po, Abram, Brahma and Eawahtah

23/4.1. For two whole days Cpenta-armij left the people in recreation, but on the third she ascended the throne; and lo and behold, even in that same moment of time, a light spread abroad over the entire place, so that the people comprehended indeed what was meant by Jehovih's hand being upon them. And they all resumed their places; at which point Jehovih spoke through Cpenta-armij, saying:

23/4.2. Those whom I brought with Me from Haot-saiti shall be My Council during dawn; but the portals shall remain open on every side.

23/4.3. Those who are not of My Council are not bound to these, My labors, and they shall go and come as they choose, remembering the call of their respective Gods.

23/4.4. For whoever aspires to Me shall come to Me; but the nearest way for many is round about.[741] You, being above grade fifty, are already more to Me and for Me than against Me or from Me, and in equal degree are cast upon your own responsibility. For such is the light of My kingdoms, from the first to the highest: To the child, no responsibility; to grade twenty-five, one-quarter; to fifty, one-half; to seventy-five, three-quarters; but to the emancipated in My etherean realms, responsibility not only to self but to all who are beneath.

23/4.5. And that makes My highest worlds responsible for the lowest, being bound to one another through Me for the resurrection of all.

23/4.6. I come in this day to deliver My Gods down to the earth, to walk on the earth with mortals, raising them up in My name.

23/4.7. Those who shall be raised up in Me, even though still of the earth, shall also be held responsible for all who are beneath them; for with My light and power before them, and doing in My name, those who are beneath them will hold them responsible, not only on the earth, but in heaven, for their labors and words.

23/4.8. The Voice departed, and then Cpenta-armij spoke on her own account, saying: I will now travel once around earth and heaven, seeing with my own eyes and hearing with my own ears, even as is commanded of me by the Father; so I may know from my own experience the condition of mortals, and of the spirits who dwell both with them and in the lowest heavens. He who is still your God shall abide with you on this throne, until I return.

---

[739] This evidently means he was the first God who maintained Jehovih's light all around the earth during a cycle. –Ed.

[740] as in the recounting of stories and sharing of memories

[741] indirectly, circuitously, in a roundabout way

23/4.9. Cpenta-armij then descended and sat at the foot of the throne, and Owks, Ha-o-ha and See-wah-Gon with her, and God went down and took her hand, saying: Arise, O Goddess, and go your way. Then he raised up the other three in the same way, and they saluted and stood aside. Now as soon as God raised them up, the All Light settled upon him, and he again ascended the throne and sat in the middle. Then Cpenta-armij spoke, saying to God:

23/4.10. Jehovih has commanded the raising of a voice in four divisions of the earth; what is your light, O God? God said:

23/4.11. In Jaffeth I have raised up a man named Po, an I'huan of the I'hin side, of grade ninety-five. In Arabin'ya I have raised up a man named Abram, an I'huan of the I'hin side, of grade ninety-five. In Vind'yu I have raised up a man named Brahma, an I'huan of the I'hin side, of grade ninety-nine. In Guatama I have raised up a man named Eawahtah, an I'huan of the I'hin side, of grade ninety-five.[742]

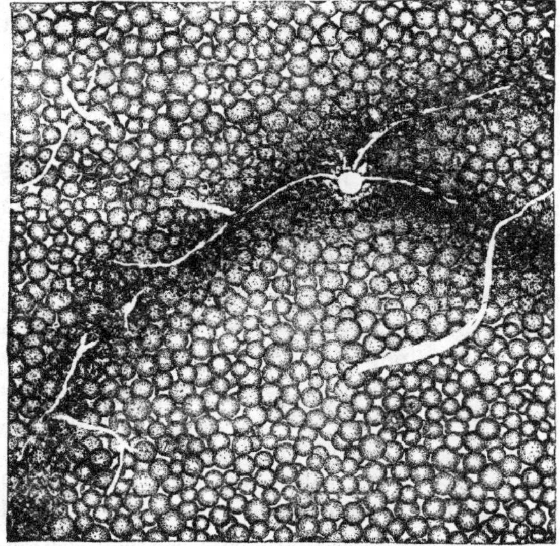

i076 **The Earth in Ocgokuk**. Jehovih said: Out of the etherean mountains of Ocgokuk I brought the earth, prepared for My four Sons: Abram, Brahma, Po and Eawahtah. And I numbered the earth at one hundred, for it had attained to fullness.

23/4.12. The loo'is who have accomplished this labor are still with their wards, but are apprised of your coming. Behold, I send messengers with you who will answer your commands. ||

23/4.13. So Cpenta-armij departed with her hosts, and entered an otevan that God had previously prepared for her; and she took one million attendants with her, going straight down to the earth. First of all she went to visit mortals and mortal kingdoms, kings and queens, temples and oracles, and then to see Po, Abram, Brahma and Eawahtah, each of whom was sufficiently illumed to see her and to know she was the person of the All Voice.

23/4.14. Next she visited all the heavenly kingdoms belonging to the earth, going first to the heavenly kingdom belonging to Japan; then to Ah'oan, of Jaffeth; then to E'chad, and so on until she saw them all.

23/4.15. After that Cpenta-armij returned to Craoshivi, making a circuit sufficient to examine all the plateaus below the belt meteoris.

23/4.16. During Cpenta-armij's absence, which was thirty-two days, God extended the receiving grounds of Craoshivi by twelve thousand miles in breadth toward the south, and founded sixty colonies. For even now, ships were arriving daily with hundreds of thousands of angels who were being prepared for the degree of Brides and Bridegrooms to Jehovih, ready for the third resurrection, and more would continue arriving for the four years to come.

23/4.17. Messengers had arrived in Craoshivi daily from Cpenta-armij, so that God knew when she would return. Accordingly he made preparations, and she was received with due ceremony in the name of the Father.

23/4.18. And Cpenta-armij ascended the throne of God and sat in the midst, and a light like a sun settled around her. Her companions, Gods and Goddesses, did not sit near her now, though on the throne to the right and left. While they were taking their respective places, the es'enaurs were chanting anthems, and the awe and majesty of the scene were magnified to the utmost.

[742] see image i076

CHAPTER 5 Cpenta-armij

23/5.1. When the light fell fully upon Cpenta-armij, the Voice of Jehovih spoke through her, saying:

23/5.2. I am well pleased with you whom I made God over the earth and her heavens; by My hand you have raised them up; through you I have maintained the Diva even to this day.

23/5.3. You shall have honor in My exalted heavens because you are the first in Spe-ta; but you shall crown your glory by descending to the earth and walking with mortals for the term of four years, with My Son, Brahma. And when your time is completed, I will come and deliver you and Brahma.

23/5.4. In My name you shall speak and establish Me among men; and I will be with you in Wisdom and Power. Take your attendants and proceed to your labor; whatever you desire of Me, call, and I will answer, for I have messengers who shall labor between us.

23/5.5. God then saluted, and withdrew. Next came Yima, and Jehovih spoke to him, saying:

23/5.6. Being one with God, you shall labor even as he labors; and you shall descend to the earth, to My corporeal Son, Po, who has been prepared in My name, and you shall walk the earth four years with him. And you shall speak in My name, establishing Me among mortals, to the end that My chosen shall be delivered into My kingdoms. For you shall lead them away from the mortal kings, and teach them to know Me as their only King.

23/5.7. Take, then, your attendants and go to your labor, and at the end of four years I will appoint a successor to you, and I will deliver you into My etherean kingdoms.

23/5.8. Yima then saluted and stood aside. Next came Vishnu, renowned for his labor in Vind'yu and her heavens. Jehovih said to him:

23/5.9. Being one with God, you shall fulfill with him the completion of Spe-ta in My name. For which purpose you shall descend to the corporeal earth, to Arabin'ya, and dwell there for the period of four years with My corporeal Son, Abram. With Abram you shall remain day and night, speaking and laboring in Me as fully as My very Self. And you shall deliver My chosen away from the kings' peoples, teaching them to have no king but Me, their Creator. To Abram you shall reveal My name, Jehovih, and establish it in secret, with due rites and ceremonies. And at the end of four years I will appoint a successor to you; and I will deliver you into My emancipated worlds. Take, then, your attendants and depart to your labor, and I will be with you in wisdom and power. Vishnu then saluted and stood aside.

23/5.10. Next came Os, who had been sent by the etherean regions of Haot-saiti to deliver the kingdoms of Japan and Heleste and their heavens, but who was now relieved by the Divan successor. To Os Jehovih spoke, saying:

23/5.11. In honor of your volunteering in the days of darkness for the relief of God and his kingdoms, I now create you God of the first Spe-ta of the red star, and crown you with My Own hand. ||

23/5.12. And lo and behold, even with these spoken words, a light descended in the form of a crown and settled upon his head; at which, Jehovih said: In which I have made you a lawful Div with corporeal power.

23/5.13. And you shall descend to the corporeal earth, to Guatama, and walk with My Son Eawahtah, whom the loo'is have bred for My Voice, staying with him day and night, for the term of four years, gathering together the remnants of My lost tribes, and establishing them in faith of the Great Spirit, in My name, Egoquim, being suitable to the utterance I have created with them.

23/5.14. And at the end of four years I will appoint a successor to you; and after that I will restore you into My etherean worlds. Take, then, your attendants and depart to your labor, and I will be with you in wisdom and power.

23/5.15. Then Os saluted and stood aside, and the Voice departed; then Cpenta-armij, on her own account, said: Now I dissolve the Diva with honor and glory to them. The kingdoms you ruled over shall be my kingdoms during dawn; in the Father's name I assume them and their affairs. Peace, love, wisdom and power be with you all, amen.

23/5.16. The four inspiring Gods then departed to the outer border of Craoshivi where they each had waiting, a fully equipped otevan, which had been prepared beforehand by their attendants, into which each God with his fifty thousand attendants, now embarked. The musicians then saluted them, even as they moved off, in direct lines for the earth.

23/5.17. Cpenta-armij then lowered the light a little, and her three visiting companions, Owks, Ha-o-ha and See-wah-Gon, sat near her on the throne, before her etherean Council of five hundred million.

23/5.18. Cpenta-armij said: I have visited the earth and her heavens, even the heavens on her very surface. By the power vested in me, I relieve from duty all Lords, Gods, sub-Gods, and sub-Lords, on the earth and in the heavens of the earth. My messengers will communicate this to them, commanding them, in my love and wisdom, which are one with the Father, to come at once to Craoshivi, so I may honor them and apportion them for the third resurrection, which will occur in four years.

23/5.19. To the Lord-dom, Maitraias, founded by Vishnu, I appoint Yugsaesu as Lord and allot him thirty million of my etherean hosts, to be chosen by him. Let Yugsaesu come before me! Yugsaesu then came before Jehovih's throne, and Cpenta-armij said to him: Go to Maitraias, taking your hosts with you. And when you arrive, possess it in Jehovih's name, and establish it in the order of a Lord-dom, providing sub-kingdoms to your place as may be required.

23/5.20. And you shall have dominion over all angels that are already with the plateau of Maitraias, or those who afterward may be sent to you from the other heavenly divisions and from the earth. And you shall provide your kingdom to the service of the Father, in ways chiefly to prevent angels from returning to the earth to obsess and pollute mortals. For you shall find hundreds of millions of them who have no aspiration other than destruction. Many of them were slain in wars on the earth, and are still seeking vengeance, and if they escape to the earth, they obsess mortals to burn cities, to murder, and to all manner of wickedness.

23/5.21. Your labor, O Lord, is not to reform them or teach them, for I shall appoint and allot others to that end; but you shall labor wholly and entirely to prevent the return of Maitraiasans to mortals. And so that you shall be strong before them, you shall draw from all other heavenly kingdoms, which I shall establish, a sufficient guard to enforce my commandments.

23/5.22. For four years you shall labor in this matter, and you shall also raise up one from within your Lord-dom, to be your successor after you. Take, then, your hosts and go to your labors, and the Father will be with you in wisdom and power.

23/5.23. Yugsaesu then made his selections from Cpenta-armij's hosts, and they came and passed before Jehovih's throne, saluting, and then withdrew and went into a ship which had been prepared for them by persons whose labor lies in that matter; and, having saluted with music, they departed, Yugsaesu and his hosts, rejoicing.

23/5.24. Cpenta-armij spoke again, saying: Behold, the time has now come upon the earth when I will divide and allot to each of its great divisions, heavenly kingdoms accordingly.

23/5.25. To Japan, because she is a remnant of the submerged continent, I establish a heavenly kingdom, and it shall be called SUASU.

23/5.26. To Jaffeth, because she has preserved much of the first language, I establish a heavenly kingdom, and it shall be called HI-JEE-TSE.

23/5.27. To Vind'yu, because she is the most advanced in holiness of all the earth, I establish a heavenly kingdom, and it shall be called VRI-MIJ.

23/5.28. To Arabin'ya, because she is the foundation of Jehovih's migratory hosts who shall go forth around the earth, I establish a heavenly kingdom, and it shall be called PARADISE.

23/5.29. To Heleste, because she was rescued from darkness by Os in time to meet this arc, I establish a heavenly kingdom, and it shall be called SPE-TA.

23/5.30. To Uropa, because she was first founded by a woman, I establish a heavenly kingdom, and it shall be called HIMMEL.

23/5.31. To South Guatama, because she is the least inhabited of all the great divisions of the earth, I establish a heavenly kingdom, and it shall be called AHDEN.

23/5.32. To North Guatama, because she is the ground on which the circumscribing of the earth by the different nations shall take place, where the revelations of heaven and earth shall be made to man,[743] I establish a heavenly kingdom, and it shall be called KOSMON.

23/5.33. To all the South Islands, I establish a heavenly kingdom, and it shall be called FLUE.

23/5.34. To all the North Islands, I establish a heavenly kingdom, and it shall be called SIN-YOT.

---

[743] Oahspe is one such revelation.

23/5.35. Now the light of Jehovih spread over Cpenta-armij, and His voice spoke through her, saying: To My ten heavenly kingdoms which I have made through My Daughter, behold, I choose ten Lords, and My ten Lords shall go to the kingdoms I apportion to them. In My name My Lords shall build to Me ten heavenly places of delight, for the spirits of the dead that rise up from the earth.

23/5.36. And in My kingdoms, My Lords shall establish places of learning, places of labor, and places for the sick and helpless angels that rise up from the earth. And My Lords shall raise them up to know Me and the glory of the worlds I have created for them; inspiring them to perfect themselves in wisdom, purity and power, so that they may arise and inherit My etherean heavens.

23/5.37. And My Lords shall appoint ashars to mortals at the time of their corporeal birth; and these ashars shall be appointed to shifts of watch, so they may relieve one another, having a time of labor and a time of rest. And My Lords shall appoint My ashars so that each and every ashar shall have a hundred changes of labor with a hundred different mortals, in order to learn all the varieties of men and women I have created. And the number of ashars shall be equal to the number of mortals dwelling on the earth.

23/5.38. And My Lords shall appoint asaphs to reside in heaven, sufficient in number to receive the spirits of all who die on the earth, which they shall receive from the ashars in My name. And the asaphs shall take these angels, thus received, and place them in the regions My Lords shall have prepared for them, where there shall be sufficient teachers, nurses and physicians in My heavenly places to administer to them.

23/5.39. And My Lords shall provide discipline to the spirits thus received, who shall be trained according to the Divan law that I established through My Gods, and this discipline shall extend beyond the es'yan even to the thirtieth grade.

23/5.40. Then My Lords shall provide for those who have attained to the thirtieth grade by sending them in suitable ships to this place, Craoshivi, and so, deliver them to My Daughter, Cpenta-armij, and to her successor God or Goddess, who shall have dominion over the whole earth and her heavens.

23/5.41. For behold, it is the nature of man on the earth to go after earthly things instead of heavenly; and it is the nature of the es'yan to strive for the earth instead of My higher heavens. Be careful, therefore, to lay a foundation to prevent angels and mortals from going downward; to provide inspiration to make them desire to ascend to My holy regions.

23/5.42. The Voice now departed, and Cpenta-armij spoke on her own account in Jehovih's name, saying:

23/5.43. Let whomever I call, come before Jehovih's throne, for they shall be the Lords whom I shall anoint for the heavenly kingdoms I have established:

23/5.44. Le-tzoo, Lord of Suasu, a heavenly place over Japan.

23/5.45. Oe-wah, Lord of Hi-jee-tse, a heavenly place over Jaffeth.

23/5.46. Loo-gam, Lord of Vri-mij, a heavenly place over Vind'yu.

23/5.47. Ha-kappa, Lord of Paradise, a heavenly place over Arabin'ya.

23/5.48. Jes-Sie, Lordess of Spe-ta, a heavenly place over Heleste.

23/5.49. Yo-han, Lord of Himmel, a heavenly place over Uropa.

23/5.50. Hinot-tse, Lordess of Ahden, a heavenly place over South Guatama.

23/5.51. Ami, Lordess of Kosmon, a heavenly place over North Guatama.

23/5.52. Horam, Lord of Flue, a heavenly place over the Southern Islands.

23/5.53. Puetse, Lordess of Sin-Yot, a heavenly place over the Northern Islands.

23/5.54. All these angels came before Cpenta-armij when called, and they now stood abreast Jehovih's throne, at which point the All Light overspread the place, and the Father's Voice spoke through Cpenta-armij, saying:

23/5.55. You are My Lords and Lordesses, by Me raised up and allotted your places. You shall labor for four years, even to the end of this dawn; and you shall provide successors to take your places after you. And in this lies your greatest glory and Mine. For they who succeed you shall hold dominion two hundred years. And they in turn shall provide successors after them, and so on; for these successions shall continue till the arc of Bon.

23/5.56. With My own hand I weave crowns, and crown you for My kingdoms!

23/5.57. When these words were spoken, the light that was now gathering quickly in a variety of colors, took the shape of ten separate crowns, and descended on the heads of the Lords and Lordesses. The Voice ceased, but Cpenta-armij spoke on her own account, in Jehovih's name, saying:

23/5.58. My Lords and Lordesses, go to your labors in the love, wisdom and power of the Father, and He will be with you; and you shall be a glory in His kingdoms. Therefore, each of you shall choose ten million of my hosts, who shall go with you to your places, to be exchanged or divided later, as I may direct. So that you may choose in order, he who was first appointed shall choose first; the second next, and so on until you have your chosen.

23/5.59. All these Lords and Lordesses were of the Higher Light, and knew beforehand, and had already chosen their attendants in that manner, so that at a given signal the chosen multitudes rose up and came before the throne, forming ten groups of ten million each. And they at once formed in line and passed before Jehovih's throne, saluting in the sign, BIRTH OF SPE-TA ON THE EARTH, and Cpenta-armij answered in the sign, JEHOVIH AND THE LOWER HEAVENS.

23/5.60. Cpenta-armij said: For the glory of this scene, I bequeath a day of rest, so that my hosts may witness the departure of the fleets of Jehovih's Lords and Lordesses. || At once the hosts joined in a mighty chorus of thanksgiving and praise; and they went out and saw the ships laden with the joyous crews; saw them set their great fleet in motion; sang and shouted to them in Jehovih's love, for the glory of His high heavens.

CHAPTER 6 Cpenta-armij

23/6.1. In the beginning of the second year of Cpenta-armij in Craoshivi, messengers came before Jehovih's throne, saluting, and greeting from Ctusk, who now lived under the name, Ahura, and submitted the following communication:

23/6.2. Ctusk, who has become Ahura, a servant of Jehovih, and is now God of Ailkin by just judgment of Jehovih, desires audience with the Most High-Raised Cpenta-armij, Daughter of the Great Spirit.

23/6.3. To this Cpenta-armij answered: Greeting, in love to my brother, Ahura. By the Grace and Power of Jehovih, come and see me, bringing your attendants. || Now, after the lapse of a few days, Ahura came to Craoshivi, attended by one million, escorted by music, and proclaimed according to the discipline of the higher heavens, with heralds and trumpeters. And Cpenta-armij's hosts received Ahura and conducted him and his hosts within the capital chamber; and Ahura went before Jehovih's throne, saluting on the sign, SECOND PLATEAU and Cpenta-armij answered in NIRVANIAN ROAD, SALKWATKA. She said:

23/6.4. In the name of the Great Spirit, Whose Daughter I am, I welcome you in love and high esteem. I know all your past record, and look upon you as the foundation of one of Jehovih's brightest suns. I have long desired that you should petition to come to see me; and I much desired to see you and greet you in the Father's name.

23/6.5. Ahura said: O Most High Chieftainess, of hundreds of thousands of years, how can I stand before you? I know you have seen many truants in your day, and watched their course thousands of years. You can see before me all that awaits me and mine; the past and the future are as an open book before you. That I have stood before you and looked upon you, I am blessed above all things since the day of my birth.

23/6.6. Behold, the hand of the Great Spirit has appeared before me; I comprehend the only road that leads to everlasting resurrections; I know that the ONE ALL PERSON must always stand as the KEYNOTE for angels and mortals. Without Him, a man is like a ship without a rudder; the seas around him drive him to ruin in the end. Blessed is he who has had the experience of this in an early day of his life. Nervous and full of fear is he who has been tried two thousand years!

23/6.7. Then Cpenta-armij spoke, saying: I perceive your desires, O Ahura! I understand why you are before me. Your wisdom is great indeed. You perceive that your plateau is in the second removal from the earth. You fear that some of your hosts will forsake Jehovih, and usurp kingdoms of their own, even as you did in the past. You desire me to raise your plateau farther away from the corporeal earth.

23/6.8. Ahura said: If it is Jehovih's will; for this is the very reason I have come before you!

23/6.9. Now a great light came, bright, like a sun, and settled over the throne, enveloping the Goddess Cpenta-armij, and Jehovih's Voice spoke out of the light to Ahura, saying:

23/6.10. My Son, My Son, why have you so little faith! Behold, I am with you even as I am with this, My Daughter. All you lack is faith. Go back to your plateau and raise it yourself. My Daughter shall come to you, and show you how, and you shall not fail. To have faith in Me is to be one with Me; to lack faith in Me is to be far removed from Me.

23/6.11. Ahura said: O Jehovih, teach me how to begin to have faith. To find the beginning, there is my stumbling block!

23/6.12. Jehovih said: By trying Me, there is the beginning. By learning to know your own power in Me; and to know My power in you; this is the sum of all power and wisdom. By the lack of faith in Me, man sets up himself; by the lack of faith in Me, the self-assuming Gods build kingdoms for themselves.

23/6.13. The failure of man is proof of My power; the failure of all kingdoms is proof of the lack of faith in Me, which proves My power is manifested over them. First, after the abjuring[744] of self, comes the constant manifestation of power through faith, the example of which holds the multitude to Me and My works.

23/6.14. Because you have allowed fear in your soul for a relapse of your kingdom, you have opened the door for disaster. Have I not proved this on earth, in which the faith of a captain leads his soldiers on to victory, and his lack of faith breaks them down in weakness and defeat? Do not think, O Ahura, that My examples are any less applicable to My Gods.

23/6.15. If, therefore, My Daughter should come to your kingdom and raise it up, behold, she would lessen your hosts' faith in you. For which reason you shall return to Ailkin, and proclaim to your people that you will raise your plateau. And though millions of them will consider it vanity, and beyond your power, behold, I will provide for you so that you shall not fail.

23/6.16. Ahura said: I perceive Your Wisdom, O Jehovih! That which You have put upon me, I know I shall accomplish through You. || The Voice departed, and Cpenta-armij spoke on her own account, saying: You shall proclaim a day for this great work; and you shall send invitations to me and my hosts, and to my Gods and Lords, Goddesses and Lordesses. Send, therefore, your surveyors and inspectors, and determine where you would raise your plateau, and you shall be provided from my hosts whatever assistance you may need.

23/6.17. Ahura then saluted, and he and his hosts departed from the capital chamber, and rested awhile in recreation with the etherean hosts; after which they entered their ship, departed and returned to Ailkin. There Ahura appointed the day for the resurrection, and sent messengers throughout atmospherea, proclaiming what he would do, inviting Gods and Lords, with their attendants, to come and spend the day with him.

23/6.18. Jehovih spoke to Cpenta-armij, saying: Send your mathematicians to estimate the grade of Ahura's plateau; and send your surveyors to the place he has chosen, so that your hosts may know the power required; and you shall provide from your own hosts, privately, suitable stationers so that Ahura shall not fail. For, in time to come, Ahura shall be one of My greatest Gods.

CHAPTER 7 Cpenta-armij

23/7.1. So on his return to his kingdom, Ahura immediately set about accomplishing this great labor.

23/7.2. Now there were many with Ahura who had been sub-Gods, captains and generals under him while he was in rebellion against Jehovih and His kingdoms; and when they heard of the proclamation they said within their souls: What, is it possible Ahura is at his old games? For they did not know of his concert with the kingdoms above, and so did not believe in his power.

23/7.3. Jehovih moved upon Ahura, and induced him to send numerators and graders throughout his kingdom, to take the measure of those who had faith, and of those who had no faith, and of those who had neither faith nor non-faith. And Ahura graded and numbered these, so when the time came he would know where to place them. Then he numbered the unlearned and dumb; and then the enthusiastic; and he graded them and arranged them also.

[744] abnegating, turning away from, renouncing

23/7.4. When he had this much accomplished, there came to him one Anuhasaj, a former sub-God, and he said to Ahura, privately: I love you, Ahura, and for that reason I have come to you. You shall meet only failure and disaster in your undertaking. How many times, in your mighty kingdom of Ctusk, did the All High fail to come to you?

23/7.5. Ahura said: Because of your love I rejoice in you; but because of your lack of faith I deplore you. How long will it be before angels and mortals understand the Father and His kingdoms? Behold, in the days of Ctusk I did not labor for Jehovih, but for myself and my exaltation, and for the exaltation of my kingdom for my own ends. Consequently the All High did not come to answer my prayers. Now in this matter, I am doing that which is not for me, nor for my kingdom for my own sake, but for the Father's sake only. And I know He will not fail me.

23/7.6. Anuhasaj said: Has it not been from the time of the ancients till now, that certain ones say that by prayer and faith all things are possible, assuring us, moreover, that by these, all things are accomplished on earth and in heaven? And yet, who has not witnessed more failure than success? I do not desire to discourage you, O Ahura, but well I know the lack of faith on the part of all men, and that to get one's self weaned away from self is the weakest talent in the soul. And, for which reason, too, it is ultimately the greatest glory. But it would seem to me to be expedient to have Cpenta-armij and her hosts do this resurrection for you.

23/7.7. Ahura said: Even your every thought I have already fulfilled. And through the Chieftainess came the Father's Voice, commanding me to do this resurrection on my own account.

23/7.8. Anuhasaj made no reply to this, but in his soul he was not free from the tetracts, being jealous that by obtaining the Father's commands Ahura had advanced beyond him. But Ahura did not perceive it, and he said to Anuhasaj: The hosts of Ailkin have been counted, and there are four billion five hundred million. And within the grades above es'yan there are one hundred and seventy thousand schools, two hundred and thirty thousand colleges, four hundred thousand factories, and two hundred thousand hospitals.

23/7.9. Behold, on the day of resurrection I shall have the Han-od-wotcha recreation for my hosts. Let this, then, be your labor, to have the matter proclaimed throughout Ailkin. Anuhasaj said: By Jehovih's leave and yours, I am satisfied.

23/7.10. Thus ended the matter; but Ahura remembered later that Anuhasaj had not answered positive acceptance, and so Ahura feared that Anuhasaj might not fulfill the task, and so to make doubly sure, he called Evasan, and committed the same charge to him.

23/7.11. Now when the time came, lo and behold, Anuhasaj did not fulfill his part, but Evasan did; and Evasan, moreover, came to Ahura, bringing answers from all the departments.

23/7.12. In the morning of the day of the resurrection, Ahura sent for Anuhasaj and inquired concerning the matter. Anuhasaj said: No, I did not issue your proclamation or your invitation, for I reasoned on the matter, saying to myself: If the resurrection is a failure, then it would indeed be better that the ignorant do not know of it.

23/7.13. Ahura said: To do one's own part well, is this not the highest? Anuhasaj said. It is the highest. And I did so; for I have done that which seemed the highest in my own sight.

23/7.14. Ahura said: The resurrection was not for you or me, but for the hosts. For you had previously admitted that the resurrection of this plateau was the highest, best thing to be done. Even though it seemed impracticable in your sight, you were not justified in withholding your hand. You should have striven to accomplish that which was for the universal good, not even whispering your distrust to anyone. Then if it had failed, your own soul would have been clear. For which reason Jehovih came to me, and I was admonished for my oversight, and so, assigned Evasan in your place, and he has fulfilled my commands.

23/7.15. Anuhasaj made no reply, but went away in displeasure, and for the present the matter was dismissed.

23/7.16. Ahura had sent invitations to the Lords of all the divisions of the earth, asking them to come, bringing their attendants with them. Of these the following came, namely: Oe-wah, Lord of Hi-jee-tse; Ha-kappa, Lord of Paradise; Loo-gam, Lord of Vri-mij; Jes-Sie, Lordess of Spe-ta; Ami, Lordess of Kosmon; Horam, Lord of Flue; and Puetse, Lordess of Sin-Yot, each bringing one million attendants, besides hundreds of thousands of visitors of lower grade.

23/7.17. Cpenta-armij, with her visitors, Owks, See-wah-Gon and Ha-o-ha, along with five million attendants and thirty-five million visitors, came from Craoshivi in an avalanza made for the purpose.

23/7.18. The place of relocation that Ahura had decided to inherit was in the second belt below meteoris, known in atmospherea at that time as Vara-pishanaha, a heavenly place, uninhabited, which lay between the land of Vind'yu and the star-region known as the HORSE AND COW AND CALF PASTURES. To travel from Ailkin to Vara-pishanaha would take fourteen hours in grade twenty-five, which was the average of Ahura's hosts; but its enlargement in the upper belt would be as fifteen to nine.

23/7.19. Cpenta-armij and her hosts were the first to arrive in Ahura's dominion, for she was determined that nothing would lead to failure in Ahura's enterprise. Following her advice Ahura stationed water-bearers along the entire distance of travel, lest, in the excitement, the drujas might run into knots or riot. For such is the nature of darkness, both on earth and in the lower heavens: The low delight to dwell in a city, or near a place of filth, for companionship, rather than go to a place of isolation where improvement is possible.

23/7.20. Jehovih had said to Ahura: Do not permit your drujas to know you will be moving them so far from the earth; confide only in the wise regarding your destination. Cpenta-armij had said to Ahura: Provide a parade holiday for your drujas, with rites and ceremonies. And Ahura perceived how the matter had to be, so he apportioned eighty million of his hosts to provide parades, rites and ceremonies for the drujas among his hosts. Of these drujas, there were one billion two hundred million ranking below grade five, being angels who did not know the left hand from the right, nor could they remember how to count to five from one day to the next. And yet the next billion, rating below grade twelve, knew only a little more, and were scarcely wiser than beasts in the field.

23/7.21. Cpenta-armij, seeing these, exclaimed: O Jehovih, how long must Ahura labor with these in order to raise them to grade ninety-nine! O if only they who set themselves up as Gods knew what lay before them! O if leaders of men knew! O if only mortal kings and queens knew the bondage that they lay down for themselves! What a work in the lower heavens for them before they can ascend! And yet, O Jehovih, You are just. Someone must labor with these unfortunates. It is well that man aspires to be king, and Lord and God.

CHAPTER 8 Cpenta-armij

23/8.1. When all the billions of angels were assembled for the resurrection, Cpenta-armij went and stood at the right hand of Ahura, and next to her stood Owks; and at the left hand of Ahura stood See-wah-Gon and Ha-o-ha, and the Voice of Jehovih fell upon Ahura, saying: Extend My lines to the four corners of the world; give the highest grades into My labor.

23/8.2. Accordingly the marshals drew the line on the plateau, and the hosts of etherea stood equally toward every corner, arranged in phalanxes of ten million each, each having the form of a quarter of a circle; leaving spaces where the lines of power ran from center to circumference, and the distance was equal to the width of Vind'yu on the corporeal earth. And the center of the plateau was high raised, so that Ahura stood on the highest place, which lay near the CAPITAL OF THE COUNCIL.

23/8.3. Now it so happened that the jealous Anuhasaj stood twelfth on the east line, being the thirteenth from Ahura's left hand. Cpenta-armij said to Ahura: Behold, the line is shattered. Ahura said: I feel nothing; what do you mean, the line is shattered? She answered him, saying: He who does Jehovih's work must deal as Jehovih deals. Only those who are in concert with you must labor with you. Otherwise your best endeavors will be thwarted. Ahura said:

23/8.4. O far-perceiving Goddess! In my much love and sympathy I admitted Anuhasaj to the lines. He has been my best friend. Cpenta-armij said: You shall know only One Friend, Jehovih.

23/8.5. Ahura perceived, and he now felt the shattered place, and he sent his chief marshal to Anuhasaj to bring him from the rank. And when Anuhasaj was before Ahura, the latter said to him: Because you serve yourself, you shall not stand in line; behold, there is only ONE to serve, even Jehovih. Anuhasaj said: A joy upon you and your scheme. Because you are powerless, you have singled me out as an excuse before these Gods and Goddesses!

23/8.6. Ahura made no answer, but spoke before Jehovih, saying: Give me strength for Your Children's sake, O Father! Behold, I have cut loose the foundations of Ailkin; with high-extending cords I have bound her to Vara-pishanaha. By virtue of Your power in me I will raise her up. In Your name, let my hosts in will command: ARISE! UPWARD! ONWARD! O AILKIN! ARISE, UPWARD, ONWARD, O AILKIN! ARISE, UPWARD, ONWARD O AILKIN!

23/8.7. With the third enunciation, which came from the billions in concert, behold, the plateau moved from her foundation; turned a little, then slowly rose upward. Loud shouts and cheers erupted from the inhabitants of that heaven; for, along with their own universal will, the Great Spirit had stretched forth His hand and raised up the heavenly continent. Even as with His hand He touches a corporeal continent and sends it beneath the ocean, so also does He raise His heavenly places toward His emancipated worlds. Yes, because of His Spirit upon His people, they desire it risen; with them and Him, ALL IS ONE.

23/8.8. And now the Gods, with unbroken will, held their places through what was daylight for the corporeal earth,[745] and not a God or Goddess strayed a moment of time from the single purpose in thought, nor did any distracting thought intervene; for such is the will and mastery of Gods over their own thoughts. Nevertheless, to keep up the concerted force joyously, those who had the drujas in charge set the games and tournaments going, with racing and music, so that there was not one idle moment for all the hosts of Ailkin, nearly five billion.

23/8.9. Upward and onward rose the great plateau, making straight course for Vara-pishanaha. Ahura stood in the eyes of the unlearned populace as the greatest and most masterly of all the Gods. One alone, even Anuhasaj, stood awhile transfixed with disappointment and chagrin,[746] even hoping some mishap to Jehovih's proceedings. And, finally, he went wandering about, sore and out of sorts with all righteousness.

23/8.10. Thus was raised the heavenly place, and no longer called Ailkin, but Vara-pishanaha, home of Ahura and his hosts. And now, when they were securely established in the new place, and the Gods and Goddesses broke from their line, they all came greeting Ahura. And, even in that same moment of time, a messenger came from God, who was with Brahma on the corporeal earth, bringing to Cpenta-armij the following commandment, by proxy, namely:

23/8.11. In Jehovih's name, give a throne and crown to Ahura for me, and in my name. I promised him thus!

23/8.12. The light came upon Cpenta-armij, and Jehovih spoke through her, saying: Behold the work of My hand, O Ahura, My Son! From the substance of heaven I fashion you a throne and high-raised capital. And with My own hands weave you a crown. From this time forth you shall be My God, and I will abide with you.

23/8.13. While the words were being spoken, the throne rose up before Cpenta-armij's hand, and a high-raised capital came and stood over the throne extending beyond it. And there descended from the heavens above bows of light and color, which in Cpenta-armij's fingers were shaped and woven into a crown, which alighted on Ahura's head. And there went up from the hosts a universal shout of praise and thanksgiving. Then seven million trumpeters broke in, and after they played a while, the es'enaurs chanted: THE CONCERTED HOSTS OF JEHOVIH!

23/8.14. Thus was founded Jehovih's heavenly kingdom, Vara-pishanaha, in which Ahura established his dominions where rebellion and secession were cut off forever. And Cpenta-armij gave to Ahura a thousand messengers, and opened a roadway to Craoshivi. Ahura ascended his throne, and the Gods and Goddesses saluted him, GOD OF VARA-PISHANAHA, and they and their attendants departed to their various places.

CHAPTER 9 Cpenta-armij

23/9.1. In the third year of dawn Jehovih spoke to Cpenta-armij, saying: Gather together the officers of your traveling hosts, and take your companions with you, and go and visit all the Lords and Lordesses of the earth, whom you appointed. And let your recorders make their accounts of the affairs of the earth and her heavenly

---

745 i.e., likely from sunrise to sunset, near summer solstice; recall it was a 14-hour journey (23/7.18)

746 wounded pride, humiliation, resentment

kingdoms, so that they may be taken to, and entered in, the libraries of the Nirvanian kingdoms.

23/9.2. Also you shall set your collectors of Brides and Bridegrooms to work in Craoshivi; and give otevans to your collectors, so that they may also visit your Lords' kingdoms and collect all the angels prepared for the next resurrection, and bring them to Craoshivi, where they shall be classified. For in the coming resurrection you shall provide twelve avalanzas for those who are to be raised to the etherean heavens; therefore, you shall cause them to be divided according to their grade and rate, in order to have them delivered after the marriage ceremony to etherean regions suitable to their advancement. ||

23/9.3. Prior to this, the Lords had contributed abundantly to Craoshivi, and already there were more than twenty billion angels capable of taking the third resurrection; and these were also classified accordingly. Now, the departure of Cpenta-armij on her impending visit was important, for it involved the selection of the next succeeding God of earth and heaven, who would sit on the throne during her absence. At this time, the reigning God was with Brahma on the earth, so Cpenta-armij sent messengers to him, acquainting him with the commandments of Jehovih.

23/9.4. God answered through his messengers, saying: Greeting, in the name of Jehovih, to Cpenta-armij, His Daughter, Chieftainess! The reigning God deputizes you, O Goddess, to make the selection instead, to be crowned at the termination of dawn. || And now, accordingly, Cpenta-armij sent forth her examiners, to search for the highest, best, most learned of all that had been raised up from the earth, capable of the God-head. For sixty days her examiners were at work, and in the evening of the sixtieth day, they had completed the search. And it fell upon Thale of Peola, whose corporeal birth had been five thousand years before.

23/9.5. Thale, a tiller of the soil in corpor, born in spirit in Yueson, ninety years; five years in es'yan; thirty years in factories; in the nurseries, ninety years; in the colleges, one hundred and eighty years; projector, seventy years; surveyor, sixty-five years; measurer, two hundred years; entered an etherean airavagna, and traveled seven hundred years; returned to the lower heavens of the earth and for twelve hundred years was Lord in six successions for each of the chief earth divisions; was called by Onavissa, Goddess of Ni-yi-ag-ag-ha to clear the roads of Chenshaya, beyond Chinvat, where he labored six hundred years. Returned again to the earth and her heavens, and served as captain and general for four hundred years; served as marshal seven hundred years under four different Gods and Lords; and the balance of the time traveled as messenger and swift messenger. Of the rates in a thousand, he was nine hundred and ninety-nine. And he knew the whole earth and her capabilities; could read a billion voices at the same time, and interpret them and answer them, and had even created plateaus. He knew the atmospherean heavens, habitable and uninhabitable; the roadways; the oceans and nebulous regions; knew the ascending and descending ethe; knew the power in the different rings of the earth's vortex; knew the c-vork-um,[747] and its times and places.

23/9.6. Cpenta-armij sent a delegation of one million angels to wait on Thale and bring him before the throne at Craoshivi, sending them in her private otevan, and under the guardianship of her chief marshal, with this commandment:

23/9.7. Thale, of Peola, greeting to you, in the name of Jehovih, Who commands your immediate presence at the throne in Craoshivi. Of all the honored in these heavens, you stand first on the list, and are appointed by our Father to be the next succeeding God, through His Daughter, Chieftainess of Haot-saiti. You shall sit on the throne in my place while I complete my labor in dawn; after which you shall be crowned Jehovih's God of the earth and her heavens!

23/9.8. Cpenta-armij knew Thale, for he had sojourned three hundred years in Otaias, in etherea, where she had been Surveyor ten thousand years. So when he came before Jehovih's throne, Cpenta-armij was rejoiced to meet him in person; nevertheless, she first saluted in rank, saying:

23/9.9. My brother, welcome in the Father's name, and joy to you. Jehovih has called you to this throne; you shall be one of the pillars of His everlasting temples. What I put upon you in the Father's name, you shall consider from Him.

23/9.10. Thale said: Before You, O Jehovih, I bow to Your decrees, which come through Your High-Raised Daughter, Chieftainess of Haot-saiti. I

[747] the path of the solar vortex

accept whatever is given me to do, that will raise up man to rejoice in his creation. By virtue of Your power in me, O Jehovih, I know I shall not fail. May Your Light be upon me!

23/9.11. Cpenta-armij now raised the light to the highest atmospherean grade, and said to Thale: Approach Jehovih's throne, O my brother, and hold up your hands toward High Noon, as the symbol of the highest light, for as the sun is to the earth and atmospherea, so is Jehovih to the soul of man and to the etherean worlds.

23/9.12. Thale stepped onto the foot of the throne, and the marshal stood at his side. The whole Council was seated, and sweet music rose from the es'enaurs, which added to the solemn scene. Thale then faced the place of High Noon in the temple and held up his hands, saying: I am in Your Will, O Father!

23/9.13. Jehovih spoke in the light over Cpenta-armij's head, saying: Thale, My Son, you are My God, and you shall have dominion over the earth and her heavens for two hundred years. Whatever you shall do shall be of Me and My doing. Your word shall be My word; your labor My labor. And you shall have Lords and kingdoms, and all manner of heavenly places; and all of them shall be My places through you.

23/9.14. And at the expiration of your service, you shall raise up a successor to you, who shall be worthy of you and Me. And he shall likewise have dominion in Me and in My places; and likewise raise up a successor to come after him, and so on until the next dawn of dan. Be joyful in dominion; My worlds are places of delight, mirth, peace, love, righteousness, and good works.

23/9.15. The Voice ceased, and then Cpenta-armij spoke on her own account, saying: He who will crown you will come at the end of dawn; till then you shall hold dominion in the RED HAT, in memory of the FEAST OF LIONS. Approach the Judgment Seat, my brother, and I will give you dominion in Jehovih's name. || Then Cpenta-armij gathered from the colored rays of light, a substance light as ethe, and made a red hat and put it on Thale's head, saying: Sit on the throne in memory of the FEAST OF LIONS, so that I may be honored because of you, and rejoice before my hosts.

23/9.16. Thale then sat down on the throne, and the Council proclaimed in the sign, LION'S DEATH! Thale answered in the sign, DOMINION OF THE LAMB! And Cpenta-armij spoke, saying: Council of Jehovih, hear my voice. I have raised up a new God to my labor. And you, O God, hear my voice. I have given a new dominion into your keeping.

23/9.17. For one year I shall now visit my Lords and Lordesses in the first plateaus of the earth, for it is a part of my labor for the Father. And when I have finished with them, I shall return to my present reigning God of the earth, who is with Brahma, and I will deliver him and Brahma, and return again to this kingdom, where the etherean resurrection will take place.

23/9.18. Provide accordingly in all things, even as I would if I were here; and count the Brides and Bridegrooms one hundred and sixty days in advance, and send swift messengers to etherea, to the Nirvanian fields and forests in Chan-us-hoag, and then through Salkwatka to Haot-saiti, in the etherean Abarom, finding six regions, suitable for grades from sixty to ninety. And you shall send greeting to my sister, Chue-in-ista, Goddess of Oambuyu, asking her to deliver us.

23/9.19. Having said that, Cpenta-armij withdrew along with Owks, See-wah-Gon and Ha-o-ha, and in their own proper way departed out of Craoshivi, and in the airavagna descended to the lowest plateau, and so, visited the Lords of the lower kingdoms.

CHAPTER 10 Cpenta-armij

23/10.1. The work of the Lords and Lordesses did not require much labor from Cpenta-armij; for they had long been high-raised Gods and Goddesses in other worlds, and knew their parts well. But Cpenta-armij sent her heralds in advance to each heavenly place, and the Lords and Lordesses in turn sent receiving escorts to meet the airavagna. And when the Chieftainess arrived, she was asked in the usual manner to honor the throne, and she thus sat on all the thrones, ruling in actual person, and in her presence the Voice of Jehovih spoke in the Light before the assembled COUNCIL OF THE HOSTS, and it was thus fulfilled in the ARC OF SPE-TA that the VOICE had circumscribed the whole earth.

23/10.2. And when Cpenta-armij was about to depart from each heavenly place, she always descended to the foot of the throne of the Lord, and sat there; and the Lord went down and took her hand, saying: Arise, O Goddess, and go your way; the Father calls you! And then she would arise and depart to another Lord or Lordess, to proceed in like manner.

23/10.3. Now for this entire trip, Cpenta-armij had taken with her three thousand angel scribes and recorders, three thousand angel artists, three thousand angel geologists and mineralogists, besides many others, all of whose trade was to make reports of the lands and waters of the earth, and the air above the earth; and they were to include pictures.

23/10.4. For Jehovih had said to Cpenta-armij: You shall make reports of the land, water and air of the earth, and of all the living, and include pictures of these things. Two copies you shall make; and when the end of dawn comes, you shall take the two copies with you in your ascension to My etherean worlds. One copy you shall put on record in the library of Haot-saiti, and the other copy you shall send to the Hyperiis Council of the United Chiefs and Chieftainesses, for their own deliberations.

23/10.5. For the Hyperiis Council shall determine from your report, what is good for the earth; as to whether she shall be changed in her course, or broken up and divided; or whether she needs a'ji or dan; and they shall send out road-makers to that end, or send vortices against her vortex, to break it or rule over it, according to My light upon them. ||

23/10.6. Besides these, Cpenta-armij had a thousand recorders, whose business it was to prepare reports of the Lords' kingdoms, and of the factories, colleges, nurseries, hospitals, the hells, if any, and knots, if any; to record the grade and number of spirits in each heavenly place; to record the earthly kingdoms, and kings and queens and their subjects, their occupations and grades, and their rate of corporeal life age. Also they were to record the percentage of familiar spirits with mortals; the fetals, the drujas; as well as the ashars and asaphs; and the temples and oracles in use by mortals; the altars and places of worship. And to record the number of I'hins still inhabiting the earth; the number of pure I'huans, who worshipped only one Great Spirit; and the druk order, who always have idols or saviors, and are given to war.

23/10.7. Cpenta-armij remained with each one of the Lords of the earth for one full moon of four quarters; and then she departed, going to all the habitable places on the earth, and into the heavens that rested on the earth. In ten moons she had completed her labor with the Lords of the first resurrection; had witnessed the manner in which the Lords sent away the upraised to Craoshivi, to enter the second resurrection. And her scribes and recorders had completed their labor also.

23/10.8. And now the Chieftainess sent her airavagna back to Craoshivi, with her visitors, Owks, See-wah-Gon and Ha-o-ha. But for herself, she had a piedmazr built; and taking ten thousand attendants, besides the workers of the boat, she descended onto the very earth, to visit the four Gods, in the four great divisions of the earth; who were with Wah-tah,[748] Brahma, Abram, and Po. With each of these she spent twelve days, and then she departed and went to the heavenly place Maitraias, the only Lord-dom of the earth, where Yugsaesu ruled, with thirty million. Here she remained twelve days also; and the inhabitants gave a tournament and festival.

23/10.9. After this Cpenta-armij departed for Craoshivi, for the end of dawn was near at hand.

CHAPTER 11 Cpenta-armij

23/11.1. In the Council of Craoshivi the Voice of Jehovih came to Cpenta-armij, saying: Behold, the time of your sun and stars rises in the Road of Salkwatka. The red star approaches the fields of Abarom; Great Oteson has filled the sinks and slues of Yosawakak; billions of My Sons and Daughters behold the Feast of Spe-ta.

23/11.2. Hear your Creator, O Cpenta-armij! For you shall spread broad the table of My hosts; to an extent never before seen in Haot-saiti. And you shall send for Obed, God of Oise; Gavaini, Goddess of Ipthor; Ab, Shriever of Riv-Sing; Raisi, Goddess of Esdras; Wish-tse, God of Zuth; Harava, God of Yon-yon; Vraga-piet, Goddess of Zoe; and Loo-chung, God of Ata-bonaswitchahaha. And you shall send for the Gods and Goddesses of the Plains of Cnoe-Chang; and for the Gods and Goddesses of the Chi-ha-wogo Roads; and for all the Gods and Goddesses in their own Nirvanian fields; and for the Great Chief, Shoo-lo, of the Roads of

[748] i.e., Eawahtah

Jini-hassij, and for all the Gods and Goddesses in his dominions in My etherean worlds.

23/11.3. And from your own memory also, you shall remember many Gods and Goddesses; and you shall charge your companions, Owks, See-wah-Gon, and Ha-o-ha, to sit in Council with you, so that you may remember any Chiefs and Chieftainesses, Shrievers, and Gods and Goddesses, who may be delightful:

23/11.4. And you shall command them in My name to meet in the Feast of Spe-ta, for it is the first in this, My new world. Make way for them; make place for them, O My Daughter! Make wide the roadways in My lower heaven; make My Holy Feast glorious.

23/11.5. Cpenta-armij said: Too wide are the dans of earth; too far apart and cumbersome, O Father! More than twenty-four billion will be my harvest to You, O Jehovih! Great is Your wisdom in Spe-ta; the time for the beginning of quarter ascensions, fifty years.

23/11.6. Your Gods and Goddesses, O Jehovih, and Your Chiefs and Chieftainesses, will bind up these loose heavens into wholesome discipline. I will send my swift messengers into Your far-off etherean worlds, and bring Your Sons and Daughters to Your Feast. ||

23/11.7. Cpenta-armij sent invitations into the wide heavens, high beyond the earth heavens, to tens of thousands of high-raised Sons and Daughters of the Great Spirit. Then she called her surveyors and table-makers before Jehovih's throne, and said to them:

23/11.8. The end of dawn is near at hand; I will give a feast, a very great feast. Go and survey the ground from Craoshivi to the Lakes of Oochi-loo, in etherea, and for the length of it, make a width in the form of Fete;[749] and the road of the Fete shall be sufficient for the passage of twelve avalanzas abreast; and the depth of the Fete shall be as from the surface of the earth to Chinvat. You shall carry the border flames to within twelve sios of Abarom, and of the height of the circuit of Bilothowitchieun; and the flames shall be of double currents, going and coming, so that the food of the feast may be brought from any region suited to the high-raised grades.

23/11.9. And the arc of the feast shall encompass the whole earth, and extend outward to the belt of Craoshivi, and then downward in two lines, east and west; and the downward lines shall be like the feet of a compass, one stationary and the other movable. And the light that extends from the arc down the movable line shall rest on the delivered hosts of Abram, and it shall bear upon his people, so that, after this, they can draw Light direct from the Father's throne in Craoshivi; and it shall move westward and be as an inheritance of Jehovih's light upon His corporeal sons and daughters.

23/11.10. But the line that stands in the east shall be a base line and center, where the Father's light shall descend upon the delivered sons and daughters of the hosts of Brahma and Po. And because of the arc of Spe-ta upon them, they shall remain in their own divisions of the earth.

23/11.11. And for the deliverance of the harvests of the quarter, the high-raised horns of the arc shall stand to the four quarters, east, west, north and south.

23/11.12. Jehovih then spoke through Cpenta-armij, saying: For I will illume the horns of the arc, and My new world, the earth and her heavens, shall rest in the light of My Roads forever. So that no man, having My examples before him, can misunderstand Me.

23/11.13. Behold, to a child, only one lesson a day is given; to a youth, two lessons a day; and to a mature adult, many lessons a day; likewise in the early creation of man, I give few lessons; then in the youthful age of the race, many more lessons; but when the race has attained to full adulthood, behold, I lay My light at their feet, so that they may take My lessons every day.

23/11.14. In one age I send the angels of the dead to lead man up to a knowledge of Me and My places; but when man has attained to think for himself, I set up My arc of Spe-ta; and it is like a candle in the firmament of heaven, from which My Light falls upon the soul of My people, without any interpreter, except My Own Voice.

23/11.15. For which reason, when one of My worlds has attained to Spe-ta, I come to deliver them from kings, queens, priests and angels, and it is like the maturity of a son in his father's house, when he invites his neighbors and spreads a feast.

---

[749] see image i033r07a, p.132

23/11.16. Open wide your places, O Cpenta-armij! A great joy is upon My etherean worlds; My high-raised Sons and Daughters shall have great glory in the earth and her heavens. Behold, I have proclaimed Myself in the words of mortals; four high-raised sons have learned to know their Father in heaven.[750]

CHAPTER 12 Cpenta-armij

23/12.1. Cpenta-armij said: Who can understand Your models, O Jehovih! Who cannot understand Your models, O Jehovih! You have shown to mortals the food of the flesh, and the source of the substance of the blood.[751] You have created Your corporean members as a symbol before them of Your es'sean worlds and Your es'sean peoples; to receive and to impart, but this is not all. You created poison, to show man that whatever does not receive, and does not impart, is death.

23/12.2. Most wisely, O Father, You have provided the degrees of subsistence to all Your creations: To the corporean, corporeal food; to the atmospherean, atmospheric food; to the etherean, ethe'ic food. Wide I will spread my tables, O Jehovih. Your Gods and Goddesses, and Your high-raised Chieftains, shall sit at the Feast of Spe-ta.

23/12.3. The Chieftainess sent five hundred thousand swift messengers into the regions of etherean worlds, near the Roadway of the Great Serpent. Down to the atmospherean regions she sent ten thousand messengers to the Gods and Lords, her laborers. To her invited guests she privileged each to bring one million attendants.

23/12.4. Next Cpenta-armij sent a message to fifty thousand arrow-ship makers in the regions of Cvent-agma, in the etherean Itis, to prepare ceremonial salvers and connecting rods, so that all the billions, being united, could hear the Voice of Jehovih from her mobile throne, in her airavagna. Twelve counterparts to these she sent down to the lowest heavenly regions, so the All Light could pierce the corporeal earth.

23/12.5. And now, when her well-skilled workmen, of tens of thousands of years' experience, had saluted and gone off to their respective labors, the Chieftainess spoke before the Council, saying: Because of my arc upon the earth and her heavens, the Light of our Father will forever remain with mortals and in the hadan fields. But, behold, even as a young man, coming to maturity, goes away on his own account, in great hope and self-conceit of his powers, to meet many misfortunes and great darkness, so will it be with the earth and her heavens after Spe-ta. Because I plant my arc in these heavens, and say to its Gods, "You are free!" behold, there shall arise numerous false Gods of great power. And as a young man going forth is puffed up with conceit, so will the atmospherean Gods believe they know all things, and so, bring great darkness and misery upon their kingdoms and upon themselves.

23/12.6. But the Light of my arc shall stand; shall grow like a small seed planted; and in time to come, both angels and mortals shall understand that there is only ONE ALL LIGHT, a very center, to Whom all Gods are only like small diadems. As a young man of the earth must have experience of his own to realize his own shortness, so must even the Gods of these lower heavens be left to run with a loose rein, for the glory of Jehovih, and for themselves in final deliverance. For which reason, starting now, the bondage of the discipline of the God and his Lords shall be as nothing.[752] From this day forward they shall use fire and water (as a method of enforcement) only for casting out hells and knots; they shall hold dominion in their respective places only by persuasion, and the example of practice.

23/12.7. As in the early days, a king rules with a rod and with tyrannous[753] laws; and as, in a riper age, the king and his armies give way to a power

[750] That is, Brahma, Abram, Po and Eawahtah. – Ed.

[751] Presumably this is a reference to the type of food a mortal eats—vegetable foods keeping the blood clean, pure and cool, and good for the spirit in keeping peaceful and content as seen by the models of herbivore animals; while making a food of animals and other flesh keeps the blood unclean, impure and hot, making the spirit contentious, impatient, predatory, etc., as seen by the models of carnivore animals.

[752] That is, the discipline of God and his Lords shall not be forced.

[753] stern, exacting, rigorous, dictatorial, strict

vested in the people, so shall my arc be the giving of the lower heavens, and the earth beneath, into the keeping of themselves. But my arc, which is the foundation of the Father's upper kingdoms within the lower heavens, shall stand forever.

23/12.8. I go now on my journey down to the earth, in my airavagna, to receive and deliver my four Gods, Os, Vishnu, Yima, and Ela-elia, God in Chief.

23/12.9. Thus saying, Cpenta-armij descended to the foot of Jehovih's throne, and the light fell upon Thale, and he rose up from the throne and descended, taking her hand, saying: Arise, O Goddess, and hear the Voice of your Father, Creator and Ruler! Behold, your labor on the earth and her heavens is near the end; and because of your steadfastness, I am honored in you, My Daughter.

23/12.10. While you are delivering My Gods, behold, I will be with you, and whatever you desire of Me I will give to you. My Sons and Daughters shall receive the visiting hosts from the high heavens, and allot them places in the feast; and My Sons and Daughters shall receive and adorn My Brides and Bridegrooms; and My trumpeters shall proclaim Me in My works, from the surface of the earth to the farthest places in Salkwatka. Yes, My Light-makers shall plant the staff of My holy fire in the throne of Craoshivi, and the foot of the staff shall pierce the earth in the land of Vind'yu, to receive and deliver My earth Son, Brahma.

23/12.11. Go, O Chieftainess, Holy One, of Great Wisdom and Power; it is the Voice of your Father!

23/12.12. Cpenta-armij stood aside, and then said: To you, my loved companions, Owks, See-wah-Gon, Ha-o-ha, when the staff of the Father's light has descended to the earth, come quickly to me then in my arrow-ship of fire, for it shall be a signal between us that in that hour I will raise up my Gods from the corporeal earth; and I will open the earth and bring forth the bodies of my son, Brahma, and his wife, Yu-tiv, whose youngest son holds the leaven of the Osirian law. And I will have the hosts of my ten Lords assembled there, and I will deliver into their hands, for their successors, the fulfillment of the Divan laws.

23/12.13. Her companions responded: In Jehovih's wisdom and power, we will be there.

CHAPTER 13 Cpenta-armij

23/13.1. The Light of Jehovih now spread over Haot-saiti and lined the Road of Salkwatka, in etherea, extending from the Orian Banks of Loo-che-wan to the Oixanian Spars of Ochesu. The Cross Roads, Chi-ea-wha-chong, and the plains of Sha-tumatz, were like seas and worlds of crystal fire. And in the piercing light, the old-time Gods, of millions of years ago, sped forth in awesome majesty, in answer to the prayers of Cpenta-armij.

23/13.2. And over the earth and her heavens, farther than Chinvat, rose a trident arc, broad as a world; of shimmering light from the countless rays of ethe, like mortals see the glimmering air on a summer's day; but the ethe was of every color, hue and tint, reflective and brilliant, the clear soul of things separate, the very breath of Jehovih. It was the beginning of the form of the arc of Spe-ta, the deliverance of the earth and her heavens into a new condition; to give, to bestow it upon itself, ratified by the ceremony of a festival for the Gods and Goddesses within the neighborhood of hundreds of millions of miles around!

23/13.3. Meanwhile, their high-raised companion, Cpenta-armij, known and loved in hundreds of etherean worlds, was down on the low earth, laying the cornerstone for Jehovih's everlasting kingdom, on which would fall, presently, from out the arc of Spe-ta, a shaft of fire, the feast for the purified Chieftainess, who had for four years subsisted on the coarse provender of the lower heavens!

23/13.4. And touched by the hand of Immortal Light, was Brahma, long trained to look toward Jehovih; for his angel wife rose upward, leading his vision toward a realm among the Gods and Goddesses, whom he saw in countless numbers receiving her most royally. Thus gazing on the glorious scene, the great man in soul came forth, leaving his corporeal part stretched on the ground. And Cpenta-armij and God took him; received the soul of Brahma, and held, in obedience to the sacred purpose, his place in the sacred circle with mortals three days.

23/13.5. Then, on the fourth, the Chieftainess signaled her swift messengers; and they touched the currents along, till they ran high beyond the earth's vortex, where the stationed Gods of etherea fastened on the ethe'ic wave, extending to the great arc over all.

23/13.6. It was the signal for the shaft of light; of which mortals have a weak and coarse symbol in the electric currents which tear things meaninglessly and without judgment; but the ethe'ic current is not so small and purposeless, but mighty, being a tool from Jehovih's fountain of All Power, and learnedly directed with skill by high-raised angels who have had millions of years of experience, and who know well what prayers deserve an answer from the Immortal spheres.

23/13.7. And Cpenta-armij's name, and word, and wisdom, had long been in fellowship with mighty works on many worlds; and her well-trained thought, so tuned to the Creator's purpose, kept ever in concert both with the ethe'ic foundation of each place and with the administration of thousands of Gods and Goddesses.

23/13.8. And when the signal shot upward, and from beyond Chinvat the shaft of light began to pierce the earth's vortex, making way for Craoshivi, it was also the signal for Owks, See-wah-Gon and Ha-o-ha, to fly instantly for their arrow-ship and make full speed for Cpenta-armij; which they did now, even as a flash of light darts forth, being guides and directors of Jehovih's flame to the grave of Brahma and Yu-tiv.

23/13.9. As Cpenta-armij, standing by her ship, saw the shaft descending, she flew forth to the center of the circle; her hand pointing to the graves, she said: There, O Jehovih! Come forth, O earth! Earth, in Jehovih's name! It is I who commands!

23/13.10. And down fell the bolt of light, piercing the newly disturbed ground, made rich with mortal tears, and thus made powerful to the soul current; and as a breath of wind would move a heap of feathers, so did the light, by the wave of Cpenta-armij's hand, blow the earth away, and lift up the buried forms of two dead lovers, Brahma and Yu-tiv, and marched them in their unspoiled and newly animated bodies before the mortal audience, together, lovingly, hand in hand, triumphant over death.

23/13.11. Then spoke Hog, the youngest mortal son, an Osirian in belief, seeing the resurrected forms, saying: It is, it is! The very Brahma! And Yu-tiv! My father and mother!

23/13.12. The great Brahma, now quickened in Cpenta-armij's arms, and in God's, spoke a few words from Jehovih's throne, to the loving sons and mortal concourse,[754] then took final leave. Cpenta-armij seized the folds of the shaft of light, as a mortal would the ropes and canvas of a toy ship, and wrapping it securely around the earthly part of Brahma and Yu-tiv, then wheeled in line her own ship and raked in the etherean current from high heavens.

23/13.13. Tossing up her hand, the prearranged signal to the great workers in the trident arc above, the exchanging currents of the traveling flame began, and raised up all the etherean hosts along with the bodies of Brahma and Yu-tiv, which had not raised a mile before they were etherealized, scattered and gone; and the souls of the two sweet loves rested in cognizance and fellowship with the millions of Jehovih's Sons and Daughters, now swiftly making way for Craoshivi.

23/13.14. Cpenta-armij's work was done. In the arc of light and companionship of her compeers,[755] the feast was open, and the billions in rapport[756] sat along the series of tables, hundreds of millions of miles, to relish soul food brought from more than a thousand worlds.

23/13.15. Meanwhile, God, to finish his labors, resumed his throne in Craoshivi just in time to receive the twelve avalanzas, sent from Yuckowts' factories, in Abarom, in etherea, which were to receive in Jehovih's name the twenty-four billion Brides and Bridegrooms, who were to take the degree of third resurrection and be raised beyond the earth's vortex and emancipated in the etherean realms of Haot-saiti.

23/13.16. Chue-in-ista, Goddess of Oambuyu, chief commandress of the fleet, having been apprised of the number of initiates, had prepared twelve thousand rings, a thousand for each avalanza; and the fleet, in turn, was in a ring, and the ring extended sufficiently wide to encircle the holy capital and throne in Craoshivi, so that when it had descended to its place, God and his officers, and the Holy Council of heaven and earth, now thirty million members, were in the center of the audience. On every side, far as the eye could see,

---

[754] gathering, assemblage

[755] peers, colleagues, associates

[756] consonance, fellowship, harmony, friendship

stood the Brides and Bridegrooms of Jehovih, arrayed in spotless white, fearless before the Light and ceremonies.

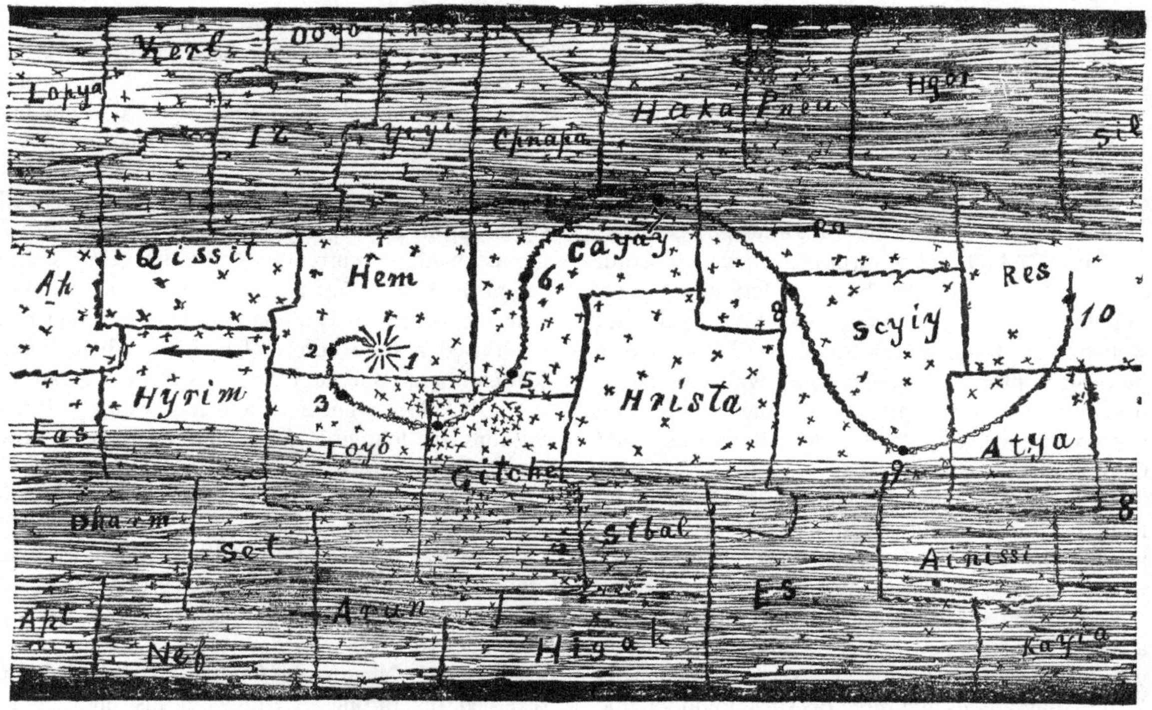

i097 **Anoad.** C'vork'um; and A'hiss'a-Corpor [Great Serpent], embracing nine phalanxes. First of Spe-ta period. Earth, 3 = 765,744. Gitche, 86. Hem, 11. Entrance to Hyrim, 6,000 years.

23/13.17. When the fleet landed, Chue-in-ista, the commandress, came forth from the east, facing God on the throne. She said: Your voice, O God, has called the name of Jehovih. Behold, I am His Daughter, sent by Him to know your will and Holy Desires?

23/13.18. God said: Behold, I am His Son! You are my Sister! Hear me, then, in our Father's name. I have here a harvest of twenty-four billion angels, pure and holy, brought up out of the earth for Jehovih's emancipated kingdoms.

23/13.19. Chue-in-ista said: Let them answer before me in His name, so I may witness their wisdom and power as being sufficient to dwell in All Purity. My Father and I are one; my hosts have crossed the Nirvanian pastures; they no longer feed on substance rising from below, but on the Light emanating from etherean realms above.

23/13.20. God said: I know You have provided for me, O Jehovih!

23/13.21. Then the hosts of Brides and Bridegrooms responded, saying: By Faith I know I am safe in Your kingdoms, O Jehovih. Take me to Your emancipated worlds; give me scope and power and wisdom, for greater works.

23/13.22. Then the full ceremony followed in the usual way of the third resurrection; and was witnessed by Cpenta-armij and other Chieftainesses and Chiefs above, who were at the feast of the arc of Spe-ta; and when it was completed and God had said: O Jehovih, give me crowns for Your Sons and Daughters, Brides and Bridegrooms for Your etherean worlds! || There were cast down by Cpenta-armij and her hosts, twenty-four billion crowns; and they alighted on the heads of Jehovih's Brides and Bridegrooms. ||

23/13.23. And now God turned to Thale, who was to be his successor for the next two hundred years. God said: In Jehovih's name, I bestow to you the crown of earth and her heavens. And I also bequeath to you the triangle, symbol of these regions, and the inqua,[757] and the trident, the latter being new in these worlds, and symbolical of the arc of Spe-ta; and the interpretation of the trident shall be the Three Lights: Jehovih; His Son, God; and the Star in the mortal soul, emblem of resurrection.

23/13.24. Thale said: In Your name, O Jehovih, I will be God of earth and her heavens till the next rise of dan! Be with me, O Father!

23/13.25. So he who had been God laid the crown and jewels on Thale, saying: Hail, O God of earth and heaven!

23/13.26. Thus ended the ceremonies. He who had been God descended to the foot of the throne and sat down; and then God (Thale), came down and took his hand, saying: Arise, O God, and go your way! || And he rose up and prepared to depart, for the ceremonies had now lasted one full day.

23/13.27. Cpenta-armij, seeing it was finished, signaled the hosts for the close of the festival, and with her airavagna passed over and above the fleet, and gave Chue-in-ista, the commandress, the sign, at which the ascent began. The tens of billions of angels entered their respective places. The music of the es'enaurs and of the trumpeters sounded and resounded, to the distance of a hundred worlds.

23/13.28. Upward rose the fleets; downward fell the showers of flowers and perfumes to those left behind. Higher and higher rose the great world of lights; higher and higher, till soon they passed beyond the earth's vortex, the boundary Chinvat.[758]

END OF BOOK OF CPENTA-ARMIJ, DAUGHTER OF JEHOVIH

[757] This would be the inqua git's'ang, see 20/43.21-22.

[758] see image i097

First Book of God

Being contemporaneous with the Book of Cpenta-armij, Daughter of Jehovih. As the latter book relates to the higher heavens, so the First Book of God deals with the lower heavens and with the earth, for the same period of time. This book treats fully of the four great persons chosen by God, namely: Po, of Jaffeth, inspired by the God Yima; Brahma of Vind'yu, inspired by the God Div; Abram, of Par'si'e, and afterward of Arabin'ya, inspired by the God Vishnu; and Ea-wah-tah, of North Guatama, inspired by the God Os. And their inspirations were for the same period of time, known in the kingdoms of heaven as the time of the arc of Spe-ta. These four Gods were the chief Divan Gods of that day, Ha'chue being Div in Chief.

CHAPTER 1 First Book God

24/1.1. The Creator of creations! Out of Whom all voices are! Of Whom all things are in semblance![759] From Him and in Him these utterances are, by His Gods and Lords, and high-raised angels and mortals.

24/1.2. Into whose dominion He gave the earth for the glory of Jehovih, Whose God came and walked and talked with those who had been prepared for the deliverance of His chosen.

24/1.3. For the four preserved divisions of the earth, He gave four Sons of holy light and power for the voice of God and his Lords:

24/1.4. Po, of Jaffeth; Abram, of Arabin'ya; Brahma, of Vind'yu; and Eawahtah, of Guatama; whose records are everlasting on the earth, which are testimony that these men were raised up by the Father for His Own glory, and for the deliverance of men (male and female).

[759] i.e., all things are like Him in some way

CHAPTER 2 First Book God

The first Chinese Bible—being of Po, an Iesu,[760] *chosen by God for the children of Jaffeth*

24/2.1. These are the generations of the Line of Light from the time of Zarathustra:

24/2.2. Shu Sa, Gwan, Loo, Sam, Dhi Jo, Wee, Him, Gow, See, Wing, He Wen, Tse Kong, Lam Ne, Moo Yow Tine, Luts, Hime, Mai Se, Hong, Ghee, Wan Ghee, Tse Loo, succeeding one another.

24/2.3. All the foregoing were seers and prophets of God (Light), having the Voice from their youth up, and were each in turn a shield and guardian to the chosen of God (Faithists).

24/2.4 God (Light)[761] said: With Tse Loo, behold, the Voice was lost. But I called aloud on the face of the earth, and my Light spread abroad. ||

24/2.5. And there came a woman of Che Song, named Ha-se, an I'hin, through whom the Voice was regained.

24/2.6. Ha-se had seven sons and seven daughters, all of whom heard the Voice, and saw the Light.

24/2.7. And God divided the fourteen sons and daughters, one from another, and sent them in different ways.

24/2.8. These, then, are the tribes that sprang from them: King, Si, Gwe, Loo, Hi-Gah, Hi-se-Gua, Yo, Ha Fung, Ne, Hi Lam, Se'ing, Yuth Lo, Jon, Ying'e and Ho Lun Gow.

24/2.9. From the line of Ha Fung sprang Enam-jo and Ze'zoo (half I'hin). From Ying'e sprang No'e and Yu Laim; also Yu'tse and He-ah. And God commanded the He-ahns to dwell toward the south, and they so dwelt.

24/2.10. From the line of King descended the We Yah-Ho; and they lived toward the north and made fellowship with the Foe-Sim, who were I'huans by blood, and also followers of the Zarathustrian law under the name Sa Sin, having rab'bahs whom they called bah, the same as to this day.

24/2.11. From the tribes of Foe-Sim sprang Han. And from We Yah-Ho sprang Hi and Te-Wing'e; both of which tribes had the Light and the Voice.

24/2.12. And all the north regions of Jaffeth dwelt in peace and happiness.

24/2.13. And God looked upon them and blessed them in all things.

24/2.14. Nevertheless, it came to pass that the tribes of Han forgot the commandments of God; and Le Han, a mighty chieftain, rose up among them, and re-established the Osirian doctrines; that corporeal knowledge should stand higher than the Ormazdian law.

24/2.15. Han usurped the central throne of Jaffeth, calling himself HAN, KING OF THE SUN. And so Han gave himself up to obtaining knowledge, and to enforcing knowledge upon the people.

24/2.16. Han issued the following decree: Han, King of the Sun! Behold, there is one sun and his satellites. There shall be only one kingdom, with satellites.

24/2.17. Behold me, I am the sun king! I will put away all other doctrines and learning. Let all the world bow down to me!

24/2.18. Han was asked: Shall a man not worship the Unseen? He answered: It is better to worship a stone, which you can see.

24/2.19. Han said: Do not worship in words, but in works; do not worship in prayer, but in doing righteously. What is prayer but crying to one's own weakness?

24/2.20. If there is an Unseen Light, He will do in His own way. What is the use of praying to Him? Rites and ceremonies to Him are the expression of folly. Rites and ceremonies to our forefathers are excusable. If their souls continue to

---

[760] Iesu means without sin, or one who has risen above sin; accordingly an Iesu is a person who moves in light. Iesu also means having no earthly desires for their own sake; and signifies having no sexual desires. Which is to say, Iesu can also refer to a person born of neutral sex, or very nearly so, i.e., was neither boy nor girl insofar as sexual organs were concerned, for these were not discernible, or not readily discernable—being undeveloped even as seedless variety of fruits can reveal undeveloped seeds within. Hence a natural-born Iesu is incapable of naturally producing offspring, as was the case with Po.

[761] With the ancient Chinese the word Light is equivalent sometimes to our English word God, and sometimes to Jehovih (Creator), just as Christians and even Jews sometimes make no distinction between the words God and Jehovih. –Ed.

exist, the rites and ceremonies may give them good pleasure.

24/2.21. So Han abolished the worship of Jehovih (Light) and His God and Lords.

24/2.22. God looked down from his holy hill in heaven, and he said: It is well; let Han have dominion. Behold, Han enraptures the multitude with his new doctrines, forgetting that these doctrines were tried thousands of years before.

24/2.23. God prophesied through his prophet Ze-wing'e, saying: Hear me, O Han, and all you people of the whole world. I prophesy by the Voice and Light; I know my words are true words: By words the soul is bent;[762] by not praying to the Unseen, the Unseen will be forgotten. By the abolition of rites and ceremonies to the Gods, the Gods will be forgotten. Man will rise up in self-conceit against his Creator, saying: Behold me; I am the highest of all things; my judgment is the greatest of all wisdom. And the tribes of men will aspire to establish opinions as fundamental doctrines. War and destruction will come upon the nations!

24/2.24. Han would not heed the prophecy of God. Han established what was called THE FIRST HAN DYNASTY, and it spread over the land of Jaffeth from center to circumference.

24/2.25. And because of the laws of Han, great persecution came against the Faithists, the worshippers of Jehovih (Light).

24/2.26. Han said: Try them by the food they eat; and whoever refuses to eat fish or flesh shall suffer death. And the favor of the courts shall be denied to any man or woman who holds sacred the life of a cow, horse, dog, or any other animal on the face of the earth, or in the waters, or in the air above the earth.

24/2.27. So the Faithists, the followers of the Zarathustrian law, were outlawed, and were tortured and put to death on every hand.[763] And the prophecy of Ze-wing'e came true.

24/2.28. God said: Behold, they have not only forgotten the Creator, and denied His Person in words, but in behavior also. For they no longer hold sacred anything He created alive, even man.

[762] i.e., words shape the direction and inclination of the soul

[763] i.e., whenever discovered

CHAPTER 3 First Book God

24/3.1. From Ze-wing'e, God raised up prophets for seven generations. Ze-wing'e begot Do Tse, who begot Yin, who begot Hi Ne, who begot Lan Se'ang, who begot Dhi Hsotch'e, who begot Ho Lon, who begot Po, who was an iesu in birth.

24/3.2. When Po was still very young, the voice of God came to him, saying: Be steadfast in the doctrines of your forefathers, eating neither fish nor flesh; your God will not only preserve you alive, but you shall gather together the scattered tribes of Zarathustrians, the Faithists, and re-establish them in this great land.

24/3.3. In those days many of the Zarathustrians were celibates; and the king saw his people being reduced by war, so he made a law against celibacy, commanding all men to marry, and all women to bring forth children, or be put to death.

24/3.4. When Po was grown up, God said to him: Behold, you cannot fulfill the law, for you are iesu-born. But I will fetch you a wife like you, who is also barren, but you two shall be blessed with three children, and you shall call them Wan-le, To-ghan and Tse Loo.

24/3.5. And it came to pass that a woman of Hong Ge, with three adopted children, escaped from the tyranny of Dhi'Wan, fleeing for the southern tribes of Hi See Gua and Yo, and Gwan Gooh; and Po married her and named her Ah T'dowh Jee.

24/3.6. Po was twenty years old when he married, and he went with his wife and three children to the country of Heng'a Di, which name signified brother land, and he labored at scutching [764] flax and hemp.

24/3.7. And God came to Po, saying: What is the extent of your fidelity to the All Highest Light?

24/3.8. Po said: I will obey Him in all things.

24/3.9. God said: Would you sacrifice your three sons, if commanded by your Creator?

24/3.10. Po said: They are the Creator's, not mine. How dare I sacrifice that which is another's?

[764] Scutching separates the fibers from the pulp by beating the stems. From the flax or hemp fibers were made cloth for blankets, clothing, tapestry; rope; and other items.

24/3.11. God said: You are wise; you know the Ormazdian law.

24/3.12. Then Po asked: Who are you? Who is this that comes upon me silently, asking questions?

24/3.13. God said: Go and visit Hi Seiang, the philosopher, and question him.

24/3.14. Hi Seiang was governor of the south province of Heng'a Di, and was also a man of great learning.

24/3.15. Po came to him and questioned him, saying: What is this that asks us questions? Why do we question and answer ourselves all day long?

24/3.16. Hi Seiang answered: Are we not two selfs? Do we not discourse within ourselves like two selfs?

24/3.17. Po asked: Which do you say is the superior self, that which questions within us forever, or that which is forever answering?

24/3.18. The governor said: That which asks questions must be the superior self.

24/3.19. Po said: Who is it?

24/3.20. Hi said: It is nothing, it is something. Po answered him, saying: It appears to me, these two selfs are two different persons; one belongs to the flesh, the other to the Creator. Because this questioning self is the same one that sees and hears Gods and angels.

24/3.21. Hi said: What did you say? God and angels?

24/3.22. Po replied: God and angels.

24/3.23. To which the governor took exception, saying: Do you too defy the law?

24/3.24. Po said: What I see I see, what I hear I hear. Something external to ourselves made us, and rules over us.

24/3.25. The governor asked: Have we not rid the world of superstition? Why do you deal with doctrines that were in the dark ages? I tell you there are only two things in all the universe; the unseen firmament, and the corporeal worlds that float within it. Their action and reaction on each other produce what we call life, which is only an effervescence that comes and goes, and there is the end.[765] The laws are right. Han has done a good thing in abolishing the doctrines of the ancients.

24/3.26. While they were still talking, God sent a blaze of fire into a bush standing nearby, and a voice spoke out of the flame, saying: Who, then, do you say I am? For truly I am!

24/3.27. The governor saw the light, and saw that the bush was not burnt; and he also heard the voice. But God suffered him to be hard of heart, and Hi said: Behold, you come to me, knowing I am a philosopher, and you cast your spell in the bush, like a magician. I am master of a thousand books, and am registered as a man of great learning. You have offended me.

24/3.28. Po said: Why accuse me? For is it not as just for me to accuse you of casting the spell? I did not cast it.

24/3.29. Again God appeared and spoke, saying: Do not accuse this, my son, Po. You shall labor with him. Behold, I give into your keeping the country of Feh, for at this hour Moo Gwon has died. The tribes of Ghan shall be gathered together in Feh and Heng'a Di.

24/3.30. Hi Seiang, the governor, was astonished at the words of the Light; and he sent a servant to ascertain if Moo Gwon was dead; and it turned out to be true, though the distance was a day's journey each way.

CHAPTER 4 First Book God

24/4.1. Hi Seiang, the governor, sent for Ah Sin to come and investigate the nature of Po. So when the three were together, God wrote in the sand the word TE-IN, and it was as if a flame of fire pierced the ground.

24/4.2. Po said: From now on, Te-in shall be the name of the tribes who have faith in the Creator only. Because He alone has written it.

24/4.3. Ah Sin said: How can you distinguish between that which is written by the spirits of the dead, and that which is written by the Creator?

24/4.4. Po said: Light comes in light; darkness comes in darkness.

24/4.5. Hi Seiang asked: Are you saying you can see the angels and the Gods?

24/4.6. Po said: I see the angels, but the Gods I cannot see. Angels are like ourselves; but the Gods are like a flame of fire.

24/4.7. Now while they were thus discoursing, a light in the form of a triangle came and rested on Po's head, and the word Te-in was inscribed on the sides of the triangle.

[765] the end of life, the end of all philosophy, the end of a person

24/4.8. The governor said: What does this signify? And Po, being under the influence of the light of God, said:

24/4.9. Call me Te-in; I am the Father (rab'bah, or bah) over all the living. I write in the sand, and speak in the mouths of My seers and prophets. He whom you call Po is My Son, begotten for the deliverance of My chosen out of the bondage of Han and his satellites (sub-kingdoms).

24/4.10. Behold, My people are imprisoned and tortured; persecuted and abused. And you two have kingdoms taxed for the glory of Han in his unrighteous work.

24/4.11. Provide yourselves with triangles also, and espouse[766] Me, and I will deliver your kingdoms also. ||

24/4.12. Hi Seiang and Ah Sin both desired some pretext to throw off the yoke of the Han dynasty, and now lent willing ears to the instruction of Po and the Voice (Te-in).

24/4.13. Accordingly, the learned men of these provinces were called together, to learn, through Po, about God and the mysteries of earth and heaven, and especially about the great monarchy.

24/4.14. When these Councils were assembled, God cast his light upon Po, and they all saw it. And the words Po spoke were called God's Words (Vede'or). And they learned the wisdom of God word by word, repeating them over and over (until memorized), which was called learning by the mouth, as distinguished from learning by books and tablets.

24/4.15. God said: Great trials will come upon my people. The kings will seek to destroy the doctrines of the Lord your God (Te-in).

24/4.16. For which reason you shall neither write nor engrave my words until I come in judgment of the world.

24/4.17. These, then, that follow, are the sacred laws given through Po, by God (Te-in):

24/4.18. Seek to bring forth heirs that will be a glory to your Creator.

24/4.19. Do not marry because of the impulse of the beast (animal nature of man),[767] but consider your own spirit and the spirit of your spouse.

[766] choose, uphold, advocate

[767] sometimes called natural man; carnal desire; impulse of the flesh

24/4.20. Do not shut yourself up in celibacy, but multiply and adorn the earth.

24/4.21. Your Creator provided milk for the infant; but with the coming of teeth, you shall provide for their service also.

24/4.22. Feed him according to the Ormazdian law. To make him a warrior, give him fish and flesh. To make him patient and strong, with docility, remember the camel and the ox, feeding on the herbs that grow on the earth. [Those of Te-in forswear the first and espouse the second, eating herbivorously. –ed.][768]

24/4.23. Ne-gwon asked: Was celibacy not the highest of all laws? Is it not so now?

24/4.24. God said: There are times for all things. In the days of Zarathustra celibacy was the first of laws. In those days man was not ready for God's laws. Yet you shall not call one law higher than the other.

24/4.25. The fullness of earth knowledge requires marriage, yet the bondage after death holds the spirit of man for six generations to his own heirs. By celibacy, a man's soul is not bound after death (by the love he bears his children) to linger on or near the earth, and he may ascend quickly into paradise.[769]

24/4.26. The man or woman who is weak (sickly, chronically infirm), or deformed, blind, deaf, with running sores, or with hidden sickness, shall not marry, nor bring forth heirs. Nor shall man take sorrow to his soul for this; for it is the testimony of the Father that his race is emancipated from the earth.

24/4.27. You shall keep the Panic language sacred; nor shall these, my holy words, be given in any other language till my time is fulfilled on the earth.

[768] Keep in mind that the Ormazdian law is given here. Note also that both the Zarathustrian law and the I'hua'Mazdian law through the Diva, would specify an herbivorous diet for mortal Faithists. (To see difference between the types of laws, see 22/1.17-37.)

[769] That is, love will bind a person to his or her child and to any descendents to six generations after oneself (about 200 years or 6 x 33 years); but the celibate in not having children, is not thus bound.

24/4.28. Your sons at the age of eleven years, and daughters at the age of nine years, shall begin to learn maxims.[770] And at that same time they shall be consecrated to the Creator and committed to His service. And of the sixth law, this is made a part, namely: Teachers in public shall be celibates; children who decide that they will become teachers, or priests, or priestesses, shall take the vows of celibacy. For such persons are married to the Great Spirit; and they shall be like Gods and Goddesses, knowing no more love to one person than another.

24/4.29. Remember that those who marry are chosen by Ormazd to raise up offspring for the glory of heaven and earth; and they shall dwell together in peace, love and harmony.

CHAPTER 5 First Book God

24/5.1. The wise shall rule over the foolish, but only to raise them up.

24/5.2. The rich shall apportion their riches for the benefit of the city.

24/5.3. The poor shall reverence the rich and take counsel from them.

24/5.4. Behold, I have given many gifts to my people: the woman to give suck; the very strong man to carry burdens; the wise man to oversee the city; the learned man to explain the ancients; the prophet to hear my voice; the magician to hear the voice of angels; the physician to heal the sick. To every single one I gave good gifts.

24/5.5. You shall not covet[771] another man's gifts, but be wise in discovering your own, and using them for the benefit of the city.

24/5.6. Neither shall you covet another man's riches, nor anything that is his. What more is a rich man than a watchdog? Behold, it is his matter,[772] whether he fulfills my commandments.

24/5.7. According to every man's gifts, so do I require of him, as to what he can do for the people of his city.

24/5.8. To the poor man, my exactions are lighter than a straw on a camel's back.

24/5.9. For the ignorant man, and for the very young child, I provided the wise and the rich as Gods to raise them up. As they minister to them, so do I bless them for their labor.

24/5.10. What they do corporeally for the resurrection of those beneath them, so do I answer them in spirit in my resurrections in the heavens.

24/5.11. You shall marry only once; neither shall you look after any other partner all the days of your life.

24/5.12. The husband shall be the master of the house; but when he is not present, the wife shall be master.

24/5.13. Seven castes I have made for my chosen: The first are the prophets; the second, those who have the highest genealogy; the third, the rab'bahs and priests; the fourth, the nuns (spe-e-su); the fifth, physicians; the sixth, the rich, and seventh, the very poor.

24/5.14. Each and every caste shall remain by itself; all of them are worthy before me, and are equally my children.

24/5.15. You shall not kill, for food to eat, anything that breathes the breath of life.

24/5.16. You shall love to search for your Creator in all things on and in the earth, in the waters, and in the air above the earth.

24/5.17. You shall love to search for all that is good in your neighbor; but to excuse all the evil that is in him.

24/5.18. You shall keep the sacred days of your God, and cause all your people to rejoice in the delightful creations of your Creator.

24/5.19. You shall obey the prophet of your God; and be obedient to the father (rab'bah) of the city. Next to these, you shall honor your father and your mother, and pay reverence to your grandfather and grandmother.

24/5.20. Remember that all men are alike in the house (temple) of your God; for even as death lays the high and the low alike, so is the standing of my people in the house I have built.

24/5.21. You shall respect the opinions of all men; for even you may be in error.

24/5.22. You shall speak only a little of yourself or of anything that is yours; for all others have a history also.

24/5.23. You shall make yourself compatible to others in all righteousness.

---

[770] concise statements of basic truths, rules of conduct, ethical behavior, morals, doctrine, etc.

[771] strong desire to want something that is another's; must have for oneself

[772] business, affair, responsibility

CHAPTER 6 First Book God

Of cities and government

24/6.1. To reinstate the Zarathustrian law, the largest city shall not exceed two thousand souls; and the smallest shall be ten families. Unless they are celibates, in which case a city may be as small as eight souls, having one rab'bah or priest.

24/6.2. The best, highest learned man, who shall be a celibate, shall be the priest and ruler of the city; and the sins of the people of the city shall be upon his head. But if it is a large city, he may choose one, or as many as six priests, to rule with him; and in that case, the sins of the city shall be upon them.

24/6.3. When a matter comes up, the priest shall call whom he will to speak on it; and when they have spoken, he shall decree by his highest light, and that shall be the law without repeal, except by himself.

24/6.4. It shall be lawful for the governor, who is the chief priest, prior to death, to repeal all his laws; so that his successor shall make new laws. For no man shall be bound after death by his own laws, because he cannot come back and repeal them.

24/6.5. But regarding the laws a governor or chief priest makes while he rules over a city, and over all persons whom he has ruled during his lifetime, he shall be responsible for them, both in this world and the next. For if a priest or governor makes a law of darkness, and his people live by that law, their souls will be in darkness in the next world through his fault, and he shall answer to them in the soul world for what he has done in this.

24/6.6. In cases where the manufacture of copper or iron, or other things, requires more than two thousand people, there shall be another city, with five breadths of the first city between them. And the government of the second city shall be like the government of the first. But in no case shall there be more than four cities nearby in the same country.

24/6.7. You shall neither hire nor be hired, either among yourselves or with the kings' peoples. Neither shall you have servants nor masters, for all shall be alike servants to Ormazd only.

24/6.8. Sin-wah inquired: Was it not taught in the Zarathustrian age to respect the caste of men according to the number of their servants? And whether, according to their genealogy, they were born of parents who had risen above servitude for many generations?

24/6.9. God said: The old law was for the past. It was a good law to improve the breed of men for special trades and learning. And that law has fulfilled its purpose. The physician has found great cures; and he knows all the parts of the flesh and the blood. The miner knows the different kinds of stone, the metals in them, and how to extract them. The farmer knows grounds, their yield, and what they will best bring forth. The spinner and weaver have found the best of fibers for paper and cloth. And so by the Zarathustrian law of caste it has come to pass, that they have perfected these things in all departments, sufficient for the requirement of man.

24/6.10. For which reason you shall teach all things to all; and they shall work with their own hands at all industries; remembering that the highest, best, most perfect man is he who can do all things.

24/6.11. Jon-Le inquired: Since a man dies in a few years at most, why shall he strive to learn things that pertain to the earth?

24/6.12. God said: All learning is like a gymnasium to the spirit. Knowledge is the strength of the soul.

24/6.13. You shall teach all things to your sons and daughters, perfecting them in the talents created with them: first, to useful labors; second, to learning; third, to music and art, in sculpture and painting; fourth, to mining; and fifth, to perfectness.[773]

24/6.14. And you shall intersperse labor and learning with recreation, not only in rites and ceremonies, but in harmless games, as in dancing, racing and playing; and for the old as well as the young.

24/6.15. Cultivating joyous hearts, for these are outspoken words of glory to the Great Spirit.

24/6.16. Every governor, priest and rab'bah shall provide for a successor; they shall be chosen according to the light of the Council of the All Highest.

---

[773] i.e., seek improvement of all talents and seek perfection in all things

i109 **Po.**

CHAPTER 7 First Book God

24/7.1. Hi Seiang became converted to the doctrines of Po as taught by God, who was called Te-in in those days in that country.

24/7.2. Ah Sin and Hi Seiang and Tse Gow entered into compact to throw off the dominion of Han, and so notified him. Han immediately declared war against them. And he pursued them cruelly, laying waste a great country.

24/7.3. Po and his followers were thus driven toward the south; and on their way they gathered up the Faithists of the tribes of He-ah.

24/7.4. Now it came to pass that Han's success in war was so great that he did not concentrate his armies, but caused them to scatter in different directions. And behold, he went so far that the barbarians fell upon his armies and destroyed them. And Han himself perished by the blow of a barbarian woman.

24/7.5. In the fourth year of Po's inspiration,[774] he returned and possessed the countries of Feh, Heng'a Di and Se Lov, and he reinstated Ah Sin and Hi Seiang as governors.

24/7.6. Hi Seiang called a council of thirteen kingdoms of Jaffeth, and after seventy days of deliberation, Hi Seiang was made ruler over Jaffeth, receiving the title, KING OF THE SUN.

24/7.7. And he established the doctrines of Po by law, changing the name of All Light, to Te-in, signifying God. And he stopped all persecution against the Faithists; and he prohibited idol worship.

24/7.8. And Po traveled east and west, north and south; teaching and displaying miraculous things. And God was with him at all times and places.

24/7.9. And wherever Po went he gathered together the chosen, explaining and practicing the commandments of God (Te-in).

24/7.10. And man ceased to worship all idols, Gods and saviors; worshipping the Creator only.

END OF THE FIRST CHINESE BIBLE

[774] see image i109 Po

CHAPTER 8 First Book God

The first Fonecean Bible—being of Abram, a man chosen by God for the children of Arabin'ya

24/8.1. Out of the hosts of Par'si'e, who were of the people of Shem, who existed since the days of the flood, came Abram, a man chosen by God, in the arc of Spe-ta, for the deliverance of the Faithists of Arabin'ya. God said: Because they have not raised up one out of the sons of Ham, your name shall become Abra-Ham, and it shall be testimony in thousands of years, of my records in the libraries of heaven.

24/8.2. And it came to pass that forgers and deceivers, not having the fear of Jehovih before them, falsely gave the interpretation of the meaning of the words Abra and Ham,[775] not knowing (in thousands of years) that in so small a matter He would display the truth and glory of His revealed word. ||

24/8.3. God led Abram away from He-sa, his native place, where he was a maker of baskets, and took him to the ancient land of Ham, which had been destroyed by druks, before the flood, as the name signifies; after which God surnamed him Abraham, and made him chief rab'bah over the Faithists of Arabin'ya.

24/8.4. These, then, are the generations of the line (of light) from whom Abram came, that is to say: of Shem and the seventy tribes, first going forth beyond the mountains of Owatchab-habal, Tur who settled in Par'si'e, and his descendants Raf-bak, and his descendants Goe, and his descendants Wawa, and his descendants Sadr.

24/8.5. In Sadr the line was lost; but through his daughter Bar-bar, regained through the I'hins in the land of Goats, where the Listians lived, having fled from the tyranny of the kings of Oas.

24/8.6. From Bar-bar was descended Egount, from him Dir, from him Wow-sha, from him He-lial, from him Rac-ca. And here the line ran by the female heirs, beginning in Rac-ca's daughter, Hess, from whom was descended Gil-gil, from whom was descended Thussa, from whom was

[775] For example, the Ezra bible, Genesis 17.5, indicates the word Abraham to mean father of a multitude of nations.

descended She, from whom was descended seven generations in su'is; and it was lost in We-ta-koo, but regained again through I'hin seed, and appeared in Re-both, and again su'is extended through these generations: Arfaxad, Sala, Eber, Pe-leg, Roo, Sa-rug, Na-hor and Terah; but in Terah the line was lost, but regained by I'hin seed, from whom sprang Geth, from whom sprang Choe, from whom sprang Gus, from whom sprang Ra-bak, from whom sprang Ya-shem, and by I'hin seed sprang Ti-lot, and by I'hin seed Shi-ar, and by I'hin seed Shir-ra, from whom descended Na-hor the second, from whom sprang Abram.

24/8.7. Abram was of pure blood, and an I'huan; and the light of su'is had been with his forefathers and foremothers since the flood, and he was large and red, like new copper, and had black hair and long beard, fierce to look upon; but his soul was gentle as a woman's.

24/8.8. Abram could see without eyes and hear without ears, knowing things by the light of God which dwelt in him. For which reason, God chose Abram[776] to gather together the Faithists in Arabin'ya and the adjacent countries, even as he had appointed Po in Jaffeth.

24/8.9. In those days, there were great kings and men of great learning, who had books of learning and instruments for measuring things far and near.

24/8.10. And Abram knew these things, for he had been a servant in a king's family where learned men and women congregated. And so, knowing the power of God was upon him, he ran away in his youth, and lived among the Listians, who made baskets and trinkets in the forests, which they sold to the kings' peoples.

24/8.11. God spoke to Abram, saying: Do not concern yourself regarding men of learning; nor long for the learning in books. The day will come when they will be forgotten, but your words and your labors will overspread the world.

24/8.12. And God lived with Abram, teaching him and working miracles through him. And it came to pass that the Listians in their rambles, selling wares, told the slaves of the kings about the wonders of Abram.

24/8.13. And the slaves fled from bondage and went into the wilderness in search of Abram. And when they came before him, he spoke to them, day by day, as they came, saying:

24/8.14. Why have you come? I did not call you! And when they could not answer, Abram said to them: God brought you. Man of himself does nothing. Search, then, the records of your generations; for you are descended from the Faithists of old.

24/8.15. And they searched and found that every one of those who had come, was descended from before the time of Zarathustra.

24/8.16. Abram said: Do not think that God comes to one man alone; when he provides a voice he also provides ears and hearts. Because you have been faithful to him, he calls you to deliverance from your enemies, who are God's enemies also.

CHAPTER 9 First Book God

24/9.1. When the number of those who had come to Abram, in She-a-do-wan, reached four thousand five hundred souls, God spoke to Abram, saying: Come now, I will lead you and your people into another country.

24/9.2. So Abram led them away, and they came into Lower Howd-Lutz. And it came to pass that in the year after they departed out of She-a-do-wan a famine came upon the land, and the enemies of God were cut off, and could not pursue Abram and his people.

24/9.3. It was after this that Abram was called Abraham, and he built altars of worship and altars of sacrifice, according to the commandments of God.

24/9.4. Now it came to pass in the early days of Abraham, he told his brothers that the light and power of God were with him; and, though others believed in Abraham, yet Lot, Abram's brother, and Lot, Abram's nephew, did not believe in Abraham, saying of him: He was born naturally, and is wise because of his own judgment.

24/9.5. God said to Abraham: Behold, it is an easy matter to commune with spirits, but to judge righteously regarding them is not so easy. For which reason you and your wife, and one hundred picked men, shall go and visit Sodom and Gomorrah in the valley of Siddim.

24/9.6. And Abraham and his people went as commanded by God, and visited the cities of Sodom and Gomorrah; and God spoke privately to

[776] see image i110 Abraham, p.402

Abraham, saying: I will destroy these cities, for they are like hells for evil spirits; but Lot (the elder and younger) shall escape for your sake.

24/9.7. And when they came to Sodom, behold, angels walked among the people, and the people knew they were angels, but were indifferent[777] regarding them. And there were laws made by Bera, king of Sodom, regarding the behavior between angels and men.

24/9.8. And Abraham, being pressed by the presence of God, said to his people: Behold, there are angels that love to dwell in lust, and to partake with mortals; to eat with them, to lie down with them, and to partake in all ungodly pleasures.

24/9.9. God, through his angels, rained down fire and brimstone on Sodom and Gomorrah, and they were burnt and destroyed. Lot, the elder, escaped, and went and lived in a cave.

24/9.10. Now after Abraham and his people had returned to Jireh, his camp, and it was night, God said to Abraham: Be steadfast, and show your people so that they may understand my words.

24/9.11. And while they were still praying before the altar, God withdrew from Abraham, and allowed the evil angels, who had followed them from Sodom and Gomorrah, to draw near the altar. And one of the angels clothed himself in a great light, and, adorned with sparkling gems and a crown, he appeared, so all the multitude of people could look upon him.

24/9.12. Abraham said: Who are you? And the spirit said: I am your God, ruler of heaven and earth! Abraham said: I am your servant; what may I do for you? And the spirit said: You shall take your only son, Isaac, and your hosts who were with you at Sodom and Gomorrah, and go with me where I will lead you, for I have a great work for you.

24/9.13. Abraham said: I will do whatever you put upon me to do.

24/9.14. So in the morning Abraham and his son Isaac, and the hosts who had been with Abraham to Sodom and Gomorrah, assembled together. And Abraham spoke, saying: Where to, O God?

24/9.15. The spirit answered, saying: Take sticks and a firebrand (torch) and come to the summit of the hill over there, for you shall restore the rites of burnt offerings. || Abraham told the people what God had said, so they began, and Isaac carried the bundle of willows, such as basket-makers use, saying: This will light the large pieces; but what will you burn for an offering, O father? And Abraham said: God will provide.

24/9.16. And when they ascended to the place, Abraham gathered logs and heaped them up, and Isaac placed the willows.

24/9.17. Then the spirit spoke, saying: What shall a man love above all things in the world? And Abraham said: God. And the spirit said: For which reason you shall offer your only son, Isaac, as a burnt offering. And it shall be testimony before your people that you will obey God even to the sacrifice of your own flesh and kin.

24/9.18. Abraham said: Show me that you are God, so that I may not err; for I have been commanded not to kill.

24/9.19. And the spirit departed away from Abraham, perceiving that he knew the higher law. And Isaac was grieved at heart, for he desired to witness what a sacrifice was. And the people, seeing a ram near at hand, went and caught it, and slaughtered it, and sprinkled the blood on the sacrifice, and they lit the fire, roasted the flesh, then took it and gave it to the poor.

24/9.20. And Abraham called the place Jehovih-Jireh, and they returned to the camp; and Abraham, being moved by God, spoke before the people.

CHAPTER 10 First Book God

24/10.1. Abraham said: This testimony I declare to you, regarding which, your own brethren are witnesses, that even the chosen of God can be deceived by evil angels; for they can take any name and form; and, having no fear of God before them, declare falsehood for truth and darkness for light.

24/10.2. And also, as you have seen, the evilest of cities, even as well as the purest, may be the abiding place of angels.

24/10.3. For which reason you shall not seek signs and miracles, for these may be from evil spirits, even though they show their bodies or converse learnedly. It is not in the power of man to know by words and signs, or by oaths or promises, what is truth.

[777] unconcerned, not caring one way or the other

i110 **Abram or Abraham.**

24/10.4. But the Father has created one thing besides, which is His Own Light. For which reason be believing toward men and angels; and when they teach you according to Jehovih, which is life to all, and happiness to all, without sacrifice to any, [778] they are holy.

24/10.5. If man or angel says: Visit the sick, and administer to the distressed, || follow his advice, for it is of the Father.

24/10.6. But if man or angel says: Do this, and you shall have profit, or glory, or applause, || do not obey him, for he advises for yourself and not for the brotherhood of man. He is not of God.

24/10.7. For spirits will come disguised as your fathers and mothers who are dead, professing love and profit to you. Do not believe them, except when they teach you to sacrifice self for the good of others.

24/10.8. The wicked in heart, having profited in herds, and in gold and silver, say: Behold, God has blessed me! But I say to you, they are cursed, and not of God. Has he gathered you together here because you were rich? You were slaves, and in poverty; sick, and in bondage. And he came and delivered you. Be like him, and he will abide with you.

24/10.9. If a man comes to you, saying: Behold, this is my coat; give it to me! You shall say: Prove yourself as to who you are. But if a man comes to you, saying: Your herd has gone astray; you shall not say to him: Prove yourself as to who you are. But go, and see after your herd.

24/10.10. If a spirit says: Behold, I am your father, say to him: It is well; what do you want? And when he answers you, consider if his words are of God, which are for the glory of the Creator. And if his words are not of God, you shall challenge him to prove himself.

24/10.11. As God is captain of heaven and earth to all righteous souls, so is there a satan who is captain over evil spirits.

24/10.12. And to the extent that the kings' peoples do not have faith in the Father, so do their souls fall prey to satan and his hosts.

[778] that is, without worshipping any God, man or angel; without demands that you follow a certain person; and without having tribute demanded of you

24/10.13. Yet, neither shall man flatter himself by saying: Behold, I have joined the Faithists (Israelites); my soul shall escape hell. || For in that day and hour God may be putting him to the test, to see if his heart is for good works and holiness. || For, because you profess God, you are doubly bound to practice godliness in your behavior toward men and angels.

CHAPTER 11 First Book God

24/11.1. When Lot the younger escaped out of Sodom, he stopped in a small city called Ben-ah, and stayed there while Sodom and Gomorrah were being consumed with fire; and because he was saved, he called the place Zoar, because he was a worshipper of the doctrines of Zarathustra, who was called in the Fonecean language Zoa-raastra. And the place was called Zoar for more than a thousand years.

24/11.2. When Lot departed out of Zoar, two tribes went with him; and there were born of the house of Lot, offspring to the two tribes who accompanied him, and these became the nations later known as Moabites and Ammonites, who were of the Foneceans, as their names show, and they followed the doctrines of Zarathustra. ||

24/11.3. In former years God appeared to Abraham in a dream and said to him: You shall be a father to many peoples.

24/11.4. When Abraham awoke he told Sarai, his wife, and she, being barren, was troubled and she prayed to God for Abraham's sake.

24/11.5. Now it came to pass that Hagar, Sarai's maid, had a son, and named him Ishmael; and Sarai, jealous of Hagar, abused her during pregnancy. And the Lord spoke to Abraham, saying: Because of the hatred between your women, Hagar's son will be like a wild man; his hand shall be against every man, and every man shall be against him.

24/11.6. Abraham said: How did this come about, O God? And God said: I told you that you would be a father of many peoples, and you told Sarai, your wife. Now Sarai has become vain in her desires for offspring, and, in her eagerness, she opened the door of your house to satan, and so this matter is upon you.

24/11.7. Go, therefore, my son, and reconcile your women. And Abraham told Sarai what God had said. And Sarai inquired of Abraham, saying: Before God, tell me, is Ishmael your son? And God shall judge between us. Abraham said:

24/11.8. Teach me, O God, to answer Sarai, so I may reconcile them. And God said: Behold, your Creator is the Father of all the living.

24/11.9. And when Abraham told Sarai God's words, she cried in sorrow and repentance, saying: You are wise, O God! For what matter is it to me, since I know that Ishmael is your son, and Hagar is your daughter?

24/11.10. And Sarai went to Hagar and said: O my sister, I have sinned before the Lord, my God. I saw your son, and knew God gave him, but I turned against my own soul, and did not love your treasure.

24/11.11. Hagar said: Did your God say that Abraham was father to my child? And Sarai said: No, O Hagar. Hagar said: Neither did I say your husband was Ishmael's father.

24/11.12. So they were reconciled, and by right of the beginning of Abraham's nations, Ishmael was Abraham's son before God, but not in the flesh.

24/11.13. Sarai had a son, and he was called Isaac, because he was born to Sarai after she had passed the time of childbearing.[779]

24/11.14. And when Hagar saw that Sarai bore a son, Hagar became jealous for Ishmael's sake, and she wept before Abraham. Hagar said:

24/11.15. I am a South Arabin'yan[780] woman, and I left my people for you. Behold, I am not favored by your God. Abraham said: Have I not been like a father to you and your son? Truly, when all people reviled you because you had a child in maidenhood, laying it on me, I did not deny you, nor justified myself before the kings' people, suffering these things for God's sake, and yours, and your child's.

24/11.16. Do not complain, then, against my house, my wife, or my son, Isaac; all things are of the Creator. And so Hagar was pacified for a season, but then returned to grief and jealousy, and finally resolved to depart away from Abraham's house.

24/11.17. Then Abraham said to Hagar: The matter lies with you. If you go, I will give you, according to the custom of the Arabin'yans, a jug with water, and bread and blankets.

24/11.18. So Hagar persisted, and Abraham provided her, and she departed, taking Ishmael with her, and she went into Par-an and dwelt there.

24/11.19. In those days Arabin'ya was divided into many kingdoms, some having one city and some two, and some as many as six cities. And they were constantly at war one with another, and the victors always changed the names of the kingdoms. The largest and most powerful always called itself the Sun Kingdom, after the manner of the Par'si'e'ans (Persians).

24/11.20. Men and women of learning dwelt in the Sun Kingdom, and they had tablets and books, and maps relating to heaven and earth, all of which were kept in a library; and in the summit of this same building was an oracle for consulting with the spirits, called Lords of heaven.

24/11.21. For which purpose, a man or woman, whose head had been flattened in infancy, sat by a

---

[779] menopause

[780] The whole of the continent of Africa plus the Arabian Peninsula and some area north of it, was known as Arabin'ya. In those regions, the area east of, say, the Sinai Peninsula, was apparently known at some point as North Arabin'ya, because it consisted of two sections, northeastern Arabin'ya and northwestern Arabin'ya. Some or all of this latter became known as Western Arabin'ya.

On the other hand the area, say, west across the land bridge of the Sinai Peninsula, was known as South Arabin'ya. In practical terms, at least insofar as the people in the region were concerned, this meant that land later called Egupt (Egypt); and so, Hagar was from this region. It is not clear from Oahspe how far up the Nile River the original allotment of Egupt extended, nor is it necessarily clear whether or not South Arabin'ya included the whole of what we today call continental Africa.

From the Post-Flood Map of the World, image i018 (p.228), and from corporeal records, northern Arabin'ya appears to have consisted of the area east of the Red Sea and Mediterranean Sea including Arabia, Mesopotamia, Syria, etc., to the Taurus Mountains in the northwest; and bounded in the north by the upper reaches of the Tigris and Euphrates Rivers; and by the Zagros Mountains in the east; and by the sea and the Sinai peninsula in the south.

table covered with sand, upon which the spirits wrote with the finger. And this person communing with the spirits was called Æ'jin (AE'jin)[781] in the South Arabin'yan language, and was next to the Sun King in rank. Now, no matter what wars took place, the library, the temple of the oracle and the Æ'jin were sacred, and never suffered harm even between enemies.

24/11.22. The kings kept scribes whose business it was to write and translate, and to keep the records of the kingdom. Besides these, there were gatherers of news, who held the second rank of scribes.

24/11.23. Now when Abraham and his people came into Arabin'ya, especially into that part later called Egupt, the matter was entered in the records of the different kingdoms, with special reference to Abraham professing to hear the voice of God, for he did not have a flat head, and moreover, had good judgment of his own, quite unlike the Æ'jins in the temples.

24/11.24. But because Abraham gave no counsel regarding war or earthly gain, he was not favored by any of the kings, and allowed to go his way unmolested.

24/11.25. When Sodom and Gomorrah were destroyed, the kings' people heaped the blame on Abraham's head, and enemies rose up against Abraham in those regions.

24/11.26. And they also accused him of attempting to burn his son, Isaac, as a sacrifice to his God, after the manner of the heathen of old.

24/11.27. And they accused Abraham of being the father of Ishmael, by his servant-maid, and of driving Hagar and Ishmael away to Par-an after he tired of her.

24/11.28. And these accusations, and many more of equal wickedness, were heard of by the news gatherers, the scribes, and they wrote them down, not knowing in truth what they were doing before God (recording lies as historical facts); and so, their records were entered in the libraries of the kings of Arabin'ya, especially in that land later known as Egupt.

24/11.29. Abraham perceived these matters, and he wept before God, saying: Alas, O God, if only I had great learning and could write my record truthfully before men! God answered him, saying:

24/11.30. Your faith being in Jehovih, it is well with you. In thousands of years, one Ezra shall send his scribes into these countries to gather news, even as the kings of this day do. And his scribes shall translate from these records, with all their errors and falsehoods, and Ezra shall publish the matter as the history of THE DELIVERANCE.[782]

24/11.31. Abraham hearing this from God, bowed down his head and wept, saying: Your will be done! And God comforted him, saying: I am the Light and the Life!

24/11.32. The God of heaven and earth will come afterward and render the records of your life, which are not dead, but of life everlasting. And so, since your people shall be honored by even that which shall come from their enemies, how much greater will their glory be, when God of heaven speaks for you and them!

CHAPTER 12 First Book God

24/12.1. Abraham inquired of God concerning the king's peoples and the Faithists. And God said: Whomever I lead to you shall be yours; from this time forward you shall be father to all men, women and children that are yours. And they shall be your family. But all other peoples shall not be yours; neither shall you be a father nor prophet to them. You shall not make laws for the kings' peoples, nor laws between your people and them. You shall be of your own people, and for your own people, forever.

24/12.2. Neither shall your people have anything in common with the kings' peoples, nor with any other people under the sun. Nor shall you enter into treaties or alliances in any way whatsoever. Both your labor and the labor of your people are for Jehovih, through the Lord your God.

24/12.3. But regarding the intercourse[783] between yours and the kings' peoples, be circumspect to give full value, to the fraction, in buying and selling. Neither permit my chosen to accept presents, nor otherwise become obligated to

---

[781] Ægian, or Eajian, or Æjin: a decree that cannot err. –Ed.

[782] This can be found in the Ezra Bible, which became the holy book for the Jews, and later, the basis for the Old Testament of the Christian Bible.

[783] contact, interaction, dealings, trade

other peoples; for it is the law of your God. For above all things, it shall not be said by the kings' peoples: Behold, I made them!

24/12.4. For I say to you, neither kings nor rich men make the people of your God.

24/12.5. Whoever would give you gifts, let him quit his people and come and dwell with my people in person and spirit. I cannot be put off with money and with gifts, like a peevish child or a wanton woman.

24/12.6. Shall a man say: Here are gifts for your God, he is a good enough God! But as for my soul it is too good to give to you or your God.

24/12.7. Nor shall you permit your people to marry with the kings' peoples, for the same reason. But whoever desires to marry my daughters, let him first come and dwell with my people, proving that he has forsaken all the idolatrous Gods for Jehovih's sake. It shall be the same with your sons; if they desire strange damsels for wives, they shall first bring them to dwell one year among my chosen.

24/12.8. Abraham inquired concerning government. And God said to Abraham: To teach people to dwell together in peace, order, harmony and love; being disciplined to these, what more is required? Government belongs to the kings' peoples.

24/12.9. Abraham said: O God, teach me more regarding these matters; for I am like one in a dark cellar groping about. Behold, my people are unlearned!

24/12.10. God said: Who is learned? I say to you, he who knows the stars, rocks, mountains, valleys, and all that is living and dead, and the languages of the ancients, but does not know the Creator, is unlearned. But he who knows the Creator is learned indeed.

24/12.11. It is better that your people dwell in tents and under trees; and their children roll on the ground, and do not die, but grow strong in person and in spirit for the glory of the Creator, than to dwell like the kings' peoples, in magnificent cities, and in lust and death. To your God, your people are a most learned people.

24/12.12. Abraham inquired of the Lord concerning servitude. And God answered him, saying: There is only one Master, even Jehovih; your people shall be His servants only. But all people have loves; a damsel says to her lover: I will be your servant, and he marries her. A man says to another: Your judgment is greater than mine; I will be your servant. And the man takes him in love to work for him.

24/12.13. Therefore, for convenience' sake, you may say, master and servant. Nevertheless, my chosen shall not, in fact, have either masters or servants; for the one shall not have authority over the other, except by love and free consent.

24/12.14. Abraham asked concerning the products of labor. God said to Abraham: What I have said regarding servants and masters also applies to the productions that come out of the earth: Nothing belongs to any man, for all things are Mine, says the Creator.

24/12.15. Nevertheless, for convenience' sake, you may say: This is his product, or that belongs to another. But still he holds it only by his Creator's consent.

24/12.16. Let all men render to the Creator his creations, for they are Jehovih's. After that, Abraham said: Some men grow flax, some wool, and some corn; but the seasons do not bring forth alike to all. Others spin and weave; and others make butter and cheese. And yet this also happens: One man is strong, another weak; one rises with the sun and toils all day; another sits on the bank, fishing.

24/12.17. Now when the products are brought in, lo and behold, there are no two that are equal.

24/12.18. And God said: Every man's matter is between him and his Creator. According to diligence and industry He rewards them in the end. He who perceives this, knows his heavenly Father; he who does not perceive it, dwells in darkness.

24/12.19. Abraham said: Shall the lazy be rebuked, and those that shirk be upbraided?

24/12.20. And God said: No. Let all your people bring their products and cast them before you, saying: This is my sacrifice to Jehovih; you distribute it. And if some do not bring anything, neither rebuke them nor pity them; they are the sons and daughters of your God. And if some decorate themselves with fine raiment, or jewels, do not censure them; your God searches their hearts.

24/12.21. Abraham asked concerning lands. God said: Consider the way of your God. Did I go to the king and to the rich man and say: Give me your sons and daughters? No, but I went to those who were despised by the king and the rich, and I said: Come! And they came.

24/12.22. And when you came here, did I say: Take the king's lands, or the rich man's? No, but I led you to that which was neglected and waste in the eyes of the kings' peoples, and I said: This is your inheritance.

24/12.23. It is sufficient for you and your people to buy burying-places for the dead, which shall not be disturbed. But neither buy nor sell any other lands.

24/12.24. And after your people have improved a place, and a king comes against you, saying: I will have this land either by purchase or by battle, you shall say: No, neither by purchase nor by battle, shall you inherit that which is Jehovih's. But if you desire the land, then I will give it to you without money and without battle.

24/12.25. And it shall come to pass that my chosen shall be driven from place to place, where I will lead them; and they shall make the waste lands bloom like gardens, and the deserts yield ample harvests; for they shall dig wells, and till the soil, and prove to the nations of the earth the glory of my works.

24/12.26. And they shall be cut down, driven away and scattered, but I will come and gather them together. Their places shall be inherited by idolaters and worshippers of strange Gods, who will build mighty temples. But my people shall not build that which endures in stone, wood or iron; for they shall go from place to place, proclaiming me and my works; but where they have been, there shall be nothing left on the earth to show their labors.

24/12.27. But when I have taken them across all the earth, and they are scattered like dust before the wind, and no man can say: Here is a nation of the children of Abraham, lo, I will raise up my voice for them, even I, the God of heaven and earth. And in that day the idolaters and worshippers of strange Gods will be on the wane; their temples of stone and mortar will still be standing.

24/12.28. But a voice shall go up from the whole earth, even from the remote nations of the earth, saying: What about those who laid the foundations of the temple of ONE GOD, EVEN JEHOVIH! Those who were the sons and daughters of Abraham! O if only my eyes could have seen the Faithists of that labor!

CHAPTER 13 First Book God

24/13.1. When Abraham's wife was getting old, her ears were opened to hear the voice of God. And God said to her:

24/13.2. Concerning your son, Isaac, hear your God, who is also the God of Abraham: My labors are not for a day, nor without judgment.[784]

24/13.3. Behold, in the land of Es-seth, the place of your husband in his youth, I have built for many generations concerning the seed of my people. For which reason your son, Isaac, shall take a wife who shall inherit my voice.

24/13.4. Before the time of your husband's father's father, I sent my angel from heaven, saying: Go and raise me up an heir to hear my voice, for I will dwell for a season with the children of men.

24/13.5. And my angel fulfilled his part, and I have come and talked with you and your husband face to face. And I can talk to your son, Isaac, in the same manner and he can hear me also. And Isaac shall raise up heirs to my voice through his wife, to whom he is not yet known.

24/13.6. Sarai told Abraham what God had said to her; and so Abraham and Sarai went to the altar that Abraham had built, and they prayed alone; and God came and spoke, saying: What is your request?

24/13.7. And Abraham said: Concerning our son Isaac's wife? And God said: Because of the blessing of Sarai, your wife, who has been upright all her days, I will give her comfort in her old age.

24/13.8. Send your servant to the land of your fathers, and I will send my angel with your servant, and he shall come to a maiden who shall be Isaac's wife. So, Abraham called his servant, who was overseer over his goods, and he said to him: Equip yourself with camels, asses, and servants; and with jewels I will give you, go to Syria, the land of my fathers, and bring a damsel here, who shall be Isaac's wife.

24/13.9. The overseer said to Abraham: Alas me! How shall your servant choose a wife for your son? Or, if choosing, how shall he induce her to come so far? Abraham said: That which God has commanded of me, I have told you, except that God says: My angel shall go with your servant, and he shall not err.

---

[784] i.e., not without foresight and wisdom

24/13.10. So the servant of Abraham, in fear and trembling, equipped himself with ten camels, twenty asses and thirty servants, taking presents and goods, and departed. The journey took twenty-two days, and all the while the overseer reasoned upon what he should say, for he had misgivings that he was on a fool's errand.

24/13.11. Nevertheless, he prayed to God that he would do his own part wisely. So when he came near Abraham's father's people, the angel of God spoke in his heart, saying: The damsel that comes with a pitcher on her head shall be Isaac's wife. Say to her: Will you give me a drink? And she will say: I will give you a drink, and also draw water for your servants and camels.

24/13.12. And the overseer looked, but saw no damsel, and he wondered; but presently he saw many damsels, one of whom had a pitcher on her head; and his heart failed him till she came near, and he said: Give me a drink? And she gave him a drink and said to him: You are a stranger; if you will allow, I will water your camels and give drink to your servants.

24/13.13. And so she gave as she said; and when she had finished, the overseer said to her: Who are you? And she answered him, and he perceived she was Isaac's niece by Abraham's father's second wife, but of no blood kin. And then she asked the overseer who he was and where he came from; and he told her he came from Abraham, whose servant he was. So she invited him to her people's houses, and she ran ahead with joy to tell who had come so far, bringing word from Abraham.

24/13.14. Now when the camels and asses had been fed, and straw spread for the travelers to lie upon, and when repast was spread for them to eat, the overseer rose up, perceiving the way of God, and he said: Till I have spoken, do not eat, but hear the words of God. So he related the object of his visit as commanded by God, and in reference to the angel of God, and the words that came to him.

24/13.15. And when he had finished, the power of God came upon the damsel, whose name was Rebecca, and she rose up and spoke, saying: Isaac shall be my husband, and I shall be his wife, for I know this matter is of God!

24/13.16. So it came to pass after some days, that Rebecca departed from her people, and by her faith in God came to Abraham's home, and Isaac took her to wife, and Sarai rejoiced before God because of the light of his kingdom through Abraham's heirs.

24/13.17. And God said to Abraham: Divide your people into families of tens, and families of hundreds, and families of thousands, and give to each family one rab'bah, and yet to all of them together one chief rab'bah. And make your will, and appoint your son Isaac and his heirs by his wife Rebecca to be your successors, so that my voice may remain with my chosen.

24/13.18. And Abraham made his will and did all things as God commanded; and he further made the rab'bahs officers in the rites of Emethachavah, [785] and communicated the sacred name of the Creator (E-O-Ih) to them, as well as the plans of the upper and lower heavens, the dominion of God and the dominion of satan, all of which were kept in secret through the rab'bahs.

* * * * *

24/13.19. God said: Behold, there is a time to clear up all things, present and past: Were Abraham father to Hagar's son, Ishmael, and had he been true to the law of sacrifice among the heathen, then, Ishmael, being first-born, would have been chosen for the burnt offering.

24/13.20. In which matter the Ezra Bible is shown to be false before Jehovih, in regard to Abraham, Ishmael and Isaac, and the burnt offering also.

24/13.21. Which words were not my words, nor the words of my angels, but the words of the Eguptian record.

END OF ABRAHAM'S HISTORY, AND OF THE FIRST FONECEAN BIBLE

[785] Order of Faithists; more is given later in Oahspe concerning the Emethachavah

CHAPTER 14 First Book God

The first Bible of Vind'yu—being of Brahma,[786] a man chosen by God for the children of Vind'yu. Giving an account of Brahma becoming an iesu; of his labors and his resurrection after death

24/14.1. These are the fore-races of Brahma: Gons, Shone, Gamma, This, Ram, Zerl, Mex, Shriv, Vat, Eun and Delta, each a thousand years. Of Gamma and Delta, in the upper country (Wa-wa-o-gan), were born Gu-sem and Hagu by Gamma; and by Delta: Yots, Rammus, Borgl, Otesiv and Riv. Gamma was of the fourth descent of Git-ow; and Delta the third descent of E'wangga, I'hins from the land of Jaffeth.

24/14.2. The ascending caste of light in the lower country (Ho-jon-da-tivi)[787] was by Ram, first; then Zerl, I'hin migrants from the land of Ham; then Shriv, then Vat, then Gons and Eun, the half-breed druks; then Shone, and then This.

24/14.3. Jehovih, Who was called Ormazd by the Brahmans,[788] sent His light to the earth world once for every hundred generations.[789] And the light fell upon His Sons, prepared from before their births by the angels of Ormazd. In the times before the submersion of Pan, each cycle was called one man, and the length of his life three thousand years.

24/14.4. But for the times after the flood, Ormazd commanded the nations of the earth to be rated as a man, and it was so. Ormazd said: So that man will not be confounded,[790] you shall count Osiris with the generations that do not believe, except in the sun; but of the Zarathustrians, their number shall be those who survived in the darkness of his cycle.

24/14.5. Which were: Zarathustra from the races of Shone and This; and of Zarathustra, Haman; of Haman, Wonchakaka, who begot Zoar, who begot Theo, who begot Andassah, who begot Mur, who begot Romsat; these were tribes of the Zarathustrian order, who rejected idols, Lords, Gods, Saviors, kings, queens, and all other rulers on the earth or in the heavens above the earth, except Ormazd, the Creator. And had faith in Him that to do righteously, and practice good works, made the best, nearest perfect man.

24/14.6. The Light by the Voice was lost in the sixth hundredth year after Zarathustra, but regained in Romsat by the I'hins, from whom came the tribe Lo-jon, who begot Thonegala-hogreif, who begot Subinij, and from him to Wowthutchi-subinij, which were forty-four generations, in which the Voice always came to the chief rab'bah.

24/14.7. In Chusa-king the Voice was lost, but again restored by the I'hins, whose heirs were called Wah-sin-chung, who begot Avar, who begot Irigavagna, who begot Ben-haoma, from whom was descended thirty generations, the chief rab'bah of whom could hear the Voice.

24/14.8. Ben-haoma counted the Faithists of his day including men, women and children, and there

---

[786] This is Brahma the First. A dan'ha later a false God, Kabalactes, using the name of Brahma, would do much destruction in India; and afterward, another self God, Ennochissa, falsely took the name Brahma.

Accordingly it should be noted that Brahma the First had nothing to do with shaping modern Brahminism, but the later false Gods would pick over the doctrines and twist or reject them according to their profitability to the false God.

[787] The student must remember that these are Vedic terms belonging to Upper and Lower Thibet [Tibet], or of what, in a general and better sense, may be called the mountains and the valleys of India. [Wa-wa-o-gan evidently refers to the Himalayas and Tibetan plateau, whereas, Ho-jon-da-tivi presumably refers to the land mass south and east of the Himalayas (see image i018 Post-Flood Outline Map of the World, p.228).] Nearly all we have left of ancient Greek sprang from these ancient histories. In the production of languages, and of Gods, India exceeds all the rest of the earth put together. –Ed.

[788] For convenience of identification, in this Oahspe the spelling, Brahmans, refers to the followers of Brahma the First and True, as described in this Vind'yu Bible. On the other hand, those who later falsely used or took on the name of Brahma, have been given the spelling Brahmin, Brahmins and Brahminism. [As with any name in Oahspe, if found in man's historical records, there spellings and even meanings, may vary.]

[789] i.e., once every dan'ha cycle

[790] confused, perplexed, bewildered

were four thousand of them, and all other nations and tribes in Vind'yu were idolaters.

24/14.9. Through the descendants of Romsat the Voice was again regained via the I'hins, through a tribe called Shriviyata, who begot Them-saga, who begot Friavamargalum, who bred with the I'hins and begot Thace, who begot with the I'hins, Anu, who begot with the I'hins, Maha, who begot with the I'hins, Brah, who had both voice and power from the Father. And he was called Brahma because of his great wisdom.

24/14.10. The angels of Ormazd had prophesied, saying: Out of your seed shall come one called BRAHMA, who shall have su'is with power. Things that were revealed in Zarathustra have been lost, but shall be recovered in Brahma.

24/14.11. Romsat had prophesied, moreover: With the coming of Brahma will come the end of the I'hin race in Shem (Vind'yu).

24/14.12. God spoke in kosmon, saying: Let no man say: The beginning of the doctrine of One Spirit began with Brahma, Abram, Po or Eawahtah. For since man walked upright on the earth, behold, I have said to him: You shall have only one God, even the Creator. And in the cycles of my times I have raised up many who have comprehended my words, but others constantly put away the I AM, and raise up idols instead.

24/14.13. But let all men understand who, and what, is meant by the terms, Po, Abram, Brahma and Eawahtah, which is, that though I walked the earth with these men, teaching and speaking through them, yet none of them was idolized by men. For the nations of the earth, in the time of these four men, comprehended that they were not Gods, but men through whom, and to whom, I, God, had spoken. ||

24/14.14. Brahma said: Do all men have stars? Behold, since my childhood, I have had a star above my forehead.

24/14.15. No man could answer Brahma. They said: Brahma is foolish, even with all his wisdom.

24/14.16. Brahma asked the star: Who are you?

24/14.17. God said: I am your star; I am the light of the second heavens.

24/14.18. Brahma asked: What is your name, O star, you mysterious light?

24/14.19. God said: Call me Ormazd; I am the same light that spoke to Zarathustra in his time.

24/14.20. Brahma asked: Who are you, O Ormazd, you voice of light?

24/14.21. God said: You shall commune with one only, even your Creator; you shall worship one only, even He Who made you alive.

24/14.22. Brahma said: Why have you taken up your abode above my head?

24/14.23. God said: Attain to be one with your Creator, in wisdom, goodness and purity, and you shall answer your own questions.

24/14.24. Then Brahma applied to the rab'bah, the Zarathustrian priests, and he learned abnegation of self, and the rites and ceremonies of the ancients.

24/14.25. When Brahma was grown up, God said to him: Arise tomorrow, my son, and I will lead you into another country, where you shall marry, and settle down for a long season.

24/14.26. Brahma said: Peaceful have been my slumbers, and joyous my wakeful hours all my life. I have made labor a pleasure, and I give all I have to the poor, doing Your commandments with all my wisdom and strength.

24/14.27. From my youth up I have not killed any living creature of Yours that goes on the earth, or swims in the waters, or flies in the air. Nor have I eaten anything that had ever breathed the breath of life; and I have been most abstemious[791] in plain food and water only, according to the Zarathustrian law. Hear me, O Ormazd; for I will open my soul to You, and hold nothing back. || Ormazd said: It is well.

24/14.28. Brahma said: Woe is me, if my soul turns toward woman! Was I not wed to You, O Ormazd? Was I not Your Bridegroom from my youth up?

24/14.29. Why, then, do You not protect me to Yourself? Ormazd said: In times past I raised up many an iesu, and they were without flesh desires all their days.

24/14.30. Such men could not perpetuate the earth; they were good for their day. Zarathustra was an iesu. My Light is now for those who can perpetuate. All things are possible in My hands. Do not grieve, nor smother out any talent I created with the pure in flesh.

---

[791] disciplined, self-restrained, moderate, sticking to bare necessities, temperate

24/14.31. Brahma said: If I love a woman, O Ormazd, might I not lose my love for You? Ormazd said: By faith in Me you shall triumph by the road I marked out for you, since before you were born. Arise, then, O Brahma, and follow your star. I will lead you.

24/14.32. Brahma said: Can there be another way other than by celibacy? Can a married man serve Ormazd?

24/14.33. So Brahma traveled, and came into the country of Etchoyosin, where lay the mountains of Talavitcha, under King Tyama, who had enforced the Zarathustrian religion with sword and spear, and with chains and death, being himself sole interpreter.

24/14.34. When Brahma came to Au'watcha, he stopped to inquire the way to the high priest's house, so that he could be absolved for twenty days in Tyama's kingdom, according to law, paying the price as apportioned for strangers.

24/14.35. In answer to his summons, there came to the gate, the damsel Yu-tiv, fairest of women, draped, also, to go before the priest for confession. Brahma inquired of her concerning the priest and the tax. Yu-tiv informed him, and, moreover, said: I am going there, and shall be delighted to lead you to the place. So Brahma went with Yu-tiv, and when they were gone a little way she said to him: Where did you come from, and what is your mission? Perhaps I may serve you. Behold, I see a star above your head!

24/14.36. Brahma said: Do you see a star? Now I say to you, there is an old legend that the pure in heart, looking upward, often see their own paroda [soul, or bird –Ed.], and think it belongs to another. || Yu-tiv reassured Brahma she saw the star, whereupon Brahma took heart[792] and said:

24/14.37. Yes, I have a star, and the Voice of Ormazd comes to me at times. For some years I strove to be a priest, for I saw the wickedness of the world, and, too, the tyranny and tortures of the church (ha'oke), and my soul cried out for the oppressed who had more faith in the Great Spirit than in the priests. And Ormazd came to me and said: Brahma, My son, forsake your studies, and take your broad-axe, and go and hew logs. Behold, I will come to you sometime later, and you shall bless the earth.

24/14.38. So I gave up my studies and became a hewer of wood, living abstemiously day and night, and praying and striving with all my soul and strength to purge myself of all earthly thoughts. So I grew, as you see, to be a large man of great strength. But, alas, evil overtook me; my soul desired a woman. And I cried out to Ormazd, saying: Why have You put this matter upon Your son? Lo, I strove to be wedded to You only; I shut my eyes to all the earth, but You have allowed me to fall. Rescue me, I pray.

24/14.39. Then Ormazd spoke to me, saying: Behold, I have revealed My word through those who have no earth desires; but that time is past. I will now prove to the nations of the earth that I have power in directing the flesh, so that heirs can be born to Me. Arise, therefore, and go where I will lead you, for you shall take a wife and raise up seven sons, and I will deliver My edifice,[793] to liberty.

24/14.40. So I rose up and followed the light of my star; I have come this far, but how much farther I must go I do not know; but I will go to the end of the earth if Ormazd requires it of me.

24/14.41. Yu-tiv said: I pity you, O man! One so holy should never wed with woman. To win such a man's love, the best of women would forget her God! To bear you one child, let alone seven, a woman would cleave the earth in two. It would be like peopling the world with Gods and Goddesses.

24/14.42. O promise me, stranger, you will turn from such unholy desires. I do not know what moves me past all modesty to speak to you like this, but I speak truly before Ormazd, Creator of heaven and earth, that before you came to my father's gate a voice spoke in my ear, saying: Quickly, put on your robes for confession, and hasten to the priest.

24/14.43. I tell you, O man, to save you, the angels of Ormazd came to me. It is true that two can see more than one.

24/14.44. Brahma said: Who are you, O woman? Yu-tiv said: A weaver of mats; no more. My father lives in that thatch[794] over there; my mother's soul ascended to heaven, giving me birth.

[792] i.e., as a consequence, Brahma became emboldened

[793] house; foundation; here meaning Faithists, the righteous

She was of the I'hins. My father and I have been driven from place to place; all the ills of earth are written on my soul. And the rudeness of men; the lightheartedness[795] of women! By day and by night my soul cries out for the miseries of the earth. O the sins of the earth! O the death of little infants! O the trials of the poor! O the suffering of the sick! O the anguish of the imprisoned! O stranger, stranger, stranger! Add no more people to this world!

24/14.45. Let us turn our souls upward; to Nirvania; to the regions of endless paradise! To the voices of angels and Gods! To wisdom that does not err; to music never discordant! To love that never separates! Never!

24/14.46. Brahma said: Now I beseech You, O Ormazd, that I may never marry! But because You have raised up here so fair a woman, and wise as well, give me leave[796] so I may dwell near at hand!

24/14.47. Then out of the midst of the voices of their stars, Ormazd spoke, saying: Hold up your hand, O man! Hold up your hand, O woman! And they held up their hands, and Ormazd said: I am the Father, and you are My children. So that I may have joy, you may dwell near together.

24/14.48. Now after this, Brahma and Yu-tiv proceeded to the priest's house and made their sacrifices, and returned and came to Yu-tiv's father's house, and her father's name was Ali-egan-is, called Ali. And Yu-tiv told her father all that had happened, but Brahma said little. Ali said: What the All Light does is well done. My house is ample. Brahma shall stay as long as he desires.

24/14.49. Brahma said: Of my own accord I am not master of many words. When it pleases Ormazd to speak with me, I will raise my voice. Then Yu-tiv spread mats and provided food, and set it before Brahma, and he ate; and after that they said prayers according to the laws of the king, and then retired to sleep.

[794] a house made of interlaced thatch (reeds, stalks, large grasses, etc.)

[795] shallowness, frivolousness, insincerity, etc.

[796] a (usually temporary) exemption from obligation; a dispensation, waiver, release, indulgence

CHAPTER 15 First Book God

24/15.1. When morning came, Brahma and Yu-tiv rose early, and came together and spoke in joyous greeting, and they were moved to shake hands, though such a proceeding was not according to the custom of the country, except between relatives. And it came to pass that they were together during much of the day, and in the evening they walked together, but did not touch each other.

24/15.2. Now on the second day, when they walked together, they held hands. And on the third day they joined arms. And on the fourth day they kissed each other. And after that they were only separated at night when they slept. But it came to pass that they were so delighted with each other that they sat up nearly all night, so as not to be separated.

24/15.3. And all the while they did not neglect their devotion to Ormazd; but finally they sat up all night, not sleeping, except in each other's arms.

24/15.4. Yu-tiv said: Since we sit up all night, it is wiser to sit on mats than on stools. Brahma said: It is wiser. So they provided mats, half raised and half spread down, for a season, and finally laid the mats full length, and they lay down together. More than that, history does not say.

24/15.5. But Brahma followed his trade in that country, and it came to pass they had a son born to them, and his name was Whe-ish; and in time another son, and his name was Vus, and then Vede, and Git-un, and Oos, and Sa-it.

24/15.6. Now after they lived together as man and wife, the voice of Ormazd no longer came to Brahma, though the angel of Ormazd remained, and at times talked to both Brahma and Yu-tiv. And during all the time, until after the birth of the sixth son, Yu-tiv had faith in Ormazd, and was a Faithist in her whole heart. But during all these years she had communion only with the angels, and had also suffered many hardships in common with Brahma.

24/15.7. And their love did not abate[797] a fraction, and Yu-tiv believed in her husband, and encouraged his aspirations. He had told her ten thousand times: I know Ormazd will come; through me He will deliver the Faithists out of bondage.[798]

[797] diminish, decline, recede, wane

[798] see image i111 Brahma and Yu-tiv

i111 **Bahma and Yu-tiv.**

24/15.8. And she believed in him; and believed these things would come to pass, and believed her sons would have the Voice of the Creator with them also. But after the birth of the sixth child, Yu-tiv lost faith in the Father! She said: All my life I have been in error. There is no All Person. There is no Voice, except the spirits of the dead. And they know little more of heaven than we. The Creator is dumb, like the wind; His voice is like the wind, it speaks nothing.

24/15.9. And after that, she ceased to use the name Ormazd, or Father, but said, Eolin, like the ancients. And Brahma ceased to speak anymore in the presence of Yu-tiv regarding the coming of Ormazd to himself; and he also adopted the name Eolin, signifying, like the wind, void of shape or person.

24/15.10. While this state of unbelief was upon them, they had another child born to them, and they called his name Hog, signifying Fact, or without inspiration; an animal that roots in the ground.

24/15.11. Yu-tiv weaned Hog when he was three years old, and, the next day the voice of God came to Brahma, saying: Brahma! Brahma! And Brahma said: Here I am, O Eolin. And the Father said: Be faithful another eighteen years! I shall be with you to the end!

24/15.12. Brahma was so delighted, he ran home and told Yu-tiv. But she did not rejoice, did not answer; silently she looked upward for a long while, and then she said: Eighteen years! Hog will be twenty-one. And you and I will be old.

CHAPTER 16 First Book God

24/16.1. So God did not speak to Brahma for eighteen years, but Brahma remained faithful, and Yu-tiv was full of hope. But when the time was fulfilled in Ormazd's own way, He came with renewed light, which was on Hog's twenty-first birthday.

24/16.2. While Brahma and his family were seated on mats, eating breakfast at sunrise, lo, a light, like that of a sun, came within the hut, passed over Brahma's head, and then disappeared. And out of the void, in the space above their heads, came these words: From this time forward, the twenty-first birthday shall be the time of maturity for man. Be watchful for the voice of Ormazd; He is Ever Present!

24/16.3. And all of them saw the light and heard the words, except Hog, for he, having been begotten in unbelief, could neither see the light nor hear the voice. And when they all had exclaimed: Behold the light! Hear that voice! || Hog spoke before them:

24/16.4. For many years you have prophesied this would come to pass when I reached my twenty-first birthday. Because of the love you all bear me, I know you would not pull a joke on me; but I am seriously grieved that you say: Behold the light, and hear the voice! For I say to you, these things are not in reason, and cannot be so. But in much hope, faith and belief, all of which you have cultivated for years, you allow your imaginings to stand for realities.

24/16.5. Now while Hog was thus speaking, the light came again and stood over Brahma's head while one might count to twenty; and the Voice said: Blessed are you, O Brahma; blessed you, O Yu-tiv! These things had to be fulfilled. I do not preach by reason alone, but provide living examples! (In his old age Brahma had attained iesu!)

24/16.6. Again all of them saw and heard the manifestation of Ormazd, except Hog, for he could neither see nor hear what came of the Spirit. Hog said: Do I not have eyes as good as the best? Show me a hair that I cannot see; let a mite fall that I cannot hear. Then Whe-ish, the first-born, answered him, saying:

24/16.7. First, my brother, I greet you with my love, for you are the fairest and best of all the great sons born of this God and Goddess, our father and mother. And I appeal to you in your great wisdom, how could we all have imagined the same light at the same time and in the same place? And greater yet, how could we have imagined the same spoken words? Hog replied:

24/16.8. How can my answers cope with one who has wisdom like you, O my brother? You have confounded me; but still I do not understand how you, and you, my most loving brothers, can see and hear things that I cannot. Do we not all have the same parts, so like one another that our neighbors can scarcely distinguish us from each other? And above all else, we are all fruit from the same father and mother, the holiest and wisest of created beings.

24/16.9. Now Yu-tiv spoke, saying: I am in Your judgment, O Ormazd! That which I have done, I have done! Deal with me for my great unbelief; I have sinned against heaven and earth. Even while You quickened into life within my womb this star of everlasting light, lo, I put out his eyes and stopped up his ears against You. The unbelief of my soul penetrated the walls of my womb and shaped the fruit of my holy husband into a man of darkness. O Ormazd, why was Your daughter born!

24/16.10. And Yu-tiv fell into tears. Hog said: O Goddess, mother! Do not weep, but rejoice for the glory of my birth. Because you and my holy father, a very God among men, brought me into life, my soul is boundless in rejoicing. I declare to you, O mother, I am not in darkness, nor am I blind and deaf. If there is another world, what does it matter to me? The glories of this one are boundless. And if there is a Great Light and a Voice, what are they to me! You have so filled my every vein of blood with your warm love, and with the sweet love of these, my holy brothers, and with the wisdom of my father, God among men, that I know nothing but to rejoice and to invent praises and thanks to you all, with all my wisdom and strength.

24/16.11. And now the Light gathered within the soul of Brahma, and he was as one with the Father. Then Ormazd, the Creator, spoke through Brahma, saying:

24/16.12. I created the earth not to be despised, as the Zarathustrians do through the hearts of monarchs and priests, but so that it should be the glory of man. This was the Zarathustrian law, but, for the sake of profit, bondage and evil, they have perverted My doctrines and bound up My peoples. They profess Me, even Ormazd; but they have turned My commandments and My doctrines upside down.

24/16.13. I came through Zarathustra and delivered those who called on Me in faith; and they became My chosen for a season; but they allowed evil to usurp[799] their hearts; they squandered My substance in building temples and providing a superabundance of priests and priestesses. They raised up the sword and spear for Me; yes, by blood and death they established kingdoms and called them by My name, Ormazd!

24/16.14. The spirit of My Voice they put aside; but the words they retained, and added earthly meaning to them, by which they proclaim darkness for light, and light for darkness. And the poor and distressed who worship Me in truth and in spirit have learned to hate the established words. For which reason they are persecuted, bound, taxed, and despitefully used.

24/16.15. Yes, they impress into service of war, those who would not kill because of their natural love for Me and for My created sons and daughters. Thus they take these from their kindred, saying to them: Come away from peace and kill! Be a slayer of men; be a soldier of death for the glory of the king.

24/16.16. I commanded them, since ancient times, to kill not at all. My words were plain. But the kings commanded the priests to interpret My words in such a way that war could be justified.

24/16.17. I commanded them against taking that which was another's. My words were plain. But the kings commanded the priests to interpret the meaning in such ways that the kings could exact tribute for their own glory. And so they levy [800] wherever and whenever they desire, saying: For the defense of the king and the country!

24/16.18. Thus they have perverted My commandments from beginning to end. But I declare to you, that in My sight, I will hold him accountable who kills one man; and ten times accountable if he kills ten men, and a hundred times for a hundred. They shall not hide death and murder from My sight by the word war.

24/16.19. Neither shall they excuse stealing by levying tax for the king or for the country's protection. For by their own evil, it has come to pass that they talk about protection. Have I made a law that one king or one country shall protect itself against another? Does any man not see that these doctrines come from the flesh and not from the spirit? (For as My kingdoms in heaven need no protection from one another; why should those on earth, who profess Me, require protection from one another, unless they are heeding the flesh and not Me?)

24/16.20. They profess to be Faithists in Me. But they immediately go and build fortifications of

---

[799] take control of

[800] impose and collect taxes, provisions, forced labor, military draft, etc.

earth, stone and wood. And as for those who know Me in spirit and truth, perceiving I am wrongly interpreted for evil's sake, being those who rebel in their souls against these iniquities—these they seize and impress as lifelong slaves, or, if refusing, they kill them.

24/16.21. And those who work such wickedness say: Behold, we have the Zarathustrian law, the I'hua'Mazdian law, the Ormazdian law; ours is the holy, the revealed word. Let no man raise up his voice against these truths, or he shall surely be put to death!

24/16.22. But I looked down from My holy heavens and saw, and My ears heard; and I cried out in My soul for the evils of the earth. I said: Behold, I will go and deliver those who have faith in Me in spirit and truth. And I went over the lands of the earth, but I found no man in whom My light could shine. So I called My holy masters of generations, My angels high raised in heaven, and I said to them: Come and dwell on the earth many generations, and by inspiration raise Me up one in whom My light shall shine, for I will surely deliver My people.

24/16.23. Now I declare to you who are assembled, the time is at hand, and you are all so many parts in My work. Even as through My angels you named these sons; so also according to their names, I will establish My kingdom.

24/16.24. Therefore, permit Vede to write down the words I have spoken, for lo, he has learning and memory provided to that end. Be watchful for when I come again!

24/16.25. Jehovih (Ormazd) ceased, and Brahma woke as from a trance, though he had heard all that was said. So Vede remembered every spoken word, and he wrote them down on cloth prepared for that purpose. And this was the beginning of a new name of a people on the earth, for though they were in fact Faithists, and nothing but Faithists, yet their neighbors sometimes called them Vedans and sometimes Brahmans.

CHAPTER 17 First Book God

24/17.1. The next morning, at sunrise, Jehovih came again, speaking through Brahma, saying:

24/17.2. As I prepared a way for My voice, be wise in laboring to show this light to all peoples. Yet do not take sorrow to your souls for the latest born, Hog (who cannot see this light); for he is also in My keeping, and his wisdom shall be the glory of the earth.

24/17.3. For is not all fact interpreted by each and every man from the light of his own standing place? In which, error comes into the world by the darkness of men, in not perceiving rightly the things I have created. Behold, one man sees the forest with reference to its value in logs; another for splints for mats; another for shade to lie in; another for its solitude; and they all see by what dwells in them, but they see through their own particular windows.[801]

24/17.4. Consider, then, the injustice of the man who says: You shall see as I see; hear as I hear; or who says: I have proven this to be true, and that to be untrue; or who says: Behold, we are many witnesses, and we attest.

24/17.5. While Jehovih was speaking so, His angel appeared and stood in the doorway of the hut, and all except Hog looked and saw the angel, and witnessed the color of the angel's hair and eyes, and the clothes he wore. And they pointed, saying in a whisper: Behold, an angel of heaven!

24/17.6. Then Jehovih spoke, illustrating, saying: While no one has yet spoken, let one at a time privately describe to Hog the appearance of My angel in the doorway.

24/17.7. Accordingly, they all, except Brahma, told Hog all that pertained to the angel, and their accounts accorded with one another. And Jehovih said: Speak, My Son, Hog. Hog said:

24/17.8. To whom shall I speak? For, whether You are my very father; or, in truth, the Creator, I do not know. God said: Who do you say the Creator is? Hog said: Even as the wind; the great void; without person, shape, or sense.

24/17.9. God said to him: For which reason I say to you, because of the unbelief of your father and your mother, while you were in your mother's womb, you are as you are. This they have attested to you thousands of times since you were weaned. And they have also attested to you as often, that during the bringing forth of your brothers, they were in the fullness of faith in Jehovih (Ormazd).

---

[801] vantage point, perspective, point of view, framework, frame of reference, standpoint, viewpoint, way of thinking

24/17.10. You were born of the earth, and can only see with earthly eyes, hear only with earthly ears, and can reason only with earthly reason. Hog said: Then in truth I shall go down to earth and there shall be no more of me; but these, my sweet brothers, and this Goddess and this God, my very father and mother, shall inherit everlasting life?

24/17.11. God said: I would place two eggs before you, with the birds within them nearly hatched; now with one you shall open the shell a little, and the young bird sees out, but the other you leave closed. Would you say one bird will have much advantage over the other when they are hatched? Or, that one shall not live, because, in fact, it did not see through the shell? Such, then, is your way to everlasting life. Of your darkness I will make light that will reach millions. Your sacrifice is the sacrifice of a very God among Gods.

24/17.12. Hog said: Because of your great wisdom, I fear to speak in your presence. But your words come out of the mouth of him who is the sweetest and holiest of created beings. Therefore I take courage in my argument.

24/17.13. Now, behold, they have all described the angel in the door; and their descriptions are alike in all particulars. And the wisdom of your words goes to the bottom of things, not like the words of man, but faultlessly. You have made me see that I am bound as if with iron hoops, and must go my way all my days. I do not complain against this; for I perceive it is not within my judgment to know even myself, as to what is good for me or not good for me. However, you have shown me this: I was molded as I am; I am as I am. If I have faults, they are not my faults. Neither are they my father's nor my mother's; for the cause of their unbelief at that time did not lie with themselves, but with you.

24/17.14. God said: Vede shall also write down your words; the glory and the wisdom of the earth shall come out of your mouth. The manner of my edifice[802] shall be shown to the inhabitants of the earth. You have seen the king's temple and how he builds it. For the fine posts he sends his best hewers into the forest, and they choose the straightest and strongest trees, and fall them and hew them,[803] and polish and engrave them, and the posts are set up in the front as strength and ornament. But for the walls of the temple, the king does not call for the best hewers, but the choppers, and they also go into the forest to fetch logs, not the straightest and handsomest, but whatever their axes come upon. And their timbers are put in the walls with mortar and withes.[804] And the temple is completed to the king's will.

24/17.15. Jehovih said: My heavenly edifice is like this also; I do not send winter to please one man, nor summer; nor the rain. I consider in what way I shall induce men to raise up one another and to be considerate. Thus through Me: Your father, mother, brothers, and all Faithists that come after these, My doctrines, shall learn to consider the unbelief of mortals, and the impossibility of one man seeing through another man's eyes.

24/17.16. For as I have raised you up in a house of love for one another, so will I show the wisdom of disbelief, and its necessity on the earth.

24/17.17. The foremost of all lessons is that all men shall have liberty; and no man's judgment shall be binding on another's; for all do not see alike, nor can they understand alike.

24/17.18. So you shall be as considerate to those who do not see My light, or My Person, as you are to those who are born in su'is; for they are of the same flesh and blood, and they have their spirits from the same Creator.

24/17.19. For in the evidence of the past and present it is before you, that men endeavor to enforce their doctrines by saying: BEHOLD THE WORD OF ORMAZD! HE HAS SPOKEN THUS! AND I AM HIS PRIEST! BOW DOWN YOUR HEADS![805]

24/17.20. Instead, man shall not bow down, but hold up his head and rejoice. Those who seek to enforce Me are My enemies.

24/17.21. Nor have I said of this man or that: Hear him, for he is Truth. || Shall the Creator make one greater than Himself, and thus cut Himself off? And yet the kings and priests of this day assume to be Truth in Ihua's (God's) name. And the mothers and fathers of many have become discouraged because of their great hardships; and they bring

---

[802] house, foundation, structure, building

[803] i.e., cut down, then trim and smooth them

[804] A withe is a supple twig, like willow, flexible enough to be used like string or twine for lashing together things such as timbers.

[805] a sign of submission and obedience

forth heirs who have eyes but do not see, ears but do not hear.

24/17.22. God said: In the days of Zarathustra, I came to deliver those who had faith but were in bondage; today I come to teach men how to bring forth heirs with eyes to see spiritual things, and with ears to hear them, and with liberty to all men.

24/17.23. And I come to prove three worlds to men. First, the earth and its fullness; second, the intermediate world of spirits, where all shall sojourn for a season; and third, the Nirvanian worlds beyond Chinvat, where, for the pure and wise, unending paradise awaits.

CHAPTER 18 First Book God

24/18.1. In the next morning, at sunrise, God spoke again to Brahma, saying:

24/18.2. Consider the fruit of the earth, and the pasturage in the fields. The male and the female feed on the same grass; yet one yields milk, and the other is for the yoke; neither can any man change these creations.

24/18.3. What man shall say to another: Feed on this, or on that? || But they take those who are born in darkness, and raise up priests! The food for the flesh, or even fasting, cannot bring su'is. The air warms the earth, and not the earth the air. The spirit enlightens the corporeal part, and not the corporeal part the spirit.

24/18.4. Light is the freedom of all; to know this is the beginning of wisdom. Nevertheless, without suffering, some who are bound would not know they are bound, or, if knowing, would not desire freedom.

24/18.5. || At this time, Hog, the youngest born, was greatly moved,[806] and so God bade him speak.

24/18.6. Hog said: O if only I could believe these things! O if only I could see! O if only I could hear! O the misery of my darkness! O the horrors of the suspense of not knowing a matter! Bitter is my soul, and full of anguish! O the madness of this hour upon me!

24/18.7. How, O Wisdom, did You forget the time of my begetting, to let me spring up as an offensive weed in such a garden of paradise! ||

24/18.8. And he bowed his head and wept; and then Yu-tiv, his mother, who had brought him forth, spoke, saying: I perceive Your light, O Father, but I cannot bear it. You unlocked my members to bring forth these seven Gods! Never has woman on the whole earth brought forth so rich a harvest; but yet my soul is tortured to its very center! O if only the light of my soul could be transferred to this God among men! And she also wept.

24/18.9. Now spoke Sa-it, saying: I am nearest born to you, O my sweet brother, Hog,. No love lies as fondly to you as mine. And as to you, Yu-tiv, my Goddess mother, you have most wisely named me ABUNDANT. For in our love, Ormazd has provided us equal to the highest of Gods. Because I have witnessed that this purest and best of brothers cannot see spiritually, my soul is mellowed toward all the world. Yes, my outstretched arms shall receive the darkest of men, and my soul shall go up in praise of Ormazd forever!

24/18.10. Oos spoke next; he said: Most wisely I am named SPACE; for it has pleased Ormazd to show me the breadth of His Creations. What belief or unbelief is there that He has not provided a glory for it! Because my sweet brother, Hog, has been thus blessed with darkness, he shall be guardian to me in earthly wisdom all my days. In my faith I know it is well with him; yet in my love I wish he could see as we all see!

24/18.11. Then spoke Git-un, whose name signified TIME. He said: Behold, I am the fourth born, and, as it were, in the middle. Whose love is so delightfully hedged around as mine is! Who is so surrounded by the Light of heaven and earth! At one end behold my father, God among men; the very voice of heaven and earth; interpreter of the Creator's words! At the other end, the best, sweetest brother ever created on the earth, with all the wisdom of men and angels. O the glory of this hour! O the delight to be with these Gods, and with Yu-tiv, Goddess among women!

24/18.12. Then Vus, the second born, spoke. He said: How shall I glorify You, O Ormazd, and not glorify myself! I am full to overflowing with delight for the love of these, my brothers and father, very Gods! But for Yu-tiv I have more than love. I perceive through my own sweet mother how the different castes of men are made! O mother, how very near the Creator dwells such a righteous woman!

24/18.13. Whe-ish said: To keep one's thoughts and desires ever high; would this not deliver the

[806] stirred, agitated, perturbed

world? Vede said: To know the truth and ever speak it in love and kindness, would this not deliver the world and establish Ormazd?

24/18.14. Brahma now woke from his trance, and he spoke, saying: To find the Father; to know Him; to reveal Him; these are all, and for His glory only.

24/18.15. Now God spoke again, saying: Wiser than all the rest is Brahma. Who of you all has not spoken of himself or herself? Who has uttered a word of praise or of thanks, and left out self? Judge, then, what is required of men so that my spirit may find utterance through their lips.

24/18.16. Then the Voice departed for that day; and the angel of God appeared in the door, so all except Hog could see him. The angel said: Come at midnight and sit in the sacred circle in the grove of Ebon so that you may see the spirits of the intermediate world. We will appear in sar'gis.

24/18.17. Hog did not hear the angel, but the others told him what the angel said. Accordingly, at midnight they sat in circle in the grove of Ebon.

CHAPTER 19 First Book God

24/19.1. And the angel of God appeared in the middle of the circle, in sar'gis, and talked with them face to face. And Hog said to the angel: In truth, I know you are not mortal, and yet you have the semblance of flesh, limbs, arms and an actual body having clothes that look just like mortal clothes.

24/19.2. Now I tell you face to face, I believe you are no angel of the dead, but actually a reflected self-substance, produced out of the substance of my father. Can you prove otherwise? The angel answered, saying:

24/19.3. Mortal words cannot convince you; nor can the words of a spirit. Behold, I will show you a friend of yours who is dead. With that, the angel showed the spirit of Hog's friend who was dead, and the man's name was Aara-acta; and so Hog said to him:

24/19.4. You are an actual counterpart of him I knew. What is your name? The spirit answered: Aara-acta! I tell you, O Hog, these things are true. I am the spirit of your friend; yes, I am that very friend. Hog said: Where do you dwell? Where have you been? Are you happy? Have you visited all the heavens?

24/19.5. The spirit answered him, saying: I live around here on the earth even as before death. I am happy; the glory of my present world surpasses the earth. I have not visited the highest heavens. I am as yet only in the first resurrection. Up above us there are heavens where all the people are Gods and Goddesses. I cannot go there; they are too white.[807] || The spirit then disappeared, and Hog said:

24/19.6. I saw what I saw and heard what I heard. Yet I do not believe that I have seen a spirit nor heard one. A spirit must by reason be thin, subtle, and air-like.

24/19.7. Then the angel of God spoke, saying: How shall I please this man, O Ormazd? This morning I showed myself in the door of the hut, thin and subtle and air-like, and he did not see or hear me. Who can find a way to open this man's soul to Your Wisdom, O Ormazd?

24/19.8. Now Yu-tiv spoke, saying: Great is the glory of Your angel, O Ormazd! Heavenly are the spirits of the dead. Welcome, O you angels of heaven! Then Whe-ish spoke, saying: Even the lowest of heavens has great glory! O what delight it would be to dwell in such a paradise! Next Vus spoke, saying: Such wisdom and truth! What are Your kingdoms, O Father, when even the first heaven has such glory. Vede said: Truth is Your mightiest work, O Ormazd! Git-un said: Because I have lived to see these things, I will proclaim Your wonders, O Ormazd, for as long as I live! Oos said: You have framed Your worlds so wisely, O Ormazd, that even Your lowest of angels are the delight of my soul! Next spoke Sa-it, he said: Give us of Your abundance, O Ormazd. Open wide the gates of the lower heavens. I will take Your angels into my arms and rejoice forever!

24/19.9. Brahma then came out of his trance, though he had heard and seen all. He said: Whoever comes that can make me better, and show me how most to benefit Your world, him, O Ormazd, send to me. || And lo, Brahma was answered first of all! A light, bright as a sun, stood in the middle of the circle, and it was higher than the clouds, and displayed a staff on which was a banner of gold and silver; and on the banner, stars

[807] This refers to their radiant spiritual light, not to skin color.

clustered to spell the words, Love, Wisdom and Power!

24/19.10. Presently the scene changed, and the angel of God said: He who spoke last (Brahma) has been answered first, because his words reached to the Fountainhead. Wherever you send your prayers, you are answered from there.[808] With that in mind, I will now open the gates of the lower heavens, and you shall witness what you may.

24/19.11. The angel withdrew all surrounding lights, so that great darkness came upon the circle. Presently, Yu-tiv started,[809] as if somewhat frightened. Then Vus sprang up, saying: What was that? And then another started, till presently all except Brahma and Hog were wild and startled, whispering: What do my eyes behold! O that foul smell! O that vulgar touch! And then one screamed; and another, and another, until all broke and fled, screaming and crying out in fear and distress; flying into the darkness of the grove, frantic; almost dead with fear!

24/19.12. Hog did not run; saw nothing to fear; heard nothing to dread; felt nothing to make him ashamed.

24/19.13. And his father, Brahma, did not run, was not afraid, and the two called to the rest, pleaded, coaxed and called in vain; could not stop them; could not find them in the darkness. They returned to the hut, Brahma and Hog; saw the torches burning brightly, and came in and found Yu-tiv and her sons huddled together in each other's arms, white and pale as death.

24/19.14. Hog asked the reason. Yu-tiv said: Shh![810] Are they gone? Shh! Keep them away! Then Vus spoke, saying: O my brother, do not ask what we saw! Do not ask what we felt, and what felt us! These things would not be lawful to mention! Say no more, in heaven's name! The air of heaven is full of demons (druj).

24/19.15. Now Vede spoke, saying: Alas, O my father, I dropped the holy book, the Veda I am writing. In my fright I let it fall. It is not sized yet, and if it rains before morning, the holy words will be lost! And not for a thousand worlds would I go back to the grove tonight. Oos said: Nor I, for a thousand worlds! Whe-ish said: For all the gold and silver in the world I would not go there tonight.

24/19.16. They all spoke in the same way except Hog, and with all the love they bore for Ormazd's words, not doubting they were His very words, not one would venture among the evil spirits they had seen, to recover the book.

24/19.17. Then Brahma spoke, saying: For many generations Ormazd has labored for this; I will go myself; I know He will protect me at all times and in all places. And Brahma rose up to depart; but then Hog spoke, saying: No, father; you are old; I am fresh and young, and besides, I know there are no spirits but in the imagination of men. I will go alone!

24/19.18. Neither will I carry a lantern or a torch; nor will I whistle or sing. I will confront all the evil spirits of hell and their captains. I will recover that book tonight even if I have to scrape every leaf from Ebon grove! And mark my words, I will return unscathed; nor will I see or hear a spirit all the time I am gone. || So, only Hog and Brahma were fearless.

24/19.19. With that, Hog departed, and after a while he returned, rejoicing, bringing the book; and he said: I neither saw nor heard a spirit, and I declare to you that none of you saw or heard them, for there are none. The extreme bent of your minds makes these imaginings seem real. And as to the great Light, with the words, Love, Wisdom and Power, which I also saw, I say to you, it is some emanation from this, our holy and most loved father. How often have we heard him use those same words! And as to those figures that talked, and had the semblance of men and women, even to the detail of their garments, I say to you all, they emanate from the same source, from our father, Brahma.

24/19.20. Now Yu-tiv spoke, saying: O happy unbelief, my son! O if only I had been born as you! O if only I had never seen such sights as I saw tonight!

24/19.21. Then Oos said: O happy brother, our youngest born! If only I were like you! O the vulgarity of those hands that came upon me tonight!

24/19.22. Vus said: O if only I had never known the unseen world! O if only I had been born in darkness like you, our most favored brother! ||

---

[808] That is, the focus of your prayer determines the place from which a response comes.

[809] reflexively recoiled in alarm, jolted, startled

[810] urgent request for silence; shush, hush, lower the volume of your voice

24/19.23. Similarly the rest of them, except Brahma, spoke deploringly of their gift of su'is; and when they had finished speaking, the angel of God spoke through Brahma, saying: While it is yet night, I speak. With the dawn, at sunrise, comes the Father's Voice. Hear me, then, briefly, without expecting much wisdom, for I am not long born in heaven:

24/19.24. The Creator created two great men, the Faithist and the unbeliever; the first has passed through the trials of the flesh, and attained to the Father's Voice; for in becoming one with the Father, he no longer stands in fear of anything in heaven or earth. The glory of constant resurrection is before him forever.

24/19.25. All men who have not attained to this may be compared to a man going up a slippery hillside, who often rises high, but suddenly slides low. They glorify themselves for their own light, wisdom and good gifts, rejoicing for self's sake for the glories that have fallen upon them. But they are cowards.

24/19.26. Nevertheless, the Creator created a great man among these; and that is the unbelieving man. He has neither gold nor silver, nor house nor land; and he is without spiritual sight or spiritual hearing; but his glory is in understanding his own understanding.

24/19.27. He is the one who subdues the forest, and tames the beasts of the field to man's service. He goes alone in the dark, fearing nothing. He does not follow the course of any man, but searches for himself; the priest cannot make him believe, nor can the angels of heaven; none can subdue his judgment. He sees the glory of the earth and manhood. He calls to the multitude, saying: Why do you permit others, even priests, to think for you? Arise, and be a man! Arise, and be a woman!

24/19.28. He inspires of the earth and for the earth; through his arm tyrants and evil kings are overthrown. Through him doctrines and religions are sifted to the bottom, and the falsehood and evil in them cast aside. Yes, who but Ormazd could have created so great a man as the unbeliever?

24/19.29. And these two men, the Faithist and the unbeliever, do most of all the good that is done in the world; one labors at the top of the hill, calling upward; the other labors at the bottom of the hill, pushing upward.

CHAPTER 20 First Book God

24/20.1. On the next morning, at sunrise, Ormazd spoke again through Brahma, and Vede wrote down the words; and on the succeeding morning, the same; and so it continued for forty days; and in forty days, behold, the Veda was completed; the holy words of Brahma were written.

24/20.2. God said to Brahma: Go now, and preach my gospel to whoever will listen, proclaiming liberty to all who will follow you. I will be with you to the end. And you shall take Yu-tiv, your wife, and all your sons with you, even Hog, the youngest born.

24/20.3. So Brahma went forth preaching by day, and exhibiting the spirits of the dead by night. But to the chosen he spoke at dawn, in the early morning, the time the All Light was upon him. And his sons also preached and explained; and Yu-tiv explained to all women how it was with her when pregnant with her sons. Only Hog did not preach; nor did he open his mouth before the populace as to his unbelief. In his soul he said: These things may be true, and if they are true, it is well. If they are not true, still, the believing of them, by the populace, works righteousness and goodness. With all my philosophy, I cannot move the multitude to righteousness. But my father makes them like a flock of sheep; they cease from evil, and they practice good fellowship. Therefore, I will stand by my father to the end.

24/20.4. When Brahma came near a city, he halted outside the walls because there, according to law, the kings could not restrain his speech. And the multitude came out of the city to hear him, and many did not return, preferring to remain with Brahma and his sons in their camp. And when Brahma moved to another city they went with him. And in a little while the hosts of Brahma were as an army of thousands.

24/20.5. And not a few of them were men and women of wealth, and they cast their treasures at Brahma's feet, saying: Take this trash, and give me of everlasting life instead. || But men of learning did not come to Brahma; nor did the priests, kings, magicians, or consulters of oracles.

24/20.6. God said: Take your hosts and establish them in families of tens, and of twenties, hundreds, and thousands, and give a head father to each and every family. And your people shall be a people to themselves, having nothing in common with the kings' peoples.

24/20.7. Behold, my angel will go with you, and show you the wastelands, those that the kings' peoples do not desire; and you and your people shall possess the lands and dwell together in love and wisdom, doing good to one another.

24/20.8. So Brahma did as commanded, and he established the mountains of Roam, and the valleys in the mountains of Roam; and his people dwelt there, being six thousand eight hundred and twenty, men, women and children.

24/20.9. And there came to Brahma a certain captain-general of the army of King Syaythaha, of the West Kingdom of Vind'yu, in which lay the city of Gowschamgamrammus, of a million inhabitants, and he said to Brahma:

24/20.10. In the name of the king, mightiest of men, Syaythaha, I am before you, O Brahma. Behold, the king sends you gold, silver and copper, saying: Brahma is good! Brahma shall give me the blessing of heaven!

24/20.11. Brahma answered the captain-general, saying: Brahma salutes the king, mightiest of men, Syaythaha, in the name of Ormazd, the Creator, in love and in these wise words that come to the soul of Brahma. Brahma sends the king's servant, who is the captain-general, back to the king, with his gold, silver and copper, saying: Deal with your Creator and not with men! The Great Spirit holds all blessings in His own hands. Give Him your treasures!

24/20.12. The captain-general departed and returned with his gold, silver and copper to the king, and told the king Brahma's words. The king was pleased with the wisdom of Brahma, but also felt rebuked and sore at heart. So Ormazd allowed satan to possess the king for a season; and the king resolved to destroy Brahma and all his people. And he commanded the captain-general to assemble together fifty thousand men, with arms, ready for battle. And when they were thus prepared, and started on their journey, which would require seven days, the king thought to inquire of the oracle as to his best mode of success.

24/20.13. Now the angel of God had taken possession of the oracle, but the magi did not know it, nor did Syaythaha. So the king came before the sand table, and the spirit wrote these words: He who has become one with Ormazd is mightier than an army. Take off your crown, O king, mightiest of men, and your golden robes, and all that is fine and fair to look upon, and clothe yourself in the poorest of garments, like a druk who wanders about. But your crown and your costly robes, and your raiment, fine and fair to look upon, put them on your body servant. And the pair of you shall go in advance of the army, as you come before Brahma.

24/20.14. And you shall witness that man who professes to labor for the poor, fall on his belly before the man of riches and power. And behold, O king, you shall feel justified in destroying him who falls before the crown and robes, knowing he is a hypocrite.

24/20.15. The king was pleased with this, and he fulfilled all that was commanded by the oracle; and when he came near Brahma's camp, a man came before the king's servant, saying: Behold, O king, command me as you will! And he prostrated himself on the ground before the king's servant. At which the king, dressed as a druk, came to him and said: Who are you? And the man answered: Be gone, beggar! My matter is with the king! (For he mistook which was which.)

24/20.16. The king ordered the man to be seized and taken away and put to death; and the advance guard fell upon the man and slew him with war clubs. And when the man was quite dead, behold, Brahma came, and the king did not know him, nor did any of his advance guard. And Vus and Whe-ish were with their father, and the three came and stood by the dead man. Brahma then took the king's hand, saying: You, dressed in the garb of a druk, come here, for you have flesh and blood toward holiness. Lay one hand on the dead man; put your other hand on my head, for I will prove Ormazd before your eyes. Behold, you who have tried to kill Brahma, killed another person!

24/20.17. And when the king's hands were placed, Brahma stood by the head of the dead man, and his two sons by the heart; and Brahma said: In Your name, O Ormazd, and by Your power in me, return to life, O man! And arise! Arise! Arise!

24/20.18. And behold, the man was brought to life, and rose up and stood before the multitude.

24/20.19. The king trembled with fear, and the guard stood aback,[811] amazed. And as for the servant arrayed in the king's garb, he cast aside the crown and robes, and fled into the forest.

24/20.20. Brahma said to the king: Here stands the angel of Ormazd, and the angel says you are the king in disguise, and, moreover, that he, the angel, commanded you here for this purpose, saying to you in the oracle: He who has become one with Ormazd is mightier than an army!

24/20.21. The king said: This is true. I swear before You, O Ormazd, from this time forward I will wear such garments as these I have on, and my life shall be given to Your service. Let who will, take my kingdom and all I called mine.

24/20.22. So Syaythaha joined Brahma's hosts; and with Syaythaha came his brothers and their sons and daughters. And those who came, cast into a heap whatever goods or moneys they had, and the head fathers of the families divided and distributed the same according to their best wisdom. And Brahma's people, by commandment of Brahma, called themselves not Brahmans, but Vedans, that is, Truth-followers.

24/20.23. In those days the language of the kings of Vind'yu, and of men of learning, was All-ao, signifying, OUT OF ALL THAT IS GOOD. But the Vedans were the unlearned, and their language was imperfect, and had many meanings for every spoken and written word.

24/20.24. And God foresaw the liability[812] to corruption of the Brahman religion, and he spoke to Brahma, saying: Behold, I have given you seven sons, six of light and one of darkness. Your six sons of light shall each establish a school among my chosen, and teach my scriptures by word of mouth. And all who afterward become rab'bahs shall be capable of repeating every word of the Veda by heart. And if, in later times, the plates and the books of my holy religion are destroyed by war, it will not matter. The substance of your labors shall live.

24/20.25. Then Brahma's sons did as commanded, each and every one becoming a teacher. And again God spoke to Brahma, saying: Arise, and go where my angel will lead you, taking your wife and your son Hog, with you. And you shall travel from place to place for two years, and then return here, for your labor will be completed.

CHAPTER 21 First Book God

24/21.1. The place thus founded by Brahma was called Haraoyo, and his people, at this time, extended to seven cities and thirty villages, and possessed all the country of Roam, which had been uninhabited for hundreds of years. And the Vedans cultivated the lands, living on fruits, roots, and bread made from wheat grown in the fields; but they ate neither fish nor flesh, nor anything that had breathed the breath of life.

24/21.2. Brahma, Yu-tiv and their youngest son, Hog, departed from Haraoyo, accompanied by seven disciples, and they went forth under the direction of the angels of Ormazd, to preach and explain the Veda, carrying one book with them. And they first went to the northeast, through the kingdoms of Haomsut, Ali-oud, Zeth, and Wowtichiri; then westerly to Hatiqactra, where the tyrant, Azhi-Aven, had built a temple of skulls, like the ancients. Azhi kept six dens of lions, for devouring his condemned slaves. So, because of oppression, the kingdom of Azhi was profitable to Ormazd. From Hatiqactra, Brahma obtained three thousand followers.

24/21.3. And when Brahma had seven thousand followers, the angel of God directed him to the plains of Cpenta-armaiti. And here he established his people, dividing them into families and villages, and appointing priests to them. And after that, Cpenta-armaiti became renowned over all the known world. ||

24/21.4. After Cpenta-armaiti had been established, the angel directed Brahma to go to the southwest, through the kingdoms of H'spor and Vaetaeyo, and Aramya, and then to Dacyama, to the city of H'trysti, where Ormazd had a host of one thousand already inspired to join Brahma.

24/21.5. And now the angel directed Brahma to take his hosts to the mountains of T'cararativirwoh, and establish them, which he did. And behold, the time of Yu-tiv and of Brahma was near an end, for they were grown quite old.

---

[811] startled or surprised, stepped back; retreated somewhat

[812] vulnerability, risk, susceptibility; (perhaps to the level of likelihood or probability)

24/21.6. The angel said to Brahma: Great has been your labor. Very great Yu-tiv's! Where else in all the world is such a woman? From the day you first saw her! For the glory of your sons! And in her old age to follow you, walking so far!

24/21.7. Behold, O Brahma! Yu-tiv is weakening fast. Rise up and take her back to Haraoyo! The mountains of Roam are calling her! And your faithful son, Hog, strong and tall. Take him back with his mother. Haraoyo is calling.

24/21.8. Brahma went and looked at Yu-tiv; and his soul spoke within him, saying: O Ormazd, have I not forgotten her in You! The mother of my Gods! O her proud young soul when first I saw her! Alas, I see, she is tottering and feeble!

24/21.9. Brahma came closer to Yu-tiv, and she spoke to him, saying: O Brahma, you God among men! I do not know if my eyes are turning dim. But O, I have had so strange a vision even toward the high sun. It was myself I saw, rising, going upward! The earth going downward! Then I called: O Ormazd! Not alone! Behold, my God is over there! Let me go back to Brahma! Then I thought the Creator brought me back and said: Go quickly and see your godly sons in Haraoyo, for your time has come!

24/21.10. Brahma said: My angel says: Go back to Haraoyo, your labor is nearly finished. || This is why I came to you just now. It is well, therefore, for us that we return, taking Hog with us.

24/21.11. So Brahma, Yu-tiv and Hog, with five remaining disciples, departed for Haraoyo, which lay a three days' walking journey away, and they did not know how Yu-tiv would make it, for she was worn to the last step, and, above all, her shoes were worn out, and she had only pieces of cloth on her feet.

24/21.12. And while they were deliberating, having gone only a short distance, Hog spied a score of soldiers going in another direction, mounted on horses; and they were leading a number of spare horses with them. Then spoke the soul of Hog within him, saying to him:

24/21.13. Behold, my father has made many converts in his day, made good men out of bad ones. And he has always refused money, gifts and presents. Now, wherever justice lives I do not know; but many of the rascals who became followers of my father were conscience-stricken with ill-gotten gains, and, finding that my father would not receive their stuff, they tried me, and behold, my pockets are full of gold and diamonds. In truth, it may have been a very devil that prompted me; but I am not supposed to know the higher light, but to know the lower. Of myself and for myself I do not want these things. If they belong to Ormazd, it follows I should not keep them. Therefore, if I give some gold or diamonds to those soldiers, they will give me a horse for my angel mother to ride on. Who knows but the nearest road for this gold to find its way to Ormazd is by way of those soldiers?

24/21.14. So Hog went away and purchased a horse, and brought it to his mother, saying: Behold, a man gives you a present in the name of Ormazd, but forbids you to retain it except to ride to Haraoyo, where you shall sell it and give the money to the poor.

24/21.15. Yu-tiv said: A good man he was, and wise, for only on those conditions could I have accepted the horse. Accordingly, Yu-tiv was mounted on the horse, and they proceeded on their way, going slowly, for Brahma was also near the end. And after seven days they arrived at Haraoyo, where they were received by Brahma's sons, and by all the multitude of disciples.

24/21.16. But owing to Yu-tiv's deep love for her sons, and also being worn out, and having witnessed the glory of righteous works fulfilled through her husband and her sons, the strain was too much for her corporeal parts. And they brought straw and laid her on it, putting a bundle of straw under her head. Then she spoke, saying:

24/21.17. First to You, O Ormazd, my blessing, because You created me alive, to enjoy Your glories. Next, O Brahma! My husband, my blessing on you, God among men! You have taught me the fullness of earth and heaven! O the glory of having been your wife!

24/21.18. Then she called Whe-ish and said: O my son, my first-born! My blessing on you. Because I have watched you from the hour of conception, I have had the wisdom of creation demonstrated before me. O the joy when my eyes first saw you; I am going now, to prepare a place in heaven for you!

24/21.19. And, after that, Yu-tiv blessed all her sons, and coming to Hog she said: My blessing on you, O my latest born, God among men! To all my other sons I have told my love, but to you my soul so overflows, I am nearly speechless. You have been a very God in all your ways, and yet do not believe in Ormazd; nor in heaven nor angels! For which reason I look upon you as the highest of all creations. You are good for goodness' sake; wise for wisdom's sake, happy in finding a way to master all unhappiness!

24/21.20. And these were Yu-tiv's last words; she shut her eyes. She was dead! So they took her body, and robed it in white, and on the fourth day buried her in the forest of Roam.

CHAPTER 22 First Book God

24/22.1. On the day of Yu-tiv's death, Brahma said: Sing no songs; pray in silence only. Let her soul be in quiet with Ormazd.

24/22.2. On the second day Brahma said: Pray in whispers, praise in whispers, the best, good deeds of the dead.

24/22.3. On the third day Brahma said: Burst forth a song of praise to Ormazd; extol the virtues of the dead.

24/22.4. On the fourth day Brahma said: In song and in prayer bid the dead arise and go onward, upward!

24/22.5. Thus on the fourth day they put Yu-tiv's body in the ground; and then they went and sat in the sacred circle and sang and prayed for her soul to go on to Nirvana (paradise). And when they had finished, a light came down in the middle of the circle, and an angel in white appeared. It was Yu-tiv; the soul of Yu-tiv in the glory of Ormazd, the Creator!

24/22.6. Then the angel Yu-tiv spoke, saying: The spirit is born from out of the head of the corporeal body; and angels stand around, where they receive the spirit of the dead onto a spirit blanket. For one day, in quiet, they keep the spirit, teaching it to reconcile and understand. On the second day, the spirit hears the prayers of the earth-people coming upward; and on the third day, the spirit understands death and birth of spirit.

24/22.7. And on the fourth day, when you sang: O Goddess, arise from the dead! The Father calls you from on high! Arise, O Goddess, and go your way! Then my spirit was free from the earth, resting in the arms of Gods and Goddesses who had come from on high to receive me. Thus, O my beloveds, the first resurrection is on the third day; and, to the holy, the second resurrection begins on the fifth day. After the fifth day do not call me back again! My labor lies up there! I must build houses for you all. Thus Ormazd sends me on before! If it is His will for me to return to you at times, I will return. His will above all—this is the greatest wisdom.

24/22.8. Whe-ish, her first-born, asked: What about the angels of the intermediate world, O mother? Then his angel mother answered, saying: They were shown to us in Ebon grove! Alas, some of them do not begin the resurrection for a thousand years!

24/22.9. Then Yu-tiv, the angel, came over near Hog, her latest born, whom she loved so much. She said: Can you see me, my son? Hog answered: No, I only faintly see a glimmering light: I hear a voice, but it does not sound like my mother's voice. Yet, if it is true that there is a soul that lives after death, and if in truth you are the very spirit and soul of her who brought me forth, do not be unhappy because of my unbelief. As for myself, I am happy because you brought me forth in unbelief; nor would I choose to be any other way. Whether our eyes are blue or black, or whether we are tall or short, believers or disbelievers, or however we are created, to fill our place in doing good to others with all our wisdom and strength, is this not glory enough?

24/22.10. Yu-tiv said: O you wisest of men! In the day you are born in heaven, you shall not linger long in the intermediate world, but be crowned a very God indeed! Here ends my labors with the earth, O, my beloveds! An otevan above waits for me to ascend; the Gods and Goddesses are calling me! Farewell, my beloveds! Farewell!

24/22.11. And now the music of heaven descended, and even while the mortals sang, the very gates of heaven opened, and the angel Yu-tiv rose upward in a sea of fire!

24/22.12. But behold, the love of great Brahma was too much for him! His eyes raised upward after the ascending light, and his soul burst within him. He fell down and stretched himself on the cold earth! He, too, was dead.

24/22.13. Then burst the mighty hearts of Brahma's sons. The whole earth shook with the wail of Gods. The wind, the air above the earth, stood still, and the forest of Roam shuddered as if the earth were broken in two. Then wailed the sons and daughters of Haraoyo. Though no man uttered it, yet all knew that great Brahma was dead.

CHAPTER 23 First Book God

24/23.1. The angel of God came in the sacred circle and stood in its center. He said: Greeting, in the name of Ormazd! In His name I speak before you. First, then, who of all that was dearest to Brahma, he or she, shall arise!

24/23.2. And lo and behold, there arose every man, woman and child, more than ten thousand. The angel said: You, his most beloved, shall bury his body by the side of Yu-tiv. You shall bury him on the third day after his death, even at the hour of his death. And you shall sit around the grave three times a day, morning, noon and night, for one hour each time, singing and praying for the soul of Brahma; and you shall do this for two days.

24/23.3. And behold, on the evening of the second day you shall see the graves of both Brahma and Yu-tiv opened, and their very bodies will come forth, and Brahma shall speak with you face to face. || The angel then disappeared.

24/23.4. And the people did as commanded; and they sat around the graves in a circle, at a distance of ten paces from the graves, watching. And the brothers favored Hog above all the rest, so that he might be converted. And it came to pass, in the evening of the second day, two hours after sunset, there descended into the center of the circle a light, bright as the sun, so that the multitude held their hands before their eyes; and it was so bright that even the graves could not be seen, and the graves burst open.

24/23.5. And after a moment, the light was lowered so all could look upon the scene; and, lo and behold, Brahma and Yu-tiv stood arm in arm, in the middle of the circle, in their own flesh and bones wearing their burial robes.

24/23.6. Brahma said: Have faith in the Creator; with Him all things are possible. He is the All Master of all things. Never accept any God, Lord, Savior, priest, or king, but Him only, the everlasting All One, the Person.

24/23.7. Practicing good works to all men; abjuring self in all things; and Ormazd will dwell with you and in you forever.

24/23.8. Then Brahma and Yu-tiv came near Hog, so that he could see clearly. Hog said: Are you truly Brahma, my father; and you, Yu-tiv, my mother? Yu-tiv did not speak, but Brahma said: I am your father, even Brahma. To practice the highest light a man has; this is all that is required of any man.

24/23.9. Hog said: In truth it is my father! In truth it is my mother!

24/23.10. Brahma said: We are blessed! This is the first belief: to believe in the spirit surviving the corporeal body; the second belief is to learn the All Person. After this comes faith.

24/23.11. Hog said: You have proven the first; but as to the All Person, I cannot understand.

24/23.12. Brahma said: As I and your mother have revealed ourselves to you, and so proven ourselves, so in due season Ormazd will reveal Himself to you.

24/23.13. And these were the last words. Brahma and Yu-tiv rose up in the sea of fire, smiling and waving their hands in love to those beneath, rising higher and higher, till they disappeared in the sky.

24/23.14. Then the people went and witnessed that the graves were open and the bodies gone. They filled up the places, and set a post inscribed: TOMB OF BRAHMA AND YU-TIV, GOD AND GODDESS.

END OF THE HISTORY OF BRAHMA

CHAPTER 24 First Book God

The first Bible of Guatama (America)—being of Eawahtah, a man chosen by God for the children of Guatama[813]

24/24.1. In Guatama, in the Middle Kingdom (Central America), by the sea of So-ci-a-pan (Gulf of Mexico), down from heaven came Gitchee, the Creator, the World-Maker, Manito! With silence, speaking in the soul of things. He said: Speak, O earth! Have eyes, O earth! Have ears, O earth! Behold Me, your Maker!

24/24.2. The earth answered Him, not with words, boasting, but raised up man!

---

[813] That is, this is the first bible for a race of Guatamans other than the I'hin, the latter having had many bibles over the cycles.

24/24.3. Man said: Here I am, O Gitchee! The Creator looked, and lo and behold, the I'hins of Guatama stood before Him, the little people, white and yellow. Gitchee (God) said: Because you have answered me in faith, O earth, your ong'wee (talking animals) shall be called I'hin. Thus was named the first talkers; men with mouths for words, ears for words.

24/24.4. Then Gitchee (God) called the I'hins together, and said they were good; the handsomest of all created creations. And he commanded them to marry, male and female, and beget heirs.

24/24.5. And they obeyed God's commands; but the dumb earth cast clouds upward, and blinded the ways of the I'hins, so they strayed away from the mounds, and came to the black druks,[814] which do not speak; have no words; being dumb like the black mud of the earth where they burrowed.

24/24.6. In the darkness of the earth the I'hins mingled with the druks, and lo and behold, a second-born speaking animal (ong'wee, man) stood upon the earth, tall and red, and strong, swift and handsome. Gitchee (God) said:

24/24.7. I do not blame you, O I'hin! I saw the darkness; saw your straits! But you shall never again dwell with druks, nor with the new red-born, those with faces like new copper. Call them I'hua, for they shall be protectors over my chosen, the I'hins, forever. The I'hua shall drive away the baugh and mieu[815] and great serpents, and all man-slaying beasts; for I will make mighty nations out of the seed of the I'huans.

24/24.8. The first I'huan's name was O-e-du, and his wife's name was Uh-na; and they begot Owena, Dan and Shu-sa, but they had no more heirs. At a time soon after, the second man, whose name was Ka-ka-ooh, and whose wife's name was Wees, begot Somma, Pan-ah, Kac-ak, Ku-bak and Jessom.

24/24.9. And these were the first tribes of I'huans in the land of Guatama (after the flood), and they dwelt together, marrying and begetting offspring, dwelling in peace. And the I'hins taught them about all things, so that they became an honor on the earth and a glory to the Creator; but they were so mixed together that one tribe had no preference over another. So, by commandment of God, they were called the tribe of Oedukakaooh,[816] of the middle kingdom, Waneopanganosah (Central America).

24/24.10. In the valley of Owak, by the river Ho-e-jon-wan, Gitchee (Jehovih) created another tribe called Bak-Haw-ugh, and to the north of them, in the mountains was the tribe Meiu-how-an-go-to-bah; and their tribes commingled, and Gitchee (God) named them, Bakhawughmeiuhowangotobah.

24/24.11. Jessom, son of Kakaooh, married Wepon, daughter of Bakhawughmeiuhowango-tobah, and they begot Sto-gil-bak, and he begot Kom, and he begot See, and she married Ban, son of the tribe Kakaooh, and Ban's first-born son's name was La-ban-a-see.

24/24.12. And Labanasee was born in su'is of the second order, and could hear the voice of the Creator, Gitchee, the Great Spirit. And the Voice remained with Labanasee during his lifetime, which was one hundred and twenty-five years. And the Voice descended to Labanasee's son,

[814] Again, this must be the statistical mode. Interestingly, while in Guatama those of the druk race were thus chiefly black, yet we learn shortly in Oahspe that in Arabin'ya, Par'si'e and Jaffeth, their mode was brown. Keep in mind, though, that in these modern times of Kosmon, skin color alone is neither sufficient to determine lineage, nor is it determinative of spiritual grade, and, moreover, every person alive today has both druk and I'hin lineage in them.

[815] lion and tiger, respectively

[816] Pronunciation guide: O-e-du-ka-ka-o-oh, that is, Oedukakaooh is a combination word (Yi-ha language) referring to the commingling of two tribes, the Oedu + Kakaooh, and their descendants (see verse 8). That is, the compounded names in this Guataman history portion are in the Yi-ha language (see 19/2.5), and many of the lengthy words found in these Guataman chapters are compounded from earlier mentioned tribes. Too, the reader should note that the hyphens in the words are there as pronunciation aids, and as such can be removed as shown in some instances throughout this book. For examples, Ka-ka-ooh in verse 8, is the same as the Kakaooh portion of Oedukakaooh of verse 9; and La-ban-a-see and Labanasee of verses 11 and 12 refer to the same person.

Hootlabanasee, who lived one hundred and one years, and the Voice descended to his son, Hatapanagooshhootlabanasee; and then to his son after him, named Arapanseekasoodativhatapana-gooshhootlabanasee.[817]

24/24.13. Thus were represented the eighteen tribes of Gitchee's chosen among the I'huans who would become everlasting heirs to the Voice.

24/24.14. And God said to Ara: Arise and go forth; my hand will steer you. So Ara rose up and departed by the hand of the Creator, and came to the valley of Owg, broad and sweet-smelling, full of health-giving food, air and water. And there came with Ara into Owg one thousand men, women and children; and they built a city and called it Eftspan, signifying place of beauty.

24/24.15. And these took the name of the tribe of Ara, which name survived one thousand seven hundred and fifty years. And their people were tens of thousands.

24/24.16. After the tribe of Ara lost the Voice, there was raised up Sho-shone, of the tribes of Sto-gil-bak. And Gitchee raised His hand before Sho-shone and pointed the way, and Sho-shone departed out of the country of Tabachoozehbakkankan and came to Owg, and took to wife Hisam, daughter of Ooeguffanauha, and they begot E-a-ron-a-ki-mutz, a son of great beauty and strength, a swift runner.

24/24.17. And the voice of Gitcheemonihtee (Son of Jehovih[818]) came to Earonakimutz and remained with him during his natural lifetime, which was ninety years; and passed to his son, Fassawanhootaganganearonakimutz, and then to his son, Monagoamyazazhufassawanhootagan-ganearonakimutz.[819]

24/24.18. And Monag inhabited the regions of the plains of Yiteatuazow (Arkansas), and his people became mighty in cities and agriculture. For four thousand years the Voice of the All Father remained with the regular succession of the heirs of Monag, but their names and their cities' names became so long that no man could speak them or write them.

24/24.19. So Gitchee (Jehovih) raised up Honga, son of Ab, of the tribe of Oedu, of the land of the Middle Kingdom. And Honga went into the mountains of Ghiee (Rocky or Eagle Mountains),[820] sloping to the east.

24/24.20. Gitchee (God) spoke to Honga, saying: You shall take Oebe for your wife; out of your seed I will raise up a greater tribe than all other tribes; and your first-born son shall have your name; and your son's son shall be called Honga also; and your son's son's son, and so on forever. For I am wearied with the burden of names; your Great Creator has spoken.

24/24.21. Then Honga asked, saying: What if I have no son, but only daughters? Or what if my son or my son's son (my lineage) ceases to have a son, but only daughters?

24/24.22. Then Gitchee spoke, saying: The wife's first daughter shall take the name Honga. || So it came to pass that Honga married and begot heirs; and the Voice of the Great Spirit remained with the tribes of Honga. And it came about that he who heard the Voice, who was always the chief high prophet for the tribe, was called Hoanga; but the peoples themselves were called ong'wee, the same that has endured to this day, and is called Indian [Native American –ed.].

24/24.23. And the generations of Honga were called: first Honga; second Honga; third Honga; and so on. And this was the beginning of the counting of time in Guatama. Nor did any man know the number of generations before the time of Honga the first.

24/24.24. And the land became full of cities, from the east to the west, and from the north to the south, and the people all over the land dwelt in peace, tribe with tribe. Then came the God of evil, I'tura (Ahura), sowing evil in the temples and on the altars. With a false tongue and cunning, he came before the prophets, stealing their eyes away, stealing their ears away; holding up his hand, saying: It is the Great Spirit's hand.

24/24.25. And I'tura obsessed the nations and tribes of men to worship him;[821] infatuating them

---

[817] shortly referred to simply as Ara

[818] i.e., God

[819] for convenience' sake, called Monag

[820] literally, Eagle mountains, but known today as the Rocky Mountains that run like a spine up the western half of North America

[821] The name I'tura is still known among some American tribes. –Ed. [Note it was not Ahura in person, in Guatama, but his emissaries doing in his name.]

with the stories of far-off countries, and the glory of kings and queens. And he set on foot a war of plunder; brought ten thousand times ten thousand evil spirits to aid and abet[822] mortals in war.

24/24.26. And I'tura, the God of evil, taught mortals to flatten the head, to make prophets, and, lo and behold, the land of Guatama became a land of seers, prophets and conjurers, seeking evil for sake of evil; consulting the spirits of the dead for war and for earthly glory in blood and death.

CHAPTER 25 First Book God

24/25.1. These, then, were the principal kings of that day (before I'tura's attack): Lanoughl, king of Eboostakgan, a city of tens of thousands, in the valley of Aragaiyistan. Lanoughl was the son of Toogaoogahaha, who was the son of Eviphraiganakukuwonpan, who was the son of Oyoyughstuhaipawehaha, who built the canal (oseowa) of Papaeunugheutowa, which extended from the sea of Hoola'hoola'pan (Lake Superior) to the plains of Aigonquehanelachahoba (Texas), near the sea of Sociapan, where dwelt Heothahoga, king of kings, whose temple was roofed with copper and silver. Ten thousand boats (canoes) plied the canal, extending along, carrying copper and silver from the north regions to the cities of the valley of Hapembapanpan, and to the cities of the mountains of Oaramgallachacha, and to Ghiee, home of Honga the first, the mightiest of red men.

24/25.2. Next in power to Lanoughl was Tee-see-gam-ba-o-rakaxax, king of the city of Chusanimbapan, in the plains of Erezehoegammas (Central America), with twelve tributary cities extending along the river Akaistaazacha-haustomakmak, to the mountains of Nefsaida-wowotchachaeengamma.

24/25.3. And the third king in power was Chiawassaibakanalszhoo, of the city of Inuistahahahacromcromahoesuthaha, and tributary to him were twenty-seven cities and their kings.

24/25.4. Chiawassaibakanalszhoo was the son of Tenehamgameralhuchsukzhaistomaipowwassaa, who was son of Thusaiganganenosatamakka, who built the great east canal, the Oseowagallaxacola, in the rich valley of Tiedaswonoghassie, and through the land of Seganeogalgalya-luciahomaahomhom [most likely Louisiana and Mississippi –Ed.], where dwelt the large men and women, the Ongewahapackaka-ganganecola-bazkoaxax.

24/25.5. The fourth great king of Guatama was Hooagalomarakkadanapanwowwow, king of the city of Itussakegollahamganseocolabah, which had seventeen tributary cities of tens of thousands of people. And his kingdom extended from sea to sea in the Middle Kingdom (Panama). Here stood the temple of Giloff, with a thousand columns of polished mahogany [Pharsak –Ed.], and with a dome of copper and silver. And within Giloff dwelt the Osheowena, the oracle of the Creator, for two thousand years.

24/25.6. The fifth great king was Penambatta, king of the city of Liscararzakyatasagangan, on the High Heogula Ophat (Tennessee), with thirty tributary cities of tens of thousands of inhabitants. Here was situated the school and college of great learning, the Ahazahohoputan, where tens of thousands of students were taught. Penambatta was learned, and had traveled far, devoting his life to imparting knowledge. He had six thousand attendants, besides six hundred and forty officers.

24/25.7. The sixth great king was Hoajab, son of Teutsangtusicgammooghsapanpan, founder of the kilns of Wooboohakhak. Hoajab's capital city was Farejonkahomah, with thirty-three tributary cities, having tens of thousands of inhabitants, on the plains of He'gow (Southeastern Ohio).

24/25.8. The seventh great king was Hiroughskahogamsoghtabakbak, and his capital city was Hoesughsoosiamcholabonganeobanzhoh-ahhah, situated in the plains of Messogowanchoola [Indiana, North Ohio and Pennsylvania –Ed.], and extending eastward to the mountains of Gonzhoowassicmachababdohuyapiasondrythoajaj, including the valleys of the river Onepagassatha-lalanganchoochoo, even to the sea, Poertha-wowitcheothunacalclachaxzhloschistacombia (Lake Erie). Hiro had forty-seven tributary cities of tens of thousands of inhabitants.

24/25.9. Between the great kings and their great capitals were a thousand canals, crossing the country in every direction, from east to west and from north to south, so that the seas of the north were connected with the seas of the south. The people traveled in kanoos (canoes), and carried the

[822] support, urge, incite, encourage, assist, help, approve, promote

products of the land to all directions. Besides the canals mentioned, there were seven other great canals, named after the kings who built them, and they extended across the plains in many directions, but chiefly east and west.

24/25.10. These were: Oosgaloomaigovolobanazhooegollopan, and Halagazhapanpanegoochoo, and Fillioistagovonchobiassoso, and Anetiabolalachooesanggomacoaloabonbakkak, and Ehabadangonzhooeportalicha-boggasa-megitchee-papa, and Onepapollagassayamganshuniatedoegonachoogangitiavatoosomchooibalgadgad, and Hachooaolagobwotchachabakaraxexganhammazhooelapanpan.

24/25.11. In those days the kings and learned men set their hearts on building canals and finding places and roadways for them, and the great glory and honor of man at that time lay in this achievement.

24/25.12. And God (Gitchee), perceiving the virtue and wisdom of men, sent his angels to teach man the mystery of canal-making; to teach him to compound clay with lime and sand, to hold water;[823] to teach man to find the gau,[824] the level, and the force of water. The angels also taught man to make pots and kettles; to burn the clay in suitable shapes; to find copper ore and silver ore, and gold and lead for the floors of the oracle chambers, clean and shining white, suitable for angels.

24/25.13. And they taught man how to soften copper like dough; how to harden copper like flint rock, for axes and mattocks for building canals;[825] taught man how to work the ore in the fire and melt (smelt) it; and how to make lead into sheets, like cloth.

24/25.14. Taught man to till the soil and grow wheat and corn; taught the women how to grind it and make bread. Taught the hunters how to slay the lion, the tiger, and the mastodon, the HOGAWATHA, THE ROOTING ANIMAL OF WISDOM.[826]

24/25.15. Besides all these inhabited regions there lay another country to the far west, fifty days' journey, the land of Goeshallobok [Utah –Ed.], a place of sand and salt, and hot, boiling waters. And the breadth of this region took twenty days' journey east and west, but its span north and south took fifty days' journey.

24/25.16. In the High North lay the kingdom of Olegalla, the land of giants, the place of yellow rocks and high spouting waters (geysers). It was Olegalla who gave away his kingdom, the great city of Powafuchawowitchahavagganeabba, with the twenty-four tributary cities spread along the valley of Anemoosagoochakakfuela [Yellowstone Valley –Ed.]; gave his kingdom to his queen Minnegane-washaka, with the yellow hair, long, hanging down. And the queen built two hundred and seventy temples, and two adjacent to the spouting waters, where her people went every morning at sunrise, singing praise to Gitchee, Monihtee, the Creator.

24/25.17. South of Olegalla lay the kingdom of Onewagga, surrounding the sea of Chusa-mangaobe hassahgana-wowitchee [the salt lake –Ed.], in the valley of Mauegobah, which is to say, CONSECRATED PLACE OF THE VOICE, a kingdom of forty cities. Here reigned for twenty generations the line of kings called Wineohgushagusha, most holy and wise, full of manliness and strong limbed. To the east of the lake lay the Woohootaughnee, the ground of games and tournaments, where tens of thousands came every autumn to exhibit their strength, carrying horses and oxen, and running and leaping, and running races with the trained aegamma [deer –Ed.]. And to the strongest and the swiftest, the king gave prizes of handsome damsels, with straight limbs and shapely necks, proud, who loved to be awarded handsome, mighty husbands.

24/25.18. To the south of Onewagga lay the kingdom of Himallawowoaganapapa, rich in legends of the people who lived here before the flood; a kingdom of seventy cities and six great canals coursing east and west, and north and south,

---

[823] that is, to make concrete from hydraulic cement

[824] i.e., to find the amount of slope (drop or rise in elevation)

[825] A mattock has a handle like an axe, but with its flat blade oriented at a right angle to that of an axe blade or the handle. It is typically used to break up soil and cut through roots.

[826] The legends of China, India and America all give the same name, Hog-a-wat-ha, for the mastodon. And the legends make the beast not like the elephant in its habits, but a rooting animal, like a swine. –Ed.

from the Ghiee Mountain, in the east, to the west mountain, the Yublahahcolaesavaganawakka, the place of the king of bears, the Eeughohabakax (grizzly). And to the south, to the Middle Kingdom, on the deserts of Geobiathaganeganewohwoh, where the rivers do not empty into the sea, but sink in the sand, the Sonagallakaxax, creating prickly Thuazhoogallakhoomma, shaped like a pear.

CHAPTER 26 First Book God

24/26.1. I'tura, God of evil, dweller in hell, looked over the broad earth; saw the land of Guatama, the mighty races of I'huans. And his mouth watered, like a lion's when a lamb stands before him. I'tura called his legions, tens of thousands of drujas, devils from the regions of hell: Come, he said, I have found a rich feeding place. Behold, I will make my kingdoms wider; spread out the walls of hell and gather in this great harvest of innocent souls.

24/26.2. Then came I'tura's hosts of evil, ten times tens of thousands, for such is the nature of spirits and men;[827] call for ten thousand to do a righteous work, and only a hundred come; call for ten thousand to do an unholy work, and behold, ten times ten thousand come. They said to I'tura:

24/26.3. How shall we proceed? Where shall we strike? And I'tura, wise in wickedness, said: Go to the temples, the places of shining copper and silver, and obsess every one of their oracles. And when the kings and the learned men come to consult Gitchee, my deadly enemy, you shall assume to be Him, and answer them with lies and all types of unprofitable speculation; turn them upside down; make them curse Gitchee; make them ask for I'tura. And when madness comes upon them, follow them to their sleeping couches and whisper in their souls that their neighbors are their deadly enemies. Incite them to war and to all manner of deeds of death; and when they overturn each other's kingdoms and houses, and their dead lie like ashes over all the land, gather in their distracted spirits to fill my mighty kingdom with Gitchee's harvest!

[827] i.e., the general mass of both unripe spirits in the intermediate world (atmosphereans) and unripe mortals

24/26.4. Then answered the hosts of I'tura (who was known in heaven as Ahura): Most mighty God, what are your prizes, for the souls of men, for souls to extend your heavenly kingdom?

24/26.5. I'tura answered, saying: According to the number of subjects any angel brings me, so will I exalt him to be a captain, or a general, or a Lord, or a God, and he shall have a sub-kingdom in my heavenly regions, with thousands of servants to do his bidding.

24/26.6. With that the evil God and his evil spirits fell to work, night and day; and lo and behold, the fair land of Guatama was overspread with human blood. Fell war[828] spread throughout all the mighty kingdoms; kingdom against kingdom; city against city; man against man.

24/26.7. And the holy temples were pulled down or burnt; the canals broken and wasted; the cities set ablaze; and the fields laid desolate. With no grain growing, the grinding mills of the women lay silent, like the dead stretched over all the fields!

24/26.8. Into the far-off forest fled the women with the children, hungry, weeping, starving. And the cities went down; the nations went down; the tribes of men were broken up; only remnants here and there remained. And where once had been great and mighty peoples, lay only heaps of ruins, past the power of man to rebuild.

24/26.9. Then the Creator, the Great Spirit, looked down from the highest heaven; saw the work of desolation; saw I'tura at his bloody work.

24/26.10. And the Great Spirit cried out with a loud voice, so that earth and heaven shook with the power of His voice, sifting all things, as a woman sifts meal. And He found one grain of corn not ground by the God of evil, found Honga! The tribes so firmly sworn to the Great Spirit that the words of the evil Gods and evil spirits rolled off and took no hold on them.

24/26.11. The Great Spirit saw the tribes of Honga, they who stuck most to the I'hins, the sacred little people, white and yellow, often marrying with them, thus preserving the stock to the Hand and Voice. And He called loud and long: Honga! Honga! Honga!

24/26.12. The Creator would not be put off with silence; called again: Honga! Honga! Honga! But He heard only His Own Voice resounding far;

[828] i.e., unusually harsh, fierce, cruel, and dire

knew only His mighty Power! Again He called: Honga! Honga! Honga!

24/26.13. In the first call, I'tura and his evil hosts ran away. In His second call, it was like springtime, after heavy winter. And in the third call, it was like budding summer. And from the seed of Honga a sprout came up, an I'huan; taller than any other man with a bright shining face of copper; shining as if all the destroyed temples glistened in his broad head.

24/26.14. And he spoke, saying: Here, O Great Spirit, here I am! And the Great Spirit said: Who are you, My Son? And he answered: I am Son of the Creator. Then asked the Great Spirit: Of what tribe? And he answered: My flesh is nothing; my genealogy is of the spirit. Of the I'hin my mother; of the I'huan my father.

24/26.15. Then said the Creator: For which reason, I name you Eawahtah, spirit and flesh evenly balanced, best of men. Come with Me; walk along with Me; you shall reinstate the tribes of men; deliver them out of darkness; make them worshipful.

24/26.16. Eawahtah said: I am Your servant, O Great Spirit. What shall I call You, so that the tribes of men shall no longer be distrustful? Then answered the Creator: Call Me after the wind, O Eawahtah!

24/26.17. Eawahtah said: How after the wind? The Great Spirit said: Come with Me, My Son. Then Eawahtah walked along and came to a place where the wind blew in the leaves.

24/26.18. The Creator said: Tell Me, My Son, what does the wind in the leaves say? And Eawahtah answered: E! Then the Creator took Eawahtah to the big sea water, and asked: What does the wind in the water[829] say, My Son?

24/26.19. And Eawahtah answered: Go! Then the Creator took Eawahtah to the high crags, the rocks above the clouds, piercing, where the wind whistled; and He said: What does the wind say, My Son? And Eawahtah answered: Quim!

24/26.20. And the Great Spirit said: Call Me Egoquim, O My Son. I am three in One; the earth and all that is in and on the earth, and all the stars, moon and sun; they are one of My members. And the air above the earth, the Atontea, is another member of My Person. And higher yet; in the high place above the air, is the ether; the great penetrator; and that is the third member of My Person. I am everywhere, far and near; all things your eye sees, all things your ear hears, are of Me and in Me.

24/26.21. Whatever is one with Me has no hard labor. Behold the flowers of the field; I color them. Behold the ant and the honeybee; I lead them; the bird I teach how to build.

24/26.22. Man alone is stubborn, setting up ways of his own. O if he could learn to be one with Me! To move and labor with Me! Then spoke Eawahtah, saying: Holy Egoquim! I will go and teach man, give him Your words; make him understand.

24/26.23. Egoquim said: For that labor I called you forth, made you tall and handsome, with strong limbs, and broad shoulders. Come, then, My Son, I will go with you; into all the lands; among all the scattered tribes; your voice shall be My Voice. Do not fear, for I will stand so close to you, that when you open your mouth to speak, I will give you words; you shall not err.

24/26.24. Eawahtah inquired: What shall I say; how should I teach the sons and daughters of men; give me a synopsis?

24/26.25. Egoquim answered Eawahtah, saying:

CHAPTER 27 First Book God

24/27.1. One Great Person, even Egoquim, Creator and Ruler over all in heaven and earth.

24/27.2. You shall have Him, and no other God, Lord, idol, man or angel to worship, forever!

24/27.3. You shall love Him above all things in heaven above, or on the earth, or in the waters of the earth!

24/27.4. And you shall teach Him to your children, and command them to teach Him to their children, and so on forever!

24/27.5. And you shall swear against all other Gods, Lords and idols, to never serve them! And the same to your children, and to their children after them, forever!

24/27.6. And this is the first Egoquim law.

---

[829] i.e., in the surf

i112 **Eawahtah.** [Known later as Hiawatha. –ed.]

24/27.7. And you shall deal with all men, women and children, as justly and as kindly as with your own mother, out of whose breast you were fed when you were helpless and weak.

24/27.8. Teaching this to your children, and to their children after them, forever.

24/27.9. And this is the second Egoquim law.

24/27.10. And to the sick and helpless; to the stranger and the man who comes from far away; to the widow who is destitute; and to the child who has no father; you shall be both father and mother to them; and take them into your house and feed them; and give them skins and cloth to wear; and if they are lost you shall go with them and show them the way.

24/27.11. Commanding these things to your children, and to their children after them, forever!

24/27.12. And this is the third Egoquim law.

24/27.13. And you shall not tell lies; nor speak falsely against any man, woman or child; nor break your word of promise, even if threatened with death. The word of your mouth shall be as unchangeable as the setting and rising sun!

24/27.14. And you shall command this to your children, and to their children after them, forever!

24/27.15. And this is the fourth Egoquim law.

24/27.16. And you shall not take and possess that which is another's; nor allow your children to do so, nor their children after them, forever.

24/27.17. Which is the fifth Egoquim law.

24/27.18. And you shall respect the times of woman; and when she is pregnant with child, you shall not lie with her;[830] nor give her heavy labor, nor angry words, nor fret[831] her; but be obedient to her, doing whatever she asks you to do, for it is her time, and she is your queen.

24/27.19. Teaching this to your young men and women, and to theirs that come after them, forever; for their young are begotten of Me, and I will have them shapely, strong and brave!

24/27.20. Which is the sixth Egoquim law.

24/27.21. You shall labor six days, but on the seventh day it is the moon's day, and you shall not labor, hunt or fish, but go to the altar of your Creator and dance and sing before Me; and sit in silence to hear My words, which I speak into the souls of men, women and children.

24/27.22. Teaching this to your children, and to their children that come after them, forever.

24/27.23. Which is the seventh Egoquim law.

24/27.24. You shall restore the rites and ceremonies of Choe-pan and Annubia-pan;[832] except you shall not flatten the head to make a seer, a Haonga, to drive the judgment of the brain away to the prophetic regions; and this procedure you shall swear to Me to never restore.

24/27.25. Teaching these things to your children, and to their children after them, forever!

24/27.26. Which is the eighth Egoquim law.[833]

24/27.27. Then Eawahtah, Son of Egoquim, rose up, saying: I am Your servant! Lead me, for I am going in Your name, even to the end of the world![834]

24/27.28. When Eawahtah, Son of the Great Spirit, thus spoke, a Light came over him, dazzling, brilliant, lighting the way, showing him the way.

24/27.29. And the spirit upon Eawahtah was so powerful, that when he came to the river, he rose up like an angel and sailed over, landing safely on the other side.[835]

---

[830] i.e., not have sex with her

[831] provoke or agitate to anger, wear her down (irk), disturb to displeasure, try her patience, etc.

[832] Most likely the rites referred to were similar to Port-pan and Anubis [shown later in Oahspe]. The word Annubia is known among some of the western tribes. The pipe of peace is known to all of them. And this was part of the Egyptian ceremonies also. –Ed.

[833] These people lived and practiced this religion when the Christians came to inhabit it. They welcomed the Christians and fed them, and divided their substance with them. Their corn-fields spread over all the present northwestern states [now called the Midwest]. They had state organizations, and their united states were called after the name of the Great Spirit, Agoquim, or, as improperly called, Algonquin. But because of their religion, the Christians raised the cry of "heathen," and fell upon them, and killed them, men, women and children, three millions of them! Destroyed their corn-fields, and said they were too lazy to work! –Ed.

[834] see image i112, p.433

[835] I have myself seen persons floated and carried in the air by angel power. And there are now thousands of men and women who have seen

24/27.30. Nor did he know where he was going; did not know the places of the scattered, destroyed peoples.

24/27.31. And the angels of Egoquim went before him; went into the forests and valleys, calling to the souls of the suffering, starving, and dying, saying to them in their despair:

24/27.32. Egoquim, the Mighty, is coming! His Son! Behold Him! He holds the keys of Yaton'te, the heavenly hunting ground. Come forth from your hiding! Come forth, O My beloved! It is your Heavenly Father calling.

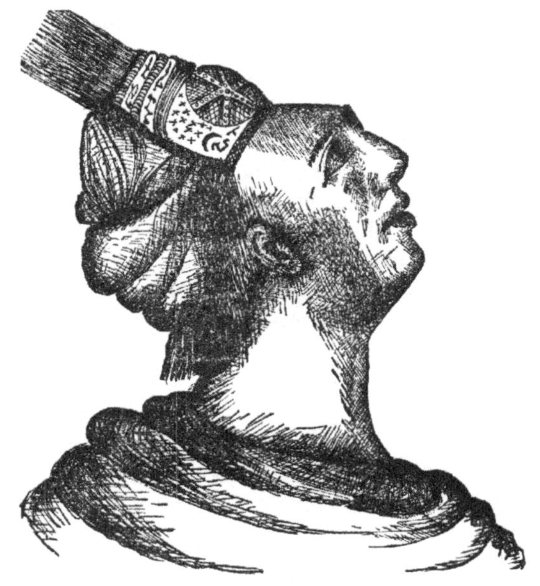

i023 **Took-shein.**

24/27.33. And the women heard! The little children, with sore, bleeding feet, heard! The proud, brave men listened! They said: Why do we fight? Why do we destroy? It was a wicked God! He called himself the Savior—the wicked monster, I'tura!

24/27.34. Then came Eawahtah; came first to the kingdom of Took-shein, and to his queen, Che-guh, in the land, Anagoomahaha, the flat-heads.[836] Told them all the words of the Great Spirit, Egoquim.

24/27.35. Then spoke Took-shein, saying: To me the Great Spirit has spoken; told me all the words as you have spoken. I know all you have said is true. Then spoke Che-guh, saying: Gitchee, the Great Spirit, spoke to me. All your words are true, O Eawahtah. All the scattered tribes will be gathered together by you. There will be many tribes of the red man; Egoquim will be the center, the Mighty Spirit!

i024 **Che-guh.**

24/27.36. Then Eawahtah spoke, saying to his good host and hostess: Your place shall be the center; from your place I will shoot out in different directions, always returning, bringing in followers.

24/27.37. While they thus talked, a Light appeared above them. Look, said Took-shein: It is the hand of Egoquim! Look, said Che-guh: It is the Voice of Gitchee! Then Eawahtah, seeing more clearly, raised up expressly,[837] and said: It is a ship of fire coming down from heaven! I hear the voice of the angel of Egoquim, the Mighty!

---

the same things, knowing the possibility of all that is here related. –Ed.

[836] see images i023, i024

[837] purposefully rose to attention, inspired –ed.

24/27.38. Then Eawahtah went and stood between Took-shein and Che-guh, holding their hands, so the Voice of Egoquim could speak plainly; so he could hear.

24/27.39. And Egoquim spoke out of the ship of fire, saying:

24/27.40. Yes, My beloved! I am with you! Behold, My worlds are wide and many. When My back is turned, evil Gods come to steal My children; tell them lies to win them; tell them they are My Sons coming to save them!

24/27.41. Hard is the fate of those who worship one God only;[838] but they are Mine. I look around at times; I set the evil Gods flying. Be of strong heart, O My beloved! Many races will come and go on these lands. But the red man shall possess it; inhabit it far and near. Then another evil God [Christ was called an evil God by the Indians –Ed.] shall come, to flay and destroy My sons and daughters, to cover all the lands over with pure blood. Then I will come again and rout the evil God, and raise up My sons and daughters, full of glory.

24/27.42. I will bring their kindred (Faithists) from far across the water; a wise speaking people, who worship none born of woman; a people who do not war; who do not kill off weaker nations.[839] I will come in the Tenonachi, and the Hoochiquis [Mahican (Mohican) and Iroquois confederacies – ed.]; My hand shall reach around the earth in that day.[840] I will chase away all Gods and Saviors born of woman. And all men shall worship the Great Spirit only.

24/27.43. Go forth, My son; build wide My foundation; I will found My earthly kingdom in this land.

24/27.44. Then upward rose the ship of heaven; and Eawahtah buckled on his traveling slippers; said goodbye to Took-shein; filled his pockets with the bread of Che-guh; kissed her hand goodbye, and started forth.

24/27.45. For many years Eawahtah traveled, over all the regions of Guatama, teaching, gathering together, swearing the people to be forever firm to the Great Spirit; made them swear solemn oaths that never again would they listen to any God except the Creator; made them swear they would never be caught by another cunning Savior, like I'tura, whose people delight in war.

24/27.46. Eawahtah gathered the frightened tribes into villages, and taught them writing and engraving; taught them the secret name of the Great Spirit, Egoquim; and explained the moon to them and how to keep the seventh day for worship.

24/27.47. The Creator saw the great work of Eawahtah; saw the people gathered together in tens of thousands of places. Then the Creator spoke to Eawahtah, saying:

24/27.48. You shall found forty mighty nations, O My Son; and every nation shall be an independent nation; but all the nations shall be united into a brotherhood of nations, as ONE mighty people, and that one shall be called O-pah-E-go-quim,[841] signifying ONE. For when I come in kosmon, My people shall have many states, like yours, and their combination shall be called UNION, signifying ONE. Build a model for them, O Eawahtah. For, although when they come they will overthrow your people on the earth, the angels of your holy ones (Native American spirits firm in adherence and obedience to the Great Spirit

---

838 Recall that Gitchee meant both Creator and God, see 24/24.1-5.

839 This refers to the early Faithist emigrants in aggregate and who essentially were the descendents of the seed of Ham, and who generally were Faithist in heart—although not necessarily in all aspects. Accordingly, these new arrivals included but were not limited to the pilgrims who worshipped God (but not Christ), Quakers, Masons, Jews, and others of similar nature who were brought to America in the early days, including from Africa.

840 This began around 1450 and lasted to about 1850 c.e., when the four heads of the beast were cast out of heaven. From then till the time of this editing [c.150 ak], on earth the beast struggled on; but without a unified heavenly head, it shall ultimately whither away upon the earth as man grows into his birthright.

841 The union of Indian states was first called as stated, but after it became an Anglicized word it was called Algonquin. –Ed. [That is, Egoquim eventually became Agoquim, which, when the Native American said it, to the European ear it sounded like Algonquin, and it was spoken so and written so in the English language.]

Jehovih) shall come and purge them of their Savior, and make them clean in My sight.

24/27.49. Then Eawahtah made the nations; united them into one mighty people, and called them the nations of Opahegoquim. And they planted the country over with cornfields, and dwelt in peace.

END OF EAWAHTAH'S HISTORY

CHAPTER 28 First Book God

24/28.1. God said: Be wise, O man, in the words of your God. My records do not come up out of the ground, nor from the books of mortals.

24/28.2. I open my heavenly libraries, and find my living sons and daughters who once trod[842] the earth.

24/28.3. Their light I recast down again to mortals in a stream of fire, and lo, my words are rewritten (translated, formed into corporeal words).

24/28.4. Search for the evidence of my footsteps on the earth; find the people who stand by the Creator, the All One, God of All! Who can shake their faith, or feed them with your story of a Savior born of woman?

24/28.5. Listen to the voice of the millions of Chine'ya and Vind'yu, and the remnants of the Algonquins! Their bibles are a power to this day. Their people are appalled at the work of your bloody sword.

24/28.6. They will not fall down and worship as you decree; they know that Jehovih is mightier than you.

24/28.7. Be considerate of all the races of men, and their doctrines, rites and ceremonies.

24/28.8. Behold, I raise up the nations of the earth in my own way. According to the times and conditions of mortals, so do I administer to them from my heavenly kingdoms.

24/28.9. You have tried to convert all my people, but have failed utterly. Behold, I come now with a new book; and they will accept it from my hand.

24/28.10. I prophesy this to you, beforehand, so that you shall witness in time to come, that I, God of heaven and earth, have spoken.

[842] walked, spent time on

24/28.11. Nor shall you say: Man of himself progresses; and that such and such would come of a natural order.

24/28.12. I say to you, man does not progress, except by me, through my angel hosts in heaven.

24/28.13. In testimony of which, I have left many peoples before you, for hundreds of years. Your natural order is laziness and uncleanness. When you are quickened in spirit, behold, it is the heavens upon you that stirs you up.[843]

[843] Recall the sentiment: Progress comes of a natural order (24/28.11). This is the claim of many philosophers, especially the Evolutionists. For theories of natural selection, evolution, survival of the fittest, and enlightened self-interest, exampled in works such as Adam Smith's 1776 *Wealth of Nations* and Darwin's 1859 *On the Origin of Species by Natural Selection*, were, and are, taken as substantiating the notion that progress is the natural order of life.

While that may seem to hold true for the animal and plant creation and other biological organisms, yet were man to solely follow that, he would not progress but devolve into ever worsening animal behavior.

Fortunately man has a Higher Cause as well, and this Higher Cause inspires him to progress.

But the materialist or Osirian denies any cause of progress except what man himself generates or "invents." Thus, he allows for some combination of psychological causes, social causes, and natural causes, as in biological and environmental causes, based on the "laws" of physics or other constants in the universe. And the actions of these, he would assert, bring about necessity, which is then looked upon as a "mother" of invention; or, "nature" shows example, which man then exploits.

So he attributes all progress to man's ingenuity, or else to dumb luck. But, according to the Osirian, even if the triggering event were accidental (by chance, random), yet it was man alone, not some supposed Creator or God, responsible for useful explanation or application.

Hence, in general:

MATERIALISTS, at best, define progress as a subjective judgment; and to the extent that they acknowledge the concept of progress, they attribute the source either to the natural course of events (scientific cause and effect), or else to man's

24/28.14. You shall not mistake the teaching of your God; which was manifested the same in the ancient days as in this day, which is: to worship your Creator only; to not bow down to any other God or Lord; to love your neighbor, and to do good to others with all your wisdom and strength, having faith in the Almighty!

END OF FIRST BOOK OF GOD

intelligence taking advantage of and building upon chance occurrences (resulting in, e.g., inventions and innovations); thus making "progress" possible.

IDOLATERS, to the extent that they believe in progress, attribute the source to their idol, perhaps through his underlings (angels, saints, avatars, etc.).

FAITHISTS understand that progress comes from Jehovih the Great Spirit, including through His kingdoms, officers and hosts, the least of which is individual initiative and effort inspired by the light of Jehovih; and progress increases in effectiveness as compact (organic unity) is achieved, and grows as greater compact is reached.

Book of Wars Against Jehovih

Or, God's labors in atmospherea. Containing an account of the establishing on the earth the names: Lord God, De'yus,[844] Dyaus, Deity, Te-in, Sudga, Osiris, Baal, and Ashtaroth. Covering a period of two thousand four hundred years, that is, from the time of Abraham, Brahma, Po, and Eawahtah, to the time of Moses, Chine, and Capilya. This book of God pertains to both the earth and lower heavens, and contains an exposition of the labors of the above false Gods; and their fall and environment in hells, all except Baal and Ashtaroth.[845]

CHAPTER 1 Wars

25/1.1. Jehovih spoke to God on the throne, in Craoshivi, saying: These are My divisions in the cycle of My Daughter, Cpenta-armij: Two hundred years; four hundred years; five hundred years; three hundred years; four hundred years, and six hundred years; after which I shall send dawn. You shall have five successors, and their reign shall be according to the divisions I have made.

25/1.2. My Son, I have allotted to you forty years' indulgence in a great light, so that you shall perfect all the orders of Lords and Lordesses in the lowest lower kingdoms of these My heavens. Nor shall it be dark during your reign; and your labor shall produce a great harvest for My etherean worlds. Accordingly, you shall prepare to reap in fifty years, and again in fifty years, and again in fifty years, and again in fifty years.[846] And for each reaping, My daughter Cpenta-armij will send you

[844] Among the ancient Greeks, the name of this false God was pronounced Theos and Zeus.

[845] Note that these were not wars BY Jehovih, not wars WITH Jehovih's participation, but wars waged AGAINST Jehovih by those who sought to destroy worship of Him on earth and in the hadan heavens.

[846] quarter harvests, i.e., four harvests during this first dan of 200 years

ships of deliverance for all you have prepared as Brides and Bridegrooms.

25/1.3. And behold, I give you a new law, which is, that you shall have your Lords deliver to you, for your kingdoms, all whom they have raised to grade fifty, doing this in advance of your reapings (ascensions to etherea), and in the same divisions of time as yours.

25/1.4. And once every reaping, you shall call to your capital, your Lords from all the divisions of the earth; and together you shall sit in Council of Div for seven days each time, and you shall constitute My Holy Eleven; nor shall the Div be larger or smaller than eleven during its lifetime. And the Div shall make laws relating to the affairs of each of the heavenly places, to make them harmonious with each other, and these shall be called Divan Laws.

25/1.5. God inquired concerning the light and darkness of the cycle. Jehovih said: The first division shall rate seventy; the second, fifty; the third, forty; the fourth, eighty; the fifth, thirty, and the sixth, twenty.

25/1.6. God inquired concerning the Lord of the Lord-dom. Jehovih answered him, saying: Because he is not a teacher, he shall not be eligible to the rank of Div. But he shall have the benefit of all the decrees, and all the kingdoms of My other Lords; for he is the earth's bodyguard, and a beneficent[847] to them.

CHAPTER 2 Wars

25/2.1. When the Diva was assembled, God propounded the duties of Lord-dom. On which the members spoke at length, and then God decreed:

25/2.2. First: From this time forth forever, the Lord God of Maitraias shall not use force to enforce, except in delivering hells or knots where the use of violent force by fire or water may be permitted.

25/2.3. Second: By the Arc of Spe-ta: By the decree of the Most High: The Lord God of Maitraias is bound by the same rule as the Lords of the lowest heavens; whose walls and pillars of fire are abolished, except on special occasions; thus making their respective kingdoms open and free for all spirits above the es'yan grade.

25/2.4. Third: The Lord God of Maitraias' times and successors shall be the same as the Diva. And the stations of the hosts of the Lord God shall be according to the heavenly realms of the Lords, with Maitraias as the Lord-dom in chief.

25/2.5. Fourth: The hosts of the Lord God shall be distinguished from ashars and asaphs by the name Mishm, but a single one shall be called Mishm-ah. And their leaders shall be called captains and generals.

25/2.6. Fifth: The labor of the Lord God shall be to prevent drujas returning to the earth to dwell with corporeans; to capture drujas on the earth and carry them off to the nearest Lord's heavenly place, and there deliver them. Force by violence or without consent being abolished, the mishm shall devise stratagems, such as games and tournaments, to persuade the drujas to go with the mishm.

25/2.7. Sixth: The mishm shall not arrest fetals, infants, the wards of ashars, or spirits in chaos on battlefields; for these labors belong to the Lords and their hosts.

25/2.8. Seventh: Where there are companies of millions of drujas, and the Lord God does not have a sufficient number of mishm, the Lord God shall summon the nearest Lord for help, and it shall be given to him.

25/2.9. Eighth: In no case shall it be the labor of the Lord God to teach the captured drujas, or to house them, or to provide them with schools, factories, hospitals, or nurseries, for these labors are the Lord's, to whom the Lord God of Maitraias shall deliver them.

25/2.10. Ninth: To prevent the establishing of heavenly kingdoms by self-constituted Lords and Gods, otherwise false Lords and false Gods; the Lord God of the Lord-dom of Maitraias shall be the central head, in conjunction with all the Lords of the lowest heavens; and his voice will be the rule and guide as to how to deal with them.

25/2.11. Tenth: The Lord God shall have one hundred thousand messengers; and he shall determine their stations and routes of travel.

25/2.12. This was the first section of Divan Law in the heavens of the earth for this cycle.

[847] A person who is an opposite of beneficiary, and yet not a benefactor. One whose passive presence is of benefit, though he gives nothing [directly pertaining to the beneficiary's business]. –Ed.

CHAPTER 3 Wars

25/3.1. In God's heavenly place, Craoshivi, Jehovih said: For My chosen on the earth, of Abram, Po, Brahma and Eawahtah, provide a place in Craoshivi for when they die, for they shall not dwell in the lowest heavens.

25/3.2. And for the infants of My chosen, who die in infancy, do not allow them to be engulfed in hada, but bring them also to the place of My God.

25/3.3. The Diva then decreed: First, lines of roadways to be established from the earth up to the kingdom of God for such transport, and second, appointed officers and laborers to prevent the spirits of God's chosen from falling into the hands of the drujas, and to bring the chosen to Craoshivi. The Diva said: On the third day after the death of such a mortal, his spirit shall be borne to the home of God. And it was so.

25/3.4. But as to the heathen, the Diva decreed: The labor of the Lords of all the divisions of hada and of the earth shall be with the undelivered sons and daughters of the earth and her heavens; but in no case shall they labor anymore with the Faithists; for the Faithists, mortals and spirits, come under the higher law, which is of Jehovih, through His Son, God of Craoshivi. This was the second section of the Divan law.

25/3.5. And from this arose the saying: The believers go to God, but the unbelievers go to his Lords; they who live the higher law on earth, escape hada. And after some years the Diva passed a law, according to the saying, and called it the third section of the Divan law, and it was proclaimed as such throughout heaven and on earth.

25/3.6. Now it came to pass in course of time, that some corporeans, who did not belong to the societies of Faithists of any of the tribes of Jehovih's chosen, became believers in the All Person, and believed that to live by the All Highest light was the fulfillment of the Divan law. And they did not join the Faithists, or follow the rites and ceremonies.

25/3.7. God propounded this in Diva: Where shall the spirits of these be delivered? Behold, even on the earth they have delivered themselves away from the druks; shall we now suffer them to fall into the kingdoms of mixed company in hada?

25/3.8. Upon this the Diva decreed: A separate kingdom shall be prepared for those who believe, but have lived isolated, and who do not know the rites and ceremonies. This was the fourth section of the Divan law. The fifth was like it, but explanatory, which was:

25/3.9. To have faith in One Great Person, the Ever Present Spirit; Creator and Ruler, is well; but to have such faith, and yet not commit one's self to an association of brethren of like faith, proves a lack of discipline; and that requires beginning at the fifth grade in the es'ean world.[848]

25/3.10. The sixth section of the Divan law provided: The kingdom, for those who profess faith in the Great Person, Jehovih, but are without practice, shall be called Me-de,[849] and its place shall be in the first remove from the earth.

CHAPTER 4 Wars

25/4.1. Jehovih spoke to God, saying: Because you have founded Me-de you shall make Me-de-ci laws; and you shall send your surveyors down to hada and to the earth also, and they shall choose a heavenly place for your new kingdom. And there you shall go and create a plateau and holy place and capital, and provide a throne for it.

25/4.2. And when you have completed your work you shall appoint a sub-God to the throne, who shall rule in the place with wisdom, power and love, in My name.

25/4.3. But since many of My chosen forget Me, and so, apostate[850] themselves, your sub-God shall also receive their spirits, and his kingdom

---

[848] i.e., above the grade of helplessness but below that of association

[849] Medes, half-way between savageness and civilization. A name given to a land by the Caspian Sea, and to its people. Medes is from the Greek language; the word in the Panic should be, Me-de; and if applied to earth, Me-de-ya. In China it is Me-de, and in Algonquin, Me-dah, and in Phoenician, Me-dwe. –Ed.

[850] abandon some or all of one's religion, e.g., faith, practices, vows, rites and ceremonies, etc.; to backslide; to become a skewed believer, misbeliever

shall be their kingdom till they are purged of their sins.[851]

25/4.4. God spoke in the Council of Craoshivi, relating what Jehovih had said to him, and the Council then ratified the commandments of Jehovih. And A-chung-le was selected and made sub-God of Me-de, with the title Anubi, signifying mediator, and judge of grades.

25/4.5. God said: Anubi shall have a badge, and a pair of scales; with my own hands I will invest him. And, accordingly, through his kingdom of Craoshivi, God, under the commandment of Jehovih, duly established the place, kingdom, person, and the badge of office. And the term of office was made to correspond with God's and his Lords'.

25/4.6. Thus put upon the throne in the heavenly place, Me-de, was Anubi, who had been A-chung-le, an angel of a thousand years in the colleges of Jehovih, most wise and full of love, and industrious also.

25/4.7. Again Jehovih spoke to God, saying: From this time forward My colleges shall be in Craoshivi; and from this time forward My schools and primaries shall be in the kingdoms of My Lords. || The Diva afterward made this another section of the Divan law.

25/4.8. So God and his Lords removed all his colleges and places of great learning to Craoshivi; but the schools and primary educationals were left in their heavenly places in the dominions of the Lords.

25/4.9. Now during the dawn of dan, four etherean Gods had sojourned on the earth, walking with four mortals, namely, with Po, of Jaffeth; Abram, of Arabin'ya; Brahma, of Vind'yu, and Eawahtah, of Guatama. And the four Gods preached through these four men, explaining Jehovih and His kingdoms; and the angels of Jehovih inspired many followers to them. For four years these Gods dwelt on the earth, and then ascended into the upper regions.

25/4.10. Jehovih spoke to God concerning the matter, saying: For four years I bestowed My light in Person on the corporeal earth, and then I departed; for it is well that men and angels learn to be self-raising. For which reason I left four substitutes, Lords of heaven, on the earth, with My four peoples whom I delivered. And I commanded these, My substitutes, to abide upon the earth for forty years, in order to indulge My chosen in a surety in My creations founded in corpor.[852]

25/4.11. Because My substitutes are ethereans you shall provide for them; and (at the end of forty years) you shall have their places filled by atmosphereans from the highest grades. ||

25/4.12. The Diva then made a section of the Divan law, providing for the four who stood highest in the grades in Craoshivi to take the places, to dwell with the Faithists in the names of the Great Spirit; and the names of the Great Spirit given were: to Jaffeth, Te-in; to Arabin'ya, Jehovih; to Vind'yu, Ormazd; to Guatama, Egoquim; according to the languages and capabilities of mortals to pronounce words.

25/4.13. The Diva then made another section of the Divan law, which was the title to be given to the four angels thus provided to bestow the Voice of Jehovih on mortals, and the title was O-yra; that is, O the High Heaven; and Y, going to; and ra, the earth.[853]

25/4.14. The twelfth section of the Divan law provided for each O-yra to have ten thousand attendants—angels from above the eightieth grade, from the colleges of Craoshivi. And the attendants were to sojourn on the earth with the Faithists as inspiring spirits and protectors.

25/4.15. The thirteenth section of the Divan law made the term of office for the O-yra eleven years each; and the same for their attendants.

25/4.16. The fourteenth section of the Divan law explained the duties of the O-yra and their attendants, which were: That the O-yra was to reside with the chief rab'bah or high priest, and be his inspirer; being with him day and night; and by virtue of his presence make the chief rab'bah know the Voice of the All Highest. And the attendants first in rank were to dwell in the same way with the ordinary rab'bah, and for the same purpose. And the other attendants were to dwell with the multitude in like manner, and for the same purpose. And each O-yra was to have a heavenly place in

[851] Here we have the origin of purgatory. –Ed.

[852] That is, to securely establish via the Faithists, the anchorage of Jehovih's light within the corporeal creation, so as to make it irrevocable, irreversible, sealed, permanent.

[853] This is the origin of the word oracle. –Ed.

the mortal temple, where he could meet his attendants in Council in reference to the Faithists and their affairs.

25/4.17. The fifteenth section of the Divan law made the O-yra and his attendants the heavenly kingdom for the ashars of the Lords who dwelt with mortals.

25/4.18. The sixteenth Divan law provided for the O-yra to increase the number of his attendants, according to the increase of the number of Faithists in each of the four divisions of the earth.

25/4.19. Such, then, were the chief of the Divan laws made in heaven in the cycle of Cpenta-armij, during the first two hundred years. And all the kingdoms of atmospherea were established and officered; and all the people in these heavens became organic as soon as they passed the es'yan age. Nor was there any dissatisfaction among any of the Gods or Lords, or other officers, or in any of the colleges, or hospitals; and never since the foundation of this world had there been such prosperity in the resurrections of the inhabitants in heaven.

CHAPTER 5 Wars

25/5.1. And the harmony of heaven reigned on earth; war ceased among men on all the divisions of the earth. And man began to esteem wisdom, truth, virtue, and industry. The inspiration of the angels set man to imitating the affairs of heaven. He built schools and colleges, nurseries and hospitals; and factories for cloths of silk, linen and cotton, and for paper, and for making glass, and leather, and for smelting iron, copper, silver and gold.

25/5.2. Three great peoples sprang up on the earth within two hundred years; in Jaffeth, in Vind'yu, and in Arabin'ya; and a fourth great people were overspreading Heleste in every quarter. And the kings of Heleste were sending emigrants by thousands and thousands into Uropa.

25/5.3. The Lords sent ashars of great wisdom to dwell with mortals, to teach them by inspiration in regard to all knowledge; to teach them to spin and weave finely; to teach them the seasons, the times of the earth, moon, sun and stars; and to observe them with lenses, as had been the case in the cycle of Osiris, but was lost on the earth. || Yes, the spirits who had been mortal thousands of years before were brought back to the earth to reveal to mortals the lost arts and sciences.

25/5.4. By night and by day these angels remained in the presence of mortals, and by virtue of their presence spoke to the souls of men, and thus made them understand.

25/5.5. And the Lord God of Maitraias restrained the drujas of heaven from coming back to afflict mortals or lead them astray. He guarded the earth around on all sides, so that, in heaven, the Lords and the Divan hosts, in mirth, styled him THE SAVIOR OF MEN!

25/5.6. Jehovih rebuked them, saying to God: They who sow in mirth often reap in sorrow. But even the Lords, with all their wisdom, did not see what was in store for their successors.

CHAPTER 6 Wars

25/6.1. The O-yra, the four angels with their thousands of assistant angel hosts, dwelt on the earth, with the Faithists; inspired them in peace, and rites, and ceremonies; inspired them in prayers, and psalms,[854] and sacred dances; dwelt with them day and night; talked to their spirits when they slept; led them by inspiration to happy marriages, so that they might beget offspring capable of the Voice.

25/6.2. And in each of the four countries the Faithists became as bands[855] of brothers and sisters. And there came to them from the kings' peoples tens of thousands, who joined them, living as Faithists, casting their wealth into the rab'bahs' hands, for the benefit of the poor.

25/6.3. In two hundred years there were in Jaffeth three million Faithists. In Arabin'ya there were two million Faithists, In Vind'yu there were four million Faithists. In Guatama there were one million Faithists.

25/6.4. But the Faithists were mostly poor people, and inhabited many far apart regions.

25/6.5. But the kings' peoples were rich; had large cities, and an abundance of elephants, horses, camels, asses and cheetahs.

25/6.6. The Faithists had little learning as to books and instruments for measuring the stars,

[854] sacred songs (hymns, anthems), some perhaps not unlike chants

[855] groups of people, associations, clans

moon and sun; they derived their knowledge from the angels of the Lords. The Faithists' knowledge pertained mostly to perfecting the soul; but the knowledge of the kings' people pertained mostly to earthly matters, and to the gratification of self.

CHAPTER 7 Wars

25/7.1. The Anubi's labor on earth was to win the disaffected of the kings' peoples into association; and as far as possible bring them to the rites of Faithism.

25/7.2. Anubi sent tens of thousands of angels into all the regions of the earth. By inspiration and otherwise, these angels established the rites of Anubi.[856]

25/7.3. By these rites even kings were converted to Faithism and the full ceremonies of the brethren.

25/7.4. And by the same means the Maichung, of Jaffeth, were made into Faithists; and by the same rites the Effins, of Vind'yu, were converted into Faithists, adopting all the rites and ceremonies of Emethachavah afterward.

25/7.5. And it came to pass in course of time that there were no suffering poor in the world. The Faithists had gathered them all up and made brethren of them; and the contributions to the Faithists by the kings' peoples rendered all the people comfortable.

25/7.6. || Anyone (who desired to learn heavenly things) was eligible for the degree of Anubi. The rites and ceremonies were in dark chambers; and the angels of heaven, clothed in sar'gis, took part in them. And the angels taught mortals, by the voice, the mysteries of spirit communion; how to sit in circles and in crescents; taught the four dark corners, and the four bright sides; taught them how to ascertain from what grade in heaven the spirits came; how to keep off evil spirits; how to attract righteous spirits; taught them how to develop in su'is and sar'gis; the secrets of falling water; and the application of lotions to the skin, that would make poundings and rappings.[857]

25/7.7. The second degree taught the people of the Great Spirit and His secret names; taught them His high holy heavens, where all is rest and happiness forever. Whoever took the second degree had to live one year with the poorest of the poor, going about soliciting alms, reserving only the poorest of things for himself. And if he found a person naked he must take off his clothes and give them to that person. Men and women alike served the same conditions.

25/7.8. The third degree taught the dominions of God and the Lords, the place of their abiding, and their respective labors in heaven. And the members had to learn the names of the God or Gods, Lord or Lords, and the Divan laws; the words of salutation; the anthems; the prayers; the praise; the positions of utterance [oratory –Ed.]; the orders of marching; to write sacred names; the secret of begetting pure offspring, and the key to the two preceding degrees.

25/7.9. The fourth degree taught the arrangement of the heavens; the places of the sun, stars and moon; the places and grades of the unseen worlds; the localities of the lower and higher heavens; the places and dominions of false Lords and false Gods; the places in hada, and of hells and knots; of familiar spirits, and also of fetals, both the harmless and the destructive vampires, that live on mortals and in swine and cattle, that induce mortals to eat flesh food for that purpose; the key to the place of the north star; the position of the earth's vortex; the vortices that move the corporeal worlds and hold them in place; and the rules for building temples and pyramids, with their spirit chambers.

25/7.10. Besides this there was the fifth degree, which reached the secret of life in the flesh; the power of will and how to use it far and near; how to rule over others without their knowing it; to cast spells; to enter the prophetic state; to estimate numbers without counting; to find proportions and distances without measuring;[858] to forecast the time of things; to find the weight of things without weighing; to find the power of the capstan before it is made, and of the lever and screw; to find the

[856] A later version of part of the Anubi degree is given further on in Oahspe.

[857] These rappings and poundings were caused by spirits (a spirit rap is sharp sounding, like rapping a knuckle against a door; a spirit pounding is dull sounding, like pounding the fleshy part of the fist on a door).

[858] Mathematics was at that time taught in colleges as a branch of prophecy. –Ed.

friction of things before they were moved, in order to know the power required. The fifth degree was called the degree of prophecy; and the place of initiation was called the college of prophecy.

25/7.11. In this degree the angels came in sar'gis and taught these things orally, and initiated mortals thus learned them. But no one could take the fifth degree without having become proficient in all the four preceding degrees, and without the recommendation of the rab'bah (or priest) who had charge of the college.

25/7.12. And such was the wisdom of God that only Faithists could receive the degrees, except the first degree; and, therefore, the greatest knowledge of the earth was kept in secret with the Faithists. And the kings' people, even the richest and most powerful, were beholden to the sons and daughters of the Faithists. To build a palace or a temple, or an aqueduct or canal, or a ship, or any great affair, the kings and the kings' people were obliged to employ Faithists of the fifth degree to superintend the work.

CHAPTER 8 Wars

Of Anuhasaj; who, by treachery, becomes Lord God, second in rank to God, Son of Jehovih

25/8.1. Jehovih spoke to God in Craoshivi, his heavenly place, saying: Behold, I have given great light to the earth and her heavens for hundreds of years; and My Gods and Lords are becoming conceited in their own power and wisdom to rule in heavenly places.

25/8.2. Now I will try them for a season, by sending them a'ji'an darkness; for My Gods and Lords must learn to master the elements I have created in the firmament.

25/8.3. So Jehovih brought the earth and her heavens into a dark region for a season.

25/8.4. Anuhasaj, a one-time sub-God under Ahura, the false, had been cast into hell, and then delivered out of hell, at which time he repented, and became a Faithist in heaven; serving many years in holy works in Ailkin, a heavenly place of great wisdom.

25/8.5. And it came to pass that Ailkin was raised into a new heavenly place, called Vara-pishanaha; and in the removing, behold, Ahura ordered Anuhasaj from the line because of his disharmony. And Anuhasaj allowed himself to become angered.

25/8.6. Satan (self) said to Anuhasaj: Who are you, that one of less wisdom orders you? Anuhasaj said: Alas, I am a fool, and without will to assert myself.

25/8.7. For many years afterward Anuhasaj became a wandering spirit in heaven, going from kingdom to kingdom, doing nothing; and at times descending to the earth, observing the kingdoms of the earth.

25/8.8. Satan came again to him and said: Listen to my voice, and you shall triumph over all other Gods. Anuhasaj said: What shall I do? And satan said: Go to Ahura, who offended you in presence of the Chieftainess, Cpenta-armij, and say to him: O God, I crave[859] your forgiveness. You were right, and I was wrong. I have repented most bitterly. Now I come to you, with faith in Jehovih. I will serve Him forever. Do not turn me away, O Ahura; remember your own onetime shortness; and the high Gods above you accepted you.

25/8.9. Satan continued: Ahura will delight in you and take you at your word. And you shall enter Vara-pishanaha, asking for the lowest of places; practicing humility in all your behavior. But be fruitful in making acquaintances with those who shall serve you afterward.

25/8.10. Satan continued: And whether it takes fifty years, or a hundred, or even two hundred, bide your time. But the time will surely come when you shall be exalted; and you shall solicit and accept a place in the dominions of the Lord God in the Lord-dom of heaven and earth, Maitraias.

25/8.11. Satan continued: And whether it takes one hundred years more, or two hundred years, it does not matter to you; but you shall finally attain to the Lord-dom, and be duly installed and crowned Lord God of heaven and earth.

25/8.12. And when you are thus exalted, you shall seek to have appointed to the ten divisions of earth those Lords who are your own special friends. And it shall come to pass that the whole earth and her heavens shall be yours, and your title shall be Lord God, and all people on earth and in heaven shall be your servants.

[859] desire deeply, ask humbly for

25/8.13. Anuhasaj said: You are the wisest of Gods, O satan. All you have advised, I will do; nor shall anyone in heaven or earth know my designs.

25/8.14. And it came to pass in course of another hundred years, Anuhasaj was promoted on the staff of the Lord God, the guardian, where he served the Lord God one hundred and seventy years. So the Lord God named Anuhasaj for his successor.

25/8.15. So God came from Craoshivi and crowned Anuhasaj Lord God of heaven and earth; with great pageantry and display, God gave him a throne and placed him upon it. And from this time onward Anuhasaj was known and saluted as Lord God, which is the first rank below God.

25/8.16. The Lord God said to satan: Who first shall I bring into my favor? Satan said: You shall first bring into your favor Anubi, MASTER OF THE SCALES OF HEAVEN, and when you have this to your liking, you shall call him YOUR SON and SAVIOR OF MEN!

25/8.17. The Lord God said to satan: Who next shall I bring into my favor? Satan said: You shall next bring into your favor the ten Lords of the heavenly kingdoms of the earth. And when you have them to your liking, you shall exalt the chief one of them to be above the rest; and you shall call him Osiris, for it is a name loved on earth and in heaven.

25/8.18. Satan said: You shall re-establish your Lord-dom and call it Hored, and it shall be the central kingdom of all the heavens belonging to the earth.

25/8.19. And Anubi shall send the spirits of his department to your heavens; and Osiris and all the other Lords shall send the spirits of their departments to your kingdom. And in no case shall any more spirits be sent to Craoshivi; for all people in heaven and earth shall be taught that your kingdom is the All Highest Place; and that you are the All Highest God, even the Creator of all things; and all angels and mortals shall be your servants.

25/8.20. Then the Lord God went to work earnestly, but slowly and surely. The Lords of all the divisions of the earth were his special friends, and the type who would willingly do his bidding. And they were learned and of high grade, having heavenly experience of more than a thousand years each.

25/8.21. And the Lord God told no one in heaven or on the earth about his designs; gave no sign or token in his behavior that would make messengers or swift messengers look at him to read him; and he passed for the meekest and holiest of Gods.

25/8.22. But the time came at last for which the Lord God had labored hundreds of years; and he gave a festival in his heavenly place, inviting the Lords, captains, generals and marshals, whom he knew would willingly do his bidding.

25/8.23. And they came even as the Lord God had planned, and it was a time of great joy. And when the feast had ended, the Lord God spoke before them, speaking as one moved in sorrow to do a solemn duty for the sake of Jehovih.

25/8.24. The Lord God said: O my brothers, hear the words of your Lord God! Behold, I have charge of the Lord-dom of heaven and earth, I am like a guardian that stands by a cornfield to see that the corn grows unmolested. My experience is not of a year, nor of a hundred years, but of thousands of years.

25/8.25. In Jehovih's name I speak before you; for the love I bear for the souls of men and angels. I do not belong to the Diva as you Lords do; my voice finds vent in the fullness of the Father in me.

25/8.26. Who is here who has not seen in these heavens during the last hundred years, great decline in the faith of angels in the All Person? Speak then, O Lords; and if you have hearts for more energetic service for the Father and His kingdoms, now let your tongues have full liberty, as becomes[860] Gods.

25/8.27. Anubi said: You are wise, O Lord God. God of Craoshivi lays the blame on a'ji.

25/8.28. Then spoke Hi-kas, whose heavenly place was over Jaffeth, he said: My Lord God and my Lords, before your wisdom I bow. I am barely a child in heaven, little more than a thousand years. My tongue should be silent before you, my long-experienced Lords. Hear me though in my little wisdom, and pity me for it.

25/8.29. To the east or west, or north or south, all things grow [progress –Ed.], in heaven and on the earth; I have seen no greater wisdom than this. One thing does not grow, the Diva. Behold, the Diva made laws hundreds of years ago, and they were wise laws at the time they were made. You

[860] as is fitting for, right for, suitable for

and I, all of us, are bound by the old Divan laws. The laws have not grown.

25/8.30. Gods older than I am, and Lords also, tell us that the All Light is a Person and has Voice; and, moreover, that long ago He spoke to high-raised Gods, saying: These things, shall be thus and so.

25/8.31. I appeal to your judgment, O my Lord God and my Lords, was that not a wise doctrine for the ancients? For on this authority angels and mortals fell down and worshipped Him Whom they did not see. And they where obedient to do the will of their masters and teachers on this self-asserted authority of a Person no one had seen!

25/8.32. Which is to say: It is wiser to worship Him we do not know, and cannot comprehend, and is therefore as nothing before us, than to hearken to the words of most wise Gods and Lords.

25/8.33. If to worship 'that which we are ignorant of' is the highest of worship, then the fool is the greatest of worshippers. For he is ignorant of all things. And by virtue of this reason, he who is the wisest must be the poorest of worshippers. And in truth, is it not so, both in heaven and on earth?

25/8.34. With the acquisition of knowledge, they all put away the Unknowable;[861] the ignorant are devout worshippers. Shall we hold our tongues, saying: Wh-ce, wh-ce![862] The ignorant must not hear the truth; the whole truth!

25/8.35. Are we not hypocrites in doing this? Some have come to us from far-off regions, saying there are more delightful heavens, much higher! Why, then, shall we not all run away and leave this?

25/8.36. My Lord God, and my Lords, these heavens are good enough, if improved. The earth is good enough, if improved. We want larger kingdoms and more adorned thrones in our heavens and on the earth.

25/8.37. Next spoke Che-le-mung, whose heavenly kingdom was over Arabin'ya. He said: My Lord has spoken soul words. With knowledge obtained, what more do angels or mortals need? What value is it to them to say: Beware! The Unseen hears and sees! or, Stop and consider the Divan laws!

25/8.38. My Lord God, for the wisest, best and most honest to assume dominion—this I have not seen. Your kingdom should be the largest and most adorned of all kingdoms. And you should have, to labor with you, Lords with kingdoms greater than all Craoshivi. Can our Gods and our Lords not make these heavens the greatest of all regions in the universe? Shall we and our people continually run off to etherea in search of higher heavens? And not improve our own? To exalt a place by going away from it, who has seen this done?

25/8.39. Arc-wotchissij, whose heavenly kingdom was over Vind'yu, spoke next. He said: O if only I had not struggled so long to put away wisdom like this! All that has been spoken I have understood. But I curbed my soul; I thought I was alone in such reason. Now, so suddenly, I do not have words well schooled. I speak little, lest I later trip myself up. It is the joy of my life to listen to such wise arguments. Another time I will say more.

25/8.40. After him spoke Baal, whose heavenly kingdom was over Heleste and the south end of Jaffeth to the sea, a young Lord of great promise. He said: How shall one of my inexperience speak before such Gods as are here! But because you have touched upon a matter dear to my soul, my words will come forth. I have seen all these heavens, and even Craoshivi, waning for hundreds of years. Our kingdoms are like old women, resigned to routine, living, but dead.

25/8.41. We have the same rites and ceremonies as the ancients; parades, salutations, and anthems sung for thousands of years; and to whom? A figurehead that is void of shape and person and sense. Who is here that has not deserved honor more than such a being? My Lord God has labored two thousand years! I have seen him in Vara-pishanaha for more than a hundred years, stooped to the vilest labor, over bad-smelling drujas, teaching them, washing them!

25/8.42. The Lord God should have a kingdom wide as the earth, and a million attendants to do him honorable parade. And when he goes forth he

---

[861] Note that this is an Osirian (materialist) speaking, and truly for him, at that time, Jehovih was Unknowable. But for the Faithist, the understanding or experience is that Jehovih is KNOWABLE, but never in His entirety.

[862] Equivalent to shh... or shush or hush—the sound of the wind. Thus: Shall we keep quiet, saying, hush, the ignorant must not hear... [Note this seems to be said in mockery of Eolin, Eolin being taught as being like the wind.]

should have hundreds of thousands of heralds and trumpeters to proclaim he is coming. We need such. We need wider fields and more pomp and glory in our heavens; and kingdoms with great capital cities, and thrones arrayed in splendor.

25/8.43. Then rose Ashtaroth, assistant to Baal, and Lordess of the East Wing of his heavenly place. She said: Here are other Lordesses who can speak wisely. As for me, my words are few. The ancients have taught us to be plain in all things. And we have made our heavens like orchards stripped of leaves and blossoms. As fast as angels are made bright and useful, they are persuaded to become Brides and Bridegrooms to Jehovih, and fly off to remote worlds. Our own beloved earth, that brought us forth, together with her heavens, are thus forever stripped of the most valuable fruitage and ornament.

25/8.44. We all know that atmospherea is extensive enough to contain all the angels the earth will bring forth in millions of years! I appeal to you, my Lord God, and to you, most wise Lords, are these Brides and Bridegrooms not hoodwinked [863] by the tales of the etherean Gods? And by the parade and pageantry of the marriage ceremony? And by the fire-ships, and pomp and splendor of the marshals, and trumpeters, and music, and the high-raised Gods?

25/8.45. Behold, we have one here who can invent all these glories, even our Lord God. He should have such a heavenly place of splendor that the Brides and Bridegrooms would fly to him instead of the far-off heavens.

25/8.46. The other Lords and Lordesses spoke similarly, and when they had all spoken, Anuhasaj, currently the lawfully anointed Lord God, rose up. He said:

CHAPTER 9 Wars

25/9.1. Most wise Lords, in words you have done me great honor. There let the matter end. I perceive what anyone can understand, which is that the center of the heavens should be here. Why should the heirs of the earth and atmospherea be carried off to other heavens? It is sufficient for us that we cultivate our own. I am not competent for so great a work. Rather you should choose from among yourselves the highest and best wise man, and make him your God. I will be his servant to do whatever he puts upon me.

25/9.2. I have traveled far, and took the measure of many worlds. I declare to you there are no glories in the far-off worlds (etherea), that cannot be built up in these heavens, and even on the very earth.

25/9.3. Hear me then and judge me, not for my fitness, but for my unfitness, and so dismiss me except to make me your servant.

25/9.4. Do not send off the highest raised angels, but make these heavens suitable to them.

25/9.5. Make this kingdom the All Highest heavenly kingdom; and make your God the highest of all Gods, even the Creator. You shall surround him with a capital city, a heavenly place paved with diamonds and most precious gems. And his throne shall be the most exalted, highest of all glories. To which none can approach, except by crawling on their bellies. Yes, such majesty should surround your God as befits[864] a Creator, and such newly-invented rites and ceremonies as will dazzle beyond anything in all the worlds!

25/9.6. The rites and ceremonies should be carried to the highest.[865] Without rites and ceremonies a people are like a dead people; they are like an army without discipline. In fact, discipline is void without the formalities of rites and ceremonies. To not have these is to have everyone do for self, which is the dissolution of all union. Baal has spoken wisely on this; we need new rites and ceremonies, adapted to the highest grades. We shall no longer bow to a God we do not know, a scattered substance wide as the universe!

25/9.7. Because you have spoken, I am pleased. Because you have come to my feast, I am delighted. To be with one's own loves, what is greater than that? It has been said, man shall love all alike; but I say to you that this is impossible. We have our preferences, and we delight to come together. Who shall tell us not to?

25/9.8. And yet, my Lords and Lordesses, shall we not deliberate on these things? And council with

[863] misled, deceived, tricked, cheated, duped

[864] is appropriate for, corresponds to, comports with

[865] highest perfection, highest degree, highest potency, highest priority, suitable even for the highest persons, etc.

our best loves upon it; for such is the construction of the mind that it often sees better through others' eyes. And, above all, shall we not mature the subject to know if in our own souls we are sincere, doing all things for the good of heaven and earth, and not for ourselves.

25/9.9. You know how Ahura's kingdom prospered until he began to work for his own glory; let us not, then, fall into his errors, but from his errors learn to avoid similar ones. And now, since the time of the feast has ended, and our respective kingdoms await us, I declare the assembly dissolved. Arise, then, my Lords and Lordesses, and go your ways. And if you desire further communication with me regarding this matter, do so through messengers, which you already have.

CHAPTER 10 Wars

25/10.1. Satan[866] went to all the Lords and Lordesses in hada, and said to each and every one: Yours shall be exaltation without labor; because you are wise, others shall serve you; and great shall be your glory. As you have witnessed the rites and ceremonies, in Craoshivi, of the high-raised Gods, even so shall it be with you. Behold, the heavens of the earth shall become the brightest and most glorious of all heavens. Be patient, enduring anything, for you shall surely, in time to come, be second to none, the highest of Gods!

25/10.2. And your name shall be sung in the ceremonies, and shall be honored even in the far-off heavens. It shall be said of you that you are among the youngest of Gods, who, by your own self-will, mastered all things so suddenly that even the oldest of Gods stood appalled at your daring.

25/10.3. Be patient, and seeming most humble, and bide your time; you were born to be a leader even among Gods. Be secret, disclosing nothing. ||

25/10.4. Satan said to Anuhasaj, who was Lord God: Be dignified, and by your much-professed love, like a father to all the others. And it shall come to pass that they will thrust these great dominions upon you.

25/10.5. Now while these matters were with these Lords, behold, in far-off Craoshivi Jehovih spoke to God on the throne, before the Council of Jehovih's Son, saying: Because I indulged your Lords and Lordesses in prosperous places, they are becoming forgetful of Me.

25/10.6. For so I created man: In prosperity he idolizes himself. He says: Behold me! What great things I can do: Yes, I am wise; I perceive the nothingness of the Creator! || And he builds to his own ruin. I created life and death all around him, so that he might learn My power before he quits the earth. And hada I made wide, with a place of ascent and a place of descent. Upward I placed My holy lights, saying: Come! Downward, I made darkness, saying: Beware! Hell lies here! But they plunge headlong into misery.

25/10.7. God said: What have they done, O Jehovih? Jehovih said: They are laying their heads together to rebel against the manner of My everlasting kingdoms. Summon the Diva before you, and bid them speak outright as to what they desire.

25/10.8. God sent messengers into all the divisions of the lowest heavens, to the kingdoms of Jehovih's Lords and Lordesses, as the Father had commanded, summoning them to Craoshivi. On the other hand:

25/10.9. Satan spoke to Anuhasaj, the plotter of the mischief, saying: Lest God in Craoshivi get wind of this matter, and so bring to nothing your long-laid plans, send word to him, saying: Greeting, in love to you, Son of Jehovih, God of the heavens of the earth. From the light before me I am resolved to resign the Lord-dom. Search, therefore, and provide one in my place. ||

25/10.10. Satan continued speaking to Anuhasaj: Send word to your Lords and Lordesses, saying: Greeting in love to you, Lord of Jehovih. I foresee that many will desire me to take the place of God of the earth and her heavens. Seek to relieve me of this, and choose one less radical, so that you may more fully endorse him. Behold, I am about to resign the Lord-dom, and desire to see you. ||

25/10.11. The Lords and Lordesses received the two communications at the same time; and they each laid the matter before their Holy Councils; and great was their excitement. That which had

[866] Satan here is not in the figure of a person, but as the expression of coherent darkness within the souls of the unripe that inspires the self toward self-serving ends.

been planned to be in secret was thus made public before billions in all the hadas in a day!

25/10.12. The Lords and Lordesses hastened at once to Anuhasaj's capital, each attended by ten thousand attendants.

25/10.13. Now when they were assembled, perceiving that God in Craoshivi knew of the matter, and with their own shame over disobeying the Divan summons further inciting them, they at once proceeded to found a consolidated kingdom, with Anuhasaj at the head. Anuhasaj made believe he did not desire the Godhead, and only agreed to serve provided they installed him with oaths of fidelity. And this they did.

25/10.14. So, after a session of three days, Anuhasaj was elected and enthroned in Hored, a new heavenly place, and crowned OUR GOD of the earth and her heavens, the VERY LORD GOD IN JEHOVIH. Thus he became a false God.

25/10.15. But they did not crown him with the true crown, for that was with God in Craoshivi; but they made one, creating it in the sacred circle. But since he could not be crowned by those beneath him, they were in a quandary how to proceed. Then satan spoke to Anuhasaj, saying: Command them to lie on their bellies in token submission to you, and say to them: Lay the crown at my feet, and I will stand with my head bare; and when you have prostrated yourselves, I will command the crown in my own name to rise up and lie on my head; and if it so rises, then you will know in truth our work is the highest, best work.

25/10.16. Anuhasaj then repeated this to the Lords and Lordesses, and they laid themselves down on their bellies, each being anxious to show fidelity, in hope of exaltation. And when they were down and could not see, Anuhasaj, having no power in Light, said: Crown of these most holy, wise Lords and Lordesses of heaven and earth, arise and lie on the head of him who shall have dominion on earth and in these heavens!

25/10.17. And with that, he stooped down on the sly, and with his own hand raised it up and crowned himself, and commanded the Lords to rise up. And lo and behold, some of the Lords and Lordesses said they saw with the second sight of the soul, and that the crown rose of its own accord, being under the will of the circle!

25/10.18. And they clapped their hands, saying: ALL HAIL, OUR GOD! ALL HAIL, OUR GOD! ALL HAIL, OUR GOD! Proclaiming him in the east and west and north and south.

25/10.19. He responded: THE LORD, YOUR GOD, REIGNS! Peace be yours. Behold, the heavens and earth are mine; be steadfast to me, and you shall be glorified in my name. You who have been Lords and Lordesses shall be Gods and Goddesses, with great powers and with mighty kingdoms. As I foresaw this, so have I provided for you beforehand. In this very time and place I will crown you and apportion you with great glory. Yet do not think that this is the last; it is only the first, and temporary until the new heavens are founded with broader boundaries.

CHAPTER 11 Wars

Of the Deity, alias Dyaus, alias De'yus, alias Deus; origin and power in the heavens and on earth

25/11.1. Anuhasaj said: I, the Lord, your God, being the All Highest, through your choice, decree, for the sake of harmony and concert in our labors, the establishment of a De'yus [Congress –Ed.].

25/11.2. As the Craoshivians have had a Diva (Divinity), so will I have a De'yus. And by virtue of my own authority I proclaim you, my Lords and Lordesses, as its holy members.

25/11.3. As the Diva has been taught in these heavens, so also shall be taught the De'yus, in which I assume the rank of chief head.

25/11.4. As the Diva had laws, so also shall our De'yus; and they shall be promulgated on the earth, and taught to mortals as the laws of De'yus (Deity).[867] Therefore by my own voice I dissolve the Diva of heaven; and it shall not exist from this time

[867] This [explanation] corresponds with the sacred books of India and China, Dyaus and D-yin being the words they use. Our term, Deity, is most likely from the Greek Zeus or [Latin] Deus. There is no word in Hebrew corresponding; this shows that the Jews [i.e., the Israelites] were protected from the word. Only idolaters have ever substituted this name for Jehovih. The Greeks rated Zeus as the All Highest God, i.e., a person in figure of a man. The word Jehovih has never had any such signification. He is co-extensive with the universe. –Ed.

forward forever. And whoever of you are its members, shall this day resign from the Diva, and send word to the ruler of Craoshivi, for his benefit, and for his kingdom's benefit.

25/11.5. And the ruler of Craoshivi shall continue in his own place and kingdom; for it is his.

25/11.6. And the ruler of Vara-pishanaha, called Ahura, shall continue in his own place and kingdom, for it is his.

25/11.7. First, then, I take to myself Anubi, the Lord loved by you all, and he shall be my associate, and his title shall be MASTER OF THE SCALES OF HEAVEN, for he shall determine the grades of the spirits and send them to their respective departments. On earth his title shall be SAVIOR OF MEN, SON OF DE'YUS.

25/11.8. Second, you, Hi-kas, shall be RULER OVER JAFFETH and its heavenly kingdom; and your title shall be TE-IN, and of the first rank of GOD OF THE EARTH.

25/11.9. Third, you, Wotchissij, shall be ruler over Vind'yu and her heavenly kingdom, and your title shall be SUDGA,[868] and of the first rank of GOD OF THE EARTH.

25/11.10. Fourth, you, Che-le-mung, shall be ruler over Arabin'ya and her heavenly kingdom, and your title shall be OSIRIS, and of the first rank of GOD OF THE EARTH.

25/11.11. Fifth, you, Baal, shall be ruler over Heleste and her heavenly kingdom, and your title shall be BAAL, and of the first rank of GOD OF THE EARTH.

25/11.12. Sixth, you, Ashtaroth, shall be ruler over Parsa,[869] and its heavenly kingdom, and your title shall be ASHTAROTH, of the first rank of GODDESS OF THE EARTH.

25/11.13. Seventh, you, Fo-ebe, shall be ruler over Uropa and her heavenly kingdom, and your title shall be FO-EBE, and of the first rank of GODDESS OF THE EARTH.

25/11.14. Eighth, you, Ho-jab, shall be ruler over Japan and her heavenly kingdom, and your title shall be HO-JAB, and of the first rank of GOD OF THE EARTH.

25/11.15. After that the false God made appointments for the other divisions of the earth and their heavenly places, and then he said to them:

25/11.16. All my Gods and Goddesses shall have thrones in their places, and holy councils and attendants, as is fitting for Gods of the first rank. And every one shall have a capital city, with subsidiaries according to the number and place of their spirits and mortal subjects.

25/11.17. And every God and Goddess shall manage his or her own kingdom in his or her own way; but every one shall nevertheless be tributary to my kingdom, according to the exactions I put upon him or them.

25/11.18. So that you may resign the Diva, and choose your assistants, before being crowned, I declare a day of recreation, to assemble at the trumpeter's call. ||

25/11.19. And so the hosts relaxed from duty and made their resignations from the Diva, sending these with messengers to God in Craoshivi, but not one of them mentioned the new state of affairs resolved upon. On the next day, at the trumpeter's call, they assembled again; and Anuhasaj said to them: Come with me, and I will show you the place of Hored and its boundaries; for it shall not be my kingdom alone, but yours also, for my kingdom shall be the kingdom of your kingdoms.

25/11.20. And they entered an otevan, and arrived in the fourth belt below meteoris, in the sign of the twelfth arc of Chinvat; and Anuhasaj said: From this time forward this belt shall be called Hored, and it shall be my place forever. It shall be the central kingdom of all the earth's heavens.

25/11.21. And the multitude said: HAIL, KINGDOM OF HORED, THE HOLY HILL, PLACE OF THE MOST HIGH GOD! And after that it was known as the belt of Hored, hill of God. It was a three-quarters belt,[870] and its base was ten thousand miles from the earth, and the summit was fifteen thousand miles high; habitable within and without. And its ascending rank in the grades was twenty, that is, it was easily habitable by spirits who had attained to that grade; being above the grade of infants and

---

[868] Sudga means Apollo.

[869] The word, PARSEE, and the country, PERSIA, and the tribe, PARSIE, and, in Vedic, Par-su, are all confined to the same region of country. –Ed.

[870] That is, it extended three-fourths the way around the world (but above it).

drujas, and above the region of hells and knots, except in cases of great panic. Now, from the first place of Hored, where Anuhasaj crowned himself, which was the eastern base of the hill, to the place for his capital city, he made a roadway and called it Loo-hored, and it was the only opened roadway to the kingdoms below.

25/11.22. So it came to pass that Anuhasaj had two capital cities; and the first was called the City of the Gate of Heaven, that is, Anubi; and the other was called the Place of Everlasting Rest, that is, Sanc-tu. Anuhasaj said to Anubi: Behold, the City of the Gate of Heaven shall be your place. And you shall determine the rate of all souls who desire to enter the Place of Everlasting Rest. You shall be judge over them. And whoever is not for me shall not enter, but shall be cast into the kingdoms of hada (the lower plateaus). And those who are for me, you shall send to me.

25/11.23. And you shall have a Holy Council of one hundred thousand; and you shall have one million examiners. And your capital shall be guarded on every side but one, with pillars of fires, so that none can pass except by the Gate of Heaven. And you shall have seven million guardsmen, divided into seven watches, one for each day. You shall have ten thousand messengers between your place and mine; but between you and the Gods and Goddesses of the lower kingdoms, you shall have five hundred thousand. But the number of es'enaurs, trumpeters, marshals, and your attendants, shall be left to your own choice.

25/11.24. And all Gods and Goddesses coming to me, or sending messengers to my holy place, shall come through your city, even through the Gate of Heaven; and they shall come according to certain rites and ceremonies, which I will give to you. Come, therefore, and receive your crown.

25/11.25. Anubi was thus crowned; and after him the other Gods and Goddesses were crowned; and Anuhasaj bequeathed to each one his own kingdom, according to the custom of the ancients. And when these matters were completed, he again spoke before them, saying: Behold the example I have made before you; even before I provided myself for my own kingdom I have given to every one all things required. It is fitting and proper, therefore, that you contribute to me and my place workmen and materials, so that I may build in great glory also.

25/11.26. For, as I am exalted, and my kingdom made glorious, so do you have something to preach gloriously about to your inhabitants regarding the place in store for them. || In that way Anuhasaj put Gods and Goddesses under obligations to himself, and they acquiesced in his proceedings, saying: No, we will not only contribute men and women for this purpose, but we will labor with our own hands for the space of twenty days, helping to build the capital city, and to open roads, in all directions.

CHAPTER 12 Wars

Anuhasaj, the false God, declares himself against Jehovih

25/12.1. Anuhasaj never established the De'yus as projected at first, but took the name De'yus upon himself, and became known in the heavens by that name. When he had thus established Hored in its entirety, he gave a feast to the Gods and Goddesses; and after it had ended, he spoke before them prior to their departure, saying:

25/12.2. The time of duty is now upon you, and upon me, the Lord your God, also. Be, then, solicitous of[871] these things I speak of, so that in the everlasting times we may be brethren, and there shall be no other Gods but ourselves, forever.

25/12.3. Behold, I have given into your hands to manage your own kingdoms in your own way; for which reason I can no longer say, do this, or do that, for my affairs are in my own kingdom. But if I have wisdom I shall freely impart, and the choice is yours, whether you will follow my advice or do otherwise, for you are of equal rank with me. And, moreover, my kingdom is dependent upon you, and not yours upon mine. Hear then my words as if I were merely one in a Council with wise Gods:

25/12.4. To overturn Jehovih and His dominions on the earth and in these heavens will be your first labor. And whenever corporeans embrace Him, calling themselves Faithists in the Great Spirit, or Faithists in Jehovih, or Faithists in Ormazd, or by any other name signifying the All Light, or Unseen, or Person of Ever Presence, you shall pursue them, and destroy them off the face of the earth. To accomplish this you shall use the

[871] attentive to, seeking toward, considerate of, ask questions concerning

oracles, prophets, seers, magicians, or inspiration; and you shall set the kings and queens of the earth to war upon them, and not spare them, man, woman or child.

25/12.5. And those spirits of the dead who are Faithists and fall into your respective kingdoms, bring them before Anubi and his hosts, and he shall send them into regions of darkness, saying to them: Behold, you have your Jehovih! And Anubi shall place guards over them, and they shall not know where to go, but will cry out in their darkness.

25/12.6. At which time they shall be sworn into servitude in Hored to the Lord your God forever, and become slaves within your kingdoms.

25/12.7. And you shall teach both mortals and spirits that Hored is the All Highest heaven, and that it is the place of the All Highest God, even De'yus. Which for them to attain, you shall exact servitude from them in your heavens accordingly as you may desire.

25/12.8. In the rites and ceremonies, both in your heavens and on the earth, you shall enforce the exchanging of words signifying Great Spirit to words signifying Lord God, who is of the form and size of a man, declaring in truth that I sit on my throne in judgment of the world, for it is mine, and you are one with me.

25/12.9. And all songs of praise, prayers and beseechings shall be changed to your God, instead of Jehovih, or Ormazd, or the Great Spirit. For both mortals and angels shall be made to know that He is my enemy, leading my people astray. And as to the prophets and seers on the earth, who will persist in preaching or singing to the Great Spirit, you shall incite torture, punishment and death to them.

25/12.10. And whether I am called De'yus, or God, or the Lord God, or the All Perfect, they shall worship me only, forever. And my place, Hored, shall be the sacred hill of God forever! And none shall approach me except by crawling on their bellies; for I will so exalt my lights that none can stand before me.

25/12.11. When the Lord God had finished his discourse, the other Gods responded in love and adoration. Thus ended the feast, and, similar to the rites in other heavens, the Gods and Goddesses went and sat at the foot of the throne, and De'yus came down and took them by the hand, one at a time, and raised them up, saying: Arise, O God, and in my name, wisdom and power, go your way. And they departed.

25/12.12. Accordingly, regarding the earth, great havoc and persecution were visited upon the Zarathustrians and Israelites, being put to death by hundreds of thousands.[872]

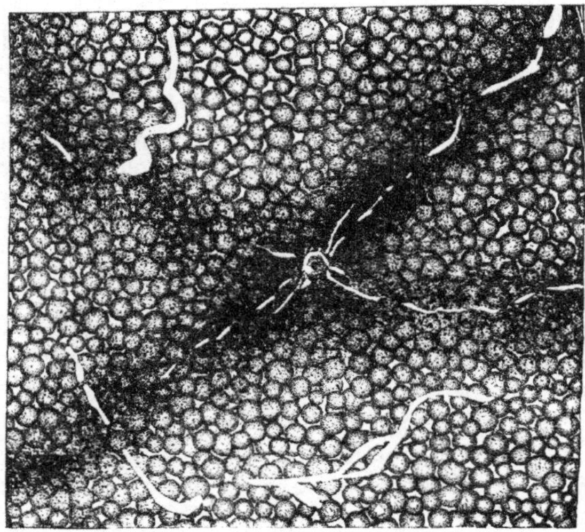

i077 **The Earth in Kas'kak.** Jehovih said: So that My Gods could learn to master the elements of My heavens, I brought the earth into the etherean Forest of Kas'kak. And lo and behold, angels and mortals fell in the darkness. And Anuhasaj established the names Lord God and De'yus (Dyaus) (Deity) as worshipful on the earth. Before that time, man worshipped Me under the term Great Spirit. And man built the great pyramid as a monument of his own darkness.

CHAPTER 13 Wars

25/13.1. Swift messengers coursing the heavens, from far-off etherean worlds, bound for destinations remote, passed over the regions of Hored; and the high-raised travelers felt the discordant plots of satan's Lord God and his hosts, thus bent to overthrow the Great Spirit's happy world. And so they sent word of it to Cpenta-armij, through whose fields the great serpent moved along. And her Most High Council, one with the Creator, cast about to know the cause and treatment of the dastardly outrage.

---

[872] see image i077

25/13.2. Then Jehovih spoke to His Daughter, Chieftainess, saying: The Lord God was duly honored in My name, and swore before Me to serve faithfully, forever, by his highest light. Hold him to his purpose, and bind him in the world he has assumed to rule for his own glory. And to his fellow-Gods, conspirators against Me, Who brought them into being, give them full sway to destroy My worshippers. Let them raise the name of their God, and bait mortal kings and queens to glut themselves in the havoc of My chosen, the Faithists.

25/13.3. The earth nears her greatest corporeal growth, and these self-assuming Gods, through their mortal emissaries shall, in the greatest divisions of the earth, build monuments: temples, pyramids, and oracle-palaces, which shall stand thousands of years as testimonies of the audacity of Gods and Saviors. To honor whom, the Lord God has sworn to make angels and men suppliant slaves in heaven and earth.

25/13.4. For I will use the corporeal temples and pyramids they shall build on the earth at the expense of My chosen, as testimony, in coming ages, of the oppression in the hadan heavenly kingdoms of these self-Gods. Till that time, I cannot teach mortals of the vanity of the lower heavens, except in the deserted ruins of their moldering monuments.

25/13.5. For in kosmon, mortals shall know that even as the earth has been a place of foolish sacrifice to persons born of woman, so were My heavens debauched in that day by similar oppression and cruelty.

25/13.6. Let him who is falsely crowned Osiris, build in the Osirian field,[873] and him who is proclaimed De'yus, build in the hadan field,[874] for the time shall come when these testimonies shall be required in the sum of earth and heaven.

25/13.7. For I will show them that without an All Highest Person there is no resurrection for angels or men. Regarding which, the ten billion who are slaughtered and bound by the Lord God, shall swear in kosmon, the fall of all things except Me. ||

25/13.8. Down to the lower heavens, to God in Craoshivi, Cpenta-armij sent swift messengers, with the words of Jehovih, comforting to God and his hosts, as to the wide plans on which the Father lays the destinies of worlds. And God received them, and now comprehended why, alas, his Diva did not come, nor answered his call except by resigning.

25/13.9. But God, the true ruler of heaven and earth, now saw how the prosperity of the indulged heaven had made bad men out of most holy Gods, even as prosperity on the earth closes up man's eyes against his Creator, making himself an egotist in self, and vociferous[875] as to Jehovih's shortcomings, according to man's views. And God remembered how he had prayed for the continuation of the light in heaven, which Jehovih granted him; and he repented now, saying:

25/13.10. O Jehovih, why did I not say: Your will be done; let darkness come! || Had I not seen on the earth how night must follow day, and winter after summer; and yet I prayed for endless light in a heaven where Your sons and daughters are as yet only babes in the time and course of worlds. My own judgment should have shown me that spells of darkness should follow seasons of light in Your lower heavens. For, then, these half-tried Lords and Gods would have stopped to consider before they rushed into so mad a scheme.

25/13.11. God called together the Holy Council in Craoshivi, and told them about the words of the Creator, through His High-Raised Daughter. Then within the Council, all who chose to, spoke, and the thirty million listened. And, meanwhile, messengers fresh from Hored, the seat of rebellion, came in, bringing full news to Craoshivi of the proceedings of the Lord God, alias, De'yus, and his self-Gods and Goddesses.

25/13.12. When the full particulars had been related, and the Council had spoken upon it, then the light of Jehovih came upon God, and God said:

25/13.13. In the name of our Father, I will speak to these Gods and Lords and acquaint them

[873] OSIRIAN FIELD, here as elsewhere, seems to mean materialism, or that material philosophy which maintains that materiality rules over spirit, and not spirit over matter. –Ed.

[874] HADAN FIELD, here seems to mean spirit world, and without a Great Spirit or All Person. –Ed.

[875] vigorously raising voice; loud and conspicuous outcry; speaking up against; intensely calling attention

with Jehovih's words. Yes, I will entreat[876] them to return even as they were.

25/13.14. Then God was overwhelmed by the terrible adversity of the heavens entrusted into his keeping. As in a small degree the captain of a merchant's ship, far out at sea, meeting with a mishap of broken masts, stripped to the hulk, and rudder gone, powerless to save, feels the burning shame of incompetence before mariners, so God, before the High-Raised Chiefs of the etherean worlds, must helplessly view his shattered kingdoms.

25/13.15. With great sorrow God sent word of Jehovih's warning to De'yus and his Gods; and he pleaded for them to return, as a father pleads to a wayward son. Off went the messengers swiftly; and God, even though long schooled to adverse trials and suspensions, burned with impatience for his messengers to return, hoping that his sweet pleadings might yet reverse the scenes.

25/13.16. Then the messengers came back, empty-handed! Not one of the truant Gods had deigned[877] to answer him. And God wept, scarcely believing his messengers, that so great an insult could be heaped upon him, who had done nothing anyone could complain about. Then Jehovih came and spoke to God, saying: Do not weep, My Son! He who follows his highest light from day to day—great is his glory; and in whatever he loses he shall regain a thousand-fold. Behold, I will bring love to you that you do not know of: Remember, as this season is upon the earth and her heavens, even so do I send a season like it upon all My worlds.

CHAPTER 14 Wars

25/14.1. In course of time, word came to Ahura, in Vara-pishanaha, of the proceedings of the Lord God, now styled De'yus, and of the revolt of all the lowest heavens in one fell swoop.[878] And Ahura remembered his own shortcomings, thousands of years ago, and the terrible bondage that came upon him in the end. And he knew De'yus, who had been a sub-God under him for hundreds of years, under the name Anuhasaj, who had tried to break the lines in the arc of Spe-ta, in the resurrection of Ailkin.

25/14.2. So Ahura prayed to Jehovih, before the Holy Council in Vara-pishanaha, to know what he should say or do in the matter, or if he should do nothing at all. Jehovih answered him, saying:

25/14.3. My Son, you are no longer a child. Address the Lord God, or not, as seems fit in your own eyes. Behold, I allowed you to try the same road, so that you could understand Me and My kingdoms.

25/14.4. So Ahura decided to send, in his own name, and in his own way, word to De'yus. This, then, is what he sent:

25/14.5. To Anuhasaj, my one-time sub-God, greeting to you in justice and wisdom. If you were inexperienced, I would treat you with respect. But you know you are false. And because you are false, you shall reap in falsehood.

25/14.6. Behold, the day shall come when your Gods will desert you; for such is the tree you have planted in your kingdoms. This rule holds on earth and in all the heavens. Can that which is unborn, restrain its own birth? Or that which is not quickened into life, restrain the Creator's hand?

25/14.7. So also does it hold true for him who sows for self: He shall reap a harvest of selfs.[879] And your Gods will be for themselves, and your marshals, and all your hosts; every one pulling in an opposite way.

25/14.8. Not suddenly will these things come upon you; for you shall have a mighty kingdom and great honor and glory, like no other God before you has had in these heavens. And your people shall be jealous to serve you, striving with all their might to outdo one another in worshipful obedience to you. And your name, even the names De'yus and Lord God, shall stand for a season as the highest on the earth of all the names that have ever been.

25/14.9. And yet the time shall come when your names shall be cast out of earth and heaven. And it shall be the deeds that you shall do, that shall be the means of making your names execrable.[880]

---

[876] earnestly request, implore, appeal to, beseech

[877] vouchsafed, lowered themselves, stooped, condescended

[878] in one deadly, descending, sudden sweep, seizure, or snatch

[879] In other words, by setting up his kingdom for himself, Anuhasaj could no more prevent this ultimate harvest of selfs than a fetus can stop its own birth.

25/14.10. Do not think, O my Lord God, that you will deal righteously, and keep yourself holy. Behold, I, too, was a revolted God who set up a kingdom for my own glory. And at its beginning I was most resolute to practice righteousness in all things.

25/14.11. But the surroundings overcame me; for as I was allied to self, so selfish officers under me beset me on all occasions, and I was forced to find new places and new glories for them, or, by their grumbling, they would sow my fields with mutiny. I was powerless in the great kingdom I built up. You know the result.

25/14.12. Do you think the larger your kingdom, the greater will be your power to avert your fall? My experience was the opposite of this.

25/14.13. I admonish you in wisdom and justice; I know you are doing these things not for the raising up of the fruit of the earth, but for your own aggrandizement and glory. And I say to you, the time will surely come when your Gods will do the same things against you. And in that time the wise and learned and truthful will fly from you, but the drujas and slaves will not leave you; but you shall be environed[881] with them, and cast into hell.

25/14.14. You shall heap misery upon millions of your subjects, but you shall not escape the hand of justice: You shall reimburse every one of them. You have cast your net in shoal water;[882] your own feet shall be tangled in its meshes.

25/14.15. Behold, I, too, once craved a great heavenly kingdom; now I weep day and night because I have it. And you, too, shall experience the time of scalding tears, to be rid of that which you crave even now.

25/14.16. Yet, how else shall the dumb be raised in heaven? Who else shall minister to the wandering spirits that overspread the earth; and the evil drujas; and the lusters; and the foul-smelling? Shall I say to you: Go on, you self-presuming Lord God, the Great Spirit has a rod in pickle[883] for you!

25/14.17. Yes, He answers the ambition of men and Gods sooner or later; in a way they do not think of, He brings them up with a round turn.[884]

25/14.18. You are like a man who, desirous of great bulk, shuts up the pores of the skin of his flesh; you seek to shut up the course of the heavens that rises out of the earth, upward forever. And as the man chokes up with a foul smell, and dies, so shall it be with your kingdom. Behold, the way of everlasting light is outward, onward, away from the corporeal worlds; but the way of darkness is toward the earth.

25/14.19. Do you say the spirits of the dead shall not rise away from the earth? And, in their ignorance of the higher heavens, become guides to mortals!

25/14.20. Behold, you have traveled far; and you strut about, saying: It is enough; I, the Lord God, have traveled in the far-off heavens (etherea); stay at home, and work for me forever, so that I may be glorified!

25/14.21. Will you say: I, the Lord God, I, De'yus, am the only Son of the Void! Behold, my kingdom lies in a little corner! Come and worship me, the Lord God, and you shall see me on my throne!

25/14.22. Or will you say: The impersonal space, senselessness, by accident fructified itself in corporeal substance, and became me, the Lord God, in the form of a full-grown man, and then I created all the creations! For which reason let men and angels fall down and worship the man, De'yus, who dwells in Hored, a ripple in the lowest heavens!

25/14.23. I am not professing love to you, Anuhasaj, but justice toward those beneath you. For you shall hoodwink mortals, and even angels of little experience, to believe you were the very Creator; but your Gods know who you truly are, and the Gods above you know also. All your days at most have been only two thousand and seven hundred years! And the time shall come upon you when you shall be forced, by your own fault, to assert you were the very Creator, Whose worlds

[880] offensive, repulsive, deplorable, loathsome, fit to be excreted (cast out)

[881] bound on all sides; trapped; imprisoned; obliged; beset; surrounded; girdled; hemmed in

[882] shallow water, often with sandbars (ridges of sand) that lie hidden just beneath the surface, difficult, even dangerous to navigate, and can become turbulent compared to the deeper waters

[883] in storage; has preserved a rod for you

[884] a full turn; like an anchor being lifted up by the turn of a capstan

have run billions of years! Who can carry so great a falsehood as this! And not carrying it, it shall fall down on you and on your people, and take root and spread abroad, till your place and your Gods' places are the foundations of nothing but lies.

25/14.24. For the rule holds in all places, high and low, that according to the seed sown so shall be the harvest, whether good or bad. Nor can any man or God alter this rule, or bend it to the right or left.

25/14.25. If it is Jehovih's decree that someone shall make the names of God, and Lord God, and De'yus, execrable on earth and in heaven, it may well be that you have put yourself into the yoke to that end. Yet I would not have you so, if I could prevent it.

25/14.26. You were once my sub-God, and I remember you well; you were young and full of promise. My judgment spoke to me of you, saying: A sub-God to be proud of for thousands of years! But my judgment was not Jehovih's. My love for you was early nipped in the bud, for you were forever talking about yourself. You made your neighbor Gods sick by forever relating your experiences and your prophecies as to what you would do.

25/14.27. And when Jehovih encompassed me about in my own evil, you tormented me because I had not followed your advice. Now I repeat to you, I could not follow anyone's advice. And you too shall be environed about and unable to follow anyone's advice; for such is the bondage of the Godhead, unless we cut ourselves loose making Jehovih the Head and Front, and ourselves His servants. For the God should not only be the greatest in his kingdom, but the most menial servant of his people; forever casting off responsibility,[885] and forever urging his subjects not to idolize him, but Jehovih! Forever showing them that their God is nothing more than they are; that they must stand alone, and become, not slaves to their God, but independent beings full of manliness,[886] having faith in the Great Spirit only.

25/14.28. By which the God binds neither himself nor his people; giving full sway to the love of liberty in every soul, but in tenderness and love that harmonize with Jehovih's proceedings.

25/14.29. Now when you came back to me after I was delivered out of hell, and my kingdoms raised to Vara-pishanaha, you did profess to understand these things, and, in truth, to love this philosophy. And you prayed fervently to Jehovih, repenting of your former ways, and taking part in the rites and ceremonies.

25/14.30. Then I opened my heart to you. My much love for you, as when I first knew you, returned upon me a thousand fold. In joy and in tears I fell upon you, and I praised Jehovih that He had sent me so sweet a love.

25/14.31. In each other's arms we repented, and we swore our mutual love forever. Then we both saw the way of Jehovih clear, and He made us strong and wise, full of rejoicing.

25/14.32. And we fell to work, hand in hand, laboring with drujas, dark and most foul, teaching them day and night, forever repeating to their stupid minds. And when we were both nearly exhausted thousands of times, and we slacked up, and withdrew for a short spell, we rested in each other's arms!

25/14.33. Then we reasoned and philosophized on the plans and glories of Jehovih's works; watching hopefully for signs of progress in our wards. O the glory of those days! O the richness of your wisdom and love to me in those days of darkness! For a hundred years we toiled thus, and I was blessed, and my people were blessed, by you, you star of our love.

25/14.34. When we raised up my four billion wards a small way up out of darkness, our far-off Goddess, Atcheni, needed one who was great, like you, to travel in other regions. And I parted with you. My soul was as if divided in two.

25/14.35. For hundreds of years you traveled and became rich in knowledge; but did not return to me, to my bursting heart! What more can I say? You are in your place, and I am in mine; but Jehovih is with Wisdom, Love, Truth and Fidelity,[887] for these are His abiding places. ||

---

[885] That is, to direct the petitioner to Jehovih; and to induce the petitioner to take responsibility and make his own decision in the light of Jehovih, and within the parameters of His kingdom.

[886] having the attributes of a wholesome developed man (male or female); see e.g., 20/24.16<fn-make>

[887] faithfulness; e.g., to Jehovih; and to one's own holy vows and obligations

CHAPTER 15 Wars

25/15.1. De'yus did not reply to Ahura, God of Vara-pishanaha, but sent the messenger away without a word. And satan came again to De'yus, saying: Send word to your Gods to be firm, for today Ahura and the God of Craoshivi have beset them to return to Jehovih's worship.

25/15.2. De'yus feared nevertheless, so he inquired of satan what was the best great thing he could do. Satan said: O Lord, my God, this is the best thing you can do: For all the Divan laws you have destroyed, make De'yus laws instead. Why shall you follow in the footsteps of the ancients?

25/15.3. The Lord God said: Yes, yes! I will not be bound by the laws of the ancients, but I will have laws of my own, and they shall be called the Laws of the Lord God.

25/15.4. Satan (self) said: These, then, shall be your words, O Lord God, which shall be the laws of De'yus, namely:

25/15.5. I, the Lord God, have made self-preservation the first law.

25/15.6. You shall love the Lord your God with all your soul, heart and mind.

25/15.7. You shall worship only him, now and forever.

25/15.8. You shall not worship Jehovih; He is void; He is nothing.

25/15.9. Nor shall you worship any idol of anything, on the earth or in the heavens of the earth.

25/15.10. Whoever worships anything except me, the Lord God, shall be put to death.

25/15.11. Behold, I am a God of justice and truth; I am a God of anger; vengeance is mine.

25/15.12. I have a gate at the hill of Hored; my guardians are cherubims and seraphims, with flaming swords.

25/15.13. Whoever raises his arm against me shall be destroyed; to do my will is the sixth law.

25/15.14. Whoever puts the mark of the circumcision on a male child shall be put to death.

25/15.15. No man shall do evil for evil's sake; nor by violence oppress any man, woman or child.

25/15.16. Whoever exalts me on earth, him I will exalt in heaven.

25/15.17. Whoever overthrows other Gods, except the Lord God, who is the De'yus of heaven and earth, him will I exalt in heaven. ||

25/15.18. Now it came to pass that these decrees of the false God were established on the earth. And the name of Dyaus became paramount[888] to all other Gods in Vind'yu and eastern Par'si'e; and the name Te-in, in Jaffeth, and the name Lord God, in Arabin'ya. And these peoples now had a new sacred book given to them. And yet all of these names represented one angel only, Anuhasaj, a one-time mortal.

25/15.19. Prior to this the Faithists on earth were taught non-resistance; to ignore leadership; to return good for evil, and to dwell together as brethren.

25/15.20. But now, because of the decrees of Anuhasaj, alias De'yus, Faithists were led astray, becoming warriors, and aspiring to become kings and rulers.

25/15.21. Nevertheless, many of them still called themselves by names signifying Faithists, but changing their belief from the Great Spirit to a God in shape and figure[889] of a man, with attributes like a mortal.

25/15.22. And mortals in these countries made images of cherubims and seraphims, having flaming swords; and images of Anubis holding a pair of scales; the same as is made to this day, and called Justice.

25/15.23. In addition to these earthly decrees, Anuhasaj, alias the Lord God, made heavenly decrees between his own kingdom and the kingdoms of his Gods. The chief decrees were: That, for the first one hundred years, all angels borne up out of the earth shall fall into their respective divisions, and shall belong as subjects to my Gods, to be appropriated by them in their own way.

25/15.24. That after the hundredth year, my Gods shall deliver to me one-tenth of their subjects of the highest grades.

25/15.25. De'yus made two hundred laws in reference to the kingdoms of his Gods, concerning such things as their boundaries and ornamentation, providing great pageantry and countless numbers of heralds, staff-bearers, musicians, and players of oratory (theatricals), besides innumerable servants

---

[888] highest ranking; first; chief; dominant; foremost

[889] likeness, representation

and decorators, so that the pageantry could be in great splendor.

25/15.26. When he had completed these forms and system of government, he sent an invitation to his Gods to again feast with him, so that they might ratify his laws and receive them.

25/15.27. And it came to pass that the laws of De'yus were thus ratified and accepted by the Gods; and they went away rejoicing, returning to their respective kingdoms, where they fell to work at once to provide themselves in their glory.

CHAPTER 16 Wars

25/16.1. Thus was established the CONFEDERACY OF SELFS; that is, the false Lord God, and his false Gods, were as many kingdoms united into one; yet every God was secretly sworn to himself, for his own glory.

25/16.2. The time from the beginning of the revolt until it was completed as a confederacy was sixty-four days, and the number of inhabitants in these heavens at that time was eight billion men, women and children. And they were well ordered, in nurseries, hospitals, schools, colleges and factories, and in surveying, building ships, road-making, and all other types of occupations that belong to the lower heavens, objective and subjective. Four billion of these were presently sent to Hored, to De'yus.

25/16.3. De'yus at once began the work laid out, and issued a decree commanding the destruction of all otevans and other vessels plying to the upper plateau, Craoshivi; and commanding the seizing and destroying of fire-ships or other vessels that might come from the upper regions down to the lower. De'yus said: My people shall not ascend to other heavens. I have made the earth and this heaven sufficient for all happiness and glory. Whoever builds a vessel, saying: I will ascend; or if he does not say, but my judges discover him, he shall be cast into the hadan region prepared for him. And if a man or a woman preaches in my heavens, saying: Behold, there is a higher heaven, that person shall be cast into hell, as my son (Anubi) judges.

25/16.4. And I, De'yus, command the locking up of all the books in the libraries of my heavens that in any way teach of Jehovih or Ormazd, or of heavenly kingdoms above mine or greater. For I, the Lord God, will have only one kingdom, and I will draw all people into it to abide with me forever.

25/16.5. And my Gods, marshals, generals and captains, shall take their hosts and go throughout the regions of Hored, and make a clean roadway, and cut off all connection with the outer kingdoms. And they shall place in the roadway around my heavens a standing army, sufficient to guard my kingdom and my Gods' kingdoms forever. And no man-angel, nor woman-angel, shall pass outward beyond my roadway forever. ||

25/16.6. These things were carried out, except for the libraries. But four thousand otevans and other ascending ships were destroyed; and of places for manufacturing ships for the outer heavens, more than seven hundred were destroyed. Consequently, seven hundred million men and women were thrown out of employment! And many of these were compelled to go to Hored, where they were sorted by grade, and put to work, beautifying the capital, the Council house, and the palace of the false Lord God. Others were impressed into the standing army, being allotted seasons and years.

25/16.7. After the outward extreme of hada was thus secured in every way, De'yus turned to the interior. He said: Now I will hide away any textbooks in my heavenly places that relate to higher kingdoms or to Jehovih; for, from this time forward, He is my enemy and I am His. Upon my own self I have sworn it; the name of Jehovih and of Ormazd shall be destroyed in heaven and earth; and my name, De'yus, even the Lord God, shall stand above all else.

25/16.8. For sixty days, the armies of destruction traversed the lowest heavens, high and low, far and near; and they hid away many of the records, books and maps relating to the higher atmospherea and to the etherean worlds beyond; and in sixty days the work of destruction was complete in these heavens, and there was nothing left within sight to prove or to teach of the higher heavens, or of Jehovih, the Ormazd.

25/16.9. The Lord God, the false, said: Let my name and my place, Hored, replace those destroyed, for I will make the name De'yus rule in one-half of the world, and the name Lord God rule in the other half.

25/16.10. The inhabitants of heaven and earth shall know where to find me, and shall behold my person, and witness the strength of my hands. Yes, they shall know my pleasure and my displeasure, and serve me in fear and trembling.

25/16.11. And the books in the schools and colleges of these heavens were thus made to rate De'yus and the Lord God as the All Highest, Most Sacred, Most Holy.

25/16.12. When these things were established thus far, De'yus gave a great feast, and he invited all the valorous fighters and destroyers that had proved themselves great in fulfilling his commandments. In the meantime, the laborers and officers in charge had extended and beautified the palace and capital of the Lord God in Hored beyond anything ever seen in these heavens, so that at the time of this feast, the place was already one of magnificence and glory. And so great were the order, temper and discipline of the more than one million officers and servants who had charge of preparing and conducting the feast, that the assembled Gods, great generals, governors, marshals and captains did nothing for a long while but ejaculate applause and astonishment.

25/16.13. Besides these, De'yus had provided fifty thousand receiving hosts, five hundred thousand es'enaurs and trumpeters, and one hundred thousand proclaiming heralds; and these latter, when conducting the distinguished visitors into the presence of De'yus, proclaimed them amid the applause of the Holy Council, such honor surpassing anything that any of them had ever witnessed.

25/16.14. The substance of the feast, being above grade twenty, which was above the animal region, was, consequently, of vegetable and fruit es'pa[890] from the earth, previously brought by trained shippers and workers, for this special occasion. But there was no es'pa of flesh or fish present on the tables; but an abundance of the es'pa of wine, and this was called Su-be (Nectar of the Gods).

25/16.15. The walls of the chamber of the feast were ornamented with sprays of colored fire, and from the floor of the chamber innumerable fountains of perfume rose upward, which were also es'pa brought up from the earth, and forced up in the fountains by more than one million servants, impressed into service from the regions of shippers, which had been previously destroyed.

25/16.16. The number of guests at the feast totaled one thousand two hundred, aside from the Lord God and his Gods; and the feast lasted one whole day, and the Gods and guests ate and drank to their hearts' content, and there were not a few who felt the intoxication of the rich nectar.

25/16.17. When the feast was over, De'yus, through his marshals, signified that he would speak before them; and when quiet was restored, he said: What greater joy has anyone in a matter than to make others happy! Because you served me, doing my commandments, behold, I have served you. My feast has been your feast; I have given my substance to you, so that you may rejoice in the glory I have received from your hands.

25/16.18. Yet do not think that the Lord, your God, ends this proceeding so: I will not end it so. I have commanded you here so that I may honor those who deserve honor from me, your God. My Gods also have great exaltation in the labor you have done in my heavens, for my heavens are their heavens, and yours also. Because you have destroyed the ascension, the most worthless and foolish of things, and cleared away the rubbish of my heavens, you have also prepared a place for endless glory for yourselves.

25/16.19. For which reason, and in justice to you, I have appointed this time to promote all of you, according to your great achievements. Nor shall you fall back on my promotion, resting in ease; for I have a greater labor for you, as well as greater honor and glory.

25/16.20. Behold, I have commanded the earth and her dominions; and you, my Gods, shall subjugate her to my name and power. And you who have proved yourselves most valiant in heaven shall be their chosen officers to go down to the earth in my name, with millions of my heavenly soldiers, to plan and fix the way of mortals to my hand. As you have cast out the names Jehovih and Ormazd in heaven, even so shall you cast them out on the earth.

25/16.21. Remember, I am a God of anger; I have declared war against all ungodliness on the earth. Whoever worships the Great Spirit under the

---

[890] spiritual food carried up from the earth. – 1891 glossary. [The spiritual emanation of earthly fruits is sometimes called es'pa. –Ed.]

name Jehovih or Ormazd, shall be put to death, both men and women. Only little children shall be spared, and of them you shall make slaves and eunuchs and whatever else that shall profit my kingdoms.

25/16.22. All idols shall be destroyed, whether they are of stone, wood, gold or copper. Neither shall it save them to make an idol of the Unseen; for that is even more offensive in my sight than the others. Nor will I leave one Faithist alive on the face of the earth.

25/16.23. To accomplish this, my Gods shall select from you who are here at my feast; they shall choose according to their rank; and when you are thus divided and selected, you shall receive badges from my hand, and go with my Gods to the places and service they desire.

25/16.24. And when you get down to the earth, you shall possess the oracles and places of worship, driving away all other angels, Gods, Lords and familiars. And when mortals come to consult the spirits you shall answer them in your own way in order to carry out my commandments.

25/16.25. And when you find prophets and seers, who accomplish by the Unseen, who have with them spirits belonging to the kingdom of Craoshivi, you shall drive away such spirits and obsess the prophet or seer in your own way. But if you cannot drive away the Ormazdian angel, then you shall go to the depths of hell in hada and bring a thousand spirits of darkness, who are foul and well skilled in torment, and you shall cast them upon that prophet until he is mad. But if the prophet or seer is so protected that spirits of darkness cannot reach him, then you shall send evil spirits in advance of him to the place he frequents, and they shall inoculate the place with virus that shall poison him to death.

25/16.26. But if a prophet of Jehovih repents and renounces the Great Spirit, and accepts De'yus, or the Lord God, then you shall drive all evil away from him, and put a guard around him, for he shall be my subject in time to come.

25/16.27. And whether you reach a king of the earth by means of the oracles, or through prophets and seers, or by obsession, it does not matter; but you shall come to him by some means, either when he lies asleep, or is awake, and you shall inspire him with the doctrines and the love of the Lord your God. And he shall rise up in great war, and pursue all people who do not profess De'yus, or the Lord your God; for he shall be an instrument in your hands to do my will. ||

25/16.28. When De'yus ceased speaking, the Gods immediately made their selections, and the generals and captains were thus allotted to new places. And now the attendants carried away the tables of the feast, and the Gods, each with his captains and generals, formed twelve rows facing De'yus; and De'yus conferred badges upon them, as previously promised.

25/16.29. De'yus then departed to the Council chamber, and took his seat on the throne. The guests, and Gods and Councilors, entered the south gate, and went and stood in the middle of the floor of the chamber; here the Lord God saluted them, WARRIORS OF GOD, and they embraced in the SIGN OF TAURUS, signifying, TO ENFORCE RIGHTEOUSNESS, for the image of a bull was one of the signs above the throne. (And this was called the EDICT OF THE BULL.)

25/16.30. These, then, are the names of the Gods and Goddesses, with their generals and captains, who were empowered in heaven to go down to the earth to subjugate it to the false Lord God:

25/16.31. The Gods and Goddesses were: Anubi; Hikas, now called Te-in; Wotchissij, now called Sudga; Che-le-mung, now called Osiris; Baal, Ashtaroth, Foe-be, Hes-loo, He-loo, Orion, Hebe and Valish.

25/16.32. Their generals were: Hoin, Oo-da, Jah, Knowteth, June, Pluton-ya, Loo-Chiang, Wahka, Posee-ya-don, Dosh-to, Eurga-roth, Neuf, Apollo-ya, Suts, Karusa, Myion, Hefa-yis-tie, Petoris, Ban, Ho-jou-ya, Mung-jo, Ura-na, Oke-ya-nos, Egupt, Hi-ram, T'cro-no, Ares, Yube, Feh-tus, Don, Dan, Ali-jah, Sol, Samern, Thu-wowtch, Hua-ya, Afro-dite, Han, Weel, Haing-le, Wang-le, Ar-ti-mis, Ga-songya, Lowtha, Pu, Tochin-woh, To-gow, Ben, Aa-ron, Nais-wiche, Gai-ya, Te-sin, Yu-be, Argo, Hadar, Atstsil, E-shong, Daridrat, Udan, Nadar, Bog-wi, She-ug-ga, Brihat, Zeman, Asrig, Oyeb, Chan-lwang, Sishi, Jegat, At-ye-na, and Dyu.

25/16.33. Their captains were: Penbu, Josh, Yam-yam, Holee-tsu, Yoth, Gamba, Said, Drat-ta, Yupe-set, Wag, Mar, Luth, Mak-ka, Chutz, Hi-rack-to, Vazenno, Hasuck, Truth, Maidyar, Pathemadyn, Kop, Cpenta-mainyus, Try-sti-ya, Peter, Houab, Vanaiti, Craosha, Visper, Seam,

Plow-ya, Yact-ta-roth, Abua, Zaotha, Kacan-cat, Hovain, Myazd-Loo, Haur, Abel, Cpenista, Isaah, Vazista, Potonas, Kiro, Wiska-dore, Urvash, Ashesnoga, Cavo, Kalamala-hoodon, Lutz-rom, Wab, Daeri, Kus, Tsoo-man-go, and Le-Wiang.

25/16.34. Besides these, there were one thousand officers of lower rank; and now, when they were sealed as to rank and place and allotment, they withdrew; and De'yus gave a day of recreation so that the Gods with their officers could select from the multitude, their private soldiers.

25/16.35. And in one day's time the armies were made up, totaling three billion angels, and they departed down to the earth to destroy the Faithists and the names Jehovih and Ormazd, and establish De'yus, otherwise the Lord God, the false.

CHAPTER 17 Wars

25/17.1. God, in Craoshivi, bewailed heaven and earth. He said: Great Jehovih, how I have failed in Your kingdom! Behold, You gave into my keeping the earth and her heavens, and they have gone astray!

25/17.2. Jehovih said: Behold the plan of My government; which is, to come against nothing in heaven or earth; to seize nothing by the head and turn it around by violence to go the other way.

25/17.3. Though I am the power that created them, and am the Ever Present that moves them along, I gave to them to be Gods, like Myself,[891] with liberty to find their own direction.

25/17.4. I created many trees in My garden, the greatest of which is the tree of happiness. And I called out to all the living to come and dwell in the shade of that tree, and partake of its fruits and its perfumes. But they run after prickers[892] and they scourge[893] themselves; and then, alas, they fall to cursing Me, and accusing Me of shortness in My government.

25/17.5. I confined them in their mother's womb [i.e., the earth –Ed.] for a season, showing them there is a time for all things. But they run forward hurriedly, desiring speedy happiness and wisdom, without halting to observe My glories by the roadside.

25/17.6. I said to them: Even as I have given liberty to all My people, so shall you not impress (force) into your service your brothers and sisters. But the self-assuming Gods make slaves of their fellows; they build roads round about,[894] and station armies of soldiers to prevent My newborn from coming to My most glorious kingdoms.

25/17.7. They go down to the earth and inspire kings, queens and rich men, to do the same things. And they portion out to their servants, saying to them: Serve me, and I will provide for you. Little do they think their servants will become like thorns, stones, chains and spears against them in the far future. They build up a justice of their own, saying: To the extent that my servants labor for me, so will I render to them. || But I have said to them, that no man shall serve another except for love, which shall be his only recompense.

25/17.8. The king and the queen of the earth, and the rich man, shut their own eyes against Me, thinking that by doing so, I cannot see them; they flatter themselves that in heaven they will give the slip to[895] their servants. But I sowed a seed of bondage in My garden, and I said: Whoever binds another, shall himself be bound. And behold, when they are risen in heaven, their servants and their soldiers come upon them; their memory is like a troubled dream that will not depart from them.

25/17.9. Nevertheless, even with these great examples before them, there are still angels in hada who have not learned from this. For they say to themselves: I will build a great kingdom in heaven; I will become the mightiest of Gods; millions of angels shall serve me; I will shut out the Great Spirit and His distant heavens; I will wall my place

---

[891] Note this does not mean that Jehovih is a God per se, which is, after all, merely an office and rank of great attainment, but rather that He encompasses the highest best attributes of a God, and, so, becomes the model upon which Gods base themselves. And in that sense, He is the God of Gods—but not in their form and figure (i.e., He is neither shaped like an angel nor is He an angel).

[892] prickles, thorns, barbs, thistles, briars

[893] inflict pain and suffering onto

[894] here and there; in the vicinity; surrounding

[895] smoothly outmaneuver in a deft and stealthy way; to escape from

around with an army of soldiers, and with fire and water.

25/17.10. As a libertine steals an unsuspicious damsel to abuse her; and, in time, she wakes up to the matter only to curse him, so do the false Gods steal upon the inhabitants of My places and carry them into bondage. But the light of My understanding dwells in the souls of My little ones; it waits for the spring sun; and it will spring up and grow into a mighty tree to accuse these Gods. ||

25/17.11. God inquired concerning warfare.

25/17.12. Jehovih said: I answer all things by good. To the good at heart I give good thoughts, desires and holy observations. To the perverse of heart I hold up My glories and the beneficence[896] of virtue and peaceful understanding. To those who practice charity[897] and good works to others, not laboring for self, I give the highest delight. Though they are pricked in the flesh with poverty and wicked persecutions, yet their souls are like the waters of a smooth-running river. Among those who practice evil, destruction and war, I send emissaries of benevolence and healing, who have plenteous[898] words of pity.

25/17.13. These are My arrows, spears and war-clubs, O God: Pity, gentle words and the example of tenderness. Sooner or later, these shall triumph over all things in heaven and earth.

25/17.14. Behold, these wars in hada and on the earth will continue more than a thousand years. And the inhabitants will go down in darkness, even to the lowest darkness. For which reason, you and your successors shall not provide hastily, as if the matter will change with the wind. But you shall organize a new army of deliverers for My Faithists, and it shall have two branches, one for the earth and one for hada. And the business of your army shall be to rescue My people from those who seek to destroy them. And as to the spirits of the dead who were Faithists on the earth, you shall provide means of transportation and bring them to your new kingdom, which you shall call At-ce-wan, where you shall provide a sub-God, and officers, and attendants, hundreds of millions.

25/17.15. And in At-ce-wan, you shall provide the sub-God with nurseries, hospitals, factories, schools, colleges and such other houses and places of instruction as are required in the kingdoms of My Lords in hada.

25/17.16. And when you have this matter in good working order, you shall speak before your Holy Council; in My name you shall speak to them in this manner: Jehovih has called for two hundred thousand volunteers; I am commanded by Him to find them; and they shall be wise and strong, and without fear. For they shall be angel-preachers in Jehovih's name to go down to Hored, the place of De'yus, the Lord God the false, and to the kingdoms of his Gods; and their labor shall be to preach and proclaim the Father and His glories in the etherean worlds.

25/17.17. And my preachers shall not say one word against the Lord God nor his Gods; but rather the other way; by majesty of Jehovih's love, be loving towards them and their officers and subjects. For by this means my preachers shall have peaceful dwellings in these warring kingdoms; and thus their voices shall have great weight. For the greatest wisdom of a great diplomat is not to be too opposite or too vehement, but conciliating.[899]

25/17.18. Jehovih said: And your preachers shall travel constantly in the lowest kingdoms, teaching and explaining My boundless worlds, sowing the seed of aspiration with the wise and with the ignorant, and especially with the enslaved.

25/17.19. And to as many as become converted, and desire to ascend to Craoshivi, you shall say: Go to the border of your kingdom, where the Father's laborers have a ship to take you to His kingdom. But your preachers shall not go with them, lest they excite suspicion or hate, but continue on preaching

---

[896] blessings, benefits, unselfishness, giving nature, generosity, kindness, good feelings, goodness

[897] upliftment, warm-heartedness, kindness, understanding, tolerance, empathy, aid, relief, helpfulness, refreshment, generosity, compassion, altruism, goodwill, benevolence, sympathy, consideration, magnanimity, mercy, forgiveness, comfort, supportiveness, courtesy, politeness, attentiveness, responsiveness, pity, caring, mildness, tenderness, gentleness, temperance, self-control, virtue, love, etc.

[898] plentiful, ample, copious

[899] to win over by pleasant demeanor, friendly actions, agreeable reasoning and mutual concessions; conciliatory; and being respectful, patient, peaceable, inoffensive and reconciling

and inciting the slaves to ascend to higher and holier heavens. ||

25/17.20. Then God, of Craoshivi, fell to work to carry out the commandments of Jehovih. And his Council labored with him. At-ce-wan was established and Yotse-hagah was made the sub-God, with a Holy Council of one hundred thousand angels, and with a thousand attendants and fifty thousand messengers. He was provided with a capital and throne, and with one million ship-makers and builders of mansions.

25/17.21. After that, God and the Council of Craoshivi organized all the armies as commanded by Jehovih. And in these armies, all told, there were one billion seven hundred million two hundred and eight thousand five hundred and sixty, [900] all of whom were above grade fifty, and some as high as ninety.

25/17.22. And it so happened that these organizations were completed and in working order two days prior to De'yus and his hosts beginning their war on the earth. But the Faithist angels were distributed mostly in hada and the regions above. So that when the three billion hosts of De'yus descended to the earth, only four hundred thousand Faithist angels were there, in addition to the ashars who were in regular service.

CHAPTER 18 Wars

Of the battles of the Gods for the dominion of the earth and the lowest heavens; and these were called battles of a thousand years

25/18.1. De'yus was no slow hand; not a dull God. He had two thousand seven hundred years' experience, and his soul was quick and strong in mighty works. He did not rush in without first measuring the way, most deliberately and with great wisdom.

25/18.2. At first he felt his way along, doing as if by proxy Jehovih's commands,[901] in order to humor[902] the populace, till his flattered Gods and officers safely fell into his dominion and power, then boldly launching forth: I, the Lord God, command!

25/18.3. The very audaciousness of which overcame his friends' judgment, and made them believe for a fact that De'yus was the foremost and greatest, mighty God. To do whose will, and reverently applaud his name, was the surest road to home laurels.[903]

25/18.4. To win great majesty to himself, and after having sworn to devastate the whole earth in order to establish the name De'yus, and Lord God, he called to his side his five chief friends: the Gods, Hikas, falsely named Te-in; Wotchissij, falsely named Sudga; Che-le-mung, falsely named Osiris; and Baal and Ashtaroth. And in dignity De'yus spoke to them:

25/18.5. It is well, my Gods, that you stand about and watch the battles; but let your generals and high captains go forth and mingle in the bloody work. In your kingdoms be constantly upraising your magnificence, and at times sallying forth to the earth valiantly, as when kings, queens and prophets are about to win a victory, or be plunged into mortal death, to show how your august presence turned the tide of battle. Then immediately return in dignity to your thrones, leaving your officers and inspiring hosts to continue on in the game of mortal tragedy.

25/18.6. Then he who was falsely named Osiris, spoke, saying: To exalt your name, O De'yus, my Lord God; and to persuade mortals that you, of all created beings, can stand in Hored, and by your will, control the victory to whoever applauds you and praises your name. You will be the bond of my solemn oath, so that I will lose or win battles on the earth according to whether they honor you, and despise the Great Spirit or any other God or Lord.

25/18.7. Then Te-in, also falsely named, said: To keep mortals in constant war for a thousand years; to teach them that battles are won or lost according to the loudest call and praise to you, O De'yus, I will be like an ever-renewed oath taken under your thigh.

25/18.8. Sudga,[904] the false, said: By all my parts, in order to shape the arms and legs of the

---

[900] i.e., 1,700,208,560; this is one of the few places where the Oahspe authors give an exact figure rather than rounding off

[901] that is, he acted as if he were doing what Jehovih would do, or would approve of

[902] cater to the sentiments of; generally please

[903] honor and glory; recognition bringing fame and (self) advancement

[904] recall that Sudga means Apollo

unborn in comeliness, my legions shall drum into the ears of pregnant women for a thousand years, swearing them to your name, O De'yus; or, if refusing, to curse with crookedness all their progeny. And when these mothers sleep, my legions shall find their souls in their dreams, and give them delight or torment, according to whether they, when awake, applaud you, my most mighty Lord God.

25/18.9. Baal said: To overturn the oracles of Jehovih, and to make the prophets and seers receive and announce your name, O De'yus, my Lord God of heaven and earth, I have already sworn more than ten thousand oaths.

25/18.10. Ashtaroth said: The work of my legions shall be to deal death to your enemies, O De'yus. To those who raise the name Jehovih, or Ormazd, or Great Spirit, my legions shall carry foul smells into their noses while they sleep. And to your enemies, who happen to win a battle against your people, my legions shall carry inoculation from the rotten dead; they shall carry the virus in the air to the breath of those who will not bow down to the name, Lord God!

25/18.11. De'yus answered them, saying: As spoken, so shall these things be; I, the Lord your God, command. Send forth your generals and high captains thus decreed; to each and every one sufficient armies to make manifest[905] these, our high resolves. Into three great armies my legions shall be divided for the earth battles: one to Jaffeth, one to Vind'yu, and one to Arabin'ya and the regions lying west and north.[906] Of the latter, you, Osiris, shall have chief command; and you, Baal, and you, Ashtaroth, you two, so linked in love and one purpose, shall be the earth managers to Osiris' will. For your efficient service, behold, I have given you these high-raised generals and captains: Jah, Pluton-ya, Apollo-ya, Petoris, Hi-ram, T'cro-no, Egupt, Ares, Yu-be, Ali-jah, Afro-dite, Ar-ti-mis, Ben, Aa-ron, Argo, Atstsil, Nadar and Oyeb, besides Peter, Yact-ta-roth, Haur, Abel, Said, Josh and Wab, who shall be the conquering spirits to play on both sides in battles, urging stubborn mortals on to religious feud till both sides fall in death, or till one bows down in fear and reverence to me and my Gods. And they shall sing their names in mortal ears day and night, and teach them to live in praise of the Lord, your God, the De'yus of heaven and earth, and to be most daring in the overthrow of Jehovih, most hated of Gods.

25/18.12. To you, Te-in, another third of my legions is committed, to deal with the land of giants (Jaffeth), and urge them on in the same way, to greatness or to death, doing honor and reverence to me and my kingdoms. High raised are your generals: Wah-ka, Ho-jou-ya, Oke-ya-nos, Thu-wowtch, Haing-le, Tochin-woh, To-gow and Eurga-roth, besides Yam-yam, Hi-rack-to, Kacan-cat, Isaah, Lutz-rom and Le-Wiang, and others of high grade and power.

25/18.13. And to you, O Sudga, in like manner I have given another third of my legions to play battles with mortals for a thousand years. Like Osiris and Te-in, to set mortals up in war, and move them one way and then another, and thus plunge them into each other's bloody arms and death. So that they may learn to know in truth they are only machines and playthings in the hands of angels and Gods; that they are worked like clay in a potter's hand, till they cry out: Enough! I will bow my head to God, who is Lord over all, great De'yus. Yes, more, I will fight for him and drink even my brother's blood, if only De'yus will prosper me and mine in slaying Faithists, fool-worshippers of Ormazd, the Unseen and Scattered Wind. To De'yus, in likeness of a man, with head, legs and arms in boundary and size of a man, sitting on a throne in Hored; to him, the great Lord God, I will always bow in reverence.

25/18.14. And you, O Sudga, shall play war in Vind'yu with the most numerous, highest learned people of the earth. For which purpose you shall have these, my high-raised generals and captains: Asrig, Gai-ya, Nais-wiche, Samern, Yube, Sol, Mung-jo, Don, Hefa-yis-tie, Lowtha, Daridrat, Udan, Brihat, Bog-wi, E-shong, Weel, Vanaiti, Plow-ya, Vazista, Kiro, Cpenista, Visper, Cpenta-mainyus and Urvash, and many others, most determined to rescue the earth from the dominion of far-off Gods.

25/18.15. De'yus continued: Go forth you Gods, and in majesty build your thrones; in great splendor ornament your high places, so that even the magnificence shall be like a million preachers' tongues proclaiming the heavens' well-chosen Gods. And as fast as mortals fall in battle, gather

[905] real, demonstrable, concrete, substantial

[906] Heleste and Par'si'e

the spirits of the dead into groups, not letting them lie in chaos, but for pity's sake bring them to your kingdoms in easy riding ships. And once there, apply your physicians and nurses diligently, to restore them to their senses and new condition; and when they wake up in the heavens,[907] seeing the great glory of your thrones and kingdoms, initiate them by solemn rites and ceremonies to sworn servitude to yourselves and to me, your Lord God, to inherit such bounteous kingdoms.

25/18.16. And as you shall thus despoil those of earth, to make them know my power and yours, so shall you pursue those newly arrived in heaven, to make them swear solemnly against Jehovih, the Great Spirit, the Ormazd, and against all other Gods; but if they stubbornly refuse, though in heaven, even as they did on earth, take them before my son, Anubi, who shall further examine them; but if they still refuse, then Anubi, with his strong guard and brands (sticks) of fire, shall send them down into hell.

25/18.17. I, the Lord God, have spoken; my commandments have gone forth in heaven and earth; whoever praises and glorifies me, with everlasting service for the exaltation and glory of my kingdoms, shall enter into everlasting happiness; but whoever will not bow down to me shall be cast into everlasting torments.

CHAPTER 19 Wars

Of the hosts of Osiris, the false

25/19.1. Now sallied forth the captains, generals, and well-disciplined hosts of hada, the angels of De'yus, bent on independence for the earth and heaven from all other rulers except the Lord God, and to establish him forever. Foremost of the three mighty divisions was Osiris' army, of more than a billion angels, going forth boldly to cover the great lands of the earth: Arabin'ya, Par'si'e and Heleste.

25/19.2. In the front, dashing madly on, was Baal, and next to him, his assistant Goddess, Ashtaroth, followed by their first attendants and high exalted officers. Some of whom displayed: Great maps of mortal cities and cultured lands, where the peaceful worshippers of Jehovih dwelt, hundreds of thousands of them. And the lists of altars and temples to the Great Spirit, where the righteous came daily and deposited their earnings and products as sacrifices for benefit of the weak and helpless. And the wide fields, where toilers religiously brought out of the earth, wheat, flax, cotton and barley, as gifts from the Great Spirit. And the canals filled with boats, carrying produce, fruit and cloth, in interchange, one district with another. And the mounds and tree-temples of the I'hins, the sacred people, small, white and yellow;[908] the forefathers and foremothers of the great I'huan race, the half-breeds between the brown burrowers in the earth and the I'hins.

25/19.3. Over these maps, charts, and lists, the generals and captains discoursed as they descended to the rolling earth; most learnedly laying plans to overturn Jehovih's method, and build up De'yus, the God of Hored.

25/19.4. Osiris himself, to display such dignity as becomes[909] a great God, halted in his heavenly place, now headquarters of the belligerents. And so he rested on his throne, with his tens of thousands of messengers ready to answer his summons, and bear his will to the remotest parts of his mighty army, and to return, bringing him news of the nature of the proceedings. And between Osiris' and De'yus' thrones another long line of messengers extended, being a thousand angels, high raised and resolute, suitable to travel in the ever-changing atmospherean belts of great velocity.

25/19.5. Beside Baal, on the downward course to the earth, but a little behind him, woman-like, was Ashtaroth, with her thousand attendants, all accoutered[910] to show their high esteem for their warring Goddess. By the often-changing wave of her hand, her part of the army had learned to know her will, and most zealously observe her commands.

25/19.6. And now, on every side, farther than the eye could see, the billion rushed on, some in boats, some in ships and otevans, and others in single groups, descending. As one can imagine an earthly kite sufficient to carry its holder high up in

[907] i.e., as each awakes in one of the various false heavens

[908] Again, this is a generalization; recall, e.g., that Arabin'ya had I'hins of all colors (see 19/3.4).

[909] suits, befits, matches, puts in the best light, reveals, shows, demonstrates

[910] equipped and outfitted

the wind, so, reversed, and single-handed, hundreds of thousands flew toward the earth by ballast flags, the most daring of angels.[911]

25/19.7. Toward the earth they came as if on a frolic, full of jokes and loud boasting, sworn and swearing to forever clear the earth of Jehovih's worshippers. Many of them, long trained in the schools, colleges and factories of heaven, were only too glad for a change of scenes and labor, all having been promised by their superiors that with this campaign, they were taking their first lessons in becoming Gods and Goddesses; and thousands and thousands hoped to accomplish some daring deed, in order to gain sudden promotion.

25/19.8. To the east and west, and north and south, Baal and Ashtaroth spread out their armies, wide as the three great lands they had sworn to subdue to the Lord God, who, of woman born, was the most presuming son the earth had yet brought forth. And the theme and project was to alight on the earth, to flood the temples and altars with so great an abundance of spirits as would drive Jehovih's ashars into disastrous confusion, and vanquish them. The temptation of promotion caused the warriors on every side to strive with their utmost speed and power, desiring to be foremost[912] in so great a work.

25/19.9. Which Jehovih foresaw, and so, spoke to God in Craoshivi, warning him. Accordingly, due observance of the danger had been communicated, by messengers, to the managing angels in the altars and temples of worship. And these, through the rab'bahs and the oracles, had spread the caution far and wide among mortals regarding the threatened dangers.

25/19.10. Thus Jehovih's angels fortified themselves, through the faith of mortals, and held on, bringing together their scanty numbers, knowing well that by Jehovih's law they must not resist by arms, but only through words and good example, high-toned by faith in the Father over all.

[911] When Oahspe was written, parachutes, hang gliders (and flying machines) had not been invented, yet here they are described as we know them today. –cns ed.

[912] first, at the front, eye-catching, outstanding, distinguished above all others, most important, indispensable, dominant

25/19.11. Down, down, down on these, on every side came the billion destroying hosts; with oaths and loud clamor rushing for the altars and temples; flying suddenly to the holy arcs; in hundreds of thousands of places, shouting:

25/19.12. Leave this arc! Vacate this altar! Depart this temple! You Jehovihian usurpers, be gone! In the name of the Lord our God! We command!

25/19.13. But alas for them, every arc, every altar, and every temple to Jehovih was invincible. So strong in faith stood His angels, unmoved and majestic, that even the assailing spirits halted, overawed. And as they stood a moment contemplating, wondering where such great majesty came from that it could manifest in such a lowly place, the Jehovihians made this reply:

25/19.14. We bow in adoration to none but Great Jehovih! Whose Very Self contributed to make us what we are, His servants in doing good to others with all our wisdom and strength! In Him we stand to shield His helpless ones by virtuous peace and harmonious love. For what reason, then, do you come in arrogance, demanding our wards to service of your God, born of woman?

25/19.15. The Osirians said: Fly, O sycophants![913] You who bow down in fear and trembling to One as hollow as the wind, and Personless. Too long have earth and heaven been cajoled[914] by far-off foreign Gods, who come here to win subjects for their kingdoms' glory, using that pitiful tale of an Ever Presence Over All, Whom none have seen or known. Be gone! Give us these earthly anchorages! To build earth and heaven in unity, ruled over, along with ourselves, by Gods we know and revere!

25/19.16. The Jehovihians said: Is this your only power? By threats and commands? O harmless words, in mockery of truthful Gods! You of no good works or promises, except to exalt the self of earth and hada, and glorify your masters, born only equal with yourselves. Why not rush in and carry us off, you who are a thousand to one, and by your deeds prove the great source from which you draw your power?

[913] overly servile persons given to hollow flattery; obsequious dupes; fawning parasites

[914] wheedled, sweet-talked, coaxed, inveigled, lured, enticed, tricked

25/19.17. The Osirians said: To give you a chance of liberty, to save you from the Savior's judgment, Anubi, who shall cast you into hell, we hoped to find your willing departure in peace. Behold, then, we will wall this altar around and shut off the attendant ashars with mortals, and flood the place with drujas, to obsess them to total madness. If, then, you love your wards as you profess, abandon all to us, for the glory of De'yus, whose son is Osiris, our commanding God.

25/19.18. The Jehovihians said: Words! Words! Words! You had no explanation at first, only your command. Now, behold, an argument! And presently you will withdraw, deceived in what your commanding Gods told you would result. We tell you we will not leave, except by orders from our superiors, who are Jehovih's, rightly raised to precedence.[915]

25/19.19 The Osirians said: For which reason, behold our Lord God, who was honored in the title through Jehovih's hand; whom you should obey according to your oaths.

25/19.20. The Jehovihians said: Until the Lord God put aside Jehovih, we were his; but when for his self-glory he denied his Creator, his false position freed us from obligation to him. To obey him now, would make us false to Jehovih, and forever weaken us in reaching the Nirvanian kingdoms.

25/19.21. But now the clamoring Osirian angels in the background crowded forward menacingly, and the tide rose to the highest pitch. The morning sun was dawning in the east, a most wonderful assistant to Jehovih's sons in time of battle; and their messengers brought from the fields and country places many ashars who had been on watch all night with sleeping mortals. The Osirians saw them coming; knew the turn, one way or another, was at hand! But by the audacity of the Jehovihians, outnumbered one to a thousand, the Osirians were kept looking on in wonder till the sun's rays pierced their weapons and melted them in their hands.

25/19.22. First one and then another of the Osirians, then tens and hundreds and thousands, turned away or looked about, discomfited, like a host of rioters attempting to assault a few well-trained soldiers, and, becoming frightened, turn and flee harmlessly. So Jehovih's sons and daughters won the victory in the first assault, except in rare instances, one in a hundred, where the Osirians triumphed and got possession.

CHAPTER 20 Wars

25/20.1. All over all the lands, east and west and north and south, of Arabin'ya, Par'si'e and Heleste, stood the discomfited Osirian angels, in groups, tens of thousands, unseen by mortals, and considering how best to proceed to overthrow Jehovih and His worshippers.

25/20.2. Meanwhile, messengers and mapmakers bore the disastrous news to Osiris, who in turn sent word on up to De'yus, the self-Lord God, who now, through Osiris, his most favorite God of power, sent these commands:

25/20.3. When night comes and mortals sleep, my hosts shall fall upon the ashars, the guardian angels, and drive them away, obsessing every man, woman and child, in these great divisions of the earth. What do I care about altars, temples, oracles and arcs? Possess the mortals before tomorrow's morning sun. Hear the command of De'yus, the Lord your God, through his high-raised son, Osiris!

25/20.4. And the well-stationed messengers plied all day long to the near and remote parts of the assaulting armies, giving De'yus' commands. And before the sun went down, the whole billion knew their work, and were wheeled in line, to march with the falling darkness, and pounce furiously upon the ashars of Jehovih.

25/20.5. But the true God, in Craoshivi, had been warned by Jehovih's Voice of the course of events, and he had sent his messengers with all speed down to the earth to warn them of the enemy's designs for that night; which the messengers only just accomplished, for when they completed their most exhaustive work, the sun had already dropped below the west horizon.

25/20.6. So, at the midnight hour, the terrible approach began on all sides; and to each and every guardian spirit, enemies came, in tens, and hundreds, and thousands, shouting: Be gone, you Jehovihian fool! The Lord our God and his son, Osiris, command! Away from your sleeping mortal ward, or by the voice of God we will cast you, bound, at Anubi's feet, food for hell! Be gone!

[915] higher rank; a command office

25/20.7. Each Jehovihian answered: To Great Jehovih I am sworn! Though you bind me and cast me into hell, by the Great Spirit's hand I will free myself and come here again and teach His sacred name. And repeat forever my peaceful mission to raise up this heir of Jehovih!

25/20.8. Again the threatening adversaries stormed, and wondered while they stormed, how one alone could stand so boldly in the face of such great odds and not fly away at once. And every ashar laid his hand on the sleeping mortal in his charge, for by this, his power was multiplied a thousand-fold, and raising up his other hand, he addressed the All Highest: By Your Wisdom and Power, O Jehovih, circumscribe this, Your sleeping heir, so that whoever touches the mortal part shall cut himself off from Your everlasting kingdoms!

25/20.9. And, with the words, a circle of light fell about the place, bewildering to the assaulters, who, having once halted, opened the way to recoil within them, their own cowardice, a most valiant warrior against unrighteous deeds. And so a war of words and arguments ensued, till again the morning sun rose upon the almost harmless assault, and left the Osirians discomfited and ashamed.

25/20.10. Though not in all places, for in some extremes they did not wait for words but rushed in and laid hands on the mortals, gaining sufficient power to hurl clubs, stones, boards, stools or tables about the house, and so roused to wide awake, the mortal occupants. Who, seeing things tumble about by some unseen power, were quickly up and frightened past composure. Some hurried off to the rab'bahs, some to the oracles and temples, to inquire about the trouble between the ruling Gods. ||

25/20.11. And in these few places, once De'yus' spirit-soldiers gained possession, they fastened on in thousands, even quarreling as to who had most honor in the hellish work. And yet not one of the ashars in all the lands was seized or borne away.

25/20.12. And now, as the sun rose, the messengers of the Lord God flew hastily to Osiris' kingdom, where he sat on his throne, expecting news of an overwhelming victory. And when they told him about the most pitiful failure, except in so small a degree, Osiris raved and swore: By my soul, I swear an everlasting curse, that I will fill all the hells in hada with these foolhardy ashars! Yes, even if I have to go down to the earth in person, and with Baal and Ashtaroth go from house to house throughout the world!

25/20.13. Osiris again sent word to De'yus, who was of vast experience, and not so hasty; a wiser God, and better acquainted with the tides in mortal energy to serve Jehovih. So De'yus sent back word to this effect: To rest the soldiers three days, so that the surveyors could measure the stature of mortal faith, and so make the third attack more successful. And he concluded with these words:

25/20.14. Because of the long spiritual peace among mortals, there must be many grown to intellectual disbelief in an All Highest. By groveling down[916] in the earth to measure the rocks, and to study the habits of worms and bugs, for generations, their seed has brought forth many skeptics, believing nothing of spiritual kind, but rating high their own judgment. With these, because of their lack of faith in Jehovih, the ashars are powerless to ward off my soldiers. Mark them out in every city and in all the country places, and again at midnight, fall upon them, crowding away Jehovih's ashars.

25/20.15. Besides these, find the ignorant and superstitious among mortals, who are lazy and of lustful desires, because by their habits the ashars have little power in their presence. Mark these also, and, at midnight, fall upon them and possess them.

25/20.16. And go among the rich, whose sons and daughters are raised in idleness and pleasure; whose thoughts seldom rise to heaven; for the ashars are also weak to protect them, they being most excellent subjects to spirits fond of sporting[917] pleasures. Mark them also, and at midnight fall upon them, driving away the ashars.

25/20.17. For the present, abandon the altars, arcs, temples, oracles and all the strongest, most zealous Faithists; except those few who still flatten the head and are dull in judgment, whom you shall also possess. ||

25/20.18. Accordingly Osiris, Baal and Ashtaroth prepared for the third assault on Jehovih's angels and mortals. Their millions of groups were kept in constant drill, ready for the

---

[916] wallowing or crawling, with faces downward

[917] mischievous; making jest with; to treat as a pawn or plaything; to play for a fool; perhaps engaging in dalliance, libertinism, philandering

work. The first fire and flush of boasting was already gone from them, except for a few, and the serious aspect of a long war stared them in the face.

CHAPTER 21 Wars

25/21.1. Thus lay the three great countries, Arabin'ya, Par'si'e, and Heleste, of which Par'si'e was mightiest, peopled with very giants; lofty-bearing men and women, who were red, copper colored; with an abundance of long black hair; high in the nose and cheek bones; with determined jaws, and eyes to charm and command; mostly full-blooded I'huans, half-breeds between the I'hins and the burrowers in the ground, the brown people, dull and stupid.[918] The Par'si'e'ans were a proud race, built up in great comeliness by the God Apollo (the first), whose high-raised office was to fashion the breeds of mortals into noble forms. Par'si'e was foremost in all great deeds in the world, and in men of learning, and in ancient wars. It was here that great Zarathustra was born and raised for Jehovih's Voice and corporeal words. Here the first great City of the Sun was built, Oas, whose kings aspired to rule the entire world; and it was here where great riches among men were first tolerated by the Gods.

25/21.2. A strip of Par'si'e'an land cut between Jaffeth and Vind'yu, and extended to the sea in the far east; but the great body lay to the west, covering the Afeutian Mountains, still plentiful in lions, tigers and great serpents. Into these mountains the I'huan hunters came to catch lions and tigers to fight in the games, where unarmed men often went into the arena, and fought them with their bare hands, choking them to death before applauding multitudes. From these mountains the hunters supplied the private dens of kings and queens with lions, whose duty was to devour thieves and other prisoners, according to mortal law.

25/21.3. And these traveling hunters often dwelt with the sacred little people in the wilderness, the I'hins, whom Jehovih had taught to charm even the great serpents and savage lions and tigers to be their friends and worshippers. And from these sprang a people called Listians, who, living mostly in the forests, went naked, to whom the I'hins taught the secret of charming and sacred hand power,[919] who worshipped Jehovih, having no man or God as master, for which the Great Spirit named them Shepherd Kings, for they ruled over flocks of goats, which supplied them with milk, butter, cheese, and wool for cloth for crotch-clothes, the only covering they wore.

25/21.4. These Shepherd Kings, the Listians, lived in peace, wandering about, making trinkets, which they often exchanged with the inhabitants of cities and the agricultural regions. One-fourth of the people of Par'si'e were Listians, who were well guarded by Jehovih's angels. And De'yus meant to obsess these for future use in terrible wars; but the other three-fourths of the population lived in the fertile regions of Par'si'e, lands rich in yielding

[918] Again, these are generalizations, being the modes of certain peoples from the distant past; and much commingling has happened since then even as before then. Because every person alive today has all three of I'hin, I'huan and druk lineage in them (whether from the Par'si'e region or from elsewhere), skin color is not indicative, much less determinative, of spiritual grade or intelligence; nor is skin color alone sufficient to determine lineage (see 06/1.16<fn-war>; 06/2.4<fn-stout>; 19/3.4<fn-knowledge>; 22/11.18<fn-years>; 24/24.5<fn-burrowed>).

Note that in Par'si'e, Jaffeth and Arabin'ya, the color of druks was generally brown. And the I'huans were generally copper colored; copper being reddish brown, and somewhere on a continuum from copper brown (brownish copper) to orange-ish copper to yellowish copper to pinkish or reddish copper. Now recall that Ahura in the previous cycle (Fragapatti's cycle) promoted or allowed mixing of races.

Therefore it is wise to keep in mind that there was some mixing between the I'huan and the druk; and although the tendency of this line was to degenerate, nevertheless if the offspring of such a combination was wedded to another I'huan, this could and would bring about brown I'huans capable of upward inspiration. (Recall that by the end of the cycle of Fragapatti, all the races of man were now capable of eternal life, 22/18.13).

[919] To charm is to bring into an agreeable mood, to soothe, to enchant, to captivate, to enthrall, to entrance—perhaps by a chant or song, amulet or talisman, or by using hand motions.

ample harvests. The cities were filled with mills, factories, colleges and common schools, free for all people to come and learn; and altars, temples of worship, and oracle structures made without windows, so Jehovih's angels could come in sar'gis and teach His Holy Doctrines. Also there were temples and observatories for studying the stars, which were mapped out and named even as their names stand to this day. And next to these were the HOUSES OF PHILOSOPHY, in all the cities; where great and learned men undertook to examine into the things of earth, to learn their character and properties. And whether of fish, worm, stone, ores, iron, silver, gold or copper, they had learned to read its worth and nature. And their houses were well filled for the benefit of students and visitors, with things dead and extinct from the earth, and with strange stones, and skins and bones of animals. It was these people that De'yus meant to have his armies possess, body and soul, for his own glory, knowing that by their researches in such matters for many generations they had strayed away from Jehovih. For such is the rule pertaining to all children begotten on the earth. If the father and mother are on the downward road in unbelief, the child will be more so; but if on the upward way, to glorify an All Highest, the child will be holier and wiser than its parents.

25/21.5. In ancient days the Gods had inspired the Par'si'e'ans to migrate toward the west and inhabit the lands of Heleste, also a country of giants, but less given to rites and ceremonies; and they carried with them three languages: the Panic, of Jaffeth; the Vedic, of Vind'yu, and the Par'si'e'an; and because they mostly used the same sounds, but different written characters, a confused language sprang out of these, and was called Fonece, and the people thus speaking were called Foneceans,[920] that is to say: We will use the same sounds, but use whatever written characters we choose according to our judgment. || Hence, Fonece is the first and oldest of mortal-made languages; and this was styled in heaven as the period of the emancipation of mortals from the dictatorship of angels in regard to written signs, characters and words. Jehovih had said: In that respect man on earth has advanced enough to stand alone; and it was so, for, from that time to this, neither Jehovih nor His angels have given any new language or written characters to mortals. And all languages that have come from that time onward, are only combinations, branches, amalgamations and malformations of what existed then on the earth.

25/21.6. The Helestians were rich in agriculture, and in herds of cattle and goats, both wool goats and hair goats; for it was in this country that the angels first taught man how to breed the goats for hair or for wool, accordingly as he desired. And these people were also mostly worshippers of Jehovih, and had many altars and temples; dwelling in peace, and loving righteousness.

25/21.7. Arabin'ya had four kinds of people within her regions: the I'huans, the Listians, the I'hins,[921] and the brown burrowers in the ground, with long noses and projecting mouths, very strong, whose grip of the hands could break a horse's leg. The brown people, though harmless, were naked, living mostly on fish, worms, bugs and roots; and they inhabited the regions of the great river, Tua [Nile –Ed.]. Over these people, to subdue them and destroy them, Osiris allotted his great angel general, Egupt, servant of De'yus. Egupt called the region of his allotment after himself, Egupt, the same that is corruptly called Egypt to this day.

25/21.8. In the time of Abraham this country was called South Arabin'ya; but when, in later years, the great scholars entered the records in the kings' libraries, the later names were used,[922] being

[920] Today's historians, what little they know of them, know these people as the Phoenicians.

[921] Recall that the I'hins, being the little sacred people, the people of spirit light, of Arabin'ya, were of all skin colors, and this included brown I'hins and black I'hins. || The Listians were apparently immigrants from regions east.

[922] This replacing of the old geographical, regional and city names with the Fonecean equivalents is not unusual; in our own corporeal records, when discussing things of Egypt, the Greeks often used the Greek equivalent word instead of the Egyptian word. Historians and writers of Latin and English also did the same thing, as did those of other countries. Thus, for examples, España is what the Spanish call their country, but in English it is called Spain; Deutchland is what the Germans call their country,

written in the Fonecean language and not Eguptian, which was the language of the unlearned.

25/21.9. But the majority of the people in Arabin'ya were I'huans, being similar to the Par'si'e'ans in color, size and figure,[923] for they also were the offspring of the I'hins and the brown earth burrowers,[924] the hoodas, from whom they inherited corporeal greatness, even as from the I'hins they inherited holiness of spirit. But the flat heads had mostly disappeared from Arabin'ya.

Summary Table of Skin Color Modes*

Region	I'hin Color	Druk Color	I'huan Color 6000 bk	Man's Color c.300 bk
Jaffeth	white & yellow	brown	copper-brown	yellowish copper-brown
Par'si'e	white & yellow	brown	reddish copper	light brownish copper
Guatama	white & yellow	black	reddish copper	reddish copper
Arabin'ya	all colors	brown	reddish copper	darkish

* Compiled by the present editor. While this chart cannot show all the range of color, it can serve as an indicator of approximate differences between regions. (See footnote #924.)

---

while in English it is called Germany.

[923] See 25/21.1, which indicates reddish copper; copper is defined in 25/21.1<fn-stupid>.

[924] Looking at statistical modes of color, Oahspe says the druks were black and brown; and one supposes a range or continuum ran from black to brown, although how light the brown was, is not specified; and while I'hins were mainly white and yellow, some were darker-skinned, and these latter inhabited Arabin'ya to such great extent, that no statistical mode regarding skin color could be stated for there.

Now post-Flood, the Lord took the I'hins to all divisions of the world (13/1.2). Could it be that the darker-skinned I'hins, because they would suffer less from the heat, were brought to live in the warmer climates? (Oahspe speaks later on light skin suffering from heat.) While the lighter-skinned I'hins were brought to cooler climates? If so, we can thus perceive a cause for darker-skinned people in the warmer zones. If we compare the people around the world in the time world-wide exploration began (circa 1500's c.e.), in general, those with darker skins would be found in more abundance in the warmer climates, while in the temperate zones, those with comparatively lighter skins would predominate.

What is their lineage? Around 6000 years before kosmon, Jaffeth, Par'si'e, Guatama and Arabin'ya all had copper I'huans. Jaffeth had brown druks as well as white and yellow I'hins; Par'si'e had brown druks as well as white and yellow I'hins; Guatama had black druks and white and yellow I'hins; and Arabin'ya had brown druks but I'hins of all skin colors including dark (24/24.5; 25/21.1,9; 25/24.15).

Yet around the time of world exploration (1500's; c. 350–250 bk), the Jaffethans, Par'si'e'ans and Guatamans, all had lighter skin colors, in general, than the Arabin'yans. Since in 6000 bk, ALL the mentioned regions had similar colored I'huans, besides brown or black druks, this suggests that the later Arabin'yans had darker skins because their I'hin forebears were darker skinned than I'hins elsewhere.

Thus the difference in skin color of the darker Arabin'yans would seem to come from the relative abundance of dark-skinned I'hins. Indeed we are told that the I'hins of Arabin'ya mated significantly with the I'huans (19/5.13). And more, this mixing was likely greatly increased during the cycle of Spe-ta, for the line of I'hins was prophesied to end shortly after.

In conclusion, from the evidence presented, the many dark-skinned Africans owe their dark skin color chiefly to the dark-skinned I'hins. As to the druks' contribution to color, there is nothing in Oahspe to suggest it was more than other regions; in fact, 27/21.7 suggests it could be less. So while all people today have I'hin heritage in them, in those mortals with dark skins, should we not consider contribution from the dark-skinned I'hins? –ed.

See Summary Table above.

25/21.10. And here, even as in Par'si'e and Heleste, were thousands of cities, great and small; [925] and like Par'si'e, they also had colleges and houses of philosophy, besides thousands of public libraries, which supplied books freely to the poor, who came here to be taught in the sciences, and in the arts of painting, engraving and sculpture, and in astronomy, mathematics, chemistry, minerals, assaying, and in the rules for inventing chemical combinations. But the Listians were the only people who dealt in charms and the secrets of taming serpents and beasts by virtue of the hand, and by curious scents, prepared secretly. And the Listians maintained the fifth rite in the resurrection, by which on the fifth day after death, the soul of the dead appeared in mortal semblance to his living people, and advised them lovingly, after which he ascended in their burning incense going to Jehovih!

25/21.11. These, then, were the people over whom De'yus, named Lord God, had set his billion, to subdue them for his own glory. And so it came to pass that Jehovih spoke in Craoshivi, saying: The time shall come when angels and mortals shall know in truth that the Lord God is a false God, and a vain-glorious usurper. For I will leave one race of I'huans on the earth, in Guatama [the North American Indian –Ed.], even till the era of Kosmon. And men and angels shall see and understand that man of himself never invents a God in the figure of a man born of woman. And that only through the inspiration of My enemies, who build kingdoms in hada for their own glory, has any people ever fallen from My estate to worship a God in image of man.

CHAPTER 22 Wars

25/22.1. And now came the third assault of Osiris' legions of angels, inspired to desperate madness by the harangues of their generals and captains. And every mortal was marked out, and his degree of faith in the Great Spirit known; so the destroyers knew well where to strike effectively.

25/22.2. At midnight, again came the Osirians, rushing on; and by force of numbers laid their hands on millions of mortals! Held fast, and hurled missiles furiously about in the bedrooms, to rouse from sleep their mortal victims, who, waking and seeing no cause for the whirling stools and tables, and the terrible noises and blows in every corner of their houses, sprang up frightened, and at a loss to know what to do. In many places the angels of De'yus spoke audibly in the dark, saying: There is only one God, even the Lord your God, great De'yus, on the throne of Hored. Bow down in reverence before him, or destruction and death shall be your doom!

25/22.3. The Osirian angels, gloating in their much success, now filled every house where they had fastened on, and made all those places headquarters for their captains and generals, and thousands and tens of thousands of angel servants, who were proud and boastful, most hilarious[926] in knocks and hideous noises about the house walls.

25/22.4. In many instances the ashars, the guardian angels, were overpowered and crowded off; for their power was weak and scattered because of the small faith and little spirituality in the mortals captured.

25/22.5. But the Osirians did not win in all cases, for in hundreds of thousands of families, they were overcome or baffled till the rising sun, which drove them off, leaving the Jehovihians still victorious. But the glory (victory) to Osiris and his legions was sufficient enough, that messengers were sent to De'yus speedily, with most exaggerated tales of the victories won.

25/22.6. In Par'si'e this night, one million two hundred thousand men, women and children, fell into the clutches of the hosts of De'yus, the Lord God, the false. In Arabin'ya, the fallen victims numbered two million; and in Heleste, one and a half million! But as yet, the captured mortals did not realize what had happened; they only knew frantic noises and flying missiles, disturbing them all night long. Many rushed out to the oracles and altars to learn the cause, and to know if, in truth, the angels of heaven were at war; or if Gods had come, as had been told in the old legends, to afflict mortals. The learned did not acknowledge the cause to be angels, but looked for cracks in the wood, or concealed persons, or cats, or dogs. But not finding the cause excited their disbelieving souls, so that they proclaimed before all people

[925] Note that as well as the Fertile Crescent, this includes all of Africa; see e.g., 25/50.22<fn-interior>.

[926] boisterously merry, celebratory

each special wonder, exaggerated a hundred times over.

25/22.7. The unlearned believed in the angels thus suddenly come upon them; and cultivated their coming, and believed their words: to put away Jehovih and accept De'yus; or otherwise, after death, their souls would be weighed by Anubi, and, for lack of faith in the Lord God, instead of Jehovih, cast into everlasting hell.

25/22.8. And such mortals, willing tools to follow spirits' advice instead of Jehovih's light within their own souls, were led through the Anubian ceremonies, which were now malformed by substituting words to glorify De'yus, and Osiris, his so-called son.

25/22.9. But the philosophers searched deeper, to find if, in truth, the soul was immortal; and to find if it was really true that the souls of the dead come back in such a way, defying nature's laws, as they called the common occurrences all around them. If true, then what were the sum and substance of the created worlds; and what was the ultimate end, the all highest place for man?

25/22.10. And these questions the Osirian angels answered, explaining that the first heavenly place was hada, where there were many hells; and that the all highest heaven was Hored, where the Lord God sat on his throne in great glory. And around him on every side were billions of angels who had attained to everlasting peace, with nothing more to do but to bow and sing praises to their God forever!

CHAPTER 23 Wars

25/23.1. Not many more days passed before Osiris called his legions together, and gave them four days' recreation and a great heavenly feast. And after the feast was over, he spoke from his temporary throne on Mount Agho'aden, situated in the sky over the earth mountains of Aghogan, in Par'si'e; complimenting them, saying:

25/23.2. In the light and power of life and death I speak! Greeting, in De'yus' name, highest of Gods! In his love, to glorify you all for your great victory, this feast was spread, and my voice upraised in your praise.

25/23.3. First, to you, Baal, wise and powerful among Gods, for your great energy and glorious success, I bestow the Sign of the Sacred Bird, Iboi, [927] to be yours forever. And next, to you, Ashtaroth, the Goddess who never tires, or is without a stratagem, for your glorious success I bestow you with the fete, the circle and the true cross, to be yours forever.

25/23.4. To you, Hermes, most unflinching of generals, second in rank to Lord, for your victories, I bestow the Inqua.[928] To you, Apollo-ya [Apollo –Ed.], I bequeath a bow and arrow, for you shall break the bonds of the creed of circumcision, and tempt mortals to wed by no law but by the impulse of the heart. For as the Faithists have been bound by their sign (circumcision) to not marry outside their own people, so shall you teach the opposite; for by crossing the breeds of men, they shall be broken off from Jehovih.

25/23.5. To you, Posee-ya-don [Poseidon –ed.], I bestow a model ship, for you shall have dominion over sea-faring men in all these divisions of the world. To you, Hefa-yis-tie [Hephaestus –ed.] I bestow a forge and tongs, for your dominion over mortals shall be with the workers of metals and weapons of war.

25/23.6. To you, Pluton-ya [Pluto –Ed.], I bestow a torch and brand of fire, for you shall rule over mortals for the destruction of cities and houses, belonging to whoever will not bow down to De'yus as the highest God. To you, Ura-na, queen of the es'enaurs, the very stars of my armies, I bestow a quill and staff, for you shall have

---

[927] Ibis, Iboi, a Phoenician word. Though the Parsees who migrated to Egypt in early times also used the same word, originally signifying A FLYING BEAUTY. The bird was named afterward. –Ed.

[928] See Inqua [image i033, row 3 end, vol.2 p.227]. The planet Mercury was supposed by the ancients to run on the circle nearest the sun. The inside circle. We have a vulgarism in the English to the same effect, saying of any one: He is the swiftest because he has the INSIDE TRACK. The fastest horse gets the inside track, hence he was called, in Phoenician, INQUA, from which the word EQUESTRIAN came to us. The medal is usually engraved with an outer and an inside circle, with a star in the center, representing the place of the sun. The medal is no longer sacred, but is often used by horse jockeys on the brow-band of the bridle. And it thus came from Osiris, the false, as seen above. –Ed.

dominion over the songs of the earth, inspiring mortals to sing praises to the Lord our God. ||

25/23.7. In that way Osiris went through the list, bestowing and assigning medals, signs, symbols and emblems upon the generals and captains, and exalting many of the privates for daring deeds done, and for victories. And then Osiris allotted to the generals and captains tens of thousands of spirits specially adapted to their respective work; and he placed Baal and Ashtaroth as chiefs over them. Next Osiris organized a new division of angels, an army of one hundred million, distributed into one hundred parts, and called this army See-loo-gan, signifying spirits who travel about among mortals in systematic order, to measure them as to how best they can be used for the glory of the heavenly kingdoms; and to possess them, or hand them over to be obsessed, as may be deemed profitable.

25/23.8. At Pluton-ya's request, Osiris made his selection for him, and then further explained, saying: To you, all privilege in your line.[929] If you find fire is not well suited to destroy a city, even though thousands of mortals are obsessed at the same time to set it afire, then you shall have your spirits carry virus and inoculate mortals so they die; or have them fill the city with epidemic air, well poisoned, throwing mortals into fevers so they shall die. For in all cases, whether Baal or Ashtaroth, or any of your superior officers, says to you: Destroy that city, or this city, or that family, or this family, or that man or this man; then you shall fall upon the place, family or man as commanded and accomplish it. ||

25/23.9. And now, with due ceremonies, and with excellent music, the assemblage was commanded back to the earth to resume work. And Osiris' messengers bore the news to De'yus, well exaggerated, extolling the fidelity of Osiris to the highest.

25/23.10. From this time forward the Osirians made no more masterly raids, but they took advantage of the well-adapted times to give mortals an abundance of wonders in angel manifestations; which bait mortals eagerly took. And they were, for the most part, easily persuaded to follow angel advice, and so fell to work and built temples and established oracles of their own, obliterating the doctrine of the Great Spirit, and substituting the words: The Lord God; and De'yus; and Anubi, his holy Son and Savior and Judge of the world; and Osiris, God's commanding Lord of the earth. And mortals traveled throughout all regions, preaching and explaining spirit communion, and establishing the Anubian rites and ceremonies, but never using the names Great Spirit or Jehovih, except to deride and accurse. The rites taught virtue, love, truth, and the acquisition of knowledge, but did not teach peace, but war, which was maintained to be justifiable if done for the glory of the Lord, or for the Lord God, or for the Son, the Savior, Anubi, whose sign was a pair of scales, and who was sometimes called Judge, and Keeper of the Gate that led to the upper heaven, Hored.

25/23.11. So for those reasons it came to pass, that the mortal adherents of Osiris began to war on the Faithists and take their possessions. And because the Faithists, by their pledges to Jehovih, dared not resist by weapons of death, but only by walls around their cities, and by stratagems, and by running away, the Osirians had easy victories in most instances.

25/23.12. In ten years the Osirians began to build great cities, as the ancients had; and to gather in their plunder taken from the Faithists.

25/23.13. And Osiris, Baal and Ashtaroth, through their angel hosts, chose from among mortals the largest and strongest, most war-like, and by means of the oracles declared them kings and queens, and instructed them in building palaces and having thrones, after the manner of Lords and Gods. And they directed mortals how to make themselves powerful by organization and obedience to the kings and queens, who were recognized as adopted sons and daughters of the Lord God.

25/23.14. Now it came to pass, in course of time, that in consequence of the great abundance of angel manifestations, mortals sought by this means to obtain knowledge of heaven and earth, and especially in regard to the purpose of man.

25/23.15. And the Osirian hosts, being the only angels engaged in the matter of establishing De'yus, answered them, saying: The life and the

[929] That is, Osiris gives Pluton-ya discretion in deciding the best way to carry out his mission, but as to what the mission is, he must look to his superiors.

purpose of man is to glorify God, who is Lord of heaven and earth.

25/23.16. And the mortals pressed the matter further, asking: Who is God? What are the worlds? Where did all things come from? How was it with the creation and the Creator?

25/23.17. For an answer to these questions, Osiris sent messengers to the Lord God in Hored; so De'yus called a Council of his Gods and Lords, to meet in Hored, to solve the matter, so that a uniform answer could be given to all the divisions of the earth.

25/23.18. After the invitations were sent, but before the Council assembled, the self (satan) of De'yus spoke to him, saying: If you admit a Creator except yourself, you are undone. For is this not the point on which hangs the power and dominion of Jehovih? The Lord God inquired of satan, saying: Why did you not speak of this before? Behold, the Great Spirit signifies everywhere. But I am only as a man, small, compared to the size of the worlds!

25/23.19. Satan said: It does not matter; you shall say you were the Creator of heaven and earth.

25/23.20. De'yus said: But this is not truthful? When you persuaded me to assume dominion of earth, you said: Be truthful in all things. How, then, shall I say, I created heaven and earth? Satan said: When Osiris comes before you, ask him: Who have you found among mortals to be the greatest, wisest and best su'is? And when he tells you, say to him: Osiris, my son, you yourself shall inspire the one whom you say is the greatest su'is. And you shall cause him to write answers to the questions of mortals, so that the learned and the ignorant alike may know me and my kingdoms. Behold, before my time both heaven and earth were void as to a Godhead, except for the servants of Jehovih. And because they (heaven and earth) were void in this respect, you shall persuade your seers to know I created them (heaven and earth) from voidance to my own glory.

CHAPTER 24 Wars

Of the Jaffethan assault

25/24.1. Anuhasaj, alias the Lord God, had said to Te-in, the false, into whose charge he gave Jaffeth and her heavenly places: At the same time that Osiris and his hosts fall upon his divisions of the earth, even in that day and hour you and your hosts shall fall upon Jaffeth (China), possessing the temples, altars, and places of oracles, where they serve the Great Spirit under the name Ormazd, and you shall subdue them to me under the name Joss, who is and ever shall be Ho-Joss[930] of heaven and earth.

25/24.2. So Te-in, the false, with his billion warriors sped forth, downward, to the earth, having spread his army wide, to cover the whole of Jaffeth, hoping to capture it suddenly. And, even as Osiris had, he plunged into the temples and oracle-houses, and surrounded the altars, in the dead of night, to drive away Jehovih's guardian angels, and like Osiris, but even worse, Te-in was baffled and repulsed, and saw the morning sun arise upon his shame in total failure. And then he, too, with his mighty legions, went stalking about[931] all day long on the earth, waiting for the next night's assault on sleeping mortals, and to receive new orders from the Lord God, as to the next proceeding.

25/24.3. So when the second night came, Te-in went in with his army, furious because of the previous night's cowardly failure. And to the sleeping mortal men, women and children, his army rushed in with oaths and loud boastings, threatening Jehovih's angels with the tortures of

---

[930] Joss is the Panic word for God. It is pronounced in three syllables, G-o-ce, long sound. God is also a word of three syllables, and pronounced, G-o-d. These are called the three primary sounds of the wind. The making of one word out of God, or of Joss, is a vulgarism. Ho-Joss is the same as Lord God. In some parts of China it is pronounced, Ha-Joss. The "o" is a long sound, like "o" in God. Joss and God are synonymous, and are the vulgarism of the Panic word, Zhe-ode-de, or nearly as one would pronounce the letters in spelling God, and it is from the same source as E-O-Ih, i.e., the three primary sounds the wind makes. Ghad, (a, short) became confounded with God and Joss. The Chinese were most probably given the word Joss because, in that age, they could not say God. Elohim, and its vulgarism, Elah, have the same origin. –Ed.

[931] angry and frustrated at being humiliated

hell if they did not instantly resign all to Ho-Joss, the all highest ruler, dweller in Hored.[932]

25/24.4. But faithful stood the Jehovihians; laid their hands on the sleeping mortals, and became all powerful against the terrible odds, and held them in abeyance again, till the sun arose and scattered Te-in's hosts, ashamed and sulky, in most pitiful defeat. Of which news Te-in now, most painfully, sent word to his commanding God.

25/24.5. De'yus sent word to him, even as he did to Osiris, to next attack the houses of the men of learning, the unbelievers; and the ignorant, and the superstitious; to abandon, for the present, the arcs, temples, oracle-houses, and the firmly sworn Faithists. De'yus said: Send your numerators and mathematicians; and measure and mark all mortals in Jaffeth, as to their vulnerable points, and map their localities; and when you have completed this work, set apart another night for an attack upon them. And your hosts shall not fall upon the Faithists who are firm in the Great Spirit, Ormazd, but upon the weak and disbelieving, the skeptical and much learned philosophers, who are weak in spirit, and you shall not fail.

25/24.6. So Te-in enumerated the Jaffethans, as commanded, marking them as to their vulnerable points, whether in disbelief in spirit, or if given to lust, or to hasty passions, or to telling lies, or to stealing, or to murder, or to hypocrisy, or to desire for leadership. And before the time of battle, Te-in knew the grade of every mortal in Jaffeth. And he called his generals and captains before him in his heavenly place, Che-su-gow, over the Chesain Mountains, twenty miles high, showing them the lists and maps.

25/24.7. Take these, he said, and distribute them to my mighty armies, and before tomorrow night they shall learn every mortal's place and quality; and in the night my legions shall rush upon the places, laying hands on the sleeping mortals, thus gaining power; and they shall hurl missiles, with terrible noises, through the houses of the sleepers, and so rouse them to awaken and experience the war of heaven carried to their homes.

25/24.8. The generals and captains took the lists and maps, and had millions of copies made, and then sent them into all the regions of De'yus' militants; and sent, too, millions and millions of proclaimers, with terrible oaths against the Great Spirit, but who extolled[933] the munificence[934] of De'yus to the utmost; appealing to their love of independence, and to their power to cast off all other rulers forever, except Ho-Joss.

25/24.9. And now, when the night of battle came, the infuriated angel warriors of Te-in marched in lines, millions strong, toward the sleeping mortals. Their great armies spread broad, covering the land of Jaffeth from east to west and from north to south. Over Flang'e'loe, the City of the Sun, thirty million of Te-in's warring angels were sent, sworn to subjugate the people of great learning, alive or dead, and scatter the angels of Jehovih, or bind them and cast them into hell. And over the city of Pen Goo twenty million of Te-in's hosts were sent; while the cities of Tsee, Wung, Ha-tzo, Ne King, and Zoo Wun, each had over them twenty million of Te-in's angels of war.

25/24.10. Besides these there were millions and millions stationed over the great valley of Wan, and in the mountains of So Jon. In the plains of Wow Gan seventy million were stationed. Five million were allotted to each of the following cities: Sum Conc, Ah-gee, Ah-sin, Chang-ha, Ge Oooh-young, Gwan Gouk, Na'tji, Yuk Hoh, Ah Tosh, Ah Koan, Chaung, Shon, Nufow, Zow, Lin, Gee Bak, Ow-wa, Tdong, King-do, Ghi Sam, Seung, Chog, Doth, Jawh, Bing-Tah, Gha, Haih, Huug, Wing-tze, Ni Am, Ah Sam, and Zow-lin.

25/24.11. In the mountains of Witch How Loo were stationed eighty million, set to fall upon the Listian breed of men. On the borders of the sea, for sea-faring men, and for their wives and children, were one hundred and ninety million of Te-in's angel soldiers, ready for the assault. Besides these there were tens of thousands of smaller armies, stationed in the small cities and country places, waiting for the signal. ||

25/24.12. Now in this age, Jaffeth had attained to great wisdom in many things, but in war her people were as babes. More than half her people were Faithists, followers of Po, worshippers of the Great Spirit. And they practiced peace and dwelt in communities. Many of the cities were in families of

[932] In Chinese the equivalent word is Hoe-Leb-e. –Ed.

[933] praised highly and enthusiastically

[934] liberality, generosity, openhandedness, unselfishness, consideration

tens, and hundreds, and thousands,[935] but nowhere more than two thousand. And the city families were ordered in this manner: The manufacturers of wool cloth, one family; of linen cloth, another family; of silk cloth, another family; of leather, another family; of paper, another family; of transportation, another family; and so on, till all departments were full; and of these combinations there were cities of fifty thousand, and a hundred thousand, and two hundred thousand inhabitants.[936] And in the country places there were small cities, whose people tilled the soil and gathered the fruits of the earth, and they exchanged goods with the manufacturers who dwelt in large cities.

25/24.13. The government was by priests, one for each communion family; and the priests, who were called Wa-shon, were the receivers and distributors of goods, and they ministered in the temples and at the altars of worship in the name of the Great Spirit, Ormazd, sometimes called Po-e-tein, and sometimes E'O'lin, and by other names also.

25/24.14. Besides the schools and colleges there were HOUSES OF PHILOSOPHY, and HOUSES OF PROPHECY, and HOUSES OF ASTRONOMY, thousands and thousands.

25/24.15. The Jaffethans were large, being I'huans, with one degree more of the brown people's blood in them than the Par'si'e'ans. Nor was there in all the world, at that time, so strong a people, and clean and jovial, high aspiring, with great gentleness. And because the land was tilled and made to bloom on every side, the angels of heaven named it the FLOWERY KINGDOM; and because the people reveled in song, and poetry, and oratory, they were called, LAMBS OF THE GREAT SPIRIT IN THE FLUSH OF SPRINGTIME.[937]

25/24.16. And these things were well known to De'yus, and to Te-in, the false, and to hundreds of millions of the assaulting angels, sworn to subdue them to Ho-Joss or to everlasting destruction.

25/24.17. But, as previously described, because of the power of Jehovih with the most faithful of the Faithists, the arcs and temples of worship had stood unharmed by the satanic raid; equally so the Te-ins failed to overpower the Great Spirit's guardian angels. So now, after due preparation, the time came for another contest, this time upon the least Jehovih-like of mortals.

25/24.18. On the other hand, the true God, Son of Jehovih, sent word from his throne in Craoshivi to the guardian angels dwelling with these mortals, who were so unmindful of the Father's care. He said: Come defeat, disaster or terrible darkness, overpowering your utmost strength, still struggle on, in the name of Jehovih. The true Faithist knows nothing impracticable, but does his utmost for his highest light, though failure stares him in the face.

25/24.19. For once distrust of weakness enters the human soul, the man slides backward down the hill of faith; while he who will not consider results, except to serve Jehovih right on, fail or not, rises, even though his project fails. ||

25/24.20. With this and no other word from Jehovih, the Faithists stood by their weak and helpless wards on the low earth, waiting for the billion Te-ins. But not in any lengthened suspense, for when the sun stood with the widest part of the earth between, being the midnight hour, the militants came rushing on, with oaths most hideous, and by their dense flood of numbers reached the sleeping mortals and laid hands on them.

25/24.21. Then, with joy run to mania because of triumph, hurled objects about in the dwellings. And, in many places, they spoke in the dark with audible speech to the frightened mortals:

25/24.22. From Sanc-tu I come, to lay in the dust every mortal born who will not bow down in reverence to Ho-Joss, ruler of worlds. Give ear,[938] O man; the anger of heaven's Creator is let loose upon a disobedient race!

25/24.23. And then, to give semblance of truth to the words, the angel intruders let fly such knocks and poundings that they moved many a house on its foundation,[939] and roused the mortals,

---

[935] Family here must be equivalent to House, meaning a very extended family, a clan, a family line tied to a common ancestor, as in the House of David, or the House of Lot.

[936] For example, if a city had 200,000 inhabitants, comprising 2000 families, this would make the average size of a family or House, a hundred people.

[937] Oh ne spe bah'e, oe tong su da'e. –Ed.

[938] Listen; Listen up; Be attentive

panic-stricken, to find the cause or to hasten quickly to repentance and prayers.

25/24.24. But it was not a complete victory; for the Jehovihians firmly held the power in hundreds of thousands of places. And yet the Te-ins had a great victory.

25/24.25. Te-in quickly sent word to De'yus, exulting, and exaggerating the victories won. And in turn, De'yus congratulated him and his army of one billion, who, now anchored on the earth, and with mortals, frolicked about in all regions.

25/24.26. And in course of time, the same questions arose in Jaffeth as in Arabin'ya; questions from mortals to the spirits; as to the destination of the soul of man; as to the origin of things; as to the heavenly places? And Te-in in turn sent word on up to De'yus, in Hored, as to what answer should be given. It was thus, that he, too, was summoned to Sanc-tu, in Hored, to meet with Osiris, Baal, Ashtaroth, and Sudga, subduer[940] of Vind'yu.

CHAPTER 25 Wars

Of the Vind'yuan assault

25/25.1. Sudga, the false, sent by De'yus to overturn the Great Spirit's dominion in Vind'yu, and to establish the highest heavenly place, Urvatooz [Hored –Ed.], was wiser than Osiris or Te-in in his wicked work. For he did not permit his army of one billion to immediately rush for the places of worship and for the oracle-houses. But most deliberately he halted his forces in Haroyu, the lowest heavenly place over the mountains of Vivrat, in Vind'yu. Situated three miles high, and broad as the earth, it offered a commanding situation.

25/25.2. From this place, in a sure way, he sent his measurers on ahead down to the earth, to measure mortals, as to their weakness or strength of faith in Jehovih (Ormazd), and in other heavenly rulers; and then to map, mark and number them.

25/25.3. Great was the peace, beauty and glory of Vind'yu in that day. Her rivers and canals coursed the country over, and her industrious sons and daughters, two hundred million, were, in the eyes of the angels, the pride and glory of the earth. Hundreds of thousands of her people were prophets and seers. And so abundant was spiritual light among the people, that even those who had learned only one language, could understand and speak other languages with people from remote parts; using words and sentences they had never heard, even when first meeting strangers. The Vind'yuans lived like the inhabitants of Jaffeth in government and industry, their economy being mostly by the exchange of goods, and not by buying and selling. This was their weakest point, as to an assault.

25/25.4. Sudga said to his generals and captains: Only by confounding the languages of these people can they be broken up and subdued. Behold, they are becoming like Gods; knowing and understanding in advance of the words spoken. Does this not, then, become their greatest liability, if we confound them suddenly in the meaning of words? Therefore fall upon them, possessing and obsessing all who are easily captured. Get a foothold here and there in the first place; and then cripple them in their commerce.

25/25.5. Sudga said: It is a strong city that makes all kinds of goods; it is a weak place indeed that depends on another which is far off. Such people are easily tripped up. Behold, I will teach these people that I am the militant before whom every knee shall bow; or, in failing to win them in that way, I will set city against city, and country place against country place; all against one another, for which their superabundant languages will furnish excellent material.

25/25.6. Sudga opened the door at night for his hosts to fall on mortals who were weakest in faith in Ormazd, Who, to hundreds of thousands of men and women, had become like a stale story. In Vind'yu woman had risen in knowledge, higher than the highest of women in other parts of the world. In the HOUSES OF PHILOSOPHY and HOUSES OF SCIENCE women were foremost, compared to men, and skeptical as to the Ormazdian power.

25/25.7. On rushed Sudga's legions; and even as Osiris and Te-in won in the third assault, so now Sudga won in the first. And he too sent word to De'yus, and exaggerated his victories beyond all

---

[939] Many Spiritualists have witnessed the oscillation of houses by the spirits. I have witnessed the shaking of large brick houses, and seen the walls and ceilings cracked across by the spirits in the same way. –Ed.

[940] one who wins by overpowering; one who subdues; vanquisher, conqueror, subjugator

bounds of truth. Nevertheless, his hosts were sufficiently anchored on the earth to claim an everlasting victory for De'yus and to establish his name.

25/25.8. And here, also, after a few years, the questions came from mortals, such as: Behold, you cut off the heavens of the ancients, the Nirvanian regions beyond Chinvat. You teach us that De'yus is the ALL HIGH RULER. What, then, is the all highest for man? How did the worlds come about? Where did man come from? How was the creation created?

25/25.9. To answer which, Sudga sent to De'yus for instructions. And De'yus sent to Sudga, even as to the other Gods, an invitation to meet in Hored, to hear the words of the Lord God, to learn his commands.

25/25.10. Thus invited, the five great warrior Gods went before De'yus, each taking with them ten thousand attendants, besides thousands of trumpeters. De'yus had a good feast prepared for them, and sent receivers forth to meet them and conduct them to Sanc-tu in great splendor.

CHAPTER 26 Wars

25/26.1. Great was the feast, the pomp, parade and glory in Hored, when De'yus' victorious Gods and their companions and attendants came in answer to the summons of Anuhasaj, alias the Lord God. The trumpeters of Hored were stationed along more than a thousand miles on the heavenly roadways, and in turn, the trumpeters and heralds of the visiting Gods extended in advance of the Gods themselves an equally great distance.

25/26.2. The roads were lined all along the way with flags and banners, and with millions of spectators, the same who had formerly been in schools and colleges in heaven, but were now emancipated from the restrictions of self-improvement, and used as applauders, to sing and shout praises to De'yus for his own glory.

25/26.3. The table of the feast was private and in secret, and only prepared for the Gods and their close companions, one hundred all told, but the serving host numbered more than one million souls.

25/26.4. While at the feast, De'yus said to Osiris: Tell us about your exploits, and about Baal and Ashtaroth and their valorous legions.

25/26.5. Then Osiris explained the nature of the earth countries, and the battles and incidents, well exaggerating these latter. After Osiris had finished his story, De'yus said to Te-in: Tell us about your exploits, and those of your generals and captains, and your valorous legions.

25/26.6. So Te-in displayed the maps of the earth regions where he had been, told of his battles and final success, also much exaggerated. And now, after he had finished his story, De'yus said to Sudga: Tell us about your generals and captains and your valorous legions.

25/26.7. Then Sudga explained the earth region where he had fought and won, extolling his generals and captains, and his hosts, well exaggerated also.

25/26.8. When they had all finished their hilarious[941] accounts, and applauded one another in sufficient zeal, in that same time the feast of eating and drinking was ended also. Anuhasaj rose up and said:

25/26.9. I now declare the feast ended. Let the tables be removed. Behold, I will speak from the throne, in private, before my five Gods only, plus my own marshals. But to all others I declare a time of recreation and sport, to be called again to duty when I have finished with my Gods, at which time my marshals will inform the trumpeters, who shall sound the call.

25/26.10. Speedily now, the attendants took away the tables; and the hosts all withdrew except the Gods and De'yus with his marshals. So De'yus ascended the throne, and then spoke, saying:

25/26.11. I, the Lord your God, who am De'yus of heaven and earth, declare to you, my Gods and earth rulers, in my own name, and with love abounding:

25/26.12. My purpose for calling you together is to declare my doctrines and creations before you, so that all the earth may be subdued alike to me and mine forever. Here is the foundation:

25/26.13. Not to surpass my own age in my doctrines, nor to explain my axioms. But to surpass the understanding of mortals sufficiently in their earthly knowledge, so as to appease their curiosity, as revealed in the questions they put to you, my Gods.

---

941 lively, amusing, entertaining, humorous

25/26.14. Neither will I bind myself as Ahura did; for I will not explain who I am, except that man is in my own likeness; nor will I explain when the beginning of things was.

25/26.15. I created this heaven; and you also bear witness that I have established the earth in me, through your valorous deeds.

25/26.16. I, who am your God, do not look to matters of a day, or a year; my times are as one time, for from this time forward forever, this heaven and the earth are mine, time without end.

25/26.17. In which you behold the days, years, and generations of men on the earth pass rapidly. Who, then, shall think seriously of the inhabitants that now are yours and mine?

25/26.18. Behold, the earth is fruitful; a thousand years are only as one day; and in that time, billions of newborn souls shall spring up out of the earth. For them my answers are shaped, more than for those who are living now.

25/26.19. In the beginning I created this heaven and the earth (to my own name and glory). For they were void and without order; darkness was upon them. So I moved upon them, saying: Let there be light; and there was light. And I drew a line between darkness and light (for they had worshipped the void instead of me).

25/26.20. And so I declare this the morning and evening of the first day. And I have divided those who were void, and established my firmament between them, like land between water and water.

25/26.21. And my firmament is heaven, and I have made it to be over those who were void, like water.

CHAPTER 27 Wars

25/27.1. Osiris, being commanded by the Lord God to speak, said: Give us one day, O De'yus, so that we may digest this matter.

25/27.2. So the Lord God gave them one day; and on the next day, when they were assembled, the Gods ratified every word De'yus had spoken. And it was called the morning and evening of the second day.

25/27.3. Again De'yus spoke, saying: Let the waters of the earth be in one place, and the land appear to itself, for it was so. And I saw that the earth was good (and that heaven could reign on it). And I saw that the earth brought forth grass and trees, and fruit and seeds, everything after its own kind; and I said: Behold, they are good. (Neither did I attribute evil to anything on the earth, or in the waters, or in the air above. But I separated the light from darkness; this was the substance of my creation.)

25/27.4. Again Osiris asked for a day, so the Gods could weigh the words of the Lord God; and this was the evening of the third day. And God gave them a day; and when they were assembled again, De'yus said:

25/27.5. Let there be Gods in the firmament above the earth; and they shall separate the darkness from the light of the earth (so that man may know me and my kingdoms).

25/27.6. And my Gods shall teach signs and seasons, and days and years, forever, to the sons of men. And I made myself to rule the light of the world; but Osiris I made to rule the darkness of the world, which is the earth, my footstool.

25/27.7. Again De'yus gave the Gods one day, to weigh the matter of his words, and to ratify them; which they did. And this was the morning of the fourth day.

25/27.8. Again De'yus said: Let the waters of the earth bring forth abundantly the moving creatures that live; and let the fowl fly above the earth in the air of the firmament. For they are good. Let every living creature be fruitful and multiply, and fill the earth, and the waters of the earth, and the air above the earth, every creature after its own kind. For which reason my blessing is upon them.

25/27.9. Again the Lord God gave his Gods a day to weigh his words and ratify them, which they did; and this was the morning of the fifth day. And then De'yus said: And now, my Gods, let us make man[942] in our own fashion;[943] and in likeness of ourselves (who have dominion over angels and mortals), let them have dominion also, but over the fish in the waters and the fowl in the air, and over the cattle, and over the earth, and over every living creature upon the earth. And you shall go to them and say to them: In our own likeness you are created, male and female, and God's blessing is upon you. Be fruitful, and multiply, and replenish

---

[942] See Ezra Bible, Genesis, chapter i, verse 26. And God said: Let us make man, etc. Query: Who was God talking to? Who was helping him? –Ed.

[943] in our own image, as we see fit

the earth and subdue it; and have dominion over the earth, and the fishes and fowl, and every living creature on the earth, for they are yours forever! And behold, you have every herb, seed and fruit, which is on the face of the earth, and the roots that grow in the earth, and they shall be your food. But whatever has breathed the breath of life, man shall not eat. ||

25/27.10. Again De'yus gave the Gods a day of rest, in order to weigh the matter and ratify it; and this was the morning of the sixth day.

25/27.11. And again De'yus spoke, saying: The Lord your God said to you, Osiris, and to you, Te-in, and to you, Sudga: Search among mortals for one high in su'is, for when I announce my doctrines, you shall go to that mortal and cause him to write my words, saying: These are the words of the Lord, your God. || To answer if you have found such a su'is, I bid you all to speak now before me.

25/27.12. Osiris said: According to your commandments I have searched and have found Thoth the highest man in su'is, and he dwells in Arabin'ya.

25/27.13. Then spoke Te-in, saying: In like manner, I also searched, and found Hong, in my division of the earth, the highest man in su'is; and he dwells in Ho'e Sin.

25/27.14. Then answered Sudga, saying: Even so have I accomplished in Vind'yu, and I have found one Anj-rajan.

25/27.15. De'yus said: To these mortals go and give my doctrines in your own ways; according to the languages of mortals, and their capacity to understand. Neither do I bind you to my exact words, nor limit you, except that which I have spoken shall be the foundation.

25/27.16. Then De'yus concluded, saying: Here, then, ends the feast; and behold, it is the seventh day; for which reason I sanctify it and declare it a day of recreation.[944]

CHAPTER 28 Wars

25/28.1. On the following day the Gods departed, with due ceremonies, in the manner they came, and returned to their kingdoms, and then descended to the earth, each one to his own division.

25/28.2. And each of the three Gods went to his own chosen mortal (who had power to see and hear spiritual things). And the Gods possessed them by their presence, and inspired them to write the words of Anuhasaj, alias the Lord God, word for word; and they were written so, in the three great divisions of the earth. And copies of them were made and filed in the libraries, and in the houses of philosophy of mortals.

25/28.3. But when these matters were thus entered, in answer to the queries of mortals, as to the origin of man and his destiny, they were not deemed sufficient by the learned men. Many of them said: The Lord God has evaded our questions.

25/28.4. Then satan came to each of the three Gods who had the matter in charge, and he said to them: Consult with one another as to what shall be done. So Osiris sent messengers to Te-in and to Sudga, asking them to come to Agho'aden, his heavenly place, for consultation. And, in due course of time, Te-in and Sudga came to Osiris, to his throne, where they were received in great honor and glory. And presently Osiris' marshals cleared the place, and the interview was private, for even the marshals stood far away.

25/28.5. Osiris said: What shall we do without a Creator in fact? I do not know if my judgment is beside itself, for it is said they who lose their reason are the last to discover it. The time was, when De'yus, our much-loved Lord God, said: While you labor on the earth for me and my kingdoms, behold, I will reciprocate in all things. Ask for anything and it shall be granted to you.

25/28.6. Hear me then, O my brothers, in my complaint; mortals have asked us, to know the origin of man, and his destination; and to know the cause of good and evil. These things I submitted to our Lord God, in Hored, to learn his will and decree.

25/28.7. And he sent messengers to me announcing a feast, promising that then he would answer satisfactorily the questions of mortals. You and I went to the feast, only to have De'yus furnish us with something that is nothing. For mortals can also perceive that what the Lord God has said is one and the same thing that was said by the Gods through Zarathustra; and, moreover, that the questions are still unanswered.

[944] This completes the first chapter of Genesis and three verses of the second chapter [of the Ezra Bible]. –Ed.

25/28.8. De'yus is my friend, and I do not desire to press him further on the subject; and so I have called you, to learn from you how you managed the same issues?

25/28.9. Te-in said: Before our heavenly kingdoms were confederated, Anuhasaj professed that he would announce himself the head and front of all created creations. Shall we say his courage is not up to the task? And so excuse him?

25/28.10. Sudga said: When he should have said: I created man in my own image, behold, he has weakly said: LET US MAKE MAN! Is it not clear, then, that he shirks from the responsibility, and desires to commingle us into the pitiful story? Hear me, then, my brothers; I am asked how I have answered the issues with my own division, and I say to you, I have been in the same quandary, and have not answered at all.

25/28.11. Te-in said: Neither have I. But that we may be justified in doing so, behold, the Lord God said to us: I do not bind you to my words, nor limit you, except that which I have spoken shall be the foundation. Now it is clear that if we admit that sin is in the world, then we must find a way to justify the Lord God, whose servants we are. If he is not justified, then sin is justified.[945]

25/28.12. For mortals perceive good and evil understandingly; but to justify a good God for permitting evil is not an easy matter. For in the breath we praise him, we must praise his works; of which sin is apparent; and in the same breath that we condemn sin, how shall we glorify De'yus? For have we not proclaimed him the foundation of all things; the head and front, before creation was created? Was this not our battle-cry, to urge our angel warriors on to overthrow Jehovih? And has our loud-praised Lord God not said: LET US MAKE MAN! A child would have more courage than this!

25/28.13. Sudga said: It is plain we all understand these issues, and perceive, also, what is required of us. For, since De'yus has left us liberty to add to his doctrines, according to our own judgment, is it not well that we agree upon a doctrine, even as prior to the confederacy De'yus professed he would do? And so, give it to mortals?

[945] For example, if the Lord God is not made blameless, then sin is defensible because sin might not be the mortal's fault, but the Lord God's fault.

25/28.14. Osiris said: This is wisdom, O my brothers. To make our Lord God the Creator, we must accredit all things to him, both good and evil. For this reason we shall give two masters to man, one being the serpent, the earth, the lowest inspirer; and the other the voice of our Lord God.

25/28.15. Sudga said: My brother has spoken wisely. And yet, is the term two masters the wisest term? For in declaring the Lord God the highest, we must make him master over the earth also.

25/28.16. Te-in said: Why shall we not adopt the E'O'LIN of the ancients, substituting the words Lord God? And make a commandment over man, forbidding him to listen to the serpent, lest he be led away from the Lord God; and thus throw the cause of sin upon man, for violating the Lord God's commandment.

25/28.17. Osiris said: Most wisely spoken, my brothers. For by accusing man, through the serpent, we clear the Lord God unscathed.

CHAPTER 29 Wars

The Osirian Bible of Arabin'ya, Vind'yu, and Jaffeth

25/29.1. On the following day the three false Gods, Osiris, Te-in and Sudga, wrote their account, each one in his own way. And when they were read, Osiris' stood clearer than either of the others'; but nevertheless, Te-in's and Sudga's had much of merit. So it came to pass that Osiris' account was adopted, with interpolations from the others'.

25/29.2. This, then, is the completed report:

25/29.3. These are the times of earth and heaven when created; the time the Lord God created them. And the Lord God formed man out of the dust of the earth, and quickened him through his nostrils with the breath of life, and man became a living creature.

25/29.4. And God caused mists to rise up from the waters, and spread over the earth, and rain upon it. And he caused trees and herbs to grow up out of the ground; everything that is pleasant for the sight and good for food. Thus out of the ground the Lord God caused man to come forth, being of the earth, of the land of Eden (Spe-a).[946]

[946] Eden, Aden, Haden, Ah-den, Jeden, are of the same meaning in the Vedic, Phoenician and

25/29.5. The Lord God commanded man to dress[947] the land and keep it pleasant, saying: This shall be your labor, in which you shall be perfected to everlasting life. You may freely take and enjoy all things that are in the land of Eden.

25/29.6. And man prospered on the earth for a long season; and he was naked and not ashamed. And God planted the tree of knowledge in the land of Eden, and he said to man: I have planted this tree; do not partake of it, for it pertains to life and death.

25/29.7. And God called the name of the first man A'su (Adam). And the Lord God caused man to name all things on the earth, and in the waters, and in the air above the earth, and whatever man called every living creature, that was its name.

25/29.8. And the Lord God caused A'su to fall into a trance; and an angel of heaven came and stood by his side. And the Lord God drew from the flesh, and from the bones, and from the blood of A'su, and thus made woman, and brought her to A'su.

25/29.9. And the Lord God repeated his commandment to woman, saying: You shall dwell for a season on the earth, and cleave to A'su, for he is your husband, and you are his wife; and you shall partake of all things on the face of the earth, except for the tree of life, which is of both good and evil, for in the day you eat of it you shall surely die.

25/29.10. But because of the serpent (the earth) of the woman, she listened to him [her flesh –Ed.], and he said to the woman: I say to you, in the day you eat of the tree of knowledge you shall have your eyes opened, and shall become like a Goddess, creating offspring.

25/29.11. And the woman was more easily persuaded than man, for she had confidence in the serpent; and they partook of the fruit of the tree of knowledge; and, in truth, their eyes were opened, and they saw their nakedness.

25/29.12. And presently they heard the Lord God walking in Eden, and they hid themselves in the bushes. And the Lord God said: Where are you, A'su? And A'su said: When we heard you walking, we hid ourselves, for we are naked.

25/29.13. The Lord God said: Who told you that you were naked? Have you eaten from the tree, which I told you that you should not eat from? A'su said: The woman you gave me to be with me, led me, saying: Behold, it is good fruit; and we ate it.

25/29.14. The Lord God said: Woman, what have you done? And the woman answered, saying: The serpent [her earth body –Ed.] beguiled[948] me. And the Lord God said to the serpent [the flesh –Ed.]: Because you have done this, you are accursed, and you shall not rise up from the earth, but return to dust from which you came.

25/29.15. The Lord God said to the woman: Because you have conceived, you shall have great sorrow; in sorrow bring forth children; your desire shall be to your husband, and he shall rule over you. And I will put enmity[949] between the serpent and your offspring; and the flesh shall call one way, which is to earth, but the soul of man shall call to me, the Lord God. And though the serpent bites, yet man shall bruise him, and subdue him.

25/29.16. And God taught man to make coats of skins and be clothed. And the Lord God said: Lest man partake further, becoming as one of us, he shall go out of Eden, where I created him. So he drove man out of Eden backward,[950] and gave him cherubims[951] to hold him on every side, to preserve to man the tree of life, so that man might not only fulfill the spirit, but the flesh also. ||

25/29.17. When Osiris had gone thus far, Sudga interposed, saying: If we say, Becoming as one of us, || will man not say: Behold, there are more Gods than the Lord God?

25/29.18. Te-in said: Because De'yus said: Let us make man, shall we not use us in this instance?

25/29.19. Osiris said: Hear me further, my brothers, for I previously found a way out. For I have divided the Lord from God; that is to say:

Chinese languages, and are from the Panic word Spe-a, or, rather, S'pe-a; i.e., a heavenly place on earth. –Ed.

[947] cultivate, till, fertilize, make pleasant, improve, groom, adorn

[948] charmed, lured, deluded, deceived

[949] opposition, enemy-like; irreconcilable differences; deep hatred

[950] i.e., to the east, or from his spiritual condition. –Ed.

[951] Kerub or Kerubim, in Hebrew, signifies GRASPED AND HELD FAST. Laws are cherubim, and so are guardian angels. –Ed.

25/29.20. And the Lord God said: Because man has learned good and evil, I am like two entities to him, for I am Lord of the earth and God of heaven. And that which is on the earth is the Lord's, and that which is in heaven is God's.

25/29.21. And A'su called his wife's name Eve (We-it), for she was the fountain of all men. And Eve brought forth a son, Cain, saying: I have begotten a son from the Lord. And she brought forth another son, Abel. And the firstborn was begotten in darkness, but the second in the light of the Lord. And the Lord had more respect for the second, Abel, than for the first, Cain.

25/29.22. In course of time Cain brought forth the fruit of the ground and offered it to the Lord. And Abel brought the firstlings of his flocks as his offerings for the Lord. And Cain perceived that the Lord had more respect for his brother, and Cain was angered, and his countenance fell.

25/29.23. And the Lord said to Cain: Why are you jealous? If you do well, shall you not be accepted? And if you do not do well, sin lies at your door.

25/29.24. But Cain would not be reconciled (because of the darkness in him), and when he and his brother were walking in the fields, Cain turned upon Abel and slew him.

25/29.25. God said: Behold, darkness is between men; the son begotten in darkness falls upon the one begotten in the light. And it shall come to pass on the earth from this time forward that the righteous shall be persecuted by the unrighteous.

25/29.26. And the Lord said to Cain: Where is Abel, your brother? And he said: I do not know. Am I my brother's keeper? The Lord said: The voice of your brother's blood cries out to me from the ground. Now you are accursed from the earth, for it has opened to receive your brother's blood from your hand. In my sight you shall be a fugitive and a vagabond upon the earth. And because you have shed blood, blood shall not cease to flow from your sons and daughters forever.

25/29.27. Cain said: O Lord, my punishment is greater than I can bear. For I have become the first foundation of all the wars on the earth; for you have hidden your face from me; and it shall come to pass that everyone who finds of me in them shall be slain also.

25/29.28. And the Lord said to Cain: Whoever slays you or yours, vengeance shall be upon him sevenfold. And the Lord wrote upon Cain's forehead the word Asugsahiben, signifying, BLOOD FOR SAKE OF SELF, a mark, lest any finding him might kill him.

25/29.29. And from this time forth Cain lost the voice of the Lord, because he went off into Nod (darkness).[952] And Cain took a wife and begot heirs to himself, who were like him in manner, and they were called Cainites, and their heirs were called the tribe of Cainites, which survived him nine hundred and ten years, after which they were divided into twenty-six tribes. (And the name Cain was lost. But the people survived, and are known to this day as THE WORLD'S PEOPLE.)

25/29.30. And We-it bore another son, Seth, in place of Abel, whom Cain slew. And after these came the generations of men, good and evil. And the Lord God said: Behold, I created man without sin, and I gave him warning, so that he could remain holy on the face of the earth. But woman did not listen to my counsel, but to the serpent, and sin came into the world. Therefore in pain woman shall bring forth all the generations of the earth.

25/29.31. Thus it was that the Lord God created man in the likeness of God.

25/29.32. And the sons of Cain were called tribes, even to this day, but the sons of the righteous were sons of God; and for that reason it was said of old: Behold the sons of earth and the sons of heaven.

25/29.33. And the Lord said: Shall I not accord to myself[953] to choose what I will? For this right I gave to man also. And from that time forward the sons of God were called God's chosen.

25/29.34. And it came to pass that man multiplied on the face of the earth; and the tribes were mightier than the sons of the Lord God, and the wickedness of man became great in the earth, and the desires of his heart were continually evil.

25/29.35. And the Lord God repented that he had made man on the earth, and it grieved him in

---

[952] Nod, in Phoenician, is equivalent to M'hak in Chinese. All persons who cannot recognize conscience, that is consciousness of right and wrong, are in Nod; that is, cannot hear the voice of the Lord. –Ed.

[953] i.e., give myself the right

his heart. And the Lord God said: I will destroy man whom I have created; neither will I spare beast nor creeping thing in the place I gave.

25/29.36. Behold, I will bring a flood of waters upon the lands of the earth, and I will destroy all flesh which has the breath of life. But my covenant is with my chosen, who shall not be destroyed by the flood of waters.

25/29.37. And God's sons in Noe[954] took with them pairs of the living, of both beasts and birds, according to the commandments of God, to keep their seed alive on the earth.

25/29.38. And when the earth was six hundred years in Noe, the flood of waters came upon the earth. And for forty days and forty nights the rain fell, and the fountains of the sea came upon the lands of the earth. And man and beast alike that drew the breath of life, died, for the land was no more.

25/29.39. But the heirs of Noe did not suffer; and the ships of the arc, where the Lord had concealed them, rode upon the waters. And God made a wind to pass over the earth; and the fountains of the deep were stopped, and the rain of heaven restrained, and the ships of the arc brought to dry land.

25/29.40. And the Lord God said: Behold, I will build a new earth and a new heaven. For these, my sons, have proven their faith in me. Never will I again destroy the tribes of men because their hearts are set on evil. And the Lord God swore an oath by the bow of the arc, saying: This is the token of the covenant which I have established between me and all flesh that is upon the earth. || And the sons of Noe spread over the whole earth, and the Lord blessed the earth, and said: Every moving thing that lives shall be meat for man; even as the green herb I have given. But flesh with the life[955] in it, which is in its blood, man shall not eat.

25/29.41. For if you do, I will surely require your blood from your lives; no matter the type of beast thus eaten, I will require it. By the hand of every man's brother I will take the life of man who feeds on living flesh and blood.

[954] Noe, one of the arcs of light in etherea. –Ed.

[955] In olden times some tribes of men cut flesh out of living animals and ate it raw. –Ed. [But now under this present edict, any creature that had blood in it was not to be eaten while it was alive.]

25/29.42. And he who sheds man's blood, shall have his own blood shed by man; for I made man in my image. So be fruitful and multiply, and bring forth harvests abundantly from the earth, and inhabit it, for it is yours for perpetual generations. ||

25/29.43. Thus ended the words of Osiris. Te-in said: Because of flesh blood, you are wise, my brother. Sudga said: The glory of our enterprise hangs on this. For man being less restrained than in the Divan laws, will readily accept the new.

25/29.44. After this, Osiris prepared a book of generations of men on earth. And with that, the substance of the doctrines of De'yus and his Gods was finished. So Osiris, Te-in and Sudga departed, and descended to the earth, to their mortal wards, and by virtue of their presence inspired their wards to write the doctrines in mortal words, according to the languages in the places where they lived. And after these seers finished the writing, copies were made and put on file in the libraries containing the records of the kings and queens of earth, in Arabin'ya, Jaffeth and Shem. And these became the bible of that day.

CHAPTER 30 Wars

25/30.1. Now, after the three false Gods, Osiris, Te-in and Sudga, had revealed these things to mortals, they sent messengers to the Lord God, requesting audience with him, so as to disclose to him what they had done. Anuhasaj, alias De'yus, therefore appointed a time of meeting, and the Gods came before him and made their report. After which De'yus said:

25/30.2. In all you have done I acquiesce; neither have you said anything that I would not have said, except that I did not desire to laud myself with my own mouth. || And thus ended the matter of how mortals were taught to worship the names Lord and God, Lord God, Ho-Joss, Joss, De'yus, Deity, Dyaus, Zeus, and various other names, according to the languages of the people of Jaffeth, Vind'yu, Arabin'ya, Par'si'e, and Heleste. And billions of angels of the Lord God and his Gods, who were sent down to mortals, inspired them and taught them the same things through seers, prophets, magicians, and through other people also, by dreams and visions.

25/30.3. And mortals were taught the secret of spiritually going out of their own corporeal bodies, and returning safely; and in this state they were taken subjectively to the kingdom of the Lord God, where they saw him as a man, sitting on a throne; and saw the great glory of his kingdom, and the millions of worshippers, glorifying De'yus, the false Lord God. And these persons became preachers on the earth; enthusiastically stirring up men on every hand to draw the sword, the spear, the sling, to go forth in battle, to overthrow the doctrine of the Great Spirit and establish the De'yus.

25/30.4. And it came to pass that they thus accomplished the will of the Lord God in all these divisions of the earth. The Jehovihians, being non-resistants, were powerless before them. Kings and queens on the earth accepted these doctrines, and they marshaled their armies in all directions to establish the Lord God, who had said to them: To the extent that you exalt me and my kingdoms, so will I exalt you. When I see you have become wise and powerful in ruling over many on the earth, so will I give you large kingdoms in heaven.

25/30.5. As to the false Lord God and his false Gods, they and their kingdoms prospered in earth and heaven for nine hundred years, and by then the Faithists of the earth had been reduced to a small fraction of people, mostly hidden away, like sheep from wolves.

25/30.6. But in nine hundred and fifty years, behold, the worshippers of the false Lord God began to quarrel and fight among themselves. Even as by blood they had established him, so by blood the kings and queens of the earth were overthrowing one another.

25/30.7. Because of the warfare: schools, colleges and houses of philosophy were wasted away; the factories for spinning and weaving were destroyed; and the lands not tilled.

25/30.8. And now this is what became of the heavenly kingdoms of Anuhasaj and his Gods: They had accumulated twenty-eight billion spirits, all of whom were servants to De'yus and his Gods. For the most part they were below grade ten, while three billion were below grade five, which is helplessness.

25/30.9. Jehovih had so made man and angels that, whoever had learned to abnegate self and to labor for the good of others, was already above grade fifty, and his ascension should be perpetual ever after; while those who were below grade fifty, who had not put away self (satan), incline downward, toward the earth. Accordingly it had come to pass that the false Lord God and his false Gods were burdened with their kingdoms.

25/30.10. And though they were adorned to the utmost, having vast cities for their heavenly capitals with millions of attendants, and millions of musicians, who were forever inventing new and wonderful music, and playing and singing, millions and millions in concert, with millions of trumpeters, near and far off, to fashion echoes beautiful to the ear; and though they had decorators forever inventing and changing their billions of flags and banners, and the ornaments for the pageantry; though they had millions of heavenly cities, built with heavenly precious stones and gems of splendor, and with roadways and streets paved with heavenly diamonds and pearls; and though they had heavenly tournaments and games, rites and ceremonies, prostrations[956] and salutations, without end; with great heavenly ships, capable of coursing atmospherea in journeys and excursions, ships to carry hundreds of millions of angels, whose chief occupation was to sing and chant the glory, power and dominion of De'yus and his Gods; yes, though a large book could not contain a description of a thousandth part of their wonderful glory, yet each and every God began to see coming danger.

25/30.11. Jehovih had said: Two precipices I have left open for testing man's strength, and they are: great prosperity and great adversity. ||

25/30.12. And behold, satan came upon them in the guise of a good friend. First, he went to Anuhasaj and said to him: You greatest of Gods! Who is like you? Behold, I came to you in the beginning, and told you what to do, even to stretch forth your hand, and heaven and earth would be yours forever, for your own glory. And lo, it has come on finely! You have routed Jehovih and His hosts in heaven and earth; they are as a remnant skulking away. Hear me, then, O De'yus, for I will not only praise you for what you have accomplished, but I will chide you for your failings.

25/30.13. De'yus said: In what have I failed, O satan? And satan answered, saying: You are too honest for your own good; too pure for your own

---

[956] A kind of glorification. –Ed.

benefit; too unsuspecting regarding your Gods. Being honest yourself, you have easily attributed honesty to others, and they have taken advantage of you.

25/30.14. Anuhasaj said: How? Satan answered, saying: From the beginning, you said to your Gods: Maintain your schools, colleges and factories, and otherwise prepare the spirits of the dead for resurrection. And as fast as they arrive at grade thirty, send them to my kingdom, so that Hored may be glorified forever. But lo and behold, your Gods used the angels as slaves, to build up the glory of their own kingdoms. They have allowed their heavenly places of education, for the most part, to be scattered and gone. Nor have they inspired mortals to educate, as I warned you at the beginning. And mortals have thrown aside their schools and colleges, and their places of art, and have become riotous, and given to gross living, and there is no resurrection in them. Which matters show you that, sooner or later, all the spirits of the earth will be of no grade at all, but as fetals and vampires to live on mortals.

25/30.15. De'yus said: Why have mortals become gross in their living? Satan answered him, saying: Behold, in your own revelation to mortals you said to them: For your food, do not eat fish, flesh, blood, or anything that breathes the breath of life. And now, behold what came to pass: Your three Gods, whom you had elevated and trusted, went to work and made other revelations, in which they said: Eat fish and flesh; for they desired to please mortals. And lo, it has come to pass that man not only wars for you, but he wars to the right and left, for it is in his blood, like beasts that feed on flesh. Your Gods had no right to give this law to man without first consulting you, to know your will and pleasure.

25/30.16. Anuhasaj said: Alas, it is true. What shall I do? Satan said: You shall call your Gods before you and chide them in your own way, and command them to go down to mortals and re-establish learning and industry, instead of war. Anuhasaj said: So shall it be; they shall come and receive my reprimand. They shall know in truth that I am the Lord their God!

25/30.17. Satan went to every one of the other false Gods, separately, saying to each: Hear me, O wisest of Gods, who, because of your great wisdom and integrity, should in fact be at the all highest Godhead in heaven. Behold, I came to you in the beginning and foretold how your kingdom would become great and glorified; and it has come to pass. When you put forth your hand to do a thing, it is done; for you were born into life different from all others, and for the highest of glories. And because of your greatness, behold, all the Gods of heaven are jealous of you and fear you, all of which you know by your own knowledge. Now, while I accredit this to you, I will also chide you for your shortness:

25/30.18. For, because you are honest yourself, you believe the same of others; and for this reason you are cheated and ill-used on all hands. From the beginning you sent your highest grades to the Lord God, to be his; yes, you have robbed your own kingdom of its finest and best subjects for the glory of De'yus. And who is De'yus more than you? Is he not a coward? For he feared to give his own doctrines to mortals; instead he abridged his words till they were worthless. And you and your fellow-Gods made his doctrines up in full for him! Yet you serve him as if he were your superior.

25/30.19. The false God said: Alas, it is true, with all my wisdom I have acted like a fool. Because I was too honest and pure for De'yus and his Gods, they have taken advantage of me. What shall I do? Satan said: I told you at the beginning, that the time would come when you would rise to be higher than all other Gods. Behold, the time is near at hand when you shall strike the blow. You shall not only have your own kingdom, but the kingdoms of your companion Gods; and even De'yus shall be tributary to you and yours.

25/30.20. The false God said: What shall I do? And satan answered, saying: De'yus will scent[957] the danger to his kingdom, and he will summon his Gods for consultation. Be ready with your answer to him and them; not hastily, for such is the manner of the weak; but most deliberately, in high holiness of purpose, for the good of mortals and spirits. ||

25/30.21. In that way satan spoke alike to all the false Gods; and they nursed the planted seed; held it in the light and shade to see it grow, till it became the very giant of each one's understanding.

---

[957] sniff, smell, become aware of, detect, sense

CHAPTER 31 Wars

25/31.1. In due course Anuhasaj called the meeting of his Gods in Hored, and Osiris and Sudga came. Great were the pageantry and show that day; and the pomp and glory, and splendor of Sanc-tu; with billions of trained slaves, with their dashing officers of high rank. For it had been nearly seven hundred years since even generals and high captains could come into the presence of the Lord God, the false, except by crawling on their bellies, even for miles.

25/31.2. And in and around the heavenly house of the capital were erected fifty thousand pillars of fire, kept forever going by the labor of his slaves, some of whom stood in their tracks laboring at one thing for more than a hundred years, without change of watch, or rest, being threatened with hell, and being too impotent to believe otherwise. No one could walk upright to the throne of the Lord God except his High Council, his high marshals, his Gods, and Anubi. And no one else was permitted to look upon him, under penalty of being cast into hell.

25/31.3. At first his Gods came to feast with him once a year, for more than a hundred years; after that, for awhile, once in six years; and afterward, only once in fifty or a hundred years; and then only by special command.

25/31.4. So it came to pass that the coming of De'yus' false Gods was an occasion of rejoicing and glory for more than twelve billion inhabitants of the kingdom of Anuhasaj. For, far and near, they were given extra clothing and food, and granted freedom for the time being.

25/31.5. On this occasion, the Gods, coming in fire-ships of great size and brilliancy, were received by hundreds of millions, called the receiving hosts, who conducted them up to the roadways of the court, nearer than which the receiving hosts dared not approach. There the Gods were met by De'yus' High Council and high marshals, and with them entered the area and walked up to the high arch of the capital, which led into the place of the throne of the Lord God. When inside of the Arch, the Council and marshals parted on either side, and, with the head bowed, chanted an anthem of praise to De'yus. The Gods also bowed with respect and friendship, and walked in the middle directly toward the throne.

25/31.6. When they were near, the vice-Gods, on either side of De'yus, rose up, saying:

25/31.7. In the name of the Lord God of the heavens of the earth, who come here, upright, and as Gods?

25/31.8. The Gods responded: Behold, we are sons of the Lord God, great De'yus, and in truth we are Gods! We demand audience with our Godhead, for the glory of our kingdoms and his.

25/31.9. De'yus said: Peace, O my vice-Gods! I recognize these, my brother Gods. Greeting, in the name of heaven and earth.

25/31.10. The Gods responded: Greeting to you, O Lord God, mightiest of Gods. In your mighty name, De'yus, we salute you worshipfully, to know your will and pleasure, so that we may serve you in wisdom, power, and love.

25/31.11. De'yus said: Welcome, O Gods; the freedom of Sanc-tu is at your hands. Behold, I will clear my palace, so that we may privately, and in a most holy manner, consult together for the good of angels and mortals.

25/31.12. So De'yus gave a signal for all his officers and attendants to retire beyond the Arch, which they did. And now that the ceremony of reception was over, Anuhasaj came down from his throne and greeted the Gods cordially by clasping hands, after which they all sat down on the foot seats of the throne; and with no others within hearing range, there were present De'yus, Osiris and Sudga; for Te-in had not come.

25/31.13. And for a while they talked together like long-separated friends; and lo and behold, the satan that was within each one of them began to fail him with regard to reproving the others. For the smothered seed of love that the Great Spirit had given them, began to swell up, as if about to burst forth a mighty power. So the time passed on, and none dared approach the subject of his soul and resolution.

25/31.14. Till at last, De'yus, the most schooled in satan's cause, put an end to their old-time stories and trivial conversation; he said:

25/31.15. I have loved you both so much, and am now so moved by your august presence, that with all my majesty and power I am weaker than a young child, who will unconcernedly reprove its own father. Or rather I am like an old man who, in the absence of his child, finds cause to quarrel with it; but on seeing it return, breaks down utterly, and turns from his previous grieving to an outburst of manifest love.

25/31.16. Osiris said: What can move you to this seriousness, O De'yus? For in speaking so, you have uttered the sentiment long lain heavily on my heart. But which now, in reverence to you and your great kingdoms, causes me to melt down like snow in a summer's sun. Please, continue!

25/31.17. Sudga said: As I live, you two, so far my superiors that I am as nothing, have spoken the very sentiment of my soul. Please, both of you continue; for so great is my love for you, that your most extravagant wish shall be answered by me, though I labor a thousand years to accomplish it.

25/31.18. So De'yus sweetly told his tale, even as satan had taught him. And then he bade Osiris to speak his mind, and also Sudga to speak his; which they did, even as satan had taught them their parts. When they had finished, De'yus, much surprised by their pitiful tales, even as the others were at his, then spoke:

25/31.19. My Gods, how much easier it is to find fault with the state of affairs than to find a remedy. I have seen those who find fault with their neighbors, or with the kingdom, or with the ancients, and yet they turned around and committed the same faults themselves. All of us know that one of the complaints we had against the old Divan laws was their bondage over the Lords and their dominions, holding them to the letter. So that, when we confederated, it was to give independence to each and every Lord to rule his own heaven and division of the earth in his own way. And this was granted to all my Lords, and to me and my kingdom likewise. And look at its harvest! In the fullness of my soul I gave you certain doctrines to give to mortals, chief of which was to make my names worshipful on the earth. But I did not bind you, saying: Do this and no more. But I said to you: Here is the substance of the foundations of my doctrines. Go to mortals and teach them these things, adding or abridging according to your own wisdom.

25/31.20. And this you accomplished, and added to it the temptation to mortals to become carnivores, by which the grades have fallen woefully. And now you find fault with me for exacting a certain number of slaves annually of a certain grade, complaining that your own kingdoms are becoming flooded with drujas.

25/31.21. Osiris said: Hear me, O Lord my God, for I have labored for you and your kingdoms many a hundred years. Nor are my words in passion, but well considered; so, if I err, I ask no excuse on account of hastiness. First, then, our confederacy was founded to make a mighty heavenly kingdom, having dominion over mortals on the whole earth; of which kingdom you were to be the chief and greatest glory, and ourselves second. To all of which our songs to this day bear testimony. But, as for songs or testimonies in the libraries of heaven, that our confederacy was founded chiefly to get rid of the Divan laws, I have not seen nor heard of one.

25/31.22. Sudga said: What I have done is done. I was commanded to a division of the earth, to subdue it to De'yus, and I have accomplished it. I have listened to your complaints but neither has offered a remedy. You are both higher in rank and wisdom than I; when you have spoken to the purpose I will also speak. For my part, I am thankful there are no Divan laws to bind me.

25/31.23. De'yus said: The remedy lies in overturning the cause of the falls in the grades. For sake of glorifying themselves, my Gods have allowed places of learning and industry to fall to pieces, both in heaven and earth. True, there are those who glorify charity, and rites and ceremonies; but I say to you, my Gods, INDUSTRY AND LEARNING stand higher than either charity or rites and ceremonies; and especially when industry yields profitable support.

25/31.24. Osiris said: Where, O Lord my God, does the difference lie between that which is written or spoken? In your opening words you have even now reiterated the bondage of the Divan laws over the Lords. And in the next breath you say: I command you to re-establish the places of learning and industry.

25/31.25. Sudga said: Are not written laws less arbitrary than spoken ones? For we see them beforehand, and are not, therefore, shocked by the sudden audacity.

25/31.26. De'yus said: In either case, is it not true that the highest in power and mightiest in the plans and arrangement of his kingdoms must either take jibes and insults from his inferiors, whom he has lifted up and made what they are, or otherwise fall broken-hearted on the loss of their love and worship? For time and again we behold, alas, beneficiaries are apt to turn like venomous serpents, and strike their benefactor, even though the blow would send themselves into destruction.

25/31.27. Osiris said: That is most especially true, O De'yus, where the highest kingdoms owe their glory and greatness to those who have been subsidiary and built them up. None are so slow to see their danger as they who are exposed to it. There are those holding high places, with slaves, and if these latter should discover their true condition and how they were deceived, they would bind the former in knots and cast them into hell.

25/31.28. Sudga said: But in such cases is it not better, my wise brothers, that the highest—who have been raised up by the toil and industry of others that labored to have them glorified—turn from their own glory and selfish ends, and divide up their ill-gotten kingdoms, and bestir their lazy carcasses by sending assistants to those who have them in their power?

25/31.29. De'yus said: Most wisely spoken, both my Gods. But how shall we teach apes and monkeys to know their masters? They crook their tails and squeal, imagining themselves great monarchs. But if they were cut off from their masters, they would come to grief most ignominiously[958] or be the first plunged into torments.

25/31.30. Osiris said: You wisest of Gods, is it not most strange, wonderful, how better we can see others' shortness than our own? Nor are we much quicker to find a way to save them, which we often could do were they not self-conceited fools; but we guard our arms, so that when they show the least sign of doing us wrong, we inwardly swear within our souls to hurl them into hell.

25/31.31. Sudga said: O my loves, it is a sad reflection, when we survey mighty kingdoms at their quarrels, knowing that, if either dares to lift a hand to destroy, we ourselves hold the key by which they both can be stripped of their highest subjects and their greatest glories, and left in the ruins of their own evil concocting. But the wise bide their time, and often are fortified when others do not know of it.

25/31.32. De'yus said: My most wise Gods, you have spoken great wisdom. I will weigh your words and be governed accordingly. For your most holy visit I am honored above all I deserve.

25/31.33. Osiris said: Words cannot express my reverence for your spoken words, O De'yus.

25/31.34. Sudga said: I am bowed with sorrow to leave the place of so much wisdom, love and power. ||

25/31.35. And now Osiris and Sudga stepped backward, four paces each, but separate from each other, with their heads still bowed. By a signal, the vice-Gods re-entered and stood beside the Gods, and then all, with heads bowed, raised their hands and saluted in the sign Central Sun. De'yus answered them on the sign Music of the Satellites.

25/31.36. Slowly now, and with measured backward step, to low sweet music, the Gods and vice-Gods crossed the area and passed the Arch, where the vice-Gods left them and returned within. But the Gods were now met by the High Council and high marshals and conducted to the entrance gate, where they left Osiris and Sudga, each being received by their respective hosts and re-conducted to their ships, with great pomp and honor, and they set sail at once for their own heavenly kingdoms.

25/31.37. Now in this whole proceeding, the Gods were all surprised that Te-in had not come, nor, by messenger or otherwise, answered the summons; nor could one of them imagine the cause.

CHAPTER 32 Wars

Of Te-in and his heavenly kingdoms

25/32.1. When Te-in, whose heavenly kingdom contained three billion angels, was informed when Osiris and Sudga were gone to Hored, satan said to him: Now is your time, call your Council together; proclaim yourself God of heaven and earth, mighty in all regions, the Central Kingdom of the Eternal Heavens! Choose from among your Council those of the highest grades, and make them Lords under you. After which you shall renew the battles in Jaffeth, on the earth.

25/32.2. Te-in said: Why on the earth? Satan said: Behold, Jaffeth must be subdued to one nation of people, and this shall be your footstool, and your heavenly kingdom's headquarters. After which your Lords shall proceed to the lands of Par'si'e, and Arabin'ya, and inspire the inhabitants to

[958] shamefully, disgracefully, degradingly

another central kingdom, and when mortals are thus subdued to limited numbers of rulers, you shall have only a few to deal with in order to make yourself God of the whole earth.

25/32.3. Te-in said: You are wiser than all Gods. Behold, my way is clear.

25/32.4. So on the same day of De'yus' meeting with Osiris and Sudga, Te-in severed the bonds between his heavenly kingdom and all others, and he chose twelve of his highest grade in the Holy Council, and made them Lords of the earth; but he allotted no portion of the earth to any one alone. He said:

25/32.5. I will not give them kingdoms; this is the strongest way; to keep everything in one's own hands. ||

25/32.6. Then Te-in, through his Lords, whom he sent down to the earth, made Kan Kwan mortal king of Jaffeth, with the title, King of the World, Sun, Moon and Stars! And the Lords caused Kan Kwan to build an oke'spe [spirit-house or oracle – Ed.], where he could receive the commandments of Te-in, the holiest, all highest ruler of heaven, as to what he should do in order to subdue the earth to himself.

25/32.7. Te-in said: And, my Gods, say to Kan Kwan when the earth is subdued to himself: Behold, I will also come down and dwell in the temples he builds for my Lords. || And when the king goes forth and subdues a place to himself, he shall immediately build a worshipful temple and dedicate it to me and my Lords, whose names you shall give alike in all places. For I will not confuse mortals with a multiplicity of heavenly Lords. And the king shall show to the people that there is only one High Ruler in heaven, whether he is called Ho-Joss or Joss, or Po-tein, or Te-in, and that I am the Person. But in no case shall the king permit the worshippers of the Great Spirit to remain alive upon the earth.

25/32.8. Te-in said: My Lords, each of you shall take with you one million angels who are strong and cunning in war; twelve million are sufficient, for you shall not scatter them about, but keep them in the vicinity of the war and the king. As when a fire burns, beginning from a spark and spreading outward till a city is consumed, likewise keep your forces concentrated and potent. This is the whole art of power. And while mortals sleep, your angels shall come upon them and give them dreams and visions of glorious success; make them see themselves in the heat of battle, rushing through the jaws of death unscathed, while on every side their manly arms slay their enemies by the score in flowing blood. For when these mortals awake and remember their dreams, they will be well prepared for the valorous work. But as to those who are to be conquered, let your angels go to them while they sleep, and give them dreams and visions of horrid deaths; make them see the heat of battle and themselves overpowered on every hand, and, pierced with sword and spear, they fall, dying in great agony. For when such mortals wake up and remember their dreams, they are half conquered already.

25/32.9. Te-in said: My Lords, you shall inspire the king to be merciful and gentle; and when his soldiers come to a place to subdue it, they shall send truce-men before them, inquiring: Who, do you say, shall be the ruler? And if the people answer: We are Kan Kwan's slaves, they shall not be slain.

25/32.10. Te-in said: My Lords, among mortals, what is righteousness? Now one Lord said: Rites and ceremonies. Another said: To worship you, O Te-in. Another said: To follow the doctrines of the ancients. Another said: To purify one's self. Another said: To do good with all one's might. Another said: To practice truth. Another said: To harm no man.

25/32.11. Te-in said: Not one of you knows righteousness. Behold how you stand: The doctrines of the ancients were their own, and they are as dead. To put on a dead man's clothes, will they make the wearer like the dead was?

25/32.12. Rites and ceremonies are what showmen train their horses with, to run or leap, or lie down, to please their masters.

25/32.13. To purify one's self! What is that? A mortal man's body cannot be purified, for it is rotten at best.

25/32.14. To do good with all one's might! Who knows the meaning of that? To cut off a crushed foot to save a man's life, gives him pain in the cutting, even while he is suffering. Then it is well that some men's heads are cut off for their own good. Yes, even nations extirpated.[959] Let him who does, then, do with all his might. Do you not see in

---

[959] uprooted; destroyed

this, that before one attempts to do good, he is his own judge, judging by his own judgment?[960]

25/32.15. To practice truth! What is that? The Jehovihians say: Jehovih is All Truth. But Jehovih is nothing, scattered as the wind. Then truth is nothing. Who has found a man who does not say: To see as I see, is to see the truth; to see as you see, is to see falsely? A man told lies knowingly, and practiced them; and he was all truth to himself, for he was a liar. Therefore, he practiced truth.

25/32.16. To worship me is unrighteousness instead of righteousness. To worship Joss is unrighteousness; to worship the nondescript, Jehovih, is unrighteousness, and to worship Po is unrighteousness also. Behold this matter: The large trees in the forest were smothering out the small ones; and the small ones said: We praise you, giant oaks, for the many blessings we have received; be merciful to us! The large trees laughed at them, and they died. Is this not Jehovih? Is this not the Gods? For all mortals, at best, are only as un-hatched eggs; and when they are dead, their souls are like hatched chickens for the Gods to play with, and to use in their own way.

25/32.17. Te-in said: Teach this to mortals; and tell them, moreover, to choose what God they will; and if it is me, then I will labor for them; if it is not me, then I am against them. This, then, is righteousness: Reciprocity[961] between Gods and mortals; reciprocity between mortals themselves; to war for opinion's sake in order to develop in steadfastness; to help the helpless; to feed and clothe the stranger, and to worship the father and mother.

CHAPTER 33 Wars

25/33.1. Te-in's Lords and their angels departed out of Che-su-gow, Te-in's heavenly place, and descended to the earth on their mission; and the following is what came of it:

25/33.2. Kan Kwan was the son of Kwan Ho, a flat-head; but because Kan Kwan's parents became converts to the Brahmin priests, Kan did not have his head flattened. But because su'is and sar'gis had been in their family for many generations they descended to Kwan all the same. And he could see and hear the angels and their Lords; hear all the words spoken to him, a most excellent thing in a king, when drujas are restrained from observing him.

25/33.3. The Lords guarded Kan Kwan on every side, day and night, and Kwan being stupid, because of the flat heads of his parents, was well suited to carry out all that was commanded of him. So he announced himself at once with all his titles, and sent heralds here and there to proclaim him and let all peoples and kings know that he was coming to subdue them to himself.

25/33.4. Kwan issued this decree: Kan Kwan, king of the world, and of the sun, moon and stars, I command! I, son of the sun, son of Te-in, behold! There is only one ruler in heaven, Te-in! There shall be only one on earth, Kan Kwan. Bow your heads down! I come! Choose to bow down, or to die. One or the other shall be. When the world is subdued to me, I will war no more!

25/33.5. In those days there were many great kings in Jaffeth, and their kingdoms were in many places, and far apart. Between them, in a sparse region, in the Valley of Lun, lay the city of Ow Tswe, and this was Kan Kwan's small kingdom, which had been known for a thousand years.

25/33.6. When other kings heard of Kwan's proclamation they laughed. And this is the vanity of mortals, for they disregard the power of the Gods over them.

25/33.7. So Kwan started with an army of four thousand soldiers, men and women, with spears, axes, scythes, swords, slings, and bows and arrows; and he marched against Tzeyot, a city of a hundred thousand people; and here king Cha Ung Chin ruled, with twenty thousand soldiers. Cha Ung Chin laughed. He said to his captain: Send a thousand women soldiers to kill Kwan and his army; they are mad, and do not know what war is.

25/33.8. The captain went forth to battle, but in addition to the thousand women soldiers he took a thousand men soldiers. But lo and behold, Kwan and his soldiers knew no drill, but ran forward so strangely that their enemies did not know how to

---

[960] And here we see a deficit that comes from not knowing Jehovih; for the Faithist, in perceiving the light and voice of Jehovih within his own soul, has Jehovih as the higher judge, indeed the highest judge.

[961] a mutual exchange, where all parties gain something of value in return

fight them, and they fled in fear, except the captain and a hundred women who were instantly put to death. But not one of Kwan's army was killed.

25/33.9. Cha Ung Chin was angry, and he sent ten thousand soldiers against Kwan's ragged army; and when the battle began, the angels cast clouds before the hosts of Cha Ung Chin, and they thought they saw hundreds of thousands of soldiers coming upon them, and they turned and fled also, except five hundred men and women, who were captured and instantly slain.

25/33.10. Cha Ung Chin said: It is time I go myself. My laziness has cost me dearly. Tomorrow I will lead thirty thousand pressed[962] men and women, and make it a day of sport to slaughter Kwan's army. So the king sent his marshals to select and summon his soldiers during the night. Many were too frightened to sleep; and those who slept had such visions and dreams that when they awoke they were as persons nearly dead.

25/33.11. Next morning, Cha Ung Chin sallied forth out of the city to battle, going before his army. When he saw the pitiful army of Kwan, he said: In truth, the world is going mad! That such fools have courage is because they do not know what a battle is. With that he rushed forward, faster and faster, calling to his soldiers. But they stretched out in a line behind him, for they trembled from head to foot, remembering their dreams.

25/33.12. Presently Kwan and his army started for them, not with orderly commands, but screaming and howling. Cha Ung Chin's soldiers took panic, broke ranks and fled in all directions, except one thousand, including King Cha Ung Chin, who were captured and instantly slain.

25/33.13. And on the same day Kan Kwan took possession of the city, Tzeyot, commanding obedience and allegiance from the people. And on the following day he put twenty thousand men to work building a temple to Te-in, pulling down other edifices for their material. Nor did Kwan have a learned man in all his army; but the Lords with him showed him how to build the temple, east and west, and north and south, and how to make the archways and the pillars to support the roof; and the sacred chambers and altars of sacrifice. Out of brick, mortar and wood he built it, and when it was completed it was large enough for twelve thousand people to do sacrifice[963] in. And it took forty days to build.

25/33.14. Besides this, Kwan put another ten thousand men and women to work clearing away houses and walls, and making new streets in many directions; so that at the time of the first sacrifice the city of Tzeyot did not look like itself; and Kwan gave it a new name, Lu An, and commanded all people to call it by that name, or suffer death.

25/33.15. Kan Kwan made the people go and do sacrifice to Te-in in the temple every morning; enforced a day of rest for each quarter of the moon; enforced worship on the part of children to their fathers and mothers, the father taking first rank.

25/33.16. Then Kwan made them pray for those who were slain in battle. And these are the words he commanded them to use: Te-in! Father of Life and Death! Who feeds on suns and stars! Whose refuse[964] is mortals. In your praise I bow my head. For your glory I lie on my belly before your altar. I am the filthiest of things; my breath and my flesh and my blood are rotten. Death would be sweet to me if you or your soldiers would slay me. For my soul would come to you to be your slave forever.

25/33.17. Behold, my brothers and sisters who fought against you are dead, and I glorify you because of that. We have buried their rotten carcasses deep in the ground; good enough for them.

25/33.18. But their spirits are howling about, lost and wild on the battlefield. O Te-in, Father, send your spirits from Che-su-gow, your heavenly place, to them, to help them out of darkness. And we will always praise you, our mightiest, all highest ruler! ||

25/33.19. When they made the sacrifice they laid down on their bellies, while certain ones

---

[962] instantly drafted, pressed into military service

[963] In Chinese and Indian literature, sacrifice does not mean killing and burning, but prayer and praise. In other words, the sacrifice of time and self-interest, to acknowledging one's own unworthiness before the God, is sacrifice per se. – Ed. [Nevertheless, killing and burning appears to have been a part of the worship (sacrifice) to De'yus at least in certain places as will be shown later in this book.]

[964] worthless item, trash, cast away, rubbish, waste matter, feculence

prompted them with the words that Kwan received from the Lords.

25/33.20. After this, Kwan appointed to them a governor, Ding Jow, who was the first governor of a province in Jaffeth, in the order of governors as they exist to this day [1882].[965] Which is to say: As a Lord is to a God, so is a governor to a king. And this was the first of that order established by the Gods of hada. Prior to this, Jehovih had given a similar government to the Faithists; even as it had been given in its purity to the pure, so now it was given in its crudity to the crude.

25/33.21. Jehovih had said: Independent kingdoms shall not exist side by side; nor shall one be tributary to another; but there shall be one whole, and the lesser shall be parts of it, not over nor under them, but as helpmates. The wicked will not see this now; but their own wickedness will bring it about in time to come. And it was so. ||

CHAPTER 34 Wars

25/34.1. Kan Kwan again went forth to conquer and subdue, going southward, to Ho-tsze, a large city having five tributary cities, ruled over by Oo-long, a king with two hundred wives and a well disciplined army of thirty thousand men and women.

25/34.2. Kwan's army was now seven thousand strong, but without discipline; and with no head except himself. And on his march through the country he compelled the farmers to embrace the Te-in religion, under penalty of death.

25/34.3. Now when he had come near Ho-tsze, he, even as he had for the previous city, sent an order for the king to surrender.

25/34.4. Oo-long laughed when told of the kind of company that had come against him, and he sent only eight thousand women soldiers to give Kwan battle. When the armies were near each other, the Lords said to Kwan: Send a truce, and call on your enemy to surrender under penalty of death; for the angels of Te-in will deliver them into your hand, and not one shall die.

25/34.5. A truce was sent, and lo and behold, the whole of Oo-long's battlefield army surrendered, and made oaths of allegiance to Kwan, and not one was slain. Oo-long, when informed of it, said: Now I will go with all my army and slay this ragged king and all his people, and also my eight thousand who have surrendered. So he marched to battle with twenty-two thousand soldiers. Kwan's army was scattered about the fields. Oo-long said to his captain: Go, tell this foolish king to set his army in line of battle; I have no desire to take advantage of a flock of sheep.

25/34.6. The captain started to go, but before he reached the place, he fell down in a swoon, for the angels overpowered him. The king saw his captain fall, and he cried out to his army: It is enough! My army has never seen such fools, and do not know how to battle with them. Come, I will lead!

25/34.7. At that, he rushed on, followed by his thousands. Instantly, Kwan's army set up their screams and howls, and ran forward in every direction; and lo and behold, Oo-long's army broke and fled, except for twelve hundred who were captured, Oo-long among them; and they were instantly slain. But of Kwan's army, only one man was killed.

25/34.8. The Lords sent messengers to Te-in in his heavenly place, informing him of Kwan's success. Te-in returned this commandment: In what has been done I am well pleased; but do not let your mortal king, Kan Kwan, win so easily from now on; but let him have losses, so that he will not forget me and my Lords and my hosts of angels. Place him in straits,[966] and cause him to pray to me; and his army shall pray also. And when they have thus sacrificed, deliver him and his army from their straits, and make him victorious for a season. ||

25/34.9. Kwan entered the city of Ho-tsze without further opposition, and possessed it. Immediately he put thirty thousand laborers to work building a temple to Te-in. Another twenty thousand he told to pull down houses and make other streets, more beautiful than before. In twenty-eight days the temple and the streets were completed; and on the twenty-ninth day the sacrifices (worship) commenced, and all the people

---

[965] This refers to a governor as an officer appointed (assigned) to govern a dependency such as a colony, a territory, a province, etc. Nowadays, in, say, the United States of America, governors of states are elected by the people; and they constitute political heads of state more or less in the manner suggested in verse 21.

[966] predicament; difficulty; crisis; distress

were obliged to swear allegiance to Kwan and to Te-in, or be slain. And on the first day there were slain four thousand men and women (worshippers of different Gods, but for the main part the Great Spirit) who would not take the oath.

25/34.10. After that, none refused, and so Kwan gave the city a new name, Tue Shon; and he appointed So'wo'tse governor, and commanded the tributary cities to come under the yoke.

25/34.11. Then Kan Kwan went forward again to conquer and subdue; and the Lords of heaven and their twelve million angels went with him and in advance of him, preparing the way. And the news of his success, well exaggerated, was spread abroad among mortals, so that the inhabitants of cities far and near feared him.

25/34.12. The Lords made it possible for Kwan to conquer and subdue three more large cities without loss to his army; and lo and behold, Kwan began to think it was he himself who possessed the power, and not Te-in.

25/34.13. The next city, Che-gau, was a small one, of fifty thousand inhabitants. Kwan did not ask Te-in (through the Lords) how to make the attack, but he went forward on his own judgment. Now over the city there ruled a woman, Lon Gwie, a tyrant little loved, and she had only four thousand soldiers, while Kwan had seven thousand.

25/34.14. Kwan, arriving near, demanded the place; but the queen did not answer him with words; but had her soldiers in ambush, who then fell upon Kwan's army, and put one-half of them to death; and yet the queen suffered small loss. Kwan, not finding his Lords with him, fled with his remaining army. But the Lords urged the queen to pursue him, and she again fell upon them and slew half while crippling hundreds more. But again the queen suffered small loss.

25/34.15. The Lords then spoke to Kwan, where he had escaped to, and said to him: Because you were vain and did not remember me, your heavenly ruler, Te-in, I have labored to show you that of yourself you are nothing. Then Kwan prayed to Te-in, saying: Most mighty ruler of heaven and earth, you have justly punished me. I pray to you now, with good repentance, in the bitterness of my shame. What shall I do, O Te-in? I am far from home, in a strange country, and my army is well-nigh destroyed. All nations are against me; a sheep is safer in a forest with wolves than I am in these regions.

25/34.16. The Lord said to Kwan: Now that you have repented, behold I, Te-in, will show you my power. For you shall gather together the remnant of your army and turn about and destroy the queen and her army, or put them to flight and possess the city.

25/34.17. So the next morning, Kwan, being inspired by his Lords, prepared for battle, though he had only seven hundred men. On the other hand, the Lords and their angels appeared in the dreams and visions of the queen's army, saying to them: The queen is deceived and has led her army into a trap. In the morning fifty thousand men will join Kwan. Prepare, therefore, to die tomorrow.

25/34.18. The next day, then, the queen's soldiers related their fearful dreams to one another; hardly had they finished when Kwan's army came upon them. And the angels, more than fifty thousand, took on sar'gis, seeming like mortals. At sight of this, the queen's army were so frightened they could not flee, except a few, but nearly the whole army surrendered, throwing away their arms and lying down.

25/34.19. Kwan and his army fell upon them and slew them, more than four thousand, who were rendered powerless by the angel hosts with them. Kwan then went into the city, doing as previously in other cities, establishing himself and Te-in.

25/34.20. Such, then, was the manner of Te-in, the false, in establishing himself in Jaffeth. Hear now of Sudga, of Vind'yu, and her heavenly kingdom.

CHAPTER 35 Wars

Of Sudga and his heavenly kingdoms

25/35.1. Sudga, the false God of Vind'yu and her heavens, whose heavenly kingdom contained more than three billion angels, said to himself on his way home from Hored: Two things I am resolved upon: to proclaim myself CREATOR AND RULER OF HEAVEN AND EARTH; and to change the name of my heavenly place and call it AHL-BURJ, THE MOUNTAIN OF THE CLOUDS.

25/35.2. Satan spoke to Sudga, saying: O all highest God, hear me. In the land of Vind'yu, down on the earth; and in the heavens above the land of

Vind'yu; what God has labored like you? You did establish De'yus, for nearly a thousand years in these regions. You possess by right that name, and you shall call yourself Dyaus[967] and Sudga; and your heavenly place shall also be Hored, because, in truth, it is also a heavenly mountain.

25/35.3. Sudga said: Most wisely said, O satan.

25/35.4. And so it came to pass that Sudga at once went to work moving his capital and throne, and founding his new place. And he also chose twelve Lords, saying to himself, like Te-in did: Though I will have twelve Lords to rule over mortals, yet I will not give to any one of them a specific division of the earth to be his.

25/35.5. And when Sudga was thus founded in his new heavenly place he called his Lords to him and said to them: Go down to mortals, to T-loyovogna, who has a small kingdom in the valley of Hachchisatij, in Vind'yu, for I will make him king of all the earth, even as I am ruler of heaven. And by obsessions and otherwise, you shall lead him forth to conquer and subdue.

25/35.6. Go ahead of him in his journeys, and cause mortals to fear him, so they may be easily overcome. Twelve million angels I allot to you as your army, nor shall you return into my presence until you have made T-loyovogna king of Vind'yu. After that I shall bestow you according to merit.

25/35.7. The twelve Lords, with their twelve million angels of war, departed for the earth, and came to Varaja, the city where T-loyovogna lived and ruled, and they covered the surrounding regions, even beyond the Valley of Hachchisatij.

25/35.8. T-loyovogna was the son of Hucrava, who was the son of Han Cyavarat, who was the son of Aipivohu, sacred in su'is to the Gods and Lords of heaven. So T-loyovogna talked with Sudga's chief Lord, who said to him: Behold, you shall proclaim yourself king of all the world; for I and the hosts of heaven are with you.

25/35.9. T-loyovogna said: Alas, mine is the weakest of kingdoms; I have less than a thousand soldiers. Other kings will laugh at me. But the Lord answered him, saying: What are mortal kings in the hands of Dyaus, he who was Sudga? I say to the nations of the earth: Go down! And they fall. I say: Rise up! And they rise. Man looks to stone, clay and water (i.e., corporeal things) for great power; but I who am unseen am greater than all the lands and waters of the earth, for I rule over them, and over heaven also.

25/35.10. I will have only one king on the earth; and as I rule the angels of heaven, even so shall you rule mortals, and establish you and me forever! For your heirs, and their heirs after them, shall have dominion over every kingdom and country in the world.

25/35.11. T-loyovogna said: I fear you, O Dyaus; I know your power. But how can a king go to war without soldiers? Or an army without arms?[968] The Lord answered him: Send your proclamation to kings far and near, commanding them to bow down to you. And presently I will come to you and lead you forth, and you shall conquer and subdue them, and not a hair of your head shall be harmed.

25/35.12. T-loyovogna did as commanded; and some days after his proclamation had been sent to the nearest kings, all of whom knew him well, he mustered his army of seven hundred men and one hundred women. And those without spears, swords, scythes, or bows and arrows, took clubs, clappers, and pans, to make noise with, and others took lanterns.

25/35.13. The first city they approached was Abtuib, ruled over by Azhis, who had an army of four thousand men and one thousand women. When near the place, T-loyovogna sent his demand for the surrender of the city. Azhis did not answer him, but said to his army: Go surround the fool, and destroy him and his army.

25/35.14. Now, behold, the night came on, very dark, before the attack was made. And the Lord said to T-loyovogna: Command your soldiers to light their lamps. T-loyovogna said: I fear, O Lord, for will lamps not expose us to death? But the Lord said: Light the lamps! So when the lamps were lit the enemy began to march to surround them, some going one way and some the other.

25/35.15. And the Lord's angels made lights also, to the left and to the right, so that the enemy, in order to surround the lights, kept extending in

---

[967] In the original this word is De'yus, and this God usurped the identical name of the God of Hored. But I, the editor, have here adopted the spelling, Dyaus, so that the student will not confound the two persons. –Ed.

[968] weapons, implements of war

two lines, away from each other. Presently, they judged by the lights that there were tens of thousands of soldiers come against them. Suddenly, now, T-loyovogna's army sounded their pans and kettles, and set up furious howls and screams; and at the same time the angels of heaven cast stars of light in the midst of Azhis' army, and they became panic-stricken and fled in all directions, except three hundred who were captured and put to death. Then T-loyovogna sent one hundred men into the city and captured Azhis and slew him. After this, T-loyovogna entered the city and declared the place his.

25/35.16. And while it was yet night, thousands and thousands of the people came and prostrated themselves before T-loyovogna, swearing allegiance. And in the morning of the next day he proclaimed himself king; and he impressed[969] thirty thousand men to build a temple to Dyaus; and another twenty thousand to change the streets and otherwise beautify the place. In forty days the temple was completed, and was large enough for eight thousand souls to do sacrifice in at one time. T-loyovogna compelled the people to prostrate themselves on their bellies and pray to Dyaus, whose home was in Ahl-burj, a high heavenly place, a mountain above the mountains.

25/35.17. After this, T-loyovogna changed the name of the city to Savazata, signifying, first fireplace; and for governor to rule over it he appointed Vistaqpa, with the right to bequeath it to his son after him.

25/35.18. For Sudga had said: To concentrate power, this is the greatest. There shall be only one heavenly ruler, and his Lords shall be his helpmates. Likewise there shall be only one king, and his governors shall be his helpmates in the same manner.

25/35.19. T-loyovogna then marched forward, to conquer and subdue another city; which he accomplished also, changing its name, appointing a governor, and making all the people swear allegiance to himself as king, and to Sudga, the Dyaus, as heavenly ruler, creator of worlds.

25/35.20. In this way, even as Kan Kwan in Jaffeth did, T-loyovogna proceeded throughout Vind'yu, from city to city, conquering and subduing. For, the Gods, Te-in and Sudga, previously had often conferred together on this subject, and had long experience in manipulating mortals in their games of life and death, nor did mortals mistrust the power above them.

25/35.21. Hear next of Osiris and his Gods, Baal and Ashtaroth, whose heavenly kingdoms contained more than twelve billion angels.

CHAPTER 36 Wars

Of Osiris and his heavenly kingdoms

25/36.1. When Osiris, the false God of Arabin'ya and her heavens, left De'yus, in Hored, the self (satan) that was in him, spoke to him, saying: Osiris, you are a fool! You deserve to be ground to dust! Behold your wisdom and power, and yet you cringe to your inferiors on every side. Were you not made as well; and too, as masterly in making others bow to your will and decrees? What more is required for Gods or men, than to make slaves of others, to do him honor and reverence? Then Osiris said:

25/36.2. O truest of Gods. If only I had struck out for myself from the beginning! But I will make up for it. When I am in my heavenly place I will send for my Gods, Baal and Ashtaroth, who are presently laboring on the earth, and I will make our three kingdoms into one, and mine shall be chief. And I will offer emoluments[970] to the best, highest grades in Hored, thereby drawing from De'yus his best fruits and flowers, and I will send him some two or three billion of my superabundant drujas.

25/36.3. Accordingly, when Osiris arrived at Agho'aden, his heavenly place, he sent messengers down to the earth to Baal and Ashtaroth, summoning them to his presence at once. And they came, each being attended with ten thousand companions, besides heralds, musicians and trumpeters.

25/36.4. Osiris had made great preparations for them. His receiving hosts, one million, were newly adorned for the occasion. The roadway, for three hundred miles, was illumed with pillars of fire. The Holy Council, half a million, were in extra session. The laborers, four billion, were granted a day of rest. So that when Baal and Ashtaroth entered the

[969] conscripted, drafted, forced

[970] enticements, incentives, rewards, bonuses, compensations, fringe benefits, advantages, perks, premiums

heavenly capital, it was a magnificent scene, and as if in fact Osiris, the false, was a mighty God.

25/36.5. Great were the ceremonies and salutations between the Gods, as also with the generals, captains, marshals and others; to describe which, a whole book could be written and yet not mention one-half.

25/36.6. After the reception, Osiris proclaimed an extra day of recreation to Agho'aden, and in that time he and Baal and Ashtaroth retired to a private chamber beyond the throne, to the east, to consult on the matters of heaven and earth.

25/36.7. Osiris said: My brother and sister, you are my loves; all else in the worlds are vain! De'yus is the most selfish of Gods, and unreasonable. He said to me: You should keep up the grades! Now, behold, his own grades are broken down. As I and other Gods send him contributions in subjects, so in their grade such subjects remain; no more education for them in Hored. Then he complains and assumes to dictate. And all this for De'yus' glory. Not a word for lifting angels or mortals up out of darkness.

25/36.8. Baal said: A most unreasonable God. Did you not say to him: O if I had the power and means you have! What great good I would do!

25/36.9. Ashtaroth said: This I have found before: The greater power a God has, the less he does for others' good. As for my part, what good can I do? I have scarcely two billion slaves, all told! If only I had a kingdom like De'yus! But what do you propose, O Osiris, you far-seeing God?

25/36.10. Baal further said: Ashtaroth, you wise Goddess, you have expressed my own soul. My own kingdom is only a little larger than yours; I am a very helpless God indeed. But once I reach De'yus' means, my soul's delight will be to fill all the heavens full of schools and hospitals! But speak, Osiris, whatever you have resolved is wise. As for myself I have spent two thousand years trying to put myself in good position first, so I could help others.

25/36.11. Osiris said: To cut loose from De'yus; this is wisdom. To send drujas into De'yus' kingdom, is greater wisdom. To establish Agho'aden as the all highest heavenly kingdom with myself at the Godhead, and you two to be my sole Gods of the earth, is the greatest wisdom.

25/36.12. Baal said: I swear, you have spoken at last what I have for five hundred years hoped to hear you say. To you I am sworn forever. Put upon me whatever you will.

25/36.13. Ashtaroth said: Now I am blessed above all Goddesses! What I have heard you speak, is what I would have spoken.

25/36.14. Osiris said: It is enough then; this I proclaim, and on our crossed hands we swear: AGHO'ADEN, ALL HIGHEST HEAVEN! OSIRIS, SON OF THE ALL CENTRAL LIGHTS! THE MOST HIGH GOD! HIS ONLY SON, BAAL, RULER OF THE CORPOREAL EARTH! HIS ONLY DAUGHTER, ASHTAROTH, RULER OF THE CORPOREAL EARTH! FIDELITY AND UNION FOREVER!

25/36.15. Thus they swore themselves into the Godhead. And the next day Osiris sent messengers to De'yus, in his heavenly place, informing him of what had been done, and adding further: But as to you, De'yus, I cut you off from these earth regions. Get your supplies where you can. Adversity does a proud soul some good.

CHAPTER 37 Wars

25/37.1. Osiris said to Baal and Ashtaroth: Go down to the earth to subdue it; and your first labor shall be in Arabin'ya, Par'si'e, and Heleste; after that you shall fall upon remote parts and subdue them to ourselves also. But do not go as the other Gods have, to destroy mortals, for we want them to propagate and make subjects for us. Nor shall you pursue them, neither tribe against tribe, nor by putting them to death if they do not worship Osiris or Baal or Ashtaroth. No, not even the worshippers of the Great Spirit, except for those whose spirits we cannot catch at the time of their death; them destroy.

25/37.2. But permit mortals to worship as they may, and if they worship the Creator, say to them: It is well. If they worship Ahura, say: It is well. If De'yus: Yes, it is well; for all of these are only one person, who is Osiris, whose high heavenly place is Agho'aden. In that way, teach them.

25/37.3. You shall also do this: re-establish places of learning, teaching the Osirian law; rebuild houses of philosophy, oracles and temples; and in all such places where mortals come to consult the spirits, provide them with spirits who shall answer through the oracles for the benefit of our dominions.

25/37.4. It was we who gave the name Lord God to the Arabin'yans; it was we who gave the name De'yus to Par'si'e and Heleste. Let us not waste ourselves away undoing what has been done, but appropriate it to ourselves. ||

25/37.5. Such, then, was the basis on which these three Gods set out to establish heaven and earth. Osiris gave to Baal and Ashtaroth, in addition to their own kingdoms, twelve Lords each, to labor with them in the earth department; and every Lord was allotted one million servant soldiers, to be under the Lord's jurisdiction.

25/37.6. With this, Baal and Ashtaroth returned to their heavenly kingdoms on the earth, and at once set about their labors; first, by inspiring mortal kings and queens to build the required oracles. And the kings and queens, thus inspired, impressed tens of thousands and hundreds of thousands of their subjects to do the building.

25/37.7. And in seven years' time there were built in Par'si'e and Arabin'ya four thousand altars for the sacred dances; seven thousand temples of sacrifice; four hundred and seventy oracle temples; and thirty-one sar'gis temples, where the Lords took on corporeal forms and talked and reasoned with mortals, especially regarding the stars, moon and the earth: teaching the philosophers the four motions of the earth: axial, oscillaic, orbitic and vorkum; the plan of the hissagow [solar phalanx – Ed.]; and the cycles of the earth; the cycles of the sun; and the cycles of the sun's sun, the north star-belt within that; and the vortices that move them all.

25/37.8. And the inhabitants of Arabin'ya, Par'si'e and Heleste began again to prosper, and became mighty. But after many years, behold, Baal and Ashtaroth rebelled against Osiris, and seceded from Arabin'ya. And this was the end of the heavenly confederacy founded by De'yus. As for the far-off Gods in other divisions of the earth, they seceded at the time Osiris, Te-in and Sudga did. And from this time on, no more spirits were sent to the Lord God, the false, the author of the name De'yus.

25/37.9. When Baal and Ashtaroth seceded from Osiris and resumed their own kingdoms, behold, in all the divisions of the earth, every God was for himself and his own kingdom. But between Osiris and Baal and Ashtaroth, a triangular war ensued in reference to the boundaries and divisions of the lands of the earth.

25/37.10. Now, therefore, since the self-Gods had become the beginning of a new order of dominion in heaven and earth, everyone in his own way, it is profitable to leave them for the present, to be resumed afterward. Hear, then, of De'yus, the false Lord God; and of God, the true Son of Jehovih:

CHAPTER 38 Wars

25/38.1. After the meeting between De'yus, Osiris and Sudga, when De'yus was left alone, he reasoned: Since Sudga and Osiris have left me, uncivilly, in the middle of a most disgusting quarrel, it must follow that on their arrival home they will secede, taking their kingdoms with them. Well, it will be well; I will all the more warmly bind my fellowship to Te-in, and we two shall overthrow Sudga and Osiris, and take all their spoils.

25/38.2. While De'yus thus soliloquized,[971] messengers came from Che-su-gow, Te-in's heavenly place, bringing this word: Greeting to you, our Lord God: Te-in has seceded, and taken both his heavenly and his corporeal dominions for himself. With an army of two hundred million angel warriors he is walling his heavenly kingdom around on every side; none can pass or re-pass without his permission.

25/38.3. Before De'yus recovered from his surprise, behold, other messengers came from Sudga's heavenly place, saying: Greeting to you, our Lord God: Sudga has seceded, taking with him his heavenly kingdom and his earth dominions, Vind'yu! With an army of two hundred million angel warriors he is walling his heavenly kingdom around on every side; none can pass or re-pass without his permission!

25/38.4. De'yus said: So, one and the same! Then these rascal Gods had this planned beforehand! || Presently other messengers arrived, saying: Greeting to you, our one-time Lord God of heaven and earth! Osiris, Baal and Ashtaroth have seceded, taking their heavenly kingdoms and their mortal dominions with them. I, Osiris, have spoken. Your higher grades I will draw to myself; my lower grades I will banish to you!

---

[971] talked aloud to himself

25/38.5. De'yus said: Well, it is well. I will now make the other heavenly divisions stronger to me; and the earth divisions, too long neglected by me; Uropa, North and South Guatama, and their heavenly places.

25/38.6. But while he thus soliloquized, behold, messengers arrived from these places, also announcing their secession in like manner. Then De'yus was silent for a long while, considering. But satan came to him, saying:

25/38.7. Darkness comes to all the great, for by this the light is made to shine brighter. Now, since all access to the corporeal earth is cut off, and since all your supplies for food and raiment must come up from the earth, it follows that you shall lower Hored, your heavenly place, nearer to the face of the earth. And once accomplished, you shall send ten billion of your warrior angels against these rebellious Gods and despoil them of their dominions, and cast them into hell, and repossess the whole earth.

25/38.8. De'yus said: It is true! My way is clear. These rascally Gods do not know how foolishly they have exposed themselves. Hored is wide enough to cover them up. And by fire I will chase the drujas upon them, ten billion strong; flood them with such foulness that their kingdoms will go to pieces under them and suffocate them in the horrid stench.

25/38.9. De'yus then called together his vice-Gods, and his Holy Council, and his highest raised officers; and he related to them what had occurred, and his plans ahead. But, so he could better deliberate and gain their acquiescence, he granted a day of recreation, to meet on the following day at the trumpet call.

25/38.10. But lo and behold, on the day of recreation, no less than seven hundred million of his highest grades left him and Hored, and descended to the heavenly kingdoms of his former Gods, some to one and some to another, while a few of them descended to the earth to found small kingdoms of their own. Danger was already staring Anuhasaj in the face.

25/38.11. Accordingly, he at once chose his officers, and set them to work, but owing to their lack of knowledge in such matters, only small sections were bound and lowered at one time, at which rate a hundred years would be required to accomplish the work. And upon realizing this, De'yus' heart began to fail him. The prophecies of the higher Gods, that he and his kingdoms would be ultimately broken up and cast into hell, began to show signs of realization fearful to contemplate.

25/38.12. Anuhasaj had no time for war, but now needed to use every stratagem in his power to prevent dismemberment in his own kingdom. In these straits, good fortune came to him in the form of a ji'ay'an harvest falling in all the atmospherean heavens, compressing and falling, so that his lowest grades were provided with sustenance from above, and they were pacified.

25/38.13. Jehovih had spoken to Cpenta-armij, in her far-off etherean worlds, saying: Behold, the earth, she enters now the ji'ay'an fields of Tu'e'vraga, in My high roads Loo-sutsk. For a little while I will feed the self-Gods of the lower heavens, and lead them on to know My power. ||

CHAPTER 39 Wars

25/39.1. Jehovih spoke to God, His Son, in Craoshivi, saying: Prepare for the fall of ji'ay in atmospherea. The earth and her heavens enter Loo-sutsk, seventy years in the rates of seven hundred; forty years in five hundred; twenty years in a'ji. Be advised; for Craoshivi shall fall to thirty, and Hored be buried in the earth. Call My Son, Ahura, and reveal My words!

25/39.2. So God, in Craoshivi, advised his High Council, and also sent messengers in haste to Vara-pishanaha, to Ahura, and acquainted him. After this, God propounded in Council: Anuhasaj, what can Craoshivi do for him? And the members spoke at great length, more than a thousand of them.

25/39.3. So God decreed: A commission to go to Anuhasaj and inform him of his danger, and offer to come to his aid and save him. This that follows is the message God sent:

25/39.4. To you, O Anuhasaj, greeting in Jehovih's name, and by our love be assured. You are adjudged to be in perilous condition. Behold, one hundred and thirty years' pressure will fall on the heavens of the earth; Craoshivi will go down to the depths of hada. Reach up your hands, and I will come and save you and your kingdom. Will you withdraw your armies and permit the resurrection of your lowest grades?

25/39.5. Anuhasaj answered this in these words: Who are you that assails my peaceful kingdom in this manner? You pretended son of the Void Nothingness? Call on me as becomes[972] one with your small kingdom, and if you need help for yourself, or for your paupers, I will give to you!

25/39.6. To that, God returned this answer: Be patient with me, O brother: If it is proved that I am in darkness, and you in the light, I will make ample amends to you. If on the other hand I am in the light and you in darkness, I will say nothing that would wound you. If you will apply yourself diligently to solve the place of the earth and her heavens you will find in truth the coming pressure of which I told you. Do not think that my words are spoken at random, but try them by prophecy and by mathematics.

25/39.7. As to the coming danger, it is an easy matter to estimate. A thousand years ago, when you first established yourself and your heaven, Hored possessed an average grade above fifty, all told. And there were four billion of them.

25/39.8. In two hundred years you had six billion, and the grade was raised to sixty-five. In the next two hundred years the number was nearly doubled, but the grade had fallen to forty. And in two hundred years later the inhabitants had nearly doubled again, but the grade had fallen to twenty-eight. In the next two hundred years, the increase in numbers was at the same rate as the decrease in the grade.

25/39.9. Now behold, your twenty-eight billion, more than half of whom are in Hored, are below grade ten. And when you first possessed Hored, a ten grade could not survive there. Do not think that some accidental thing will raise so great a weight.

25/39.10. Look into this matter, as to what you have done! You have persuaded your hosts not to look up to Jehovih and His kingdoms, and lo, they incline downward to the earth. Yes, they have already filled the earth with war and destruction.

25/39.11. You cannot hope to throw these things on your Gods, for they will turn against you and accuse you. At present they are content to found kingdoms of their own. But they will also come to an end. Because they have seceded from you, let it be evidence that all the highest grades will follow in the same way.

[972] befits, appropriate to

25/39.12. As for Craoshivi, her lowest grades are above fifty, and therefore self-sustaining; her highest grades are ninety-nine and her average eighty-eight. And hundreds of millions of these are those whom my Lords have rescued from your bondage; others, Faithists on the earth whom your false Gods put to death for refusing to bow to you. And have they not proved it is better to suffer death than to renounce faith in Jehovih? Otherwise they would now be within the company of your slaves, toiling in darkness.

25/39.13. Yes, my kingdom is made up of those who were despised and abused; and of those whom your Gods slew in war, chaotic and mad. For my asaphs followed your cruel wars and gathered in the spirits of the slain, whom you would not have. You call them poor still. Why, so they are; they are washed white as snow;[973] for they have been taught to keep casting aside all accumulation, except knowledge and goodness of heart, in which they are rich indeed.

25/39.14. They would come to you now in pity to take your people by the hand and deliver them away from you and darkness. And if your slaves are not delivered away from you, they will surely, sooner or later, turn upon you and cast you into hell. I pray, therefore, for you to assume conversion to Jehovih, and cast your kingdom upon Him while you may. For I have the power and the means to deliver you and your slaves. Yes, I will give you a new name, and hide you away, so they cannot find you. And you shall be one with me in my holy place. ||

25/39.15. To this Anuhasaj made no reply, and so the matter remained.

CHAPTER 40 Wars

25/40.1. In Vara-pishanaha Ahura had now toiled nearly two thousand years with his people, who for the most part had been drujas, but were now high in the grades. Of them, more than two billion had been raised into light, becoming Brides and Bridegrooms to Jehovih, and had been delivered into the etherean worlds.

25/40.2. But Ahura did not allow his dominions to become depleted, but like God in Craoshivi, he sent hosts down to hada and to the earth to gather

[973] This refers to the soul, not to skin color.

in both, the fallen angels of De'yus and his false Gods, and the chaotic and foul-smelling spirits, wild, frenzied, and vengeful. And Ahura had them brought to Vara-pishanaha and there treated, nursed, restored, and put to school and to factories, to be taught and developed; hundreds of millions of them becoming bright, wise and of great love and power.

25/40.3. God sent word to Ahura, saying: Greeting to you in the name of Jehovih. Because of the coming darkness that will soon press upon atmospherea from every quarter, and the trials that will be put upon Gods and angels, let us unite our heavenly kingdoms! Let us bring our plateaus together, and your kingdom shall be my kingdom, and mine shall be yours; and one of us shall be manager in heaven, and the other shall descend to hada and to the earth, when the great darkness is on.

25/40.4. To this Ahura replied: Greeting to you, God of the heavens of the earth, and with love and most high reverence. There is wisdom in your design. I will do with you whatever you demand, to fulfill this great work.

25/40.5. So God, of Craoshivi, and Ahura, brought their forces to bear on their respective plateaus, to unite them. As their places were two thousand miles apart with Craoshivi situated to the east and Vara-pishanaha to the southwest, and Vara-pishanaha standing seven thousand miles below Craoshivi, this was the proceeding:

25/40.6. Because the coming pressure would drive them both down near the earth's surface; to steer Vara-pishanaha to the eastward, and to steer Craoshivi to the south-westward, would bring one over the other; and to lower the grade of Craoshivi would bring the two in contact. And the inhabitants of both dominions were so high in power and wisdom that their presence was higher than the place they inhabited; so that the element of the plateaus was all that was required to be moved.

25/40.7. To find the power required, and to arrange the ranks for the proceeding, God appointed officers and set them to work, and the officers reported back that the work could be completed in twelve years. So Ahura united with God, and three billion angels engaged in this labor. First they made a bridge between the two plateaus, and it was completed during the first year; and it connected them in such a way that millions of angels could pass and re-pass objectively while the work was going on.

25/40.8. Yet God's labors and Ahura's labors in receiving the spirits of the earth, of the Faithists, and of others from the regions of hada, did not cease, did not lag. Their thousands of otevans sailed along the heavens in every way, gathering in the unfortunate.

25/40.9. And now that the self-Gods in hada had quarreled among themselves and separated, De'yus' blockade was broken of its own accord. His mighty standing army against Jehovih's believers had melted away; and the otevans sped here and there, unmolested. And they gathered in many thousands, indeed, tens of thousands, of De'yus' highest raised angels. The lowest would not come; they had been taught to hate with vengeance Jehovih and His worshippers; to look upon all ills as from Jehovih; to look upon all good delights and blessings as the gifts of De'yus, the Lord their God.

25/40.10. Suffice it to say, in twelve years' time the great heavens, Craoshivi and Vara-pishanaha, were united and became as one place. And there was a time of rejoicing and delight; great recreation and communion; great rites and ceremonies; and worshipping and rejoicing before Jehovih.

25/40.11. Already the pressure of ji'ay was upon the heavens and the earth. Hored was falling fast toward the earth; De'yus' highest raised had already gone; his kingdom was becoming a kingdom of fools and idlers, a most dangerous class once deprivation and starvation come upon them.

25/40.12. De'yus, still stubborn, and still hoping for a change from some unseen cause, no longer had time to quarrel with his truant Gods, but from day to day, hour to hour, was kept at maximum exertion to avert the threatened doom.

25/40.13. Meanwhile, the false Gods, his own one-time pupils, were now heaping into his distracted kingdom millions and millions of drujas, who had been taught on the earth that all that was required of them was to call on the Savior, Anubi, and the Lord God, and that when they died they would go straight to glory to dwell on the holy hill of the Lord God. And these poor creatures the self-Gods now encouraged, helping them on, saying: Yes, go on; your Savior, Anubi, will open the gate and pass you in. From now on, forever, you shall do nothing but bow to De'yus.

25/40.14. And these spirits of darkness, like idiots, were bowing all the time, day and night, doing nothing but bowing, and saying: Blessed Anubi! He can save me! Glory to the Lord our God! Then they would begin again: Blessed Anubi! My Savior! Glory be to De'yus! For this was all they knew; neither would they hear nor see anything else; they were like wild people; with out-bursting eyes, looking for Anubi; looking for De'yus; but bowing incessantly in all directions; millions of them, tens of millions—delirious angels!

25/40.15. Consequently, in fear of them, Anubi gave up his place; and his heavenly city was like a house without a keeper, where throngs go in and out, and around about, forever shouting: O my blessed Savior, Anubi! Glory be to the Lord God. ||

25/40.16. But Anubi was with the false Lord God, striving to help him find some means of escape or safety.

CHAPTER 41 Wars

25/41.1. Darker and darker, the hadan fields palled[974] before the touch of Jehovih's hand, to try the self-assumed Lord God and his heavenly works. As if an epoch[975] new and terrible had come to one so audacious, who, more than any in heaven and earth, had sought to banish the worship and the name of the Great Spirit from mortals, and give them instead a heavenly ruler in the image of man.

25/41.2. For prior to this, all nations knew the office of Gods and Lords, and reverenced them as Jehovih's high officers, raised up spirits of the dead, wise and powerful. But now, in five great divisions of the earth, satan's hadan chief had bound his name in mortals, with threatened penalties, and even death, for mentioning Jehovih's name. And, to put them to the test, made oaths on burning flesh, so that whoever would not eat of it would die.

25/41.3. For this was the criterion before the courts: That any who refused fish and flesh food, or would not pollute the body by noxious drinks and smoke, intoxicating to the senses, were possessed of Jehovihian worship, and so, deserved torture and death. ||

25/41.4. So the names of Lord, God, Lord God, and De'yus, had for a thousand years now, become fixed in mortals' minds as the Creator, a large man sitting on a throne in Hored, his heavenly seat, watched and guarded by his son, Anubi, keeper of the scales, and of the gate to heaven. To make a plausible story of which, the angels, through oracles, magicians, priests and prophets, proclaimed that in the beginning, God created the heavens and the earth, and all things in and on the earth. And he was tired, and rested; and, as if creation was a completed work, left certain laws to run the wonderful machine while he sat far off, looking on; smiling at the pranks of mortals, and their failure to understand him; and with a devil and a horrid fire to torture their souls, if they did not sing in praise of this compounded, false Lord God.

25/41.5. Thus he, their false God, turned the voice of mortals from Him Who is Ever Present, Whose speech every soul has heard, Whose Presence moves all things in heaven and earth! The false God turned them to sing and pray to himself, so he could clutch and bind their souls in endless slavery; untaught, half fed; as drudges, to bring provender and building stones into his capital, to glorify him forever.

25/41.6. Over Jaffeth, far and wide, this traitor to Jehovih had sealed in stone, papyrus, wood, and sacred cloth, his name, Ho-Joss, to suit the Panic voice; while in Vind'yu he made them engrave it Dyaus, to fit the Vedic tongue; and then in Fonece to suit the higher-spirited race, Adonia-Egad,[976] and go over to Heleste, and, in less distinct and bastard [977] Greek, whisper Zeus, saying: These words are watchwords to gain Anubi's ear, and turn the scales for endless paradise. Go slaves, engrave my names; and, in mortal libraries, register my great exploit, of how I created the world!

---

[974] lost light; became cloaked in increasing darkness, becoming saturated, satiated with it

[975] an important or noteworthy period of time; a milestone

[976] Adonia means Lord, and Egad means God

[977] hybrid, mixed, heterogeneous, motley. The word bastard here seems to mean that the language of Greece was a combination of different language groups, with no pure lineage to one group or another; thus having no distinct parent language.

25/41.7. And make me spotlessly pure, letting sin into the races of men by Osiris' cunning tale of Eve's weakness by fault of the earth. For I do not come like Jehovih's captains—spirits sent to rule men for a season; but a very God of blood and bones, who once, in terrible anger, flooded the earth to drown my disobedient sons and daughters. Make them tremble and draw long breath when my name is spoken, or, by my own soul, I will hurl heaven and earth into endless chaos! ||

25/41.8. Slowly and surely ji'ay came pressing downward, the very motion of which spoke like a million tongues, serious, awful. For on every side, many of the hosts of Anuhasaj were deserting him. As one, in a small way, may see on a sinking ship how the expert swimmers leap into the water boldly, and with strong arms swim for the far-off shore, while the helpless, in frantic rage, cluster fast upon the distracted officers, blockading them from doing good. So began the tumult in the fast-descending plateau, Hored, which was increased a hundred-fold by the flood of drujas cast upon De'yus' kingdom by his own traitorous false Gods.

25/41.9. De'yus' generals and captains first tried music to hold the forty billion to peace and order; but the es'enaurs themselves took fright, and fled by the millions, flying down to the earth, to Osiris' or Te-in's or Sudga's kingdoms, and over-flooding mortals with ghostly revelries. Next, by parades, and rites, and great processions, De'yus' officers sought to divert the panic-stricken millions.

25/41.10. Thus for years this maddened God with wonderful strength of will, almost held his own, inventing tens of thousands of stratagems. But at last, in the downward course, Hored touched upon the corporeal earth; and suddenly, as if startled by the shock, the frantic millions screamed, and then, alas, all order died.

25/41.11. The doors of hell (anarchy) were opened! The maddened mob broke loose to pillage or to destroy Anuhasaj's throne and capital, with all their splendor. And then the faultfinders rushed in, shouting: You lying God, only like a man, who are you? And you, Anubi! Deceiving judge! A thousand horrid deaths to you!

25/41.12. But the unlearned drujas did not know who was rank or officer, God or judge, but seized the pale and trembling De'yus and Anubi, and more than a million officers; overpowered them, by ten million to one, pressed on by the foul-smelling crowd. And now, with blows, kicks and cuffs, on every side the awful fray began, till, stretched as wide as the earth, the countless millions plunged into hell. So that, to right or left, unceasing combat prevailed, and all the hosts of the Lord God were sworn for vengeance against anyone they came against.

25/41.13. Then came the torturers, casting into the hells the most offensive smells and suffocating gases, crammed in the nose and mouth of their victims. No more were the Lord God and Anubi seen, but swallowed up in measureless darkness, where every soul sought nothing good, but labored hard to give others excruciating tortures for vengeance' sake.

CHAPTER 42 Wars

25/42.1. God in Craoshivi prayed to Jehovih as to what he should do to release De'yus and Anubi; Jehovih answered, saying: My Son, you shall first labor for those who desire; whoever courts darkness does not deserve your hand. Since the early days, I have proclaimed warnings to those who put Me away; but in their self-conceit they denied My person and power.

25/42.2. If you were, this day, to deliver from hell De'yus and Anubi, and their billions of self-torturing slaves, they would only use their deliverance to mock My creation, saying: It did not last; it was only a breath of wind. || For which reason you shall not yet meddle with the hells of Hored.

25/42.3. In four hundred years I will bring the earth into another dawn of light. Till then, let De'yus and Anubi and their hosts take their course.

25/42.4. God inquired concerning Osiris, Te-in and Sudga, and Jehovih answered him, saying: Sufficient for them is the light they have received. Allow them also to take their course, for they also shall become involved in hells of their own building.

25/42.5. But be attentive to My Chosen, the Faithists, in all parts of heaven and earth; not letting one of them fall into the hells of My enemies.

25/42.6. God acquainted Ahura with Jehovih's words; then Ahura prayed to Jehovih, saying: O Father, grant me permission to go to Osiris, and to

Te-in, and to Sudga, to plead Your cause. Behold, the Lord God is locked up in hell; even high-raised Gods would not find it safe to go to him.

25/42.7. Jehovih said: Why, O Ahura, do you desire to go to Osiris, Te-in and to Sudga? Do you not know how difficult it is to alter the mind of a mortal man; and yet these self-Gods are ten times more stubborn!

25/42.8. Ahura said: I know, I cannot change them. To break this matter of conceit—and all learned men are liable to fall into it—none but You, O Jehovih, have power. But these self-Gods were long ago my most loved friends; behold, I will go to them as a father would go to a son, and plead with them. || And Jehovih gave permission to Ahura to visit the three great self-Gods.

25/42.9. So Ahura fitted out an otevan, and, with ten thousand attendants, one thousand heralds and five thousand musicians, besides the officers of the fire-ship, set sail for Che-su-gow, Te-in's heavenly place, over Jaffeth. And when he arrived near the place he halted and sent his heralds ahead to inquire if he could have audience with Te-in.

25/42.10. Te-in received the heralds cordially, and being informed of their object, sent back this word: Te-in, the most high ruler of heaven and earth sends greeting to Ahura, commanding his presence, but forbidding Ahura and his hosts from speaking to any soul in Che-su-gow except himself (Te-in).

25/42.11. Ahura received this insulting message with composure, and then proceeded and entered the capital city, the heavenly place of Te-in, where he was met by one million slaves, arrayed in the most gorgeous manner. These conducted him and his attendants to the arena, where Ahura was received by the marshals, who brought him to the throne, leaving the attendants in the arena. Here Te-in saluted on the Sign of Taurus [Ex-bau –Ed.], and Ahura answered in the Sign Friendship [Aries – Ed.].

25/42.12. Te-in signaled privacy, and so all others fell back, leaving Ahura and Te-in alone. Te-in said: Come and sit beside me on the throne. Ahura said: Because you have not forgotten me I am rejoiced. And he went up and sat on the throne. Te-in said: Because you are my friend I love you; because you are beside me I am rejoiced. It is more than a thousand years since my eyes have seen you. Tell me, Ahura, how is it with yourself and your kingdom?

25/42.13. Ahura said: As for myself I am happy; for the greater part, my kingdom is happy also. My trials have been severe and long enduring. But of my four billion, more than half of them are delivered beyond atmospherea, high raised; and of the others they grade from fifty to ninety.

25/42.14. Te-in said: And for your toil of more than two thousand years, what have you gained by striving to raise up these drujas? Ahura said: Only this, O Te-in, peace and rejoicing in my soul.

25/42.15. Te-in said: On that hangs two philosophies: One seeks peace and rejoicing by laboring with the lowest of the low; the other, by leading the highest of the high. As for myself the latter suits me better than the former. I tell you, Ahura, all things come of the will; if we will ourselves to shut out horrid sights and complaints, like those the poor druk and the druj indulge in, we have joy in a higher heaven. To me it is thus: Sympathy is our most damnable enemy, for it binds us to the wretched and miserable. To put away sympathy is to begin to be a great master over others, to make them subservient to our wills.

25/42.16. Ahura said: Is it not a good thing to help the wretched? Te-in answered: To help them is like drinking nectar; it makes one's senses buoyant for the time being. That is all. They relapse and are less resolute than before, but depend on being helped again. For which reason, he who helps the wretched wrongs them woefully. To make them know their places, this is the highest. For do not even the Gods have to submit to their places? To learn to be happy with one's place and condition is great wisdom.

25/42.17. In this matter thousands of Gods have fallen; they helped up the poor and wretched; as one may, in sympathy to serpents, take them into his house and pity them; but they immediately turn and bite their helpers. But speak, O Ahura; for I have respect for your words.

25/42.18. Ahura said: If a man plants an acorn in a flowerpot, and it takes root and grows, one of two things must follow: the growth must be provided against or the pot will burst. Even in the same way, the lowest druj in heaven draws from the surrounding sources. None of the Gods can bind him forever. Alas, he will grow. All our bondage over them cannot prevent the soul, sooner or later, from taking root and growing. How, then, can we be Gods over them forever?

25/42.19. Te-in said: You are a God over them; I am a God over them. Where is the difference? Ahura said: I am not in my own name; though I am God over them, yet I am not God over them. For I teach them they shall not worship me, but Jehovih. I train them so that I may raise them away from me. Nor do my people serve me, but serve the Great Spirit. You teach your drujas that you are the all highest, and that they shall be contented to serve you everlastingly. You limit them to the compass[978] of your kingdom. I do not limit my subjects, but teach them that their progression is forever onward, upward.

25/42.20. Te-in said: How do we know that the time will not come upon them, when they shall say: Alas, I was taught in error. They told me there was a Great Spirit, a Person comprising all things, but I have not found Him. Will they not then revolt also? Was this not the cause of De'yus' fall? He had searched the heavens to the extreme, but did not find Jehovih. Then he returned, and possessed heaven and earth for himself. Although he failed, and is cast into hell, it is plain that his sympathy for drujas caused his fall. From his errors, I hope to guard myself; for I shall neither show sympathy for the poor or wretched, nor will I permit education on earth or in heaven, except to my Lords or marshals. When a mortal city displeases me, I will send spirits of darkness to overwhelm it to destruction. Yes, they shall incite mortals to fire the place, and to riot and death. Thus I will keep the drujas of heaven forever busy playing games with mortals, and in bringing provender and diadems to forever glorify my heavenly kingdom.

25/42.21. Ahura said: Where in all the world has a self-God stood and not fallen? Te-in said: You may well ask of mortals: Where is a kingdom or a nation that stood, and has not fallen? Yet you perceive that nations continue to try to establish themselves everlastingly. But they are leveled in time. Things spring up and grow, and then fall into dissolution. Will it not be so with ourselves in the far future? Will we not become one with the ever-changing elements, and as nothing, and wasted away?[979]

25/42.22. Ahura said: One might say of man and spirits: There were some seeds planted; and many of them rotted and returned to earth; but others took root and grew and became large trees. But yet, is it not also true of the trees that they have a time? For they die, fall down, rot, and also return to earth.

25/42.23. Ahura continued: Admit this to be true, O Te-in, and that the time may come when you and I shall pass out of being, then does it not follow that for the time we live we should contribute all we can to make others happy?[980]

25/42.24. Te-in said: If by so doing it will render ourselves happy, with no danger to our kingdoms, then yes, truly. For which reason, are we not forced back, after all is said and done, to the position that we shall labor for our own happiness, without regard to others? One man delights in art, another in philosophy, another in helping the poor and wretched; and another in eating and drinking, and another in ruling over others; shall they not all have enjoyment in the way of their desires? Shall you say to him who delights in eating and drinking: Stop; come and delight yourself helping the wretched!

25/42.25. Ahura said: This I have seen: The intelligent and clean have more delight than do the stupid and filthy; the rich more enjoyment than the poor. As for ourselves, we delight more in seeing the delighted than in seeing the wretched. More do we delight to see a child smile than to hear it cry; but there are those who delight more to make a

[978] reach, extent, boundary

[979] Note that this supposition by the false God is because he does not yet recognize and know that Jehovih exists within his soul; once he does, he will come to understand that a person does not lose his individual identity, that is, he does not ever cease to be a person or an individual, with life and power to move and grow.

[980] The reader should not fall into the trap of thinking that Ahura is agreeing that man does not have eternal life. Instead of countering Te-in's assumption that all angels fade away, Ahura applied another tact, that of saying in essence: Well, suppose for the moment that it is true that man shall one day fade away into nothingness—then even were that the case, he should create happiness for others in the meantime, should he not?

child cry than to see it smile; but such persons are evil and take delight in evil. Shall we, then, indulge them in their means of delight? Or is there not a limit, as when we say: All men have a right to that which delights themselves, provided it does not mar the delight of others?

25/42.26. Te-in said: You have reasoned well. We shall delight ourselves only in such ways as do not mar the delight of others. Upon which, Ahura said: Then I am not delighted with the manner of your kingdom; and you should not practice what gives me pain. Because you have resolved to not educate mortals or angels, you have raised a hideous wall in the face of Gods.

25/42.27. Te-in said: This also you will admit: That as we desire to delight ourselves we should look for the things that delight us, and turn away from things that do not delight us. Therefore, let the Gods not turn their faces this way, but to their own affairs.

25/42.28. Ahura said: You are wise, O Te-in. But this I have found; that something within us grows, that will not be put down or turned aside. In the beginning of life we look to ourselves, which is the nature of the young; but when we grow, we take a wife, and we delight to see her delighted; then comes offspring, and we delight to see them delighted. After this, we delight to see our neighbors delighted; and then the state, and then the whole kingdom. This delight to be delighted grows within us; and when we become Gods we delight no longer in the delight of a few only, but we expand to many kingdoms. As for myself, I first delighted in the delight of Vara-pishanaha; but now I delight to see other Gods and other kingdoms delighted. For that, I have come to you. I fear your fate. I love you. I love all your people, good and bad. Behold, this I have found, that it is an easier matter to suffer a river to run its course than to dam it up; but to dam up a river and not have it overflow or break the dam, this I have not found. The course of the spirit of man is growth; it goes onward like a running river. When you shut up the mouth,[981] saying: Thus far and no farther! I fear for you. I tried this matter once; I was flooded; the dam was broken. I see you shutting out knowledge from mortals and angels; but I tell you, O Te-in, the time will come when the channel will be too broad for you.

25/42.29. Te-in said: How shall I answer such great wisdom? Where find a God like you, O Ahura? And yet, behold, the Lord God, Anuhasaj, toiled with you hundreds of years, and learned all these things; yes, he traveled in the far-off heavens (etherea), where there are Gods and kingdoms which have existed for millions of years. And he came back[982] and renounced the Great Person, Jehovih. He said: All things are not a harmonious whole; but a jumble; a disordered mass, playing catch as catch can.[983]

25/42.30. Ahura said: And what has befallen him? And is this, itself, not a great argument? For we behold in all times, conditions and places, in heaven and on earth, wherever people assume doctrines like his, they begin to go down into hell. They flourish a little while, but only as a summer plant, to yield in the winter's blast. I have seen this coming for a long time against these heavens, even yours, that as darkness crushed De'yus, so will your heavenly dominions sooner or later fall, and in the shock and fray you will suffer a fate like De'yus.

25/42.31. Te-in said: For your wise words, O Ahura, I am your servant. I will consider your argument, and remember you with love. In a

---

[981] mouth of the river; where the coursing river meets a body of water such as a lake or sea

[982] Note that Anuhasaj traveled etherea as an atmospherean; he did not resurrect into etherea, did not attain to the rank of Bride and Bridegroom to Jehovih; was never an etherean. But because of his great age, high grade and good works (this was before he renounced Jehovih), and apparently because of an emergency situation, he was permitted to travel into etherea.

[983] According to the Jehovihians, the universe was governed by an overarching wisdom and order, and to good purpose; and this was said by them to be because of the presence of the Person of the Universe, Jehovih.

And those who failed to perceive the truth in this, would thus have a limited understanding of etherea. So that, knowingly and/or otherwise, Anuhasaj, when he returned, would misrepresent etherea. And this had effect among those he was grooming for self-purposes, disposing them to turn aside desire for resurrection to higher heavens, and to remain and build kingdoms in atmospherea.

thousand years from now I may be wiser; and I may have my kingdom so built up that it will be an argument stronger than words. ||

25/42.32. With that, the two Gods brought their argument to a close, and Te-in signaled his vice-Gods and marshals, and they came; and when Ahura and Te-in had saluted each other, Ahura was conducted away from the place of the throne, and after that beyond the capital. The vice-Gods and marshals delivered him to his own attendants, and with them he embarked in his otevan, and set sail for Sudga's heavenly kingdom, over the land of Vind'yu.

CHAPTER 43 Wars

25/43.1. Sudga, after assuming a heaven for himself, moved it over the Nua Mountains and called it Hridat, in which place he had eight billion angel slaves, in the same manner as Te-in's. Sudga's capital city, Sowachissa, his highest heavenly seat, was modeled in the style of Sanc-tu, De'yus' heavenly place in Hored, at the time of its greatest magnificence.

25/43.2. The capital house of Sudga was made of precious stones and gems, the work of billions of angels for many years. And when Hored was pillaged, prior to De'yus being cast into hell, millions of its most precious ornaments were stolen and brought to Hridat. The streets of Hridat were paved with precious stones; and an arena surrounded the palace on every side, set with crystals of every shade and color, and of every conceivable manner of workmanship. On the borders of the arena stood five hundred million sentinels, arrayed in gorgeousness such as only Gods had looked upon. Inside the line of sentinels were one million pillars of fire, kept brilliant day and night, by the toil of five hundred million slaves. Inside the line of the pillars of fire were one million marshals, so arrayed in splendor that one could scarcely look upon them. These were on a rotational watch with two other groups of one million each, and each group stood watch eight hours.

25/43.3. Only the vice-Gods and the high marshals were permitted to walk across the arena to the palace; all others must crawl on their bellies; and for every length crawled, they must kiss the pavement and recite an anthem of praise to Sudga, who now took both names, Sudga and Dyaus. Nor must anyone repeat the same anthem twice, but it must be a new anthem for each and every length of the person. For a tall person, a thousand lengths were required from the line of marshals to the palace, thus requiring a thousand anthems. So that, only the few, as compared to his millions, ever laid eyes on the throne of Sudga. Moreover they were only permitted to gaze no more than once on him, and even then he was at such great distance and amid such a sea of fire, that they scarcely could see him; and after they saw him on the throne, then they must re-crawl back again to the place of beginning, again reciting another thousand new anthems.

25/43.4. All of which made Sudga almost inaccessible, and permitted only those who were favored to even look upon him, which with the ignorant is a great power.

25/43.5. When Ahura came to the capital and sent word to Sudga who he was, requesting a meeting, Sudga gave orders to admit him, commanding Ahura to walk upright into his presence, along with the vice-Gods. Accordingly, Ahura came before Sudga, and saluted in LOVE AND ESTEEM, and Sudga answered in FRIENDSHIP OF OLD. The latter at once commanded privacy, and so all others withdrew, and Ahura and Sudga went up and sat on the throne.

25/43.6. Sudga said: Because you have come to see me I am overflowing with joy. Because I know you have come to admonish me for my philosophy and the manner of my dominions, I respect you. Because you did once try to found a kingdom of your own, and failed, I sympathize with you; but because you went back on yourself and accepted Jehovih, and so was rescued from your peril, I commiserate[984] you.

25/43.7. Ahura said: To hear your gifted tongue once more is my great joy. To know that no misfortune was in store for you and your kingdom would give me great delight. Because I love you, and the people of your mighty, heavenly kingdom, I have come to admonish you and plead for Jehovih's sake. As for myself, I have found that to cast all my cares on Him, and then turn in and work hard for others, these two things give me the greatest happiness.

---

[984] feel sorrow for, pity

25/43.8. Sudga said: Can a brave man justly cast his cares upon another? Was not yourself given to yourself for yourself? If so, you desire none to work for you? If so, how have you a right to work for others? If you prevent them from working out their own destiny, do you not wrong them? Moreover, you say that casting your cares on Jehovih, and working hard for others, gives you the greatest happiness. How is it, then, that you are not selfish by working for your own happiness? For is this not what I am doing for myself in my own way?

25/43.9. Ahura said: Granting all your arguments, O Sudga, where shall we find the measure of righteous works if not in the sum of great results? For you or I to be happy, that is little; for a million angels to be happy, that is little. But when we put two kingdoms alongside, and they are the same size, and have the same number of inhabitants, is it not just that we weigh them in their whole measure to find which of the two kingdoms has the greater number of happy souls? Would this not be a better method of arriving at the highest philosophy?

25/43.10. Sudga said: Yes that would be higher than logic, higher than reason. That would be the foundation of a sound theory.

25/43.11. Ahura said: And have we not found, both in heaven and earth, that all kingdoms that are overthrown owe the cause of their fall to the unhappiness and disaffection of the ignorant? As soon as the masses begin to be in unrest, the rulers apply vigorous measures to repress them, but it is only adding fuel to the fire; it deadens it awhile, but only to have it burst forth more violently afterward.

25/43.12. Sudga said: You reason well, O Ahura; go on. Ahura said: How, then, shall we determine the happiness of two kingdoms, in order to determine which has the greater happiness? Are revolts not evidence of unhappiness? Hear me, then, O Sudga; where, in all the Jehovihian heavens, has there ever been a revolt? And on the earth, where have the Jehovihians, the Faithists, rebelled against their rulers? Behold, in the far-off etherean heavens, the Nirvanian fields, never has any God or Chief been environed in tortures. As for my own kingdom, my people will not rebel against me, nor do I need to fortify myself against such disaster.

25/43.13. Sudga said: You are wise, O Ahura. The only way to judge a kingdom's happiness is by the peace, contentment and civility of its people toward one another, and by the confidence between the ruler and the ruled. He who has to guard himself lives on the eve of the destruction of his kingdom and himself. And yet, O Ahura, remember this: The Jehovihians of heaven and earth are high raised before they become such; anyone can be a ruler for them, for they know righteousness. But I have to deal with druks and drujas. How, then, can you compare my kingdom with the Nirvanian kingdoms?

25/43.14. Ahura said: Alas, O Sudga, I fear my arguments are void before you. You show me that the line between selfishness and unselfishness is finer than a spider's web. Even Gods cannot distinguish it. And yet, behold, there was a time when I said: I will be a mighty God, and not bow to the Unknown that brought me into being. For this I labored long and hard; the responsibility of my kingdom finally encroached upon my happiness. Long after that I put away all responsibility,[985] and made myself a servant to Jehovih. Then a new happiness came upon me, even when I had nothing that was mine in heaven and earth. This is also beyond my understanding; yet it is inside of me as a new tree of delight. It is this that I would tell you of, but I cannot find it; it does not fly away; it baffles words, even as a description of the Great Spirit is void because of His wondrous majesty. Such is the joy of His service that even Gods and angels cannot describe it. With its growth we look famine in the face and do not weep; we see falling ji'ay and do not fear; with the ebb and flow of the tide of Jehovih's works we float as one with Him, with a comprehensive joy.

25/43.15. Sudga said: To hear your voice is joy to me; to not hear you is great sorrow. Behold, I will consider your words of wisdom. In your far-off place I will come in remembrance and love to you.

25/43.16. Thus ended the interview, and Sudga signaled his vice-Gods and high marshal to come; so he saluted Ahura in the sign of CRAFT, and Ahura answered him in the sign, TIME.

25/43.17. And then Ahura, between the vice-Gods, led by the high marshal, departed, passing beyond the arena, where the vice-Gods and

---

[985] i.e., placed it in Jehovih's hands

high marshal delivered him into the charge of the marshal hosts, who conducted him beyond the line of sentinels, where Ahura joined his own attendants and went with them into his otevan, and set sail for Agho'aden, Osiris' heavenly place, which had been over Par'si'e, but was now moved over Arabin'ya.

CHAPTER 44 Wars

25/44.1. At this time Osiris' heavenly kingdom numbered thirteen billion angels, good and bad. And it was the largest heavenly kingdom ever established on the earth.

25/44.2. It was built looking like Sudga's; that is to say, modeled after Sanc-tu, in Hored, but more magnificent than Sudga's kingdom, and far larger. The arena-way was five thousand lengths of a man across; so that approaching visitors to the throne must crawl two thousand lengths in order to approach the throne. And they also had to repeat an anthem of praise, or a prayer, for every length crawled, going and coming. And they were, like at Sudga's, permitted to approach only to within a long distance from Osiris; meanwhile the array of lights around him were so dazzling that scarcely any could look upon him. And they who thus approached were so reverential that their minds magnified Osiris' glorious appearance, so much so, that they truly believed they had looked into the Creator's face, and saw, in truth, man was of his image and likeness. And thousands, and even millions, who thus crawled to look upon him, afterward went about in heaven preaching Osiris as the veritable All Highest Creator of heaven and earth.

25/44.3. Osiris made his Godhead consist of three persons: first, himself, as THE FOUNTAIN OF THE UNIVERSE, whose name was UNSPEAKABLE; second, BAAL, HIS ONLY BEGOTTEN SON, into whose keeping he had assigned the earth and all its mortals; and, third, ASHTAROTH, HIS VIRGIN DAUGHTER, into whose keeping he had assigned life and death, or rather the power of begetting and the power to cause death with mortals.

25/44.4. Osiris was the most cunning of all the self-Gods; for thus he appropriated the triangle of the Faithists; thus appropriated the names and powers of the false Lord God (now in hell), for only through Baal and Ashtaroth could any mortal or spirit ever attain to approach the arena of the throne in Agho'aden. And here again tested, they had to pass the high sentinel, Egupt, before they were entitled to the right to crawl on their bellies over the sacred pavement, the way to the heavenly palace.

25/44.5. Only the vice-Gods of Osiris and his chief marshal could walk upright to the capital palace, and they with heads bowed low. And when Osiris was informed of Ahura's coming he sent word that he should come upright, with head erect, but veiled from head to foot. To this Ahura gladly consented; and, being veiled by Egupt and handed over to the vice-Gods and the chief marshal, he walked upright; when he came to the high arch of the palace, they halted, and Ahura saluted on the sign OLD TIME LOVE, and Osiris answered in the sign JOY IN HEAVEN. Upon which, Ahura left the vice-Gods and walked near the throne, and Osiris came down, and they embraced in each other's arms, not having seen each other for more than a thousand years.

25/44.6. Osiris signaled the vice-Gods and chief marshal to fall back, and in privacy they ascended the throne and sat on it.

25/44.7. Osiris said: This is a great joy! To meet one's loves, is this not greater, after all, than all the pomp and glory of the Gods? Ahura said: True; but who is wise enough to live in such a way as to enjoy so cheap a glory? We run off far away; we build up mighty kingdoms, and our places are replete with great magnificence; in search of what? While that which costs nothing, love, the greatest good of all in heaven and earth, we leave out in the cold. I have more delight to look upon your buoyant face again, and hear the music of your voice, than I ever had in my heavenly kingdom of seven billion angels.

25/44.8. Osiris said: Is it not so with all Gods, and with mortal kings and queens? They boast about the extent and power of their countless millions; and yet they have no more than a handful to love them, whom they can take into their arms in the fullness of reciprocity. What, then, are pomp and glory? Are not kings and queens of earth only watchdogs, to guard the stinking flesh and bones of other mortals? And are the Gods not equally base in their dirty trade of ruling over foul-smelling drujas?

25/44.9. Ahura said: It is so. But where does this great desire to rule over others come from; to lead them; to be applauded; and to revel in the toil of the millions? Would it not be wise for the Gods who understand this, to resign their mighty kingdoms and go along with their loves to feast in the great expanse of the universe.

25/44.10. Osiris said: True, O Ahura. But who has power to do this? Certainly not the Gods. And is it not so with mortals? For thousands of years, have they not been told: Unless you give up your earthly kingdoms, and give up your riches, you cannot rise in heaven. But, behold, the rich man cannot give up his riches; the king cannot give up his kingdom. They are weak indeed! As for such souls, one might as well expect an unhatched bird to fly, than to expect these to be anything but slaves in our dominions. I also perceive this regarding my own kingdom; I cannot give it up, because, in truth, I cannot get the desire to give it up, although my judgment says it would be the highest, best thing for me.

25/44.11. Ahura said: Are great possessions not like dissipation? I have seen mortals who admit THE HIGHEST, BEST THING TO DO IS TO LIVE THE HIGHEST, BEST ONE KNOWS, who then immediately go off and pollute the body by eating flesh and drinking wine. They also know the right way, but they have not yet attained the desire to put into practice what they know to be the highest.

25/44.12. Osiris said: Yes, all this is dissipation. And if a man gives away what he has, is that not also dissipation? Can it be true, O Ahura, that even as we manipulate mortals, to drive them to war or to make them play peace, to make them destroy their kingdoms and build up others by our angel armies, which they do not know of, that we ourselves are similarly ruled over by the Gods in the etherean heavens?

25/44.13. Ahura said: It seems to me thus, Osiris, that is to say, that the etherean Gods above us rule us, but not in the same way, but by their absence from us when we do unjustly, and by their presence when we do righteously. We rule over mortals by direct action upon them, shaping their destinies by our heavenly wills, and they are often cognizant of our angel servants being with them. But when we cannot appropriate a mortal to do our wills, we withdraw our angels and suffer him to fall into the hands of drujas.

25/44.14. Ahura continued: Not that the Gods above us, O Osiris, send evils upon us; but that we foster evils within our own kingdoms, which take root like thorns and nettles in a neglected field, and they grow and environ us. Even this I have seen in your heavens in the far future. It will come upon you, O Osiris, and with all your wisdom and strength you will meet the same fate as De'yus, and be cast into hell.

25/44.15. Osiris said: Were I to judge by all the self-Gods who have been before me, I would assent to your wise judgment. But hear me, O Ahura, for mine is not like any other heavenly kingdom, nor formed for my own glory only. This, then, is what I will accomplish:

25/44.16. I will cast out sin from among mortals, and all types of wickedness; and I will give them a heavenly kingdom on earth. They shall war no more, nor deal unjustly with one another; nor have suffering, immature deaths, famines or sickness, but peace, love, righteousness, good works and nobleness.

25/44.17. For I will go down to them in person in time to come; and I will take with me angels high raised and appoint them to mortals, and give them corporeal bodies for their pleasure, and they shall be the teachers of man on the earth. And man shall put away all selfishness, deceit, lust and lying; and the races of man shall be taught how to beget offspring in purity and wisdom.

25/44.18. And in that day I will take back the drujas of heaven and engraft[986] them on mortals and re-raise them up with understanding. So for that purpose, O Ahura, though I fortify myself in all this, am I not laboring in the right way?

25/44.19. Ahura said: It seems to me a dangerous proceeding. I would compare your plan to that of a teacher who took his pupil into a place of vice to teach him virtue. How can a heavenly kingdom exist among mortals, except with celibates? And they cannot people the world. Is there any other way but by the delight of the lowest passion that man can be born into life? What belongs to the flesh is of the flesh; the spirit repudiates the earth.

25/44.20. Osiris said: It has been so said; but I will cast the higher love down into the lower.

---

[986] This by some is called reincarnation. Some who have spirits thus engrafted are said to be POSSESSED OF A FAMILIAR SPIRIT. –Ed.

25/44.21. Ahura said: Why, so you can; but, alas, will it remain down, and forever grovel on the earth? I have seen a sweet maiden wed to a vicious husband, and she did not lift him up, but he pulled her down. Will it not be so with the higher love, when you wed it to the passions? Behold the manner of the oracles! We appoint high-raised angels to answer the questions of mortals, to lead them up to virtue and wisdom; but, alas, mortals do not come to the oracles to learn these things, but to learn wickedness, war, and earthly gain. Will it not be so with your kingdom founded on earth? Instead of helping mortals up, mortals will pull down the angels to answer them in their most sinful desires and curiosity.

25/44.22. Osiris said: You have great reason on your side, and facts as well, to sustain you. Yet do not forget, O Ahura, I shall have a temple built of stone on the earth,[987] and a chamber where I can come and command the kingdom through the mortal king.

25/44.23. Ahura said: Behold, my mission is fruitless. I have now visited my three loves, Te-in, Sudga, and you. And I cannot turn one, even a fraction. In this I have great sorrow; for I fear the time may come when great darkness will be upon you all.

25/44.24. Osiris said: I will consider your wise words, O Ahura. And though you now go from me, my love will follow you.

25/44.25. With that, Osiris signaled the chief marshal and the vice-Gods, and they came. Then Osiris and Ahura embraced each other and parted, both saluting in the sign, LOVE FOREVER. Ahura retired even as he came, but walking backward, with vice-Gods on either side, and the marshal leading the way. After they crossed the arena Ahura was delivered to Egupt; and the chief marshal with the vice-Gods returned to Osiris.

25/44.26. Egupt passed Ahura on to his own attendants, who conducted him to his fire-ship, in which they embarked and set sail for his own heavenly place, Vara-pishanaha.

[987] Today this is called the Great Pyramid of Giza (Giza being the city nearby where it is located).

CHAPTER 45 Wars

25/45.1. Jehovih allowed the self-Gods to prosper for more than four hundred years; and Te-in, Sudga, and Osiris, became the mightiest Gods that ever ruled on the earth. Know, then, these things of them, in heaven and earth, conveyed in the following synopsis drawn from the libraries of Jehovih's kingdoms, which relate the subject more fully:

25/45.2. First of Te-in, then Sudga, then Osiris. Of Te-in's heavenly kingdom, two vice-Gods, Noe Jon and Wang-tse-Yot. Chief high marshal, Kolotzka, and under him thirty thousand marshals. Chief general, Ha-e Giang, and under him one hundred thousand generals and high captains. Of these, twenty thousand were allotted to the dominion of mortals in Jaffeth; the others served in heaven, mostly around the throne of Te-in. Chiefly distinguished as Gods on the earth were Te-in's fourteen chief generals: Kacan-cat, Yam-yam, Tochin-woh, Ho-jou-ya, Wah-ka, Oke-ya-nos, Haing-le, Lutz-rom, Le-Wiang, Thu-wowtch, Eurga-roth, I-sa-ah, To-gow and Ah Shung.

25/45.3. These generals were divided into two parts of seven each; and they were allotted equally of the twenty thousand rank generals assigned to the earth; and these again were allotted each thirty thousand angel warriors.

25/45.4. Te-in had said to these fourteen chief generals: When you come to the earth, and, finding two cities near each other, both of which worship Gods other than me, you shall divide yourselves into two parts; and one army shall go to one mortal city and the other to the other, and by inspiration and otherwise you shall bring the two cities to war against each other until both are broken down, or destroyed. After which you shall inspire another city that worships me, to come and possess both of those that are destroyed. It is better to make our enemies kill each other than to kill them ourselves.

25/45.5. And such was the mode of warfare by Te-in that all the land of Jaffeth was subdued to him in less than a hundred years; except the matter of a million Faithists, scattered here and there, and of the Listians who were in the mountains and wildernesses. And great and costly temples were built in all the cities of Jaffeth, and dedicated to TE-IN, CREATOR AND RULER OF HEAVEN AND EARTH.

25/45.6. Now, as to the worshippers of Joss and Ho-Joss,[988] they were not converted but subdued, and they worshipped their God in secret, and made rites and ceremonies by which they could know one another and the better escape persecution. Many of these rites were modeled on the ancient rite of Bawgangad.[989]

25/45.7. Among the great cities[990] destroyed in these wars were: Hong we, Chow Go and Sheing-tdo. For Hong we the wars lasted twenty years; and five hundred thousand men, women and children were slain within the city.

25/45.8. The wars of Chow Go lasted forty years, and three hundred thousand men, women and children were slain within her walls. For Sheing-tdo the wars lasted twenty-five years, and three hundred thousand men, women and children ware slain within her walls.

25/45.9. In the destruction of Hong we there were consigned to ashes four hundred houses of philosophy; two thousand four hundred colleges, and twelve thousand public schools. All of which had been made glorious in the reign of Hong, the king of the city. Because he worshipped Ho-Joss, his great city was destroyed.

25/45.10. In Chow Go there were destroyed six hundred houses of philosophy and two hundred colleges of Great Learning. Here was the Temple of Jonk, which was dedicated to worship of Joss (God), and which, in building, required twenty thousand men twelve years. It had two thousand pillars of polished Awana stone; and at the blood altar it had twelve thousand skulls, of which the great king Bak Ho was slaughterer in the name of Ho-Joss. The throne of worship for the king was set with diamonds and pearls; and it had a thousand candlesticks of gold and silver. And the extent of fine silk drapery and fine wool drapery within the temple was so great that, if spread out on the ground, five hundred thousand men could lie down on it and yet not cover up half of it. And the draperies were painted and embroidered with pictures of battles and wars; and of scenes in heaven. And it had taken twenty thousand men and women forty years of labor to accomplish this ornamentation of the draperies. All of which were destroyed, together with the entire city and all its riches and magnificence.

25/45.11. Sheing-tdo was a city of fashion and splendor, inhabited by the richest men in the world. She had a temple called Cha-oke-king, dedicated to learning, but in fact appropriated to the display of wealth and pageantry. It was round, with a high projecting roof, the eaves of which rested on ten thousand pillars of polished stone. There were four hundred doorways to enter the temple; but, within each doorway, one came against the square columns of precious stones that supported the roof inside; and to either side of the columns were passageways that led into the four hundred chambers within. In the center of the temple, twenty thousand artificial stalactites hung from the roof; these were made of silk and wool and fine linen, and painted, and of colors so bright that mortal eye could scarcely look upon them, and they looked like ice with the sun shining on it, forming rainbows in every direction. Kings, queens and governors, of great learning, came here; for here, copies of the greatest books in all the world were deposited.

25/45.12. Besides the temple of Cha-oke-king, there were seven great temples built to Joss, any of which was large enough for ten thousand men to do sacrifice (worship) in at one time. For twenty-five years the people of Sheing-tdo fought to save their great city from destruction, but it fell, and was destroyed along with all the temples in it. By king Bingh, it was laid low.

25/45.13. Next to these, the following great cities were destroyed: Gwoo-gee, which had one hundred houses of philosophy and forty colleges for great learning; one temple, with eight hundred polished pillars and two thousand arches; thirty temples of wheat and corn sacrifice; one food warehouse where, in case of famine, food for one hundred thousand people was stored, sufficient for eight years; and all these, and the libraries of the records of the Gods and Lords of earth, and all things in the city, were burnt to ashes.

25/45.14. The city of Young-ooh, of two hundred thousand inhabitants, which had seventy

---

[988] i.e., God and Lord God, aka Anuhasaj

[989] i.e., Baugh-Ghan-Ghad, presented later in Oahspe; presumably this included burnt offering, and evidently human sacrifice as shown later

[990] Great city in those days signified cities with tributary governors, and tributary towns. Where the city had no tributary town or governor, it was called simply a city. –Ed.

houses of philosophy, and thirty-five colleges of great learning, besides many schools; one TEMPLE OF THE STARS, where lectures were given daily to the people to teach them the names and places of the stars and their wondrous size and motion; forty temples of sacrifice, seven of which were large enough to hold all the inhabitants of Young-ooh, the great city. By king Shaing it was laid in ashes, and nothing but heaps of stone remained to tell where the city had been.

25/45.15. The city, Gwan-she, which had thirty houses of philosophy, and seventy temples of sacrifice, two Temples of the Stars dedicated to Joss; eighty-five colleges of Great Learning, and also a feed-house, stored sufficiently to feed the city seven years; and there were two hundred thousand inhabitants within the city walls. Twelve years the people of this city fought against the incited plunderers, the warriors under the God Te-in, but were conquered at last, and their city laid low.

25/45.16. And the great cities, Ghi, Owan, Chong, Goon, Ca-On, Jong-wong, Sow, Wowtch-gan, Sem-Sin, Gee, Tiang, Choe, Doth, Ah-mai, Conc Shu, Guh, Haingtsgay, Ghi-oo-yong, and Boy-gonk, all of which had houses of philosophy, colleges of great learning, public schools, temples of sacrifice, feed-houses, and hundreds of thousands of inhabitants. And all these cities were destroyed, and only heaps of stones left to tell where they had been.

25/45.17. Besides these, there were more than two thousand cities of less prominence destroyed. And yet, of the villages and small cities that were destroyed, so great was their number, that no man ever counted them.

25/45.18. It was city against city; king against king; man against man; for the inhabitants of Jaffeth were obsessed to madness, war and destruction; almost without cause they would fall upon one another to destroy; for Te-in had sent his hundreds of millions of warring angels to inspire mortals to destroy all knowledge, instruction, learning, and philosophy, and to destroy all trace of all other Gods and Lords, so that he alone would reign supreme.

25/45.19. And these angels taught mortals how to make explosive powder, and guns to shoot with, more deadly than the bow and arrow; and taught the secret of under-digging a city and blowing it up with explosive powder.

25/45.20. So the fair land of Jaffeth, with its wisdom and great learning, was reduced to a distracted and broken-up country. The bones of mortals were scattered over the lands in every direction; nor could the land be tilled without digging among the skulls and bones of the great giant race of I'huans that once had peopled it.

25/45.21. And of those who were not destroyed, one might say: They were a poor, half-starved, sickly breed, discouraged and helpless, badly whipped.

25/45.22. And the spirits of the dead were on all the battlefields, lighting up the dark nights with their spirit-fires, and in the morning and the twilight of evening they could be seen by the hundreds and thousands, walking about, shy and wild! But an abundance of familiar spirits dwelt with mortals; took on sar'gis forms, and ate and drank with them, and even did things of which it is unlawful to mention.

25/45.23. Thus was Jaffeth won to the God Te-in. Now know of Sudga.

CHAPTER 46 Wars

25/46.1. Sudga had two vice-Gods, Brihat and Visvasrij. Next to these was Sudga's heavenly chief marshal, Atma, who had four thousand marshals under him, and equally divided among them to command, were one billion heavenly warring angels. Atma had authority over thirty thousand generals and captains, to whom two billion angels were allotted.

25/46.2. Chief of the heavenly generals were: Shahara, Vasyam, Suchchi, Dev, Nasakij, Tvara, Watka, Shan, Dorh, Hudhup, Nikish, Hajara, Hwassggarom, Viji, Yatamas, Brahma,[991] Goska, Fulowski, M'Dhuhitri, Yaya-mich-ma, Hijavar, Duth, Lob-yam, Hi-gup, and Vowiska. And these falsely assumed the names of the ancient Gods and Lords of thousands of years before.

25/46.3. Sudga had said to them: So that my age may be magnified before the newborn in

[991] Note this is not the Brahma who was husband to Yu-tiv; yet this one existed prior to the false-God Brahma who established the Brahminism known to this day in early kosmon.

heaven, you shall also magnify your own names by taking the names of Gods and Lords who are revered in heaven and earth, for all things are free to you. But I give privilege to none others to choose the names of the ancients.

25/46.4. Sudga then made the following his Private Council: Plow-ya, Vazista, Kiro, Cpenista, Visper, E-shong, Bog-wi, Lowtha, Brihat, Gai-ya, Sa-mern, Nais-wiche, Yube, Sol, Don, Mung-jo, Urvash, Cpenta-mainyus, and Vanaiti; and to each of them ten thousand attendants.

25/46.5. Then Sudga made two great captains, Varsa and Baktu, and he said to them: Two billion angels I have allotted to go down to the earth, to the land of Vind'yu, to subdue mortals and have dominion over them permanently, and I divide the two billion between you two. But all other angels shall remain in my heavenly kingdom and work for me, and embellish it, and beautify my heavenly cities, especially my holy capital.

25/46.6. Now, when you two are permanent on the earth, and secured in the temples and oracles, you shall survey all the lands of Vind'yu, including the cities, large and small, and all the people. And, behold, all men shall be subdued to my two names, Sudga and Dyaus; and when a city stands, in which the people worship any other Gods or Lords, you shall destroy that city and all its people. It shall be city against city and man against man; for as I am the all highest God of heaven, so will I be the God of earth, and its Lord. And when finding two cities to be destroyed, the two of you shall divide, one going with his angel warriors to one city, and the other to the other city; and you shall inspire them against each other until death; and when they are laid low, you shall bring my worshippers into the place, to inhabit it.

25/46.7. Thus the two destroying captain Gods, Varsa and Baktu, with their two billion angel warriors, descended to the earth. And they spread out over the land of Vind'yu, where there were many kingdoms and thousands of cities; and they came to mortals asleep or awake, and inspired them to havoc and destruction, for Sudga's sake.

25/46.8. And in twelve years, four thousand cities were laid in ruins, of which thirty-seven were great cities. And chief of these were Yadom, Watchada, Cvalaka, Hoce-te, Hlumivi, Ctdar, and Yigam, each of which contained more than one million souls, and some of them two million.

25/46.9. In all of these there were places of great learning, and schools, and temples of sacrifice (worship). In Ctdar the roof of the temple was made of silver, copper and gold; and it had one thousand columns of polished stone, and five hundred pillars to support the roof. The walls were covered with tapestry, painted with written words and histories of heaven and earth, and of the Gods, Lords and Saviors of the ancients. Within the temple were seven altars of sacrifice, and four thousand basins of holy water for baptismal rites. Within the walls of the temple were niches for five hundred priests, for the confession of sins, and for receiving the money, cloth and fruits of the earth, contributed by the penitent for the remission of their sins. Through the central passage within the temple the king drove in his golden chariot, when he came for sacrifice; and the floor of this passage was laid with silver and gold.

25/46.10. In the center of the temple floor was a basin filled with water, and the diameter of the basin was equal to twenty lengths of a man. In the middle of the basin was a fountain throwing up water. And at the east, west, north and south sides of the basin were four pillars of polished stone, with stairs within them; and the tops of these pillars were connected by beams of inlaid wood of many colors, polished finely, which were called the Holy Arch of Suhhadga. On the summit of the arch was a small house called the Voice of the Oracle, for here sat the king's interpreter of heaven and earth, the reader of visions. And the spirits of the dead appeared in the spray of the fountain, sometimes as stars of light and sometimes in their own forms and features, and were witnessed by the multitude.

25/46.11. Within each of the five hundred pillars was a sacred chamber, for the benefit of the priests communing with angels. In the east pillar was an opening from top to bottom, a slatway, so the multitude could see into the pillar, which was hollow its entire height. This was occupied by the king's high priest or priestess, as the case might be, and this person had attained to adeptship, so that the angels could carry him up and down within the pillar, even to its top, which was equal to fifty lengths of a man. And the multitude thus saw him ascending and descending.

25/46.12. In the west pillar was the library of the temple, which contained a history of its important events for a period of eight hundred years; of the priest and high priests, and of the kings of the city.

25/46.13. Next to the Temple, which was called Tryista, stood the House of Learning, where the wise men and women congregated, being skilled in philosophy, music, astronomy and mineralogy. The House was made of polished stone and wood interlocked, and its front had one hundred and forty columns of polished stone and wood. The house contained the skins and bones of thousands of creatures, ancient and modern, which were classified and named; and with these were books of philosophy and history, all of which were free to the public one day in seven. Next to the House of Learning was the Temple of Death, dedicated to all kinds of battles, battles between lions and men, tigers and men, and between lions and tigers, and elephants, and between man and man. And so great was the Temple of Death that its seats could accommodate three hundred thousand men, women and children. The temple was circular, and without a roof over the arena. But the greatest of all buildings in Ctdar was the king's palace, commonly called Temple Of The Sun. This was also made of polished stone; and on the four sides had eight hundred columns of polished stone; and next to the columns were fifty pillars, on every side connected by arches twelve lengths high,[992] on which rested a roof of wood and stone; and yet on this was surmounted another row of four hundred columns of polished wood, inlaid with silver and gold, and these were connected on the top by other arches ten lengths high, and on these another roof, and on the top of this a dome covered with gold, silver and copper. From the arena to the dome the height was twenty-eight lengths, and the base of the dome across was sixteen lengths. Entering the temple from the west was a chariot roadway, so that the king and his visitors could drive up into the arena of the palace in their chariots. But as for the interior of the king's palace, a whole book could be written to describe it, and yet not tell half its richness, beauty and magnificence.

25/46.14. Besides these great buildings there were four hundred and fifty Temples of Darkness, dedicated to the spirits of the dead. These were without any opening except the door; and when the communers were within, and the door shut, they were without light. Within these temples, spirits and mortals congregated, and the spirits taught mortals the art of magic; of making seeds grow into trees and flowers; of producing serpents by force of the will; of carrying things through the air; casting sweet perfumes, and casting foul smells; of casting virus to one's enemy, and inoculating him with poison, causing death; of finding things lost; of bringing money to the poor, and flowers and food to the sick; of entering the dead sleep,[993] and of becoming unconscious to pain by force of the will.

25/46.15. Nor could any man or woman attain to be a priest in the Temple of Tryista until he mastered all the degrees in the Temples of Darkness.

25/46.16. The angels of Sudga decided to destroy this city (Ctdar); and, accordingly, they inspired a war between it and the city of Yadom, which was a close second to it in magnificence, possessing temples and palaces like it. Indeed, to describe one of these great cities was to describe the other, as to mortal glory. For seven hundred years these cities had been at peace with each other, only half a day's journey apart, on the great river, Euvisij, in the Valley of Rajawichta.

25/46.17. And the captain God, Varsa, chose one city, and the captain God, Baktu, chose the other city; and each of them took from their billion angel warriors a sufficient number, and inspired the two great cities to everlasting destruction. As mortals turn savage beasts into an arena, to watch them tear and flay each other, even so sat these captain Gods in their heavenly chariots, witnessing the two great cities in mortal combat. And when one had too much advantage, the angel hosts would turn the tide, or let them rest awhile; then urge them to it again, holding the game in such even balance as would ensure the greatest possible havoc to both.

---

[992] A length was the length of a man, but as to how many feet and inches, we are left in the dark. – Ed. [Nevertheless, using an average five-foot length (c. 1.5 meters) should give sufficient scale of the building's magnitude.]

[993] The dead sleep is still practiced in India. Some of the fakirs enter this dormant state and suffer themselves to be buried for months; and when they are dug up, come to life again. –Ed.

25/46.18. Eight years these battles lasted; and hundreds of thousands of men, women and children were slain; and when the great cities were thus reduced, the Gods let loose THE BAND OF DEATH, whose angel office was to carry poison virus from the rotten dead and inoculate the breath of the living; and then make mortals in desperate madness set fire to their cities, to keep them from falling into other hands. And in eight years the great cities, with their mighty temples, were turned to ruin and dust; and of the people left, only the ignorant few, starving, helpless wanderers, could tell the tale of what had been.

25/46.19. Sudga had said: All knowledge among mortals is inimical to[994] the Gods in heaven; therefore I will destroy all knowledge on the earth. And this was the same doctrine maintained by Te-in, God of Jaffeth.

25/46.20. The captain Gods of Sudga proceeded in that manner, over all the land of Vind'yu, laying low all kingdoms, cities, places of sacrifice, and places of learning. And in one hundred years the mighty people of Vind'yu were reduced to beggary and scattered tribes of wanderers. The great canals were destroyed, and the upper and lower country became places of famine and barrenness. And in the valleys and on the mountains, in the abandoned fields and in the wildernesses, lay the bones and skulls of millions of the human dead. And lions and tigers came and prowled about in the ruined walls of the fallen temples and palaces. Nor was there left in all the land a single library, or book, or the art of making books, or anything to show what the great history had been.

25/46.21. Thus perished the Vedic language, the language of song, poetry and great oratory. Except in a small degree, such as that preserved by the remnant of Faithists who had escaped through all these generations, still worshipping in secret the Great Spirit.

25/46.22. Hear next of Osiris and his dominions, and of Arabin'ya, Par'si'e and Heleste:

CHAPTER 47 Wars

25/47.1. Osiris, the false, on setting up a heavenly kingdom of his own, and holding dominion over Arabin'ya, Par'si'e and Heleste, said: Let Te-in and Sudga pursue their course in destroying; mine shall be in the opposite way.

25/47.2. Osiris, the false, said: Three kinds of bad people I have found in heaven and earth: Those who are forever finding fault with and putting down, what others have built up; they are most crafty in argument to find the flaws of others, the inconsistencies, errors and shortness; but there is nothing in them to build up anything in heaven or earth. The next bad man is he who finds fault, not only with all that has ever been, but with all propositions designed for a new state of affairs. He is as worthless as the shaft of a spear without a head. The third bad man I have found is he who, seeing the faults and errors of others, does not harp upon them, but plunges into work with something new and bold, involving himself and others in disaster. And these three have the great multitude, the world, to take care of! I alone am capable of destroying and building up.

25/47.3. The non-resistance of the Faithists has made them ever dependent on the mercy of their neighbors, in heaven and earth. They must be destroyed, and their doctrines also.

25/47.4. In destroying their doctrines, I must give something in its place. I have labored to put away Jehovih and establish the Lord God; now to put away the latter and establish myself as myself would take some hundreds of years more. It is better, then, that since De'yus is cast into hell, I assume the names, Lord God, De'yus, Creator, and all others that are acceptable in heaven and earth.

25/47.5. Neither will I rob them of their rites and ceremonies, but so add to them, that, by the superior glory, they will accept mine.

25/47.6. Nor will I abridge mortals of their learning; but, on the contrary, be most exacting and high in aspiration; for by this I will win the approval of the wise and learned.

25/47.7. Mortals love idols; therefore I will give them idols, both male and female. ||

25/47.8. Osiris then called Baal, Ashtaroth and Egupt into his heavenly Council chamber, and said to them:

25/47.9. Two idols you shall inspire mortals to build to me; and one shall be the figure of a male horse, with a man's head, chest and arms, and he shall point upward, signifying, heavenly rest; and the other shall be the figure of a mare, with the head, breasts and arms of a woman. And she shall

[994] detrimental to; harmful to the aims of

hold a bow and arrow before her, and behind her a sword and a rose; signifying, for righteousness' sake. And the male idol shall be called Osiris, and the female, Isis.[995]

25/47.10. For when I assert myself creator of all the living, I must show to men that I am male and female.

i025 **The False Osiris**. During the Spe-ta cycle began the heavenly reign of the false Osiris; who ultimately broke free of his God, the false De'yus, and set up under his own name, and eventually was cast into hell. This image, as well as Isis (see i026), was imparted to mortals after breaking free from De'yus.

25/47.11. Which, in truth, is the fountain of all that is in heaven and earth, of which PROJECTION and RECEPTION are the sum of all philosophy.

i026 **Isis**. The feminine aspect of the false Osiris, as promulgated by him (see i025).

25/47.12. In which you shall teach that to go forth is Osiris, and to rest in meekness is Isis; for which the ancients used the bull and the lamb.[996]

25/47.13. For I was a globe, boundless in size, and swift in motion. And I put forth a wing for flying, and a hand for labor, by which all things are conquered and subdued. And beneath the wing I set the Lamb of Peace,[997] as a sign of the flight of the defenseless; but under the hand I set the head of a bull, as the sign of my dominion.

25/47.14. And I made heaven and earth with wings flying forth, bearing the serpent and the sun. All good and powerful things I have made square with the world, and circumscribed.

25/47.15. And in man's hand I placed the key to unlock the mysteries of the firmament of heaven, as well as the power, wisdom, riches and glory of the earth. Into his hand I place a club, to slay the lion, or to subdue him.

25/47.16. For I am like man, having created him in my own image; and I hold the key of heaven and earth, and dominion over all the inhabitants I created on the earth. I am Tau, I am Sed.

---

[995] See The False Osiris, and Isis [images i025, i026]. It must be remembered that in after ages, say two hundred years, mortals lost the above interpretation, and called Osiris the Savior of men, saying he was the son of Isis, the virgin earth. –Ed.

[996] Taurus and Aries. –Ed.

[997] See image i027 Tablet of Osiris. The Lamb of Peace is depicted in Osiris' tablet as the glyph of Aries or Sed. See Sed in Se'moin tablet image i033 volume 2 p.227 (row 5, sixth to right). The head of the bull under the hand is depicted as the Taurus glyph. See Tau in Se'moin tablet image i033 volume 2 p.227 (row 5, 2nd from right).

i027 **Tablet of the False Osiris**. This Tablet belonged to the Egyptians in the mosaic cycle, and was of the established religion of that day. That is, by the time of Moses, Osiris the false God was overthrown in his heavenly kingdom, but the religion he established on earth continued on for a season with mortals.

25/47.17. I am the light, and the life, and the death. Out of myself I made all that live or ever have lived. The sun in the firmament I set up as a symbol of my power. The stars, the moon, and things that do not speak, and do not know, are the works of my hand. Without me nothing is, nor was, nor ever shall be.

25/47.18. Whoever goes forth warring for the right, is for me; and I am with him. With warriors I am a god of war; with the peaceful I am a lamb of peace. To do, is of me; to not do, is not of me, but of death. An eye for an eye, a tooth for a tooth, blood for blood, mercy for mercy; but force toward all things, with will to conquer, for in these I am manifest to men.

25/47.19. For in the beginning I created the world by my own force; and this is my testimony, justifying force even with violence when the greater good comes to the greater number. Upon this hangs my law; in which any man can understand that had the Faithists fought for righteousness, they would have long since mastered the world and subdued it to their God.

25/47.20. What, then, is the stratagem of Gods, other than, by some means, to reduce men and angels to oneness in all things? || When Osiris had thus addressed the three Gods, he waited for them to speak. Baal said: This is a foundation; we have never had a foundation for men or angels. Ashtaroth said: This is a head and front to lead the world. Egupt said: The wisdom of the Faithists was in having a direct course.

25/47.21. Osiris said: Then I will revise the doctrines of earth and heaven. I will not say this is for De'yus, nor the Lord, nor God, nor Osiris, nor Apollo, nor any other God. But I will give that which all except Jehovihians can accept.

25/47.22. For I will allot[998] all things to God, not defining which God, or what God, but God only; the rest I will manage in Agho'aden, my heavenly kingdom.

25/47.23. Go, therefore, to mortals, and revise the things of De'yus to God; and if mortals question the oracles to know who God is, reply: He is Osiris to the Osirians; Apollo to the Apollonians; Isis to the Isisians; he is the Creator, the master, the all, out of whom all things were created; he who created man in his own image; who dwells on a throne in heaven.

25/47.24. But if they question further, asking if he is the ever present, answer them: No. And if they say: Is he Jehovih, the Great Spirit? Answer them: No.

25/47.25. For I will not permit even one Faithist to dwell alive on the face of the earth.

CHAPTER 48 Wars

25/48.1. [999]In Haikwad, in Par'si'e, dwelt king Luthag, a man of great wisdom and kingly power. His capital city, Sowruts, lay on the border of Fonecea, and had twelve tributary cities, each city being ruled over by a king.

25/48.2. A great drought came upon the regions ruled by Luthag; and being a king of benevolence,

[998] assign, attribute

[999] This chapter starts out as a flashback to earlier times and then works its way toward the present of the current narrative, which it fully resumes in Chapter 49.

he sent inspectors far and near, to find a country of water and good soil. But alas, they did not find what was desired.

25/48.3. Luthag consulted the oracles, and behold, the angel, Egupt, came and answered the king, saying: Send your seer and I will lead him. So the king sent for his high seer, and told him the words of the oracle. The seer said: Wherever the God touched you, permit me to touch also, and perhaps I can hear your God speak.

25/48.4. The seer touched the king in the place, and at once the God spoke to him, and he heard. So it came to pass that the God led the seer into Egupt, which at that time was called South Arabin'ya. The seer did not know the country, and he asked the God. The spirit said: Behold the land of Egupt. Thus was named that land, which is to this day called Egypt.

25/48.5. The seer found the land fertile and well watered; so he returned to Par'si'e and informed the king. Upon hearing the report the king commanded his people to migrate to Egupt. And so in the first year fifty thousand departed; and in the second year one hundred thousand, and this many migrated each year afterward for many years.

25/48.6. || These things occurred in the seven hundredth year of the reign of De'yus in Hored. And in the space of two hundred years more, behold, the land of Egupt was peopled over with millions of people; for the drought and famines in the nearby countries drove them here. ||

25/48.7. Luthag sent his son to govern the land of Egupt, and he made it tributary to the kingdom of Sowruts. The son's name was Haxax; and when he was old and died, he left the governorship of Egupt to his son, Bakal, who broke the allegiance with Par'si'e and established all of Egupt as an independent kingdom. Bakal's son, Goth, succeeded him; and Goth enriched his kingdom with great cities and temples, and places of learning, and founded games and tournaments. Goth's daughter, Rabec, succeeded him; and was the first queen of Egupt. Rabec still further enriched the great land with cities and places of learning. Thus stood the country at the time De'yus was overthrown in his heavenly kingdom. And now for seventy years the Gods, Osiris, Baal, Ashtaroth and Egupt, did not have much power with mortals.

25/48.8. And during this short period, the shepherd kings migrated into Egupt in vast numbers; and in sympathy with these, and of kindred faith, were the followers of Abraham, the Faithists, who also migrated rapidly into Egupt.

25/48.9. Meanwhile the kingdom had passed from Rabec to her oldest son, Hwan; and to his oldest son, Naman; and to his oldest son, Sev; and to his daughter, Arma; and to her oldest son, Hotha; and to his oldest son, Rowtsag.

25/48.10. And here stood the matter when Osiris resolved to revise the records of mortals and angels regarding the history of creation by God; which he did according to his own decrees, which were as previously stated.

25/48.11. So it came to pass that through the oracles, king Rowtsag bestowed upon the libraries of Egupt the history of the creation of heaven and earth, with the origin of sin, and the creation of man, the first of whom was now called Adam, instead of A'su, adopting the Par'si'e'an word instead of the Vedic.

25/48.12. And these records were the same from which Ezra, in the next dan'ha cycle, made selections, and erroneously attributed them to be the doctrines of the Faithists, who were called Iz'Zerlites.[1000] And the records of the Faithists were neither kept nor permitted in the state records, but kept among the Faithists themselves, for they were outlawed then, even as they are to this day,[1001] because they would not adopt the Saviors and Gods of the state.

25/48.13. Rowtsag's son, Hi-ram, succeeded him; and Thammas, his son, succeeded Hi-ram. Thammas was a seer and prophet, and could see the Gods and talk understandingly with them. Thammas was succeeded by his daughter, Hannah; and she was succeeded by Hojax, who was the builder of the TEMPLE OF OSIRIS, commonly called the GREAT PYRAMID.

25/48.14. In honor of the prophet of De'yus, the first mortal servant of Osiris, whose name was Thoth, Hojax named himself, Thothma, which is to say, God-Thoth; for Osiris told Hojax: You are the very Thoth reincarnated; and behold, you shall be God of the earth.

25/48.15. Thothma could hear the Gods and talk understandingly with them. And to him, Osiris,

[1000] Isaerites –Ed. [Israelites]

[1001] i.e., the 1880s; and suppression in some parts of the world continued after that

through his angel servant God, Egupt, gave special care from his youth up. At the age of sixteen years, Thothma passed the examination in the house of philosophy, and in astronomy and mineralogy. At seventeen he passed The Builders School and the Histories of the Thousand Gods. At eighteen he was admitted as an Adept in Life and Death, having power to attain the dormant state; and to see without his mortal eyes, and to hear without his mortal ears. At nineteen, he ascended the throne at the death of his father and mother.

25/48.16. For, because Osiris desired to use Thothma, he sent his destroying angels, and they inoculated the breath of Hannah and her husband, and they died by poison in the lungs.

25/48.17. So Osiris, through his servant God, Egupt, spoke to Thothma, saying: My son, my son! Thothma said: I hear you, O God, what do you desire? Osiris said: Provide a dark chamber and I will come to you. Thothma provided a dark chamber, and then Osiris through his servant God, came to him, saying:

25/48.18. You have great wisdom, but you forget your promise! Thothma said: In what, O God? Osiris said: When you were in heaven, you said: Now I will go down to the earth and reincarnate myself, and prove everlasting life in the flesh. || For many years Osiris had told this same thing to Thothma until he believed faithfully he had been so in heaven, returned, and reincarnated himself for such purpose.

25/48.19. And he answered Osiris, saying: It seems like a dream to me, even as you speak about it.

25/48.20. Osiris asked Thothma what was the greatest, best of all things. Thothma said: There are only two things, corporeal and spiritual.

25/48.21. Osiris said: True. What then is wisdom? Thothma said: To acquire great corporeal knowledge in the first place; and in the second, to acquire spiritual knowledge. But tell me, O God of wisdom, how can a man attain the highest spiritual knowledge?

25/48.22. Osiris said: To come and dwell in heaven and see for one's self. Thothma said: How long must a man sojourn in heaven in order to learn its wisdom? Osiris said: One day; a hundred days; a thousand years; a million years, according to the man.

25/48.23. Thothma said: If one could leave the corporeal part for a hundred days and travel in heaven for that amount of time, would it profit him? Osiris said: To do that is to master death. Behold, you have already attained to power of the dormant state. To control the course of the spirit; that is the next lesson.

25/48.24. Thothma said: Behold, O God, I have attained to the power of the dormant state, even as the magicians who submit to be buried for ninety days. Yes; and I go in spirit from my corporeal part, and see many things, but my soul is like a breath of wind, and goes at random.

25/48.25. Osiris said: Provide me a temple, and I will come and teach you. Thothma said: How to preserve the body for so long, so that it is not damaged—that is the question. The magicians who have been buried long, upon being dug up and resuscitated, find their bodies so damaged that they die soon after. (And have you, O God, a remedy?)

25/48.26. Osiris said: You shall build a Temple of Astronomy, and dedicate it to Osiris, Savior of men and angels, God of heaven and earth. And it shall be built square with the world, east and west and north and south. And the observing line shall be with the apex of the Hidan vortex,[1002] which lies in the median line of the variation of the north star (Tuax).

25/48.27. In the form of a pyramid you shall build it; I will show you every part, measure for measure.

25/48.28. And you shall provide such thickness of walls that no sound, heat, or cold can enter it; and yet, you shall provide chambers within, suitable for yourself, your chiefs, and your friends, who are also adepts. For I have also provided the earth for heaven, and heaven for the earth; and my angels shall come and dwell for a season on the earth, and my earth-born shall go and dwell for a season in heaven; yes, they shall come to me on my throne and see the glories I have prepared for them.

25/48.29. Nor shall my temple be exclusive, but open to all who will pursue the philosophies of earth and heaven. For which reason you shall build it with the sun, moon and stars;[1003] and it shall be a testimony to the nations of the earth that you are the highest of all mortals, and first founder of

---

[1002] the vortex of the North Star. –1891 glossary

[1003] i.e., build it in alignment to them

everlasting life in the flesh. For as the angels of heaven can return to the earth and take upon themselves corporeal bodies for a season, so shall you master your own flesh to keep it as you will. For this is the end and glory for which I created man on earth.

CHAPTER 49 Wars

25/49.1. Osiris then instructed king Thothma to drive out of the land of Egupt all the Faithists who could not be made slaves of, especially the shepherd kings.

25/49.2. Thothma impressed an army of two hundred thousand warriors, and drove off the shepherd kings, putting to death more than three hundred thousand of them. And he took from the Faithists all their possessions, such as houses and lands, and did not allow them to hold any mortal thing in possession; neither permitting them to till the soil, except as servants, nor to engage in any other labor except as servants. And to escape the tyranny of Thothma, there went out of the land of Egupt, three million Faithists, including the shepherd kings, the unlearned. And in regard to the Faithists who remained in the land of Egupt, Osiris, through king Thothma, made the following laws:

25/49.3. You shall not possess any land, house, ox or any beast of burden, nor cow nor calf, nor shall your people possess an altar of worship, temple, or place of sacred dance. But you shall be a servant and a servant of servants all the days of your life. But in your sleeping place and in the sleeping place of your family you shall do worship in your own way, nor shall any man molest you there regarding that.

25/49.4. You shall not openly profess your doctrines under penalty of your blood and your flesh; and you shall no longer teach in the schools or colleges; nor shall your children receive great learning. And of your arts, of measuring and working numbers, you shall no longer keep them secret, or your blood shall be upon you.

25/49.5. And if you say: Behold, the Great Spirit; or Jehovih, the Ever Present, you shall suffer death, and your wife and your children with you. And if a man questions, to try you, asking: Who created the world? You shall answer: Behold, God! And if he asks further: Do you think the Creator is Ever Present? You shall say: No, he is like a man who has finished his labor, he sits on his throne in heaven. And if he asks you further: Where is God? You shall answer: On the Mountain Hored, in heaven. And if he asks you still further: Is the Ever Present a Person? You shall say: No, the Ever Present is void like the wind; there is only one ruler in heaven and earth, even Osiris, who is Lord the God, Savior of men.

25/49.6. Whoever does not do these things shall be put to death; whoever does not bow to Thothma, my earthly ruler, shall not live, says God. ||

25/49.7. These laws were entered in the libraries of Egupt, and also proclaimed publicly by the scribes and seers. And yet even with these restrictions upon them, more than two million Faithists remained in the land of Egupt.

25/49.8. And it came to pass that Thothma began the building of the Temple of Osiris (pyramid), and he impressed two hundred thousand men and women in the building of it, of which number more than one-half were Faithists. And these laborers were divided into groups of twelves and twenty-fours and forty-eights, and so on, and each group had a captain; but for series of groups of one thousand seven hundred and twenty-eight men and women, there were generals, and for every six generals there was one marshal, and for every twelve marshals there was one chief, and these chiefs were of the Privy Council[1004] of the king.

25/49.9. And the king allotted a separate work to every chief; some to dig canals, some to quarry stone, and some to hew the stones; some to build boats, some to provide rollers, and others timbers, and yet others capstans.[1005]

25/49.10. In two places the surveyors found stone with which to build the temple, one was above the banks of the great river, Egon, at the foot of Mount Hazeka, and the other was across the Plains of Neuf, in the Mountains of Aokaba. From the headwaters of Egon a canal was made, first to Aokaba, and from there it descended by locks to the Plains of Neuf, and then on to Gakir, the place chosen by the king for the temple to be built.

25/49.11. And as for the logs used in building, they were brought down the waters of Egon, from the forests of Gambotha and Rugzak. These logs were tied together and floated on the water to the

[1004] advisory council; a cabinet

[1005] a type of pulley

place required, where, by means of capstans, they were drawn out of the water ready for use.

25/49.12. Now the stones of the temple were hewn in the region of the quarries. And when properly dressed,[1006] they were placed on slides by capstans, and then, by capstans, let down the mountainsides, to the water, upon which they were to float to the place required for them.

25/49.13. The floats were made of boards sawed by men skilled in the work, and were of sufficient length and width to carry the burden they were designed for. And at the bottom of the floats were rollers, gudgeoned[1007] at the ends. Now when a stone was let down from the place of its hewing on to the float, it was ready to be carried to its destination. And when the float arrived near Gakir, ropes, made of hemp and flax, were fastened to the float, and by means of capstans on the land, the float was drawn up an inclined plane out of the water, the rollers of the float answering as wheels.

25/49.14. When all things were ready for building the temple, the king himself, being learned in all philosophies, proceeded to lay the foundation, and to give instructions as to the manner of building it.

25/49.15. These were the instruments used by the king and his workmen: the gau, the length, the square, the compass, and the plumb and line. Nor were there any other instruments of measure or observation used in the entire building of the temple. And as to the measure called A LENGTH, it was the average length of a man, after measuring one thousand men. This length was divided into twelve parts, and these parts again into twelve parts, and so on.

25/49.16. After the first part of the temple was laid, the builders of the inclined plane began to build it also, but it was built of logs. And when it was raised a little, another layer of the temple was built; then again the inclined plane was built higher, and another layer of the temple built; and so on. Thus the inclined plane, which was made of wood, was built up as the temple increased in height.

25/49.17. The width of the inclined plane was the same as the width of the temple, but the whole length of the inclined plane was four hundred and forty lengths (of a man).[1008] The floats carrying the stones were drawn up this inclined plane by means of capstans, and by men and women directly pulling also.

25/49.18. Thothma spent twenty-four years building the temple; and then it was completed. But it required another half a year to take away the inclined plane used in building it. After that it stood free and clear, the greatest building that had ever been built on the earth or ever would be.

25/49.19. Such, then, was Thothma's TEMPLE OF OSIRIS, THE GREAT PYRAMID.

25/49.20. Jehovih had said: Suffer them to build this, for the time of the building is midway between the ends of the earth; and now is the extreme of the earth's corporeal growth; so let it stand as a monument of the greatest corporeal aspiration of man. For from this time forward, man shall seek not to build himself everlastingly on the earth, but in heaven. And these things shall be testimony that in the corporeal age of the earth, man was of like aspiration; and in the spiritual age of man, in an opposite condition of corporeal surroundings; for by the earth I prove what was; and by man prove what the earth was and is at certain periods of time.

CHAPTER 50 Wars

25/50.1. When the temple was completed, and the king and his four high priests entered into the Holy Chamber, the false Osiris, through his servant God, Egupt, came in sar'gis, and spoke to the king, saying: Here I am, O king!

25/50.2. Thothma said: My labor is well recompensed. That you have come to me, O Lord my God, I am blessed. Osiris said: Keep holy my chambers; permit no man, woman or child, that dwells on the face of the earth, to know the mysteries of these, my holies, except for my adepts. Here lies the key of everlasting life.

25/50.3. Thothma said: What do you mean by, the key of everlasting life? Osiris said: In this is that which is of good and evil, as I commanded your forefathers; to eat of it, man shall become as

[1006] prepared; shaped; smoothed and finished as required

[1007] an assemblage allowing for rotation of the roller logs, each roller log probably having a pin (axel) carved out on each end

[1008] This would make the inclined plane about half a mile. –Ed. [About 670 meters]

Gods, and so live forever. For this is the triumph of man over death, even for which I created him on the earth.

25/50.4. Thothma said: Shall only we five know these things? Osiris said: Surely not; otherwise the light of my kingdom would not be full. Behold how I built the temple! Was it not in the keeping of adepts?[1009] So, then, in the same manner that I have given you knowledge of my kingdom, so shall you give it to others, not permitting these lights (to come) to them except through my commandments.[1010]

25/50.5. Now in the second month after the temple was completed, Thothma, the king, having put the affairs of his kingdom in order, went into the Holy Chamber, and from there ascended into the Chamber of Life and Death, leaving the four chief priests in the Holy Chamber. And Thothma cast himself in death (dormancy) by swallowing his tongue. And the priests closed the entrance and sealed the king within.

25/50.6. Osiris, through his servant God, Egupt, said to the priests: One of you shall remain on quarter-watch, dwelling within the Holy Chamber and I will remain also. And the four priests cast lots, selecting their order, one for each of the four watches, of six hours each; repeating their schedule every day. And Osiris sent Baal to the spirit of Thothma, and took him to Agho'aden, Osiris' heavenly place, showing his spirit the glory of the throne, saying: Behold the God of Gods. Thothma said: It is a great glory; lo, my eyes are blinded by the light of the Lord my God. After this, Baal took the soul of Thothma into a thousand heavenly places in Osiris' kingdom, and showed him its glory.

25/50.7. Thothma said to Baal: O angel of God, you have shown me that God, in truth, is in the image of man. Nor is there anyone else but one God, who rules over all.

25/50.8. Baal said: What do you say, then; who is God? Thothma said: What do you say? For behold, his glory was so great I could not look upon him.

25/50.9. Then Baal answered, saying: There are only angels and mortals; these are the sum of all things. He, you have looked upon, was even as you are, a one-time mortal, but on a far-off star-world. He attained to the Godhead to create a world for himself; even as you, who are an adept, can create flowers, plants and serpents. Thus he came into the void regions of space and created the earth and her heavens, and they belong to him, for they are his. And in like manner every star-world is created and ruled by a God like your God, who is Lord of all.

25/50.10. Thothma said: O if only all people could know these things! O that I may remember them when I am returned to earth. Baal said: You shall remember more than this; for I will now take you to the hells of the idolaters and the Jehovihians. Baal then took the soul of Thothma to the hells of De'yus, and showed him its horrors. But he did not take him to the regions of God, in Craoshivi.

25/50.11. Now when Thothma had traveled in heaven for thirty days, Baal brought his spirit back to the Chamber of Death, and showed him how to regain his corporeal part, which he did. And then Baal signaled to Egupt, and the latter spoke to the priest on watch, saying: Behold, Thothma has returned; go and fetch your brothers, and deliver him into the Holy Chamber.

25/50.12. And when they came they unloosed the sealing stones and delivered the king into the Holy Chamber, and he was awake from his trance. Now, Thothma had been in the death trance forty days, but remembered all he had seen in heaven, which he related to the high priests who were with him. And both Baal and Egupt came in sar'gis and talked in the Holy Chamber with Thothma and the priests. For one day the king remained in the Holy Chamber, so that his spirit could be reconciled to the flesh; and on the next day he and the priests came out of the temple and sealed its door, and placed the king's guard in charge, so that no man or woman would molest the place.

[1009] The degree of adepts embraced not only su'is and sar'gis, but a knowledge of astronomy, chemistry and mathematics. The power of creating plants, flowers and serpents, was not taught in any of the degrees below adepts. The power of dormancy belonged to the next degree above, called miracles. –Ed.

[1010] In other words, don't allow aspirants to learn these lights (knowledge, understandings, attainments, etc.) unless they are initiated into the order and obey the commandments of Osiris (via his priests).

25/50.13. The three angels, Egupt, Baal and Ashtaroth, came into the altar in the king's palace that night, and showed themselves to the college students who had attained ADEPT. Baal spoke orally before them, directing his words to the king, saying: Behold, I am the angel of God your Lord, whom you have seen in heaven; I am the same who traveled in heaven with you. What I speak, I say in the name of the Lord our God, whose servant I am. Tomorrow your high priests shall draw lots, and one of them shall enter the Chamber of Holies, in the Osirian Temple, and do as you have done. And after him, behold, another of the high priests shall do likewise; and so on, until all four have had your experience.

25/50.14. And it came to pass that the four priests in turn CAST THEMSELVES IN DEATH, and visited Osiris' heavenly kingdoms, and also many of the hells of De'yus, being led in spirit by Baal or Ashtaroth, Egupt being the guardian God of the temple.

25/50.15. When they had thus accumulated the same knowledge of heaven and earth, the five of them were of one mind as to attaining life everlasting in the corporeal body. Osiris said: Behold, I will bring back many who are already dead; and they shall call to their embalmed bodies and wake them up and inhabit them. Go, then, to the root of the matter, and prepare my people, for I will come in person and inhabit the temple you have built; and my heavenly kingdom shall descend to the earth. Therefore, prepare the COLUMN OF THE STARS!

25/50.16. Thothma built a column to the east line of the slat, seven lengths, and the height was thirty-six lengths; of wood and stone he built it, with an opening from the bottom to the top, and the width of the opening was six lengths. In its walls was a winding stairway, and there were windows looking out to the east and west and north and south, so that the stars from every quarter could be observed. On the summit of the column were dwelling-places for the seers and mathematicians, with places for the measuring instruments and lenses.

25/50.17. When this was completed, Thothma built an external wall of wood and stone across the slat of the temple; and within this wall were stairs also, and these led to the top of the pyramid. This wall was also provided with windows, so that the northern stars could be observed.

25/50.18. Thothma made an observing column for the sun, and it was provided with lenses of all colors, so that adepts standing at the base of the pyramid could see the sun at every hour of the day, and distinguish the spots and their changes. A gau was set within each of the angles of observation, so that the position of the sun relative to the northern stars could be determined every day.

25/50.19. By using these two columns, therefore, Thothma and his mathematicians measured the sun, moon and stars as to their distances and sizes. And Osiris commanded the king to send his wisest mathematicians into the distant lands of the earth, to observe the winds of heaven, and the drought upon the earth; and the abundance of the yield of the earth in different regions, in different years and seasons; and to observe famines and pestilences, and all types of occurrences on the face of the earth. He said to the king: When your mathematicians have returned to you with their accumulated wisdom, you, or your successor, shall examine the sun, stars and moon, and compare them to the things that the mathematicians shall relate, one year with another; and three years with another three years, and five with five, and seven with seven, and so on for hundreds of years, and thousands of years.

25/50.20. And when you have taken in the term of three thousand three hundred years, and compared the sun, moon and stars, as relate to the occurrences of the earth, you shall have the key of prophecy for three thousand three hundred years ahead. And you shall say of this land and of that land; and of this people and that people, how it will be with them, and you shall not err. ||

25/50.21. Thothma, the king, called together his mathematicians, and, according to their grade, chose from among them twelve hundred. These he divided into groups of one hundred each; and he gave them a sufficient number of attendants; and he sent them toward all the sides of the world, allotting to them sixteen years each for observation, according to the commandments.

25/50.22. And they took with them all kinds of instruments to measure with, besides scribes to make the records of those matters that came before them. And they went throughout Arabin'ya, Vind'yu, Jaffeth, Par'si'e, Heleste, and Uropa, even across to the western sea (Atlantic Ocean); and to the southern extreme of Arabin'ya (Africa), and to the great kingdoms in the interior;[1011] and to the north of Heleste, Par'si'e, and Jaffeth, to the regions of everlasting snow.

25/50.23. And in sixteen and seventeen years they returned, except some who died on the journeys. And most wonderful was the knowledge these mathematicians gained. In some countries they found philosophers who had the knowledge required even at the tip of their tongues.[1012] Thothma received them in great pomp and glory, and awarded all of them with great riches.

25/50.24. And Thothma had these things rewritten and condensed into books, and named them books of great learning, and they were deposited within the south chamber of the pyramid, where harm could never come to them.

25/50.25. And Thothma made it a law, that other mathematicians should travel over the same regions for another sixteen years and make similar observations; and after them, yet other mathematicians to succeed them, and so on for three thousand three hundred years. And accordingly, a new expedition started out. Now during the absence of the first mathematicians, Thothma and his philosophers observed the sun, moon and stars every day, and a record was made as to their places and movements, and as to occurrences on the earth in the regions of Thothma's home kingdom. And these observations were reduced to tablets and maps, and a record made of them in the Par'si'e'an language, which was the language of the learned. For the Eguptian language of that day was spoken mostly by the unlearned, and was mixed with the Fonecean, a language of sounds.

25/50.26. After the mathematicians returned, Thothma and his philosophers examined the whole matter as compared with the maps and tablets of the heavens, and the facts deduced from these comparisons were written in a separate book and called THE PHILOSOPHIES OF GOD AND HIS SON THOTHMA, KING OF EARTH!

[1011] Here we see that there were great civilizations within central Africa during the Spe-ta cycle.

[1012] i.e., they were readily conversant regarding the subject asked for

25/50.27. Copies of this book were made and sent into the lands of Arabin'ya, Vind'yu, Jaffeth, Par'si'e, Heleste and Uropa, to the priests of God, but the original book was filed in the Holy Chamber, in the Temple of Osiris.

25/50.28. Thothma applied himself to impart wisdom to all men. And during his reign he built in the land of Egupt seventy-seven colleges of Great Learning, twelve colleges of prophecy, two hundred houses of philosophy, seven adepteries, three thousand free schools, and four thousand houses of sacrifice to Osiris, Savior of men.

25/50.29. Besides those, there were constructed three hundred and forty obelisks to God; thirty triumphal arches to De'yus; and four thousand oans-nus[1013] [or nu-oan –Ed.] to the Creator (the false Osiris), and these were mounted on pedestals of polished stone, and stood at the street corners.

25/50.30. And during Thothma's reign more than four thousand men and three hundred women graduated to the rank of adept, all capable of the death trance, and of going about in spirit. And within thirty years over seven hundred of these were permitted to test the cast of the holy chambers in the pyramid. And their spirits were conducted into Osiris' heavenly regions, and sojourned there for many days, and returned to their bodies unharmed. Because of the position of the chambers, there was no action upon their bodies while in the swoon.

25/50.31. Thus Thothma proved himself to be one of the wisest and greatest men that ever dwelt on the face of the earth.[1014] He believed all things the Gods told him, believed he was Thoth reincarnated, and believed he would never die as to the flesh.

25/50.32. The false Osiris, through his servant God, Egupt, had said to Thothma: This is the manner of heaven and earth, regarding man: All men are reincarnated over and over until perfected to immortal flesh; and in that day, man has so perfected his adeptism that he can remain on earth or ascend to heaven, even when he desires. Hence of all knowledge, adeptism is the greatest.

[1013] fertility sculptures

[1014] see image i113

i113 **Thothma (Hojax)**, the builder of the great pyramid in Egypt, and one of the greatest adepts that ever lived. He could hear the Gods and talk with them understandingly.

25/50.33. Thothma asked if there were any new creations. Satan prompted Osiris, who said: No; your spirit is as old as the earth. At first it was small and round, like a grain of mustard, only it was spirit. And the multitude of these seeds comprise[1015] the All Unseen. When one of them takes root in gestation, then is the beginning. And it is born into the world a frog, or an ass, or worm, or lion, or small creeping thing; and it lives its time and dies. And the spirit dispatches itself back again into another womb, and it is born forth a man low as to knowledge, evil as to life. And he lives a time and dies again; but again the spirit hurries back to another womb, and it is born forth again, another man, but wiser as to knowledge, and less evil as to life. And this continues to hundreds of generations and to thousands. But he who has attained adeptship has it in his power to call forth out of the earth his own corporeality; he no longer needs to go through the filth of others.

25/50.34. Thothma was wise even in his belief; for when he was growing old, and seeing his flesh sunken, and his eyes growing hollow and dim, and his hands getting withered, he inquired of the Gods, saying: I know you have taught me truth, O God. As to judgment, I am weak before you, and curious in my vanity. Osiris said: Speak, O king!

25/50.35. Thothma said: By all the force of my will; and by my great learning, I cannot stop the withering of the flesh. If, therefore, I already dry up like a mummy, beyond the power of my will, how will it be with me when I am further emaciated?

25/50.36. Satan prompted Osiris to answer the king, and so he said: Until you are even more emaciated you cannot understand the power of your own soul.

25/50.37. With this the king was reconciled, and even when he was tottering on his last legs he began to build a new palace, saying: After I have changed this flesh into immortal flesh, here I will come and dwell forever. And I shall be surrounded by adepts, wise and faultless. And this shall be the first colony of the kind I will build on the earth.

25/50.38. But afterward I will build many colonies like it; more and more of them, until I have all the earth redeemed to immortal flesh. For of such shall be my kingdom, and all men and all women on the earth shall own me Lord of all. ||

[1015] make up, constitute

25/50.39. Nevertheless, with all Thothma's wisdom, and the wisdom of his Gods, he fell on a stone and died suddenly on the day he was one hundred years old.

CHAPTER 51 Wars

25/51.1. When Thothma was quite dead the priests carried his body into the temple, fully believing his spirit would return from heaven and transform the body from corruptible into incorruptible flesh to live forever. And they laid the corpse in the place previously designated by the Gods, and sealed it up according to the commands of the false Osiris, Savior of men.

25/51.2. Osiris had said: Whoever believes in me, him I will save to everlasting life, and though he lose his body, he shall find it yet again, and the corruptible flesh shall be changed in the twinkling of an eye, and become incorruptible to life everlasting, with the spirit that abides within it.

25/51.3. On the fifth day the priests opened the chamber, for according to the LAWS OF MIRACLES, on that day, the spirit should accomplish the feat; but lo and behold, it had not come to pass, and the body still lay cold and dead. But the Gods came in sar'gis and said to the priests: Seal up the body for another five days. And the priests did as commanded; and after that they examined it again, but life had not returned. Again they were commanded to seal it up for another five days, which they did, but life did not return.

25/51.4. Houaka, who was now the high priest, inquired of Osiris concerning the matter. And Osiris, through his servant God, Egupt, answered him, saying: Go fetch a young man who is warm in the blood, which is life in the flesh, and he shall be the seventh son of an adept, and know how to CAST HIMSELF IN DEATH.

25/51.5. The priests brought Xaian, who was in his twenty-fourth year, and when he came into the Holy Chamber he was told to cast himself in death for benefit of the king's soul. And Xaian thus cast himself, and he was sealed in the chamber of death for five days along with the king's corpse. And in five days the priests brought both bodies into the Holy Chamber, according to instructions. And Osiris came and commanded them to stand around the bodies, and when they had done so, the angels from Osiris' kingdom came and spirited away the dead body of the king, and they brought back the spirit of Xaian to inhabit the body of Xaian, and put it in possession of it, making believe it was the spirit of Thothma returned.

25/51.6. Houaka said to the Gods: Where is the body of Thothma? Has it been transformed? And the Gods answered: It has gone to heaven, and will return after many days. But as to the spirit of the king, behold, he is with you. And the priests spoke to Xaian, believing it was Thothma. And after three days they came out of the temple (pretending Xian was Thothma), to re-crown him as Thothma the Second, and they proclaimed it abroad that these things were true, although they knew they were not.

25/51.7. As to the spirit of Thothma, at the time of death it was taken to Agho'aden and put among the servants of Osiris' heavenly kingdom, and thus enslaved. So Xaian became king of Egupt.

25/51.8. Now, regarding the false Gods, Osiris and his confederates, they never tried to reincarnate the spirit of Thothma; but because of the virtues and the wisdom of Thothma, they used him for the benefit of Osiris' heavenly kingdom, and to establish Osiris everlastingly on the earth as the all highest God.

25/51.9. As to the kingdoms of the land of Egupt, which succeeded Thothma, the inhabitants of the earth already know the chief part. For hundreds and hundreds of years the Eguptians were the most learned people in the world, and especially in knowledge of the stars, sun and moon, and in adeptism and miracles.

25/51.10. But woe came to them; the land became flooded with hundreds of millions of drujas; and as to the people of Egupt, the chief desire was to be able to return in spirit after death and dwell with mortals. And the things which followed are not even lawful to mention.

25/51.11. Suffice it to say, these spirits lost all sight of any higher heavens than to dwell on the earth; they knew no other. And they watched for the times when children were born, and obsessed them, driving away the natural spirit, and growing up in the new body of the newborn, calling themselves reincarnated; and these drujas professed that when they previously lived on earth they were great kings, or queens, or philosophers.

25/51.12. And they taught as their master, Osiris, the false, did: That there was no higher heaven than here on the earth, and that man must be reincarnated over and over until the flesh became immortal. Not all of these spirits drove away the natural spirit; but many merely engrafted themselves on the same body; and, while such persons lived, these spirits lived with them and dwelt with them day and night; not knowing more than their mortal companion. And when such a person died, behold, the druja went and engrafted itself on another child, and lived and dwelt with it in the same way; and thus continuing, generation after generation.

25/51.13. And because of these indulgences many of the spirits came in sar'gis in the families of the Eguptians; eating and drinking with them corporeally; and even doing things of which no man may speak, by which dire disease seized upon the flesh of mortals; and their blood and their flesh became inhabited with vermin. The people became idlers and vagrants; the lands were not tilled, and the places of learning became deserted ruins.

CHAPTER 52 Wars

25/52.1. Of the land of Egupt, the above suffices; and of Par'si'e and Heleste these things are the chief part, regarding the dominion of Osiris, Baal and Ashtaroth, namely: Because of the persecutions of Faithists, shepherd kings, and Listians, these people fled into Par'si'e and Heleste for hundreds of years, and they built cities and established kingdoms.

25/52.3. And none of these accepted the Lord, or God, or De'yus, but for the most part worshipped the Great Spirit. Nevertheless, they were not Faithists in purity; for they engaged in war and did not live in communities, with rab'bahs as rulers, but dwelt together in the manner of warriors.

25/52.4. The duty of subjugating these people to Osiris, Savior of mortals, was committed to Baal and Ashtaroth. So Baal and Ashtaroth, finding them stubborn in the worship of the Great Spirit, finally resolved to make them destroy one another, in the same manner as Te-in, in Jaffeth, and Sudga, in Vind'yu; and they asked Osiris for armies of warring angels for that purpose. Osiris gave them the following great angel generals and high captains:

25/52.5. Jah, Apollon-ya, Petoris, Pluton-ya, Hi-ram, Ben, Yu-be, Ali-jah, Ares, Sa'wang, T'crono, Afro-dite, Argo, Oyeb, Nadar, Abel, Said, Ar-ti-mis, Yact-ta-roth, Wab, Josh and Haur; and besides these there were the following deserters from Te-in and Sudga, namely: Clue, Jon, I-sa-ah, Yam-yam, Luth, Bar, Hote, Ki-dom, Athena, Hira, Oke-ya-nos, Hermes, Posee-ya-don, Ura-na, Hace, T'sodus, Rac-Rom, Mi-kak, Tol, Taes, Wo-wouski, Sur, Ala-jax and Hesmoin.

25/52.6. And Baal and Ashtaroth cast lots for each of the above generals and captains, choosing by taking turns, until they were divided equally between them. And Osiris gave Baal and Ashtaroth, each five hundred million warring angels. And thus armed, they descended to the earth, to the objectionable regions of Par'si'e and Heleste. In those days, these great divisions of the earth were divided into many nations and kingdoms.

25/52.7. And a kingdom was not measured according to the land, but according to the number of cities that paid tribute to the central city; though some kingdoms had only one city.

25/52.8. These, then, are some of the largest cities that Baal and Ashtaroth decided to destroy: Su-yan,[1016] with five tributary cities; Lakao, with two tributaries; Haugun, with eight tributaries; Waas, with three; Lowga, with six; Tol, with six; Sun, with five; Tos, with four; Troy, with six; Abed, with two; Athena, with twelve; Hess, with four; Ituna, with twelve; Fado, with ten; Tuna, with seven; and Wa'ke'at, with seven. And besides these there were many large cities without any tributary cities, which were also doomed to everlasting destruction.

25/52.9. The first great cities that were turned to war on each other were Haugun and Lowga, Ashtaroth choosing Haugun and Baal choosing Lowga.

25/52.10. These two cities were both of more than four hundred years' standing, and each contained a half million inhabitants, besides their tributary cities. Tojak was king of Haugun; he was the son of Soma, who was the son of Atyis, the necromancer. And of Lowga, Turwea was king; he was the son of Diah, son of Bawn, the philosopher.

25/52.11. When Baal and Ashtaroth, with their armies from heaven, came near these cities, they halted and built a temporary kingdom in the mountains of Zoe.

25/52.12. Baal said to Ashtaroth: Behold, you have had the choice of cities, give me the first assault?

25/52.13. Ashtaroth said: On your own terms these battles shall be, and I will beat you. To it, then; set on Lowga.

25/52.14. Baal went to Turwea in his dreams and told him his son was waylaid[1017] by the people of Haugun, and, moreover, that Tojak had decided to advance upon him and possess the city. When Turwea awoke, he was troubled by his dream, and he inquired of the oracle concerning the matter. Ashtaroth had possession of the oracle, and she answered the king, saying: You are of the seed of the Faithists, why fear a dream? But be cautious regarding your dreams; do not tell your son, for today he goes on the hunt, and your words might bring about that which otherwise might not be. The king went his way, but Ashtaroth sent inspiring spirits to the king, saying: It would be wise to caution your son. And the king went and cautioned his son.

25/52.15. Ashtaroth then went to Tojak's wife, and gave her a dream in which the Prince of Lowga went on a hunt, to all appearances, but really came near Haugun for a very different reason, which was no less than the slaying of herself and husband. The queen awoke suddenly in fear, and told the king her dream. Tojak said:

25/52.16. Foolish woman; it was only the fault of your diseased blood, which, coursing the heart, gave you a foolish dream. Tojak dismissed the matter. The next day, the angels kept inspiring the queen to send her servants to the place of her dreams, to which she acceded; and her servants were armed with spears, and instructed to kill, as if by accident, whoever came their way.

25/52.17. Thus it came to pass that Turwea's son was slain. Turwea inquired of the oracle, and was answered by Ashtaroth, saying: Why do you come to me for comfort; is it not your own fault that your son is dead? I said to you: Do not

[1016] Many of these names were given in the Ahamic language, but I have used the privilege granted me, to so modernize them that the student can trace them from Hebraic, Greek and Latin down to English. –Ed.

[1017] ambushed

mention the matter of your dream to your son, for it often happens that telling of a thing brings it to pass.

25/52.18. Turwea said: I am justly rebuked, O Apollon-ya! But tell me, you who know all things, since one part of my dream has come true, may not the other part, and, in truth, Tojak comes to possess my kingdom? Ashtaroth said: If I tell you, you will blab it about, and do nothing in your own defense. Turwea then made an oath to obey the oracle; so she commanded him to march with all his army against Tojak, and demand satisfaction at once in ten thousand lives, to balance the loss of the prince.

25/52.19. This ended Ashtaroth's part with the city of Lowga; and now she went to Haugun, while Baal took charge of Lowga, sending his legions of angels to the people of Lowga, to inspire them with madness because their prince was slain.

25/52.20. Ashtaroth, on her part, now assumed control of the oracle in Haugun, and sent her warring angels to the people of the city, advising them of the justice of slaying the prince, because he had come not on a hunt, but to slay the king and the queen. And Ashtaroth, further, told the king, Tojak: Try me as to my truthfulness: Behold, in two days the warriors of Turwea will be at your city's gates; be ready for them and drive them away, or lo, your city wall will be reduced to dust and ashes.

25/52.21. Of course the prophecy of Ashtaroth came true, and Tojak now believed he was in the protection of the Gods. The queen said to him: A matter of weight is on my mind, O king: I commanded my servants to slay the prince, for the Gods showed me that only by this could your life and mine be preserved.

25/52.22. The king, Tojak, justified the queen, saying: You have been the preserver of my life and yours.

25/52.23. Baal, God of Lowga, marched the mortal armies against the city of Haugun, while Ashtaroth marched the armies of Haugun to battle against them.

25/52.24. And thus, as mortals play a game with sticks and pegs, so did this God and Goddess play a game with the mortals of these two great cities; played give and take to see the battles lost or won; and they used their legions of angels to inspire the mortals on, or to make them, at times, turn and flee. And while the Gods rested, amusing themselves by feasting and by talking over the sport of mortal death, the two great cities would also gain a little rest, but only to renew the bloody work.

25/52.25. For four years the Gods and angels kept these two mortal cities at war; and though they lay a day's journey apart, all the way in between was strewn with the bones of the slain. And in four years they were reduced to dust and ashes; and as to the people of the last year, mostly they were inoculated with the poisoned air of the dead, and they died also. And yet it came to pass that Baal beat Ashtaroth in this battle of death, for he caused all his people to be slain, while a few of Ashtaroth's remained.

25/52.26. In that manner, Baal and Ashtaroth pursued the other great cities of Par'si'e and Heleste. And the time it took to destroy any two or three cities varied from two years to ten years. But for the destruction of Athena and Troy it required twelve years. And for the destruction of Ituna and Fado it required eleven years. Between Su-gun and Lakao it required two years to bring them to war. Between Athena and Troy it required three years to bring them to war. Two hundred vampires, angels of lust, were set upon a prince of Troy, and in desperation he was driven to kidnap an Athenian princess, who was led to exposure by Baal's angel hosts. In this great battle Ashtaroth won the game, having succeeded in having all of the Trojans destroyed.

25/52.27. In the war between Tos and Sun, which lasted nine years, it was an even game, for both cities were entirely destroyed and all the people in them, and also their tributary cities as well. But the city of Tol was destroyed within itself, for there was no city near enough to war upon it. The angels brought virus from the dead of other regions, and inoculated the breath of the people of Tol, and their flesh festered, and they died of disease instead of war.

25/52.28. The whole time of destruction was one hundred and six years; and after that, Par'si'e and Heleste were wasted and desert, and wild beasts coursed the country far and near.

25/52.29. Osiris had said I will make the land of Egupt the greatest country in the world; I will have the place of my dominion near at hand. Satan had said to Osiris: If you do not destroy Par'si'e and Heleste, behold, Baal and Ashtaroth will rebel against you, choosing these lands for their own kingdoms.

25/52.30. But both satan and Osiris, who now falsely styled himself God of heaven and earth, were powerless to prevent the march of Jehovih's hand. For as He gave liberty to all His creatures, and as Osiris had fostered the idea of being sole ruler of earth and heaven, even so the seed of his own sowing took root in Baal and Ashtaroth. And they formed a compact with each other and seceded from Osiris after all. And in order to determine what share of the earth should be theirs, a war in heaven ensued between the three Gods; and Te-in and Sudga joined in also.

CHAPTER 53 Wars

25/53.1. Jehovih had said: I created man blank, as to good and evil, and gave him liberty. And I gave liberty also to the spirits of the dead. But these spirits set themselves up as Gods; and to glorify themselves used mortals in their own way. For they found that mortals could be turned to good or evil, to war or to peace, to virtue or to lust, according to the inspiration of the angels watching over them.

25/53.2. But in this I provided a remedy also, and without abridging liberty, which was, that the Gods, in contention for mortal souls, would quarrel and ultimately destroy their own heavenly kingdoms; from which, angels and mortals could escape from bondage. ||

25/53.3. And this was so. Te-in, Sudga and Osiris, even while their wars and machinations were going on with mortals, were scheming for mastery in hada, each to overthrow the others, and involve them in ruin. And it thus came to pass that a triangular war ensued in these two heavens,[1018] in which more than ten billion warring angels were engaged hundreds of years. For, as mortals engage in corporeal warfare, so do angels engage in es'sean warfare. For though they cannot kill one another, they can bind and enslave and cast one another into hells, and surround them with never-ending fire, so they cannot escape. And the warring Gods send their armies forth to make captives of their enemies, who, when seized, are either made into subjects, or else cast into torments. And these armies of warring angels, hundreds of millions strong, go into the kingdom of another God, and from its suburban[1019] districts, carry away the subjects, with all their acquisitions. And yet at times these raiding armies venture too far, and are themselves captured and cast into torments. Consequently Gods in hada wall their kingdoms around with standing armies, even as they have taught mortals to defend themselves. And their enemies seek to invent means to break through the defense lines of these standing armies, and go in to plunder and destroy.

25/53.4. In times of which madness, no voice from Jehovih's angels can gain an attentive ear among them; even the same as when mortal kings are at war: Were one to say to them: Behold, Jehovih is All Peace! they would even curse Jehovih and peace. Even so do the fighting angels threaten and curse if one of Jehovih's holy ones interposes in peace and love.

25/53.5. As like a burning fever or canker worm that needs to run its course, before a healing balm can do good, so Jehovih permits the Gods to pursue their reign, till, helpless, they fall, environed in the harvest they sowed. For to every man and woman born, a time comes on earth or in heaven, when sore disaster, if nothing else, will cast him helpless in agony, to make him own[1020] the Mighty Power Who created him; and make him supplicate in pity for some helping hand to lead him safely to the All Person's pleading Voice. Then he is ready to listen; to turn from Gods, Lords, Saviors, and Sons, who profess to save; and to stand upright before the Father, and learn to know Him, and willingly learn peace, love, reason and truth.

25/53.6. Jehovih has said: In every soul I made a door, and in this My Light shines. Here My Voice speaks; but they turn away, and go after those who speak to the external ear; a serpent bites them, and they are cast in poison and in death!

25/53.7. Man on the earth has said: I will not heed Your still small voice, O Jehovih, which speaks to the soul; I will obey the king who leads on to war, and who, with loud noises and violent oaths, pursues death-dealing as a virtuous trade.

[1018] that is, in the hadan region resting on the earth, and also in those heavens above the earth surface but close to it

[1019] outlying

[1020] acknowledge, own up to

Not You, O Jehovih, shall be my master, but the king, who has great pageantry. Behold, I will stand in his great armies, or be led on to death, even as the king wills me; for he is my Savior and my defense. His Gods shall be my Gods; his Lords my Lords; his Savior my Savior; by blood and heroic butcheries I will prove my loyalty.

25/53.8. And even so have billions of angels in hada said: Not the still small voice of my soul will I obey; but yonder gaudy God, whose sacredness is so great none can approach him except by crawling on their bellies! He shall be my Lord and Savior; his battles shall be my battles; to feed the hells of hada with his enemies shall be my trade.

25/53.9. Jehovih has said: Even to those who choose darkness and evil, I have given liberty also; for they shall learn by experience, in time to come, that all these guides and leaders, whether they are kings, or Gods, or Lords, or Saviors, are only snares, from whom, sooner or later, they must turn in order to rise out of the hells they have built for others. For, because they put Me at a distance, or denied My Person, or called Me Void like the wind, I do not cut them off; but they cut themselves off from Me, and thus fall into torments.

25/53.10. For I am as near to the corporean as to the es'sean; let them, then, disown their kings and Gods, and whoever has a kingdom to glorify; and they shall espouse Me, for I am Ever Present. For this, all people shall do, either on earth or in heaven. My kingdoms are not by violence or by war, but by liberty to every soul; and whoever practices peace, and love, and liberty to others, are My chosen. They are on the way of everlasting resurrection.

CHAPTER 54 Wars

25/54.1. About the time Baal and Ashtaroth had destroyed the inhabitants of the earth in Par'si'e and Heleste, they applied to Osiris, demanding promotion to separate kingdoms of their own. They said:

25/54.2. You know in truth that for the sake of confederacy we merged our own kingdoms into yours; to make you powerful against the wars of Te-in and Sudga in heaven. And to do your will we have laid desolate the mortal kingdoms of Par'si'e and Heleste. For which things you promised us from the beginning that we would have great kingdoms in heaven.

25/54.3. Now behold, heaven is only one vast scene of war! And this also we perceive, that the mighty contests are without any prospect of ending. As these heavenly wars raged hundreds of years ago, even so do they this day. Too, the heavenly forces are becoming less disciplined and less scrupulous from year to year.

25/54.4. By evidence of which it is plain that your heavens, and Te-in's, and Sudga's, will sooner or later be cast into interminable[1021] hells. To prevent which, we ask of you, our God, to give us each a section to ourselves, and we will subdue the places and govern them in our own way.

25/54.5. Osiris answered them, saying: Of all the Gods, who, other than I, has done a hand's turn to raise mortal subjects to a higher plane? Te-in's course was destruction; so was Sudga's. And by much importuning you two persuaded me to have the mortals of Par'si'e and Heleste destroyed. And now, in the time when most of all we should be united, you importune[1022] me to have my great kingdom disrupted and divided. Do you not perceive that we have the balance of power in our favor? And also, if in these troublous times you espouse new kingdoms, we will all be at the mercy of Te-in and Sudga.

25/54.6. For which reasons I beseech you both to postpone the matter till we have driven our enemies from our doors. Let us be faithful to the confederacy.

25/54.7. Now in this affair Baal and Ashtaroth did not come to Osiris in person, but, as if ashamed of their own proposal, sent messengers. And yet, on the other hand, Osiris did not invite them to his kingdom.

25/54.8. Ashtaroth said to Baal: See what Osiris has done! He treats us as children; giving us sweet promises if we will only keep right on serving him. I tell you, Baal, you may serve Osiris; but from this time forward I am none of his! Behold, I will mark out a kingdom of my own, and I will establish it and rule it in my own way. Moreover I will send word to Te-in and Sudga; and if Osiris balks me, they shall know his vulnerable points.

[1021] never-ending, endless, perpetual

[1022] implore, urge, beseech, press

25/54.9. Baal said: Even so will I; and I will establish a kingdom alongside of yours, and if our enemies attack us we can better defend ourselves.

25/54.10. So said, so done. And Baal marked out for his heavenly kingdom the expanse over Heleste and northwestern Arabin'ya; and Ashtaroth marked out for her heavenly kingdom the expanse over Par'si'e and northeastern Arabin'ya. And the two no sooner chose their generals and captains, and founded their heavenly thrones, than they sent word to Osiris and to Te-in and to Sudga.

25/54.11. This, in turn, triggered a general dismemberment of these mighty kingdoms. In Osiris' heaven, one Kabbath revolted, taking the name Thammus. He was a general, whom tens of thousands of angel officers delighted to serve. He marked out his heavenly place over western Egupt, and established his throne and officers, and had himself proclaimed to mortals through the oracles as THE ONLY SON OF THE GREAT SPIRIT, THE SAVIOR OF MEN.

25/54.12. Teos-judas also revolted from Osiris, and established a heavenly kingdom over South Arabin'ya (Africa). Besides these there were: Marcus, Delos, Acta, Hebron, De-bora, Julta, Wab, Thais and D'nor, great generals and captains in Osiris' heavenly kingdom, all of whom revolted and began setting up heavenly kingdoms of their own.

25/54.13. And in Sudga's heavenly kingdom more than one thousand generals and captains revolted and began to establish heavenly kingdoms of their own. Of these the most prominent were: Judsa, Vishnu, Eorata, Chrisna, Histaga, Vivaulias, Hiras, Haroyu, Ahhoma, V'ractu and Tivirassa.

25/54.14. And in Te-in's heavenly kingdom more than eight hundred generals and captains revolted, and established kingdoms of their own. Of these the most powerful were: Chong, Ho-Tain, Dyut, Cow, Ghan, Su-Lep, Djhi, Hiss, Me Lee, Wang, Hop-jee and Kaab.

25/54.15. And all the revolted ones called themselves Gods or Lord or Saviors, and endeavored to establish an earthly habitation as well. And all of them took with them millions and millions and tens of millions of angel followers; and some of them had more than a hundred million subjects to start with.

25/54.16. So anarchy began to reign in hada. Order was broken down; warfare was divided in a thousand ways, and neither angels nor Gods could discover anymore what this war or that war was about, other than to inflict torments on others. And so great was the conflict that in more than half the earth, all the lowest heaven was nothing but one continuous succession of knots and hells. To inflict pain, disorder and destruction was the work of twenty billion angels in darkness; war, war, war; hell, hell, hell!

25/54.17. And now, alas, over all the earth where war had reveled hundreds of years, billions of spirits were in chaos, not knowing in fact they were in the spirit world, but still battling against all who came along, to the left and to the right, before and behind, screaming, bawling with madness, striking out in madness, in unceasing agony, in an unending nightmare of madness.

25/54.18. And from among the mighty hosts of darkness, the drujas, deep born in darkness, now pestering the people on earth, were hundreds of millions of familiars taking to fetalism! Vampire spirits who suck the blood and the flesh of mortals till the brain and heart are wild and mad! Till the mortal is driven to nameless deeds of horrors, desperate with the foul obsession. Spirits who bring poison and horrid smells to afflict mortals; spirits who delight to feed on mortal flesh corrupted with scabs and running sores. Spirits who teach reincarnation and lust as the highest, most exalted heaven.

25/54.19. And now the mighty hosts of Anuhasaj, alias De'yus, the Lord God, the false, broke in on every side, and spread here and there, searching for foulness and for fuel to feed their thousands of hells.

25/54.20. And these, in remembrance of Osiris' hated name and treachery, went for his great kingdom, followed by billions of angels, desperate from long-continued slavery, roused for deeds of vengeance. Forth into his capital, Agho'aden, they rushed, beating down the pillars of fire and high archways, and rushing into the throne of Osiris, seized him and his vice-Gods and high marshals and dragged them off and cast them into foul-smelling hells, hideous with the wail and roar of maniacs and tormented drujas, and with kicks and blows and poundings covered them up in foul darkness, heaped deep and smothering in suffocating gases.

25/54.21. Then off ran other legions for Te-in and his high officers, and to pillage his kingdom. And him and them they seized and bore off in triumph to equally horrid hells. And then for great Sudga others ran, even more desperate for vengeance' sake; and him they also caught, despoiling his mighty kingdom, and cast him into hell.

25/54.22. And they ran for many of the lesser Gods, and broke them down utterly, and cast them into hells. Only two Gods of the past days in those regions escaped, Baal and Ashtaroth, who fled to save themselves for a more opportune season to carry out their wicked schemes.

CHAPTER 55 Wars

25/55.1. Of the self-Gods of Uropa, and North and South Guatama, little need be said. They established weak heavenly kingdoms and succeeded in inciting mortals to war, but to no great destruction. Their heavenly kingdoms were for the most part failures; their thrones were poor and dilapidated almost from the start.

25/55.2. For, the mortals of these great divisions of the earth were too scattered and few to be profitable for false Gods. In Guatama they had not forgotten the lessons of I'tura, the false God who had ruined their forefathers. They were wary, and for the most part preserved their allegiance to the Great Spirit.

25/55.3. Enough said, then, of evil; now know of the good and faithful, and of the changes of earth and heaven.

25/55.4. By the pressure of ji'ay, Craoshivi had descended near the earth, and some places bordered upon it. Darkness had overspread the land of the earth in some regions for seven hundred years, so that the sun did not shine, except as a red ball of fire. And nebula fell in many places to a depth of three lengths,[1023] so that even the places of the great cities of the earth, which had been destroyed, were covered up, and it was like a new country.[1024]

[1023] around 15 feet (4 1/2 meters)

[1024] While archaeologists dig to find earlier civilizations, they do not, as of circa 150 ak, attribute their burial to the falling of a'ji, ji'ay or nebula, those being not yet understood by present day archaeologists. –cns ed.

25/55.5. And this proved beneficial to Jehovih's angels, assisting them to deliver the hosts of chaotic spirits, whose mortal part fell in dread war. For such was the labor of the true God in Craoshivi, Son of Jehovih, and of his hosts of upraised angels: to gather in from every quarter of earth and her heavens the fallen victims of the self-Gods; to restore them to reason and to happier and holier scenes; and to teach them righteousness and good works.

25/55.6. Jehovih had said to God, His Son: Because one man cannot lift up the whole world he shall not grieve, nor cease doing what he can. For his glory lies in exerting himself to the full.

25/55.7. Because the self-Gods have come against you, they are against Me also; because they have assumed to be Creators, and thus proclaimed themselves for their own glory, they shall have their fill. Before these times, the false Gods were content to proclaim their own names; but now, lo and behold, they have made the Lord God as the Creator, and set him up as a man, on a throne, to worship him!

25/55.8. And Te-in, and Sudga, and Osiris, too! All of woman born, and knowing My breath upon them. It is sufficient for you, My Son, to gather in the afflicted and distressed, and restore them and deliver them in light and truth. Keep ready your schools and colleges in heaven, and your nurseries and hospitals, and factories, and your fleets of swift-flying otevans and airiavagnas. And send your faithful volunteers, and make the afflicted rejoice and hold up their heads in great joy.

25/55.9. But to those who will not hear; and to those who curse you and Me, seeking to destroy for their own glory; be silent. My hand is upon them. My ji'ay'an shower covers earth and heaven. In their own game they shall cast themselves in darkness and destruction. ||

25/55.10. And while the self-Gods were at their evil deeds, the Faithists, Jehovih's angels, worshippers of the Ever Present All Person, coursed throughout the heavens in their fire-ships, calling in the persecuted children of Jehovih. Calling loud and cheerfully through the heavens of the evil Gods, and over the kingdoms of the earth; calling in these words:

25/55.11. Come! Come! The Father's kingdom is free! Come! Come! In peace and quietness you shall be your own master! Behold, the Father's places rise higher and higher! Not downward to the lower kingdoms, not to the earth, not to reincarnation, the invented tale of drujas; but upward to wisdom, goodness, love and happiness.

25/55.12. Because you have put away the All Person, you have fallen in the mire; you have closed your eyes to yonder higher heaven. Come, O you who are in bondage! Cut loose from all! Fly to Him Who brought you forth to life! Disown the world! And self! And all the Gods and Saviors! Lords and kings! Be Jehovih's! Sworn to peace and love! To good works and righteousness!

25/55.13. Come! Come! Our otevans are free! Our airiavagnas full of comfort. O come and be our loves! Be fellows, one with Jehovih. ||

25/55.14. And they gathered in millions and billions! For hundreds and hundreds of years they labored in the distracted regions of hada; toiled and toiled till wearied and prostrate, tens of thousands of times; then rested awhile, invigorated for more energetic work.

25/55.15. But not alone, nor unseen, were these toiling millions, hundreds of millions, of Jehovih's angels, faithful Sons and Daughters. For the labor built up their own spirits to be as very Gods and Goddesses in noble endurance. Which was written in their fair faces, so that the high-raised messengers of far-off heavens, traveling past, saw Jehovih's soul in them. And so, bore the news to other worlds of the darkness of the earth and her evil Gods, and of the faithful, struggling hosts of Jehovih in their uphill work.

25/55.16. And now the earth and her heavens crossed the boundaries of the ji'ay'an forests, and rolled slowly towards the homes and dominions of other etherean Gods.

END OF BOOK OF WARS AGAINST JEHOVIH

Book of Lika, Son of Jehovih

Known in heaven as the Dawn of Bon, and on earth as the cycle of Moses, Capilya and Chine. Jehovih said: I gave to the earth a time of full earthhood; and, so that the generations of men might know the period, behold, I caused man to build a pyramid in the middle of the world. For it was my mark, that, from that time forward, man would turn from stone temples, and the hope of everlasting flesh-life, to rejoice in spiritual abodes in my etherean heavens. And I brought the earth out of darkness and encompassed it with the dawn of Bon.

CHAPTER 1 Lika

26/1.1. In the far-off etherean worlds the Voice of Jehovih spoke, saying: Lika, Lika, My Son! Behold the red star, the earth. She comes your way; she emerges dark and soiled from the forests of ji'ay, in the swamps of Bonassah. She will cross your etherean fields, the Takuspe, Opel, and Wedojain,[1025] dripping with the odor and dross of the ji'ay'an swamps. Go to her, and wash clean her soil and her atmospherean heavens.

26/1.2. Lika said: Alas, O Jehovih, how they have forgotten You!

26/1.3. I will go to the red star, the earth, O Father! I will deliver her into purity and faith. Your chosen shall be delivered from bondage; Your God made triumphant on earth and in her heavens.

26/1.4. Lika called his High Council, in his etherean kingdom, Vetta'puissa, in the Plains of Poe-ya, off the Road of Ahtogonassas, at the high Arc of Bon, made light by the holy angels of tens of thousands of years; and he said:

26/1.5. Behold the red star, the earth; the Voice of Jehovih came to me, saying: Go to her, O My Son, and wash clean her soil and her atmospherean heavens. And I said: I will go, O Father! I will deliver her into purity and faith.

[1025] see image i087, p.367

26/1.6. Lika said: Five hundred million etherean hosts I will take with me. For five years and forty days I and my hosts will sojourn on the red star and in her heavens. Her true God shall be restored and delivered in my name by Jehovih's hand. According to the rank of harvest of the gardens of Honyon, so shall my marshals choose and record my hosts. ||

26/1.7. Then in the Council spoke the historians of the etherean libraries of the Vorkman Road, where the earth has traveled for tens of thousands of years. And they detailed the affairs of the earth for many cycles past; made plain before the Gods assembled, all the doings of the earth and her heavens.

26/1.8. Then Lika sent swift messengers off to the earth and her heavens; in arrow-ships of fire they sped forth, twenty thousand, well skilled in both coursing the etherean heavens and in penetrating the atmospherean vortices of traveling stars; to obtain the details of her God and her false Gods, her Lords and false Lords, her hadas and her hells; to scan her libraries; and hastily return to Vetta'puissa, to lay the matters before the High Council and Lika, the Nirvanian Chief on Jehovih's throne.

26/1.9. Lika had sprung from the corporeal star Atos, which traverses the roads, Yatas-ko-owen, of the south circuit of Thoese, the vortex of another far-off sun, and was raised to etherea in the cycle of Sai-kah, one hundred and twenty-five thousand years, by Meth-ya, Goddess of Ori-iyi, afterward Chieftainess of Yeuna-gamaya.

26/1.10. And Lika rose to be God of Avalassak four thousand years; God of Kemma, six thousand years; Inspector of Judas' etherean roads at the a'ji'an swamps of Hennassit, fifteen thousand years; Surveyor of Iwalt, two thousand years; Surveyor of the Wacha excursion, four thousand years; Recorder of Hitte-somat, eight thousand years; Deliverer of Habian vortices, twenty-six thousand years; Measurer of densities in Ablank, one thousand years; Recorder of the Ratiotyivi, two thousand years; God of the Home Plains of Cteverezed, twelve thousand years; Chief of Mah-ha-dewin, twenty thousand years; and Chief of Vetta'puissa, twenty-five thousand years.

26/1.11. For his High Council Lika had thirty thousand Chieftains and Chieftainesses, of grades of more than a hundred thousand years in the etherean worlds; five hundred thousand of the rank of Inspectors; seven million of the rank of Gods and Goddesses; and of the rank of Lords and Lordesses, more than half a billion.

26/1.12. Of the Rapon hosts there were seven Chiefs and nine Chieftainesses, who were Lika's private companions. First, Rebsad, Chief of So-tissav, forty thousand years; Sufristor of Sheleves, sixty thousand years; Marshal of Zele'axi, twenty thousand years; Master of Bassaion, seventy thousand years; and he passed twenty thousand years on the journey of Loo-soit-ta-vragenea, besides thousands of other journeys of less duration.

26/1.13. Next to Rebsad was Yanodi, Chieftainess of Ure, seventy thousand years; Chieftainess of the Roads of Sallatamya, seventy thousand years; Marshaless of Petanasa, forty thousand years; Goddess of the ji'ay'an forest of Loo-loo-woh-ga, sixty-five thousand years; besides Goddess of Mor, Goddess of Chichigennahsmmah, Goddess of El, and of Raumba, and of Zee.

26/1.14. Next to Yanodi was Thazid, Goddess of Zoleth; matrusettess of Yith-kad; Chieftainess of Hagu; Chieftainess of De'baur, and of Hachull, and of the Roads of Oleaskivedho; besides Goddess of more than one hundred etherean worlds.

26/1.15. Then came Thoso, Chief of Kassarah and Dassamatz, ninety thousand years; God of Saxax, seven thousand years; God of Chennesa, God of Hoxora, God of Fiben, God of Hotab, each six thousand years; surveyor of the Lymthian Roads, twelve thousand years; marker of meteors, two thousand years; Fireman of Thostus on the Ibien excursion, thirty thousand years.

26/1.16. Next to Thoso came Miente, Chieftainess of Gawl and Sanabtis, in whose dominions the star T-lemos was uzated (dissolved out of being) when Gai-loo opened the Road of Enjxi-ustus for the Nizaigi vortices of Messak; Chieftainess of Lam-Goo and Kud; Goddess of Itzi, Goddess of Ashem and of the Baxgor Wing; Goddess of the Duik Swamps, and Lordess of Sus and Havrij; in all, one hundred and seven thousand years.

26/1.17. Chama-jius stood next; she was Chieftainess of Hors-ad and Tu and Okadad; Goddess of Asthy, Hid, Sheaugus and Jagri; surveyor of Arvat and the Vadhuan Roads; surveyor of Anchas; surveyor of the Han Mountains in the etherean Uuj of Drij-Lee; in all, two hundred and sixty thousand years.

26/1.18. Next stood Murdhana, Chieftainess of D'hup and Hen-Dhi; Chieftainess of Happa and Hirish; surveyor of Sepher and Daka; Inspector of Anachu, Zadon, Edau, Medtisha and Roth; in all, ninety thousand years.

26/1.19. Oshor stood next: Chief of Out-si and of Yotek, Samoan and Yadakha; maker of the Bridge of Weasitee; Marshal of the Honlaguoth expedition, and, besides these places, God of seven etherean worlds; in all, one hundred and twelve thousand years.

26/1.20. Next came Yihoha, Chief of Shung-how and Agon; Chief of Neo-sin; God of Izeaha, Kaon, Ahsow, Una, Yuk-Hoh and Ahgoon. He was also the builder of the Raxon etherean arches; in all, ninety thousand years.

26/1.21. Hisin was next: Chief of the Kionas Belt, where Yagota, the Orian Chief, walled the Plains of Maga, the Nirvanian home of the delivered hells of Mina half a million years before. Hisin was here nick-named Creator of Wit, because of establishing his Chieftaincy on the ruins of hell. He was also Chief of Mamsa and Jauap; God of Gah, and of Darah, the region of fountain flowers; in all, ninety thousand years.

26/1.22. Bowen was next: Chief of Apaha, formerly the Farms of Lung-wan and Srid; Chief of Vadhua, and of the Valleys of Nasqam, where a million years before, the Chief of Chaksa disrupted the Atmospherean Sakri, and liberated from its four thousand hells more than thirty billion angel slaves in chaos. Bowen had also served as God of Amaan, Havat, Shedo and Pivan; and as measurer of Pracha, Xeri and Asthus; and surveyor of Ulam, Sheyom, Chozeh and Zadark; in all, eighty thousand years.

26/1.23. Gwan Goo was next: She was Chieftainess of Andol, the place of the one-time apex of the Karowgan vortex, where the star Ogitas was formed and sent on its course by Aclon-guin, Orian hemmer of Shegoweasa. This vortex, when first formed by Aclon-guin, was three hundred billion miles long and was cometary thirty thousand years in Aclon-guin's hands. Gwan Goo was also Chieftainess of Ahsa-thah and Waegon; Goddess of Anoa, Howgil and Zahaive; in all, one hundred and ninety thousand years.

26/1.24. Geehoogan was next: Chieftainess of Sumatri in the by-roads of Yotargis; Chieftainess of the four etherean worlds, Yoni, Ogh, Theum and Wachwakags; surveyor of Unshin, Zarihea and Keanteri; Inspectress of Saguiz, Hagimal, Hafha, Borax, Rab and Shor-loo; in all, eighty thousand years.

26/1.25. Next stood Bachne-isij, Chief of Yahalom, where the Gein Maker, Tarmoth, cleared the Forests of the a'ji'an Haloth, in making a roadway for Havalad's group of Shemasian corporeal stars, in which labor he employed ninety billion Nirvanians for four thousand years, and the distance of the road was more than one hundred billion miles. Bachne-isij was Chief of Agwan, and Shoe-nastus, Hador and Ad; God of Vach, Kuja, Rai, Kathab, Cynab, Buhd and Abbir; measurer of the mountains of the etherean worlds Vijhath, Hakan and Dis; measurer of the arches in the etherean world Niksh; constructor of the Plains in the Nirvanian world Chom; in all, one hundred and thirty thousand years.

26/1.26. Rehemg was next: Chieftainess of Otaskaka, commonly called World of Shining Waters, a great visiting place in Nirvania; she was Goddess of Theasapalas and Timax; weigher of Sultzhowtcih in the Ofel Plains; in all, one hundred and ten thousand years.

26/1.27. Then stood Antosiv, Goddess of Munn, renowned because she was of two hundred and sixty thousand years, and had declined exaltation above the rank of Goddess.

26/1.28. Such, then, were the Rapon hosts.

CHAPTER 2 Lika

26/2.1. Far and wide, spread the words of Lika, words of Jehovih, over the Plains of Poe-ya, first highest light in etherea (in this region), where the earth and her heavens traveled. Far off, toward the northern group of twinkling stars, the etherean millions gazed; the voice of millions arose: Where is the red star? Where lies the earth and her troubled heavens? Is this not the young star, a satellite that travels with the hidan sun?[1026] What is the angle and course of this little traveling world, so that our eyes may feast on the road where our Chief will soon send Jehovih's redeeming ships?

[1026] North Star. –1891 glossary

26/2.2. Then they pointed, surmising by the red-like color and tedious motion, which of them was the earth, one of the small gems that Jehovih had placed in the measureless firmament. And they gazed upon it, speaking with souls of delight: Great You are, O Jehovih, to build so wide. To stud the etherean worlds with gems like these; to provide a place for the souls of men to germinate. Surely her people, the sons and daughters of the red star, must see etherea; must realize the difference between a short corporeal life and this endless paradise. Can it be that they have, in their small heavens, unscrupulous false Lords and false Gods who set themselves up to be worshipped as creators, whom mortals name with bated breath? And do they have, too, a host of Saviors, who profess to have the key to all the roads that lead into this great expanse, the etherean worlds? Mortals who are brought forth to life on the central suns have some excuse to be stubborn in their egotism of their Lords, Saviors and Gods; but on one so small as the earth, how can it be?

26/2.3. Then Lika's swift messengers returned in their arrow-ships; messengers attained to be very Gods in wisdom, and in swiftness. And they quickly told the tale, about their visit to the red star and her heavens; told how the true God, Son of Jehovih, had struggled on, but had been outmatched by all odds by self-Gods and self-Lords, who had plunged billions of hapless souls into torturing hells.

26/2.4. And Lika spread this news abroad in his etherean dominions, which only needed to be told once, for every sympathetic soul by his shocked appearance told it to others, the like of which spread instantly to billions of high-raised ethereans. And when Lika said: Five hundred million angels shall go with me to the troubled earth and her heavens, in double-quick time the volunteers were ready to be enrolled on the list.

26/2.5. Then Lika inquired for more detail from the swift messengers, and they answered him, saying: This, O Lika, Son of Jehovih! The earth has passed her corporeal maturity, and mortals have set up a pyramid to mark its time. The days of the highest, greatest audacity of the self-Gods are passed, and are memorized by the pyramid also; for in that same time, they taught mortals to worship the God and the Lord and the Savior, instead of the Great Spirit, Jehovih. But darkness is upon the self-Gods, and they are bound in hells; and mortals are also bound in hells.

26/2.6. Behold, this is the first dawn of dan on the earth since she passed the limit of her greatest corporeality.

CHAPTER 3 Lika

26/3.1. Lika said to his chief marshal: Enroll my five hundred million hosts, and appoint captains and generals to them, and grade them and apportion them. Besides these, give me one million singers, one million trumpeters, one million attendants, one million heralds, one million messengers and one million recorders and waiters.

26/3.2. Lika called his chief builder and said to him: Build me a fire-ship, an airavagna, with capacity for a billion; and provide the ship with sufficient officers and workmen. Consult with my mathematicians as to the distance to the red star, the densities through which the ship shall pass, the power required, and the time of the journey; then provide all things sufficient for that.

26/3.3. Next, Lika spoke to the High Council, saying: For the time of my absence my vice-Chief, Heih-Woo, shall hold my place. Touching any matters in which you desire my voice before I go, speak!

26/3.4. Atunzi said: Behold, O Lika, the star, Yatis, heads towards the a'ji'an Forests of Actawa, and she has not passed the esparan age! Lika said: To clear the forest Actawa I appoint Eashivi, Goddess, with three billion laborers. Eashivi, what do you say? Eashivi said: Thanks to Jehovih and to you, O Lika. I will choose my laborers immediately, and proceed to make the road.

26/3.5. Wan Tu'y said: Before your return, O Lika, the Hapsa-ogan vortex will cross the south fields of Vetta'puissa. She has twenty billion souls in grades of sixty and seventy. Lika said: To her assistance for three years[1027] I appoint Tici-king, God, with fifty million for his hosts. What do you say, Tici-king? Tici-king said: By the grace of Jehovih, I rejoice in this labor. I will prepare my

[1027] Er-a-a is equivalent to three years of the earth. To make most of these times intelligible to the student, I have reduced the Panic words to English years of earth. –Eng. Ed.

hosts in sufficient time and accomplish what you have given into my keeping.

26/3.6. Wothalowsit said: In four years the hosts of E'win will return from the double stars, Eleb and Wis, with their harvest of forty billion angels. How shall they be apportioned? Lika said: To Bonassah, six billion; to Opel, two billion; to Wedojain, five billion; to Eosta, two billion; to Feuben Roads, seven billion; to Zekel, four billion; to Huron, three billion; to Poe-ya, six billion; to Yulit, one billion, and to Zulava, four billion; and I appoint Misata, Goddess, to provide the places in these several heavens for them, and to have charge of their selection and allotment. And I give her five hundred million angels as her laboring hosts. What do you say, Misata? Misata said: It is Jehovih's gift; I am rejoiced. I will prepare myself and my hosts.

26/3.7. Ching Huen said: Behold the star-world, Esatas, in her se'muan age will cross the Roads of Veh-yuis three years from now! Lika answered Ching Huen, saying: To cross these roads of light in her se'muan age would blight her power to bring forth animal life sufficient for her wide continents. The trail must be filled with se'muan forests to preserve her gestative season. To this labor I appoint Ieolakak, God of Esatas' se'muan forests in the Roads of Veh-yuis, four thousand years. And I allot to Ieolakak six billion laborers. What do you say, Ieolakak? He answered: This is a great labor; by the wisdom and power of Jehovih, I will accomplish it.

26/3.8. Veaga-indras said: In two years the fleets of Leogastrivins will return from their voyage of four thousand years, bringing two billion guests from the Iniggihuas regions. Who shall provide for their reception? Lika said: Yeanopstan, with ten million hosts. What do you say? Yeanopstan said: A most welcome labor, O Lika.

26/3.9. Hiss-Joso said: The Arches of Rassittissa, on the etherean world of Yungtsze's Plains, will be ready to cast in four years. Lika said: To Sut-tuz six million arches, and to Iviji four million arches, and to each of them one hundred million laborers. What do you say? Then spoke Sut-tuz and Iviji, saying: By the help of Jehovih, the labor will be accomplished.

26/3.10. Sachcha said: The star-world, Neto, will need to be turned on her axis in two years, at which time she will pass through the south fields of Takuspe. Lika said: This will be a great labor, and I appoint Urassus, with Salas, to accomplish it. And I give them three years, with four billion laborers. What do you say? Then Urassus and Salas answered, saying: With fear and trembling we rejoice at this great work. By Jehovih's wisdom and power, we shall accomplish it. ||

26/3.11. In this way, Lika made more than a thousand appointments to be accomplished before his return from the earth and her heavens; but ordinary matters he left with his vice-Chief, Heih-Woo, and to the High Council, the select ten million.

26/3.12. Jehovih had said: Even as I provided a little labor for mortals to develop the talents I created with them, so similarly, and after the same like,[1028] but spiritually, I provided greater labor to the high-risen inhabitants in My etherean worlds. For which reason, let My children learn the secret of harmonious and united labor with one another. I gave labor to man not as a hardship, but as a means of great rejoicing.

26/3.13. For the talents I gave on corpor, I gave not to die on corpor, but to continue on forever. As I gave talent for corporeal mathematics, and talent for building corporeal structures, yes, a talent for all things on corporeal worlds; even so have I provided in My etherean worlds for the same talents, but spiritually. In which man on the corporeal earth, judging the adaptability of talent to corporeal things, may comprehend the nature of the labors I provided in My exalted heavens for the same talents.

26/3.14. Neither let any man fear that his talents may become too exalted for the work I have provided; for until he has created a firmament, and created suns and stars to fill it, he has not half fulfilled his destiny.

CHAPTER 4 Lika

26/4.1. Jehovih spoke in the light of the throne of Kairksak, in Vetta'puissa, saying: Lika, My Son! This is My road and My journey: With you and your hosts My Voice shall travel with power; on the

---

[1028] that is, in harmony with your tendencies, bents, aptitude, affinities, drift, penchant and temperament; and in the same field of your liking, preference, predilection

earth I will lay My foundation, in spirit and word. Your companion Chiefs and Chieftainesses shall go with you; they shall help deliver the inhabitants of the earth and her heavens.

26/4.2. My enemies have marked their labors in temples and pyramids. Because their hearts did not rise up to Me they descended into stone, the most dead (unresponsive) of all things. They have carried the inhabitants of the earth down to rottenness and to death. Let their monuments stand as testimonies of those who hated Me, who denied Me, who did not believe in Me, the All Person.

26/4.3. My building shall be the most subtle of all things, the Spirit of My Own Body. Truly it shall be a monument within the souls of My chosen. Nor will it go away again in darkness, but it shall encompass the whole earth.

26/4.4. For you shall find My chosen a scattered people, persecuted and enslaved, the most despised of all the races of men. But I will show My power with them; I will raise them up; the things I do through them, and the words I speak through them, even in their ignorance and darkness, shall become mighty. Their words shall be treasured forever; and none can match them in wisdom of speech, or in the craft of good works.

26/4.5. But the learned men of all other peoples shall be forgotten; their wisdom: like the wind that blows away. The self-Gods and self-Lords, who led them astray, shall be like a serpent that bites itself to death. Yes, as long as their pyramids and temples stand, their own falsehoods shall stare them in the face.

26/4.6. They have bound themselves in their own bulwarks;[1029] they shall yet be My laborers, thousands of years, to undo the evil they sowed on the earth. Nor shall they look down from heaven and see with joy their temples and pyramids; but as one sees a coal of fire burning in the flesh, so shall their edifices cry out to them forever: You False One. And it shall be to them a burning fire that will not die out.

26/4.7. And their great learning, even of the stars, sun, moon, and of all the things of the earth and in its waters, shall pass away and not be remembered among men. Yes, the names of their men of great learning shall go down, with none to remember them on the earth. And in time, long after, the nations of peoples will forget them and their wisdom, and even pity them, and say of them: What a foolish people!

26/4.8. But My chosen, who are their slaves, and are as nothing in the world, shall speak, and their words shall not be forgotten; shall write, and their books will be a new foundation in the world. Because My hand will be upon them, My wisdom shall come forth out of their mouths.

26/4.9. And this shall be testimony in the ages to come, as to what manner of knowledge endures forever. For as the buildings of the earth remain on the earth; and the spirits of those who incline to the earth do not rise up; so have I bound corpor in corpor; but because I planted in man a spirit quickened for spiritual knowledge, so shall spiritual knowledge look upward for an everlasting resurrection. ||

26/4.10. Lika asked: O All Highest, Jehovih, what are the preparations of Your Gods? What have they done that shall strengthen my hand on the earth? Jehovih answered, saying: For six generations My God has been preparing for you and your hosts. My voice was with My God, and I said to him: My Son, behold, the time comes in six generations, when I will bring the earth into another dawn of light. And in that day I will bring My Son, Lika, from My etherean worlds; and he shall come with a mighty host of ethereans with great power. Go, My Son, down to the earth, and with your loo'is, your masters of generations, raise up an heir to your voice. In the three great divisions of the earth, provide three servants to do My will.

26/4.11. So My Son, God of Craoshivi, has raised up to you, O Lika, three men, Capilya, Chine, and Moses, the fruit of the sixth generation in the lands of their fathers; and they are of the Faithists in Me, holy men and wise. To these you shall send the Gods of their forefathers, even those who were beaten away by the Gods of evil.

26/4.12. And Capilya shall deliver the Faithists of Vind'yu, and Chine shall deliver the Faithists of Jaffeth, and Moses shall deliver the Faithists of Egupt. And you shall also put this upon Moses and his people: He shall lead his people westward; and their heirs after them shall also go westward; yes, westward until they circumscribe the earth. Three thousand four hundred years you shall allot to them to complete the journey. And wherever they go, they shall establish My name, Jehovih; they shall

[1029] fortifications

lead all people away from all Gods, to believe in the Great Spirit, Who I am.

26/4.13. And when they have carried My name to the west coast of Guatama [North America – Ed.], and established Me, behold, I will bring the earth into Kosmon; and My angels shall descend upon the earth in every quarter with great power. And it shall come to pass that the Faithists of the children of Moses shall find the Faithists of the children of Chine and the Faithists of the children of Capilya.

26/4.14. And all these people shall cry out in that day: No God, no Lord, no Savior! For My hand will be upon them, and their words shall be My words. But they will proclaim Me, the Great Spirit, the Ever Present, Jehovih.

26/4.15. And they shall become the power of the world; and shall establish peace and put away war, leading all peoples in the way of peace, love and righteousness.

CHAPTER 5 Lika

26/5.1. Vetta'puissa, in Lika's etherean regions, made glorious by Jehovih's light, and by His purified Sons and Daughters, whose heavenly mansions matched their great perfection, was now quickened with great joy. The trained hosts of Jehovih's Son, Lika, knowing he was to take recreation by a journey to the red star, the earth, to deliver her to holiness and love, provided music, heralds and trumpeters, millions of performers, to proclaim their reverence and rejoicing.

26/5.2. The fire-ship, the airavagna, now adorned in splendor, was brought into its place, and the vast hosts for the journey entered into it. A walkway was reserved for Lika and his companion Chiefs and Chieftainesses. First to lead, of the Rapon hosts, were the Chieftainesses, Yanodi and Thazid, and they walked arm in arm. Next after them came Lika, alone. Next came Rebsad and Thoso, arm in arm. Next came Miente and Hors-ad, arm in arm. Then came Chama-jius and Murdhana, arm in arm. Then Oshor and Yihoha, arm in arm. Then Gwan Goo and Geehoogan, and after them Rehemg and Antosiv.

26/5.3. As the Chiefs marched forth, the music swelled loud; more than a billion in concerted song to Jehovih; and echoed by the far-off trumpeters. And when the Chiefs entered the ship, followed by the ship's laborers and firemen,[1030] all was motionless till the music ceased.

26/5.4. Lika walked upon the High Arch, and stretching up his hands to Jehovih, said: I go forth in Your name, wisdom, love and power, O Jehovih! Your great heavens, which you have made full of glory, shall bear me up; the spark You gave to me I will keep quickened in Your sight. Your hand is upon me. Your arm encompasses my ship of fire. In You I know it will rise and course these worlds, to the red star, and sail with Your hosts triumphantly to labor, for Your glory.

26/5.5. Arise, O palace of the firmament; by the power of Jehovih that dwells in me: Upward! Onward! Arise!

26/5.6. And now with one will the hosts joined in, and the laborers and firemen stood to their places. A moment more, and the airavagna rose from its foundation, steered toward the red star, and moved forth over the Fields of Vetta'puissa. From every side on the great ship of heaven a hundred thousand banners and flags floated and waved, answered by more than a million more in the hands of the hosts below.

26/5.7. The es'enaurs of the ship struck up a quickened march, joined by the millions beneath, while the great multitudes tossed up their hands and shouted in prolonged applause. Thus went forth Lika, Son of Jehovih, to the red star, the earth.

CHAPTER 6 Lika

26/6.1. As Lika in his ship sped on, coursing the fields of Sonasat, Hatar, and Yaax, in the etherean world Chen-a-goetha, rich in light in these regions, on the Yong-We Road, and now traversed by hundreds of vessels coursing here and there, Jehovih's light descended on the High Arch, in the midst of the Rapons; and the Voice of Jehovih spoke out of the light, saying:

26/6.2. As I taught corporeans to build ships to traverse corporeal seas, so have I taught ethereans to build vessels to course My etherean seas.

26/6.3. As I bound the corporean so that he could not rise up in the air above corpor, except by a vessel, so did I create My heavens for the spirits

[1030] The job of fireman was to keep the engines of the ship running and supplied with fuel.

of men, that by manufactured vessels they could course My firmament.

26/6.4. For I made the little knowledge I gave to corporeans to be a type of knowledge that is everlasting.

26/6.5. To the corporean I gave two kinds of presence, objective and subjective. By the latter he can imagine himself in a far-off place; and the thought that proceeds out of him goes to a friend and speaks understandingly in the distance. For, I created him so. But he who goes objectively must take his person with him, for I also created him so.

26/6.6. And I magnified these two conditions to the spirits of all men, so that they could also appear objectively and subjectively in the places known to them.

26/6.7. And this is the bondage I created to all places on the earth and in its heavens, making all men understand the power of objective association.

26/6.8. I created wide seas on the corporeal earth, so man would perceive that one person alone could not cross over; nor in a small boat, with any profit under the sun. Neither did I create My heavens in the firmament so that one angel could go alone on long journeys, becoming isolated and powerless. But I provided them in such a way that they could not escape association; yes, I created the firmament so that they must congregate together and go.

26/6.9. Nevertheless, I gave freedom to all; to him who does not go objectively, to go subjectively; but of little avail and not much truth or profit. And because I give this liberty, behold, even drujas will say: Yes, I have been there. || Nor do they know how to rise up from the earth, or go to any place, except on another's shoulders.[1031]

26/6.10. And I created man and angels in such a way that all knowledge which is to be everlasting must be obtained objectively; yes, I made him desire without end, experience by his own person.

26/6.11. And they fill My seas in heaven and earth with their great ships; yes, I created man with wants that could not be satisfied in one place. For I drive him forth on strange errands and on missions of profit and love; for I will store him with a knowledge of My works.

[1031] i.e., except with the help of one or more others who know how to accomplish objective travel

CHAPTER 7 Lika

26/7.1. Onward sped Lika with his eight hundred million; his airavagna, the ship of fire, shining like a meteor in its flight, through the sea of Enea-Wassa, the etherean realm of Haog-sa-uben. On every side, the Jehovihian worshippers' vessels, tens of thousands, coursing in myriad ways; some fast, on missions of quickened labor; some slow, as traveling school-ships, exploring the great expanse and glorious richness of Jehovih's provided worlds, always ready for the newborn; each and all the ships like studded gems in the etherean sea, moving brilliants[1032] playing kaleidoscopic views, ever changing the boundless scene with surpassing wonders. And all of these, by signs and signals, revealing the story of their place and mission to the high-raised etherean souls; ships and men as quickened living books of fire, radiant with the Father's light and history of worlds.

26/7.2. On Lika's ship, as on all the others, every soul, hundreds of millions, enraptured, stood in awe and admiration of the ever-changing scenes; some in silence, absorbed in thought; some posing with upraised hands; some ejaculating gleefully; and some in high reverence to Jehovih, uttering everlasting praise; every soul in its full bent, being the full ripe fruit of the diversified talents as they first shone forth in corporeal life.

26/7.3. Onward sped Lika's airavagna, now in the Roads of Nopita, through the a'ji'an Forest of Quion, most rich in adamantine substances, arches, stalactites, stalagmites, and in forming and dissolving scenes, a forest, a very background in the etherean worlds for the over-brilliant crystal regions of light.[1033] And here, too, were tens of thousands of ships of Jehovih's chosen; and on either side of the great roadway lay the Fields of Anutiv, inhabited by countless millions of etherean kingdoms. Along the road for hundreds of thousands of miles, stretched up the hands of millions and millions of souls, waving banners and

[1032] Brilliants is a noun here, hence: transiting ships of brilliancy, collectively displaying kaleidoscopic movements of color, speed and angle.

[1033] meaning the darkness of the a'ji'an forest created a balancing contrast to the brilliant regions of light

flags to their favored ships, which were going to some native star, from which Jehovih brought them forth.

26/7.4. Then the course of Lika's airavagna changed; by his commands, sent through the comet Yo-to-gactra, a new world condensing, already with a head of fire four thousand miles broad; a very ball of melted corpor, whirling like the spindle of a filling spool, continuously winding onto itself the wide extending nebulae. Here coursing along, were hundreds of thousands of school-ships with students and visitors, to view the scenes, most grand in rolling on, now round, now broken, now outstretched, this ball of liquid fire, whirling in the vortex, thirty million miles long. To balance against this comet's vortex many of the ships tossed and rolled, dangerously, had they not been in skilled hands, and causing millions of the students on many a ship to fear and tremble, perceiving how helpless and stupid they were compared to the very Gods who had them in charge.

26/7.5. Not long did Lika loiter to view the scenes, or to indulge his eight hundred million, but stood his course again for the red star, the earth. And while coursing the Faussette Mountains, where the God, Vrilla-Gabon, built the Echosinit kingdom whose capital was Exastras, the place where the Niuan Gods assembled to witness the first starting forth of the earth, Lika halted awhile; and down went his recorders, to gather from the Exastras libraries the earth's early history and the grade of her creation. A copy of which obtained, the recorders hastily returned; when onward again sped the airavagna, now making course across the Plains of Zed—in the middle of which lay the great sea Oblowochisi, four million miles across, and also studded over with thousands of etherean ships.

26/7.6. And now the ship sped across to Rikkas, the place of the Goddess, Enenfachtus, with her seven billion etherean souls; and here Lika and his hosts cast down millions of wreaths and tokens, while the music of the two spheres mingled together in Jehovih's praise. From here, the distance across was three million miles.

26/7.7. Now during their journey to this point, the red star had stood above the horizon, but here it began to stand in horizontal line, gleaming in more effulgent[1034] flame. And along the course where Lika's airavagna would go, the Goddess, Enenfachtus, had previously upraised a hundred thousand pillars of fire to honor him and his company; and this great respect, Lika and his hosts answered with holy salutations.

26/7.8. After this came the ji'ay'an Forests of Hogobed, three million miles across, and close for lack of etherean air and inspiration. Here stood the Province of Arathactean, where the God, Yew-Sin, dwelt with thirty billion newly-raised Brides and Bridegrooms from the star Kagados. Over these regions Lika sped swiftly, and then to the open sea, Amatapan, on the Vashuan Roads.

26/7.9. Then a sail of two million miles, in the uninhabited regions of Samma, when he reached Chinvat, the bridge on the boundary of the earth's vortex beyond the orbit of the moon.

26/7.10. And without stopping, but now coursing on a downward plane, made straight toward the swift-rolling earth, whose speed was three-quarters of a million miles a day. Through the high-floating plateaus of atmospherea came Lika with his fire-ship, with his eight hundred million hosts, rapidly descending, his ship like a meteor, large as a continent.

CHAPTER 8 Lika

26/8.1. On the uninhabited plateau, Theovrahkistan, rich, and broad as the earth, high above the lands of Jaffeth, Vind'yu and Arabin'ya, Lika alighted in his airavagna, with his hosts of eight hundred million. Here he made fast his fire-ship, and out came his hosts to found a heavenly kingdom. Lika said:

26/8.2. I hear Your voice, O Jehovih; Your hand is upon me; in Your Wisdom and Power I will build the foundations of Your kingdom in these heavens.

26/8.3. Jehovih said: Call forth your Rapon hosts, your companion Chiefs; build your throne broad for them and you. And shape the area of the capital and stand your High Council, the chosen million, to the four quarters of the heavens of the earth.

26/8.4. The legions then joyously commenced work and built a heavenly place for Jehovih, and called it Yogannaqactra, home of Lika and his eight hundred million.

26/8.5. Jehovih called out of the light of the throne which Lika built, saying: Lika, My Son, you

[1034] resplendent, splendidly gorgeous

shall build all things new on the earth and in the heavens of the earth, even as if nothing had ever been. Send your messengers in an otevan to the broken-down region of My beloved, God of Craoshivi, and bring him and his thousand attendants to your place.

26/8.6. So an otevan was sent off, well officered, and in due time it returned, bringing God to Yogannaqactra, where he was received with great joy, and greeted in Jehovih's name.

26/8.7. Lika said: Speak, O God, for I have come to deliver these heavens into Jehovih's dominion. What are the light and the darkness of the heavens and the earth that have been entrusted to your keeping, in Jehovih's name?

26/8.8. God said: Alas, how can I speak? Behold, my kingdoms are scattered and gone; I have no pride in anything I have done in heaven and earth. An exceedingly great darkness came upon my people, lasting fifteen hundred years! Your servants have been overpowered, helpless, and tossed like chaff before the wind.

26/8.9. Lika said: How many Gods? How many dans of darkness? Where have my true Gods gone?

26/8.10. God said: Four Gods have risen to etherea with their hosts, heartbroken, true Gods. Four dans have come and gone, so weak and small, like a breath of air; for the darkness brushed them away. In Savak-haben, in etherea, your Gods sojourn.

26/8.11. Jehovih's light fell upon the throne, and His Voice came out of the light, saying: O My Son Lika, send four arrow-ships with a hundred thousand attendants, to Savak-haben, for My true Gods, and bring them to Yogannaqactra.

26/8.12 Lika then sent four arrow-ships with his swift messengers and a hundred thousand attendants, to bring back the four disconcerted Gods.

26/8.13. God said: Billions of angels of darkness flood the hadan regions; and as many grovel about on the low earth. De'yus, the false Lord God is cast into hell, a hell so wide that none can approach his place of torment. Te-in, the false God, the Joss, is also cast into hell; and so is Sudga, the false Dyaus; and so are all the false Gods that encompassed the earth around; their kingdoms are in anarchy.

26/8.14. The names Lord, God, Dyaus, De'yus, Zeus, Joss, Ho-Joss, and many others, have become worshipful on the earth! Not only did the traitors labor to put away the Great Spirit, but also to establish themselves as men-Gods capable of creating; yes, even claiming to be the veritable Creator of heaven and earth!

26/8.15. Lika said: Hear, then, the Voice of Jehovih! Because they have put Me aside and assumed to be Creators under the names God and De'yus, I will magnify the Person of God and De'yus in men's understanding.

26/8.16. Nor from this time forward on the earth, for three thousand years, shall man be confined to the one name, Jehovih, or Eolin, or Eloih, but worship God, or Lord, or De'yus, or Zeus, or Dyaus, or Joss, or Ho-Joss. For since these men have cast themselves into hells, behold, the spirits of the risen shall not find them or their kingdoms. And you shall magnify to mortals that all names worshipful belong to the Ever Present, whose Person is the spirit and substance of all things. And if they inquire of you Who is Dyaus? or, Who is God? or, Who is Joss? you shall say: Has He not said: Behold, I am the Creator of heaven and earth! And I say to you, He is the Ever Present, the All Highest Ideal. ||

26/8.17. But this bondage shall come upon them, to reap the harvest they have sown. Because one has said: Build a pyramid, and your God will come and abide in it, even as a man dwells in a house, || he shall be bound while the pyramid stands. And where another has said: Behold, your God (Creator) is in the image of a man, and he sits on a throne in heaven, || he shall be bound while this belief survives on the earth.

26/8.18. Because they have sown a falsehood on the earth, the harvest is theirs. And until they have reaped their whole harvest they shall not rise into My etherean worlds.

CHAPTER 9 Lika

26/9.1. When the other four Gods, the true Sons of Jehovih, who had been discomfited in the lower heavens by De'yus and his fellow false Gods, came from etherea, the light of Jehovih came again on Lika's throne. Jehovih said:

26/9.2. I do not allow evil to triumph over good except for short seasons; and, sooner or later, My righteous Sons and Daughters rise up and rejoice in their trials, which I allowed to come upon them.

Let neither men nor angels say, because this or that happens: Lo, Jehovih sleeps at his post! or: Lo, Jehovih is the author of evil, or is impotent to avert it.

26/9.3. My times are not like the times of men or angels; nor am I within the judgment of men as to what is evil or good. When the wealth of the rich man is stolen, do mortals not say: Poor man, Jehovih has afflicted him! For they judge Me by what they consider afflictions. But they do not see that I look to the soul of man as to what is good for him. And when the assassin has struck the king to death, behold, they say: How has a good Creator done this? For they do not consider the nation or the problem of anything except their immediate affairs; nor do they consider what I do for the souls of many nations, by one small act.

26/9.4. For all people in heaven and earth are My own; they are like trees in My orchard, and I prune them not for the life of the branches, but for the benefit of the whole orchard, and for the harvest that comes after.

26/9.5. I created life, and I take away life; I do with My own in My own way. I send night to follow day; clouds to interchange with the sunshine. And likewise I give times of dan to My atmospherean heavens, to be followed by seasons of darkness.

26/9.6. It is by these changes that mortals, angels and Gods learn to battle with and overcome the elements of My worlds.

26/9.7. The true Gods said: We weep before You, O Jehovih. Long and hard we labored our allotted seasons; we were helpless witnesses to the great darkness that came upon the inhabitants of heaven and earth.

26/9.8. Lika said: To you five true Gods, who have toiled in the darkness of the earth and her heavens, I restore your old time names for the season of dawn, after which I will raise you all up, with your kingdoms restored to the full, and you shall be heirs in my Nirvanian heavens, in peace and rest.

CHAPTER 10 Lika

26/10.1. The five Gods' names were Ane, Jek, Lay, Oal and Yith. Lika said to them: You have been previously crowned as Gods; come to the foot of Jehovih's throne, for I will crown you with new names.

26/10.2. When they came to the place designated, Lika continued: Take my (newly made for you) crown upon your head, and speak in Jehovih's name in that labor which I put upon you, Jehovih in Ane, Jehovih in Jek, Jehovih in Lay, Jehovih in Oal, Jehovih in Yith.

26/10.3. And with that, Lika crowned them with a band on the head, inscribed, INANE, INJEK, INLAY, INOAL and INYITH, Panic names designating their rank and the age of the earth in which these things came to pass.

26/10.4. Lika said: To each of you I give for the period of dawn ten million laborers from my etherean hosts. And these are the labors I allot to you: To Inane, to go down to the earth, to the land of Vind'yu, and be inspirer to my mortal son, Capilya, and his followers. To Inlay, to go down to the earth, to the land of Jaffeth, and be inspirer to my son, Chine, and his followers. To Inoal, to go down to the earth to the land of Egupt, and be inspirer to my son, Moses, and his followers. And you three shall restore the Faithists in these great divisions of the earth to liberty and safety. And you, Inoal, shall deliver Moses and the Faithists out of Egupt, and shape their course westward; for they shall circumscribe the earth, and complete it by the time of Kosmon.

26/10.5. To Injek, to go down to the earth, to Par'si'e and Heleste, and provide those peoples to liberate the slaves who are Faithists, whom you shall inspire to migrate to Moses and his people. To Inyith, to go down to the earth, to Jaffeth, Vind'yu and Arabin'ya, to inspire the scattered Faithists in those lands to come together, to the great lights, Capilya, Chine and Moses.

26/10.6. And you shall take with you those from my hosts, whom I brought from etherea, and labor together as one man. And when dawn has ended, you shall return here, and be raised up into my Nirvanian kingdoms. Nevertheless, you shall not leave Jehovih's chosen alone, but provide angel successors for them. And in this I give a new law to all my angel hosts who shall dwell with the Faithists on the earth, which is, that successors shall always be provided by the retiring hosts before they have departed; for never again shall the Faithists be left alone for a long season. ||

26/10.7. The chosen five then said: In Your name, wisdom and power, O Jehovih, we go forth in joy to fulfill Your commandments. Because we lost the earth, You have given it into our hands to redeem it and glorify You!

26/10.8. And Lika proclaimed a day of recreation, so that the fifty million hosts could be selected; in which labor, the marshals helped the five Gods in their selections.

26/10.9. During the recreation, the atmosphereans explained to the ethereans the layout and nature of the lands of the earth and its heavens. And then, after a season of prayer and singing, and a season of dancing, the recreation was brought to a close.

26/10.10. After labor resumed, the chosen five, with their hosts, saluted before the throne of Jehovih, and then withdrew to vessels that had been previously prepared for them, where they embarked and departed for the earth.

CHAPTER 11 Lika

26/11.1. Jehovih spoke to Lika, saying: Appoint other servants to Me for the other great divisions of the earth, and for the islands in the oceans of the earth; and to each of them give ten million of My servants whom you brought from Nirvania. And they shall go down among mortals, and by inspiration and otherwise, collect into groups the scattered Faithists who worship Me. And your servants shall also provide successors to come after them, to abide with mortals, making short their seasons of watch, so they shall not become weary.

26/11.2. Then Lika appointed T'chow, N'yak, Gitchee, Guelf, Ah and Siwah, and allotted them to different divisions of the earth, and he gave them each ten million hosts brought from the Orian worlds. And these hosts were selected in the same manner as the previous ones; and they also saluted and departed for the earth.

26/11.3. Again Jehovih spoke in the light of the throne, saying: Because many are risen in wisdom and truth, I will have Theovrahkistan as My holy place for them; and it shall be the region for My Brides and Bridegrooms at the resurrection of dawn. But at the end of dawn it shall be divided and subdivided so that none can find the place of My standing. For it has come to pass that man on the earth, learning the name of one of My heavens, glorifies it, and aspires to rise to it, but to rise to no other heaven.

26/11.4. Because My true Gods taught man about Hored in the early days, man desired Hored. That being so, each one of My enemies, the false Gods, cried out: Behold, my heavenly place is Hored! I am the All Heavenly ruler! Come here to me! || For by this means, the name I gave in truth, was usurped, and made into a snare to enslave My earth-born.

26/11.5. And I will no longer give to mortals a name of any of My heavenly places; nor shall they be taught of any heavens except the higher and the lower heavens, which shall designate My etherean and My atmospherean heavens. And by these terms man on the earth shall be fortified against the stratagems of false heavenly rulers.

26/11.6. And man shall perceive that when angels, men, Gods or Saviors, say: Come to me, and I will give you of my heavenly kingdom! || that they are false, and nothing but tyrants to enslave My people. But if they say: Go, serve the Great Spirit, and not me, for I am only a man as you are! || then it shall be known that they are of My Nirvanian hosts.

26/11.7. And if they say: Come to this heaven or that heaven, for with me only is delight, || it shall be testimony against them. But if they say: Truly, Jehovih is with you; cultivate yourself within Him, and you shall find delight in all worlds, || then that shall be testimony they are from My emancipated heavens.

26/11.8. Lika said: You shall found seventy new kingdoms in the lowest heaven, where you shall begin again with schools, colleges and factories, teaching the spirits of the dead the requirements for resurrection.

26/11.9. Two hundred million of my Orian angels shall be allotted to these seventy heavenly places, and during dawn it shall be their work to carry out these commandments. And they shall provide for successors after them, who shall continue for another season; and they shall provide yet other successors, and so on, till the coming of the Kosmon era (in three thousand four hundred years). ||

26/11.10. Lika then selected the two hundred million angels, and divided them into seventy groups and companies around the earth, in the lowest heaven. And after they were duly officered and organized, they saluted before the throne of Jehovih and departed to their respective places.

26/11.11. Then the voice of Jehovih came to Lika, saying: Behold, one hundred and seventy-five million still remain of your five hundred million. This, then, is the work you shall put upon them: They shall begin at one end of hada and go to the other, delivering all the hells of the false Gods as they go; untying any knots and providing passage for the drujas into one great plateau. For, because the false Gods began in confederacy, I will bring back into confederacy all those cast into hell. And you shall organize them safely, providing officers; and when they are thus established, behold, you and your Rapon hosts shall go and raise them up and deliver them into the a'ji'an Forest of Turpeset, where they shall be colonized and begin a new life of righteousness and love.

26/11.12. And Anuhasaj, once-crowned Lord God, shall be over them; and Osiris, Sudga, Te-in and all the other confederated Gods shall be under him; for even as these Gods labored to cast Me out, behold, I give them their harvest. ||

26/11.13. Then Lika commissioned the one hundred and seventy-five million ethereans, officered them, and sent them into the hadan regions of the earth to deliver its hells.

26/11.14. Jehovih said to Lika: The rest of your eight hundred million shall remain in Theovrahkistan, for the labor here is sufficient for them. And so they remained.

CHAPTER 12 Lika

26/12.1. The Rapon hosts desired to see Ahura, and so Lika sent an arrow-ship, with one hundred thousand angels, properly officered, to Ahura in Vara-pishanaha, inviting him to come on a visit for ten days, bringing his ten thousand attendants with him.

26/12.2. And it thus came to pass that Ahura came to Theovrahkistan, where he was most honorably received and saluted under the Sign Morning of Jehovih's Light, and he in turn answered in the Sign My words shall serve His Sons and Daughters!

26/12.3. Accordingly, Lika came down from the throne and greeted Ahura, saying to him: Come, then, and stand in the middle of the throne, so that your voice may delight the Holy Council.

26/12.4. So Ahura ascended the throne, along with Lika, and when the latter sat down, Ahura walked to the middle and saluted the Holy Council with the Sign Fire and Water, and he spoke, saying:

26/12.5. Because You, O Jehovih, have called me in the Sign of the Morning of Your Light, behold, I am risen up before You, to speak to Your Sons and Daughters.

26/12.6. But how shall I clear myself, O Father! I am like one who had a hidden skeleton, and the place of concealment broken down. Because I was, by You, created alive in the world, why should I not have forever glorified You? This I have asked myself all the days of my life; but You did not trouble to answer me in my curiosity.

26/12.7. When I was young in life, lo, I cried out to You, complaining because You did not make me wise. I said: Behold, You created all the animals on the face of the earth to know more than I in the day of birth. Yes, I did not even know where to find suck, nor could I rise up on my feet, but lay as I was laid down by my nurse.

26/12.8. Even to the lambs, calves and young colts, You gave greater wisdom and strength than You gave Your servant. I said: Why, then, shall I glorify You or sing songs in Your praise? Why shall I pray to You; Your ways are unalterable and Your Voice does not answer me.

26/12.9. You are void as the wind; You are neither Person, nor Wisdom, nor Ignorance. And as for Your servants, who say they hear Your Voice, behold, they are mad! I said: How can a man hear You? It is the reflection of himself he hears. How can a man see You? It is the reflection of himself he sees.

26/12.10. And You allowed me to become strong, as to strength, and wise as to self, even as I called to You in my vanity. Yes, I prided myself in myself; and as to You, I sought to disprove You whenever possible. And the worthlessness of prayer to You I exposed as a great vanity. Yes, I craved wisdom for the sake of showing that You were neither wise nor good. And to this end You also gave to me. And I became conceited in hiding my conceit, even from my own understanding, so that I could carry all points.

26/12.11. I pointed to the fool, saying: Behold, Jehovih's son! I pointed to the desert place, saying: Behold, Jehovih's fruitful earth! To the mountain, which is rocks and barren, saying: Behold, how

Jehovih has finished His work! And of the evil man, who murders his brother, I said: Jehovih, good in one thing, good in all!

26/12.12. But I did not know the hand that was upon me; You were answering my prayer every day. Yes, I ventured to judge You with my eyes and my ears and my own understanding. In the place I stood, I judged You and Your works, O Jehovih! And the craft of my speech won applause; by flattery I was puffed up. And I deemed my judgment the right one; and whoever did not see as I saw, I condemned or pitied; yes, I craved great speech so that I could expose them in their folly.

26/12.13. And in this You also answered me by giving freely; and my words were reckoned great words and wise. And I was quoted and praised far and near. Yes, I practiced good works so I could show others that, even in good works, a belief in You was vanity and a waste of judgment.

26/12.14. Yes, I craved means and great treasures so that I could render good to others, in order for my own philosophy to seem the highest of the high. And even in this You rendered to me great treasures and ample means; and by my good works done to others, I was applauded as a great and good God above all others.

26/12.15. I craved a heavenly kingdom so I could prove to billions my great wisdom and power; for I pitied those whom I thought foolishly dwelt in darkness in regard to You. And even yet, You, O Jehovih, did not cut me off; but gave me a great kingdom of seven billion!

26/12.16. And I taught them my philosophy: that there was nothing above them; that You, O Jehovih, did not see, did not hear, did not answer. Yes, I made my will all-powerful so that I could cut them off from You. But alas for me.

26/12.17. I had been like the sylph[1035] of old who stole into the musical instruments and put them out of tune. My kingdom was divided into seven billion philosophers, every one mad in his own conceit, and in a different way. There was no harmony among them. Yes, they were a kingdom of growlers and cursers! I had carried away the tuning fork, for I had cast You out, O Jehovih! My own philosophy had done it all.

26/12.18. Because I set myself up as the All Highest, You indulged me; and I became the highest God of my people. Yes, they cast their plaudits[1036] on me at first, but afterward all their ills and their curses. Neither could I satisfy them in anything in heaven or earth; nor could I turn them off from me, for I had bound them to me by my great promises.

26/12.19. I became as one in a cloud, because of the great trouble upon me and because of the fear. And yet You, O Jehovih, did not forget me; but sent Your Gods' words to me, imploring me what to do, so that I might be delivered in season. But how could I hear you, O Jehovih, or listen to Your Gods? Behold, my pride had swallowed me up, I was encompassed on every side. Because I had denied You before, I must deny You still.

26/12.20. Then greater darkness came upon me; Your light was obstructed by the walls I had built up against You; truly I had cut myself off from You! Then came the crash, as if heaven and earth shattered! I was cast into the chasm; my kingdom was upon me! The leadership and vanity I had sown had cast me into hell! I was in death, but could not die!

26/12.21. A knot was bound upon me; foul-smelling slaves were clinched upon me, millions of them, tens of millions; and the shafts of their curses pierced my soul; I was as one lacerated and bound in salt; choked and suffocated with foul gases. But yet, You, O Jehovih, did not desert me; but held my judgment from flying away into chaos.

26/12.22. And Your Voice came to me in the time of my tortures; came as the argument of the Most High! It was like myself speaking to myself, saying: He who forever casts away all things, can never be bound in hell; he who craves and holds fast, is already laying the foundation for torments.

26/12.23. And I cried out to You, O Jehovih, saying: O if only I had possessed nothing! No talents, no craft, no philosophy. That I had told these wretches to go to You, O Jehovih! O if only I had told them You alone could bless them, or supply them! But I sought to lead them, and lo, they are upon me!

26/12.24. O if I could be freed from them. That I could turn about in an opposite way from my former years; having nothing, craving nothing, but a right to serve You, O My Father!

[1035] a mischievous spirit, a pixy, a sprite

[1036] approvals, applause, praise, high esteem, appreciation, accolades

26/12.25. You sent Your Gods into the depths of hell, and they delivered me. And I made an oath to You, O Jehovih, to serve You forever. And You gave me labor, and I bowed myself down to labor for Your drujas, with all my wisdom and strength forever! And Your hand came upon me and gave me great power; power even over my own soul to create happy thoughts.

26/12.26. Why should I not praise You, O my Father? You gave me liberty in all my ways, and answered me according to my desires. Not once have You turned away from me or afflicted me; but because of my own vanity I cut myself off from You. Yes, You have shown me that to glorify You is the foundation of the highest happiness; to sing to You is the greatest delight; to praise You is the highest wisdom.

26/12.27. And now Ahura halted in his speech a while, and, still standing in the middle of the throne, burst into tears. Presently he said:

26/12.28. Anuhasaj was my good friend. It was he who since then took the name De'yus, and afterward proclaimed himself the Creator. I weep in pity for him. He is in hell now!

26/12.29. He was my best friend in the time of my darkness. And after I was delivered out of hell, he came and labored with me, full of repentance and love. Often we rested in each other's arms. Afterward, he traveled far and near in Your great heavens, O Jehovih.

26/12.30. And when he returned to this earth's heavens he did not come to see me. And I was brokenhearted because of my great love for him. Then he founded his heavenly place and called it Hored. And I called out to You, O Jehovih, as to what message I should send him, for I foresaw his kingdom would be broken up and himself ultimately cast into hell.

26/12.31. And You gave me liberty to send him a message in my own way. And in the anguish of my broken heart I sent him a message, saying, in substance, I no longer have any love for you! And I chided him and upbraided him because he did not come to see me, to gratify my burning love. And I foretold him the great darkness and the hell that would come upon him, even as they now are.

26/12.32. Now I repent, O Jehovih, that I sent him such a message! For nearly two thousand years my message has been to me as if I swallowed a living coal of fire!

26/12.33. Ahura ceased. Lika spoke, saying: Because you have pleaded for De'yus, you have turned the etherean hosts to him. To you I allot the restoration of De'yus, alias Anuhasaj. In the proper time my hosts will take you to the hell where he is bound, and you shall be the first to receive him.

26/12.34. Lika then proclaimed a day of recreation, for there were millions of ethereans who desired to meet Ahura and greet him with love and praise.

CHAPTER 13 Lika

26/13.1. Lika spoke before the Rapon hosts, saying: Behold, the hosts of laborers are allotted to their places.

26/13.2. Let us go and examine the earth and her heavens. It is proper that my surveyors measure her land and water, together with all the living on and in it, and especially as to every man, woman and child, and their time of maturity, and the years of the generations of men.

26/13.3. And man that is brought forth out of the earth shall be numbered; and the grade of his understanding measured; and the nature of his desires and aspirations shall be ascertained; which reports shall be copied and sent into the Orian kingdoms, for the deliberations of the Chiefs, so they may determine the requirements of the earth, and the nature in which her roadway shall be strewn with either light or darkness for the ultimate perfection of her soul harvests.

26/13.4. And the heavens of the earth shall be measured, as to the spirits of the dead; and their grades shall be determined, together with their desires and aspirations; the lengths of the times of their bondage to the earth, the places of their habitation, and the nature of their supplies. And a record shall be made, and a copy also sent to the Orian Chiefs for their deliberations.

26/13.5. And the plateaus of the earth's heavens shall also be counted and measured, and their localities mapped out and recorded, and copies also sent to the Orian Chiefs, so that they may determine if any changes to these places are necessary. ||

26/13.6. I appoint Havralogissasa as vice-Goddess in my place during my absence from Theovrahkistan. What do you say, Havralogissasa?

She said: Jehovih's will and yours be done. I am rejoiced.

26/13.7. Lika then called Havralogissasa to the throne, and commissioned her vice-Goddess of Theovrahkistan. And after this, Lika gave instructions as to extending the capital, Yogannaqactra, and enlarging the places for reception of the higher grades; all of which were duly provided with the persons to carry out the commands.

26/13.8. And now Lika spoke to Ahura, saying: Behold, you shall return to your kingdom, Vara-pishanaha, for when I come there on my journey, I will resurrect your hosts as Brides and Bridegrooms to the etherean kingdoms. Your labor is well done; your glory is the glory of billions! May the love, wisdom and power of Jehovih be with you, now and forever!

26/13.9. So Ahura saluted, and was in turn saluted, then he advanced and met the marshals, who conducted him to the arrow-ship, where he embarked and departed.

CHAPTER 14 Lika

26/14.1. In due time Lika's otevan was completed, and he, with the Rapon hosts, as well as one million hosts in attendance to make the necessary surveys and records, entered into the ship and departed for his two years' cruise around the earth and in her heavens.

26/14.2. || Sufficient for the earth is its history which is in the libraries of the earth, including the maps of land and water; and the number of inhabitants; and the living creatures upon the earth and in its water. Therefore, suffice it to say that the revelations of the heavens upon the face of the earth, which records are in the libraries of heaven, shall be disclosed before the generations of men from the records of Lika, Son of Jehovih. ||

26/14.3. This, then, is a synopsis of the atmospherean heavens at that time, namely: In the hells of Hored, with Anuhasaj, alias De'yus, forty billion angels.

26/14.4. In the hells of Te-in, eight billion; in the hells of Sudga, twelve billion; in the hells of Osiris, seventeen billion.

26/14.5. In the smaller hells in other parts of hada, there were, in all, fourteen billion angels.

26/14.6. These ninety-one billion were not all bound in their respective hells; more than thirty billion of them surged about, from one hell to another, often in groups of a billion.

26/14.7. And these groups, at times, descended to the earth, fastening upon mortals, even casting large cities and nations in death. Because they carried the foulness of their hells with them, they impregnated the air with poison, so that mortals were swept off by the million. And these were called plagues.

26/14.8. Lika said: Behold, I will give a new grade to these heavens for a season. From this time, such angels shall be known as being in the first resurrection. But spirits who have quit their old haunts, and joined organic associations, being enlisted in companies, either for labor or for receiving heavenly instruction, shall be known as being in the second resurrection. And such spirits as have attained to etherean grades, being Brides and Bridegrooms of Jehovih, and having ascended beyond atmospherea into the etherean worlds, shall be known as being in the third resurrection.

26/14.9. Angels who engraft themselves onto mortals, becoming like a twin spirit to the one corporeal body, shall be known as reincarnated spirits. But where such spirits usurp the corporeal body, as of an infant, growing up in the corporeal body, and holding the native spirit in abeyance, such spirits shall be known as damons (which was the origin of that name) [i.e., demons –ed.].

26/14.10. Spirits who inhabit mortals in order to live on the substance mortals eat and drink, and often absorbing the strength and life of mortals, shall be known as uzians (vampires). Nevertheless, these shall not include fetals.

26/14.11. All the foregoing, who are not in the way[1037] of resurrection, shall be called drujas. ||

26/14.12. Now, behold, there were millions of angels in those days who knew no other life, but to continue engrafting themselves on mortals. And, when one mortal died, they went and engrafted themselves on another.

26/14.13. These were the fruit of the teaching of the false Gods, who had put away the All Highest, Jehovih. They could not be persuaded that etherea was filled with habitable worlds.

[1037] direction, on the path

26/14.14. And they professed that they had been reincarnated many times; and that, previously, they had been great kings or philosophers.

26/14.15. Some of them remembered the ji'ay'an period of a thousand years, and so, hoped to regain their natural bodies and dwell again on the earth, and forever. Hence was founded the story that every thousand years a new incarnation would come to the spirits of the dead.

26/14.16. Lika said: Spirits who come to mortals purposely to inflict them with pain or misfortune shall be called evil spirits.

26/14.17. And when they go in groups, having a leader, that leader shall be called beelzebub, that is, captain of evil (prince of devils). (And this is the origin of that word.)

26/14.18. In Par'si'e and Heleste there were habited with mortals one billion damons, and one billion two hundred million evil spirits; in Vind'yu there were one billion one hundred million damons, and one billion evil spirits. In Egupt there were inhabited with mortals seven hundred million engrafters (reincarnated spirits), who, for the most part, held the spirits of their victims in abeyance all their natural lives [i.e., were damons –ed.].

26/14.19. In Jaffeth there were habited with mortals more than one and a half billion damons and evil spirits, besides four hundred million vampires. So that in these three great divisions of the earth, Vind'yu, Jaffeth and Arabin'ya, there were habited more than ten billion spirits who had not attained to any resurrection.

26/14.20. Besides all the foregoing there were billions of spirits in chaos, being those who had been slain in wars. Of these chaotic spirits there were in Par'si'e and Heleste a billion; and in Jaffeth two billion; and in Vind'yu two billion. But in Egupt there were not half a million, all told.

26/14.21. So that in atmospherea at the time of Lika, there were more than one hundred and twenty-five billion angels who had no knowledge of, or belief in, any higher heaven.

26/14.22. To offset this great darkness, there were only four billion believers in, and laborers for, Jehovih and his emancipated kingdoms; and many of these not above grade fifty. And these were members of Craoshivi and Vara-pishanaha.

26/14.23. Two billion of them were ashars, laboring with the Faithist mortals of Egupt, Jaffeth and Vind'yu.

CHAPTER 15 Lika

26/15.1. After Lika had numbered all the mortals on the earth, and all the angels in the heavens of the earth, and saw their great darkness, he visited Hao-yusta, and found it a good plateau, capable of all grades up to sixty. And Lika possessed the place and consecrated it to Jehovih; and he left on it three hundred thousand Gods and Goddesses, who were of his etherean host. And after this he returned to instruct Gessica, chief God, for the deliverance of the hells of De'yus, Te-in, Osiris and Sudga.

26/15.2. Gessica had his vessels constructed with walls of fire around the margins, to prevent the drujas from escaping. And in total, there were four hundred vessels built, each capable of carrying one hundred million drujas.

26/15.3. The manner of driving the drujas into them was by leaving part of the fire-wall open, and by fire-brands in the ethereans' hands cutting off sections of drujas from the hells. In this way the ethereans drove the drujas into the vessels, at which point the doorway in the wall of the ship was closed. Then the workers of the ship put it under way and carried them up to Hao-yusta, where the Gods and Goddesses received them, placing the drujas in pens, walled with fire, where they could be treated and restored to reason, after which they were to be liberated in installments, according to their safety.

26/15.4. In the first year Gessica delivered from the hells of hada five billion drujas; but in the second year he delivered thirty-five billion; and in the third year, sixteen billion. After this the work went slowly, for the balance of the hells were mostly in knots, some of them hundreds of millions. And these had to be delivered individually, requiring great labor, power, wisdom and dexterity.

26/15.5. In the fifth month of the fourth year, Anuhasaj, alias the false Lord God, was delivered out of the great knot of hell, in which there had been eight hundred million bound for more than four hundred years. After the manner in which Fragapatti delivered knots, even so did Gessica and his hosts, with brands of fire.

26/15.6. When it was known in which place De'yus (Anuhasaj) was tied (in a knot), and when it was half delivered, Gessica sent for Ahura to come and have the honor of releasing Anuhasaj. And to this end Ahura labored on the knot fifty-five days, and then it was accomplished.

26/15.7. But lo and behold, Anuhasaj was bereft of all judgment, crying out, unceasingly: I am not God! I am not the Lord! I am not De'yus! He was wild, crazed with fear and torments, frenzied, and in agony.

26/15.8. Which Ahura, his friend, saw; and Ahura caught him in his arms. Ahura called to him: Anuhasaj! O my beloved! Do you not know me? Behold me! I am Ahura!

26/15.9. But, alas, Anuhasaj did not know him; pulled away, tried to escape in fear; his protruding eyes not seeing; his ears not hearing. And he kept forever uttering: Let me go, I am not the Lord God, nor De'yus! I am Anuhasaj! Then broke the good heart of Ahura, and he wept.

26/15.10. Then they held Anuhasaj and carried him away into the ship, and Ahura helped to carry him.

26/15.11. Then the ship rose up and sailed along higher and higher, farther and farther, till at last it came to Hao-yusta. And they took Anuhasaj to a hospital prepared for maniacs, and stretched him on his back and held him. Then Ahura called to the Gods and Goddesses to come and help him; and they came and seated themselves around, making the sacred circle.

26/15.12. And Ahura said: Light of Your Light, Jehovih! You Who first quickened him into being, O deliver him!

26/15.13. A light, like a small star, gathered before Anuhasaj's face, and this was the first thing his fixed eyes had yet seen. Then Ahura and the Gods and Goddesses sang sweetly: Behold Me! I am the light! And the life! I quicken into life every living thing. Behold Me! I am with you! I am never away from you! You are Mine now, and forever shall be! Look upon Me! I am in all things! Nothing is, nor was, nor ever shall be without Me! Hear My Love! I am your Creator! Only for love, and for love only, I created you, My beloved.

26/15.14. Anuhasaj gave a long gasp and relaxed his mighty will, then fell into a swoon, all limp and helpless. Still the Gods stood by him, waiting, watching while he slept awhile. And then, by signals to the es'enaurs, Ahura caused other music to steal upon the scene, to be answered by the distant trumpeters. For the space of seven days Anuhasaj slept; and all the while the great Gods and Goddesses did not relax their wills or steadfast positions. And at the end of the seventh day Anuhasaj began to sing in his swoon, like one weak and out of breath, but half awake.

26/15.15. How could I deny You, O Jehovih! Was the evidence of my own life not before me? I raised up my voice against my Creator! I plucked Him out of my soul; from all people in heaven and earth I dispersed Him. But those who applauded me turned against me! Even as I had turned against You, You All Person!

26/15.16. In my vanity I did not own that I was in You or of You; with my own hand I cut myself asunder from You, O Jehovih! O if only I had perceived I was going farther and farther away; if only I had known the road of life and death!

26/15.17. I see Your judgment upon me, O Jehovih! I hear Your just decree: While the name of God or Lord or Savior is worshipped on the earth I shall labor with the drujas of heaven and the druks of earth!

26/15.18. A most righteous judgment, O Jehovih! While I am in hell or in heaven, in hada or on the earth, I will pursue all peoples, mortals and angels, till I cast out the worship of a God and of a Lord and of a Savior. And You alone, You Great Spirit, Ever Present Person, Everlasting and Almighty, You shall be All in All.

26/15.19. Again Anuhasaj went off in a swoon for the space of three days, and yet the Gods and Goddesses did not cease their fixed places. And again the music was resumed till Anuhasaj awoke and again chanted in Jehovih's praise. And again he relapsed and again awoke; for many days; but at last awoke and saw first of all Ahura. Steadily and wildly he gazed upon him, until his eyes were clouded and as if dead. And he dropped again into a swoon.

26/15.20. Another day the Gods watched him, and sang for him; moved not from the sacred CIRCLE OF JEHOVIH.

26/15.21. Then Anuhasaj awoke, singing: Who was it who taught me to love? Ahura! Who first proclaimed Jehovih to my ear? Ahura! Who was the last to plead Jehovih? Ahura! Who most of all that live labored for me? Ahura!

26/15.22. I broke your heart, O Ahura! I was mad, O I was mad, Ahura! Because of your love,

Ahura, you praised me; I was vainglorious and unworthy of you, O my beloved.

26/15.23. A vision of you has raised up before me, Ahura. Second to Jehovih, O my love? O if only you knew I am here, penitent and heartbroken! I know you would fly to me, Ahura. You alone, I know, who would never desert me, sweet Ahura.

26/15.24. Then again Anuhasaj relapsed into a swoon, wilted, breathless, like one that is dead. Ahura sang:

26/15.25. Behold me! I am Ahura. I have come to you from afar, O Anuhasaj. Awake and behold your love, my love. My heart is broken for you, Anuhasaj. A thousand years I have wept for you. O if only you could awake to know me!

26/15.26. Anuhasaj looked up and saw Ahura. The latter kept on singing: It is not a dream, Anuhasaj. Your Ahura is here. Behold me! I am he. Break the spell, O Anuhasaj. By Jehovih's power put forth your soul! Ahura is here!

26/15.27. Again Anuhasaj relapsed, but not to swoon; merely closed his eyes and sang: Blessed are You, O Jehovih! You have given me a sweet vision! You have shown me the face of my love, Ahura! His sweet voice fell upon my ear! I am blessed, O Jehovih!

26/15.28. You have blessed even these hells, O Jehovih! The darkness of endless death is made light by Your Almighty touch. You alone shall be my song forever. You alone my theme of delight. Jehovih forever! Jehovih forever and ever!

26/15.29. Then Ahura, seeing the spell was broken, said: Arise, O Anuhasaj. I will sing with you. Behold Ahura, your love, is before you. This is no vision. Come to the arms of your love.

26/15.30. And he raised Anuhasaj up, and he awoke fully, but trembling and weak, and knew understandingly.

CHAPTER 16 Lika

26/16.1. In the same time that Anuhasaj was delivered out of hell, so was Anubi, and from the self-same knot. And he was carried on the same calyos to Hao-yusta, the same heavenly place. And he was also in chaos, knowing nothing, only screaming: I am not Anubi. I am not the Savior. I am plain Chesota! (his real name).

26/16.2. And he also did not see and did not hear, but was wild, desiring to fly away. And they held him fast, and, in the same way they delivered Anuhasaj to reason, they also delivered Chesota.

26/16.3. And when both of them were well restored to sound reason, though still timorous,[1038] Ahura took them in his own otevan and carried them to Theovrahkistan, before Lika, for judgment. And great was the time when they came; and especially the desire of the inhabitants to look upon Anuhasaj, the most audacious God that had ever dwelt on the earth or in her heavens, and, as well, the much-loved friend of Ahura.

26/16.4. When they came before the throne of Jehovih and duly saluted, Lika said: Where do you come from and for what purpose, O my beloved?

26/16.5. Ahura said: Hell has delivered up the bound. My friends are before you. Then Lika said: In Jehovih's name, welcome. Whatever the Father puts into your souls, utter it and be assured of His love, wisdom and power.

26/16.6. Anuhasaj said: That I am delivered out of hell it is well; that I was delivered into hell it was well likewise. Give me Jehovih's judgment. My purpose before you is to register my vows to Jehovih, so that my record and your just judgment may be carried to the heavens above.

26/16.7. Lika said: My judgment upon you, Anuhasaj, is that you shall judge yourself!

26/16.8. Anuhasaj said: Most righteous judgment, O Jehovih! (And then speaking to Lika:) But do you not know Jehovih's voice?

26/16.9. Lika said: You asked for a great heavenly kingdom. Behold, Jehovih gave it to you. As soon as order is restored, you shall have your kingdom again.

26/16.10. Anuhasaj said: I do not want it.

26/16.11. Lika said: You shall not say, I want this or that; but say that you will do whatever Jehovih has given into your hands. When you have raised up your whole kingdom, behold, you will also be raised up.

26/16.12. Anuhasaj said: Alas me, this is also just. Show me the way; I will labor from this time forth for the billions who were my kingdom.

26/16.13. Lika now bade Chesota (Anubi) to speak. Chesota said: I called myself Master of the Scales and Savior of men. Whoever called on me,

[1038] easily frightened, reticent, unassertive, timid

worshipping me and De'yus, alias the Lord God, I accepted; whoever did not worship me, or De'yus, or the Lord God, I cast into hell, saying: Depart from me, you cursed, into everlasting torments.

26/16.14. What, then, O Lika, shall be my judgment? For, behold, I cast a billion into torments.

26/16.15. Lika said: Judge yourself.

26/16.16. Chesota said: Alas, the pains I gave can never be called back and undone. Have I, then, no hope?

26/16.17. Lika said: Whom you have pained, go to, and by your good deeds done to them after this, so win their love that they will call you blessed! When all of them have accepted you, behold, it shall be well with you.

26/16.18. Chesota said: O endless task! And yet, it is just. Teach me, then, O Lika, how to carry out this great judgment.

26/16.19. Lika then asked for Anuhasaj to come forward and be crowned; and when he approached the foot of the throne Lika came down and said: Anuhasaj, Son of Jehovih, I crown you God of Hao-yusta in Jehovih's name, to His service forever. Be with him, O Jehovih, in wisdom, love and power.

26/16.20. Anuhasaj said: Into Your service, O Jehovih, I commit myself forever! Give me of Your love, wisdom and power so that I may glorify You and Your kingdoms.

26/16.21. Lika stretched up his hand, saying: Light of Your light, crown of Your crown, O Jehovih! And the light was formed in his hand, and a crown came out of the light, and Lika placed it on Anuhasaj's head. The latter then sat down on the foot of the throne, and Lika took his hand, saying: Arise, O God, and go your way, and the Father be with you!

26/16.22. With that, Anuhasaj and Chesota saluted and stood aside. And then Ahura saluted and stood aside also; after which Lika granted a day of recreation, during which time the visiting Gods departed for Hao-yusta.

CHAPTER 17 Lika

26/17.1. As this history has overlapped the running story, hear now how it was with Ahura and his kingdom, Vara-pishanaha, which Lika visited prior to the deliverance of the hells of hada.[1039] To accomplish the resurrection of Vara-pishanaha, Lika had previously sent swift messengers to Ye'a-Goo, Goddess of Ha'mistos, in etherea, to bring an avalanza capable of six billion Brides and Bridegrooms for the mid-harvest (mid-dawn).

26/17.2. Accordingly, at the time Lika and his Rapon hosts were visiting Ahura, the Goddess, Ye'a-Goo, came down in her avalanza, fully equipped. Her avalanza was egg-shaped with its outside veiled, and was seven miles high and five miles wide every way, habitable throughout. On the outer surface, but under the veil, were twelve thousand porches with banisters.[1040] The propelling vortices were within the center, and the workmen were in the summit. On the lowest porch were five hundred thousand es'enaurs, and on the highest porch one thousand trumpeters.

26/17.3. Ye'a-Goo's compartment and the place of the Holy Council were in the middle; and her throne faced to the north, like the earth's vortex.

26/17.4. Ahura said to Lika, Son of Jehovih: My Brides and Bridegrooms I give to you; honor this dissolving kingdom by performing the marriage ceremony. Lika said: Your will and Jehovih's be done. Thus it was arranged, and the two, along with the Rapon hosts, ascended the throne together and sat upon it.

26/17.5. Ahura had previously prepared his hosts, in all, four and a half billion Brides and Bridegrooms, and arrayed them in white; they anxiously awaited the coming of Ye'a-Goo, and were on the lookout to see her magnificent ship descending. A place of anchorage had also been previously made, together with accommodation for the spectators, of whom there were one and a half billion, being adopted wanderers, rescued from the various hells during the past hundred years.

26/17.6. The Brides and Bridegrooms were arranged in semi-circles facing the throne, leaving a place for the avalanza, which would be above them, so that when Ye'a-Goo descended from her ship's bottom she would be in the center of the semi-circles and before the throne.

[1039] Recall that Lika went on a two-year journey to survey earth and its heavens. During that journey he would visit Ahura to resurrect his harvest, and that story is now being told in this Chapter 17.

[1040] handrails, railings

26/17.7. While the ship's workmen were anchoring, Ye'a-Goo and her Holy Council descended to the platform, and saluted the Gods and Goddesses on the throne in the Sign, THE GLORY OF THE FATHER, and Lika and the others answered under the Sign, THE ABANDONMENT OF SELF!

26/17.8. Ye'a-Goo said: In Jehovih's name I come to answer the call of His Son, to deliver the emancipated Sons and Daughters.

26/17.9. Lika said: Behold, O Daughter of Jehovih, the Brides and Bridegrooms are before you. To you I give them in Jehovih's name!

26/17.10. Ye'a-Goo said: My beloved, do you know the resurrection of the most high heavens?

26/17.11. Response: Reveal, O Goddess; our faith is strong. ||

26/17.12. Ye'a-Goo instructed them, and then the usual ceremonies followed, but concluding with the seventh degree of emuth, in Jehovih's voice: To be My Brides and Bridegrooms forever?

26/17.13. Response: To be Your Brides and Bridegrooms forever, O Jehovih! To labor for You, and to be mouthpieces for Your commandments, and to be Your expression forever! And to be in concert with Your most high Gods for the resurrection of mortals and angels.

26/17.14. Jehovih: Whom I receive as Mine forever! To be one with Me in My kingdoms; for which glory I accept you as My Sons and Daughters, Brides and Bridegrooms forever!

26/17.15. Response: And be Your Sons and Daughters! To be one with You forever, Most High, Jehovih!

26/17.16. Ye'a-Goo said: Behold the crowns the Father bestows upon His loves, to be theirs forever. (And now the Rapon Chiefs, with Lika, gathered of the curtains of light and wove crowns and cast them forth, billions, and the power of the Great Spirit through their wills bore them upon the heads of the Brides and Bridegrooms.)

26/17.17. Response: Crown of Your Crown, O Jehovih! Glory to You, Creator of worlds!

26/17.18. Ye'a-Goo: The Father's ship has come for His chosen. Walk in and rejoice, for you are His harvest. Gods and Goddesses are waiting for you, as a woman waits for her first-born. They will receive you with joy and love. Yes, they are crying out to me, Daughter of Jehovih, why do you take so long? ||

26/17.19. Lika now saluted the Brides and Bridegrooms, and said: Arise, O my beloved, and go your ways, the Father calls.

26/17.20. The Brides and Bridegrooms saluted, saying: Alas, we have not paid our teacher, Ahura. And every one plucked from the rays of Jehovih's light a flower of love, and cast it at Ahura's feet, saying: Most blessed of Gods, love of my love; Jehovih be with you!

26/17.21. Ahura did not respond; only burst into tears. And now, while the Brides and Bridegrooms were going into the ship, Ye'a-Goo came along the platform, accompanied by the chief marshal and his staff, and these were followed by Ye'a-Goo's High Council. The Rapon Chiefs rose up and received them, and they all sat on Jehovih's throne in relaxation and fellowship.

26/17.22. Thus ended the ceremony. The music of the two spheres now commenced; Ye'a-Goo and her hosts embarked, and she gave the word, Arise! and lo, the great avalanza started from its foundation, amid a universal shout of applause from the four billion. Higher and higher rose the ship of fire, toward the bridge Chinvat, toward the etherean heavens.

CHAPTER 18 Lika

26/18.1. After the judgment of Anuhasaj and Chesota at Theovrahkistan, Ahura asked Lika for assistance to remove the remainder of Vara-pishanaha to Hao-yusta, which Lika granted, allotting ten million of his etherean hosts to accomplish it. With these Ahura, Anuhasaj and Chesota accomplished the removal.

26/18.2. Not many days after this, Sudga was delivered from the hells of Auprag, and because Ahura had been previously informed as to the time, he accordingly had gone to Auprag, to be ready to receive Sudga, and help restore him if required.

26/18.3. Sudga, on his delivery from the knot, where there had been thirty million bound, was bereft of reason, but not gentle like Anuhasaj, but fierce, battling right and left, a very maddened maniac that neither saw nor heard, but raved and cursed with all his strength, choked up with madness. For all the curses of his broken-down kingdom recoiled upon himself; the projective curses of his billions of slaves were piercing his soul from every quarter.

26/18.4. But they held him firmly and carried him into the ship, which sailed for Hao-yusta, where he was landed in the same condition. Ahura was with him, and Ahura arranged for a circle of deliverance to assemble and labor in the restoration. And it required thirty days and nights to bring him around, so he could even see and hear; but as for his judgment it was yet a hundred days more before it manifested.

26/18.5. So Ahura could not wait any longer with him, but returned to the hells where Te-in was bound, the Ak-a-loo-ganuz, for Te-in was to be delivered. But again Ahura was disappointed, for Te-in was neither frightened nor wild nor mad, but limpid, helpless as water, and with no more knowledge than a vessel of water. His energies had all been exhausted, and in a dead swoon he lay in the heart of the knot. Him they also carried to Hao-yusta, and Ahura provided for his restoration.

26/18.6. But before Te-in awoke from his stupor, Ahura departed for Osiris, who was bound in the hells of Prayogotha. Osiris had been in hell now for more than a hundred years, and in a knot for fifty years.

26/18.7. When the false Osiris was delivered he was deranged, but preaching Jehovih, calling everybody Jehovih, and everything Jehovih. Him they also carried to Hao-yusta and provided restoration for him. And Ahura went there also to assist with all his wisdom and strength.

26/18.8. Thus were delivered all the self-Gods who had rebelled against Jehovih and established the great confederacy, of which not one vestige was now left.

26/18.9. But of all the angels delivered out of the hells and knots not one in ten was of sound judgment, while more than half of them were only drujas at best.

26/18.10. Thus was founded the new kingdom of Hao-yusta, as yet in the charge of the ethereans, who were to commit it to Anuhasaj and his one-time confederates, for their deliverance.

26/18.11. It came to pass in course of time that Sudga, Te-in and Osiris were restored to judgment, and in this matter Anuhasaj, Ahura and Chesota were constant workers. And when they were all restored, they in turn set about to restore others, to which labor they were committed till the close of dawn.

26/18.12. Osiris, Te-in and Sudga desired to go before Lika, to be adjudged and sentenced; and they all sentenced themselves, which was granted to them. On this occasion Osiris said:

26/18.13. Your lessons are near at hand, O Jehovih. But who will learn them? Mortals go insane because they have not learned to throw their cares upon You. To throw government upon You, O Jehovih, is this not wisdom? To cast riches and kingdoms into Your lap; to own nothing; to have nothing; is this not the sum of the highest happiness?

26/18.14. Whoever does this will battle against no man for anything in heaven or earth. But he who does otherwise will sooner or later descend into hell. For what is hell but the opposite of bliss? What is battling against others, but sowing the seed of anarchy in one's own soul? To battle against others is to gain the lower, by sacrificing the higher, of which latter You, O Jehovih, are the summit.

26/18.15. To go against You, O Father, is to go against one's fellows; to go against one's fellows is to go against You. And who can go against You without sooner or later evolving his own fall?

26/18.16. To mortals You have given kings and queens, and shown them that sooner or later their kingdoms will fall to pieces. And yet Lords and Gods, seeing these things, will not believe. Every one, in his own conceit, imagines his particular kingdom will be governed more wisely than all his predecessors. And yet his also falls.

26/18.17. Now I will turn to find You, O Jehovih, and the search shall be everlasting. Kingdoms are nothing to me; all possessions, except wisdom and love, are but vanity and vexation. I know You are above all else, and yet You are that which has given Yourself all away, so that none can look upon Your face. Truly You have hidden Yourself away; to be like You is to hide away the self of one's self; and that which will remain will be Your mouthpiece and Your hand. ||

26/18.18. Then Sudga spoke to Jehovih, saying: Why was I puffed up, seeing that I did not even create my own self? Nor did I have anything in earth or heaven to use or to work with, except substance already made. Yes, I leapt into Your garden which You had planted.

26/18.19. I raised up my voice against You; because You were too Holy for my gross senses to perceive, I condemned You. I wanted You gross, so that I could look upon You; so that I could walk around You, and behold Your stature. I saw that all men were like me in this.

26/18.20. Therefore I made a figurehead of myself; I said to Your children: Behold me! And at first they were pleased, because they imagined they had found a Creator they could measure. But Your eye was upon me, Your hand pointed the way and the manner of my iniquity. And they searched me out and found I was only a man, like they themselves. And, so, they condemned me.

26/18.21. The fool acknowledges no person unless he can grapple with him,[1041] and find the arms, and their length, and the feet and their standing place. How vain I was in this, O Jehovih!

26/18.22. He who professed Your Person I denounced as a fool; because I did not see Your completeness, You allowed me to pursue my vanity. Because I had risen above acknowledging Your Person I was forced to make man the All Highest; and this drove me to make myself the all highest man. But You did not come against me to beat me from my iniquity, but gave me full play to do my utmost.

26/18.23. On all sides You have encompassed Your creation with liberty. Even Your enemy You have not restrained. He stands in public, saying: Jehovih, I deny You. If You are mightier than I, strike me down. Behold, I deny You and Your Person! You Void Nothingness! You fool Creator, with Your half-created world. You Who have created sin! And created misery! You Father of evil! O You dumb Nothing.

26/18.24. Yes, even to him You have given free speech; and he builds up his own soul in his own way. And for a season he is the delight of the druk and the druj; yes, they fasten upon him, and he gains a multitude of evil ones, divided one against another, but the seed of his curses takes root in them, and he becomes encompassed with foulness and bondage.

26/18.25. To find harmony in You, O Jehovih; to measure the Goodness of You; to rejoice in one's joys; to treasure Your best gifts; to laud[1042] Your love; to love You because You have given me power to love, and things to love; to rejoice in Your fruits and flowers and all perfected things; to harp forever upon Your glories and the magnitude of Your creation; to sing praises to You for harmony wherever found; to love to comprehend all good things; to find the good that is in all men and women; to rejoice in delights; to teach others to rejoice, and to search after all perfected beauties and goodness and righteousness and love; these shall be my service to You, my everlasting Father.

26/18.26. To not seek to find imperfections; to not seek to find disharmonies; to not seek to find evil; to not seek to find ugliness; to not seek to find evil in others, nor their darkness nor shortcomings; to not seek to prove imperfections upon You, O Jehovih; to find no fault with You; to not complain against You; to not complain for trials nor for hardships, nor for the evil others inflict me with; to not quibble because I cannot comprehend Your vastness; to not quibble for myself; to not speak evilly against anything You have created. O Jehovih, make me strong and wise forever. ||

26/18.27. Te-in spoke to Jehovih, saying: Where is the limit of experience, O Jehovih! And how short have I not been before You, My Father! Behold, I had learned all philosophies; I had been taught for a long season in the right way, but I rebelled against You, my Creator.

26/18.28. I had been taught to not hoard up anything; to own nothing; to desire nothing but wisdom and love. And Your teachers, O Jehovih, showed me the evidence of thousands of great rulers, and every one of them had come to evil and destruction. Why then, O Father, was I not wise in the evidence before me? But I rose up against all this testimony, and I fashioned a mighty kingdom. Yes, You allowed me to try in my own way to the full.

26/18.29. I went not by peace but by war; I raised up standing armies and great warriors without limit; by force I established myself, but only as a tree that grows up and is cut down. But what was I in Your great universe, O Jehovih? What was my experience but the repetition of others who had been before me?

26/18.30. Now I will be wise; most cautious in my wisdom, and slow to proceed. But how can I make my experience profitable to others? You have stood me far away; whoever hears me will say: Ah, if I had tried it I would have succeeded better. You

[1041] wrestle him, engage with him, interact with him, seize him, grip him

[1042] praise, extol, acclaim, glorify, cherish

prick each one to go in and try, but they all fail. Yes, they reiterate[1043] their failure; but of this experience where is the profit to others? How can I ever reach them, O Jehovih!

26/18.31. What greater profit do I have than a mortal who dwells on the earth? Have the angels not testified for thousands of years that the rich man was crippling his own soul, and that the king and queen were binding themselves with chains for the habitation of hell? But they will not heed; every one hopes he, at least, will find a way to escape; to gain prestige over others; to be a leader; to have servants; to be idle; to live at ease; to have great possessions; to revel in luxuries. Are these not more powerful motivators than another's experience; greater in the eyes of the ignorant than all the wisdom of earth and heaven?

26/18.32. You have wisely shaped Your creatures, O Father! You make great servants of us in a way we do not know of. Behold, I desired a mighty kingdom in heaven, and You gave one into my hand. Yes, I flattered myself with my success; I laughed at the Gods who had been before my time. How things are changed now, O Jehovih!

26/18.33. You have made me a servant of servants; yes, by my own hand I have bound myself. Have I not heard mortals say: O if only I had a kingdom to rule over! O if only I had great riches, how good I would be! And because You deny them for their own good, they complain against You. Who shall answer for the vanity of men and angels! They do not have patience with You, Who created them alive and know what is best.

26/18.34. One says: There is a great king, why does he not do a great good? Or, there is a rich man, why does he not do a great good also? O if only I were in their places. ||

26/18.35. How shall I show them, O Father, that to be a king is to go away from doing good; that to be a rich man is to deny goodness? Yes, by the very act of possession he is testimony in the opposite way. For he who is good gives all; even as You gave all and so, made all things. And the greater the possessions the greater the bondage. Who has so small a responsibility as he who has nothing? This is the sum of wisdom, O Jehovih; and all men and all angels sooner or later will acknowledge it.

26/18.36. Better You have made it for the servant than for the master; better for the poor than the rich; and these things will also come to their understanding in course of time. But how can I, O Father, make them know wisdom without experience, to accept the testimony of others' tortures in hell?

26/18.37. Behold, You gave me great learning when I was of the earth; and when in hada great advantages to attain to deep wisdom; but, after all, I was caught in a snare of my own setting. How much, then, O Father, must I expect of the multitude? Happy is he who has nothing, and desires only wisdom and love. To cultivate such a garden, what a harvest will ripen out to him. ||

26/18.38. When the three had thus spoken before the throne and before the High Council, Ahura stood aside and spoke also. He said:

CHAPTER 19 Lika

26/19.1. O if I could sing You a song of delight, You All Highest. Or find the words to make plain Your marvelous ways. But You have limited me as a shadow, of which You are the substance. Your causes are deep and of long times; my judgment: less than a breath of air; I resolve and reason and devise, but all is nothing before You.

26/19.2. Today my soul is buoyed up with great rejoicing; You have sent me my loves. I would bind them with sweet words; their wisdom I would feast upon forever. In Your great mercy, Jehovih, You have showed me a world of delight.

26/19.3. How can I repay You, or make Your countless millions understand the way of rejoicing? O if I could show them the secret way of bliss; or turn them in the direction of the All Highest! O if only they could be the Within; to know the delight of that which proceeds outward.

26/19.4. O if I could make them understand; to look upward instead of downward; to look inward instead of outward. And how You follow up Your wayward children; Your truants that strive to go away from You.

26/19.5. They wander off, and You give the slack of the leading line to them. They go as if around a circle, and come to the place of beginning at last. O if I could prevail upon them at the

[1043] restate, say again, go over, retrace, play back, recite

beginning; if I could save them the first journey of the circle. O if only they would go slowly and with You always, Jehovih!

26/19.6. But You enrich them with Your bounteous fields; they travel far and are footsore and weary; and the two causes are like a new book of songs. O, that experience may never die! And Your creations never cease to have adventurous Sons and Daughters!

26/19.7. O, if only I could understand Your Greatness; or find in the darkness the light that glorifies Your countenance. I drink deep of my own folly, and my eyes wander about because of the darkness. I come upon Your pathway and burst forth with a song of delight. Yes, I rejoice for the darkness I have passed through; because of it I am more buoyant in my love for You, my Creator.

26/19.8. How can I make all Your people sing songs to You; or teach them to never harp on the dark side of things? I have seen the tree of hell they planted in their own souls, and the way they cultivate it. They do not know what is meant by singing praises to You, and of Your growth in them.

26/19.9. Why will they interpret me by words, or not realize that I sing of the exuberance of the soul? O if I could inspire them to talk good of all things; to harp forever on the beauties You have made, instead of the ills and horrors around about. Can they never understand what it is to sow the seed of the tree of endless delight?

26/19.10. O if only I could call them to You, Jehovih! Or that I could lift their aspiration up from the shadows of death. I would follow them into Your two great gardens which You have created; that which is green, where they go and curse You; and that which is ripe, where I have found You full of love. Because I said: Sing to Him forever; pray to Him with great rejoicing, they interpret me to mean words uttered like a parrot. Yes, they grumble forever.

26/19.11. To find You, O Jehovih; to glorify the good that comes along, this is the salvation of the world. Of this, my songs shall never end; without a shadow of darkness You will tune my voice forever. I will sing and dance before You; the germ of happiness in my soul I will nurse as Your holiest gift. For of all the trees that You have planted in the soul of men and angels, this is the most glorious; for it is the perfection of Your Voice, which sings in all Your living creatures. ||

26/19.12. When Ahura ended his song, then Lika spoke, for the Voice of Jehovih was upon him. He said: Many leaders I have created for the earth and her heavens; but not one have I created with power to make a leader of himself. My hand is upon those whom I choose; with wisdom and power I raise them up from the beginning.

26/19.13. To a people on the earth I give a king; to the inhabitants of My heavens I give Lords and Gods.

26/19.14. Because you have tried the fullness of self, and raised up mighty realms in heaven, only to come to nothing before My hand, you are as a new power in these heavens.

26/19.15. As by the name Jehovih, I have maintained the Faithists in earth and heaven, so shall you rule over My enemies, in righteousness, love and good works, by the names Lord and God, which they shall worship until the coming of the next dawn. But I will come in that day and deliver you and them, and there shall be no more Lord or God upon the earth or in its heavens.

26/19.16. Do not grieve that you have had great kingdoms, and been overthrown and cast into torments; for you have been prepared in My works, so that through you I could reach those who are not of the flesh and blood of My Faithists. And to the extent that you have gone to the farthest limit of glory and of the darkness of hell, so will I give to you wisdom, love and power accordingly.

26/19.17. For, to make ready for the Kosmon era, I want not a few, but billions in heaven and earth, to inspire those who live in darkness.

26/19.18. As I delivered you, so shall you deliver them; because they will accurse themselves with war and with standing armies for the sake of earthly glory to their rulers, you shall encompass them, break them up, and deliver them into My kingdoms, which are peace and love.

26/19.19. As you have been delivered out of hell, so shall you deliver the kings and queens of the earth out of their kingdoms in which they will unknowingly bind themselves in condemnation before Me. They shall be made to understand that, whoever assumes a kingdom, shall not rule it to his own glory without reaping the fruits of hell.

26/19.20. When the king goes forth, he shall not be afraid he will be cut down; nor shall his marshals stand around him to protect him, for My Person shall shield him, and his people will shout with great joy when his steps draw near. To serve Me is not in prayer only, or in rites and ceremonies, but in stretching forth the hand to do good to others with all of one's might.

26/19.21. Because you have proved that force and violence only establish for a day, and are not of Me, so shall you make them understand that whoever uses force and violence or armies to sustain himself is not of Me, but is My enemy, and is on the way to destruction.

26/19.22. Whoever is a king, or a general, or a captain, and in war, either offensive or defensive, professing to serve Me by rites and ceremonies and praises, is a mocker of Me and My kingdoms; yes, a blasphemer in My sight; he provides the way of his own torments. These are My creations: to answer force with force, violence with violence, mockery with mockery; as the seed is sown, so shall the harvest come to the sowers.

26/19.23. Nor shall evil, darkness and misery cease on the earth till I have disbanded the dealers in death; by My own hand I will liberate the nations of the earth; their armies shall go away, like the winter's snow in sun of summer. To which end you shall be My workers, with wisdom, love and power.

CHAPTER 20 Lika

26/20.1. During the fourth year of dawn, the Voice of Jehovih came to Lika, saying: My Son, you shall provide yourself a sufficient army, and you shall take away from the earth all angels below the first resurrection, except those fetals who are under the dominion of My heavenly rulers.

26/20.2. And you shall provide them separate regions in My lower heavens, from which they cannot return to mortals. And you shall appoint rulers and teachers over them, to deliver them out of madness, evil and stupor.

26/20.3. You shall appoint teachers and rulers from your etherean hosts for this purpose; but at the end of dawn they shall give their places to atmosphereans selected from Theovrahkistan.

26/20.4. From this time forth My atmosphereans shall begin to help one another, not depending upon having all teachers come from My etherean heavens.

26/20.5. Lika then called up At'yesonitus and told him of Jehovih's words, and further added: I therefore allot this labor to you. And I give you twelve generals, for the different regions of the earth; and to each of the twelve I allot five million ethereans, whom you can draw from the armies that were engaged in delivering the hells and knots.

26/20.6. At'yesonitus said: In Jehovih's will and yours, I am pleased. I will divide up the regions of the earth among the twelve generals, and give to each one of them five million, according to your commandments.

26/20.7. At'yesonitus then sent officers out into different regions in atmospherea to select the sixty million deliverers, commanding them to report to Theovrahkistan, in the Valley of Tish, his heavenly place, where he took the twelve generals Lika had assigned him.

26/20.8. Lika gave At'yesonitus a list of the spirits to be taken away from mortals, that is, the engrafted, the damons, the familiars, the vampires, the lusters, and all other spirits that otherwise lead mortals into darkness and crime; showing him the regions of the earth where they were most numerous. With which list, At'yesonitus and his generals made themselves well acquainted before starting on this perilous enterprise.

26/20.9. At'yesonitus then ordered the shipbuilders to provide him twelve thousand fireboats, with bulwarks of fire, and with gateways.

26/20.10. In the meantime, Lika sent Yussamis with four hundred geographers, mathematicians and surveyors to find the necessary plateau to which At'yesonitus could send his captured hosts.

26/20.11. Yussamis therefore founded the six heavenly plateaus known as the Ugsadisspe, a name signifying the Heaven of the Destroying Serpents.

26/20.12. These, then, were the six heavens of Ugsadisspe, namely: Tewallawalla, over Arabin'ya, one thousand two hundred miles high; Setee'song, over Vind'yu, one thousand miles high; Go'e'dhi, over Jaffeth, one thousand one hundred miles high; Ellapube, over Uropa, one thousand miles high; Apak, over North and South Guatama, six hundred miles high, and bordering on Yaton'te, the subjective heaven of the ancients, which was now being re-established by Kaparos; and Fue, over Chihuahi, nine thousand miles high.

26/20.13. Yussamis provided these heavens with no roadways, in order to prevent the delivered spirits from flocking together, in which case they might run into anarchy (hells). And, accordingly, appointed to each of these heavens one ruler of the rank primal God, selecting them from the etherean hosts, but empowering them to bestow their thrones on successors at the end of dawn, giving them terms of office not less than two hundred years, but subject to the limiting power of God of Theovrahkistan.

26/20.14. Lika gave four thousand messengers to At'yesonitus, and twelve thousand messengers to Yussamis, to whom he also gave sixty million laborers. But each of them provided their own heralds, musicians, marshals and captains in their own way.

26/20.15. Now, therefore, At'yesonitus and Yussamis, receiving their armies of laborers, fell to work, the former to delivering, and the latter to receiving the drujas of the earth. And Yussamis put his hosts to building houses, hospitals and other heavenly places, and to founding cities and provinces through the primal Gods under him.

CHAPTER 21 Lika

26/21.1. Jehovih had said: All angels below the first resurrection, except infants, shall be known in heaven and on earth as drujas, for they are those who do not have capacity in knowledge or strength of individuality. ||

26/21.2. As there are paupers, vagrants, beggars and criminals, on earth, who are druks, so are there spirits in hada who are a great trial to both mortals and angels.

26/21.3. And they inhabit mortals and the houses that mortals dwell in. Some mortals have one or two of them; some a score; and some have hundreds of them. Some of them continue to inhabit mortal dwellings long after mortals have abandoned them, even till they fall in ruins. And whoever comes into such a house, the drujas come upon him to live on him and with him.[1044]

26/21.4. And if a mortal has greater wisdom and strength of soul than the drujas, he rules over them, to a good purpose, reforming them and raising them up out of darkness and helplessness.

26/21.5. But if the drujas have greater power than the mortal, then they pull him down in darkness, making him into a man who lusts after the affairs of earth. Sometimes they help man to riches and great power; and if he has sons and daughters who are brought up in idleness, ease and luxury, then the drujas fasten upon them, leading them in their own way, of lust and debauchery, or hard-heartedness.

26/21.6. The flesh-eater is their delight; and the drunkard their great joy. The man of riches, and kings, generals, fighting men, harlots and soldiers, are great treasures to them. And all manner of intoxicating things, that mortals delight in, are great feasts and rejoicings to them. The priest and the preacher who live in ease and luxury, performing showy rites and entertainments, are great harvests for them to revel with.

26/21.7. Sometimes the drujas rule over their mortal, and his neighbors call him mad, and they send him to a madhouse,[1045] which is to them a city of delight. When mortals engage in war, slaying one another, the drujas have great merriment, taking part, by inspiring the mortals into the conflict.

26/21.8. The pleader (lawyer) is a favorite to them, for his vocation brings them into the center of contention, craft and lying; he is to them a fortunate habitation.

26/21.9. The magician who works miracles and tricks is their favorite, for with him and through him, they can make themselves manifest. And when they show themselves, and are questioned as to who they are, they answer to any name that will please or flatter, even at times pretending to be Gods and Saviors!

26/21.10. The tattling woman who talks about her neighbors is a good home for drujas; and if the woman is given to talk evil, they are rejoiced beyond measure. The man who is a great boaster, and liar, and slanderer, is a choice house for them to dwell in.

26/21.11. The cheater and defrauder, the miser and the spendthrift, the curser of Jehovih, the curser of the Gods, is like a citadel for them to inhabit.

26/21.12. They do not go, for the most part, away from the mortal they inhabit while he lives;

[1044] Here we see that haunted houses, which mortals have stories about, can be worse than mortals imagine.

[1045] mental hospital, insane asylum

no, they lack the wisdom or strength to go more than one length away. Some of them have strength to go to a neighbor or to a neighbor's house. And if a mortal curses his neighbor to die, then those drujas who can go to that neighbor, seek out some poisonous infection and inoculate him to death, which is called casting spells.

26/21.13. No, there is nothing too low or foul for them; and for the most part they are no more than idiots, and deranged imbeciles,[1046] answering to any name or request, like a man who is drunk, one so very drunk that he does not know or care.

26/21.14. A large city full of crime and debauchery, with rich and fashionable people, and people of evil habits, suits them better than a country place.

26/21.15. Drujas dwell as numerously among the rich and fashionable as among the poor; they fill the bawdy-house and the temples of the idolaters; a court of justice full of pleaders (lawyers) and criminals is their delightful resort, but a battle in war is a sweet amusement to them.

26/21.16. A laboring man who is good and honest is of little value to them, unless he is a gross feeder or drinker of intoxicating beverages.

26/21.17. A man who marries a rich, lazy woman, receives with his wife a hundred drujas, or more.

26/21.18. A woman who marries a rich, lazy man, or a gambler, receives with her husband a hundred drujas, or more.

26/21.19. Drujas rule over mortals more than mortals rule over them. It was because of their abundance and their power to do evil, that Jehovih commanded His chosen to marry among themselves; and to withdraw from other peoples, and make themselves a separate and exclusive people, so that they would not be inhabited with drujas.

26/21.20. When a mortal dies, and he had dominion over his drujas, not only will his spirit rise to the first resurrection, but his drujas also, as a result of which they are all delivered into light.

[1046] In 1882 when Oahspe was published these were descriptive terms, not meant derogatorily; their literal meanings were intended and the readers of the time took them as such. Idiots are the lowest mental grade, and imbeciles the next higher of the lowest.

26/21.21. When a mortal dies, and his drujas had dominion over him, then his spirit becomes a druj also, and he becomes one with them, fastening on whoever comes along; but if it is in a house and no mortal comes, upon whom they can fasten, then they remain in that house. And here they may remain a year or ten years or a hundred years, in darkness, knowing nothing, doing nothing, until other angels come and deliver them, which is often no easy matter, requiring bodily force to carry them away.

26/21.22. Jehovih gave certain signs to both angels and mortals, by which it shall be known both on earth and in heaven, who is master over the other, a mortal or his drujas, and, consequently, such matter determines to what place the spirit of a man will most readily fall after death:

26/21.23. If the mortal cannot control his habit for intoxication, or gluttony, or avarice, or debauchery, or laziness, or lying, or hypocrisy, preaching what he does not practice, or sexual indulgence, or vengeance, or anger, or tattling mischievously, then he is, indeed, a victim in the hands of drujas, and at the time of his death he becomes one with them.

26/21.24. For if he does not have power to rule in such matters while he is in the mortal world, he will be no stronger by the loss of his corporeal body.

26/21.25. If the mortal, on the other hand, shall have risen to control himself over these habits and desires, then he will be indeed, at the time of death, already entered into the first resurrection; and the drujas, if he has any, will be delivered also.

26/21.26. And whether they are mortals or drujas, neither their words and professions,[1047] nor their prayers nor religious rites and ceremonies, are of any value to them; but by the works and behavior of mortals all things are known and proven.

26/21.27. So that Jehovih's high-raised Gods only need to pass once over a corporeal city, to determine whether it is in resurrection or declension. And such Gods put their angel laborers to work, sorting the afflicted as a mortal would his cattle.

[1047] declarations, proclamations, pretences, claims, affirmations

26/21.28. And if a city is badly cast in drujas, dragging mortals down to destruction spiritually; then the angels inspire those mortals who are on the path of resurrection to move out of the city, and after that they cast the city in fire and burn it down.

26/21.29. And while it is burning, and the drujas distracted with the show, angels of power come upon them and carry them off, hundreds of millions of them. And the mortals are thus cleared of those who would have bound them in darkness after death.

26/21.30. In this matter the infidel curses Jehovih because the houses are burned, for he judges matters by the things his soul was set upon. He says: What a foolish God! How wicked, to burn a city.

26/21.31. For he does not understand that all things are Jehovih's; and that His Gods under Him do not work for man's earthly aggrandizement, which is the curse of his spirit, but they work for his spiritual resurrection in their own way, according to the Father's light in them.

26/21.32. To accomplish the resurrection of the drujas dwelling with mortals on the earth, Lika, Son of Jehovih, had appointed At'yesonitus, with his twelve generals, very Gods in wisdom and power, each one to a certain division of the earth.

CHAPTER 22 Lika

26/22.1. Jehovih spoke to Lika, saying: These are My ways; reveal Me to them. Those who do not know Me, shall be made to know Me; My labors shall rise up before them, and their understanding shall be opened.

26/22.2. They shall know what I mean when I say I will destroy or I will build up. I have heard man in his vanity, judging Me. His eyes are on the earth only; and delighting in houses and riches. Because I take them away from him, he complains against Me.

26/22.3. I gave man an example in his own child who delights in sweets, idleness and vain pleasures. Man takes these from his child, saying: Behold, they are not good for you, except in great temperance![1048]

26/22.4. In what way have I injured you, O man? Where have I destroyed anything that contributed to your spirit? Where have I allowed destruction to come upon you, while you followed My commandments? Why shall you complain because I laid great cities in ashes? Did you see the millions of drujas you were holding down in darkness by your evil habits?

26/22.5. I am not in anger, neither do I pull down nor burn up any place in a passion. As you go forth to destroy a row of houses to stop a great conflagration (fire), shall the people murmur against you for such an act? For your hand is stretched forth to do a good work for the whole city.

26/22.6. My heavens are magnified cities, and when a mortal wing offends, behold, I clip it short. They are all Mine; and with My own, no one can question My authority, which I wield for the resurrection of the whole.

26/22.7. You have wept because of the destruction of the books of great learning of the ancients; but you do not know your own words. Did I not see, O man, that you would never wean yourself from the doctrines of the dark ages if the books of great learning were not destroyed!

26/22.8. In all ages of the world you have been bound to the ancients; you are forever searching backward for wisdom; and attentive to the angels of the dead who pretend to be ancients. I behold the latter, and that they are drujas.

26/22.9. I send wise angels down to them to deliver them out of darkness. And they come and bear the drujas away from you, for your own good and theirs. My wise angels allow mortals to burn up the books of the ancients; for I command them to make you open your understanding to the living present.

26/22.10. Jehovih spoke to At'yesonitus, and through him to the twelve Gods of deliverance, saying:

26/22.11. Go forth, My son, in wisdom and power. Your labor requires great strength and stratagems. For you shall find the drujas bound firmly to mortals and to mortal habitations (houses). As a drowning man clings to a log, so cling the drujas to mortals. As a delirious man, mad with drunkenness, in fear flies from his best friends, so will the drujas fly from you and your hosts who shall attempt to deliver them.

26/22.12. They will inspire their mortals to dread an innovation of the ancient doctrines. Yes,

[1048] moderation, self-restraint, sparingly

both of them, not knowing it, will bind themselves together with great tenacity.

26/22.13. But you shall deliver them apart nonetheless; by stratagem, or persuasion, or with a strong hand. And when you have them separated, you shall surround the drujas with flames of fire, and carry them off to the boats, which are bulwarked with fire. And you shall deliver them in the places My Son, Yussamis, has already prepared for them.

26/22.14. You shall not only deliver the drujas, but cause mortals to hate them.

26/22.15. Mortal kings shall issue edicts against magicians, prophets, seers, and priests; and the consultation of spirits shall come to an end. And man on the earth shall turn to his own soul, which is My light within him, and he shall cultivate it and learn to think for himself. ||

26/22.16. At'yesonitus prepared a record to give to mortals; and so, by inspiration it was given. And the nature of the record was to teach mortals to be guarded against drujas, and know who was afflicted with them.

26/22.17. This, then, that follows is the record, even as it stands to this day in the libraries of heaven, namely:

26/22.18. The man who says: I pity my neighbors, they are surrounded with drujas!

26/22.19. The man who says: Only fools believe in obsession!

26/22.20. The man who says: There is no All Person!

26/22.21. The man who says: My way is wisdom; yours is wicked!

26/22.22. The man who says: Let no one dictate to me! I will have nothing but liberty to the uttermost!

26/22.23. The man who says: As the priest thinks, so do I!

26/22.24. The man who says: If only you had my knowledge!

26/22.25. The man who says: The ancients were wiser than we!

26/22.26. The man who says: The ancients were fools!

26/22.27. The man who says: Whoever does not see as I do is a heathen!

26/22.28. The man who says: Whoever does not worship my God is wicked!

26/22.29. The man who says: Wisdom is book-learning!

26/22.30. The man who says: There is no wisdom in books!

26/22.31. The man who says: My book is sacred; it contains the sum of all revelation and inspiration!

26/22.32. The man who says: There is neither inspiration nor words of inspiration!

26/22.33. The followers of the ancients only.

26/22.34. He who will have nothing to do with the ancients.

26/22.35. He who ignores rites and ceremonies and prayers.

26/22.36. He who depends on rites and ceremonies and prayers.

26/22.37. Whoever denies the Ever Present Person.

26/22.38. Whoever follows the counsel of angels or men.

26/22.39. Whoever will not learn from the counsel of men and angels.

26/22.40. Whoever feels prayers and confessions to be good for others, but not necessary for himself.

26/22.41. Or says: I will lead and supervise; you be my servant!

26/22.42. Or says: Behold my rights!

26/22.43. Or: Behold my earnings!

26/22.44. Or: Behold my possessions!

26/22.45. Or talks about himself and his experiences.

26/22.46. Or tattles on others.

26/22.47. Or judges his brother, or criticizes him.

26/22.48. The self-righteous, who says: Behold me, I am holy!

26/22.49. Or who does not desire new light, or says: The old is good enough!

26/22.50. Whoever labors for himself only.

26/22.51. Whoever does not labor for others in his wisdom and strength.[1049]

26/22.52. Who seeks his own ease.

26/22.53. Who does not consider others' welfare more than his own.

26/22.54. The hypocrite preaching one way and practicing another.

[1049] i.e., wholeheartedly; not token (merely symbolic) or empty gestures, nor as a ruse or feint

26/22.55. Who does not openly speak his doctrines, lest his words jeopardize[1050] profit for his earthly means and associations.

26/22.56. At'yesonitus said: For these are all as much under the bondage of drujas as is the drunkard, harlot or murderer. And after death their spirits float into the same hada of darkness.

CHAPTER 23 Lika

26/23.1. When At'yesonitus' generals and their hosts went through Vind'yu, Jaffeth and Arabin'ya, they concerted with the Gods who had in their charge the inspiration of Capilya, Moses and Chine. And not only did the angel generals remove the drujas from mortals, but inspired mortal kings and queens in those great divisions of the earth to issue edicts against magicians and priests who consulted with spirits.

26/23.2. Jehovih had said: It shall be a testimony in the latter days (kosmon) to the inhabitants of the earth of My proceedings; not with one division of the earth only, but with all places. For they shall in after years search history and find that in the same era in these three great divisions of the earth the kings and queens issued edicts against spirit communion. And this fact shall be testimony of My cycle of Bon; in which man shall understand that I come not in one corner of the earth only, and to one people only; but that I have them all in My charge, as a Father who knows His own children.

26/23.3. Nor did I give them the same aspirations; for one I send westward to circumscribe the earth; one I build up with a multitude of languages, and a multitude of Gods; and the third one I build up without any God except Myself. And they shall understand that where there are many languages there are many Gods worshipped; where there is one language, there is only One worshipped, even I, the Great Spirit.

26/23.4. For in kosmon I will bring them together; and these diversities shall be a key to unlock the doctrines and languages of times and seasons long past.

26/23.5. Man living away from other men becomes conceited in himself, deploring the darkness of others, and great nations likewise become conceited of themselves and their doctrines.

26/23.6. Each one of the great peoples saying: Behold those barbarians! I was the chosen of His special care. Those others are only heathens, and have not been worthy of the Great Spirit's concern.

26/23.7. But in this day I plant the seed of My testimony, which shall come up and blossom, and bear fruit in three thousand years. ||

26/23.8. At'yesonitus and his generals, with their millions of angel hosts, cleared off the drujas of the earth, the angels of darkness. They extended east and west and north and south, around all the earth, in all its divisions, into every nook and corner.

26/23.9. Day and night At'yesonitus and his armies labored, neither ceasing nor resting, but in good method went right on, filling all the lowest place of heaven with their transport boats of fire.

26/23.10. And the boats sped here and there without ceasing, loaded in their ascent with the screaming, frightened drujas, all under guard, and duly preserved against accident or harm by the wise angels over them.

26/23.11. Some drujas were easily captured and carried away; others were weak, helpless and harmless; but hundreds of millions of them were mad, and most desperate; and yet others were evil, fearful in their desperate oaths, and in foul talk; and dangerous.

26/23.12. But others were most pitiful in their love to linger with their mortal kindred; mothers, whose children dwelt on the earth; and children spirits, whose mothers dwelt on the earth. To separate them and carry away such drujas was a most heart-rending task, requiring Godlike souls to accomplish it.

26/23.13. Jehovih had said: As a mortal mother will cling to the mortal body of her dead child, till her friends must tear them apart, while all souls who look on are brokenhearted because of her love, even such is the bond between the spirit of the dead and the mortal left behind.

26/23.14. But when My wise angels look upon them, and perceive they are carrying each other down in darkness, then they shall be torn asunder; and the spirit shall be taken away and provided for ultimate resurrection, and only permitted to visit the mortal kin under due guardianship. ||

[1050] put at risk, endanger, imperil, injure, harm, hurt

26/23.15. On the battlefields of the earth were hundreds of millions of spirits in chaos, still fighting imaginary battles, not knowing their bodies were dead; knowing nothing but to curse and fight; roving over the battlefields; and they would not leave, except by capture and being carried off.

26/23.16. Thus did At'yesonitus and his mighty hosts clear the earth. But of their great labors and wonderful adventures a thousand books could be written, and thousands of heroes singled out, whose great achievements overwhelm one's belief because of the manifested love and power.

26/23.17. And yet not much less were the labors and adventures of Yussamis in Ugsadisspe and her six heavenly places, where his etherean hosts labored unceasingly, preparing places, keepers, nurses, physicians, and teachers, for the delivered drujas, the billions.

26/23.18. Jehovih said to Yussamis: You shall sort the drujas; the peaceful to themselves; the dumb to themselves; and then the mad, the chaotic, and all other of My afflicted ones; providing sections and places for them. And provide them teachers, nurses and physicians; for they shall be delivered out of darkness also. Yes, every one of them shall become as a star of glory in heaven.

26/23.19. And Yussamis and his Gods developed the six heavens of Ugsadisspe; established places for the tens of billions of drujas; and provided order and discipline, and altars of worship, schools, colleges, factories, and all things required in a primary heaven.

CHAPTER 24 Lika

26/24.1. Jehovih spoke to Lika, saying: Behold, the end of dawn draws near; go once more around the earth and her heavens, and examine into the labor of your Gods. And you shall take with you your Rapon hosts, and a sufficient number of heralds and attendants, and such musicians and messengers as you desire.

26/24.2. And when you have come to Yaton'te, My subjective heaven, you shall stay a while with Kaparos, and re-establish it in greater holiness and efficiency. For this is My only subjective heaven in the regions of the red star.

26/24.3. Behold, the spirits of those who die in infancy call out to Me, saying: Tell us, O Creator, how is it with the earth? How is it with mortals who dwell on the earth? What do they toil at? Do they have schools, hospitals and factories, like ours? Do mortals have mishaps and trials? And do they have roadways, and oceans of water on the hard earth?

26/24.4. How can these things be, O Jehovih? Why is it that mortals cannot go down into the earth and to the bottoms of their oceans, even as we do in the heavens?

26/24.5. How did You create us alive in the earth? What was the place like? Why do mortals carry around with them such earth-houses (bodies)? Can they not go in them and out of them at pleasure?

26/24.6. What do mortals mean, O Jehovih, by mortal life and mortal death? Does the clay and stone and water they dwell in (the earth body) have life and death? What do they mean by: This is mine and that is yours?

26/24.7. Shall everyone retain his own body? How do the earth bodies grow? Do they eat clay and stone? And water? Where do they get their blood? And do they eat hair, so that they may have earth hair?

26/24.8. Why is it that they do not bring up their bodies with them when they are dead? Do they wear clothes over the spirit body only, or over the earth body also?

26/24.9. Great are Your works, O Jehovih! Take me to Yaton'te, Your great subjective heaven. We would learn by figures in pantomime the illustrations of the earth. We would learn by Your panoramic heaven what mortals do. How they live and what their schools are like. How they have contrived to teach the corporeal senses by corporeal things. How their boats are made and propelled; how their vehicles travel along upon the solid earth. ||

26/24.10. Jehovih said: For which reason, O Lika, you shall see to it that Yaton'te is perfected to this instruction, as well as to arouse from stupor, the spirits of the dead who do not desire to rise up from the earth.

26/24.11. Lika told the Rapon hosts Jehovih's words; and he also gave command to his chief marshal to provide the necessary otevan with officers, heralds, musicians and messengers.

26/24.12. Accordingly, as soon as all things were ready, Lika committed the throne of Jehovih, in Theovrahkistan, to his vice-Goddess, and Lika and the Rapons, with their attendant hosts, departed on their journey.

26/24.13. Now since Lika first came to the plateau of Theovrahkistan, it had become inhabited by billions of angels, and they were high in the grades.

26/24.14. So much so, that the officers of selection were already preparing them by the millions for Brides and Bridegrooms to Jehovih. And there were thousands of heavenly cities besides Yogannaqactra, which were now in beauty, gaiety, refinement and delight, with music, and most magnificent rites and ceremonies.

26/24.15. Then there were officers over these officers, whose place it was to sort and arrange the inhabitants of cities; and others over these for each one hundred and forty-four cities; and yet another over these officers, and he was called MARSHAL OF THEOVRAHKISTAN. And he was of the same rank as the marshals of the hosts of Lika, conferring with the MARSHAL IN CHIEF OF JEHOVIH'S THRONE.

CHAPTER 25 Lika

26/25.1. Jehovih said to Lika: Finish your visit and your inspection, My Son, in all the places of hada on the earth, leaving the land of Jaffeth to the last. And you shall go there, at the time of Chine's resurrection, and descend with your ship and take him up from the earth.

26/25.2. And you shall bring him with you to Yogannaqactra, where he shall remain the few days that dawn remains; and when your hosts ascend to etherea you shall take Chine with you and make your home his home until such time as he is taught the ways and powers of the higher heavens.

26/25.3. For, since his corporeal life is a sacrifice for the resurrection of men, he shall receive special care and assistance in heaven. ||

26/25.4. Lika had been previously informed by the God of Chine as to the time Chine would die, and be burnt up, with his ashes scattered to the four winds; and the re-gathering up of a corporeal form of Chine; and the seven days' duration prior to being taken up into the otevan. So Lika shaped the course of his otevan, according to the instruction of his messengers, who had been appointed for that purpose, so that he would reach the field in time to raise up Chine before the multitude.

26/25.5. The God of Chine had prophesied to mortals, through his ward, that a fire-ship would descend from heaven on a given day, and take Chine up to heaven.

26/25.6. Accordingly, a great multitude of mortals were assembled in the ash-field, where they cast the ashes of the dead, watching for the heavenly ship.

26/25.7. Of which matters, Lika had been previously informed by his messengers; and Lika had in turn informed the God of Chine as to the time he would appear with the ship, so that he (God) could cause Chine to walk in the middle of the field and so, be caught up.

26/25.8. And in the hands of these great Gods, all these matters were carried out to the hour and minute. And Lika caused the fire of the ship to be made visible to mortals. And the size of the ship was ten times larger than the field of the dead, so that when the people saw the light of the ship they feared and trembled, and many of them fell down bewailing that the world was coming to an end.

26/25.9. So God caused Chine to walk out in the field, and Lika sent down a whirlwind and took him up into the ship, in the presence of tens of thousands of mortals assembled.

26/25.10. And now Lika bore his course for Yogannaqactra, for the end of the dawn of Bon was at hand.

CHAPTER 26 Lika

26/26.1. Lika sent messengers to all his Gods and Lords, to install their successors, and to bestow them; after which, the Gods and Lords were to report in Theovrahkistan ready for the cyclic resurrection. And he commanded them to bring their etherean hosts with them, except those who volunteered to remain the next dan of two hundred years.

26/26.2. Lika had previously sent word to etherea by his swift messengers, to Lissa, Goddess of Teannakak, in etherea, next to Howgil. And he said to Lissa: My resurrection will be eight links, each one equal to eight billion Brides and Bridegrooms. Send a cowppon to deliver them.

26/26.3. Lissa sent word back to Lika, saying: O Jehovih, I am delighted with the command of Your Son, Lika, Chief of Vetta'puissa! I will deliver the chain of cowppon.

26/26.4. Then Lissa gave her commands in Teannakak, to have her builders construct the cowppon; and she also set her officers to work selecting the hosts she would need for her great undertaking. For she had been notified in sufficient time, as it was a matter of great magnitude even in etherean realms.

26/26.5. And so perfectly were Lissa's commands carried out, that all was ready not one day too much or too little wide of the mark. And then she embarked with her hosts for the red star, the earth, with her billion trained resurrectionists; on her long journey, twenty billion miles!

26/26.6. Jehovih had said: Carry far My Brides and Bridegrooms; make them know the magnificence of the heavens I have created. House them not together in a small corner. Let them feast their souls on the splendors of My great heavens!

26/26.7. Meanwhile Lika and his hosts in Theovrahkistan were getting ready for the ceremonies and for the ascension.

26/26.8. The Gods, with their hosts, were now coming in from every quarter of the lower heavens, bringing in their harvests and quartering[1051] them in the places allotted by the marshals.

26/26.9. Most conspicuous and beloved of all was Ahura. Next to him were the five true Gods: Inane, Injek, Inlay, Inoal and Inyith, with their heavenly hosts restored to them; for it was through these five Gods that the three mortals, Capilya, Moses and Chine, had delivered the Faithists of Vind'yu, Jaffeth and Arabin'ya. These five Gods had in five years changed the mortal dominions and laws of Vind'yu and Jaffeth, and sent four million Faithists on a westward journey across the earth; and, along with the Lord God Gitchee of Guatama, had firmly established the All One [the Everpresent Great Spirit] in the four great divisions of the earth, and had delivered from bondage all the Faithists on the face of the earth.

26/26.10. Great also was the work accomplished by At'yesonitus, and by Yussamis; and by the Gods who had delivered the hells and the knots; and by many others. So good and great were the works of them all, that a history of any one of them in the five years' labor, would make a book that a man could not read in a lifetime.

[1051] lodging them; providing temporary living quarters

26/26.11. And they had left successors to carry out what they had founded; so that all the lower heavens were in order, system and discipline, the like of which had not been for two thousand years.

26/26.12. The drujas of the earth were removed away from mortals; the battlefields of the earth were cleared of the chaotic spirits slain in wars.

26/26.13. Thus the whole earth and her heavens were delivered into a new condition, in the way and form of Jehovih's light.

26/26.14. And this was the Arc of Deliverance in Bon.[1052]

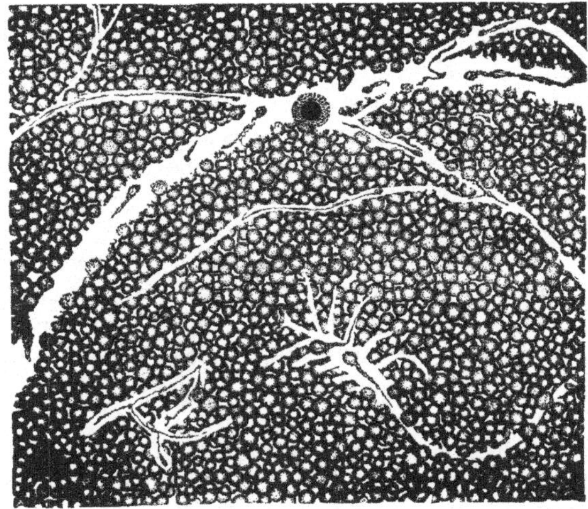

i078 **The Earth in the Arc of Bon**. Showing the arc through which the earth traveled in the cycle of Moses, Capilya and Chine. And Jehovih made a sign of the triumph of light to endure four hundred years. Jehovih said: Let the period of four hundred years be a sign to those who come after. || And it was so. For at the termination of that time, both Israelites and Brahmans abandoned the higher law and established kings and rulers among themselves. And this is also one of the numbers of the prophets to this day.

26/26.15. Then descended Lissa with her chain of cowppon; with her ships of fire stretched wide as the earth. And the hosts of Theovrahkistan, the Brides and Bridegrooms, sixty-four billion Sons and Daughters of Jehovih, stood, waiting, watching, nervous, but filled with inexpressible delight.

[1052] see image i078

26/26.16. And they saw the cowppon coming; knew the mission of the mighty Goddess, Lissa, Daughter of Jehovih!

26/26.17. Arrayed in spotless white, the sixty-four billion stood; shuddered at the etheric current, the whirlwind of the higher heavens; stood pure, the exalted affianced[1053] of Great Jehovih!

26/26.18. Nearer and nearer came the mighty sea of etherean fire; and nearer, till it landed at the plateau of Theovrahkistan.

26/26.19. Then Lissa came forth, saluting; and, being answered by great Lika, Jehovih's Son, proceeded before Jehovih's throne.

26/26.20. Then Lissa demanded in the usual form, why she had been summoned in Jehovih's name. Lika also answered in the usual form: To bestow Jehovih's affianced Sons and Daughters.

26/26.21. After this, each of the five Gods of the earth took their hosts and bequeathed them to Jehovih, through Lissa, His Daughter.

26/26.22. But so great and grand were the ceremonies that mortal words cannot describe them. And as for the awe and magnificence, together with the music, could they be described to mortals, understandingly, they scarcely could live, because of the enchantment.

26/26.23. But there is a time, and a limit, and an end to all such matters; and so there was to the labor of Lika, Son of Jehovih. The hosts were wed, and they marched aboard the great etherean ships, the cowppon. Lika and his hosts went into his own airavagna. And, as it were, with a thread of light he made fast to the cowppon, and gave the word, the command to go.

26/26.24. Then up rose the mighty seas of fire, the eight-linked cowppon and the airavagna! Slowly, steadily moving onward, upward, higher and higher, faster and faster, and still higher. And thus departed Lika with his billions of upraised Sons and Daughters of Jehovih. And thus ended the dawn of Bon.

END OF BOOK OF LIKA, SON OF JEHOVIH

[1053] betrothed, engaged to be wed

Book of the Arc of Bon

Being a history of Capilya, Moses and Chine, the three great leaders-forth of the Faithists in the time of Lika, Son of Jehovih. As Lika's book is of the heavens, so is this book chiefly of earthly affairs in the administration of God.

CHAPTER 1 Arc Bon

History of Capilya

27/1.1. In the mountains of Dharma, in the high country of Yatinghadatta, in Vind'yu, God, Son of Jehovih, chose the family of Capilya for gathering together the scattered Faithists, and establishing them in safety and prosperity.

27/1.2. Six generations previous to the time of Capilya, God came down from his holy hill in heaven to visit the land of Shem, now called Vind'yu.

27/1.3. And God called aloud over all that land, but no man could hear his voice.

27/1.4. Then God called his angels, saying: Come here. Behold, here is a great country, with millions of people, but they cannot hear the voice of God.

27/1.5. God commanded the angels to go down among mortals, and to dwell with them for six generations.

27/1.6. To the angels God said: By inspiration and otherwise, lead man and woman together as husband and wife, to the profit of the voice of God. Raise me up a man who can hear me, for I will deliver the Father's chosen.

27/1.7. The angels of God, half a million of them, then came down to the earth. The angel, Hirattax, was commander over them. He divided his angel hosts into groups, and allotted them certain places in the land of Vind'yu, where they were to dwell and to labor.

27/1.8. In those days the Faithists were known by the names Vede, Par'si'e, Hiyah, and Syiattahoma, beside various other names of less note.

27/1.9. In some places they were slaves; in other places serfs; and in still other places, hidden away in wildernesses and among the mountains; being nonresistant and timorous, having suffered great persecution by the idolaters of Dyaus and other false Gods and Lords.

CHAPTER 2 Arc Bon

27/2.1. These are the generations of the scattered tribes, contributory to the bringing forth of Capilya:

27/2.2. In Brahma, begotten of the Lord, Hathiv, who begot Runoad, who begot Yaid, who begot Ovarana, who begot Chesam, who begot Hottaya, who begot Riviat, who begot Dhor, who begot Avra, who begot Lutha, who begot Jaim, who begot Yanhad, who begot Vravishaah, who begot Hoamya, who begot Wothcha, who begot Saratta, who begot Hriviista, who begot Samatrav, who begot Gatonat, who begot Thurin, who begot Vrissagga, who begot Hesemwotchi, who begot Ratha, who begot Yoshorvat, who begot Capilya.

27/2.3. Know, then, the way of God through his holy angels, and profit in the light of his revelations.

27/2.4. Capilya was a natural born iesu; and also a natural born su'is and sar'gis.

27/2.5. God said: Behold, man shall not only learn to bring forth seedless fruits in his garden, but also learn that all flesh tends in the same direction, toward barrenness.

27/2.6. And as man draws nearer and nearer toward the light of Jehovih, so does his race become less prolific. And when man attains to be one with the All Light, behold he is iesu also.

27/2.7 God said: By diet and by fasting, iesu can be attained, even by many who do not have it. But the natural born iesu stands more to the way of Jehovih.

27/2.8. When Capilya was born, a light in the form of a crescent appeared above his head, and the voice of God spoke out of its light, saying: This is my son. By him I will overthrow the governments of the tyrants who have persecuted my people.

27/2.9. When Capilya's mother was pregnant, the angels of Jehovih, under the archangel Hirattax, stood guard over her, thinking holy thoughts night and day, by which the mother's soul ran constantly to heavenly things.

27/2.10. And when Capilya was born, behold, Hirattax appointed a host of one hundred and forty-four angels to be with the child day and night. Into four watches of six hours each, he divided the guardian angels.

27/2.11. So the angels of God taught Capilya from the time of his birth, and he became wise above all other children.

27/2.12. || But, of the way in which God rules over nations for the glory of the Creator, consider the history of this deliverance. ||

27/2.13. Jehovih had allowed the power of the kings of Vind'yu to become centered chiefly in Yokovrana, king of Hafghanistun, of the capital, Oblowski, a great city dedicated to Dyaus. Yokovrana held forty provinces and four hundred cities tributary to himself, and every city furnished one governor, and these were the Royal Council of king Yokovrana.

27/2.14. By the laws of Hafghanistun, the oldest male heir succeeded to the throne; but in case the king had no male heir, then the king's oldest brother's male heir succeeded to the throne. Therefore, every king desired a son, but Yokovrana was frustrated by the plans of the loo'is, the angels of Jehovih.

27/2.15. For Hirattax, chief loo'is, had said: I will not only raise up an heir to You, Jehovih; but I will have dominion over Your enemies, to Your own glory. For by inspiration, I will lead the king of kings to marry with a barren woman; and because he shall have no heirs, he shall become a tool in my hands for the deliverance of the Faithists, who are persecuted and outlawed.

27/2.16. And in those days, whoever was of the seed of the worshippers of the Great Spirit, Ormazd, was outlawed from receiving instruction. So that the chosen, the Faithists, were held in ignorance, lest a man of learning might rise up among them and deliver them. And the angel of Jehovih foresaw that Capilya should be a learned man, and acquainted with the cities and the Royal Council. For which matter the angel, Hirattax, provided the chief king, Yokovrana, to be childless, and to desire an heir as successor to the throne.

27/2.17. When the king consulted the oracle, behold, the angels of Jehovih had possession, and they answered the king, saying: Put your wife away in a dark chamber for nine months, and she will deliver into your hand a male child, who shall save the crown from your brother's child.

27/2.18. The king told the queen, who was near the time of limit for women (menopause), and she would not believe. Nevertheless, she also went to consult the oracle, and to her the angel of Jehovih said: Have not kings killed their wives in order to obtain one who shall birth an heir to the throne?

27/2.19. The queen acknowledged this, adding: What, then, shall I do, for in truth I know I shall bear no child.

27/2.20. The angel said: Do as the king has said, and the angels will bring a male child to you in your dark chamber; and your maids and your servants shall see to it that no other woman enters into your place; and they will testify that the child is your own. Neither shall you, under penalty of death, inform the king otherwise.

27/2.21. On the other hand, the angels of Jehovih foretold the father and mother of Capilya, even before his birth, that the child would be carried away and given to the king, Yokovrana, known for his cruelty and the most hated of men. And the angels said, moreover: Neither shall you grieve the loss of the child, for Ormazd will make him a deliverer of his people. And it shall come to pass that on the day the child is delivered to the queen, its own mother shall become its nurse.

27/2.22. Thus it came to pass; and, at the time of the birth of Capilya, the angels carried him into the city of Oblowski, into the king's palace, and to the queen's arms, in the dark chamber. And in that same instant of time, the angels illumined the chamber, so that all the maids and servants saw the child and the light, and they were frightened, and fell down, beseeching Dyaus for protection.

CHAPTER 3 Arc Bon

27/3.1. When Yokovrana went to the temple to do sacrifice, the high priest implored him to consult the oracle in reference to the child, and for his kingdom's sake. And so he consulted the oracle, and the angels of Ormazd said to him: O king, before whom all people fear, hear the angels of heaven and be wise, for your kingdom's sake, and for Capilya. Behold, you have maintained the custom of your forefathers, and caused to be slain on the altar of your God, Dyaus, twelve young men and twelve virgins for every day of the twelfth new moon, so that by blood your God would triumph on the earth, and that you would be the most feared of kings. And you have subdued all the regions of the rich earth to honor you and your laws.

27/3.2. Therefore, the God of heaven says you shall no longer pursue the sacrifice of human blood, but instead you shall make the blood of the lamb sacred, and the sacrificial lamb shall be called the Lamb of your God. And on the day of your first sacrifice, you shall bring Capilya to the altar, and sprinkle upon his head, as a blood offering to your God, the blood of the lamb you have slain. And he shall be called CAPILYA, THE LAMB OF HEAVEN.

27/3.3. To this the king assented, and Capilya was accordingly sprinkled with the blood of a lamb, which was sacrificed in the altar of the king. Thus ended the first of the evil edicts of the evil Gods of Vind'yu; and from that time, mortals were no longer sacrificed to the Gods by consent of the kings.

27/3.4. Capilya was called Yokovrana's son; and he was taught all things that were lawful in those days to teach a prince; and because he was prepared for the throne, he was made acquainted with the kings and governors of all the tributary cities and countries in the land of Vind'yu.

27/3.5. || Of the matters concerning Capilya revealed in this history, know that in all things he was directed by the angels of Jehovih (Ormazd).[1054] ||

27/3.6. When Capilya had attained maturity, he asked the king for leave to travel, saying to the king: Is the greatest wisdom not that which comes by the eye and the ear? And is it not wise that he who may some day become king should acquaint himself with his kingdom while he is yet young? For then, he will not only see and hear better than if he were old, but he will have time to weigh the nature of the government, as to its best adaptation to the people.

27/3.7. To this the king replied: You are already wise, my son; you know enough about the earth and her people according to the laws of the ancients. Therefore to travel for wisdom's sake would be great folly. Your eyes and ears are too sharp already; it is better for you that you do not see the people of your kingdom. For the time may come when you shall need to use great severity

---

[1054] see image i114

upon them; therefore, if they remain strangers to you, your sympathy will not lead you away from justice.

i114 **Capilya**, of India, an i-e-su, living three thousand four hundred years before kosmon in the cycle of Lika.

27/3.8. Capilya said: You reason well, O king; and because you are wise, I have no credit in being wise also. For it must be true that a son has his wisdom from his father. And since you have so wisely put me off with your arguments, answer me this: Is it not profitable to a young prince, before he has the cares of a mighty kingdom, to go abroad and enjoy the pleasure of the world?

27/3.9. The king said: There are only three pleasures in all the world: eating and drinking is one; sleeping is another; the presence of women is the third. Why, then, shall a man go abroad?

27/3.10. Capilya said: And yet you hide the true reason as to why you desire your son not to travel.

27/3.11. The king said: If you tell me the true cause, then you shall go wherever you desire.

27/3.12. Capilya said: First, then, I will say to you that I rejoiced because you did deny me; for I so loved you, O king, that I knew no joy but to remain with you. And, moreover, you so love your son, you would not have him go far from you?

27/3.13. The king was so delighted with this answer, he said: In truth, O prince, you have guessed rightly. And if you find it in your heart to leave me for a season of travel, then I will indeed bear with your loss until you return.

27/3.14. Capilya traveled for nine years, and he went to the uttermost extent of the land of Vind'yu, east and west, and north and south. And because his nurse, who was in fact his real mother, had told him thousands of tales about the persecution of the Faithists, and their sufferings, he sought to obtain information about these scattered people, but as yet he did not know he was of that race.

27/3.15. At the end of nine years Capilya returned to Yatinghadatta, rich in knowledge about the inhabitants of Vind'yu. And when he came before the king, Yokovrana, where he was received in great honor, he related the knowledge he had obtained concerning the country, its extent and grandeur, and its hundreds of great cities and innumerable people. To all of this wisdom the king lent a willing ear; and he declared Capilya was the wisest and most learned man in all the world.

27/3.16. And now the time had come when God, Son of Jehovih, came to establish Jehovih, and begin the deliverance of the Faithists, and to collect them together in the places designed for them.

CHAPTER 4 Arc Bon

27/4.1. The word of Jehovih (Ormazd) came to Capilya, saying: Son of heaven, hear the Voice of the Ever Present! Capilya asked: What do You mean, the Ever Present?

27/4.2. Jehovih (Ormazd) said: Behold Me; I am not of the king's laws; I am the Maker of kings. They have made a law against Me, the Ever Present. They have scattered My people. They have denied My people the right to obtain knowledge.

27/4.3. Capilya said: My eyes and ears have proved these things. What shall Your servant do?

27/4.4. Jehovih said: You shall deliver the slaves to freedom, and provide them places to dwell together, according to the laws of the ancients.

27/4.5. Capilya said: O Ormazd (Jehovih), why have You put this upon me, Your servant? Why did You not place this matter into the hands of the Vrix? [Faithists –Ed.]

27/4.6. Jehovih said: You are yourself of the race of Faithists [Vrix'Vede –Ed.], and have been prepared for this labor from the time of your birth. Go and find your nurse who cared for you in infancy, and when you have her alone, say to her: Nurse, the voice of heaven has come to me, saying "Capilya, you are of the race of Faithists," what do you say? And the nurse will say to you: My son! My son! Alas me! Do you think I would be the cause of your death, or your mother's death? For is that not the law?

27/4.7. Capilya went and inquired of the nurse, and she said to him: My son, my son. Alas me! Do you think I would be the cause of your death, or your mother's death? For is that not the law? Capilya answered: That is the law. But tell me the truth, and I swear to you, both under the name of Dyaus and under the name of your God, Jehovih (Ormazd), that your words shall be secret with me, as the God's will. Am I an adopted Vrix?

27/4.8. The nurse said: Behold, you have loved me all your days; from my own breasts you were fed. Shall I then lose your love, and so, die of a broken heart?

27/4.9. Then Capilya made an oath before the Gods, and after that she answered him, saying: I am your mother, O prince! The angels of the Ever Present came to me in the moment you were born, and carried you into the queen's arms; and the king did not know, even to this day, that you were anything other than his.

27/4.10. Capilya said: Why has this been done to me?

27/4.11. The nurse said: Hear me, O prince! The king's wife was barren; the king desired a son who would be heir to the throne.

27/4.12. Capilya interrupted: And you bartered your flesh and blood with the queen for this?

27/4.13. The nurse said: Patience, O prince! I am of a race that owns only One King, the Ever Present! Respect me, therefore, till you have learned the whole truth. The angels of Ormazd came to me before your birth, saying: Alas, the Chosen People are persecuted and abused, scattered and despised; but because they are faithful and most virtuous, the Ever Present will come and deliver them. Then I said to the angels: What is this matter to me? Behold, I am myself only a servant, and can do nothing.

27/4.14. Then the angel answered, saying: You shall have a son and name him Capilya; and he shall be the deliverer of your people. For which purpose he shall receive great learning. But because great learning is denied to your people, your son shall be adopted by the queen; and the king, believing it is his own son, will render to the child learning, and power also.

27/4.15. And I said to the angel: Flesh and blood of me are nothing if by this I can serve Jehovih (Ormazd).

27/4.16. Capilya said: Since you committed me to your God, then I am indeed His. || Now while they were yet talking, Jehovih spoke to Capilya, saying: I come not to give new doctrines to men, but to rescue My people from bondage, and to restore equal rights to the inhabitants of the earth. For this purpose you, O Capilya, were sent into the world. Because you were of the race of the Faithists, My voice has come to you.

27/4.17. Because the king imagines you are his son, and loves you dearly, you shall not suffer from his hand. Go, then, where I will lead you, and it shall be testimony to you, that I am the Ever Present, moving the Faithists by means of the spirit to come to you. ||

27/4.18. In due time the prince departed from home, not advising the king of his purpose; and he went as Jehovih led him, and came to Hosagoweth, near the river Vesuthata, where there was a forest, with meadows interspersed, and he found a camp of four families of wandering Faithists, and they were famished with hunger, and ragged.

27/4.19. The prince, seeing they feared him, said: Do not be afraid; I am not here to persecute or drive you away. As you perceive by my dress, I am a prince, yet do not judge me to be your enemy come to destroy you. For, by the same power you were led here, I was also led. And I bequeath to you this land, to be yours forever. Cease, therefore, traveling about, but stay and begin tilling the soil.

27/4.20. Yatithackka, the rab'bah, said: What do you mean you were brought here by the same God? Then, in truth, you know the signs and passwords?

27/4.21. Capilya said: I have learned none of these things; but even as there is a legend among your people that one would come of Jehovih and restore His chosen people, so do I declare to you, I am he. So you may know your Ruler is my Ruler, take me in private with you, O rab'bah, and the Ever Present will give the signs and passwords, and thus prove me.

27/4.22. Moreover, I say to you in prophecy, that before three suns have risen and set, there shall come to this place hundreds and hundreds of your people. || Now when the rab'bah had examined Capilya, and found that he had the signs and passwords, he wondered exceedingly. The prince then had the Faithists lay wood and stone in the form of a crescent, and its size was sufficient to seat one hundred people. He said: This is the altar of Jehovih (Ormazd). Let us sit here tonight, for the Father's voice is with me.

27/4.23. During the day, many more came; so by nightfall there were one hundred, men, women and children, and the prince commanded them to sit on the altar of Jehovih (the crescent). And presently the Voice spoke in the middle of the altar, saying: This is My Son, about whom it has been prophesied, that one would come to restore My people. Behold, I am the Ever Present, and not in the figure or image of a man, but I am the All Space and Place, doing My will through My angels and through the souls of men. Be steadfast in righteous works and love toward one another; and most just to a fraction with all other peoples. I will establish Myself with you, even as I was in the ancient days with your forefathers.

27/4.24. Capilya then appointed the oldest rab'bah as chief of the altar; and this was the first established family [community –Ed.] since many hundreds of years, that was assured by a prince that they would not be driven off.

27/4.25. The next day the prince took the people a little way off, about half an hour's walk, and he said to them: Build here another altar, for again, before nightfall, others shall come, but here. Let the Ever Present have an altar provided for them. Accordingly the people labored in faith, and built another altar; and when it was finished, and before the sun had set, many wanderers, Faithists, came to the place.

27/4.26. Capilya said to them: Come to the altar of Ormazd, for He desires sacrifice [worship –Ed.] of all whom He blesses. And they went in and sang, and prayed, giving thanks to God. Jehovih said: Permit Capilya, whom I have sent to you, to build three more altars at like distances apart; for I will bring My people together for the three places of sacrifice.

27/4.27. The next day, many more wanderers came, who had escaped from the province of Anassayon, where a war was being carried on against raiders from Tubet, the high mountain region. And Capilya built altars for them also; and he also appointed rab'bahs and chief rab'bahs to them.

27/4.28. Now, behold, they were without food, and many had been famished for many days. Capilya, perceiving that some of the people were suspicious of him, said to them: Whoever has faith in me that I am of Jehovih, let him stand with me tonight, for the Father will manifest to us.

27/4.29. Not more than forty came to the place designated; for they feared Capilya was an impostor. And when they were assembled, Capilya tried them, and found, in truth, they had faith. And he said to them: Stand in a circle and join hands, and I will stand in the center. Yet I do not know what the Great Spirit will do for us.

27/4.30. And when they were standing thus, Jehovih sent a cold wind, and down from heaven came an abundance of Ahaoma,[1055] enough to feed all the people for many days. Nor did any man know what ahaoma was made of; but it was savory and nutritious.

27/4.31. And the people came and ate, and also gathered up the ahaoma, and carried it home. Capilya said to them: Because Ormazd has done this, go into the altars and return thanks to Him.

27/4.32. And the people did as commanded; and from this time forth not one of them lacked faith in Capilya. And so he said to them: This place shall be called Maksabi, for it is the first colony (Tarag-attu) in all the world where the Father has fed His people with His Own hand. So the place was called Maksabi, which, in Vedic, would be Suta-ci-ci (I speak with food!).

CHAPTER 5 Arc Bon

27/5.1. For forty days Capilya remained in Maksabi, teaching and helping the people; and on the fortieth day he said to them: I go now; the Father desires me. Be faithful to Jehovih, and maintain the sacrifices (worship). The eye of Jehovih is upon you; His ear hears not only your spoken words, but the thoughts in your hearts. I will come again to you at a later time, and restore your rites and ceremonies.

27/5.2. Jehovih said to Capilya: Even as you have done in Hosagoweth, so shall you do in Tibethkilrath; for there I will also bring My chosen from the Province of Yusitra.

27/5.3. So Capilya went to Tibethkilrath, where more than seven hundred Faithists were assembled; and they feared him, saying to one another: Is this not someone sent by the king to entrap us?

27/5.4. But when Capilya saw they feared him, he said to them: He who has faith in Ormazd fears nothing in heaven or earth. For the Father appoints a time to all peoples; nor can they make it more or less. Throtona, one of the rab'bahs, said to Capilya: Are you indeed one of us? Capilya said: Because I am as I am, I cannot answer you. If I say I am of your race, then your people will not be restored to liberty; for I would suffer death, being a teacher of your people. If I say I am not of your race, then your people will not have faith in me.

27/5.5. I say to you, I am only a man, even as you are; neither am I pure and good; for there is only One pure, the Creator. Therefore, put your faith in Jehovih, and where my words and my labors are good, render to me even as to any other

[1055] Haoma signifies spiritual food. From this it would appear that ahaoma meant earth food. I have myself stood in the spirit circle when various kinds of fruits and flowers were brought by the spirits and cast in the midst of the circle. And it is always preceded by a cold wind. Hundreds of thousands of Spiritualists have now witnessed this manifestation. –Ed.

man, no more no less. And yet, even as you believe in the Ever Present, so do I; and even as you do not believe in a man-God, so also do I not believe.

27/5.6. Are all men not brothers, and created by the same Spirit? Because the kings do not acknowledge this doctrine, they persecute and outlaw your race. To restore your people, who are my people also, for this reason I am sent into the world. My labor is now upon me; and for that purpose I am here with you and your people.

27/5.7. This land, around about, I bequeath to the Faithists; and they shall settle here and till the soil, and reap the harvests, and shall not be driven away. And in time to come I will provide teachers, and the Faithists shall have the right to obtain knowledge.

27/5.8. Capilya built altars for the multitude, saying to them: First of all, you shall dedicate to God all things you put your hands to, for without the rites of bestowal upon the Great Spirit, your people cannot be in harmony. To neglect the rites is to neglect all things. Do you know the doctrines of the ancients?

27/5.9. None of the rab'bahs could answer Capilya, and so he said: Ormazd provided your servant with great learning. For this I am sent to you. Know, then, the doctrines of the ancients, even from the time of Zarathustra and Brahma:

27/5.10. To rise with the sun; to bathe the body once every day; to eat no flesh nor fish; to pray to Ormazd at sunrise, at high noon, at sunset, and before lying down to sleep.

27/5.11. Certain philosophers, wise in vanity, said: To rise an hour after the sun is no sin; to bathe one day in seven is sufficient; to eat fish-flesh, which is of cold blood, is no sin. Now, behold, it came to pass that they lay in bed two hours; they ceased to bathe altogether, and as to eating, they did not stop with fish-flesh, but ate of all flesh. And sin came upon them; by their behavior they cut themselves off from the Father.

27/5.12. Be scrupulous in following the texts; and as to him who opens the door for disobedience, have nothing to do with him or his philosophy.

27/5.13. Capilya asked: Why does one man do a good act rather than a bad act? Why does another man commit a bad act rather than a good one? The rab'bahs said: The first is the speech of Ormazd; the second is the speech of satan; for as these dwell in men, so do they manifest.

27/5.14. Capilya said: I am pleased with the answer; for which reason I have previously commanded you to build altars and do sacrifice; for these are the expression of your souls, which testify you would rather serve the Creator than the destroyer.

27/5.15. This was also of the ancient doctrines of Zarathustra; but certain other philosophers, vain in self-knowledge, said: Can a man not worship in the soul, and without building an altar of stone and wood? And the multitude listened to them; but afterward they went further, and said: Why worship at all? So, they fell in darkness. A soul without an outward expression of worship stands on the brink of hell.

27/5.16. To see an altar, as we pass along, enforces upon us the thought of worship, and of Ormazd, the Creator; it leads the soul upward. To see evil, or the temptation of it, is to lead the soul toward darkness. Therefore, let men and women be discreet of their persons; but make the altars of sacrifice numerous.[1056]

27/5.17. Capilya asked: What is the first poison? The rab'bahs did not know how to answer, perceiving Capilya had great learning and wisdom. Capilya said: The first poison is self. One man says: Rites and prayers are good for the stupid and unlearned; I do not need them. || I say to you that such a man is drunk on the first poison; do not let his breath breathe upon you; for here enters the wedge of destruction.

27/5.18. Capilya said: What is the second poison? But when he perceived no one would answer, he said: The first leads to the second, which is desire to lead others and rule over them. Htah-ai, one of the rab'bahs, asked: How can we get on without leaders?

27/5.19. Capilya said: Allow no man to lead you; good men are expressions of the All Light. Capilya asked: What is the best and yet the most dangerous thing? Some replied as to one thing, and some as to another. Capilya said: The best and yet most dangerous thing is speech. To talk of good things; of delights; of love; of Ormazd and His wonderful creations; of life and death; of

[1056] That is, be discreet in their dress and behavior; instead of drawing attention to themselves, set out plenty of altars to raise the soul upward.

everlasting happiness; these are good speech, and give the soul great happiness. To talk of evil; of dark deeds; of one's neighbors; of disgusting things and words; these enrich satan's harvest.

27/5.20. Certain three men traveled through a great city, and when they returned home, and the neighbors assembled to hear the story of their travels, one of the travelers related all that he saw, good and bad; another one related only all the bad things he saw; and the other one related only the good things he saw, the delights and most beautiful things. Now which of the three would you say does most for the Father's kingdom? The rab'bahs said: The last one. Capilya said: True! Be, then, like him, even to one another; for by this course only, is speech not dangerous, but of profit to the world.

27/5.21. Sufficient is the number of evil men to relate the evils in the world; instead, relate the good, for by constantly walking in clean ground you shall remain clean, in word and deed.

27/5.22. Search both spirits and men, not for the brilliancy of speech, for often its brilliancy hides its poison, or steals on the senses unawares;[1057] but search their words as to holy ideas and good delights, to make man rejoice in his life. He who harps on deceivers, liars and debauchees, is a fireman for satan's hells. Do not reply to him, lest your speech becomes a snare to entrap yourselves.

CHAPTER 6 Arc Bon

27/6.1. For three years Capilya traveled over the land of Vind'yu, east and west and north and south, establishing the Faithists wherever he found them; and he donated to them whatever lands lay waste and untilled;[1058] but he did not touch any land on which other people dwelt and tilled the soil.

27/6.2. And it came to pass that the servants in the provinces fled from their masters and went and dwelt in the places of Jehovih, to so great an extent that the governors and sub-kings complained against Capilya, and he was reported to Yokovrana, the king in chief, Capilya's foster-father. And the king sent a commission summoning his supposed son to the capital, to answer the charges against him.

27/6.3. When Capilya was before the Royal Council, and demanded by the king why he had come, Capilya said: The servant of the great king answers; his words are bound words. Whatever comes out of Capilya's mouth, Capilya holds as his. There are those who maintain that man, whose tongue is moved by the spirits of the dead, is not responsible for his words. Capilya creeps not through so small a hole. To be master of one's flesh, and desires, passions and words, these are great gifts indeed. Capilya professes these. Therefore, Capilya binds himself in every word.

27/6.4. Know, then, Most Royal Council, servants to our Great King, Yokovrana, Capilya was summoned here by the king, to answer certain charges made by members of the Royal Council. These charges prefer[1059] that Capilya has founded certain colonies, which have attracted away the servants of the sub-kings and of the rich, and by this, sowed disobedience in the remainder.

27/6.5. Capilya has come to answer these charges. Hear, then, Capilya's answer: Capilya being heir to the throne, asked the king for leave to travel, and the king said to him: Do whatever your soul observes that may be good for the United Kingdoms. Did the king not say this?

27/6.6. Yokovrana said: Yes, my son. So Capilya continued his answer: When Capilya traveled near and far, for nine years, his heart was sick because of the misery of the poor and the glory of the rich. He saw many forests and many plains where no man dwelt; and he said to himself: Let the poor come here and live. Yet he did not call any poor man. Was it, then, an evil for Capilya to say this to himself?

27/6.7. The king said: Surely not. Then Capilya went on: After a long season of idleness Capilya went the second time to travel, and when he came to the forests and plains, behold, the poor were gathered together, with still more coming. So Capilya went among them to show them how to dwell together wisely. Was this an evil in Capilya?

27/6.8. The king said: No; in truth it was good. Then Capilya said: In a little while they discovered it was good for them to dwell together and to help one another; and the news spread abroad, and soon the servants of the governors, and the rich, ran

---

[1057] without being noticed; unexpectedly

[1058] uncultivated, un-worked, inactive, unused, wild

[1059] submit, present for remedy, accuse, lodge a complaint

away from them. Is it not just to say of the king, governors and rich men, that they are driving their servants away from themselves, because of hardships that are greater than the hardships of the Gods?

27/6.9. The king said: A good proof. But why do you say, the Gods? These people for the most part do not believe in the Gods. And many of them, I hear, are believers in the Great Spirit! Capilya said: You speak the truth, O king. But that is their matter, and not Capilya's. The king said: You are right, my son. But what do you say about education? Shall the laws not be maintained?

27/6.10. Capilya said: Are you the king? Or merely the servant of the dead? Shall Capilya call him father who is only a servant to carry out the laws of the dead? If so, then Capilya has sinned against the law. But listen, you who are of great learning; do you obey one law of the ancients and not another? The law of the ancients was that with the death of the king all laws died, and whoever became king afterward must by necessity make new laws of his own. The law against educating the Faithists is a law of the ancients. Let Capilya's accusers find that which they will; for if they stand by the laws of the ancients, then, indeed, have we no laws, and no king nor sub-kings. If they repudiate the laws of the ancients, then Capilya has not sinned against any law.

27/6.11. Yokovrana said: You are acquitted, Capilya. The laws of the ancients cannot bind your king nor the king's kings. Touching these matters, then, the Royal Council shall make new laws. And since Capilya has not contravened any law, the new laws shall not interrupt the orders of the state as they now are. ||

27/6.12. Because of Capilya's presence in the Royal Chamber, the power of Jehovih and His angels was great in that house.

27/6.13. The speeches of the sub-kings and governors were in the following manner: To permit great learning to the Faithists is to overthrow Dyaus and his reigning Gods and Lords; for by great learning the Faithists will ultimately become members of the Royal Council; therefore, at all hazards,[1060] great learning must be prohibited. Great learning is inimical[1061] to good servitude.

27/6.14. Jehovih said to Capilya: Be present when these laws are passed; for by this means My holy angels will rule over the Royal Council for the good of all men.

27/6.15. For one hundred days the Royal Council discussed the matter, but the angels of heaven kept them divided as to opinion and belief, so that no law was passed by them. Now after they had thus wasted much time to no purpose, Capilya asked permission to speak before the king and Council as to what was wisdom in the government of the nations; and it was granted to him. This that follows is, then, the substance of Capilya's speech:

CHAPTER 7 Arc Bon

27/7.1. Whoever is born into the world is, in part, possessor of the world by fact of his birth. All come into the world naked and helpless, and they deserve our assistance because of helplessness. To help the helpless is the highest virtue.

27/7.2. Two wise men are greater than one; a nation of wise men, what could be greater than this? Yet all men come into the world knowing nothing; to give them great wisdom is to make the nations wise and great. To open the avenues on every side to great learning, this is the foundation for a great kingdom.

27/7.3. To have the soil tilled, is this not greater than hunting and fishing? To throw the lands open in the east and west, and north and south, to the tiller of the soil, this is the foundation of plenty. When the poor and ignorant are supplied with necessities, to eat and to wear, with a place to live, there is little crime, but great virtue; and such people are a great strength in that kingdom.

27/7.4. To hold more land than one can till is to sin against those who have none, who do not have the means to live or to earn a living. Yes, such a one is an enemy to the nation.

27/7.5. There are two kinds of governments, one is government for the government, and the

[1060] no matter what the detriment, harm, loss, disadvantage; no matter what the cost; at all costs; no matter the circumstances

[1061] against the interests of, contrary, adverse, detrimental, harmful

other is government for the people. The latter government the people will endorse, and by their wills make it mighty. The former government seeks to make itself mighty at the expense of the people. Such a government is in the throes of death.

27/7.6. To make government and people one, as to prosperity and peace; this is the highest government. For the government to render to the people bountifully, as to land and water, and as to great learning, and to music,[1062] this is the wisest, best government.

27/7.7. What man is there who does not love liberty, the chief of all desires? Can a government abridge this without crippling itself or forfeiting the love and cooperation of its people? To bestow liberty, and to maintain liberty to all people, this is the greatest good thing a government can do.

27/7.8. But who shall say what liberty is, and its limit? A man who makes offense[1063] against his neighbor, or deprives him of virtuous livelihood, shall not have liberty. No man should run naked; nor should a man have liberty to go into another's field and take his harvest. How, then, shall a government take a man's possessions against his will? But he who has received great learning will not offend by nakedness, nor by taking that which is another's.

27/7.9. What, then, is greater than for a government to bestow great learning on the people? It is not enough to say to the poor: Here is land; feed yourselves. But men of great learning shall be sent among them, showing them how to till the soil, and how to build, and to keep themselves pure in soul and body. For great learning is not in the books only; no, there are men of great knowledge as to books, who are themselves gluttons and debauchees, and bigots, and tyrants, and base authority. Such men do not have great learning, in fact, but great vanity.

27/7.10. Two kingdoms, lying side by side; in the one are great philosophers and colleges, but the multitude are in need; in the other kingdom there are no philosophers, as such, nor colleges; but the multitude have plenty: The latter is a kingdom of greater learning than the former. For what does great learning consist of, if not in knowing how to live wisely? A few philosophers are not a nation. To bestow such knowledge on the people as will enable them to live wisely and be happy to a good old age, this is the labor of the best, great government.

27/7.11. It is a common saying that such and such a king[1064] is a great king, because, behold, he has founded colleges. And this is no small matter. But how much greater is the king who has founded a thousand poor families, and taught them how to live wisely? (And so, in this way, is casting out poverty from his kingdom, enriching it, strengthening it.)

27/7.12. To make a law to prevent liberty; to bind slaves more rigidly, is to weaken the nation; to weaken the kingdom. For example, a man had ten servants, and they were free; then he bound nine of them with chains, and complained because they did not serve him well. He was a fool.

27/7.13. To labor for one's self at the expense of the state, is to rob the state; to hoard up possessions is to rob the poor. What treasure has any man that he can take out of the world? It is better to give it while one may, for tomorrow we die, leaving it to them who did not earn it.

27/7.14. The highest peace is the peace of the soul, which comes of consciousness of having done the wisest and the best in all things according to one's own light. For after all, is not the earth-life only the beginning, in which we are as in a womb, molding our souls into the condition which will come upon us after death? In which case we should with alacrity[1065] seize upon the passing time and appropriate it to doing righteous works to one another.

CHAPTER 8 Arc Bon

27/8.1. When the king and the Royal Council saw the great wisdom of Capilya, they were struck dumb in their seats. After a while the king said: Was it not by blood that our forefathers established

[1062] Under the head of [definition of] music is reckoned in India the same as in ancient Greece; i.e., everything that contributes to harmony between individuals, and between individuals and the state, is music. –Ed.

[1063] evil-doing, sin, wrong-doing, attack, assault, crime

[1064] i.e., a non-specified king, being any king applicable to the situation

[1065] all due speed, eagerness, ready willingness

Dyaus? Scattering the Faithists with great havoc? Shall we gather up the escaped races and nurse them only to have them turn upon us and bite us? Shall we not with our valiant arms defend Dyaus?

27/8.2. To this Capilya answered: Sufficient for his own battles is the God of Vind'yu. If the king must by necessity fight Dyaus' battles, then Dyaus is a weak God indeed. Heaven forbid that Capilya believe in such a God, or labor for one so weak!

27/8.3. But you are right, O king; by blood our forefathers established Dyaus; but where is there, either in ancient or modern learning, a commandment that Dyaus shall be maintained by blood? Did you yourself not receive a commandment to stop the sacrifice of human blood on the altar? Is it, then, indeed a holier place on the battlefield, that these things must continue?

27/8.4. Man loves vengeance; and more for this than for righteousness he desires to inflict or destroy others. Nevertheless, all things are answered accordingly as they are; vengeance answers vengeance; blood answers blood; war answers war. And the same rule applies to virtue, which begets virtue; love, which begets love; peace, peace; good works, good works. For in these things our souls play a greater part than do our external bodies. ||

27/8.5. One of the Royal Council said: What do you say about rites and ceremonies? Capilya answered: Without rites and ceremonies the spiritual person of the state and of the community, and of the nation, is like a man that has thrown away his clothes, and then, with disgust, drowned himself. As the soldiers of the army have drill, which is discipline, so shall the worshippers have rites and ceremonies, which are the drill to keep one's soul in reverence for the Creator.

27/8.6. But it does not fall to my lot to say to you what rites or what ceremonies; for these also come under the head of LIBERTY.

27/8.7. Another one of the Royal Council asked: Some men, who are bad men, have great pleasures and enjoyments; some men, who are virtuous and wise, have great trials and misery: What, then, is the prize that your philosophy offers to those who practice righteousness and good works?

27/8.8. Capilya said: If your eyes could see as mine have seen, or your ears hear as mine have heard, then it would be easy to answer you. Nevertheless I declare to you a great truth, which is also revealed in the doctrines of the ancients, that this is not the real life, but the embryonic state. And many who have great pleasures and enjoyments in this life, wake up only as babes in heaven; while many who are virtuous and wise, but suffer great misery in this life, wake up in heaven in strength and glory. More are trials and exertions to be desired than ease and enjoyment; for the former causes the soul to look upward; but the latter causes the soul to look downward. Nevertheless, severe trials are a great injustice to any man. ||

27/8.9. When the king and Royal Council perceived that Capilya had greater wisdom than any other man, the king said to them: No man in all the world has enough wisdom to try my son. What do you say? And they answered: That is true. So the king said: Capilya, hear the king's decree, and it shall be a law to you in all the kingdoms of the world, which is, that you have been tried by the greatest king on the earth, and are acquitted and declared to be above the dominion of mortals. And you shall go wherever you will in any land, doing whatever you desire, and no man shall arrest you or forbid you in anything at all. And whatever law you make, no king shall make another law above yours, to set yours aside. If you were not my own son I would say you were begotten[1066] by the Gods!

27/8.10. The king's decree was recorded in the House of Records, and copies of the decree sent to the tributary cities and kingdoms throughout Vind'yu. Yokovrana also had a copy made of Capilya's speech, and it was also recorded and signed by the king and Council, under the name, THE FOUNDATION OF LAWS.

27/8.11. Jehovih said to Capilya: I have allowed this land to endure war for hundreds of years, so that they would be ready for this. Behold, they are not slow to accept doctrines of peace and liberty.

27/8.12. Capilya inquired concerning the laws, and Jehovih said: Do not trouble yourself anymore with this; My hand is upon the king and Council. They will pass laws endorsing what you have said. Go forth, then, My son, among My chosen, and you shall establish them anew in rites and ceremonies.

[1066] sired, fathered

CHAPTER 9 Arc Bon

27/9.1. When Capilya had come to Wes-tu-chaw-aw, Jehovih said to him: Send messengers into twelve colonies which I will name to you, to its chief rab'bahs, summoning them here, for you shall teach them all alike.

27/9.2. The colonies were: Tahdayis, L'wellaat, Ha'darax, Thowaka, Dormstdatta, Ghiballatu, Yhon, Themmista, Vrach'hao, Ebotha, Ewen and Sravat, and each of them sent the high priest (rab'bah) with three accompanying rab'bahs, so that in all, there were thirteen chief rab'bahs, and thirty-nine rab'bahs. And Capilya had them put on red hats, without brims, after the custom of the ancient Zarathustrians.

27/9.3. Jehovih said to Capilya: Choose twenty damsels who are young and well grown; and twenty dames who have borne children. And these you shall adorn with blue hats with earflaps, after the manner of the Daughters of the Zarathustrian law.

27/9.4. When Capilya had them clothed with hats and aprons, he had the rab'bahs and the women go with him to the summit of a mountain, so that they could not be approached by idlers or spectators without due warning. And on the summit of the mountain Capilya said: When you were babes I prayed for you; now that you are mature, you shall worship the Creator with your own words. Bring, therefore, every one a stone, and cast it down, for it shall be an altar before Jehovih for our sacrifice. And as I do, you do.

27/9.5. They all took stones and cast them into a pile; and when they were still standing near, Capilya raised his hands to heaven and said: Father, when I was weak, You provided for me. My mother and my father and my rab'bah prayed for me, and taught me of You. And for that reason I praise You with thanks and glorification. Now that I am strong, I stand upright before You and praise You and pray to You with my own words, and not as the heathen who have priests to pray for them.

27/9.6. Because You made me a man I will labor to prove myself before You.[1067] As I have here cast down this stone, let it stand as my covenant to You that I will, from this time forward, cast away earthly passions and desires. And because I have raised up both my hands to You, lead me, O Father, in the right way!

27/9.7. When they had all repeated these words, Capilya walked once around the altar, followed by the others, and he said: Jehovih (Ormazd) Almighty, glory to You forever! You are on the mountaintop and in the valley; Your circle is the circumference of the world. I walk in the circle with You; You are forever by my side; Your light, the glory of my soul. Praise Him, O you mountains and valleys; sing to Him, you moon, and you stars; His hand holds you up; His breath moves all things!

27/9.8. In You I live; of Yourself You made me! O that I may not dishonor Your handiwork; or make myself ashamed before You. Because You are Ever Present, I fear You; because I cannot hide from You, I will be most circumspect in my behavior.

27/9.9. Capilya then sat down on the altar, saying: Go out a little way, and then return, so that I may teach you how to approach the altar of Jehovih. The people did as commanded, and when they came near, Capilya said: Who comes?

27/9.10. Now here are the questions and answers as Jehovih taught His children through Capilya:

27/9.11. A worshipper of Jehovih (Ormazd): Behold the altar of my people, who are known by their piety and good works, and in helping one another.

27/9.12. Who is Jehovih?

27/9.13. The Ever Present. He fills all place and space. He created me alive, and taught me to adore Him and His works.

27/9.14. Why do you come to this place above any other? If He is Ever Present why not worship Him in any other place?

27/9.15. He sends guardian angels to abide with His children who are pure and good. These angels desire certain places and times, in which my soul may be given to Jehovih. Through His holy angels He teaches me in wisdom and love.

[1067] That is, Jehovih made humans with capacity to contribute to their growth; and it is up to each person, male or female, to prove that he or she is more than an animal, and worthy of emancipation in the order of man.

27/9.16. Why not worship the angels themselves, since they are your guardians and benefactors?

27/9.17. To not call on the name of any angel who is Lord or God, is my religion; but to call on Jehovih, the Great Spirit. Whoever calls on the name of angels, or Lords, or Gods, will be answered by them, but whoever calls on the Creator will be answered by Him, Who is the All Highest.

27/9.18. How can Jehovih answer you? Does He have lips, and tongue, and mouth?

27/9.19. Jehovih is the Soul of all things; He speaks to soul. His voice has had many names; by the heathen and the idolater He is called Conscience.

27/9.20. What profit do you have in worshipping Him?

27/9.21. I am created so; because of the fullness of Him in me, I desire to express my adoration, and to commune with Him. Whoever does not have this desire is an evil man.

27/9.22. Will He answer your prayers? Turn aside from His usual course and come especially to you more than to another?

27/9.23. As a horse drinks water from a trough and so enlarges himself, so does the soul of the righteous man drink from the everlasting Fountain, Jehovih, and the soul of man thus enlarges and accomplishes in answer to its own prayer; nevertheless, it all comes from Jehovih. Nor does He turn aside from His usual course, for He is Ever Present, and thus answers the prayer of the soul of man.

27/9.24. What prayers does He answer? And what prayers does He not answer?

27/9.25. He answers the prayer for purity, and for love, and wisdom, and virtue. Whoever prays to Him for permission to do good to others, He answers without fail. He does not answer selfishness, or the prayers of the wicked. And for this reason the wicked say: He does not answer prayer. ||

27/9.26. Capilya said: My beloved, when you approach the altar of Jehovih, you shall repeat the wise words I have taught you; but not aloud like the idolaters, but in whisper or low voice.

27/9.27. What is the worship of Jehovih's chosen? And how does it differ from the heathen's?

27/9.28. Jehovih's chosen stand equal before the Father, and every one shall work out his own resurrection, both in this world and the next. Hence they are direct worshippers, being taught to worship Jehovih with their own prayers and songs. The heathen have priests to do worship for the people, who contribute to them in money for the service. The heathen priests worship the spirits of the dead, who call themselves Lord, and God, and Savior. The chosen children do not war, do not resent by violence, but answer evil by good, and practice charity and love. The heathen, the worshippers of God, and of Lord, and of Dyaus, and all other idols, practice war, and maintain armies of soldiers, who are taught the art of killing with great havoc. They build monuments to men, and otherwise blaspheme against Jehovih. They teach that Jehovih is void, but that He made Himself into Dyaus, a large man, and then created all things, after which He retired to His throne, leaving certain laws to govern His works.

27/9.29. What is the Zarathustrian law of life?

27/9.30. To not eat flesh of anything Jehovih created with the breath of life. To bathe once every day. To rise with the morning sun, and be temperate in all things.

27/9.31. What is the Zarathustrian fatherhood and motherhood?

27/9.32. To have only one wife; to have only one husband; to maintain sacred the maternal period.

27/9.33. What was the Zarathustrian compensation?

27/9.34. All things belong to Jehovih; man is only His servant. The fruits of the earth and of all labor shall be cast into the rab'bah's house, and by him delivered to the needy.

27/9.35. Why were the Zarathustrians persecuted and destroyed?

27/9.36. Because they did not resist by violence, and because they did not worship the idols of the heathens.

27/9.37. Had they no way of saving themselves?

27/9.38. To that end Jehovih gave them certain signs and passwords, by which they could know one another, and in time of distress assist one another to flee away.

27/9.39. Why did Jehovih not preserve His chosen people?

27/9.40. By the laws of the circumcision the Faithists could only marry among themselves, in order to preserve a knowledge of Jehovih (Ormazd) among mortals. Those who were holy were preserved; those who went after earthly things, and after the idolaters, were cut off. But even in this Jehovih profited the seed of the Faithist, by raising up heirs of su'is among the heathen.

27/9.41. Capilya said: Teach these things to your children from their youth up, and enjoin it upon them to teach these to their children.

CHAPTER 10 Arc Bon

27/10.1. Jehovih said to Capilya: You shall remain with My chosen until they have learned these rites and ceremonies and doctrines; after which you shall go to another region where I will lead you, and there teach the same things, and in the same way. || And Capilya obeyed the commandments of the Great Spirit in all these things.

27/10.2. In the fifth year of Capilya's preaching, the voice of Jehovih came to him saying: Behold, your foster-father is near death's door. Go to him and have the law of protection established before his death; and when you are king after his death, you shall ratify the law, and then abdicate the throne.

27/10.3. So Capilya returned to Yokovrana, the king, who was ill with fever. The king said: O my son, my son! I feared I might die before my eyes could gaze upon you once again. A few days more, and it will be over with me. You will be king. Think now, what would you ask of me, while I may yet accomplish it.

27/10.4. Capilya said: Call your Royal Council and pass a law guaranteeing Brahmans, the Zarathustrians (Faithists), the lands they have possessed and tilled and are now dwelling upon, to be theirs forever.

27/10.5. The king assented to this, and the law was so enacted; and this was the first law made by any king in all the world granting land to the Faithists, to be their own. And the law stipulated that the Faithists could worship in their own way; nor could they be impressed into any army as soldiers of war.

27/10.6. After the law was established, Yokovrana said to Capilya: I was wondering why you did not wait till you were king, and then enact the law yourself, and it could not be set aside during your lifetime? I will die soon, and the law will die with me.

27/10.7. Capilya answered: I shall ratify your law on the day I ascend the throne, which is binding, according to the rules of the ancients. Had I waited until I was king, then I would have been bound, according to my religion, which is that no one individual possesses land, except what he tills, and then only by donation from the community in which he dwells, and only during his lifetime, after which it reverts to the community.[1068]

27/10.8. Yokovrana said: You are wise, O my son! What is it that you do not understand? After the king rested a while, he said: Capilya, you have often said you have seen the angels of heaven: Who do you say they are?

27/10.9. Capilya said: Persons who once inhabited this earth. Some of them once lived on the stars.

27/10.10. The king said: Since you say so, it must be so. I thought, sometimes, they might be different beings that dwell in the air, and never dwelt here. Do you say, Capilya, that all souls are immortal?

27/10.11. Capilya said: They are born so into life; nevertheless, not all inherit everlasting life. Even as the body goes into destruction, so can the spirit of a man dissolve out of being. The fruit of those who have attained to faith in everlasting life are safe; but for those who have fallen from faith in everlasting life, and from faith in the Creator, I pity them and their heirs.

27/10.12. The king said: Why do the oracles tell lies? They are the words of angels.

27/10.13. Capilya said: If a man will not think for himself, examine for himself, the Creator allows him to be the recipient of lies. He is a wise man who has attained to disbelief in angels and men; for then he will turn to the Creator, Who is All Truth. This is the beginning of wisdom. Some fair men, with stunted souls, who fail to look to doing good in the world, require the serpent's fang in order to make them think.

[1068] This land law is still in existence in rural districts in India. –Ed. [Keep in mind '–Ed.' refers to the 1882 editor.]

27/10.14. The king said: I have killed many men in my day; do you say I have sinned? Capilya said: Inquire of your Creator. I am not your judge, nor any man's. The king asked: If a man is killed and his soul lives, then the killing amounts to little. We put away the body, but the soul may come back and retaliate. Is it not so? Capilya said: Yes, O king.

27/10.15. The king reflected a while, and then he asked: My son, can the spirits of those we have slain catch us in heaven and injure us? Capilya said: Yes, O king. The king said: And they, having been in heaven first, would have the advantage in battle. And if they go in gangs and have a leader (beelzebub), they might do great hurt. Know O, Capilya, I have a great secret for your philosophy; which is: When death draws near, we begin to shake in the soul as to what we have done all our lives. Sometimes I think of saying to Dyaus: Here, I will pray to you! But then I remember I have no merchandise that he would accept. How strong we are in health and prosperity, and how weak in adversity and in death! Do you think prayers would make my case stand better in heaven?

27/10.16. Capilya said: I am not master in heaven; or if I were, my love for you would shield you from all darkness. The king said: The priest says if I pay him money he can intercede with Dyaus and so, secure me a high seat in heaven. I think he falsifies, for Dyaus owes him nothing. Two things I have found, even with my little wisdom: Both the caterer to the king and the caterer to Dyaus[1069] make great pretenses, but actually do little regarding their promises. These two men, O my son, beware of them.

27/10.17. I owe my greatness to this discretion more than to wisdom. They are at the bottom[1070] of all the wars and evils in this world. They can deceive even the Gods, I am told. When you are king, Capilya, apply your wisdom to this matter; do not spare them; they are the curse of the world. I regret that I did not slay more of them; my conscience pricks me for this.

27/10.18. Capilya said: Since man's conscience is only part of the man, might it not err? Is the conscience not dependent on other things for wisdom? And after all, if we have done that which seemed the highest, best thing at the time, have we not fulfilled the law?

27/10.19. The king said: It would seem so. Conscience must depend for its errors or its justice on the education it has received. But is it possible that conscience is a disease in the heart? To regret over not having done a thing; to regret over having done a thing, these are irreparable complaints. Whoever can say beforehand, and yet not err, is wise indeed. I find that no man brought himself into the world; nor can he live except for a short period at most. When we are young we dislike to die; but at my great age I desire not to live. Evidently He Who created us has more mastery over us than we have over ourselves.

27/10.20. Capilya said: That is true; at best, man has no more than half mastery of himself. Yokovrana interrupted, saying: I interrupt you, my son, because my time is short. I would ask you what is the greatest consolation to a dying man?

27/10.21. Capilya said: There are two consolations that are great to a dying man; one is to know that he left no heirs after him; and the other is, that he leaves after him a noble son. The king said: You are wise, my son. I asked the priest in the oracle-house the same thing, and he said: For a dying man to have faith that his soul will enter paradise. So I said to him: No honest man can have such faith; for such a fate would be cheating heaven with one's sins. If I were the Creator, I would break the necks of half the world. Still, it may please a foolish dying man to tell him such a tale regarding his soul. You alone, my son, have told me the greatest consolation to a dying man.

27/10.22. My slaves may have faith that they will be kings, but they will wake up in their folly. A man may have faith that his soul will enter paradise, and he may wake up and find it was a mistake. Faith without a guarantee is folly.

27/10.23. Capilya said: A man who of his own knowledge knows a thing, has the greatest of all wisdom. To be as you are, a philosopher in time of death, is evidence of a great soul. Few have attained to this.

[1069] A caterer to the king is what we call a politician. A caterer to Dyaus is a priest. –Ed. [The editor's generalization seems too broad; and instead of ALL politicians, Yokovrana appears to be talking about panderers to the king, being flatterers, sycophants, yes-men, self-serving opportunists and similar ilk, but not those who are statesmanlike in their demeanor and conduct.]

[1070] the underlying cause

27/10.24. The king said: Compared to you I am nothing as to wisdom. You are a mystery to me. Your mother, whom the doctors slew to put her out of her misery from long sickness, was not wise. And as to myself, I am only great, not wise. I can make men fear me; but you know the secret of love, which is a great thing. Your name, O Capilya, will be honored long after mine is forgotten, even though I am the greatest king in all the world. O Capilya, my most wonderful son!

27/10.25. Capilya said: Because you gave me great learning and a father's kingly care, why should I not be an honor to you, O king? When you are in heaven, and can look upon me, I hope you may not lose your hope for me.

27/10.26. The king said: It does not seem wise to me that angels should see too closely their mortal kin, or else, in truth, they would never rise up to higher heavens. The seers say heaven and angels are around us all the time. I think this is a lie, otherwise it would be more hell than heaven to them.

27/10.27. After the king rested a while he said: I have been surmising what to say to you, for I feel the blood in my veins is nearly stopped. And this makes me think more than ever that man at best is only a gaming ball for the Gods to play with. Who knows, perhaps even now they laugh up their sleeves as to how they have used me for some hellish game! O if only man had some standpoint to judge things by! O if only he had a measure and a foundation to stand upon! I have searched the spirits of the dead, and the Gods of the oracles, and they are lies, lies, lies!

27/10.28. Capilya said: The small spark of light within our souls is right at the start; and if it is rightly cultivated it will grow brighter and clearer every day. For is it not in the nature of all things to grow by culture?

27/10.29. The king said: To rightly cultivate! There is the matter, O my son. To settle that point the world has been washed all over with man's blood. Rightly! Who knows that word? O if only my enemies were mistaken, and that I was clear in perceiving what was right!

27/10.30. Again he rested a while and then he said: I had hoped that when death came on, I would get glimpses of what is in store for me; but even death is silent, dark and deceiving. My members weaken evenly. This shows I was born from good blood. Had you not been my son, I would rejoice more than I do. For then I would know that my family line had run out, and so I could have ascended to the higher heavens. Now I may be obliged to dwell on the earth for a long season. As I understand myself now, even with all your wisdom and your love, I would rather you had been some other man's son. Then I could die easier and not care so much about leaving you. I have no other kin.

27/10.31. Capilya said: O king! You have torn my heart in two! In truth I am not your son! When your wife lay in the dark chamber, the angels of heaven stole me and brought me there. She who nursed me was my mother; and her husband was my father. I am a Brahman of Zarathustrian blood, a Faithist!

27/10.32. The king said: Is this true? It cannot be! Go call your nurse! Capilya called in the nurse, and the king said to her: Before I doom you to death, I command you to answer: Is this your son, and is your husband his father? She answered him: I am sworn to Jehovih and cannot answer you. Therefore sentence me, for I have carried a great load for many years. Behold! An angel of heaven appears!

27/10.33. Jehovih's angel appeared before the king, and they all saw the angel, who said: Capilya is not your son, O king! And yet no sin has been committed! And at that, the angel vanished.

27/10.34. The king said: If this was not a counterfeit made by the Gods, then it was my angel wife. So, Capilya! Must our love end here? The earth is going fast from me now! Capilya said: Our love will never die! For the good you have done for the Zarathustrians, the Great Spirit will provide you a home suited to your great soul. If you had any faults, you have more than balanced them.

27/10.35. The king beckoned for Capilya and the nurse to come to him, and then he said, feebly: It seems to me I hear the Gods laughing! Keep up the joke! My brother's oldest son knows nothing of it! A kingdom is but a farce. Hold me up, Capilya. I would have my eyes feast on the sky only, after having seen your sweet face.

27/10.36. Capilya lifted him up, and the king said to the nurse: I bless you! You brought forth a good prop! O aden (sky), Aden! All is something! All is nothing!

27/10.37. And the breath went out of him; he was dead.

CHAPTER 11 Arc Bon

27/11.1. Jehovih said to Capilya: My chosen shall not have kings; I, Jehovih, am King. As through Zarathustra I gave rab'bahs and chief rab'bahs, so have I done the same through you; and their families are My families.

27/11.2. To the unrighteous I give kings and kingdoms of men; for they who do not perceive Me, Who am the higher law, shall have that which they can perceive, which is the lower law.

27/11.3. A kingdom is thrust upon you; what will you do? Capilya said: What shall I do, O Jehovih? Jehovih answered, saying: Permit yourself to be proclaimed at home and in the provinces, after which, you shall ratify the laws, and then abdicate, and the kingdom shall fall into other hands.

27/11.4. Capilya was proclaimed, and known as king Capilya, and he abdicated, and then Heloepesus became king, and he became obligated to Capilya, so that the latter, though not king, stood as a protector over the Faithists, even greater than Heloepesus; nor could any laws be enacted affecting the Faithists without the consent of Capilya.

27/11.5. Jehovih had said: My people shall be a separate people; they shall live under My laws, for I am their King.

27/11.6. Now the whole time, from Capilya's first beginning of the restoration of the Zarathustrians (Faithists), until establishing a protectorate for them, was five years. After this, Capilya traveled about, east and west, and north and south, collecting together the scattered remnants of his people; and he established them in colonies, and taught them not only rites and ceremonies, but also taught the lost arts of tilling the soil and of making fabrics out of hemp, wool and silk; and he established schools and provided teachers for the people.

27/11.7. Capilya said: The first virtue is to learn to find Jehovih in all things, and to love and glorify Him.

27/11.8. The second virtue is Cleanliness; all people, old and young, shall bathe once a day.

27/11.9. The third virtue is to eat no fish nor flesh, nor other unclean thing; for what profit is it to bathe the outer part if one puts filth within?

27/11.10. The fourth virtue is Industry. Because the Father gave man neither feathers, nor hair nor wool; let it be testimony of His commandment that man shall clothe himself. To clothe one's self, and to provide one's self with food; these are the enforced industry upon all people. In addition to these, to labor for the helpless; to bathe them and feed them, and house them and clothe them; these are the volunteer industries permitted by the Father, so that you may prove your soul's worthiness before Him. Without industry no people can be virtuous.

27/11.11. One of the rab'bahs asked him what Industry was? To this Capilya replied: To keep one's self in constant action to a profitable result. To rise before the sun and bathe and perform the religious rites by the time the sun rises; and then to labor, not severely but pleasantly, until sunset. This is Industry. The industrious man finds little time for satan's inspiration.

27/11.12. The fifth virtue is of the same kind, which is Labor. There shall be no rich among you; but all shall labor. As reasonable labor develops the strength of your corporeal bodies, so also by the act of labor, the spirit of man develops beneficial growth for its habitation in heaven. For I declare to you a great truth, which is, that the idle and the rich, who do not labor with the corporeal body, are born into heaven helpless as babes.

27/11.13. The sixth virtue, which is greater than all the rest, is Abnegation of one's self. Without Abnegation no man shall have peace of soul, either on earth or in heaven. Consider what you do, not that it shall profit yourself, but whether it will benefit others, even as if you were not one of them. Without the sixth virtue no family can dwell together in peace.

27/11.14. The seventh virtue is Love. When you speak, consider whether your words will promote love; if not, then do not speak. And you shall have no enemies all the days of your life. But if you can justly say a good thing about any man, do not be silent; this is the secret to win many loves.

27/11.15. The eighth virtue is Discretion, especially in words. Consider well, and then speak. If all men would do this, you would be surprised at the wisdom of your neighbors. Discretion is a regulator; without it, man is like a tangled thread.

27/11.16. The ninth virtue is System and Order. A weak man, with System and Order, does more than a strong man without them.

27/11.17. The tenth virtue is Observance. With Observance a man accepts from the ancients those things that have been proven to be good, such as rites and ceremonies. Without Observance a man begins back even with the earliest of the ancients, and thus casts aside his profit in the world.[1071]

27/11.18. The eleventh virtue is Discipline, the Discipline for the individual and the family. He who does not have Discipline is like a racehorse without a rider. A time to rise; a time to eat; a time to pray; a time to dance; a time to labor; these are good in any man; but the family that practices them in unison with one another has Discipline.

27/11.19. The twelfth virtue is like discipline, and is Obedience. All good and great men are obedient. He who boasts about his disobedience to discipline is a fool and a mad man. Greater and better is the weak man of obedience, than the strong man of defiance; for the first promotes the harmony of the family; but the other ruptures it.

27/11.20. Consider these twelve virtues; they are sufficient laws for the whole world. Man may multiply books and laws forever, but they will not make the family, or colony, or state, happy, without the adoption of these twelve virtues.

[1071] That is, casts aside his advancement in the world. This can be likened to casting aside wheels and therefore anything that depends on wheels. If continued, man could lose knowledge of wheels, including their desirability; and eventually, if he would advance, would have to reinvent the wheel, inventions built with it (gears, transportation, etc.) and the social order built upon them.

Observance concerns beneficial spiritual practices. So that man, in casting them aside, foregoes not only their immediate benefit, but eventually loses knowledge of them, of their purpose, benefits, and advances built upon them, thus casting aside his profit, advancement and accumulated benefits in the world; and so if he would advance, he must start again from a rudimentary and undeveloped state.

CHAPTER 12 Arc Bon

27/12.1. Capilya (being inspired of Jehovih) said: Let your life be your preacher. The behavior of one good man, even in a sparse country, is of more help than a thousand preachers.

27/12.2. The clamor of the tongue makes speedy converts, but it does not change the blood. Those thus converted perform the rites and ceremonies, but their behavior is not of the twelve virtues.

27/12.3. One community (family) of a score of men and women, who dwell together in peace and love, doing good toward one another, is the manifestation of more wisdom than all the books in the world.

27/12.4. A man who has learned sympathy is better learned than the philosopher who will kick a cat or a dog. Great learning is not only in books; he who has learned to harmonize with Jehovih has great learning.

27/12.5. The doctrine of the idolater is war; but My Sons and Daughters practice peace, not resisting any man with weapons of death, says Jehovih.[1072]

27/12.6. My sermons are not in wordy professions, but in the souls of My people who practice My commandments.

27/12.7. You have witnessed that Sudga's followers said: Behold, Sudga is our Lamb of Peace! But they were nations of warriors; they built monuments to glorify their greatest slayers of men.

27/12.8. My people say little; profess little, regarding their virtues; but their practice is My Voice!

27/12.9. Capilya said: Whatever the character of one man should be, so the character of the family (community) should be, and likewise so the character of the state should be. Because harmony in a man's soul is his greatest blessing, even so

[1072] The resistless character and refinement of Capilya's doctrines in India attained to so great an extent, that when the Christians, under the guise of the East India Company, began the enforcement of Christ and plunder, thousands of them submitted to be shot down rather than take up arms to shed human blood. And the missionaries and the British press published this doctrine of peace among the East Indians as evidence of foolish idolatry. –Ed.

harmony in the family soul is its greatest blessing; likewise of the state and its soul.

27/12.10. Whoever will sacrifice self-gratification for the good of the family is the greatest, best one in the family. Whoever triumphs in self-desire, or in inflicting on others his opinions or doctrines, is the worst, bad man in the family.

27/12.11. My Father in heaven, is your Father also; all men and women are my brothers and sisters. To magnify one's soul so as to realize this brotherhood, is a great virtue. No matter what name He has, there is, nevertheless, only One Creator; and all peoples are His children. Call Him whatever name you will, I will not quarrel with you. I am a child of His love; by love I will prove it to you. No man can prove this by war.

27/12.12. At death the real life begins; mold yourself well while your soul has a good anchor (the physical body). The highest, best life in this world, finds the highest best life in heaven. To love your Father Who created you; virtuous happiness is little more than this. The happiness of lust, is hate to your Creator.

27/12.13. The man learning to swim had better go in with corks, till he finds the stroke; your Creator gave you a corporeal body, which is like the corks, to sustain you while you grow in spirit. Do not be in haste to enter the unseen world; make sure that you have learned the stroke of the resurrection before you put aside your flesh and bones.

27/12.14. Religion is the learning of music (harmonious flow) in a community, in which the rab'bah is the keynote. Music is of two kinds, sounds and assimilation. Dumb instruments may make sound-music; but assimilation comes to the real matter of putting one's behavior in harmony with the community.

27/12.15. Good works! Who knows the meaning of these words? King Yokovrana judged the good works of a man by the number of bad men he had slain. When alms-houses promote laziness they are not good works. Preaching, praying, and singing, are not works; they are the blossoms, and with enticing fragrance. Yet satan persuades man that these are good works. Nevertheless, all fruit is preceded by blossoms. The most learned man, the most pious man, and the greatest philosopher cannot tell what is the meaning of the words, good works. But a mother, with a child one day old, can tell; a farmer, who has sowed and reaped one harvest, and given half of it away to the less fortunate, can tell also.

27/12.16. To bring forth out of the earth food or clothing, these are good works only so far as they exceed one's own requirements and are given to others. To live on the earnings of others, except in time of helplessness, is evil. To preach and not produce substance for others; such a man is a vampire. He sells sermons and opinions to the ignorant, making believe his words are Jehovih's concerns.

27/12.17. The preacher shall dwell with the poor, taking hold with his own hands; teaching and helping; he who gives words only, and not labor, is a servant of hell. He finds honeyed words, and drawls his voice; he lives in ease and plenty; he stretches out a long face seriously; he is a hypocrite and a blasphemer against his Creator.

27/12.18. With love and rejoicing, and with willing hearts, stand upright before Jehovih; for your preaching shall bear evidence of joyful light; and your presence give to the weary and disconsolate assurance that you are the Creator's son, come in earnest to glorify Him by righteous works and a helping hand. ||

27/12.19. Besides Capilya's book of maxims, the quarter of which is not here related, he also restored the Zarathustrian commandments and the songs of Vivanho. Not since two thousand years were the children of Jehovih so well standing before the world. And peace and plenty came upon the land of Vind'yu, even greater than in the days of Brahma.

27/12.20. Thus closes the history of Capilya, who was led in all things by Jehovih, through His angels, even to the words he uttered, though often he did not know it. Such it is to walk with the Creator. Now while this was going on in Vind'yu, the Creator also labored through His angels in the land of Egupt, with Moses, about whom, hear the following:

CHAPTER 13 Arc Bon

History of Moses of Egupt

27/13.1. God commanded his loo'is, in the high heavens, saying: Descend to the earth, to the land of Egupt, and raise me up a son capable of my voice.

27/13.2. The angels descended as commanded, and searched over the land of Egupt and the adjoining countries, examining into the flesh and souls of men. And they called to God, saying: The land of Egupt is overrun with spirits of darkness (drujas), and mortals have attained to see them; and they dwell together as one people, angels and mortals.

27/13.3. God said: Go among my chosen until you find a man capable of understanding between truth and fable; and inspire him to an I'hin woman for my voice.

27/13.4. In Ellakas the loo'is found a man, Baksa, a Fonecean Faithist, born a su'is, and they said to him: Why are you alone in the world? Baksa said: Alas, my eyes have never seen God; my ears never heard him. I am searching for God in the life of a recluse.

27/13.5. The loo'is perceived what manner of man he was, and they led him to take an I'hin woman to wife, and she bore him a son, Hasumat.

27/13.6. The loo'is guarded Hasumat till he was grown, and they spoke to him, trying him also as to his power to distinguish angel voices.

27/13.7. Him they also inspired to take an I'hin woman to wife, and she bore a son, Saichabal, who was guarded in the same way. And the angels inspired Saichabal, to marry Terratha, of the line (house) of Zed. Terratha bore a daughter who was named Edamas. And Edamas bore a son by an I'hin father without marriage, and she called his name Levi, signifying, joined together (because his toes were not separate on the right foot, nor the fingers separate on the right hand). And Levi grew to be a large man, larger than two large men.

27/13.8. Levi, being of the fourth birth of I'hin blood, was not acknowledged an heir of the chosen race, the Faithists. Therefore Levi established a new line, which was called, the House of Levi.

27/13.9. Levi, not being eligible to a Faithist wife, was inspired by the loo'is to take an I'hin, Metissa, to wife. Metissa bore him a son, Kohath, who, at maturity, was admitted to the Order of Avah, the third degree of Faithists, at which time he was circumcised, and afterward called an Israelite, the name given to the Faithists of Egupt.

27/13.10. Kohath took to wife, Mirah, a devout worshipper of Jehovih. Mirah bore him a son, Amram, who took to wife Yokebed, sister-in-law to Kohath, and she bore him a son, who was Moses.

27/13.11. Before Moses' birth the loo'is perceived that he would be capable of the Father's voice, and they called to God saying: In the next generation, behold, your son will be born.

CHAPTER 14 Arc Bon

27/14.1. In these days in Egupt there were houses of records, where the affairs of the state, and of the king and governors, were recorded; and there were recorded also the births, marriages and deaths of people.

27/14.2. The languages of the learned were Fonecean and Par'si'e'an; but the native languages were Eguptian, Arabaic, Eustian, and Semis. The times (calendar) of the learned gave two suns (365 days) to a year, but the times of the tribes of Eustia gave only six months to a year. Accordingly, in the land of Egupt, what was one year with the learned was two years with the Eustians and Semisians.

27/14.3. God said: My people shall reckon their times according to the place and the people where they dwell. And this they did. Therefore, even the tribes of Israel had two calendars of time, the long and the short.

27/14.4. For events of prophecy there was also another calendar, called the ode, signifying sky-time, or heavenly times. One ode was equivalent to eleven long years; three odes, one spell, signifying a generation; eleven spells, one Tuff. Thothma, the learned man, and builder of the great pyramid, had said: As a diameter is to a circle, and as a circle is to a diameter, so are the rules of the seasons of the earth. For the heat or the cold, or the drought or the wet, no matter which, the sum of one eleven years is equivalent to the sum of another eleven years. One SPELL is equivalent to the next eleventh spell. And one cycle matches every eleventh cycle. Whoever will apply these rules to the earth shall prophesy truly regarding drought, famine and pestilence, except where man contravenes by draining or irrigation. And if he applies himself to find the light and the darkness of the earth, these rules are sufficient. For as there are three hundred and sixty-three years in one tuff, so are there three hundred and sixty-three days in one year, besides the two days and a quarter when the sun stands still on the north and south lines.

27/14.5. In consequence of these three calendars, the records of Egupt were in confusion. The prophecies and the genealogies of man became worthless. And as to measurements, some were by threes, some by tens, and some by twelves; and because of the profuse number of languages, the measurements became confounded; so that with all the great learning of the Eguptians, and with all the care bestowed on the houses of records, the records themselves became the greatest confounding element of all.

27/14.6. Jehovih had said: For two thousand years I gave My enemies a loose rein; and they have the longest line of kings in all the world; and yet in the midst of their prosperity they fall down like a drunken man. Even their language has become like a pearl that is lost in a mire.

27/14.7. Jehovih said: Because the kings of Egupt have outlawed My people, and denied them the right to obtain great learning, behold, My people are divided also. One tribe has one speech, another tribe another speech, and so on, till they cannot now understand one another; except, in fact, in their rites, and signs, and passwords.

27/14.8. Yes, the kings have perceived that to keep My people in ignorance is to keep them forever in bondage. But I will raise up a leader, Moses, among My chosen, and I will send him even into the house of the king, and the king shall give him great learning; he shall master all languages, and be capable of speaking with all My people. ||

27/14.9. Because the Israelites (Faithists) did not worship the Gods and Lords, but the Great Spirit only, and because they did not resent injury done by another, they had been limited to servitude by the Eguptian laws, which had stood for fifteen hundred years. These laws were called the Sun laws, after the manner of the division of the Osirian system, which was:

27/14.10. The sun is a central power; its accompanying planets are satellites. In like manner the king of Egupt was the Sun King, and his sub-kings (governors) were satellites. Osiris, the highest angel in heaven, was the Sun God, that is, God of Gods; for all other Gods were his satellites. He revealed certain laws to mortals, and these were Sun laws; and all minor laws were satellites. A Sun law extended over all of Egupt, but a satellite law pertained to the minor affairs of a city or province; but it must conform to the Sun laws. For in those days, the spirits of darkness taught that the sun once whirled so fast it cast off its outer extreme, and so, made the earth, moon and stars; and this was the accepted philosophy of the learned Eguptians of that period. Because the worlds run in circles [orbits –Ed.], the circle was the highest measure, or sun measure; and the diameter of the circle was called, the ode, a Fonecean word, signifying short measure. And this name, ode, was applied to the Israelites in satire, as the Anglo-Saxon word, odious, is used to this day. But the Israelites made sweet songs and called them odes also.

27/14.11. Among the Sun laws were the following, namely: The God of Gods (i.e., Osiris) decrees: Whoever does not bow down to me, shall not partake of me. Behold, mine is the sign of the circle! My enemies shall not receive great learning.

27/14.12. They shall not hold sun places (be employers), but be servants only, all their lives. And these signs shall reveal them:

27/14.13. If they do not worship me, but the Great Spirit;

27/14.14. If they deny that the Creator is in the image of a man;

27/14.15. If they circumcise; and will not serve as soldiers;

27/14.16. Then their possessions are forfeited already; nor shall they possess houses in their own names; nor send their children to the schools; for they shall be servants and the servants of servants forever. ||

27/14.17. Under the Eguptian laws, to worship the Great Spirit, Jehovih, was accounted a sufficient crime of idolatry, meaning the Israelites were not even admitted to the courts to be tried for an offense, but fell under the jurisdiction of the master for whom they labored, and his judgments were beyond appeal.

27/14.18. Now at the time of the birth of Moses, there were thirteen million inhabitants in Egupt; and of these, four million were Faithists (Israelites), more or less. For among the Israelites not all were of full faith, but many, to shirk the rigors of the Sun laws, professed to be worshippers of God (Osiris), and they would also enlist as soldiers, and otherwise connive in the ways of men, for sake of favors.

27/14.19. For which reason, the Sun King (Pharaoh[1073]) feared the time might come when the Israelites would revolt against the Sun laws, or become soldiers and confederate with foreign kingdoms for the overthrow of the Eguptian dynasty.

27/14.20. For more than three hundred years, the God Baal and the Goddess Ashtaroth had driven the foreign kingdoms to war; and as a consequence of these wars the Faithists had fled into Egupt, and even accepted servitude rather than be slain elsewhere.

27/14.21. Jehovih had said: Behold, My enemies in killing one another, frighten off My chosen. Now I will lead them into Egupt together, and give them a great leader, who shall restore My doctrines to them, and afterward I will deliver them into lands of their own.

CHAPTER 15 Arc Bon

27/15.1. The king's palace and pyramids were surrounded by a wall of stone; with twelve gates, made of wood and iron. The wall was sufficiently wide for twelve men to walk abreast on it, and the height of the wall was equivalent to twelve squares.[1074] On the summit of the wall were twelve houses for the accommodation of the soldiers who patrolled the walls. And in each and every gateway were houses for the keepers of the gates. So that no man, woman or child could come into the palace or palace grounds without permission.

27/15.2. And it came to pass that when Leotonas, the king's daughter, walked near the river, accompanied by her maids, she saw a child in a basket among the bulrushes. Leotonas commanded her maids to fetch it to her; and when she looked upon it, and saw it was an Israelitish child, she said: The Gods have sent him to me, and he shall be my child.

27/15.3. And they carried the child into the palace, and Leotonas said to the king: Behold, a wonder of wonders! I have found an Israelitish child in a basket in the rushes, and only Gods know how it came, or how it scaled the walls. The king said: Keep the child, and it shall be both a brother and a son to you. Nevertheless, my guards shall find the way my grounds are entered, or blood will be upon them.

27/15.4. Now after some days, and when the search had been completed, and no way discovered as to the manner of the child's ingress, the king issued a decree commanding a thousand Israelitish male children to be put to death, Moses among the rest, unless the mother of the child, Moses, came and confessed as to the manner of ingress. The king allotted three days in which time the matter should culminate; but nevertheless the mother did not come and confess.

27/15.5. And the king called his daughter, and said to her: What shall be done? Leotonas said: The king's word must not be broken; nevertheless, you gave the child to me, saying: Keep it, and it shall be a brother and a son to you. And immediately I sent my maids and procured an Israelitish woman as nurse for the child. And I set my heart upon the child, nor can I part with it and live. Last night I consulted the oracle concerning the matter, for I saw that your mandate must be fulfilled.

27/15.6. The king said: And what did the oracle say? Leotonas said: Proclaim word abroad that the nurse of the child is its mother. Now I beseech you, O king, let it be heralded abroad that all is confessed.

27/15.7. The king, seeing the child, relented; and word was proclaimed as Leotonas had desired. And, moreover, the matter was entered in the recorder's house that the mother of the child had made the basket and placed it where it was found, though no reason was assigned for the action. Such, then, was the Eguptian explanation.

27/15.8. Now the truth of the matter was, the angels of Jehovih came to Yokebed and said: Your son's name shall be Moses, signifying, a leader-forth,[1075] for he shall deliver the Israelites

---

[1073] The word Pharaoh is Phoenician for Sun King. –Ed.

[1074] This would make it about thirty-two feet. –Ed. [circa 9 1/2 meters]

[1075] The etymology of the Hebraic word, Moses, is A LEADER-FORTH, and has no reference to being drawn out of the water. Hence the Ezra account must fall to the ground [see Book of Exodus, Ezra Bible, chap ii, v.10], except so far as the facts corroborate the Israelitish account. –Ed. [Exodus 2.10: And the child grew, and she [Moses' mother]

out of bondage. But he shall be taken from you, and you will not find him. For the angels of Jehovih will deliver him into Leotonas' hands. And she shall adopt him as her brother and son, and bestow upon him the education of a prince.

27/15.9. Yokebed feared, for in those days male children of Israelitish parentage were outlawed,[1076] nor could any man be punished for slaying them. And Yokebed prayed to Jehovih, saying: Your will be done, O Jehovih, for I know Your hand is upon my son. But I ask of You, O Father, that I may come to the princess and be her nurse for the child. The angel of Jehovih said: Swear before Jehovih you will not tell the child that you are his mother!

27/15.10. Yokebed said: Though I am commanded by the king, yet I will not admit that I am the mother, and it is Your will, O Jehovih!

27/15.11. And Jehovih's angels fashioned a basket; and carried the child and placed it where it was found by Leotonas and her maids.[1077] And Leotonas, seeing it was a Hebrew child, commanded one of her maids to go and bring an Israelitish woman to nurse it. And the maid went out beyond the Utak gate and found and brought Yokebed, the child's mother, but no one knew she was its mother.

27/15.12. And when Yokebed had come before the princess, the latter said to her: Nurse the child, for I will be its mother and its sister, for the Gods have delivered it into my hands. And Yokebed said: It is a goodly[1078] child; I will nurse it for you.

27/15.13. Moses grew and became a large man, being a pure I'huan, copper-colored and of great strength. And Pharaoh, having no son, bestowed his heart on Moses, and raised him as a prince, having provided him with men of great learning to teach him. Moses was master of many languages, and also made acquainted with kings and queens and governors, far and near. And he espoused the cause of the king, whose dominions held seven kingdoms beyond Egupt as tributary kingdoms, which paid taxes to Pharaoh.

27/15.14. So Pharaoh made Moses ambassador to the foreign kingdoms, in which capacity he served twelve years. But because of the prejudice against him, for being of Israelitish blood, the court of Pharaoh importuned[1079] the king for his removal, and so Moses was removed from office under the king.

27/15.15. The king said to Moses: My son, this is a double infliction on me in my old age; in the first place, it is as a sword-thrust, to cut off my love to you, lest you someday become king; and in the second place, it is hard for a Pharaoh to be dictated to by his own court.

27/15.16. Moses replied: Fear not, O king, that my love and yours can be severed. Often it happens that men are tried in a way they do not know the wisdom of, but which, afterward, we realize to be the best thing that could have taken place.

27/15.17. As for myself, I think this rebuke is put upon me by Jehovih because I did not labor for my own people.

27/15.18. The king said: How so? Moses replied: For many days a great heaviness has come upon me; it is as if the wind of heaven bore down on my heart, saying: Moses, Moses, lift up your

---

brought him to the Pharaoh's daughter, and he became her son; and she named him Moses, for she said, "Because I drew him out of the water."]

[1076] This would define them to be outside the scope of the law, which probably meant that they were not protected by law, but moreover, their very existence was against the law. And so when a de facto attitude of leniency was practiced, the male children remained at risk at all times. Note that Pharaoh's decree to kill a thousand Israelitish male children came after and as a consequence of, Moses being found among the bulrushes (not the other way around as is related in the Ezra Bible).

Such a decree or one similar, as a way of controlling and punishing the Israelite slaves, must have been common not only from the Pharaoh, but other sub-rulers and slave owners as well. This is evidential from statements in Oahspe and from recent archeological excavations. –cns ed.

[1077] According to the account in the Ezra Bible there was an edict to kill male Hebrew children. If so, why did Moses' mother put him in this most dangerous of places? Would any mother resort to so foolish a stratagem? As to the angels carrying the child, as also in the case of Capilya, sufficient evidence is at hand now, in this country [USA] and in England, of hundreds of full-grown people being carried by the angels. –Ed.

[1078] wholesome-looking, healthy, pleasant to look at, handsome

[1079] persistently pressed; repeatedly troubled

voice for your people. For, behold, the king, your father, will favor you!

27/15.19. Pharaoh said: What would you ask, my son? And if it is possible it shall be done.

27/15.20. Moses answered: Until I have gone among them and ascertained their grievances, I do not know how to answer you. The king said: Go, and keep your counsel to yourself till you are returned.

27/15.21. So Moses departed and traveled over the land of Egupt, and was four months absent, and then returned to Pharaoh. And Moses related to him all the grievances of the Israelites; explaining the tasks put upon them; their denial before the courts; their forbiddance to education; but also extolled[1080] them highly for being a peaceful and virtuous people.

27/15.22. The king said: It is a pity; it is a great pity. But what can I do, O Moses? You see how even you yourself are chastised by the king's court. If I demand the repeal of the laws, the court will heap coals of fire on your head and on mine.

27/15.23. Moses said: Neither do I know, O king, what to do. And Moses was greatly troubled in his soul; and after he waited a while for his thoughts to come to him, he said: O king, tonight you and Leotonas shall reason with me, for I feel it incumbent[1081] because of the pressure on my soul.

27/15.24. When the three were alone that night, lo and behold, it was the beginning of the dawn of light. And Moses' ears were opened, and he heard the Voice of Jehovih (through His angels), saying:

27/15.25. Behold, O king, and you, Leotonas, and you, Moses, now is the beginning of My power on the face of the earth. Moses, My son, you shall take your people out of the land of Egupt; and I will bestow upon them the lands of the ancients, even where I will lead you. Do not change your laws, O king; let Egupt have her way; and let the Israelites have their way also.

27/15.26. The king said: To deliver four million people! O what a labor!

27/15.27. The next day Moses walked out, going into the woods to be alone, for heavy trouble was upon him. And an angel of Jehovih appeared in a flame of fire in a bush, calling: Moses, Moses, My son! And Moses saw that the bush was not burnt, and he said: Here I am, and I heard Your Voice.

27/15.28. The Voice said: I am the God of Abraham, and of Isaac and Jacob. Moses said: What may I do for You?

27/15.29. The Voice said: Go once more among your people, and say: I, Moses, have come to deliver you out of the land of Egupt, and into an inheritance which shall be your own.

27/15.30. Moses said: My people will ask of me: By whose authority do you speak? What, then, shall I answer them? The Voice said: Say to them: The I AM sent me. And if they question further, saying: You have a deceiving spirit, like the Eguptians, then you shall say to them: How can you distinguish one spirit from another? And they will say: Whoever labors for himself will deceive us. And you shall say to them: Whoever has faith in Jehovih, let him give up all, even as I do; and let them follow me; for if a multitude goes forth in Faith in the Father, then the Father will provide for them. (For this is the meaning of Faith, from which you were named Israelites.[1082])

27/15.31. So Moses and his brother, Aaron, traveled about in the land of Egupt, calling together Raban families,[1083] explaining to them, and urging the people to get ready for departure out of Egupt. For three years they labored thus, and it became known far and near that the project was on foot.[1084]

27/15.32. And the oracles of the Eguptians prophesied that when the Israelites were once out of the country they would unite with the kingdoms where Moses had been ambassador, and then return and overpower the Eguptians.

27/15.33. And in order to stigmatize Moses they said he fled away from Pharaoh's palace because he had seen two men, an Eguptian and an Israelite, fighting, and that Moses slew the Eguptian and buried him in the sand. And the recorders thus entered the report in the Recorder's House.

[1080] spoke enthusiastically and approvingly, complimenting and commending them, dignifying them

[1081] necessary, obligatory, urgent

[1082] Iz-zerl. –Ed.

[1083] A family of ten, i.e., thirty people; a small community. –Ed. [Here 'family of ten' probably means ten households or thereabouts.]

[1084] in preparation, going to occur

27/15.34. Moses was of tender heart and he inquired of the Great Spirit, saying: Will a voice of justice ever speak on my behalf? Jehovih, through His angel, answered Moses, saying: Suffer your enemies to put on record what they will, for the time will surely come when the truth shall be revealed to men. Pursue your course; for it shall be shown that you do still visit the king; yet, had you fled as the records state, you would not have returned, with the report hanging over your head. [1085]

27/15.35. In those days Egupt was a land of glory and of misery. Hardly is it possible for words to describe the splendor in which the nobles lived. Of their palaces and chariots a thousand books might be written, and yet not reveal all. And as to the members of the king's court, so grand were they that many of them did not stand on the ground from one year's end to the other; but caused carpets to be spread wherever they desired to walk. And as to their chariots, they were bound with silver and gold, and set with precious stones.

27/15.36. Of the royal court and the nobles, there were two thousand four hundred and eighty, and they owned and possessed everything in Egupt, which was the richest country in the world.

27/15.37. The next in rank were the masters, who were servants and tenants to the courtiers and nobles; and the third in rank were the Faithists, called Israelites, who were servants under the masters.

27/15.38. And it was against the law for anyone to call a meeting of Israelites, or to incite them against servitude to the masters; for which reason Moses and Aaron violated the law of the land, nor did any man dare to arrest them, because Moses carried with him the king's seal.

27/15.39. Of the miseries of the land of Egupt, half has never been told, nor ever shall be; for they were of the nature of the flesh, and of such kind that one may not mention them fully, for the history would also involve the beasts of the fields, and dogs, male and female, and goats also.

27/15.40. Suffice it to say that the people were victims of evil spirits, and had descended to such unnatural practices as poisoned the flesh, which became inhabited with vermin; and they had running sores; and only evil practices alleviated the pains. The people were subject to entrancement by evil spirits, and the latter appeared among the people, taking to themselves corporeal forms for evil's sake, also eating and drinking with mortals daily.

27/15.41. When Moses saw these things he prayed to Jehovih for wisdom and strength; for thousands and thousands of the Israelites were becoming afflicted in the same way. Jehovih answered Moses, saying: Because of the abundance of evil angels in this land it is impossible for My chosen to dwell here and escape affliction. Moses explained this matter to the Israelites.

27/15.42. Jehovih said: Moses, you and your brother shall return to the king, for he is worried concerning you and your labors. Behold, the nobles have complained before the king against you.

27/15.43. Moses visited the king, who was sick with a fever; and the king was on his divan at the fountain in the palace grounds, and the men servants were forcing water. When the king saw it was Moses, he raised up, rejoicing, and called Moses to come and sit with him. And servants ran in and told Leotonas that Moses had returned, and Leotonas came also and rejoiced to see Moses. Now while they were talking the king was overcome and fell in a faint, at which, Moses raised him up and restored him; and then in his arms he carried the king to the palace.

27/15.44. Leotonas said: Moses, my son and brother, you shall not leave us alone anymore? Behold, my father is old, and he gave his heart to you when you were a child. Be to him his son. Behold how he revives in your strong hands!

27/15.45. Then spoke the king, saying: My son, with all your wisdom, can you understand a woman? Moses said: Alas, O king, except the princess, I have not studied them. But why do you ask?

27/15.46. The king replied: Leotonas has not said one word about the affairs of the kingdom! What is uppermost in a woman's heart, that she speaks first; but as to man, he speaks first that which lies at the bottom of his heart. I love you, Moses, and delight in your presence; but my

[1085] It is strange indeed that the world has endorsed the [Ezra] Bible account for two thousand years, overlooking this fearful blunder. Nevertheless, we see now that we have not had the Mosaical account at all, but the Egyptian. –Ed.

kingdom concerns me deeply. The nobles have complained against you for meddling with their slaves, and for this reason I have desired to see you.

27/15.47. Moses said: The Voice came to me, informing me of what you say, and then commanded me to come to you, for you were ill with fever. And the king replied, saying: If I should die before you have accomplished the migration of your people, I fear my successor, Nu-ghan, will make it hard for you. Tell me, therefore, how matters stand with you?

27/15.48. Moses said: Jehovih has planned this migration; it cannot fail. For, witness what proof I have found: The Israelites were looking for a leader-forth, even as I was named in the basket. And wherever I have gone, the rab'bahs and their families are acquainted with the matter as if it were born in their souls.

27/15.49. The king said: Everywhere the oracles declare against you and Jehovih; saying you are in the hands of evil spirits.

27/15.50. Moses said: What are the oracles to me? To feel assured one is in a good work; this is better than oracles.

CHAPTER 16 Arc Bon

27/16.1. The Voice of Jehovih came to Moses, saying: Have the king give you commissioners who shall go in advance and examine the countries where I will lead you; and when the commissioners have returned, you shall proclaim to My people what the commissioners say, and the people will be convinced, and rise up and follow you. So Moses asked the king for a commission of Eguptians, and the king appointed thirty-three men, and allotted them seven months to accomplish the inspection; and he gave the commission camels and asses to ride upon, and to carry food to eat on the journey.

27/16.2. Meanwhile, Moses sent Aaron throughout Egupt, to inform the people of the commission, and also as to how they should make their outfits.[1086] And Aaron said to the rab'bahs: Be circumspect as to the outfits of our people; observing that they do not carry away with them anything that is another's, even to a fraction; for Moses has commanded me to say this to you.

27/16.3. When the commissioners returned and made their report, which was favorable, Moses had the report sent among the Israelites; and Moses added: For there are those who, having little faith in Jehovih, will have faith in the words of the commissioners.

27/16.4. The Gods of the Eguptians were not idle, and they sent word by way of the oracles to the courtiers and nobles to the effect that Moses had persuaded the king to hand the kingdom over to the foreign nations, knowing the king had no son eligible to the throne.

27/16.5. The courtiers and nobles, therefore, importuned the king to choose one of two things: Either to banish Moses out of the country, and put aside all arrangements for the migration of the Israelites; or, on the other hand, to abdicate the throne in favor of Nu-ghan. In the meantime, a whole year's drought came upon Egupt, and the rivers failed to overflow, so that a famine was sure to fall upon many parts of the country.

27/16.6. The king answered the demand of the courtiers and nobles with these words: I am Pharaoh, king of Egupt! Look to the threatened famine; provide the stores for my people. I declare to you all, a new thing has come to the world, which is: MIGRATION FROM BONDAGE! Nor is it in the power of nobles or courtiers or kings to stop this invention.

27/16.7. When the courtiers received this answer they said to one another: These are Moses' words, fashioned for the king's mouth. Certainly he has lost the fear of the Lord, and listens to the Great Spirit of the Israelites!

27/16.8. Jehovih, through His angels, spoke to Moses, saying: Now is your time. Go to the Heads whom you have chosen and appoint a time to them of one place, and a time to others of another place, and so on, to all the Heads. And you shall make the armies (unarmed multitudes) going forth so numerous that the Eguptians will be overwhelmed.

27/16.9. These, then, were the Heads, the chief rab'bahs appointed by Moses, and the places in Egupt where they were to depart from:

27/16.10. Rasak, son of Ubeth, of the place Hagor; Ashimel, son of Esta, of the place Ranna; Gamba, son of Hanor, of the place Nusomat; Bothad, son of Nainis, of the place Palgoth;

[1086] i.e., the goods, possessions, baggage, gear, personal effects, etc., they would be carrying away with them

Amram, son of Yoth, of the place Borgol; Lakiddik, son of Samhad, of the place Apau; Jokai, son of Keddam, of the place Hasakar; Jorvith, son of Habed, of the place Oeda; Sattu, son of Bal, of the place Harragatha; Tussumak, son of Aban, of the place Ra; Makrath, son of Filatti, of the place Nabaoth; Hijamek, son of Tor, of the place Nu'joram; Fallu, son of Hagan, of the place Ennitz; Shutta, of the place Romja; Jokkin, son of Rutz, of the place Moan; Tudan, son of Barrahha, of the place Hezron; Osharrak, son of Libni, of the place Raim; Thammas, son of Rodaad, of the place Sakaz; Misa, son of Tiddiyis, of the place Tessam; and Sol, son of Zakkaas, of the place Annayis.

27/16.11. Jehovih said: And the Heads shall have seventy-seven days notice; and they shall notify the rab'bah of their places, so that due preparation shall be made for the start. Nevertheless, the time appointed to your people shall be kept secret with the Heads and with the rab'bahs. And whatever number the rab'bah can send forth, he shall notify the Head; and when all things are ready, that number shall go forth on the day appointed, everyone on the same day.

27/16.12. And Moses appointed the tenth day of the month Abib, when all the people should start; and moreover, he said to the Heads: You shall see to it that the night before they start, at the hour of sunset, in the very moment the sun sets, every family shall offer a lamb in sacrifice, and every man, and every woman, and every child that can speak, shall covenant to Jehovih in the blood of the lamb.

27/16.13. When the time of the slaughter is at hand, the family shall stand around, and the lamb shall be in their midst, bound head and foot; and, when the knife is raised for the blow, no one shall speak, for that which is to be, shall be the covenant of the blood of the lamb against Egupt. And when the throat is cut across and the blood flowing, they shall all say: In Egupt the lamb of Jehovih is dead; His God shall go from here with Israel, but Egupt shall be accursed from this night! Accept this, my covenant, with You, O Jehovih (E-O-Ih!), for innocent blood has been shed as a testimony before You that, with tomorrow's rising sun, I rise to never again lie down in Egupt!

27/16.14. Thus went Aaron and Akad, bearing this message in secret to the Heads of the Houses of Israel, saying to them: Thus says Moses: This is the commandment of Jehovih, Who is Almighty!

27/16.15. And now, on the eve of success to the Israelites, the king of Egupt, being at the point of death, sent for Moses, and Moses went to him. The king said: If it should be the Lord's will to take me off before your people are gone, you will have great bother; for my successor, Nu-ghan, has a great hate toward Israel.

27/16.16. Moses said: What, then, shall be done? The king said: Behold, the pestilence has overspread Najaut and Arabenah. Your people will be cut off from traveling that way. Nu-ghan and his courtiers dwell in Harboath. Moses replied: My people shall march through Najaut and Arabenah; neither shall the pestilence come upon them, for the hand of the Almighty is in this matter.

27/16.17. Leotonas, learning that Moses was with the king, went in to see him. She said: O my son and brother, you are welcome. Behold, the trials of the royal court, and the persistence of the nobles, are the death of the king. To this the king said: And still I live, Leotonas! But, alas, these were his last words, for he laughed, and the blood burst through his heart, and he died then and there, in Moses' arms.

CHAPTER 17 Arc Bon

27/17.1. Jehovih, through His angels, said to Moses: When the body of the king is embalmed and put away, you shall go quickly to your people; for he who comes to the throne is under the voice of the Lord, Baal, and he will try to prevent the departure of My chosen. So Moses left the capital, and did as commanded.

27/17.2. On Nu-ghan's being crowned he at once issued the following decree: Behold me, I am Pharaoh, King of Egupt, and Ruler of the World. God has raised his voice in my dominions, saying: Hail, Sun King of the corporeal world: Behold, I gave you all the living that are on the face of the earth, and in the waters of the earth, to be yours, to keep forever. And I say to you, what is your own is your own, and you shall have dominion in your own way, for I made all that are alive on the earth to be yours forever!

27/17.3. Whether of beasts of the field, or fish in the waters, or man on the earth; all the living I created for you, and you shall possess them from everlasting to everlasting. And the life of the living I gave into your keeping; and I said to you: The house of Pharaoh I have created, and it is my house also.

27/17.4. And whoever rules on the throne of this land, the same is my son, and is the possessor while the breath of life is in him. But when he dies, and the throne falls to his successor, the rights and the powers and possessions of your kingdom shall not die nor be set to nothing. But the successor shall be my Pharaoh whom I raised up to my dominions; thus says the Lord.

27/17.5. Now, therefore, I, Pharaoh, who am king and possessor of all the world by commandment of God, and by his son (Osiris), who is dead and risen, being myself God of the earth, into whose hands are bequeathed all the living, am today, yesterday, and forever, the same everlasting king and Lord of all. And I decree to my people, who are mine by virtue of my authority from God, that only by my gracious indulgence has any man or people the right to put one foot before the other, on this my sacred earth.

27/17.6. And whoever goes here or there, except by the sign of the signet of my seal, shall surely be put to death.

27/17.7. And any multitude of my people, who are my servants, whom the God of Gods has given into my hands to do my works, to till my earth, or to build my houses, or dig ditches, or make bricks, or gather harvest, or make cloth, or attend flocks, and to do any works whatsoever, who may design to escape out of Egupt, to go to my enemies, the foreign kings, shall be deemed guilty to death. And if such people start forth, to quit my service, to go out of my holy land, then my loyal slaves shall fall upon them and slay them, right and left, sparing neither man, woman nor child. For thus commands the Lord God, whose son I am. ||

27/17.8. Jehovih, through His angels, spoke to Moses, saying: Take Aaron your brother, and go before the king and plead your cause. Moses said: O Jehovih, You Almighty, why have You said this to me? I have no argument in me, like other men. Nor have I courage to confront a man or woman. My tongue is slow to find words till after the opportunity. From my youth up I have known this man, Nu-ghan, who is king, and if he merely stamps his foot at me I am helpless before him.

27/17.9. Jehovih said: For that reason, My son, I can give you My words. Go, and do not fear.

27/17.10. Then Moses went before Pharaoh, taking Aaron with him. The king asked: What is your will? And Moses said: I have come to beseech you to allow my people to depart out of Egupt. The king replied: The Lord is with me; he says you shall not go; and I repeat the words of my God.

27/17.11. Then spoke Moses, the power of Jehovih being upon him: Do not think, O king, that bondage is for this world only; here the matter does not end. You have said here in your decree, you have spoken from the Lord, saying: The life of the living I gave into your keeping. Did the Lord say this to you? Where, then, is justice, since pestilence and death are coming upon your people? Do you call this keeping them? I declare to you, that even in the words of your own God you have failed utterly, and this sin is upon you. Permit, then, my people to depart, so that your own shortness may not be multiplied, in the afflictions that will surely spread over this land.

27/17.12. The king said: You have no authority; you are a frozen serpent that was taken into the house of the king; and being thawed out, you turn to bite your benefactors. You are outlawed by men and accursed by the oracles. It is said of you, you have been to Hored, and there wed for sake of alliance with my high priest, Jethro, for conveyance of my lands to your people. Who are you, that pretends to hear a voice, and to be led by the Unseen? You slave!

27/17.13. Moses said: I am not here to plead my own cause, O king, but my people's. Suffice it, though, that even as your Lord God stands upon miracles, I do not bow down before him. For these are evidence that your God and your Lord are only angels of the dead, who labor for you and your aggrandizement, and not for all men's welfare.

27/17.14. For I have miracles also; and whatever your magicians can do, I can do also; do I not have eyes and ears, even as the oracles? Now I declare a miracle to you, which is that you yourself shall yet not only consent to my people going out of Egupt, but you shall send armies to drive them out. To turn a rod into a serpent, or water into wine; or to show the spirits of the dead, alas, O king, even those who are of rotten flesh can do such things!

27/17.15. Pharaoh said: If the oracle hears God, is this not the greatest? Moses replied: He who utters what an angel bid him is that angel's servant; he who utters a good truth has spoken with Jehovih's voice. Pharaoh asked: Do you say your words are the Creator's?

27/17.16. Moses replied: I am like all good men who speak truth; all that is good, and all truth, are Jehovih's words. In a rose He finds expression in perfume; in the lightning His words are thunder; in a bird His words are songs; but in man, His voice is in man's words; for every living creature, and every dead thing on the earth, or in the waters, or in the air above the earth, gives expression in its own way; because the Father's hand is the foundation of all that is good and true. He is the I Am who sent me to you; by His command I open my mouth before you. And in His name I declare to you that you shall not only allow my people to depart out of Egupt, but you shall send your armies to drive them out.

27/17.17. The king said: Moses, Moses, you are mad! For even if all Egupt runs with blood, yet I will not do as you have said. Then Moses replied: I tell you, O king, there are two powers in heaven: that which is for Justice and Goodness, even Jehovih; and that which is for sin and death. And if the Creator lifts His protecting hand from Egupt, she shall in that day become the plague spot of the earth. You do remember, when, in the ancient days great Thothma built the first pyramid, your forefathers decried[1087] the power of heaven; and immediately all the land, and the great pyramid itself, was flooded over by evil spirits. And then came foreign kings, who robbed and plundered Egupt. Do not think, O king, these legends are only idle tales; there are Gods and Lords in heaven who could sweep the sea up, and drown all this country. Behold, a day is set; a night is marked out when the lamb of peace shall die. And in that night the first-born of every woman, and the first-born of every beast in the fields, shall die for all the Eguptians; but in that same night not one of the Israelites shall go down in death. Jehovih says: I will show My power through My people in the time of My covenants.

27/17.18. Pharaoh said: Were these things to be, God would have come to more noble quarters. You are beside yourself.[1088] And I banish you; nor will I again look upon your face.

27/17.19. Moses said: Whether in this world or the next, you shall yet call to me to deliver you from torments. Nevertheless, I do your bidding; neither will I come to you again; nor shall you look upon my face for a long season. With that, Moses and Aaron saluted the king and departed.

CHAPTER 18 Arc Bon

27/18.1. Pharaoh called his chief superintendent and said to him: As to the Hebrew brick-makers, you shall no longer supply them with straw, but they shall gather stubble themselves, and they shall continue to make the same number of bricks. And as to the tillers of the soil, you shall no longer permit them to have cattle to draw the plows, but they shall draw the plows themselves, and they shall likewise break the same quantity of ground. And in this way the king put extra hardships upon the Israelites because he was angered at what Moses said.

27/18.2. Moses perceiving this, cried out to Jehovih, saying: O why did You send me before Pharaoh? Behold, matters are worse than before. Oh, if only I had guarded my tongue and been of persuasive speech!

27/18.3. Jehovih said to Moses: Do not rebuke yourself, for you have done My commands. And it shall come to pass now, what otherwise would not. For those Israelites who hesitated about going out of Egupt, will now decide for themselves as to what they will do. And the hardships that Pharaoh has newly added, shall be a blessing to your people.

27/18.4. And it came to pass that the Israelites went away from their taskmasters, and the rab'bahs sent them to the Heads; and the people of Israel were stirred up from one end of Egupt to the other. And as for the Eguptians, except the courtiers and nobles, they were likewise stirred up, but without any purpose or order; so that all the great land of Egupt had neither tillers nor builders; and cleanliness departed away from them; and the

[1087] denounced, condemned, depreciated, belittled

[1088] not thinking clearly; crazy, insane, mad

country stank like a dead carcass, so that insects and vermin filled all that air of heaven.

27/18.5. But the flesh of the Faithists was good; and vermin did not come upon them; nor were they stricken with fevers, or leprosy, or scabs, like the Eguptians.

27/18.6. Pharaoh ordered his army of two hundred thousand men to take the field, but lo and behold, they were scattered and afflicted so that they were only as vagrants, without head or discipline.

27/18.7. Jehovih spoke to Moses, saying: Now I will show her philosophers a miracle in the air above the earth. Have they not said: All things come up out of the earth? For they have tried every way to put Me aside, and to explain My creation away as an idle tale. They shall look and see the sun, and declare that in truth there is no cloud; but while they look up, they shall see a cloud high up in the heavens, a very black cloud, and it shall be broad as the land of Egupt. And it shall descend to the earth, and it shall prove to be locusts, come without any seed; and they shall be so numerous that in three days they will eat up every green leaf of every tree and herb in all the land. Nor shall they be like any other locusts that have been on the earth or ever shall be; for man shall comprehend that they are not of the seed of the earth.

27/18.8. Moses sent a herald with this prophecy to the king, and he added to it: Why have you put more hardships on my people? Do you not see that the evil you had hoped to accomplish has cured itself even before it came to pass? For now the Israelites do not work at all, and their taskmasters are left in the lurch. Again I call upon you to let my people go.

27/18.9. The king did not reply to this, but silently put his officers to work, drilling and equipping his armies and collecting them together; which, when Moses saw it, he understood to be the sign, as the Great Spirit had previously said, when the cloud would appear. And it came to pass on a very clear day, at noon, a cloud formed high up in the firmament, and it grew blacker and blacker, until it descended upon the earth; and it was locusts; and like a snowstorm they covered the land of the earth, in places to the depth of the shoes and ankles. And they hungered, eating every green leaf, and herb, and grass, so that in two days not a leaf could be found far or near. And on the third day, the hunger of the locusts remained unappeased, and they leapt upon the Eguptians, old and young, feeding upon their clothes, and even upon the flesh of the Eguptians.

27/18.10. And on the fourth day Jehovih caused a great wind to come, and it blew the locusts off into the sea. And again Moses sent heralds to the king, saying: Consider my words now and be wise. I have told you that the hand of the Creator is upon this land. In your heart you say: Moses is a fool! Only a windstorm fetched the locusts from a far-off country.

27/18.11. But I say to you, O king, this is not so. And you shall still further witness Jehovih's power. For as the locusts came down out of the firmament, and you have a philosophy for the occurrence, behold, now another miracle shall come in another way: For frogs and reptiles shall suddenly come up out of the water, and they likewise shall be so numerous on the land that man shall not find a place to put his foot where it shall not tread upon them. And the first day they shall be harmless; but on the second day they shall crawl upon the people, and under their clothes, and in their houses; and on the third day they shall eat the flesh of the Eguptians. But they shall not touch one Hebrew in all the land.

27/18.12. Nor shall any man find where so many frogs and reptiles came from; for they shall not be like the seed of other frogs and reptiles. And on the fifth day all the frogs and reptiles shall suddenly disappear, neither by wind nor rain. But a stench, like rotten flesh, shall nearly suffocate the Eguptians to death.

27/18.13. Again I appeal to you, O king, to permit my people to depart out of Egupt in peace. This is the last time I shall solicit you. And if you do not answer me, then it shall come to pass that on the ninth day and night in the month of Abib, Jehovih will raise His hand over Israel; but as for Egupt, your Lord shall strike her in death. For on that night, in every family of Eguptians, far and near, the first-born shall fall dead; and so that you shall not say the prophecy killed them [by suggestion –ed.], behold, the first-born of every beast shall die also, including goats, sheep, cattle, asses, dogs, cats, and every living creature man uses. For on that night, behold, four million Israelites shall make with Jehovih the covenant of death. And when morning comes, they will rise up to not lie down again in Egupt. And this shall be the testimony of innocent blood against yourself and all your people, for what the Hebrews have suffered.

27/18.14. The king did not answer Moses; and it came to pass that Egupt was overspread with frogs and reptiles, to every detail even as Moses had prophesied. Nevertheless, Pharaoh pursued his course.

27/18.15. Jehovih spoke to Moses, saying: Moses, My son, look upon man and pity him, for he does not believe in Me, though I multiply signs and omens continually, and give him prophecies without end. One thing only turns man's eyes inward; and that is flesh of his flesh, lying dead before him.

27/18.16. Now on the night of the passover, when the Israelites made the covenant on the blood of the lamb, a hot wind blew upon the face of the earth; and the first-born of the Eguptians fell dead, both man and beast. And Pharaoh's son died, and his brother's son; and the first-born of every courtier, and every noble's first-born, and all other people, their first-born, so that in every family there lay one dead.

27/18.17. Pharaoh was now stricken, but not to repentance, for evil was in his heart, and he cursed Moses and the Israelites, and swore an oath to destroy Israel, man, woman and child, so that never again would there be one on the earth. And he sent his officers such a commandment, and to mobilize and begin the slaughter.

27/18.18. As for the Faithists, not many of them had slept during the night, but were providing for the journey, so that when morning came, every one of them started forth with the sunrise. From all the different regions of Egupt they went forth toward Sukkoth, westward [of Sukkoth]. The Heads led the way, and every commune was led by a rab'bah, and every man's family by the father of the family or by the eldest son. And at the start they spoke through their leaders, saying: In Your name, O Jehovih, we depart out of the land of our birth, where we were born, and our sons and daughters were born, to never return! Neither shall Egupt prosper again till You have subdued the whole earth to You. ||

27/18.19. But things had changed wonderfully with the Eguptians, for when they saw the Israelites were indeed going, and knew the miracles that had taken place, they relented, and brought them gifts of gold and silver; and also asses and camels for the Hebrew women and children to ride upon; and gave them food to eat. But the Israelitish women said: No, if we take these things we will be under obligations to the Eguptians. The Israelites do not accept what they cannot pay for. Then the Eguptians bewailed in fear, saying: So that we will not be accursed by the Gods, take them, we beseech you in the name of your God also.

27/18.20. So the Faithist women accepted the presents of asses, camels, and other things besides; and they mounted the asses and camels, and rode them.

27/18.21. When Moses heard of this afterward he rebuked Israel, saying: Because you have accepted these things it will be said, you borrowed and begged them so as to despoil the Eguptians.

27/18.22. When they arrived near Sukkoth, Jehovih spoke to Moses and Aaron, saying: Stand here for twelve days, so that you may see My people as they pass, and that you in turn may be seen by them. So Moses and Aaron pitched their tents on a high piece of ground off to the side, and remained there twelve days, and Moses showed himself before them, speaking and encouraging.

27/18.23. After this the Israelites passed through Etham, on the borders of the wilderness, and then on toward Migdol, near Baal-zephon, the place of the oracle of the God, Baal, and they encamped before Pi'hahiroth, where Moses commanded them to remain some days to rest.

27/18.24. Now as for Pharaoh, he had not made any attack on the Israelites, for Jehovih's Lord held his army in confusion. Pharaoh, finding that the Israelites were not injured, decided to take to the field himself; and accordingly, having impressed all the chariots of Egupt, went ahead, leading his army in person. The Israelites were wearied and footsore, and, discovering that Pharaoh was after them, many of them complained and grumbled, saying: O Moses, why did you bring us from home? It would have been better for us to remain in servitude to the Eguptians than to be slain.

27/18.25. Moses rebuked them, saying: You profess to be Faithists but yet have no faith in Jehovih? Put your trust in Him; for He will deliver you safely, as He has promised.

27/18.26. Jehovih spoke to Moses, saying: They shall witness the salvation of My hand; for the

Eguptians who pursue them this day shall never again pursue them. For when you lead them to the sea, you shall lift up your rod, and I will divide the sea, and My people shall walk across on the land of the bottom of the sea. And Pharaoh's army shall pursue, but be swallowed up in the waters. And so it came to pass:

27/18.27. Jehovih brought a strong wind and divided the waters of the sea and swept them back, and the Israelites went over on land. But Pharaoh's army, who were in pursuit, were caught in the flood of the tide and were drowned.

27/18.28. Thus Jehovih delivered the Israelites out of Egupt; and Israel believed in Him and in Moses, His servant.

27/18.29. Now from the place Sukkoth to the other side of the sea, a pillar of cloud preceded the Israelites by day, and a pillar of fire stood over them by night, and the people looked and everyone saw the cloud and the light. And the name of the place they reached when they crossed over was Shakelmarath; and they camped there many days.

27/18.30. From the time Moses began to prepare for the migration of Israel[1089] until he reached Shakelmarath, was four years two hundred and seven days. And the number of Israelites who went forth out of Egupt was three million seven hundred and fifty thousand, men, women and children. And the number of other people who accompanied them was four hundred thousand; and because they were of the uncircumcised tribes of ancients, the Hebrews nicknamed them Levites, i.e., imperfect flesh.

27/18.31. And Moses commanded the Levites to camp aside, and not to mix with the Israelites, and they obeyed him in all things, maintaining that they were the true descendants of Abraham.

27/18.32. And Moses made a song to Jehovih, and Miriam, his sister, sang it and played on the timbrel,[1090] and the women of Israel danced before Jehovih.

27/18.33. This, then, is the song of Moses:

[1089] Recall this was when the Voice came to Moses, with Pharaoh and Leotonas (27/15.24-29).

[1090] A timbrel is similar to a tambourine, a percussion instrument with jingling bells.

CHAPTER 19 Arc Bon

27/19.1. Eloih, Almighty, You, my God, Who have delivered my people! I will sing to You a song; and the children of Israel to You, O Eloih!

27/19.2. You are a great strength and salvation; for You, Eloih, I will build my habitation; You, my father's God, O Eloih!

27/19.3. You are my Warrior; Eloih is Your name, forever!

27/19.4. You have encompassed Pharaoh and his hosts; they are swallowed up in the sea; his chosen captains and his warriors in the Red Sea.

27/19.5. The depths covered them up; they sank to the bottom like a stone, O Eloih!

27/19.6. Almighty Eloih; Glorious in power in Your right hand that passed over innocent blood!

27/19.7. You my God, Eloih; Wise in majesty, in Your right hand that dashed in pieces Your enemy!

27/19.8. Excellency, You O Eloih; Who in graciousness came upon those who rose up to block Your way; You sent Your breath upon them; as stubble they were cut down by Your righteous sword!

27/19.9. By the breath of Your nostrils, You heaped up the waters of the sea; and the floods stood upright by Your voice, to entrap them in the heart of the sea!

27/19.10. Your enemy said: I will pursue; I will overtake them; the spoil shall be mine; I will draw the sword; my hand shall destroy them!

27/19.11. You blew with Your wind; the sea covered them; they sank like lead in the mighty waters.

27/19.12. Who is like You, Eloih, among the Gods? Who is like You, Glorious in Holiness, fearful in praise and wonders, O Eloih! You stretched out Your right hand, and they went down into the earth.

27/19.13. Merciful Almighty, Eloih, my God, and God of my fathers; Who has led forth Israel and delivered her into the land of her fathers, O Eloih! Who has guided them to a holy and peaceful habitation.

27/19.14. All people shall hear and be afraid; sober thought shall take hold on the inhabitants of Palestina. And the nobles of Edom shall be amazed! Trembling shall take hold of the warrior of

Moab; and the wild men of Kana'yan shall melt away!

27/19.15. You, O Eloih, shall strike them with fear; by the magnitude of the strength of Your arm they will be amazed and helpless as stone. For this land is Your purchase, O Eloih; in the passover of the blood of the lamb You purchased it; and Israel shall pass over it in fear.

27/19.16. And You shall bring them to the mountain of their inheritance, to Your place, Our God, Eloih. To dwell in Your sanctuary, which You have established for Your reign, forever and forever.

CHAPTER 20 Arc Bon

27/20.1. Moses called together the Heads and the rab'bahs, privately, and spoke before them, saying:

27/20.2. What have I taken upon me, O Jehovih? Behold Your sons and daughters have followed me out of Egupt; how shall I bind them to You and not to me, O my Father in heaven?27/20.3. Jehovih said to me: Moses, Moses, what I say to you, say to the rab'bahs and to the Heads; saying to them: Not Moses, nor the Heads, nor the rab'bahs, brought you out of Egupt; you were brought out by the Creator, Jehovih, Who is God of all, Captain of all, Head of all, Rab'bah of all.

27/20.4. For in this I have drawn the line between My people and My enemies, the idolaters of men. Because of signs and miracles, the idolaters make a man-God of their magician and worship him. But who is like you, Moses, My son; in miracles, who can match you in the magnitude of your proceeding?

27/20.5. Who led forth My millions; and delivered them out of a great power without loss of a man, woman or child?

27/20.6. But I declare to you, you shall do a greater miracle than any of these; for you shall preserve yourself from becoming an idol before men. For you shall proclaim Me to your people in all things; teaching them that you are only a man. And your Heads and your rab'bahs shall likewise teach them the same, for I will put away all idolatry from the face of the earth.

27/20.7. Neither will I have kings nor queens; I am sufficient for all men.

27/20.8. As Abraham apportioned My people into families [communities –Ed.], with rab'bahs and with chief rab'bahs, so shall you re-establish them.

27/20.9. And My commandments, which I gave to Abraham, I will give to you; and I will re-establish My crescent with My rab'bahs. And My crescent shall be the fullness of My law for the rab'bahs and chief rab'bahs.

27/20.10. Moses said: I cried to Jehovih, saying: How shall it be with the square and at high noon? And the angel of Jehovih, speaking in the Father's name, said: To the northeast God; to the southwest Lord; to the northwest Baal; to the southeast Ashtaroth. For Osiris is dead already.

27/20.11. To this end, then, prepare a place for tonight, so that the Great Spirit may bless us. The rab'bahs and the Heads said: It is well.

27/20.12. And when it was night Moses with the rab'bahs and the Heads went aside, placing sentinels so they would be alone. And when they were thus prepared, the light of Jehovih came upon Moses, and the books of the ancients were opened before him. And he administered Emethachavah upon them; by the voice of Jehovih he re-established it; with all the rites and ceremonies as they are to this day. And after that the Heads were no longer called Heads, but Chief Rab'bahs; for Moses anointed them by command of Jehovih.

27/20.13. And in not many days, Moses wrote the Levitican laws; for the inner temple of Jehovih was in spoken words only; but the outer temple was written. So that it was said: The Hebrews have two laws; one which no other man knows, and one for those who are not eligible by faith, being those who were called Leviticans; but not Leviticans in fact, but hangers-on, who had followed the Israelites out of Egupt and who for the most part had no God, little judgment and no learning.

27/20.14. But regarding all that Moses did, and taught, and how he labored with his own hands, many books could be written. And it is doubtful if the world ever produced another so good and great a man.[1091]

[1091] see image i115 next page

i115 **Moses**. He rebuilt what had been lost since Abram's time.

27/20.15. At the time Moses reached Shakelmarath he was forty-four years old by the Hebrew sun (solar year), but by the Eguptian calendar he was eighty-eight years old.

27/20.16. As for Pharaoh and those of his hosts who were not destroyed in the sea, they returned home to their places. And not long after that, Pharaoh banished God (Osiris) from the earth, declaring himself the SAVIOR OF THE WORLD, and VICE-GERENT[1092] OF THE HOLY GHOST.

27/20.17. Pharaoh's scribes and recorders assembled in Kaona, and they appointed Feh-ya (an Eguptian), to write the departure of the Israelites out of Egupt. And Feh-ya wrote the account and called it the EXODUS OF THE HEBREWS, and it was recorded in the king's House of Records. And copies of it were sent to the large cities, and there recorded also, for such was the law of Egupt. Feh-ya's record was afterward accepted by Ezra, and is that which is known to this day as the First Book of Exodus.

27/20.18. The Book of Genesis, as it stood in the Eguptian records, was written by Akaboth and Dueram and Hazed, and was the substance from which Ezra copied it through his scribes, even as it is to this day. The inspiration of Genesis was from the God Osiris, the false, and his emissaries, chief of whom were Yotabba and Egupt, who were angel servants to Osiris. And so far as the records now stand, the spirit of both books was the Eguptian version of the whole subject.

27/20.19. Touching genealogies, in which men seemed to have lived to so great an age, this, then, is the explanation for it:

27/20.20. Thothma had said to his recorders: In searching for the truth of legends, give the latitude of it. For one legend will say, such a man lived seven hundred years ago; another legend will say he lived one thousand fifty years ago. The latitude between them is, therefore, three hundred fifty years, which shall be the time of that man's life. || And in this way latitude became confounded with fact,[1093] and with no intent to deceive.

[1092] one who acts in the place of another; a viceroy; a deputy

[1093] In the example the man lived sometime between a span of 350 years; that is, he lived, for some unspecified duration, sometime between 700 and 1050 years before the date of recording; and this 350 years of latitude (range; extent of applicability) during which a person lived, became confused with a person's age at death; that is, the lower and upper limits of the latitude incorrectly became thought of as the points of birth and death of that person. As a result, such a person was mistakenly thought to have been 350 years old when he died.

27/20.21. And behold, it came to pass that the records were worthless; and to make matters worse the records were so voluminous, being more than six thousand books, that the scribes of Ezra could make neither head nor tail of them. Nevertheless, they were all written, in the first place not by the Israelites, but by their enemies, where, even so, the testimony of the miracles is none the weaker.

27/20.22. Thus ends the history of Moses' deliverance of the Faithists out of Egupt.

27/20.23. Hear now of Chine of the land of Jaffeth:

CHAPTER 21 Arc Bon

History of Chine (Tschin'e), of Jaffeth, Founder of China

27/21.1. These are the generations of the seven antecedents of Chine, the chosen of the Great Spirit, Ormazd, otherwise, in Fonecean, Eloih; that is to say:

27/21.2. Tse'wong begot Hi-gan, who begot Ah So, who begot T-soo Yong, who begot Ah Paing, who begot T-chook Lee, who begot Tschine Loo, who begot Ah Sho'e, who begot Tschin'e (Chine), gifted in su'is and sar'gis of six generations.

27/21.3. Of these, T-soo Yong and Ah So were prophets of Jehovih (Ormazd), and Ah Sho'e was a seer; but the six generations could hear the Voice, and they walked upright, keeping the commandments of Jehovih as revealed in the Zarathustrian laws.

27/21.4. Ah Sho'e was a basket-maker, and was like the man Zarathustra; and Chine, his son, was the fourth birth of Ah Sho'e's wife, Song Heng. Like Moses, Chine was of copper color, and very large, but his hair was red, like a fox, and he was bashful and of few words.

27/21.5. Ah Sho'e, i.e., Chine's father, said: I have had other sons; my words are wise and true; Chine was unlike any child born in the world; for boy child, or girl child, no physician could tell which, but rather to the boy kind was he. The angel of Jehovih (Ormazd) came to me before the birth and said: The child shall be called Chine, signifying no sex; as it is written among the ancients, i-e-su, having no earthly desires. For, he shall restore the chosen people of Jehovih.

27/21.6. Before the birth I told the physicians of this prophecy, but they would not believe. Nevertheless, by command of Jehovih, I sent for seven physicians to witness the birth, lest it be said afterward the surgeons have dealt wrongly with the child at its birth.

27/21.7. The following physicians came: Em Gha, Tse Thah, Ah Em Fae, Te Gow, T'si, Du Jon, Foh Chaing, and Ah Kaon, and they witnessed the child being born, to which they made oath,[1094] and a record of it, touching the strangeness of such a birth, and of the prophecy of its coming into the world; this record was put in the Ha Ta'e King (library) of records belonging to the Sun King [state records –Ed.].

27/21.8. Being now in my old age, I, Ah Sho'e, put these things on record, of which hundreds have come to ask me concerning the growing up of Chine.

27/21.9. First, that he was the laziest of all children, and dull past belief. For his brothers and sisters mocked him, concerning my prophecy, as to becoming a great man.

27/21.10. Second, he ate less than a small bird (Fa'ak), and grew so thin we were ashamed of him in his childhood; truly he was nothing but skin and bone, with a large head.

27/21.11. Third, when he walked about, the stools and tables moved out of his way; and yet no hand touched them.

27/21.12. Fourth, the angels of Jehovih often carried him about the hut, and would lift him up to pick fruit from the trees.

27/21.13. Fifth, he never laughed, but was serious and pleasant, like an old man who had abandoned the world. But he spoke so little no man knew whether he was wise or stupid.

27/21.14. When he was three years old his mother weaned him, or rather he weaned himself. And from that time on, he never ate anything but fruit and nuts and grains of rice. When he was sixteen years old he began to grow suddenly large and strong, and of deep color. After which I procured a teacher for him; but lo and behold, he could learn a whole book in a day. He learned by hearing once; nor did he forget anything he learned.

[1094] sworn statement; attestation; written testimony

27/21.15. In his twenty-second year he began to talk, and the angels of heaven spoke through him also. And his speech was full of wisdom.

27/21.16. From sunrise in the morning until late at night his tongue did not cease speaking. And his mouth was as if it were the mouthpiece of heaven. For after one angel had discoursed before the audience for a while, another came, and then another, and so on; and when none came, then Chine himself spoke.

27/21.17. And there came before him men of great learning, and philosophers, to try him as to his knowledge; but they all went away confounded, as if they were fools. Nor was it possible to ask him a question that he could not answer correctly. Whether it was to read a tablet or to reveal the size and design of a temple he never saw; or the sickness of a man who was far away; for all things were like an open book to him.

27/21.18. For four years this great wisdom remained in him, and his fame spread from the east to the west, and from the north to the south; no man knew how far. When he was asked how far he could see and hear, he said: Over all my land. And he marked with his finger, saying: On this tablet, Chine land! ||

27/21.19. Thus was the country named Chine (China), which it bears to this day.

27/21.20. Ah Sho'e said: Suddenly Chine's abundant speech ceased, and he answered only yes and no to all things. And he was thus silent for seven years and eighty days. And then the angels from the second heaven (etherea) came to him. After that he did not speak as man (except in private), but he spoke as the All Light, of which the world knows the rest.

CHAPTER 22 Arc Bon

27/22.1. Chine said: I am a man only. I am the All Light. My voice is that which lives forever. Do not worship me; do not worship man; worship All Light. I am Jehovih (Ormazd) Ever Present. Because of My abundance in man, man opens the mouth; makes words.

27/22.2. To know Me is to know all things; he who strives to Me is My chosen. He who does not know Me, does not prove Me; he who knows Me cannot prove Me. To every self I am The Self of that self. To perfect that self which is in all selfs;

such a man is one with Me. To travel on such a road; that is the right road.

27/22.3. Hear Me, O man! I come every three thousand years; I newly light up the world. My voice comes upon the souls of men; your All Highest is Me; your all lowest is sin. Two things only I set before you, O man; the Self that is Myself, and the self that is yourself. Which will you serve? For on this hangs either your resurrection or your hell.

27/22.4. In the time of the first of ancients I asked the same questions. Whoever said: I will serve You, Ormazd, You All Self, || he was My chosen. Whoever answered: I will serve the self of myself, was satan's. The latter went on the wrong road. Their trail was blood and death; war, their glory.

27/22.5. They fell upon My chosen; like tigers they have pursued them. I called out in the ancient days: Why do you persecute My chosen and destroy them? And they answered: They will not war; they do not serve our king; they serve the King of kings; they practice peace; they do not uphold our God.

27/22.6. But I stretched forth My hand from the second heaven; I bowed down to My virgin daughter, the troubled earth, Ma-lah. And I took My chosen and put them in Brahma's hand; and they were shapely and fleet-footed, valiant in love and good works. And I sent great learning to the sons of men, and wisdom and peace, and great rejoicing.

27/22.7. And Ma-lah blossomed and was fragrant as new honey, and clean and full of virtue. Her daughters hid the thigh and the ankle; their full breasts were concealed and their words were of modesty.

27/22.8. Her sons were early to rise; producing abundance, and with songs of rejoicing, and with dancing. For My beloved shaped the ways of man; their progeny were like the sweet blossoms of an orchard; like the fragrance of red clover. I said to them: Do not fear; your sons and your daughters are a great glory to you. Count the days of your wife; and rejoice when the birth draws near; for it is fruit of Me and of you.

27/22.9. And they taught the little ones to clap their hands and rejoice; I made them for this. Sing, O earth! Hold up your head, I said to My beloved, for Mine is a place of glory and sweet love, sparkling with good delights. || None could restrain them; like young colts and young lambs at play; their capers were unceasing and most tender.

27/22.10. This was My good creation; the bliss of My chosen; this was My shapely earth in the days of peace; in the times of My chosen. Neither war nor weeping was there; nor hunger, thirst, nor famine; nor fields lying waste; nor sickness, nor evil diseases; nor cursing, swearing, lying nor deceit; nor hardships and sore toil, nor any evil thing under the sun.

27/22.11. I, the All Light, Jehovih, have spoken. Will they hear My words? How will man judge Me, the Creator? Has he gone among My beloved; and My upraised who obey My commandments? Has he seen the beauty of the earth in the hands of My chosen?

27/22.12. O man! You fool! You go into a dark corner and say: How dark! You go before My enemies and say: What a vain creation! Or search among those who do not serve Me, and say: Miserable world! Or among those who hate Me, and say: How wickedly they kill one another. Oh, if only Jehovih had made a better creation!

27/22.13. You cry out: There is no happiness on the earth; all is misery, sorrow, pain and death! And this is your standard, O man, to judge your Creator! You say: There is no peace, no delight, no love, no harmony on the earth!

27/22.14. Stubborn man! And contrary, and of narrow judgment! O if you would stand in a clean place and high, and then judge! Have you measured My chosen, who have faith in My Person? Why have you treasured yourself? And put yourself uppermost of all things? Who have you found that denied My Person, who did not dwell in lust and self-conceit?

27/22.15. Where is your standard, if not the All High? What is your dispute about the all low? If I call Myself the All High, are you better pleased? If satan calls himself the all low, will you be satisfied? Or shall a man not speak of the All High? Nor of the all low? Are there not such things? And shall they not have names?

27/22.16. Your wicked hand rises up against My chosen, to lay them in death. And when you have trailed the earth over in blood; and your hand is wearied with destruction, and your little ones have nothing to eat, you pray: O Father, help Your little ones!

27/22.17. I have spoken!

CHAPTER 23 Arc Bon

27/23.1. Chine spoke Jehovih's words, saying:

They have sought after pleasure, and after you, O earth! They have bowed down to men, to the king and the rich man, and now, behold their misery! The king said: Come serve me. Take your spear, and your strong bow and arrow, and come with me. I will show you great delights; you shall slaughter my enemies; and I will give you wages.

27/23.2. And they ran to serve the king; yes, they washed their hands in the blood of My innocent ones. Because the king said: Brave! Good slaughterer! || Then they were pleased, highly recompensed!

27/23.3. I have said: You are on the wrong road; serve only Me, for I am Good Delights. Because you slay one another, the land will not be tilled; you are hungry and ragged. And they queried: What will Jehovih give for wages? More than the king?

27/23.4. Your weakness lies in this, O man! You say: Wait a little while; I will serve the man first; and afterward Jehovih!

27/23.5. What profit do you have in your brother's death? With all his treasures of gold and silver, what do you really have?

27/23.6. Behold, you will not allow to live in peace even those who choose Me and My ways. Because they say: My Creator is my King; I will serve Him. || the king says: Go for them; slaughter them! They put Jehovih higher than me!

27/23.7. And you say: It is a good and wholesome thing to serve the king, and kill his enemies. To serve my country by killing men, this is great glory!

27/23.8. But the voice of My beloved rose up to Me; yes, My lambs flee before the wolves, being driven away from My goodly pastures. Behold Me, I have come to them, to the lovers of peace and virtue and loving kindness. My hand is stretched over them in great power; My word is given to them, and is not dead.

27/23.9. I will call them together; they shall again hold up their heads and rejoice because of My Presence. ||

27/23.10. After Jehovih's voice came to Chine he traveled far and near; and because of his wonderful wisdom, men of great learning and even kings sent for him. And wherever he went he preached the same, for peace and love, and against war.

27/23.11. For three years Chine traveled, proclaiming the Creator above all else in heaven and earth. And then he rested one hundred and forty days, sleeping like a young child, saying nothing more than a child would say.

27/23.12. Then a change came upon Chine; he was like a new man in the world, and not as a God. And he rose up, saying: My Father, Creator of men, calls me. I hear His voice. It is like a burning fire in my soul, moving me. Not with pain, but with great power. He says:

27/23.13. Chine, My Son! Chine, My Son! My house is on fire! My little ones are burning. Go to them, Chine. They are in fear and trembling; they do not know what way to turn. The kings of the earth have outlawed them; they are hunted down, and are famished. Go to them, O Chine! For that end I created you alive in the world; you shall be My Voice to them.

27/23.14. Chine said: Jehovih says: Who can overcome the fire when he remains in the house? He goes outside where there is water. Call My people out of the house of My enemies. Give them a wellspring of clean water; they are parched[1095] and thirsty. Say to them; Jehovih lives! His love abounds. || Come to My fountains that are not dried up. Come and hear the covenant of My Son, Chine: [1096]

27/23.15. I swear to You, O Jehovih, my Almighty! I will have no other God but You, Creator! All Light, Most Glorious! You are my King! Holy, Holy, Ever Present! O my Captain, my All Highest Captain! I salute You in the Rising Sun! In the High Noon, most Mighty! And in the sweet Setting Sun!

27/23.16. I know nothing but You; to You I swear this, my most solemn oath, O Jehovih! Call up Your angels, holy and most wise; Your recording angels! They shall hear my covenant to You, My Creator! They shall write it in the books of heaven, O my Master! And while the sun, moon, earth and stars stand, my oath to You shall stand up against me:

[1095] dry, withered, lacking vitality

[1096] see image i116

i116 **Chine**. The founder of China, and who restored the rights of the believers in Jehovih throughout that great country.

27/23.17. You only shall be my King; You only shall be my God and Heavenly Ruler. All other kings I forswear, and all other Gods, captains, and great rulers. I will not bow down to any of them, nor worship them, forever. I, Chine, have spoken.

27/23.18. I swear to You, O Great Spirit, You are my bond to the end of the world. I will neither war nor abet war; to peace forever I am sworn. And though they impress (draft) me and torture me, or slay me outright, they shall not force me; I will not draw one drop of blood in any man, woman or child whom You have created alive on the earth.

27/23.19. I swear to You, You All Person—You Who are so large that the earth and sun and stars would not fill the hollow of Your hand—to be like You, O Jehovih: Fair dealing to all men, as You would; good, forgiving, and without anger forever; and to share equally in all possessions with Your chosen, O Jehovih.

27/23.20. To raise up those who are cast down; to deliver the afflicted and helpless; to never render evil, nor the fruit of anger, to any man, O Jehovih; but good to those who abuse me; and in my actions, steadfast in Your course, my Creator.

27/23.21. In my blood I covenant with You; by the veins in my flesh, make oath forever: To never wed out of Your Order, the Hi-tspe.[1097] Blood of the blood of Your chosen my heirs shall be and their heirs after them, forever.

27/23.22. Hear me, O Jehovih: I make a new covenant; it shall be written upon the firmament of heaven. I will do good with all my might; the tears of the suffering poor shall be like scalding blood in my veins; I will not sit down and rest, nor take my ease, nor hold possessions while they are in want.

27/23.23. Prick me, O my Father in heaven; sharpen my conscience keener than a sword; drive me to labor for the poor and afflicted, give me no rest, except while I am doing good to them.

27/23.24. O if only my covenant was set with swords, pointing every way; so that I could find no peace but in serving You, my Creator, Ormazd; and that I was pure, strong, wise, and swifter than life and death, and as unfailing.

27/23.25. And that my oath reached to Your chosen, and they heard me; that my voice was sweet to them, and enticing like an early love.

27/23.26. If only they would come forth from their hiding places, Your faithful children, and not be afraid.

27/23.27. I would go to them like a lover, and bow my head down to them, for their long suffering and their faith to You, Jehovih.

27/23.28. Like a father who has lost his son and found him again, I would take them in my arms, Your worshippers, You All One, Everlasting Spirit.

27/23.29. As a rosebush trampled in the mire, O how they have been scourged, O Jehovih. Destitute,[1098] ragged and scattered. But I would wash them clean, and give them new soil; so their voices in song and praise would gladden the whole earth.

CHAPTER 24 Arc Bon

27/24.1. The great cities of the ancients in Jaffeth had been destroyed by Joss (Te-in) and his evil spirits, who inspired mortals to war. And for the most part it was a land of ruins, but now thousands of cities, standing beside the broken walls, were spread over the entire breadth of the land.

27/24.2. Jehovih spoke to Chine, saying: Now is a good time for My chosen. Behold My enemies, the idolaters; you can recognize them by their soldiers. They are weak now. They pant with the labor of their great battles. Let My people come out of their quarters and hold up their heads.

27/24.3. Say to them, O Chine: There is no Joss, no Ho-Joss, no Te-in, no Po, no Po-Te-in, to make you afraid. || And while the enemy rests, bid My sons and daughters arise! They shall inhabit the land that is spoiled, and cause it to bloom and bring forth abundantly. Call up My outlawed race; the enemy is sick of his wounds; his heart is ashamed and disconsolate; he is cast down.

27/24.4. Chine went to A'shong and gathered up many converts, descendants of the Faithists, the pure Brahmans, the line of Zarathustra, the people of the Great All One, who did not accept Gods and Lords. And he established them, and invented plows and mattocks for digging the ground; for these implements had been lost and destroyed,

[1097] One of the orders of Faithists in China. Equivalent to Hi-dang in some regions. –Ed.

[1098] utterly without means; tenuous subsistence; deathly poor

since hundreds of years, and no man knew how to make them.

27/24.5. Chine said to them: This is a good philosophy: Do not wait till you are well fed and clothed before you bow your heads down at the altar of Jehovih. When you have prayed and sung before Him, then go forth into the field to work. And He will bless you.

27/24.6. Remember the heathen, they say: First provide the natural body, and then the spirit. But I say to you, Jehovih created them both together. And he who says: First provide the natural body, never looks to his spirit afterward.

27/24.7. In all things give precedence to the spirit; as the Creator is over all His works, so should the spirit of man be over man's works, and over his corporeal body also.

27/24.8. In that lay the foundation of the wisdom of your forefathers, the Zarathustrians. For the heathen and the idolater, who labor for self, what are they but servants to the flesh?

27/24.9. Those people who labor for the raising of the spirit, which is through purity, love, goodness and justice, are on the right road to become a great people. But when they strive, every man for himself, such people are beginning to fall.

27/24.10. Her boundaries may be large, and her people increasing, but she has a cankerworm within that, sooner or later, will let her down suddenly.

27/24.11. Two extremes meeting are always dangerous: great wealth and extensive poverty. It not only devolves on the rich to give their substance to the poor, but they shall go among them, teaching them and lifting them up.

27/24.12. He who does not do this, consider how vain it is for him to pray to Jehovih. His prayer does not rise upward. Let him first answer the poor himself. This is the opening of his own soul, so Jehovih can reach him.

27/24.13. Remember that all men have judgment, and that they should be perfected to see things from their own standpoint, and not from yours. Consider, then, how unjust it is to foist on any man your opinions, uncalled for. ||

27/24.14. Chine established families of the chosen, but limited them to two hundred; and to each family he gave one priest. But he set a limit of four thousand people to dwell in any one city.

27/24.15. Chine said: You have been afflicted with Gods; I was sent into the world by the Creator to deliver you to liberty in the family. I am only a man. I have no authority in myself. Jehovih, the Creator, dwells freely in me. You can attain the same.

27/24.16. Because He is within me, this shall be called Chine-land [Chine'ya –Ed.]. There is a time for this. My name is like a post to mark the time when the Creator began His temple of peace, which shall extend over all these people.

27/24.17. Jehovih says: Why will man be vain about himself? Truly I have not have created one man on the face of the earth who is composed of himself. Instead he is made up of all oddities, soul and body. Consider his flesh, where he received it from, and how he sustains it. Not so much as one hair on his head is of his own making; neither is it made out of new material, but has been used over and over forever.

27/24.18. Nor is even his mind his own; not even his simplest thought; but he is made up of borrowed things from beginning to end, for so I created him.

27/24.19. He imagines I, Who created him, am nothing; but even his imagination he picked up from someone else. He gathers a little here, and a little there, and then proclaims what he knows.

27/24.20. Chine said: One man says: I am normal; neither angels nor mortals rule over me! Yet he has only boasted like a crazy man, who will say the same thing. Another says: Behold my wisdom! The highest of angels discourse through me. Yet he does not know whether it is true or not. Nor do any of them know the fountainhead. For if an angel says it, the angel himself is made up of borrowed knowledge.

27/24.21. Chine said: I saw a great mathematician one day, and he said: There are no Gods, no Lords, no angels, no All Person. Everything is void. He showed me a book he had, and I asked: Who made the book? He said: I made it; no, I did not make the cloth, nor the binding; I mean, I made the philosophy that is in the book; no, I did not make the philosophy, but found it; no, it was not lost; I mean I led myself to find the philosophy; no, a man cannot lead himself; I mean that I searched and found what was new to me. || So, very little of that book was his, after all.

27/24.22. I saw three angels standing beside that man, and they were laughing at him. If I had asked the angels, they might have said: No, the thoughts were ours. And had I looked further I would have seen angels behind them, claiming the same things. Yet, even they are not the highest.

27/24.23. So that I say to you: All things come from an All Highest, name Him what you will. The one who says: Jehovih spoke to me; || he, of all, is nearest the mark. For all good knowledge that comes to man is Jehovih's word to that man. Whether it comes by an angel or by another man, or by the commonest corporeal thing, it is nevertheless from the All Highest.

27/24.24. For which reason do not bow down in worship to man or angels, but only to the Highest, Jehovih, for He is the Figurehead and Pinnacle of the All Highest Conceived Of. And in contradistinction, the all lowest; the foot of the ladder; call it darkness and evil, and wickedness and sin, and death and satan.

27/24.25. Do not attribute this or that to men or angels, for they themselves are not first causes, nor responsible except in part; but attribute all good, high, best and wise things to Jehovih; and all evil, dark, wicked, low things to satan.

27/24.26. By these terms you shall make plain to one another what you mean; and it is an easy matter to look into your own souls and comprehend as to which of these two you most incline.

27/24.27. The soul may be likened to a vine, which can be trained either upward or downward. And if you desire to know if a vine is up or down, you look for the fruit, and not to the fragrance. Some men pray much, but as to good works they are like a vine without fruit, but with plenty of fragrance.

CHAPTER 25 Arc Bon

27/25.1. Chine said: One man waits till he is rich, before helping the poor; another man waits for the angels to inspire him, and give him wonders, before he teaches the unlearned; another waits for the multitude to join in first; and yet another waits for something else. Beware of such men; or put them in scales where straw is weighed.[1099]

[1099] i.e., be careful, they lack substance; don't give much weight to their declarations; be circumspect in giving latitude; don't be fooled by pretense, etc.

27/25.2. The sons and daughters of Jehovih go right on. They say: It is the highest, best! I will go in! Though I do not accomplish it, yet I will not fail [to do the best I can to fulfill my highest light. –ed.].

27/25.3. Consider the foundation of things at all times. Jehovih says: I created all the living to bring forth after their own kind. Therefore be perceptive as to whom you marry; and consider the All Highest inspiration common to your choice. ||

27/25.4. Judge the All Highest inspiration of any man or woman not by their words, but by their works. For the raising up of the world shall be mostly accomplished by the fruit of judicious marriage.

27/25.5. Chine said: I declare a bondage to men that they do not know of, for it belongs in the next world; which is the begetting of selfish offspring in this world. For while their heirs are in darkness they themselves cannot rise in heaven.

27/25.6. Yet, I also declare a glory in heaven to those who wed in self-abnegation,[1100] who do good to others constantly and with delight; for they bring forth heirs to glorify Jehovih in good works also.

27/25.7. For this reason the mark of circumcision was given to your forefathers, lest the Faithist women be led astray by idolaters. And yet, despite all precautions, many fell, being tempted by the flesh. And their heirs descended lower and lower in darkness, until they lost sight of the All Person, and did not believe in Him.

27/25.8. The hand hardened from toil will ensure a better heir than the dimpled hand of a proud woman. The latter has a soul of passions, and her offspring will have souls like a mixture of gall and sugar; though they are sweet, they will prove to be bitter in time to come.

27/25.9. Consider your heir; show him an orderly house with a head; so that he may grow up understanding the discipline of earth and heaven.

27/25.10. The father shall be master in all things; and the mother shall be vice-master in all things, to rule in his absence.

27/25.11. For each family shall be a kingdom of itself; but no one shall be a tyrant, though he has precedence in all things.

[1100] set aside self; willing to set aside self-interest for the sake of Jehovih

27/25.12. Do not sit down at the table to eat until all stand gathered about it; and when they are seated, you shall say: In Your praise, O Jehovih, we receive this, Your gift; be with us for Your own glory, forever, amen!

27/25.13. For the chief virtue of the words lies in the discipline for the young mind; holding him steadfast in the orderly manner of the angels in heaven. And because he speaks the prayer with you, he learns to honor you with good rejoicing.

27/25.14. And when the sons and daughters are yet small, you shall teach them to work; inspiring them above all things not to fall into idleness, which lies at the borders of hell.

27/25.15. But do not overburden them, nor give them pain; remembering they are to be your glory, which Jehovih bestowed to you to be in your keeping, not for your self-aggrandizement, but for their own delights and holy pleasures.

27/25.16. For they shall sing and play, and clap their hands and rejoice and dance, for these are their thanks to the Creator; and the earth shall be glad because they came into the world.

27/25.17. Remember that labor shall be delight, and toil a great delight; to have it otherwise for your children and for yourself, is to prostitute man to be like a beast of the field. But you shall bring them into groups, and their labor shall be a frolic and full of instruction.

27/25.18. And even your little ones shall learn that you are only a brother, an elder brother, and one of the children of the same Creator; teaching them that one who hoards and keeps things as his own possessions is like a cannibal who eats the flesh and blood of his kindred.

27/25.19. Above all things you shall teach them to keep holy and pure the body created with them; for in this lies health and strength. To be foul is to be sick, to be sick is to be foul. Behold the heathen and idolater, the feeders on flesh and blood; in the time they boast of health they stink like a carcass; their flesh is congested and puffed up, their breath like a kennel of dogs. How can their souls be pure or their understanding clear? They have made themselves a festering stink-house for the spirit to dwell in.

27/25.20. And they say: Bah! I see no Jehovih! I know no All Person! I deny the soul of things! Where is the spirit? I cannot see it! Or the sound of its voice? I cannot hear it! And if there is a Great Spirit, let Him come before me! I would see Him. || Yes, in their filthy bodies they say this. Let them be pure and they will understand the vanity of such words.

CHAPTER 26 Arc Bon

27/26.1. Jehovih said to Chine: Now I will stir up the nations. Through you I will show them the glory and dominion of My kingdoms.

27/26.2. For you shall walk without feet; write without hands; hear without ears; see without eyes; and you shall rise in the air like a bird; by your own will, go wherever you choose.

27/26.3. And you shall bring down the thundercloud, and at the sound of your voice the rains shall fall.

27/26.4. And you shall say: Go away, you clouds; and the sun will shine in their place.

27/26.5. And you shall come to some who are hungry, and your voice shall rise up to Me, and I will send down from heaven the food of heaven (haoma); and your people shall eat of it and be appeased.

27/26.6. And you shall stretch up your hand over the dead that are ready for the furnace, and they shall come to life again and be made whole.

27/26.7. For these are the testimonies that you are My servant, and have kept My commandments.

27/26.8. In which you shall say to them: Behold me; I am only a man! Why do you fall down (prostrate) before the Gods and worship them? For I charge, O all you people, that you shall not worship me nor call me anything but a man striving to do the will of my Father, the Creator.

27/26.9. For whoever becomes one with Him; to such a person many miracles are possible; although, I declare to you, they are not miracles in fact; but possibilities granted by Jehovih to the upright, who serve Him in act and truth.

27/26.10. Jehovih said to Chine: And when you have shown these things to many, know, then, your time on the earth is finished. For I will cast you in a trance, and the people shall bewail, saying: Alas, he is dead! And they shall cover you and cast your body into the furnace as is done with the dead; and the fire shall blaze and consume your body before them. But you shall have previously bid them watch by the furnace, for you shall gather together the elements of your burnt body and restore them, and again inhabit it and go about, preaching before men.

27/26.11. Therefore get ready; declaring these prophecies beforehand, so that they may be testified to by men, and so be recorded in the libraries of the kings and queens.

27/26.12. Chine conveyed to the congregations of Faithists, the true Zarathustrians, what Ormazd (Jehovih) had said, and many of them wept bitterly.

27/26.13. In years prior to this, when Chine had traveled and preached by the voice of Jehovih, he visited the kings, princes and rich men in many regions; and while he was thus speaking, rebuking them for their governments and for their possessions, they took no part against him. But afterward, when he was gone, the kings, queens and nobles said: Chine has preached a dangerous doctrine; for he said: You shall have no king but the Creator, Who is King over all. Will this not set our slaves against us? And if the people go into communities of their own, ignoring the king, where will the king find his revenue?

27/26.14. And there were priests of Dyaus and of other Gods, and speakers in temples (oracles) where the Gods wrote on sand tables. Besides these there were countless seers and prophets. And the kings, being on the alert, investigated the matter, inquiring of the spirits as to whether the doctrines of Chine were true.

27/26.15. And some of the spirits said: There is no All Person. Behold, we have visited the stars and the sun, and looked far and near, and we did not see any Creator, or All Person. There is no Great Spirit, except Te-in, who was a onetime mortal, but has risen to all power in heaven and earth.

27/26.16. And other spirits said: There is nothing in heaven that you do not have on earth. How shall we find Ormazd? Do not waste your time with Chine and his doctrines; he will overthrow your kingdoms. Eat, drink and satiate your desires; for these are the sum and substance of all things in heaven and earth.

27/26.17. Te-zee, king of A'shong, the capital city of the Province of Aen-Na-Po'e, who was also a great philosopher, had previously heard Chine preach, and was greatly interested. Sometime after this a magician, Loo Sin, visited Te-zee, who told the magician about the wonders of Chine. The magician listened to the king's story, and the king asked the magician whether he could himself, in addition to his sleight-of-hand, manifest wisdom in words, like Chine, and if so, how could it be attained?

27/26.18. Loo Sin, the magician, answered: Te-zee, O king, you do not know how you have embarrassed me, your servant. For when we are young, and finding we have the natural powers for a magician, we go before an adept to be taught all the mysteries of the order; and here we take a most binding oath never to reveal by hint, word, mark, or written character, anything that will reveal any of our signs and mysteries, binding ourselves under great penalties, which I cannot name to you.

27/26.19. Know then, O king, I can answer all your questions, and am desirous to serve you, but what shall I do?

27/26.20. The king said: I, being king, absolve you from your oath. The magician said: Compared to my power, though I only beg from door to door, your power, O king, is only as chaff before the wind. In my subtle realms are the keys of all dominions. Not only do I and my craft rule over mortals, but over the spirits of the dead. My oath, then, is too great for you to absolve, for I cannot even absolve it myself!

27/26.21. Te-zee, the king, said: Since, then, you cannot do all things, and, especially, absolve an oath, you are not sufficient for me to deal with. Loo Sin, being desirous of earning something, said: As for that, O king, I tell you I cannot reveal all, for the virtue of my art depends much on its secrets and mystery. Nevertheless, as I am very poor, I might reveal an index[1101] to you, by which, if you would apply yourself diligently, you could attain the remainder.

27/26.22. So the king commanded him to perform before him, agreeing to award him according to the decree of the fates (spirits). And Loo Sin at once went to work, performing wonderful feats, such as causing the tables, seats and desks, to move about and to roll over; and he caused voices to speak in unseen places. He also changed rods into serpents, and caused birds to sit on the king's shoulder; and he changed water into wine, and also brought fish and laid them on the floor at the king's feet.

[1101] a key; a hint; a pointer

27/26.23. The king said to him: All these things I have witnessed from my youth up. Show me now, while you remain here, how you can see into my neighbor's house?

27/26.24. The magician said: Yes, O king; but for that feat it is necessary to enter the state of the holy ghost (trance), and the price is expensive!

27/26.25. The king said: I will pay you; therefore enter into the state of the holy ghost.

27/26.26. Loo Sin turned up his eyes and gave a shudder, as one dying, and having stretched himself on the floor, bade the king to question him.

27/26.27. The king said: Here is chalk; mark on the floor the character that is on the top of my tablet, on the left of the throne! Almost immediately the magician marked correctly. And now again the king tried him as to his power to see without his eyes, and in far-off places; and, having proved him in many ways, the king said: Can you also show the spirits of the dead?

27/26.28. Loo Sin said: In truth I can, O king. But that requires me to enter the sublime state of creation, and is even yet more expensive!

27/26.29. The king said: Have I not said I will pay you? Get moving, then. Enter the sublime state of creation at once!

27/26.30. Loo Sin then went into a dark corner and laid himself down on the floor, and then swallowed his tongue, and was motionless and stiff, like one that is quite dead. Presently a light like a thin smoke rose up from the body and stood a little aside, and a voice spoke out of the light, saying:

27/26.31. Who are you that calls up the spirits of the dead? Beware! He whose body lies stiff and cold beside me, is one of the heirs of the immortal Gods! What do you ask, man of earth?

27/26.32. The king said: Who are you? The voice answered: I am Joss, Te-in! Ruler of heaven and earth! The Great Spirit personified! Creator of all things!

27/26.33. The king in satire[1102] said: You are welcome, O Te-in! I am one of the most blest of mortals, because you have made my place a holy place.

27/26.34. The spirit then assumed mortal shape and stood before the king, even while the magician's body lay on the floor in sight also. The spirit said: What question troubles you, O king? Speak, and I will answer you, for I am all Wisdom and Truth personified.

27/26.35. The king said: Why have you not appeared to me before this? Why have I been left in the dark as to your real existence? Answer me this? For it is the foundation on which I desire to rest many questions.

27/26.36. The spirit said: My son, Te-zee, I have been with you since your youth, watching over you, for you shall become the greatest king in all the world. Yes, there are great works for you to do. And if you desire to extend your kingdom, or to gain great battles, I will show you the way, yes? Or if you desire another woman to wife, I will find her for you, yes?

27/26.37. The king said: You are a great heavenly ruler, I fully believe, but you did not answer my question. Moreover, you question me about my kingdom and about another woman to wife, and these things are not what I desire of you. And as for the matter of women, I do not yet have one wife; consequently I do not desire another.

27/26.38. The spirit said: Who do you say I am? The king replied: I am at a loss to know if you are a fool or a devil; and I say that I have either seen one like you, or else you, through many magicians. But, alas, there all knowledge ends.

27/26.39. The spirit said: You said you would pay what the fates decreed. Hear me then, O king; you shall give to Loo Sin four pieces of gold. And after that I will explain all things to you.

27/26.40. The king then cast the four pieces of gold to Loo Sin, and demanded the knowledge as promised. The spirit then said: And on your oath you will not reveal?

27/26.41. The king said: I solemnly swear to reveal nothing of what you teach Me. The spirit said: Know, then, O king, I am Loo Sin, the magician! By long training, the magician attains to go out of his own body in spirit, and to appear in any form or shape desired. Will you try me? The king said: Show me the spirit of king Ha Gow-tsee.

27/26.42. The spirit walked back to the body of Loo Sin, and presently returned before the king, looking like the spirit of Ha Gow-tsee. The king said: It is like the king! The spirit answered: Here then, O man, is the end of philosophy. Behold, I am Loo Sin also. Some men are one spirit, some two,

[1102] in sarcasm or ridicule

some three, and some four, to one corporeal body. And yet there is only one person in fact.

27/26.43. The king asked: What becomes of the spirit when the corporeal part is dead? The spirit answered: One of two things is possible to every man: His spirit will either dissolve into non-existence, and be scattered and void like the air of heaven, like the heat of a fire that is burnt out; or else it will reincarnate itself in the body of a child before it is born, and so, live over again.

27/26.44. All people came into the world this way. A child that is stillborn is one in whose body no spirit reincarnated itself. There are no new creations. The same people live now on the earth that always lived on it; nor will there be any others. They go out of one body when it is old and worn out; and then enter a young one and live over again and again, forever. Nor is there anything more or less for any man, woman or child in all the world.

27/26.45. The king asked: What, then, is the highest, best thing for a mortal man to do during life?

27/26.46. The spirit said: To eat and drink, and sleep and rest, and enjoy begetting numerous offspring.

27/26.47. The king asked: How long would a spirit live if it did not reincarnate itself? The spirit said: If the mortal body is burnt to ashes, then that is the time; if the body is buried, and rots, and returns to earth, then that is the time; if the body is embalmed, and keeps well, the spirit goes back into the embalmed body and remains till that body is moldered into dust. When the body is moldered into dust, or burnt to ashes, then the spirit is set free, and ready to either reincarnate itself or to dissolve and disappear forever.

27/26.48. The king asked: As it is with you, is it the same with all magicians? The spirit said: You have only given four pieces of gold; if you would have more, the price is expensive. The king said: I have told you I would pay whatever the fates decreed; therefore, proceed. The spirit said: It is even so with all magicians. The king asked: Show me now that you can preach like Chine?

27/26.49. The spirit said: You shall ask me questions, and I will preach on them. ||

27/26.50. The king asked many questions, and the spirit spoke on them. Finally the king said: That is sufficient; I will pay you; go your way. As for your preaching and your doctrines, they are nothing. || Now I will send and find another magician; for out of a counsel with many I shall arrive at the truth.

CHAPTER 27 Arc Bon

27/27.1. Te-zee, the king, sent for another magician, Wan-jho, who came and was commanded to exhibit his powers; but he also demanded a high price; which the king agreed to pay, and Wan-jho exhibited. First he caused a rose to come within a glass bottle while it was shut; then he created a small serpent out of a rod, and caused birds to come and sing to the king; then changed vinegar into water; then wrote on a stone tablet without touching the tablet, and even while the tablet lay under the king's foot.

27/27.2. Now after he had exhibited many more similar feats, he demanded his money, saying: The angels are gone; I can do no more. The king said: And do you not have power to fetch them back?

27/27.3. Wan-jho said: How much would you give? The king answered: Three pieces of gold. And Wan-jho said: Ah, in that case, behold, they have come again! What do you wish? The king commanded him to show the spirits of the dead, so he could converse with them.

27/27.4. Wan-jho went into the same place where Loo Sin had exhibited, and, lying down, cast himself into the death trance. Presently an angel, robed in white, appeared, and came and stood before the king, saying: Most mighty king, what do you ask? Behold me, I am the Goddess, Oe-tu Heng, come from my throne in high heaven. And if you are desirous of conquest in war, or to attain great riches, or more wives, most beautiful, then by my most potent will, I will give to you.

27/27.5. The king said: I am blest, O Goddess, because you have come to see me. But alas, none of the things you have mentioned suits me. I desire nothing regarding this world. Give me light concerning the place in heaven where king See Quan dwells?

27/27.6. The spirit said: Was he your friend or your enemy? The king answered: He was my deadly enemy. The spirit said: I asked you if he was your friend or your enemy, because I saw one See Quan in hell, writhing in great agony. And yet I saw another See Quan in paradise. So, then, I will go and fetch him who is in hell.

27/27.7. The spirit passed over to the corner, and presently returned, saying: O, O, O, O, O! Horrors! Demons! Hell! and such like, pretending to be in torments, as if it were See Quan in torments.

27/27.8. After this the king called for many different spirits, whether they had ever been, or whether fictitious, and they came all the same. Finally Te-zee, the king, said: Bring me now the wisest God in heaven, for I would question him. So, the spirit went again toward the corner, and then approached, saying: Man of earth! Because you have called me I have come. Do you know that when I come, I decree four gold pieces to Wan-jho, my prophet?

27/27.9. The king said: Most just, God! I will pay him. Tell me now where man comes from, and what is his destiny?

27/27.10. The spirit said: First, then, the air above the earth is full of elementary spirits; the largest are as large as a man's fist, and the smallest not larger than the smallest living insect on the earth. Their size denotes their intelligence; the largest being designed for human beings. These fill all the air of the earth, and all the space in the firmament above the earth; they have existed from everlasting to everlasting, for they were without beginning.

27/27.11. Now while a child is yet within the womb, one of these elementaries enters into the child, and in that instant there is the beginning of the man. And all things that live on the earth are produced like this.

27/27.12. The king asked: Before the time when man begins, while these elementaries are floating about, do they know anything? The spirit said: Many of them have great wisdom and cunning, but are also great liars, thieves and rascals. Do you know Loo Sin, the magician? The king answered: Yes. And then the spirit said: Well, Loo Sin is obsessed by the elementaries, and they are all great liars, pretending to be spirits of the dead! As for myself, I am a most virtuous Goddess, from the highest heavenly spheres. I tell you, O king, these elementaries are the curse of the world; they are anxious to be born into life, so they may obtain souls, and they inspire mortals to paternity and maternity so that they may have an opportunity for incarnation.

27/27.13. The king said: You have answered well, O Goddess. I will pay according to your decree. And with that, the spirit departed. King Te-zee sent for another magician, Hi Gowh, of the rank of priest, and having bargained with him as to his price for exhibiting, commanded him to proceed.

27/27.14. Hi Gowh then exhibited in the same fashion as the others, doing great wonders. And the king also commanded him to show the spirits of the dead. Hi Gowh complained about the price; but being assured by the king that his demands would be paid, the magician went into the same corner and cast himself in the holy ghost (trance); and, presently, a spirit appeared, saying: Greeting to you, O king! Whether you desire conquest, riches, or more women, name your desire, and I will give abundantly. For, I am the spirit of the great Zarathustra.

27/27.15. The king said: Great Zarathustra, you are most welcome. But, alas, none of the things you have named are what I desire. Tell me, O Zarathustra, what is the origin and destiny of man?

27/27.16. The spirit said: First, then, O king, in days long past, the sun turned round so swiftly it threw off its outer rim, and the rim broke into a million pieces, flying every way, and these pieces are the stars and the earth and the moon.

27/27.17. And for millions of years the earth was only a stone, melting hot; but it cooled off in time; and the outer stones on the earth were oxidized, and this made moss; then the moss died; but the spirit of the moss reincarnated itself, and this made grass; and the grass died; but the spirit of the grass lived and reincarnated itself, and thus made the trees.

27/27.18. Then the trees died; but the spirit lived, and it reincarnated and became animals; and they died, but their spirits lived and reincarnated and became man. After that the spirit no longer reincarnates itself, but floats upward into peace, and rests for a long time, when it finally merges back into the sun and is extinct, like a lamp burnt out.

27/27.19. The king asked: How, then, is it with yourself? The spirit replied: I was the original Sun God, who came away from the sun to take charge of this world. It is in my keeping. The king asked: Who, then, is the All First that still stays with the sun?

27/27.20. The spirit answered: Because you ask many questions, O king, you shall pay more money. The king assured the spirit that the money, to any amount, would be paid; so the spirit said: Ahura-Ormazd was the original of all; but when the sun threw off its surface Ahura-Ormazd was thrown into pieces, one piece going to every star, except the earth, and I came here of my own accord, because it was larger and better than any other world.

27/27.21. The king dismissed the spirit and the priest, and sent for another, a magician also of the rank of priest, Gwan Le. And Gwan Le, being assured that his price would be paid, proceeded to exhibit also. And he performed feats like the others. Then the king commanded Gwan Le to call the spirits of the dead.

27/27.22. The priest apologized about the expense of the death trance (holy ghost power), but being further assured that his demands would be paid, he went into the corner and cast himself into the swoon, becoming stiff and cold.

27/27.23. Presently an angel appeared, saying: Behold me, O king, I am Brahma. And if you desire conquest in war, or greater riches, or more women, I will grant your wish. I can tell you about hidden treasures, and rich mines, and desirable women. Also I can tell you how your armies can overcome your enemies with great slaughter.

27/27.24. The king said: I am delighted, O Brahma. But I desire nothing of which you have mentioned. Tell me about the origin and destiny of man?

27/27.25. The spirit said: Know then, O king, all things alive have two parts, the corporeal and the spiritual; all dead things are but one, which is the spirit. You, O king, were first a stone, a very large stone; then when it moldered into dust your soul went into silver, a very large piece; but when the silver rusted away, your soul went into gold; and when the gold was worn away, your soul began to run into vegetable life; and after that it ran into animal life, then into a low order of man, then into the high order of man, as you now are. Thus man came up from the beginning, reincarnating himself over and over, higher and higher and higher. And when he is perfected in spirit as you are, he no longer returns to reincarnate himself. The king asked: What does the spirit do after leaving this world? The spirit replied: You shall then meet your sexual partner, your soul wife; and shall do nothing ever after but have sexual indulgence, peopling the spirit realms with delightful spiritual offspring.

27/27.26. The king said: It is well; you have a wonderful doctrine. And with that, the spirit departed, and the priest also. And the king sent for still another priest, Tseeing, a Brahmin prophet. And the king asked him: What do you see for your king?

27/27.27. The priest said: By the rites of my order I cannot disclose any of the secrets of heaven or earth until you have paid the price of indulgence, which is two pieces of gold. So the king paid him. Tseeing said: And if you desire riches, or success in war, or new wives, speak, and I will grant to you according to the price. The king said: Alas, Tseeing, I desire none of these indulgences; tell me the origin and destiny of man, for I would learn why I am, and the object and end?

27/27.28. Tseeing said: The first of all was Brahma, which was round like an egg. Then Brahma broke open, and the shell was in two halves, and one half was the sky and the other half was the earth. Then Brahma incarnated himself in the earth; but he did not come up as one only, as he expected, but he came up in ten million and one million parts, and every part was a living thing, a tree, or a plant, or a fish, or a bird, or a beast, or a man. And this is all there is or was or ever shall be.

27/27.29. But Brahma looked over the world and he saw that some men were good and some evil. And he said: I will separate the good from the evil. And so that justice would be done he called all the nations and tribes of men before him. And when they had come, he said to them:

27/27.30. Whoever delights in the earth, it shall be his forever. And though he does die, his spirit shall have power to reincarnate itself in another unborn child, and so live over again, and so on, forever. And he shall have great indulgence in the earth, in eating and drinking, and with women, and in all manner of delights, for they shall be his forever.

27/27.31. But whoever delights in spirit shall be blest in spirit. He shall not, after death, reincarnate himself and live over again, but shall dwell forever in heaven and have heavenly delights. But since heavenly delights are different from earthly delights, then as a mortal the spiritual chooser shall not live like earth-people.

27/27.32. But he shall live secluded, and shall torment his flesh with fastings and with castigations.[1103] Neither shall he marry nor live with woman, nor beget children, nor have any indulgence on the earth whatsoever, except merely to live; for the earth is not his, nor is he of the earth. And the more he tortures the flesh, the higher his bliss shall be in heaven.

27/27.33. Now, when Brahma had stated the two propositions to the children of the earth, he further added: Choose now which you will; for after you have chosen, behold, there is the end. For you who choose the earth shall be of the earth, even to all succeeding generations. But whoever chooses heaven, to him and his heirs it shall be final, and forever.

27/27.34. And so mortals made their choice, and lo and behold, nearly all of them chose the earth. But in thousands of years and millions of years afterward, Brahma repented of his former decree, for he saw the earth became too full of people, and they were sinful beyond bounds. And Brahma sent a flood of waters and destroyed a trillion times ten millions of them. And he sent Zarathustra into the world to give new judgment.

27/27.35. Zarathustra opened the door of heaven anew, saying: Whoever after this chooses Brahma, and will torture his flesh, and hate the earth, and live away from the world, him I will save from the earth and from hell also, for I am very efficient and influential with the Creator.

27/27.36. Such, then, O king, is the origin and destiny of man. Some are born for the earth forever, and some are born for heaven. Nevertheless, the way is open to all, to choose that which they will, earth or heaven.

CHAPTER 28 Arc Bon

27/28.1. Te-zee pursued his researches for a long while, and with many prophets, magicians, seers and priests. Afterward he said:

27/28.2. All is vanity; all is falsehood. No man has answered me correctly as to the origin and destiny of man. Even the angels, or whatever they are, can only inform me of the things of earth; they only see as man sees. And it may be true that these angels are nothing more than Loo Sin said, that it is the spirit of the magician only. Because his body enters this trance it seems reasonable.

27/28.3. Now, therefore, I will put a stop to these magicians and priests; they are of no good under the sun. So Te-zee issued a decree covering his own province, commanding magicians and priests to leave the province, under penalty of death. And so they departed out of his dominions.

27/28.4. Now it so happened that in four other great provinces, the kings did precisely the same (questioned magicians and priests), and at about the same time. And these were the provinces, namely: Shan Ji, under king Lung Wan; Gah, under king Loa Kee; Sa-bin-Sowh, under king Ah-ka Ung; Gow Goo, under king Te See-Yong; and these five provinces [which included Te-zee's province of Aen-Na-Po'e –ed.] comprised the chief part of Jaffeth. And all these kings issued similar edicts. So that the magicians, seers, and priests, were obliged to abandon their callings or go beyond these provinces, where barbarians dwelt.

27/28.5. Jehovih commanded Chine to go before king Te-zee, and when he had come, the king said to him: It has been some years since I heard you, and you were profound. I am delighted you have come before me again, so that I may question you.

27/28.6. Chine said: When you heard me before, the Great Spirit spoke through me. Now I am well learned, and He commands me to speak from my own knowledge.

27/28.7. First, then, I am a man as you are; yet every man has a different work. You are king of this province, and I am told, moreover, you are good and wise. I hope you are. Otherwise my words will not please you. As for myself, I was sent into the world to mark out this land and name it Chine'ya (Chine-land), and to establish anew those who accept the Great Spirit. For Chine'ya and her people shall remain a different country and different people from all the world.

27/28.8. Know then, O king, I do not come in vanity, boasting that I, Chine, am much or can do much; on the contrary, I say to you, I am one of the weakest of men; and yet I have more power than any other man in the world. And yet, mark you, of

[1103] In some ascetic orders, these were severe and frequent rebukings, with punishments sometimes extreme (like whippings) even for petty offences, in order to gain and prove mastery over the flesh and flesh desires.

myself there is nothing to boast about; for I am only as a tool in the hands of Jehovih (Ormazd), and I myself do not do anything, but He through me.

27/28.9. I look upon you and see you have been questioning magicians and priests, and that you are unsatisfied. Know then, O king, your error is in not magnifying your judgment.

27/28.10. You have worked with magicians who are under the power of angels of the first resurrection, and even angels below them.

27/28.11. All such angels teach according to their own individual understanding; as wandering individuals they go about. And their miracles are of the same order, merely individual miracles.

27/28.12. He Whom I teach, works miracles not in a small corner, but in the affairs of kingdoms and nations; and not through magicians only, but through kings and queens, and even through common people. You yourself are an instrument in His hand.

27/28.13. Behold, when you issued your decree against magicians and asceticism, even in that same time four other great kings did the same thing! This is a miracle indeed! No man can counterfeit His miracles. Do not flatter yourself that such matters occur by accident. They do not occur by accident; but by Jehovih. For His angels in the second resurrection are organized, and work in mighty armies.

27/28.14. Te-zee said: You are great, Chine; or else your sudden philosophy turns my brain! Go on! How shall we know, first, that there are angels who are really the spirits of the dead? Second, how shall we distinguish between the first and second resurrections?

27/28.15. Chine said: Only by seeing and hearing with the natural eyes and ears, and with the spiritual eyes and ears, can any man attain to know anything either on earth or in heaven. When these senses are pure and clear, then a man knows that the spirits of the dead do live. For I declare, O king, in truth, that the spirit of my body has emerged from my body on many occasions, sometimes going subjectively and sometimes objectively. Nor is this a special creation meant for me only; but it is that which thousands and tens of thousands can attain to by discipline.

27/28.16. Touching the first and second resurrections, know, O king, spirits that dispose individual things, or earthly things; or propose riches or personal gain, or marriage, discanting (lecturing) to this man or that man about what is good for him as an individual; spirits giving great names, professing to be this or that great person long since dead; all these are deceivers and have not advanced beyond the first resurrection. They deny the I Am, the Great Spirit, the All Person. Their highest heaven is re-engraftment on mortals, and the reveling in lust. They flatter you, telling you, you were this or that great man in a former reincarnation. They manipulate you to make profit for their own magician; they are without truth or virtue, and of little wisdom.

27/28.17. The second resurrection does not come to an individual as an individual; it comes as an army, but not to an individual, but to a kingdom, a nation, a community. For as such angels belong to organized communities in heaven, so does that organization work with virtuous organizations of mortals.

27/28.18. This is wisdom, O king; to get away from the individual self; to become one with an organization, to work with the Great Spirit for the resurrection of men. For as you make yourself one with many to this end, so does the Father labor with you and them. As you keep yourself as an individual self, so do individual angels come to you as individuals.

27/28.19. Individual answers to individual; the first resurrection to the first; the second to the second. Moreover, the All Person is over all, and works each in its own order, to a great purpose.

27/28.20. Do not think, O king, I am making a new doctrine; I am only declaring that which was also proclaimed to the ancients. And those who came forward and had faith were called Jehovih's chosen people, because, in truth, they chose Him.

27/28.21. Recognize, then, that whoever denies the All Person is not of His order; nor does such a one have the light of the Father in him. But he who has attained to understand that all things are really one harmonious whole, has also attained to know what is meant by the term, All Person, for He is All; and, consequently, Ever Present, filling all, extending everywhere.

27/28.22. In contradistinction from Him, two other philosophies have run parallel, which are darkness and evil. One says the All is not a person, being void, and less than even the parts thereof; the other says the only All High is the great angel I worship, who is like a man, and separate from all things.

27/28.23. These three comprise the foundation of all the doctrines in the world, or that have ever been or ever will be. The lowest is idolatry, which is evil; the second, unbelief, which is darkness; and the first is faith, truth, love, wisdom and peace.

27/28.24. Jehovih and His angels classify all men under one of these three heads. And they may be compared to three men looking across a field; one sees a light and knows he sees it; another hopes he sees it, but he only sees a white leaf; but the third sees nothing at all.

27/28.25. As a witness, therefore, the last one is worthless; the second is a circumstantial witness; but the first is positive, and stands the highest and firmest of all. He knows his Heavenly Father. He sees Him in the flowers; in the clouds, and in the sunshine; yes, in the fruits and herbs; in the beasts of the field, and in every creeping thing; and beyond, in the stars, moon, earth and sun. In sickness, in health, in sorrow and in rejoicing; truly he finds Jehovih in all things; he knows Jehovih's eye and ear are forever upon him; and he walks upright in fear,[1104] but in truth and faith and pride and rejoicing!

27/28.26. Te-zee, the king, asked: Tell me, O Chine, what is the origin and destiny of man?

27/28.27. Chine said: The Ever Present quickens him into life in his mother's womb;[1105] and he is then and there a new creation, his spirit from the Spirit Jehovih, and his body from the earth; a dual being the Father creates him.

27/28.28. His destination is everlasting resurrection; in which matter, man can have delightful labor as he rises upward forever and ever.

27/28.29. The king asked: If Jehovih is creating all the time, will the firmament not become too full of angels?

27/28.30. Chine said: A thousand men read a book, and yet that book is no fuller of ideas than at first. The corporeal man is not divisible, and so, fills a place. Thought, which may be compared to the soul, is the opposite of this. Ten thousand men may love your flower-garden, yet your garden is no fuller because of their love. Exalted souls in the upper heavens are without bulk and substance; and even so are the regions they inhabit, as compared to corporeal things.

27/28.31. The king said: I wish I were as you are! For which matter, if you will use your wand and make me even half as wise, I will give away all my kingdom!

27/28.32. Chine said: You cannot bargain for Faith, or purchase it, like a coat or sandals. And yet, until Faith is attained there is no resurrection. No bird ever flew from its nest without first having faith it could fly. And when you have Faith, you will cast away your kingdom and choose heavenly treasures instead. Until you have attained Faith you will retain your kingdom. This is a judgment to the rich man in the same way.

27/28.33. Riches and a king's kingdom may be compared to balls of gold tied to a man's feet in deep water; he cannot rise until he cuts himself loose, and casts away that which binds him. So, also, are men bound in spirit, and until they put their own hands to the matter, there is no resurrection for them.

CHAPTER 29 Arc Bon

27/29.1. Te-zee, the king, said to Chine: Because you have given me this great light, it seems to me I should issue a decree commanding all my people to accept your doctrines?

27/29.2. Chine replied: O man! How short you are in understanding our Father! Violence is His enemy. Such a decree would be no better than a decree establishing any other heavenly ruler. It would thwart itself. He does not come with sword and spear, like the idol-Gods; He comes with education, the chief book of which is the example of good works, and of peace and liberty to all.

[1104] The context seems to imply that Jehovih's eye and ear, being always upon one, plays a role in this feeling. Thus, for example, one might fear the doing of something wrong, or fear failing Jehovih, fear falling from His Countenance (grace), fear the prospect of temptation, fear Jehovih's power, etc. And this is a foundation. Yet to walk in fear can mean more; it can mean acknowledging one's vulnerabilities, but not letting these turn one aside from doing the right thing, and so, remain upright; thus one walks amid fear and faces fear.

[1105] We learn elsewhere in Oahspe this happens at conception (see e.g., 04/6.21; 10/5.10; 24/21.18).

27/29.3. Te-zee said: You reason well. Hear me, then, you greatest of men; command me even as if I was the lowliest[1106] of servants, and I will obey you.

27/29.4. Chine said: O king, you torment me with my own inability to make you understand! You shall not make yourself servant to any man, but to Ormazd, the Great Spirit.

27/29.5. The king said: Then I will put away my kingdom. But Chine said: Consider first if you can best serve Him by doing this way or that way, and then follow your highest light, and you shall not err.

27/29.6. The king asked: What do you think, shall I put aside my kingdom and my riches and do as you do?

27/29.7. Chine said: You shall be your own judge. If I judge for you, and you follow my judgment, then I am bound to you. Allow me to have my liberty also.

27/29.8. Te-zee said: If the Great Spirit would give me your wisdom, then I would serve Him. How long, do you say, a man shall serve Him in order to reach great wisdom?

27/29.9. Chine said: Suppose a man had several pieces of glass; some clear, some clouded with smoke and grease; how long, do you say, would it require to make them all clear? For such is the self in man; it clouds his soul; and when he has put self away, then his soul is clear, and that is wisdom, for then he beholds the Father through his own soul; yes, and hears Him also. And until he does this, he does not believe in His Person or Presence, no matter how much he professes.

27/29.10. The king kept Chine many days, and questioned him with great wisdom and delight. One day Chine said to him: Jehovih says to me: Go quickly to the four other great provinces of Chine'ya, and explain to their kings who I am. Chine added: Therefore, O Te-zee, I must leave you, but after many days I will return to you and exhibit to you the testimony of immortal life.

27/29.11. The king provided camels and servants, and sent Chine on his way. And, after Chine was gone, Te-zee said to himself: Although I cannot decree Chine's doctrines, I see no reason why I cannot decree the extinction of Te-in and other idol-Gods. And so he did as he thought best, prohibiting the priests from doing sacrifice [worship –Ed.] to Joss (God), or Ho-Joss (Lord God), or Te-in, or Po, or any other ruler in heaven, except the Great Spirit.

[1106] lowest ranking; most subservient and compliant; most menial

CHAPTER 30 Arc Bon

27/30.1. In course of time Chine completed his labor with the kings of Jaffeth, and returned to Te-zee, to die.

27/30.2. At this time more than a thousand families (communities) of Faithists had been established in different places, either through Chine or his followers, the chief rab'bahs. And when Chine returned before the king, Te-zee, men and women came there from every quarter of the world to meet him and learn wisdom.

27/30.3. And all who were in any way sick, lame, blind, or deaf, he cured by pronouncing the word E-O-Ih over them. And persons who were obsessed with evil spirits he healed by permitting them to touch his staff. And many that were dead he brought to life; for in man's presence, he showed power to accomplish anything whatsoever. Indeed, he even rose up in the air and walked in it and on it over the heads[1107] of the multitude.

27/30.4. And while he was up in the air he said to the multitude: I will now come down among you and die, as all men do die. And you shall let my body lie five days, so that the eyes become sunken and black, showing that I am truly dead.

27/30.5. And on the sixth day you shall cast the body into the furnace and burn it to ashes. And you shall take the ashes into the field and scatter them this way and that, so that no more of me is seen or known on the earth.

27/30.6. And on the seventh day, which shall be a holy day for you, behold, you shall witness a whirlwind in the field of my ashes, and the whirlwind shall gather up the ashes of my body; and my soul shall inhabit it and make it whole, as you now see me, and I will break the whirlwind and descend down to the earth and abide with you for another seven days, and then you shall see a ship descend from heaven in an exceedingly great

[1107] Thousands of Spiritualists have witnessed this feat to a certain extent within their own houses. –Eng. Ed.

light, and I will enter it, and ascend to the second heavens (etherea).

27/30.7. Neither shall any man, woman or child say: Behold, Chine was a God. Nor shall you build an image of me, nor a monument, nor in any way do more for me or my memory than to the least of mortals. For I say to you, I am only a man who has put away earth possessions, desires and aspirations.

27/30.8. And whatever you see me do, or know of my having done, the same is possible to all men and women created alive on the earth.

27/30.9. Remembering that all things are possible with Jehovih (Ormazd); and to Him only is due all honor and glory forever.

27/30.10. So Chine died, and was burnt to ashes on the sixth day, under the superintendence of king Te-zee, and the ashes were scattered in the field as commanded.

27/30.11. And on the seventh day, while the multitude surrounded the entire place, a whirlwind came and gathered up the ashes in a small degree; and the ashes were illumed, and the soul of Chine went into them; then he burst the whirlwind and came down, even at the king's feet.

27/30.12. And Chine said: Do you know who I am? And the king answered, saying: In truth you are Chine. And because this has come to pass I decree that this, your native land, shall now and forever be called Chine'ya! And I will send word to the other kings also, and they will decree the same thing.

27/30.13. Chine said: Yes, do so. And since the Father has allotted me seven days to remain with His chosen and with you, O king, apprise those, whom I will name to you, to come and see me. So Chine told the king whom he desired to come.

27/30.14. And Chine walked about on the earth, even the same as before death, nor could any man tell by looking at him that he had passed through death. Nor were his clothes different, although they were made out of the ashes in the whirlwind.

27/30.15. On the last day that he was to remain, he called together Te-zee and the persons he had selected, and spoke to them, saying:

CHAPTER 31 Arc Bon

27/31.1. My brothers and my sisters, in the name of the Great Spirit, hear me: These are Chine's last words, for the Father calls me. Be attentive, so that you may remember my sermon; also consider and reason regarding my words, for I am no more nor less than one of you.

27/31.2. I was sent into the world to wall this great people around with Jehovih's hand. I have made you an exclusive people for three thousand years to come. I give to you peace and liberty; I have drawn a veil over the bloody past, and taught you to love and respect one another.

27/31.3. Chine'ya shall become the most populous nation in the entire world; this is the miracle of the Father to you. Your doctrines now and forever shall rest on the foundation I have given you.

27/31.4. Be watchful against Gods (Josses) and Saviors, and especially wary of spirits of the dead who do not profess the Great All Person.

27/31.5. All such are instigators of war, and lust after earthly things.

27/31.6. Be exclusive to one another; neither permitting outside barbarians to come among you, nor, especially, to marry with my people.

27/31.7. Yet you shall not war against them.

27/31.8. But it is lawful for you to build walls around your land, to keep them away. And these walls shall stand as the Father's judgment against all people who molest or injure you.

27/31.9. And at every change of the moon you shall renew your covenant, which was my covenant, with Jehovih. (See 27/23.15-29.)

27/31.10. Teaching it to your children, and commanding them to teach it to theirs after them, and so on forever!

27/31.11. Swearing yourselves to the Great Spirit to ignore all heavenly rulers but the Creator, the I Am who is everywhere.

27/31.12. And if idolaters come among you, proclaiming their God, or their Lord, or their Savior, do not listen to them. But nevertheless, do not persecute them or injure them, for they are in darkness.

27/31.13. Neither be conceited over them; for your forefathers were like them.

27/31.14. The Father has made a wide world, and fruitful and joyous, and He gives it to man's keeping.

27/31.15. To one people one country; to another people another country, and so on, over the entire world.

27/31.16. He gives Chine'ya to you, and He says:

27/31.17. Be as brothers and sisters in this, My holy land.

27/31.18. Which in the ancients' days was made to bloom as a flowery kingdom by My chosen, the Faithists of old.

27/31.19. But they were neglectful of My commandments.

27/31.20. Idolaters came upon them and destroyed them, and laid waste their rich fields; yes, the bones of My people were strewn over all the land.

27/31.21. But now you are delivered once more, and you shall make Chine'ya bloom again as My celestial kingdom.

27/31.22. And you shall multiply, and build, and plant, and make this heritage, which I give to you, into an example to all peoples, of industry, peace and thrift.

27/31.23. And of the multitude that can dwell together in one kingdom, manifesting love, patience and virtue, you shall be an example before all the world.

27/31.24. And by your neglect of war and of war inventions, you shall be a testimony of My presence in this day.

27/31.25. For the time shall surely come when I will put down all unrighteousness, and war, and idolatry, and I will be the All Person to the whole world.

27/31.26. Chine has spoken; his last words are spoken. Jehovih's ship of fire descends from His highest heaven!

27/31.27. Chine will rise up in this; and even so shall you who are pure and good and full of love. ||

27/31.28. A light, like a great cloud, but brilliant, blinding with holy light, descended over the entire field where the multitude were.

27/31.29. Many fell down in fear; and many cried aloud in great sorrow.

27/31.30. Then Chine went and kissed Te-zee, and immediately walked toward the middle of the field, and was lost in the exceedingly great light.

27/31.31. And the light turned around like a whirlwind, and rose up, higher and higher, and then was seen no more.

27/31.32. Chine was gone!

27/31.33. And now the power and glory of Jehovih were manifested. Te-zee at once made special laws protecting all persons who rejected Gods, Lords and Saviors, but worshipped the All Light (Jehovih). Four other kings followed with the same edicts and laws.

27/31.34. The Faithists were safely delivered into freedom throughout Chine'ya.

Thus end the revelations of the three contemporaneous Sons of Jehovih, Capilya, Moses and Chine.

END OF BOOK OF THE ARC OF BON

END OF VOLUME 1
OAHSPE MODERN LANGUAGE EDITION

Made in the USA
Las Vegas, NV
18 March 2023